READINGS IN

INFORMATION VISUALIZATION

USING VISION TO THINK

The Morgan Kaufmann Series in Interactive Technologies

Readings in Information Visualization: Using Vision to Think
Written and edited by Stuart Card, Jock Mackinlay, and Ben Shneiderman

The Design of Children's Technology
Edited by Allison Druin

The Usability of Engineering Lifecycle: A Practitioner's Guide
Deborah Mayhew

Contextual Design: Defining Customer-Centered Systems
Hugh Beyer and Karen Holtzblatt

Human-Computer Interface Design: Success Stories, Emerging Methods, and Real-World Context
Edited by Marianne Rudisill, Clayton Lewis, Peter Polson, and Tim McKay

Readings in

Information Visualization

Using Vision to Think

Written and Edited by

Stuart K. Card

Xerox Palo Alto Research Center

Jock D. Mackinlay

Xerox Palo Alto Research Center

Ben Shneiderman

University of Maryland

Morgan Kaufmann Publishers, Inc.

San Francisco, California

Senior Editor	Diane D. Cerra
Director of Production and Manufacturing	Yonie Overton
Production Editor	Cheri Palmer
Production Assistant	Pam Sullivan
Assistant Editor	Marilyn Uffner Alan
Editorial Assistants	Belinda Breyer and Sarah Luger
Cover Design	Ross Carron Design
Cover Photo	Michael McGovern/Nonstoc
Text Design, Composition, and Pasteup	Christine Cotting, UpperCase Publication Services
Color Preparation	Mark Ong, Side by Side Studios
Copyeditor	Gary Morris
Proofreader	Jennifer McClain
Indexer	Ty Koontz
Printer	Courier Corporation

Morgan Kaufmann Publishers, Inc.
Editorial and Sales Office
340 Pine Street, Sixth Floor
San Francisco, CA 94104-3205
USA

Telephone 415 / 392-2665
Facsimile 415 / 982-2665
Email mkp@mkp.com
WWW *http://www.mkp.com*
Order toll free 800 / 745-7323

03 02 01 00 99 5 4 3 2 1

Library of Congress Cataloging-in-Publication Data

Card, Stuart K.
Readings in information visualization : using vision to think / written and edited by Stuart K. Card, Jock D. Mackinlay, Ben Shneiderman
p. cm.
Includes bibliographical references and index.
ISBN 1-55860-533-9
1. Information display systems. 2. Computer graphics. 3. Visualization. 4. Image processing. I. Mackinlay, Jock D. II. Shneiderman, Ben. III. Title.
TK7882.I6C36 1999
621.39′87—dc21 98-53660
CIP

TO OUR FAMILIES:

JJ, GWYNETH, TIFFANY

POLLE, MOLLY, GAVIN

JENNY, SARA, ANNA

Brief Contents

Detailed Contents

You can observe a lot by watching.

– Yogi Berra

Preface

Advances in science and commerce have often been characterized by inventions that allowed people to see old things in new ways. Telescope, microscope, and oscilloscope are obvious instrument examples. But invented visual representations, such as maps, statistical diagrams, and PERT charts, also qualify. Computers can combine both new instrument and new visual representation, resulting in the emerging field of information visualization.

The foundational period of information visualization is now ending. Computer hardware developments provide neat bookends to this period. One bookend is the introduction of the Silicon Graphics workstation in the mid-1980s. This machine (and its competitors) brought advanced, real-time interactive graphics for animation, geometric transformations in 2D and 3D, and new visual effects down to around \$40,000–\$100,000 per workstation and allowed exploration of visualization techniques for abstract information. The other bookend is the absorption of these advanced interactive graphics capabilities into the standard PC computer platform at the end of the 1990s. PCs are coming to support real-time, dynamic, interactive visual representations. The path is now clear for information visualization to be used in mass-market products. For example, we had the satisfaction of seeing the work at our institutions result in the launch of companies: Inxight Software, Inc. for the Xerox PARC work and Spotfire, Inc. for the University of Maryland work.

As this 15-year period draws to a close, there is a need for collecting together the results to date, organizing them, understanding the essence of this field, and providing materials for teaching. In the next period, information visualization will pass out of the realm of an exotic research specialty and into the mainstream of user interface and application design. There will be a shower of products using its techniques. It especially seems likely that techniques from information visualization will be important in creating interfaces to large-scale databases and document collections, most notably applications, services, and electronic commerce for the Internet and its successors. But advances in information visualization are scattered throughout the research literature. There is a lack of materials for teaching courses now springing up in information visualization and for professionals wanting to catch up on what has been done to exploit it for their own work. Students, researchers, software designers and programmers, scientific data users, digital library managers, financial analysis, and other professionals all have need of sources beyond the raw conference and journal research literature.

The purpose of this book is to help take the next step—to organize the rationale and structure of the field, to make accessible a selection of classic papers as well as a sampling of current work, to point to lines of application, and to provide materials for teaching. To accomplish these aims, the book follows a certain plan. First, it attends to the rationale, the problem that information visualization is trying to solve, and introduces a reference model for information visualization as a framework (Chapter 1). The next set of chapters organizes papers and commentary around different parts of the reference model. We proceed from how space is used in information visualization (Chapter 2), to the addition of interaction (Chapter 3), to how interaction allows space to be used nonuniformly (Chapter 4). We then shift gears and look at how information in one particular domain, document collections, can be transformed and visualized (Chapter 5). This naturally leads to the visualization-based user interfaces of the World Wide Web, information workspaces, and visualization-enhanced objects in those workspaces (Chapter 6). Finally, we shift gears again and consider information visualization theoretically (Chapter 7) and in terms of its potential applications (Chapter 8).

As part of the plan, we enhanced the book with features for education, research, and application. The first of these is to print as much of the material in color as possible. This is a larger, more perilous—and more expensive—undertaking than many readers will realize. It required courage on the part of our editor Diane Cerra and our publisher Mike Morgan. It also required considerable effort tracking down source material by Marilyn Uffner Alan and occasional heroics by our production editor Cheri Palmer. Even better than seeing information visualization in color is seeing it in color in action. This is especially important for designers and programmers. For this reason we included an appendix listing a selection of videotapes and their sources. These can be ordered for class or personal use. We are indebted to Catherine Plaisant at the University of Maryland for collecting the list.

Because we strongly believe a good bibliography is an important part of a book like this, we produced a unified bibliographic index. All works referenced in any of the papers or in our discussion are part of a single bibliography, and that bibliography is indexed back to all the places where a particular work is referenced. Even in a rather large readings book such as this one, many interesting and good papers must be left out. The bibliography allows many of these to be identified and for the reader to notice papers and authors heavily cited by this corpus. The 700 references are not a complete bibliography of information visualization, but it is the most comprehensive we know of so far. We hope it will be useful for research and education. We thank the PARC Information Center for its help. In particular, Mina Malaki and Jeannine Torres transcribed the list.

The collaboration on this book began when Card and Mackinlay at Xerox PARC and Shneiderman at the University of Maryland discovered they were each working on a book of readings and commentary on information visualization. We decided we could do a better job if we joined forces. This resulted in a more unified view of the field and a richer set of acknowledgments.

XEROX ACKNOWLEDGMENTS

Of course, books are the result of a process that involves critical help and influences of people who are not the editors, both for the production of the book and for the development of the ideas on which it is based. On the research front: Card and Mackinlay's deepest acknowledgment must go to their colleague for many years, George Robertson. George brought his ability to conquer any machine (quickly) and his vast experience with exotic systems programs to bear, providing the anchor for our exploration of the information visualization space. He influenced us so profoundly and in so many ways, it is hard to even realize them all. Many of whatever insights we have into this area are jointly his. Ramana Rao, a later member of the team, brought his background in object-oriented programming, his gunslinger programming speed, his skills as a designer, and his ability to understand the industry. Part of the conceptual insights in this book also derive from him. He later lead the creation of the Inxight Xerox start-up business. Bill York and Eric Hoppe provided key leadership in translating technical ideas to the PC. Mary Beth Erickson, Kevin Walters, and Alex Matic translated ideas in information visualization to the product world. Our close research partners at Xerox PARC, Peter Pirolli, Rich Gossweiler, Edward Chi, James Pitkow, Mark Stefik, Polle Zellweger, and Dan Russell have been influential through many discussions and meetings around these ideas. Among our many colleagues outside Xerox who have influenced us, we want to specially mention Bob Spence, George Furnas, Steve Eick, Lisa Tweedie, Nahum Gershon, and Mei Chua.

Several managers at Xerox played critical roles. John Seely Brown, who always seems to know the future before anyone else, introduced us to Silicon Graphics machines (when they were a start-up), helped us horse-trade ourselves into one, and provided critical support over the years. Robert Bauer made the critical decisions to build the team and to provide the capital for visualization machines. Per-Kristian Halvorsen supported the effort with good advice, hiring, and capital and took crucial risks to make commercialization possible. It is a pleasure to acknowledge the support of the Office of Naval Research for support of part of the theoretical activity on this book.

In preparing the manuscript, we appreciate very much Katy Moore's help as well as the help of the patient editorial staff at Morgan Kaufmann.

UNIVERSITY OF MARYLAND ACKNOWLEDGMENTS

Among the great professorial pleasures are collaborating with colleagues and creating with students. The lively atmosphere at the Human-Computer Interaction Laboratory has been inspiring and nurturing to me (Shneiderman) for its 16 years. The continuing partnership with Catherine Plaisant and Kent Norman has been intellectually stimulating and personally satisfying. Gary Marchionini was a vital colleague for a decade until his recent departure. Anne Rose's energetic contribution during the past five years has added much to our community, and Ben Bederson's recent arrival has already enriched us.

Memorable participants in our early visualization work were students Brian Johnson, Christopher Williamson, and Christopher Ahlberg. They were followed by important contributors such as Harsha Kumar, Marko Teittinen, and Christopher North. Other contributors to our visualization research (*http://www.cs.umd.edu/hcil*) include Toshiyuki Asahi, Richard Beigel, Tom Bruns, David Carr, Richard Chimera, Khoa Doan, Jason Ellis, Stephan Greene, Vinit Jain, Ninad Jog, Eser Kandogan, Anita Komlodi, Jia Li, Brett Milash, David Nation, Egemen Tanin, David Turo, and Degi Young. Jenny Preece provided thoughtful comments on the manuscript and supportive encouragement.

Each personality added fresh perspectives, challenged our beliefs, and pushed forward our adventure of innovation. I am grateful to each person for the thrilling moments of discovery.

Acknowledgments

FIGURES

Chapter 1 Opening Image: Courtesy of Inxight, a Xerox New Enterprise Company.

1.5: © 1996 MIT Press, Cambridge, MA.

1.8: © 1987 Scientific American Library Inc., New York.

1.9: © 1987 Scientific American Library Inc., New York.

1.11: © 1997 IEEE.

1.12: © 1992 Association for Computing Machinery, Inc.

1.14: © 1997 Kluwer Academic Publishers.

1.30: © 1996 Cambridge University Press.

1.34: © 1993 IEEE.

1.39: © 1995 IEEE.

Chapter 2 Opening Image: Risch et al. (1996) IV'97. Copyright 1997 IEEE.

2.3a: © 1995 American Association of Artificial Intelligence.

2.4a: Christopher Ahlberg, IVEE Development AB. *http://www.ivee.com.*

2.4c: © 1996 Association of Computing Machinery, Inc.

Chapter 3 Opening Image: Courtesy University of Maryland.

Chapter 4 Opening Image: Courtest Xerox PARC.

4.5: © 1997 IEEE.

Chapter 5 Opening Image: Wise et al. (1995) IV'97. Copyright 1997 IEEE.

Chapter 6 Opening Image: Courtesy Xerox PARC.

6.2b: © 1996 Association of Computing Machinery, Inc.

6.2c: © 1992 Association of Computing Machinery, Inc.

6.4b: Reprinted by permission from Kahn (1998). Dynamic Diagrams. *http://www.dynamicdiagrams.com.*

Chapter 7 Opening Image: Courtesy William Wright, Visible Decisions.

7.1: © 1998 IEEE.

Chapter 8 Opening Image: Courtesy University of Maryland.

8.1: Courtesy of Christopher Ahlberg, Spotfire. *http://www.spotfire.com.*

8.2: A. Buja, D. Cook, D. F. Dwayne (1996). © 1996 American Statistical Association.

8.3: William Wright, Visible Decisions. *http://www.vdi.com.*

8.5: © 1995 Association for Computing Machinery, Inc.

8.6: D. A. Nation, C. Plaisant, G. Marchionini, and A. Komlodi (1996). © 1996 US West Communications.

Chapter 9 Opening Image: Courtesy Bell Labs, Lucent Technologies.

PAPERS

DeFanti, T. A., Brown, M. D., and McCormick, B. H. (1989). Visualization—Expanding Scientific and Engineering Research Opportunities. *IEEE Computer, 22*(8), 12–25. © 1989 IEEE. Reprinted with permission.

Bertin, J. (1981). *La Graphique et le Traitement Graphique de l'Information.* (English version: *Graphics and Graphic Information Processing.* Translated by Walter de Gruyter, Berlin, 24–31.) © 1981 Flammarion, Paris. Reprinted with permission.

Mackinlay, J. D. (1986). Automating the Design of Graphical Presentations of Relational Information. *ACM Transactions on Graphics, 5*(2), 111–141. © 1986 by the Association for Computing Machinery, Inc. Reprinted with permission.

Wright, W. (1995). Information Animation Applications in the Capital Markets. *Proceedings of IEEE Information Visualization'95,* 19–25, 136–137. © 1995 IEEE. Reprinted with permission.

Feiner, S., and Beshers, C. (1990). Worlds within Worlds: Metaphors for Exploring *n*-Dimensional Virtual Worlds. *Proceedings UIST'90,* 76–83. © 1990 by the Association for Computing Machinery, Inc. Reprinted with permission.

Inselberg, A. (1997). Multidimensional Detective. *Proceedings IEEE Information Visualization'97,* 100–107. © 1997 IEEE. Reprinted with permission.

Mihalisin, T., Timlin, J., and Schwegler, J. (1991). Visualizing Multivariate Functions, Data, and Distributions. *IEEE Computer Graphics and Applications, 11*(13), 28–35. © 1991 IEEE. Reprinted with permission.

Keim, D. A., and Kriegel, H.-P. (1994). VisDB: Database Exploration Using Multidimensional Visualization. *IEEE Computer Graphics and Applications,* September 1994, 40–49. © 1994 IEEE. Reprinted with permission.

Spoerri, A. (1993). InfoCrystal: A Visual Tool for Information Retrieval. *Proceedings of IEEE Visualization'93,* 150–157. © 1993 IEEE. Reprinted with permission.

Johnson, B., and Shneiderman, B. (1991). Treemaps: A Space-Filling Approach to the Visualization of Hierarchal Information Structures. *Proceedings of IEEE Information Visualization'91,* 275–282. © 1991 IEEE. Reprinted with permission.

Baker, M. J., and Eick, S. G. (1995). Space-Filling Software Visualization. *Journal of Visual Languages and Computing, 6,* 119–133. By permission of the publisher Academic Press Limited, London.

Jin, L., and Banks, D. C. (1997). TennisViewer: A Browser for Competition Trees. *IEEE Computer Graphics and Applications,* July/August, 63–65. © 1997 IEEE. Reprinted with permission.

Fairchild, K. M., Poltrock, S. E., and Furnas, G. W. (1988). SemNet: Three-Dimensional Representations of Large Knowledge Bases. In R. Guindon (ed.), *Cognitive Science and Its Applications for Human-Computer Interaction,* 201–233. © 1988 Lawrence Erlbaum Associates, Inc. Reprinted with permission.

Eick, S. G., and Wills, G. J. (1993). Navigating Large Networks with Hierarchies. *IEEE Proceedings Information Visualization'93,* 204–210. © 1993 IEEE. Reprinted with permission.

Becker, R. A., Eick, S. G., and Wilks, A. R. (1995). Visualizing Network Data. *IEEE Transactions on Visualization and Computer Graphics, 1*(1), 16–28. © 1995 IEEE. Reprinted with permission.

Shneiderman, B. (1994). Dynamic Queries for Visual Information Seeking. *IEEE Software, 11*(6), 70–77. © 1994 IEEE. Reprinted with permission.

Ahlberg, C., and Shneiderman, B. (1994). Visual Information Seeking: Tight Coupling of Dynamic Query Filters with Starfield Displays. *Proceedings CHI'94,* 313–317, 479–480. © 1994 by the Association for Computing Machinery, Inc. Reprinted with permission.

Eick, S. G. (1994). Data Visualization Sliders. *Proceedings UIST'94,* 119–120. © 1994 by the Association for Computing Machinery, Inc. Reprinted with permission.

Fishkin, K., and Stone, M. C. (1995). Enhanced Dynamic Queries via Movable Filters. *Proceedings of CHI'95,* 415–420. © 1995 by the Association for Computing Machinery, Inc. Reprinted with permission.

Chuah, M. C., Roth, S. F., Mattis, J., and Kolojejchick, J. A. (1995). SDM: Selective Dynamic Manipulation of Visualizations. *Proceedings UIST'95,* 61–70. © 1995 by the Association for Computing Machinery, Inc. Reprinted with permission.

Tweedie, L., Spence, R., Dawkes, H., and Su, H. (1996). Externalizing Abstract Mathematical Models. *Proceedings CHI'96,* 406–412. © 1996 by the Association for Computing Machinery, Inc. Reprinted with permission.

Plaisant, C., Milash, B., Rose, A., Widoff, S., and Shneiderman, B. (1996). LifeLines: Visualizing Personal Histories. *Proceedings CHI'96,* 221–227. © 1996 by the Association for Computing Machinery, Inc. Reprinted with permission.

Kumar, H. P., Plaisant, C., and Shneiderman, B. (1997). Browsing Hierarchical Data with Multi-Level Dynamic Queries and Pruning. *International Journal of Human-Computer Studies, 46*(1), 103–124. By permission of the publisher Academic Press Limited, London.

Furnas, G. W. (1981). *The FISHEYE View: A New Look at Structured Files.* © 1981 Bellcore. Reprinted with permission.

Spence, R., and Apperley, M. D. (1982). Data Base Navigation: An Office Environment for the Professional. *Behaviour and Information Technology, 1*(1), 43–54. © 1982 Taylor & Francis, UK. Reprinted with permission.

Rao, R., and Card, S. K. (1994). The Table Lens: Merging Graphical and Symbolic Representations in an Interactive Focus + Context Visualization for Tabular Information. *Proceedings CHI'94,* 318–322. © 1994 by the Association for Computing Machinery, Inc. Reprinted with permission.

Leung, Y. K., and Apperley, M. D. (1994). A Review and Taxonomy of Distortion-Orientation Presentation Techniques. *ACM Transactions on Computer-Human Interaction, 1*(2), 126–160. © 1994 by the Association for Computing Machinery, Inc. Reprinted with permission.

Carpendale, M. S. T., Cowperthwaite, D. J., and Fracchia, F. D. (1997). Extending Distortion Viewing from 2D to 3D. *IEEE Computer Graphics and Applications,* July/August, 42–51. © 1997 IEEE. Reprinted with permission.

Lamping, J., and Rao, R. (1996). The Hyperbolic Browser: A Focus + Context Technique for Visualizing Large Hierarchies. *Journal of Visual Languages and Computing, 7*(1), 33–55. By permission of the publisher Academic Press Limited, London.

Salton, G., Allan, J., Buckley, C., and Singhal, A. (1995). Automatic Analysis, Theme Generation, and Summarization of Machine-Readable Text. *Science, 264*(3), 1421–1426. Reprinted with permission. © 1995 American Association for the Advancement of Science.

Eick, S. G., Steffen, J. L., and Sumner, E. E. (1992). SeeSoft—A Tool for Visualizing Line Oriented Statistics

Software. *IEEE Transactions on Software Engineering, 18*(11), 957–968. © 1992 IEEE. Reprinted with permission.

Lin, X. (1992). Visualization for the Document Space. *Proceedings of IEEE Visualization'92,* 274–281. © 1992 IEEE. Reprinted with permission.

Wise, J. A., Thomas, J. J., Pennock, K., Lantrip, D., Pottier, M., Schur, A., and Crow, V. (1995). Visualizing the Non-Visual: Spatial Analysis and Interaction with Information from Text Documents. *Proceedings of IEEE Information Visualization'95,* 51–58, 140. © 1995 IEEE. Reprinted with permission.

Rennison, E. (1994). Galaxy of News: An Approach to Visualizing and Understanding Expansive News Landscapes. *Proceedings of UIST'94,* 3–12. © 1994 by the Association for Computing Machinery, Inc. Reprinted with permission.

Bray, T. (1996). Measuring the Web. *Fifth International World Wide Web Conference'96.* © 1996 Elsevier Science, UK.

Andrews, K. (1995). Visualizing Cyberspace: Information Visualization in the Harmony Internet Browser. *Proceedings of IEEE Information Visualization'95,* 90–96. © 1995 IEEE. Reprinted with permission.

Hendley, R. J., Drew, N. S., Wood, A. M., and Beale, R. (1995). Narcissus: Visualizing Information. *Proceedings of IEEE Information Visualization'95,* 90–96, 146. © 1995 IEEE. Reprinted with permission.

Robertson, G. G., Card, S. K., and Mackinlay, J. D. (1993). Information Visualization Using 3D Interactive Animation. *Communications of the ACM, 36*(4), 57–71. © 1993 by the Association for Computing Machinery, Inc. Reprinted with permission.

Bederson, B. B., and Hollan, J. D. (1994). Pad++: A Zooming Graphical Interface for Exploring Alternate Interface Physics. *Proceedings of UIST'94,* 17–22. © 1994 by the Association for Computing Machinery, Inc. Reprinted with permission.

Card, S. K., Robertson, G. G., and York, W. (1996). The WebBook and the Web Forager: An Information Workspace for the World-Wide Web. *Proceedings of CHI'96,* 111–117. © 1996 by the Association for Computing Machinery, Inc. Reprinted with permission.

Risch, J. S., Rex, D. B., Dowson, S. T., Walters, T. B., May, R. A., and Moon, B. D. (1997). The STARLIGHT Information Visualization System. *IEEE Proceedings International Conference on Information Visualization'97,* 42–49. © 1997 IEEE. Reprinted with permission.

Robertson, G. G., and Mackinlay, J. D. (1993). The Document Lens. *Proceedings of UIST'93,* 101–108. © 1993 by the Association for Computing Machinery, Inc. Reprinted with permission.

North, C., Shneiderman, B., and Plaisant, C. (1996). User Controlled Overviews of an Image Library: A Case Study of the Visible Human. *Proceedings of ACM Digital Libraries'96,* 74–82. © 1996 by the Association for Computing Machinery, Inc. Reprinted with permission.

Card, S. K., Pirolli, P., and Mackinlay, J. D. (1994). The Cost-of-Knowledge Characteristic Function: Display Evaluation for Direct Walk Information Visualizations. *Proceedings of CHI'94,* 238–244. © 1994 by the Association for Computing Machinery, Inc. Reprinted with permission.

Furnas, G. W. (1997). Effective View Navigation. *Proceedings of CHI'97,* 367–374. © 1997 by the Association for Computing Machinery, Inc. Reprinted with permission.

Pirolli, P., and Rao, R. (1996). Table Lens as a Tool for Making Sense of Data. In Catarci, T., Costabilem, M. F., Levialdi, S., and Santucci, G. (eds.), *Workshop on Advanced Visual Interfaces: AVI-96,* 67–80. © 1996 by the Association for Computing Machinery, Inc. Reprinted with permission.

Tweedie, L. A. (1997). Characterizing Interactive Externalizations. *Proceedings of CHI'97,* 375–382. © 1997 by the Association for Computing Machinery, Inc. Reprinted with permission.

CHAPTER 1

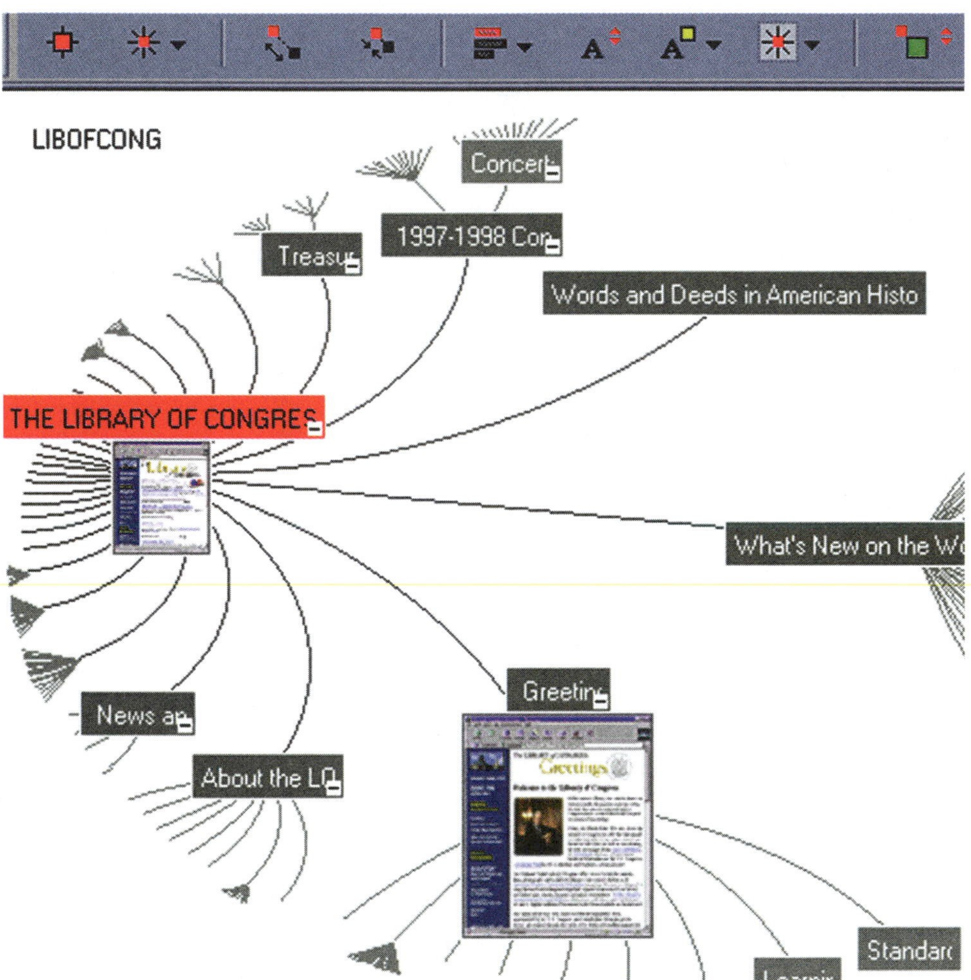

Graphics is the visual means of resolving logical problems.

– *Bertin (1977/1981, p. 16)*

Information Visualization

To understand something is called "seeing" it. We try to make our ideas "clear," to bring them into "focus," to "arrange" our thoughts. The ubiquity of visual metaphors in describing cognitive processes hints at a nexus of relationships between what we see and what we think. When we imagine someone hard at mental work, we might picture a scholar drawing a diagram, a book of sources open at her side. Or we might imagine a stockbroker, watching computer displays of financial data, rushing to act on events. Whatever the activity, mental work and perceptual interactions of the world are likely to be interwoven.

This interweaving of interior mental action and external perception (and manipulation) is no accident. It is the essence of how we achieve expanded intelligence. As Norman says,

> *The power of the unaided mind is highly overrated. Without external aids, memory, thought, and reasoning are all constrained. But human intelligence is highly flexible and adaptive, superb at inventing procedures and objects that overcome its own limits. The real powers come from devising external aids that enhance cognitive abilities. How have we increased memory, thought, and reasoning? By the invention of external aids: It is things that make us smart.* (Norman, 1993, p. 43)

An important class of the external aids that make us smart are graphical inventions of all sorts. These serve two related but quite distinct purposes. One purpose is for communicating an idea, for which it is sometimes said, "A picture is worth ten thousand words."[1] Communicating an idea requires, of course, already having the idea to communicate. The second purpose is to use graphical means to create or discover the idea itself: using the special properties of visual perception to resolve logical problems, as Bertin (1977/1981) would say. *Using vision to think.* This second sense of graphics is the subject of this book.

Graphic aids for thinking have an ancient and venerable history. What is new is that the evolution of computers is making possible a medium for graphics with dramatically improved rendering, real-time interactivity, and dramatically lower cost. This medium allows graphic depictions that automatically assemble thousands of data objects into pictures, revealing hidden patterns. It allows diagrams that move, react, or even initiate. These, in turn, create new methods for amplifying cognition, new means for coming to knowledge and insight about the world. A few years ago, the power of this new medium was applied to science, resulting in scientific visualization. Now it is possible to apply the medium more generally to business, to scholarship, and to education. This broader application goes under the name of *information visualization.* The purpose of this book is to introduce information visualization, to collect some of the important papers in the field, and to give samples of some of the latest work.

EXTERNAL COGNITION

To understand the intuition behind information visualization, it is useful to gain an appreciation for the important role of the external world in thought and reasoning. This notion is sometimes called *external cognition* (Scaife and Rogers, 1996) to express the way in which internal and external representations and processing weave together in thought. As Norman suggests, the use of the external world, and especially the use of cognitive artifacts or physical inventions to enhance cognition, is all around us.

Multiplication Aids

Take multiplication, one of the most mental of activities. Have a person multiply a pair of two-digit numbers, such as 34 × 72, in his or her head and time how long it takes. Now repeat the experiment with another pair of numbers, in longhand using pencil and paper.

$$\begin{array}{r} 34 \\ \times 72 \\ \hline 68 \\ 23^{2}80 \\ \hline 24^{1}48 \end{array}$$

[1]According to Paul Martin Lester, professor of communications at the University of California at Fullerton, this quotation was simply made up by ad writer Frederick R. Barnard and included as an invented "Chinese proverb" in a streetcar advertisement for Royal Baking Powder. The ad writer wanted to make the point that pictures can attract attention faster than other media. See *http://www5.Fullerton.edu/les/ad.html* and *Printers' Ink*, March 10, 1927.

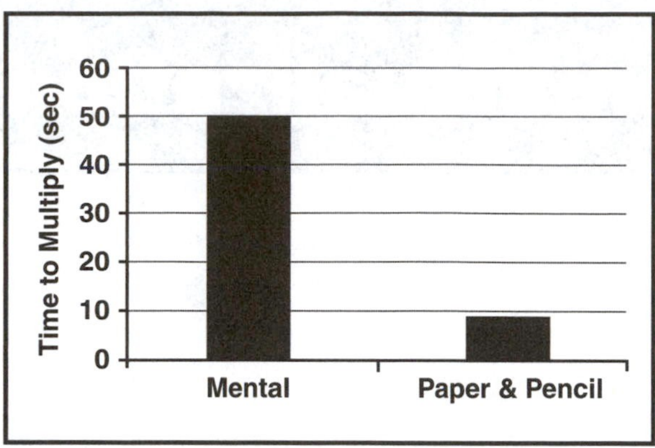

FIGURE **1.1**

Use of external aids amplifies ability to do multiplication.

Figure 1.1 shows the result of trying this experiment on a hapless colleague: pencil and paper reduced the time by a factor of five. (Too keep the story simple, we made sure that none of the digits was 0 or 1 and that the colleague did not know the Tractenberg or other special system for mental multiplication). As this informal demonstration shows, visual and manipulative use of the external world amplifies cognitive performance, even for this supposedly mental task. And if we had chosen to multiply 3- or 4-digit numbers—or 25-digit numbers—then the task would have quickly become impossible to do mentally at all (at least without special methods).

Why does using pencil and paper make such a difference? Quite simply, mental multiplication is not itself difficult. What is difficult is holding the partial results in memory until they can be used. The visual representation, by holding partial results outside the mind, extends a person's working memory. Applying this principle backwards, people can learn apparently astonishing feats of mental arithmetic by learning special algorithms like the Tractenberg system that minimize internal working memory (Cutler and McShane, 1960). The cost is in the extra effort to learn the algorithms.

Manipulable, external visual representations like long-hand arithmetic with paper and pencil work a different way from the algorithmic tricks. By writing intermediate results in neatly aligned columns (plus little numbers for carries), the doer of multiplication creates a visual addressing structure that minimizes visual search and speeds access. An internal memory task is converted to an external visual search and manual writing task.

External visual representations for multiplication can work in other ways as well. The slide rule is an analogue interactive visual device that represents quantities as scales with length proportional to their logarithms. Sliding the scales adds these lengths and hence multiplies the quantities (Figure 1.2). Instead of aiding cognition by extending working memory, the slide rule actually does the visual computation (except for placing the decimal point). There are no partial results at all. Slide rules are devices for interactive manipulation of good visual representations.

Nomographs are visual devices that allow specialized computations. The nomograph in Figure 1.3 allows visual calculations and trade-offs for the design of a water conduit. Water needs to be conveyed from a storage pond to a powerhouse by a ditch or a pipe. At the powerhouse, it will be converted to mechanical rotational energy and then to electric energy. The ditch will absorb some of the energy from the water. Suppose we want to know what slope to give a

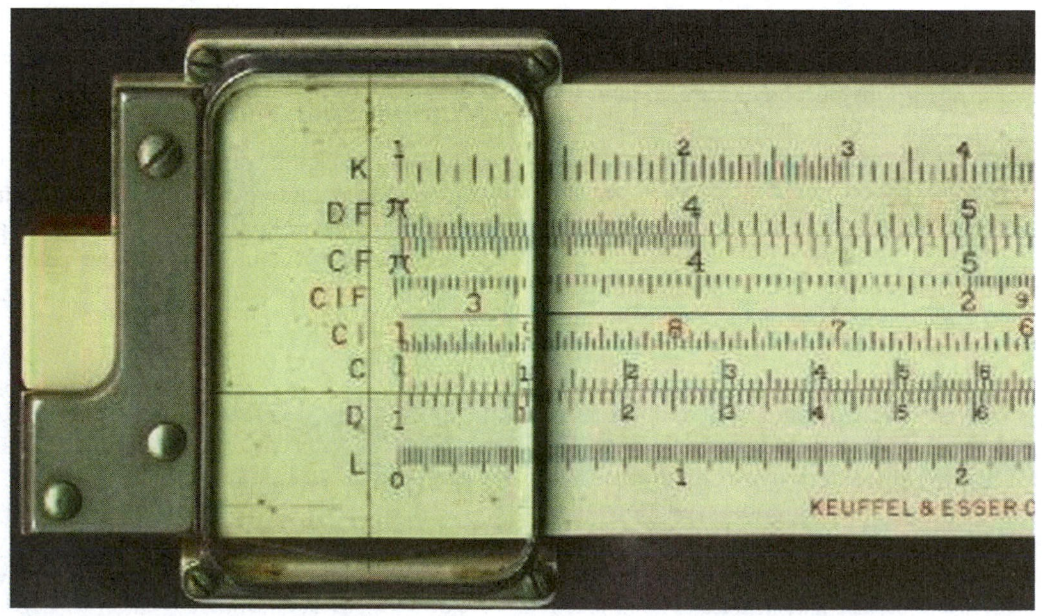

FIGURE **1.2**

Section of a slide rule.

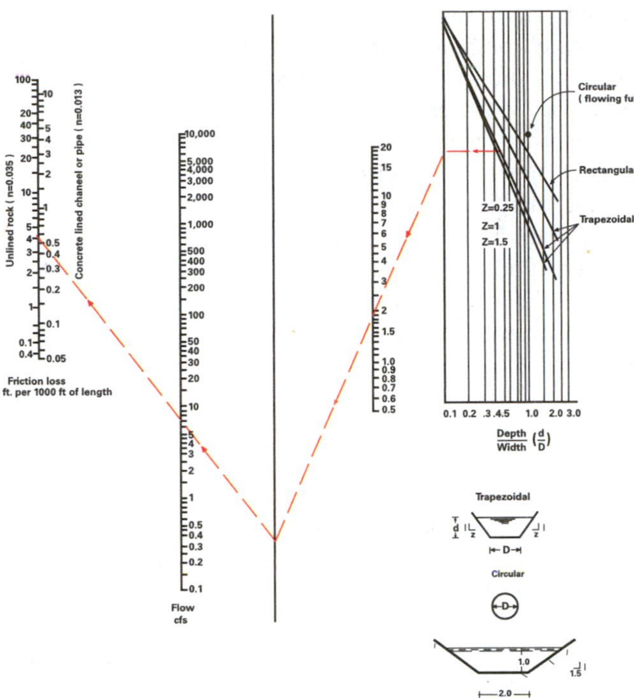

FIGURE **1.3**

Nomograph for determining friction loss in a conduit (Leckie et al., 1975, p. 66).

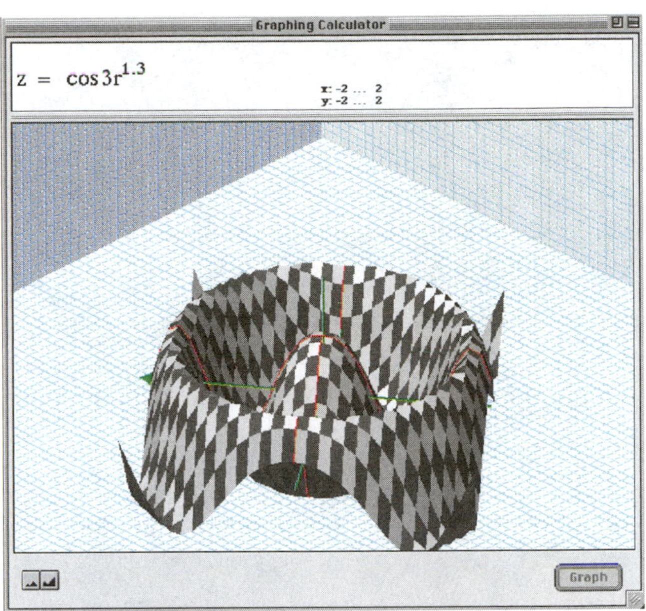

FIGURE **1.4**

The Apple Graphing Calculator.

trapezoidal rock ditch in order to overcome frictional losses and deliver 7 cubic ft/sec to the powerhouse. The base of the ditch is $D = 2$ ft. Its sides are inclined at 1:1.5. Water is to be carried at a depth of $d = 1$ ft. We use the nomograph as follows:

1. On the right side of the nomograph, we locate the point corresponding to a ratio of $d/D = 1/2 = 0.5$ and the line $Z = 1.5$ for the slope of the sides of the ditch.
2. With a ruler, we determine a line between that point and $D = 2$ ft on the next scale. This determines a point on the Center Reference Line of the diagram.
3. We now use that point and the required flow rate of 7 cfs on the Flow cfs scale to determine a new line.
4. We read our answer on the Friction Loss scale of about 4 ft drop/1000 ft of ditch length, which equals 0.4% slope.

We could easily do "what if" calculations, just by adjusting slightly the position of the ruler. What happens if we make the ditch rectangular? if we use a pipe? if our requirements for flow are changed? This reasoning, trivial with the nomograph, would be difficult to do in the head (unless you were a specialist) or even with a calculator.

Slide rules were superseded as computational devices by pocket calculators. The lesson is that although visually based devices can aid mental abilities, they are not the only means of augmentation. Direct computational devices may do as well or better. But then the direct computational devices may themselves become a component of an even more powerful visually based system. An example is the Graphing Calculator (Avitzur, Robins, and Newman, 1994). In Figure 1.4, the user has typed in a simple trigonometric formula to evaluate $z = \cos 3r^{1.3}$. Instantly, a visualization is displayed involving perhaps millions of computations of the sort that would be done by a slide rule or a simple pocket calculator. The user could not quickly absorb this many calculations. Figure 1.4, on the other hand, produces insight that occasionally surprises even people with some mathematical sophistication. The visualization is designed with skill. The muted background provides orientation. Lighting is used to give the different axes identity. The graph itself uses a checkered pattern and lighting effects that enhance contours. The user can set the figure into spinning animation, highlighting the 3D effect and revealing the figure from different angles. If the number 3 in the formula is replaced by n, a slider control appears. The slider can vary n, showing its effect on the graph. The slider can even be put into automatic animation.

Navigation Charts

Let us consider another example of a visual aid to cognition, navigating at sea. Virtually all computations of a ship's position are done using a nautical chart (see Hutchins, 1996) of the sort shown in Figure 1.5. The chart is a navigator's main representation of position, even though the chart shows a view that no navigator ever sees. In fact, because the earth is round and it is convenient to use flat charts, compromised projections of the round earth on the flat chart must be used such that graphical operations performed on the charts will work.

A navigation chart is really a sort of visual analogue computing device for navigation. With the chart, the navigator can compute a ship's compass heading to its destination if the destination is not too far. If the trip is long, however, a

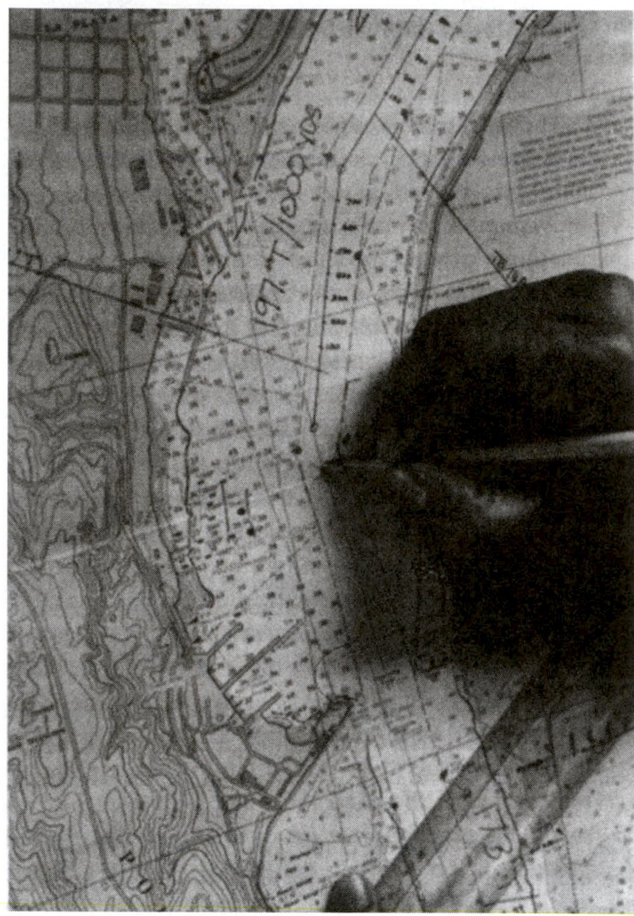

FIGURE **1.5**

Navigation chart in use (Hutchins, 1996, Figure 1.3).

constant heading becomes a spiral around the pole. A Mercator projection transforms this spiral back into a straight line. But radio beacons and the shortest line to distant points follow a great circle route, which is not a straight line on either projection. A straightedge ruler can, however, be used to plot a great circle route as a straight line on a Lambert projection. Each type of map sacrifices accurate representation of some physical property of the earth, because its true purpose is to support specific calculations. Of course, irregular features on the earth's surface can modify a straight route: coastline shapes, ocean depths, political ownership of territory, navigational beacons. The map is not just a calculator but also a storage device, storing for access enormous amounts of information about the earth's irregular features naturally located near where they are needed for calculation.

Diagrams

Diagrams are another important class of visual aids, although they are usually not interactive. Diagrams can lead to great insight, but also to the lack of it. Tufte (1997) cites as an example the accident of the space shuttle *Challenger*. There was a question whether the shuttle should be launched on a cold day. The decision depended on whether the temperature would make the O-rings that sealed the sections of the booster rockets unsafe. Figure 1.6 reprints one of the diagrams used for this decision by the booster rocket manufacturer to analyze earlier launch damage to the booster seals. On the chart, boosters are shown in historical order of launch. The choice of presentation obscures the important variables of interest: temperature is shown textually rather than graphically; degree of damage is not mapped onto a natural graphical scale (and there is no legend). Diagrams of the rockets clutter the chart, making other patterns difficult to see. Consequently, the diagram reveals no obvious patterns. It seems to show that the incidents of damage are relatively few.

Tufte's chart of the same data (Figure 1.7) tells a different story. It uses a simple scattergraph depicting the relationship between the two major variables of interest. Different types of damage are combined into a single index of severity. The proposed launch temperature is also put on the chart to show it in relation to the data. The diagram reveals a clear pattern of damage for launches below 65°. In fact, the new diagram shows that there was always damage below 65° and that the most serious damage occurred at the lowest temperature. It shows that the proposed launch is *very* much

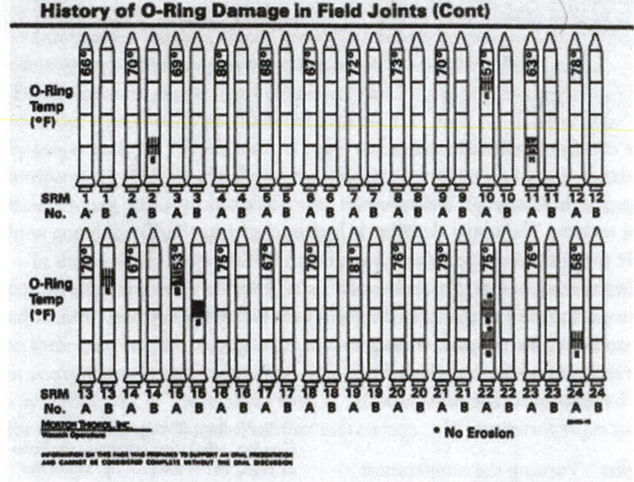

FIGURE **1.6**

One of the diagrams of O-ring damage used to make the decision to launch *Challenger* (Nielson, Hagen, and Muller, 1997, vol. v, p. 896).

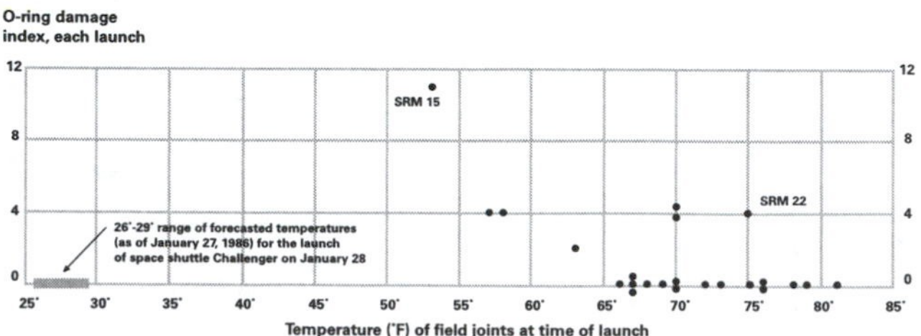

FIGURE **1.7**

Scattergraph of O-ring damage index as a function of temperature (Tufte, 1997, p. 45).

colder than this previous lowest temperature. Had the engineers seen this diagram instead of Figure 1.6, it is difficult to believe they would have recommended launch. The diagram illustrates how the right representation of a problem, often the right visual representation, can make a problematic decision obvious. It also illustrates Tufte's point that "There are right ways and wrong ways to show data; there are displays that reveal the truth and displays that do not" (Tufte, 1997, p. 45).

A related but different lesson comes from the next two diagrams. The first of these, Figure 1.8, shows the sleep/wake cycles of a newborn infant (Winfree, 1987). In these diagrams, a good representation reveals surprisingly simple patterns embedded in massive data and great complexity. Each line in Figure 1.8 represents time sleeping, and each dot is a feeding. In the weeks after birth, the sleep cycle shows considerable irregularity, but we can detect the natural 25-hour patterns exhibited by humans when they are isolated from the light/dark cycle of the day. Around the 17th week, the infant's sleep/wake cycle synchronizes with the 24-hour solar day. The diagram presents every one of some three million observations, yet allows the large-scale pattern to be detected.

The second diagram, Figure 1.9, shows another time cycle aggregated from massive data and calculations. Tides at any given point on earth generally have a cycle of around 12 h 26 m. A more complex picture emerges if we ask what are all of the points on the earth that are in the same tide phase at a given time. High tide cannot be everywhere at once, since there is only a fixed amount of water in the ocean. While some places on earth are in high tide, others must be in low tide or in between the two. The figure plots the tidal phase of each point of earth relative to Greenwich, England, by mapping tidal phase onto the color wheel (used because the color wheel is circularly continuous without a zero point). The figure reveals the surprising existence of singularities called *anphidromic points,* points at which there are no tides at all. *Cotidal lines* (contour lines consisting of points at the same tide phase) circulate around these anphidromic points, some clockwise, some counterclockwise. The diagram makes it possible to comprehend this phenomenon, which is unintuitive and made more complicated by the irregular shape of the earth's landmasses.

As our brief examination illustrates, visual artifacts aid thought; in fact, they are completely entwined with cognitive action. The progress of civilization can be read in the invention of visual artifacts, from writing to mathematics, to maps, to printing, to diagrams, to visual computing. As Norman says, "The real powers come from devising external aids that enhance cognitive abilities." Information visualization is about just that—exploiting the dynamic, interactive, inexpensive medium of graphical computers to devise new external aids enhancing cognitive abilities. It seems obvious that it can be done. It is clear that the visual artifacts we have discussed so far have profound effects on peoples' abilities to assimilate information, to compute with it, to understand it, to create new knowledge. Visual artifacts and computers do for the mind what cars do for the feet or steam

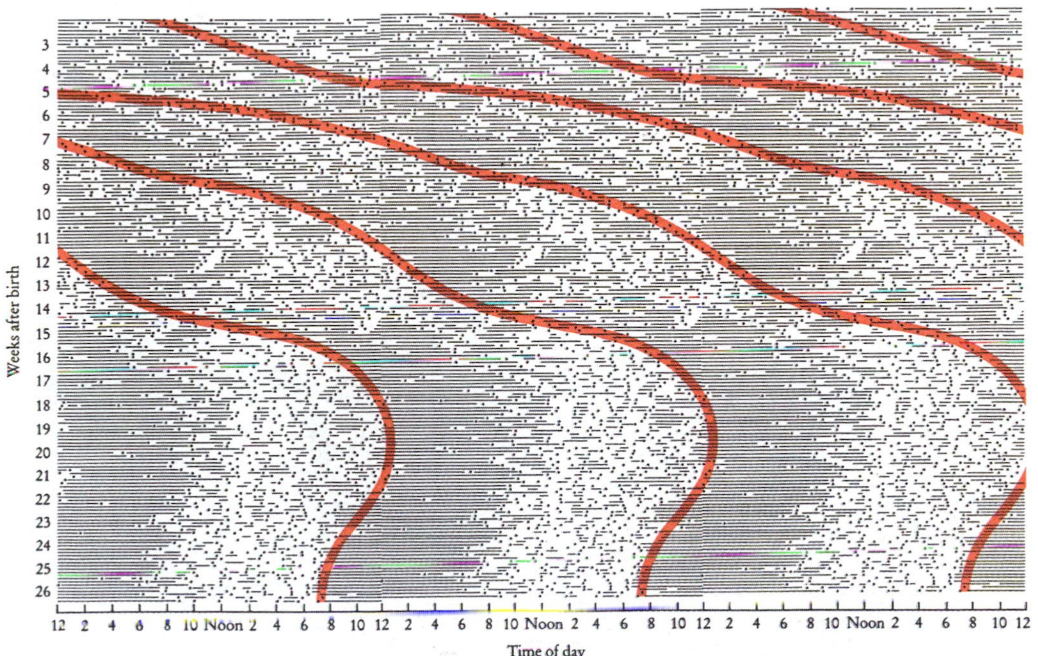

FIGURE **1.8**

Sleep/wake cycles of a newborn infant. To make the cycles easier to see, each line starts a new day, but three days are plotted on each line. The infant transitions from the natural human 25-hour cycle at birth to the 24-hour solar day (Winfree, 1987, p. 31).

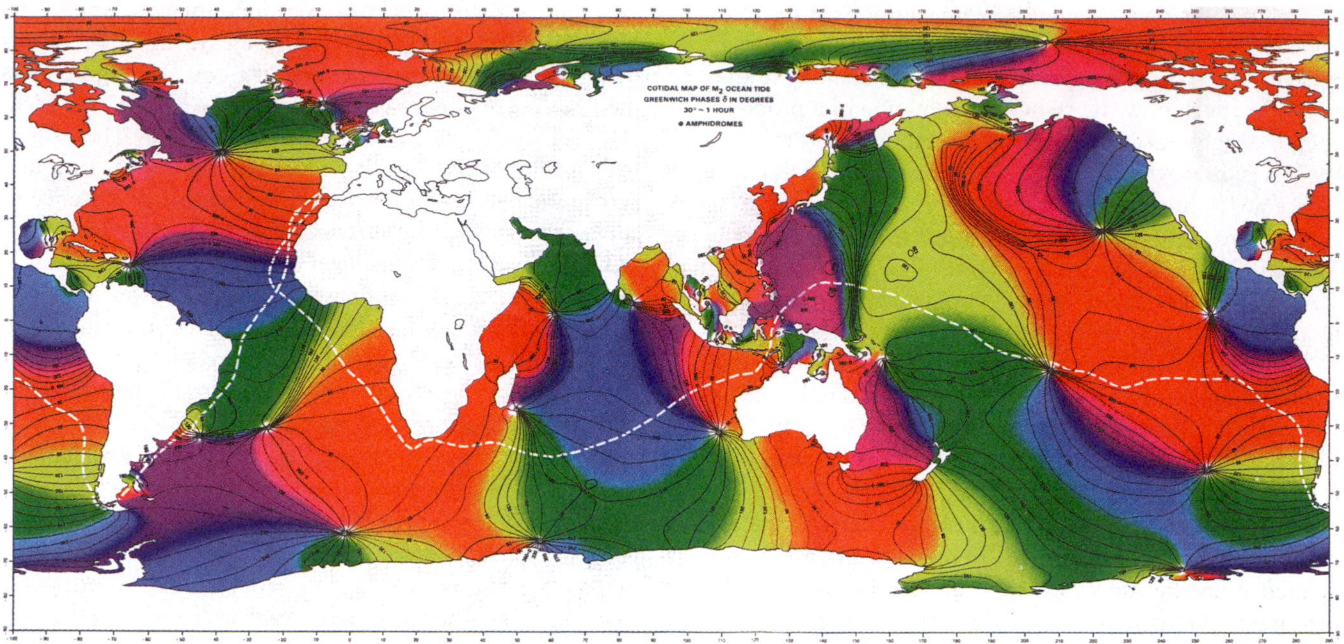

FIGURE **1.9**

Cotidal chart. Tide phases relative to Greenwich are plotted for all the world's oceans. Phase progresses from red to orange to yellow to green to blue to purple. The lines converge on anphidromic points. The dotted white line shows the route of Magellan's ship (Winfree, 1987, p. 17).

shovels do for the hands. But it remains to puzzle out through cycles of system building and analysis how to build the next generation of such artifacts.

INFORMATION VISUALIZATION

Several activities are concerned with the creation of visual artifacts, and we need to disentangle their relationships in order to set information visualization in context. Let us start with the notion of visualization itself, which we define as follows:

VISUALIZATION:

> The use of computer-supported, interactive, visual representations of data to amplify cognition.

Cognition is the acquisition or use of knowledge. This definition has the virtue of focusing as much on the purpose of visualization as the means. Hamming (1973) said, "The purpose of computation is insight, not numbers." Likewise for visualization, "The purpose of visualization is insight, not pictures." The main goals of this insight are *discovery, decision making,* and *explanation.* Information visualization is useful to the extent that it increases our ability to perform these and other cognitive activities.

Visualization dates as an organized subfield from the NSF report, *Visualization in Scientific Computing* (McCormick and DeFanti, 1987). There it is conceived as a tool to permit handling large sets of scientific data and to enhance scientists' ability to see phenomena in the data. Although it is not a necessity of the original conception, scientific visualizations tend to be based on physical data—the human body, the earth, molecules, or other. The computer is used to render visible some properties. While visualizations may derive from abstractions on this physical space, the information is nevertheless inherently geometrical. For example, in Figure 1.10, a visualization of ozone concentration in the atmosphere, the visualization is based on a physical 3D representation of the earth. In Figure 1.11, a visualization of fluid flow around a hemispherical surface, the colors of the tubes show changes in the eigenvector of the stress tensor of flow.

Both of these visualizations show abstractions, but the abstractions are based on physical space. Nonphysical infor-

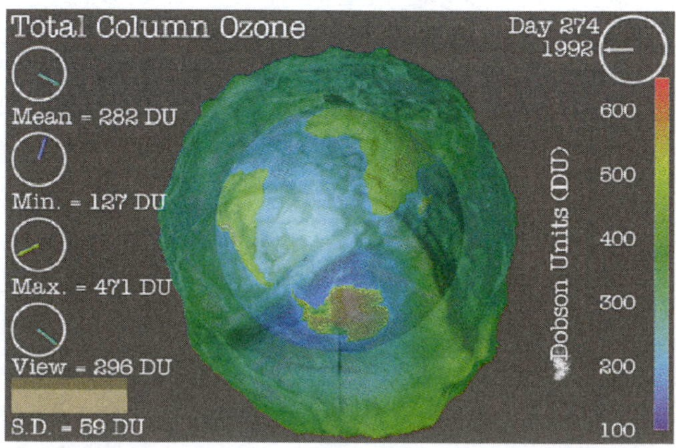

FIGURE **1.10**

Ozone layer surrounding earth. L. Treinish, IBM. Used with permission.

FIGURE **1.11**

Stress tensor in a flow past a hemisphere cylinder (Lavin, Levy, and Hesselink, 1997, Figure 5).

mation—such as financial data, business information, collections of documents, and abstract conceptions—may also benefit from being cast in a visual form, but this is information that does not have any obvious spatial mapping. In addition to the problem of how to render visible properties of the objects of interest, there is the more fundamental problem of mapping nonspatial abstractions into effective visual form. There is a great deal of such abstract information in the contemporary world, and its mass and complexity are a problem, motivating attempts to extend visualization into the realm of the abstract (Card, Robertson, and Mackinlay, 1991). As we saw before, visual aids to cognition benefit from good visual representations of a problem and from interactive manipulation of those representations. We define *information visualization* as follows:

> **INFORMATION VISUALIZATION:**
>
> The use of computer-supported, interactive, visual representations of abstract data to amplify cognition.

In Table 1.1, we have recorded a number of working definitions to clarify the relationships among concepts related to information visualization. *External cognition* is concerned with the interaction of cognitive representations and processes across the external/internal boundary in order to support thinking. *Information design* is the explicit attempt to design external representations to amplify cognition. *Data graphics* is the design of visual but abstract representations of data for this purpose. *Visualization* uses the computer for data graphics. *Scientific visualization* is visualization applied to scientific data, and *information visualization* is visualization applied to abstract data. The reasons why these two diverge are that scientific data are often physically based, whereas business information and other abstract data are often not. It should be noted that while we are emphasizing visualization, the general case is for *perceptualization.* It is just as possible to design systems for information *sonification* or *tactilization* of data as for multiple perceptualizations. Indeed, there are advantages in doing so. But vision, the sense with by far the largest bandwidth, is the obvious place to start, and it would take us too far afield to cover all the senses here.

Origins of Information Visualization

These distinctions carry with them some of the historical evolution of this area. Information visualization derives from several communities. Work in data graphics dates from about the time of Playfair (1786), who seems to have been among the earliest to use abstract visual properties such as line and area to represent data visually (Tufte, 1983). Starting with Playfair, the classical methods of plotting data were developed. In 1967, Bertin, a French cartographer, published his theory of graphics in *The Semiology of Graphics* (Bertin, 1967/1983; Bertin, 1977/1981). This theory identified the basic elements of diagrams and described a framework for their design. Tufte (1983) published a theory of data graphics that emphasized maximizing the density of useful information. Both Bertin's and Tufte's theories became well known and influential in the various communities that led to the development of information visualization as a discipline.

Although the data graphics community was always concerned with statistical graphics, Tukey (1977) began a movement from within statistics with his work on *Exploratory Data Analysis.* The emphasis in this work was not on the quality of the graphics but on the use of pictures to give rapid statistical insight into data. For example, "box and whisker" plots allowed an analyst to see in an instant the most important four numbers that characterize a distribution. Rocking displays allowed an analyst to see 3D scatterplots without special glasses. Cleveland and McGill (1988) wrote an influential book, *Dynamic Graphics for Statistics,* explicating new visualizations of data in this area. A problem of particular interest was how to visualize data sets with many variables. Inselberg's parallel coordinates method (Inselberg

TABLE **1.1**

Definitions.

External Cognition	Use of the *external world* to accomplish cognition.
Information design	Design of *external representations* to amplify cognition.
Data graphics	Use of *abstract, nonrepresentational* visual representations of data to amplify cognition.
Visualization	Use of *computer-based, interactive* visual representations of data to amplify cognition.
Scientific visualization	Use of interactive visual representations of *scientific data,* typically *physically based,* to amplify cognition.
Information visualization	Use of interactive visual representations of *abstract, nonphysically based data* to amplify cognition.

and Dimsdale, 1990) and Mihalisin's technique of cycling through variables at different rates (Mihalisin, Timlin, and Schwegler, 1991 ●) were important contributions here. Eick's group worked on statistical graphics techniques for large-scale sets of data associated with important problems in telecommunications networks and in large computer programs (Becker et al., 1995 ●; Eick, Steffen, and Sumner, 1992 ●). The emphasis of the statisticians was on the analysis of multidimensional, multivariable data and on novel sorts of data.

In 1985, NSF launched an important new initiative on scientific visualization (McCormick and DeFanti, 1987). The first IEEE Visualization Conference was in 1990. This community was led by earth resource scientists, physicists, and computer scientists in supercomputing. Satellites were sending back large quantities of data, so visualization was useful as a method to accelerate its analysis and to enhance the identification of interesting phenomena. It was also promising as part of an effort to replace expensive experiments by computational simulation (e.g., for wind tunnels).

Meanwhile, there was interest by the computer graphics and artificial intelligence communities in automatic presentation, the automatic design of visual presentations of data. The effort was catalyzed by Mackinlay's thesis APT (Mackinlay, 1986a), which formalized Bertin's design theory, added psychophysical data, and used it to generate presentations. Roth and Mattis (1990) built a system to do more complex visualizations, such as some of those from Tufte. Casner (1991) added a representation of tasks. The concern for this community was not so much in the quality of the graphics as in automating the match between data types, communication intent, and graphical representations of the data.

Finally, the user interface community saw advances in graphics hardware opening the possibility of a new generation of user interfaces. These interfaces focused on user interaction with large amounts of information, such as multivariate databases or document collections. The first use of the term "information visualization" to our knowledge was in Robertson, Card, and Mackinlay (1989). Feiner and Beshers (1990b) presented a method, worlds within worlds, for showing six-dimensional financial data in immersive virtual reality. Shneiderman (1992b) developed a technique called *dynamic queries* for interactively selecting subsets of data items and treemaps, a space-filing representation for trees. Card, Robertson, and Mackinlay presented ways of using animation and distortion to interact with large data sets in a system called the *Information Visualizer* (Card, Robertson, and Mackinlay, 1991; Robertson, Mackinlay, and Card, 1991; Mackinlay, Robertson, and Card, 1991). The concern was again not so much the quality of the graphics as the means for cognitive amplification. Interactivity and animation were more important features of these systems.

These initial forays were followed by refinements and new visualizations, the different communities mutually influencing each other.

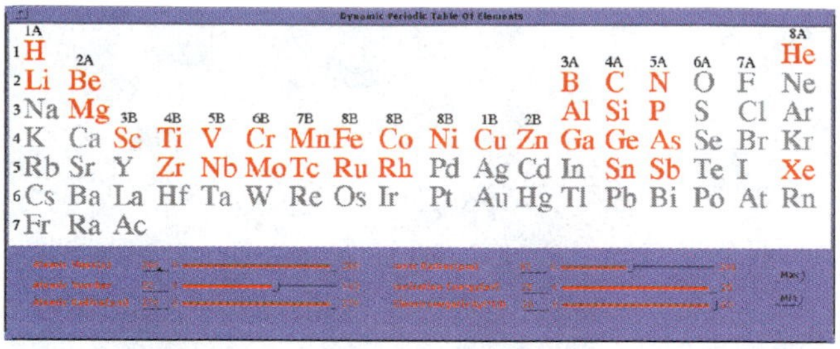

FIGURE **1.12**

Periodic table with dynamic queries sliders (Ahlberg, Williamson, and Shneiderman, 1992, Figure 2).

Active Diagrams

Let us consider some examples of information visualization to make clear what we mean. Our first example amplifies the effect of a good visual representation by making it interactive. The periodic table, created by Mendeleyev, is an important diagram in the development of chemistry. In the periodic table, elements are arranged by the number of protons in the atomic nucleus. The way the table is broken into rows and its nonrectangular appearance result from the order in which electrons populate electron subshells. Many physical and chemical properties, such as boiling point and chemical valence, form visual patterns when arranged by the periodic table. In fact, in Mendeleyev's lifetime, three elements whose properties were predicted from the periodic table were discovered: gallium, scandium, and germanium (Moore, 1962).

Figure 1.12 shows an information visualization based on the periodic table (Ahlberg, Williamson, and Shneiderman, 1992). The user can set sliders that control which of the elements in the table will be highlighted. For example, the user can indicate interest in ionic radii between 93 and 206 and instantly those values will be highlighted on the table. The sliders can be used to find specific values or to see the trends with the change of some variable. Since the periodic table is already an excellent visual organizer of chemical properties, adding dynamically created patterns on the table is effective.

Large-Scale Data Monitoring

The second example uses information visualization to monitor and make sense of large amounts of dynamic, real-time data. Figure 1.13 (see Wright, 1995 ●) is a depiction of visualization used in a decision-support application. This is an interest-rate, risk-hedging application for a broker-dealer's inventory of fixed-income instruments. The visualization is connected to a real-time database and analytical engine. It replaced 100 screens of rows and columns of numbers in a traditional database reporting system. The visualization shows a thousand bonds arranged by subportfolio along the left and time to maturity along the front. Bonds are shown as vertical

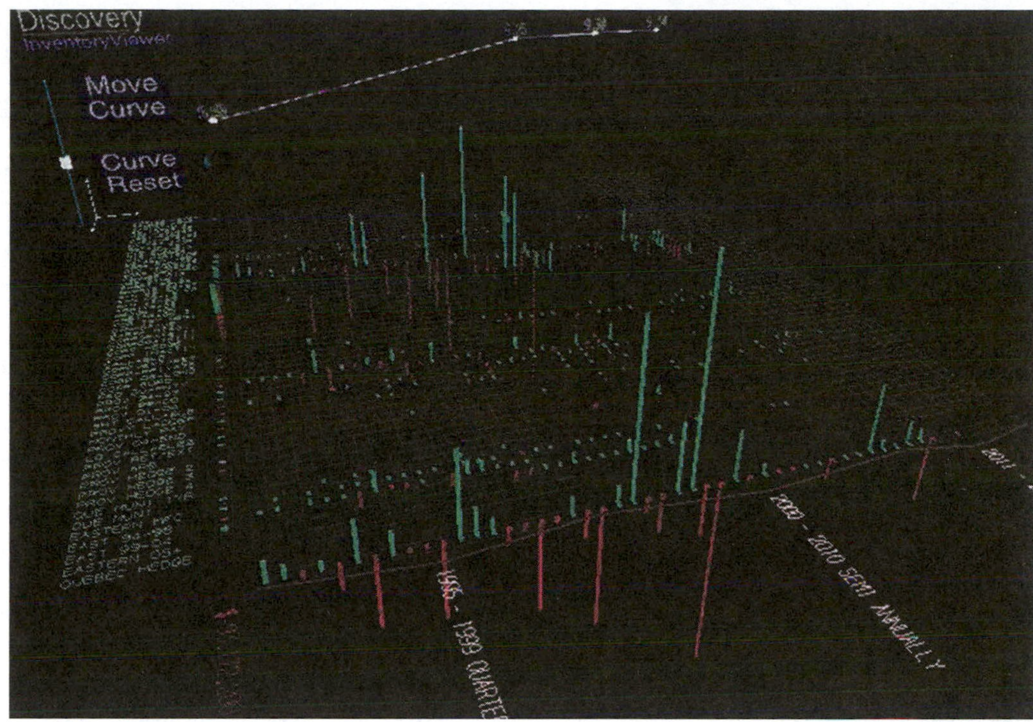

FIGURE **1.13**

Positions on the Toronto Stock Exchange. Used by permission of Visible Decisions, Inc.

bars—the higher the bar, the larger the amount of that bond in the portfolio. A total line along the front sums across all subportfolios. Different types of bonds are color coded. At the back is a yield curve. By simply grabbing the yield curve with the mouse and moving it, the user can interactively apply what-if interest rate risk scenarios across the bonds.

Presented as a set of numbers, it would be difficult for a human to monitor these positions and react quickly. Presented visually, it is easy both to spot the items of interest and to tell how these relate to similar stocks or the entire market at a certain point in time. Information visualization is particularly useful for monitoring large amounts of data in real time and under time pressure to make decisions.

Information Chromatography

Our third example uses a very abstract visualization of real-time data to detect complex new patterns in very large amounts of data: Visualization is used to detect telephone fraud. Figure 1.14 shows a visualization of 40,000 telephone calls, selected by region out of a data set of 20 million international telephone calls. The callers are laid out on a hexagonal grid. Display parameters have been adjusted to call links in a certain frequency range from the call and caller log time histograms in the lower left part of the figure. Figure 1.14 shows the visualization of a set of related calls. By interacting with the set of visualizations, the analyst in this case identified a pattern in which third parties would route calls from callers in two countries through the United States, charging a fee but then abandoning their phones before paying the bill. Telephone fraud perpetrators change

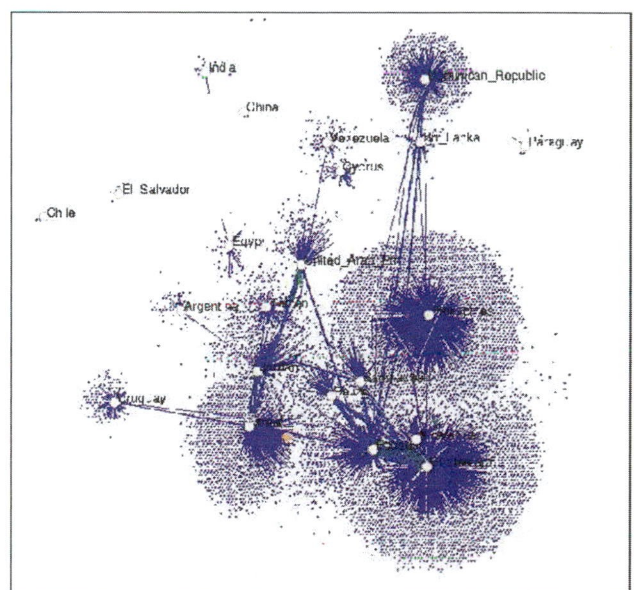

FIGURE **1.14**

Visualization used in detecting telephone fraud using Lucent Technologies NicheWorks program (Cox, Eick, and Wills, 1997, Figure 1). Used by permission of Lucent Technologies, Inc.

their patterns of activity frequently to avoid automatic detection algorithms. However, humans with visualization displays are good at picking out new patterns as they occur and thus can respond to changes in the patterns quickly. Information visualization allows human adaptivity to be brought to bear for large data sets under time pressure. We might think of this use as a kind of *information chromatography:* patterns in the data are revealed by laying them out on a particular visual substrate.

The examples of information visualization shown here make use of the power of diagrams, but they add the ability of computers to be interactive and to map large amounts of data into visual forms automatically. As we can see in the examples, the improvement in cognitive performance that occurs can happen for several reasons.

COGNITIVE AMPLIFICATION

Knowledge Crystallization

We have said that the purpose of information visualization is to use perception to amplify cognition. Let us give an example of a scenario in which this might happen:

> Sue is assigned to buy a laptop computer for a workgroup. If she wishes to make an intelligent choice, it is necessary to understand the purchaser's needs as well as what is on offer in the market. Sue consults the Internet and by a combination of search and browsing acquires documents and data sets relevant to the purchase. In addition, the purchaser acquires information from colleagues and trade magazines.
>
> The next step is to identify from materials found attributes of interest like processor speed, weight, thickness, and cost—a simple *schema.*
>
> The attributes are laid out in a table: products in rows, features in columns. The table rows and columns are reordered and some data is used to make charts. In the process of doing this exercise, the purchaser notices that some machines have interesting new features like high-speed infrared communication and "fire-wire" high-speed communication support for which there is no column. The table is amended with a new column for each of these. The exercise also reveals a lack of information on some of the models. This leads the user to retrieve more information to fill in the table. Using visualizations of table data, the user realizes that the various models represent trade-offs among processing power, multimedia, and portability.
>
> The purchaser then prepares a graphical presentation of two slides to the workgroup presenting the main trade-off (a decision for the group) and the best purchase for each of these trade-offs.

This scenario is an example of a *knowledge crystallization task* (see Figure 1.15). A knowledge crystallization task is one in which a person gathers information for some purpose, makes sense of it (Russell et al., 1993) by constructing a representational framework (which we will refer to as a *schema*), and then packages it into some form for communication or action. The results could be a briefing, a short

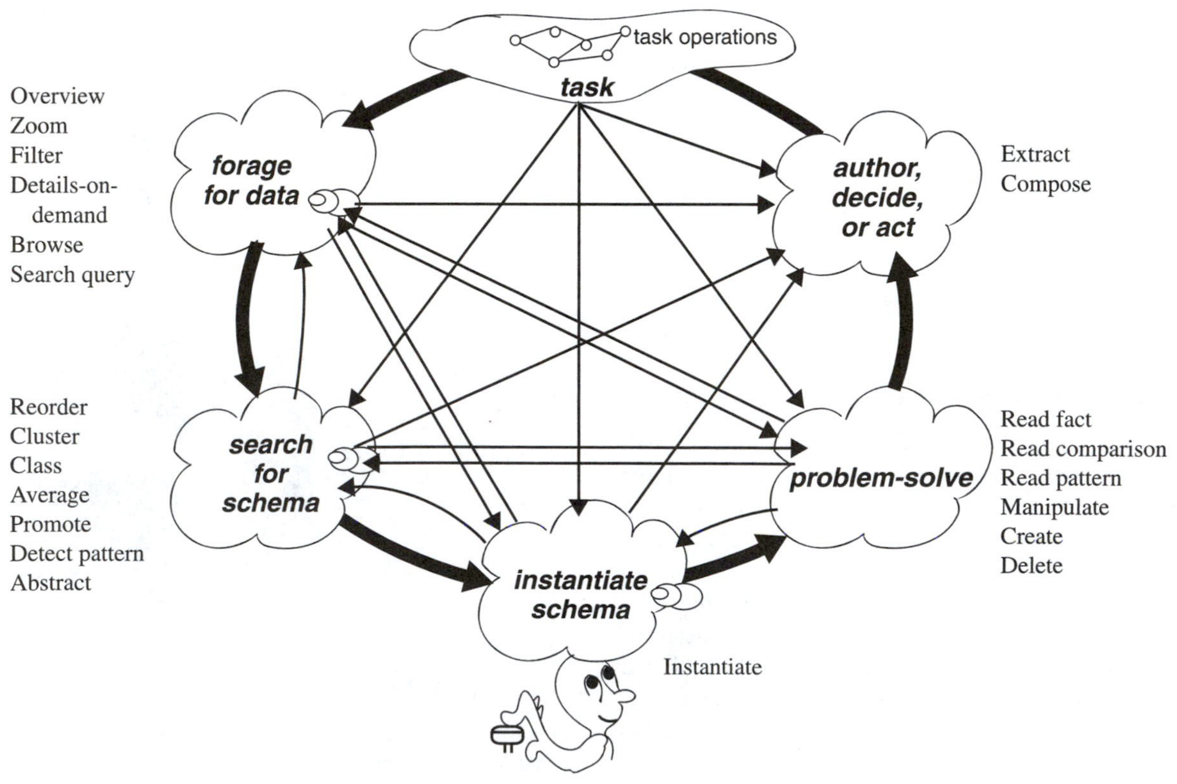

FIGURE **1.15**

Knowledge crystallization.

paper, or even a decision or action. Knowledge crystallization tasks are characterized by the use of large amounts of heterogeneous information, ill-structured problem solving, but a relatively well-defined goal requiring insight into information relative to some purpose. Knowledge crystallization tasks are one form of information-intensive work and can themselves be part of more complex forms of knowledge work, such as design. They are an important class of tasks that motivate attempts to develop information visualization.

The preceding scenario has many elements typical of knowledge crystallization as summarized in Figure 1.15. Let's take a closer look at these elements.

1. Information foraging.	Collecting articles and data on laptop computers.
2. Search for schema (representation).	Identification of attributes on which to compare laptops.
3. Instantiate schema with data. Residue is significant data that do not fit the schema. To reduce residue, go to Step 2 and improve schema.	Make table of laptops × attributes. Use a "remarks" column to record interesting properties that don't fit into table.
4. Problem-solve to trade off features.	Reorder rows and columns of laptop table. Create plots. Delete or mark laptops that are out of the running.
5. Search for a new schema that reduces the problem to a simple trade-off.	Cluster into three groups by rearranging the rows in the table, one each for power, multimedia capability, and portability. Within each cluster, delete all but the top one or two machines.
6. Package the patterns found in some output product.	Create concise briefing on decision for workgroup.

Knowledge crystallization involves getting insight about data relative to some task. This usually requires finding some representation (schema) for the data that is efficient for the task. Data are coded in the representation. This encoding leaves residue data that are unencoded or encoded inefficiently. If the residue is too important to ignore, then we search for a better schema. Otherwise, the residual data are omitted. This process of abstraction (that is, schematization) and omission of information is a fundamental principle of how an information processing organism or machine reduces the otherwise unmanageable glut of information to "an amount that can be processed by mental computing equipment with sufficient rapidity to be useful for responding to changing environmental circumstances" (Resnikoff, 1987, p. 9). As Resnikoff puts it:

> *[T]here appears to be a general* Principle of Selective Omission of Information *at work in all biological information processing systems. The sensory organs simplify and organize their inputs, supplying the higher processing centers with aggregated forms of information which, to a considerable extent, predetermine the patterned structures that the higher centers can detect. The higher centers in their turn reduce the quantity of information which will be processed at later stages by further organization of the partly processed information into more abstract and universal forms.* (Resnikoff, 1987, p. 19)

Information visualization simply abets this process of producing patterns that can be detected and abstracted.

In order to do knowledge crystallization, there must be data, a task, and a schema. If the data are not to hand, then information visualization can aid in the search for it. If there is a satisfactory schema, then knowledge crystallization reduces to information retrieval. If there is not an adequate schema, then information visualization is one of the methods by which one can be obtained.

The HomeFinder (Williamson and Shneiderman, 1992), as shown in Figure 1.16, for instance, allows us to describe home prices directly as a scattergraph on location and by looking at certain ranges of house parameters such as number of bedrooms or price. The mappings of variables into visual forms constitute an initial schema. But out of the interactive examination of the relationships, more expensive and larger houses, say, appear in the NW quadrant of Washington. It is possible to create a more sophisticated description of the housing data than is directly visible at any instant: the relative distribution of luxury apartments and low-cost apartments in the city, where the affluent neighborhoods are, what type of housing suitable for a single person can be found within a 15-minute commute of the Capitol building. This new compact description of the data is a new schema. In principle, we could *reexpress* the data in terms of derived concepts like "type of neighborhood," "housing category," or other concepts discovered in the initial analysis.

Roughly, we want to get the most compact description possible for a set of data relative to some task (Gell-Mann, 1994). The saying "a picture is worth ten thousand words" is a statement claiming a particular compaction ratio (although it does not state the comparison units for the picture or the task). More precisely, what we want is a representation that allows large increases in processing efficiency relative to some task (there may be a trade-off between supporting a single task versus a set of tasks).

Figure 1.15 also shows the subtasks of knowledge crystallization supported by information visualization. This is intended as an approximate and suggestive list, since much research remains to be done to understand the task itself and the effects of information visualization design and user behavior. We have associated subtasks with particular main tasks of knowledge crystallization; however, many of the subtasks could be associated with more than one task.

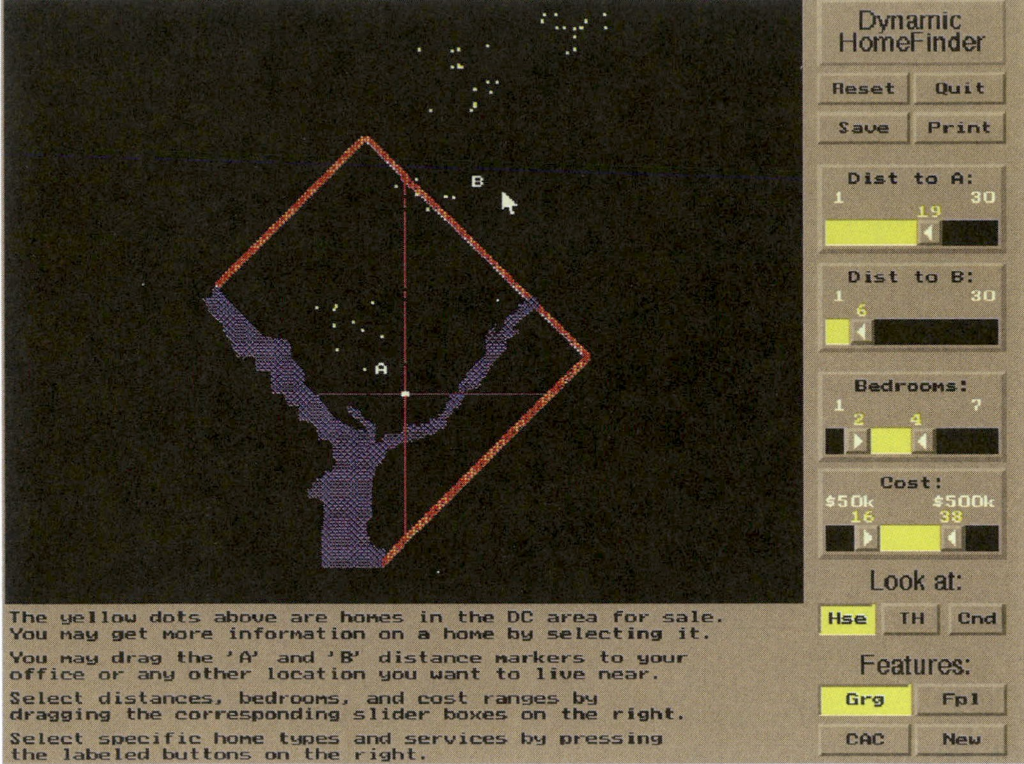
Dynamic HomeFinder
Reset
Quit
Save
Print
Dist to A:
1
30
19
Dist to B:
1
30
6
Bedrooms:
1
7
2
4
Cost:
$50k
$500k
16
38
Look at:
Hse
TH
Cnd
Features:
Grg
Fpl
CAC
New
B
A
The yellow dots above are homes in the DC area for sale.
You may get more information on a home by selecting it.
You may drag the 'A' and 'B' distance markers to your office or any other location you want to live near.
Select distances, bedrooms, and cost ranges by dragging the corresponding slider boxes on the right.
Select specific home types and services by pressing the labeled buttons on the right.

FIGURE **1.16**

HomeFinder (Williamson and Shneiderman, 1992). Courtesy of the University of Maryland.

Applying information visualization to knowledge crystallization really means using it to do these different subtasks. Bertin (1977/1981), for example, has called attention to the three levels of "reading" that a diagram can serve. These appear on our diagram as *Read Fact, Read Comparison,* and *Read Pattern.* Read Fact is visual access to a particular data value—the price of a home, for example. Read Pattern uses the whole diagram and picks out the largest-scale pattern—that expensive houses occur in NW Washington, for example. Read Comparison is at an intermediate level between these two.

Information visualization can be applied to most parts of knowledge crystallization. To illustrate, a few representative systems are given in Figure 1.17. Figure 1.17(a) shows an attempt to aid foraging by visualizing a portion of the Internet. The diameter of the base represents the number of pages in the site. The height represents the number of other sites pointing to it. The size of the globe represents the number of links to other sites. Figure 1.17(b) shows another aid for foraging by providing a workspace where pages collected from the Web can be arranged and grouped. To help search for a schema, Figure 1.17(c) shows clustering of retrieved data. Figure 1.17(d) shows a table visualization tool that can be used to instantiate a schema and to manipulate cases and variables as part of problem solving. Figure 1.17(e) shows a database visualization tool being used to find logistics resources for emergency planning. Figure 1.17(f) shows a human body made up of many thin slices, each individually photographed and indexed and available for retrieval.

Visualization Levels of Use

Figure 1.17 also illustrates the application of visualization on at least four levels of use (Card, 1996): (1) visualization of the infosphere, (2) visualization of an information workspace, (3) visual knowledge tools, and (4) visual objects. (See Table 1.2.)

Visualization can be combined with information access techniques to help the user find information. By the *infosphere,* we mean information outside of the user's work environment. This could be information on the World Wide Web, or it could be information in a specific organizational document collection or digital libraries. The visualization could take the form of a virtual place as in Figure 1.17(a) that contains all the documents, or it could be more abstract.

Visualization of an *information workspace* as shown in Figure 1.17(b)(c) is the use of visualization to organize possibly multiple individual visualizations or other information sources and tools to perform some task. The desktop metaphor for graphical user interfaces (GUIs) performs a similar function. Because information needed is at hand and findable, the time cost of doing some task is reduced, just as a carpentry workbench reduces the time cost of woodworking.

Most visualizations fall at the level of *visual knowledge tools,* as shown in Figure 1.17(d)(e). Either they arrange information to reveal patterns, or they allow the manipulation

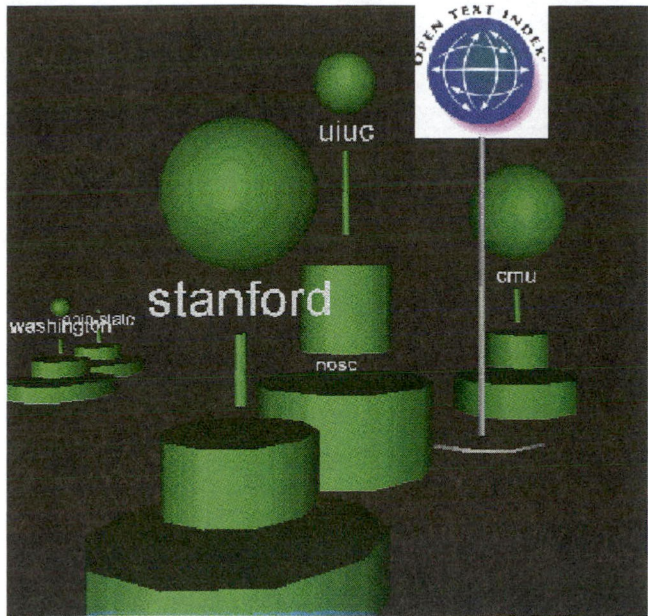

(a) View of sites on the World Wide Web (Bray, 1996 ●, detail from Figure 11).

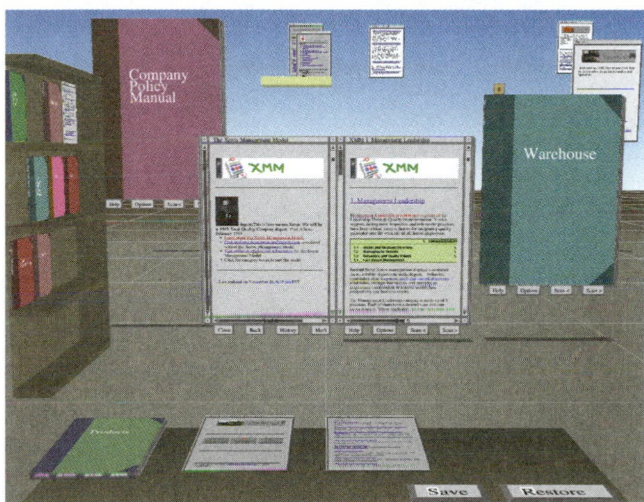

(b) Workspace of Web page. Courtesy of Xerox Corporation. See Card, Robertson, and York (1996 ●).

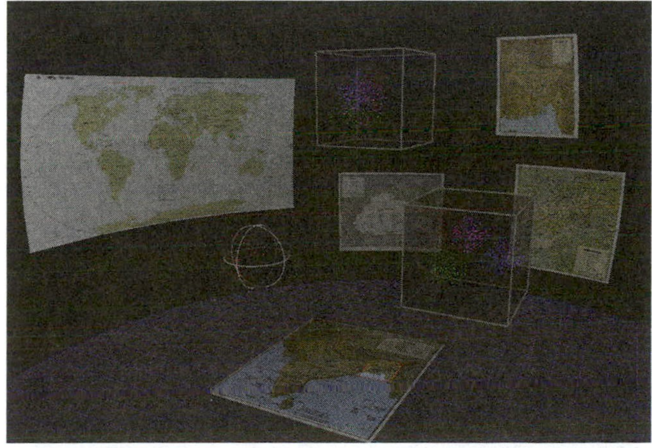

(c) Workspace for document (Risch et al., 1997 ●, detail from Figure 1).

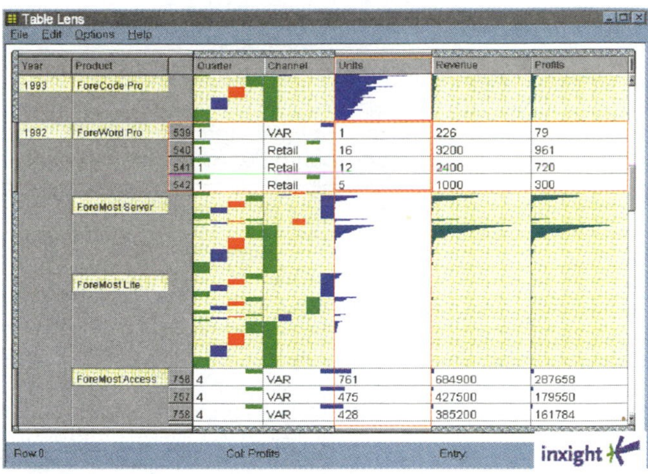

(d) Table Lens tool for data. Courtesy of Inxight Software. See Rao and Card (1994 ●).

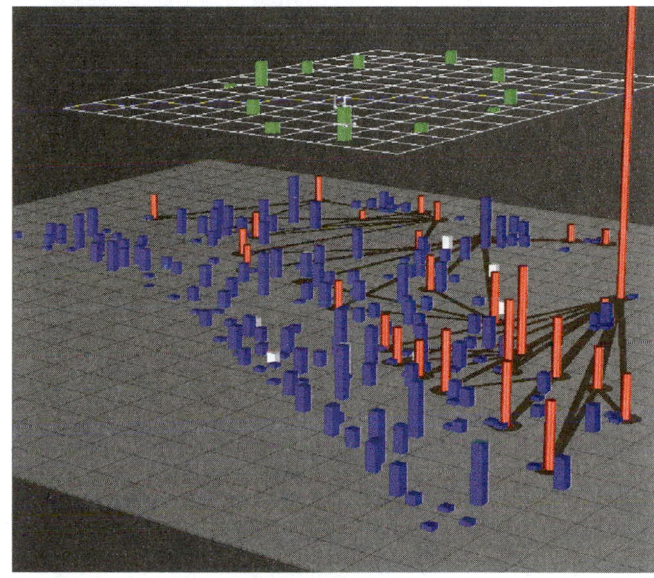

(e) SDM tool for logistic data (Chuah et al., 1995a ●).

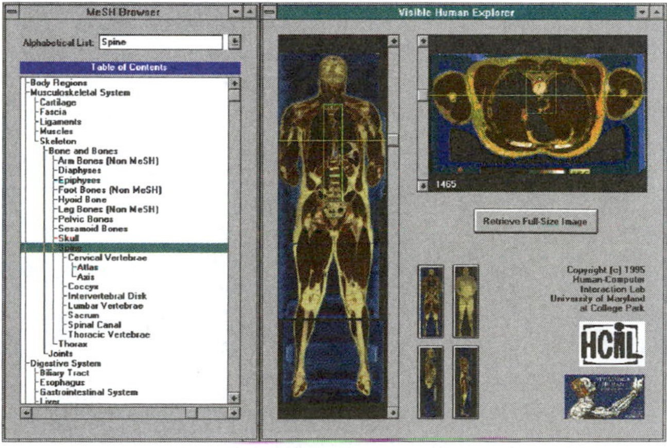

(f) Human anatomic data packaged as a visualization. Courtesy of the University of Maryland. See North, Shneiderman, and Plaisant (1996 ●).

FIGURE **1.17**

Examples of information visualization.

TABLE **1.2**

Levels at which visualization can be used.

	CONTENTS	EXAMPLE	PRIMARY USE
Infosphere	Information outside the user's environment.	Figure 1.17(a)	Place to find information needed for work.
Information workspace	Information with which the user is interacting as part of some activity.	Figure 1.17(b)(c)	Place to hold work in progress. Used for reducing cost of work, reminding user of work materials.
Visual knowledge tools	A data set.	Figure 1.17(d)(e)	Substrate into which data is poured and/or tool for manipulating it. Used for pattern detection, knowledge crystallization.
Visual objects	One or more data sets packaged for convenience.	Figure 1.17(f)	Packaging of data (data often known in advance). Used to enhance objects of interaction.

of information for finding patterns, or they allow visual calculations. Visual knowledge tools are sometimes called *wide widgets* to emphasize that they are often not just presentations but also controls.

Visualization can also operate at the level of *visually enhanced objects.* These refer to objects, especially virtual physical objects such as the human body or a book, that have been enhanced with visualization techniques to package collections of abstract information. The anatomic browser in Figure 1.17(f), for example, allows both conceptual and spatial browsing of data on a human body.

Cost Structure

Figure 1.15 lists some of the principal steps in knowledge crystallization. Each of those actions has a cost associated with it based on the means available for carrying it out. The costs are affected by the representation of information, by the operations available for acting on that information, by various resource capacities affecting the representations and the operations, and by the activity statistics of how often various operations are needed. Together these costs form a *cost structure* of information, a kind of information cost landscape.

Let us illustrate by some examples. Figure 1.18(a) shows a portion of a map of downtown San Francisco. On the map, we have drawn iso-cost contours representing the minimum time to walk to different locations. The operation of walking and the map of San Francisco induce a basic cost structure on the city. In Figure 1.18(b), we have induced a different cost structure by driving. The iso-cost contours are farther apart, since we can go farther for a given amount of cost (in time). Notice also that because there are freeways in the city, the speedup is nonuniform. Representations, defined as data structures + operations + resource constraints, induce different cost structures relative to some task we wish to perform. A rough index of this cost structure is to plot the number of places we could get to for a given cost. That would be a graph with number of places that could be visited increasing approximately as the square of the cost for Figure 1.18(a). The line would be higher for Figure 1.18(b).

The same sort of analysis can apply to the world of information (Card, Pirolli, and Mackinlay, 1994; Card, Robertson, and Mackinlay, 1991; Pirolli and Rao, 1996). Consider, for example, an office worker as shown in Figure 1.19. Information is available in the desk-side diary, through the computer terminal, in the immediate files on the desktop,

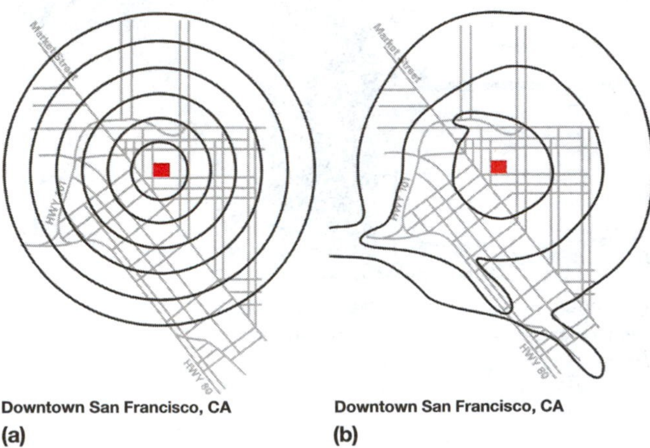

FIGURE **1.18**

Cost structure for driving and walking in San Francisco.

FIGURE **1.19**

Idealized office layout for optimizing the cost structure of information.

through other people using the telephone, in the books in the bookcase, and in files in the filing cabinet.

The cost structure of the information in the office has been arranged with care. A small amount of information (either frequently needed or in immediate use) is kept where the cost of access is low—in an immediate workspace area, principally the desktop. Voluminous, less used information is kept in a higher-cost, larger-capacity secondary storage area. More information is available in the library and other tertiary storage areas. In addition to these simplified categories, the information is linked and otherwise structured to aid in its retrieval. We could plot the number of documents a user could reach as a function of time (Figure 1.20). We call this diagram a *Cost-of-Knowledge Characteristic Function.* When visualizations are used to help foraging, then the point of a visualization is to raise this curve. If the curve is raised, users can either find the same amount of information in less time or more information in the same amount of time.

The Cost-of-Knowledge Characteristic Function can help us to understand the cost structure of visualizations that aid foraging. Figure 1.21 shows the Spiral Calendar (Mackinlay, Rao, and Card, 1995). In this visualization, calendar representations at different levels of granularity are linked together in such a way that the user can see current information plus information at all higher levels simultaneously. Clicking on a part of a calendar causes that part to expand into a more detailed calendar. The current calendar fragment (and its parents) spiral into the background.

Figure 1.22 shows the Cost-of-Knowledge Characteristic Function for this calendar in comparison to a conventional one on the Sun computer. The comparison is for using only direct point-and-click methods and does not consider string search techniques. The analysis shows that although the Spiral Calendar is superior for very large calendars, the multiple-month technique of conventional calendars results in a lower cost structure for recent dates. The dotted lines in the figure are the calculated effects for improvement proposals (some of which were successfully implemented). The Cost-of-Knowledge Characteristic Function is one way to measure the benefits of visualization at least for navigation. The example shows that making effective visualizations is not necessarily easy, even if the visualizations themselves are visually appealing.

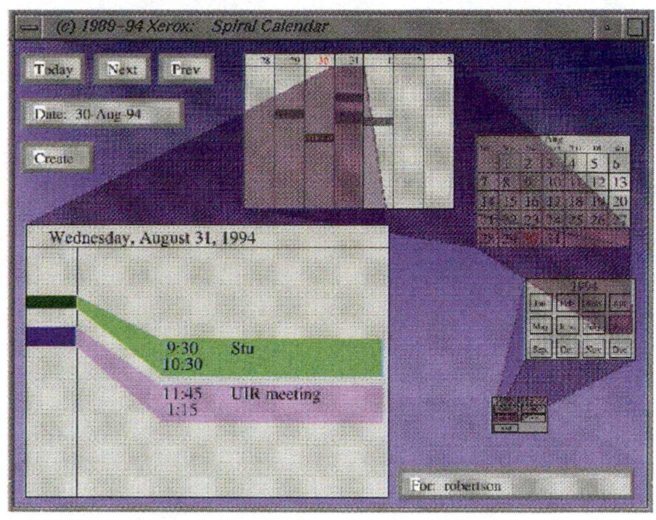

FIGURE **1.21**

Spiral Calendar (Card, Pirolli, and Mackinlay, 1994, Figure 2). Courtesy of Xerox Corporation.

How Visualization Amplifies Cognition

How does visualization amplify cognition? A classic study by Larkin and Simon (1987) illustrates some reasons why visualizations can be effective. Larkin and Simon compared solving physics problems using diagrams versus using non-diagrammatic representations. Specifically, they compared

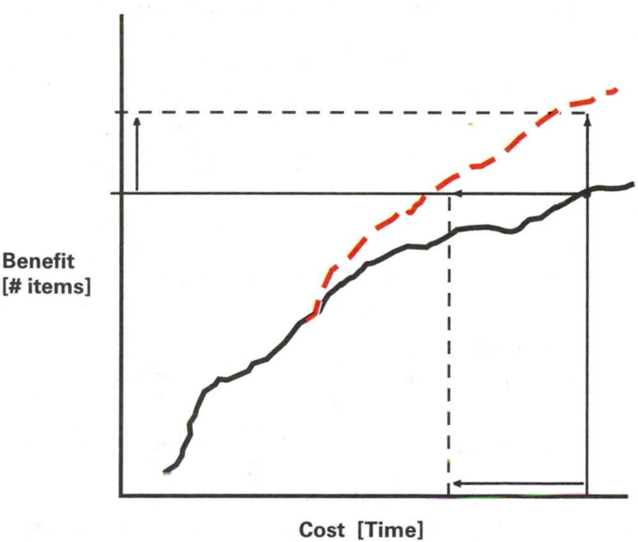

FIGURE **1.20**

Cost-of-Knowledge Characteristic Function.

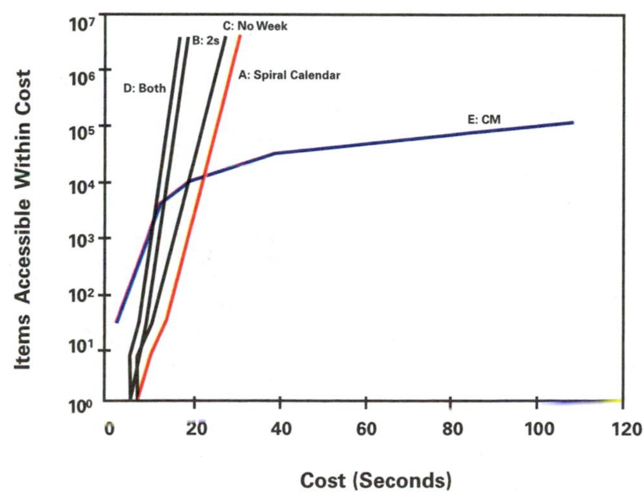

FIGURE **1.22**

Cost-of-Knowledge Characteristic Function (Card, Pirolli, and Mackinlay, 1994, Figure 5).

the effort that had to be expended to do search, recognition, and inference with or without the diagram. Their conclusion was that diagrams helped in three basic ways: (1) By grouping together information that is used together, large amounts of search were avoided. (2) By using location to group information about a single element, the need to match symbolic labels was avoided, leading to reductions in search and working memory. (3) In addition, the visual representation automatically supported a large number of perceptual inferences that were extremely easy for humans. For example, with a diagram, geometric elements like alternate interior angles could be immediately and obviously recognized. Two of these ways essentially improve the Cost-of-Knowledge Characteristic Function for accessing information. The third reduces costs of certain operations. The key to understanding the effectiveness of information visualization is understanding what it does to the cost structure of a task. Depending on the task, visualization could make a task better—or it could make the task worse.

We propose six major ways in which visualizations can amplify cognition (Table 1.3): (1) by increasing the memory and processing resources available to the users, (2) by reducing the search for information, (3) by using visual representations to enhance the detection of patterns, (4) by enabling perceptual inference operations, (5) by using perceptual attention mechanisms for monitoring, and (6) by encoding information in a manipulable medium.

Visualizations can expand processing capability by using the resources of the visual system directly. Or they can work indirectly by offloading work from cognition or reducing working memory requirements for a task by allowing the working memory to be external and visual. They can also allow the environment to store details, like a map stores details, close to where they need to be used. As we saw before, if a navigator draws a course on a chart and the course hits a rock, just those depth soundings of most relevance lie near the line he or she has drawn.

Visualizations can reduce the search for data by grouping or visually relating information. They can compact information into a small space. They can allow hierarchical search by using overviews to locate areas for more detailed search. Then they can allow zooming in or popping up details on demand. They can essentially index data spatially by location and landmarks to provide rapid access.

Visualizations can allow patterns in the data to reveal themselves. These patterns suggest schemata at a higher level. Aggregations of data can reveal themselves through clustering or common visual properties.

Visualizations allow some inferences to be done very easily that are not so easy otherwise. This is why all physics

TABLE **1.3**

How information visualization amplifies cognition.

Increased Resources	
High-bandwidth hierarchical interaction	The human moving gaze system partitions limited channel capacity so that it combines high spatial resolution and wide aperture in sensing visual environments (Resnikoff, 1987).
Parallel perceptual processing	Some attributes of visualizations can be processed in parallel compared to text, which is aerial.
Offload work from cognitive to perceptual system	Some cognitive inferences done symbolically can be recoded into inferences done with simple perceptual operations (Larkin and Simon, 1987).
Expanded working memory	Visualizations can expand the working memory available for solving a problem (Norman, 1993).
Expanded storage of information	Visualizations can be used to store massive amounts of information in a quickly accessible form (e.g., maps).
Reduced Search	
Locality of processing	Visualizations group information used together, reducing search (Larkin and Simon, 1987).
High data density	Visualizations can often represent a large amount of data in a small space (Tufte, 1983).
Spatially indexed addressing	By grouping data about an object, visualizations can avoid symbolic labels (Larkin and Simon, 1987).
Enhanced Recognition of Patterns	
Recognition instead of recall	Recognizing information generated by a visualization is easier than recalling that information by the user.
Abstraction and aggregation	Visualizations simplify and organize information, supplying higher centers with aggregated forms of information through abstraction and selective omission (Card, Robertson, and Mackinlay, 1991; Resnikoff, 1987).
Visual schemata for organization	Visually organizing data by structural relationships (e.g., by time) enhances patterns.
Value, relationship, trend	Visualizations can be constructed to enhance patterns at all three levels (Bertin, 1977/1981).
Perceptual Inference	
Visual representations make some problems obvious	Visualizations can support a large number of perceptual inferences that are extremely easy for humans (Larkin and Simon, 1987).
Graphical computations	Visualizations can enable complex specialized graphical computations (Hutchins, 1996).
Perceptual Monitoring	Visualizations can allow for the monitoring of a large number of potential events if the display is organized so that these stand out by appearance or motion.
Manipulable Medium	Unlike static diagrams, visualizations can allow exploration of a space of parameter values and can amplify user operations.

students are taught to start with a diagram of a problem and high school math students are now taught with graphing calculators. Visual representations can themselves be used for specialized operations.

Thus, as Table 1.3 argues, visualization can enhance cognitive effort by several separate mechanisms. These all depend on appropriate mappings of information into visual form.

MAPPING DATA TO VISUAL FORM

We can think of visualizations as adjustable mappings from data to visual form to the human perceiver. Figure 1.23 is a diagram of these mappings, to serve as a simple reference model. Using a reference model allows us to simplify our discussion of information visualization systems and to compare and contrast them. Other attempts at reference models are discussed in Robertson and Ferrari (1994).

In Figure 1.23, arrows flow from Raw Data on the left to the human, indicating a series of data transformations. Each arrow might indicate multiple chained transformations. Arrows flow from the human at the right into the transformations themselves, indicating the adjustment of these transformations by user-operated controls. *Data Transformations* map *Raw Data,* that is, data in some idiosyncratic format, into *Data Tables,* relational descriptions of data extended to include metadata. *Visual Mappings* transform Data Tables into *Visual Structures,* structures that combine spatial substrates, marks, and graphical properties. Finally, *View Transformations* create *Views* of the Visual Structures by specifying graphical parameters such as position, scaling, and clipping. User interaction controls parameters of these transformations, restricting the view to certain data ranges, for example, or changing the nature of the transformation. The visualizations and their controls are used in service of some task.

The core of the reference model is the mapping of a Data Table to a Visual Structure. Data Tables are based on mathematical relations; Visual Structures are based on graphical properties effectively processed by human vision. Although Raw Data can be visualized directly, Data Tables are an important intermediate step when the data are abstract, without a direct spatial component. To give an example, text Raw Data might start out as indexed strings or arrays. These might be transformed into document vectors, normalized vectors in a space with dimensionality as large as the number of words. Document vectors might, in turn, be reduced by multidimensional scaling to create Data Tables of x, y, z coordinates that could be displayed. Whatever the initial form, we assume in our discussion that Raw Data are eventually transformed into the logical equivalent of Data Tables.

The terminology of data in the literature is not consistent (Gallop, 1994; Wong, Crabb, and Bergeron, 1996), since it has been created by many disciplines—mathematics, statistics, engineering, computer science, and graphic design. Consequently, we set out in this section to create a data terminology to be used in the remainder of this book. We have attempted here to strike a balance between formality and clarity (for a more formal treatment see Card and Mackinlay, 1997; Mackinlay, 1986b ●; Mackinlay, Card, and Robertson, 1990b). A formal treatment has the virtue that it is precise, which is critical when discussing data, because subtle differences in data often result in large differences in visualization choices. However, clarity is just as important when visualization techniques are being introduced and compared.

Data Tables

Raw Data comes in many forms, from spreadsheets to the text of novels. The usual strategy is to transform this data into a relation or set of relations that are more structured and thus easier to map to visual forms. Mathematically, a relation is a set of *tuples:*

$$\{<Value_{ix}, Value_{iy}, \ldots >, <Value_{jx}, Value_{jy}, \ldots >, \ldots\}.$$

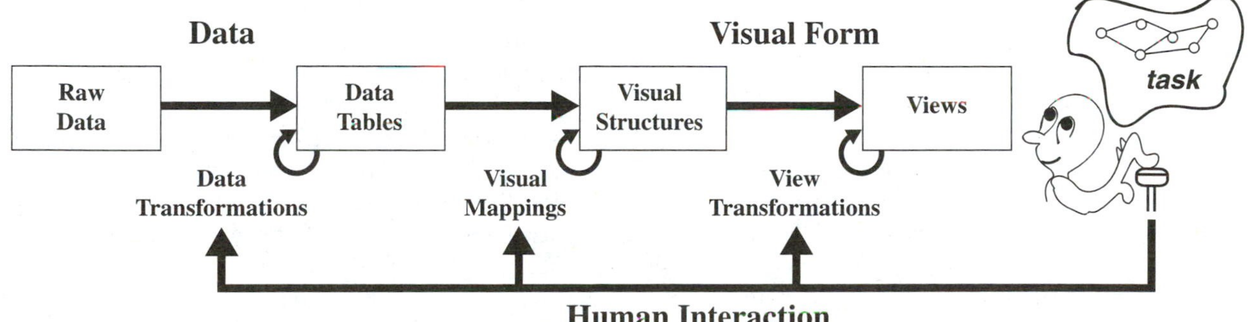

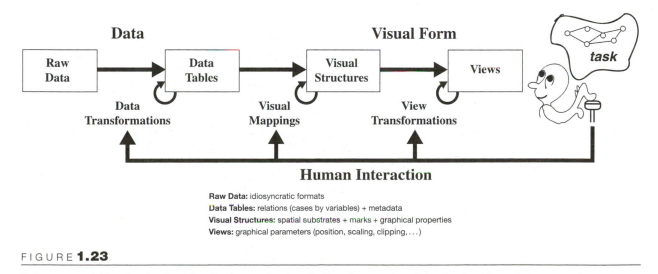

Raw Data: idiosyncratic formats
Data Tables: relations (cases by variables) + metadata
Visual Structures: spatial substrates + marks + graphical properties
Views: graphical parameters (position, scaling, clipping, . . .)

FIGURE **1.23**

Reference model for visualization. Visualization can be described as the mapping of data to visual form that supports human interaction in a workspace for visual sense making.

Because this mathematical treatment omits descriptive information that is important for visualization, we create the notion of a *Data Table*. A Data Table (see Table 1.4) combines relations with *metadata* that describes those relations:

TABLE **1.4**

A depiction of a Data Table.

	$Case_i$	$Case_j$	$Case_k$	
$Variable_x$	$Value_{ix}$	$Value_{jx}$	$Value_{kx}$	...
$Variable_y$	$Value_{iy}$	$Value_{jy}$	$Value_{ky}$	...
...	...	...	...	...

An example of metadata in Table 1.4 are the labels for the rows and columns. The rows represent *variables*, sets that represent the range of the *values* in the tuples. The columns represent *cases*, sets of values for each of the variables. To distinguish a Data Table from other tables (used as presentations of data), we mark Data Tables with a double vertical line on the left of the values. As we shall see, the ordering of the rows and columns in the Data Table may or may not be meaningful. This ordering is another example of metadata that is important for visualization.

Tables of data are often called "cases by variables arrays," where the cases are the columns in Table 1.4. Cases by variables arrays are often depicted with the cases as rows and the variables as columns, the opposite of our convention here. This is because there are usually many more cases than variables and it is convenient to let the cases expand onto other sheets of paper. On the other hand, when cases are years, as in a budget, the cases are usually laid out as columns. Furthermore, our focus here is on the variables, which are important when selecting visualizations (the cases are important when analyzing data). Therefore, for expository convenience (large numbers of cases are not necessary in examples), we have chosen to depict Data Tables with the cases as columns and variables as rows. Bertin (1977/1981) also follows this Data Table convention and depicts the cases as columns and the variables as rows, but he calls the cases "objects" and the variables "characteristics." His terminology, however, focuses on a specialized form of relation called a *function*, which has the mathematical property that variables are divided into *inputs* and *outputs* and the input variables uniquely determine the output variables. Functions from objects to their characteristics are very common in the tasks associated with visualization. They have one input variable and an arbitrary number of output variables, where each case represents a unique object:

$$f(Case_i) = \langle Value_{ix}, Value_{iy}, \ldots \rangle.$$

We depict functions in Data Tables by separating the input variables from the output variables with a thick line as shown in Table 1.5. In this table, since *Case* is a variable in the Data Table, it is no longer metadata.

TABLE **1.5**

A function described in a Data Table with input variables shown above the output variables. $Case_i$ represents a unique object and the corresponding values represent the characteristics of that object.

Case	$Case_i$	$Case_j$	$Case_k$	...
$Variable_x$	$Value_{ix}$	$Value_{jx}$	$Value_{kx}$	...
$Variable_y$	$Value_{iy}$	$Value_{jy}$	$Value_{ky}$	...
...	...	...	...	...

One of the advantages of Data Tables is that they clearly depict the number of variables associated with a collection of data, an important consideration when selecting visualizations. "Dimensionality" is one of those terms used in different ways by different authors (Wong, Crabb, and Bergeron, 1996). Dimensionality is used to refer to the number of input variables, the number of output variables, both together, or even the number of spatial dimensions in the data. The term is also commonly used to describe the type of spatial substrate of a Visual Structure. The dimensionality of space, whether it describes data or Visual Structures, is the most popular use of this term and how we generally use it in this book. Two-dimensional Visual Structures are the largest we can visualize before we have to worry about occlusions, for although we live in a 3D world, our vision (unless we move) sees something like the inside surface of a 2D sphere. Three-dimensional Visual Structures are the largest we can access with our specialized human perceptual operations. We follow common usage of the term "multi" and apply *multivariable* to data (as opposed to visualizations), specifically to Data Tables that have too many variables to be encoded in a single 3D Visual Structure. Visualizations that are specifically designed to encode such multivariable Data Tables are called *multidimensional* visualizations.

Now that we have established some data terminology, we can use Data Tables to clarify some issues associated with visualizing data. Table 1.6 describes a Data Table for films where the cases (columns) represent films and the variables (rows) represent properties of those films:

TABLE **1.6**

A Data Table about films.

FilmID	230	105	540	...
Title	Goldfinger	Ben Hur	Ben Hur	...
Director	Hamilton	Wyler	Niblo	...
Actor	Connery	Heston	Novarro	...
Actress	Blackman	Harareet	McAvoy	...
Year	1964	1959	1926	...
Length	112	212	133	...
Popularity	7.7	8.2	7.4	...
Rating	PG	G	G	...
Film Type	Action	Action	Drama	...

This table could have been written without any input variables, but we have included one, *FilmID,* which is a set of unique numbers identifying the films. The other properties (for example, *Title*) do not have unique values for each case. Such identifiers or codes are often maintained as a key by relational databases when there is no other key for a record. Because it is unique for a case, *FilmID* can be used to index a mapping from films to marks on a spatial substrate that encodes them.

Most tables used to present data are not Data Tables. Take Table 1.7, a Data Table that describes distances between cities:

TABLE **1.7**

Data Table for distances.

Start City	Basel	Basel	Berlin	...
End City	Berlin	Bern	Bern	...
Distance	860	90	930	...

Table 1.7 is an example of a function with two input variables. Such data is often presented as a two-way table (Table 1.8). Table 1.7 is a Data Table, whereas Table 1.8 is not. It is an instance of a table presentation.

TABLE **1.8**

A table presentation for the same distances. This is not a Data Table.

	Basel	**Berlin**	**Bern**	...
Basel	0	860	90	...
Berlin	860	0	930	...
Bern	90	930	0	...
...	...	...	...	...

Table 1.8 is effective for seeing the distances between cities. Considered as a presentation, Table 1.7 is effective for seeing the structure of the data.

Data Tables can undergo data transformations that affect their structure. For example, Table 1.7 could have been derived by a data transformation from Table 1.9.

TABLE **1.9**

Possible earlier form of Data Table 1.7.

City	Basel	Berlin	Bern	...
Latitude	47.33N	52.32N	46.57N	...
Longitude	7.36E	13.25E	7.26E	...
Country	SWTZ	GER	SWTZ	...
...	...	...	...	...

In Table 1.9, the input variable *City* is mapped to various output variables, including *Latitude* and *Longitude,* which can be used to calculate the *Distance* variable in Data Table 1.7. Thus, the transformation from Data Table 1.9 to Data Table 1.7 involves both new *derived values* and new *derived structure.* It involves new derived values because the *Distance* values have been computed from other values. It involves new derived structure because the numbers and identities of input and/or output variables have changed between the two Data Tables. In fact, some output variables have been used to create a new input variable. Such Data Table transformations are common as data are mapped to visual form.

Data Tables can describe hierarchical and network data. To do this, a variable is used to describe the links between cases. For example, in Table 1.10 the variable *Links* describes the relationship among hypertext documents:

TABLE **1.10**

Data Table describing the links among hypertext documents.

DocID	D_i	D_j	D_k	D_l	D_m	D_n
Length	235	54	127	341	102	186
Links	$\{D_k, D_n\}$	$\varnothing$	$\{D_j\}$	$\varnothing$	$\varnothing$	$\{D_l, D_m\}$
...	...	...	...	...	...	...

These links form the following hierarchy:

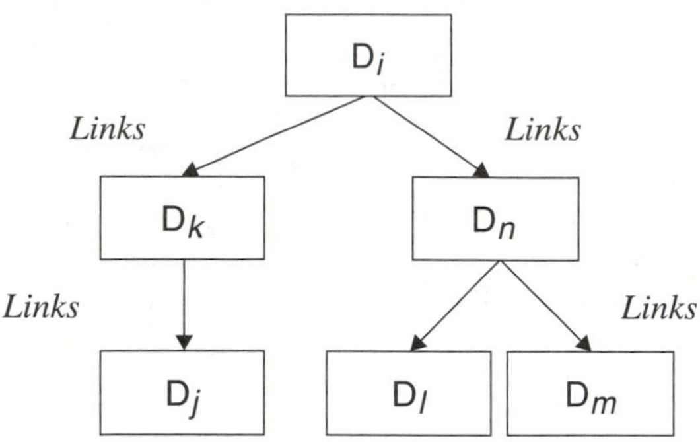

Hierarchies are specialized networks with one root and with each child having exactly one parent. Notice that the values of *Links* are sets that contain the *DocIDs* of the cases (or the null set ∅) and that this variable represents a mapping from a set of cases back into itself. This self-referential property of *Links* is included in the metadata associated with Data Table 1.10.

Variable Types

Variables come in three basic types:

N = *Nominal* (are only = or ≠ to other values),
O = *Ordinal* (obeys a < relation), or
Q = *Quantitative* (can do arithmetic on them).

A *nominal variable* N is an unordered set, such as film titles {Goldfinger, Ben Hur, Star Wars}. An *ordinal variable* O is a tuple (ordered set), such as film ratings <G, PG, PG-13, R>. A *quantitative variable* Q is a numeric range, such as film length [0, 360]. These distinctions are important, because they determine the type of axis that should be used in a Visual Structure.

Elementary choices for data transformations derive from the variables types. For example, quantitative variables can be transformed into ordinal variables

$$Q \rightarrow O$$

by dividing them into ranges. Film lengths (type Q)

$$[0, 360]$$

can be broken into the ranges (type O)

<Short, Medium, Long>.

This common transformation is called *classing,* because it maps values onto classes of values. It creates an accessible summary of the data, although it loses information. A more sophisticated variation creates an additional variable that counts the values in the ranges, leading to a histogram. A less common transformation converts ordinal variables into nominal variables O → N by ignoring the ordering. In the other direction, nominal variables can be sorted to create ordinal variables

$$N \rightarrow O.$$

For example, film titles

{Goldfinger, Ben Hur, Star Wars}

can be sorted lexicographically

<Ben Hur, Goldfinger, Star Wars>.

In addition to the three basic types of variables, there are subtypes that represent important properties of the world associated with specialized visual conventions. We distinguish the subtype

$$Q_s = \textit{Quantitative Spatial}$$

for intrinsically spatial variables common in scientific visualization, and the subtype

$$Q_g = \textit{Quantitative Geographical}$$

for spatial variables that are specifically geophysical coordinates.

Other important subtypes are the temporal variables

$$Q_t = \textit{Quantitative Time}$$

and

$$O_t = \textit{Ordinal Time.}$$

Temporal variables have associated data transformations, such as collecting days into weeks, months, or years. Of course, natural numbers, used as counting numbers, are another important subtype.

Metadata

Metadata is descriptive information about data (see Tweedie, 1997 ●). Metadata can be important in choosing visualizations. For example, Table 1.11 (Gallop, 1994) describes a function from map locations to numbers.

TABLE **1.11**

Data Table for map numbers.

Latitude	Y_i	Y_j	Y_k	...
Longitude	X_i	X_j	X_k	...
Numbers	Q_i	Q_j	Q_k	...

If the *Numbers* variable represents height above sea level, the relation represents samples from a continuous real function, which can be interpolated to approximate a surface. On the other hand, if *Numbers* represents car accidents, that is to say, natural numbers, it is not permissible to interpolate.

An important form of metadata is the *structure* of a Data Table (Tweedie, 1997 ●), which is depicted as the rows and columns in our Data Table examples. Data transformations often change the structure of a Data Table. A document's location in a semantic space could be represented using three variables X, Y, and Z or described by a single vector variable *Location.* A group of survey respondents could be individual cases described by output variables *Age* and *Sex,* or alternately the group could be classed into "cases" *Age<20, Age20-35, Age>35* with *Age* and *Sex* as input variables whose values were sets of respondent identifier codes.

Additional metadata could be added explicitly to the Data Table by adding, for example, a column for data type as in Table 1.12.

TABLE **1.12**

A Data Table with metadata describing the types of the variables.

FilmID	N	230	105	...
Title	N	Goldfinger	Ben Hur	...
Director	N	Hamilton	Wyler	...
Actor	N	Connery	Heston	...
Actress	N	Blackman	Harareet	...
Year	Q_t	1964	1959	...
Length	Q	112	212	...
Popularity	Q	7.7	8.2	...
Rating	O	PG	G	...
Film Type	N	Action	Action	...

Additional columns could be added for cardinality or range of the data. Data Tables can also include relationships between variables that are not easily depicted. For example, a business database may contain two relations: employees and sales. The sales relation will have a variable for the person who made the sale, which will be a subset of an employees variable.

Data Transformations

The transformation of Raw Data into Data Tables typically involves the loss or gain of information. Often Raw Data contains errors or missing values that must be addressed before the data can be visualized. Statistical calculations can also add additional information. For these reasons, Data Tables often contain derived value or structure. There are four types of these data transformations (Tweedie, 1997 ●):

1. *Values → Derived Values*
2. *Structure → Derived Structure*
3. *Values → Derived Structure*
4. *Structure → Derived Values*

Examples of these occur in Table 1.13.

TABLE **1.13**

Examples of data transformations.

	Derived Value	Derived Structure
Value	*Mean*	*Sort* *Class* *Promote*
Structure	*Demote*	$X,Y,Z \rightarrow P_{xyz}$

Statistical calculations, like *Mean,* are an example of derived values. Sorting variables or cases is an example of derived structure (Bertin, 1977/1981).

Transformations that switch between value and structure are more complex. Data transformations can be concatenated to form chains of aggregation and classing as part of the knowledge crystallization process shown in Figure 1.15. Patterns can be discovered and brought forward as new schemata by encoding them in the variables of the Data Table. Visualizations of the Data Table can be used to detect more patterns. User-operated controls on structural transformations of the Data Table can be used as controls on the visualization. An example of chained value and structure transformations is the "aggregation cycle" described by Bertin (1977/1981): Data Table 1.14 describes individuals and their ages, income, and profession:

TABLE **1.14**

A Data Table describing individuals and their ages, incomes, and professions.

Individual	I1	I2	I3	I4	I5	I6	I7	I8	...
Ages	55	18	22	51	34	50	28	17	...
Income	1	6	8	10	4	7	3	1	...
P1	0	0	0	0	1	0	0	0	...
P2	1	1	0	0	0	0	0	0	...
P3	0	0	0	0	0	0	0	0	...
P4	0	0	1	0	0	0	1	0	...
P5	0	0	0	0	0	0	0	1	...
P6	0	0	0	1	0	1	0	0	...
P7	0	0	0	0	0	0	0	0	...
P8	0	0	0	0	0	0	0	0	...

Ages and *Income* are quantitative variables. Variables *P1* through *P8* represent different professions, with a "1" value indicating that individual has that profession.

The first step in the aggregation cycle is to transform the quantitative variables of *Ages* and *Income* into ordinal variables of age classes and income classes, creating the Data Table 1.15 consisting entirely of binary data values:

Class (Table 1.14) *on Ages and Income* → Table 1.15,

where, to keep the example simple we omit specification of the obvious parameters for specifying class boundaries, scope of aggregation, and so on.

TABLE **1.15**

The age and income classes derived from Table 1.14.

Individual	I1	I2	I3	I4	I5	I6	I7	I8	...
Age>40	1	0	0	1	0	1	0	0	...
Age20-40	0	0	1	0	1	0	1	0	...
Age0-20	0	1	0	0	0	0	0	1	...
Inc7-10	0	0	1	1	0	1	0	0	...
Inc4-6	0	1	0	0	1	0	0	0	...
Inc2-3	0	0	0	0	0	0	1	0	...
Inc0-1	1	0	0	0	0	0	0	1	...
P1	0	0	0	0	1	0	0	0	...
P2	1	1	0	0	0	0	0	0	...
P3	0	0	0	0	0	0	0	0	...
P4	0	0	1	0	0	0	1	0	...
P5	0	0	0	0	0	0	0	1	...
P6	0	0	0	1	0	1	0	0	...
P7	0	0	0	0	0	0	0	0	...
P8	0	0	0	0	0	0	0	0	...

This transformation involves *Structure* → *Derived Structure* with the creation of the new variables for the ranges, whose rows are ordered. It also involves *Values* → *Derived Values* with the calculation of the binary values for each individual to indicate their age and income ranges.

We next generate the new Table 1.16 by aggregating individuals into their professional groups. The professions become the cases and the number of individuals in each age and income class become the new Data Values. We call this operation *promotion,* meaning that a variable is promoted into being a case (i.e., the level of the case has been promoted to a higher level of aggregation):

Promote (Table 1.15) *on Professions classes* → Table 1.16.

TABLE **1.16**

Promotion of professions to cases.

P-ID	P1	P2	P3	P4	P5	P6	P7	P8
Age>40	0	0	1	0	2	2	1	1
Age20-40	3	1	0	0	0	0	0	2
Age0-20	0	2	1	1	3	1	0	1
Inc7-10	1	0	0	1	2	2	0	1
Inc4-6	2	2	0	0	1	0	0	2
Inc2-3	0	1	1	2	0	1	1	1
Inc0-1	0	1	0	3	1	0	0	0

This transformation involves *Structure* → *Derived Values* when the professions become the values for a new input variable.

A new cycle can start from Data Table 1.16 by calculating the mean *Age* and *Income* of each profession:

Mean (Table 1.16) *on Age and Income* → Table 1.17

TABLE **1.17**

Average age and income of the professions.

P-ID	P1	P2	P3	P4	P5	P6	P7	P8
Avg Age	33	29	17	34	25	40	58	31
Avg Income	6.3	3.7	3	2.7	3.5	6.6	2	5.7

Again, this is a *Values* → *Derived Values.*

These quantitative variables can then be transformed to ordinal variables representing classes of median age and income:

Class (Table 1.17) *on AveAge and AveIncome* → Table 1.18.

TABLE **1.18**

Classing of average age and income.

P-ID	P1	P2	P3	P4	P5	P6	P7	P8
Avg Age>35	0	0	0	0	0	1	1	0
Avg Age20-35	1	1	0	1	1	0	0	1
Avg Age0-20	0	0	1	0	0	0	0	0
Avg Inc>6	1	0	0	0	0	1	0	0
Avg Inc5-6	0	0	0	0	0	0	0	1
Avg Inc4-5	0	0	0	0	0	0	0	0
Avg Inc3-4	0	1	1	0	1	0	0	0
Avg Inc<3	0	0	0	1	0	0	1	0

This is another *Structure* → *Derived Structure* transformation.

We can then treat average income as a case (Bertin calls these statistical objects) resulting in a cross-tabulation table:

Promote (Table 1.18) *on AveAge and AveInc classes* → Table 1.19

TABLE **1.19**

Promotion of average income classes.

Avg Inc-ID	AI>6	AI5-6	AI4-5	AI3-4	AI<3
Avg Age>35	1	0	0	0	1
Avg Age20-35	1	1	0	2	1
Avg Age0-20	0	0	0	1	0

This cycle can be continued. The example, summarized in Figure 1.24, also illustrates the complexities of data transformation and the kinds of transformations we would like to be able to visualize and maybe control through visualizations. Each of these Data Tables reveals a different aspect of the data and may lead to a different choice of Visual Structure. We return to the problem of choosing visualizations after discussing Visual Structures and View.

VISUAL STRUCTURES

In visualization, Data Tables are mapped to *Visual Structures*, which augment a spatial substrate with marks and graphical properties to encode information. To be a good Visual Structure, it is important that this mapping preserve the data (Mackinlay, 1986b ●). Data Tables can often be mapped into the visual representations in multiple ways. A mapping is said to be *expressive* if all and only the data in the Data Table are also represented in the Visual Structure. Good mappings are difficult, because it is easy for unwanted data to appear in the Visual Structure. For example, the visual presentation in Figure 1.25 is not expressive. It uses an ordinal axis in the Visual Structure to express a nominal relationship in the Data Table. It expresses visually a relationship not in the data.

The mapping must also be one that can be perceived well by the human. A mapping is said to be more *effective* if it is faster to interpret, can convey more distinctions, or leads to fewer errors than some other mapping. In Figure 1.26, the mapping of the sine wave into position is more effective than the mapping into color.

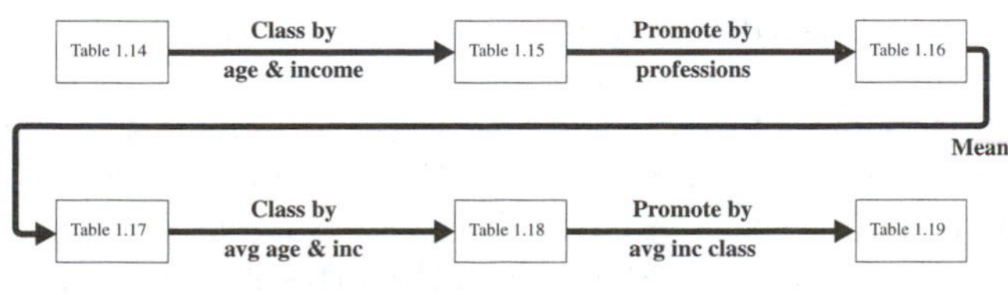

FIGURE **1.24**

Cascaded data transformations.

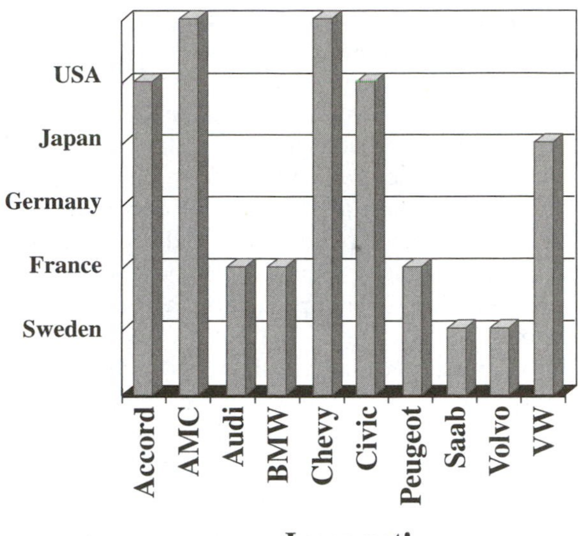

FIGURE **1.25**

This Visual Structure is not expressive, because it implies incorrect ordinal relationship among countries.

(a)

(b)

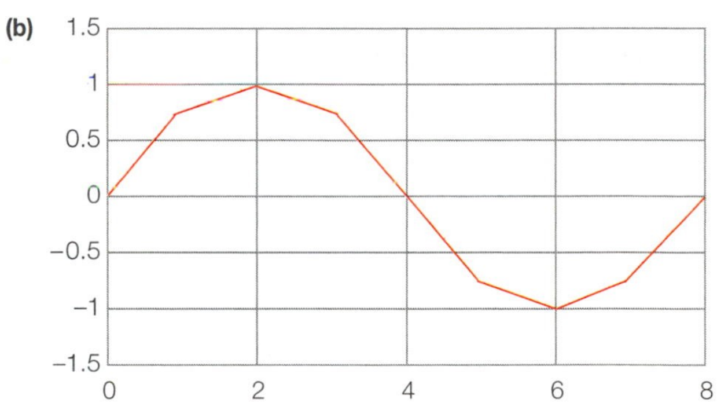

FIGURE **1.26**

Effectiveness of visual representations. (a) is less effective than (b) for communicating a sine wave.

To understand effectiveness, we have to understand a few rudimentary facts from perception. One set of such facts concern perceptual characteristics of the different graphical representations. But another set of facts concern the way in which perception itself is an active system of shifting attention, a characteristic we can attempt to play to in information visualizations.

Perception

Information visualization is clearly dependent upon the properties of human perception. Perception is a vast and studied subject (see, for example, Atkinson et al., 1988; Boff, Kaufman, and Thomas, 1986; Kosslyn, 1994; Tovée, 1996). Until recently, however, the connection between perception and cognitive activities has been tenuous (Elkind et al., 1990), making external cognition (such as the tasks of information visualization) difficult to study with any precision. While summarizing the literature of perception and addressing the integration of perceptual and cognitive theories are clearly beyond the scope of this book, we can give here a few selected facts about perception that are useful for visualization.

It is the job of information visualization systems to set up visual representations of data so as to bring the properties of human perception to bear. At the most basic level, the visual perceptual system uses a three-level hierarchical organization to partition limited bandwidth between the conflicting needs for both high spatial resolution and wide aperture in sensing the visual environment (Resnikoff, 1987). It is possible to exploit this organization in designing visualizations.

Figure 1.27 shows the human eye. A movable lens is imaged onto a substrate of 125 million photoreceptors, comprising 6.5 million color-detecting cones and the rest black and white detecting rods. Distribution of these photoreceptors is nonuniform (Figure 1.28). In a central area, called the *fovea,* cones are dense. In outlying areas, rods with larger receptive fields predominate.

Figure 1.29 shows a logical map of the eye. The first level of the visual system (see Resnikoff, 1987) is the retina. The retina has an area of about 1000 mm^2 = 10^9 μm^2 and covers a visual field of about 160° wide (since the two eyes are set horizontally and their visual fields only partly overlap, together they cover a visual field at the extremes roughly 200° horizontally and 135° vertically). The density of cones in the nonfoveal portions of the retina is about 0.006 cones/μm^2. The organization of this part of the retina is good at detecting

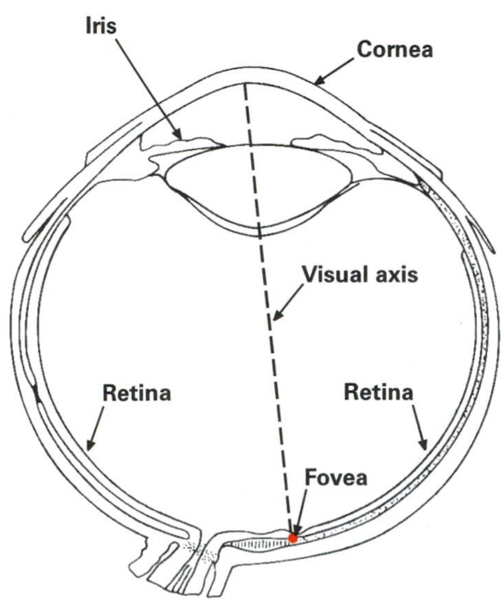

FIGURE **1.27**

The human eye. By permission of Resnikoff (1987, Figure 5.3.2).

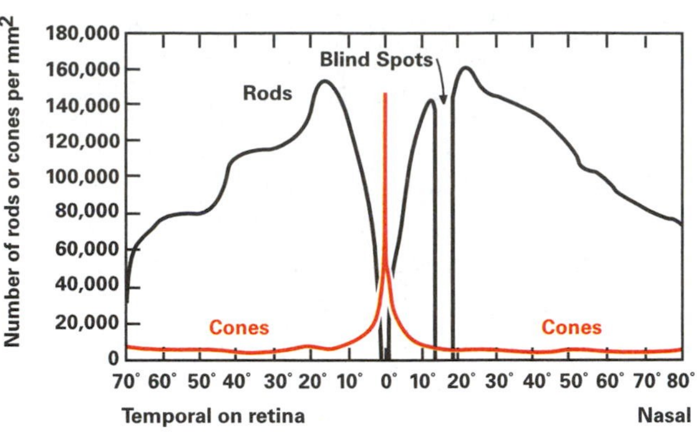

FIGURE **1.28**

Distribution of photoreceptors in the human eye. By permission of Resnikoff (1987, Figure 5.3.3).

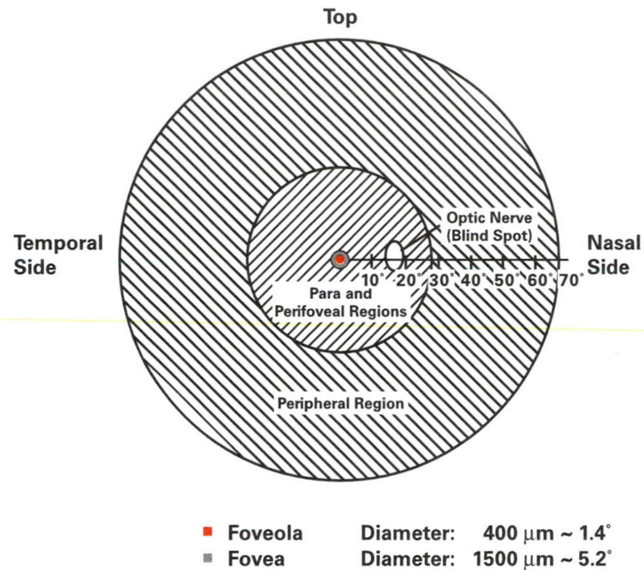

FIGURE **1.29**

Logical map of photoreceptors in the eye. By permission of Resnikoff (1987, Figure 5.3.4).

movement or other changes in the visual environment and in visually maintaining a rough representation of the location of shapes previously examined. Just how little detail is available peripherally can be seen in Figure 1.30, a photograph of a scene processed to simulate the information available in the various parts of the visual field.

The second level of the visual system is approximately the *foveola* (the inner part of the fovea), the 400 μm^2 (about 1.4°) in the center of the visual field. The entire retinal field is the equivalent of 7950 ≈ 8000 foveolae. This high-resolution field is moved to points of interest about 1 to 5 times/sec at rates of up to 500°/sec, during which vision is suppressed.

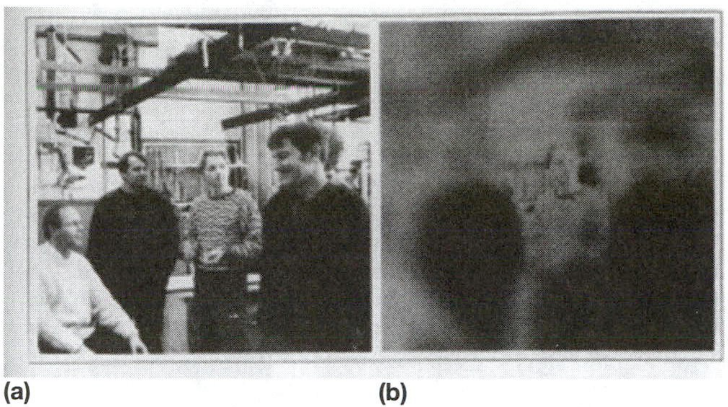

(a) (b)

FIGURE **1.30**

The visual field at any instant in time. The photograph in (a) has been processed to simulate in (b) the level of detail available at different places in the visual field. While little detail can be seen in the periphery, the general shapes and positions are preserved (Tovée, 1996, Figure 10.1).

(The eye also has tiny movements—as many as 70 times/sec —and slow pursuit movements that keep images steady.) In fact, the eye movement mechanism is part of a more complex attention mechanism including head movements and a variable-size attention window working on the visual buffer (Kosslyn, 1994). Automatic, stimulus-based attention shifting causes this mechanism to shift toward either movement or areas where preattentive features have identified strong patterns of color, intensity, or size contrast. Stereoscopic processing on the differences between the images of the two eyes gives depth information, as does *head parallax,* the moving of the head to disambiguate images. Information on configurations of interest are sent to two separate systems, one that encodes spatial properties such as location, size, and orientation, and another that encodes object properties such as shape, color, and texture (Kosslyn, 1994).

The third level of the hierarchical visual system is the set of receptors themselves within the foveola. In the foveola, the density of cones is something like 27 times greater than in the periphery. In fact, since the number of cones per neuron is around 8:1 in the periphery versus 1:1 in the foveola, the information density may be as much as 200 times greater (Resnikoff, 1987).

Thus, the system maintains a constant, computationally parallel surveillance over the entire visual field. At the same time, it is constantly moving the position of the foveola, sampling from the visual field to build up a percept or to attend to areas of high information content, such as moving objects. Visual perception is an active process in which head, eye, and attention are all employed to amplify information per unit time from the visual world.

The visual system does not work like a photograph developing in a camera but like a flying-spot scanner. It trades off time resolution to reduce the bandwidth by something like a factor of 8000 foveolae equivalents $\times$ 200 times greater information density = 1.6×10^9 (or put differently, it increases the resolution for a given available bandwidth). The visual system knits together a remarkable illusion of continuity from the succession of saccades, extracting interpretations from high-information features like sharp corners and gestalt continuity, and making invisible the missing array of receptors where the optic nerve is attached (the "blind spot").

To get a sense of how different a percept is than a photograph, imagine a person driving a car down the freeway. The driver looks ahead, into the rearview mirror, and occasionally to the side, aware of the traffic ahead, that there is a car too close behind, that another is passing on the right. At any particular moment, the driver *perceives* more than he or she instantaneously *sees,* because the percept of the traffic situation is built up from discrete visual samples of the environment. In fact, the driver will tend to sample the different visual sources roughly proportionally to the amount of information contained in them (if there is not an information overload). A car changing lanes will get more attention than one whose relative position is constant.

Visual information can be processed in two different ways, sometimes called controlled and automatic processing. *Controlled processing,* like reading, uses mainly the fovea. The processing is detailed, serial, low capacity, slow, able to be inhibited, conscious. *Automatic processing* in contrast is superficial, parallel, can be processed nonfoveally, has high capacity, is fast, cannot be inhibited, is independent of load, unconscious, and characterized by targets "popping out" during search. Actually, the contrast is not quite so crisp as this comparison suggests (see Shiffrin, 1988), but the general distinction is still important and practical. While visualizations can be designed so that detail, such as textual description, is accessible by controlled processing, coding techniques to aid search and pattern detection should use features that can be automatically processed. Color and size are typical features used to code data visually in a form capable of automatic processing, but the literature suggests more exotic features as well (these are discussed later on in Table 1.22). Many of these coding methods have not yet been tried, but because they are known to be automatically processable, they are candidates for constructing new visualization techniques.

There can be interaction among the visual codings of information. Indeed, part of the point of coding information visually is to produce patterns that the eye detects from ensembles of components. If these interactions are unintended, however, the user will be misled. The gestalt principles shown in Table 1.20 collect some well-known interactions. For example, objects near each other will tend to be seen as a cluster. Causing related objects to cluster tightly enough for this visual effect to occur may be a reason for choosing a particular layout algorithm. Eick and Wills (1993 ●), for example, argue that the "spring model" for object layout on a display is not as good as their own model, because it makes groups harder to spot.

The fact that human perception divides into focus and periphery can be exploited, not just in coding objects but also in setting up visual frames that serve as a substrate for the encoding of objects and patterns. As objects are examined, their locations become visually indexed so that search

TABLE **1.20**

Gestalt principles of organization. After Tovée (1996, Table 8.2). Used with permission.

RULE	BOUNDARIES
Pragnanz	Every stimulus pattern is seen in such a way that the resulting structure is as simple as possible.
Proximity	The tendency of objects near one another to be grouped together into a perceptual unit.
Similarity	If several stimuli are presented together, there is a tendency to see the form in such a way that the similar items are grouped together.
Closure	The tendency to unite contours that are very close to each other.
Good continuation	Neighboring elements are grouped together when they are potentially connected by straight or smoothly curving lines.
Common fate	Elements that are moving in the same direction seem to be grouped together.
Familiarity	Elements are more likely to form groups if the groups appear familiar or meaningful.

time to relocate them is reduced. The dimensions of space or patterns on the space itself, such as lines joining nodes, may be assigned meanings. As a result, objects may form a spatial external working memory. Enlarging working memory can lead to dramatic improvements of cognitive functions (see, e.g., Figure 1.1). Visualizations can also be used to store large numbers of detailed facts for rapid access (e.g., the periodic table or a ship chart).

Spatial Substrate

Not only are there characteristic limits to the perceptual system, there are also representational limits to graphics as a medium. The number of basic mappings of Data Tables to Visual Structures is actually smaller than might be supposed, because there are a limited number of components from which Visual Structures are composed. Visual Structures are made from *spatial substrate, marks,* and the marks' *graphical properties* (Mackinlay, 1986a). This limited set was identified by Bertin (1977/1981), expanded by Mackinlay (Card and Mackinlay, 1997; MacEachren, 1995; Mackinlay, 1986b ●), and expanded further here. Other properties, as we shall argue, are possible, but most visualizations will probably continue to be made from this basic set.

The most fundamental aspect of a Visual Structure is its use of space. Space is perceptually dominant (see MacEachren, 1995). Spatial position is such a good visual coding of data that the first decision of visualization design is which variables get spatial encoding at the expense of others. One reason for the effectiveness of Tufte's *Challenger* diagram is that he maps the most important variables onto spatial position in X and Y, the most potent representation properties of the Visual Structure. Like other visual features, spatial position can be used to encode the variables of Data Tables. But because of its dominance, we treat it separately from these other features as a substrate into which other parts of a Visual Structure are poured.

Empty space itself, as a container, can be treated as if it has metric structure. We describe this structure in terms of *axes* and their properties. There are four elementary types of axes:

U = *Unstructured Axis* (no axis) (Engelhardt et al., 1996),

N = *Nominal Axis* (a region is divided into subregions),

O = *Ordinal Axis* (the ordering of these subregions is meaningful), and

Q = *Quantitative Axis* (a region has a metric).

Further subdivision of the quantitative axis is possible, namely, whether the quantitative axis has interval or ratio properties. There are also important specializations to physical coordinates (a quantitative axis with physical units) or geographical coordinates (the specialized physical coordinates of latitude and longitude). But this simple division suffices for our present purposes. Axes can be linear or radial.

Axes are an important building block for developing Visual Structures. The FilmFinder (Ahlberg and Shneiderman, 1994b) in Figure 1.31 augments a scatterplot with a collection of user interface sliders and radio buttons. These allow rapid query specification through direct manipulation, which is coupled with instantaneous feedback. Based on the Data Table for the FilmFinder in Table 1.6, we represent the scatterplot as composed of two orthogonal quantitative axes:

$$Year \rightarrow Q_x,$$
$$Popularity \rightarrow Q_y.$$

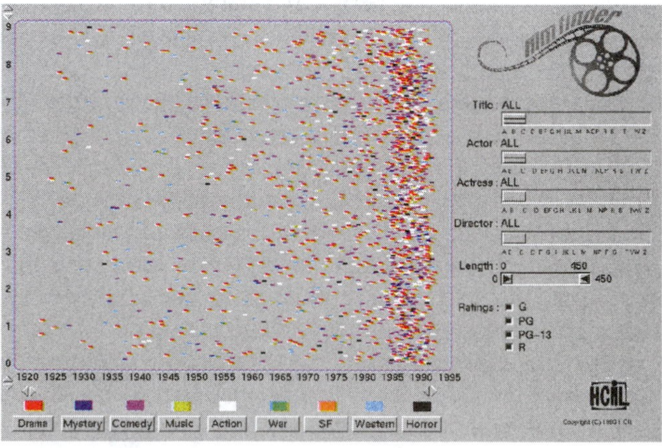

FIGURE **1.31**

The FilmFinder. Courtesy of the University of Maryland. See Ahlberg and Shneiderman (1994b).

The notation states that the *Year* variable is mapped to a quantitative X-axis and the *Popularity* variable is mapped to a quantitative Y-axis. Information is encoded by mapping the cases, which are represented by the *FilmID* variable, to points:

$$FilmID \rightarrow P.$$

Positioning these points on the axes:

$$FilmID(Year,\ Popularity) \rightarrow P(Q_x,\ Q_y)$$

encodes the year and popularity of the films.

Other axes are used for the FilmFinder query widgets. For example, an ordinal axis is used in the radio buttons for film ratings,

$$Ratings \rightarrow O_y.$$

A nominal axis is used in the radio buttons for film type,

$$FilmType \rightarrow N_x.$$

Since spatial position is such a good encoding, several techniques have been developed to increase the amount of information that can be encoded with it:

- Composition
- Alignment
- Folding
- Recursion
- Overloading

Composition (Mackinlay, 1986b ●) is the orthogonal placement of axes, creating a 2D metric space. The FilmFinder scatterplot in Figure 1.31 creates such a space where a person directly perceives relationships between film popularity and their year of production. This technique is powerful for up to two variables and still potent up to three dimensions. Even at three dimensions, if the content of the resulting cube is dense, we have the problem of seeing inside.

Alignment (Mackinlay, 1986b ●) is the repetition of an axis at a different position in the space. For example, the bond market visualization in Figure 1.13 shows the alignment of two Visual Structures on a common X-axis, representing time. The Visual Structure on the floor representing individual bond performance is aligned with the yield curve on the back wall.

Folding is the continuation of an axis in an orthogonal dimension. Figure 1.32 is a visualization of a large computer program. Each software module is represented as an axis consisting of line marks to represent the text lines of the program. These axes (oriented in the Y-direction) are folded when they are too long to fit in the window by using space

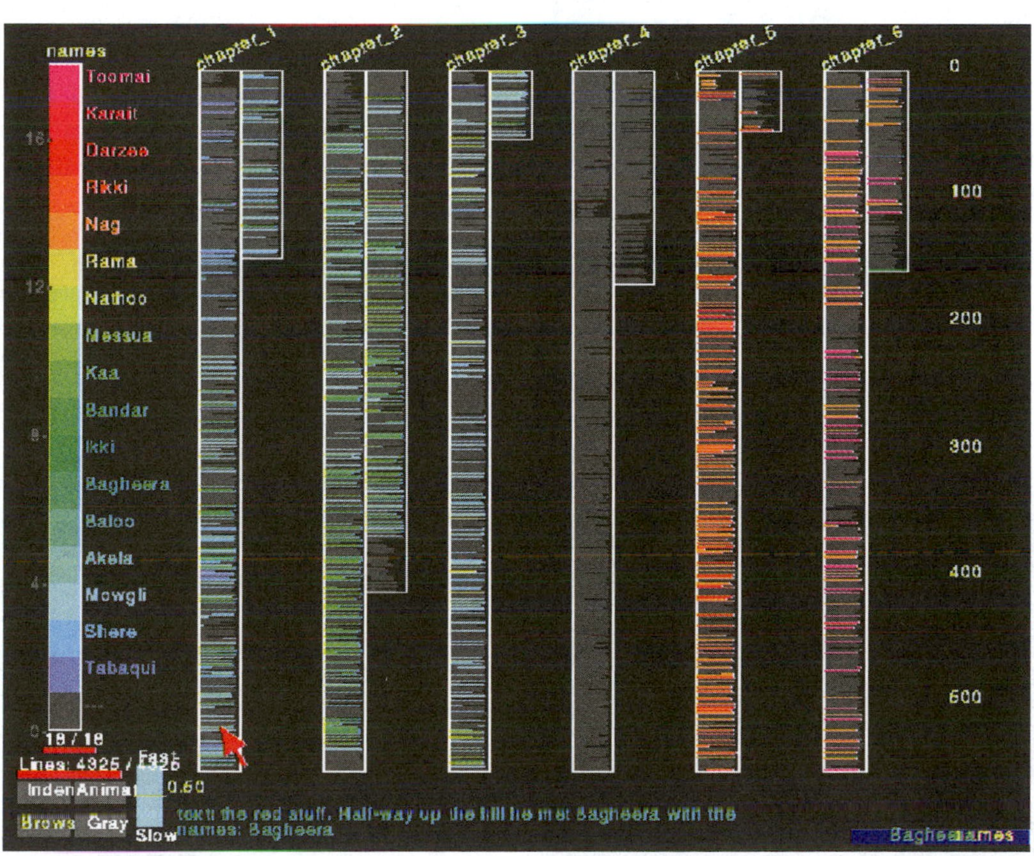

FIGURE **1.32**

SeeSoft uses a folded axis when a software module is too large to fit in the height of the window. Courtesy of Lucent Technologies. See Eick, Steffen, and Sumner (1992●). Used with permission of Lucent Bell Laboratories.

offset in the X-direction from the already used space. This visualization is also an example of axis alignment because of the alignment of the ordinal position of the text lines.

Recursion is the repeated subdivision of space. Figure 1.33 is a screen shot from Pad++ (Bederson and Hollan, 1994 ●) that provides interactive zoom into a recursive space of directories and files. A folded axis creates the top-level partitioning of the space into a set of rectangles that represent directories. Inside each of these regions are additional axes that recursively partition the space.

Overloading is the reuse of the same space for the same Data Table. In the worlds within worlds technique (Feiner and Beshers, 1990b ●), shown in Figure 1.34, the meaning of one coordinate system is determined by its placement inside another. The technique plays heavily on the fact that the data occupies only a portion of the committed space, allowing that space to be recommitted to a second use. Because this overloading is dynamically controlled by the user in this application, the user may be willing to accept some occlusion.

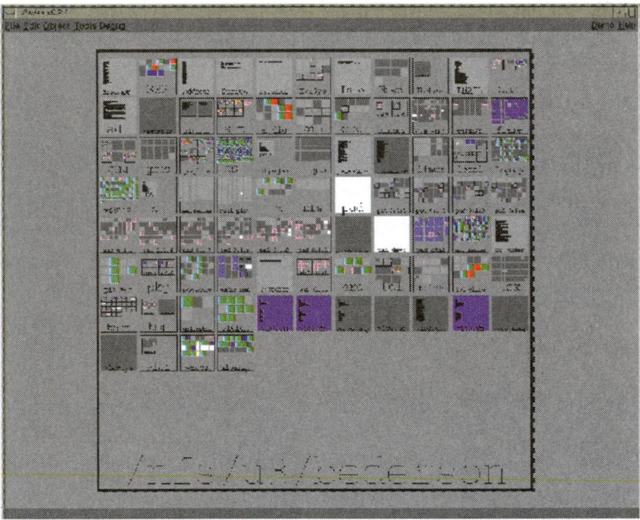

FIGURE **1.33**

Pad++ provides interactive zoom into a recursive space of directories and files. Courtesy of Jim Hollan. See Bederson and Hollan (1994 ●).

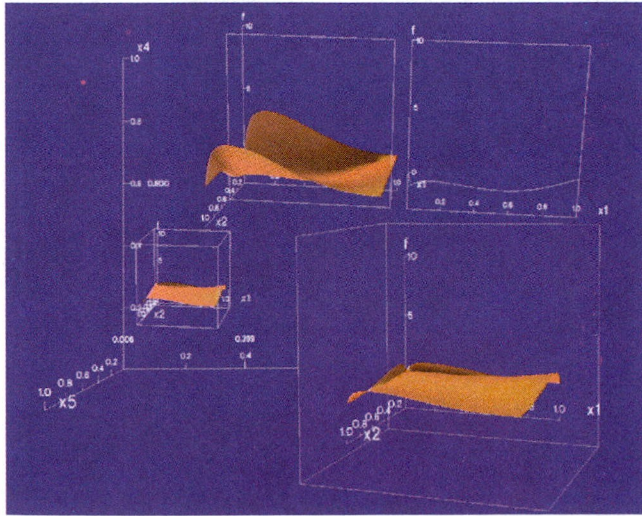

FIGURE **1.34**

Worlds within worlds (Feiner and Beshers, 1993, Figure 2) overloads space to visualize multivariable data tables.

Marks

Marks are the visible things that occur in space. There are four elementary types of marks (Figure 1.35):

P = *Points* (0D or zero dimensional),

L = *Lines* (1D),

A = *Areas* (2D), and

V = *Volumes* (3D).

Area marks include surfaces in three dimensions as well as 2D-bounded regions.

Unlike their mathematical counterpart, point and line marks actually take up space (otherwise they would be invisible) and may have properties like shape. They take up space to signify something that does not.

Connection and Enclosure

Point marks and line marks can be used to signify another sort of topological structure: *Graphs* and *Trees*. These allow relations among objects (e.g., Table 1.10) to be shown without the geometrical constraints implicit in mapping variables onto spatial axes:

Links → *Connection*.

Figure 1.36 is a screen shot of the hyperbolic tree (Lamping and Rao, 1996 ●), a visualization that uses a hyperbolic projection to show more detail in the vicinity of some focal point. The position of the nodes is used to make the objects more visually salient rather than encoding information directly.

Trees and graphs also use position to create gestalt properties such as proximity or closure (see Table 1.20). Because these are easily picked up as perceptual features, they can encode additional information such as clustering or partial trends. Trees typically start with a root node and continue with levels that represent the generations of children nodes.

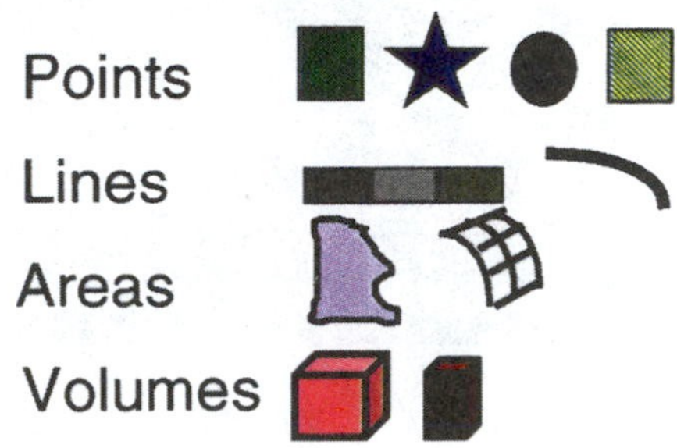

FIGURE **1.35**

Types of marks.

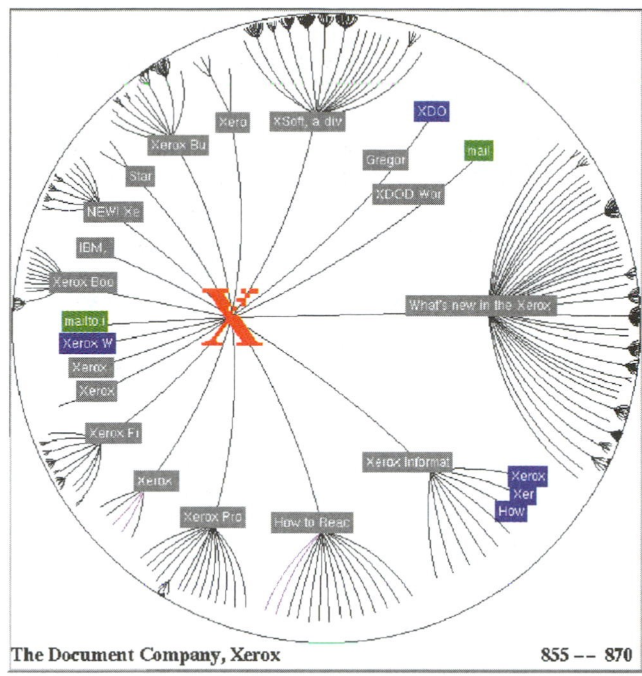

FIGURE **1.36**

Hyperbolic tree. See Lamping and Rao (1996●). Courtesy of Xerox Corporation.

These levels form an implicit ordinal axis that encodes the distance of a node to the root even when the Raw Data does not include this information explicitly, as in the radial axis in the hyperbolic tree. Constellations of data relations can trigger these as emergent visual properties, signaling the existence of the underlying data relation. However, as we have noted, care must be taken not to inadvertently express incorrect information (Mackinlay, 1986b●).

Enclosure can also be used to encode hierarchies:

Links → Enclosure.

Figure 1.37 is a treemap (Johnson and Shneiderman, 1991), mapping a library system into nested rectangles. The size of the rectangles is determined by the number of books. The hierarchy determines the nesting. Color indicates frequency of use (redder is more frequent).

Retinal Properties

Other graphical properties were called *retinal properties* by Bertin (1967/1983), because the retina of the eye is sensitive to them independent of position. For example, the FilmFinder in Figure 1.31 uses color to encode information in the scatterplot:

FilmID(FilmType) → P(Color)

This notation says that the *FilmType* attribute for any FilmID case is visually mapped onto the color of a point.

Table 1.21 shows Bertin's six "retinal variables" separated into spatial properties and object properties according to

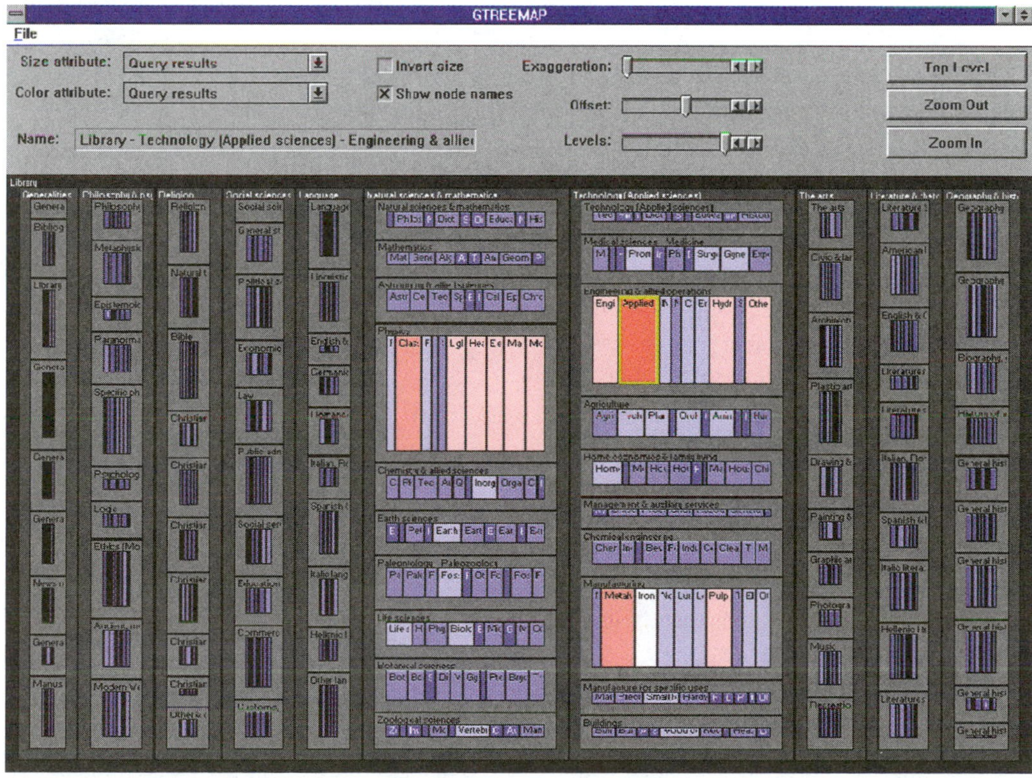

FIGURE **1.37**

Treemap of Dewey decimal classification. Courtesy of the University of Maryland.

TABLE **1.21**

Retinal properties.

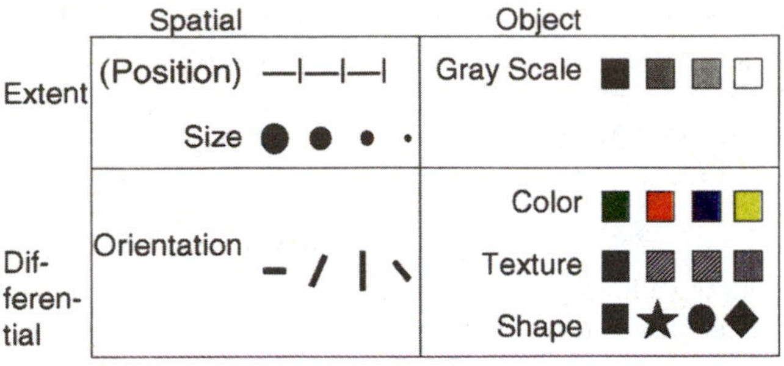

which area of the brain they are believed to be processed (Kosslyn, 1994). They are cross-separated according to whether the property is good for expressing the extent of a scale (has a natural zero point) or whether its principal use is for differentiating marks (Bertin, 1977/1981). Spatial position, discussed earlier as basic visual substrate, is shown in the position it would occupy in this classification.

Other graphical properties have also been proposed for encoding information. For example, MacEachren (1995) proposes *crispness* (the inverse of the amount of distance used to blend two areas or a line into an area), *resolution* (grain with raster or vector data will be displayed), *transparency,* and *arrangement* (e.g., different ways of configuring dots). He further proposes dividing color into *value* (essentially the *gray level* of Table 1.21), *hue,* and *saturation.* The usefulness of these requires testing. On the other hand, graphical properties from the perception literature that can support automatic visual processing (or at least preattentive processing) are other obvious candidates for coding variables. Several of these are collected in Table 1.22 from Healy, Booth, and Enns (1995). For example, lighting direction might be usable as a visual coding dimension in a Visual Structure, although to our knowledge this has not yet been attempted. We will use the retinal properties in Table 1.21 because they are a good basic set for our purposes, but it should be remembered that there are other possibilities.

Some retinal properties are more effective than others for encoding information. Position, for example, is by far the most effective all-around representation. Many properties are more effective for some types of data than for others. Grayscale, for example, is effective when used comparatively for ordinal variables, but is not very effective for encoding

TABLE **1.22**

Visual features that can be automatically processed (Healy, Booth, and Enns, 1995).

Number	Terminators	Direction of motion
Line orientation	Intersection	Binocular luster
Length	Closure	Stereoscopic depth
Width	Color	3D depth cues
Size	Intensity	Lighting direction
Curvature	Flicker	

TABLE **1.23**

Relative effectiveness of different retinal properties. Data based on MacEachren (1995, Figure 6.30). Q = Quantitative data, O = Ordinal data, N = Nominal data. Filled circle indicates the property is good for that type of data. Half-filled circle indicates the property is marginally effective, and open circle indicates it is poor.

	Spatial	Q	O	N	Object	Q	O	N
Extent	(Position)	●	●	●	Grayscale	◑	●	○
	Size	●	●	●				
Differential	Orientation	◑	◑	●	Color	◑	◑	●
					Texture	◑	◑	●
					Shape	○	○	●

absolute quantitative variables. Table 1.23 gives the relative effectiveness of different retinal properties.

Temporal Encoding

Visual Structures can also encode information temporally: Human perception is very sensitive to *changes* in mark position and their retinal properties. We need to distinguish between temporal Data Tables that need to be visualized, as in

$$Q_t \rightarrow \text{some visual representation}$$

and animation, that is, time used as part of a Visual Structure:

$$\textit{some variable} \rightarrow \text{Time}.$$

Time as animation could encode any type of data (whether it would be an effective encoding is another matter).

Time as animation, of course, can be used to visualize time data:

$$Q_t \rightarrow \text{Time}.$$

This is natural but not always the most effective encoding. Mapping time data into space allows comparisons between two points in time. For example, if we map time and a function of time into space (e.g., time and accumulated rainfall),

$$Q_t \rightarrow Q_x \text{ [make time be the X-axis]}$$
$$f(Q_t) \rightarrow Q_y, \text{ [make accumulated rainfall be the Y-axis]}$$

then we can directly experience rates as visual linear slope, and we can experience changes in rates as curves. Tufte (1994) shows a more sophisticated variant in which miniature visualizations are arranged along an axis of time. This display then becomes a control for controlling an animated sequence. Another use of time as animation is similar to the unstructured axes of space. Animation can be used to enhance the ability of the user to keep track of changes of view or visualization. If the user clicks on some structure causing it to enlarge and other structures to become smaller, animation can effectively convey the change and the identity of objects across the change, whereas simply viewing the two end states is confusing. Another use is to enhance a visual effect. Rotating a complicated object, for example, will induce 3D effects (and hence allow better reading of some visual mappings).

VIEW TRANSFORMATIONS

View transformations interactively modify and augment Visual Structures to turn static presentations into visualizations by establishing graphical parameters to create Views of Visual Structures. Visualizations exist in space-time. View transformations exploit time to extract more information from the visualization than would be possible statically. There are three common view transformations:

1. Location probes
2. Viewpoint controls
3. Distortions

Location Probes

Location probes are view transformations that use location in a Visual Structure to reveal additional Data Table information. Figure 1.38 shows the FilmFinder after the user probes a point in the scatterplot. The resulting details-on-demand pop-up window gives details about the film mapped to the point. Brushing is a form of probe where the cursor passing over one location creates visual effects at others' marks (McDonald, 1990).

Probes can also augment the Visual Structure. Scientific visualizations use slicing plane probes to access the interior of 3D solid objects (DeFanti, Brown, and McCormick, 1989). Streamlines are a probe that renders vector fields visible. *Magic lenses* (Fishkin and Stone, 1995) are probes that give an alternate view of a region in the Visual Structure. Objects in the region reveal additional properties of the Data Table.

Viewpoint Controls

Viewpoint controls are view transformations that use affine transformations to zoom, pan, and clip the viewpoint. These transformations are common, because they magnify Visual Structure or change the point of view, which makes the details more visible. For example, Figure 1.38 shows the FilmFinder zoomed into a small part of the scatterplot.

The problem with zooming is that the surrounding area (the context) disappears as the details are zoomed. One strategy, explored by the Pad (Perlin and Fox, 1993) and Pad++ systems (see Figure 1.33), is to make the zoom rapid and easy to invoke (they assign it to mouse buttons) (Bederson and Hollan, 1994 ●). However, this requires the user to remember information not visible.

Another viewpoint control technique is called *overview + detail* (Shneiderman, 1996). Two windows are used together: an overview of the Visual Structure and a detail window that provides a magnified focus for one area. The overview provides a context for the detail view and acts as a control widget to change the detail view. Figure 1.39 shows a visualization of an algorithm using an Information Mural (Jerding and Stasko, 1995a). The lower window gives an overview of the entire set of messages. The upper window shows the detail in the area indicated by the rectangle in the lower window. The message types are associated with a color resulting in characteristic color patterns in the overview window. Zoom factors of between 5 and 30 seem to work best, with larger zoom factors requiring an intermediate view (Shneiderman, 1998; Plaisant, Doan, and Shneiderman, 1995).

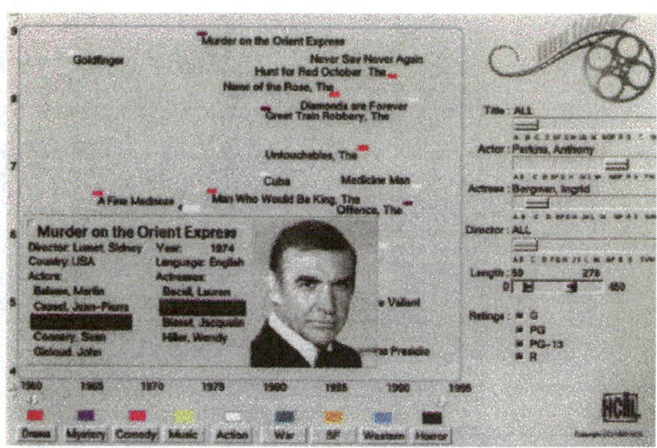

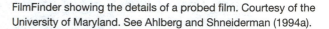

FIGURE **1.38**

FilmFinder showing the details of a probed film. Courtesy of the University of Maryland. See Ahlberg and Shneiderman (1994a).

The overview + detail technique has both strengths and weaknesses. One strength is that it is simple to implement and understand. Another strength is that it can provide rapid access to the details of a visualization that is too large to fit on a computer display. Its primary weakness is that comparison may require the movement of the detail window, including disrupting shifts of attention to the overview window. Overview analysis may require Visual Structures that do not fit in the overview window, which is typically much smaller than the detail window.

Distortion

Distortion is a visual transformation that modifies a Visual Structure to create focus + context views. Overview and detail are combined into a single Visual Structure. The *hyperbolic tree* (Figure 1.36) distorts a large tree layout (actually it distorts the space on which the tree is laid out) with a hyperbolic transformation that maps a plane to a circle, shrinking the nodes of the tree far from the root. The *perspective wall*, shown in Figure 1.40, shows when files in a computer system were modified. Clicking on the file symbols in the bent part of the wall slides the wall so as to bring them into the central focus area.

Distortion is effective when the user can perceive the larger undistorted Visual Structure through the distortion. For example, the *bifocal lens* (Spence and Apperley, 1982 ●) supports the perception of linear sequence, although objects

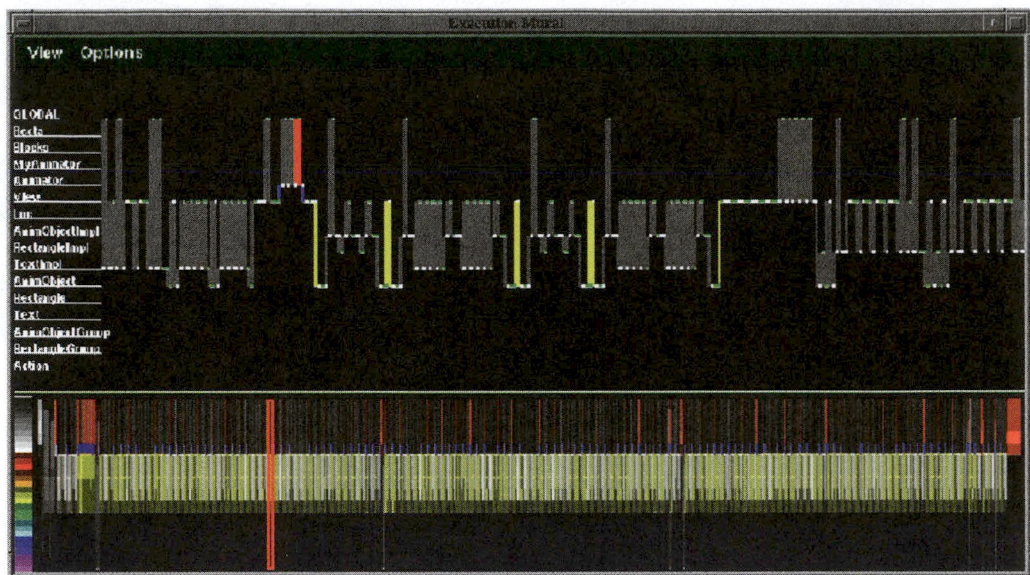

FIGURE **1.39**

Information Mural (Jerding and Stasko, 1995a, Figure 2) used overview + detail to view a long sequence of messages in a program performing a bubble sort.

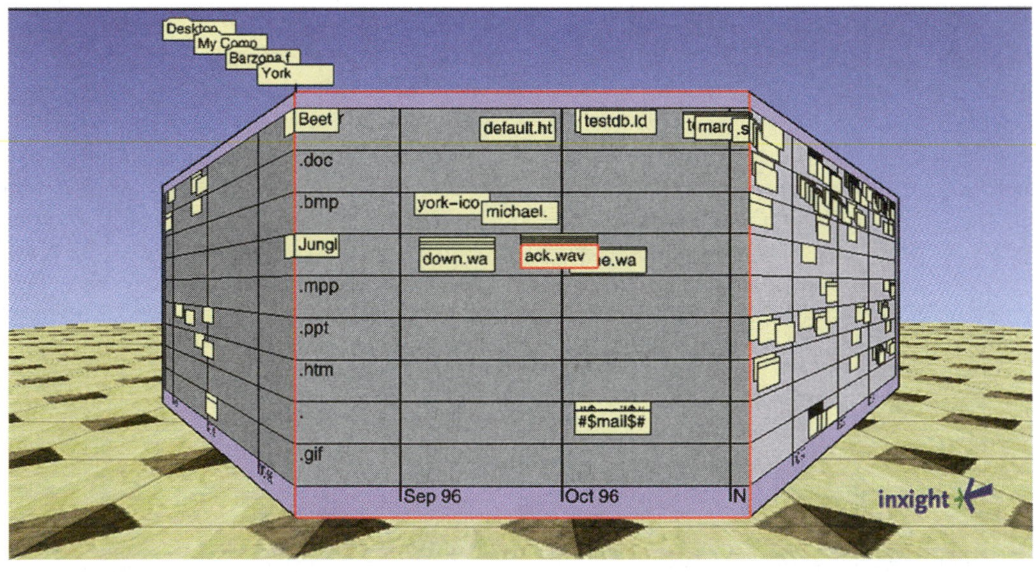

FIGURE **1.40**

Perspective wall. Courtesy of Inxight Software and Xerox Corporation. See Mackinlay, Robertson, and Card (1991).

outside the focal area have distorted aspect ratios. Distortions can be roughly classified by what the human perceives as invariant. The perspective wall (Mackinlay, Robertson, and Card, 1991) is similar to the bifocal lens, but the human perceives the linear sequence as folded, which means it is a distortion that leaves even the metric information invariant (Mackinlay, 1986b ●). The bifocal lens is an example of a 1D distortion that leaves ordering invariant. The *table lens* (Rao and Card, 1994 ●) is an example of a 2D distortion that leaves ordering invariant. Three-dimensional distortions are also possible (Carpendale, Cowperthwaite, and Fracchia, 1997 ●). The next most general type of distortion leaves topological relationships invariant, e.g., the hyperbolic tree (Lamping and Rao, 1996 ●). Distortion is not effective when the features or patterns of use to the user are distorted in a way harmful to the task.

INTERACTION AND TRANSFORMATION CONTROLS

The final part of our reference model (Figure 1.23) is human interaction, completing the loop between visual forms and control of visualization parameters in the service of some task. The most obvious form of interaction is direct manipulation. For example, the nodes in a hyperbolic tree (Figure 1.36) can be dragged with the mouse to the center of the display.

Interaction includes techniques for controlling mappings in Figure 1.23:

Raw Data → Data Table. The FilmFinder (Figure 1.31) is an example of the interactive control of data mappings. The sliders filter cases from the complete Data Table of films, selecting those that appear in the Visual Structure scatterplot. The resulting query is a conjunct of ranges specified using the user interface widgets shown in Figure 1.31. The resulting tight coupling between query and result is more effective than entering query commands.

Data Table → Visual Structure. Interactive control of the mapping from Data Table to Visual Structure can be provided in a separate user interface or integrated with the Visual Structure. Many scientific visualization systems use a separate dataflow window for their controls. Data Tables and Visual Structure are represented in this window as rectangles that have input and output spots. The user controls the mapping by connecting inputs to outputs. In contrast, integrated techniques allow the user to click on parts of the Visual Structure to change the mapping. In the FilmFinder, the user might click on the Y-axis to change *Popularity* to *Rating*.

Visual Structure → View. Interactive control of the view can also be a separate or integrated interface. Probes and viewpoint manipulations are typically integrated. Distortion techniques often have a more global impact that may require an external user interface, but they can be integrated. For example, the table lens provides small handles on the focal region for making changes.

CONCLUSION

The reference model of information visualization developed in this chapter approximates the basic steps for visualizing information: The first step is to translate Raw Data to a Data Table, which can then be mapped fairly directly to a Visual Structure. View transformations are used to increase the amount of information that can be visualized. Human interaction with these Visual Structures and the parameters of the mappings create an information workspace for visual sense making.

In real life, visual sense making usually combines these steps into complex loops. Human interaction with the information workspace reveals properties of the information that lead to new choices. Designing means for carrying out these mappings leads to a number of techniques. Table 1.24 lists some of these in summary. The rest of this book collects examples in detail.

In the papers that follow, we use the reference model to follow the literature in this newly emerging area. Chapter 2 surveys mappings of abstract data into spatial form. Chapter 3 considers methods for interacting with these mappings.

TABLE **1.24**

The components of the reference visualization model shown in Figure 1.23. Specific techniques are also included in the table. The specific techniques for Data Tables, discussed in the text, are a list of common data types that have well-known Data Tables. Tasks are operations that a user may want to do with the visualization.

DATA TABLES	VISUAL STRUCTURES	VIEWS	HUMAN INTERACTION	TASKS	LEVEL
Cases Variables Values Metadata	Spatial Substrate Marks Graphical properties	Location Probes Viewpoint Controls Distortion	Data Tables Visual Structures Views	Forage for Data Problem Solving Search for Schema Instantiate Schema Author, Decide, or Act	Infosphere Workspace Visual Knowledge Tools Visual Objects
			Specific Techniques		
Spatial (Scientific) Geographic Documents Time Database Hierarchies Networks World Wide Web	Position: NOQ Marks: PLAV Properties: Connection, Enclosure, Retinal, Time Axes: Composition Alighment Folding Recursion Overloading	Brushing Zooming Overview + Detail Focus + Context	Dynamic Queries Direct Manipulation Magic Lens	Overview Zoom Filter Details-on-Demand Browse Search Read Fact Read Comparison Read Pattern Manipulate Create	Delete Reorder Cluster Class Promote Average Abstract Instantiate Extract Compose Organize

Chapter 4 then looks in more detail at methods that dynamically focus on part of the space while maintaining a constant context, much like the visual system. Given the important role of text in knowledge crystallization, Chapter 5 focuses on methods for visualizing text. Chapter 6 is about visualization at other levels: infosphere, workspace, and visual object. Chapter 7 introduces some theory of information visualization. Finally, Chapter 8 discusses applications of information visualization and their implications.

Information visualization is a body of techniques that eventually will become part of the mainstream of computing applications just as computer graphics became part of the mainstream with the advent of bitmapped displays. At certain points, the development of technology crosses barriers of performance and cost that allow new sets of techniques to become widely used. This, in turn, has effects on the activities to which these techniques are applied. We believe this is about to happen with visualization technology and information visualization techniques. Information visualization is a new upward step in the old game of using the resources of the external world to increase our ability to think. As Norman says,

> *One method for expanding the power of the unaided mind is to provide external aids, especially notational systems, ways of representing an idea in some external medium so it can be maintained externally, free from the limits of working memory.* (Norman, 1993, p. 246)

Information visualization can help make us smart. Of course, leverage works both ways. It can also make us stupid by misadvised mappings and unworkable user interfaces just as "chart junk" graphics makes information harder to comprehend. This set of readings is about efforts to puzzle out the difference between these two outcomes by invention and analysis. Not every idea in these papers is a good idea. But collectively they are part of the exploration of the space of possibilities for using visual computing to think.

CHAPTER 2

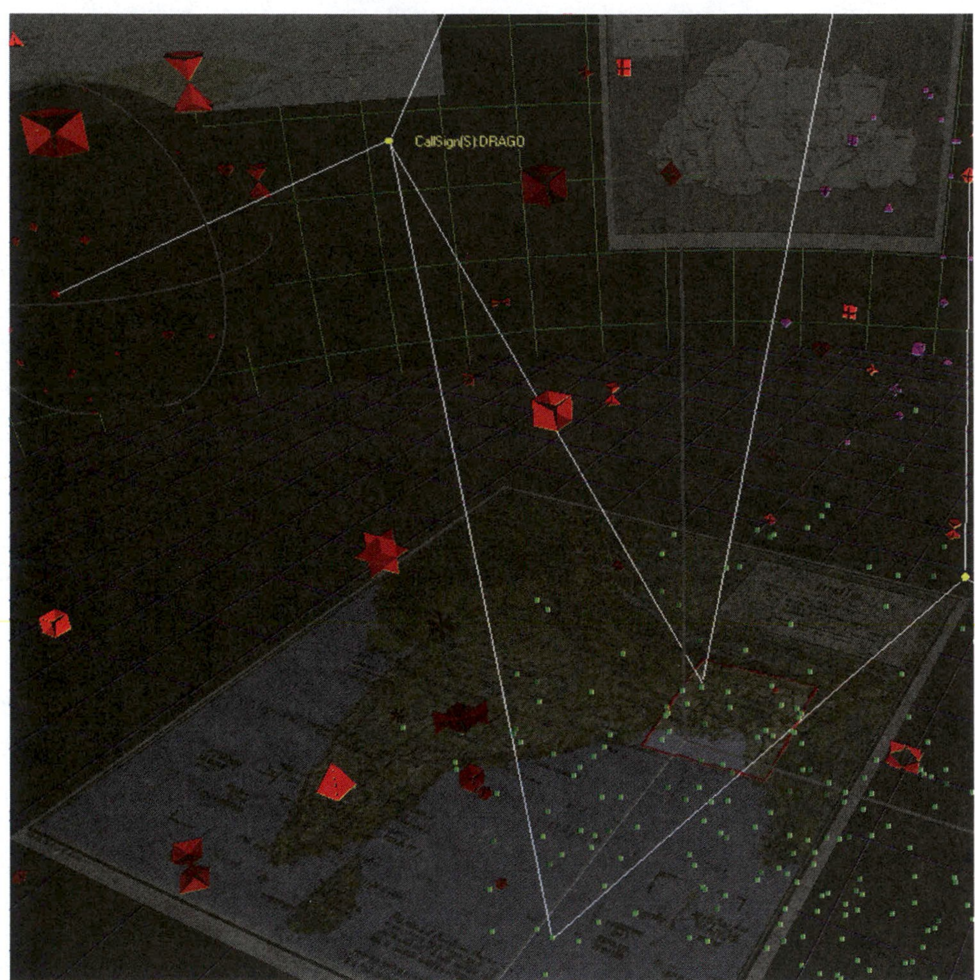

Genius seems to consist merely in trueness of sight.

– Ralph Waldo Emerson (1840)

Space

The fundamental strategy of visualization is to convert data to a visual form that exploits human skills in perception and interactive manipulation. Chapter 1 described this process with the reference model that maps Data Tables to Visual Structures. The focus of this chapter is on these Visual Structures. Visual Structures begin with the use of space.

The most frequent use of space is to mirror the physical world. Consequently, the chapter starts with a brief discussion of Visual Structures that encode physical data, a very common occurrence in scientific visualization. The remainder of the chapter discusses four ways space is used to encode abstract data, a common occurrence in information visualization:

1. 1D, 2D, 3D (orthogonal axis composition)
2. Multiple dimensions >3 (many axes or complex use of space)
3. Trees (connection or enclosure)
4. Networks (connection)

1D, 2D, 3D refers to visualizations that encode information by positioning marks on orthogonal axes. These Visual Structures are well known and are quite effective for Data Tables with only a few variables. Multiple dimensions >3 refers to the harder problem of multidimensional visualizations where Data Tables have so many variables that an orthogonal Visual Structure is not sufficient. Various techniques are employed including multiple axes and complex axes. Tree and network Visual Structures refer to use of connection and enclosure to encode relationships among cases.

Superficially, our organization is similar to Bertin's taxonomy for graphic constructions, which is described in the excerpt from his book in this chapter (Bertin, 1977/1981 ●). However, his organization is based on the number of variables in the Data Table. Shneiderman used a similar Data Table organization in a recent discussion of information visualization (Shneiderman, 1996). Basing a taxonomy on the number of variables in the Data Table is an excellent way to organize the general space of graphic constructions, particularly when focusing on multivariable data and 2D static graphic constructions. However, the Visual Structure organization used in this chapter is better for organizing information visualizations, which use computational techniques to create interactive environments not contemplated by Bertin. Consider the document lens visualization shown in Figure 2.1, which uses a focus + context technique to distort a 2D surface that holds an array of pages from a document (Robertson and Mackinlay, 1993 ●). This visualization involves 1D data (the sequence of document pages), a 2D Visual Structure (the surface), and a 3D spatial substrate (for the distortion). We classify the document lens as a 2D visualization that uses a 3D distortion to increase the amount of information. Data Table taxonomies, on the other hand, would focus on the 1D data of the document pages. The advantage of the organization used here is that it clearly indicates that the document lens is a 2D Visual Structure. Any data that maps to a 2D Visual Structure can be mapped to the document lens. Furthermore, new information visualizations can be placed into the organization by looking at their Visual Structure.

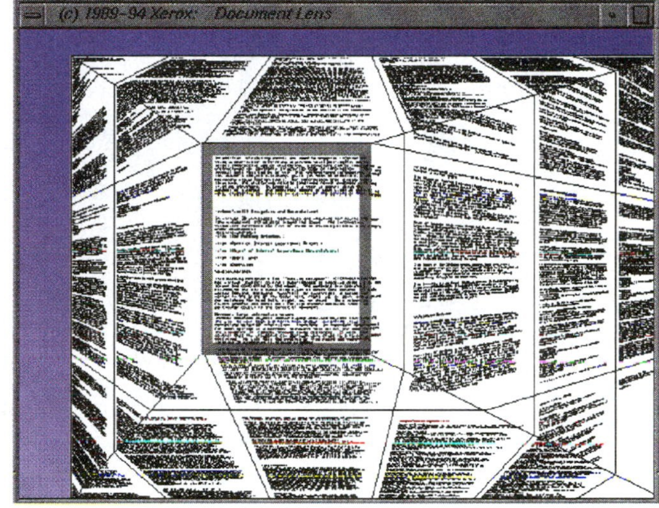

FIGURE **2.1**

The document lens.

2.1 Physical Data

SCIENTIFIC VISUALIZATION

Our first paper is a version of the NSF report that established the term "visualization" in computing. The National Science Foundation's Division of Advanced Scientific Computing convened a meeting in October 1986 of its newly organized Panel on Graphics, Image Processing, and Workstations to provide advice on graphics hardware and software for computer centers. The panel's conclusion was that visualization in scientific computing was a major emerging computer-based technology, deserving significant additional federal support. On the panel's recommendation, NSF sponsored a Workshop on Visualization in Scientific Computing in February 1987 bringing together computer scientists, computer vision experts, and scientists from various disciplines working in universities, industry, and federal agencies. The resulting NSF report was republished in *Computer Graphics* (McCormick and DeFanti, 1987). Reprinted here is a version of that report, prepared for *IEEE Computer.*

The authors of the NSF report were convinced visualization was a new scientific instrument that could accelerate progress in science. Data volumes were getting enormous, and more direct couplings between these volumes and the pattern recognition capabilities of the eye could help across many fields. In the panel's words, "As a tool for applying computers to science, [visualization] offers a way to see the unseen. . . . The gigabit bandwidth of the eye/visual cortex system permits much faster perception of geometric and spatial relationships than any other mode . . . " (DeFanti, Brown, and McCormick, 1989 ●, p. vii).

One context for the NSF report was the supercomputer centers that NSF had established. These had successfully made massive computing power available to more scientists, but scientists were asking for more graphical capabilities with which to examine the results they had computed. This was probably to be expected, since developments in science have long been coupled with the development of visual forms, as books like Robin's *The Scientific Image* (Robin, 1992) show.

But another technical context was the newly emerging capabilities of graphical computing. Figure 2.2 shows that graphical performance was increasing by about a factor of 10 every four years, making possible the computation of visual images at interactive time rates.

The report successfully identified and accelerated an important development in science. Ironically, progress in visual computing has been so great that the technical parts of the report now seem dated. Graphics performance measured in triangles/sec is roughly 1000 times greater than when the 1987 workshop did its work, making some of the arrangements in the report seem slightly quaint, even though it is just over a decade later. The link between graphics workstations and supercomputers is still important for some areas of science, but the increase in processing power and graphical processing capability means that most scientific visualization can be done without supercomputers. Commodity graphics accelerators can now perform at 1 to 5 million triangles/sec for a cost of around $25 (Hanrahan, 1997). This is roughly the performance of a 1992 SGI Reality Engine at a lag in time of about six years between high-end and commodity systems. The consequence is that the power of visual computing recognized in this report can now be applied to a wider set of problems and many scien-

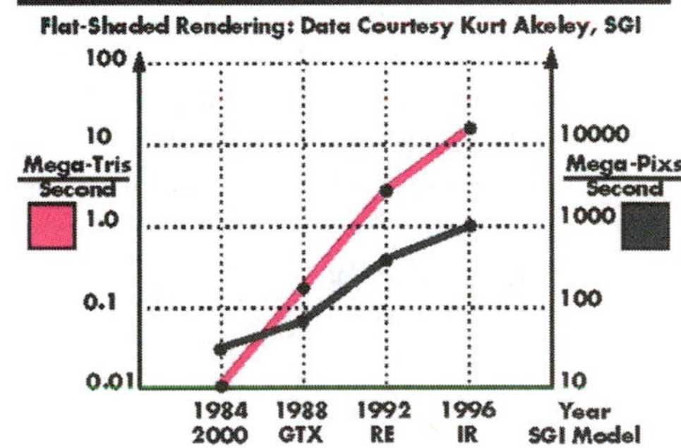

FIGURE **2.2**

Growth in performance of graphics computers as a function of year. Data are for leading models of Silicon Graphics computers. From Hanrahan (1997). Used with permission.

tific visualization problems can be done with commodity hardware.

The NSF report established a national agenda to fund the use of computer graphics and supercomputer simulation for scientific tasks and triggered extensive investment in scientific visualization. Scientists now routinely use graphical computers to access simulations on supercomputers much as the report suggested. In 1990, IEEE started the annual Visualization conference. The IEEE Visualization conference now has a companion symposium on Information Visualization. In 1995, the IEEE established a journal oriented toward scientific visualization, the *IEEE Transactions on Visualization and Computer Graphics*. The literature on scientific visualization has grown extensively, with several books published on the subject (Nielson, Hagen, and Muller, 1997; Rosenblum et al., 1994).

PHYSICAL DATA

The NSF report contains examples of the use of scientific visualization, all involving the visualization of physical data: molecules, medical images, brain structure, meteorology, space exploration, astrophysics, finite element mechanics, even mathematics. This is the second reason we have included this article: it is a convenient summary of the visualization of data that is spatial (which we notated as type Q_S in Chapter 1) or geographical (Q_g).

Physical data have the property that they contain spatial variables that can be mapped directly to the spatial substrate of a Visual Structure $Q_S \rightarrow Q_S$, or more explicitly,

$$Q_x \rightarrow Q_x$$
$$Q_y \rightarrow Q_y$$
$$Q_z \rightarrow Q_z$$

This concern with physical data leads to the development of grids that efficiently sample measurements or simulations. For example, the edges of an airplane wing may require a fine grid to sample microvortexes, whereas the surface of the wing may only require a coarse grid to sample a laminar flow. Many physical visualizations involve large computations of model values at many grid points. Previously, these were computed in batch mode and the scientist would have to redo the calculation to change the parameters of the model. But if the visualization can be seen while it is being calculated, the parameters of the calculation might be changed while the calculation is in progress. For example, the fineness or coarseness of the grid in some area might be altered. This control of simulations using visualization is called *steering*.

Although physical data can be easily mapped to a visual substrate, the resulting mapping may not be effective. In particular, physical data often involve spatial variables that map directly to dense 3D volumes—medical imaging, geosciences, computational fluid dynamics, and related disciplines. Common problems in making the visualization of 3D physical data effective have led to considerable work on volume and flow visualization.

VOLUME VISUALIZATION

Volume visualization addresses the problem of representing dense 3D volumes and providing techniques for seeing inside them. The medical images of Mosher and Johnson in the DeFanti et al. paper are examples. One approach is to divide a volume into small cubes called *voxels*, adjusting the transparency of the voxels to reflect the density of the material. In this way, bones might be seen under muscles. Probe techniques such as cut planes through the human head in the DeFanti paper are also used to see inside volumes. A related approach is to derive structure from the volumetric data. For example, algorithms can sample the volume to generate contours to form polygonal surfaces that can be rendered as geometric objects with material properties and lighting characteristics. Graphically agile computers render such surfaces efficiently. The geosciences example in the DeFanti paper shows that careful color choice can reveal additional information in a dense 3D Visual Structure. The finite element example shows how transparency can be used effectively.

FLOW VISUALIZATION

Flow visualization involves physical data that combine spatial variables with temporal variables, such as liquid or gas flows in a container. One technique is to introduce objects into the visualization that get their shapes or positions from the flow data. Streamlines work well for steady flows. Consider the space exploration example in the DeFanti paper showing lines representing the magnetosphere of Uranus. When an unsteady flow makes streamlines too visually confusing, a related technique is to introduce particles into the visualization that show the flow by their animated behavior. Abstract objects have also been used to encode variables such as velocity, acceleration, shear, and convergence (Leeuw and Wijk, 1993).

DISCUSSION

Physical data are an excellent source of visualization techniques, some useful only in a specific scientific discipline and some, such as volume and flow visualization, more generally useful. Furthermore, the scientific community has had the resources and skills to acquire and utilize graphically powerful computers when they were expensive and difficult to use. Information visualization is likely to mimic the successes of scientific visualization. As this book shows, abstract data can also be mapped to spatial substrates. In addition, the system requirements itemized in the DeFanti paper are becoming common in workstation and even commodity computers.

Visualization
Expanding Scientific and Engineering Research Opportunities

Thomas A. DeFanti and Maxine D. Brown, University of Illinois at Chicago
Bruce H. McCormick, Texas A&M University

Computational science and engineering (CS&E) describes a researcher's use of computers to simulate physical processes. CS&E parallels the development of the two other modes of science: theoretical and experimental/observational.

In addition to new methodologies, new technologies or mathematical tools have spurred the scientific revolutions. For example, calculus allowed Newton to codify the laws of nature mathematically and develop analytic methods for solving simple cases. Similarly, the development of the von Neumann computer architecture gave scientists the ability to solve the discretized laws of nature for general and complex cases.

CS&E now relies heavily on scientific visualization to represent these solutions, enabling scientists to turn mountains of numbers into movies and graphically display measurements of physical variables in space and time. This article explores the convergence of science and visualization, in support of its successful growth and development.

Visualization holds great promise for computational science and engineering, provided we can meet the immediate and long-term needs of both toolmakers and tool users.

What is scientific visualization?

Computer graphics and image processing are technologies. *Visualization*, a term used in the industry since the 1987 publication of the National Science Foundation report *Visualization in Scientific Computing*,[1] represents much more than that. Visualization is a form of communication that transcends application and technological boundaries.

A tool for discovery and understanding. The deluge of data generated by supercomputers and other high-volume data sources (such as medical imaging systems and satellites) makes it impossible for users to quantitatively examine more than a tiny fraction of a given solution. That is, it is impossible to investigate the qualitative global nature of numerical solutions.

With the advent of raster graphics, researchers can convert entire fields of variables (representing density, pressure, velocity, entropy, and so on) to color images. The information conveyed to the researcher undergoes a qualitative change because it brings the eye-brain system, with its great pattern-recognition capabilities, into play in a way that is impossible with purely numeric data.

For example, an observer instantly sees the vortices, shock systems, and flow patterns in a visualization of a hydrodynamic calculation, while these same patterns are invisible in mere listings of several hundred thousand numbers, each representing field quantities at one moment in time. When computing a space-time solution to the laws of physics, the particular numeric quantities at each event in time-space are not important; rather, what is important is understanding the global structure of the field variables that constitute the solution and the causal interconnections of the various components of that solution.

A tool for communication and teaching. Much of modern science can no longer be communicated in print. DNA sequences, molecular models, medical imaging scans, brain maps, simulated flights through a terrain, simulations of fluid flow, and so on, all need to be expressed and taught visually over time. To understand, discover, or communicate phenomena, scientists want to compute the phenomena over time, create a series of images that illustrate the interrelationships of various parameters at specific time periods, download these images to local workstations for analysis, and record and play back one or more seconds of the animation.

According to the visualization report, "We speak (and hear) — and for 5000 years have preserved our words. But, we cannot share vision. To this oversight of evolution we owe the retardation of visual communication compared to language. Visualization by shared communication would be much easier if each of us had a CRT in the forehead."[1]

Our CRTs, although not implanted in our foreheads, are connected to computers that are nothing more than extensions of our brains. These computers, however, might not be in the same room with us. They could be down the hall, across town, or across the country. Hence, the ability to communicate visually — and remotely — with computers and each other depends on the accessibility, affordability, and performance of computers and computer networks.

The visualization report recommends the development of a federally funded initiative providing immediate and long-term funding of both research and technology developments (see Table 1).[1] Research developments are the responsibility of tool users — experts from engineering and the discipline sciences who depend on computations for their research. Technology developments are handled by toolmakers — the visualization researchers who can develop the necessary hardware, software, and systems.

Tool users' short-term needs

Every researcher requires a personal computer or workstation on his or her desk connected with a remote supercomputer. However, not all scientists require the same level of computing power. Hence, a three-tiered model environment is beginning to emerge that categorizes visualization systems by such factors as power, cost, and software support.

Table 1. Recommendations for a national initiative on visualization in scientific computing.

	Short-term Needs	Long-term Needs
Tool users: Computational scientists and engineers	Funding to incorporate visualization in current research	Funding to use model visualization environments
Toolmakers: Visualization scientists and engineers	No funding necessary	Funding to develop model visualization environments

Table 2. Visualization facility three-tiered hierarchy.

	Model A	Model B	Model C
Hardware	Supercomputer or super image computer	Minisupercomputer or image computer	Advanced workstations (mini-/ micro- image computer
Bandwidth (potential interactive rates, bits/second)	$>10^9$	10^7-10^8	10^3-10^6
Location (where users interact with the display screen)	Machine room (at the center)	Laboratory on a high-speed local area network	Laboratory on a national/ regional network
Software (in addition to discipline-specific data generation and processing)	Commercial packages for output only (no steering). Research required to develop interactive steering capabilities	Commercial packages are mostly output only. Some interaction is becoming available. Research required to improve discipline-specific interaction	Commercial packages and tools are widely available for both computation and interaction. Research required in languages, operating systems, and networking
Administration			
Strength:	Support staff	Discipline-specific visualization goals	Decentralization
Weakness:	Centralization	Small support staff	No support staff

Workstations. Researchers need workstations with access to supercomputers for

- immediate access to local graphics capabilities,
- networked access to supercomputers, and
- hard-copy recording.

Local graphics. Workstations, minicomputers, and image computers are significantly more affordable than supercomputers, and they are more powerful and effective visualization tools. There are already some 20 million personal computers and workstations in the United States, compared with about 200 supercomputers. Workstation users are increasingly treating supercomputers as one of many windows on the screen, and scientists must be able to "cut and paste" between the supercomputer and applications running on their local machines.

Access to supercomputers. Scientists need to transfer data to and from a main computation device, but today's networks are too slow for use in visualization. Some temporary techniques reduce the demand for high bandwidth, such as off-peak image transmission, image compression, image reconstruction from abstract representations, and local image generation. Networking is therefore as critical as computer power in helping scientists.

Hard-copy recording. Whether the visuals are for personal analysis, information sharing among peers, or presentations in formal surroundings, equipment for producing photographs, slides, videotapes, or laser disks needs to be in place and as easy to use as sending text files to a laser printer.

Scientists need the ability to create ad hoc graphics to verify the integrity of their simulations, gain insights from their analyses, and communicate their findings to others. Low-cost animation facilities should be connected to every user workstation so researchers can make scientific "home movies" with little effort. High-end visualization capabilities and facilities also should be available at all research centers; high-end graphics become important for presentation and publication of

Low-cost, visualization-compatible workstations and networks

Our ability to communicate visually and remotely with supercomputers and each other depends on

(1) the ease with which we can use our office/home computers to connect with the outside world, receive and transmit visual information, and record this information on videotapes or slides, and

(2) the cost/performance of today's networks.

The Electronic Visualization Laboratory (EVL) at the University of Illinois at Chicago is doing research in both areas. We are designing as our scientific animation workstation a low-cost computer system with a well-integrated visualization programming environment.

Users at the National Center for Supercomputing Applications (NCSA) — or any of the National Science Foundation-funded supercomputer centers, for that matter — cannot do graphics remotely due to slow network speeds, centralized and expensive graphics equipment, lack of graphics software tools, and the need for specialists in film/video production. Our research is motivated by the recent availability of low-cost graphics hardware and a good PC-based visualization toolkit, coupled with a growing awareness that scientists need visualization more for personal/peer analysis than for presentations.

EVL is integrating affordable commercial equipment with specially designed graphics software to make visualization a reality for computational scientists — whether they use their computers on a stand-alone basis or connected to supercomputers over networks. (Regarding affordability, academicians can generally receive $10,000 in equipment monies from their departments or colleges without applying for external grants — our yardstick is that equipment should cost no more than a three-year-old Buick.)

EVL's scientific animation workstation, shown in the accompanying figure, has hard-copy recording capability and an easy-to-use visualization environment to facilitate scientists' needs. The following list corresponds to items 1-6 in the figure.

(1) Supercomputer access. Supercomputers are most efficiently used to run complex simulation codes, the output of which is numbers. With access to graphics, researchers can convert numbers to pictures to qualitatively examine the global nature of their simulation output. Graphics can be made available on the host machine or, more efficiently, on the local workstation.

(2) Televisualization: graphical networking. As images require more colors, higher resolution, or larger volumes of data, they need more memory and become more impractical to transmit over networks or phone lines, to store on disks, or to convert and display on different frame buffers. EVL's Imcomp compression and conversion software converts images consisting of 24, 16, or 8 bits per pixel to 16 or 8 bits per pixel, then compresses them further to 2 or 3 bits per pixel while maintaining a reasonable full-color representation.[1,2] The program takes only 0.4 seconds to run on the Cray X-MP at NCSA, and it converts and transmits a 512 × 512 × 24-bit image from NCSA to EVL over a 56-kilobyte line within a few seconds.

Moreover, visuals must be transmitted from memory to memory (that is, from supercomputer memory to frame buffer memory in the local computer), not just from file to file as in electronic mail-type networks. NCSA's Telnet communications software has been modified to do this and expanded to include Imcomp routines that automatically compress images.

In addition to compression, value-added nodes speed up graphical transmission by balancing transmission costs with local computing costs. Model data is sent over networks and then rendered or reconstructed at the scientist's end. EVL is currently investigating the use of its AT&T Pixel Machine as a graphics server that would render model data transmitted over the network from the supercomputer and then transmit the resulting images over a local area network to individuals' desktop computers.

(3) Truevision Vista graphics board. Scientists need to be able to preview, record, and play back animations at any speed and in cyclical fashion to examine the dynamics of their data changing over time, to spot anomalies, or to uncover computation errors. The Vista board's large configurable memory allows us to get anywhere from 32 screens at 512 × 512 pixels to 128 results once researchers conclude their work.

Three-tiered model computational environment. Observations of the way scientists use visualization suggest that a three-tiered model environment is evolving, as defined in Table 2. Each model is distinguished by hardware costs, computing power, bandwidth, location, software support, and administrative considerations.[1]

This model environment assumes that scientists want as direct a visual connection to their computations as possible. While supercomputers (model A) provide scientists with powerful number-crunching tools for generating data, they currently do not produce graphics; they do fill arrays with information that somehow gets piped to display devices. (Table 2 assumes that supercomputers and super image computers have equivalent power. Super image computers, although not commercially available today except in the form of a special-purpose flight simulator, will provide the specialized processing necessary for real-time volume visualization.)

Workstations give scientists more control over their visual output (models B and C). A workstation typically addresses its display memory the same way it addresses regular memory, incurring essentially no hardware overhead to display computed results. (Table 2 also assumes that minisupercomputers and image computers have equivalent power, and that advanced workstations and mini-/micro- image computers have equivalent power.)

Scientists should be able to select either more-expensive workstations with powerful visualization potential (model B) or less expensive ones (model C) while maintaining network connections to larger machines (model A) to do computations when necessary. This interdependency can work quite well. For example, a scientist can calculate 20-60 frames of a simulation sequence on a supercomputer, download the images to a workstation to create a minimovie, and then play back the sequence at any speed under local control.[2,3] (See sidebar, "Low-cost, visualization-compatible workstations and networks.")

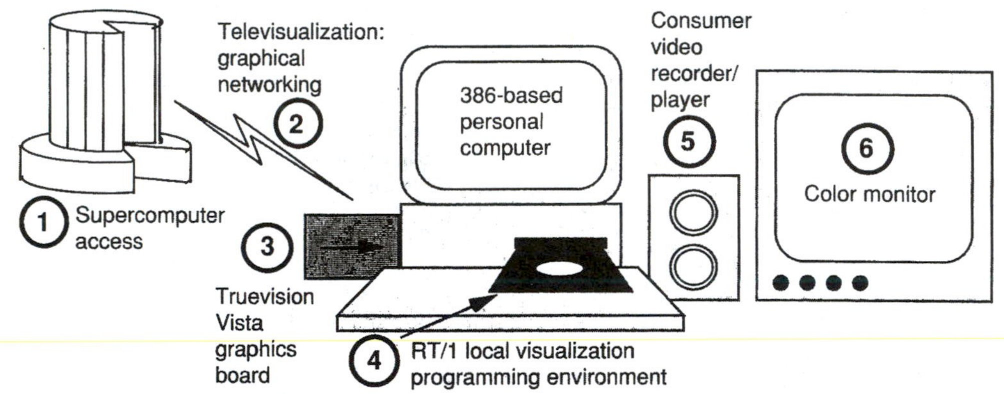

The Electronic Visualization Laboratory's RT/1 graphics language, an 80386-based personal computer, the Truevision Vista board, and consumer video gear comprise a scientific animation production facility that is economical enough to be made available to research scientists and engineers on a broad scale.

screens at 128 × 128 pixels, all at 8 bits per pixel. The board is also video compatible, so images can be recorded directly to videotape.

(4) Real Time/One (RT/1) local visualization programming environment. Scientists need a set of tools for picture composition, picture saving/restoring, fonts and text, resizing, rotation, moving, copying, hand retouching (painting), color manipulation, etc. They also need a local graphics programming environment in which to develop new tools or extend the capabilities of existing ones.

RT/1, an easy-to-use graphics programming language developed by EVL faculty and students, meets the criteria required of a visualization system environment. The language, written in C and running under Unix and MS-DOS, runs on all of EVL's workstations and personal computers. EVL is porting RT/1 to new workstations as they are acquired, extending the capabilities of the language, and developing application programs tailored to the needs of scientists.

(5) Consumer video recorder/player. If it's not recordable, it's not science. Moreover, the equipment for producing videotapes needs to be as easy to use as sending text files to a laser printer. We are integrating low-cost consumer video equipment into the workstation so scientists can quickly and easily preview and record frames of animation.[3] This equipment also comes with a built-in microphone so scientists can add narration or other sounds to visual recordings.

(6) Color monitor. Today's consumer video systems not only record but also can be attached to any television for immediate viewing of recorded material. Scientists can take a small video unit to a conference and plug it into a television there to share findings with colleagues. Should peers in other towns have similar equipment, colleagues could mail tapes to each other for viewing.

References

1. M.D. Brown and M. Krogh, "Imcomp — An Image Compression and Conversion Algorithm for the Efficient Transmission, Storage, and Display of Color Images," *NCSA Data Link*, Vol. 2, No. 3, National Center for Supercomputing Applications, June 1988, pp. 11-24.
2. G. Campbell et al., "Two-Bit/Pixel Full Color Encoding," *Computer Graphics* (SIGGraph Proc.), Vol. 20, No. 4, Aug. 1986, pp. 215-223.
3. T.A. DeFanti and D.J. Sandin, "The Usable Intersection of PC Graphics and NTSC Video Recording," *IEEE Computer Graphics and Applications*, Oct. 1987, pp. 50-58.

Table 3. Total corporate computing needs. (Source: Larry Smarr, NCSA, Sept. 1988.)

	Computational Science and Engineering	Data Processing
Corporate officer responsible	Vice president of research or long-range planning	Vice president of management information systems (MIS)
Tiered architectures	Personal computers and graphics workstations; midrange machines (mainframes/minisupercomputers; supercomputers *Need exists for multivendor, networked, hierarchical computing.*	Personal computers; minicomputers; mainframes *Software portability only partially exists between these levels, and then only within one vendor's product line.*
	Open systems *No vendor has emerged who offers integrated systems and end-to-end solutions. As a result, end users are faced with a confusing set of products from various vendors and nowhere to turn for advice on how to integrate them.*	Closed systems *IBM and Digital Equipment Corporation manufacture all levels of computers and the connections between them.*
Vendors	Fragmented market populated by start-ups and extremely high-growth companies: Workstations (Sun, DEC, Apollo, IBM, Hewlett-Packard, Apple, Silicon Graphics, Ardent, Stellar, AT&T Pixel, etc.); Midrange (DEC, IBM, Alliant, Amdahl, Convex, Scientific Computing Systems, Multiflow, Elxsi); Supercomputers (Cray, IBM).	Mature, slow-growth marketplace dominated by a few giant vendors, such as IBM and DEC.
Operating Systems	Unix	MVS, DOS, VMS (proprietary)
Networking protocols; telecommunications; speeds	Open network standards; Long-haul telecommunications; High speed = 1,000 Mbits/second *Because of the scarcity of $20 million supercomputers, most universities and corporate CS&E users are remote and must gain access to supercomputers over long-haul telecommunication lines.*	SNA, DECnet (proprietary); High speed = 50 Mbits/second *Within a corporation, most networks hook many "dumb terminals" up to a central mainframe where all the computing power resides. PCs are generally used stand-alone; those networked to a mainframe generally use the network to download or upload files, and computing is decoupled.*
Common unit of information	Image (megabyte) *Supercomputer simulations produce such enormous amounts of data that visualization is essential.*	Number (byte)
Common unit for computation speed	Mflops	MIPS

Additional models D, E, and F, corresponding to personal computers, alphanumeric CRT terminals, and batch output, respectively, also exist. They do not represent advanced visualization technology, so they are not included in our model environment. Note, however, that model F has been used to produce a great deal of animation for both the scientific and commercial entertainment industries for the past 20 years.

Tool users' long-term needs

CS&E is emerging as a new marketplace with needs distinct from those of data processing, as shown in Table 3. Success in the CS&E marketplace of the 1990s will depend on a commitment to standards, ease of use, connectivity, open systems, integrated systems, software portability, multivendor environments, leading-edge technology, and customer service and support.[4]

The list of research opportunities for visualization in scientific computing is long and spans all of contemporary scientific endeavor. The sidebar "Scientific and engineering research opportunities" presents specific examples of advanced scientific and engineering applications to show

Scientific and engineering research opportunities

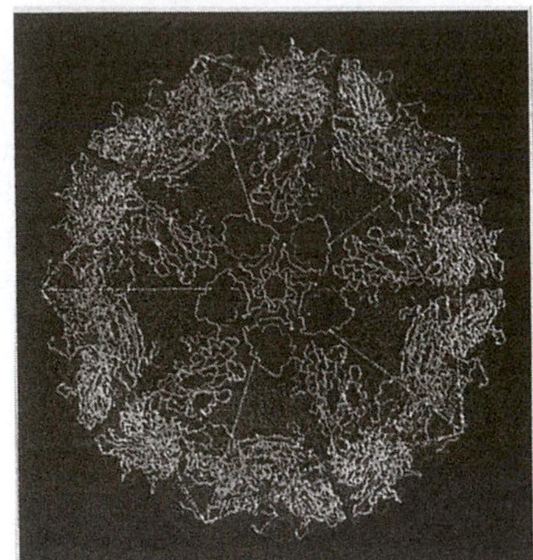

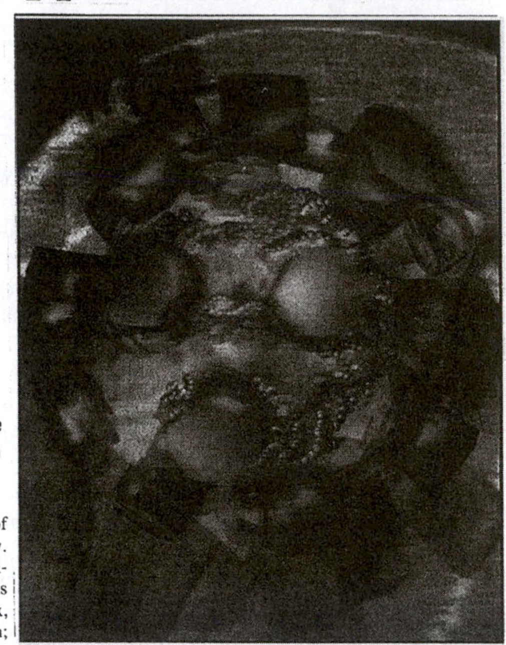

Molecular modeling. The use of interactive computer graphics to gain insight into chemical complexity began in 1964. Interactive graphics is now an integral part of academic and industrial research on molecular structures, and the methodology is being successfully combined with supercomputers to model complex systems. Two types of images can currently be generated: realistic pictures of molecules and 3D line drawings. Raster equipment is used to create realistic representations and animations, while vector hardware, used for real-time display and interaction, creates line drawings.

The image at left is a 3D line drawing of the rhinovirus, the common cold virus, showing its geometric structure and complexity. The image at right is an artistic rendering of the human papilloma virus (HPV). It was done by a group of Chicago-area artists who appreciate the underlying mathematics of nature and the complexity of the inner workings between atoms.[1]

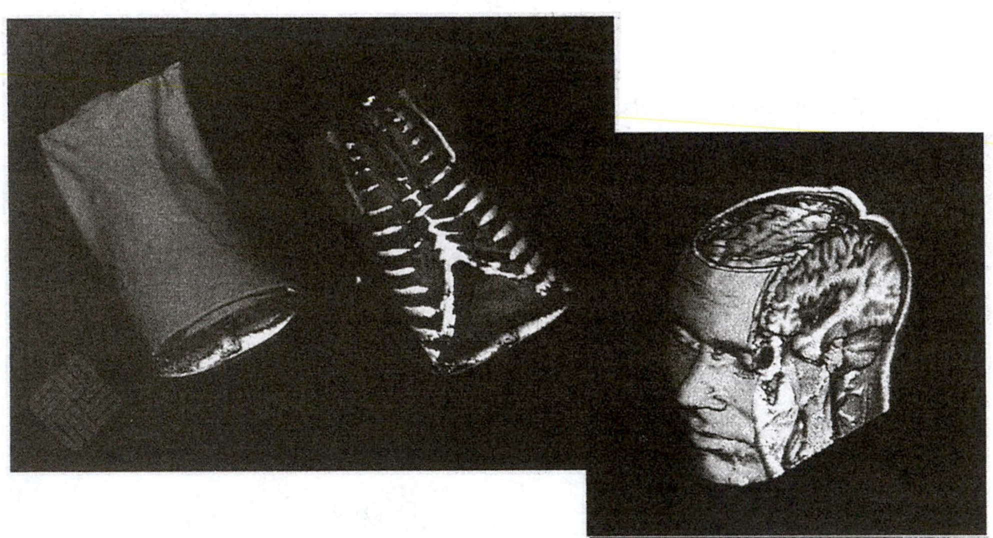

Medical imaging. Scientific computation applied to medical imaging has created opportunities in diagnostic medicine, surgical planning for orthopedic prostheses, and radiation treatment planning. In each case, these opportunities have been brought about by 2D and 3D visualizations of portions of the body previously inaccessible to view.

The above-left image is a shaded surface volume rendering of a 128 × 128 × 197 computerized tomography scan of a tree sloth. The opacity of various structures can be interactively modified to show the skin surface or to reveal internal structures. The bones of the rib cage, shoulder blades, and spine can be seen in the image on the right, as well as the trachea, lungs, heart and diaphragm.

The above-right image is a shaded surface volume rendering of a 256 × 256 × 61 magnetic-resonance imagery (MRI) scan of a human head. The rendering shows a mixture of surface and slice-based techniques, where external structures such as the skin are rendered with surface shading, while slice planes are voxel-mapped to reveal the original MRI data. Physicians can use this technique to relate the position of internal structures such as tumor sites to external landmarks. These images were generated using the Voxvu volume rendering tool on a Sun workstation with the TAAC-1 Application Accelerator.

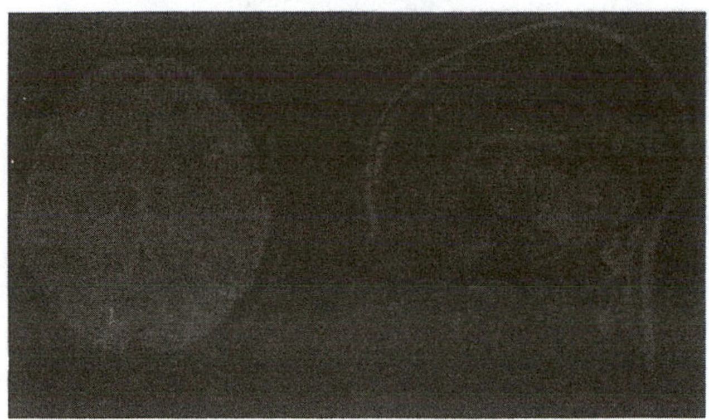

Brain structure and function. Rutgers University is using computer vision and visualization methods to automatically detect white-matter lesions in MRI scans of the human brain.

In the above-left image, low-level vision methods locate the outline of the brain, landmarks such as the interhemispherical fissure plane, and suspected lesions. The system calculates the orientation of the brain and uses the segmentations provided by the low-level methods to fit a deformable model to each patient's brain to determine the position and shape of difficult-to-identify organs or regions of interest. This customized model, shown in the above-right image, is used to obtain information about the anatomical position of the suspected lesions so that the system can reject false positives and determine the affected organs. The system has been tested on more than 1,200 images from 19 patients, producing good results.

Mathematics. These images illustrate a type of fractal known as the Julia set. A filled-in Julia set is a set of points that do not converge (or diverge) to infinity after repeated applications of a function, such as $f(z) = z^2 + c$. These functions are often investigated in the complex plane, but they also exist in the quaternions, a coordinate system that spans one real and three imaginary axes. Visualization helps mathematicians understand these equations, which are too complex to conceptualize otherwise.[2]

The above-left image is a quaternion filled-in Julia set minus its front-upper-left octant; the inner components of the four-cycle are revealed, defining its basin of attraction. The above-right image is a visualization of a dendritic quaternion Julia set in the complex plane; the unusual lighting uses a 3D gradient in the complex plane.

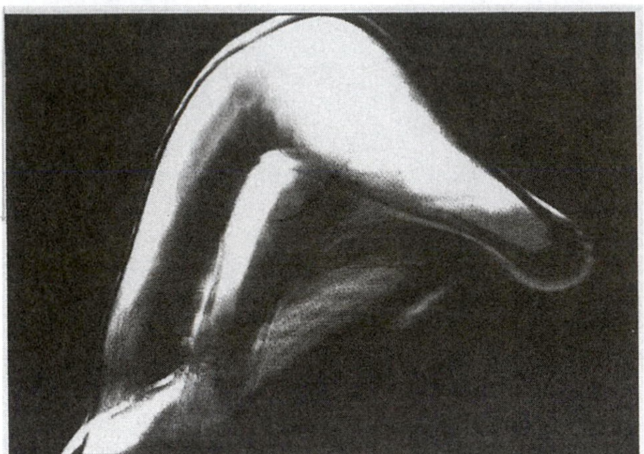

Geosciences: meteorology. The study of severe storms through observation and modeling helps research meteorologists understand the atmospheric conditions that breed large and violent tornadoes and the mechanisms by which tornadoes form and persist.[3] Theoreticians and field workers obtain information on behavior that cannot be safely observed; study the interactions of various environments, characterized by differing vertical wind, temperature, pressure, and moisture structures; and obtain useful guides for future research.

Transparency and volumetric rendering are used to view multiple surfaces; shading is used to display individual solid surfaces.

The above-left image uses voxel (grid cell) data to display rainwater and vertical vorticity information about a storm,[4] providing scientists with more information than if they had observed the storm with their eyes. The fuzzy region indicates low rainwater amounts while the bright white regions indicate large amounts of rainwater within the cloud. The vertical vorticity is texture mapped onto the rainwater with color; purple indicates dominant positive vorticity and blue indicates dominant negative vorticity.

The above-right image is from an animated simulation of a storm over Kansas, in which the rainwater surface was polygonized (tiled) and then rendered. The simulation clearly reveals substantial variations in the structure of the rainwater field not apparent earlier.

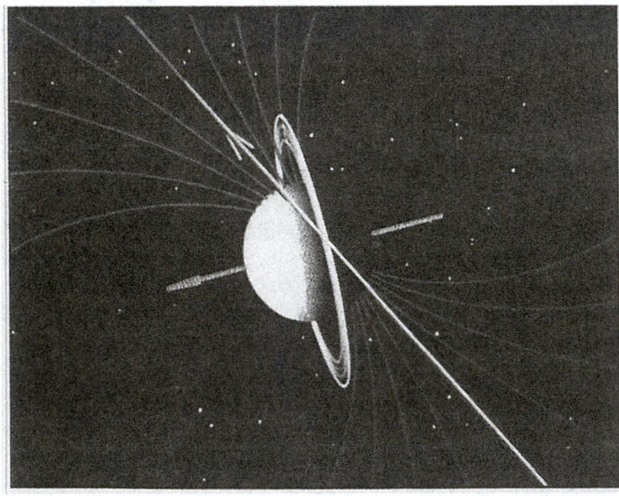

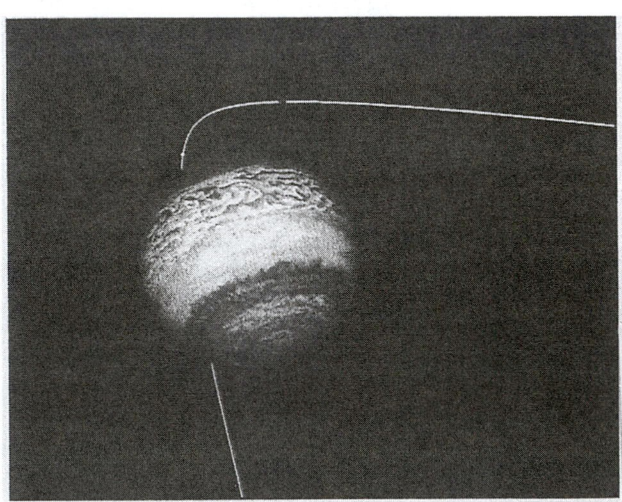

Space exploration. The field of planetary study involves the accumulation of huge volumes of data on the planets in the solar system. Enough data is now available that scientists are beginning to integrate observed phenomena and theory from other fields involved in planetary study: meteorology, geography, planetary physics, astronomy, and astrophysics.

The above-left image is from an animated simulation of the dynamics of Uranus' magnetosphere. The simulation shows that the angle of the dipole axis (purple arrow) is offset from the planet's angle of rotation (aqua arrow). The above-right image is from a simulation of the Voyager 2 Neptune encounter to occur in late summer of 1989. This image illustrates the path of the Voyager 2 as viewed from Earth.

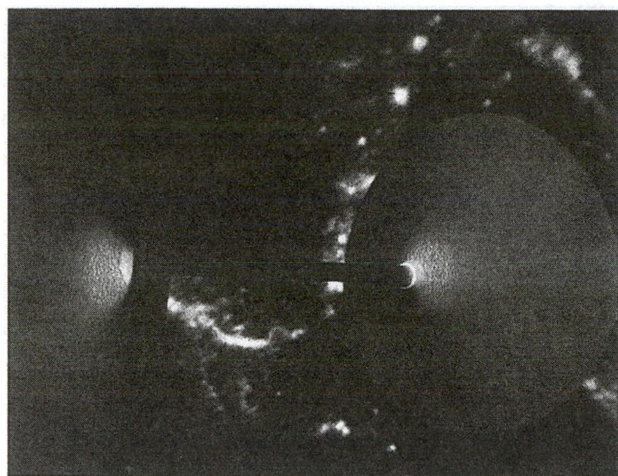

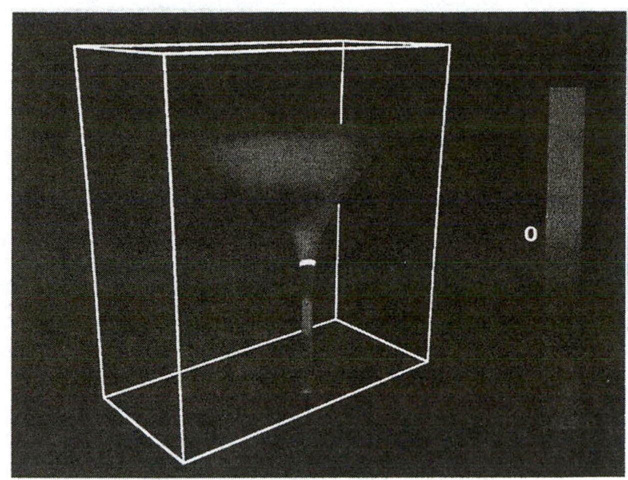

Astrophysics. Computational astrophysicists at the NCSA work with artists in an attempt to see the unseen and create visual paradigms for phenomena that have no known visual representation.

An embedding diagram of a Schwarzschild black hole and the behavior of its gravitational field, illustrated in the above-left image, was obtained from a numerical solution of Einstein's numerical relativity equations. The surface of the diagram measures the curvature of space due to the presence of the black hole, while the color scale represents the speed at which idealized clocks measure time (with red representing the slowest clocks and blue representing the fastest).

A black hole emits gravitational radiation after it has been struck by an incoming gravity wave. The above-right image is from an animated sequence that shows, for the first time, the influence of the curved space on the propagation of the radiation. Through the use of an isometric embedding diagram, the curvature of the space surrounding the black hole is represented by the surface on which the waves propagate. The white ring locates the surface of the black hole, and the regions above and below represent the exterior and interior of the black hole, respectively.

Computational fluid dynamics. Computational astronomers rely on supercomputing and visualization techniques to understand why jets from some galaxies flare dramatically. Magnetohydrodynamics code is used to solve equations that describe the flow of a fluid or gas with magnetic fields using finite differences.

The above image is a visualization of a cosmic jet traveling at Mach 2.5 passing through a shock wave (located at the left of the image). The jet abruptly slows and breaks up into a broadened subsonic plume whose morphology, or shape, is strikingly similar to that of a radio lobe of a wide-angle tailed galaxy. The morphology of the jet after impact is emphasized through the use of pseudocolor. This research has given astronomers important clues about why jets from some radio galaxies flare into broad plumes while jets from others remain remarkably straight and narrow.[5,6]

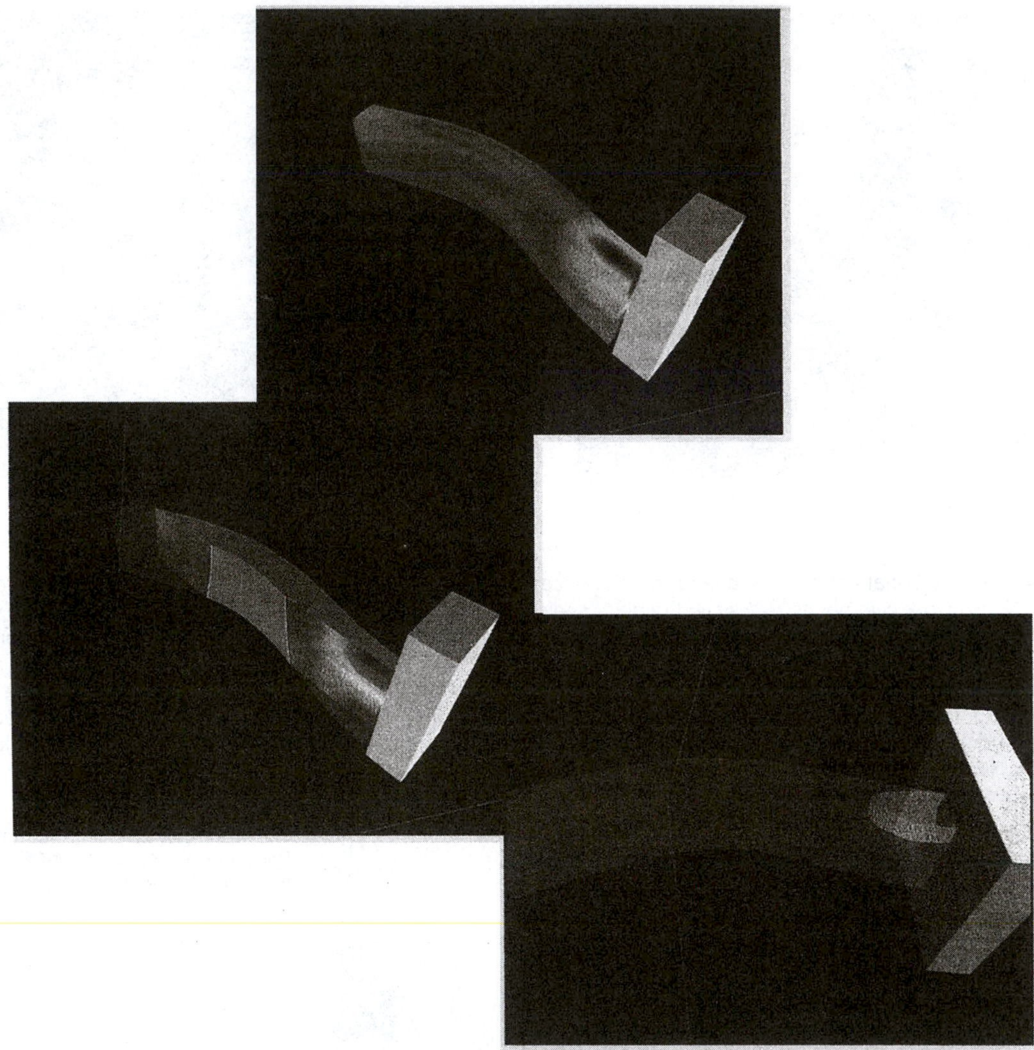

Finite element analysis. Finite element analysis is used in this example to show the stress distribution in a beam at its maximum tip displacement in the third eigenmode. The results were computed using linear elastic elements and a lumped-mass approximation.

The top image uses a conventional approach of displaying the stress values on the outer surface of the deformed shape. The middle image uses a cutting plane to look at the stress values on a cross section of the root of the beam. The bottom image shows a different view of the beam and uses an iso-contour stress surface to convey the three-dimensional nature of the stress concentration at the root of the beam. These images are still frames from fully animated and interactive models. They were computed and rendered on a Silicon Graphics 4D/120 GTX workstation using the SolidView program to perform real-time cutting and iso-contour surface generation.

References

1. R.P. Feynman, *Surely You're Joking, Mr. Feynman! Adventures of a Curious Character*, Bantam Books, 1986, pp. 236-253.

2. J.C. Hart, D.J. Sandin, and L.H. Kauffman, "Ray Tracing Deterministic 3D Fractals," to be published in *SIGGraph 89 Conf. Proc., Computer Graphics*, Vol. 23, No. 4, Aug. 1989.

3. R.B. Wilhelmson, "Numerical Simulations of Severe Storms," *Proc. Fourth Int'l Symp.: Science and Engineering on Cray Supercomputers*, Cray Research, Oct. 1988.

4. C. Upson and M. Keeler, "VBuffer: Visible Volume Rendering," *SIGGraph 88 Conf. Proc., Computer Graphics*, Vol. 22, No. 4, Aug. 1988, pp. 59-64.

5. K.-H.A. Winkler and M.L. Norman, "Munacolor: Understanding High-Resolution Gas Dynamical Simulations Through Color Graphics," *Astrophysical Radiation Hydrodynamics*, D. Reidel Publishing, 1986, pp. 223-243.

6. N.J. Zabusky, "Computational Synergetics," *Physics Today*, July 1984, reprint.

how visualization tools are helping researchers understand and steer computations. Our examples fall into the following categories:

- Molecular modeling,
- Medical imaging,
- Brain structure and function,
- Mathematics,
- Geosciences (meteorology),
- Space exploration,
- Astrophysics,
- Computational fluid dynamics, and
- Finite element analysis.

Toolmakers' short-term needs

Commercial industry currently supports visualization hardware and software, as listed below. There is a pressing need to educate the scientific and engineering research communities about the available equipment.

Software. Commercial visualization software exists in the following categories:

Lines. The earliest software for graphics drew lines in three dimensions and projected them onto a two-dimensional plane, offered viewing transformations for looking at the result, and offered transformations (scale, rotate, and translate) for describing the line objects. The theory and practice of drawing lines, expressed in homogeneous coordinates, and the control and display of lines using 4×4 matrices, represented a major development in computer graphics.

A variety of current standards incorporate these basic principles, and the CAD/CAM industry has embraced this level of the art. It is cheap enough to put on every engineer's desk and fast enough for real-time interaction.

Polygonal surfaces. The next level of software — surfaces represented by polygons — has only recently been built into hardware. Polygon filling, or tiling, is commonly available in hardware and software. Hidden surface removal is included, and antialiasing of polygon edges is sometimes provided to remove distracting stair-steps, or jaggies. Light sources can be incorporated into the rendered image, but they are usually point sources at infinity emitting white light.

Patches. The next level of sophistication represents surfaces as curved surface pieces called patches. This is still largely a software domain, although we expect hardware to appear soon. The most advanced software packages handle a variety of patch types. They also provide very sophisticated lighting models with multiple-colored lights and distributed or point sources located either at infinity or in the scene.

Antialiasing is assumed, and the packages handle optical effects such as transparency, translucency, refraction, and reflection. Research software provides even more features that produce greater realism, such as articulated motion blur, depth of field, follow focus, constructive solid geometry, and radiosity.

The software contains no practical limit on scene complexity (such as the number of allowable polygons), but computation of highly complex scenes on a supercomputer can take anywhere from 0.5 to 1.5 hours per frame.

Image processing. Image processing software has followed a separate path over the last 15 years. The elaborate software packages now available provide functions such as convolution, Fourier transform, histogram, histogram equalization, edge detection, edge enhancement, noise reduction, thresholding, segmentation, bicubic and biquadratic warping, and resampling.

Many of these functions have been hard-wired into special boards. General-purpose processors have only recently become powerful enough to make software competitive with hardware while maintaining generality. Image computers can run both computer graphics and image processing software packages.

Animation. In its broadest sense, animation means movement. It frequently connotes the complex motion of many objects, possibly articulated, moving simultaneously, and interacting with one another. Animation is desirable for the visualization of dynamic, complex processes. Basic animation control routines should be part of any standard visualization tool kit.

Glue. A class of software appreciated by visualization professionals but not necessarily by scientists is the "glue" used to combine images generated or analyzed by the packages described above. For convenience, a user must have tools for picture composition, picture saving/restoring, fonts and text, resizing, rotation, moving, copying, hand retouching (painting), color manipulation, etc. Together, these functions comprise a visualization environment system, which is to visualization what an operating system is to general computing.

Window systems. Windowing systems are commonplace in black-and-white bit graphics and are being extended to color graphics. Visualization software must incorporate and remain consistent with windowing concepts.

Volume visualization. Volume visualization software is still rudimentary. Algorithms for rendering lines, curves, surfaces, and volumes into volume memories are only now becoming available.[5,6] Hidden volume removal is unknown, the compositing of volumes is yet to be fully addressed, 3D paint programs (sculpting programs) have yet to be written, and general utilities for arbitrary rotation and size change of volumes do not exist. In other words, there is much research to be done in this field.

Hardware. The following are available commercial visualization hardware tools:

Input devices. Current digital input devices include supercomputers, satellites, medical scanners, seismic recorders, and digitizing cameras. The rapidly increasing bandwidth of these devices emphasizes the need for work in volume visualization.

We expect continued improvement in the resolution and bandwidth of input devices. Supercomputers will get faster and the resolution of images from satellites will increase. Real-time video digitizers already exist. Monochrome digital digitizers with $2,048 \times 2,048$-pixel resolution are becoming quite fast, although they do not yet operate at real-time speeds. Print-quality input scanners are still quite expensive, but we expect the prices to fall as digital technology cheapens and competing scanning technologies mature. CCD (charge-coupled device) array input scanners will improve in resolution and become serious candidates for input devices in high-resolution work.

Interactive input devices are continually improving. Common 2D devices include knobs, switches, pedals, mice, and tablets. Tablets are the most general and also need the most improvement; they need higher resolution, higher speed, and more degrees of freedom.

Six-dimensional interactive devices are also available, providing the usual 3D positional information plus three degrees of orientation information (yaw, pitch, and roll). Higher-dimensional devices, such as the data glove, have begun to appear. These will improve to offer higher resolution, higher speed, and lower cost.

Output devices. Raster displays of 2D frame buffers have improved steadily to offer more colors, higher resolutions, and less flicker. A typical color raster display today offers a 1,280 × 1,024-pixel display at 60 frames per second and 24 bits of color per pixel (16 megacolors).

High-definition television (HDTV) — a proposed standard that will offer larger, brighter, sharper pictures than currently available in video — will affect visualization. Also, video is moving toward an all-digital format, designated 4:2:2, to standardize digital interconnections of diverse video products.

Color raster displays will evolve toward 2,048 × 2,048 pixels in the next several years. The displays themselves already exist in limited quantities, but the computational bandwidth required to feed them is still lacking. Black-and-white 2D raster displays already have resolutions greater than 2,048 × 2,048 pixels with enough bandwidth to feed them. These displays will certainly reach even higher resolutions in the next five years.

Stereo displays are also beginning to appear commercially, and we confidently predict that these will improve in screen size, resolution, brightness, and availability. These displays will be quite helpful in volume visualization.

Other output devices are similarly improving. HDTV will spur the development of compatible recorders. Film recorders will become cheaper as the technology becomes cheaper and the competition matures. Should stereo become a widely accepted mode of presentation for volume visualizations, then stereo film and video standards will have to be developed.

Workstations. Fast vector machines are now common and have extensive use in such areas as CAD/CAM and real-time 3D design. Recently, they have improved to offer color vectors and perfect end-matching. Frame buffers have been added so that surface raster graphics can be combined with vector displays.

Also, fast surface machines are about to arrive. They exist in simplified forms already and in more advanced states as firmware in special machines. Chips are now being built to speed up certain aspects of surface rendering, particularly the tiling of polygons. By 1990, full hardware support of surface graphics will be available, offering rendering features such as texture mapping, bump mapping, antialiasing, reflections, transparency, and shadows.

Vector machines will initially serve as powerful, real-time front ends to surface machines. Eventually, surface machines will be cheap and fast enough to permit scientists to do real-time design using surfaces rather than lines.

Among image processors, fast planar machines have existed for some time. These machines contain special boards for certain aspects of image processing, such as fast Fourier transforms. Faster versions are becoming available that have wider processing capabilities and higher resolutions. In fact, the notion of a general-purpose image processor that can implement any image processing algorithm as a program is becoming common.

Toolmakers' long-term needs

Raw computing power would be more effectively harnessed than it is today if calculations could be understood pictorially and their progress guided dynamically. Modern modes of computing involve interactive, extemporaneous generation of views from masses of data and exploration of model spaces by interactive steering of computations.

A scientist's ability to comprehend the results of his or her computations depends on the effectiveness of available tools. To increase that effectiveness, we need to

- encourage the production of documented, maintained, upward-compatible software and hardware;
- motivate manufacturers to solve network bottleneck problems;
- encourage universities to incorporate CS&E and visualization in computer science, engineering, and discipline-science curricula; and
- guarantee the publication and dissemination of research and results on a variety of media.

Hardware, software, and systems. General visualization issues that need to be supported include:

- Interactive steering of simulations and calculations
- Workstation-driven use of supercomputers
- Graphics-oriented programming environments
- Higher-dimensional visualization of scalar, vector, and tensor fields
- Dynamic visualization of fields and flow
- High-bandwidth picture networks and protocols
- Massive data-set handling, notably for signal and image processing applications
- Vectorized and parallelized algorithms for graphics and image processing
- Specialized architectures for graphics and image processing
- A framework for international visualization hardware and software standards

Networking. The application of networks to visualization, called *televisualization*, encompasses much more than text transfer (such as electronic mail) and gateway protocol decoding. It also involves image transfer, which entails compression, decompression, rendering, recognizing, and interpreting. Televisualization requires a major enhancement over existing network capabilities in the following areas:

Increased data rates. The sheer scale of graphics and imaging data sets challenges the current bandwidth and interactivity of networks. Networks handle screenfuls of textual information well; network nodes are simply gateways that neither add nor detract from the quality of the message. But a 512 × 512-pixel image with 8 bits per pixel has approximately 100 times more information than a screen of text with 25 rows and 80 characters per row. A 1,024 × 1,024 × 1,024-voxel volume with 48 bits per voxel contains 16,000 times more information than a 512 × 512-pixel image. Gigabit speeds are sufficient to pass volumes of the current size of 256 × 256 × 256 voxels with 4 bytes per voxel, but this rate will have to be extended within several years to 1-gigabyte/second channels.

Compression/decompression algorithms. Compression improves the speed with which visual data is transmitted. Current schemes for full-color image compression work well,[7] but other forms of compression must be researched, and comprehensive protocols must be developed for managing all these capabilities:

Table 4. The evolution of communication tools.

Communications media	Number of years old
Sight	5×10^8
Speech	5×10^5
Writing	5×10^3
Print broadcasting	5×10^2
Visual broadcasting	5×10^1
Visualization	5×10^0

- Transmit the procedures to create the images rather than the images themselves.
- Transmit endpoints of vector images.
- Transmit polygonal, constructive solid geometry, or bicubic patches of surface models.
- Transmit semantic descriptions of the objects.

Value-added processing at nodes. Value-added nodes also speed up graphical transmission. Computers process text and numbers in main memory, occasionally transmitting some of them to peripherals. Images, however, often must be transferred to special memories for rendering, 3D imaging, or viewing. Each instance of transferring and processing an image aims to increase its visualization value to the scientist. The ability to process images at various nodes along a network embraces the central concept of distributed processing.

In distributed computing, transmission costs are balanced with local computing costs. It sometimes makes more sense to send model data over networks and then render or reconstruct the data at the scientist's end. This presumes that there is appropriate equipment at both ends, that the various software modules are compatible with one another, and that the software can run on a variety of equipment types.

A televisualization network for image passing between machines is analogous to the software paradigm of message passing between process layers. This type of networking, combined with interaction, cannot be achieved using conventional Fortran subroutine calls. Significant software development and protocol standardization are necessary to bring televisualization to the discipline sciences.

Interaction capabilities. Interactive visual computing is a process whereby scientists communicate with data by manipulating its visual representation during processing. The more sophisticated process of navigation allows scientists to dynamically modify, or steer, computations while they are occurring. This lets researchers change parameters, resolution, or representation, and then see the effects.

Teaching CS&E and visualization. The principal barrier to growth in the CS&E market is the fact that corporate researchers and managers lack education and training in CS&E technologies and methodologies. Few industrial researchers know how to use distributed CS&E to do their work and, more importantly, they do not know how to think computationally and visually. Other roadblocks include the following:

- The Association for Computing Machinery's approved computer science curriculum lists computer graphics as merely one of many optional topics; image processing is not mentioned at all.
- Engineering accreditors do not require computer graphics or image processing.
- Many engineering school deans are unaware of the importance of visualization or cannot justify the hardware and software expense involved in teaching the subject.
- The number of tenured faculty teaching computer graphics in American universities is about the same today as 15 years ago, and they are roughly the same people.
- Scientists, while educated to read and write, are not taught to produce or communicate with visuals.

Publication and dissemination. Contemporary scientific communications media are predominantly language-oriented. Printed media are coupled weakly, if at all, to the visual world of space-time. By contrast, half the human neocortex is devoted to processing visual information. In other words, current scientific communication leaves out half — the right half — of the brain. An integral part of our visualization task is to facilitate visual communication from scientist to scientist, engineer to engineer, through visualization-compatible media.

Publication and grants, and therefore tenure, rarely come to researchers whose productivity depends on or produces visualization results. Superiors evaluate scholarly work by counting the number of journal articles published; publications are text, and visual media do not count. Funding itself is based on the careful preparation and evaluation of proposals, which are documents full of words and numbers.

As scientists depend more and more on the electronic network than on the printed page, they will need new technologies to teach, document, and publish their work. Until scientists can build on each other's work, productivity will lag. Publishing (specifically textual materials) has always been a critical part of this building process, and it is one of the primary bottlenecks in CS&E's progress.

Reading and writing were only democratized in the past 100 years. Today, they are the accepted communication tools for scientists and engineers. Table 4 shows that, in time, visualization will also be democratized and embraced by researchers.

Electronic media, such as videotapes, optical disks, and floppy disks, are now necessary for the publication and dissemination of mathematical models, processing algorithms, computer programs, experimental data, and scientific simulations. The reviewer and the reader need to test models, evaluate algorithms, and execute programs themselves, interactively, without an author's assistance. Similarly, scientific publication must extend to use visualization-compatible media.

The use of visualization in scientific computing — in academia, government research laboratories, and industry — will help guarantee

- US preeminence in science and technology,
- a well-educated pool of scientists and engineers with the quality and breadth of experience required to meet the changing needs of science and society, and
- American industries that can successfully compete in the international economic arena.

The information age has yet to deal with information transfer. Visualization technologies can help lead the way to better global understanding and communication. □

References

1. B.H. McCormick, T.A. DeFanti, and M.D. Brown, eds., "Visualization in Scientific Computing," *Computer Graphics*, Vol. 21, No. 6, Nov. 1987.

2. T.A. DeFanti and M.D. Brown, "Scientific Animation Workstations: Creating an Environment for Remote Research, Education, and Communication," *Academic Computing*, Feb. 1989, pp. 10-12, 55-57.

3. T.A. DeFanti and M.D. Brown, "Scientific Animation Workstations," *SuperComputing*, Fall 1988, pp. 10-13.

4. T.A. DeFanti and M.D. Brown, "Insight Through Images," *Unix Review*, Mar. 1989, pp. 42-50.

5. R.A. Drebin, L. Carpenter, and P. Hanrahan, "Volume Rendering," *Computer Graphics* (SIGGraph Conf. Proc.), Vol. 22, No. 4, Aug. 1988, pp. 65-74.

6. C. Upson and M. Keeler, "VBuffer: Visible Volume Rendering," *Computer Graphics* (SIGGraph Conf. Proc.), Vol. 22, No. 4, Aug. 1988, pp. 59-64.

7. G. Campbell et al., "Two-Bit/Pixel Full Color Encoding," *Computer Graphics* (SIGGraph Conf. Proc.), Vol. 20, No. 4, Aug. 1986, pp. 215-223.

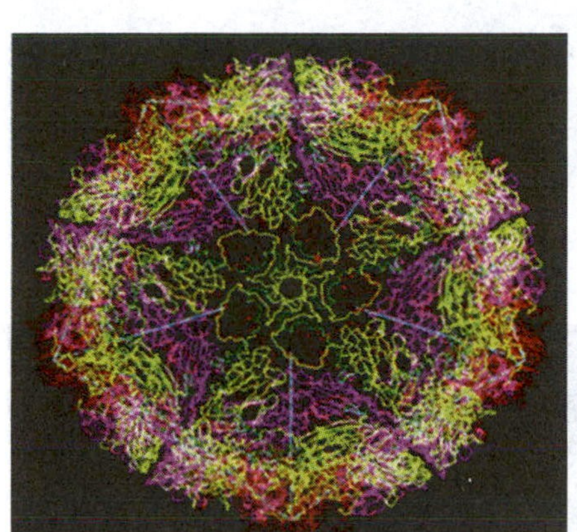

Molecular modeling.

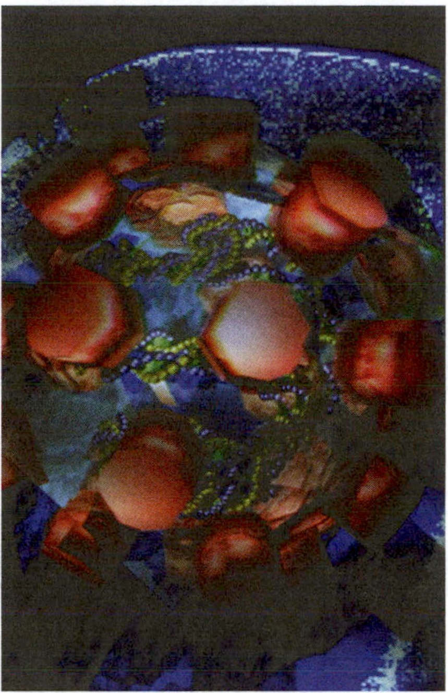

Molecular modeling.

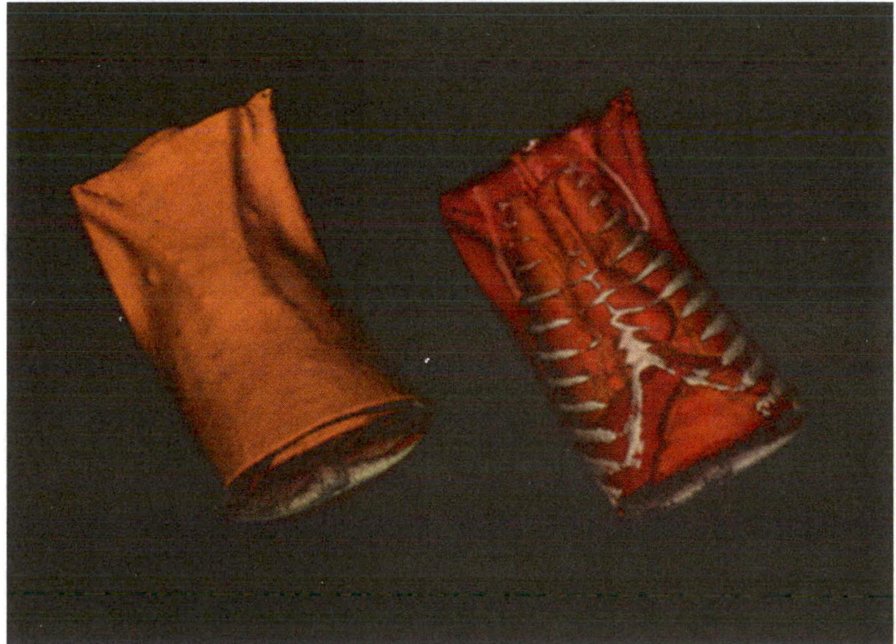

Medical imaging.

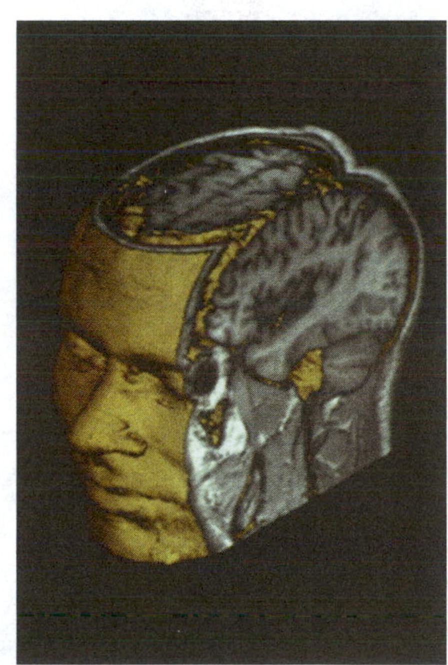

Medical imaging.

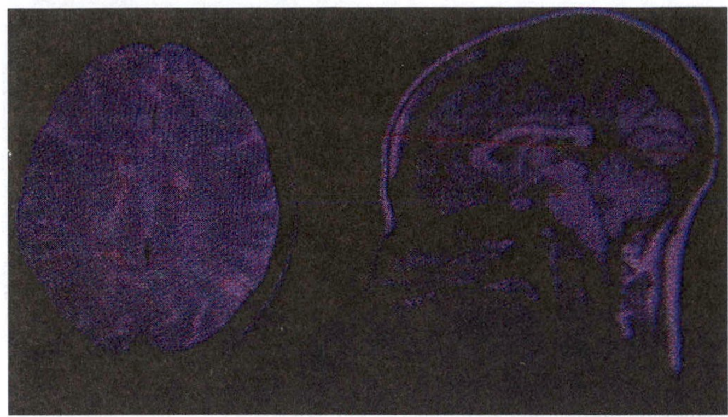

Brain structure and function.

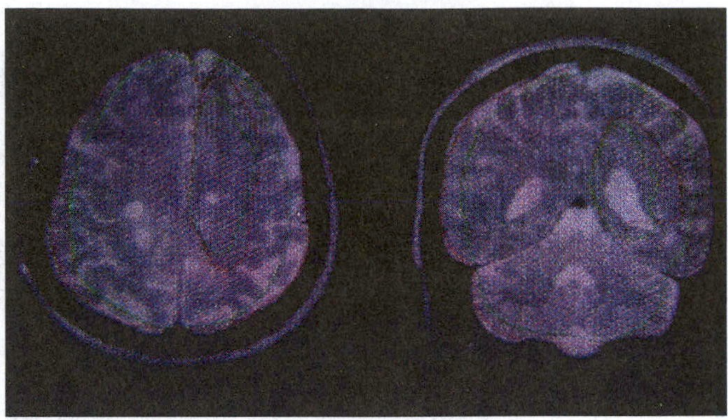

Brain structure and function.

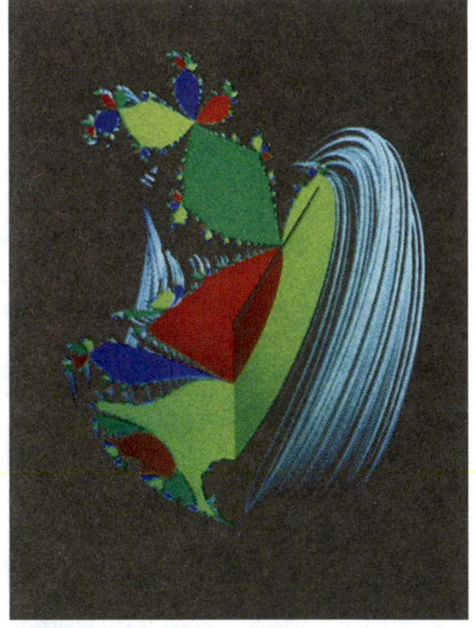

Mathematics.

Mathematics.

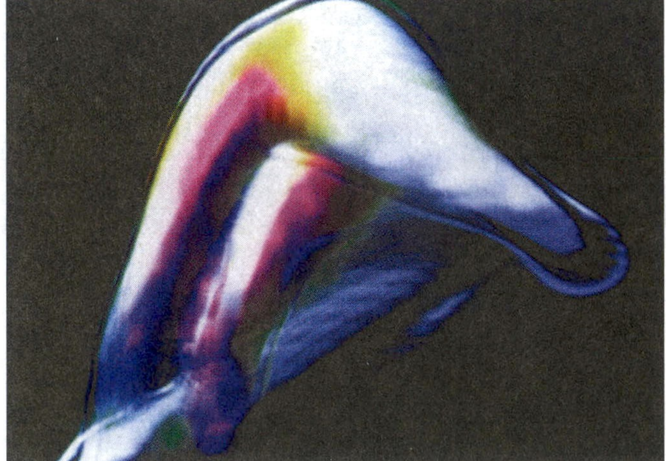

Geosciences: meteorology.

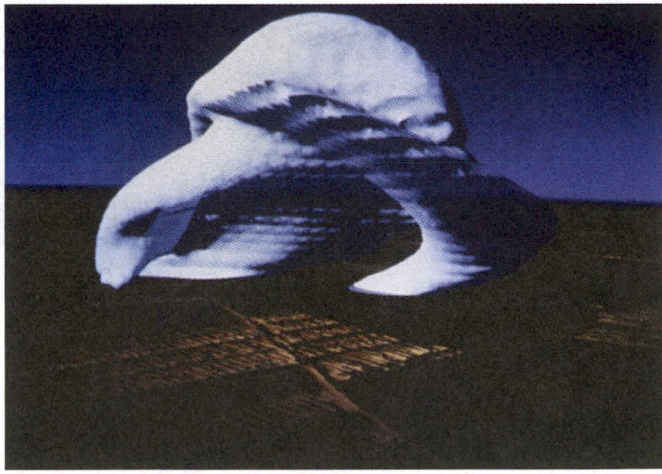

Geosciences: meteorology.

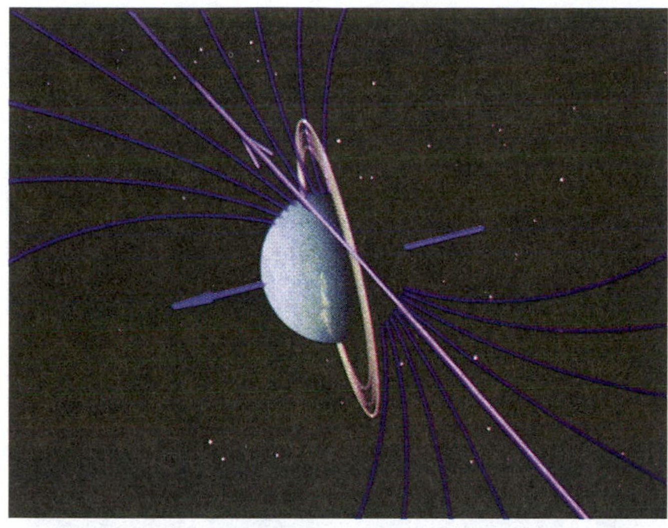

Space exploration.

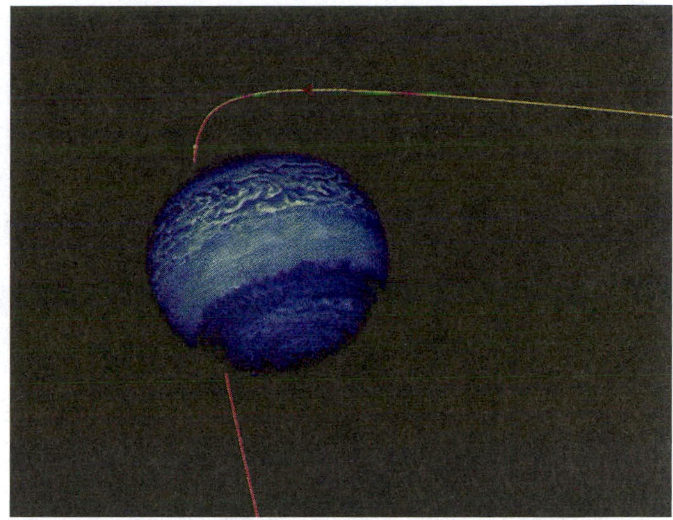

Space exploration.

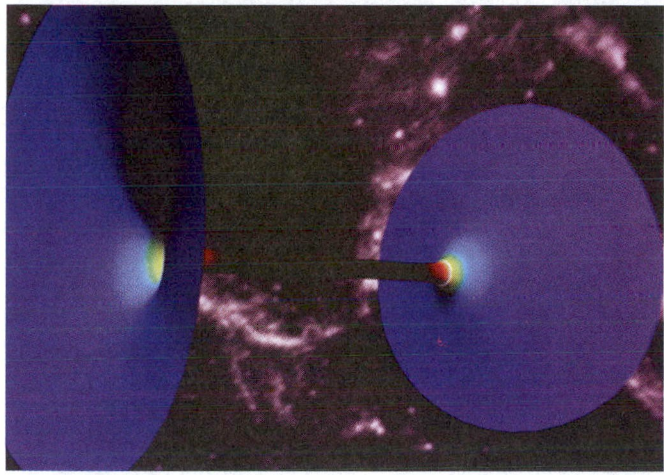

Astrophysics.

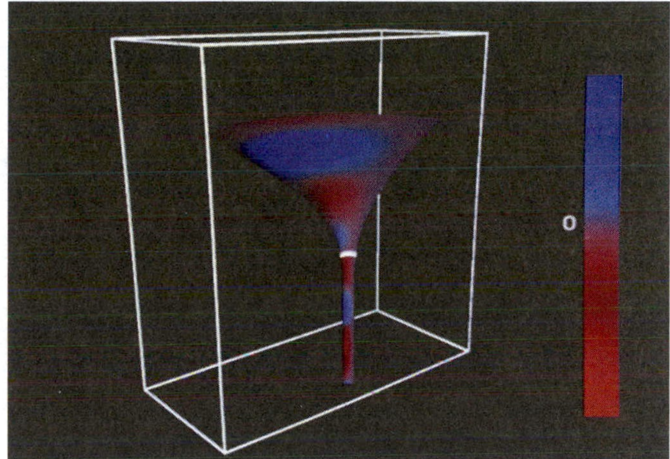

Astrophysics.

Computational fluid dynamics.

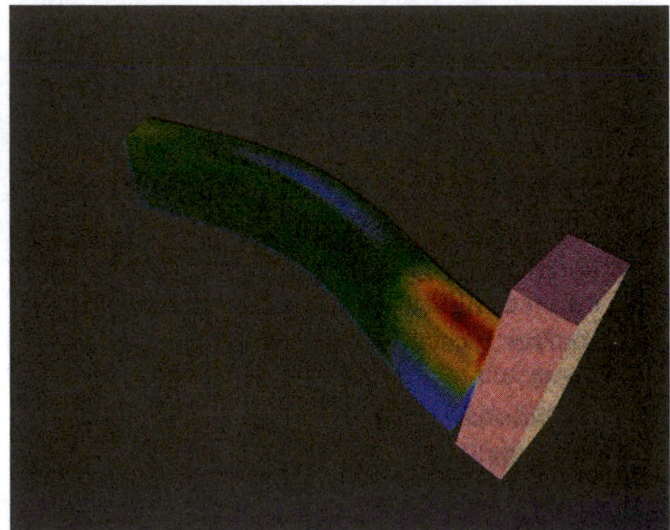

Finite element analysis.

Finite element analysis.

Finite element analysis.

2.2

1D, 2D, 3D

SPACE

In Chapter 1, we said that the axes of space are the most effective dimensions of coding data. How they are used is an important source of technique for visualizations. The FilmFinder, as we have seen, maps two of the variables from its Data Table into quantitative X- and Y-axes, a 2D Visual Structure

$$\begin{aligned} \textit{Years} &\rightarrow Q_x \\ \textit{Popularity} &\rightarrow Q_y. \end{aligned}$$

Alternative Visual Structures could be specified by making changes to this visual mapping. For example, an ordinal axis might be used for *Popularity* or an additional axis might be added to create a 3D scatterplot. The papers in this section are about the nature of the axes of graphical space and their use in representing data. The papers were chosen to suggest the theme and variation in using orthogonal axes to encode information.

The first selection is by Jacques Bertin (1977/1981 ●), a French cartographer who did what is now considered classic work in graphical semiotics. This selection, an excerpt from his book *Graphics and Graphic Information Processing,* summarizes concisely part of his theory of graphical representation. For Bertin, the standard form of the graphical problem is how to represent *n* variables of data graphically, where *n* is usually > 3. In the special cases where *n* is 1, 2, or 3, there are direct solutions. Beyond *n* = 3 variables, there is an *impassable barrier* for representation and the presentation will be some sort of composite. The only fully general solution for *n* > 3 is a *perturbation matrix*, by which Bertin means a particular graphical construction in which each row of a Data Table is represented in bar chart form. A key distinction concerns the type of the spatial axes, whether the axes are nominal (notated as ≠ by Bertin), ordinal (notated as O), or quantitative (notated Q). Space can also be used topographically as in a map (notated T). An important property of some axes (usually nominal) is that they can be permuted, thus producing new visual patterns. From these distinctions, Bertin derives the basic forms of graphical presentation. By permuting and reclassing the matrix, patterns may be detected in the data that can then be expressed by these graphical presentations.

The next selection is by Mackinlay (1986b ●). Mackinlay takes Bertin's scheme and formalizes it. In doing so, he is led to distinguish between the expressiveness of a presentation based on its logical ability to represent the data and its effectiveness based on psychological performance. With these figures of merit he is able to use a theorem-prover to generate good presentations of data by machine in a program called APT. The significance of this paper (and the more extensive treatment in Mackinlay (1986a)) is that it showed the theoretical analysis of graphical presentations were an adequate basis for partial mechanization. Data are decomposed into Data Tables that are mapped to Visual Structures that are, in turn, composed into complex presentations. For example, two variables from a Data Table might be mapped to two 1D Visual Structures and then composed to create a 2D Visual Structure. The paper represents a step from the static presentations analyzed by Bertin to the computer-supported visualizations that are the subject of this book. In particular, the theory used to develop APT is a predecessor to the reference model for visualization that is described in Chapter 1.

The selection by Wright (1995 ●) extends the discussion beyond the 2D focus of the Bertin and Mackinlay papers by adding examples of 3D Visual Structure. Wright describes a compelling strategy for visualizing large collections of financial data by arranging 1D, 2D, and 3D Visual Structures on the "walls and floors" of a virtual 3D space. The Wright paper is an example of one of the most popular ways of using 3D space, *information landscapes,* in which an output variable is graphed in the third dimension as a function of 2D input variables.

There are many more examples of axis composition in the literature and the remainder of the book. Here we take note of a few ways visualizations are based on 1D, 2D, or 3D orthogonal axes of space.

1D VISUAL STRUCTURES

One-dimensional Visual Structures are typically used for timelines and text documents, particularly as part of a larger Visual Structure. The use of a 1D visual structure is often embedded in the use of a second or third axis to accommodate large axes or to show comparison values. An example is Lifestreams (Freeman and Fertig, 1995) in Figure 2.3(a), which essentially uses the Z-axis

$$\mathit{Time} \rightarrow O_Z$$

to represent a series of events. The events are arranged ordinally, instead of on a strict timeline. The X and Y dimensions are used to provide space for seeing a particular event in detail. Mandler, Salomon, and Wong (1992) use piles similarly for arranging information in a workspace.

SeeSoft (Eick, Steffen, and Sumner, 1992 ●) (see Figure 2.3(b)), on the other hand, maps program text to its position on the line

$$\mathit{TextPosition} \rightarrow Q_X$$

folding it over to the next line, just as text is folded on a page. This gives the text a 2D character, using Y for different lines. When there is no more room in Y, the text is folded again, starting a new place in X. Additional data dimensions are coded using color, and brushing can be used to look for patterns. This method of taking a variable with long extent in one dimension and using the other dimensions to fold it in is a common technique. Folding is one solution to the *high cardinality problem,* where a variable has a large number of values that are to be displayed. Another solution to this problem is to show *overview + detail.* The SeeSoft visualization does this for text in Figure 2.3(b). Gray, Badre, and Guzdial (1996) visualize computer log files by displaying an overview at a coarse resolution and a detailed version at higher resolution.

Cardinality can also be compressed by aggregating information into higher-level meaningful units, such as paragraphs or topics. This is what Hearst does with tilebars (Hearst, 1995) in Figure 2.3(c). The user issues a response query containing several terms. The document is displayed as a 1D axis, where each paragraph has been assigned a grayscale value according to how well it matched that term.

$$\mathit{TextPosition} \rightarrow O_X$$

Again, the Y-axis has been used, one position for each query term.

One-dimensional visualizations lend themselves to being used as controls, such as sliders or scroll bars, as several researchers have noted. (Chimera, 1992; Eick, 1994a ●; Hill et al., 1992). The slider or scroll bar indicates all of the values that a parameter may have. The visualizations superimposed on it serve as landmarks and other information, such

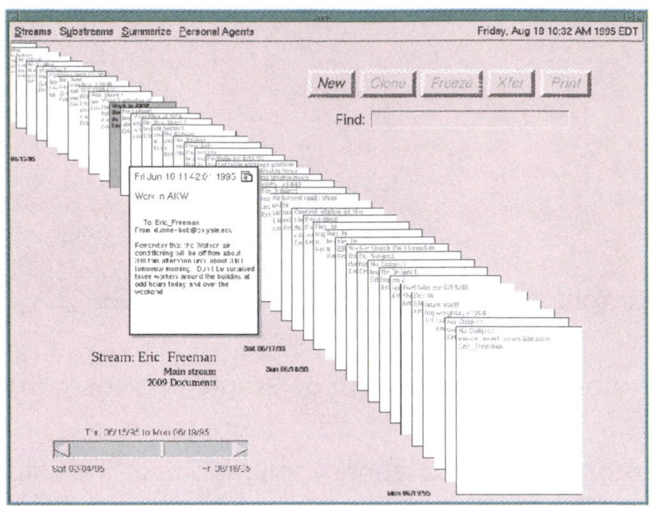

(a) Lifestreams (Freeman and Fertig, 1995, Figure 1).

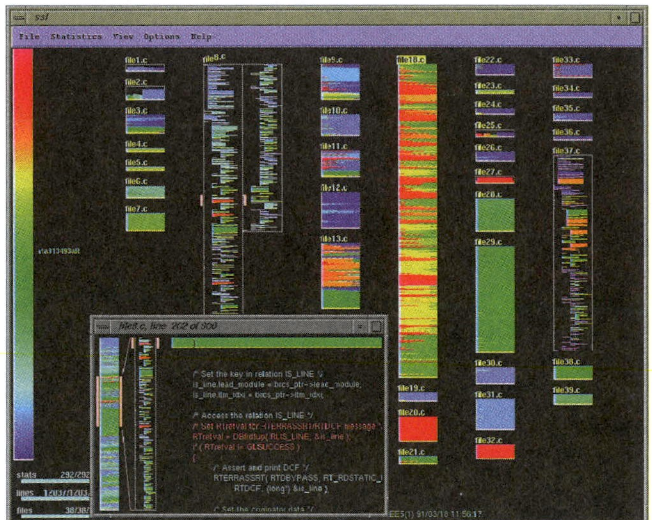

(b) SeeSoft. Courtesy of Lucent Technologies. See Eick, Steffen, and Sumner (1992 ●).

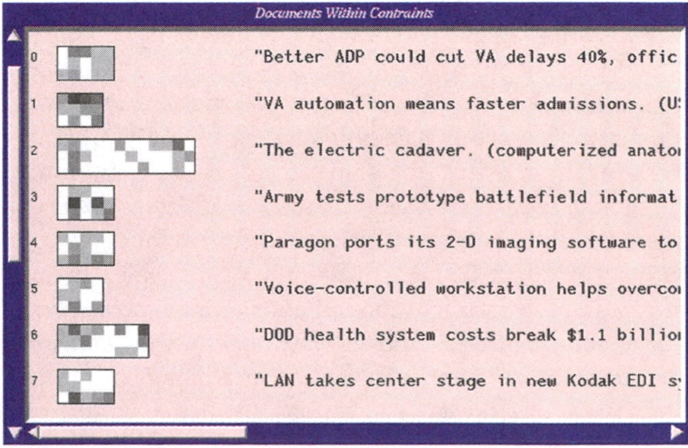

(c) Tilebars. Courtesy of Marti Hearst. See Hearst (1995).

FIGURE **2.3**

Visualizing information using 1D axes.

as a variable's distribution, that can help the user understand the effect of the variable.

One-dimensional visualizations do not need to be straight orthogonal axes. Salton's paper (Salton et al., 1995 ●) describes a very interesting 1D visualization of text axes bent into a circle to represent passages of text. This visualization is augmented with connections to show the relationships among the passages.

2D VISUAL STRUCTURES

Two-dimensional Visual Structures are typically used for chart and geographic data but have also been developed for document collections. Two-dimensional scattergraphs are one common form of visualization. Figure 2.4(a) (Spotfire, AB, see Ahlberg and Wistrand (1995a))[1] is a scattergraph of two variables. Each mark is a box whose *X* and *Y* dimensions encode two additional variables. The FilmFinder and HomeFinder discussed earlier are other examples of this technique. Yet another variable is encoded with color. Figure 2.4(b) is a matrix of scattergraphs for all possible pairwise combinations of a set of variables. In this "prosection matrix" (Tweedie et al., 1996 ●), each of the points is colored according to whether it indicates a design in or out of an acceptable range. The 2D axes are used both for the individual graphs and to compose the graphs in space.

A different sort of use of 2D axes is shown in Figure 2.4(c). The 2D axes are used to create a topography, in this case a graphical table of contents (Lin, 1996). For this topography, Kohonen maps are used to generate spatial regions for different topics. The technique is applied to document collections in Lin (1992b ●). Of course, the X- and Y-axes could represent the real topography as in a geographical information system.

3D VISUAL STRUCTURES

Three-dimensional Visual Structures are of course common for physical data, but they are also used for composing 2D visualizations or for some true 3D representations. DeFanti's paper (DeFanti, Brown, and McCormick, 1989 ●) in the previous section describes a scientific visualization system, especially for flow and volume visualization using 3D physical axes. The visualization of physical objects can become the substrate on which abstract information is organized. Figure 2.5(a) shows part of a human brain constructed from volumetric data and processed to bring out features. These features then become the basis for an elaborate labeling scheme as part of an anatomical atlas. In essence, the physical object becomes the overview for organizing abstract information.

Figure 2.5(b) shows the use of 3D for depicting an "information landscape" called themescapes (Wise et al., 1995 ●). Two axes are used for input variables, forming a sort of topography. The third axis is used for an output variable.

[1]http://www.ivee.com/corporate/index.html

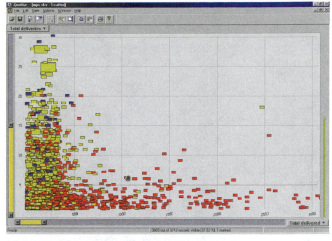

(a) Spotfire. Courtesy of Spotfire, AB.

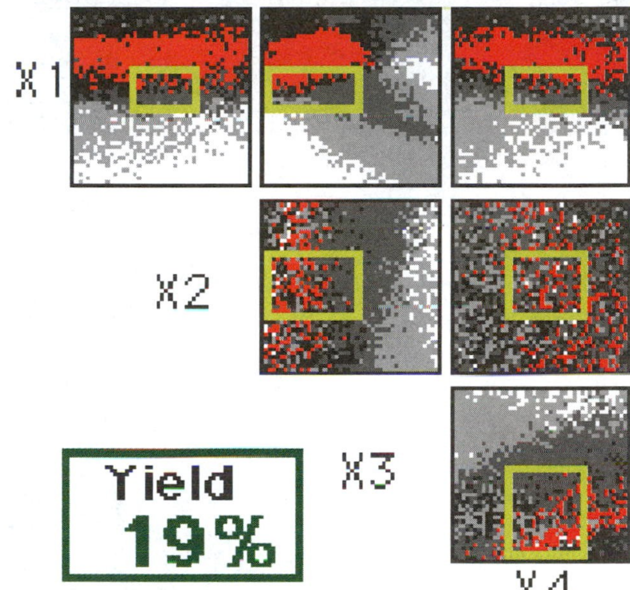

(b) Prosection matrix (Tweedy et al., 1996 ●, Figure 13).

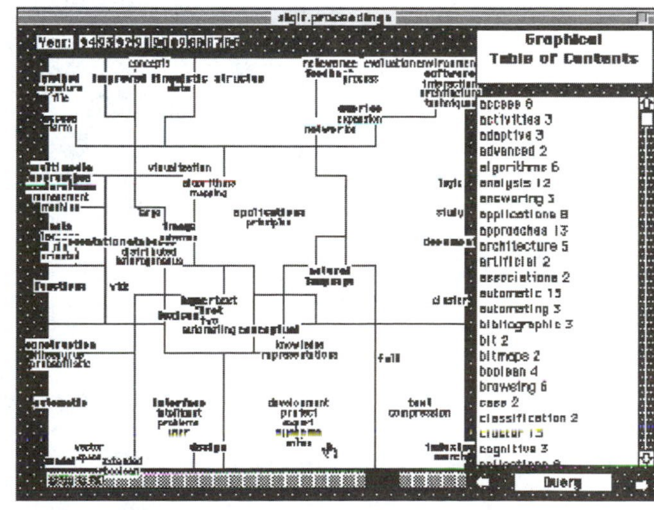

(c) Graphical table of contents (Lin, 1996, Figure 1).

FIGURE **2.4**

Visualizing information using 2D axes.

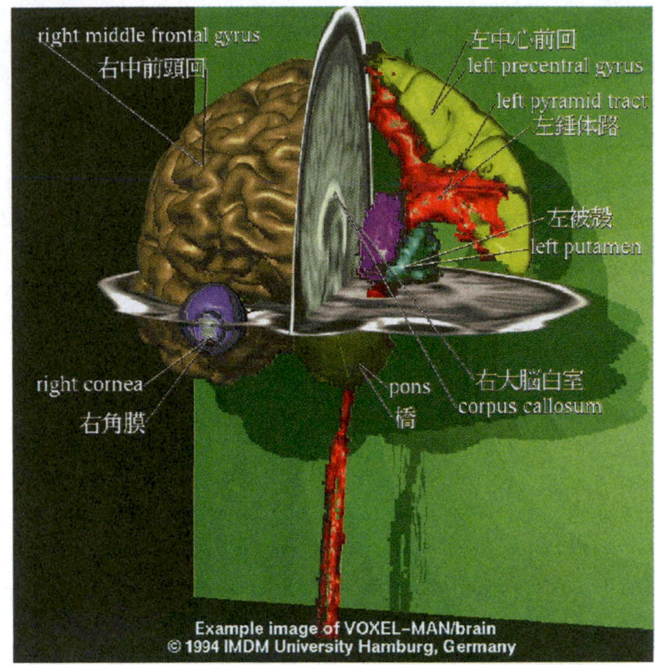

(a) Voxel-Man. Courtesy of UMDM, University of Hamburg.

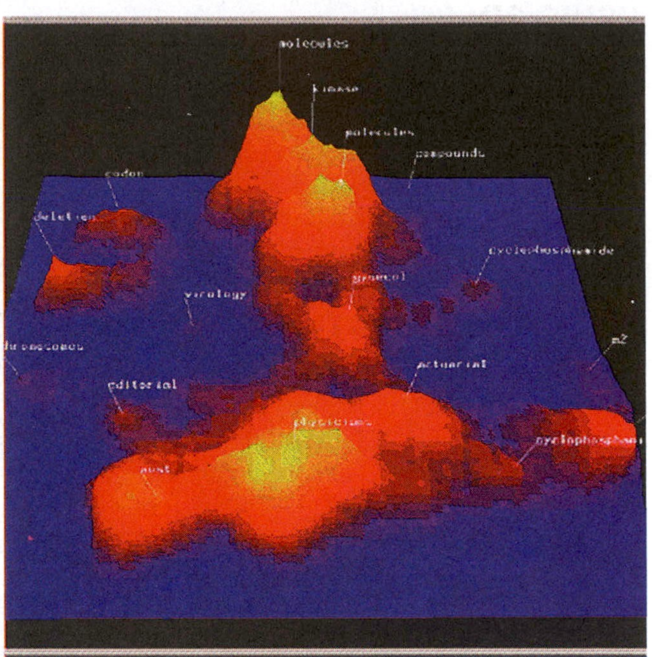

(b) Themescapes. (Wise et al., 1995 ●, Figure 3).

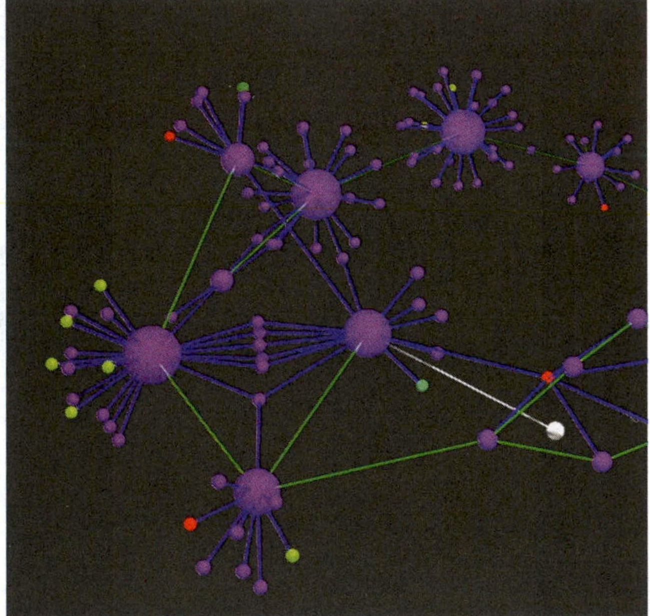

(c) Narcissus. Courtesy of the University of Birmingham. See Hendley et al. (1995 ●).

FIGURE **2.5**

Visualizing information using 3D axes.

Color is used redundantly with the third axis to increase the precision with which the height can be perceived. Themescapes can be thought of as extending the Kohonen map idea onto a 3D surface, making the clusters in the document more visible.

All three axes can be used abstractly, of course. Narcissus, in Figure 2.5(c) (Hendley et al., 1995 ●), defines a set of attractive and repulsive forces among objects in the World Wide Web. The net effect of these forces defines positions in an abstract 3D space, related objects being closer together. Rennison (1994 ●) has defined a more dynamic 3D Visual Structure in a system called *Galaxy of News.* Documents are processed to generate a 3D space of keywords. As the user zooms toward a specific keyword, more specific keywords become visible and the associated papers also move toward that keyword.

USING 3D: PROS AND CONS

Given the option of 1D, 2D, or 3D, a central question is which type of Visual Structure to use. Two-dimensional Visual Structures are the most common. One-dimensional Visual Structures are typically used when space is at a premium. Three-dimensional Visual Structures are visually exciting, but it is an open question under what conditions 3D Visual Structures are better than 2D Visual Structures for information visualization. While 3D is clearly more effective for physical data that includes 3D spatial variables difficult to map to 2D, 2D has a long and effective history for abstract data.

There are greater implementation challenges for 3D than for 2D. Because 3D implementations require significantly more processing power, 3D has been limited to expensive computers used primarily in exploratory research or niche markets such as movie production. This barrier is now being removed for the mass market. However, disagreements over standards make 3D implementation more risky than for 2D. In addition, 3D implementation involves many more parameters including lighting, texturing, and at least six degrees of freedom for movement. One area of continuing concern for information visualization is the rendering of effective 3D text since abstract data often involves textual values. Three-dimensional fonts must often be larger to achieve the same legibility, partly because of rasterization effects.

Also, 3D involves additional design challenges. On a standard computer display 3D requires additional elements such as shadows, lighting, and a ground plane to foster the perception of 3D. Another problem is occlusion. Foreground objects can hide distant objects, and dense collections of objects can obscure their centers.

Although the challenges associated with 3D have made it less desirable to many people, there are also good reasons to use 3D to visualize information. Perhaps the most obvious advantage is the additional dimension to encode information. However, a subtler but profound advantage is that this additional dimension projects from the viewpoint toward infinity, creating a large visible workspace for holding visualizations and the results of information work. With the advent of mass-market graphically agile computers, 3D visualization is likely to become more common.

DISCUSSION

Orthogonal axis composition is a powerful and ubiquitous technique for information visualization. Unfortunately, we are limited to three orthogonal axes and most Data Tables have many more than three variables. Much of the history of presentation and visualization is an attempt to get beyond this fundamental limitation. Static presentations often use retinal properties such as color to add an additional variable to a Visual Structure. Visualizations exploit the power of the computer, such as interactive animation, to make more data accessible to an information worker. However, there is a limit to what we can pack into a single orthogonal axis composition. The next section describes visualization techniques that have been specifically designed to deal with Data Tables that overwhelm orthogonal axis composition.

Graphics and Graphic Information Processing

J. Bertin

B. GRAPHIC CONSTRUCTIONS

B.1. A "SYNOPTIC" OF GRAPHIC CONSTRUCTIONS

B1.1 An impassable barrier

With up to three rows, a data table can be constructed directly as a single image, producing a *scatter plot* or correlation diagram, in which the objects are in *z*. However, an image has only three dimensions. And this barrier is impassable. Consequently, with more than three rows, there are only two ways of denoting comprehensive information:

- constructing several scatter plots and sacrificing the overall relationships of the entire set;
- placing the objects on *x* and the characteristics on *y*, that is, *constructing a matrix*. The overall relationships are then discovered through permutations.

Let us consider, for example, a table with two rows **(4)**: towns A, B, C, etc., for which we know the price of bread and the cost of housing. Two constructions are possible:

- placing the objects A, B, C on *x* and the characteristics on *y* **(5)**, a *matrix* construction. It involves classing A, B, C according to a characteristic (∼∼);
- placing the objects in *z*. They become points, which enables us to place the two characteristics along *x* and *y*, respectively **(6)**. This is a *scatter plot*. It classes the objects directly and makes apparent both their groupings and the relationship between the two characteristics.

The same applies for a table with three rows **(7)**. In scatter plot **(9)** the third row is expressed by the size of the points.
These two types of construction distinguish a "repartition" **(2)** from a "distribution" **(3)** for tables having one row.

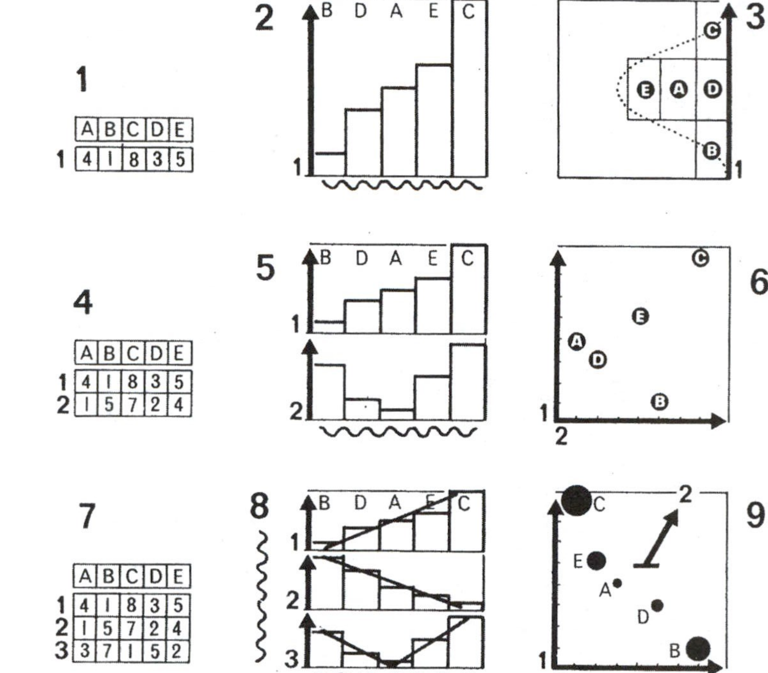

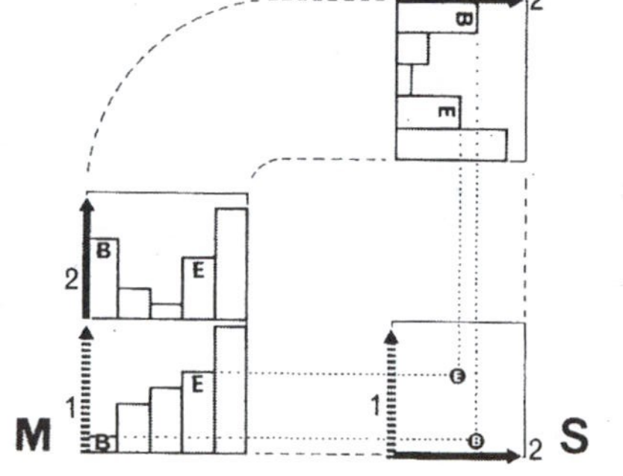

Relationship between the matrix construction and the scatter plot. This figure shows how columns B and E in the matrix construction (M) become points B and E in the scatter plot (S).

Yet, a table with more than three rows **(10)** cannot be constructed *directly* set up as a single signifying image. What we have to construct will be a series of scatter plots two by two **(12)**, or a series of scatter plots with three characteristics **(13)***, or a superimposition of scatter plots, which means a superimposition of images **(14)**. In all these cases, the overall relationships are lost. The image has only three dimensions.

There remains only the matrix construction **(11)**, which enables us to discover the overall relationships *through permutation* (∼∼∼). And this is dynamic graphics, the extension and fulfillment of static graphics.

B1.2 The unity of a problem.

The impossibility of *directly* constructing a table having more than three characteristics in a single image often leads to sub-dividing a given problem. Take the study of prices in thirty-one major cities (p. 43). This study has been commented on throughout the world, but the commentaries are all anecdotal: two towns or two products compared in relation to the seventeen published tables. However, the information itself is a unified whole, constructing only one table, one matrix that reveals the overall relationships, such as the socio-economic systems and ways of life that give each anecdote its full meaning.

And this is the real problem: is the anecdote significant or is it an exception? And if an exception, an exception in relation to what? In relation to general tendencies, to overall groupings? It is these that our memory searches for. It is these that we must SEE.

Thus the main problem we have to work at is a problem with n *characteristics. The principal construction is the matrix construction. Scatter plots are merely exceptional constructions; above all,* a problem with n characteristics is not the sum of n problems with two characteristics.

This is the reason that the classification of the *synoptic* on p. 29 is based on problems with n rows, since problems with one, two or three rows are only special cases of a problem with n rows. The habitual going from what seems the simplest (a table with one row) to what seems the most complicated (a table with n rows) only results in the subdivision of research and decision-making, and destroys our vision of the overall problem: a complaint which can well be lodged against classical graphics.

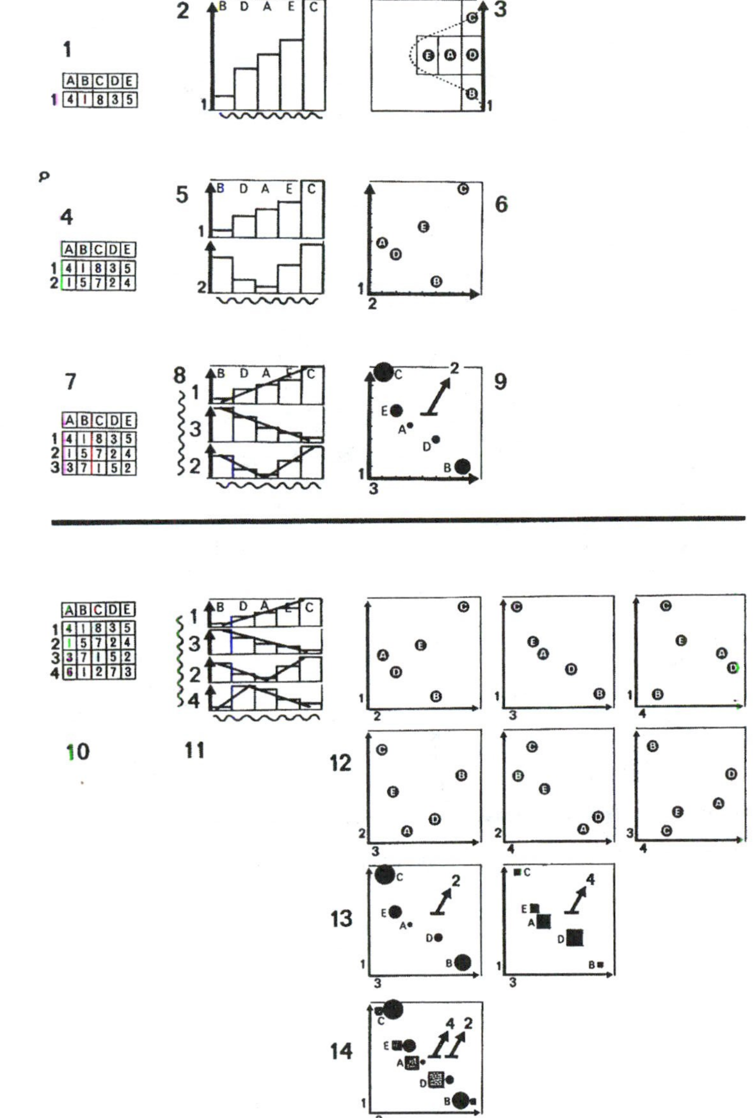

* For a table with n rows there are $\frac{n(n-1)}{2}$ scatter plots with two characteristics and $n - 2$ comparable scatter plots with three characteristics, two of which are held constant.

B.1.3 The synoptic

The synoptic on the facing page displays all the basic graphic constructions as they relate to the data table.
Take a data table containing objects A, B, C . . . along x and characteristics 1, 2, 3 . . . of these objects along y.
From this data table it is easy to observe:
1) the number of rows, that is, the number of characteristics;
2) the nature of the series of "objects," which, for example, is ordered, (0), for months; reorderable, (≠), for individuals; or topographic, (T), for townships. The synoptic classifies graphic constructions according to these two principles.

Tables with more than three rows

A table with more than three rows (n) leads to permutable matrix constructions (∿∿), in which the characteristics are always reorderable (≠).
If the objects are ≠, it is a table (≠ ≠). The construction is the reorderable matrix, **(1)**, permutable in x and y. *The "weighted matrix" and the "matrix-file" are special cases of it (pp. 61 and 86).*
If the objects are ordered, **(0)**, it is a table (≠ 0) which has two basic constructions: the image-file **(2)** and the array of curves **(3)**, applicable when the slopes are meaningful.

The ordered table **(9)**, like the map **(18)**, constructs a fixed-reference image. *A collection of tables* **(4)** or a *collection of maps* **(5)** enables us to class the images according to a given similarity as well as to define groups of characteristics and objects. Remember that the superimposition of several tables or maps in a single figure leads to elementary reading and does not answer the fundamental question: what groups are formed by the x's and/or the y's of the data table?

Tables with one to three rows

Tables with one to three rows offer two basic constructions: *the matrix construction* places A, B, C on x and leads to matrices with three, two or one row **(6, 7, 8)**, all of which entail a reclassing of the objects. Constructions **(13, 14, 15)** are arrays of curves; *the scatter plot* places A, B, C in z; when the data are quantitative, it makes a *direct construction*, without reclassing possible, **(9, 10, 11, 12)**.
In topographies, bi- or tri-chromatic superimposition **(16, 17)** reveals the overall relationships.

Networks (N) and topographies (T)

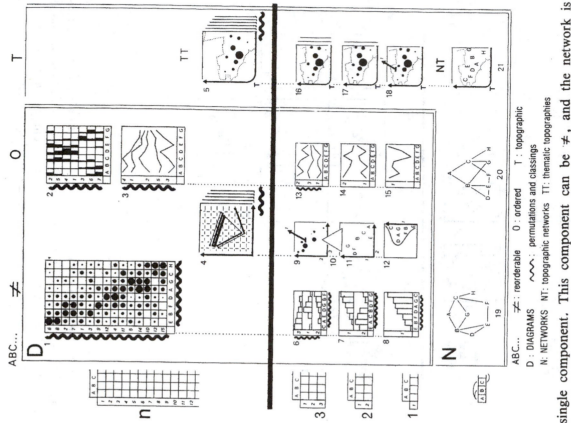

A network portrays the relationships which exist among the elements of a single component. This component can be ≠, and the network is transformable on the plane **(19)**. It can be 0, and the network is transformable on one dimension of the plane **(20)**. Finally, it can be a topography **(21)**, that is, a non-transformable network: an ordered network.

But any network can be constructed in a matrix form. The elements are transcribed twice: once along x, and once along y. The relationships become points, and the matrix is permutable.

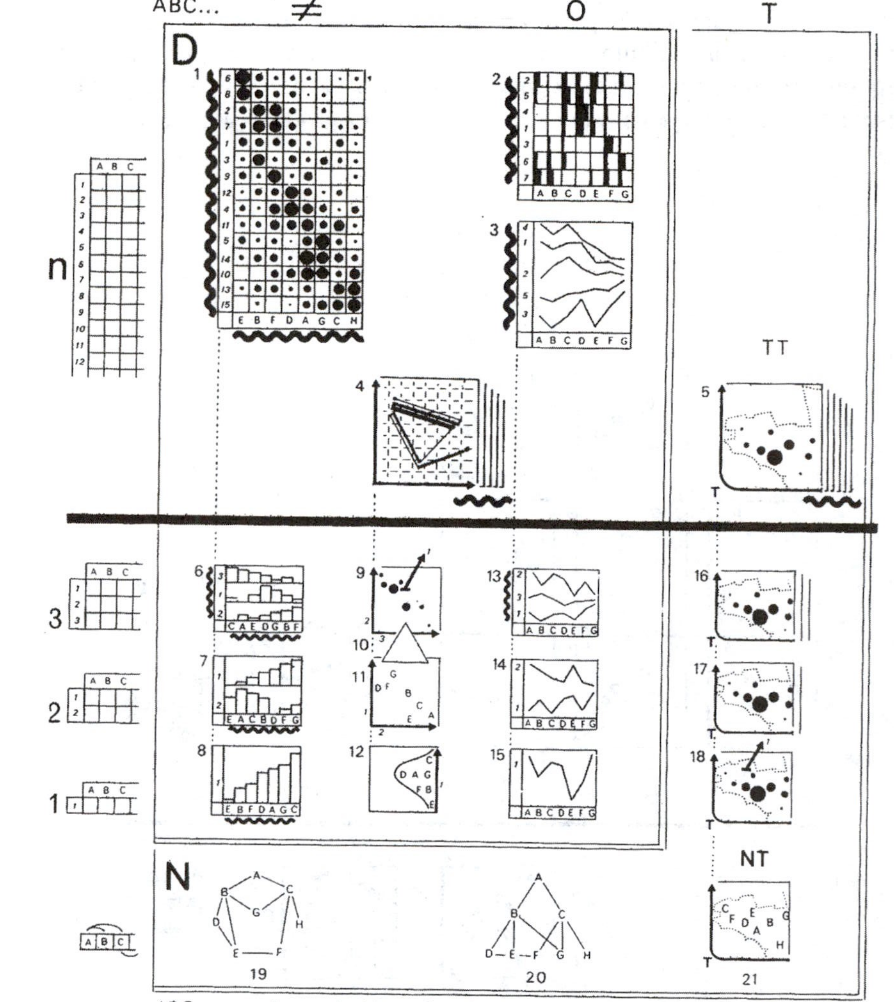

ABC... ≠: reorderable 0: ordered T: topographic
D: DIAGRAMS ∿∿: permutations and classings
N: NETWORKS NT: topographic networks TT: thematic topographies

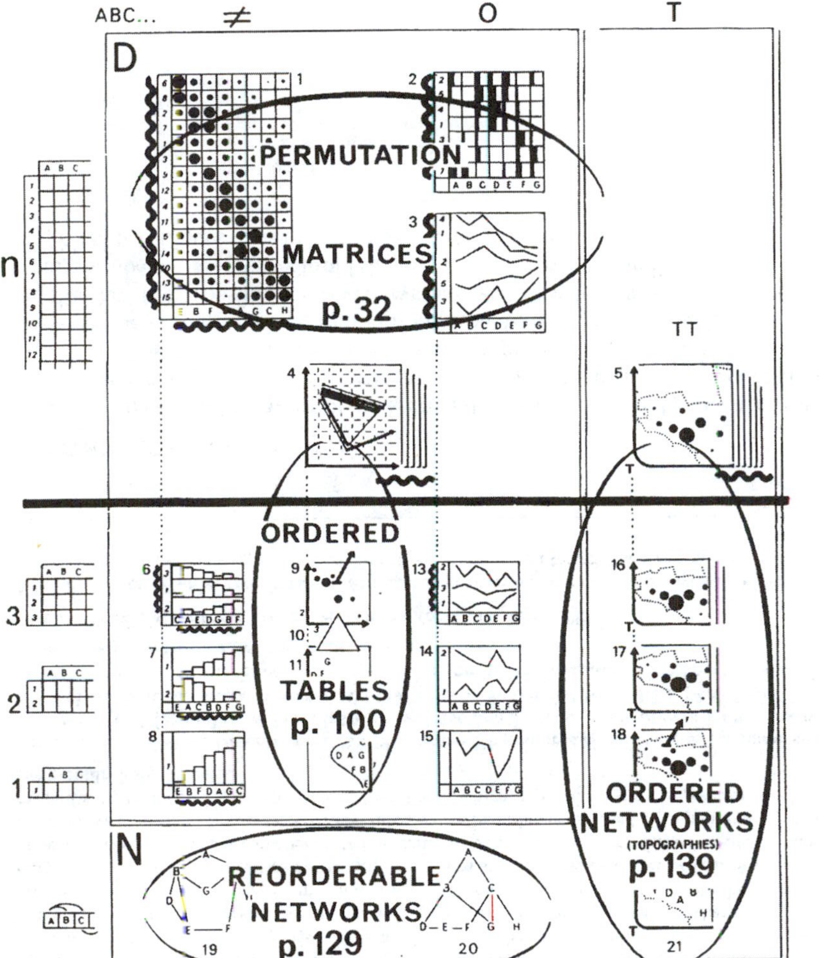

ABC...≠: reorderable O: ordered T: topographic
D: diagrams ~~ permutations and classings
N: networks NT: topographic networks TT: thematic topographies

The table above refers to the pages in this book which discuss the various constructions.

B.1.4. Utilization of the synoptic

First let us remember that the cells of the data table must only include yes/no answers, ordinal numbers, or quantities. However, the scatter plots corresponding to one, two and three rows imply that these rows do not have yes/no answers.

All the tables can contain symbols indicating the absence of data— which is different from zero—or "inapplicable" data.

To refer to the synoptic we start with the number of rows and the nature of the components in the data table. The synoptic then indicates the basic construction corresponding to the structure of the data.

The choice of a different construction must be justified. The constructions given on the synoptic are those capable of reaching the overall level of information. To adopt a different construction amounts to a shift in relation to the synoptic and a reduction in the perceptible information level. A problem involving *n* rows does not correspond to *n* problems involving one row. Consequently, a shift must be justified by the analysis of which questions will not be answered rather than by acquired habits. In any case the synoptic provides a reference point for discussing a given shift.

The choice between a map and a diagram rests on the balance between the length of the topographic component A, B, C and the number *n* of characteristics. A large number *n* leads to a matrix, a more powerful, supple and precise instrument for processing than the map, which can only be introduced at a later stage. To manifest relationships of proximity, the groupings discovered through processing are projected onto the map (pp. 50, 83, 138, 167).

On the other hand, if A, B, C is extensive, even infinite (as with a topographically continuous phenomenon), a series of maps combined with tri-chromatic superimposition is justifiable as a processing instrument.

The limits of graphic information-processing. Permutations are difficult when the following orders of magnitude are exceeded:

- reorderable matrix (≠) 120 × (≠) 120
- (experimental equipment) (≠) 500 × (≠) 100
- matrix-file (≠) 1000 × (≠) 30 non-permutable
- image-file, array of curves (≠) 1000 × (0) unlimited
- collections of tables or maps (≠) unlimited

Combinations of graphic processing

In order to reduce information to the dimensions of a reorderable matrix, we must discover about 100 objects representative of all the objects. *The matrix-file* enables us to proceed with this selection (page 87) but with a maximum of about thirty characteristics. *The image-file* (page 70) and the *array of curves* (page 90) allow us to proceed with an ordered characteristic of any length whatever. Collections of tables and maps have no limits.

Automating the Design of Graphical Presentations of Relational Information

JOCK MACKINLAY
Stanford University

The goal of the research described in this paper is to develop an application-independent presentation tool that automatically designs effective graphical presentations (such as bar charts, scatter plots, and connected graphs) of relational information. Two problems are raised by this goal: The codification of graphic design criteria in a form that can be used by the presentation tool, and the generation of a wide variety of designs so that the presentation tool can accommodate a wide variety of information. The approach described in this paper is based on the view that graphical presentations are sentences of graphical languages. The graphic design issues are codified as expressiveness and effectiveness criteria for graphical languages. Expressiveness criteria determine whether a graphical language can express the desired information. Effectiveness criteria determine whether a graphical language exploits the capabilities of the output medium and the human visual system. A wide variety of designs can be systematically generated by using a composition algebra that composes a small set of primitive graphical languages. Artificial intelligence techniques are used to implement a prototype presentation tool called APT (A Presentation Tool), which is based on the composition algebra and the graphic design criteria.

Categories and Subject Descriptors: D.2.2 [**Software Engineering**]: Tools and Techniques—*user interfaces*; H.1.2 [**Models and Principles**]: User/Machine Systems—*human information processing*; H.3.4 [**Information Storage and Retrieval**]: Systems and Software; I.2.1 [**Artificial Intelligence**]: Applications and Expert Systems; I.3.6 [**Computer Graphics**]: Methodology and Techniques—*device independence*; *ergonomics*

General Terms: Algorithms, Design, Human Factors, Languages, Theory

Additional Key Words and Phrases: Automatic generation, composition algebra, effectiveness, expressiveness, graphic design, information presentation, presentation tool, user interface

1. INTRODUCTION

Computer-based information plays a crucial role in our society. As a result, an important responsibility of a user interface is to make intelligent use of human visual abilities and output media whenever it presents information to the user. For example, a color medium makes it possible to use graphical techniques based on the fact that the human visual system is very effective at distinguishing a small number of distinct colors [13, 23]. A monochrome medium requires other graphical techniques that utilize other capabilities of the human visual system.

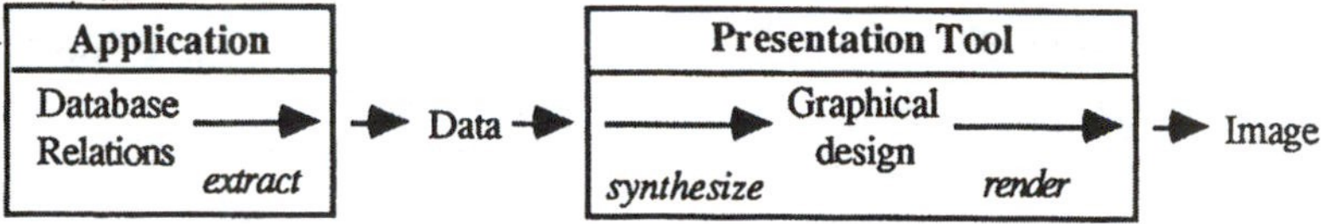

Fig. 1. A linear model for generating presentations. This simplified model, which does not include feedback loops that are required for difficult design problems, describes the fundamental process of generating a graphical presentation. A graphical design synthesized by a presentation tool describes the basic structure and meaning of a graphical presentation. The rendering process fills in the details that are required to form the final image.

Building user interfaces that intelligently present information is a difficult task. At the current time, application designers are forced to anticipate every presentation situation that might arise in an application and decide which graphical techniques are most effective in each situation. Not only do application designers have to "predesign" the presentations, but they must be graphic design experts to ensure that the resulting presentations are effective.

An obvious solution is to build a system, called a presentation tool, that automatically designs graphical presentations of information. Using such a system, application designers need not predesign the presentations, and the graphic design issues are the responsibility of the presentation tool. Figure 1 illustrates how application designers would use such a tool. The application extracts some information from its database (perhaps using statistical analysis). The presentation tool then synthesizes a graphical design and renders an image that presents this information. A *graphical design* is an abstract description of an image that indicates the graphical techniques (such as color variation or position on an axis) that are used to encode information.

There are two open problems that must be solved before such a presentation tool can be constructed: Graphic design criteria must be codified before the presentation tool can synthesize effective designs, and a wide variety of designs must be generated before the presentation tool can handle a wide variety of input.

This paper describes research that begins to solve these problems by focusing on automating the design of two dimensional (2-D) static presentations (such as bar charts, scatter plots, and connected graphs) of relational information. The cornerstone of this research is the development of precise definitions of graphical languages that describe the syntactic and semantic properties of graphical presentations. The framework established by these definitions addresses the two problems mentioned above. Graphic design issues are codified with expressiveness and effectiveness criteria. *Expressiveness criteria* identify graphical languages that express the desired information. *Effectiveness criteria* identify which of these graphical languages, in a given situation, is the most effective at exploiting the capabilities of the output medium and the human visual system. A wide variety of designs is systematically generated using a *composition algebra*, which is a collection of primitive graphical languages and composition operators that can form complex presentations. This framework is implemented with artificial intelligence techniques. A prototype application-independent presentation tool called APT (A Presentation Tool) has been built. Even though only the basic framework has been implemented, APT can synthesize a wide variety of useful designs.

The paper is a top-down description of the two types of graphic design criteria and the composition algebra mentioned above. Related work is described in Section 2. Section 3 uses three examples to motivate the development of the criteria and algebra. Section 4 gives a detailed overview of the results described in this paper. The core of the paper is contained in Sections 5–7, which describe the details of the expressiveness and effectiveness criteria and the composition algebra. Sections 8 and 9 describe how APT uses these results to synthesize presentations. Finally, Section 10 considers how the research can be extended.

2. RELATED WORK

The automatic design of graphical presentations of information is a relatively unexplored research area. As a result, existing work has focused on restricted aspects of the problem. Aside from the early unfocused work, the following three foci categorize the existing work: content issues, graphic design issues, and design variation issues. Content issues are central to systems that automatically determine the content of presentations, such as adding or removing details to generate an effective presentation or developing a sequence of related presentations. The graphic design and design variation issues have already been described. Another useful categorization is the graphical techniques used by the system (2-D, 3-D, animation).

Two of the early, less focused pieces of work deserve mention. The first developed the AIPS system, which was one of the earliest attempts to separate the presentation process from the rest of an application [24]. AIPS used the KLONE representation system to specify and refine a high-level specification of a 2-D information display. The second piece of early work studied automatic animation scripting and the rule-based layout of node-link diagrams [12].

Content issues were the primary focus for the work on two systems. The first was the VIEW system developed by Friedell, which automatically generated 2-D icons describing the properties of ships stored in a naval database [10]. A stepwise refinement of icon templates, using subicon templates, terminated when sufficient detail was generated for a given icon size. The templates were designed by hand rather than by the system. The second was the APEX system developed by Feiner, which automatically generated a sequence of images that describe actions in a 3-D world consisting of some sonar cabinets [8]. The system carefully tailored the sequence of images to omit irrelevant or redundant details. The graphic design issues surrounding the merging of icons and 3-D images were also considered.

Two other pieces of work focused on graphic design issues. The first was the BHARAT system developed by Gnanamgari, which was an early effort at the automatic generation of 2-D presentation graphics [11]. It selected a pie chart, bar chart, or line chart design for a single unary function, which could have multiple numeric ranges. BHARAT was based on a simple design algorithm. When the function was continuous, a line chart design was used. When the user indicated that the range sets could be summed to a meaningful total, a pie chart design was used. Bar chart designs were used in the remaining cases. Although multiple designs were generated, BHARAT's range of designs was limited. It could not present a collection of relations or nonfunctional relations. Gnanamgari's discussion focused on graphic design issues. However, her effectiveness criteria about issues such as font and color choice were "wired" into the code that rendered the design, making it difficult to extend the system to a broader range of input.

The second piece of work that focused on graphic design issues was Beach's system, which automated the low-level layout and design of 2-D tables whose high-level topology was specified by the user as a matrix of rows and columns [1]. This research utilized a specification called a *graphical style* [2], which allowed the explicit description of the graphic design properties of the table, such as line widths, background tints, and size constraints. As a result, the user could control parts of the design while the remainder was controlled by the existing default style. Explicit graphical styles made it possible for the system to format the table in different ways for different output media. Although the graphical styles had to be specified by hand, care was taken to make sure that graphic design issues could be addressed in the specification.

Design variation and graphic design are the primary foci of the work described in this paper. This work differs from the previous work in that it focuses directly on the generation of a comprehensive variety of designs for 2-D static presentations of relational information. The APT system uses artificial intelligence techniques to implement a "generate and test" search for a design: The composition algebra generates design alternatives, and the graphic design criteria test the generated alternatives.

3. THE GRAPHICAL PRESENTATION PROBLEM

The graphical presentation problem is to synthesize a graphical design that expresses a set of relations and their structural properties effectively. This problem is illustrated in this section by three examples that describe the desired behavior of a presentation tool. These examples describe the basic concerns that led to the criteria and algebra discussed in the remainder of the paper.

Given the process model in Figure 1, the examples of presentation tool behavior begin with the application's database. Figure 2 describes a collection of relation tuples about automobiles that might be contained in such a database. The structural properties of these relations, which might be in the database schema, are shown in Figure 3 using standard database notation [22]. Structural properties include the domain sets and their functional relationships. Given such a database, a typical input from the application to the presentation tool would be the following:

Present the Price and Mileage relations.
The details about the set of Cars can be omitted.

Note that the application can include additional requests, such as asking that the *Cars* details be omitted.

Given this input, a presentation tool produces two outputs: a graphical design and an image rendered from that graphical design. A graphical design, which is the primary concern of this paper, consists of a set of encoding relations between

Price(Accord, 5799)	*Price*(AMC Pacer, 4749)
Mileage(Accord, 25)	*Mileage*(AMC Pacer, 17)
Weight(Accord, 2240)	*Weight*(AMC Pacer, 3350)
Repair(Accord, Great)	*Repair*(AMC Pacer, Terrible)
Nation(Accord, Germany)	*Nation*(AMC Pacer, USA)
Price(Audi 5000, 9690)	*Price*(BMW 320i, 9735)
⋮	⋮

Fig. 2. Relation tuples about 1979 automobiles. This is an example of a table of relation tuples that might be generated by a database system in response to a query. A presentation tool can do much better than this.

Price: *Cars* → [3500, 13000]
Mileage: *Cars* → [10, 40]
Weight: *Cars* → [1500, 5000]
Repair: *Cars* → ⟨Great, Good, OK, Bad, Terrible⟩
Nation: *Cars* → {USA, Germany, France, ...}
Cars = {Accord, AMC Pacer, Audi 5000, BMW 320i, ...}

Fig. 3. Structural properties of the automobile relations. The arrow (→) indicates a functional dependency between domain sets. The square brackets ([ ]) describe domain sets that are quantitative ranges, the angle brackets (⟨ ⟩) describe domain sets that are ordered sets, and the curly braces ({ }) describe domain sets that are unordered sets.

a graphical image and the information it presents. For example, Figure 4 describes a scatter plot design for the price/mileage input. Graphical objects, such as points and line segments, encode the domains of the relations. Properties of those objects, such as their position, encode the functional information. The *Encodes* predicate is used to indicate these encoding relationships for both the graphical objects and their properties. Figure 5 contains the scatter plot image that APT rendered from this design.[1]

The following three price/mileage examples illustrate the expressiveness, effectiveness, and design variation concerns mentioned above. The scatter plot in Figure 5 illustrates the importance of the expressiveness concern. If the application had not requested that the details about the cars be omitted, the scatter plot in Figure 5 would not have expressed all the input. Without this request, the scatter plot would have had to include labels, as shown in Figure 6. These scatter plot labels, however, illustrate the importance of the effectiveness concern. The labels obscure the mark positions, and it is difficult to find individual cars. If the details about the cars are important, there are more effective design alternatives. For example, when the details of the cars are to be presented, the presentation tool should synthesize the aligned bar chart design

[1] In this paper, an *apt* in the lower right corner of a figure indicates that APT designed and rendered the diagram. Such diagrams are intended to illustrate APT's ability to deal with coarse-grained graphic design issues, such as the choice of the graphical techniques to encode information. Fine-grained rendering issues, such as line width, font choice, and precise graphical object placement are not a focus of this research. A production presentation tool will certainly be able to generate more graphically interesting diagrams than the ones shown here.

Encodes(*VertAxis*, [3500, 13000], *ScatterPlot*)
Encodes(*HorzAxis*, [10, 40], *ScatterPlot*)
Encodes(*Points*, *Cars*, *ScatterPlot*)
Encodes(*Position*(*Points*, *VertAxis*), *Price*(*Cars*), *ScatterPlot*)
Encodes(*Position*(*Points*, *HorzAxis*), *Mileage*(*Cars*), *ScatterPlot*)

Fig. 4. The graphical design for a scatter plot of the price mileage input. The *Encodes* relation indicates the relationship between graphical objects or properties and the information encoded. For example, the first line says that the vertical axis encodes the range of prices, and the fourth line says that the position of the points on the vertical axis encodes the prices of cars. The input relations are written as functions to simplify the description.

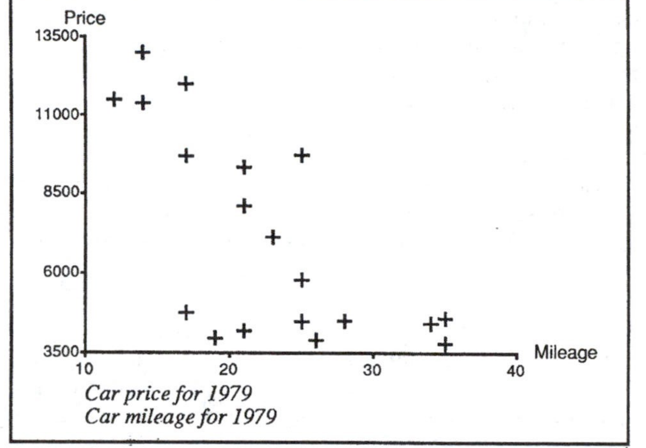

Fig. 5. Scatter plot of the price/mileage input. The graphical design for this image is in Figure 4. The design expresses the relations only if the application permits the details about the cars to be omitted. The *apt* in the lower right corner indicates that APT designed and rendered this diagram.

used to render Figure 7, rather than the scatter plot design. The aligned bar chart design makes it easy to find values associated with an individual car. The existence of this alternative design illustrates the importance of the design variation concern. A presentation tool should be able to generate an expressive and effective design for each presentation situation.

The following rough estimate indicates that there are many possible inputs to a presentation tool. The price/mileage input consists of two binary relations that share the same first domain set and are functional dependencies from a qualitative domain to a numeric range. The structural properties of the input relations are important factors for designing a graphical presentation. Different structural properties require the presentation tool to synthesize different designs. Furthermore, the ability to vary these properties independently leads to a combinatorial

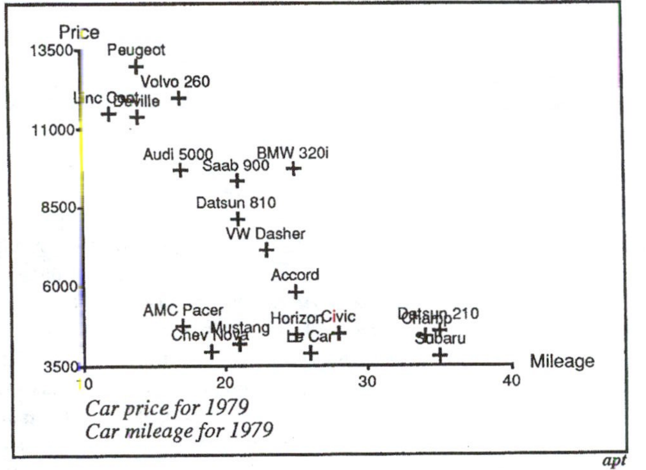

Fig. 6. Labeled scatter plot for the price/mileage input. Although a more sophisticated rendering could avoid the overlapping of the labels, two basic problems of a labeled scatter plot design reduce its effectiveness. First, labels make it difficult to perceive the positions of the points. Second, a given label is difficult to find.

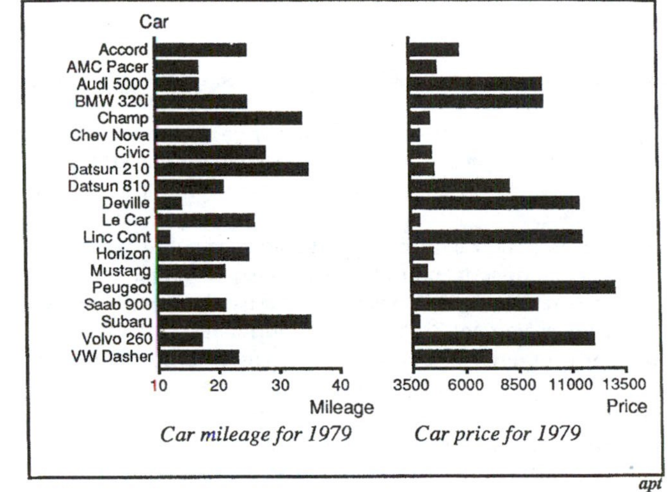

Fig. 7. Aligned bar chart for the price/mileage input. This diagram shows the detailed properties of the cars better than a scatter plot. However, the general relationships are not so easy to see.

explosion in the number of inputs that might be given to a presentation tool. To see this, abstract the two binary relations by ignoring the functional dependencies, the sharing of domain sets, and the properties of the domain sets:

$$\left.\begin{array}{lcc} & \overbrace{\hphantom{A\quad B}}^{d} \\ R: & A & B \\ S: & C & D \end{array}\right\} r.$$

Given that there are on the average d domain sets for each relation and r relations in the input, there are

$$(2^d - 1)^r \times (dr)! \times 3^{dr}$$

different possible design problems. The $(2^d - 1)^r$ factor is based on the fact that each relation can be a functional dependency from 1 through d domain sets to the remaining domain sets and is equivalent to the number of nonempty subsets of the set of domain sets of the relation. The $(dr)!$ factor is based on the number of canonical permutation cycles that can be formed by the sharing of all the domain sets [14]. The 3^{dr} factor is based on the fact that each domain set can be one of the following three types [20]: A domain set is *nominal* when it is a collection of unordered items, such as {`Jay, Eagle, Robin`}. A domain set is *ordinal* when it is an ordered tuple, such as ⟨`Monday, Tuesday, Wednesday`⟩. A domain set is *quantitative* when it is a range, such as [`0, 273`].

The preceding formula indicates that there can be many inputs to the presentation tool. For two binary relations, there are over 17,000 possibilities. However, the input can include more relations or relations with more domain sets. For example, four binary relations (similar to the automobile data presented in Figure 30) can generate over 21 billion different inputs. Furthermore, this estimate does not include other factors that increase the number of designs that must be generated by a presentation tool, such as application requests or properties of the output media.

4. APPROACH

The fundamental assumption of the approach described in this paper is that graphical presentations are sentences of graphical languages, which are similar to other formal languages in that they have precise syntactic and semantic definitions. The three concerns described in the previous section are handled by a careful analysis of the properties of these definitions. This analysis leads to expressiveness and effectiveness criteria for evaluating graphical designs and a composition algebra for generating design alternatives.

An expressiveness criterion, which is derived from a precise language definition, is associated with each graphical language. A graphical language can be used to present some information when it includes a graphical sentence that expresses *exactly* the input information, that is, all the information and only the information. Expressing additional information is potentially dangerous because it may not be correct.

Effectiveness criteria can be based on a number of different factors. For example, a design can be judged effective when it can be interpreted accurately or quickly, when it has visual impact, or when it can be rendered in a

Fig. 8. Bertin's graphical objects and graphical relationships.

Marks:	Points, lines, and areas
Positional:	1-D, 2-D, and 3-D
Temporal:	Animation
Retinal:	Color, shape, size, saturation, texture, and orientation

cost-effective manner. This paper concentrates on generating designs that can be accurately interpreted. Dealing with multiple, perhaps conflicting, effectiveness criteria is beyond the scope of this research.

Given the focus on accuracy, effectiveness criteria are based on the observation that a graphical language uses specific graphical techniques to encode information. When interpreting a graphical sentence, a person is confronted with perceptual tasks that correspond to these graphical encoding techniques. Since some perceptual tasks are accomplished more accurately than others, effectiveness criteria can be based on the comparison of the perceptual tasks required by alternative graphical languages.

Since most graphical presentations of relational information are based on a general vocabulary of graphical techniques, a wide variety of designs can be generated with a composition algebra that describes this graphical vocabulary. Figure 8 summarizes graphic designer Jacques Bertin's vocabulary of the graphical techniques commonly used to encode information in presentation graphics [3]. Graphical presentations use graphical marks, such as points, lines, and areas, to encode information via their positional, temporal, and *retinal* properties.[2] The composition algebra consists of a *basis set* that contains primitive graphical languages, each of which embodies one of Bertin's graphical techniques for encoding information, and *composition operators* that are able to generate a wide range of presentations by composing the primitive languages.

5. EXPRESSIVENESS

All communication is based on the fact that the participants share conventions that determine how messages are constructed and interpreted. For graphical communication these conventions indicate how arrangements of graphical objects encode information. This section shows how to formalize these conventions by taking the view that graphical presentations are actually sentences of graphical languages that have precise syntactic and semantic definitions. Such definitions make it possible to determine the expressiveness and effectiveness properties of graphical languages.

Intuitively, a set of facts is expressible in a language if there is a sentence of the language that encodes every fact in the set. The difficulty with this intuition is that the sentence may encode additional incorrect facts (this is discussed in detail elsewhere [17]). Therefore, the expressiveness criteria for languages contain two conditions:

A set of facts is *expressible* in a language if it contains a sentence that
(1) encodes all the facts in the set,
(2) encodes only the facts in the set.

This section presents two examples that demonstrate the importance of these two conditions. The first example shows a case in which position on an axis cannot express a one-to-many relation. The second example shows a case in which a bar chart expresses additional incorrect facts. Before the examples can be given, however, it is necessary to develop some formal machinery for defining the syntax and semantics of graphical languages. Such machinery makes it possible to determine what information is encoded by the sentences of a language. Evaluating expressiveness requires this ability.

The formal machinery required to define a graphical language is fairly straightforward. A *graphical sentence* s is defined to be a collection of tuples:

$$s \subset \{\langle o, l \rangle \mid o \in O \wedge l \in L\},$$

where O is a set of graphical objects and L is a set of locations. Each tuple, which is called a *located object*, indicates the placement of an object at a given location. The syntax of a *graphical language* is defined to be a set of well-formed graphical sentences. This paper assumes that O and L are restricted to the standard 2-D Cartesian plane, such that the objects in O are 2-D graphical objects that have a finite, nonzero height and width, and the locations in L are the conventional binary tuples that represent the x and y positions in the Cartesian plane.[3] The height and width of a sentence is determined in the normal manner from the size and location of the objects that make up that sentence. This paper uses a variety of intuitively named functions to describe geometric properties. For example, the functions *Xmin*, *Xpos*, and *Xmax* identify the x position of the left, center, and right of a located object. Precise definitions of these functions can be found elsewhere [16].

The syntax of a language can be described with a predicate that identifies the well-formed sentences of the language. Systematic syntactic conventions can be captured by conditions that indicate when this predicate is true. For example, consider the diagram in Figure 9 that encodes the *Price* relation. Intuitively, it is an example of a set of graphical sentences (i.e., a graphical language) that is based on the syntactic convention of placing a plus object above an axis. The syntax of this "horizontal position" language can be formalized with the unary predicate *HorzPos*, which is true for any graphical sentence that consists of a horizontal axis and a set of tuples placing a plus object at a constant height somewhere above the axis.

More formally, a graphical sentence s is a legal sentence of the horizontal position language when it consists of the union of a horizontal axis set h and a set of marks m such that each located object $\langle o, l \rangle$ in m is a plus object *plusobj*

[2] The *retinal* properties are so called because the retina of the eye is sensitive to them, independent of the position of the object. Although they are included in the list of encoding relationships, 3-D position and animation are beyond the scope of this research.

[3] The resolution of a device can be represented by replacing the Cartesian plane with a grid of pixels [16].

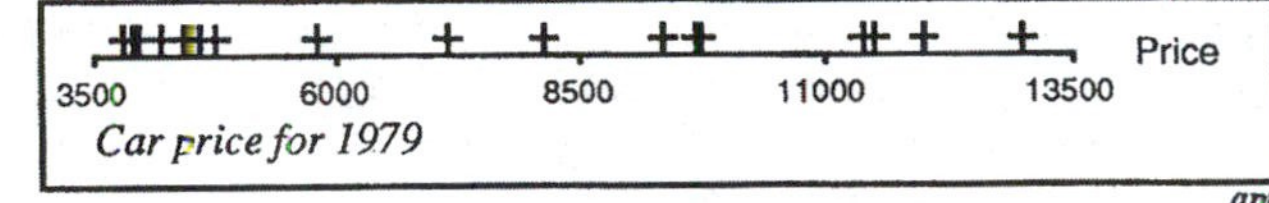

Fig. 9. The horizontal position sentence of the *Price* relation.

located at a constant height *const* above the axis:

$$\begin{aligned}&HorzPos(s) \Leftrightarrow\\&\quad s = h \cup m \wedge \langle o, l\rangle \in m \Rightarrow [\\&\qquad o = plusobj \wedge\\&\qquad Ymax(h) \le Ypos(l) = const \wedge\\&\qquad Xmin(h) \le Xpos(l) \le Xmax(h)].\end{aligned}$$

The symbols in this formula are used in a similar manner throughout the paper. In particular, the symbol h always stands for a horizontal axis,[4] and the symbol m always stands for a set of located objects (called *marks*) that have a related set of properties, such as objects positioned against the same axis.

Given a precise syntactic definition, the semantics of a graphical language can be specified using established formal techniques, such as denotational semantics [7]. A collection of located objects representing a graphical sentence can have a denotation in the same way as a collection of characters representing a logic formula. However, a presentation tool designs graphical sentences. It must be able to describe the semantic relationships between a graphical sentence and the encoded facts. For example, the *HorzPos* language encodes a binary relation with an axis, a set of marks, and the position of the marks on the axis. Formally, a relation called *Encodes(s, facts, lang)* is used to describe the semantic relationship between the objects and properties of a graphical sentence s and the set of *facts* that are encoded, given the semantic conventions of the language *lang*.[5] For example, given a relation r consisting of tuples $r(a_i, b_i)$, the following is a formal description of the three basic *Encodes* relationships for a sentence of the *HorzPos* language (see Figure 10 for an abstract description of these encodes relations). The axis h encodes the second domain of the relation, $Dom_2(r)$:

$$Encodes(h, Dom_2(r), HorzPos). \tag{1}$$

For the *Price* relation, the horizontal axis encodes the range [3500, 13000] of prices. Each located object o_i of the set of marks m encodes a unique domain value a_i of the first domain set of the relation $Dom_1(r)$:

$$Encodes(o_i, a_i, HorzPos). \tag{2}$$

Since this is true for every located object in the mark set m, the *Encodes* relation can be extended to the entire set:

$$Encodes(m, Dom_1(r), HorzPos).$$

For the *Price* relation, the marks encode the set of *Cars*.

[4] The symbol v stands for a vertical axis.

[5] Since an image might be a well-formed graphical sentence of more than one language, the *Encodes* relation includes the name of the language to indicate which semantic conventions are being described.

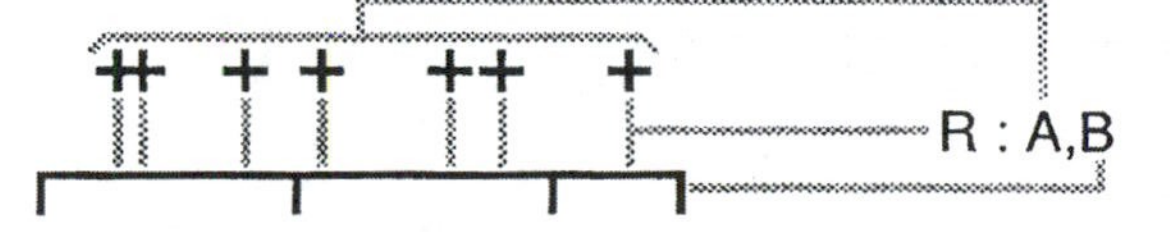

Fig. 10. The *Encodes* relationships for the horizontal position language. The graphical sentence is on the left, and the relation is on the right. The gray lines indicate that the domain sets are encoded by the objects, and the tuples of the relation are encoded by the relative positions of the marks.

Given the semantics for the objects in a graphical sentence, it is straightforward to describe the semantics for arrangements of objects. For the *HorzPos* language, the position of marks on the axis encodes the tuples of the r relation. That is, the first domain value a_i of a tuple $r(a_i, b_i)$ corresponds to a mark o_i as described in (2), and the second domain value b_i corresponds to the position of the mark o_i on the axis h, which is described with the binary function $Position(o_i, h)$. More formally, there exist two constants, *scale* and *offset*, that equate the domain value b_i with the axis position of the mark o_i for the domain value a_i:

$$\begin{aligned}&Encodes(o_i, a_i, HorzPos) \Rightarrow\\&\quad b_i = scale \times (Position(o_i, h) + offset) \wedge\\&\quad Encodes(Position(o_i, h), r(a_i, b_i), HorzPos).\end{aligned} \tag{3}$$

Since this is true for every mark in the mark set m, the *Encodes* relation can be extended to the domain sets. The positional encoding for the entire relation r can be described as follows:

$$Encodes(Position(m, h), r, HorzPos).$$

The presentation tool APT uses the domain set versions of these *Encodes* relations in the designs that it develops.

The formal machinery for describing the syntax and semantics of a graphical language leads to a precise statement of expressiveness:

$$\begin{aligned}&Expressible(facts, lang) \Leftrightarrow \exists s[lang(s) \wedge \forall f[\\&\quad f \in facts \Rightarrow Encodes(s, f, lang) \wedge\\&\quad f \notin facts \Rightarrow \neg Encodes(s, f, lang)]].\end{aligned} \tag{4}$$

The remainder of this section gives two examples that illustrate these two conditions of expressiveness.

The first example, which focuses on expressing all the facts, is based on the *HorzPos* language. It turns out that it is possible to prove that one-to-many relations cannot be expressed in the *HorzPos* language.

THEOREM 1. *When r is a one-to-many relation, it cannot be expressed in the HorzPos language*:

$$\begin{aligned}&r(a_i, b_j) \wedge r(a_i, b_k) \wedge b_j \ne b_k \Rightarrow\\&\quad \neg Expressible(r, HorzPos).\end{aligned}$$

PROOF. A proof by contradiction is straightforward, given the obvious geometric fact that a mark cannot have two positions on an axis. Assume that there

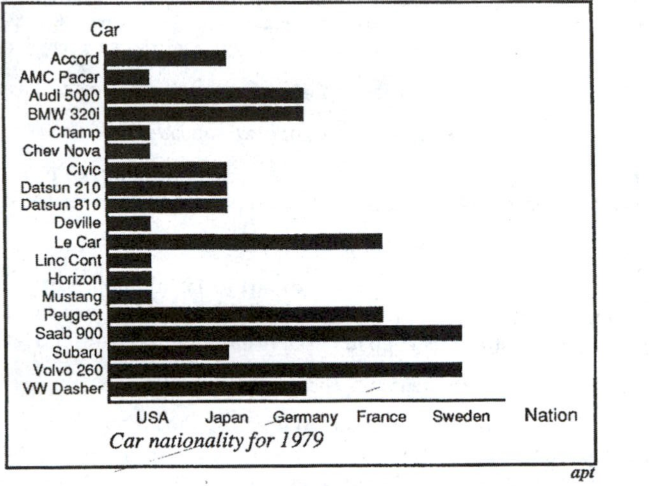

Fig. 11. Incorrect use of a bar chart for the *Nation* relation. The lengths of the bars suggest an ordering on the vertical axis, as if the USA cars were longer or better than the other cars, which is not true for the *Nation* relation.

exists a sentence s that satisfies (4) for the *HorzPos* language and relation r, which means that both tuples mentioned above are encoded in s. In particular, (2) indicates that there exists a mark o_i that is paired with the domain value a_i, and (3) indicates that $b_j = scale \times (Position(o_i, h) + offset) = b_k$, which contradicts the assumed inequality of the two domain values in the one-to-many relation. □

Although the previous theorem is not particularly deep, it illustrates the importance of precise definitions of the graphical conventions used to design and interpret information presentations. Not only do precise definitions make theorems possible, but they make clear which conventions are being used. Different conventions lead to different theorems. For example, the *HorzPos* language is based on the convention that the marks are uniquely paired with the domain values of the first domain set. Occasionally, graphical presentations use a different convention, that of pairing marks with the tuples rather than with the domain values of the first domain set. Given such a convention, the previous theorem is no longer valid because $r(a_i, b_j)$ and $r(a_i, b_k)$ can be encoded by the positions of different marks. However, this alternative convention is not so common as the *HorzPos* convention because it is natural to assume that marks are associated with domain values. For example, it is natural to assume that each mark in Figure 9 represents a unique car.

A second example, which focuses on the second expressiveness condition, illustrates the fact that some graphical languages encode additional information in the geometric relationships of the objects in a graphical sentence. Consider the bar chart diagram of the *Nation* relation in Figure 11. Most people perceive the lengths of the bars as an encoding of an ordered or quantitative set. That is, given domain tuples $r(a_i, b_i)$ and $r(a_j, b_j)$ and the corresponding bar objects bar_i and bar_j, an ordering relationship among the bar lengths encodes an ordering relation among the domain values b_i and b_j:

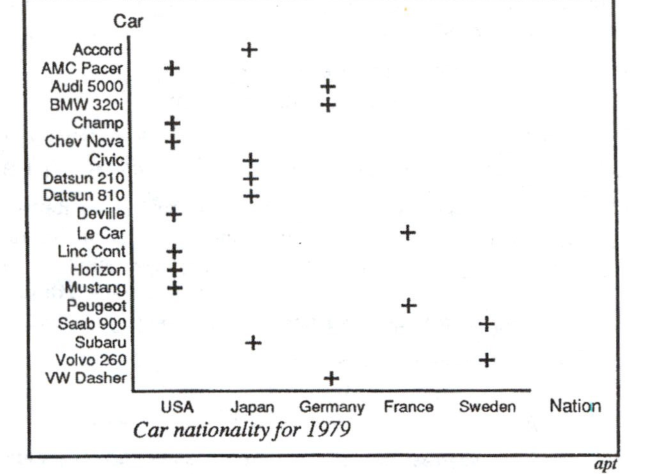

Fig. 12. Correct use of a plot chart for the *Nation* relation. Since bar charts encode ordered domain sets, plot charts are conventionally used to encode nominal domain sets. The ordering of the labels on the axes is ignored.

$$Encodes(Length(bar_i) > Length(bar_j),\ b_i > b_j,\ BarChart),$$

where the rest of the *Encodes* relations for the *BarChart* language are similar to the ones for *HorzPos*. Given this *Encodes* relation, it is easy to prove that the bar chart in Figure 11 does not express the *Nation* relation because it expresses the fact that the countries are ordered, which is not correct (see Figure 3).

The plot chart of the *Nation* relation in Figure 12, which is an alternative design for encoding the *Nation* relation that avoids the bar length problem, also illustrates the importance of precise language definitions. Sometimes, people use the convention that the sequence of labels on an axis indicates an ordered domain set, which would ruin the expressiveness of the scatter plot design for Figure 12. However, the standard convention is to ignore this sequencing encoding. After all, when the second domain set is ordered, a bar chart can be used. This means that the precise definition for a plot chart language should not include an *Encodes* predicate for the ordering of the second domain set. Therefore, the plot chart in Figure 12 does *not* encode additional incorrect facts.[6]

[6] The rendering of the plot chart in Figure 12 has the independent domain set of the *Nation* function on the vertical axis, which does not conform to the often ignored convention of encoding the independent domain set of a function with the horizontal axis. In this case the rendering code flipped the axes to make the rendering of the car labels more legible, and it did not take into account the fact that such a flip might confuse the reader of the diagram about which domain set was the independent one. (The recent development of the Dot Chart design deals with this problem [5].) Trade-offs between conventions and rendering constraints often occur. In the future, the rendering component will also have to be involved in the search for the most effective design.

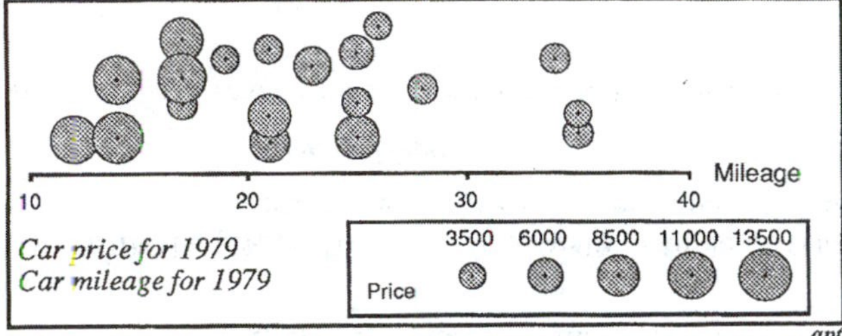

Fig. 13. Area/position presentation of the *Price* and *Mileage* relations. The vertical positioning of the marks reduces the chance that a mark is covered. This technique is called jittering; the vertical positioning does not encode any information.

6. EFFECTIVENESS

Given two graphical languages that express some information, the obvious question is which language involves a design that specifies the more effective presentation. For example, Figure 13 expresses the same price/mileage input as the scatter plot in Figure 5, but the prices are encoded with the area of the marks rather than with their position on a vertical axis. Which presentation is more effective?

Unlike expressiveness, which only depends on the syntax and semantics of the graphical language, effectiveness also depends on the capabilities of the perceiver. The difficulty is that there does not yet exist an empirically verified theory of human perceptual capabilities that can be used to prove theorems about the effectiveness of graphical languages. Therefore, one must conjecture a theory of effectiveness that is both intuitively motivated and consistent with current empirically verified knowledge about human perceptual capabilities. This section describes such a conjectural theory.

The core of this conjectural theory is an observation, made by Cleveland and McGill, that people accomplish the perceptual tasks associated with the interpretation of graphical presentations with different degrees of accuracy [6]. Cleveland and McGill focused on the presentation of quantitative information. They identified and ranked the tasks shown in Figure 14. Higher tasks are accomplished more accurately than lower tasks. Furthermore, they have some experimental evidence that supports the basic properties of this ranking.

Although the ranking in Figure 14 can be used to compare alternative graphical languages that encode quantitative information, it does not address the encoding of nonquantitative information, which involves additional perceptual tasks and different task rankings. For example, texture is not mentioned in Figure 14, and color, which is at the bottom of the quantitative ranking, is a very effective way of encoding nominal sets [23]. Therefore, it was necessary to extend Cleveland and McGill's ranking, as shown in Figure 15. Although this extension was developed using existing psychophysical results and various analyses of the different perceptual tasks, it has not been empirically verified [16].

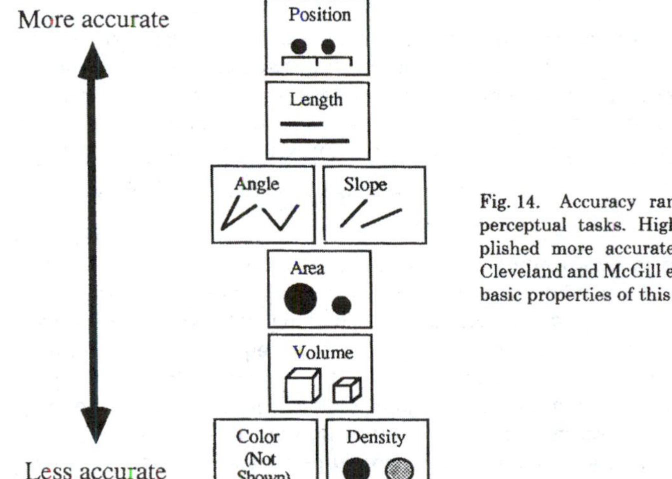

Fig. 14. Accuracy ranking of quantitative perceptual tasks. Higher tasks are accomplished more accurately than lower tasks. Cleveland and McGill empirically verified the basic properties of this ranking.

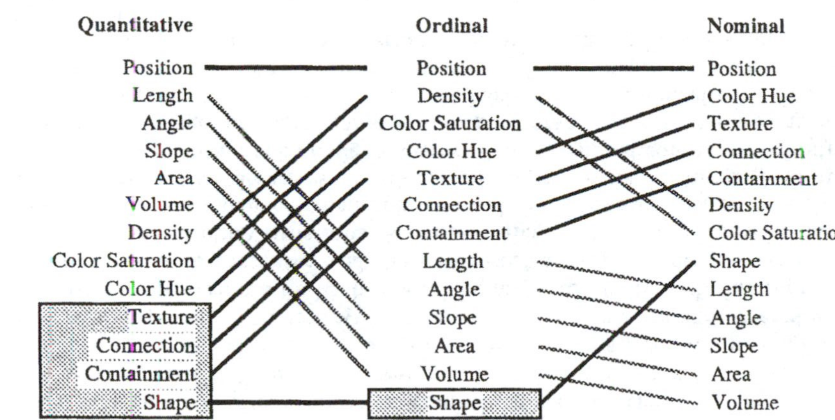

Fig. 15. Ranking of perceptual tasks. The tasks shown in the gray boxes are not relevant to these types of data.

An example analysis for area perception is shown in Figure 16. The top line shows that a series of decreasing areas can be used to encode a tenfold quantitative range. Of course, in a real diagram such as Figure 13, the areas would be laid out randomly, making it more difficult to judge the relative sizes of different areas accurately (hence, area is ranked fifth in Figure 14). Nevertheless, small misjudgments about the size of an area only leads to small misperceptions about the corresponding quantitative value that is encoded. The middle line shows that area can encode three ordinal values. However, one must be careful to make sure

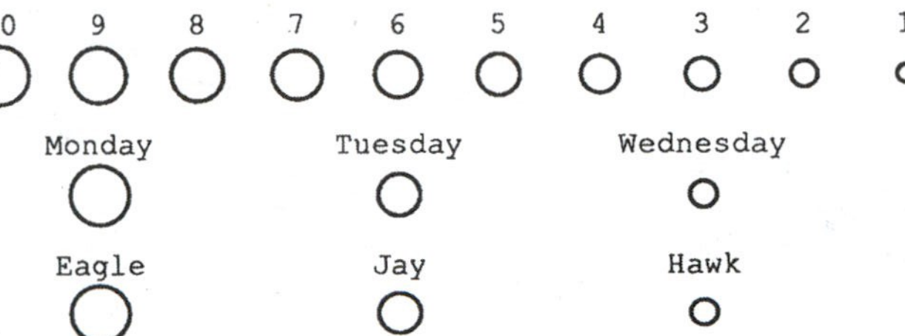

Fig. 16. Analysis of the area task. The top case shows that area is moderately effective for encoding quantitative information. The middle case shows that it is possible to encode ordinal information as long as the step size between areas is large enough so that the values are not confused. The bottom case shows that it is possible to encode nominal information, but people may perceive an ordinal encoding.

that ordinal areas are different enough so that they are not confused with each other. This is indicated by the fact that only three days of the week are encoded. If more days of the week were encoded, the step size between Tuesday's area and Monday's area would get small enough for people to start confusing them, which is quite different from confusing two quantitative values that are almost equal. The bottom line shows that area can encode three nominal values. Besides the fact that stepping is also required for nominal information, this case illustrates the additional problem that people often perceive area as an encoding of ordinal information. This analysis indicates that area should have a moderate quantitative ranking and a low nonquantitative ranking.

The ranking in Figure 15 can often be used to determine the relative effectiveness of different graphical languages. For example, Figure 17 compares the scatter plot and area/position designs for the price/mileage input. Since position has a higher ranking than area for quantitative data, it is clear that the scatter plot is a more effective design.

The ranking in Figure 15, however, does not specify a total ordering on the effectiveness of graphical languages. For example, Figure 18 compares two encodings of the *Price*, *Mileage*, and *Weight* relations. Both designs are scatter plots with information also encoded in the area of the marks. Since both designs require the same perceptual tasks, the ranking in Figure 15 does not indicate which design is more effective. The ranking can be extended to generate a lexicographic ordering with the following principle:

> *Principle of Importance Ordering*: Encode more important information more effectively.

That is, the input to the presentation tool is actually a tuple of relations that indicates the relative importance of the relations. For example, the input

$$\langle \textit{Price}, \textit{Mileage}, \textit{Weight} \rangle$$

should be presented with scatter plot 1, which has the *Weight* relation encoded with area.

	Price	*Mileage*
Scatter plot	position	position
Area/Position	area	position

Fig. 17. Comparison of perceptual tasks for the price/mileage designs.

	Price	*Mileage*	*Weight*
Scatter plot 1	position	position	area
Scatter plot 2	area	position	position

Fig. 18. Example of designs not ordered by the effectiveness ranking.

7. COMPOSITION

Expressiveness and effectiveness criteria, which were described in the previous two sections, are not very useful without a method for generating alternative designs. The naïve approach is simply to develop an ad hoc list of graphical languages that can be filtered with the expressiveness criteria and ordered with the effectiveness criteria for each input. The major difficulty with this approach is that there is no guarantee that there will exist appropriate designs for a wide variety of presentation situations. A minor difficulty is that the entire list must always be considered, even when only a few alternatives are suitable for a given input. This section describes an alternative approach based on the idea of a composition algebra. Such an algebra consists of a basis set containing primitive graphical languages and some composition operators that can generate composite designs. Described is a specific choice of basis set and composition operators that generate many of the designs commonly found in presentation graphics [3–5, 15, 19, 21]. The study of alternative composition algebras is an open area of research.

The idea of a composition algebra occurred to me when I looked at a diagram that was very similar in design to the diagram in Figure 19. The design used in Figure 19 combines two encoding techniques that are generally not seen together. First, the prerequisites among computer science classes are encoded with links that connect nodes that encode the classes. Second, a class schedule is encoded by the position of the nodes on a vertical axis. This diagram is an example of a composite design. The primitive languages used to form this composite design are a node/link language (see Figure 20) and a vertical-axis language (see Figure 21). Given this unusual example of a composite design, I realized that many presentations could be described as compositions of a set of primitive languages.

7.1 A Basis Set of Primitive Graphical Languages

A basis set of primitive graphical languages derived from Bertin's vocabulary of graphical encoding techniques (see Figure 8) is listed in Figure 22. The primitive languages have been classified by their primary encoding technique. *Single-position languages* encode information by the position of a mark set on one axis. *Apposed-position languages* encode information by a mark set that is positioned

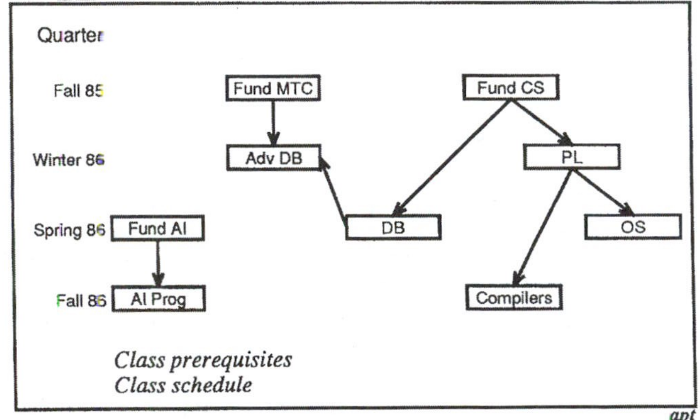

Fig. 19. Composite presentation for the prerequisite and schedule relations. The links encode the prerequisite relationships between computer science classes. The position on the vertical axis encodes the scheduling of the classes. Note that the advanced database class is scheduled before its prerequisite.

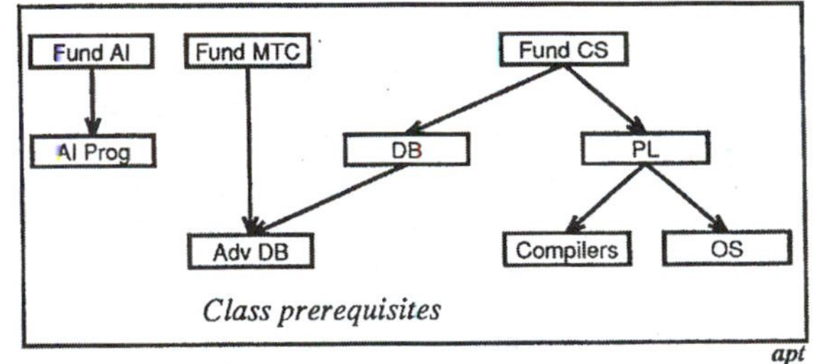

Fig. 20. Network presentation for the prerequisite relation.

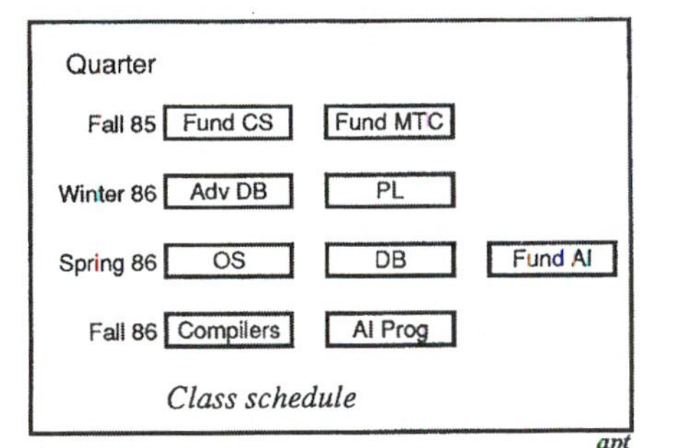

Fig. 21. Vertical-axis presentation for the schedule relation.

Encoding Technique	Primitive Graphical Language
Single-position	Horizontal axis, vertical axis
Apposed-position	Line chart, bar chart, plot chart
Retinal-list	Color, shape, size, saturation, texture, orientation
Map	Road map, topographic map
Connection	Tree, acyclic graph, network
Misc. (angle, contain, . . .)	Pie chart, Venn diagram, . . .

Fig. 22. A basis set of primitive graphical languages.

Encoding Technique	Syntactic Structure
Single-position	$h(m)$ or $v(m)$
Apposed-position	$vh(m)$
Retinal-list	m
Map	$vh(m)$
Connection	$m_n(m_l)$
Miscellaneous	$vh(m)$

Fig. 23. Syntactic structure of primitives. The notation is described in the text.

between two axes.[7] *Retinal-list languages* use one of the six retinal properties of the marks in a mark set to encode information. Since the positions of these marks do not encode anything, the marks can be moved when retinal list designs are composed with other designs. *Map languages,* which have fixed positions, encode information with graphical techniques that are specific to maps. *Connection languages* encode information by connecting a set of node objects with a set of link objects. *Miscellaneous languages* encode information with a variety of additional graphical techniques.

Figure 23 summarizes the basic syntactic structure of the primitive languages. The notation used in this figure is based on the fact that graphical sentences are sets of located object tuples. Except for connection languages, it turns out that every sentence of the primitive languages described in Figure 22 can be divided into the disjoint subsets

$$m \cup v \cup h,$$

where m is a set of marks, v contains at most a vertical axis, and h contains at most a horizontal axis. Furthermore, both the objects and positions of the mark sets have additional properties. The objects are either a collection of points, lines, or areas, and their positions are always fixed relative to the existing axes.[8] The notation always uses m for a set of marks, v for a vertical axis, and h for a

[7] It turns out that apposed-position languages can be described as the composition of single-position languages [16].

[8] This assumes that languages that restrict the positions of mark sets without a visible axis object, such as maps, define their sentences as having invisible axis objects.

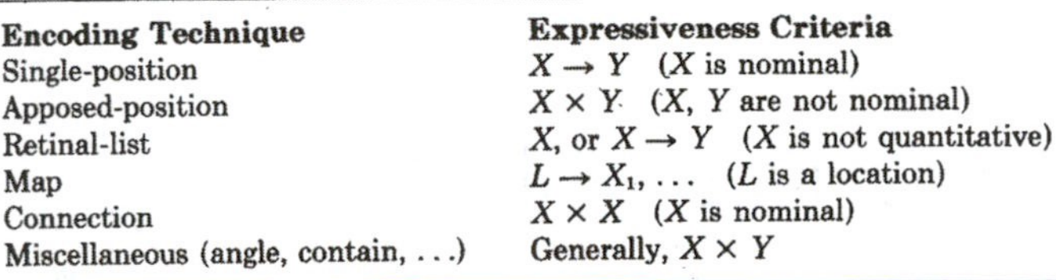

Encoding Technique	Expressiveness Criteria
Single-position	$X \to Y$ (X is nominal)
Apposed-position	$X \times Y$ (X, Y are not nominal)
Retinal-list	X, or $X \to Y$ (X is not quantitative)
Map	$L \to X_1, \ldots$ (L is a location)
Connection	$X \times X$ (X is nominal)
Miscellaneous (angle, contain, . . .)	Generally, $X \times Y$

Fig. 24. Expressiveness criteria for the primitive languages. These are the general restrictions. Specific languages can have additional restrictions.

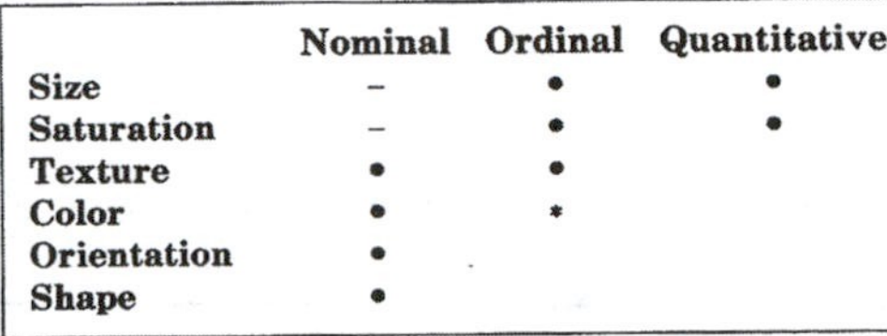

	Nominal	Ordinal	Quantitative
Size	–	•	•
Saturation	–	•	•
Texture	•	•	
Color	•	*	
Orientation	•		
Shape	•		

Fig. 25. Expressiveness of retinal techniques. The – indicates that size and saturation should not be used for nominal measurements because they will probably be perceived to be ordered. The * indicates that the full color spectrum is not ordered. However, parts of the color spectrum are ordinally perceived [23].

horizontal axis. The notation also uses parentheses to indicate that there is a positional constraint on a set of marks. For example, the positional constraints of bar charts are described by $vh(m)$, where v and h are not empty. Sentences of connection languages consist of two sets of marks: the set of nodes m_n and the set of links m_l. The nodes constrain the position of links. The notation can also be extended to more complex designs. For example, the two bar charts in Figure 7 that are aligned on their vertical axes have the structure $v(h_i(m_i), h_j(m_j))$.

An analysis of the semantic properties of these languages leads to the expressiveness criteria shown in Figures 24 and 25. Figure 24 describes the basic expressiveness criteria for each type of primitive language. For example, single-position languages can only express binary relations that have a functional dependency. Figure 25 describes the expressiveness criteria of various retinal techniques for nominal, ordinal, and quantitative information. There are additional requirements not mentioned in Figures 24 and 25. For example, line charts can only be used when a relation describes values of a continuous function.

7.2 Some Composition Operators

The composition operators associated with the primitive languages in Figure 22 are based on a single principle:

Principle of Composition: Compose two designs by merging parts that encode the same information.

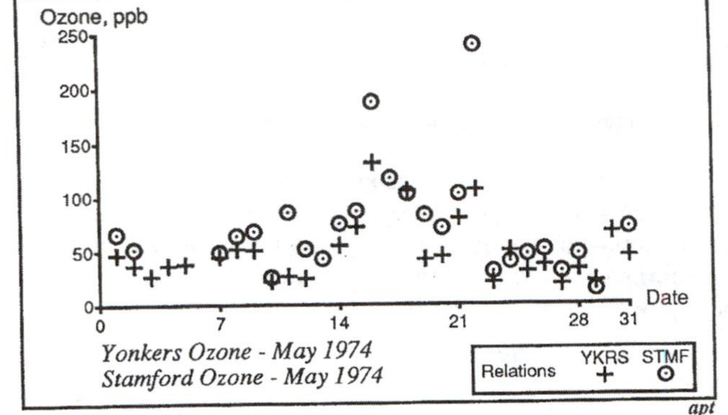

Fig. 26. Example of double-axes composition. The diagram describes a month of ozone measurements for two cities. The reason that a line chart design was not used for these data is that there are missing measurements for some of the days; a line chart is only used for continuous functions.

This principle leads to three composition operators that are based on the objects used by the primitive languages: *double-axes composition* $\bowtie_d$, *single-axis composition* $\bowtie_s$, and *mark composition* $\bowtie_m$. The following description of these composition operators gives an informal and formal definition of each of them.

Double-axes composition can compose graphical sentences that have identical horizontal and vertical axes. The multiple scatter plot in Figure 26 is an example of double-axes composition. The component designs are two plot charts that describe ozone measurements in two different cities. Since the measurements were taken in the same month, the axes of these two plot charts are identical. The composite is generated by merging the identical axes and copying the mark sets from the two component designs.

Formally, the double-axes composition $s_i \bowtie_d s_j$ is well defined if s_i contains $v_i h_i(m_i)$ and s_j contains $v_j h_j(m_j)$ such that the axis sets are not empty and encode the same information. That is, given that s_i is a sentence of language l_i and s_j is a sentence of language l_j, the *Encodes* relations indicate that both horizontal axes encode the same domain set x and both vertical axes encode the same domain set y:

$$\begin{aligned} & v_i = v_j \neq \{\ \} \wedge h_i = h_j \neq \{\ \} \wedge \\ & Encodes(h_i, x, l_i) \wedge Encodes(h_j, x, l_j) \wedge \\ & Encodes(v_i, y, l_i) \wedge Encodes(v_j, y, l_j). \end{aligned}$$

The composite contains $v_i h_i(m_i', m_j')$. The prime is required when the marks are changed by the composition. For example, composed bar charts move the bars next to each other. When the prime is not needed, double-axes composition is commutative. It is always associative.

Single-axis composition aligns two sentences that have identical horizontal or vertical axes. The diagram in Figure 7 is an example of single-axis composition.

The two component designs are bar charts that describe the price and mileage of some cars. Since the vertical axes encode the same set of cars, the composite can be generated by placing one diagram next to the other such that the vertical axes are aligned.

Formally, the single-axis composition $s_i \bowtie_s s_j$ is well defined if s_i contains $v_i h_i(m_i)$, s_j contains $v_j h_j(m_j)$, and the following condition is satisfied:

$$[v_i = v_j \neq \{\ \} \wedge Encodes(v_i, y, l_i) \wedge Encodes(v_j, y, l_j)] \vee$$
$$[h_i = h_j \neq \{\ \} \wedge Encodes(h_i, x, l_i) \wedge Encodes(h_j, x, l_j)],$$

where x, y, l_i, and l_j are defined in the same manner as for double-axes composition. The composite contains $v_i' h_i' (m_i')$ and $v_j' h_j' (m_j')$, where the positions of the objects are modified to place the diagrams next to each other in the viewing area. Single-axis composition is not commutative because the positions of the diagrams reverse. However, it is associative.

Mark composition is more complicated than the axis composition operators because it actually merges mark sets. For example, a mark set of uniform size that encodes information with color can be merged with a mark set of uniform color that encodes information with size. The resulting mark set uses both color and size to encode information (see Figure 30 for an example).

Mark composition merges mark sets by pairing each and every mark of one set with a compatible mark of the other set. The diagram in Figure 19 is an example of mark composition. The component design is a directed-acyclic-graph design for the prerequisite relation, which is rendered in Figure 20, and a vertical-axis design for the scheduling relation, which is rendered in Figure 21. The two mark sets are compatible because they encode the same information, and any shared positional or retinal constraints are identical. The composite is generated by merging the mark sets. That is, the composite includes a mark set that corresponds to the two mark sets of the components. The position and retinal properties of this composite mark set are based on the constrained position and retinal properties of the component mark sets. Compatibility makes sure that the component's properties do not conflict. Additional properties and objects in the component sentences are copied over into the composite. For example, the composite in Figure 19 includes the vertical-axis object from the diagram in Figure 21.

Formally, the mark composition $s_i \bowtie_m s_j$ is well defined if s_i contains $v_i h_i(m_i)$, and s_j contains $v_j h_j(m_j)$, and the marks in m_i and m_j can be paired such that each pair of located objects o_i and o_j encode the same domain value a:

$$[Encodes(o_i, a, l_i) \wedge Encodes(o_j, a, l_j)].$$

Furthermore, the position and retinal properties of these mark pairs must encode the same information. For position, an existing pair of axes means that the positions must be identical:

$$[v_i = v_j \neq \{\ \} \Rightarrow Position(o_i, v_i) = Position(o_j, v_j)] \wedge$$
$$[h_i = h_j \neq \{\ \} \Rightarrow Position(o_i, h_i) = Position(o_j, h_j)].$$

For the retinal properties, a little more formal machinery is required. A set of marks can have retinal constraints based on the six retinal properties identified

Fig. 27. The interaction of size and shape.

by Bertin. For example, the size of the marks in Figure 13 encode the values of the *Price* relation. Six functions identify the six retianl values of an object. These functions can also be used to indicate when the retinal properties of a mark set are constrained. Given a retinal function f, a set of marks m, and a graphical sentence s that contains m, the relation $Rt(s, m, f)$ is true when the retinal properties corresponding to f encode information for the mark set m. Given this relation, the following indicates that the paired marks must have the same constraints on their retinal properties:

$$Rt(s_i, m_i, f) \wedge Rt(s_j, m_j, f) \Rightarrow$$
$$f(o_i) = f(o_j).$$

That is, when a retinal property is used by two mark sets to encode information, the objects for each pair of marks must have identical retinal properties.

The composite sentence $vh(m)$, generated by the mark composition $v_i h_i(m_i) \bowtie_m v_j h_j(m_j)$, is constructed in the following manner. The vertical axis v is v_i if it is not empty and v_j otherwise. The horizontal axis h is h_i if it is not empty and h_j otherwise. For each pair of marks, construct a composite mark from the constrained retinal and position properties of the component marks (which must be identical) and any remaining properties from m_i. The final condition means that $\bowtie_m$ is not commutative. It is easy to show that $\bowtie_m$ is associative.

The conditions for using these three composition operators are sufficiently general for them to be used together. The major difficulty is specifying exactly how the parts of the component sentences that are not part of the composition should be handled. The best approach is to merge pairs of axes or mark sets of the component sentence that satisfy the conditions of the composition operators. This will reduce redundancy in the composed diagram.

A rough effectiveness ranking can also be assigned to the composition operators. Mark composition is the most effective because it merges the component sentences in such a way that the number of graphical objects does not increase. Single-axis composition is the least effective because it does not actually merge the designs, which makes it harder to perceive all the information at once.

Composition can have side effects that must be addressed. For example, when size and shape are composed together, the perception of shape is made difficult when the sizes are small. For example, the marks in Figure 27 are a composition of shape and size. The shapes of the small objects begin to look the same. Therefore, care must be taken to avoid situations in which such interactions reduce the effectiveness of a composite design. APT's rendering component makes sure the marks do not get too small.

8. IMPLEMENTATION

The theoretical results described in the previous three sections have been combined in a synthesis algorithm that generates designs in order of the effectiveness criteria described above. The synthesis algorithm has been implemented in APT, which consists of a design component followed by a rendering component (see Figure 1). The design component uses logic programming techniques to implement the synthesis algorithm. The rendering component uses object-oriented programming techniques and a device-independent graphics package to render the resulting designs. The rendering component, which was not the focus of this research, places an implementation restriction on the set of primitive languages in Figure 22 that can be used by APT to generate presentations. As of this writing, the following primitive languages remain unimplemented: orientation, texture, line charts, maps, and miscellaneous. Even with these restrictions, the prototype can generate a wide range of useful presentations. The diagrams in this paper with *apt* in the lower right corner are examples of APT's output.

APT's synthesis algorithm is based on a divide-and-conquer search strategy. The algorithm has three steps: partition, selection, and composition. These steps, which are described below, involve choices. When a particular set of choices does not lead to a composite design, backtracking is used to consider other choices. APT uses depth-first search with simple backtracking.

(1) *Partitioning.* The set of relations to be presented is divided into partitions that match the expressiveness criteria of at least one of the primitive languages. This is done recursively. For example, the input

⟨*Price, Mileage, Repair, Weight*⟩

can be partitioned into the sets

⟨*Price*⟩ and ⟨*Mileage, Repair, Weight*⟩.

The right partition must be recursively divided because it does not match any of the primitive languages.

The principle of importance ordering is addressed by making sure that the choices among alternative partitionings give preference to the important information. The input shown above is a tuple that indicates the importance ordering for the automobile relations. It is partitioned so that the most important relation, which is the *Price* relation, will get first chance at being matched to an effective primitive language.

Since relations, as well as sets of relations, can be partitioned [16], it is possible for the input to include relations that have more than two domain sets. The cumulative bar chart in Figure 28 is an example of a design that is generated by relation partitioning. The input is a ternary relation, which is a function of years and quarters, to the Ph.D.s conferred in each quarter for a range of years. Binary relations are generated by fixing the year. The stacked bar designs corresponding to the binary relations are composed with single-axis composition to generate the cumulative bar chart.

(2) *Selection.* Given expressiveness and effectiveness criteria, selection is straightforward. For each partition generated by the previous step, the primitives are filtered, with their expressiveness criteria used to generate a list of candidate designs. For example, the list of candidate designs for the *Price* partition does not include maps because the *Price* relation does not satisfy the map expressiveness criterion (see Figure 24).

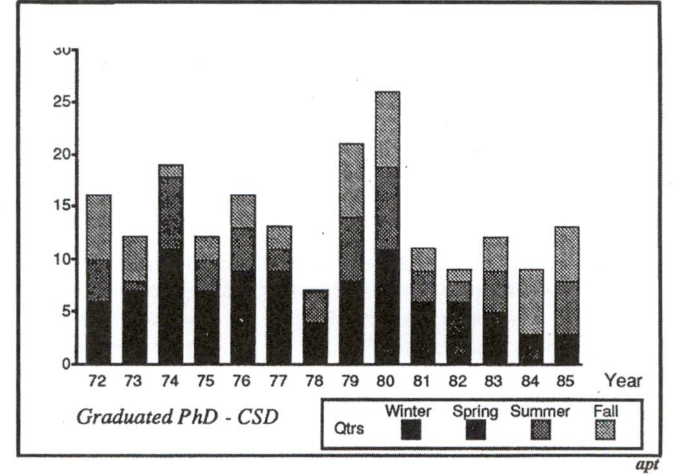

Fig. 28. A relation partitioning example. The cumulative bar chart describes the number of Ph.D. students that graduated each quarter for a range of years. The input is a relation of three domain sets, which are partitioned into a set of binary relations. The composite is generated by the single-axis composition of the stacked bar design chosen for each of these binary relations.

The effectiveness criteria are used to order the candidate designs so that the most effective design will be the first choice. For the *Price* relation the effectiveness ordering depends on whether the application has requested that the details about the cars be placed in the background. Apposed-position languages are the most effective when the details are required, and single-position languages are the most effective otherwise. The other primitive languages are less effective because position is at the top of the perceptual task ranking shown in Figure 15.

(3) *Composition.* Composition operators are used to compose the individual designs into a unified presentation of all the information. Given designs for two partitions, the three composition operators are checked to see if they can be applied. During the generation of the composite designs, additional conditions, such as the interaction of shape and size, can be checked.

The synthesis algorithm involves choices that might not lead to a design, which means that backtracking will occur. When backtracking occurs, the next most effective primitive language or composition operator is chosen until a design is found for all the information. For example, given a request to omit the details about the cars, APT processes the automobile input shown above as follows. The partitioning step generates a partition for the *Price* relation and a partition for the *Mileage* relation. The first selection choice is the vertical-axis primitive

$$
\begin{array}{ll}
rel = x \rightarrow y \wedge \neg Numeric(x) \wedge Numeric(y) \wedge & \text{Expressiveness} \\
Cardinality(x) < 20 \wedge & \text{Effectiveness} \\
LineObjs(barchart, lines) \wedge VertAxis(barchart, vaxis) \wedge & \\
Encodes(lines, x) \wedge Encodes(vaxis, y) \wedge & \text{Assumables} \\
Length(lines, len, vaxis) \wedge Encodes(len, rel(x)) \wedge \cdots & \\
\quad \Rightarrow Presents(barchart, rel) &
\end{array}
$$

Fig. 29. APT's bar-chart rule. The expressiveness conditions state that the relation must be a functional dependency from a nonnumeric set to a numeric set. The effectiveness condition limits the number of bars because too many bars make the presentation difficult to read. The assumables are *Encodes* relations that connect the relation and the presentation. The independent set is connected to the bar lines and the dependent set is connected to the vertical axis.

language for both of these partitions (because the relations have the same structure). However, the composition step fails to compose the resulting designs because mark composition, which is the only applicable operator, cannot merge marks that have two different positions on an axis. This failure triggers backtracking. The next most effective choice for the *Mileage* partition is the horizontal-axis primitive language. Mark composition succeeds for this choice, and the search proceeds to deal with the remaining relations in the input. (Given an indication from the application that the output medium includes color, the resulting design for the four automobile relations is the scatter plot rendered in Figure 30.)

The logic program implementing the synthesis algorithm is based on a depth-first[9] backward chaining version of a deductive algorithm called Residue [9]. Residue is useful for design problems because predicates describing the design can be declared to be assumable. During a deduction, an assumable predicate can be assumed to be true to make the deduction proceed. At the end of the deduction, all assumed predicates are returned as conditions that must be satisfied. For design problems, these conditions are exactly the design constraints. For example, Figure 29 describes APT's bar chart rule. The assumables are the *Encodes* relations of the bar-chart primitive language. When these predicates are assumed, they can be used to compose this design with others and to render the final image.

APT was deveoped on a Symbolics LISP Machine using MRS, a representation and logic programming system [18]. APT is a functional prototype, and no effort has been made to make it efficient, although designs are typically generated in 1–2 minutes, and images are rendered in less than a minute. The logic program is about 200 rules, and the rendering system is about 60 pages of LISP code.

APT demonstrates that a synthesis algorithm based on composition can be used to generate automatically effective designs that can express a wide variety of input. Although inefficient, the deductive search strategy used in APT has a number of advantages that recommend it over more procedural approaches. APT can be sensitive to many factors while generating designs. The next section describes how APT is sensitive to the output medium. APT is also sensitive to requests from the application. An application can indicate that a particular primitive language should be used, even when it contradicts the effectiveness ranking that APT would normally use. This makes it possible for an application to tailor a presentation to fit the profile of a particular user. Another advantage of the logic programming approach is that it is flexible. The range of designs that can be generated by APT can be modified by changing the rules associated with the primitive languages and the composition operators. The search order can also be modified by changing the expressiveness and effectiveness criteria. This is important because presentation graphics and human perceptual abilities are not yet well understood. As our understanding advances, it will be possible to make modifications to APT that will enable it to generate even more effective designs.

9. MEDIA SENSITIVITY

Since the synthesis algorithm searches for designs, it can be sensitive to the capabilities of the output medium. For example, when the application indicates that the output medium includes color, APT designs the scatter plot shown in Figure 30 for the automobile input, which is the mark composition of two single-position designs and two retinal-list designs. When the application restricts APT to a monochrome medium, APT designs the aligned bar chart shown in Figure 31, which is the single-axis composition of four bar-chart designs.[10] Given a color medium, the *Repair* relation can be encoded by the color-list primitive language. However, given a monochrome medium, the only available retinal-list primitive languages for ordinal information are texture, saturation, and size (see Figure 25). The texture primitive language was rejected because the rendering portion of APT does not implement texture. The saturation primitive language was rejected by its effectiveness criterion because five levels of gray blend together, making the repair values blend together. The size primitive language can be selected. However, the scatter plot design requires that size also be used for one of the other relations in the input, and mark composition cannot merge two designs that use size to encode different domain sets. APT ultimately settles on the aligned bar chart shown in Figure 31.

10. DISCUSSION

The research described in this paper sets the framework for the development of presentation tools that can automatically design effective graphical presentations for a wide variety of information. The formalization of graphical presentation as a collection of graphical languages makes it possible to develop expressiveness

[9] Depth-first search can be used because the effectiveness criteria place a total ordering on designs that are understood by APT. As the theory of effectiveness becomes more sophisticated, it is likely that the control strategy will also have to become more sophisticated.

[10] APT always generates the aligned bar design before the scatter plot design when the application does not indicate that the details about the cars can be omitted, because the bar charts contain the names of the cars. Labels on points in the scatter plot obscure information. When the output device is a computer monitor, however, it is generally better to omit detail, because omitted details can be obtained by interacting with the display through the use of techniques such as pick-sensitive objects and pop-up windows.

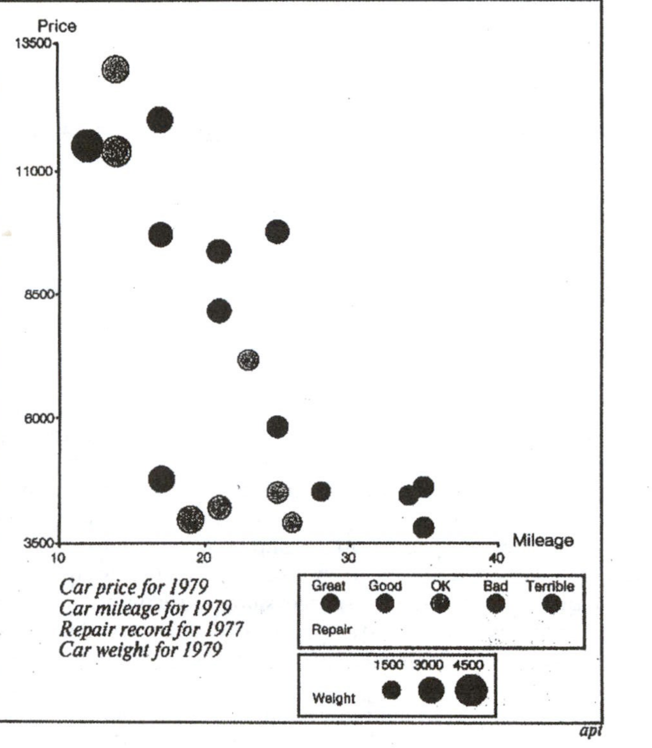

Fig. 30. Color scatter plot for four automobile relations. The design expresses the relations only if the application permits the details about the cars to be omitted.

and effectiveness criteria and a composition algebra. This formalization provides the basis of a logic program that designs presentations automatically. The prototype implementation, called APT, demonstrates the feasibility of this approach.

Many problems associated with the automatic generation of graphical designs remain to be solved. The engineering of robust presentation tools will raise many questions about the correct search criteria. Animation and 3-D presentation appear to be very powerful techniques for presenting symbolic information and should be incorporated into future tools. Larger search spaces, which can be generated with finer grained sets of primitive languages, make it more difficult to search for an appropriate choice in real time. However, it may be possible to build a discovery system that searches this larger space for unusual but effective

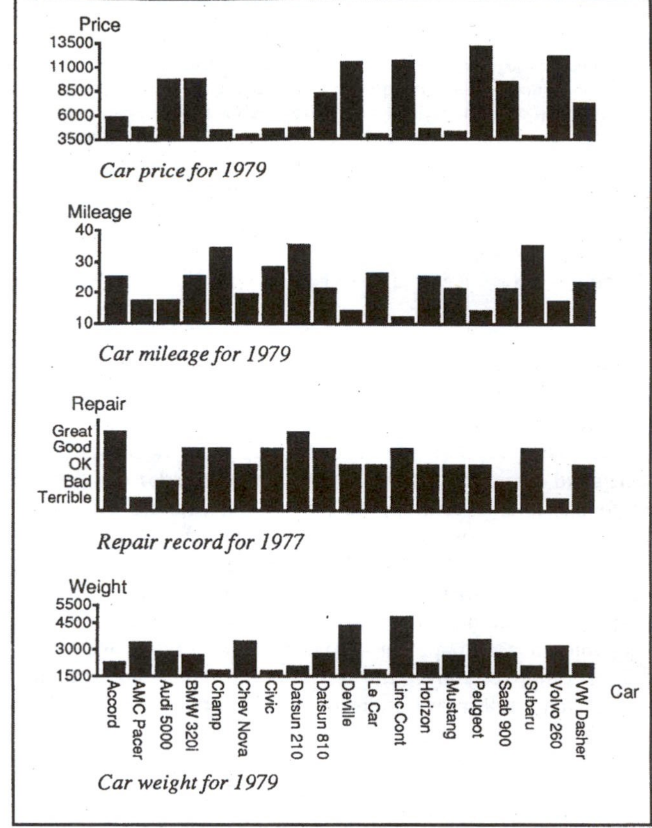

Fig. 31. Aligned bar chart of automobile data. This diagram shows the details about the car domain set. However, the general relationships are not so easy to see as in the scatter plot design.

designs. These designs can then be cached along with the primitive languages described in this paper to form a small but comprehensive search space.

This research on intelligent presentation applies artificial intelligence techniques to part of the user interface design problem—that of choosing an appropriate graphical presentation of relational data. Graphic design issues are an important concern of user interface design. This presentation research incorporates a formalized body of graphic design knowledge. Future work with these techniques can address other aspects of user interface management systems, perhaps choosing or adapting the dialogue specifications appropriate to the observed skill level of the user. When research develops theoretical results, such as the graphic design criteria and composition algebra described in this paper.

from a careful analysis of user interface systems, artificial intelligence techniques can be used to develop an intelligent user interface.

ACKNOWLEDGMENTS

I would like to thank the following people: Polle Zellweger for her inspired suggestions that improved every draft of this paper, Rick Beach for his constructive suggestions just before the submission deadline, Matt Ginsberg and Eric Bier for their helpful suggestions on early drafts, and Michael Genesereth, my advisor, for his encouragement and suggestions throughout the research. The suggestions of the referees are also appreciated.

REFERENCES

1. BEACH, R. J. Setting tables and illustrations with style. Ph.D. dissertation, Dept. of Computer Science, Univ. of Waterloo, Waterloo, Ont., Canada, 1985. Also Xerox PARC Tech. Rep. CSL-85-3.
2. BEACH, R., AND STONE, M. Graphical style—towards high quality illustrations. *Computer Graph. (SIGGRAPH) 17*, 3 (1983), 127–135.
3. BERTIN, J. *Semiology of Graphics*, W. J. Berg, Tr. University of Wisconsin Press, Milwaukee, Wis., 1983.
4. BOWMAN, W. J. *Graphic Communication.* Wiley, New York, 1968.
5. CLEVELAND, W. S. *The Elements of Graphing Data.* Wadsworth Advanced Books and Software, Monterey, Calif., 1980.
6. CLEVELAND, W. S., AND MCGILL, R. Graphical perception: Theory, experimentation and application to the development of graphical methods. *J. Am. Stat. Assoc. 79*, 387 (Sept. 1984), 531–554.
7. ENDERTON, H. B. *A Mathematical Introduction to Logic.* Academic Press, Orlando, Fla., 1972.
8. FEINER, S. APEX: An experiment in the automated creation of pictorial explanations. *IEEE Comput. Graph. Appl. 5*, 11 (Nov. 1985), 29–37.
9. FINGER, J. J., AND GENESERETH, M. R. RESIDUE—A deductive approach to design synthesis. Tech. Rep. KSL-85-1, Computer Science Dept., Stanford Univ., Stanford, Calif., Jan. 1985.
10. FRIEDELL, M. Automatic graphics environment synthesis. Ph.D. dissertation, Dept. of Computer Engineering and Science, Case Western Reserve Univ., Cleveland, Ohio, 1983. Also Computer Corporation of America Tech. Rep. CCA-83-03.
11. GNANAMGARI, S. Information presentation through default displays. Ph.D. dissertation, Dept. of Decision Sciences, The Wharton School, Univ. of Pennsylvania, Philadelphia, Pa., May 1981.
12. KAHN, K. M. Creation of computer animation from story descriptions. Ph.D. dissertation, MIT-AI-540, Massachusetts Institute of Technology, Cambridge, Mass., Aug. 1979.
13. KAHNEMAN, D., AND HENIK, A. Perceptual organization and attention. In *Perceptual Organizaton.* M. Kubovy and J. R. Pomerantz, Eds. Lawrence Erlbaum, Hillsdale, N.J., 1981, pp. 181–211.
14. KNUTH, D. E. *The Art of Computer Programming*, vol. 1. Addison-Wesley, Reading, Mass., 1973, pp. 176–179.
15. LOCKWOOD, A. *Diagrams: A Visual Survey of Graphs, Maps, Charts and Diagrams for the Graphic Designer.* Watson-Guptill, 1969.
16. MACKINLAY, J. Automatic design of graphical presentations. Ph.D. dissertation, Computer Science Dept., Stanford Univ., Stanford, Calif., 1986. Also Tech. Rep. Stan-CS-86-1038.
17. MACKINLAY, J., AND GENESERETH, M. R. Expressiveness and language choice. *Data Knowl. Eng. 1*, 1 (June 1985), 17–29.
18. RUSSELL, S. The compleat guide to MRS. KSL-85-12, Computer Science Dept., Stanford Univ., Stanford, Calif., June 1985.
19. SCHMID, C. F. *Statistical Graphics: Design Principles and Practices.* Wiley, New York, 1983.
20. STEVENS, S. S. On the theory of scales of measurement. *Science, 103* 2684 (June 1946), 677–680.
21. TUFTE, E. R. *The Visual Display of Quantitative Information.* Graphics Press, Cheshire, Conn., 1983.
22. ULLMAN, J. D. *Principles of Database Systems.* Computer Science Press, Rockville, Md., 1980.
23. WARE, C., AND BEATTY, J. C. Using colour as a tool in discrete data analysis. Tech. Rep. CS-85-21, Computer Science Dept., Univ. of Waterloo, Waterloo, Ont., Canada, Aug. 1985.
24. ZDYBEL, F., GREENFELD, N. R., YONKE, M. D., AND GIBBONS, J. An information presentation system. In *7th International Joint Conference on Artificial Intelligence* (Vancouver, Canada, Aug.). AAAI, Menlo Park, Calif., 1981, pp. 978–984.

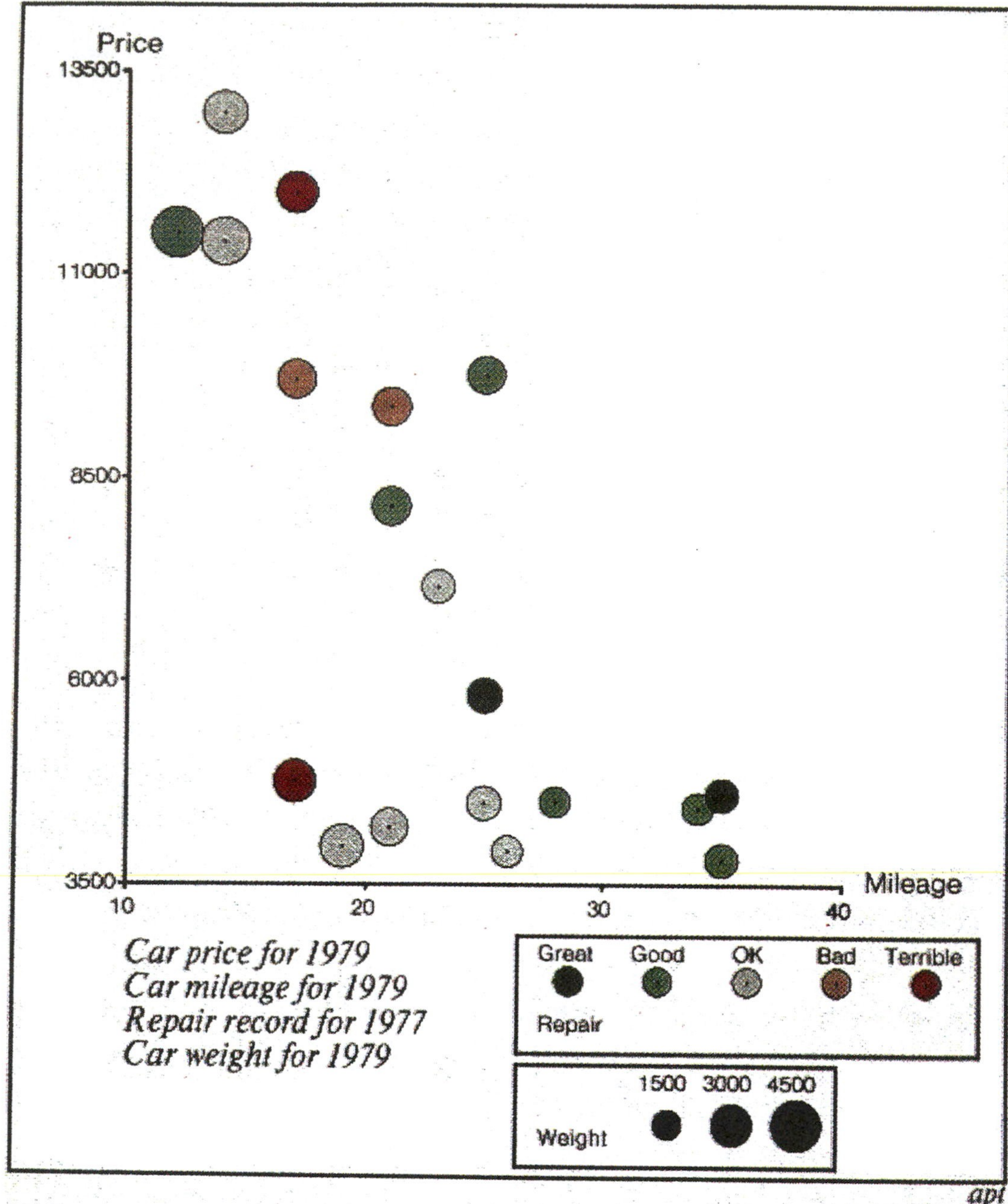

FIGURE **30**

Color scatter plot for four automobile relations. The design expresses the relations only if the application permits the details about the cars to be omitted.

Research Report
Information Animation Applications in the Capital Markets

William Wright
Visible Decisions Inc.
Toronto, Canada
wwright@vizbiz.com

Abstract

3D computer graphics can be extremely expressive. It is possible to display an entire securities market, like the S&P 500, on a single screen. A complex inventory of 3,000 positions can also easily fit on a single screen. With the correct approach to the visual design of the layout, these massive amounts of information can be quickly and easily comprehended by a human observer. By using motion and animated interaction, it is possible to use 3D as a reliable, accurate and precise decision-support tool.

Information animation applications are particularly suited to the securities industry because that is where we find huge amounts of data, the value of which declines rapidly with time, and where critical decisions are being made on this data in very short periods of time. Information animation technology is an important new tool for the securities industry, where people need to be in the decision-making loop without suffering from information overload.

Several examples are discussed including equity trading analytics, fixed income trading analytics and fixed–income risk viewing. Risk viewing is generalized to include instruments and markets beyond fixed–income, namely equities, derivatives, and foreign exchange. In each case, the common elements are positions, models of asset value, parameterized models of risk sensitivity, and scenario projections. These visual risk models more easily allow control and guidance of risk exposure over a wide variety of scenarios and stress tests.

1 Introduction

Three–dimensional computer graphics can be extremely expressive. With the correct approach to the visual design of the layout, massive amounts of information can be quickly and easily comprehended by a human observer.

Data visualization has reached a new level of capability which can be described as Information Animation™. Graphics display technology and applications have moved beyond the static or interactive 2D bar charts, line charts and pie charts, and beyond the interactive 3D scatter plots and contour plots of statistical and scientific visualization. It is now possible, on an inexpensive workstation, to build, display and have updated in real time, visual scenes comprised of abstract 3D geometrical forms. The viewer's point of view can move through these 3D scenes, which have been constructed of simple and/or complex objects, and the objects themselves can move within the scenes. Desktop workstations can now move hundreds of thousands of independent 3D polygons per second on a display console.

Military and industrial simulations make use of this computer graphics power in applications that portray realistic visual scenes showing tank combat in urban centers, or merchant marine vessels docking in busy harbors. However this same hardware technology can be used in management and knowledge worker tasks. "Information animation" is the application of this level of computer graphics power to data intensive, time critical, decision making tasks where the 3D landscape comprises numerical / textual data and analytical models.

To support decision making tasks, information animation uses 4D (3D plus motion) graphics. By itself, 3D is not sufficient. The 3D display of data is not a new concept and has often been used as a communication medium when more emphasis on impact rather than insight is desired. 3D does not lend itself to rigorous comparative analysis because of the distortions arising from a perspective view and occlusion. However, by using motion and animated interaction, it is possible to use 3D as a reliable, accurate and precise decision-support tool. To quote James Clark, the founder of Silicon Graphics Inc., "To make 3D work, you need to make it move."

This new 3D and motion capability, which we call information animation, allows a higher level of expression, a significant increase in the amount of data displayed, and a broader scope of application.

This paper provides a number of examples of information animation applications in the securities industry. These examples are drawn from equity trading analytics and fixed-income risk management. Many other applications are suggested as well, including OTC trading, equity trading execution and equities risk viewing. Before the discussion of these various applications, there is a brief review of how data visualization has been used in the past, why it works so well, and the importance of graphic design.

2 Origins of Data Visualization

The origins of data visualization are in the statistical and scientific disciplines. The majority of early work involved 2D analysis of multidimensional and multivariate data sets via static images and graphs. These static 2D images are useful in analysis but have more merit in the presentation of final results. Prominent statistician John Tukey [9] was a pioneer of exploratory data analysis.

More recently, dynamic graphics have been used in, for instance, spinning 3D data plots. "Dynamic" in this context also means direct manipulation by the user, where the user interacts directly with the graphics by use of the mouse. Dynamic graphics much more readily supports the process of finding and understanding patterns and anomalies in the data, as shown by Cleveland [1].

In the sciences, 3D visualization is typically used in analysis and presentation. Faced with understanding the large amounts of data generated in simulations and computational experiments, scientists often turn to visualization as the only practical way to digest the stacks of output created by overnight runs on supercomputers. Converting the stacks of output into a static 3D image is a useful way to sift through the information overload and pick out the patterns and anomalies of interest. Visualization broadened the scope of scientific exploration by expanding the horizon of what could be understood.

The National Center for Supercomputing Applications has created innovative 3D animations for data visualization [4]. One of the most well known animation studies was of the smog formation in the Los Angeles area. The techniques makes use of traditional frame-by-frame animation methods. Each frame is rendered and then transferred to video tape, where motion can be viewed at the standard video rate of 30 frames per second. While motion is achieved, it is not interactive. The viewer is limited to a pre-determined set of presentations and the communication of pre-conceived messages. These visualizations do not support data analysis because the relationships and features have already been identified, and the information has been extracted and prioritized for communication purposes.

In scientific visualization, the 3D image is always based on an underlying physical structure. For example, the smog study presents data overlaid on a 3D map of the Los Angles basin. Whether in physics, molecular, chemical or biological studies, the images use the physical structure of the elements themselves. Coherent data sets with an underlying xyz arrangement of positions provides a natural and easily understandable framework for a 3D image.

Information visualization using 3D animation is a current research area for Xerox PARC. This work by Card, Mackinlay and Robertson [3, 5] provides some of the best examples of interactive 3D information visualization. Numerous prototypes have been constructed. These examples allow users to better understand the structure of large datasets by allowing viewing from different angles, by flying through the data, and by interactively examining and re-arranging information objects. In these examples, the structure of the visual presentation is provided by the hierarchical or linear structure of the data itself. This provides a natural data-oriented framework and is a step forward in providing an application that is aligned to the decision making task.

In financial data visualization, there is no physical geography to provide an organizing structure. Dimensions corresponding to variables in mathematical functions can provide an organizing structure. One of the first examples of financial data visualization was the work done by Steven Feiner and Clifford Beshers [2] on exploring the value of a portfolio of options by interactively manipulating the option market value function of six variables in a 3D space. Higher dimensionality is achieved by embedding one 3D space into another. This provided a mathematically correct coherent framework but perceptually still proved to be not as natural and easy to understand as a geographical structure.

For abstract information visualization, we believe process and decision models provide a more natural framework. A visual layout that corresponds to the rationale underlying a decision blends human perceptual strengths with the exercise of human judgement. Information visualization expands to include decision visualization.

3 Human Visual Perceptual and Cognitive Abilities

Anne Treisman describes it well [7]. If you were to step outside in an unknown city, you would immediately recognize objects organized in a coherent meaningful framework. You would see people, cars, buildings, trees. You would not be aware of detecting colors, edges, movements and distances and of assembling them into multidimensional wholes for which you would retrieve identities and labels from memory. Meaningful wholes seem to precede parts and properties. This apparently effortless achievement is repeated continuously.

Visualization works because the visual cortex dominates perception, and because key aspects of the perception process occur rapidly without conscious thought. This human visualization power can be harnessed to allow the presentation of massive amounts of data and to highlight patterns hidden in that data. Used effectively, visualization can accelerate perception of data. By designing visualizations with human strengths and weaknesses in mind, it is possible to exploit people's natural ability to recognize structure and patterns, and circumvent human limitations in memory and attention.

The human brain excels at processing images and recognizing patterns. Contrast this with how the brain handles rows and columns of numbers and letters. In a stressful, time-critical environment, such as a trading desk, it would be easy to miss a crucial number displayed among dozens in rows and columns. It takes a good deal of precious time to digest a set of interrelated numbers. Using information animation, the size, color, shape, and motion of the data can all be used to indicate the information you want and its significance.

Scientific study of perception and cognition have established some explanations for why visualization is so powerful, but much still remains to be understood

Certain aspects of visual processing seem to be accomplished simultaneously for the entire visual field at once. Some aspects of visual processing are also automatic in that it does not require attention to be focused on any one part of the visual field. Other aspects of visual processing seem to depend on focused attention and are done serially, or one at a time, as if a mental spotlight were being moved from one location to another. Visualization tasks involve a combination of preattentive and attentive human behaviors. Psychological research, see Rogowitz, et al [6], has shown that certain visual stimuli attract attention, can be searched in parallel, and are perceived effortlessly by observers. These extremely efficient preattentive visual competencies are engaged before conscious or attentive thought is required. In fact, Zeki [10] discusses how four parallel systems within the visual cortex have been identified, each concerned with a different attribute of vision: one for motion, one for color, and two for form.

Powerful visualizations are designed to enlist both preattentive and attentive processes. A preattentively encoded attribute may be used to identify a region in the visualization which demands further attentive scrutiny.

There is virtually unlimited freedom in how we represent data. The difficult question is how best to represent it. The study of graphical perception needs to be expanded to examine the effectiveness of new representational techniques such as new forms of 3D geometry, animation, transparency, depth cues and connections. In the absence of scientifically derived rules, it is necessary to depend on the graphics design profession.

4 Graphics Design

While science can not always explain the functions and provide explicit rationales, the graphics design profession has developed highly effective guidelines and heuristics. There is a rigor and discipline in the graphics design process whose intent is to reveal and not obscure. Graphics design methods have largely evolved from dealing with 2D graphics used in the print medium. However, their spirit and mandates are directly applicable to a 4D medium.

In 4D information animation applications, the success of the graphics visual design (i.e. the shapes, layout, colors) is critical to the success of the application. Graphical elements need to be carefully selected and arranged to reveal data and relationships. Poor graphics design will obscure the data and its meanings. The visual design simply needs to be perfect. Users must see the message and not the medium.

Edward Tufte [8] articulates this discipline best. According to Tufte, excellence in graphics consists of complex ideas communicated with clarity, precision and efficiency. Graphical displays should induce the viewer to think about the substance, present many numbers in a small space, make large data sets coherent, encourage the eye to compare different pieces of data, reveal the data at several levels of detail, from a broad overview to the fine structure. Graphics reveal data, and can be more precise and revealing than conventional numerical computations and displays.

5 Information Animation Examples in the Securities Industry

Information animation applications are particularly suited to the securities industry because that is where we find huge amounts of data, the value of which declines rapidly with time, and where critical decisions are being made on this data in very short periods of time. Information animation technology is an important new tool for the securities industry, where people need to be in the decision-making loop without suffering from information overload.

As outlined earlier, 3D seems to hold some promise as a general decision support tool – but we need to determine exactly what it means to put abstract information in 3D, and what benefits it provides. These are key questions, and to help answer them, several prototypes, or "dynamic illustrations," were built to provoke business thinking regarding benefits, and to help further develop the basic technology.

This paper will discuss examples of work from 1992 created and operated on a Silicon Graphics workstation based on a MIPS R4000 CPU with a graphics hardware accelerator. The underlying software provides a 3D animation engine allowing data–driven and user–driven animation. Each 3D scene is completely open to interaction at any point in time. None of the interactions or animations are predefined or precalculated. Animation frame rates of four to six frames per second are achieved.

6 Equity Trading Analytics

Figure 1 shows a two dimensional image of the equities in the Toronto Stock Exchange index of 35. The Toronto Stock Exchange makes available each equity's order book (i.e. all the current bids and offers and their price and size). For each equity, we are showing the depth of the book. The baseline is the price of the last trade. The offers are above, and the bids are below the baseline. The height above or below is proportional to the price of the bid or offer. The length of a bid/offer's bar is proportional to the size of the bid/offer. This display immediately shows where bids and offers are unbalanced (e.g. more bids than offers) and where there is liquidity.

Figure 2 is a 3D extension of Figure 1. The area of each bid and offer is proportional to the size of the bid and offer. We can use Figures 1 and 2 to do a side-by-side comparison to see what added value a 3D layout provides. The 3D layout in Figure 2 appears to provide faster comprehension, and an accelerated perception. A 3D layout also provides more display area - more elbow room, so to speak. However, 3D is not sufficient. It is not possible to precisely compare two equities, and it is not possible to exactly see the book for an equity located towards the rear of the display. To make 3D work, it must be able to move. To be precise with comparisons, the view of the landscape and elements within the landscape need to move so that the user can see exactly what the values are. The prototypes allow a user to move the landscape and to zoom in to any area of interest.

In the next prototype, we explore how much information can be usefully displayed in a single screen. The landscape in Color Plate 1 shows the TSE 300 with the TSE 35 along the right forward edge. The landscape is arranged in an neutral fashion - by industry subgroup and alphabetic order within each subgroup. An actual user would order the landscape to correspond to particular interests and models of value. Several different forms of mouse and keyboard driven navigation are supported, including zooming to a point of interest, walking, running and moving to preset fixed points of view.

The TSE 300 landscape can be connected to a live data feed, and can display in real time the liquidity of the most significant portion of the Toronto market. With real time data, the landscape bubbles as trades occur and as the bids and asks are updated. Compared to existing quote screens which can display 20 or 30 equities at one time, this landscape provides an order of magnitude more information.

Of course, liquidity is just one attribute of an equity's performance. Others include net change on the day, volume on the day, volume at a price, trades at the bid, trades at the offer, etc. For each attribute, it is possible to develop a graphical icon or glyph which will visually and precisely communicate the value of the attribute. These graphical elements can be called "signs" because they are designed to display significance. For example, Color Plate 2 shows a trade by trade sign for each equity.

Color Plate 3 shows a bid/offer sign for an equity with numerical data displayed beside the sign. This is an important requirement for information animation applications. Visual perception can be used to quickly see anomalies and patterns. However, at some point, detailed data is needed. The user must be able to point at signs and retrieve the numerical and textual data behind the signs. This capability is called brushing (Cleveland, 1988).

7 Fixed–Income Trading Analytics

The next prototype, in Color Plate 4, shows the Canadian federal bond market. The green yield curve along the left edge shows the Federal benchmark issues as of early January 1992. The first yield curve in red, along the front edge shows the Federal curve as of early February 1992. Using the slider bar, we can play back in a sequence, the values for each day's closing yield curve from January to February. Whatever day is currently displayed is shown in the second yield curve (yellow) along the front edge. At the beginning of the sequence the yellow curve is the same as the green curve. At the end, the yellow is the same as the red. Rotating the scene so that we have a 2D view of the yellow yield curve (Color Plate 5), we can play back each day's yield curve. As we do that, the yellow curve moves and changes over time.

This period of time captures an interesting event - the U.S. Federal Reserve cut interest rates by a full percent. As we playback the data, we see the impact of this event on the Canadian Federal bond market. In the animation, you can see that the curve experiences a large drop, and then recovers to near previous levels.

In the center of the scene, spreads (i.e. differences in yield) are being displayed. The spreads are taken between the start date (green curve) and the current date (yellow curve). Positive spreads are gray, and negative spreads are purple. As we animate the scene, all the spreads move up and down with time.

Several useful conclusions can be made with this prototype. First of all, it becomes readily apparent that the Federal bond market is not an entirely orderly market. Our expectation was that the Federal bond market should be a liquid market with few discontinuities or anomalies. However, as you can see the boundary between positive and negative spreads is ragged. There are positive spreads located among the negative spreads. Further, these anomalies persist for several days at a time.

It is also interesting to note what is happening in this prototype from a human perceptual and cognitive point of view. This is a 20x20 spread matrix displayed over 20 days for a total of 8000 spreads. Compared to a trader's traditional quote screen or spreadsheet display which would show at most perhaps 80 spreads, this is a two order of magnitude improvement in displaying information. The display allows the user, in just a few seconds, to pick out the items of interest. Further, these items are presented in a context which supports informed evaluation. Related instrument spreads are shown in the same landscape neighborhood. At any time, the user can click on an anomaly and retrieve numerical and textual data describing the issues and their values.

Another conclusion is that the prototype has the entire field of "spreads" moving. One of the objectives of information animation is to be able to imbed information in motion. The user can see waves move across the surface of the spreads. Subtle differences in the waves, which indicate delays and anticipations in several spread regions, can be perceived and detected quickly.

8 Fixed–Income Risk Management

The next example is a fixed income inventory application. Color Plate 6 shows on a single screen a bond inventory with over 3,000 positions in it. Long positions are in green; short positions are in pink. The left axis shows portfolios and trading groups. The front axis shows time to maturity. Height is used to show the value of the positions. Along the front of the landscape is a total line that totals across trading groups. At the rear is a yield curve based on the bid yield of a set of benchmarks.

Color Plate 6 is displaying a profit/loss for each position for a yield curve shift scenario. Other models of asset value can also be displayed (e.g. weighted price value of a basis point or benchmark equivalent).

The user can point at one of the positions and retrieve fully detailed descriptive numerical and textual details related to that position's size, issue and issuer..

Animation is used in this landscape to help assess market risk (i.e. risk due to change in interest rates). The yield curve can be moved, in even or uneven shifts, and as it moves, the impact on the inventory's projected profit and loss can be assessed. Projected P+L values change by increasing or decreasing in size. Users can quickly see where the inventory is hedged (i.e. insensitive to changes in rates) or where it is exposed and by what degree.

Projected P+L is calculated using pre-computed fixed income analytical parameters such as the dollar value of an 01 (i.e. unit value for a change of 1/100 of a percent in interest rates) and convexity (i.e. second order approximation for sensitivity due to change in interest rates). The scenario P+L calculations are done rapidly so that the P+L value changes interactively with a change in the yield curve.

There are several ways a user may interact with this landscape. One or several bond issuers can be selected from a list of all issuers. The corresponding positions in these issues are then highlighted within the inventory so that the user can see what is held and where it is held. The total line then shows the total for the selected set of issuers. The market risk scenarios can be performed on the selected set.

Another type of query example is a filter based on size of position and implemented using a slider bar. The user can filter out all small long and short positions, so that landscape displays only the large magnitude positions.

This risk viewing landscape provides several conclusions. An on-line system could display perhaps 20 to 40 positions per screen. A 3D landscape displays 3,000 or more positions per screen. Using query and filtering, it is possible to highlight patterns that may be hidden in a numerical display. We believe a 3D visual approach provides more insight in minutes than traditional computer numerical displays could provide in hours.

9 Additional Examples

Information animation applications can provide significant value in many areas of the securities industry. The risk viewing application can be expanded to instruments and markets beyond fixed–income, including equities, derivatives, and foreign exchange. In each case, the common elements in the application are positions, models of asset value, parameterized models of risk sensitivity, and scenario projections. Risk viewing starts with being able to quickly see thousands of positions on a single screen. Effective risk visualization requires direct manipulation of such risk parameters as interest rate risk, volatility risk, currency risk, and credit risk. These visual risk models more easily allow control and guidance of risk exposure over a wide variety of scenarios and stress tests. Simple combinations of changes to risk parameters will quickly reveal exposed positions and help suggest more effective risk management strategies.

Another information animation application can be developed for trading in the OTC (over–the-counter) market. NASDAQ level 2 market–maker data provides bid and ask information for all market makers in an equity. Generally, there are 10 to 50 market makers per equity. Numerical equity trading displays now in use are limited to showing market–maker activity for just one equity at a time. Further, the user is able to see only 15- to 20 market makers at once, and must page back and forth to see other market makers. Considering that an individual trader makes a market in approximately 10 equities, the trader is left with the choice of either continuously flipping through 20 or 30 screens, or just not being able to see what the other market makers are doing. An information animation landscape can easily show on one screen all the market makers for a watch list consisting of 10 equities. Each market maker's current activity, their activity since market open, and several other analytics can all be seen simultaneously.

Similar concepts apply to trading on the Toronto and London stock exchanges. Both exchanges publish broker identifications on bids, asks and trades. An information animation landscape can show who is trading what equity and at what price levels. For 50 or more equities, it is possible to see on one screen for every broker, who is trading at the bid or offer, their volume weighted average price (VWAP), and how their trading has changed over the day. This is simply impossible to do any other way. This kind of display can provide a new level of intuitive insight and improved trading performance.

Equity trade execution is another task that could benefit from information animation. In any given asset management firm, hundreds of buy, sell, sell short orders may need to be executed in one day. These orders need to be optimally managed across different sources of liquidity, such as POSIT, DOT, and Reuters Instinet. An information animation landscape allows order aggregation from many portfolios, and then allows those orders to be routed to appropriate trading systems. The status of each order and the quality of execution can be displayed for hundreds of orders simultaneously on one screen.

In fact, information animation can be used in general to unify and simplify diverse sources of trading data. It is possible to integrate on a single screen market data, news, positions, P+L, order management, order routing, portfolio allocations, and historical time series data. Only the expressive power of 4D graphics has the display capacity to do this. Only the human visual perceptual channel has the bandwidth to assimilate this volume of data.

10 Conclusions

Rows and columns of numbers are a representation appropriate for machine processing but do not draw upon human perceptual and cognitive strengths. With 3D and 4D graphical representations, people can see more information, more quickly, with more comprehension. These 4D graphical applications are a significant technological advance and can be thought of as a new type of decision support medium. Information animation applications combine large amounts of rapidly changing data with interactive decision–making models. The most effective landscapes encapsulate and simplify complex decision making process models. Information animation technology will evolve into a powerful new decision–making medium, which will unify disparate sources of data and disconnected task processes.

At this point, we can summarize a number of key components used in any information animation application.

Signs. A sign is a graphical geometrical object that represents a set of related data elements, and is transformed as the data changes. For example, the current bid and ask of an equity can be represented by one sign. Each sign needs to be optimally designed to portray the significance of the data. "Sign" is preferred over the word "glyph" because it stresses the need for effective illustration.

Controller signs. This is a sign that maps a set of related input/output process control parameters to a geometrical object. For example, an interactive yield curve used to assess market risk on an inventory is a controller sign.

Landscapes. Each information application is based on one or more landscapes. A landscape consists of an arrangement in xyz space of signs and interactive controller signs. Effective landscapes reinforce – or make apparent – information attributes, decision models and the task process.

Navigation. Information animation applications require new user interface methods to allow users to move through the landscapes. These include zooming in and out, walking and running along an xyz vector, returning to predetermined fixed points of view, and a local heads–up capability to allow quick controlled viewing in the immediate neighborhood of a landscape.

Brushing. Users need to be able to point the cursor at a sign and retrieve the precise numerical and textual information behind it.

Queries. Landscapes need to be searchable, and to allow the display of the results of those searches. Users must be able to select any data attribute, whether it is price movement or size of position, and filter the landscape so that only those qualifying signs are displayed in the landscape. Query results can be displayed either by removing any signs that do not meet the search criteria, or graphically highlighting just the signs that do meet the criteria.

As with any new technology, there are a number of challenges in developing information animation applications. Perhaps the most significant is the choice of the geometrical representations for the signs, and the layout within an application landscape. The semantic challenge is to illustrate large, multidimensional and multivariate data sets without compromising the dimensionality or granularity of the data. Every variable for every data point must be able to be shown without invoking summary or reduction methods. The design challenge is to clearly and intuitively present the data.

Another challenge in building landscape applications is to effectively incorporate process models and decision models. Landscapes support decision making tasks, and much labour intensive knowledge engineering is required to identify and represent the underlying task domain. To bypass this development bottleneck, information animation tools will need to be developed which will allow end users to create their own landscapes.

Two other technology challenges are worth mentioning. A high level of animation performance is required. A large amount of 3D geometry in the landscape needs to be updated with new data and redrawn in subseconds to achieve animation frame rates of at least four frames per second. Considerable effort and insight into new data structures and rendering algorithms were required in the prototypes to reach the frame rate achieved. Even higher performance levels are required as larger volumes of data are input into landscapes, as 3D landscapes become larger in scope, and as signs make more use of motion as a representation medium.

Finally, ease of use and user interface design are crucial to application success. Information animation is a new way of working with information and requires innovative user interface techniques. Several new techniques have been developed in the prototypes, and more are being tested. Much more work needs to be done in this area. The expressive power of information animation provides an opportunity to dramatically simplify user interfaces.

Information animation has an important role within organizations. With significant investments made in computing infrastructure over the last decade, organizations have vast amounts of business data available to support decision making. So much data, in fact, that some current conditions might be described as information overload. Used effectively, information animation can accelerate perception, provide insight and control, and allow this flood of valuable data to be harnessed for competitive advantage in business decision making.

References

[1] Cleveland, W.S., and M.E. McGill, eds. Dynamic Graphics for Statistics, Belmont, CA, Wadsworth Inc., 1988.

[2] Feiner, S., and C. Beshers, "Worlds within Worlds - Metaphors for Exploring n-Dimensional Virtual Worlds", ACM Symposium on User Interface Software, 1990.

[3] Mackinlay, J.D., G.G. Robertson and S.K. Card, "The perspective wall: Detail and context smoothly integrated", Proceedings of the ACM SIGCHI Conference on Human Factors in Computing Systems, ACM, April, 1991.

[4] NCSA - National Center for Supercomputing Applications, Video, "Smog - Visualizing the Components", University of Illinois at Urbana-Champaign, Visualization Services and Development Group, 1990.

[5] Robertson, G.G., S.K. Card, and J.D. Mackinlay, Information visualization using 3D interactive graphics, Communications of the ACM, 36(4), 1993.

[6] Rogowitz, B.E., D.T. Ling, and W.A. Kellogg, "Task Dependence, Verdicality, and Pre-Attentive Vision: Taking Advantage of Perceptually-Rich Computer Environments", Human Vision, Visual Processing and Digital Display III, SPIE Vol. 1666, 1992.

[7] Treisman, A., "Features and Objects in Visual Processing", Scientific American, Nov., 1986.

[8] Tufte, E.R., The Visual Display of Quantitative Information, Chesire, CT, Graphics Press, 1983.

[9] Tukey, J.W., "Exploratory Data Analysis", Reading, MA, Addison-Wesley, 1977.

[10] Zeki, S., "The Visual Image in Mind and Brain", Scientific American, September, 1992.

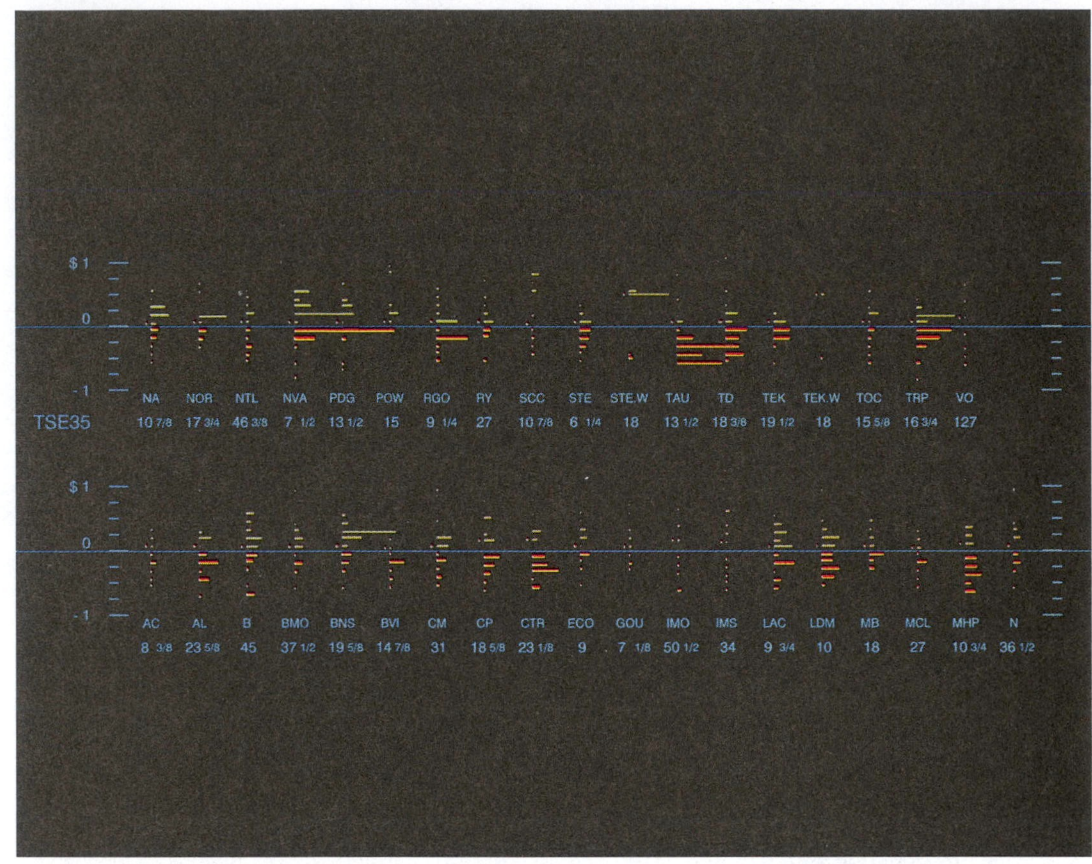

FIGURE **1**

Toronto Stock Exchange Index of 35 Equities—2-D View.

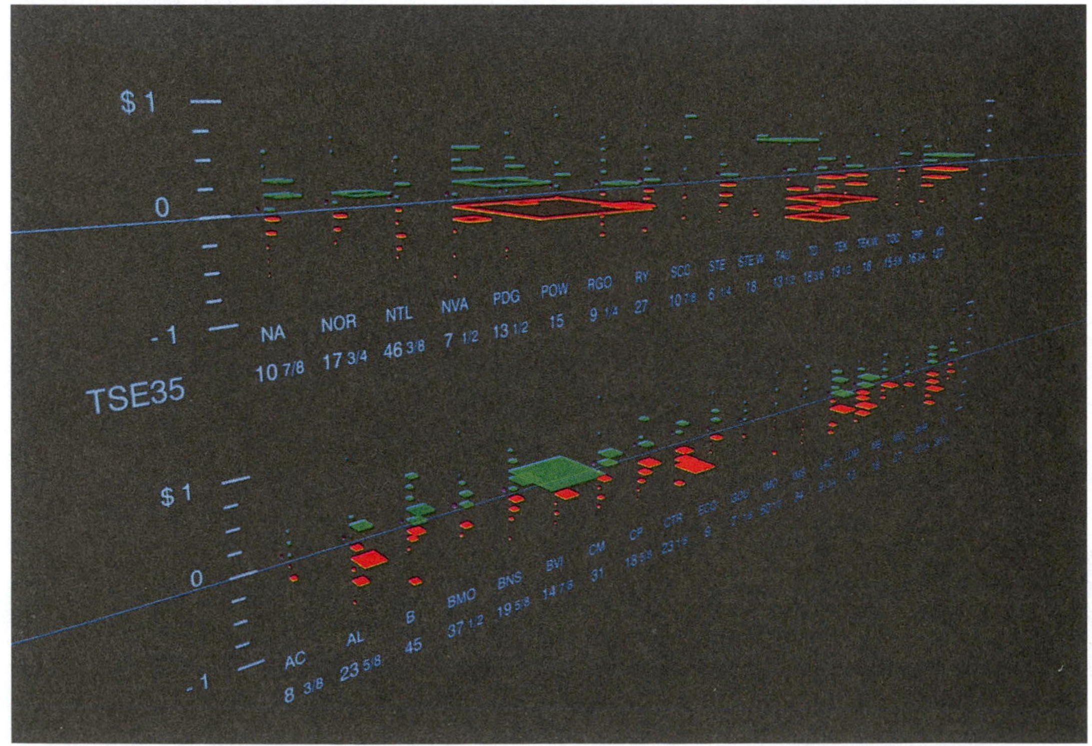

FIGURE **2**

Toronto Stock Exchange Index of 35 Equities—3-D View.

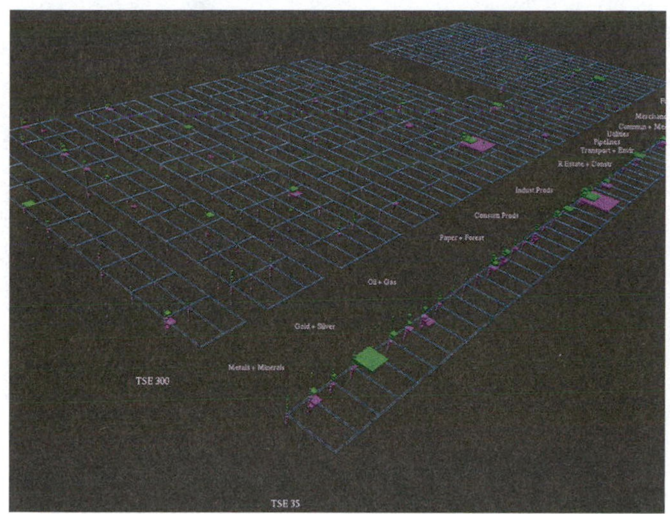

PLATE **1**

Toronto Stock Exchange Index of 300 Equities.

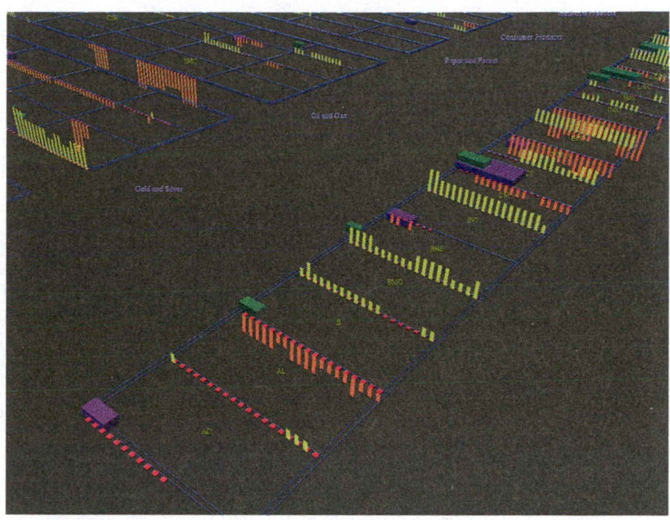

PLATE **2**

Closeup of Trade by Trade Sign.

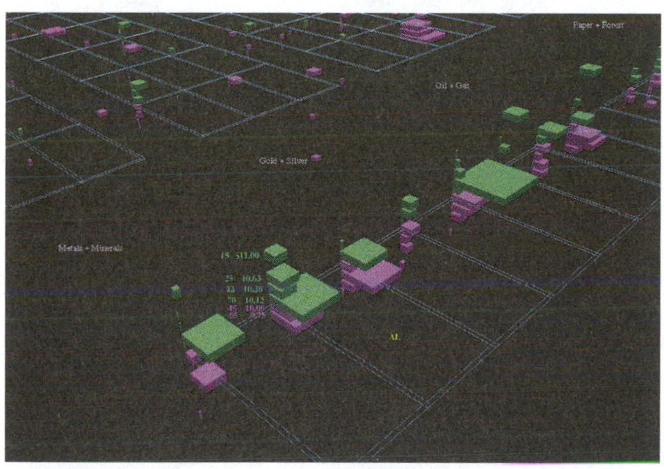

PLATE **3**

Closeup of Bid/Offer Sign.

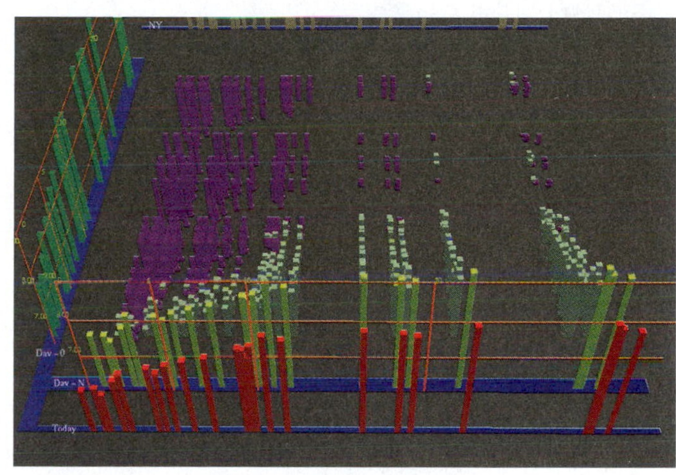

PLATE **4**

Federal Bond Market Landscape.

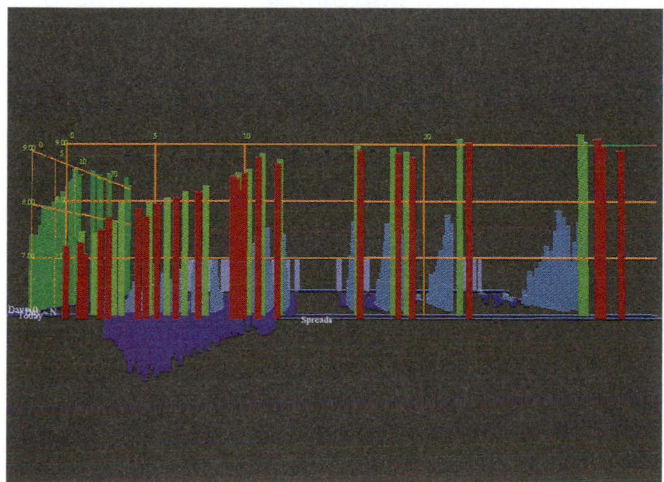

PLATE **5**

Federal Bond Market—Rotated to 2-D View.

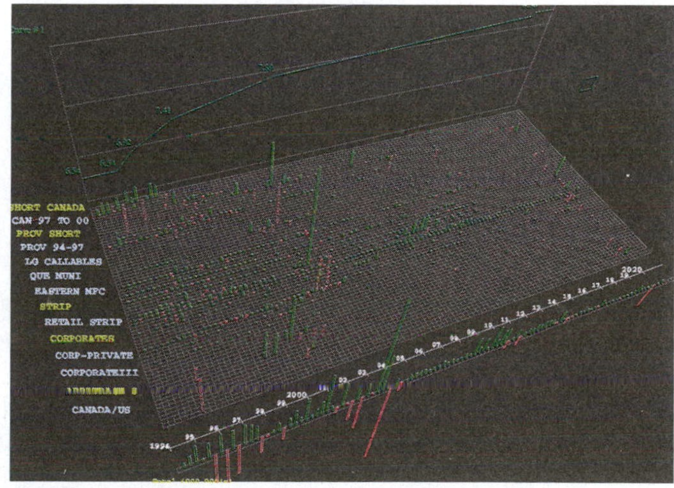

PLATE **6**

Market risk on an Inventory of 3000 Positions.

2.3

Multiple Dimensions > 3

Most visualizations start with multivariable Data Tables that have too many variables to be encoded directly in the 1D, 2D, and 3D Visual Structures of the last section. A new set of techniques is needed to encode these Data Tables. Bertin (1977/1981 ●) developed a direct technique for creating multidimensional Visual Structures from multivariate Data Tables called *permutation matrices*. The technique, developed before computers were used to support visual thinking, involves representing rows of data as bar charts and sorting them. Graphical depictions of data values were placed on cards and permuted with metal rods. When computers became available, his implementation became an early example of information visualization.

The goal of the permutations is to form patterns, typically to place the large values on the diagonal of the matrix, thereby clustering similar cases with their representative variables. For example, Table 2.1 is a hypothetical permutation matrix of people P1 through P9 on a set of variables. The black cells show values that are significant. Table 2.2 is the same data sorted with the significant values on the diagonal. In this hypothetical example, Table 2.2 ends up grouping the people (and the variables) by where they live. That is, the variables (*V8, V7, V3*) identify the city people (P5, P8, P2), and the variables (*V5, V1, V4*) identify the country people (P4, P9, P3, P7).

Permutation matrices have been the basis for some information visualizations—for example, the table lens (Rao and Card, 1984 ●)—but other researchers have tried other techniques for getting around the barrier of three dimensions.

TABLE **2.1**

Black cells represent significant values on various variables (V1) for a set of people (P1).

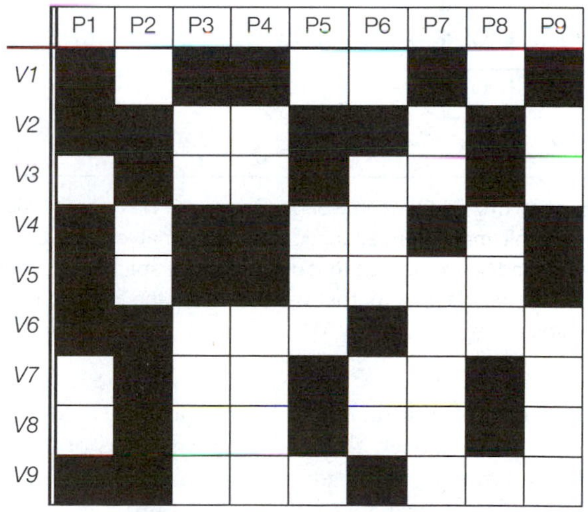

The first paper in this section describes a technique called *worlds within worlds* (Feiner and Beshers, 1990b ●), a multidimensional Visual Structure based on overloading. Input variables are mapped into a coordinate system of axes. The entire high dimensional function is visualized by placing each coordinate system inside another. As is clear from Figure 2.6, the visual axes are overloaded by reusing them. Moving the inner coordinate system with respect to the outer

TABLE **2.2**

Rows and columns of Table 2.1 are permuted to put significant values on the diagonal. This groups people and variables by where they live.

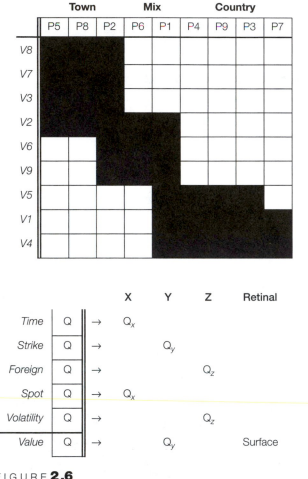

	Town			Mix		Country			
	P5	P8	P2	P6	P1	P4	P9	P3	P7
V8	■	■	■						
V7	■	■	■						
V3	■	■	■						
V2	■	■	■	■	■				
V6			■	■	■				
V9			■	■	■				
V5					■	■	■	■	
V1					■	■	■	■	■
V4					■	■	■	■	■

			X	Y	Z	Retinal
Time	Q	→	Q_x			
Strike	Q	→		Q_y		
Foreign	Q	→			Q_z	
Spot	Q	→	Q_x			
Volatility	Q	→			Q_z	
Value	Q	→		Q_y		Surface

FIGURE **2.6**

Description of worlds within worlds (Feiner and Beshers, 1990b ●). This example maps from a function with six variables about currency trading to six axes that overload a 3D spatial substrate. A surface is used for the output variable, since the function is continuous.

has the effect of shifting the surface displayed, since three of its variables have been changed. The paper has provocative examples; however, overloading can result in occlusions such as placing two coordinate systems in the same place. The paper describes how occlusions can be reduced with virtual reality techniques for manipulating the Visual Structures.

The second paper, by Inselberg (1997 ●), describes *parallel coordinates,* a technique that involves the parallel placement of axes in 2D. In drawing each axis separately, the paper is reminiscent of Bertin's permutation matrices. As shown in Figure 2.7, each case is a batch of VLSI chips that is encoded as a line. Each line connects axes that represent process parameters. Correlated cases often create recognizable patterns between adjacent axes. The challenge with parallel coordinates is to recognize these patterns. Interaction allows the user to reduce the complexity by limiting the

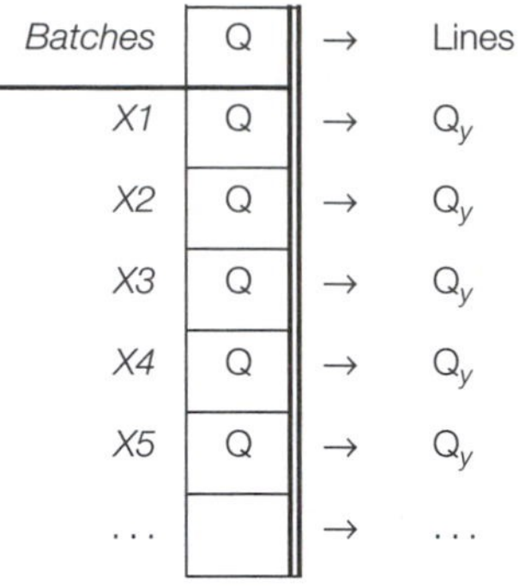

FIGURE **2.7**

Description of parallel coordinates (Inselberg, 1997 ●).

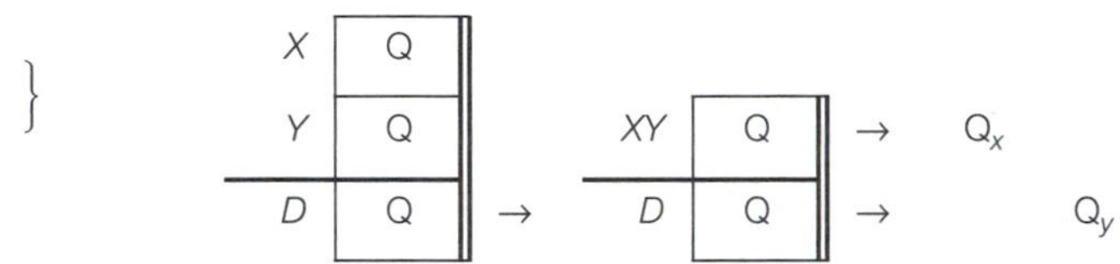

FIGURE **2.8**

Description of Mihalisin, Timlin, and Schwegler (1991 ●), which transforms multivariable data tables by sampling variables at different frequencies and mapping the results to a single axis.

range of an axis or brushing specific lines. The paper makes a convincing case that this visualization in the hands of a skilled user supports complex visual thinking.

In the third paper, by Mihalisin, Timlin, and Schwegler (1991 ●), the axes of the input variables are combined, but sampled at slow, medium, and fast frequencies to create a new variable. For example, Figure 2.8 describes his first figure where a new *XY* variable is created that has fast samples from the *X* variable and slow samples from the *Y* variable. The resulting visualization requires skillful interpretation, but the examples show that it is effective.

The fourth paper, by Keim and Kriegel (1994 ●), proposes VisDB, a more radical method of presenting the multidimensional results of database queries. The central idea of VisDB is to use each pixel of a square to represent a data item that comes from a query composed of a set of selection predicates. Figure 2.9 shows that the mapping from data items to pixels is based on a "relevance factor" that is the combination of the distances between data items and the query predicates. The layout is done on an ordinal axis that spirals from the center of the square. Items close to the query are mapped close to the center of the square. Related layouts are also discussed in the paper. The visualization consists of the square repeated for each selection predicate and the entire query. The coloring of the pixels in each square describes the distance of the data items from the corresponding selection predicate. One of the challenges of VisDB is comparing the squares for the selection predicates.

The final paper, by Spoerri (1993a ●), describes the InfoCrystal, a generalization of Venn diagrams to more than three variables. Instead of axes, the essence of Venn diagrams is enclosure. Variables are mapped to the corners of a regular polygon, and each subset of variables is assigned to a unique location inside the polygon. The size of the subset is shown with a disk at that location. Figure 2.10 shows InfoCrystal's mapping for query results from databases, which is the same application as VisDB. However, the approach is different. VisDB calculates the distance to predicates, whereas InfoCrystal only considers whether the predicate is satisfied. On the other hand, VisDB has a different Visual Structure for each predicate, whereas InfoCrystal has a single Visual Structure for the power set of the predicates. Both techniques require sophisticated reading, and it is interesting to consider whether the techniques might be combined into a single visualization.

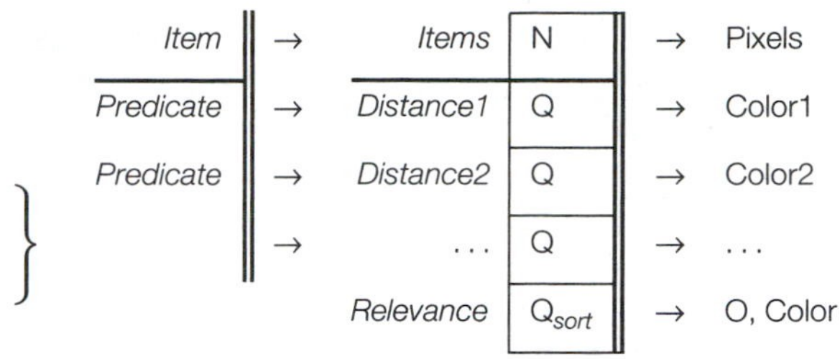

FIGURE **2.9**

Description of VisDB (Keim and Kriegel, 1994 ●). The relevance factor for items from a database query is calculated and used to sort the items onto a radial ordinal axis of pixels.

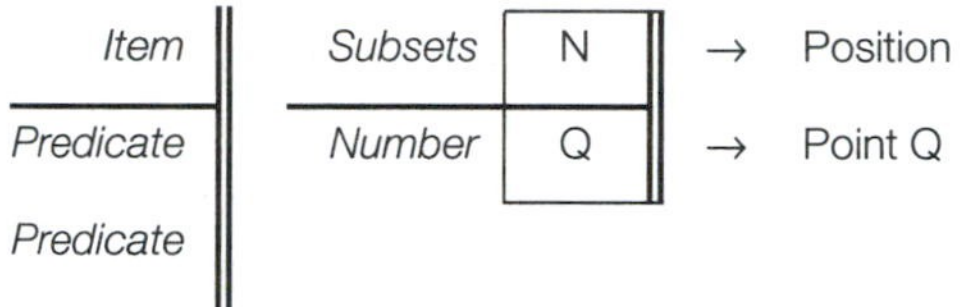

FIGURE **2.10**

InfoCrystal (Spoerri, 1993a ●) maps items into subsets that correspond to the predicates they satisfy. Each subset has a unique position in a regular polygon, and the number of items mapped to that subset is shown with a point of the correct size.

DISCUSSION

Since Tukey's seminal book (1977) on exploratory data analysis, the statistical community has been working on multidimensional visualization. This work is often referred to as data visualization, given its focus on statistical data. In addition to the overlapped and multiple axes techniques described in this section, the data visualization community has developed a variety of techniques for visualizing multivariable Data Tables. Asimov (1985) proposed an influential idea called a *grand tour,* which animated the iterative projection of variables from a multivariable Data Table to orthogonal axes in a 2D or 3D spatial substrate. Buja et al. have been developing interactive controls of these tours (Buja, Cook, and Swayne, 1996; Cook and Buja, 1997). Another important theme of the data visualization community is the arrangement of multiple views that are linked (Buja, Cook, and Swayne, 1996; Cleveland and McGill, 1988). The technique for accessing the links is commonly called *brushing* (Becker and Cleveland, 1987).

Worlds within Worlds
Metaphors for Exploring *n*-Dimensional Virtual Worlds

Steven Feiner
Clifford Beshers

Department of Computer Science
Columbia University
New York, New York 10027

feiner@cs.columbia.edu
beshers@cs.columbia.edu

Abstract

n-Vision is a testbed for exploring *n*-dimensional worlds containing functions of an arbitrary number of variables. Although our interaction devices and display hardware are inherently 3D, we demonstrate how they can be used to support interaction with these higher-dimensional objects. We introduce a new interaction metaphor developed for the system, which we call ''worlds within worlds'': nested heterogeneous coordinate systems that allow the user to view and manipulate functions. Objects in our world may be explored with a set of tools. We describe an example *n*-Vision application in ''financial visualization,'' where the functions are models of financial instruments.

n-Vision's software architecture supports a hierarchy of arbitrarily transformed, nested boxes that defines an interactive space within which information is displayed and input obtained. Our design, modeled in part after the hierarchical 2D windows of the X Window System, is intended to provide an environment that is well suited to the use of true 3D input and stereo display devices. Boxes are associated with event handlers that support 3D motion, enter, and leave events, and provide recognition of finger gestures.

CR Categories and Subject Descriptors: D.2.2 [**Software Engineering**]: Tools and Techniques—*User interfaces*; I.3.5 [**Computer Graphics**]: Computational Geometry and Object Modeling—*Hierarchy and geometric transformations*; I.3.6 [**Computer Graphics**]: Methodology and Techniques—*Interaction techniques*

General Terms: Design, Human Factors

Additional Keywords and Phrases: virtual worlds, financial visualization

1 Introduction

One common problem in graphical user interface design has been the need to manipulate and view 3D environments using inherently 2D interaction devices and displays. Although graphics researchers have long been developing true 3D interaction and display devices [SUTH65; VICK70; KILP76], it is only over the past decade that high-performance 3D graphics workstations have been coupled with commercially available 3D devices such as polarized liquid crystal shutters for stereo viewing [TEKT87; STER89], head-mounted displays [VPL89], and the DataGlove [ZIMM87]. While the use of 3D devices for 3D data seems a natural match, there are many applications in science, mathematics, statistics, and business, in which it is important to explore and manipulate higher-dimensional data. In these applications, data can be defined by points in Euclidean *n*-space. A point's position is then specified with *n* coordinates, each of which determines its position relative to one of *n* mutually perpendicular axes. One goal of our research has been the development of interaction techniques and metaphors for the 4D and higher-dimensional worlds that this data represents.

2 The *n*-Vision Testbed

n-Vision is a testbed that we are developing for exploring *n*-dimensional virtual worlds. Input is provided largely through the use of an inherently 3D interaction device, the VPL DataGlove [ZIMM87]. The DataGlove uses a magnetic sensor to sense the 3D position and orientation of the user's hand. Fiber optic cables running along each finger monitor an additional ten degrees of freedom, determined by the positions of two joints on each of the five fingers. Output is displayed on a monitor viewed with liquid crystal stereo glasses [STER89] that make it possible for the user to have a strong sense of the three-dimensionality of the virtual space in which they interact. Interaction in *n*-Vision may also be controlled through mouse-operated control panels, and dial and button boxes. *n*-Vision is implemented using a hierarchy of nested boxes whose architecture is discussed in more detail in Section 4.

We have developed a set of interaction and display metaphors in the course of using *n*-Vision to investigate an example of what we call ''financial visualization,'' in analogy to scientific visualization. Our users are interested in exploring the value of a portfolio of *options* to buy or sell foreign currency on a specified

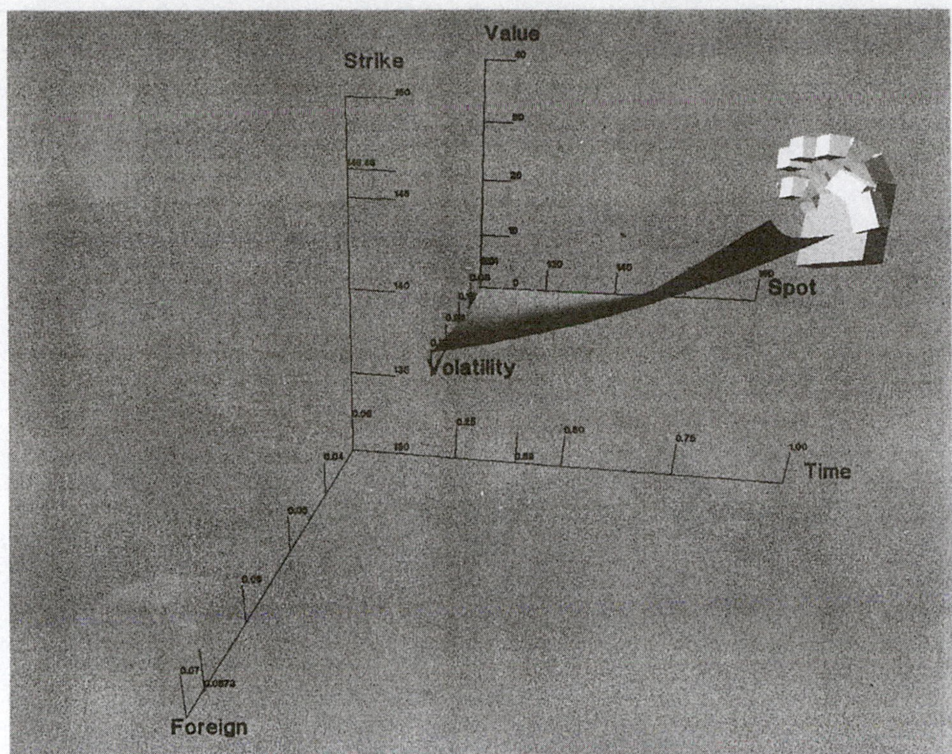

Figure 1 Value of a single call option.

date at a specified price. An option to buy is referred to as a *call*, while an option to sell is known as a *put*. Options that may only be exercised at a specified date are called *European options*. Each European option has a value that may be modeled as a function of six variables: the price at which the currency can be bought or sold at maturity (''strike price''), the price at which the currency is selling now (''spot price''), the time remaining to the date at which the option may be exercised, the interest rates for the domestic and foreign currencies, and the volatility of the market [HULL89]. These functions of six variables define surfaces in 7-space. Investors typically buy and sell combinations of different options that have been selected as part of an investment strategy that trades off risk against profit.

3 n-Dimensional Interaction Metaphors

Perhaps the simplest way to control the n values that define a point in n-space is to assign each value to its own valuator device. For example, a knob box may control as many independent variables as it has knobs. Similarly, the values of each of these n variables may be displayed by assigning each to its own numeric string or one-dimensional variable-length bar. In 2D and 3D applications, we commonly take advantage of our experience manipulating and viewing real objects, and instead use interaction and display devices that treat these objects as if they were part of a virtual 3D world. Our spatial positioning experience, however, is inherently limited to 3D. Therefore, from the standpoint of the user interface, the straightforward generalization of specifying a point in 2D by pointing in a plane, to specifying a point in 3D by pointing in space, does not extend to higher dimensions. What can we do instead?

In some cases, the multivariate data being presented has a familiar interpretation in our 3D world. For example, Ouh-young, Beard, and Brooks [OUHY89] allow users to explore a 6D space to find the energy minimum of positioning and orienting a rigid object in 3-space operated on by forces and torques. This task can be performed using visual and/or force-feedback presentations of the user's position in 6-space (3 dimensions each of position and orientation). The user sees a representation of the forces and torques as vectors of varying length or actually feels them by using force-feedback manipulators. Another approach is presented by Bly [BLY82], who demonstrated the ability of users to distinguish between multivariate data presented sonically by varying seven characteristics of a note: pitch, volume, duration, attack envelope, waveshape, and the addition of fifth and ninth harmonics. When presenting abstract multivariate data graphically, however, we must resort to visual displays that map abstract, nonvisual properties to visual properties, such as position, color, and texture, that can be represented in the display. Thus, real-world metaphors are still relevant, allowing us to map an abstract world into a concrete one. One possibility is to generalize 3D modeling transformations and viewing projections to higher dimensions [NOLL67]. Although systems based on these concepts are useful research tools [BANC78; FEIN82; BESH88], an intuitive understanding of these projections is often hard to acquire.

3.1 Worlds within Worlds

One common approach to reducing the complexity of a multivariate function is to hold one or more of its independent variables constant. Each constant corresponds to taking an infinitely thin slice of the world perpendicular to the constant variable's axis, reducing the world's dimension. For example, if we reduce the dimension to 3D, the resulting slice is a 3D height field. It represents a function of two variables that can be manipulated and displayed using conventional 3D graphics

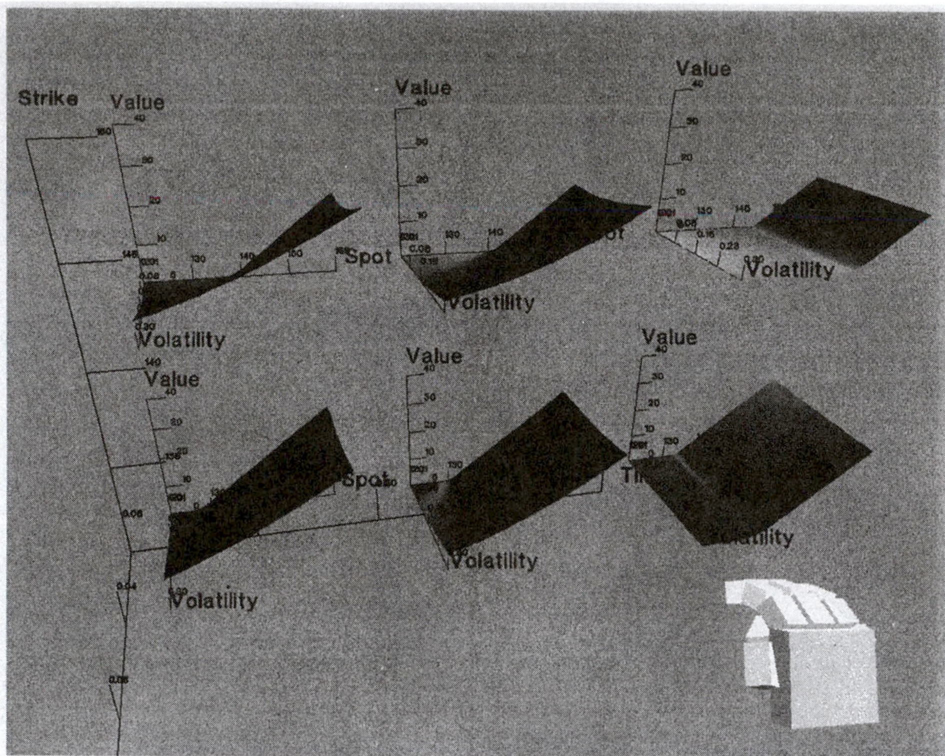

Figure 2 An array of call options.

hardware.

Although this simple approach effectively slices away the higher dimensions, it is possible to add them back in a controlled fashion. For example, if we *embed* a 3D world in another 3D world, we can represent three additional higher dimensions. The position of the embedded world's origin relative to the containing world's coordinate system specifies the values of three of the inner world's variables that were held constant in the process of slicing the world down to size. This process can then be repeated by further recursive nesting of heterogeneous worlds to represent the remaining dimensions.

Figure 1 is an example of a call option whose value is represented as a height field in a 3D inner world, plotted as a function of spot price and volatility. The outer world has axes of time to maturity, strike price, and foreign interest rate. The domestic interest rate has been held constant and is not assigned to an axis. Thus, the position of the inner world determines the time to maturity, strike price, and foreign interest rate used in evaluating the function.

In n-Vision, each world is contained within a rectangular box oriented with and containing its coordinate system. The lowest-level world in the hierarchy that contains the user's gloved hand is selected for manipulation, and its axes highlighted. Highlighted axes are drawn in black in the accompanying figures. (We also make it possible for a world to be selected and deselected for manipulation even when the hand is not inside it.) The action performed on a selected world depends on the "posture" that the user's hand assumes. One posture allows the user to translate the world. Translating a world that is embedded in an outer 3D world will change up to three otherwise constant variables, causing the object(s) within the world to change accordingly. Additional postures allow the user to rotate or scale a selected world about its origin, which makes it possible for the world to be viewed from another angle or at another size, without modifying its variables.

The kinesthetic feedback provided by an interactive system provides users with a feel for the functions being explored that they would not get from static displays.

The position of the origin of the selected world's coordinate system is shown with selectable tick marks on the axes of its containing world's coordinate system. A user can constrain the motion of an inner world along a single outer-world axis by selecting and translating the appropriate tick mark.

We can deposit multiple copies of the same world or copies of different worlds within a containing world, to allow the copies to be compared visually. Each copy, based on its position, has a different constant set of values of the containing world's variables. For example, Figure 2 shows an array of six inner worlds, each of which represents a call. A comparison of the calls, which vary only in strike price and time to maturity, indicates how market volatility has successively less effect as the time to maturity decreases, and how an increase in the price at which the currency can be bought ("strike price") makes for a lower profit, all things being equal.

Figure 3 is a stereo pair (with the left eye's image at the left) that shows a collection of worlds within a common containing world. The worlds include a put (in the foreground), two calls, and a "butterfly spread" (the surface at the left). The butterfly spread is a trading strategy in which call options for the same currency and maturity date are bought and sold. Two call options are sold with a strike price that lies within a range of strike prices established by buying one call with a lower strike price and one with a higher strike price. The strike price axis here controls only

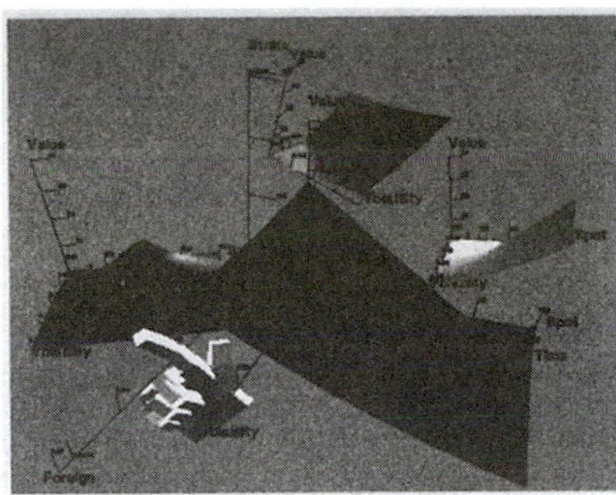
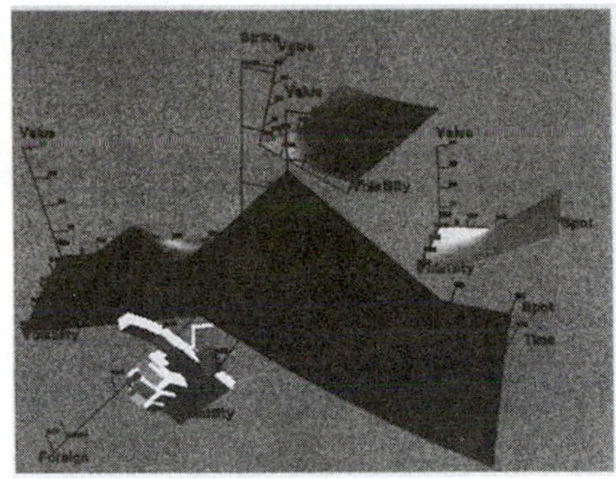

Figure 3 Stereo pair of multiple worlds. (Left eye's image is at left.)

the price of the call options being sold. This strategy effectively limits the amount of money that can be lost (while also limiting the amount of money that can be made).

Note that the order in which variables are assigned to the nested coordinate system axes has a profound effect on the surface displayed. The two variables assigned to an innermost 3D world's axes determine the shapes produced, whereas the order in which variables are assigned to the ancestor worlds' axes determines the ease with which variables may be manipulated. For example, if multiple worlds are nested directly inside another world, then translating the common containing world modifies all of the nested worlds in the same way. Thus, the easiest way to restrict a set of worlds to share the same variables is to nest them inside a world whose ancestry defines the desired variables. In order to avoid the effects of translating one or more worlds, they can be nested directly inside of a world whose coordinate system has no variables assigned to its axes. These first-level inner worlds can then be positioned without changing their contents, for example to place them next to other worlds for comparison. Rather than being limited to 3D worlds, *n*-Vision provides support for worlds of from one to four dimensions, relying, in part, on techniques we have developed for transforming and displaying 4D objects in real-time using 3D graphics hardware [BESH88].

We have found that the combination of the DataGlove and stereo display is particularly powerful for picking and manipulating one of a number of worlds. The DataGlove's direct positional control allows the user to reach out and "grab" a world, rather than "steer" toward it. The stereo display provides visual feedback that makes 3D positioning significantly easier, while also resolving ambiguities in the projections of individual surfaces. For example, the inner world in Figure 1 is quite close to the nearest face of its containing world's box, as indicated by its tick marks. Disregarding the tick marks or any knowledge of the function's expected appearance, a user may be easily convinced that the Spot–Value plane is coplanar with the Time–Strike plane, based on the single projection shown here. When viewed in stereo, however, the discrepancy in their distances becomes obvious.

3.2 Tools

Users may explore worlds by using *tools* that are implemented by a kind of box called a *toolbox*. A toolbox is usually associated with a set of glove postures that specify when the user starts and stops using its tool. Each toolbox has access to all of the interaction device settings. We currently support a small collection of tools that include a *dipstick*, *waterline*, and *magnifying box.*

The *dipstick* is a small probe that the user may pick up and move within a surface. The 3D dipstick is sensitive to motion parallel to the plane above which the function is displayed, and displays the value of the function at the point it intersects. Figure 4 shows a dipstick being used to sample the value of a butterfly spread.

The *waterline* is a plane that is perpendicular to one of the axes in a world. It may be raised or lowered to slice a surface. Since it is processed by the same visible-surface algorithm as is the rest of the world, it can be used to locate local minima and maxima visually. Figure 5 shows a waterline being used to explore the value of a put option.

The *magnifying box* is a 3D version of the familiar 2D "detail" window that provides a higher-resolution display of part of another window [DONE78]. When a magnifying box is associated with another box, the actions performed in any one of the boxes are reflected in the other.

3.3 Metamorphosis

Using a stylized hand as a cursor provides a familiar mechanism for displaying the sixteen degrees of freedom that the DataGlove supports. Although graphics researchers using the DataGlove seem to be uniform in interpreting the glove data quite literally as a hand [STUR89; WEIM89], a graphical hand is not always the best way to interact with data. For example, feedback on all sixteen degrees of freedom is usually unnecessary; When the user has selected an object to rotate or translate it, the precise position of the fingers is of little consequence. Furthermore, there are some situations in which control of multiple degrees of freedom could be exploited better than by positioning and orienting a virtual hand and its wiggling fingers. In contrast, consider the commonplace use of multiple cursor definitions in 2D mouse-driven systems. The potential is even greater when a more powerful control mechanism with a larger number of degrees of freedom can be harnessed.

We exploit this capability in a limited way in *n*-Vision by allowing *metamorphosis*, turning the hand into one or more tools, instead of just attaching the tools to the hand. For example, turning the hand directly into a dipstick eliminates the visual interference of having the full hand rendered on the display, possibly obscuring part of a surface, when we need only to probe the surface at a specific point. Mapping the hand to other more exotic tools could eventually allow hand and finger motion to control nonanthropomorphic tool parts that move (or otherwise

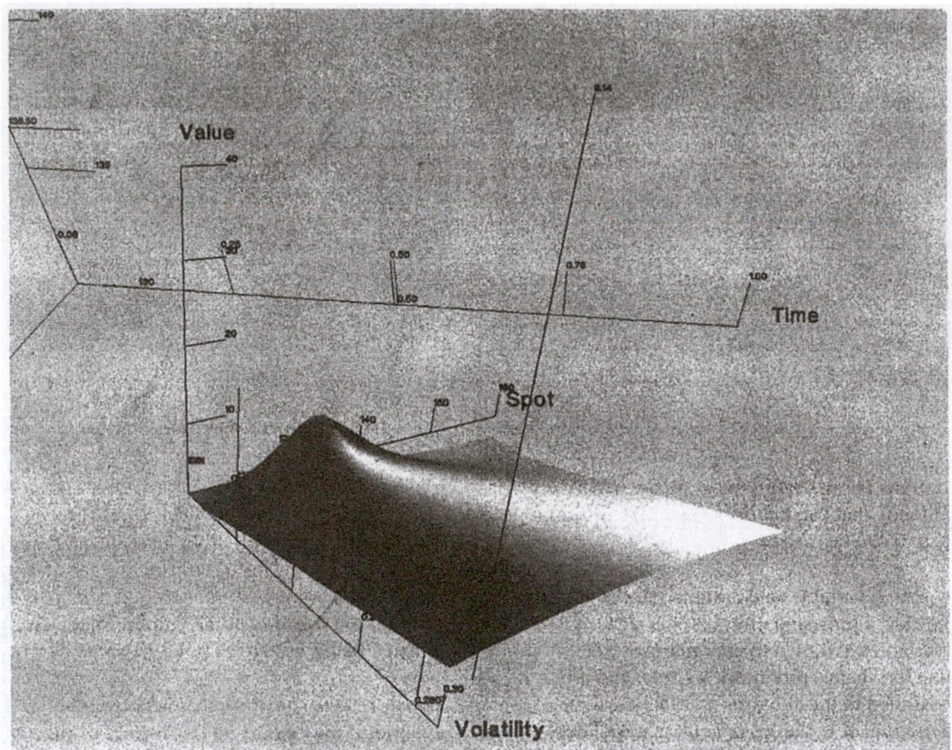

Figure 4 Sampling a butterfly spread with a dipstick.

change) differently than the user's hand and fingers.

4 Implementation and Architecture

n-Vision is implemented in C++ and runs under HPUX on an Hewlett-Packard 9000 375 TurboSRX workstation. which has hardware support for scan-conversion, shading, and *z*-buffer visible-surface determination.

The underlying structure that we have chosen for *n*-Vision is similar in spirit to that used in the X Window System [SCHL88]. Our world is a 3D hierarchy of nested boxes, each of which may be arbitrarily translated, scaled, and (unlike X) rotated relative to its parent. The hierarchy is an oriented tree: siblings are assigned relative priorities that determine the order in which they are rendered and picked in case of overlap. Rubin and Whitted [RUBI80] used a similar hierarchical structure to make possible fast 3D rendering. We have adopted this approach in an attempt to provide an understandable way to partition the space in which our users interact.

4.1 The Box Hierarchy

Boxes serve as containers for presenting graphical output and capturing graphical input. A box's coordinate system represents a transformation relative to that of its parent. Each box is an instance of a class that may be associated with event handlers that allow it to register for and react to a variety of different events. A box can map and unmap itself from the display. Mapped boxes are displayed and receive events for which they have registered; unmapped boxes are not displayed and do not receive events. By providing mapping and unmapping, we allow the creation of a controller box that owns a child box, and maps and unmaps it as it sees fit. This makes it possible to implement a low-resolution or schematic stand-in for a more complex object. For example, a box that is being moved may unmap its children during the motion and remap them only after the motion has ceased.

Each box has a list of associated event handlers, which are objects that request specific event types and are notified whenever a requested event occurs and is routed to that box. Event types are carefully designed to allow the application to track changes in the state of the system, including input arriving from a device, modifications to the box configuration, cursor movement across boxes, and box exposure. We use event handlers to implement data dependencies among boxes and to support graphics that are rendered within the box.

The body of the system's main loop performs the following series of tasks:

Sample the 3D pointer
Update the cursor
Find the regular box containing the cursor
Sample all other input devices
Dispatch all events
Redraw display

n-Vision has a 3D pointer that may be connected to any interaction devices, typically the DataGlove's position sensors. Whenever the 3D pointer moves, a special box, called the *cursor box*, is notified of the change. The cursor box differs from the other boxes in that it has a distinguished "hot point" that determines where input events are routed, and a function that sets the cursor box geometry according to the state of the pointer. The cursor box can also be set directly by the application.

Events are routed to the deepest box in the hierarchy on the

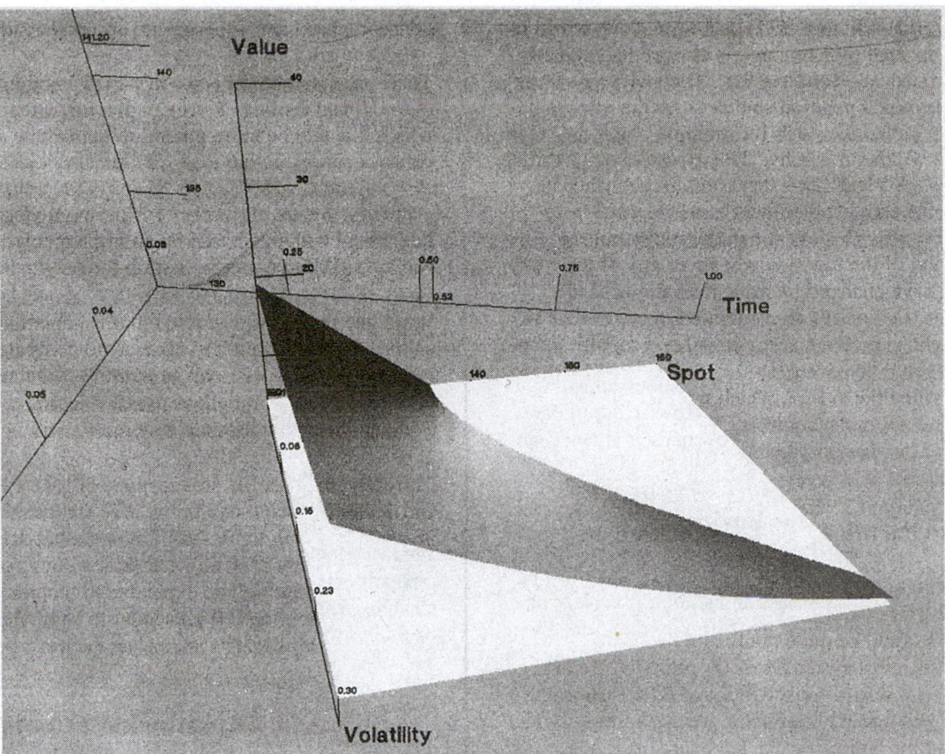

Figure 5 Examining a put option with a waterline.

highest priority branch that contains the cursor's hot point, excluding unmapped boxes and the cursor box. This is the *current box*. The box system begins at the current box and searches upward in the hierarchy until it finds a box with at least one event handler for the desired event type. It then dispatches the event to all interested event handlers attached to this box (except in the case of "grabs," which are described below.)

We also support X Toolkit events to make available standard input devices and techniques. These events are routed in the same way as other events, but only if no toolkit widget is interested in them. This gives priority to the toolkit for devices supported by X, and ensures that the box system does not interfere with the toolkit.

Events are generated by the server when a box changes state. *Mapping* events are generated whenever a box is mapped or unmapped, whereas *geometry* events are generated whenever a box is scaled, translated, or rotated.

The application can also track the path from the hierarchy's root to the current box by enabling *enter* and *leave* events. These are similar to the enter and leave window events of X, and are useful for providing graphical feedback. An event is generated for each box whose boundary is crossed by the pointer. The events indicate whether the pointer entered or left the box, and whether or not the box is or was the current box or one of its ancestors. All boxes between the old and new current box are notified of the change in status. An enter or leave event is routed first to the box for which it was generated, and then up the hierarchy to the lowest ancestor that has an event handler for the event.

The DataGlove can generate *posture* events that are triggered as it moves in and out of a set of user-definable postures that are maintained in a posture table. Each posture consists of a set of ranges for the finger bend sensors [STUR89]. One can enter or leave a posture, much like pressing or releasing a button. Unlike conventional button events, however, we do not currently support the ability to be in more than one posture at a time. Entry into or out of a posture event is used by box event handlers to allow interaction device settings (such as the DataGlove's position and orientation) to control the transformation of one or more boxes.

An event handler may "grab" a particular event type, such as pointer motion events. All grabbed events are routed exclusively to that event handler, rather than through the normal chain of event routing. This makes possible operations that control input events as long as they are active. We usually write posture-event handlers so that the box to which the posture event is routed grabs the DataGlove motion events until the posture is exited. This allows the user to assume rotation and translation postures that retain control of the box, even though the cursor may exit the box. This can occur if the box's movement is constrained (e.g., to rotate only about its origin and to maintain its origin within its parent).

The final step of the main loop is to redraw the display. This is accomplished with a depth-first traversal of the box hierarchy. *Expose* events get propagated down the box hierarchy for each new frame, with parents rendered before their children, and siblings rendered in order of increasing (higher) priority. Even though we rely on a hardware-supported z-buffer visible-surface algorithm, we must be able to specify the order in which objects will be rendered, because two objects whose projections overlap on the display may have identical z values at some shared pixel. Therefore, enforcing priority when rendering allows conflicts to be resolved consistently.

To implement the worlds-within-worlds paradigm, each world in the hierarchy is represented by a box that is assigned a geometry-event handler and an expose-event handler. The geometry-event handler constrains the box's position so that its origin always lies within the parent's box, and forwards information about the geometry changes down the hierarchy. The expose-event handler draws the box's axes. A "leaf" box that contains a surface is assigned an additional event handler that draws the surface in response to expose events. This event handler recomputes a sampled representation of the function whenever any of the function's variables have changed by more than a specified amount. The dynamic tick marks are contained in boxes that are siblings of the box whose position they control and report. Each tick-mark box has a geometry-event handler that supports constrained motion along the axis on which it is located and that propagates an event to the box it controls. Likewise, a regular box's geometry-event handler propagates events to the tick marks that represent its position.

4.2 Using Boxes to Partition the Environment

Although arbitrarily complex nested hierarchies of boxes can be constructed, each with its own interaction handler, it is clear that a complex environment could be quite confusing to the user. Even in 2D window systems, most system builders provide similar support for interaction inside of most windows. There are some places, however, in which providing spatial modes is important. For example, in using the buttons, dials, keyboard, or mouse while wearing the DataGlove the user may inadvertently enter or exit a posture. We could (and typically do) include in the posture table postures that turn posture recognition on and off. Rather than relying on the user remembering to issue these commands, we instead arrange a set of boxes that surround each of the real interaction devices, including the space needed for the hand using them. Each of these boxes has a handler for enter and leave events that turns posture recognition off and on, respectively.

While the stereo display system can provide a compelling sense of three-dimensionality, the effect is spoiled if the user reaches their hand out toward to the screen to interact with the environment. Unlike the rendered objects being displayed, the user's hand doesn't participate in the visible-surface determination algorithm; consequently, it can visually obscure parts of objects that are intended to be closer than it—an extremely disconcerting effect. Therefore, we box the view volume in front of the display, disabling both posture recognition and tracking to discourage the user from entering the volume. Unlike conventional interaction devices, the DataGlove continuously monitors a part of our bodies that we routinely use in communication with other people. This can result in the distracting effect of the user's glove cursor bouncing around on the display, while the user converses with others. Thus, disabling the glove in the view volume also ensures that gestures made when pointing at the screen are seen and interpreted only by other users, not by the system.

5 Conclusions and Future Work

We have described a new approach to visualizing and manipulating abstract n-dimensional worlds, and have discussed the software architecture underlying its implementation. The result is an environment, designed for true 3D input and output devices, that we feel provides familiar behavior when exploring quantitatively and qualitatively what are often unfamiliar objects. In contrast to generalized n-dimensional transformations and projections, the worlds-within-worlds metaphor encourages the user to think in terms of nested worlds, each of which is conceptualized and experienced as a physically realizable space.

There are a number of ways in which we would like to improve our n-Vision testbed. For example, there are many situations in which it would be more natural to demarcate arbitrary, possibly concave spaces, rather than rectilinear ones. Much as window systems such as NeWS and X11 provide arbitrary 2D window geometry, we are currently considering replacing our rectilinear box model with one based on an implementation of Thibault and Naylor's BSP tree representation for polyhedra [THIB87].

While the functions discussed in this paper have closed-form expressions that are relatively easy to compute, we are interested in exploring more complex equations. Since interactive performance is essential, we are developing a server that will evaluate the equations on a faster processor.

Currently, the user has sole responsibility for designing the world and deciding how to explore it. We are interfacing n-Vision to Scope [BESH89], a rule-based system that designs user interface control panels by choosing and laying out appropriate widgets. Scope's rule base will be expanded to include rules that we are developing for choosing presentation techniques, assigning variables to coordinate systems, and selecting tools.

Acknowledgments

This work is supported in part by a gift from Citicorp, by the Hewlett-Packard Company under its AI University Grants Program, and by the New York State Center for Advanced Technology under Contract NYSSTF-CAT(89)-5. We wish to thank Dan Schutzer for sharing his financial expertise with us, David Sturman for providing us with drivers for the VPL DataGlove, and Scott Novack for assistance with the implementation.

References

[BANC78] Banchoff, T. "Computer Animation and the Geometry of Surfaces in 3- and 4-Space." *Proc. Int. Cong. of Math*, 1978, 1005–1013.

[BESH88] Beshers, C. and S. Feiner. "Real-Time 4D Animation on a 3d Graphics Workstation." *Proc. Graphics Interface '88*, Edmonton, June 6–10, 1988, 1–7.

[BESH89] Beshers, C., and S. Feiner. "Scope: Automated Generation of Graphical Interfaces." *Proc. ACM SIGGRAPH Symposium on User Interface Software and Technology*, Williamsburg, VA, November 13–15, 1989, 76–85.

[BLY82] Bly, S. "Presenting Information in Sound." *Proc. CHI '82*, 1982, 371–375.

[BROO88] Brooks, F., Jr. "Grasping Reality through Illusion—Interactive Graphics Serving Science." *Proc. CHI '88*, Washington, DC, May 15–19, 1988, 1–12.

[DONE78] Donelson. W. "Spatial Management of Information," (Proc. ACM SIGGRAPH 78) ,*Computer Graphics*, 12(3), August 1978, 203–209.

[FEIN82] Feiner, S., D. Salesin, and T. Banchoff. "DIAL: A diagrammatic animation language." *IEEE Computer Graphics and Applications*, 2:7, September 1982, 43–54.

[HULL89] Hull, J. *Options, Futures, and Other Derivative Securities*, Prentice-Hall, NJ, 1989.

[KILP76] Kilpatrick, P.J. *The Use of a Kinesthetic Supplement in an Interactive Graphics System*, Ph.D. Thesis, Univ. of North Carolina, Chapel Hill, 1976.

[NOLL67] Noll, M. "A Computer Technique for Displaying *n*-Dimensional Hyperobjects." *CACM*, 10:8, August 1967, 469–473.

[OUHY89] Ouh-young, M., D. Beard and F. Brooks, Jr. "Force Display Performs Better than Visual Display in a Simple 6-D Docking Task." *Proc. IEEE Robotics and Automation Conf.*, May 1989, 1462–6.

[RUBI80] Rubin, S.M. and T. Whitted. "A 3-Dimensional Representation for Fast Rendering of Complex Scenes," *Proc. SIGGRAPH 80, Computer Graphics*, 14(3), July 1980, 110–116.

[SCHL88] Scheifler, R.W., J. Gettys, and R. Newman. *X Window System C Library and Protocol Reference*, Digital Press, Bedford, MA, 1988.

[STER89] StereoGraphics, CrystalEyes product literature, StereoGraphics Corp., San Rafael, CA, 1989.

[STUR89] Sturman, D., D. Zeltzer, and S. Pieper. "Hands-on Interaction with Virtual Environments," *Proc. ACM SIGGRAPH Symp. on User Interface Software and Technology*, Williamsburg, VA, November 13–15, 1989, 19–24.

[SUTH65] Sutherland, I. "The Ultimate Display." *Proc. IFIP 65*, 1965, 506–508

[TEKT87] Tektronix. "3D Stereoscopic Color Graphics Workstation (TEK 4126 product literature)." Beaverton, OR, 1987.

[THIB87] Thibault, W.C. and B.F. Naylor, "Set Operations on Polyhedra Using Binary Space Partitioning Trees," *Proc. SIGGRAPH 87, Computer Graphics*, 21(5), 153–162.

[VICK70] Vickers, D.L., "Head-Mounted Display Terminal." *Proc. 1970 IEEE International Computer Group Conference*, 1970. Reprinted in J.C. Beatty and K.S. Booth, *Tutorial: Computer Graphics, 2nd Ed.*, IEEE Computer Society Press, Silver Spring, MD, 1982.

[VPL89] VPL Research Inc. "EyePhone System Preliminary Specification v.4." Redwood City, CA, July 1989.

[WEIM89] Weimer, D., and S. Ganapathy. "A Synthetic Visual Environment with Hand Gesturing and Voice Input." *Proc. CHI '89*, Austin, TX, April 30–May 4, 1989, 235–240.

[ZIMM87] Zimmerman, T., J. Lanier, C. Blanchard, S. Bryson, and Y. Harvill. "A Hand Gesture Interface Device." *Proc. CHI + GI 1987*, Toronto, Ontario, April 5–7, 1987, 189–192.

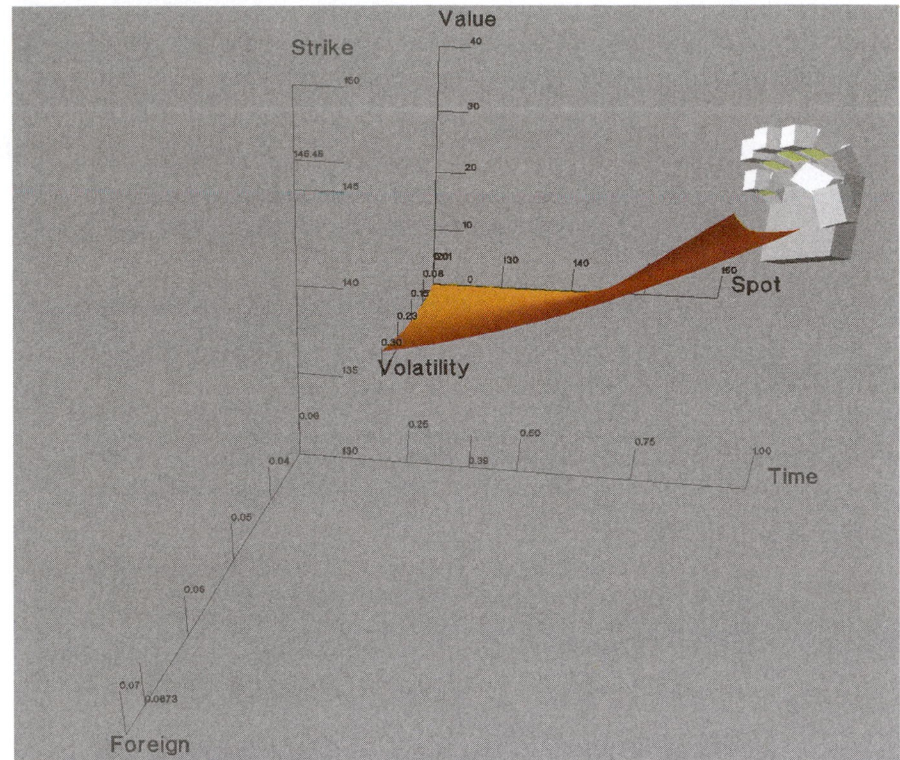

FIGURE **1**

Value of a single call option.

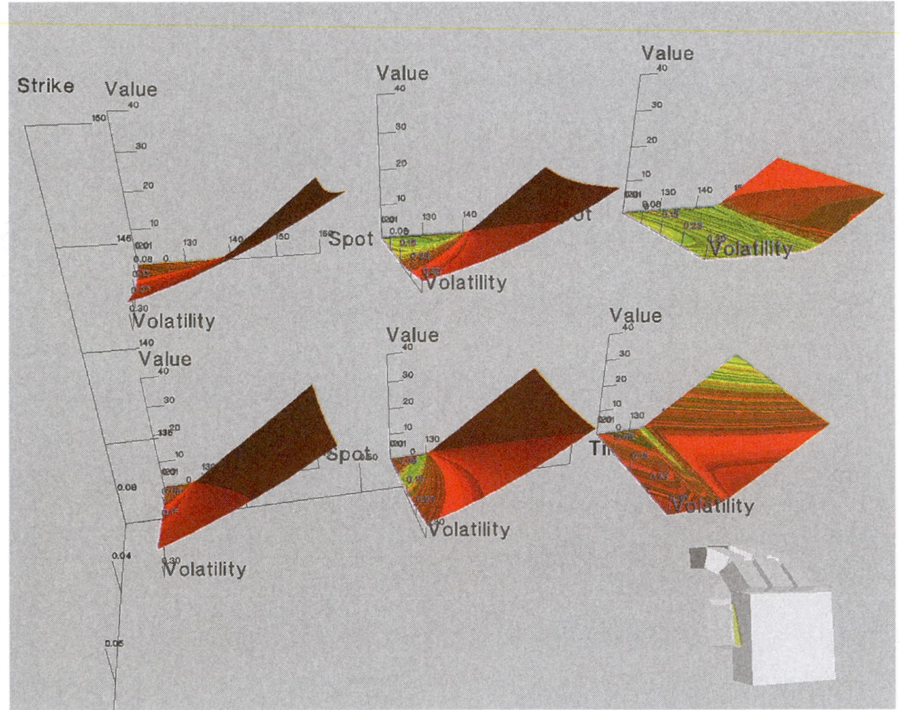

FIGURE **2**

An array of call options.

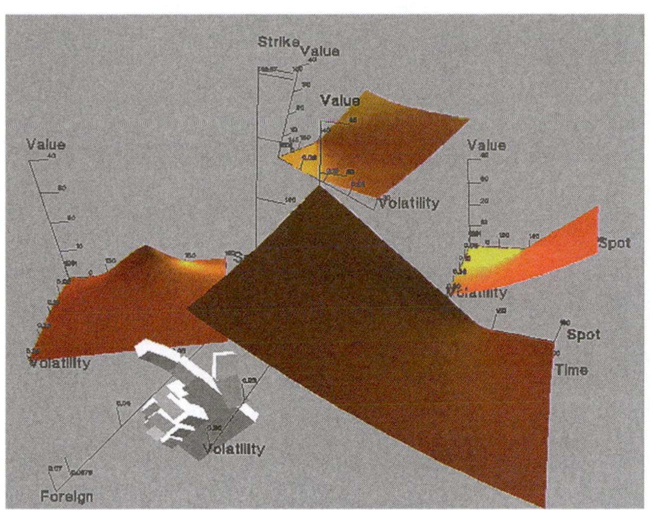

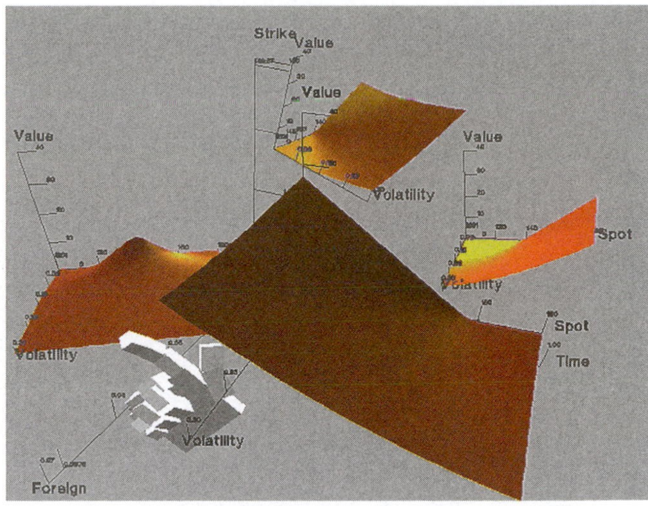

FIGURE **3**

Stereo pair of multiple worlds. (Left eye's image is at the left.)

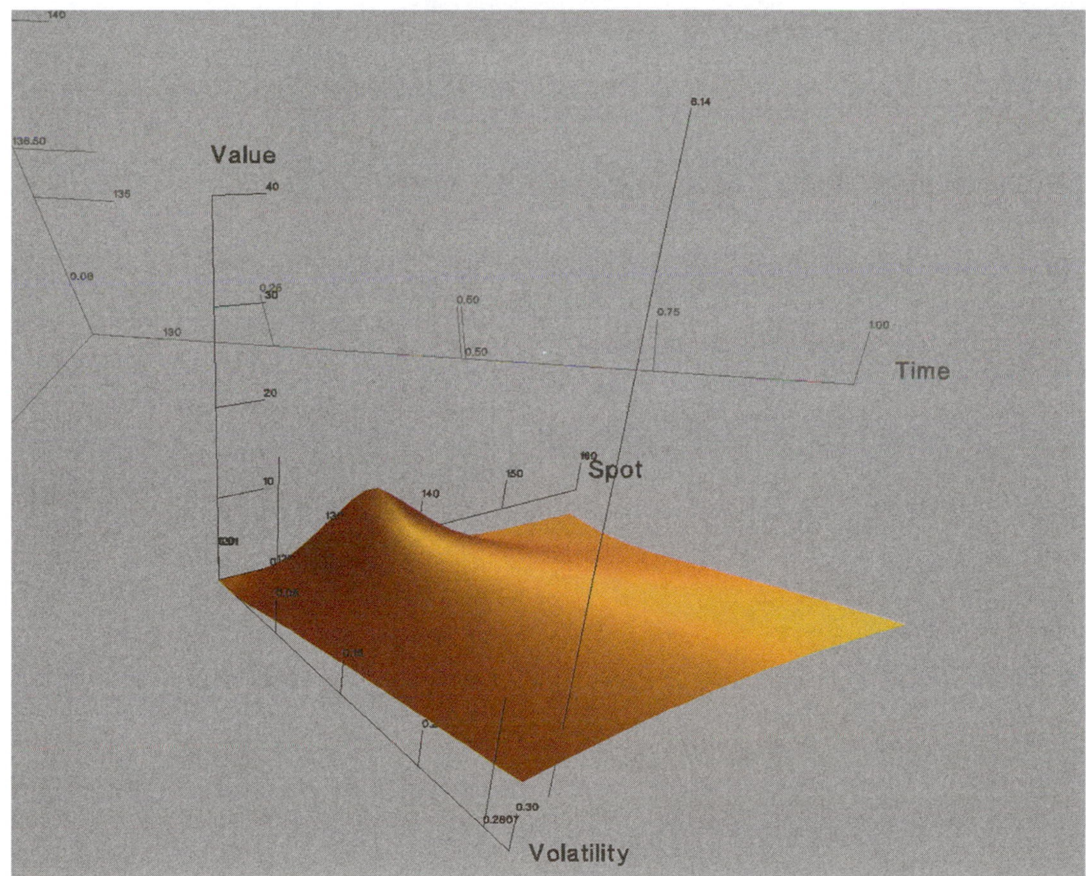

FIGURE **4**

Sampling a butterfly spread with a dipstick.

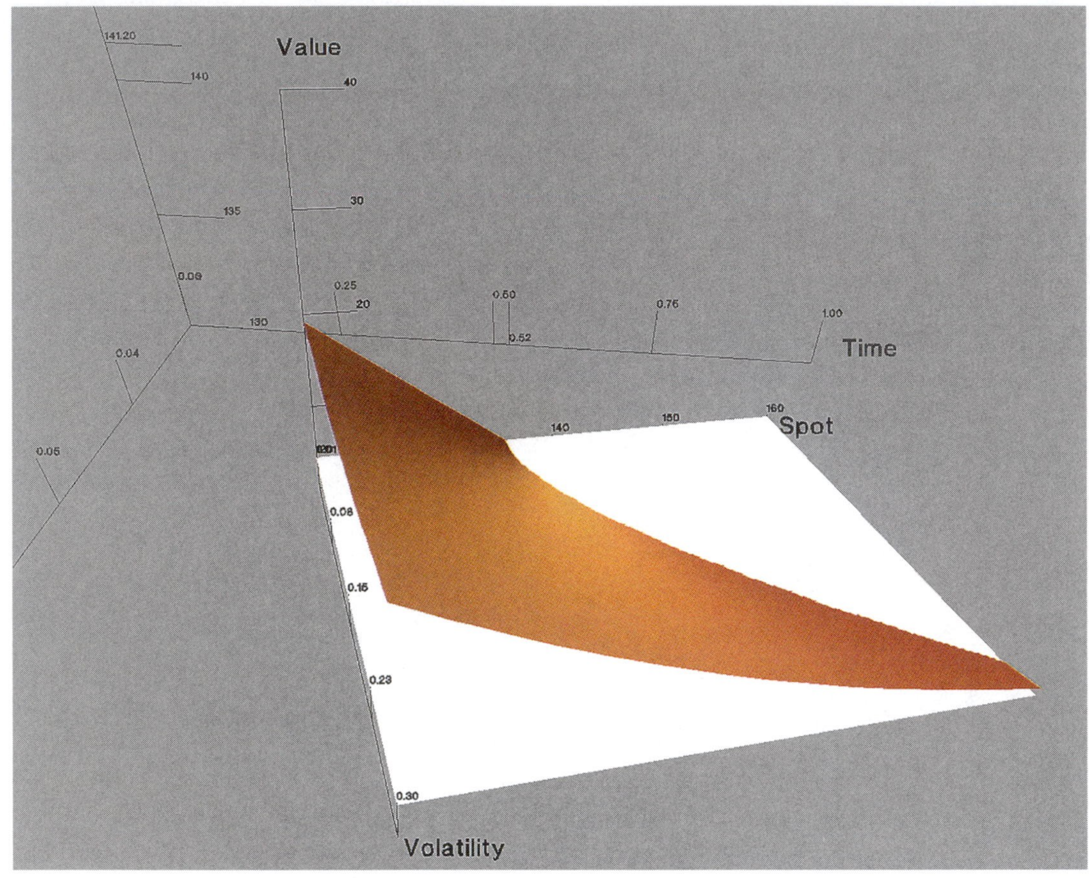

FIGURE 5

Examining a put option with a waterline.

MULTIDIMENSIONAL DETECTIVE

Alfred Inselberg,* Multidimensional Graphs Ltd†
&
Computer Science Department
Tel Aviv University, Israel
aiisreal@math.tau.ac.il

Abstract

The display of multivariate datasets in parallel coordinates, transforms the search for *relations* among the variables into a 2-D pattern recognition problem. This is the basis for the application to *Visual Data Mining*. The Knowledge Discovery process together with some general guidelines are illustrated on a dataset from the production of a VLSI chip. The special strength of parallel coordinates is in modeling **relations**. As an example, a simplified Economic Model is constructed with data from various economic sectors of a real country. The visual model shows the interelationship and dependencies between the sectors, circumstances where there is competition for the same resource, and feasible economic policies. Interactively, the model can be used to do trade-off analyses, discover sensitivities, do approximate optimization, monitor (as in a Process) and Decision Support.

Introduction

In Geometry parallelism, which does not require a notion of angle, rather than orthogonality is the more fundamental concept. This, together with the fact that orthogonality "uses-up" the plane very fast, was the inspiration in 1959 for "Parallel" Coordinates. The systematic development began in 1977 [4]. The goals of the program were and still are (see [6] and [5] for short reviews) the visualization of multivariate/multidimensional problems without loss of information and having the properties:

1. Low representational complexity. Since the number of axes, N equals the number of dimensions (variables) the complexity is $O(N)$,
2. Works for any N,
3. Every variable is treated uniformly (unlike "Chernoff Faces" and various types of "glyphs"),
4. The displayed object can be recognized under projective transformations (i.e. rotation, translation, scaling, perspective),
5. The display easily/intuitively conveys information on the properties of the N-dimensional object it represents,
6. The methodology is based on rigorous mathematical and algorithmic results.

Parallel coordinates (abbr.||-coords) transform multivariate relations into 2-D patterns, a property that is well suited for Visual Data Mining.

*Senior Fellow San Diego SuperComputing Center
†36A Yehuda Halevy Street, Raanana 43556, Israel

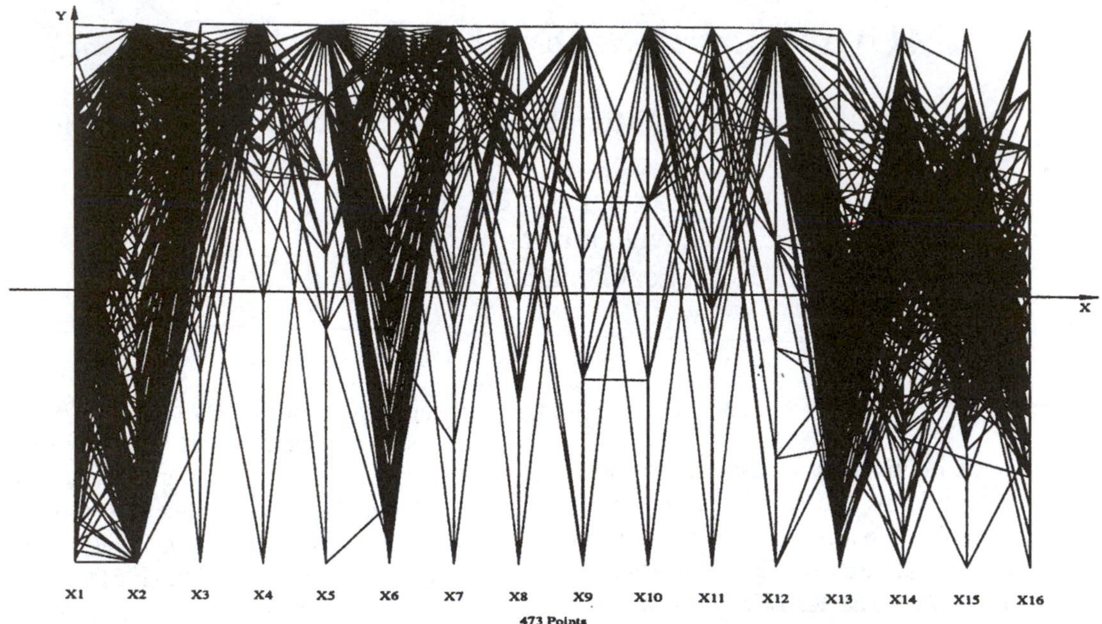

Figure 1: The full dataset consisting of 473 batches

Several Data Mining tools EDA (Chomut [2]), Finsterwalder[3], VisuLab(Hinterberger[10]), ExplorN(Carr et al), Influence Explorer(Spence & Tweedie [11]), WinViZ(Eickemeyer), VisDB(Keim [7]), Xmdv(Ward[8]), XGobi(Buja), Strata(||-coords by Gleason), Diamond(Rogowitz et al [9]), PVE(Inselberg, Adams, Hurwitz, Chatterjee, Austel) etc. include ||-coords. Here we focus on the Data Mining application and describe:

- A scenario for the discovery process,
- Guidelines for using ||-coords in Data Mining, and
- The construction and use of visual models for multivariate relations.

There are certain basics (see references) which have important ramifications. For example, due to the Point $\longleftrightarrow$ Line *duality*, some actions are best performed in the dual and their opposite in the original representation. Another important matter is the design of queries. The task is akin to accurately cutting complicated portions of an N-dimensional "watermelon" (i.e. the N-dimensional representation of the dataset). The "cutting tools" are the queries which must also operate in the dual (i.e. the ||-coords display). They need to be few, exquisitely well chosen and intuitive. This requires an efficient and convenient way of combining the *"atomic"* queries to form complex queries, corresponding to more intricate "cuts" of the dataset; and there are other issues. These points are not often appreciated and, as a result, software usually mimic the experience derived from the standard and more familiar displays (i.e. not the dual), rather than exploit the special strengths of the methodology and avoid its weaknesses.

Without the proper **geometrical** understanding and queries, the effective use of ||-coords becomes limited to small datasets. By contrast, skillful application of the methodology's strengths enables the analysis of datasets consisting of thousands of points and hundreds of variables. The intent here, is not to elaborate on the design and implementation criteria but rather to provide some insights on the "discovery process". The paradigm is that of a detective, and since many parameters (equivalently dimensions) are involved we really mean a "multidimensional detective".

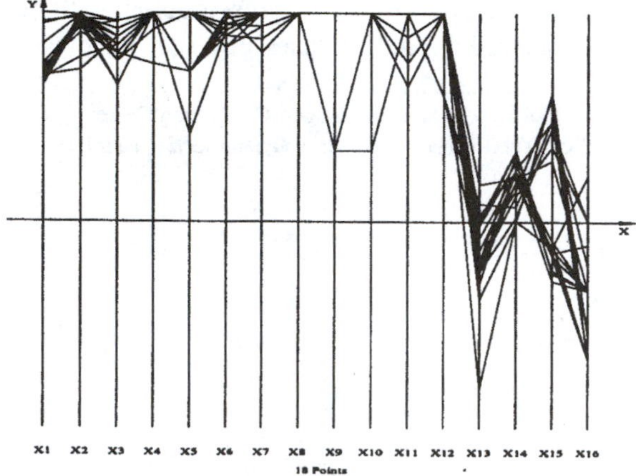

Figure 2: The batches high in Yield, $X1$, and Quality, $X2$.

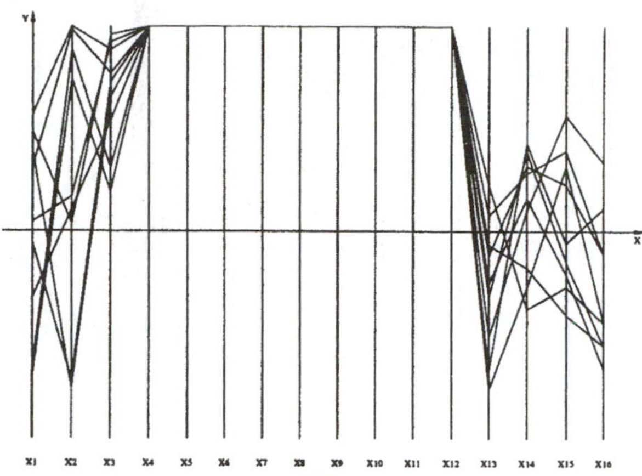

Figure 3: The batches with zero in 9 out of the ten defect types.

The Problem

Aside from starting the exploration without bias, together with some healthy scepticism about the "convictions" of the domain experts, the first admonition is:

- **do not let the picture intimidate you,**

as can easily happen by taking an uninformed look at Fig. 1 where our subject's dataset is displayed. It pertains to the production data of 473 batches of a VLSI chip with measurements of 16 process parameters denoted by $X1, X2, \ldots, X16$. The *yield*, as the % of useful chips produced in the batch, is denoted by $X1$, and $X2$ is a measure of the *quality* (in terms of speed performance). Ten different types of *defects* are monitored and the variables' scales of $X3$ through $X12$ are inverted so that 0 (zero) amount appears at the top. The remaining, $X13$ through $X16$, denote some physical parameters. We emphasize that this is a *real* dataset and in order to protect the innocent, as well as confuse the competition, it is not possible to give a more explicit description or show numerical values; for our purposes it is also not necessary. Prior to embarking on our exploration it is essential to

- **understand the objectives and use them to obtain "visual cues".**

Here the objective is to raise the yield, $X1$, and maintain high quality, $X2$, a multiobjective optimization (since more than one objective is involved). Production experts believed that it was the presence of defects which hindered high yields and qualities. So the goal was to achieve *zero defects*.

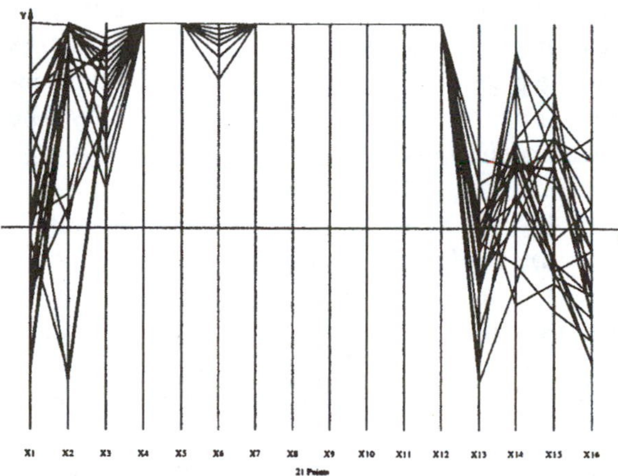

Figure 4: The batches with zero in 8 out of the ten defect types.

Discovery Process - How to be a Multidimensional Detective

The keen observer can ascertain from Fig. 1 the distributions, with $X2$ being somewhat bipolar (having higher concentrations at the extremes), and $X1$ having something like a normal distribution about it's median value. This brings us to the next admonition. Namely, no matter how messy it looks,

- **carefully scrutinize the picture**

and you are likely to find some patterns, let's call them *visual cues*, which hint at the relations among the variables.

We embark on our quest and the result of our first query is shown in Fig. 2 where the batches having the highest $X1$ and $X2$ have been isolated. This in an attempt to obtain *clues*; and two real good ones came forth (the visual cues we spoke of). Notice $X15$ where there is a separation into two clusters. As it turns out, this gap yielded important (and undiscloseable) insight into the physics of the problem.

The other clue is almost hidden. A careful comparison – and here interactivity of the software is essential – between Fig. 1 and Fig. 2 shows that some batches which were high in $X3$ (i.e. and due to the inverted scale low in that defect) *were not included in the selected subset*. That casts doubt

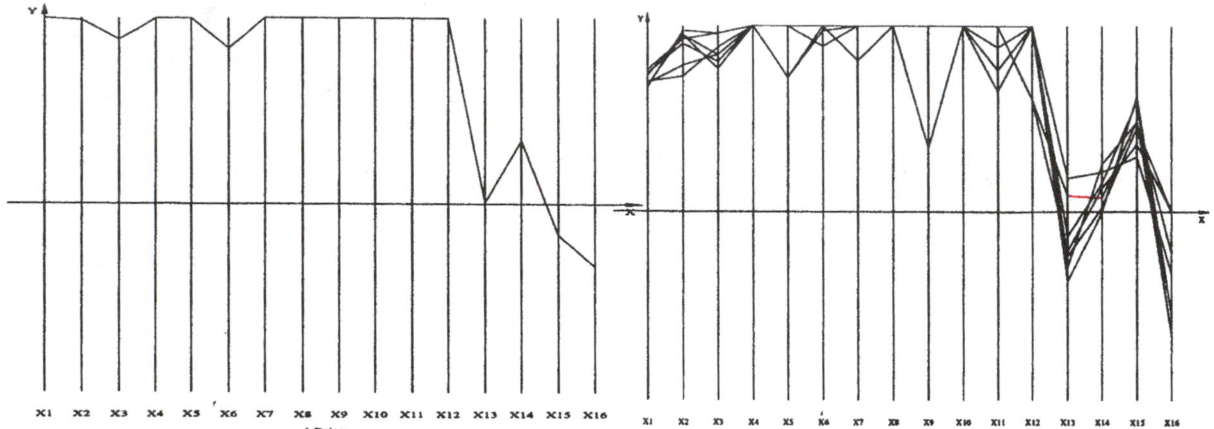

Figure 5: The best batch. Highest in Yield, $X1$, and very high in Quality, $X2$.

Figure 7: Upper range of split in $X15$

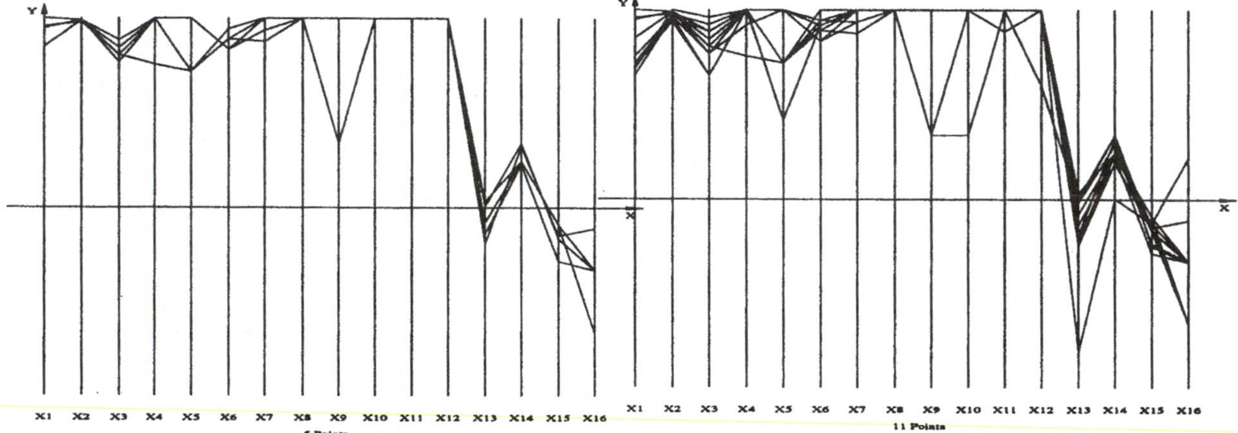

Figure 6: Batches with the highest Yields do not have the lowest defects in $X3$ and $X6$.

Figure 8: Batches with the lower range of $X15$

into the belief that zero defects are the panacea, and motivates the next query where we search for batches having zero defects in at least 9 (excluding $X3$ where we saw that there are problems) out of the 10 categories. The result is shown in Fig. 3 and is a shocker. There are 9 such batches and *all of them have poor yields and for the most part also low quality*! What is one to do? Refer again to the previous admonition and scrutinize the original picture Fig. 1 for visual cues relevant to our objectives and our findings so far. And ... there is one staring us in the face – the visual difference between $X6$ and the other defects. It shows that the process is much more sensitive to variations in $X6$ than the other defects. We chose to treat $X6$ differently and remove its zero defect constraint. The result is seen in Fig. 4 and, remarkably, the very best batch (i.e. highest yield with very high quality) is included. This is an opportunity to learn, so when that batch is highlighted with a different color (can't be seen in black and white) *it does not have zeros (or the lowest values) for $X3$ and $X6$* as shown separately in Fig. 5. A "heretical" finding, but perhaps this is due to measurement errors in that one data item. We return to the full dataset and isolate the cluster of batches with the top yields (note the gap in $X1$ between them and the remaining batches). These are shown in Fig. 6 and they confirm that small amounts (the ranges can be clearly delimited) of $X3$ and $X6$ type defects are *essential* for high yields and quality. The moral of the story is

- **test the assumptions and especially the "I am really sure of ..."s.**

Let us return to the subset of data which best satisfied the objectives, Fig. 2, to explore the gap in the range of $X15$. In Fig. 7 we see that the cluster with the high range of $X15$ gives the lowest (of the high) yields $X1$, and worse it does not give *consistently* high quality $X2$. Whereas the cluster corresponding to the lower range, Fig. 8, has the higher qualities and the full range of the high

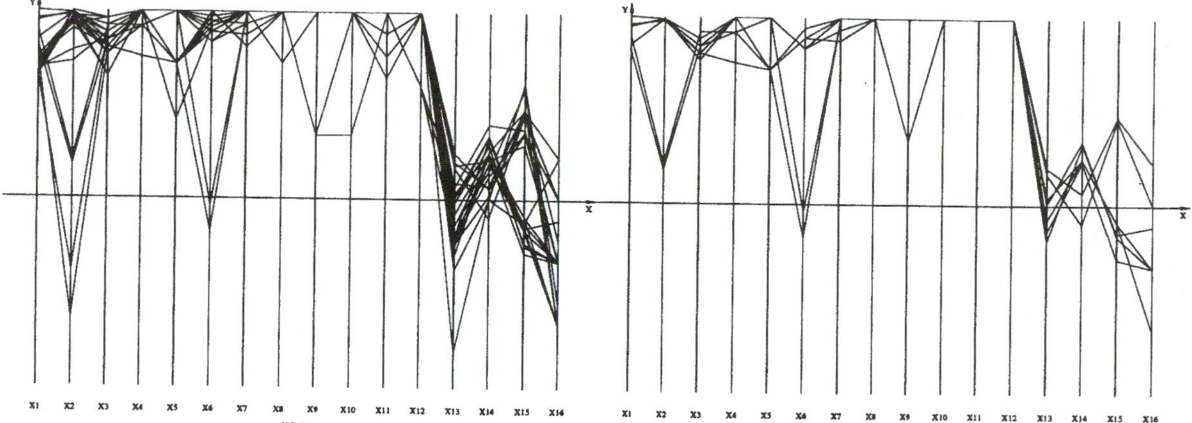

Figure 9: Top Yields produce split in $X15$

Figure 11: Top Yields, note two batches with lower Quality

yield. It is evident that the small ranges of $X3$, $X6$ close to (but not equal to) zero, together with the short (lower) range of $X15$ provide *necessary* conditions for obtaining high yields and quality. Using a characterization algorithm it can be shown that these conditions are also *sufficient*. Given any subset of the data the algorithm finds:

1. the smallest subset of variables which describe the data without loss of information, and

2. orders the variables in terms of their predictive power.

In our case these are the 3 parameters $X3$, $X6$ and $X15$ which are needed for the characterization of a very good batch. By a stroke of good luck these 3 can be checked *early* in the process avoiding the need of "throwing good money after bad". Looking again at Fig. 1 we notice a gap in $X1$ between the top 5 batches and the rest. The high cluster consists of *only* those having the small amounts of $X3$ and $X6$ and lower range of $X15$. This bit of serendipity provides an instance of my favorite "stochastic" theorem :

- **you can't be unlucky all the time!**

Some Deeper Insights

Why the gap in $X15$? It was obtained by imposing *simultaneously* the constraints for top yields and quality. Fig. 9 shows the result of constraining only $X1$ and the resulting gap in $X15$, whereas the high $X2$ by itself does not yield a gap as shown in Fig. 10. And this, I am told, provided further insights into the physics of the problem.

Just for fun we look next into the very top yields

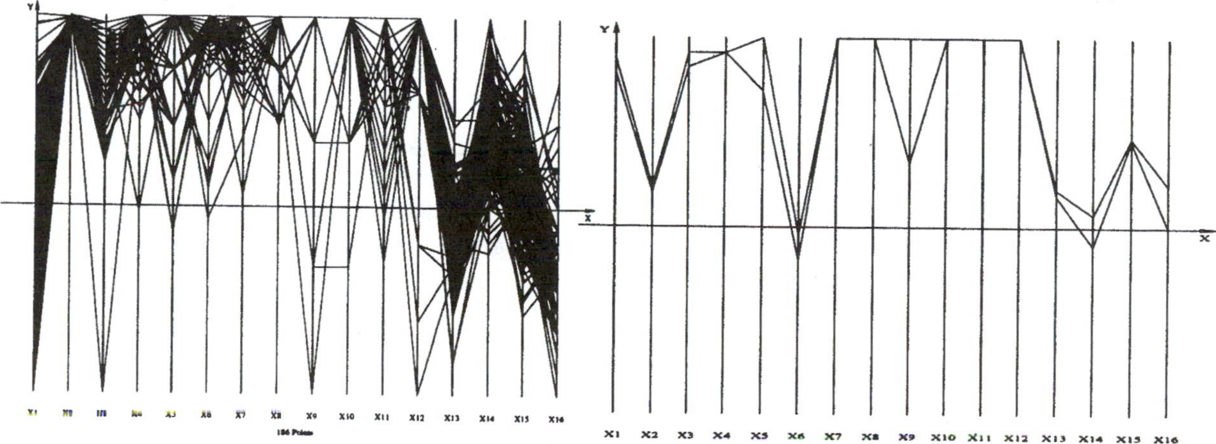

Figure 10: High $X2$ does not cause split in $X15$

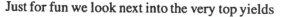

Figure 12: The two batches with high $X1$ and lower $X2$

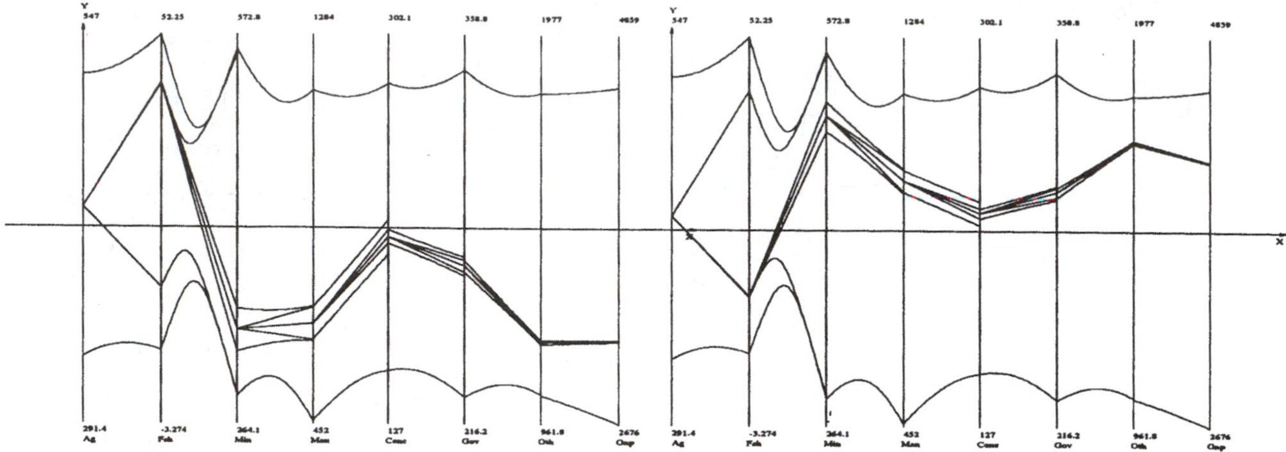

Figure 13: Model of a country's economy

Figure 14: Competition for labor between the Fishing & Mining sectors – compare with previous figure

Fig. 11 and see that except for two batches the others also have very high $X2$. Isolating the lower quality batches turns out to be very informative. The picture, Fig. 12, suggests that high yields and lower quality may be due to the different ranges of $X6$, whose influence we have already seen elsewhere, and specific ranges of $X13$, $X14$, $X15$, $X16$. This observation suggests that it may be possible to partition this multivariate problem into sub-problems pertaining to the individual objectives. The wide variation of $X9$ for these two batches, as seen in Fig. 12, lead to further testing and the conclusion that $X9$ is a "junk variable" with respect to the objectives. The observations and conclusions here involved a relatively small number of variables and should be cross-checked with larger datasets. In general, a dataset with P points has 2^P subsets anyone one of which can be the "interesting" one (with respect to the objectives). Our approach can provide a powerful tool for coping with this combinatorial explosion. The **visual cues** obtained can help to rapidly focus on the interesting portions of the data. In this sense, it can serve as a **preprocessor** to other methods, in addition to providing unique insights on its own.

After this analysis, it was revealed that this was a well studied problem and dataset, and our findings differed markedly from those found with other methods for process control [1]. This is not an isolated case and there have been other successful application of this approach in the manufacture of printed card boards, PVC and manganese production, retailing, finance, trading, insurance, seasonal weather forecasts, risk analysis, determination of skill profiles" (i.e. as in drivers, pilots etc) and elsewhere. The results frequently surprised the domain experts.

Visual & Computational Models

We have outlined a process for discovering interesting, with respect to the objective, **relations** among the variables in multivariate datasets. The real strength of the methodology is the ability to construct and display such relations in terms of hypersurfaces – just as we model a relation between two variables by a planar region. Then by using an interior point algorithm with the model we can do trade-off analyses, discover sensitivities, understand the impact of constraints, and in some cases do optimization. We just want to indicate how this works. For this purpose we use a dataset consisting of the outputs of various economic sectors and other expenditures of a particular (and real) country. It consists of the monetary values over several years of the **Ag**ricultural output, outputs of the **Fish**ing, **Min**ing, **Man**ufacturing and **Con**struction industries, together with **Gov**ernment, Miscellaneous spending and resulting GNP; eight variables altogether.

We will not take up the full ramifications of constructing a model from data. Rather, we want to illustrate how ||-coords may be used as a **visual** modeling tool. Using a Least Squares technique we "fit" a function to this dataset; for our purposes here we are not concerned whether the choice of function is "good" or not. The specific function we obtained bounds a region in R^8 and is represented by the upper and lower curves(envelopes) shown in Fig. 13(the interested reader may want to refer to the previously cited references).

The picture is in effect a visual model of the

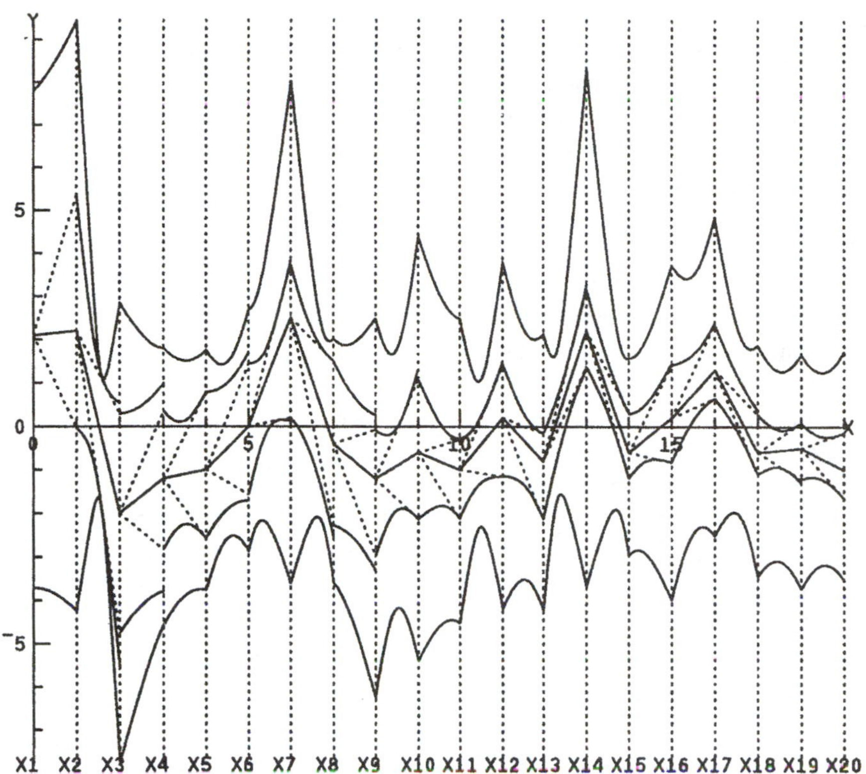

Figure 15: A Convex Hypersurface in 20-D and Interior Point Algorithm.

country's economy, incorporating it's capabilities and limitations, interelationships among the sectors etc. A point interior to the region, satisfies all the constraints simultaneously, and therefore represents (i.e. the 8-tuple of values) a *feasible economic policy* for that country. Using an interior point algorithm (see previously cited references) we can construct such points. It is done interactively by sequentially choosing values of the variables and we see the result of one such choice in Fig. 13. Once a value of the first variable is chosen (in this case the agricultural output) within it's range, the dimensionality of the region is reduced by one. The upper and lower curves between the 2nd and 3rd axes correspond to the resulting 7-dimensional hypersurface and show the *available* range of the second variable (Fishing) reduced by the constraint (i.e. fixing the value of the first variable). In fact, this can be seen (but not shown here) for the rest of the variables. That is, due to the relationship between the 8 variables, a constraint on one of them impacts all the remaining ones and restricts their range. The display allows us to experiment and actually see the impact of such decisions "downstream". By interactively varying the chosen value for the first variable we found, from this model, that low values for Agriculture correspond to low ranges of values for Fishing, and similarly corresponding to high values occurring together. So it is not possible to have a policy that favors Agriculture without also favoring Fishing and vice versa. The algorithm fails where at any stage the polygonal line crosses an intermediate curve, and that is very informative.

Proceeding, a very high value from the available range of Fishing is chosen next. It corresponds to very low values of the Mining sector. By contrast in Fig. 13 we see that a low value in Fishing yields high values for the Mining sector. This inverse relation was investigated and it was found that the country in question has a large number of migrant workers. When the fishing industry is doing well most of them are attracted to it leaving few available to work in the mines and vice versa. The comparison between the two figures shows the *competition for the same resource* between Mining and Fishing. It is especially instructive to discover this interactively. The construction of the interior point proceeds in the same way.

Let us move over to Fig. 15 where the same construction is shown but for a more complex 20-dimensional hypersurface ("model"). The intermediate curves (upper and lower) also provide valuable information and "previews of coming attractions". They indicate a neighborhood of the point (represented by the polygonal line) and provide a feel for the local curvature. Note the narrow strips between $X13$, $X14$ and $X15$ (as compared to the surrounding ones), indicating that for this choice of values these 3 are the *critical* variables where the point is "bumping the boundary". A theorem guarantees that a polygonal line which is in-between all the intermediate curves/envelopes represents an interior point of the hypersurface and all interior points can be found in this way. If the polygonal line is tangent to anyone of the intermediate curves then it represents a *boundary point*, while if it crosses anyone of the intermediate curves it represents an *exterior point*. The latter enables us to see, in an application, the first variable for which the construction failed and what is needed to make corrections. By varying the choice of value over the available range of the variable interactively, sensitive regions (where small changes produce large changes downstream) and other properties of the model can be easily discovered. Once the construction of a point is completed it is possible to vary the values of each variable and see how this effects the remaining variables. So one can do *trade-off analysis* in this way and provide a powerful tool for, Decision Support, Process Control and other applications.

It should be self-evident that the efficacy of a visual data mining tool needs to be judged by applying it to **real** and necessarily challenging datasets. Flashy demos based on artificial or small datasets can be very impressive but misleading. Each multivariate dataset and problem has its own "personality" requiring substantial variations in the discovery scenarios and calls for considerable ingenuity – a characteristic of good detectives. It is not surprising then that the most frequent requests are for tools to, at least partially, automate the exploration process. Such a development is under way and will include a number of new features, including **intelligent agents**, gleaned from the accumulated experience.

References

[1] E.W. Bassett. Ibm's ibm fix. *Industrial Computing*, 14(41):23–25, 1995.

[2] T. Chomut. *Exploratory Data Analysis in Parallel Coordinates*. M.Sc. Thesis, UCLA Comp. Sc. Dept., 1987.

[3] R. Finsterwalder. *A Parallel Coordinate Editor as a Visual Decision Aid in Multi-Objective Concurrent Control Engineering Environment 119-122*. IFAC CAD Contr. Sys., Swansea, UK, 1991.

[4] A. Inselberg. *N-Dimensional Graphics, Part I – Lines and Hyperplanes, in IBM LASC Tech. Rep. G320-2711, 140 pages*. IBM LA Scientific Center, 1981.

[5] A. Inselberg. *Parallel Coordinates : A Guide for the Perplexed, in Hot Topics Proc. of IEEE Conf. on Visualization, 35-38*. IEEE Comp. Soc., Los Alamitos, CA, 1996.

[6] A. Inselberg and B. Dimsdale. *Parallel Coordinates: A Tool For Visualizing Multidimensional Geometry, in Proc. of IEEE Conf. on Vis. '90, 361-378*. IEEE Comp. Soc., Los Alamitos, CA, 1990.

[7] D. A. Keim and H. P. Kriegel. Visualization techniques for mining large databases: A comparison. *Trans. Knowl. and Data Engr.*, 8-6:923–938, 1996.

[8] Ward M. O. *XmdvTool: integrating multiple methods for visualizing multivariate data, Proc. IEEE Conf. on Visualization, San Jose, CA, 326-333*. IEEE Comp. Soc., Los Alamitos, CA, 1994.

[9] M. Schall. Diamond and ice : Visual exploratory data analysis tools. *Perspective, J. of OAC at UCLA*, 18(2):15–24, 1994.

[10] C. Schmid and H. Hinterberger. *Comparative Multivariate Visualization Across Conceptually Different Graphic Displays, in Proc. of 7th SSDBM*. IEEE Comp. Soc., Los Alamitos, CA, 1994.

[11] L.A. Tweedie, R. Spence, H. Dawkes, and Su H. *Externalizing Abstract Mathematical Models, Proc. CHI, Vancouver, Can., 406-412*. ACM Press, 1996.

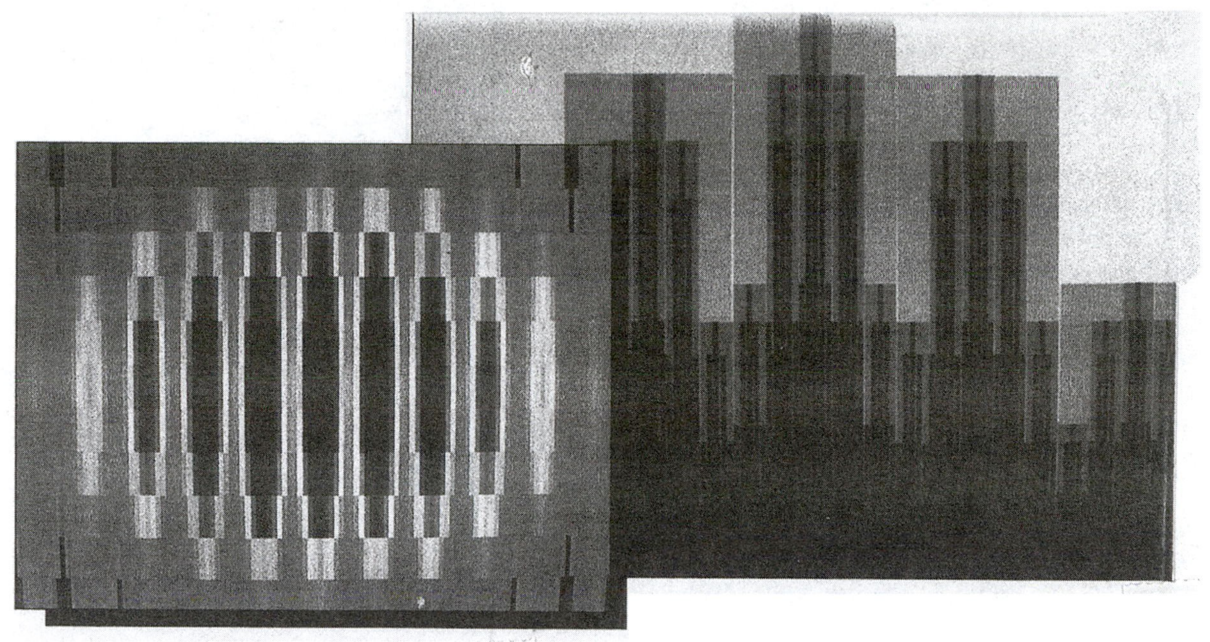

Visualizing Multivariate Functions, Data, and Distributions

Ted Mihalisin, John Timlin, and John Schwegler
Mihalisin Associates

The three real-time hierarchical methods presented here can display multidimensional data involving two, three, or more independent variables and millions of points.

Recently various authors in a special visualization issue of *Computer* (Aug. 1989) noted the need to visualize scientific data involving large data sets and/or high dimensionality. In this article we will address the problem of visualizing a scalar dependent variable that is a function of many independent variables. In particular, we will focus on cases with three or more independent variables. Hence, including the single dependent variable, we will tackle the problem of "plotting" 4D data and data of dimensionality exceeding four.

Our technique is totally distinct from other multivariate graphing methods.[1-9] Although in some sense closer to Feiner and Beshers' method[6] than to the others, our method's use of a hierarchical axis employing different metrics for each independent variable and of hierarchical data symbols makes it radically different. We will describe the technique for the case where each independent variable is sampled in a regular grid or lattice-like fashion (that is, in equal increments). However, we can also generalize it to a variety of less restrictive domains.

The number and spacing of values may differ for each variable. Hence, the N independent variable values form a hyper-rectangular lattice in the N-dimensional space within a hyper-rectangular parallelopiped domain. We can describe our technique in either an active or a passive manner. In the active view the points of the N-dimensional independent variables lattice are mapped to a single horizontal axis in a hierarchical manner, while in the passive view an observer samples the points of the N-dimensional lattice in a prescribed fashion and notes the values of the dependent variable. In the passive view a plot of the dependent variable versus a single parametric variable (which is simply the sampling number) forms the multidimensional graph.

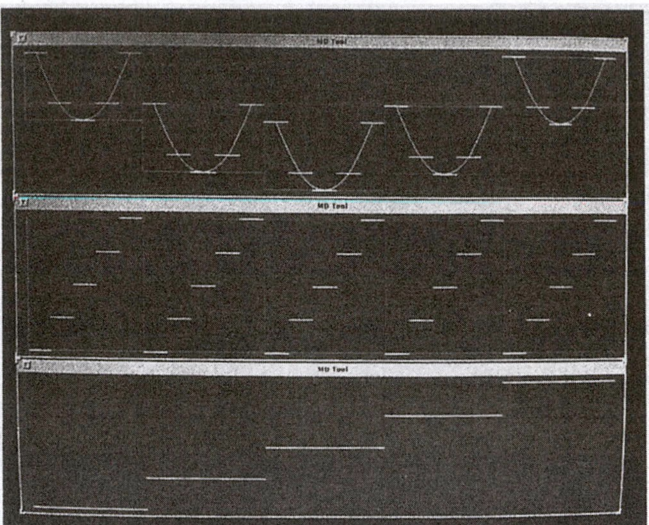

Figure 1. The top panel shows $D = x^2 + y^2$, the middle panel shows x variation, and the bottom panel shows y variation.

The first technique

In this article we want mainly to demonstrate that our techniques for plotting scalar fields on an N-dimensional lattice work for a variety of data visualization tasks, such as the location of maxima, minima, saddle points, and other features, as well as visually fitting multivariate data and the visual determination of dominant and weak or irrelevant variables. Hence, rather than presenting a formal mathematical description, we will use a visual means of describing the technique for a simple 3D data case, then demonstrate by example how to extend it to higher dimensions.

Figure 1 shows three vertically stacked X windows or panels. The problem at hand is to plot the simple function $D = x^2 + y^2$ over the domain $x = -2, -1, 0, 1, 2$ and $y = -2, -1, 0, 1, 2$. The middle and bottom panels show how x and y are sampled. For instance, the middle panel shows white horizontal lines, which you should think of as rectangles of zero height, on blue backgrounds. The white rectangles show x varying from -2 to 2 in a sawtooth fashion with five cycles. The bottom panel shows one cycle for the y values, again running from -2 to 2. The horizontal axis then corresponds to moving through the 5×5 square lattice of x and y by cycling through the five x values with y fixed at -2, then incrementing y to -1 and cycling x again and so on.

We say that x is the fastest running variable and y is the second fastest. The top panel shows the resulting graph. The dependent variable D is plotted on the vertical, and both x and y lie on the horizontal as described. First focus your attention on the 25 white rectangles (of zero height). They clearly show that the data consists of five parabolic sections, one for each y value. We added the splines to guide the eye. The five blue "background" rectangles correspond to the five y values. Their width is determined by the number of x values, while their height is $\Delta D = D_{max} - D_{min}$. Their horizontal location is tied to the value of y. Clearly the vertical location of the ith rectangle depends on $D(x, y_i)$. That is, the blue rectangles circumscribe the data for fixed y but varying x. Think of them as data symbols representing data not at a point but over a one-dimensional data line. The pattern of blue rectangles also forms a parabola.

We can extend the technique to higher dimensions. For example, for a third independent variable, z, you would sample the data with x as the fastest running variable, then y, and finally z. Then you would have white rectangles representing points in the independent variable space, blue rectangles (with nested white rectangles) representing lines in the space, and red rectangles representing planes in the space, circumscribing the blue rectangles. Hence, for any dimension you form a hierarchical horizontal axis and a set of hierarchical, nested, data-driven symbols that represent the dependent variable D at points, along lines, on planes, in volumes, in four-spaces, and so forth, in the space of independent variables. The second technique (discussed below) differs in respect to how we draw the top and bottom of the hierarchical rectangles.

Before moving to higher dimensionality and large data sets, it will help to consider a variety of functions with two independent variables for small data sets. This helps us establish pattern recognition rules.

Functions and modulations

Let's take a look at additive and multiplicate functions and frequency and phase modulation. In the example in Figure 1, we see a special case of the more general form $D(x, y) = f(x) + g(y)$. For fixed $y = y_i$, $D(x, y_i) = D(x) = f(x) + O_i$ where the offset $O_i = g(y_i)$. While O_i clearly affects the vertical location of the ith blue rectangle, it does not affect its height (vertical size) $\Delta D = D_{max} - D_{min} = f(x)_{max} - f(x)_{min} = \Delta f$. Hence, for functions of an additive form $f(x) + g(y)$ all blue rectangles have the same height, given by Δf, while their vertical locations are driven by

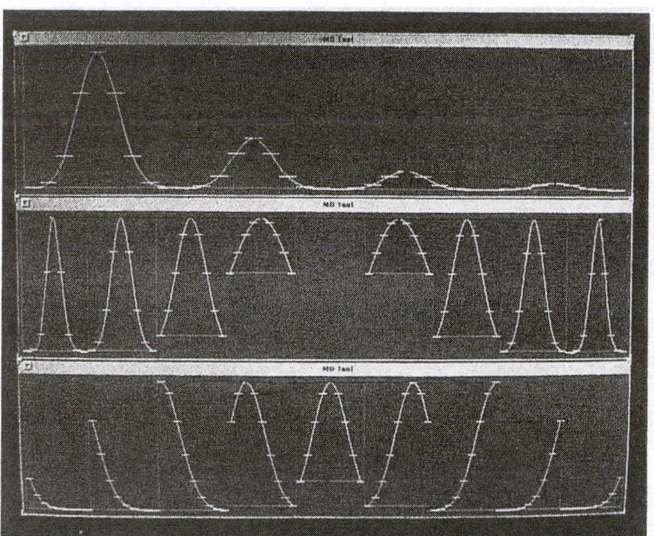

Figure 2. Amplitude modulation (AM), frequency modulation (FM), and phase modulation (PM) functions appear in the top, middle, and bottom panels, respectively.

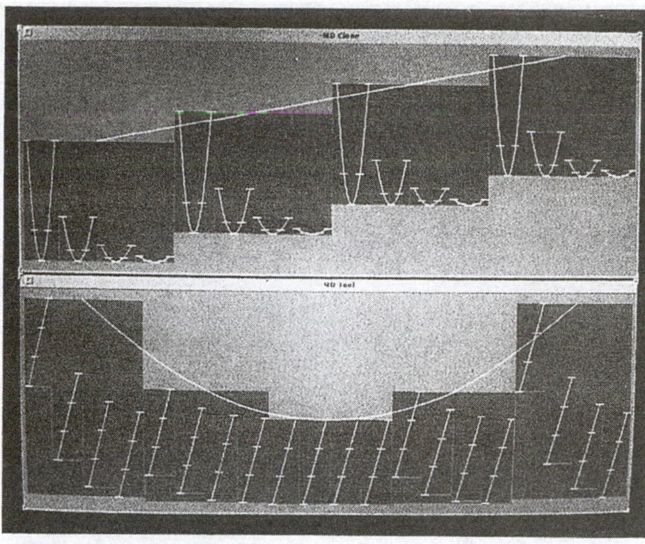

Figure 3. Plot of $D = x^2e^{-y} + z$ with x (white) fastest and z (red) slowest in the top panel and with z (white) fastest and x (red) slowest in the bottom panel.

$g(y)$. It helps to think of $g(y)$ as performing transformations on the blue rectangles, namely, offsetting them vertically.

Figure 2 shows examples of the forms $D(x, y) = f(x) \cdot g(y)$ (top panel), $D(x, y) = F(x \cdot g(y))$ (middle panel), and $D(x, y) = F(x + g(y))$ (bottom panel). In the top panel of Figure 2 $D(x, y) = f(x) \cdot g(y)$ with $f(x) = e^{-x^2}$ and $g(y) = e^{-y}$. For fixed $y = y_i$, $D(x, y) = f(x) \cdot A_i$, where $A_i = g(y_i)$. Hence, $\Delta D = D_{max} - D_{min} = A_i\,(f(x)_{max} - f(x)_{min}) = A_i\,\Delta f$. Hence, $g(y)$ provides amplitude modulation (AM) for $f(x)$. Thus $g(y)$ provides amplitude modulation for the heights of the corresponding blue rectangles. This contrasts with the $D(x, y) = f(x) + g(y)$ case, where the heights of all blue rectangles were identical (see Figure 1). Note that neither the range of x, that is, $\Delta x = x_{max} - x_{min}$, nor the phase of $f(x)$ as reflected by the value of x_{min}, have changed, in contrast to the middle and bottom panels of Figure 2, respectively.

In the middle panel of Figure 2 $D(x, y)$ has the form $D(x, y) = F(x \cdot g(y))$. In particular, $D(x, y) = e^{-(x \cdot y)^2}$, that is, $g(y) = y$ and $F(u) = e^{-u^2}$, and $u = x \cdot g(y) = x \cdot y$. If F were a periodic function, you would normally refer to this type of behavior as frequency modulation (FM). More generally, we can think of $g(y)$ as scaling (multiplying) the range of u where u is the argument of F. In the bottom panel of Figure 2 $D(x, y)$ has the form $D(x, y) = F(x + g(y))$. In particular, $D(x, y) = e^{-(x+y)^2}$, that is, $g(y) = y$ and $F(u) = e^{-u^2}$ and $u = x + g(y) = x + y$. If F were a periodic function, you would normally refer to this type of behavior as phase modulation (PM). More generally, we can think of $g(y)$ as offsetting (shifting) the range of u where u is the argument of F.

4D and the permute tool

Figure 3 shows the appearance of 4D data following $D = x^2e^{-y} + z$ for five values of x, four values of y, and four values of z. Note that in the top panel x runs fastest (white), followed by y (blue), then by z (red), which varies the most slowly, while in the bottom panel z is the fastest running variable, followed by y, and finally by x, the slowest. That is, we have permuted x and z in relation to how we move through the multidimensional space (or equivalently, how we set up the hierarchical axis). However, the function D remains $D = x^2e^{-y} + z$. Although you can deduce the mathematical structure of D from either the top or the bottom panel, the top panel makes it easier to recognize the pattern.

Large data sets

Now let's look at 7D data and the subspace zoom and clone tools. The upper left panel of Figure 4 shows a 7D graph. That is, the horizontal includes six independent variables plus the dependent variable. The fastest running independent variable is white, the second fastest is blue, the third is red, then violet, turquoise, and yellow. The white variable has nine values, the blue five, the red seven, the violet five, the turquoise six, and the yellow five, for a total of 47,250 points. This number greatly exceeds the number of horizontal pixels assigned to the upper left panel (approximately one-third of the screen or 430 pixels). As a result only the yellow and turquoise rectangles can be displayed.

Each of the five yellow rectangles corresponds to a 6D subspace containing the dependent variable on the vertical and the five remaining independent variables—white, blue, red, violet, and turquoise—on the horizontal, with the yellow variable fixed at the appropriate value. Similarly, each turquoise rectangle corresponds to a 4D space, and so forth.

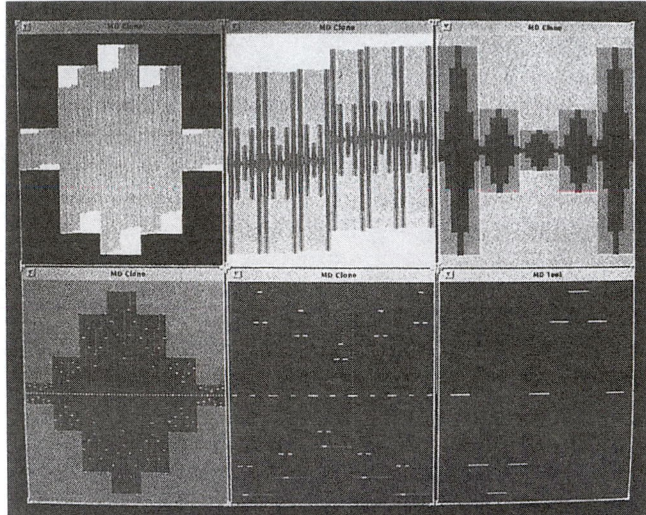

Figure 4. $D = -y^2[\arctan(t) + (1 + v^2)(e^{-r^2}) \cdot (1 + b^2)\sin(w)]$ **in the upper left panel and 6D, 5D, 4D, 3D, and 2D subspaces (see the explanation in text).**

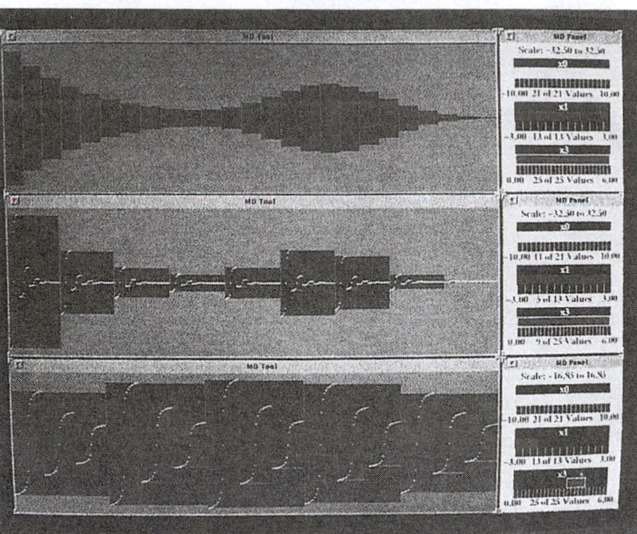

Figure 5. Full data set (top), decimated data set (middle), and zoomed view (bottom). See the explanation in text.

A tool that we have named the subspace zoom tool allows us to point to a particular rectangle and zoom to the corresponding subspace of one smaller dimension. We can perform the zoom with autoscaling for the vertical or D axis turned on or off. In Figure 4 we will locate maxima by using the subspace zoom tool with autoscaling on. If you click on the third yellow rectangle in the top left panel, you obtain the top middle panel. Note that the smaller turquoise rectangles in fact overwrite a large fraction of each yellow rectangle's area. You can identify the third yellow rectangle by focusing your attention on the tops of the rectangles. If you then click on the sixth turquoise rectangle in the top middle panel, you obtain the top right panel. Clicking on either the first or last violet rectangle, you obtain the bottom left panel. Clicking on the fourth red rectangle, you obtain the bottom middle panel. Finally, clicking on either the first or last blue rectangle, you obtain the bottom right panel. You can quickly locate maxima in this manner. A similar procedure helps locate minima and saddle points.

If you want to display all of the panels on the monitor at once, you can use a movable and scalable "clone" tool that allows you to "clone" the current panel. We used this tool to display each of our subspace zooms shown in Figure 4.

To visually fit the 7D data, let's repeat the subspace zoom operations just described. We will again start at the upper left panel. Each succeeding panel (reading left to right and top to bottom) will correspond to performing the subspace zoom as before, again with the autoscale on. Note that autoscaling of D renders identical results—no matter which rectangle we select for a zoom—if the variations in D are of the vertical offset type (see Figure 1) or the amplitude modulation type (see Figure 2, top panel). This does not happen in the frequency modulation (Figure 2, middle panel) or phase modulation (Figure 2, bottom panel) cases, nor in general for more complex forms.

However, if you inspect the slowest running variable in each of the first five panels of Figure 4, you see

- an amplitude modulation of the form $-y^2$ (here we use the abbreviations y = yellow, t = turquoise, v = violet, r = red, b = blue, and w = white) in the first (upper left) panel;
- a vertical offset of the form $\arctan(t)$ in the second panel;
- an amplitude modulation of the form $1 + v^2$ in the third panel;
- an amplitude modulation of the form e^{-r^2} in the fourth panel;
- an amplitude modulation of the form $1 + b^2$ in the fifth panel; and
- a $\sin(w)$ form in the sixth and last panel.

The formula used to generate the data of Figure 4 is $D = -y^2 [\arctan(t) + (1 + v^2)(e^{-r^2})(1 + b^2) \sin(w)]$. Thus, aside from a vertical scaling factor, all six possible yellow rectangles corresponding to the six values of the yellow variable contain an identical set of turquoise rectangles. Similarly, except for vertical offsets, each of the $6 \times 5 = 30$ possible turquoise rectangles contains an identical set of violet rectangles, and so forth. Of course, this simple behavior does not occur for more general functions—only for those involving independent variables that enter D in either an additive or multiplicative (amplitude modulation) manner.

Identifying interesting regions

The top panel of Figure 5 shows 4D data: three independent variables and a scalar dependent variable. The white variable has 17 values, the blue variable 15, and the red variable 25, for a total of 6,375. As a result, very little detail shows up in the top

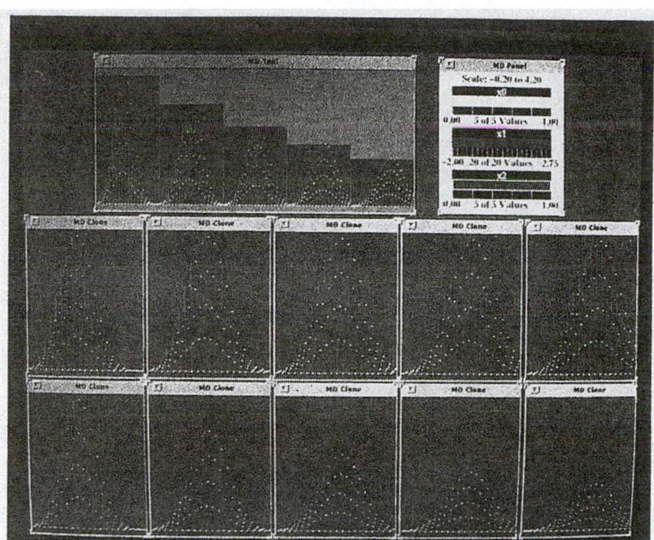

Figure 6. Plot of $D = we^{-r(b-r)^2}e^{-r}$ and the white, blue, and red widgets (top); animation frames for varying red with autoscaling on (middle); and animation frames for varying red with autoscaling off (bottom).

panel. Another tool we have implemented, a decimate tool, allows us to span the same range for each variable but to sample on a more coarse-grained grid by displaying only every other value, every third value, and so forth. You can apply the tool to as many or as few variables as you desire.

The middle panel of Figure 5 shows the result of reducing the red variable to nine values (every third) and the blue variable to six (every third). The bottom panel shows the results of applying a general zoom tool, which lets us look at a contiguous subset of variable values (that is, a subrange). To the right of each panel are slider-like widgets. These widgets indicate the subrange of each variable in view and the degree of decimation. For example, in the bottom panel all 17 values of the white variable are shown. We display three of the 13 values of the blue variable (the first three) and five of the 25 values of the red variable (the 15th through the 19th).

The animation tool

The top panel of Figure 6 shows a 4D graph involving the three independent variables white, blue, and red. The slider-like widgets next to the top panel indicate spanning of the entire range of white, blue, and red. Originally, there were 20 values for white, 17 for blue, and 20 for red, for a total of 6,800. The white and red variables have been decimated to five values each, while the number of blue remains at 17 to clearly define the Gaussian shape. The middle panels show five frames corresponding to animating through the five values of the red variable with the vertical autoscaling turned on. The bottom panels show the same animation frames with the autoscaling turned off.

The exponential decay of the heights of the nine red rectangles (amplitude modulation) is obvious both in the static top panel view and in the animation frames of the bottom panel, but it has been removed via autoscaling in the frames of the middle panels. A careful examination of both the static top panel and the unscaled bottom panels' animation frames reveals that the blue Gaussians are moving to the right (phase modulation) and broadening (frequency modulation). These latter points are perhaps more apparent in the scaled animation frames shown in the middle panels, where the distracting exponential decay has been removed via the vertical autoscaling. The function used to generate Figure 6 has the form $D = we^{-r(b-r)^2}e^{-r}$ where w = white, b = blue, and r = red.

We have not yet implemented a robust method for extracting phase modulation and frequency modulation (that is, independent variable offset and scaling) information and generating new dependent variables. Nor have we yet implemented the ability to collapse two or more independent variables to a lesser number, such as $xy \rightarrow x'$ or $x + y \rightarrow x'$. These transformations require support for missing values, which we have not yet implemented in our tree arithmetic and permutational algebra, but can be supported by the basic techniques.

Transformations of *x* and/or *y*

When plotting 2D data, it often proves useful to allow transformations of x and/or y. Our earlier discussions focused on transformations for the dependent and independent variables (that is, offset and scaling operations) involving the mathematical form of $F(x, y, \ldots)$. Although at this point we have not implemented transformation tools for the independent variables, since in general they would require support of missing values, we have implemented a means for transforming the dependent variable D. We generated the data used for all the figures in this article, except for Figures 8 and 9, with an equation parser. The addition of noise, as well as transformations on the dependent variable D, results simply from operating on the

When dealing with data involving many categorical variables, a primary consideration is the ability to view a variety of distribution functions and cumulative distribution functions.

stream of D values located at the bottom of the tree and replacing the original stream by the modified stream. Figure 7 shows 4D data generated by the function $D = e^{-w^2}e^{-2b^2}e^{-3r^2}$ (w = white, b = blue, and r = red.) The top panel of Figure 7 shows D on the vertical axis, while the bottom panel shows $D' = \ln D = -w^2 - 2b^2 - 3r^2$.

Note how the log transformation has effectively removed the amplitude modulation and rendered all variables additive, as indicated by the fact that all red rectangles are of the same

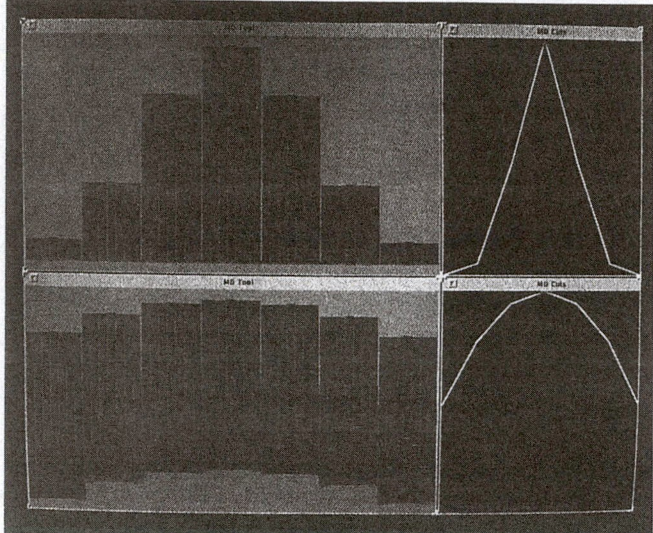

Figure 7. $D = e^{-w^2}e^{-2b^2}e^{-3r^2}$ and expansion of D in white, blue, and red directions at the maximum point (0, 0, 0) with a linear D scale (top) and a logarithmic D scale (bottom).

height. To the right of each panel appears the result of using yet a final tool, which we call the expander. You can use the subspace zoom to select any point in the space. Then the expander tool will expand D about that point by plotting the D variation in all variable directions (in this case white, blue, and red), using a uniform metric for all variables. This tool is quite useful since a direct visual reading of the metrics for white, blue, red, and other independent variables is not easy due to the hierarchical nature of the horizontal axis.

Experimental data

Up to this point we made all graphs using data generated from mathematical functions. Figure 8 shows experimental data for the specific heat anomaly of an alloy system undergoing an antiferromagnetic transition in zero and nonzero applied magnetic fields. The magnetic component of the specific heat is the dependent variable plotted vertically. The independent variables plotted horizontally go from fastest to slowest: temperature in white (decimated to 12 values), alloy concentration in

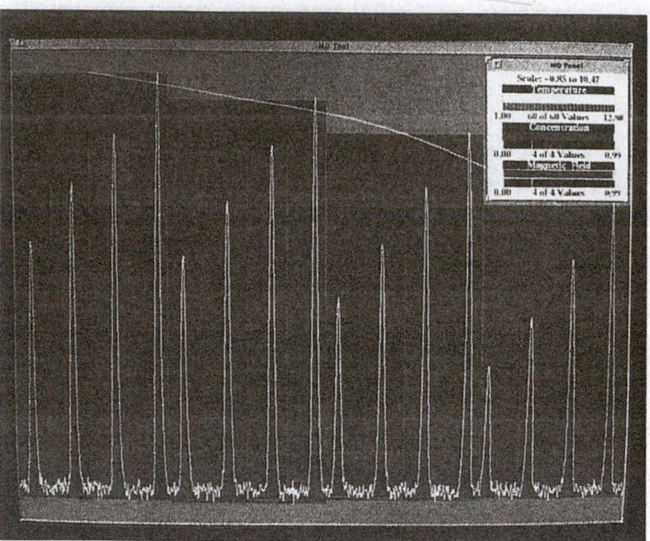

Figure 8. Specific heat versus temperature in white, alloy concentration in blue, and magnetic field in red.

blue (decimated to four values), and magnetic field in red (decimated to four values). The noise measures about 1 percent of the peak value.

You can see that for each concentration and magnetic field the specific heat versus temperature shows a more or less Gaussian peak. As we increase the alloy concentration, the height of the specific heat peak increases linearly, as does the Neel temperature (the temperature at which the specific heat is maximum). As we increase the magnetic field, we observe a nonlinear decrease in both the height of the peak and the Neel temperature. Both decreases appear to be quadratic in the magnetic field.

The second technique

The social sciences, business, finance, marketing, and a number of other areas deal with data involving many categorical variables. The data often involve populations, such as the number of households, persons, or stocks that have the nth value of the first categorical variable, the mth value of the second categorical variable, and so on. U.S. census data provides a well-known example. When dealing with this type of data, a primary consideration is the ability to view a variety of distribution functions and cumulative distribution functions.

The second technique ideally suits handling this type of data analysis visually. Otherwise identical to the first technique, it differs in that the bottom of each hierarchal rectangle lies at the vertical zero while the top is drawn at a vertical value equal to the sum of the vertical values of the set of largest rectangles within it (except for the fastest running rectangles, where the vertical location of the rectangle's top simply equals the value of the dependent variable, that is, the population). Thus, the height of each of the fastest running rectangles equals a popula-

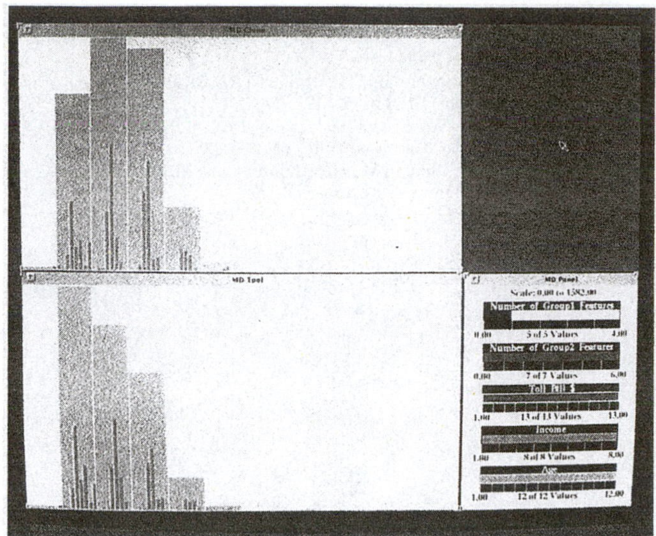

Figure 9. Distributions of households by five categorical variables (see text for explanation).

Figure 10. $D = x^2 + u^2 + y^2 + v^2$ **plotted using the two hierarchical axes techniques (see text).**

tion with all categorical variables fixed. Hence, the collection of such rectangles (white in color) represents a distribution.

Each of the second fastest running rectangles' height equals a population summed over all values of the fastest running categorical variable, but with all other variables fixed. Hence, the collection of such rectangles (blue in color) represents a cumulative distribution. Similarly, the red rectangles represent a doubly cumulative distribution, since both the fastest and second fastest running variables have been summed over, and so forth.

Figure 9 shows a sample of customer information from a national telecommunications database provided by PNR & Associates of Jenkintown, Pennsylvania. The data consists of five categorical variables for each of a total 9,631 households: the number of group 1 features chosen by each household (white), the number of group 2 features chosen by each household (blue), the monthly bill bracket (red), the income bracket for the household (violet), and the age bracket for the head of household (turquoise). These variables have five, seven, thirteen, eight, and twelve values, respectively. Thus, the total number of points in the 5D independent variable space is 43,680.

The value for the dependent variable—the number of households—is zero at many points in the 5D space. The top panel shows the distribution by age (in turquoise), summing over all values for the four faster running variables. In particular, the top panel includes all values for the number of group 1 features (including zero). Also visible in the top panel are the distributions in income bracket for each age bracket (shown as violet rectangles). The red, blue, and white rectangles are not visible, since the $12 \times 8 \times 13 = 1{,}248$ pixels required to show even the red rectangles exceeds the number of pixels along the horizontal extent of the window.

The bottom panel of Figure 9 shows a similar graph, except that the fastest running white variable runs from one to four group 1 features, as indicated by the white slider. That is, we have excluded zero for group 1 features. Note that the age distribution in the bottom panel differs significantly from that shown by the turquoise rectangles in the top panel, indicating that older heads of households are reluctant to try group 1 features. Note also that the distributions by income for each age bracket (violet rectangles) are essentially identical for the top and bottom panels, indicating that the cost of the group 1 features is not a factor.

All of the tools discussed in connection with the first technique also apply to the second technique. The zoom and permutation tools allow us to look at all possible distribution and cumulative distribution functions.

The third technique

We have investigated a wide variety of generalizations of these techniques, including new rendering techniques, extensions of applicability to include non-grid-like data and non-scalar data, and an extension to the case of two hierarchical independent variable axes with the dependent variable value represented by color or gray-scale.

We can view the last extension as a hierarchical-axes generalization of a 2D color map (normally used to represent single-valued 3D data in a planar fashion) to the case of four or more dimensions. We form a regular rectangular grid or, equivalently, a collection of contiguous rectangles. The width of the rectangles is given by the interval on the hierarchical horizontal axis that corresponds to an increment of the fastest running horizontal independent variable. The height of the rectangles is given by the interval that corresponds to an increment of the fastest running variable on the vertical axis.

We can form a hierarchy of larger rectangles of widths and heights corresponding to one increment of the second fastest running variables, the third fastest, and so forth. We can think of these sets of progressively larger rectangles as hierarchical data symbols for the behavior of the dependent variable over 2D, 4D, 6D, etc. subspaces if we prescribe a rule to render (in this case, color) all, or a portion, of the larger rectangles based on the colors of the smaller rectangles that each encloses, thus based on the encompassed set of values of the dependent variable. For example, we could determine the color of the larger rectangle from the minimum, maximum, sum, or average of the dependent variable over the corresponding subspace.

Figure 10 shows $D = x^2 + u^2 + y^2 + v^2$ for a simple case where x, u, y, and v range from -10 to 10 in integer steps. Hence, there are $21^4 = 194{,}481$ points in the 5D space. The variables x and u lie along the horizontal and y and v along the vertical. The fastest running variables are x and y. The value of D, represented by colors, increases as we move from red to violet.

LeBlanc, Ward, and Wittels[10] have also developed a two-hierarchical-axes technique starting from our earlier work.[11] Their approach differs from the one just described in that no rule is prescribed for making the rectangles hierarchical. As a result, if the number of data points exceeds the number of pixels, you must pan a larger virtual rendering to view the entire data set. Our hierarchical technique allows us to view the overall behavior of the minima, maxima, sums, or averages over subspaces for arbitrarily large data sets. A zoom tool then allows us to obtain a detailed view of any subspace of interest. A decimate tool allows us to obtain a coarse-grained view of the data over the full n-dimensional space. In summary, the hierarchical plotting methods presented here allow you to visualize and to visually analyze multivariate functions, data, and distributions in various ways. ❑

References

1. R.A. Becker, W.S. Cleveland, and A.R. Wilks, in *Dynamic Graphics for Statistics*, W.S. Cleveland and M.E. McGill, eds., Wadsworth & Brooks/Cole, Belmont, Calif., 1988, pp. 1-12.
2. J. Beddow, *Proc. IEEE Conf. Visualization*, Oct. 1990, CS Press, Los Alamitos, Calif., pp. 238-246.
3. A. Inselberg and B. Dimsdale, *Proc. IEEE Conf. Visualization*, Oct. 1990, CS Press, Los Alamitos, Calif., pp. 361-375.
4. R.D. Bergeron and G. Grinstein, "A Reference Model for the Visualization of Multidimensional Data," *Proc. Eurographics 89*, North Holland, Amsterdam, 1989, pp. 393-399.
5. E.J. Farrel, "Visual Interpretation of Complex Data," *IBM Systems J.*, Vol. 26, No. 2, 1987, pp. 174-200.
6. S. Feiner and C. Beshers, "Visualizing n-Dimensional Virtual Worlds with n-Vision," *Computer Graphics*, Vol. 24, No. 2, March 1990, pp. 37-38.
7. E.R. Tufte, *The Visual Display of Quantitative Information*, Graphics Press, Cheshire, Ct., 1983.
8. G. Kolate, "Computer Graphics Comes to Statistics," *Science*, Vol. 217, Sept. 1982, pp. 919-920.
9. R.C.T. Lee, J.R. Slagle, and H. Blum, *IEEE Trans. Computers*, Vol. C-26, No. 3, March 1977, pp. 288-292.
10. J. LeBlanc, M.O. Ward, and N. Wittels, *Proc. Visualization 90*, Oct. 1990, CS Press, Los Alamitos, Calif., pp. 230-237.
11. T. Mihalisin, "Graphing in Multiple Dimensions with MGTS," *Suntech J.*, Vol. 3, No. 1, Winter 1990, pp. 25-31.

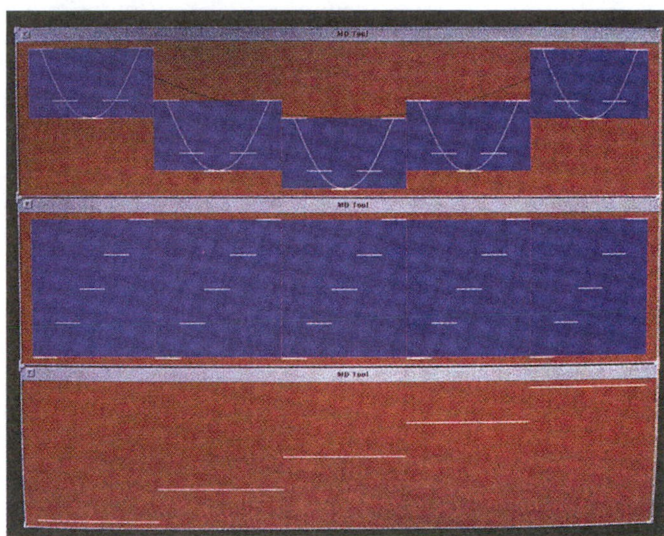

FIGURE 1

The top panel shows $D = x^2 + y^2$, the middle panel shows x variation, and the bottom panel shows y variation.

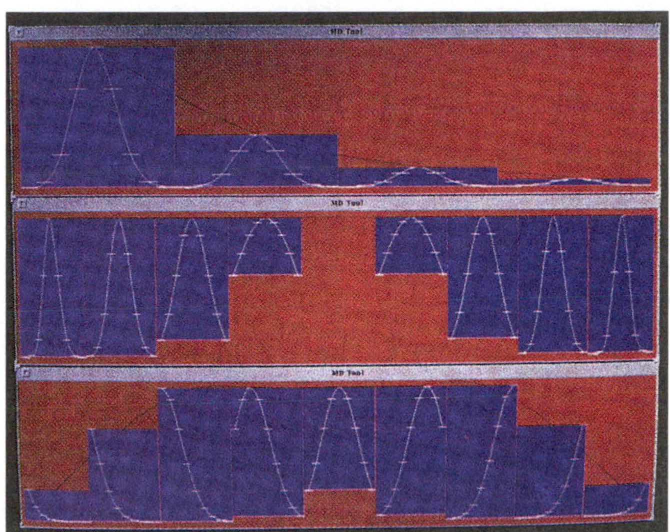

FIGURE 2

Amplitude modulation (AM), frequency modulation (FM), and phase modulation (PM) functions appear in the top, middle, and bottom panels, respectively.

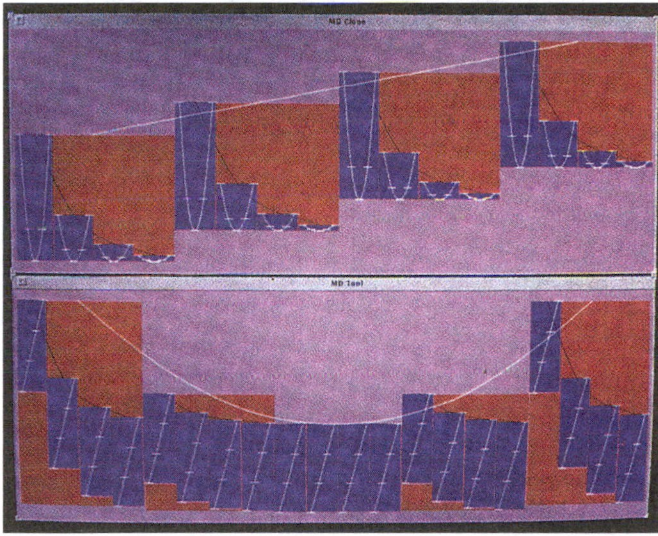

FIGURE 3

Plot of $D = x^2e^{-y} + z$ with x (white) fastest and z (red) slowest in the top panel and with z (white) fastest and x (red) slowest in the bottom panel.

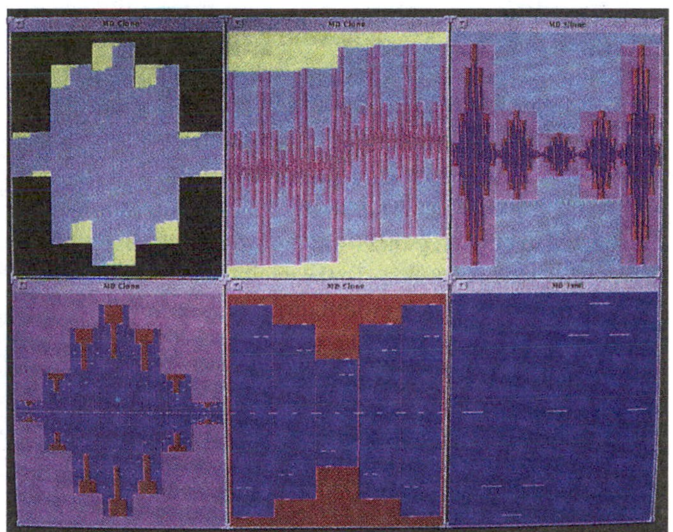

FIGURE 4

$D = -y^2[\arctan(t) + (1 + v^2)(e^{-r^2}) \cdot (1 + b^2)\sin(w)]$ in the upper left panel and 6D, 5D, 4D, 3D, and 2D subspaces (see the explanation in text).

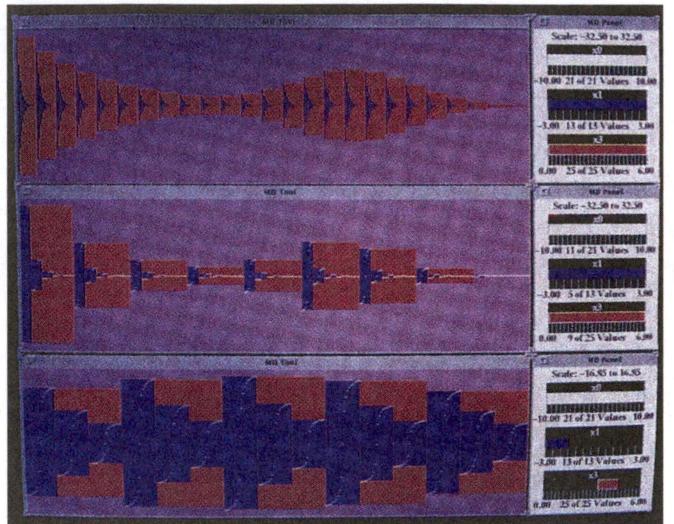

FIGURE **5**

Full data set (top), decimated data set (middle), and zoomed view (bottom). See the explanation in text.

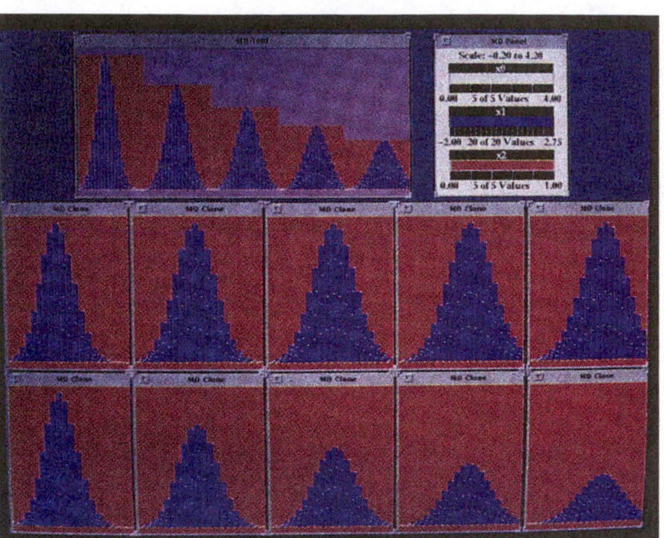

FIGURE **6**

Plot of $D = we^{-r(b-r)^2}e^{-r}$ and the white, blue, and red widgets (top); animation frames for varying red with autoscaling on (middle); and animation frames for varying red with autoscaling off (bottom).

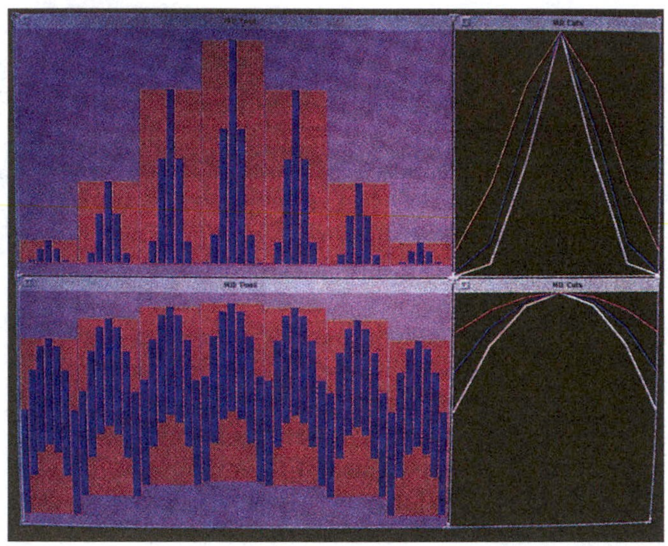

FIGURE **7**

$D = e^{-w^2}e^{-2b^2}e^{-3r^2}$ and expansion of D in white, blue, and red directions at the maximum point (0,0,0,) with a linear D scale (top) and a logarithmic D scale (bottom).

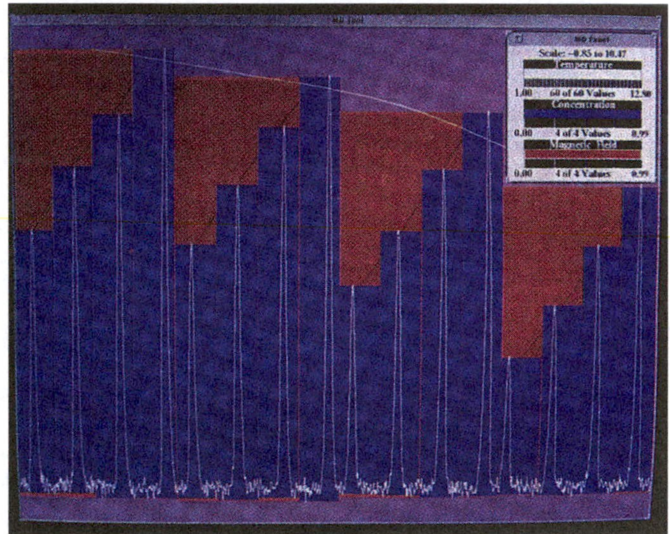

FIGURE **8**

Specific heat versus temperature in white, alloy concentration in blue, and magnetic field in red.

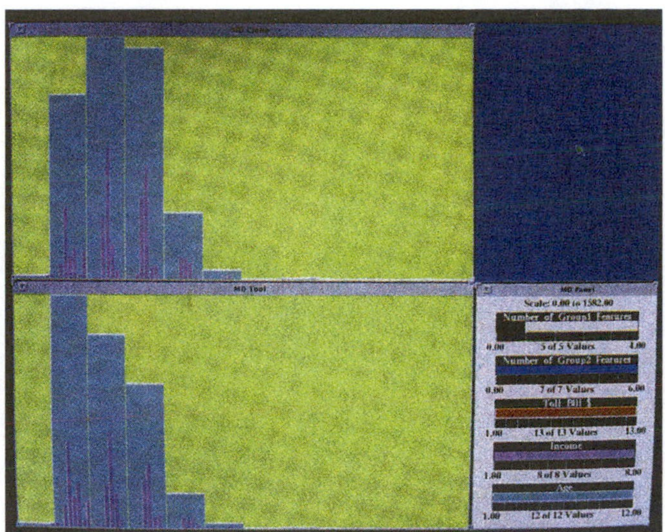

FIGURE **9**

Distributions of households by five categorical variables (see text for explanation).

FIGURE **10**

$D = x^2 + u^2 + y^2 + v^2$ plotted using the two hierarchical axes techniques (see text).

VisDB: Database Exploration Using Multidimensional Visualization

Daniel A. Keim and Hans-Peter Kriegel
University of Munich

In this system, each display pixel represents one database item. Pixels are arranged and colored to indicate the item's relevance to a user query and to give a visual impression of the resulting data set.

Scientific, engineering, and environmental databases can contain data collected automatically and continuously via sensors and, for example, satellite monitoring systems. Finding the data you want in these very large databases—with tens of thousands or even millions of data items—can be very difficult. Even researchers experienced in using a database and query system have trouble "mining" these databases for the interesting data sets. Users who do not know the data and its distribution exactly might need dozens of queries to get started.

The query specification process is the core of the problem. With today's database systems and query interfaces, users must issue queries one at a time. Generally, you cannot change a query slightly or express vague queries. Most importantly, you get no feedback on the query except in the form of the resulting data set—which may contain either no data items, and thus no hint for continuing the search, or too many data items to browse efficiently.

Researchers have developed many approaches to improve the database query interface so that it gives better feedback when the query yields unexpected results. For example, graphical database interfaces let users browse the data visually.[1,2] These interfaces either sort the data for users or provide direct hypertext-like access to more detailed versions of it. Another approach uses cooperative database interfaces[3] that try to give "approximate answers" when the original queries do not provide a satisfactory answer. This approach employs such techniques as query generalization, which drops or relaxes a selection predicate when the original queries fail, and statistical approximations or intensional responses—instead of full enumeration—when the query results are very large. Joshi, Kaplan, and Lee[4] first presented the key ideas for these techniques. Cooperative systems mainly help the user understand the results and refine erroneous queries; they do not help find interesting properties of the data such as functional dependencies, local correlations, or exceptional data items.

Information retrieval is another area that relates to our work. A lot of research in this area has been done to improve recall and precision in querying databases of unstructured data such as full text. For example, one approach employs user-provided relevance assessments of results to rerank the results or rerun adapted queries.[5]

The VisDB system supports the query specification process by representing the result visually. The main idea behind the system stems from the view of relational database tables as sets of multidimensional data where the number of attributes corresponds to the number of dimensions. In such a view, it is often unclear which dimensions are independent and which are dependent. In most cases, only a limited number of the dimensions are of interest in a certain context. In the VisDB system, we therefore restrict the number of visualized dimensions to those that are part of the query. In other words, the dimensionality of our visualizations corresponds to the number of selection predicates.

Researchers have proposed many approaches to visualizing arbitrary multivariate, multidimensional data. The well-known books of Bertin[6] and Tufte[7] include many examples. More recent techniques include shape coding,[8] worlds within worlds,[9] parallel coordinates,[10] iconic displays,[11,12] dimensional stacking,[13] hierarchical plotting,[14] and dynamic methods.[15] In developing a system to handle databases consisting of tens of thousands to millions of data items, our goal is to visualize as many data items as possible while, at the same time, giving the user some kind of feedback on the query. The obvious limit for any kind of visualization is the resolution of current displays, which is on the order of one to three million pixels. For example, our 19-inch displays with a resolution of $1,024 \times 1,280$ pixels has about 1.3 million pixels.

To explore large data sets efficiently, a system must be interactive. Empirical studies show that interactive, slider-based interfaces considerably improve efficiency and accuracy in accessing databases.[16] Equally important is the possibility of getting immediate feedback on the modified query. By playing with such a system, users can learn more about the data than they can by issuing hundreds of queries.

A new query paradigm

In today's database systems, users specify queries in a one-by-one fashion. This is adequate if you can specify the desired data exactly and access a clearly separated data set. Many database applications work this way. For example, accounting and reservation systems base their queries on keys that access the desired data exactly. If you search transactions for a specific account, the resulting data set is clearly separated. Therefore, one query generally suffices to get the desired data.

In other application areas, however, especially those with very large data volumes such as scientific, engineering, and environmental databases, it is often difficult to find the desired data. Problems occur if the database contains data different from what the user expects or if the user does not know exactly what to look for. In the latter case, querying the database is like an inexact search. If a query does not provide the desired result, the user must query the database again, usually by a similar query that differs in just one detail. Often, the user must issue many similar queries before finding the desired result.

Users have problems in querying a database when they do not know the database system, the data model and query language, or the database schema. But even if they have perfect knowledge in all these domains—that is, their queries are both syntactically and semantically correct—users can still get query results that do not correspond to their intentions, simply because they do not know the specific data in the database. In this case, they will find it very difficult to estimate the amount of data that will be retrieved, especially for range queries and complex queries with many selection predicates.

The VisDB query interface uses visualization techniques to give users more feedback on their query results. For example, environmental scientists searching a huge database of test series for significant values might be looking for some correlation between multiple dimensions for a specific period of time and geographic region. Since none of the query parameters is fixed, finding the desired information is generally very difficult. Therefore, researchers might start by specifying one query that corresponds to some assumption, but they might not find an interesting correlation until they issue many refined queries and apply statistical methods to the results.

The VisDB system simplifies the query specification process. To begin, users still have to specify one query. Then, guided by the visual feedback, they can interactively change the query according to the impression they get from the visualized results. In exploring very large databases, the visualization of results coupled with the means of incrementally refining the query offer an effective way to find interesting data properties.

The key idea of VisDB is to use the phenomenal capabilities of the human vision system for analyzing midsize amounts of data efficiently and immediately recognizing patterns that would be difficult, even impossible, for computers to find. One major research challenge is to find visualization techniques that support the user in analyzing and interpreting large amounts of multidimensional data.

Visualizing large data sets of multidimensional data

The basic idea underlying our visualization techniques is to use each pixel of the screen to visualize the data items resulting from a query. The query results thus give the user not only the data items fulfilling the query but also a number of data items that approximately fulfill the query. The approximate results are determined by calculating distances for each selection predicate and combining them into the *relevance factor*. The distance functions are data-type and application dependent, so the application must provide them. Example distance functions include the numerical difference (for metric types), distance matrices (for ordinal and nominal types), and lexicographical, character, substring, or phonetic difference (for strings). The sidebar titled "Calculating the relevance factors" describes important aspects of this procedure.

Basic visualization technique

Our basic technique for visually displaying the data on screen is to sort them according to their relevance with respect to the query and to map the relevance factors to colors. The sorting is necessary to avoid completely sprinkled images that would not help the user understand the data. One question in designing the VisDB system was how to arrange the relevance factors on the screen. We tried several arrangements such as top-down, left-

Calculating the relevance factors

The procedure for calculating relevance factors addresses the issues described here.

Calculating the distance. The first step is to determine the distance between the attribute and the corresponding query values for each data item. The distance functions used in this step are data-type and application dependent. In some cases, even for a single data type, multiple distance functions can be useful.

For number types such as integer or real and other metric types such as date, we can determine the distance of two values easily by their numerical difference. For nonmetric types such as enumerations with a noninterpretable distance between values (ordinal types such as grades) or with noncomparable values (nominal types such as professions), there is no obvious way to determine the distance. For ordinal types, the distance might be defined by some domain-specific distance function or by a distance matrix containing the distances for all pairs of values. A distance matrix can also be useful for nominal types, but even a constant value can be an adequate distance in some cases. There are many possibilities for calculating the distance of string data types. Depending on the application and the retrieval context, the user might want to choose between lexicographical, character, substring, or even some kind of phonetic distance.

Combining distances into the relevance factor. The next step combines the independently calculated distances of the different selection predicates. This is not straightforward, however, because we must consider the distances for the different selection predicates with respect to the distances of the other selection predicates.

One problem is that the relative importance of the multiple selection predicates is highly user and query dependent. Only user interaction can solve this because only the user can determine the priority of the selection predicates. Therefore, the user must provide weighting factors w_j, representing the order of importance of the selection, where $j \in 1, \ldots, \#sp$, and #sp is the number of selection predicates.

A second problem is that the values calculated by the distance functions may be in completely different orders of magnitude. For example, in a medical application, a distance of 1 gram per deciliter for hemoglobin may be very high, and a distance of 1,000 erythrocytes per deciliter may be very small. We solve this problem by normalizing the distances. We can define a simple normalization as a linear transformation of the range (d_{min}, d_{max}) for each selection predicate to a fixed range such as (0, 255).

For combining the independently calculated and normalized distances of multiple selection predicates into a single distance value, we use numerical mean functions such as the weighted arithmetic mean for AND-connected condition parts and the weighted geometric mean for OR-connected condition parts. More exactly, for each data item x_i the combined distance is calculated as

$$\text{Combined Distance}_i = \sum_{j=1}^{\#sp} w_j * d_{ij} \text{ in case of 'AND'}$$

$$\text{Combined Distance}_i = \prod_{j=1}^{\#sp} d_{ij}^{\,w_j} \text{ in case of 'OR'},$$

After calculating the combined distance for the whole condition, we determine the relevance factor as the inverse of that distance value. The relevance factor thus combines information on how well a data item approximates the query into one value representing a data item's relevance with respect to the query.

Note that special applications may use other specific distance functions, such as the Euclidean, L^p, or Mahalanobis distance in n-dimensional space, to determine the distances of multiple selection predicates.

Reducing the amount of data to be displayed. Since the number of data items in the database may be much higher than the number of data items that can be displayed on screen, we had to find adequate heuristics to reduce the amount of data and to determine the data items whose relevance should be displayed. The most exact way uses a statistical parameter, namely, the α-quantile. The α-quantile is defined as the lowest value ξ_α such that

$$F(\xi_\alpha) = \int_{-\infty}^{\xi_\alpha} f(x)dx = \alpha$$

where $0 \le \alpha \le 1$, $F(x)$ is the distribution function and $f(x)$ is the density function.

Let r be the number of distance values that fit on the screen, #sp the number of selection predicates, and n the number of data items in the database. Then only data items with an absolute distance in the range $[0, r/(n * (\#sp + 1))$-quantile] are presented to the user. If negative and positive distance values are used, then the range of values presented to the user is given by $[\alpha_0 * (1 - p)$-quantile, $(\alpha_0 * (1 - p) + p)$-quantile] where $p = r/(n * (\#sp + 1))$ and α_0 is determined by α_0-quantile = 0.

In the special case of two dimensions assigned to the two axes, we can use the combined α-quantiles for two dimensions. For the grouping arrangement, the number of data items that can be displayed on the screen is lower since each data value requires multiple pixels.

to-right, and centered, and found that arrangements with the highest relevance factors centered in the middle of the window seemed the most natural. As shown in Figure 1, we color the 100-percent-correct answers yellow and place them in the middle of the visualization with the approximate answers creating a rectangular spiral around this region.

The colors range from yellow to green, blue, red, and almost black to denote increasing distance from the correct answers. We chose this color scale empirically (see the sidebar "Coloration of the relevance factors"). To relate the visualization of the over-

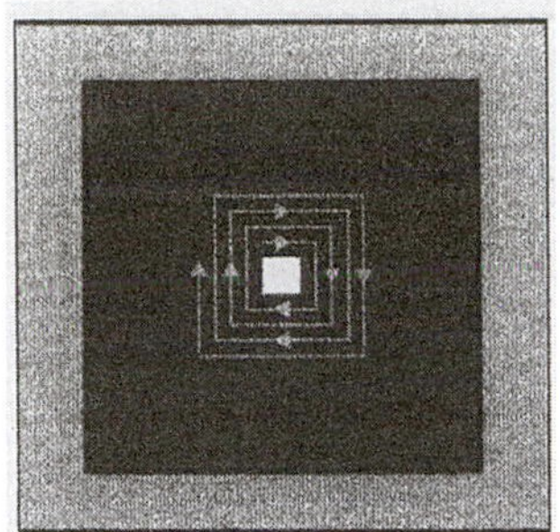

Figure 1. Spiral-shaped arrangement of one dimension.

Figure 2. Arrangement of windows for displaying five-dimensional data.

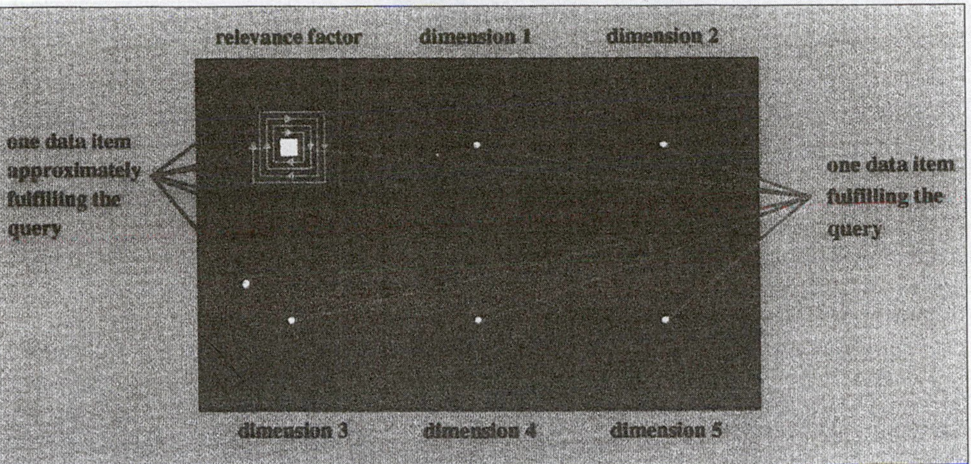

all result to visualizations of the different selection predicates (dimensions), we generate a separate window for each selection predicate of the query and arrange the windows next to each other, as shown in Figure 2. In the separate windows, we place the pixels for each data item at the same relative position as they appear for that data item in the overall result window.

All the windows together make up the multidimensional visualization. By relating corresponding regions in the different windows, the user can perceive data characteristics such as multidimensional clusters or correlations. Additionally, the separate windows for each selection predicate provide important feedback to the user, for example, on the restrictiveness of each selection predicate and on exceptional data items.

Mapping two dimensions to the axes

We also experimented with other screen arrangements of the data items. One straightforward idea was to display the data in 2D or 3D with selected dimensions assigned to the axes. Such arrangements, however, can cause many data items to concentrate in one screen area while other areas remain virtually empty. These arrangements can also cause some data items to be superimposed on others, thereby making the latter items invisible.

Although 2D or 3D visualizations might be helpful in cases where the data have some inherent 2D or 3D semantics, we did not pursue this idea for several reasons. First, in most cases, the number of data items that can be represented on the screen at the same time is quite limited. This conflicted with our goal of presenting as many data items as possible on screen. Second, in most cases where a 2D or 3D arrangement of the data really makes sense, systems using such arrangements have already been built. For example, a 2D visualization is obviously the best support for spatial queries of 2D data, and basically all geographical information systems provide such visual data representations.

However, for all cases where no inherent 2D or 3D semantics of the data exists, our visualization technique can provide valuable visual feedback when querying the database. We decided to improve our interface by including some feedback on the direction of the distance into the visualization. We assigned two dimensions to the axes and arranged the relevance factors according to the direction of the distance. As shown in Figure 3 on the next page, we arrange negative distances to the left and positive distances to the right for one axis dimension; for the other

Coloration of the relevance factors

Visualizing the relevance factors using color corresponds to the task of mapping a color scale to a single parameter distribution. The advantage of color over gray scales is that the number of just noticeable differences (JNDs) is much higher. The main task is to find a path through color space that maximizes the number of JNDs but is, at the same time, intuitive for the application domain.[1]

In designing the VisDB system, we experimented with different color maps. We found that coloration has a high impact on the system's intuitivity. The user may, for example, implicitly connect good answers with light colors and bad answers with dark colors, or green colors with good answers and red colors with bad answers (like the colors used for traffic lights). We tried many variations of the color map to enhance the usefulness of our system and selected a color map with constant saturation, increasing value (intensity), and hue (color) ranging from yellow over green, blue, and red to almost black to denote the distance from the correct answers.

The color model used in the VisDB system is a variation of the hue, saturation, value (HSV) model. Instead of the hexcone in the HSV model, we use a circular cone with the intensity defined as the Euclidean distance to the black axis and the saturation defined as the Euclidean distance to the gray axis. In the HSV model, both parameters are determined by using the maximum of (r, g, b). In contrast to color scales generated according to the HSV model, our model provides color scales whose lightness ranges continuously from light to dark colors.

Since the usefulness of color maps varies depending on the user and the application, the VisDB system lets users define their own color maps and employ them instead of our standard color map.

Reference

1. G.T. Herman and H. Levkowitz, "Color Scales for Image Data," *IEEE CG&A*, Vol. 12, No. 1, Jan. 1992, pp. 72-80.

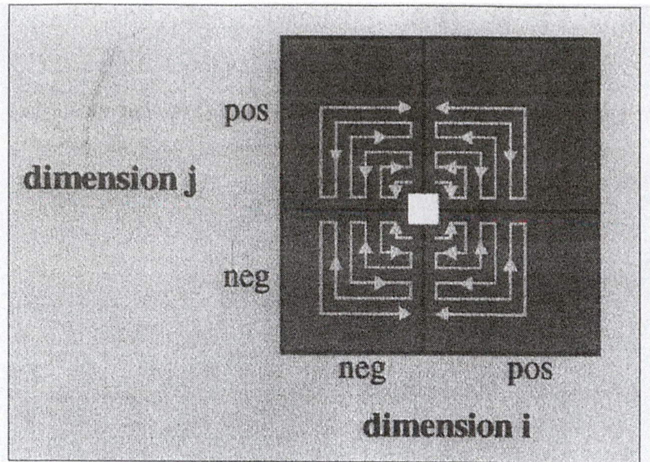

Figure 3. 2D arrangement of one dimension

Figure 4. Grouping for five-dimensional data.

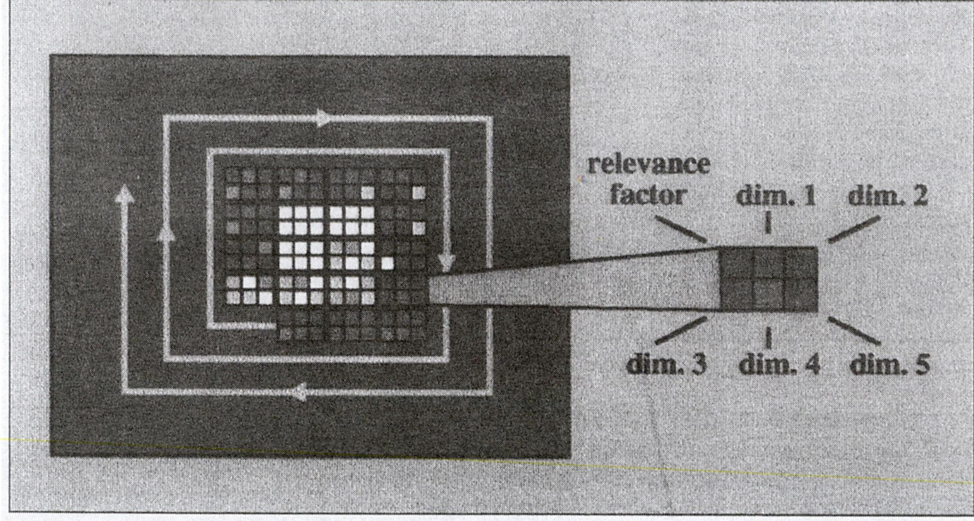

axis dimension, negative distances are to the bottom and positive ones to the top.

With this kind of representation, we do not show the distance of data items directly by their location. Instead, we denote the absolute value of their distance by color and their direction by the location relative to the correct answers (colored yellow). Thus, each data item can be assigned to one pixel, and no overlay occurs between data items with the same distance. A problem may arise in some special cases, for example, if there are no data items having a negative distance for both axis dimensions but there are many data items having a negative distance for one axis dimension and a positive distance for the other. In this case, the bottom left corner of the window would be completely empty.

In the worst case, two diagonally opposite corners of the window could be completely empty and, as a result, only half as many data items as possible presented to the user. Even in this case, the user gets valuable information on how to change the query to get more or fewer results.

Grouping the dimensions

In both the original and 2D arrangements, the pixels corresponding to the different dimensions of one data item are distributed in different windows for each dimension. In contrast, the grouping arrangement places all dimensions for one data item in one area. The idea of grouping the dimensions into one area is similar to the shape-coding approach described in Beddow.[8] In our approach, however, we do not focus on shape to distinguish the data items, and we manage the criterion and arrangement of the data items differently. As shown in Figure 4, we arrange each area in a rectangular spiral shape according to the combined relevance factor of the considered data items. The coloring of distances for the different dimensions can be the same as in the original or 2D arrangement. The generated visualizations, however, are completely different.

Preliminary experiments show that the grouping arrangement requires more pixels per data value. In the original and 2D arrangements, we used one pixel per dimension per data item. Empirical tests show that the grouping arrangement requires an area of at least 2×2 pixels per dimension per data item for the visualization to provide useful results (3×3 or 4×4 pixels provide better results). This implies that only one-fourth (or even one-ninth or one-sixteenth) of the data items can be displayed on screen at one time, making the grouping arrangement suitable only for a focused search on smaller data sets. Note that this arrangement also calls for additional pixels in the area surrounding each data item. Otherwise, it would be impossible to know which pixels belong to which data item.

Even though it may visualize fewer data items, the grouping arrangement provides more useful visualizations for data sets with larger dimensionality. In the original and 2D arrangements, the pixels for each dimension of the data items are related only by their position. For relatively small dimensionality (fewer than eight dimensions), humans seem to relate the different portions of the screen quite easily. The higher the dimensionality, the more difficult it becomes. The grouping arrangement does not require the user to make these correlations and therefore seems advantageous for larger dimensionalities.

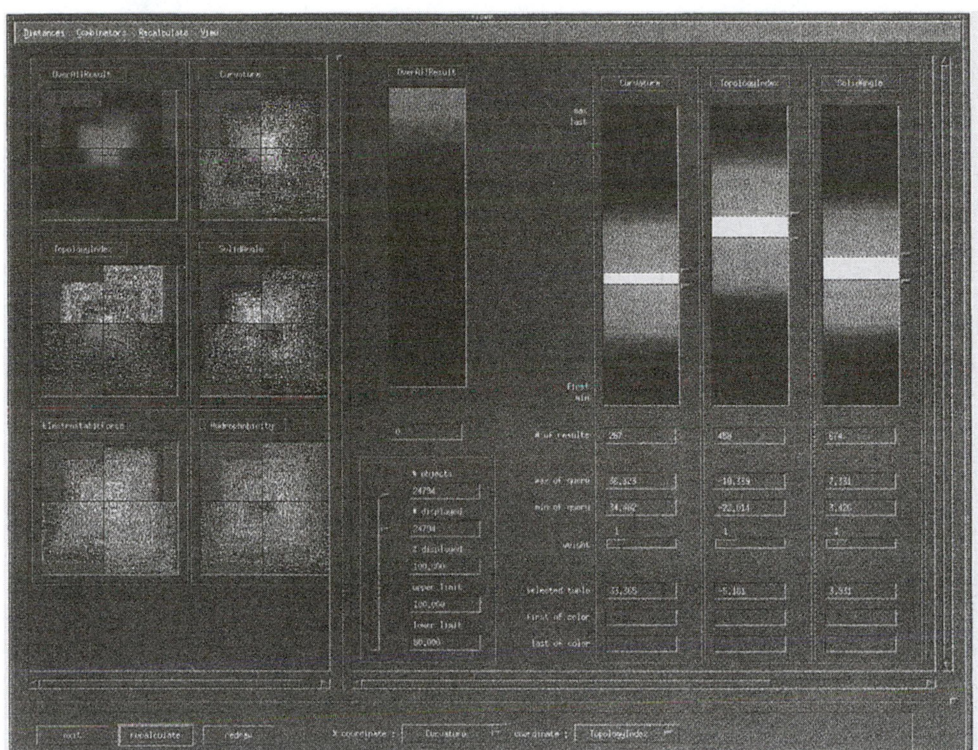

Figure 5. The VisDB system interface.

For example, sliders for non-metric types (ordinal and nominal data types) can display enumerations of the possible values and allow users to select the values. Users can design special sliders for special data types and distance functions, such as strings with different distance functions.

Below the three sliders on the far right, the interface lists several parameter fields for each selection predicate, namely, the number of results, query range (min and max), weighting factors, data values of a selected tuple, and data values corresponding to a selected color range (first and last). The possibility of correlating data values to some color or color range for each selection predicate might help the user understand the visualization and modify the query accordingly. Users can focus on sets of data items with a specific color by selecting a color range with one of the sliders. VisDB will then retrieve only those data items in the corresponding visualization window that have the selected color for the considered attribute. The other visualization windows will also display these same data items, allowing the user to easily compare the values of the other attributes of those data items.

Also helpful in understanding the visualization and finding interesting data spots is the possibility of selecting a specific data item in one of the visualization windows, highlighting it in all visualization windows, and displaying the values for the attributes in the selected tuple field. This option lets the user focus on exceptional data items or get an example of a data item from an interesting region in one of the windows.

Below the color spectrum for the overall result, there are fields for the number of data items in the database, the number of data items displayed in the visualization window (absolute value and percentage), and the number of resulting data items presented to the user. Using a slider, the user can change the percentage of data displayed or the allowed range. (In the latter case, the percentage is determined using the heuristics described in the sidebar "Calculating the relevance factors.") Changing the percentage of data displayed can completely change the visualization, since the distance values are normalized according to the new range.

In the normal mode, the system recalculates the visualization after each query modification. The user also has the option of having the system recalculate queries only on demand. This option is useful for large databases with many data items or for complex distance functions that take a considerable amount of time to recalculate. Other menu options let the user choose dif-

Interactive data exploration

To give users immediate feedback on query changes, VisDB needs dynamic query modification capabilities. The visualizations provide feedback on the amount of data retrieved, the restrictiveness of conditions, the distribution of distances for each condition, and special areas the user might be interested in. For example, if the yellow region in the middle of each window grows larger, it means that more data items are fulfilling the condition (and vice versa). If a window becomes darker, the corresponding selection predicate is becoming more restrictive. If the overall structure changes, the distribution of distances for the corresponding selection predicate is changing, and so on. These visual indicators help users understand the effects of query modifications quickly and learn more about the data in the database, especially in the context of large databases with millions of data items.

In the VisDB system, users initially specify their queries through graphical user interfaces such as Gradi[2] or traditional query languages such as SQL. As a result of this query, they get the VisDB interactive query and visualization interface shown in Figure 5. The interface features a "Visualization" portion on the left and a "Query Modification" portion on the right. The Visualization portion displays the data set resulting from the query, including a certain percentage of approximate answers, by using one of the three visualization methods described in the previous section.

The Query Modification portion provides sliders for modifying the selection predicates and weighting factors as well as some other options. Different kinds of sliders are available for different data types and distance functions. Sliders for numbers, for example, allow graphical manipulations of either the lower and upper limits or the medium value and some specified deviation. Sliders for discrete types reflect the discrete nature of the data by allowing only discrete movements of the slider.

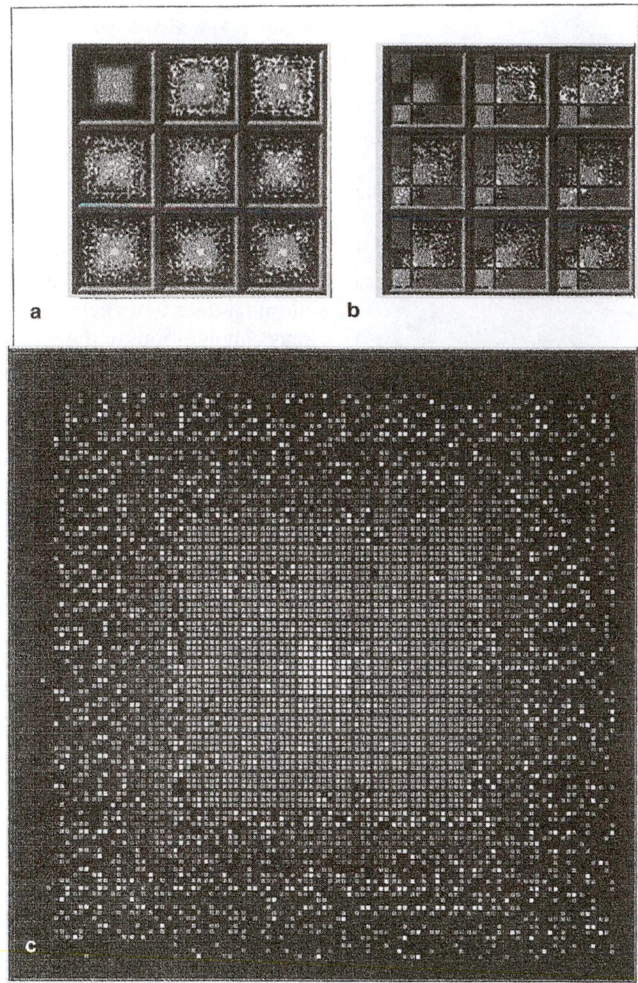

Figure 6. Eight-dimensional data displayed with the three different visualization methods (1,000 data items): (a) basic visualization technique, (b) 2D arrangement, and (c) grouping arrangement.

Figure 7. Eight-dimensional data displayed with the three different visualization methods (7,000 data items): (a) basic visualization technique, (b) 2D arrangement, and (c) grouping arrangement.

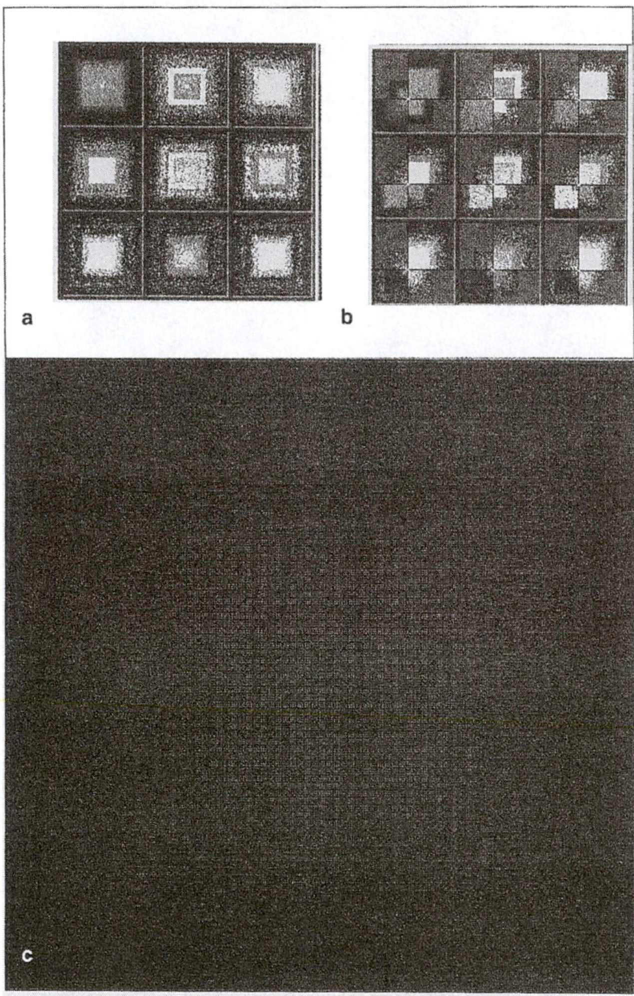

ferent distance or combinator functions, select a different visualization technique or slider type, add or delete selection predicates, extend the query, or issue a new query.

Examples

Figures 5 through 8 display several visualizations of query results. We generated the visualization in Figure 5 by using surface point data from a large molecule complex (subtilisin carlsberg with eglin). In our molecular biology project, we have used the VisDB system to find regions where molecules can dock by identifying sets of surface points with distinct characteristics.

In evaluating our visualization techniques, we currently explore other data sets including a large database of geographical data, a large environmental database, a NASA earth observation database, and artificially generated data sets. Artificial data sets are crucial for comparing different visualization techniques to find their strengths and weaknesses.[17] They let us vary the number of data items, number of dimensions, and data properties (for example, the distribution of each dimension and the number and size of clusters) for controlled comparisons.

The visualizations displayed in Figures 6 through 8 use artificially generated data consisting of a uniformly distributed base data set and multiple clusters. The data set used for Figure 6 consists of 1,000 eight-dimensional data items with five clusters. The data set used for Figure 7 is similar, except it consists of 7,000 data items. Figure 8 is generated from a database with 100,000 five-dimensional data items containing five clusters. In the visualizations, many regions of different colors are clearly identifiable and denote clusters of data items with a comparable distance. There are interesting correlations between the windows for different selection predicates. For example, regions that have a specific color in the window for one selection predicate have a different color in the window for another selection predicate. Corresponding regions with different colors denote clusters of data items with similar characteristics. The color of the region for some dimension corresponds to the cluster's distance from the reference region in that dimension.

In Figure 8, the red region for selection predicate 3 corresponds to the green region for selection predicate 2, which means there is a cluster of data items with distinct characteristics for these two dimensions. The colors denote the distance from the specified values for both dimensions, which is higher in the case

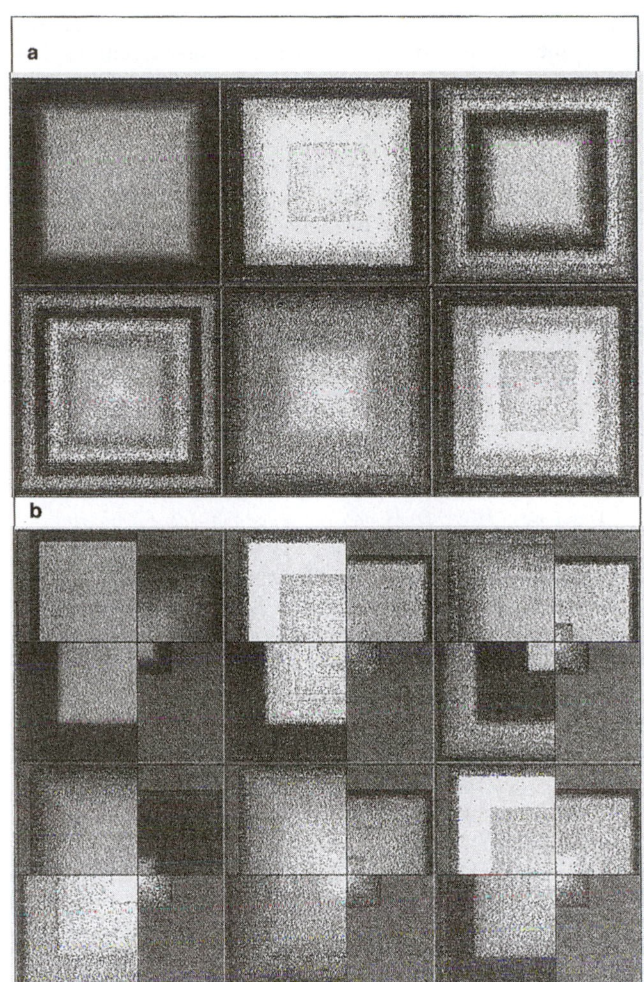

Figure 8. Five-dimensional artifically generated data items (100,000 data items): (a) basic visualization technique and (b) 2D arrangement.

of selection predicate 2, as indicated by the darker color (red).

Another interesting observation shows up in comparing the visualizations in Figure 7a and b and Figure 8a and b. The colored regions of the basic visualization technique often cluster in one quadrant of the 2D arrangement (for example, see the brown region for selection predicate 8 in Figure 7a and b). This provides additional information on the position of the cluster with respect to the two dimensions assigned to the axes. It might also help the user in modifying the query. Also interesting, but not easily identifiable in the printed version of our visualizations, are hot spots—that is, single exceptional data items in otherwise homogeneous regions.

Much of the information users get from the visualization is related to the data semantics. Due to space limitations, we do not elaborate on these aspects here. To do so would require introducing the schema and instances of the databases used. In the case of the artificial data sets, this would mean at least a specification of the base data set and all clusters.

The VisDB system is useful not only for such data mining tasks as finding hot spots, groups of similar data, and correlations among different dimensions. It also addresses such tasks as similarity retrieval and finding adequate query parameters and weighting factors. For example, in large CAD databases of 3D parts, it is not obvious how to formally describe similarity. Usually, there are many parameters describing the parts (in one real-world mechanical engineering application, we had 27 parameters), and each parameter might be important for a part to be similar. In CAD databases, you would issue a query searching for similar parts by using fixed allowances for some of the parameters. As a result, the query would get only the information concerning whether or not a data item fulfills all allowances. However, you could miss a part that exactly fits in all but one parameter. Therefore, in similarity retrieval, it seems important to provide approximate responses and let the user adjust the allowances and weighting parameters. Our system provides features that exactly support these tasks, making it a promising candidate for use in similarity retrieval.

Our system also helps find corresponding data items in multiple independent databases. If the user can define a distance function for the two attributes to be joined, our system may help identify closely related data items and find adequate parameters for approximately joining the databases.

Visualizing the results of complex queries

In addition to supporting simple one-table queries, where all selection predicates are connected by the same Boolean operator, our visualization techniques also support complex queries, such as queries with arbitrarily connected selection predicates (nested ANDs and ORs), multitable queries, and some types of nested queries (for details, see Keim, Kriegel, and Seidl[18]). VisDB uses multiple layers of windows for different parts of these queries. This gives users visual feedback for each part of the query and helps in understanding the overall result.

Multiple layers of windows are sufficient for queries with nested Boolean operators, but to support multitable and nested queries requires a mechanism for joining tables and dealing with the cross product. To support multitable queries, VisDB considers all data items of the cross product that approximately fulfill the join condition. The user obtains a separate window for the join condition wherein all data items of the cross product fulfilling the join condition are yellow and all others are colored according to their distance.

If tables are connected by foreign keys, it does not make sense to consider approximate results because the distances on foreign keys may not have any semantics. In such cases, VisDB considers only those data items that fulfill the join condition; it generates no visualization for the join condition. In many other cases, however, it is helpful to consider data items that approximately fulfill join conditions. For joins on numerical attributes, for example, we can use the numerical difference between the considered data items of the two relations as an approximation of the join condition to be fulfilled. In a similar way, we can determine the distances for non-equijoins ($a1 < a2$) or parametrized (non-equi)joins ($a1 - a2 < c$).

In the case of nested queries, VisDB provides separate visualizations for each selection predicate, including the subqueries involved. In the visualization corresponding to the overall result of a subquery, the user sees yellow when the subquery condition is fulfilled and otherwise the color corresponding to the distance of the data item most closely fulfilling the subquery condition. We determine the data item most closely fulfilling the subquery condition by the minimum distance resulting from an approximate join of the inner and the outer relation(s).

Instead of displaying a single value for the whole subquery, the system might give users the option of selecting a single data item and getting the complete subquery with all its selection predicates, including the join of inner and outer relation(s) presented in a separate window.

Implementation

The visualizations presented in Figures 5 through 8 are screen dumps from working with the VisDB system. We have implemented the system in C++/Motif running under X Windows on HP 7xx machines. The current version is main memory based and supports interactive database exploration for databases containing up to 50,000 data items (on HP 735 workstations). We find this performance very encouraging since we have not yet optimized our algorithms. The implementation runs into performance problems, however, when interfacing with current commercial database systems because they offer no access to partial query results and no support for incrementally changing queries. Nor do they use multidimensional data structures for fast secondary storage access.

We are currently working on improving the performance in directly interfacing with database systems. In the future, we plan to implement the VisDB system on a parallel machine that will support interactive query modifications even for midsize to large amounts of data and complex distance functions.

Future extensions

Inspired by our prototype, we have several ideas to extend the VisDB system. One extension is automatic generation of queries that correspond to some specific region in a visualization window. The user will identify the region graphically. The system will then find adequate selection predicates to provide the desired data items. Another idea is to generate time-series visualizations corresponding to queries changed incrementally. By changing the query, different portions of multidimensional space can be visualized, allowing even larger amounts of data to be displayed. To further improve our system, we intend to apply it to many different application domains, each having its own parameters, distance functions, query requirements, and so on. In addition to real-world data, we will also use artificially generated data sets that allow controlled studies on the effectiveness of our visualization techniques.

Conclusions

Visualization techniques can help researchers explore very large amounts of arbitrary, multidimensional data and find interesting data sets—hot spots, clusters of similar data, or correlations between different dimensions. Our approach to these "data mining" tasks combines traditional database querying and information retrieval with new data visualization techniques. The VisDB system can visualize at once the number of data values equal to the number of pixels on current displays, providing valuable feedback on the database query and helping users find results that would otherwise remain hidden. The system's interactivity lets users focus on interesting data.

We believe that query and visualization systems like ours are valuable for many applications. They may be the starting point for new visual solutions to problems that have proved very difficult. Querying large databases is just one example. ❑

Acknowledgments

We want to thank all the people who contributed to the VisDB system, especially Thomas Seidl, who implemented the first prototype of the system, and Juraj Porada, who implemented the current version.

References

1. A. Motro, "Flex: A Tolerant and Cooperative User Interface to Databases," *IEEE Trans. on Knowledge and Data Engineering*, Vol. 2, No. 2, 1990, pp. 231-246.
2. D.A. Keim and V. Lum, "Gradi: A Graphical Database Interface for a Multimedia DBMS," *Proc. Int'l Workshop on Interfaces to Database Systems*, in *Lecture Notes in Computer Science*, Springer, London, 1992, pp. 95-112.
3. S.J. Kaplan, "Cooperative Responses from a Portable Natural Language Query System," *Artificial Intelligence*, Vol. 19, 1982, pp. 165-187.
4. A.K. Joshi, S.J. Kaplan, and R.M. Lee, "Approximate Responses from a Data Base Query System: Applications of Inferencing in Natural Language," *Proc. 5th Int'l Joint Conf. on Artificial Intelligence*, 1977, pp. 211-212.
5. G. Salton and M.J. McGill, *Introduction to Modern Information Retrieval*, McGraw-Hill, New York, 1983.
6. J. Bertin, *Graphics and Graphic Information Processing*, Walter de Gruyer & Co., Berlin, 1981.
7. E.R. Tufte, *The Visual Display of Quantitative Information*, Graphics Press, Cheshire, Connecticut, 1983.
8. J. Beddow, "Shape Coding of Multidimensional Data on a Microcomputer Display," *Proc. Visualization 90*, IEEE Computer Society Press, Los Alamitos, Calif., 1990, pp. 238-246.
9. S. Feiner and C. Beshers, "Visualizing *n*-Dimensional Virtual Worlds with *n*-Vision," *Computer Graphics*, Vol. 24, No. 2, 1990, pp. 37-38.
10. A. Inselberg and B. Dimsdale, "Parallel Coordinates: A Tool for Visualizing Multidimensional Geometry," *Proc. Visualization 90*, IEEE CS Press, Los Alamitos, Calif., 1990, pp. 361-370.
11. R.M. Pickett and G.G. Grinstein, "Iconographic Displays for Visualizing Multidimensional Data," *Proc. IEEE Conf. on Systems, Man and Cybernetics*, IEEE Press, Piscataway, N.J. 1988, pp. 514-519.
12. R.D. Bergeron, L.D. Meeker, and T.M. Sparr, "Visualization-Based Model for a Scientific Database System," in *Focus on Scientific Visualization*, H. Hagen, M. Miller, and G. Nielson, eds., Springer, Berlin, 1992, pp. 103-121.
13. J. LeBlanc, M.O. Ward, and N. Wittels, "Exploring *N*-Dimensional Databases," *Proc. Visualization 90*, IEEE CS Press, Los Alamitos, Calif., 1990, pp. 230-239.
14. T. Mihalisin et al., "Visualizing Scalar Field on an *N*-dimensional

Lattice," *Proc. Visualization 90*, IEEE CS Press, Los Alamitos, Calif., 1990, pp. 255-262.

15. F. Marchak and D. Zulager, "Effectiveness of Dynamic Graphics in Revealing Structure in Multivariate Data," *Behavior, Research Methods, Instruments and Computers*, Vol. 24, No. 2, 1992, pp. 253-257.
16. B. Shneiderman, "Dynamic Queries for Visual Information Seeking," to appear in *IEEE Software*, 1994.
17. D. Bergeron, D.A. Keim, and R. Pickett, "Test Datasets for Evaluating Data Visualization Techniques," in *Perceptual Issues in Visualization*, G.G. Grinstein and H. Levkowitz, eds., Springer, Heidelberg, 1994.
18. D.A. Keim, H.-P. Kriegel, and T. Seidl, "Supporting Data Mining of Large Databases by Visual Feedback Queries," *Proc. 10th Int'l Conf. on Data Eng.*, IEEE CS Press, Los Alamitos, Calif., 1994, pp. 302-313.

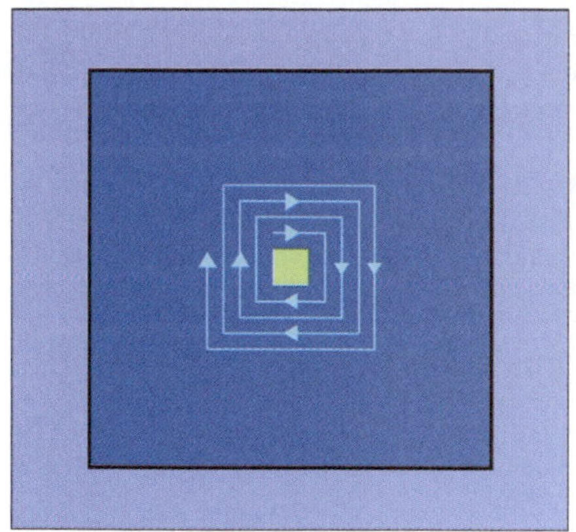

FIGURE 1

Spiral-shaped arrangement of one dimension.

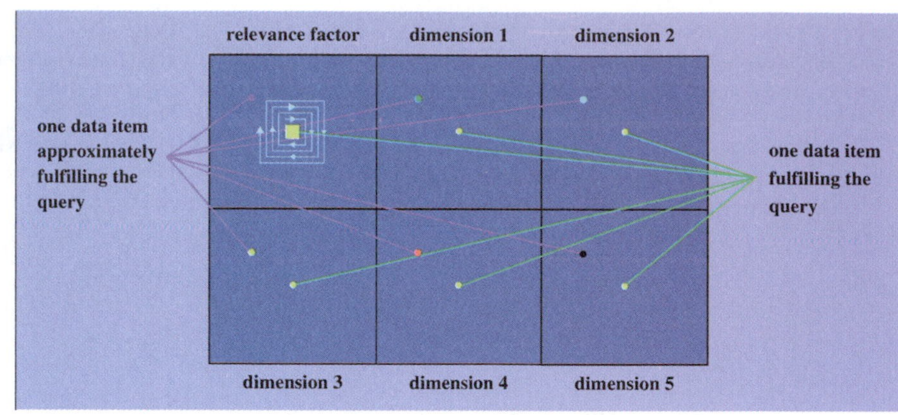

FIGURE 2

Arrangement of windows for displaying five-dimensional data.

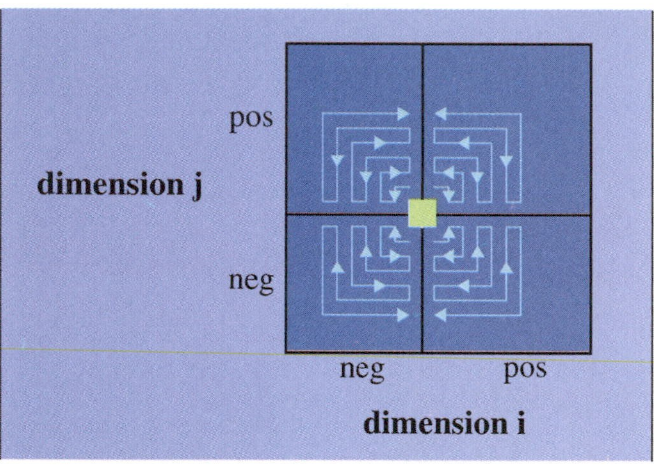

FIGURE 3

2D arrangement of one dimension.

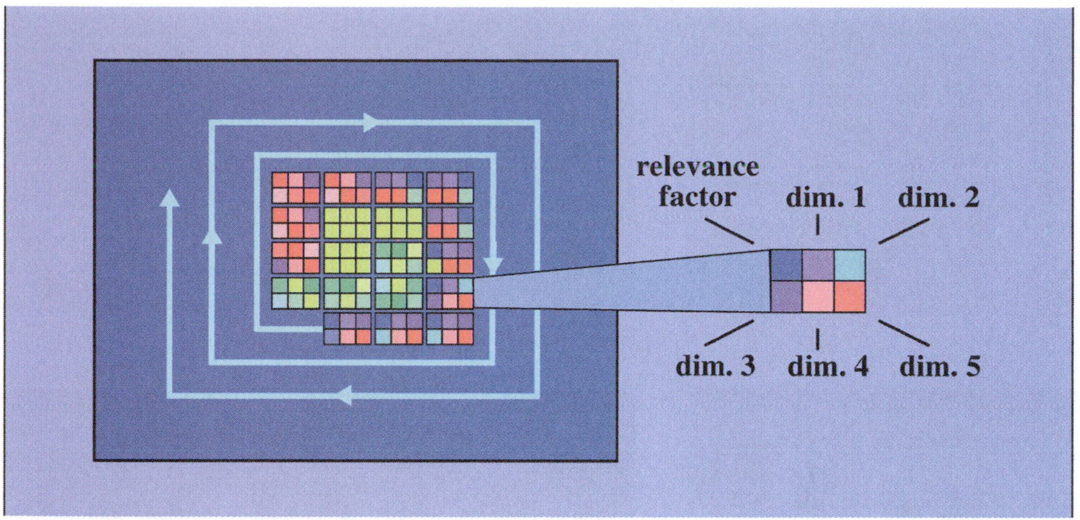

FIGURE 4

Grouping for five-dimensional data.

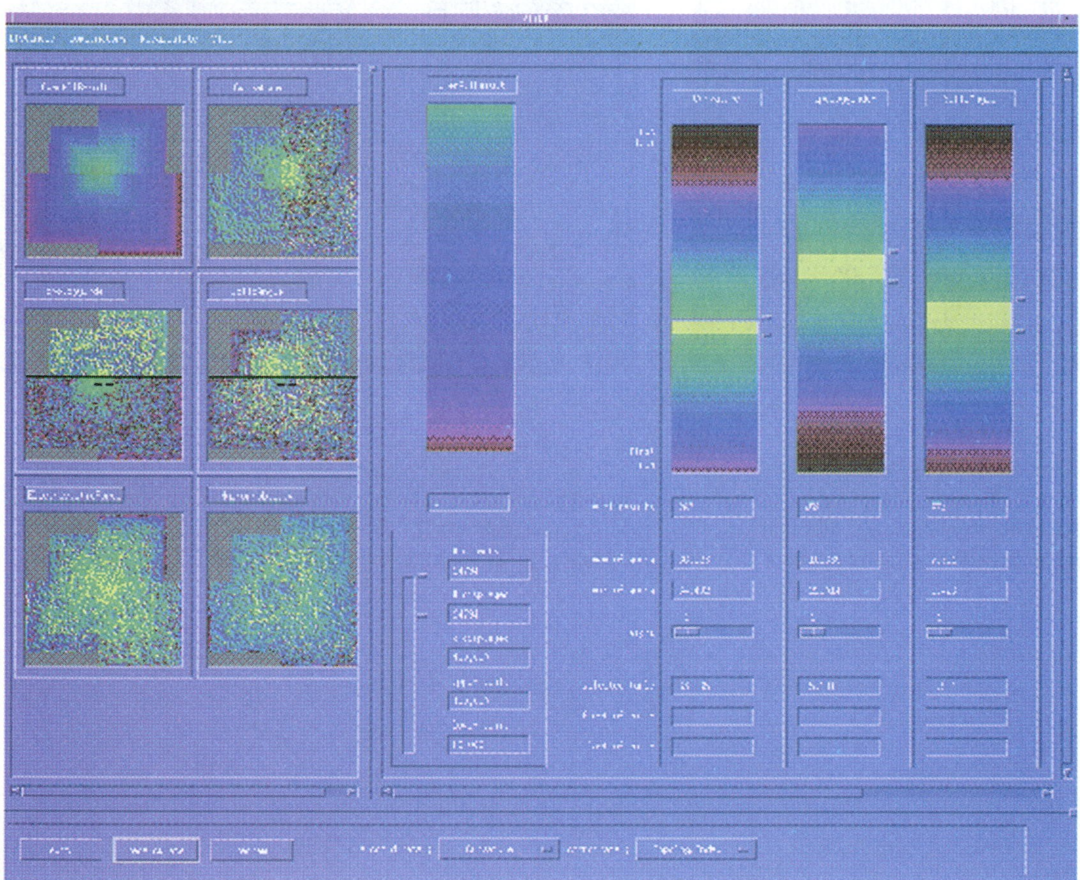

FIGURE 5

The VisDB system interface.

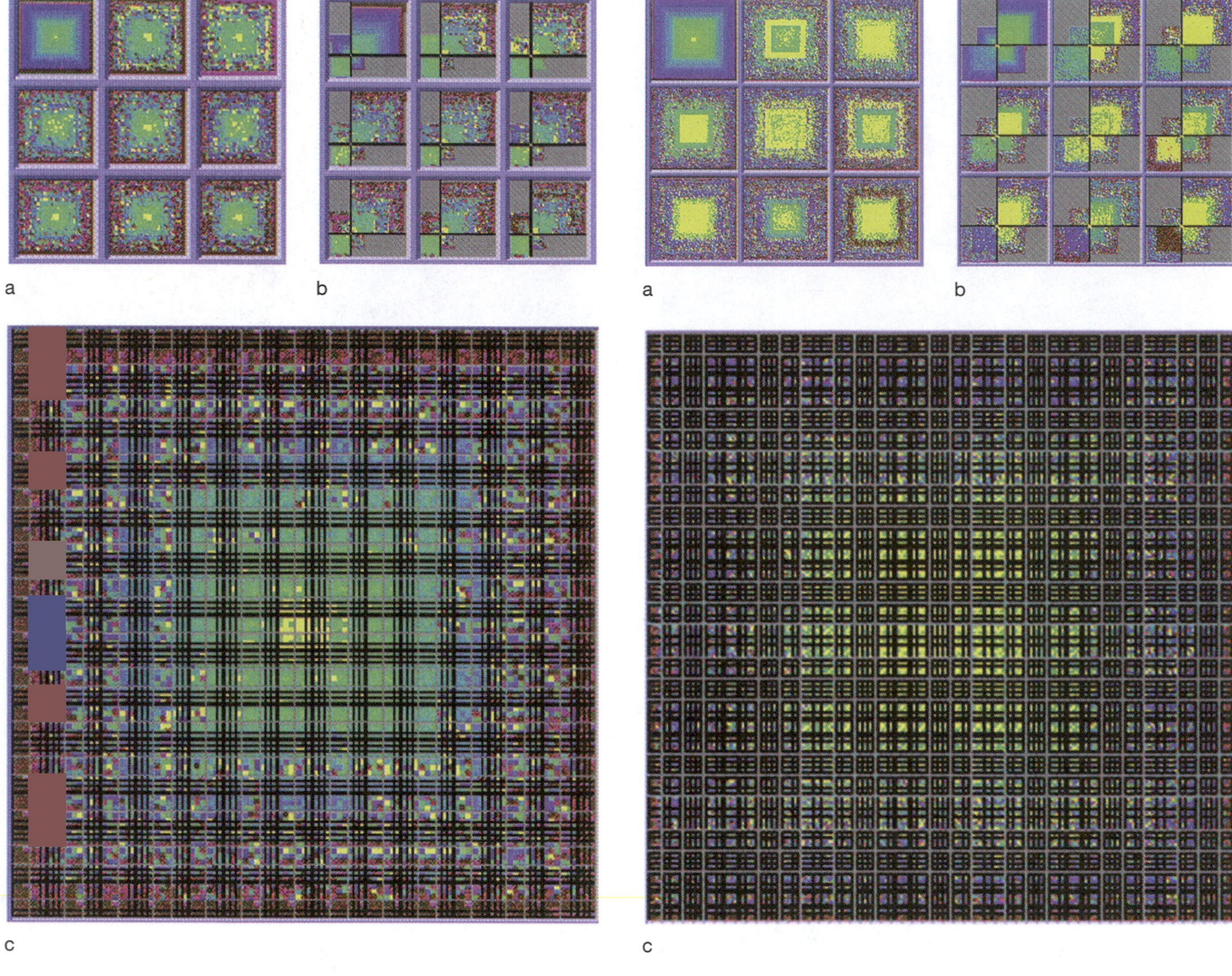

FIGURE 6

Eight-dimensional data displayed with the three different visualization methods (1,000 data item): (a) basic visualization technique, (b) 2D arrangement, and (c) grouping arrangement.

FIGURE 7

Eight-dimensional data displayed with the three different visualization methods (7,000 data items): (a) basic visualization technique, (b) 2D arrangement, and (c) grouping arrangement.

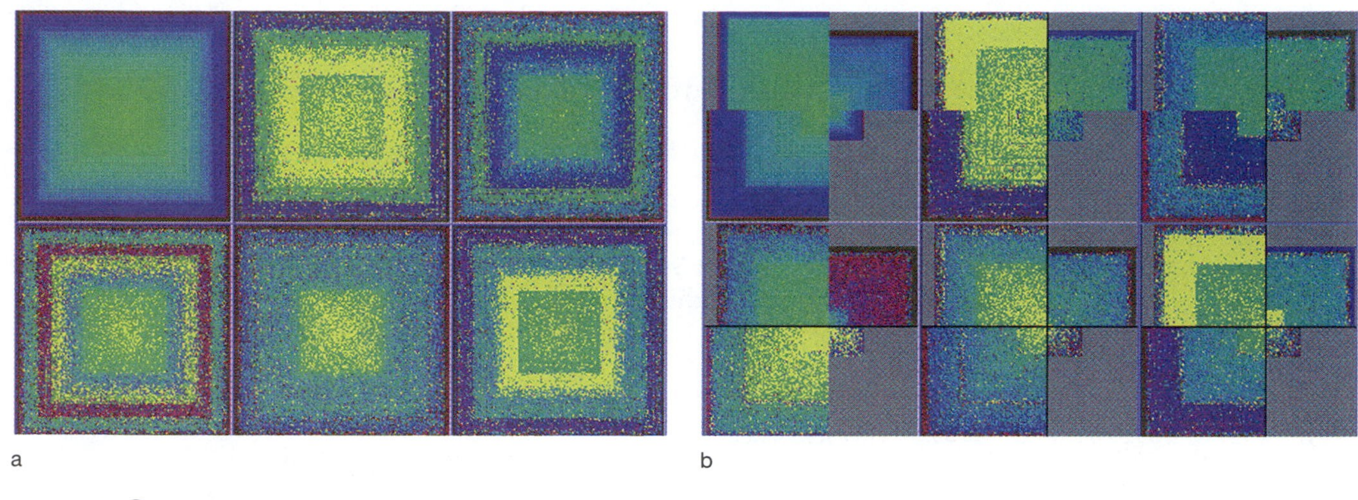

FIGURE 8

Five-dimensional artifically generated data items (100,000 data items): (a) basic visualization technique and (b) 2D arrangement.

InfoCrystal:

A visual tool for information retrieval

Anselm Spoerri

Center for Educational Computing Initiatives
Massachusetts Institute of Technology
Building E40-370, 1 Amherst Street, Cambridge, MA 02139
aspoerri@athena.mit.edu

Abstract

*This paper introduces a novel representation, called the **InfoCrystal™**, that can be used as a **visualization tool** as well as a **visual query language** to help users search for information. The InfoCrystal visualizes all the possible relationships among N concepts. Users can assign relevance weights to the concepts and use thresholding to select relationships of interest. The InfoCrystal allows users to specify **Boolean** as well as **vector-space** queries graphically. Arbitrarily complex queries can be created by using the InfoCrystals as building blocks and organizing them in a hierarchical structure. The InfoCrystal enables users to explore and filter information in a flexible, dynamic and interactive way.*

Keywords: Information visualization, visual query language, information retrieval, graphical user interface, human factors.

1.0 Introduction

Information is becoming available in ever growing quantities as the access possibilities to it proliferate. However, better methods are needed to filter the potentially unlimited influx of information. Researchers at Xerox PARC, for example, believe that managing large quantities of information will be the key to effective computer use in the 1990s and that visual interfaces that recode the information in progressively more abstract and simpler representations will play a central role [Card 91].

Recent work in scientific visualization shows how large data sets can be visualized in such a way that humans can detect patterns that reveal the underlying structure in the data more readily than a direct analysis of the numbers would. Similarly, information visualization seeks to display structural relationships between documents and their context that would be more difficult to detect by individual retrieval requests [Card 91].

Most of the visualization problems that are currently being investigated involve continuous, multi-variate fields that vary over space and time. Hence, the transformation problem is simplified, because the data has an explicit spatial structure that can be exploited. This paper, however, will address the problem of how to visualize abstract information, such as a document space, that does not have explicit spatial properties.

1.1 Problem Statement

This paper addresses the problem of how to enhance the ability of users to access information by developing better ways for both visualizing abstract information and formulating queries graphically. As the amount of available information keeps growing at an ever increasing rate, it will become critical to provide users with *high-level visual retrieval tools* that enable them to explore, manipulate, and relate large information spaces to their interests in an interactive way. We use the term "high-level" because these tools are designed to give users flexibility with both how to retrieve and how to explore information. These tools provide users with a visual framework that enables them to integrate and manipulate information that has been retrieved by different methods or from different sources.

The InfoCrystal is an example of such a high-level retrieval tool and it has the following functionality: 1) Users can *explore* an information space along several dimensions simultaneously without having to abandon their sense of overview. 2) Users can *manipulate* the information by *creating useful abstractions*. 3) Similar to a spreadsheet, users can ask *"what-if"* questions and observe the effects without having to change the framework of a query. 4) Users receive *support* in the search process because they receive *dynamic visual feedback* on how to proceed. They can selectively emphasize the *qualitative* or the *quantitative* information provided by the feedback to help them decide how to proceed. 5) Users can formulate queries *graphically*, and they have *flexibility* in terms of the particular methods used to retrieve the information. For example, users can seamlessly move between a *Boolean* and a *vector-space* retrieval approach, or they can easily switch from a keyword-based to a full-text retrieval approach.

This paper is organized as follows: 1) We will consider a concrete retrieval example to set the stage. 2) We will introduce the *InfoCrystal*. 3) We will review and compare relevant previous work with the developed tool. 4) We will provide a brief summary and talk about the research currently underway.

1.2 Concrete Example

It is best to consider a concrete example to describe some the problems a user currently faces when searching for information. For example, if we are interested in documents that talk about "visual query languages for retrieving information and that consider human factors issues" then the following concepts could capture our interest: *(Graphical OR Visual)*, *Information Retrieval*, *Query language*, *Human Factors*. Most of the existing on-line retrieval systems use Boolean operators to combine the identified concepts to form a query. On the one hand, the most exclusive query would join the concepts by using the AND operator. We performed such a query, using a CD-ROM version of the INSPEC Database for the years 1991-92. Only one document was retrieved that contained all the four concepts. On the other hand, the most inclusive query would join the concepts by using the OR operator; it retrieved 19,691 documents. Hence, we are presented either with too few documents or too many documents. How should we proceed and modify the exclusive query or narrow the inclusive query to retrieve more relevant documents? We will revisit this example after we have introduced the InfoCrystal and we will show how it could help users to modify the query successfully.

2.0 The InfoCrystal

In this section we describe how we propose to help users search more effectively for information. We will first address the question of how to visualize all the possible relationships among N concepts. Towards that end we will develop the *InfoCrystal*, whose elements can be selectively visualized to emphasize the *qualitative* or the *quantitative* information associated with them. Second, we will demonstrate how the InfoCrystal can be used to formulate *Boolean queries* graphically. We will also show how the InfoCrystals can be used as building blocks and integrated in a hierarchical structure to formulate arbitrarily complex queries. Third, we will show how users can assign *relevance weights* to the concepts and use *thresholding* to select relationships of interest. We will describe the *rank layout* and the *bull's-eye layout* principle that visualize an InfoCrystal so that the relationship with the highest rank or the one with the largest relevance score, respectively, will lie in its center. Fourth, we will show how the InfoCrystal can be generalized so that *vector-space* queries can be specified graphically. Finally, it is worth mentioning that the InfoCrystal can be integrated with a query outlining and a navigation tool, as described in [Spoerri 93a], to enable users to create and maintain complex search queries.

2.1 Visualizing Relationships

How can all the possible combinations or relationships among several search criteria be visualized in a two-dimensional display ?

A common approach is to use Venn diagrams to visualize set relationships by intersecting geometric shapes that represent each set. However, it is difficult to represent all the possible relationships among more than three sets in a visually compact and simple way. We will now demonstrate how we can move beyond the Venn diagram approach so that all the possible relationships among N variables can be represented at same time in an elegant way. Figure 1 shows how a Venn diagram of three intersecting circles can be transformed into an iconic display. We start out by exploding the Venn diagram into its disjoint subsets. Next, we represent the subsets by icons whose shapes reflect the number of criteria satisfied by their contents, also called the *rank* of a subset. Finally, we surround the subset icons by a border area that contains icons, also called *criterion icons*, that represent the original sets.

The goal is to arrive at a visual representation that lets users use their visual reasoning skills to establish how the interior icons are related to the criterion icons, and the following visual coding principles are used in a redundant way:

- **Shape Coding**: is used to indicate the number of criteria that the contents associated with an interior icon satisfy (i.e., one -> circle, two -> rectangle, three -> triangle, four -> square, and so on).
- **Proximity Coding**: The closer an interior icon is located to a criterion icon, the more likely it is that the icon's contents are related to it.
- **Rank Coding**: Icons with the same shape are grouped in "invisible" concentric circles, where the rank of an icon is equal to the number of criteria satisfied and it increases as we move towards the center of an InfoCrystal.
- **Color or Texture Coding**: is used to indicate which particular criteria are satisfied by the icon's contents.
- **Orientation Coding**: The icons are positioned so that their sides face the criteria they satisfy.
- **Size or Brightness & Saturation Coding**: is used to visualize quantitative information, i.e. the number of elements represented by an icon.

Figure 1 shows the InfoCrystal that involves three concepts. Figure 2 shows an InfoCrystal for four search criteria. Figure 3 contains a schematic representation of an InfoCrystal for five criteria (for a detailed rendering, see [Spoerri 93a]). The number of possible combinations or relationships among N different criteria grows exponentially and it is equal to $2^N - 1$ (excluding the case where documents are not related to any of the criteria). We have developed a layout procedure that enables us to generate InfoCrystals with N inputs (for a detailed discussion and examples with N > 5, see [Spoerri, 1993a]). The objective of this algorithm is to create a layout of the interior icons that ensures that none of their locations coincide. We call it the *rank layout* principle, because it strictly enforces the rank coding principle. However, it also attempts to resolve the conflict between the rank and the proximity coding principle for the icons with rank two as follows: We will represent icons that involve relationships between two non-adjacent criterion icons twice and we will place them in such a way that they are close to their related criterion icons as well as at the correct distance from the center (see Figure 2).

The user can selectively render the interior icons to emphasize the *qualitative* or the *quantitative* information associated with them: If the user is interested in how the interior icons are related to the inputs then they are displayed as shown in Figure 1. If, however, the user wants to visualize the number of documents associated with the interior icons then the icons are represented as circular pie chart icons whose size and brightness reflect the numerical information (see Figure 3). The pie chart icons are similarly oriented as the polygon icons and the colors or textures of their slices indicate which criteria are satisfied.

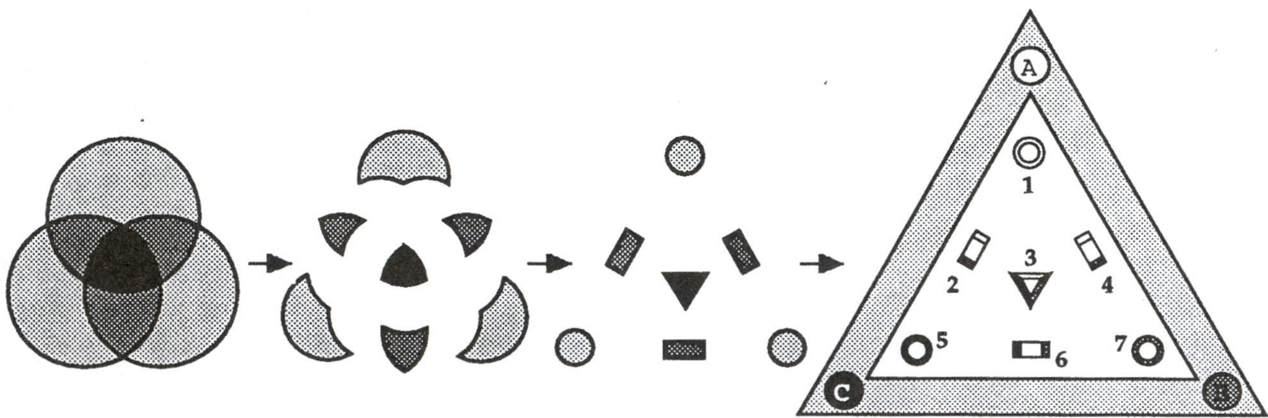

Figure 1: shows how to transform a Venn diagram into an iconic display, called the *InfoCrystal*, which represents all the possible Boolean queries involving its inputs in a normal form (see section 2.2). The interior icons have the following Boolean meanings: 1 = (A and (not (B or C), 2 = (A and C and (not B), 3 = (A and B and C), 4 = (A and B and (not C), 5 = (C and (not (A or B)), 6 = (B and C and (not A), 7 = (B and (not (A or C)).

2.1.1 Example Revisited

In this subsection we show how the InfoCrystal could help users modify the query example introduced earlier so that they do not retrieve either too few or too many documents. Figure 2 displays how the contents of the INSPEC Database (1991-92) relate to our four stated interests.

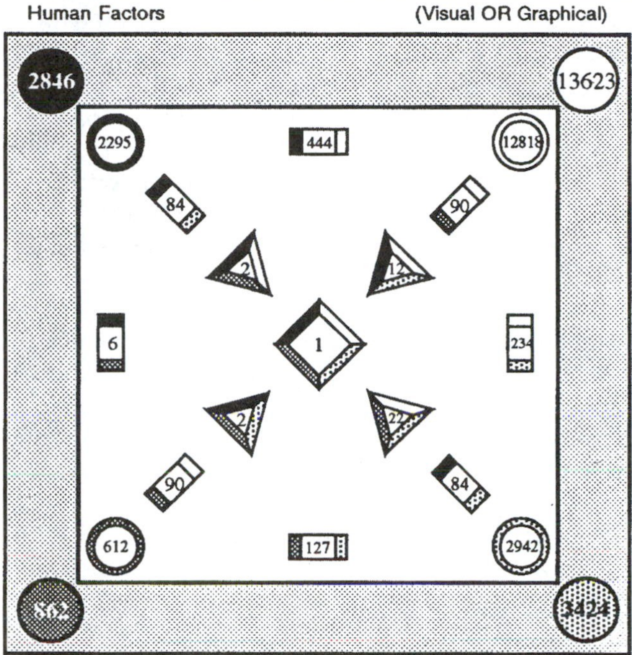

Figure 2: The number associated with an icon indicates how many of the retrieved documents satisfy the conditions represented by it.

The center icon of the InfoCrystal represents the documents that satisfy all the four criteria. In our example there is just one document. We can easily broaden our focus of interest by examining the icons that surround the center icon and satisfy three of the four concepts. For example, there are 22 documents that are indexed under and are related to the *(Graphical OR Visual), Information Retrieval,* and *Query Language* concept but not to the *Human Factors* concept. If we wanted to move further away from our initial interest then we could explore the 6 documents that have been indexed under the *Query Language* and *Human Factors* concept but not under the *(Graphical OR Visual)* or *Information Retrieval* concept. Hence, the InfoCrystal enables us to explore an information space in a flexible and fluid way. The organization of the InfoCrystal ensures that we can easily infer how the retrieved documents relate to our stated interests.

2.2. Visual Query Language

The InfoCrystal has the desirable property that each of its interior icons represents a distinct Boolean relationship among the input criteria (see Figure 1). Hence, the InfoCrystal can be used by users to specify Boolean queries by interacting with a direct manipulation visual interface. Users do not have to use logical operators and parentheses explicitly. Instead they need to recognize the relationships of interest and select them. Users just have to click on an interior icon to select or deselect the Boolean expression associated with it.

In an InfoCrystal we partition the space defined by its N inputs into $2^N - 1$ disjoint subsets or *constituents* in such a way that no information is lost. It can be easily shown that any Boolean query that involves the inputs of an InfoCrystal and that applies the Boolean operations of union, intersection or negation can be represented by the union of a certain number of the constituents (i.e., all the possible queries are represented in *normal form* by the InfoCrystal). Hence, users can specify graphically any Boolean query that involves the inputs by selecting the appropriate interior icons, because each of the constituents is represented by an interior icon. We establish the intuitive convention that the elements associated with the selected interior icons are combined to form the output of an InfoCrystal. We do not have to worry that certain elements appear more than once because we are merging disjoint subsets.

It is worth stressing that users can select a subset of interior icons in multiple ways: 1) They can select specific relationships by clicking on the appropriate interior icons. 2) Users can select subsets of interior icons by clicking on the criterion icons, thereby performing complex Boolean operations with only a few mouse clicks. 3) They can activate the appropriate interior icons by interacting with a threshold slider and/or the weighting sliders for the inputs (see Section 2.3 for explanation).

Existing visual query languages allow users to formulate specific queries, but the proposed visual query language enables users to formulate a whole range of related queries by creating a single InfoCrystal. For N inputs there are 2 to the power of $2^N - 1$ possible queries and each of them can be specified by just selecting the appropriate interior icons. Hence, in the case of five inputs there are over 2 billion possible queries and they are all represented compactly by an InfoCrystal !

2.2.1 Creating Complex Queries

The InfoCrystals can be used as building blocks and organized in a hierarchical structure to create complex Boolean queries. First, an InfoCrystal can be thought of as having several inputs, represented by the criterion icons, and as having an output that is defined by the selected interior icons. Second, the output of one InfoCrystal will be one of the inputs to an InfoCrystal one level up in the query hierarchy.

The hierarchical query structure differs from a simple tree structure as follows: The parent nodes do not just inherit the data elements associated with their children's nodes. Instead there is an intermediary step where the relationships among the children's nodes are represented by an Info-Crystal. Users have to select the relationships that should be included in the InfoCrystal's output that is passed on to the parent.

Figure 3 shows how the InfoCrystals can be "chained together" to form a hierarchical query structure. Similar to a spreadsheet, users can ask "what-if" questions by changing which interior icons are selected in one InfoCrystal and observe how the contents of the dependent icons higher up in the hierarchy change dynamically. Further, users can build a library of queries in an incremental fashion, where they can create complex queries by integrating simpler ones.

2.2.2 Interfacing with the Retrieval Engines

The atom or "leaf" nodes of the query structure represent the criteria that the user has decided not to break down any further (see Figure 3, where the atoms are represented by circular InfoCrystals). The atoms specify the query statement that a retrieval engine will use to search for information in the selected database(s). Users can also specify at the atom level whether to search the author, title, keywords or abstract field, or whether to use proximity or stemming as a search strategy.

A key feature of the InfoCrystal is that it works with any data type, provided its corresponding retrieval method returns unique data identifiers, which are then used to initialize the query structure. Hence, at any point in the search process users could switch from a keyword-based to a full-text retrieval approach by replacing an input criterion with a particular document that better captures a specific interest.

2.3 Relevance Weights & Thresholds

There will be situations where the search criteria are not of equal importance to a user. Further, users can find it initially easier to retrieve information by using a vector-space approach, where they can assign relevance weights to their search interests [Belkin 92]. We will now show how the InfoCrystal can be generalized so that users can seamlessly move between a Boolean and a vector-space retrieval approach. As a first step, we show how users can assign relevance weights to the inputs of an InfoCrystal to reflect the degree of importance they assign to them (see Figure 3). By interacting with a slider, they can choose values between -1 and 1, where negative weights indicate that users are more interested in documents that do *not* contain the concept represented by the input (i.e., the weight -1 is equivalent to the logical NOT). The assigned weights can be used to compute a relevance score for each interior icon by taking the dot product between the vector of the input weights and a vector, whose values are equal to 1 or -1 depending on whether the corresponding criteria are satisfied or not by the icon. By interacting with the threshold slider, users can select only the interior icons whose relevance score is above the threshold.

2.3.1 Bull's-Eye Layout

The key design principle used in the layout of the interior icons of an InfoCrystal is to ensure that users will find towards its center the relationships that they consider as more important. So far we have considered the *rank layout* that enforces that the number of criteria satisfied by an icon increases as we move towards the center of an InfoCrystal. We will now describe how users can display the interior icons to reflect the current setting of the relevance weights. This mapping, called the *bull's-eye layout*, causes the relationships with a higher relevance score to be placed closer to the center (see Figure 3.b). We use a novel polar representation to determine the placement of the interior icons. The radius value is determined by the relevance score. The angle, however, is not affected by the weights. It is a function of the line that passes through the InfoCrystal's center and the center of mass of the criterion icons that is computed as follows: a vector pointing towards a criterion icon that is satisfied by an interior icon receives a positive mass of 1, whereas the vector pointing towards a criterion that is not satisfied receives a negative mass of -1. Thus, an interior icon is closer to those criterion icons that it satisfies than to those it does not.

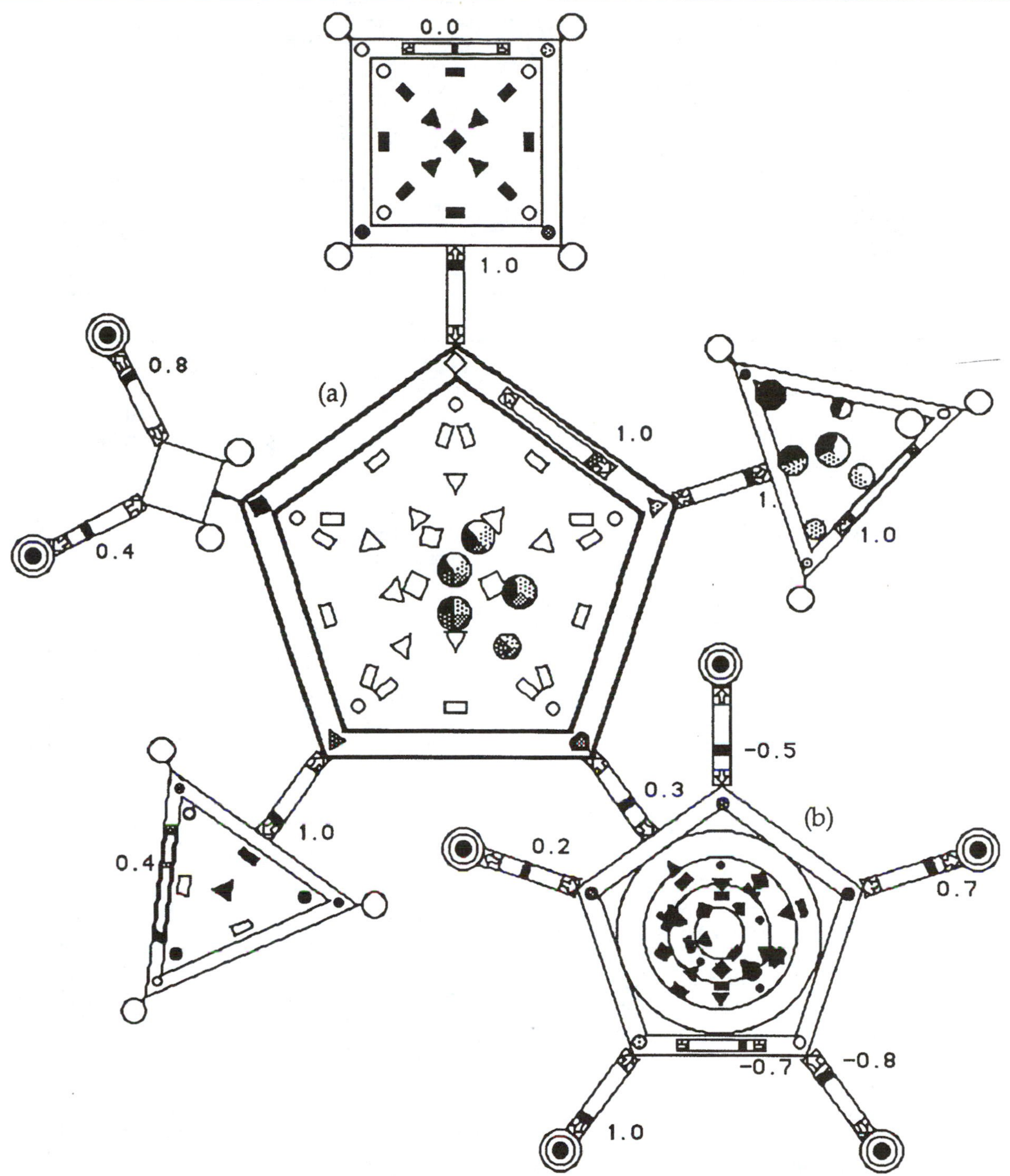

Figure 3: shows how the InfoCrystals can be organized in a hierarchical structure. Users can interactively change the way the InfoCrystals filter their inputs and they can dynamically observe how the information coming in through the circular InfoCrystals is propagated through the query structure. The interior icons that are shown in solid black indicate that they have been selected by the user to define the output of an InfoCrystal. Some of the InfoCrystals are displayed only as an outline, but the user can just click on them to view them in full detail. (a) Shows the top-level InfoCrystal, using the *rank layout* principle, where the selected icons are rendered, using a pie chart representation, to emphasize the quantitative information associated with them. (b) Shows the *bull's-eye layout* of the interior icons when the input weights are set to -0.5, 0.7, 0.8, 1.0 and 0.2; and it shows which icons will be selected if the threshold is set to -0.7 (in this case all of them).

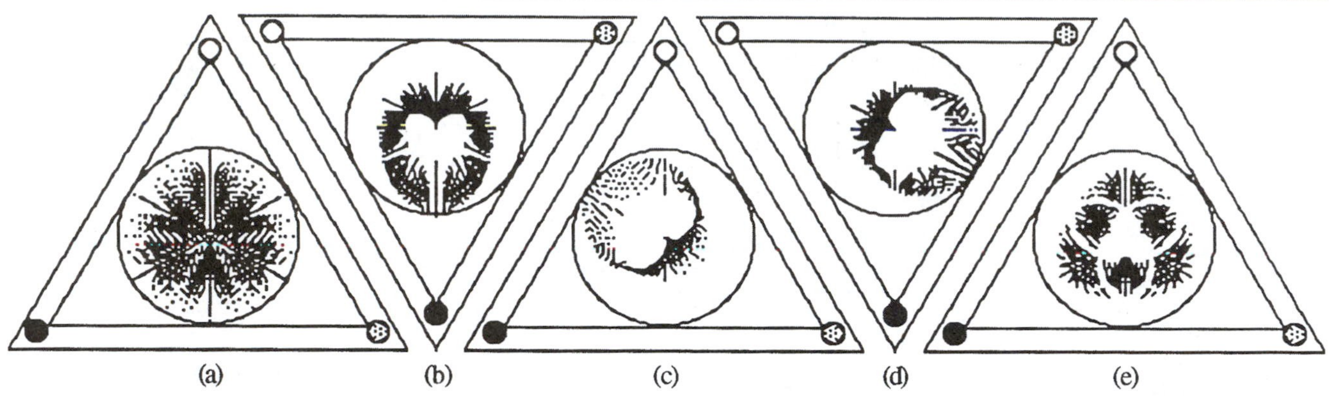

Figure 4: shows the distribution pattern of the relevance scores of all the document vectors that lie in the cube {[-1, 1]; [-1, 1], [-1, 1]}, using the bull's-eye layout principle that takes into account the particular values of the input weights. (a) - (d) Show the distribution patterns for input weights (1,1,1), (1,1,-1), (-0.75,1,-0.25), and (0.85,-0.6,-0.4), respectively. (e) Shows the clustering of the relevance scores of the documents that satisfy one or two of the input criteria, respectively, where the input weights are (1,1,1).

2.4 Visualizing Vector-Space Queries

So far we have considered the discrete case where a document either satisfies a criterion or not at all. We can generalize the InfoCrystal so that we can consider the continuous case where documents have a value between -1 and 1 to reflect the degree to which a criterion is satisfied or not. This allows us to specify vector-space queries graphically, since the vector-space approach computes the relevance of a document by taking the dot-product of the vectors of the index terms that represent the query and the document respectively [Belkin 92].

We can apply the bull's-eye layout principle to visualize how the retrieved documents satisfy the input criteria to varying degrees, where the vector pointing towards a criterion icon is now scaled by the degree to which the criterion is (not) satisfied by a document (see Figure 4). When mapping an N-dimensional space into a two-dimensional space, we are faced with the challenge of how to compress the information in such a way that it still captures what we are interested in. The polar transform used to map the documents has the attractive feature that it not only visualizes the ranking, but it also provides users with a qualitative sense of how the ranked documents are related to the input criteria (for a more detailed discussion and further examples, see [Spoerri 93b]. In Figure 4.b the input weights are equal to (1,1, -1), and as expected the documents with the lowest score are displayed close to the third & black criterion icon. Figure 4.e shows that the documents, which satisfy the same criteria and are therefore represented by the same interior icon in the discrete mode, will cluster in an orderly fashion when shown in the continuous mode.

3.0 Comparison with Relevant Previous Work

In this section we will briefly review and compare the developed tool with relevant previous work (for a more detailed discussion, see [Spoerri 93a]). We will focus on the shortcomings of existing proposals and indicate how the InfoCrystal addresses them. We hope this type of exposition will better motivate the approach taken in this paper.

Current on-line retrieval systems require users to use Boolean operators to formulate queries, but such queries can be difficult to generate [Belkin 92]. Further, either too few or too many documents are retrieved, and a pure Boolean approach does not rank the retrieved documents [Salton 88].

The InfoCrystal enables users to specify Boolean queries graphically. Users select relationships of interest instead of having to use logical operators and parentheses. The InfoCrystal displays the retrieved documents in a ranked order that enables users to control the output.

Best-Match models use statistical techniques and vector-space models to compute the similarity between documents and they rank the retrieved documents based on some relevance measure [Belkin 92]. However, a ranked linear list provides users with a limited view of the information space and it does not directly suggest how a query could be modified.

The InfoCrystal does not lock users into just one way of viewing the data. It helps users decide how to proceed in the search process because the quantitative information associated with an interior icon tells them how much additional items they can expect if they select it. Further, the bull's-eye layout shows users in a qualitative way how the ranked items are related to the input criteria.

Several researchers have developed overview maps that attempt to visualize the similarity between documents [Lin 91, Chalmers 92, Korfhage 91]. However, these maps can not visualize multiple relationships between documents and they become hard to interpret as the size of the document space increases. Further, these maps can not be used to formulate queries graphically.

The InfoCrystal is designed to visualize the similarity and the possible multiple relationships between the contents of an information space and N search criteria. It is both a visualization tool and a visual query language, and it scales well, because its organization is size independent.

Existing visual query languages suffer generally from the limitation that the organization of a query needs to be modified to generate a different query [Michard 82, Anick 90, Young 92].

The InfoCrystal represents all the possible Boolean queries involving its inputs in normal form. In the case of vector-space queries, users can interactively assign *relevance weights* to the concepts and use *thresholding* to select documents.

4.0 Conclusion & Future Work

This paper has presented a novel representation, called the *InfoCrystal*™, that can be used both as a *visualization tool* and a *visual query language*. The InfoCrystal can be used to visualize all the possible discrete as well as continuous relationships among N concepts. In the discrete case, the InfoCrystal uses proximity, rank, shape, color and size coding to enable users to see in a single view how a large information space relates to several of their interests. In the continuous case, a novel polar representation has been presented that visualizes the relevance scores of the retrieved documents and provides users with a qualitative sense of how the ranked documents are related to the input criteria. Further, the InfoCrystal allows users to specify *Boolean* as well as *vector-space* queries graphically. Complex queries can be created by using the InfoCrystals as building blocks and organizing them in a hierarchical structure.

The InfoCrystal is an example of a high-level visual retrieval tool that is designed to give users flexibility with both how to retrieve and how to explore information. It provides users with a visual framework that enables them to integrate and manipulate information that has been retrieved by different methods or from different sources in a flexible, dynamic and interactive way.

We are currently completing the implementation of the InfoCrystal on the Macintosh. We are also in the process of integrating some of its functionality with the CONIT expert retrieval assistant system [Marcus 91]. Further, we will conduct user studies to test the effectiveness of the InfoCrystal.

Acknowledgments: Support for the research described in this paper has been generously provided by the Union Bank of Switzerland (UBS). We would like to thank especially: Dr. Marty and Dr. Frei at UBS, the members of CECI at MIT; Prof. Lerman, Prof. Resnick and Mr. Marcus; the MIT Patent & Licensing Office; and Pamela Robertson-Pearce.

5.0 References

Anick, P.; Brennan, J.; Flynn, R.; Hanssen, D.; Alvey, B. & Robbins, J. (1990) "A Direct Manipulation Interface for Boolean Information Retrieval via Natural Language Query," Proc. ACM SIGIR '90.

Belkin, N. & Croft, B. (1992) "Information Filtering and Information Retrieval: Two Sides of the Same Coin" Comm. of the ACM, Dec., 1992.

Chalmers, M. & Chitson, P. (1992) "BEAD: Exploration in Information Visualization," Proc. ACM SIGIR '92.

Card, S.; Robertson, G. & Mackinlay, J. (1991) "The Information Visualizer, an information workspace," Proc. CHI'91 Human Factors in Comp. Systems, 1991.

Korfhage, R. & Olson, K. (1991) "Information display: Control of visual representations," Proc. IEEE Workshop on Visual Languages, Oct., 1991.

Lin, X.; Soergel, D. & Marchionini, G. (1991) "A Self-organizing Semantic Map for Information Retrieval," Proc. ACM SIGIR '91.

Marcus, R. (1991) "Computer and Human Understanding in Intelligent Retrieval Assistance," American Society for Information Science, 28, 1991.

Michard, A. (1982) "Graphical presentation of Boolean expressions in a database query language: design notes and an ergonomic evaluation," Behaviour and Information Technology, 1:3, 1982.

Salton, G. (1988) "A simple blueprint for automatic boolean query processing," Information Processing & Management, 24:3, 1988.

Spoerri, A. (1993a) "Visual Tools for Information Retrieval," Proc. IEEE Workshop on Visual Languages, 1993, and MIT-CECI-TR 93-2.

Spoerri, A. (1993b) "InfoCrystal: a visual tool for information retrieval," MIT-CECI -TR 93-3.

Young, D. & Shneiderman, B. (1992) "A Graphical Filter/Flow Representation of Boolean Queries: A Prototype Implementation and Evaluation, " Uni. of Maryland Report.

2.4 Trees

Tree Visual Structures encode hierarchical data, typically by using connection or containment. Connection is used to create node-link diagrams, a well-known technique for encoding relationships between cases. Node-link diagrams are also used to encode network data. Enclosure, a less well-known technique, is the focus of the three papers included in this section.

CONNECTION

Trees link cases to subcases (Figure 2.11). A natural way to do this is by drawing lines between the cases. But while logically correct, a tree with properly drawn links to randomly positioned nodes would be visually unreadable. For a tree used as a Visual Structure, the way space is used to position nodes is very important. Figure 2.12 is a typical tree Visual Structure. Tree depth is mapped onto an ordinal Y-axis, while the X-axis is nominal and used mainly to separate the nodes into their own positions. Trees can also appear as indented outlines—that is, the X-axis represents tree depth, whereas the Y-axis is just used to separate the nodes. Another variant is for trees to be circular, in which case the R-axis represents depth and the θ-axis is used to separate the nodes. Other variants are possible. The point is that whereas node positioning is irrelevant for the logical definition of a tree, it is very important for tree Visual Structures (as the use of the spatial axes always is for information visualization).

Trees have the virtue that because there can be no cycles and because one spatial axis is usually used to separate levels in the tree, trees are easy to lay out and interpret. General networks, on the other hand, are not. A good strategy for visualizing a network is to see if it can be made into a tree, even if a little violence is required. One of the main disadvantages of trees is that as they get large, they acquire an extreme aspect ratio. Even a tree with a branching factor of 2 gets wider approximately proportionally to 2^n though only taller proportionally to n. This means that almost all sufficiently large trees (say > 1000 nodes) come to resemble a straight line. The other disadvantage is that they often contain considerable empty space, because it requires a lot of space to visually organize the nodes. Some information visualizations have addressed this problem by using interaction and distortion to enhance traditional node-link diagrams.

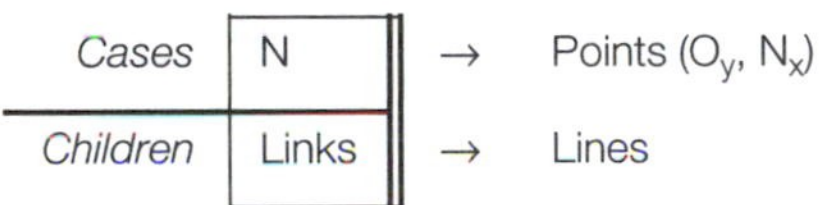

FIGURE **2.11**

Visual mapping for node-link diagrams.

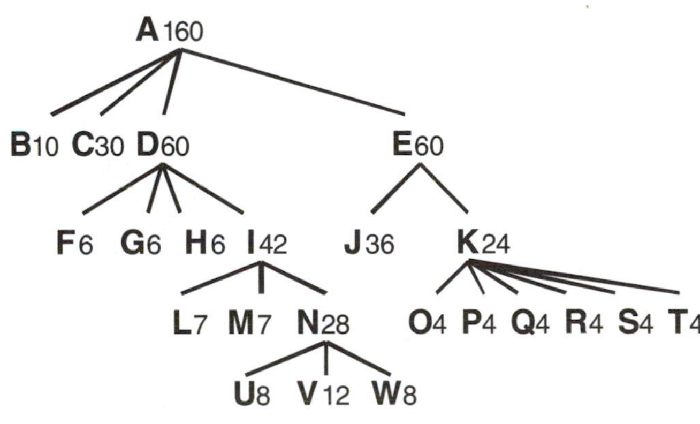

FIGURE **2.12**

Vertical tree (Johnson and Shneiderman,1991 ●).

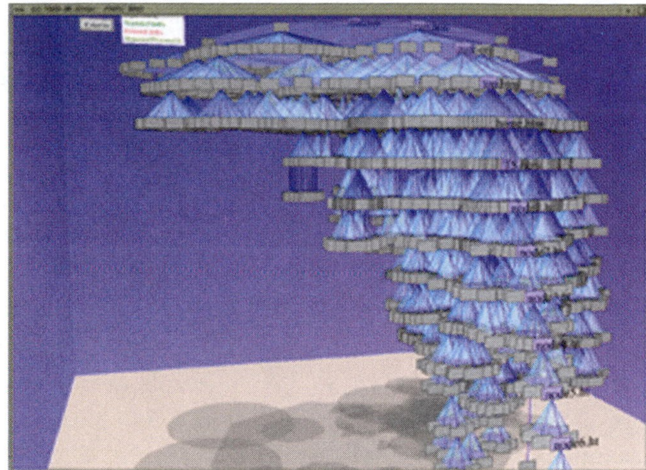

FIGURE **2.13**

Cone tree of 10,000 nodes in the Xerox PARC Web.

Recent work on node-link diagrams has used interaction to access dense node-link layouts that contain more data than would be effective in static node-link diagrams. The WebTOC system automatically expands and contracts a tree in the form of a 2D nested table of contents (Nation et al., 1997). Exploration is supported with graphical cues that describe the contracted parts for the table of contents. Kumar, Plaisant, and Shneiderman (1997 ●) describe node-link diagrams that are enhanced with overview + detail and dynamic queries techniques. Finally, the cone trees visualization addresses the problem that hierarchies grow very wide (Robertson, Card, and Mackinlay, 1993 ●; Robertson, Mackinlay, and Card, 1991). Figure 2.13 shows that cone trees address this problem by wrapping subtrees into 3D cones. The resulting visualization dramatically increases the amount of nodes that can be included in a square-shaped aspect ratio. This technique is particularly effective for showing the overall structure of a tree. Cone trees have the problem that some of the nodes are occluded. The animated visualization, on the other hand, uses interactive technique to tap human perceptual skills that let the user see the entire tree even though parts of it are occluded at any given moment.

ENCLOSURE

Another way to visualize trees is to use enclosure. Unlike connection, enclosure fills the space. The first paper in this section, by Johnson and Shneiderman (1991 ●), describes a system called *treemaps,* which introduced a method of using enclosure to visualize trees. Figure 2.14 shows that each case is mapped to a rectangular area, then that area is subdivided in X or Y to show the relative size of the children of the case. The process is recursively applied to the children cases with the subdivisions on the X- or Y-axis.

Treemaps are particularly useful for finding large cases. Consider the introductory example in the paper, which is repeated in Figures 2.12 and 2.15. The large nodes C30 and

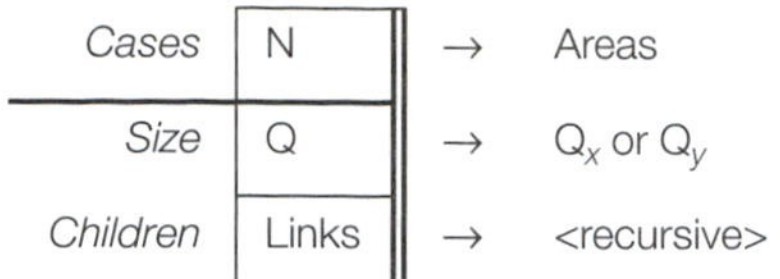

FIGURE **2.14**

Description of treemaps (Johnson and Shneiderman, 1991 ●).

J36 are clearly visible in Figure 2.15. However, comparisons of sizes can be difficult when they occur at different levels in the tree. The node B10 is larger than U8 and W8 but smaller than V12. However, it is mapped to a long, thin rectangle because it has a small value and is close to the root of the tree. The area of this thin rectangle is hard to compare with the relatively square rectangles for U8, V12, and W8. Nodes U8, V12, and W8, on the other hand, all occur at the same level in the tree and are easy to compare. The problem is that rectangles for different levels in the tree have different aspect ratios. When the aspect ratio is held constant, the width or height of a rectangle can be used to compare values. Experiments show that perception is much more accurate for length estimation than area estimation (Mackinlay, 1986b ●).

The next paper by Baker and Eick (1995 ●) describes how treemaps can be extended to encode statistical data. Their SeeSys system is designed to visualize statistics associated with software that is hierarchically divided into subsystems, directories, and files. Their major contribution to the treemap idea is to encode statistical data by filling the rectangles in lengths, which can be more accurately estimated. For example, a common software statistic is the amount of newly developed code. The area of the fill encodes the amount of new code, and the height of the fill encodes the relative proportion of new code to old code for each directory or file. Since estimating lengths is much easier than areas, Baker and Eick's method makes it easier to see what modules have changed substantially or stayed the same.

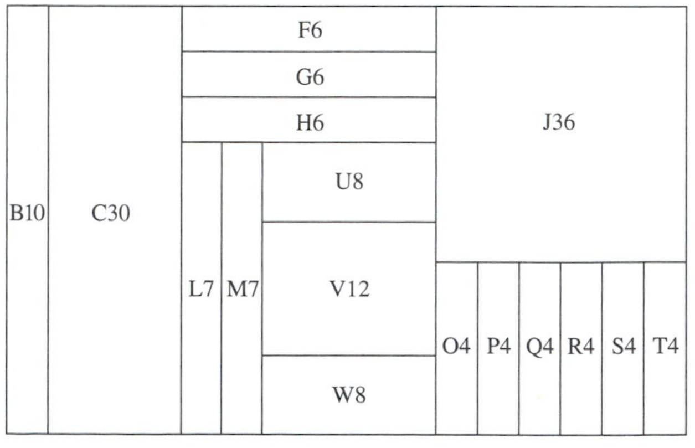

FIGURE **2.15**

Treemap based on tree in Figure 2.12. See also Johnson and Shneiderman (1991 ●, Figure 5).

The final paper, by Jin and Banks (1997●), applies treemaps to a novel application, visualization of a tennis match in a system called TennisViewer. TennisViewer uses color to encode the winner of each point. A tree describing a tennis game has three levels: match, set, and game. Color is used to show the winning player for each level. Transparency is used to show the influence of the child on the parent. As a result, the user/fan can see results of the entire game or zoom into details such as ball traces for the individual games.

DISCUSSION

Node-link diagrams and treemaps are both effective techniques for visualizing trees. Which one we use depends primarily on the properties of the data (compare Figures 2.11 and 2.14). Node-link diagrams are effective for trees that have an uneven shape such as the cone tree shown in Figure 2.13. Treemaps are effective for trees where the cases include a quantitative variable, particularly when large values are important. If the tree is balanced and the sizes of the leaf nodes are fairly homogeneous, the aspect ratios will also support effective comparison, which is the case for the SeeSys and TennisViewer examples. These applications are also not bothered by the X and Y alternation in the subdivision of the rectangles, because the levels of their trees represent distinct types of information. SeeSys's levels are subsystems, directories, and files, and TennisViewer's are match, set, and game. In these cases, rectangles are only going to be compared within level, which means they have similar aspect ratios. Johnson's dissertation (1993) also includes empirical studies that show the efficacy of using treemaps after 15 minutes of training.

Tree-Maps: A Space-Filling Approach to the Visualization of Hierarchical Information Structures

Brian Johnson
brianj@cs.umd.edu

Ben Shneiderman
ben@cs.umd.edu

Department of Computer Science & Human-Computer Interaction Laboratory
University of Maryland, College Park, MD 20742

Abstract

This paper describes a novel method for the visualization of hierarchically structured information. The Tree-Map visualization technique makes 100% use of the available display space, mapping the full hierarchy onto a rectangular region in a space-filling manner. This efficient use of space allows very large hierarchies to be displayed in their entirety and facilitates the presentation of semantic information.

1 Introduction

A large quantity of the world's information is hierarchically structured: manuals, outlines, corporate organizations, family trees, directory structures, internet addressing, library cataloging, computer programs... and the list goes on. Most people come to understand the content and organization of these structures easily if they are small, but have great difficulty if the structures are large.

We propose an interactive visualization method for presenting hierarchical information called Tree-Maps. We hope that the Tree-Map approach is a step forward in the visualization of hierarchical information, and that it will produce benefits similar to those achieved by visualization techniques in other areas.

As humans we have the ability to recognize the spatial configuration of elements in a picture and notice the relationships between elements quickly. This highly developed visual ability allows people to grasp the content of a picture much faster than they can scan and understand text [12].

The Tree-Map visualization method maps hierarchical information to a rectangular 2-D display in a space-filling manner; 100% of the designated display space is utilized. Interactive control allows users to specify the presentation of both structural (depth bounds, etc.) and content (display properties such as color mappings) information. This is in contrast to traditional static methods of displaying hierarchically structured information, which generally make either poor use of display space or hide vast quantities of information from users. With the Tree-Map method, sections of the hierarchy containing more important information can be allocated more display space while portions of the hierarchy which are less important to the specific task at hand can be allocated less space [9,10].

Tree-Maps partition the display space into a collection of rectangular bounding boxes representing the tree structure [20]. The drawing of nodes within their bounding boxes is entirely dependent on the content of the nodes, and can be interactively controlled. Since the display size is user controlled, the drawing size of each node varies inversely with the size of the tree (i.e., # of nodes). Trees with many nodes (1000 or more) can be displayed and manipulated in a fixed display space.

The main objectives of our design are:

Efficient Space Utilization
Efficient use of space is essential for the presentation of large information structures.

Interactivity
Interactive control over the presentation of information and real time feedback are essential.

Comprehension
The presentation method and its interactive feedback must facilitate the rapid extraction of information with low perceptual and cognitive loads.

Esthetics
Drawing and feedback must be esthetically pleasing.

Hierarchical information structures contain two kinds of information: structural (organization) information associated with the hierarchy, and content information associated with each node. Tree-Maps are able to depict both the structure and content of the hierarchy. However, our approach is best suited to hierarchies in which the content of the leaf nodes and the structure of the hierarchy are of primary importance, and the content information associated with internal nodes is largely derived from their children.

2 Motivation: Current Methods and Problems

This work was initially motivated by the lack of adequate tools for the visualization of the large directory structures on hard disk drives.

Traditional methods for the presentation of hierarchically

structured information can be roughly classified into three categories: listings, outlines, and tree diagrams. It is difficult for people to extract information from large hierarchical information structures using these methods, as the navigation of the structure is a great burden and content information is often hidden within individual nodes [23].

Listings are capable of providing detailed content information, but are generally very poor at presenting structural information. Listings of the entire structure with explicit paths can provide structural information, but require users to parse path information to arrive at a mental model of the structure. Alternatively, users may list each internal node of the hierarchy independently, but this requires users to manually traverse the hierarchy to determine its structure. Outline methods can explicitly provide both structural and content information, but since the structural indentation can only be viewed a few lines at a time, it is often inadequate [4].

The number of display lines required to present a hierarchy with both the listing and outline methods is linearly proportional to the number of nodes in the hierarchy. These methods are inadequate for structures containing more than a few hundred nodes. A great deal of effort is required to achieve an mental model of the structure in large hierarchies using these methods.

Tree drawing algorithms have traditionally sought efficient and esthetically pleasing methods for the layout of node and link diagrams. These layouts are based on static presentations and are common in texts dealing with graph theory and data structures. They are excellent visualization tools for small trees [2,10,12,13,17]. However, these traditional node and link tree diagrams make poor use of the available display space. In a typical tree drawing more than 50% of the pixels are used as background. For small tree diagrams this poor use of space is acceptable, and traditional layout methods produce excellent results. But for large trees, traditional node and link diagrams can not be drawn adequately in a limited display space. Attempts to provide zooming and panning have only been only partially successful [10].

Another problem with tree diagrams is the lack of content information; typically each node has only a simple text label. This problem exists because presenting additional information with each node quickly overwhelms the display space for trees with more than just a few nodes.

The presentation of content information in all of these traditional methods has usually been text based. Although tree diagrams are a graphically based method capable of making use of visualization techniques, and many of the ideas presented in this paper. Unfortunately, global views of large tree diagrams require the nodes to be so small that there is virtually no space in which to provide visual cues as to node content.

Tree-Maps efficiently utilize the designated display area and are capable of providing structural information implicitly, thereby eliminating the need to explicitly draw internal nodes. Thus much more space is available for the rendering of individual leaf nodes, and for providing visual cues related to content information.

Tree-Maps provide an overall view of the entire hierarchy, making the navigation of large hierarchies much easier. Displaying the entire information structure at once allows users to move rapidly to any location in the space. As Beard states in his paper on navigating large two-dimensional spaces [1], "If the two-dimensional information space fits completely onto a display screen, there is no navigation problem ... Users are never lost because they can see the complete information space."

3 A Directory Tree Example

Obtaining information about directory trees was the initial motivation for this research and provides a familiar example domain. For illustrative reasons, the hierarchy in this example is small and nodes have only an associated name and size. While reading through this example, think about how the techniques described would scale up to a directory tree containing 1000 files. An Apple Macintosh screen snapshot showing a Tree-Map of 1000 files from one of our laboratory's hard disk drives follows this example.

Presenting directory structures is a very practical problem. The following are the methods widely available today:

- Command Line Listing (e.g. UNIX "ls", DOS "dir");
- Outlines (e.g. UNIX "du", Microsoft Windows)
- Windowing (e.g. Macintosh Finder)
- Tree Drawings (e.g. OpenWindows File Manager)

We are not aware of approaches that provide a visual representation of the relative sizes of files or directories.

Even moderately sized directory trees are difficult to visualize using standard operating system interfaces. With command line interfaces such as UNIX "ls" or DOS "dir", only the immediate children of any directory are listed. An overall view of the directory tree must be pieced together by traversing the various paths and listing the immediate children of the currently active directory.

Desktop metaphors and their windowing strategies are another alternative. One of the problems with windows is that they often obscure each other, and users may spend much of their time may be spent arranging windows. Also, the tree structure is not apparent unless windows have been carefully placed. Desktop icons generally show only the type of the file. Much richer visual mappings are possible but are currently not available, for instance, the depth of an icon's shadow could be used to indicate file size.

We will use a small directory tree hierarchy as an example. Tree A depicted in Figures 1 through 7 contains 23 nodes, of these 6 are directories (internal nodes) and 17 are files (leaf nodes). This tree is structured such that among siblings, file nodes always precede directory nodes.

In Figure 1 we see an outline view similar to the presentations provided by PCShell under DOS, the UNIX command "du", or Microsoft Windows 3.0. This presentation requires 23 lines; a structure with 1000 files would require a minimum of 1000 lines in order to present both directories and files.

Figure 2 presents a typical tree diagram, such drawings can be found in graph theory textbooks. This tree drawing approach is similar to the presentation method used by the OpenWindows File Manager. Directory trees with 1000 files cannot be drawn all at once on a typical screen (if all files are at the same level, each file node will have less than one pixel in which to draw itself). The problem becomes even more severe when real file names are used as node labels.

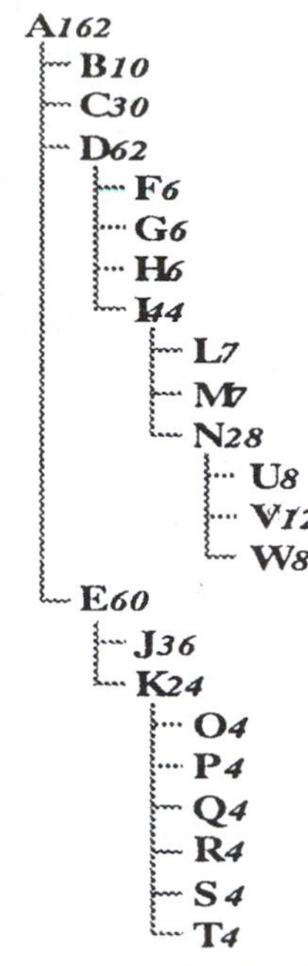

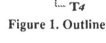

Figure 1. Outline

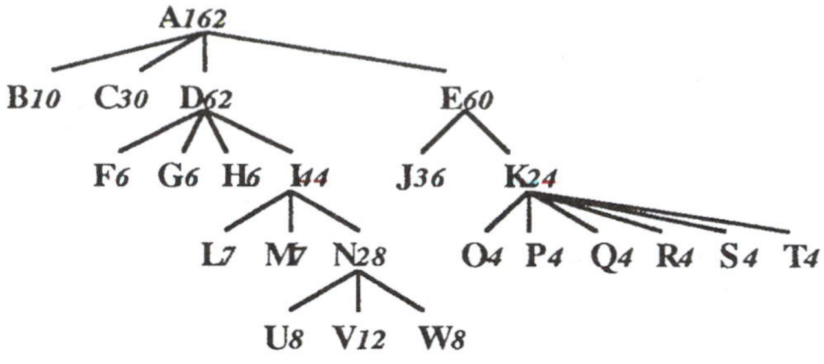

Figure 2. Tree Diagram

Figure 3 presents the same information in yet another manner, as a Venn diagram. We use this figure for illustrative purposes as a familiar and often used set theoretic visualization technique. It is an intermediate step which facilitates the transition from traditional presentations to Tree-Maps. This is an odd use of Venn diagrams, as one does not usually think of files and directories as sets. However, simple directory structures can be thought of as set theoretic collections of files, using only the containment (subset) property. Note that each node has been drawn proportionate to its size.

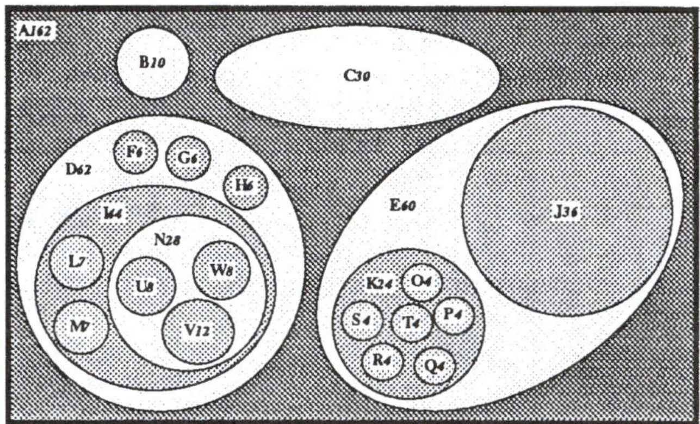

Figure 3. Venn Diagram

The space required between regions would certainly preclude this Venn diagram representation from serious consideration for larger structures. Note that this "waste" of space is also present in traditional tree diagrams. Using boxes instead of ovals and a bin-packing algorithm could partially solve this space problem. But bin-packing is an NP-complete problem and does not preserve order.

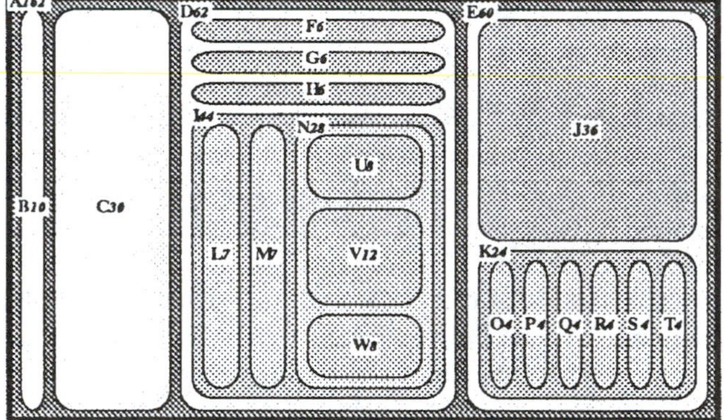

Figure 4. Nested Tree-Map

Figure 4 is a box-based Venn diagram which illustrates a more efficient use of space and is an excellent tool for the visualization of small hierarchies. But even the small degree of nesting present in this technique renders it unsuitable for the presentation of large hierarchies. Fortunately space efficient results can be achieved without bin-packing, using our "slice and dice" Tree-Map approach, a simple linear method in which the algorithm works top-down. An analogy should quickly illustrate this concept. If the hard disk drive were a large, flat, rectangular cheese, one could certainly slice it into chunks representing the size of each top level directory. Applying this slice and dice algorithm recursively to each piece of the cheese, and rotating the slicing direction 90 degrees at each recursive step, would result in the Tree Map

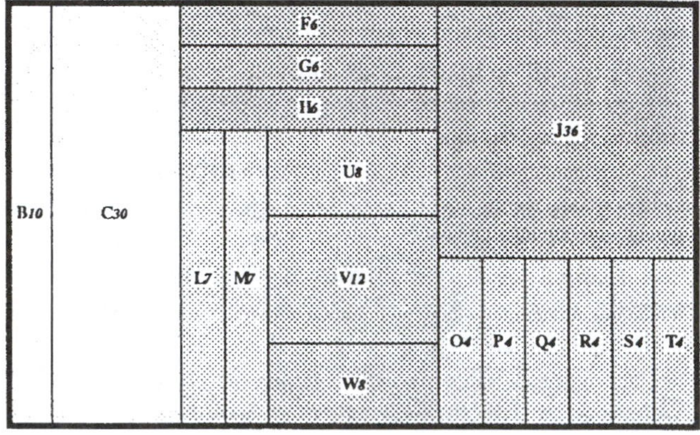

Figure 5. Tree-Map

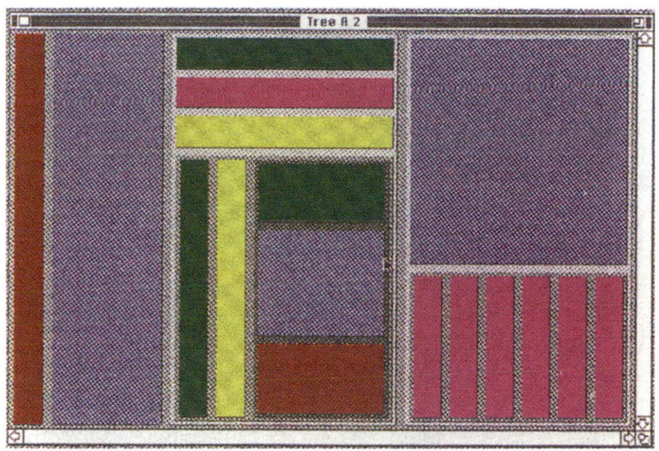

Johnson Figure 6 (Color). Nested Tree-Map

Johnson Figure 7 (Color). Non-nested Tree-Map

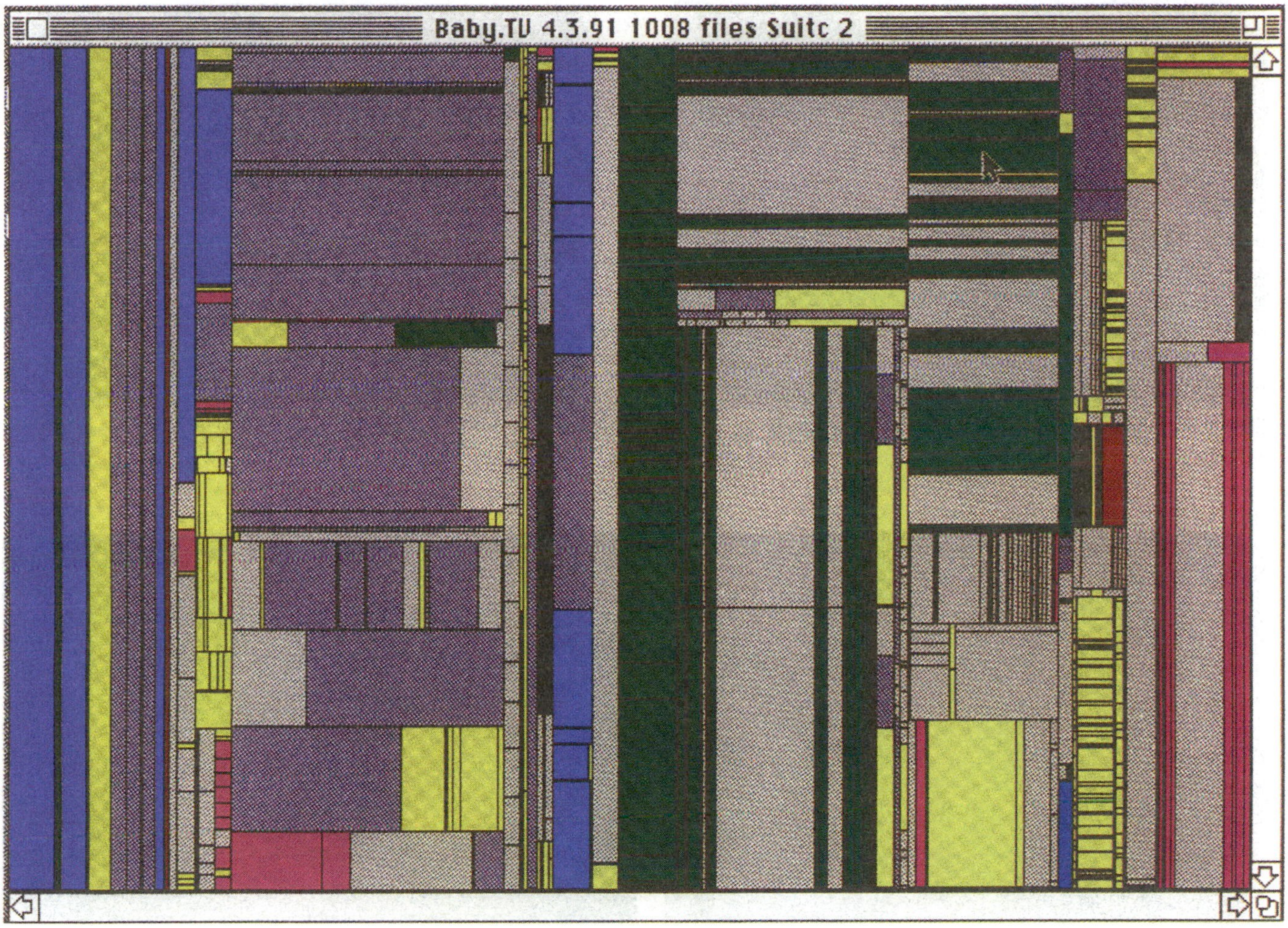

Baby.TU 4.3.91 1008 files Suitc 2

Johnson Figure 8 (Color). Tree-Map with 1000 Files

of Figure 5.

Figure 5 simply eliminates the nesting offset used to seperate objects at each level. If we wanted to distribute our cheese to 17 people based on their weights, Figure 5 would give us a slicing diagram. This weight-proportionate distribution is one of the important features of Tree-Maps. The Tree Map snapshots of Figures 6 and 7 (see color plates) are the full color, machine generated screen snapshots of Figures 4 and 5. All screen snapshots in this paper have been made while using our TreeViz application on an Apple Macintosh II.

Figure 8 (see color plates) is a screen snapshot showing a Tree-Map of 1000 files. A simple color mapping has been used to code some of the various Macintosh file types: Tree-Map applications are red; all other applications are purple; system files are green; picture files are magenta; text files are yellow; archive files are cyan; and all other file types not currently of primary interest are gray. This Tree-Map shows 21 root level files on the left, followed by 19 root level directories moving across to the right. Detailed file information is displayed in a pop-up dialog window as the mouse is dragged over files in the display.

In this directory structure it can be observed that purple application files are generally the largest files on this disk, and take up relatively the same percentage of overall disk space as system related (green) files. A duplicate set of files exists just to the right of the vertical green bar. The files in this root level folder can be seen duplicated one level down in subfolders, as repeating geometric patterns offset 90° from their parent.

Since this Tree-Map portrays the overall allocation of disk space, the largest files can be located quite easily. Sorting a large directory listing by size would also make finding the largest files easy, but these files would not be presented in their original context. In addition, sorting a list on two or more properties (i.e. size and type) makes presentation of the results difficult. Tree-Maps make finding the largest system, application, and picture files on the disk as easy as finding the largest green, purple, and magenta rectangles in Figure 8. This is one simple example of the visual display properties possible; further discussion is contained in section 4.2.

4 The Tree Map Method

Displaying a directory tree while fully utilizing space and conveying structural information in a visually appealing and low cognitive load manner is a difficult task, as these are often opposing goals. Our interactive approach to drawing directory trees allows users to determine how the tree is displayed. This control is essential, as it allows users to set display properties (colors, borders, etc.) maximizing the utility of the drawing based on their particular task.

4.1 Structural Information: Partitioning the Display Space

Tree-Map displays look similar to the partition diagrams of quad-trees and k-D trees. The key difference is the direction of the transformation. Quad-trees create hierarchical structures to store 2-D images efficiently [18] while Tree-Maps present hierarchical information structures efficiently on 2-D display surfaces.

Tree-Maps require that a weight be assigned to each node, this weight is used to determine the size of a nodes bounding box. The weight may represent a single domain property (such as disk usage or file age for a directory tree), or a combination of domain properties (subject to Property 4 below). A nodes weight (bounding box) determines its display size and can be thought of as a measure of importance or degree of interest[9].

The following relationships between the structure of the hierarchy and the structure of its Tree-Map drawing always hold:

Properties

1) *If* ***Node1*** *is an ancestor of* ***Node2****, then the bounding box of* ***Node1*** *completely encloses, or is equal to, the bounding box of* ***Node2****.*
2) *The bounding boxes of two nodes intersect iff one node is an ancestor of the other.*
3) *Nodes occupy a display area strictly proportional to their weight.*
4) *The weight of a node is greater than or equal to the sum of the weights of its children.*

Structural information in Tree-Maps is implicitly presented, although it may also be explicitly indicated by nesting child nodes within their parent. Nesting provides for the direct selection of all nodes, both internal and leaf. Although the space required for nesting reduces the number of nodes which can be drawn in a given display space, and hence reduces the size of the trees that can be adequately displayed compared to non-nested drawings [21].

A non-nested display explicitly provides direct selection only for leaf nodes, but a pop-up display can provide path information as well as further selection facilities. Non-nested presentations cannot depict internal nodes in degenerate linear sub-paths, as the bounding boxes of the internal nodes in the sub-path may be exactly equal. Such paths seldom occur and tasks dependent on long chains of single child nodes will require special treatments.

4.2 Content Information: Mapping Content to the Display

Once the bounding box of a node is set, a variety of display properties determine how the node is drawn within it. Visual display properties such as color (hue, saturation, brightness), texture, shape, border, blinking, etc. are of primary interest, but the interface will not limit users to purely visual properties [6]. Color is the most important of these visual display properties, and it can be an important aid to fast and accurate decision making [11,15,16]. Auditory properties may also be useful in certain circumstances. Nodes may have many domain dependent properties, in which case a rich set of mappings exists between content information and display properties.

The drawing of individual nodes within their bounding boxes determines the content information statically presented in a Tree-Map. The number and variety of domain properties that can be statically coded in the drawing of the tree is limited. As Kuhn states, "Since human perception imposes an upper bound on the complexity of graphic representations, only a small number of relations can be shown."[7,14] Interactive control of the drawing is therefore critical because the mapping of content information to the display will vary depending on the information users require. Dynamic feedback is provided by a pop-up window which displays information about the node currently under the cursor.

For example, files could have weights (display size) proportional to their creation date, color saturation dependent on their last modification date, and pitch (tone heard while crossing border) based on size. Using this scheme it is easy to locate old files which have changed recently, and as the cursor crosses into their bounding box a deep tone tells users that the file is large even before they read the information about that file.

5 Algorithms

Algorithms are given to draw a Tree-Map and to track cursor movement in the tree. The algorithms may be applied to any tree, regardless of its branching degree. Both algorithms appear on the following page as Figures 9 and 10.

The basic drawing algorithm produces a series of nested boxes representing the structure of the tree.

The cursor tracking algorithm facilitates interactive feedback about the tree. Every point in the drawing corresponds to a node in the tree. While the current tracking point (from a mouse or touchscreen input device) is in a node, the node is selected and information about it is displayed.

5.1 Drawing Algorithm

The Tree-Map can be drawn during one pre-order pass through the tree in O(n) time, assuming that node properties (weight, name, etc.) have previously been computed or assigned. The current algorithm has been implemented in object-oriented Think C on a Macintosh II. The drawing algorithm proceeds as follows:

1) The node draws itself within its rectangular bounds according to its display properties (weight, color, borders, etc.).

2) The node sets new bounds and drawing properties for each of its children, and recursively sends each child a drawing command. The bounds of a node's children form either a vertical or horizontal partitioning of the display space allocated to the node.

5.2 Tracking Algorithm

The path from the root of the tree to the node associated with a given point in the display can be found in time proportional to the depth of the node.

In our implementation, when a node draws itself it stores its bounding box in an instance variable. Every point in the Tree-Map corresponds to a node in the hierarchy, in addition every node is contained in the bounding box of the root node. Recall that each node's bounding box completely encloses the bounding boxes of its children, and that the bounding boxes of sibling nodes never overlap. Finding the path to a node containing a given point thus involves only a simple descent through one path in the tree, until the smallest enclosing bounding box is found.

6 Coping with Size

A typical 13 inch display has a resolution of 640 x 480, or roughly 300,000 pixels. Drawing an 80mb directory tree (weight = disk usage) on such a display requires that each pixel represent 260 bytes, i.e., there are roughly 4 pixels per Kilobyte. Assuming that such a directory structure may contain roughly 3,000 files (as on one of our lab's hard disks) implies that there are approximately 100 pixels per file on average. A box with 10 pixels per side (roughly $4mm^2$) is easily selectable using a standard mouse or touchscreen device [19]. This average case analysis is only part of the story since file sizes may vary widely.

The range of file sizes on our hard disk varied from a few hundred bytes to well over one million bytes. In the Tree-Map of Figure 8, groups of very small files often become completely black regions as there is only enough space to draw their borders. Magnification over these regions or zooming can provide access to these files. But since the assignment of node weights can be user controlled, presumably the nodes with the greatest weights are of greatest interest and the nodes with the smallest weights are of least interest.

7 Future Research Directions

Further research includes the exploration of alternate structural partitioning schemes, appropriate visual display of both numeric and non-numeric content information, dynamic views such as animated time slices, and operations on elements of the hierarchy. Standard operations such as zooming, marking, selecting and searching also invite designers to explore variations on the Tree-Map strategy.

Dr. Ram Naresh-Singh, a visiting research scientist in our lab, is working on an alternate directory only approach to partitioning the display which we have termed "top-down". His implementation on a Sun Sparcstation preserves the traditional notion of having the root node at the top and the leaves at the bottom.

Animation, or time-sliced displays, could provide insight into evolving structures. For example, the hierarchical organization of a university could be mapped from the university level (root), to the college level, to the department level, to the research lab level. If weights were assigned based on personnel resources, it would be easy to see the structure of the university based on the distribution of employees, and hence understand its strengths and weaknesses. Furthermore, if the saturation of red was proportionate to the funds spent at each node, and the saturation of cyan (the inverse of red) was proportionate to the funds allocated, nodes (labs, departments, colleges) which were on budget would be shades of gray (equal amounts of red and cyan), nodes over budget would become increasingly red, and nodes under budget would become increasingly cyan. The magnitude of the nodes funding would range from black (small budgets and expenditures) to white (large budgets and expenditures). If a series of these displays are generated based on data over the last ten years, it would be possible to see how funding and personnel resources have evolved and been distributed within the university.

The range and variety of potential applications of this

```
DrawTree()      The node gets a message to draw itself          The Root node is set up prior to the original recursive call
{   doneSize = 0;                                               The percent of this nodes subtree drawn thus far
    PaintDisplayRectangle();                                    The node sends itself a Paint Message
    switch (myOrientation) {                                    Decide whether to slice this node horizontally or vertically
        case HORIZONTAL:
            startSide = myBounds.left;                          Set start for horizontal slices
        case VERTICAL:
            startSide = myBounds.top;                           Set start for vertical slices
    }
    if (myNodeType == Internal) {                               Set up each child and have it draw itself
        ForEach (childNode) Do {
            childNode->SetBounds(startSide, doneSize, myOrientation); Set childs bounds based on the parent partition taken by previous
                                                                children of parent
            childNode->SetVisual();                             Set visual display properties (color, etc.)
            childNode->DrawTree();                              Send child a draw command
}}}

SetBounds(startSide, doneSize, parentOrientation)
{   doneSize = doneSize + mySize;                               How much of the parent will have been allocated after this node
    switch (parentOrientation) {                                Decide which direction parent is being sliced
        case HORIZONTAL:
            myOrientation = VERTICAL;                           Set direction to slice this node for its children
            endSide = parentWidth * doneSize / parentSize;      How much of the parent will have been sliced after this node
            SetMyRect(startSide + offSet,                       Left side, Offset controls the nesting indentation
                parentBounds.top + offSet,                      Top
                parentBounds.left + endSide - offSet,           Right
                parentBounds.bottom - offSet);                  Bottom
            startSide = parentBounds.left + endSide;            Set start side for next child
        case VERTICAL:
            myOrientation = HORIZONTAL;                         Set direction to slice this node for its children
            endSide = parentHeight * doneSize / parentSize;
            SetThisRect(parentBounds.left + offSet,             Left side
                startSide + offSet,                             Top
                parentBounds.right - offSet,                    Right
                parentBounds.top + endSide - offSet);           Bottom
            startSide = parentBounds.top + endSide;             Set start side for next child
}}
```

Figure 9. Drawing Algorithm

```
FindPath(point thePoint)
{   if node encloses thePoint then
    foreach child of thisNode do {
        path = FindPath(thePoint);
        if (path != NULL) then
            return(InsertInList(thisNode, path));               Add child to path
    }
    return (NULL);                                              Start path, thePoint is in this node, but not in any of its children
}
```

Figure 10. Tracking Algorithm

technology is vast. For instance, stock market portfolios are often hierarchically structured, animations over time of financial portfolios could be a valuable application of this technology.

8 Conclusion

We believe that space-filling approaches to the visualization of hierarchical information structures have great potential. The drawing algorithm we have given is quite general, and the numerous possibilities for mapping information about individual nodes to the display are appealing. The Tree-Map approach to visualizing hierarchical structures enables meaningful drawings of large hierarchies in a limited space.

Acknowledgments

We would like to acknowledge the support of the members of the Human-Computer Interaction Lab, whose suggestions and criticisms have been greatly appreciated. They have forced us to prove the value of Tree-Maps and allowed us to hone our presentations of the idea.

References

[1] David V. Beard and John Q. Walker II. Navigational techniques to improve the display of large two-dimensional spaces. *Behavior & Information Technology*, 9(6):451-466, 1990.

[2] A. Brüggemann-Klein and D. Wood. Drawing trees nicely with tex. *Electronic Publishing*, 2(2):101-115, July 1989.

[3] Stuart K. Card, George G. Robertson, and Jock D. Mackinlay. The information visualizer, an information workspace. In *Proceedings of ACM CHI'91 Conference on Human Factors in Computing Systems*, Information Visualization, pages 181-188. 1991.

[4] Richard Chimera, Kay Wolman, Sharon Mark, and Ben Shneiderman. Evaluation of three interfaces for browsing hierarchical tables of contents. Technical Report CAR-TR-539, CS-TR-2620, University of Maryland, College Park, February 1991.

[5] Donna J. Cox. The art of scientific visualization. *Academic Computing*, page 20, March 1990.

[6] Chen Ding and Prabhaker Mateti. A framework for the automated drawing of data structure diagrams. *IEEE Transactions on Software Engineering*, 16(5):543-557, May 1990.

[7] Richard Ellson. Visualization at work. *Academic Computing*, page 26, March 1990.

[8] Steven Feiner. Seeing the forest for the trees: Hierarchical display of hypertext structures. In *ACM Proc. COIS88 (Conf. on Office Information Systems)*, pages 205-212, Palo Alto, CA, March 1988.

[9] George W. Furnas. Generalized fisheye views. In *Proceedings of ACM CHI'86 Conference on Human Factors in Computing Systems*, Visualizing Complex Information Spaces, pages 16-23. 1986.

[10] Tyson R. Henry and Scott E. Hudson. Viewing large graphs. Technical Report 90-13, University of Arizona, May 1990.

[11] Ellen D. Hoadley. Investigating the effects of color. *Communications of the ACM*, 33(2):120-139, February 1990.

[12] Tomihisa Kamada. *On Visualization of Abstract Objects and Relations*. Ph.D. thesis, University of Tokyo, Department of Information Science, 7-3-1 Hongo, Bunkyo-ku, Tokyo, 113 JAPAN, December 1988.

[13] Donald E. Knuth. *Fundamental Algorithms, volume 1 of the Art of Computer Programming*. Addison-Wesley, Reading, MA, 2nd edition, 1973.

[14] Werner Kuhn. Editing spatial relations. In *Proceedings of the 4th International Symposium on Spatial Data Handling*, pages 423-432, Zurich, Switzerland, 1990.

[15] Lindsay W. MacDonald. Using colour effectively in displays for computer-human interface. *DISPLAYS*, pages 129-142, July 1990.

[16] John F. Rice. Ten rules for color coding. *Information Display*, 7(3):12-14, March 1991.

[17] George G. Robertson, Jock D. Mackinlay, and Stuart K. Card. Cone trees: Animated 3d visualizations of hierarchical information. In *Proceedings of ACM CHI'91 Conference on Human Factors in Computing Systems*, Information Visualization, pages 189-194. 1991.

[18] Hanan Samet. *Design and Analysis of Spatial Data Structures*. Addison-Wesley Publishing Co., Reading, MA, 1989.

[19] Andrew Sears and Ben Shneiderman. High precision touchscreens: Design strategies and comparisons with a mouse. *International Journal of Man-Machine Studies*, 34(4):593-613, April 1991.

[20] Ben Shneiderman. Tree visualization with tree-maps: A 2-d space-filling appoach. Technical Report CAR-TR-548, CS-TR-2645, University of Maryland, College Park, September 1990. to appear in *ACM Transactions on Graphics*.

[21] Michael Travers. A visual representation for knowledge structures. In *ACM Hypertext'89 Proceedings*, Implementations and Interfaces, pages 147-158. 1989.

[22] E. R. Tufte. *The Visual Display of Quantitative Information*. Graphics Press, Cheshire, CT, 1983.

[23] Kim J. Vicente, Brian C. Hayes, and Robert C. Williges. Assaying and isolating individual differences in searching a hierarchical file system. *Human Factors*, 29(3):349-359, 1987.

Space-Filling Software Visualization

Marla J. Baker and Stephen G. Eick*
AT&T Bell Laboratories

3 August 1994

Abstract

SeeSys™ is a system embodying a technique for visualizing statistics associated with code that is divided hierarchically into subsystems, directories, and files. This technique can display the relative sizes of the components in the system, the relative stability of the components, the location of new functionality, and the location of error-prone code with many bug fixes. Using animation, it can display the historical evolution of the code. Applying this technique, the source code from a multi-million line production software product is visualized.

1 Introduction

The software industry produces the most complicated data-driven systems ever created. A single software system may contain millions of lines written by thousands of programmers. Now, as larger and larger systems are built, the problems of understanding their increasing complexity threaten to set a limit on system size.

One solution employs data visualizations [Tuf83] [Tuf90] to help software engineers understand the code they are working on. Making data or graphical representations of software, known as software visualization, is well-known and has produced useful tools for developing code [Ebe92]. Previous work in software visualization had its roots in academia and has focused on data structure and algorithm visualization. Notable examples include Baecker's seminal work on sorting [BM88], Brown's work on algorithm animation [BH92], North et al.'s displays of software graphs [GKNV93], Price et al.'s taxonomy of software visualization [PSB93], Stasko's research in visualizing parallel computation [KS93], and Roman and Cox's visualizations of specifications [RCWP92].

Unfortunately, current graphical techniques are ineffective for large software systems. When applied to production-sized systems, routines for producing flow charts, function call graphs, and structure diagrams [You89] often break because the display is too complicated. Or they produce displays that contain too much information and are completely illegible. For many existing systems, even system structure diagrams are impossible to create because the original abstractions have been forgotten or are inapplicable after years of software modifications. And for large software projects, management issues (involving the human aspects of the project rather than the execution of the code), are often more challenging than the technical issues. For example, project managers need to know where new development activity is occurring and which modules are error prone so they can assign them to their best engineers.

To deal with these problems we have developed a space-filling technique for displaying source code related software statistics. We have focused on visualizing program source code in files, directories, and subsystems. In previous work, based on a reduced representation, Eick et al. [ESS92] and [Eic94] presented a method for visualizing statistics associated with lines of code in files. The technique, implemented in a system called *SeeSoft*™, fits up to

50,000 lines of code on a high-resolution (1280x1024) display using a reduced representation. In Seesoft each line of code is displayed as a color-coded row within columns corresponding to the files, with the row indentation and length tracking the actual code. Therefore, to visualize larger systems using that technique, the code must be divided into 50,000 line chunks. The presented work generalizes the previous technique from displaying lines within files to files in directories within subsystems. This generalization is based on Johnson and Shneiderman's fundamental work using treemaps to show hierarchical data [JS91].

Our motivation for studying source code visualization came from the source code database for a large communications software system at AT&T. This software system is continually being modified for customers world-wide. Several million lines of code are organized hierarchically into tens of subsystems, several thousand directories, and hundreds of thousands of files. Software releases occur about once a year, each built on the previous release by making changes such as adding new functionality or hardware support. The database for each software release contains detailed information on all files, directories, and subsystems, including

- non-commentary source lines (NCSL),
- software complexity metrics,
- number and scope of modifications (e.g. which files are affected),
- number of programmers making modifications, and
- number and type of bugs (a subcategory of modifications),

and other statistics. This information raises five questions for project managers:

1. Which subsystems are the largest? Where is the new development activity?
2. Where are the large directories? Are the large and small directories distributed evenly throughout the subsystems? Is the new development distributed evenly between directories? Which directories are stable and which have the most activity?

3. Which subsystems are unusually complex or error-prone? Are there any problematic directories? How is the development activity apportioned between fixing bugs and adding new functionality?

4. Are bug fixes a reoccurring problem? What components would make good candidates for code restructuring projects?

5. What were the dates of the major releases? Have any subsystems shrunk or disappeared? What is the rate for growth of different subsystems?

   Which subsystems are growing at the fastest rates? Have any subsystems remained at the same size or grown at a steady rate? Where has the development work been done historically?

Statistical methods for analyzing the distributions of subsystem, directory, and file statistics are well-known [CM88]. For software engineering, however, it is equally important to understand the context in which the statistics relate to the code. By itself, the bug rate for a directory may not look like a sign of trouble. Only when we can see most of the other directories do we realize that something may be wrong in the subsystem. Similarly, scatterplots are useful for identifying unusual files and directories. But using this information is difficult. The unusual directories must be related to the subsystem to which they belong, and for a system with hundreds of thousands of files, even relating only the worst 1% of them to their respective directories involves correlating thousands of files.

Another problem with methods of statistical analysis to study software involves incorporating domain knowledge. Experienced software engineers often have detailed knowledge and explanations that must be included in the analysis to properly interpret the data. For example, one-time events with known explanations may not indicate general trends.

To address these problems, we have developed a graphical technique that visualizes subsystem, directory, and file statistics, but does so in context. Our method, implemented in a system called *SeeSys*™, preserves the hierarchical relationships in the code, making it easy to relate the statistics to the components. SeeSys accomplishes all this by means of space-filling representations. On a single computer monitor, it can easily show directory level statistics for a system with thousands of directories.

The approach we took in SeeSys is discussed below in Section 2, applications of SeeSys in Section 3, and factors that make SeeSys a powerful visualization tool in Section 4.

2 Approach

The visualization technique used in SeeSys is based on the idea that a software system can be decomposed into its individual components. For example, the NCSL for a directory is the sum of the NCSL's for the individual files in the directory, and the NCSL for a subsystem is the sum of the NCSL's for its individual directories.

Figure 1 shows the visual technique used in SeeSys. The left pane represents the entire software system, and X, Y, and Z represent its three subsystems. The area of each subsystem is based on some subsystem statistic, such as NCSL. The subsystems are each partitioned vertically to show their internal directories. In the left pane of Figure 1, the rectangles labeled *1*, *2*, *3*, *4*, and *5* represent the directories in subsystem X. Each vertical rectangle's area is proportional to the directory's NCSL, and so the sum of the areas over the directories equals the area of the subsystem.

This technique allows for a straight-forward visual comparison of directories within a subsystem because area of each visual component is always proportional to the statistic for the corresponding software component.

The middle pane in Figure 1 shows additional information by vertically filling each rectangle. The fill might indicate the NCSL which correspond to newly developed code. The fill provides a visually pleasing display of a second statistic, and a convenient method for cross directory comparisons. It is clear from the middle pane in Figure 1 that directory *5* has had the highest percentage of new code added to subsystem X, although not necessarily the the largest amount of new NCSL. In fact, directory *1* has the most new lines of code because it has the largest area.

The right pane in Figure 1 shows a zoom view of the Y subsystem from the middle pane in Figure 1. Each directory now has been partitioned horizontally to represent its internal files. Again, as with the directories, the rectangle sizes are proportional to the file-level statistics. The leftmost directory contains files *file1*, *file2*, *file3*, *file4*, and *file5*, and the average fill for the files reflects the fill for the directory level. As in the previous example,

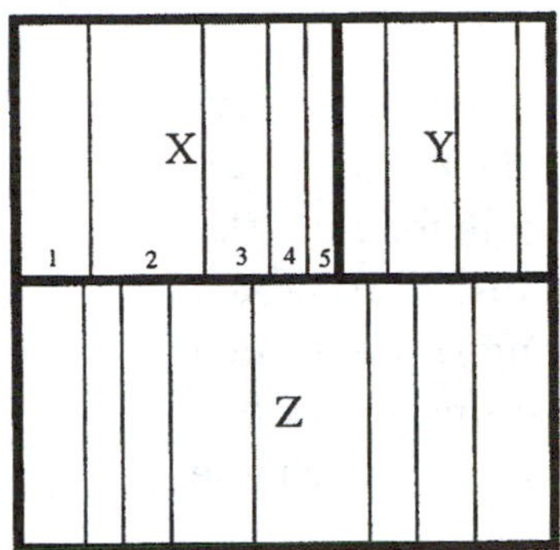

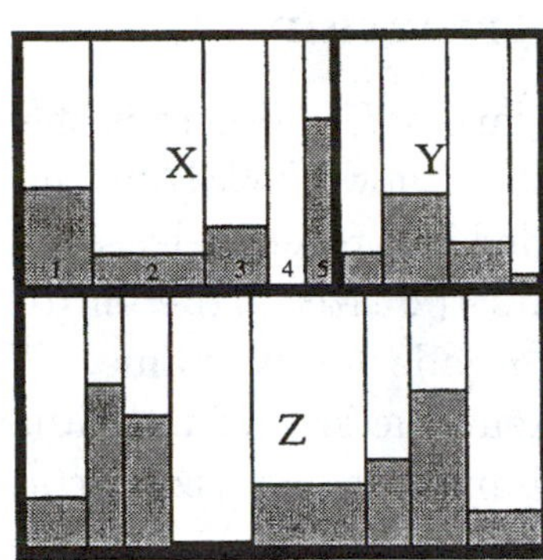

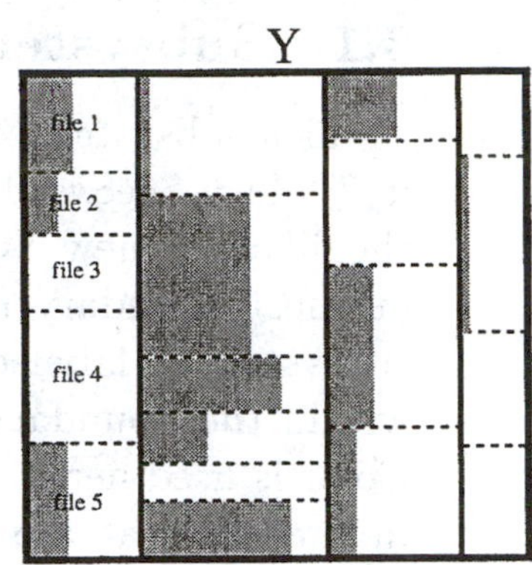

Figure 1: Left pane: subsystem and directory statistics. Middle pane: a fill statistic for directories. Right pane: a zoomed view on subsystem *Y* showing file level statistics.

at the directory level, the fill might display newly developed code in a recent release.

This technique is effective for showing software statistics that accumulate from files to directories to subsystems. These include NCSL, number of bugs, complexity metrics, fix-on-fix rates, and so on. The hierarchical decomposition immediately relates the files to their directories and the directories to their subsystems, making cross unit comparisons easy. The fill provides a visual representation of percentages, enabling quick identification of outlyers, such as directory *5* in Figure 1. The fill, for example, could be the NCSL fixing bugs, or the number of comments in the code, or in general, a percentage associated with each code unit. We also use color and interaction to overlay additional information onto the display.

3 Applications

The following illustrates the effectiveness of SeeSys by showing how it can be used to answer the questions listed in Section 1 for the software system.

3.1 Subsystem Information

"Which subsystems are the largest?" "Where is the new development activity?" In a SeeSys display that shows NCSL for subsystems (see Figure 2), the fill shows new NCSL added in a recent release. The rectangle forming the outmost boundary represents the size of the entire system in NCSL. Each subsystem is labeled with a code for its name. The rectangles contained within the boundary represent the size of individual subsystems in NCSL. Color is used here to redundantly encode size according to the color scheme in the slider at the bottom of the screen. Two medium sized subsystems, *A* and *B*, appear in the upper left-hand corner. Note that subsystems are shown in alphabetical order so they can be located easily.

What does the figure show? It is immediately clear that the three largest subsystems are *D*, *d*, and *n*, because their rectangles are visually the most prominent and their colors are towards the brighter end of the spectrum. The fill (light gray rectangles at the bottom of each subsystem rectangle) shows that *t*, *k* and *E* had the largest percentage increases in code size during the release. *t* is a new subsystem that was created in release 14. The number of NCSL [1] for *t* for recent releases is shown in the lower left-hand corner, *74,279* in release 15, *17,131* in release 14, and *0* in all previous releases. The percentage increase, *74%*, is shown in the color scale.

3.2 Directory Information

"Where are the large directories?" "Are the large and small directories distributed evenly throughout the subsystem?" "Is the new development distributed evenly between directories?" "Which directories are stable and which have the most activity?" Figure 3 shows directory statistics added to the display. The area of the subsystem rectangles is the same as in Figure 2, but each subsystem is partitioned vertically to display these internal directories. The area of each directory rectangle is proportional to its size in NCSL. Again, the fill is proportional to new development while the color redundantly encodes the size of the directory.

The largest directories are highlighted according to a color spectrum at the bottom of the display: pink for the biggest, through yellow, green, and finally blue for the smallest. We can see that the two largest directories are

[1] Data values, names, and release numbers have been altered.

in subsystems *e* and *Z*, and that subsystems *n* and *D* have no large directories since all of their directories show colors towards the blue end of the spectrum.

We refer to Figure 3 as the "software" skyline. It shows the sizes of the subsystems and directories, the new development, and even which directories are new or unchanged. The fill shows the NCSL added in release 15. For new directories the entire directory space is filled in gray; for directories with 50% new code, the gray area fills half of the directory space. In *t*, for example, we can see that almost all the directories are being actively developed, but that in *X* there has been almost no new development.

By zooming, we can obtain more information about any particular subsystem. In Figure 4, a zoom view of subsystem *t* makes the directory divisions more clear. The darker gray fill in each directory represents the new development. Thus we can see only one directory, *t7*, has been stable (1% new code), while all of the others have had significant activity during this software release.

3.3 Error-Prone Code

"Which subsystems and directories have the most bugs?" "Are there any problematic directories?" "How is the development activity apportioned between fixing bugs and adding new functionality?" In Figure 5, the size of each subsystem and directory is the new NCSL and the fill is the new NCSL added to fix bugs (directory color is uniform, no longer encoding any information). The largest subsystems are *k*, *d*, *Z*, and *t*. These subsystems have had the most new development. The light gray rectangle within each subsystem (obscured by the directory fill spikes) represents the bug fixing NCSL for the subsystem, while the directory spikes represent directory bug fixing NCSL detail. The *t* subsystem now takes up a larger portion of the display because it has had so much new development. The small light gray rectangle for *t* shows that almost all of the new development has added new functionality. Only a small percentage of the new NCSL fixed bugs in most of the *t* directories.

In contrast, subsystem *g* has a very high bug rate. The light gray subsystem rectangle shows that about 50% of the development activity in *g* has been fixing bugs. In several of the directories in *g*, the blue directory spikes that extend to the top of the rectangle indicate that all of the new NCSL involved bug fixes.

3.4 Recurring Problems

"Are bug fixes a recurring problem?" "What components would make good candidates for code restructuring projects?" A *fix-on-fix* bug is a software bug correction that modifies an earlier bug fix. A high fix-on-fix rate may indicate unstable or unmaintainable code. In Figure 6, the area representing each subsystem and directory is proportional to the number of bugs, while the fill area is proportional to the number of fix-on-fix bugs in each subsystem and directory. Again, the light gray rectangle represents the subsystem average while the spikes across the subsystems represent directory level detail. Subsystems i and K have the highest fix-on-fix rates. Some directories in these subsystems have relatively high fix-on-fix rates, making them good candidates for code restructuring projects.

3.5 System Evolution

"Which were the major software releases?" "Have any subsystems shrunk or disappeared?" "What is the rate of growth for different subsystems?" "Which subsystems are growing at the fastest rates?" "Have any subsystems remained at the same size or grown at a steady rate?" "Where has the development work been done historically?" To address these questions, SeeSys animates the display over the historical evolution of the code.

Although it is impossible to get the full effect of the animation from a static display, some ideas can be conveyed. Figures 7, 8 and 9 shows three frames from an animation. The animation depicts the NCSL growth through various software releases of the software. The bounding rectangle for each subsystem represents the maximum size of the subsystem across all software releases in the dataset, while the filled portion of the display represents the size of the system in the software release, as seen in the frame slider on the left of the screen. The frame slider controls which frame (or software release) is displayed. It will be described in more detail later. Color is again redundantly encoding the size of each subsystem, changing in relation to the size of the subsystem for each software release in the dataset. Figure 7 shows the earliest software release in the dataset. Note that subsystem t was not yet in existence while other subsystems, such as d and W, had almost reached their maximum sizes. Figure 8 shows a frame from the middle of the dataset, and Figure 9 shows the most recent software release in the dataset. At the end of the animation, most of the subsystems have reached their maximum size. A few subsystems (e.g., *W* and *f*) have decreased in size and others have disappeared completely (e.g., *O*).

From watching the animation we have discovered the following about changes in the size of subsystems:

- several of the subsystems are stable;
- subsystem *O* grew and shrank before it finally disappeared;
- subsystems *F* and *J* have shrunk;
- subsystem *D* grew slowly at first but fast recently;
- subsystems *t*, *k*, and *Z* are currently growing fastest and at similar rates.

4 SeeSys Visualization System

SeeSys is a visualization system for displaying software metrics. There are two requirements that must hold for a metric to be displayable. It must be a quantitative measure, and it must be additive (the sum of the measure for the parts must equal the measure for the whole). In the examples above, the software metrics used were NCSL, newly developed NCSL, number of bugs, and number of fix-on-fix bugs. But SeeSys lends itself to the use of other software metrics as well. For example, the number of modifications is another valid measure. In that case, the area of the rectangles would be proportional to the number of modifications in each component, and the bounding rectangle would represent the total number for the whole software system.

The SeeSys visualization system may be extended to display software complexity metrics such as Halstead's program volume measure [Hal77] or McCabe's cyclomatic complexity [McC76]. The color or texture of each rectangle could encode the complexity of the corresponding subunit, with red indicating the most complex units and blue indicating the least complex units.

4.1 User Interaction

User interaction via a mouse is a powerful means of retrieving information visually. SeeSys tracks mouse movements over the display area, conveying additional information about whichever component the mouse is touching at that time. This is called the *active component* and is indicated by a red highlighted boundary. The active component may be either a subsystem or a directory and a subsystem. In Figure 3, subsystem *I* and directory *I17* are the active components. The directory's name and current statistic appear above the slider at the bottom of the screen, with a vertical bar marking its place in the slider according to the current statistic. Components can also be activated by placing the mouse in this slider.

The available statistics are shown on the lower left side of the screen. Clicking the mouse on one of these statistics causes the display to be redrawn with that statistic. On the display in Figure 3 the user may call up information on the NCSL, on newly developed NCSL, and on software faults or bugs.

There are also five buttons (*No Mod Lines*, *No Mod Names*, *Colors*, *Fill*, and *Zoom*) that appear on the upper left corner of the screen. The first button turns directory bounding lines *on* and *off* (turned *on* in Figure 4). The second button toggles the directory colors (turned *off* in Figure 5 and Figure 6). The third button turns on and off the fill for the directory level. The fourth button activates a zoom feature which allows the user to zoom in on a particular subsystem (see Figure 4). The user clicks on the zoom button and then on one of the subsystems to bring up a zoom window. Zoom windows and the main display are linked so that operations on either one will affect the other. The buttons can make the display simpler or more customized to user preferences.

The slider labeled *ROWS* is used to control the number of rows in the display. One may click at any point in the slider to change to the corresponding number of rows or drag through the slider to find the optimal layout.

Figures 7, 8, and 9 have two additional sliders, used to control the animation, on the left side of the screen. The *speed slider* controls the animation speed (the delay in milliseconds between frames) when the animation is active, and the *frame slider* controls which frame is displayed. Clicking the mouse anywhere in the frame slider causes the display to change to the corresponding frame and, as a result, the display space is redrawn. The *play button* activates the animation and may be used interactively to stop at places of interest. Dragging the mouse through the slider shows the animation at the drag speed.

An effective interactive technique during animation is to put the mouse on one subsystem and watch the active bar move in the slider below. Each bar represents a subsystem, and is placed in the slider according to that subsystem's value. Since the bar moves across the slider during the animation, a user can see the active subsystem's evolution both in the color scale and in relative size, providing two different perspectives. In Figures 7, 8, and 9 the active subsystem, K, can be viewed in two ways throughout the animation. In the display area, one can see that K is about 50% of its maximum size in the first software release of the dataset, 75% its maximum size in the middle release, and finally, K reaches its maximum size in the last release. Looking at the color slider at the bottom of the screen offers another perspective. Here K begins towards the lower end of the spectrum (at 203,902 NCSL), along with most of the other subsystems. It then moves to the middle of the spectrum, with an increase to 270,653 NCSL. Finally, in the last software release, K moves towards the top end of the spectrum (356,070 NCSL), distinguishing itself as a relatively large subsystem. Although it is difficult to see in only three frames from the animation, K grows at a relatively constant rate.

4.2 Display Principles

The visualization approach used in SeeSys is based on three principles:

1. The individual components can be assembled to form the whole. This allows the user to easily see relationships between them.

2. Pairs of components can be compared to understand how they differ. In Figure 2, it is obvious that subsystem D is much larger than subsystem t.

3. The components can be disassembled into smaller components. In Figure 3, the vertical bars clearly show the division of the subsystems into directories. This important feature of the components allows the structure of the display to reflect the structure of the software.

4.3 Screen Real-Estate

In visualizing large software systems, it is important to utilize screen real-estate efficiently. Objects placed on the screen must be large enough to convey information, but small enough to allow room for many other objects. SeeSys does this by placing rectangles next to one another so that 100% of the display area is utilized.

When using area, components with large statistics become visually dominant, making the technique effective when the components representing the larger directories are the most interesting while de-emphasizing the small components. For example, in Figure 3 it is difficult to see the small directories. SeeSys overcomes this difficulty with a zoom feature that allows the user to zoom in on any subsystem (see Figure 4).

4.4 Spatial Relationships

It is important that the screen real-estate technique used lends itself to the rapid transfer of information. Simply packing data onto the screen is not necessarily helpful. The viewer must be able to process the information rapidly for the visualization technique to be useful. SeeSys speeds the transfer of information by taking advantage of the human ability to recognize spatial relationships. People naturally make inferences from the configuration of components and can relate each component to the whole.

It is easier to see relationships between components if the heights of the rectangles are approximately equal. We use an algorithm to equalize the heights while retaining the easy comprehensibility of the display (for example, by preserving the alphabetical ordering). If the heights were exactly even, it would be necessary to split subsystems between rows, leave ragged "margins," or have spaces of variable width between the subsystems. In Figure 2, subsystem D might have to be partially split between the first and second row. This would undermine the basis of the approach because all individual parts would not always represent one component in the system, making it harder to see relationships between individual components. To deal with this problem, we introduced a slider that allows the user to control the number of rows in the display. By changing the aspect ratio, the user can find the optimal display for gaining insight into a particular characteristic. In Figure 10, the number of rows has been reduced to just one so the user can easily compare the percentage of new development across the subsystems.

Although we have chosen to order components alphabetically to facilitate rapid location of specific components, one can foresee other useful ordering techniques such as by area, complexity metric, percentage changes, or other statistic values. Future version of SeeSys will include controls to reorder the components alphabetically, by area, and according to a specified statistic.

4.5 Color

Color[2] is another visualization technique used to convey yet more information. In the previous examples, color was used to redundantly encode size, with the brighter colors denoting larger components. We use a perceptually uniform color spectrum [LH92] [LHMR92] to encode information, but other spectrums with fewer, greater, or differing colors could be used to make distinctions between components. Color can also be used to encode other information, such as age, complexity, activity (code churn), or number of programmers.

4.6 Implementation

SeeSys is implemented in C++ using AT&T Bell Laboratories' Vz graphics library™[Gro94]. Vz is a cross-platform class library forming a computational infrastructure for producing innovative, novel, production-quality visualizations of large datasets. Vz uses C++'s object-oriented capabilities, factors out common code, embodies direct manipulation, and data abstractions in a selective manner for building highly-interactive visualizations of large datasets based on linked views.

SeeSys consists of four linked views of data: the colorful space-filling display, the leftspace containing controls, buttons, and sliders, the bottom space containing the color scale and statistics, and the zoom view showing details of a particular subsystem. Each mouse-sensitive view is implemented as Vz class, is tied together though Vz's linking, and united through the use of a perceptually uniform color scale. Each view is highly-interactive and continuously responds to mouse and keyboard input in any of the views. On

[2] In the black and white version of this paper color is mapped to gray level.

a Silicon Graphics Iris workstation screen updates occur in real-time and appear continuous.

In total SeeSys is about 3,000 lines of delicate C++ code that runs on workstations supporting X11 and Motif or Silicon Graphics's GL graphics language [Boa92].

5 Summary

SeeSys is a system implementing a graphics technique for displaying large volumes of information about software. The SeeSys visualization technique can display code for any existing software system that is organized hierarchically into subsystems, directories, and files by representing the whole system as a rectangle and recursively representing the various subunits with interior rectangles. The area of each rectangle is proportional to a statistic (for example, NCSL) associated with its subunit. SeeSys then uses color, zooming, a fill statistic, and interactive techniques to layer additional information onto the base display.

Applying SeeSys to display the source code from the system we can

- show the sizes of the subsystems and directories and where the recent development activity has been;
- zoom in on particularly active subsystems;
- discover how much of the development activity involves bug fixes and new functionality;
- identify directories and subsystems with high fix-on-fix rates;
- locate the historically active subsystems and find subsystems that have shrunk and even disappeared.

The SeeSys visualization technique can display source code statistics for an entire software system in terms of the code structure, complexity, and evolution. Three principles should be adhered to when creating visualizations of large software systems:

1. The structure of the display should reflect the structure of the software.

2. The individual components should be visually comparable and decomposable.

3. Animation can be used to depict the evolution of the software.

Potential users of SeeSys include Project Managers, Feature Engineers, and Software Developers. Project Managers can use SeeSys to help track the evolution of the code and understand how each subsystem, directory, and file fits into the whole system. Feature Engineers may use SeeSys to help determine which components of the system will be impacted by planned enhancements. And, finally, Software Developers can use SeeSys to identify error-prone subsystems that are candidates for reengineering.

Acknowledgments

We gratefully acknowledge Haim Levkowitz for providing the perceptually uniform color scales, the many helpful suggestions made by David Weiss, Brian Johnson's careful proofreading, and suggestions from two anonymous referees. An early version of this paper appears in the ICSE16 proceedings. This research was conducted while Marla Baker was a summer employee at AT&T Bell Laboratories.

References

[BH92] Marc H. Brown and John Hershberger. Color and sound in algorithm animation. *IEEE Computer*, 25(12):52–63, December 1992.

[BM88] R. M. Baecker and A. Marcus. *Human Factors and Typography for More Readable Programs.* Addison-Wesley, Reading, Massachusetts, 1988.

[Boa92] OpenGL Architecture Review Board. *OpenGL Reference Manual.* Addison-Wesley, Reading,Massachusetts, 1992.

[CM88] William S. Cleveland and Marylyn E. McGill, editors. *Dynamic Graphics for Statistics.* Wadsworth & Brooks/Cole, Pacific Grove, California, 1988.

[Ebe92] Christof Ebert. Visualization techniques for analyzing and evaluating software measures. *IEEE Transactions on Software Engineering*, 11(18):1029–1034, 1992.

[Eic94] Stephen G. Eick. A graphical technique to display ordered text. *Journal of Computational and Graphical Statistics*, 3(2):127–142, June 1994.

[ESS92] Stephen G. Eick, Joseph L. Steffen, and Eric E. Sumner. Seesoft™-tool for visualizing line oriented software software. *IEEE Transactions on Software Engineering*, 11(18):957–968, 1992.

[GKNV93] Emden R. Gansner, Eleftherios E. Koutsofios, Stephen C. North, and K.P. Vo. A technique for drawing directed graphs. *IEEE Transactions on Software Engineering*, 19(3):214–230, March 1993.

[Gro94] Visualization Group. *Vz Visualization Library: User's Guide Version 1.0.* AT&T Bell Laboratories, 1000 E. Warrenville Road, Naperville, Illinois 60565, 1994.

[Hal77] M. H. Halstead. *Elements of Software Science.* Elsevier, New York, 1977.

[JS91] Brian Johnson and Ben Shneiderman. Tree-maps: A space-filling approach to the visualization of hierarchical information structures. In *IEEE Visualization '91 Conference Proceedings*, pages 284–291, San Diego, California, October 1991.

[KS93] Eileen Kraemer and John T. Stasko. The visualiztion of parallel systems: An overview. *Journal of Parallel and Distributed Computing*, 18:105–117, 1993.

[LH92] Haim Levkowitz and G. T. Herman. Color scales for image data. *IEEE Computer Graphics and Applications*, 12(1):78–80, 1992.

[LHMR92] Haim Levkowitz, Richard A. Holub, Gary W. Meyer, and Philip K. Robertson. Color vs black and white in visuzliation. *IEEE Computer Graphics and Applications*, 12(4):20–22, 1992.

[McC76] T. J. McCabe. A complexity measure. *IEEE Transactions on Software Engineering*, 1(3):312–327, 1976.

[PSB93] Blaine A. Price, Ian S. Small, and Ronald M. Baecker. A taxonomy of software visualization. *Journal of Visual Languages and Computing*, 4(3), 1993.

[RCWP92] Gruia-Catalin Roman, Kenneth C. Cox, C. Donald Wilcox, and Jerome Y. Plun. Pavane: a system for declarative visualization of concurrent computations. *Journal of Visual Languages and Computing*, 3(2):161–193, 1992.

[Tuf83] Edward R. Tufte. *The Visual Display of Quantitative Information.* Graphics Press, Cheshire, Connecticut, 1983.

[Tuf90] Edward R. Tufte. *Envisioning Information.* Graphics Press, Cheshire, Connecticut, 1990.

[You89] Edward Yourdon. *Modern Structured Analysis.* Yourdon Press/Prentice Hall, 1989.

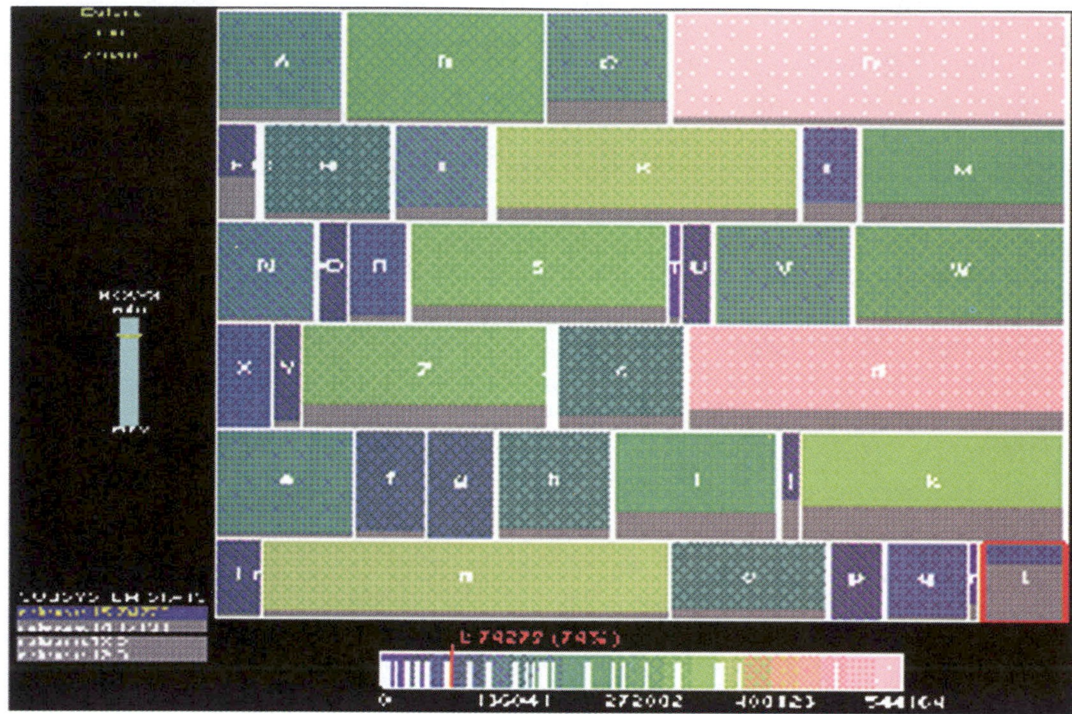

FIGURE 2

NCSL and new development by subsystem in a recent release.

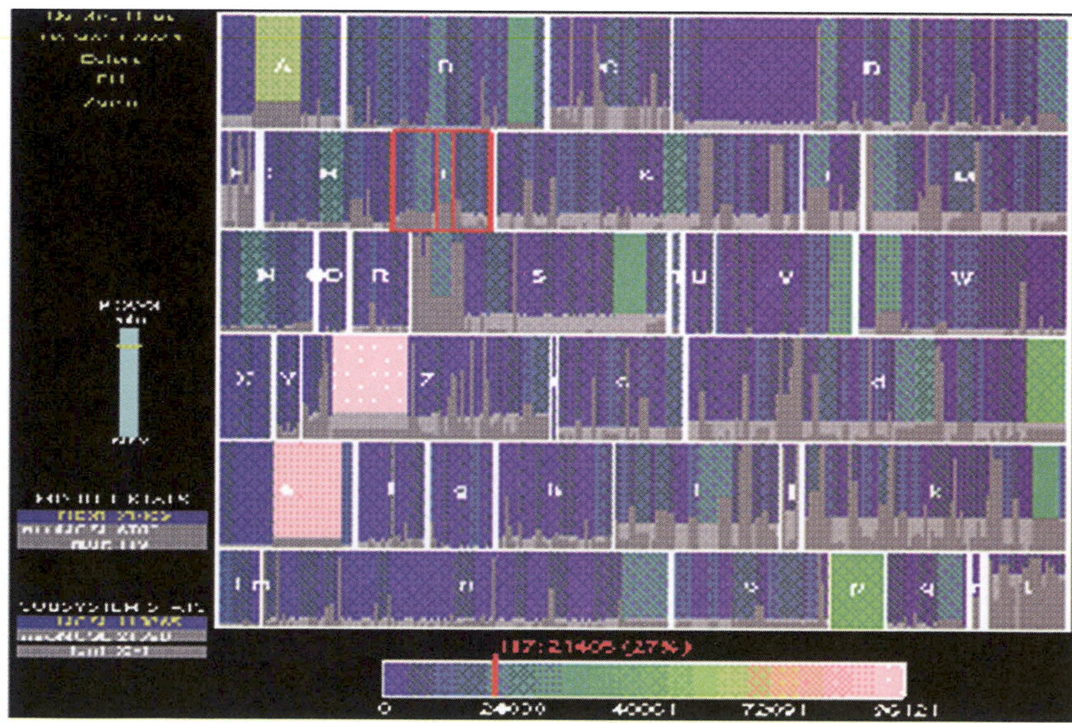

FIGURE 3

Directory level detail.

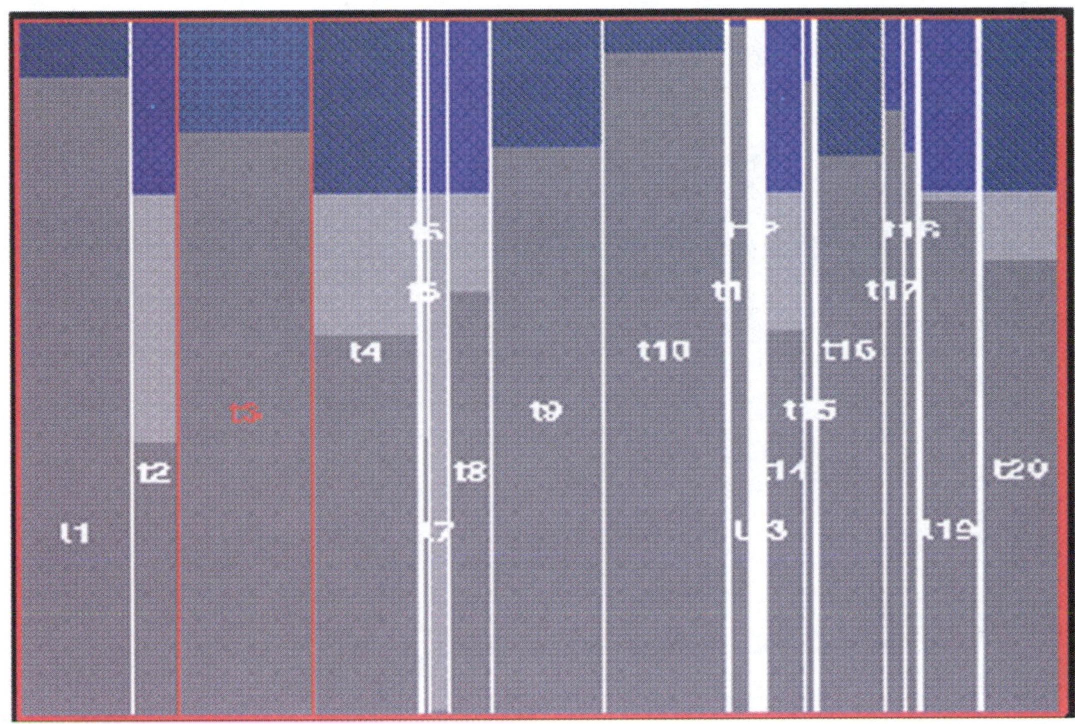

FIGURE **4**

Zoomed view of subsystem *t*.

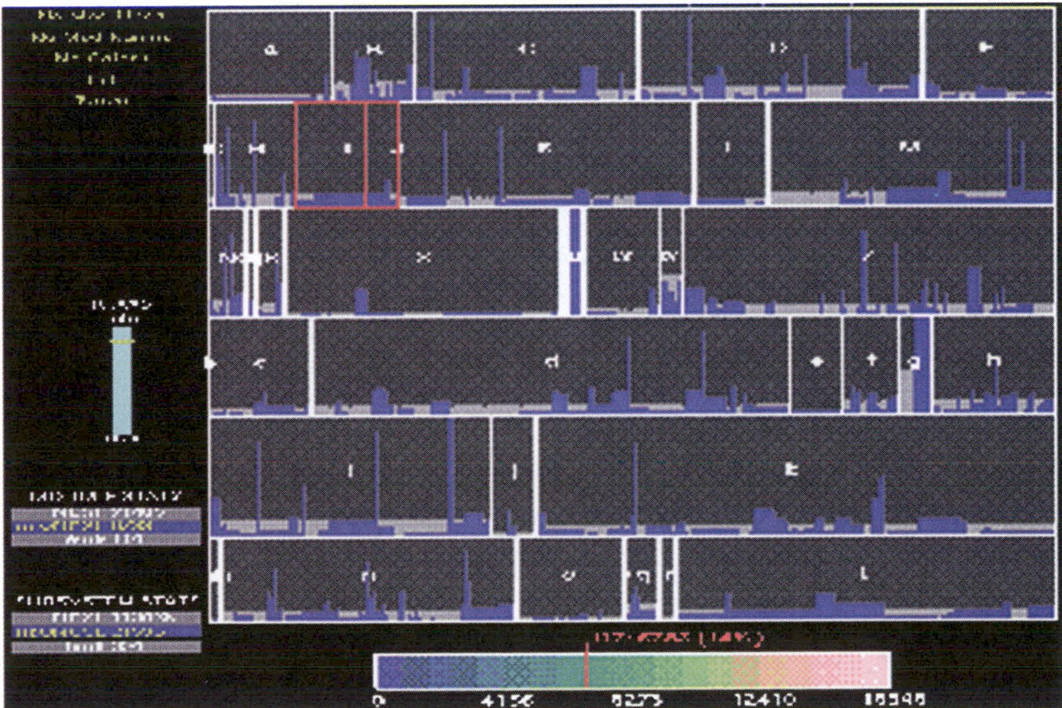

FIGURE **5**

Bug rates by subsystem and directory.

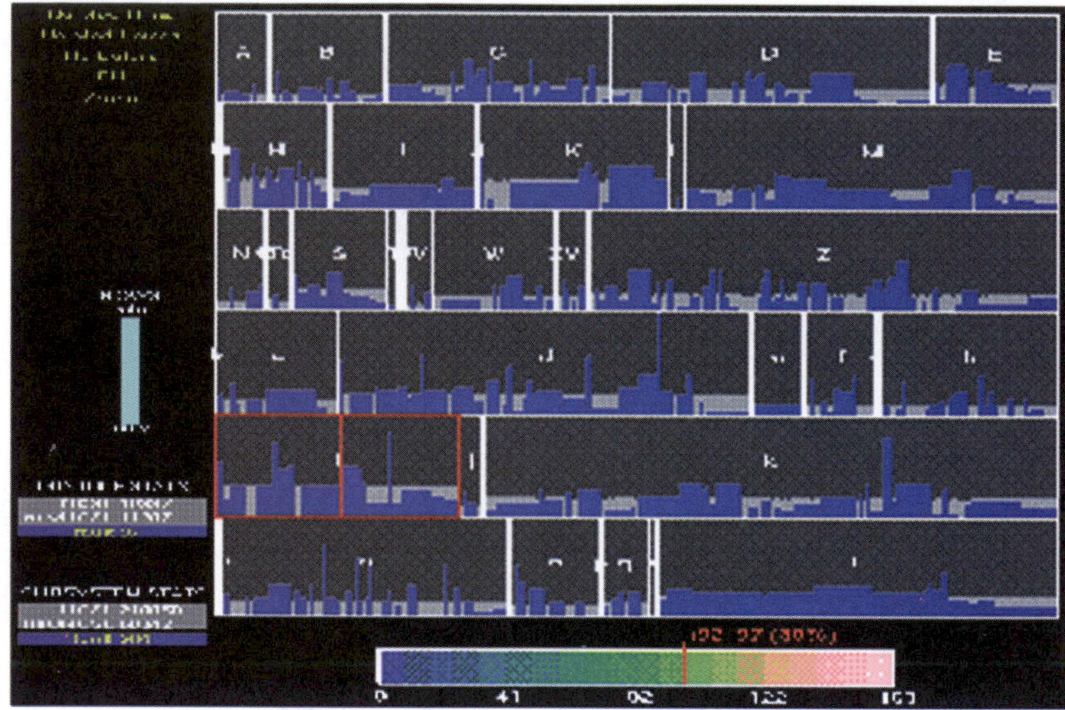

FIGURE 6

Fix-On-Fix rates.

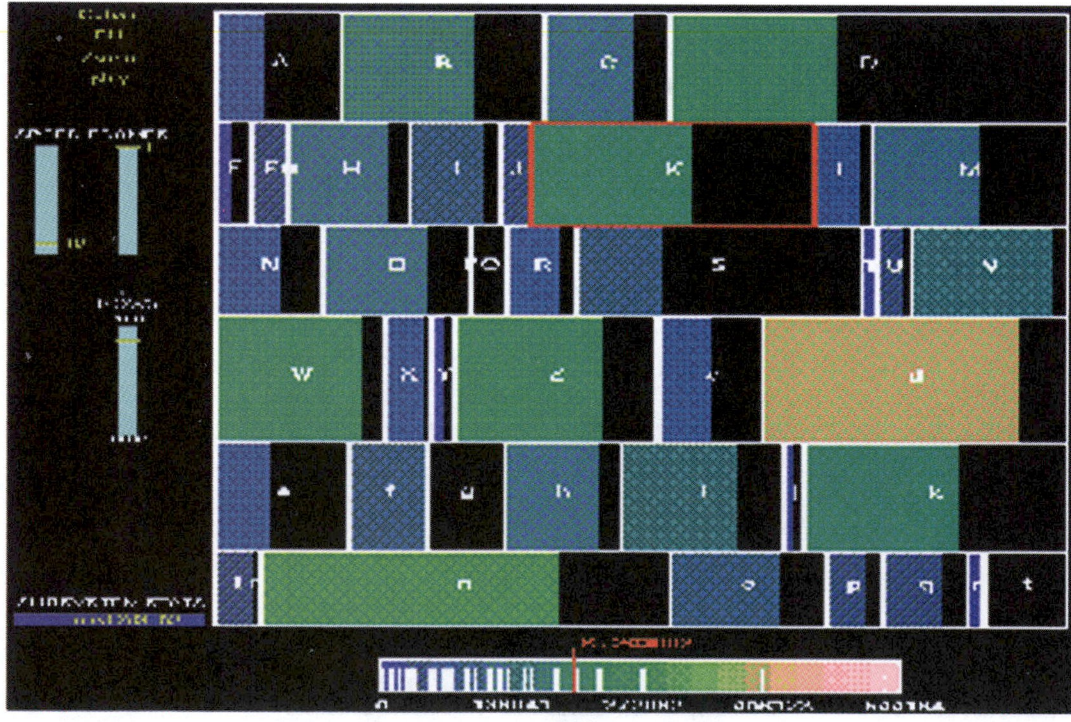

FIGURE 7

Frame 1 from an animation showing code growth.

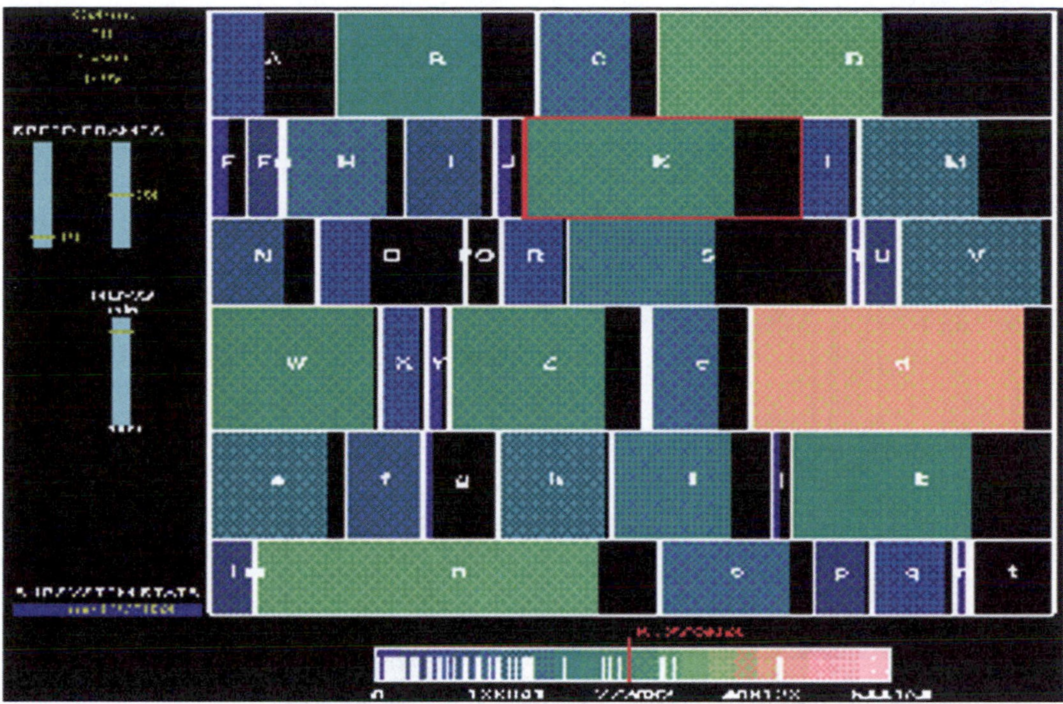

FIGURE **8**

Frame 2 from an animation showing code growth.

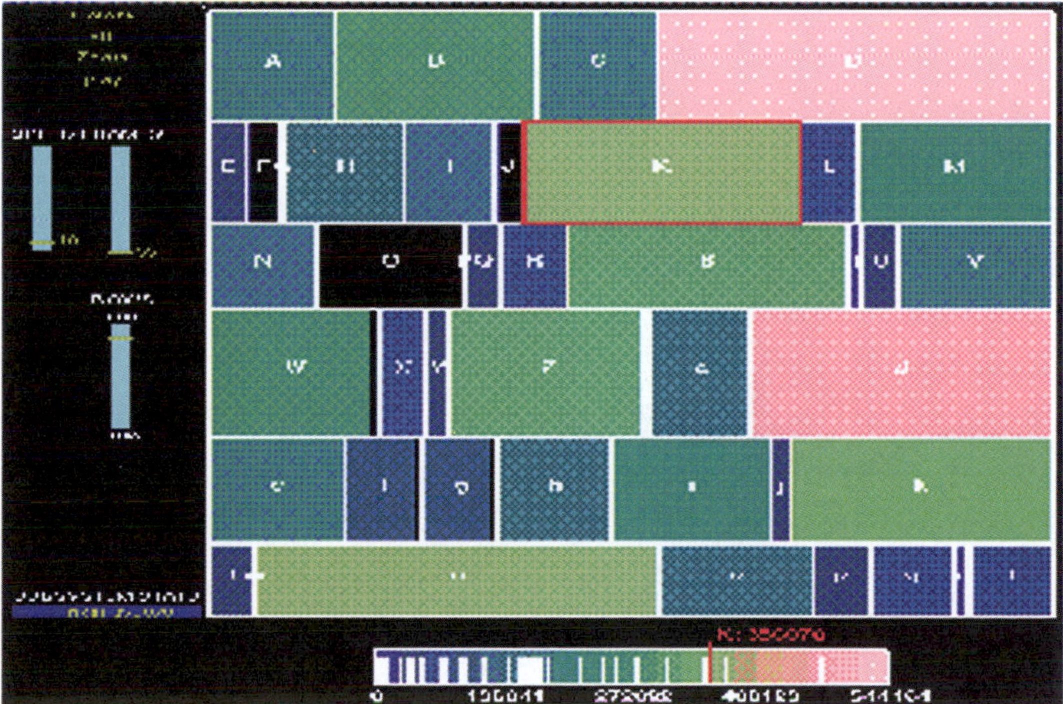

FIGURE **9**

Frame 3 from an animation showing code growth.

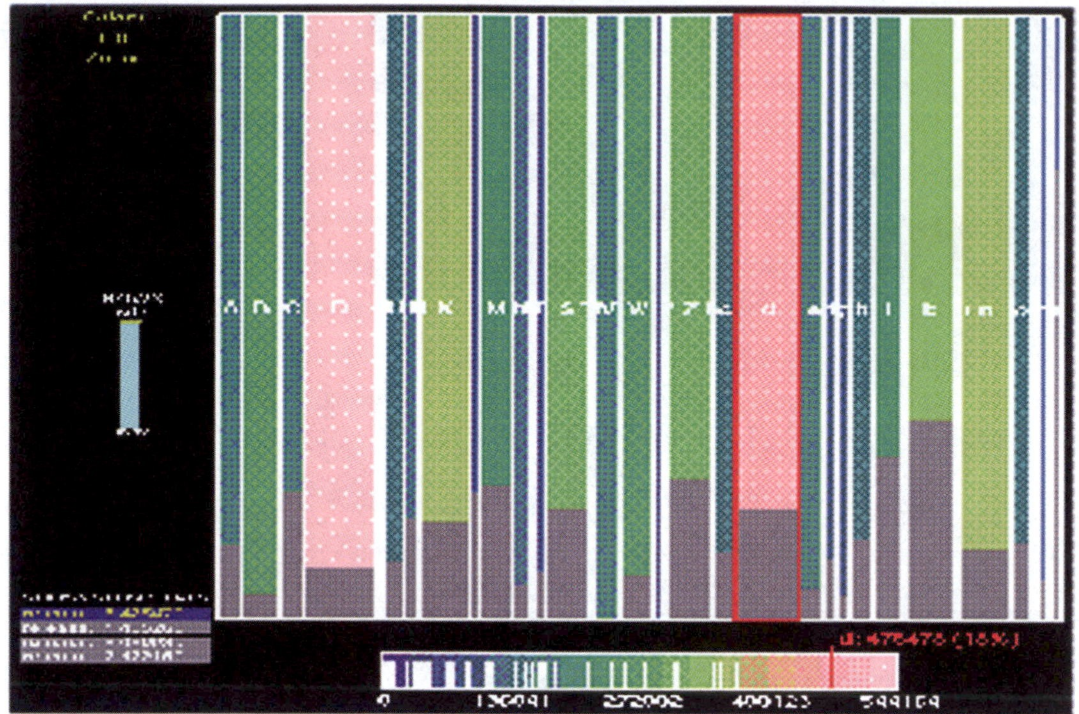

FIGURE **10**

New development by subsystem.

TennisViewer: A Browser for Competition Trees

Liqun Jin
Thomson Electronic Information Resources

David C. Banks
Mississippi State University

A tennis novice watching a match for the first time might be surprised that the crowd erupts with cheers when a player wins one point, then barely applauds when he wins the next. The crowd is not necessarily fickle; some points are genuinely more important than others because a tennis match is hierarchically structured. One match consists of several sets. One set consists of several games. One game consists of several points. The match-winning point is the most important one.

How can we make that importance visible? Our goal is to let a fan, a player, or a coach examine tennis data visually, extract the interesting parts, and jump from one item to another quickly and easily. The visualization tool should help parse the elements of a match.

We developed an interactive system called TennisViewer to visualize the dynamic, tree-structured data representing a tennis match. It provides an interface for users to quickly explore tennis match information. The visualization tool reveals the overall structure of the match as well as the fine details in a single screen. It uses a 2D display of translucent layers, a design that contains elements of Tree-Maps[1] and of the Visual Scheduler system,[2] which was designed to help faculty and students identify mutually available (transparent) time slots when arranging group meetings. TennisViewer provides Magic Lens filters[3] to explore specialized views of the information and a time-varying display to animate all or part of a match.

Competition trees

A tennis match is a tree-building process. When a player wins the last point of a game, he claims a node that lies one level higher—the game node. The game node inherits all his point nodes as its children. Both players always compete for the next higher available node, but only one of them can claim it. A player completes the tree by claiming the match node at the top level. The trees built by the two players together form a competition tree, which captures the hierarchical structure and the competitiveness of the tennis matches.

The Tree-Map offers a way to visualize hierarchically structured information with a k-D tree,[4] which is a general version of the orthogonal recursive bisection used in n-body simulations.[5] A Tree-Map depicts the hierarchy's structure and the content of the leaf nodes by using nested rectangles. We modified the Tree-Map so that each rectangle has a title bar to show the score in the corresponding node of a tennis match. The match node is a rectangle the size of the whole display. The region under its title bar subdivides vertically into subrectangles for sets. A set subdivides horizontally for each of its games. The process continues level by level, alternating the orientation of subdivisions at each level, to build a top-nesting layered map.

TennisViewer employs competition trees to organize information on a tennis match. Magic Lenses magnify details, and an animated display depicts the dynamic nature of the game.

Colors assigned to the rectangles represent node ownership: red nodes are owned by player one and green ones by player two, for example. When a player claims a node in the competition tree, his color is assigned to the corresponding rectangles. A child rectangle is layered over its parent rectangle so that its translucent color combines with the color of its parent, providing a more global context for the node. A red node in a red parent cell looks different than it does in a green parent cell. The former case corresponds to a point that contributed to a winning effort by player one. The latter indicates that the point was part of a losing effort.

The upper image in Figure 1 shows the result of blending the game layer and the set layer into the match layer at the bottom. The translucent layers provide local information (who won the point) with global context (who won the match).

Figure 2 shows the result of visualizing one simulated tennis match. J. Bond wins the match, 3 sets to 2. The color of the underlying match rectangle is red. Bond wins the first, third, and fifth sets, so their colors are red on red. M. Michel wins the second and fourth sets, so those rectangles' colors are green on red. When J. Bond

1 The top plane is constructed by projecting the two translucent planes onto the bottom plane.

wins the match, all the information in the display becomes tinted by the global outcome, "winner = red," visible through the intervening layers.

We synthesized data for a tennis match between two players by simulating strokes subject to prescribed probabilities. The simulation demonstrates that the outcome of a match is very sensitive to the probabilities at the point level. For example, player one, who won 46 percent of the points in 10,000 simulated matches, only won 40 percent of the games, 24 percent of the sets, and 9 percent of the matches. A small departure from 50 percent probability at the point level produces increasingly exaggerated effects higher up the tree, a behavior that we wanted TennisViewer to reveal. The translucent layers produce this desired effect.

Magic Lenses

To reveal the information at the low layers of the hierarchy, we must magnify the image. A fisheye view[6] is one method—it enlarges the image near the interesting parts. The Table Lens[7] uses the fisheye method to browse large tables. The Document Lens[8] uses the fisheye method to browse large documents. A Magic Lens opens a window over the image and re-displays the contents beneath it. By moving a Magic Lens on the image, the user can quickly explore the information underneath in greater detail.

We adopted Magic Lenses in our system to support exploring information at the lowest layers. The Magic Lens is a natural choice in a window system that supports rectangular viewports, and manipulating them is easy and fast. Moreover, Magic Lenses can easily be laid atop each other to produce deep zooming; for example, the tennis match information in Figure 2 includes one match, five sets, 51 games, 332 points, 446 serves, and more than 2,800 strokes (including the ball traces).

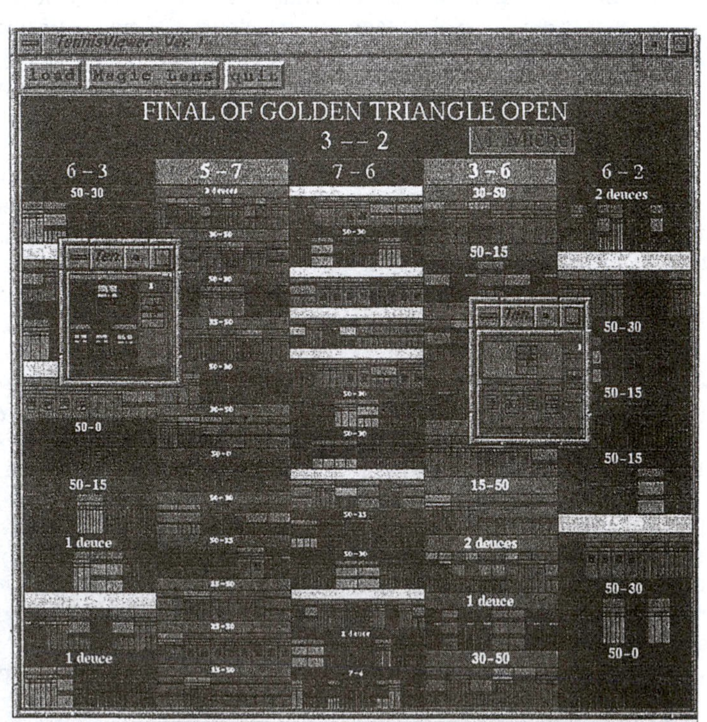

(a) (b)

2 TennisViewer displays a computer-generated tennis match. (a) A serve (top) is returned out of bounds (bottom). (b) One Magic Lens filter lies on top of another, revealing ball traces within a point.

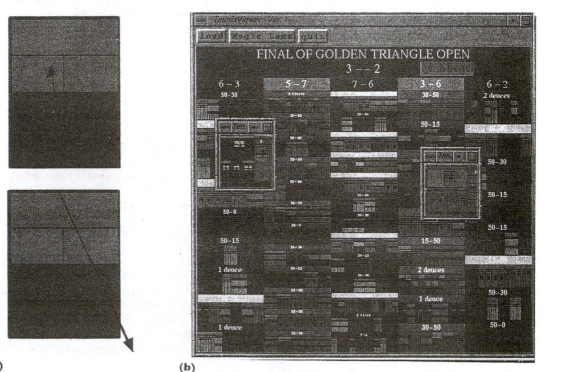

Conclusion

We developed TennisViewer to give coaches, players, and fans a new way to analyze, review, and browse a tennis match. We chose tennis because of its popularity, because a tennis match includes so much information, and because tennis is organized in an obvious tree structure of points, games, sets, and match.

Translucent coloring of the nodes provides a multiresolution view showing which player won the various nodes. The user can quickly locate the interesting sets, games, points, services, and strokes, can determine the winners of each node according to colors, and can locate the long rallies based on the repeated occurrence of nodes belonging to a given player. Animation shows abrupt and global color changes after a crucial point (like winning a match point), which visually indicates the point's importance. The user can apply Magic Lens filters to explore the details of the match.

We envision the use of video at the map's lowest levels to permit an actual replay of specific parts of the match. Future work includes installing statistical lenses (like spreadsheets) to operate on the match data and lenses to show stroke details (top-spin, under-spin, volley) of interest to coaches, players, and fans.

TennisViewer runs under X/Motif on Unix platforms. We are working with ESPNet[9] to develop a Java version that runs in a Web browser to supplement conventional multimedia reporting of tennis matches. ■

References

1. B. Johnson and B. Shneiderman, "Tree-Maps: A Space-Filling Approach to the Visualization of Hierarchical Information Structures," *Proc. IEEE Visualization 91*, IEEE Computer Soc. Press, Los Alamitos, Calif., Oct. 1991, pp. 189-194.
2. D. Beard et al., "A Visual Calendar for Scheduling Group Meetings," *Computer Supported Cooperative Work (CSCW)*, ACM Press, New York, 1990, pp. 279-290.
3. E. Bier et al., "Toolglass and Magic Lenses: The See-Through Interface," *Proc. Siggraph 93*, ACM Press, New York, 1993, pp. 73-80.
4. J.L. Bentley and J.H. Friedman, "Data Structures for Range Searching," *ACM Computing Surveys*, Vol. 11, No. 4, Dec. 1979, pp. 397-409.
5. M. Berger and S. Bokhari, "A Partitioning Strategy for Nonuniform Problems on Multiprocessors," *IEEE Trans. on Computers*, Vol. C-36, 1987, pp. 570-580.
6. G.W Furnas, "Generalized Fisheye Views," *Proc. ACM SIGCHI Conf. on Human Factors in Computing Systems*, ACM Press, New York, Apr. 1986, pp. 16-23.
7. R. Rao and S.K. Card, "The Table Lens: Merging Graphical and Symbolic Representations in an Interactive Focus+Context Visualization for Tabular Information," *Proc. ACM SIGCHI Conf. on Human Factors in Computing Systems*, ACM Press, New York, Apr. 1994, pp. 318-322.
8. G.G. Robertson and J.D. Mackinlay, "The Document Lens," *Proc. ACM Symp. on User Interface Software and Tech.*, ACM Press, New York, Nov. 1993, pp. 1-4.
9. *ESPNet*, http://espnet.sportszone.com.

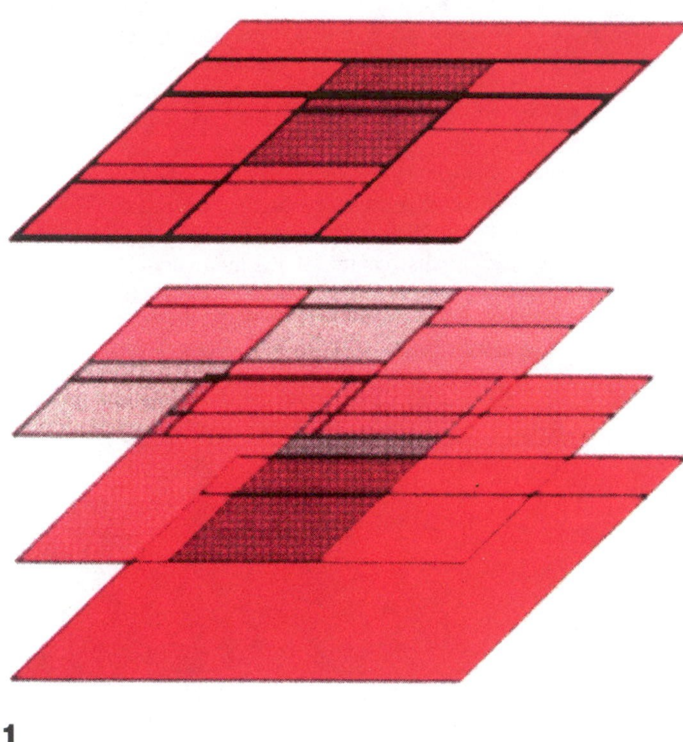

1

The top plane is constructed by projecting the two translucent planes onto the bottom plane.

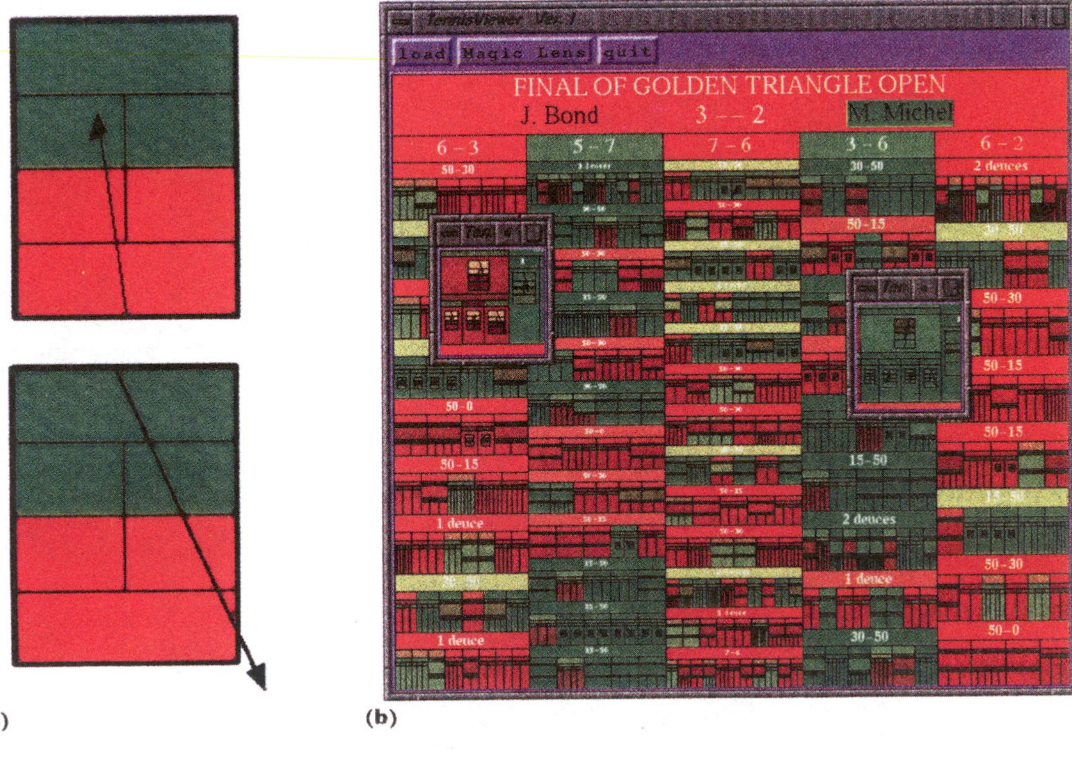

2

TennisViewer displays a computer-generated tennis match. (a) A serve (top) is returned out of bounds (bottom). (b) One Magic Lens filter lies on top of another, revealing ball traces within a point.

2.5 Networks

Network Visual Structures are often used to describe communication networks such as the telephone system or the World Wide Web. Abstractly, a network consists of nodes, links, and additional information associated with the nodes and links. Unlike trees, networks have cycles and other complexities that preclude containment as an effective encoding technique.

We can distinguish the same types of nodes and links in network Visual Structures that we did for spatial axes. Nodes and links can be unstructured (unlabeled), nominal (labeled), ordinal (have an ordinal quantity associated with them), or quantitative (e.g., weighted links). In addition, links can be directed or undirected. The usual retinal properties can be used to encode information about links and nodes, such as color or size. From combinations of these types of nodes and links, and from constraints on them (e.g., the sum of the values on the links must sum to 1), we can generate many of the common network representations.

The links in networks are an additional spatial dimension. Close relationships can be indicated between cases that are not spatially contiguous. In fact, the connectivity of objects with more than three dimensions can be presented. This flexibility comes at a cost, however. Visual presentations of generalized graphs of even modest size tend to look like a ball of tangled string. While the indicated relationships may be logically correct, they may also be visually impenetrable.

The papers in this section develop new techniques for visualizing information expressed as network Visual Structures, especially for large networks. The first paper, by Fairchild, Poltrock, and Furnas (1988 ●), describes SemNet, one of the earliest systems to explore these issues. The problem is to build a tool for constructing, debugging, and understanding large semantic networks. The significance of this paper is that SemNet was one of the first systems to benefit from the new interactive graphics of Silicon Graphics computers. The ability to generate real-time interactive presentations of large networks changes the problem, and this paper was one of the first to identify the new problems to be solved and suggest solutions in this new paradigm. Two major themes are present in the study that are important enough to merit chapters later in this book: the power of interaction and the power of variable-resolution fisheye or focus + context displays. Furnas, one of the authors, had previously invented the concept of fisheye displays (Furnas, 1981 ●), and it was natural to apply them to the problem of large networks. Later systems have attempted to improve on the solutions of Fairchild et al. The second paper in this section, by Eick and Wills (1993 ●), uses their system HierNet to develop further the notion of networks that can be defined hierarchically. It also proposes an improved way to lay out the nodes. The third paper, Becker, Eick, and Wilks (1995 ●), uses interaction to improve on methods for visualizing the network links in a system called SeeNet.

The papers address four important problems for visualizing large networks: (1) Positioning nodes, (2) Managing the links so they convey actual information, (3) Handling the scale of graphs with thousands or millions of nodes, and (4) Interacting with and navigating through large networks of information. First, the problem of positioning nodes is key to network Visual Structures, even more than for trees. But in the case of networks, the relationships are more complex, and there is no automatic tree depth property to help. The design of network Visual Structures starts with decisions about how the spatial axes that define node position will be defined.

The one approach to positioning the nodes is to use spatial variables associated with the nodes (Figure 2.16). This is what Becker, Eick, and Wilks do (1995 ●). The nodes in their paper are telephone switches located in American

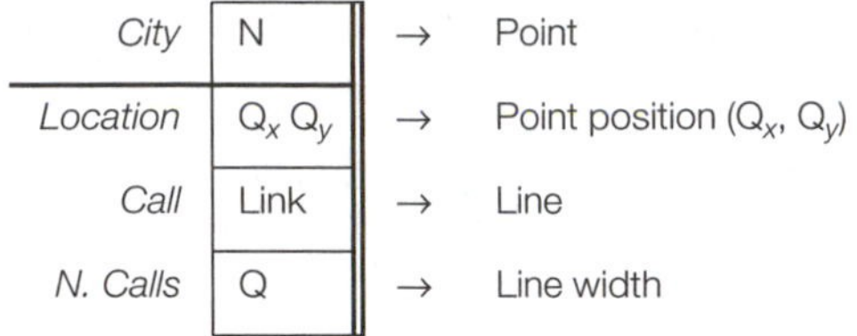

City
N
Point
Location
Q_x Q_y
Point position (Q_x, Q_y)
Call
Link
Line
N. Calls
Q
Line width

FIGURE **2.16**

SeeNet visual mapping of telephone traffic. Geographic data is used for node placement. Line width encodes the number of calls between cities.

cities. The positions of the nodes are determined by the cities' positions on a map. While this makes the node positions instantly meaningful, it can also have unfortunate consequences. In their study, California is at the edge of the map, and the links between it and eastern cities tend to obscure the Midwest and waste space. Three-dimensional versions of this geographical approach have also been developed (Eick and Cox, 1995; Munzner, Fenner, and Hoffman, 1996).

Another way to position the nodes is to use graphical layout algorithms that produce well-organized layouts from their graph properties. There exists a specialized literature devoted to the derivation of mathematical algorithms for laying out generalized graphs given assumptions of what constitutes a desirable layout, such as the minimization of link crossings in 2D. Some of the methods are elegant, but they generally handle fewer than 100 nodes. For an exceptionally clear tutorial on graph-drawing methods, see Cruz and Tamassia (1998). For a comprehensive bibliography of the literature, see Battista et al. (1994). For a review on the state of the mathematical underpinnings for graph drawing, see Tamassia (1996).

The papers in this section develop yet another approach for positioning the nodes of large graphs—using algorithmic scaling techniques to place nodes near that are similar (Figure 2.17). Fairchild, Poltrock, and Furnas (1988 ●) construct a similarity matrix among elements by tallying the number of slots that point from one element to another. They then use a statistical technique called *multidimensional scaling* (MDS) to assign X, Y, and Z coordinates to each node. The axes of space are, for this method, defined abstractly, although sometimes they can be given an interpretation. Eick and Wills (1993 ●) argue that the MDS technique places too much emphasis on smaller links. They examine two other techniques, the "spring technique," in which nodes are positioned as though they had springs relative to the strength of connection to other nodes, and an algorithm of their own. They prefer their own algorithm, because it clusters strongly related nodes more compactly instead of filling space uniformly, as the other algorithms do. This allows clusters to be perceived more easily according to gestalt principles. Positioning techniques must still address the sensitivity of final solution to the initial node starting positions and the fact that the solutions may settle into local minima. Becker, Eick, and Wilks (1995 ●) handle these problems in their SeeNet system by using "simulated annealing," in which the randomization is introduced in early iterations and gradually reduced.

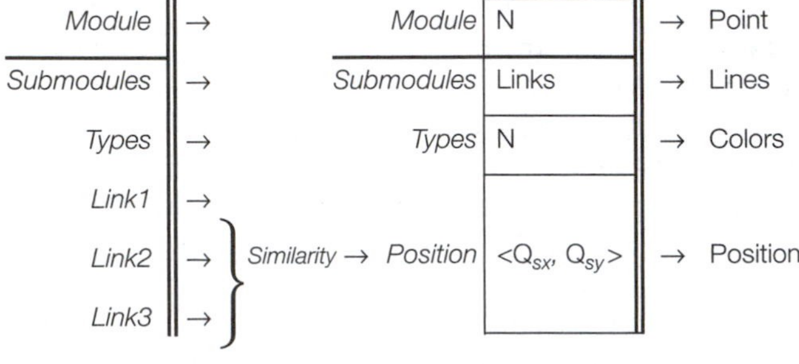

FIGURE **2.17**

SemNet is a 3D node-link diagram. Modules are mapped to nodes (points), and the module/submodule relationships are mapped to the links (lines).

Notice that if the positioning corresponds too perfectly with the linkage relationship, the links add little information. On the other hand, if there is no relationship, the linkages appear random and obscure. In a good visualization, node position and links will add information to each other.

This observation is related to the second problem, how to manage the links so that they do not create merely a tangled ball of string, but convey actual information. Fairchild, Poltrock, and Furnas (1988 ●) color their links according to link type. Becker, Eick, and Wilks (1995 ●) propose other methods. One is to select only links in some time interval or geographical region or strength by means of sliders. Another is to represent a pair of directed arcs by a single arc in which the arc is only drawn part way out from the node. This technique brings back the Midwest. Other strategies use the height and width of nodes to represent the number of in-links and out-links, without actually drawing the links. They also propose a version of the permutation matrix, but with the color of the cell indicating quantity.

A third problem is how to handle the scale of graphs with thousands, maybe millions, of nodes. All these papers propose some sort of differential aggregation. In Fairchild, Poltrock, and Furnas (1988 ●), hierarchical clustering is applied to the positions of the nodes. Multiple nodes in a neighborhood are represented by a single cluster node when the user's point of view is distant. In Eick and Wills (1993 ●), software comes with a natural hierarchy of subsystem, module, and file. File-file links within a module are retained, but other links are used to compute file-module links (to outside modules) and module-module links. This reduces the number of links by a factor of 32. Only retaining the strongest 1% of these links reduces the number of links by a further factor of 100. In this way, 8 million links in a large programming project are reduced to 2500 links. Becker, Eick, and Wilks (1995 ●) use geographical region for aggregation. Hierarchical substructures are very common in network visualization. For example, Mukherjea, Foley, and Hudson (1995) developed a system for automatically extracting hierarchies from networks. To visualize large networks, aggregation is necessary. Using fisheye techniques, this aggregation can be nonuniform and interactively progressive.

Finally, there is the problem of how to interact with and navigate through large networks of information. Fairchild, Poltrock, and Furnas (1988 ●) experiment with a number of techniques. They are hampered somewhat by the lack of good 3D input devices, but even more by the fact that the hardware of the time was not capable of speed adequate for the large number of nodes they wished to display. Also, this early 3D visualization did not have a ground plane of visual landmarks, commonly found on later systems. One of the techniques they do try is overview + detail, in which both comprehensive and detailed views are paired.

DISCUSSION

The visualization of large general graphs is a difficult problem. The easiest method is often not to try it at all, but rather to transform the generalized graph into a tree and mark it in some way to indicate discrepancies. If that method is unsatisfactory, these papers point the way to other techniques. Several themes arise out of these attempts that we will see in more detail in later chapters of this book.

One theme is the importance of node positioning, that is, the search for spatial substrates on which to project the graph. Visual axes for graphs are just as important as for other forms of visualization.

Another theme is the usefulness of interaction, as opposed to static presentations, for the analysis of and navigation through large networks. Interaction allows the user to examine successively smaller groups of nodes and so build up an understanding of the larger network. Interaction helps with the link occlusions that almost instantly arise in large networks. We pick up this theme of interaction in Chapter 3.

A final theme is the importance of aggregation, in fact, different levels of aggregation depending on the user's momentary focus of attention. These techniques are so important that we devote Chapter 4 to them.

Advances in digital libraries and the Internet mean that the visualization of hyperlinked networks of document repositories is a hot topic. Chapter 5 includes a discussion of the layout of text documents. Chapter 6 includes examples of network visualization as applied to the World Wide Web.

Finally, visualization techniques have also been used to increase the size of the network that can be effectively visualized. Bartram et al. (1995) developed a very interesting network visualization based on a fisheye scaling of nodes or groups of nodes.

5
SemNet: Three-Dimensional Graphic Representations of Large Knowledge Bases

KIM M. FAIRCHILD
STEVEN E. POLTROCK
GEORGE W. FURNAS

In the last decade, computers have increased the information available to people by many orders of magnitude. The rate of this information explosion is continuing to increase, straining the ability of computer users to comprehend or manage the available information. To help users interact with immense knowledge bases, we propose SemNet, a three-dimensional graphical interface. SemNet presents views which allow the users to examine local detail while still maintaining a global representation of the rest of the knowledge base. SemNet also provides many semantic navigation techniques such as relative movement, absolute movement, and teleportation. SemNet is an exploratory research vehicle to address questions such as: How should large data bases of knowledge be presented to users? How should users explore, manipulate, and modify these knowledge bases? Alternative answers to these questions were implemented in SemNet and informally evaluated by using SemNet as an interface to large knowledge bases.

1. Introduction

In a few decades, computers have increased the information available to people by many orders of magnitude. The rate of this information explosion is continuing to increase, straining the ability of computer users to comprehend or manage available data. Fifth-generation computers are expected to intensify this problem, but simultaneously help manage the information. With their ability to quickly access and manipulate a large amount of symbolic knowledge, fifth-generation computers should revolutionize problem solving and data management. But symbolic knowledge is also a kind of information, different from numeric data, and poses new problems for computer users. How should large data bases of symbolic knowledge (i.e., knowledge bases) be presented to users? How should users explore, manipulate, and modify these knowledge bases? SemNet has been developed to address these questions.

SemNet is an exploratory research project undertaken to advance understanding of the problems facing both users and developers of large knowledge bases. The immediate objective of the SemNet project is to identify important problems and a collection of possible solutions to these problems. The problems and solutions that have been investigated, reflecting the disciplines of the authors, derive from the convergence of computer science, measurement and scaling, and cognitive psychology. Because this research explores uncharted territory, our emphasis is on identifying and informally evaluating many alternatives instead of conducting formal evaluations of a few alternatives. A longer term objective is to develop a generic approach to knowledge-base browsing and editing by combining and optimizing the best solutions.

The major problem addressed in the SemNet project is how to present large knowledge bases so they can be comprehended by a user or developer. To comprehend a knowledge base, we hypothesize, a user must recognize (1) the identities of individual elements in the knowledge base, (2) the relative position of an element within a network context, and (3) explicit relationships between elements. Consequently, research has been focused on ways to represent elements and their interrelationships within the context of a large knowledge base.

SemNet represents knowledge bases as directed graphs in a three-dimensional space (Fairchild, 1985; Fairchild & Poltrock, 1986). SemNet represents knowledge bases graphically because knowledge bases represent information about relationships between symbolic entities, and graphics are an effective way to communicate relationships among objects. Furthermore, we want to exploit the skills that people have already developed for recognizing visual patterns and moving in three-dimensional space.

Figure 1-1 shows how SemNet represents part of a knowledge base containing Prolog rules. SemNet represents elements of the knowledge base as labeled rectangles connected by lines or arcs. The arcs are color coded to represent specific kinds of relationships between the knowledge-base elements. (The color information is not available in any of the figures in this chapter). In Figure 1-1 the rectangles represent Prolog modules (set of rules) labeled with the module names. The arcs show the modules that each module can cause to execute. The knowledge base is explored by traveling through the three-dimensional space. A user of SemNet manipulates information in the knowledge base by direct manipulation of knowledge-base objects, either the rectangles or the arcs, or by manipulation of tools, which are the (blue) rectangles at the top and bottom of Figure 1-1.

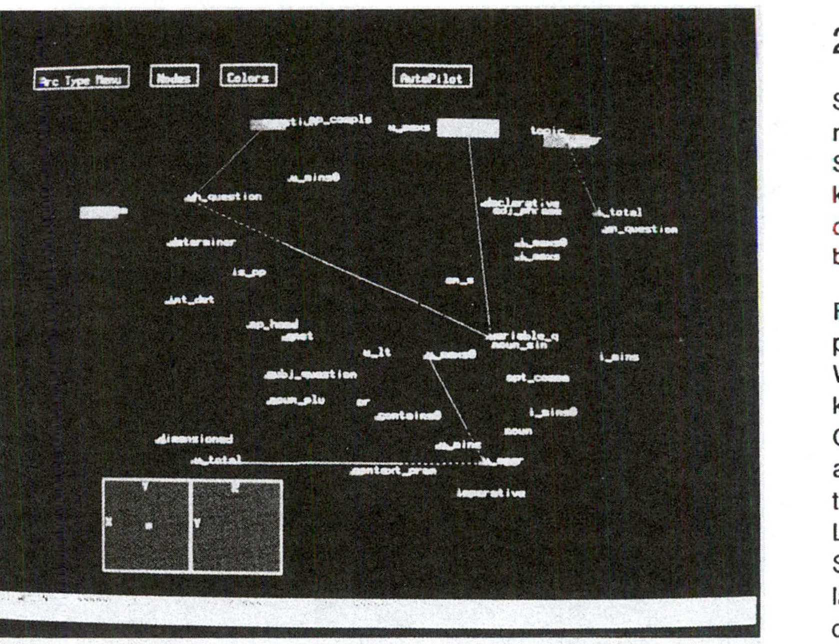

Figure 1-1: Part of a knowledge base consisting of Prolog modules

Three-dimensional graphic representations of knowledge bases, such as the one shown in Figure 1-1, can help reveal the organization of the knowledge base. However, graphic representations do not automatically solve all problems associated with exploring, manipulating, and modifying very large knowledge bases. They simply transform very large knowledge bases into very large directed graphs. The major emphasis of research with SemNet has been to investigate solutions, or partial solutions, to the problems that arise when working with three-dimensional graphic representations of large knowledge bases. In this chapter, the major problems are defined, some potential solutions are explored, and the particular solutions implemented in SemNet are described. Another approach to management of large amounts of information is presented in the chapter on the Memory Extender by Jones.

2. SemNet's Implementation

SemNet is intended to be a general purpose tool for exploring and manipulating arbitrary knowledge bases represented as directed graphs. SemNet can be used as an interface, or part of an interface, to arbitrary knowledge-base applications. This section describes how applications communicate with SemNet, how different kinds of knowledge bases may be represented, and the hardware required for SemNet.

Figure 2-1 shows the components of the SemNet system. These components are implemented on two machines, a Silicon Graphics IRIS Workstation and a machine containing the application program and the knowledge base. In the IRIS, the SemNet user-interface layer, written in C, controls the display and allows the knowledge base to be explored and edited through direct manipulation of graphic objects. In the application machine, the SemNet knowledge-base interface layer, written in LISP, connects arbitrary LISP applications and knowledge bases to the SemNet user-interface layer through a control language. These two layers (the user-interface layer and the knowledge-base interface layer) comprise a general purpose system, and may be attached to arbitrary knowledge-base applications.

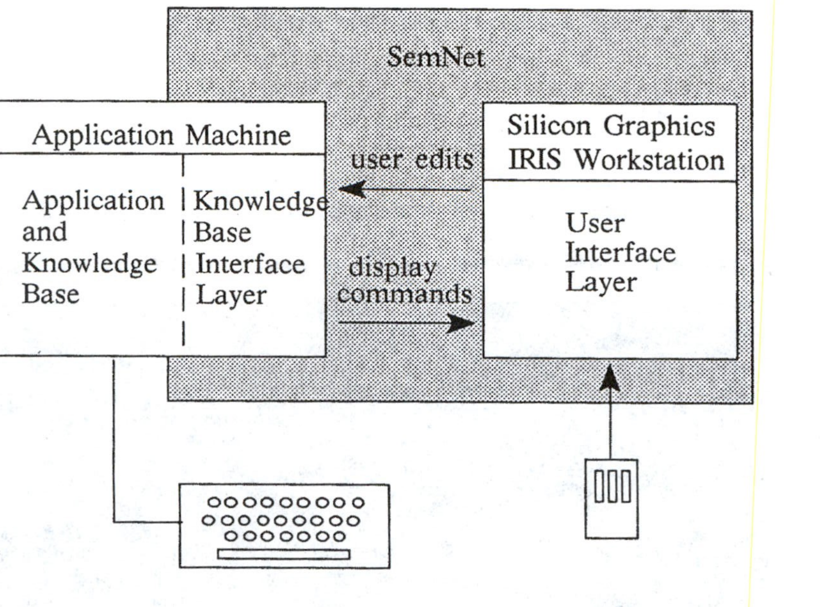

Figure 2-1: Conceptual architecture of SemNet

When the system is initialized, pointers to every element of the knowledge base are sent by the knowledge-base application to the knowledge-base interface layer. The knowledge-base interface layer constructs a description of each of the elements and their interconnections and sends these descriptions via ethernet or a serial connection to the SemNet user-interface layer. The user-interface layer generates the SemNet graphical display. The user, via the mouse, edits the graphic representation as desired. The resulting changes are sent to the knowledge-base interface layer, which in turn passes them to the application for interpretation. The resulting knowledge-base modifications are then sent back through the knowledge-base interface to the SemNet user-interface layer for modification of the graphic display.

All the components shown in Figure 2-1 are required to use SemNet with arbitrary knowledge-base applications. However, for many purposes the SemNet user-interface layer can be used in a stand-alone mode. The SemNet user-interface layer can read a file containing descriptions of the knowledge base like the descriptions generated by the interface layer. The user can browse and manipulate the graphic representation of the knowledge base, but all editing functions that require the application are disabled. This stand-alone mode is useful for training new users, investigating new graphic techniques, and for demonstrations.

When SemNet is integrated with a knowledge-base application, a mapping must be defined between elements of the knowledge base and the graphical objects that represent these elements in SemNet. This mapping defines a graph structure representation of the knowledge base. For a knowledge base represented using frames, this mapping is straightforward. Each frame is represented as a labeled rectangle (the nodes of the network) and slots of the frames are represented as lines (or arcs), color coded to indicate slot type. For a knowledge base represented using rules, defining the mapping requires some ingenuity and analysis of the task to be performed using SemNet. For example, the nodes of the network could represent the antecedents and consequents of rules with arcs representing implication.

SemNet has been used by linguists in the Natural Language Project at Microelectronics and Computer Technology Corporation (MCC) (Slocum & Cohen, 1986) to debug the morphological analyzers that they are developing. These morphological analyzers are knowledge bases expressed as rules organized into groups. SemNet represents each group as a node. The arcs connecting the groups represent paths for messages passed between the groups. Messages passed from one rule group to another are represented as labeled objects that travel along the arcs connecting nodes, providing a dynamic simulation of the morphological analysis. A formal evaluation of SemNet was conducted in this setting (Shook, 1986) and served as the foundation for many of the evaluative statements that follow.

3. Positioning Knowledge Elements

A principal reason that SemNet represents a knowledge base as a graphical network is to reveal the organization or structure of the knowledge base. One of the obstacles to comprehending the organization of the knowledge base is the large number of arc crossings in any large knowledge base. An arbitrary graph cannot, in general, be embedded in a plane without some arcs intersecting. In a flat display, such intersections impede the eyes' efforts to trace interconnections, and crossing points may also be visually confused with nodes. Fortunately, if three dimensions are available, nodes can always be assigned to positions such that no arcs intersect. Of course, arcs still intersect in two-dimensional views of the knowledge base, but when the viewpoint moves, users perceive a three-dimensional space, and the arcs no longer appear to intersect. The resulting visual simplification of the structure was one of the primary motivations for choosing a three-dimensional representation for the SemNet interface.

The positions of the knowledge elements in three-dimensional space also influence how effectively the knowledge base organization is revealed. In Figure 1-1 the assigned positions do not seem too important because relatively few nodes are displayed; Figure 1-1 shows only a small part of a much larger knowledge base. The entire knowledge base is displayed in Figure 3-1 with each knowledge element randomly assigned to a position. In Figure 3-1 the labels have been removed from the nodes and the node size has been reduced. No clear organization emerges in Figure 3-1; randomly assigned positions cause a dense maze of interconnections and obscure relationships among the elements.

The problem is how to assign positions to knowledge elements so that the organization or structure of the knowledge base is maximally apparent to the user. A general solution to this problem probably does not exist; the optimal method of position assignment for one knowledge base may be totally inappropriate for another. Some knowledge bases may contain information that can be used to compute effective positions. For other knowledge bases, the user may have information that is not stated explicitly in the knowledge base, and this information may allow the user to assign effective positions.

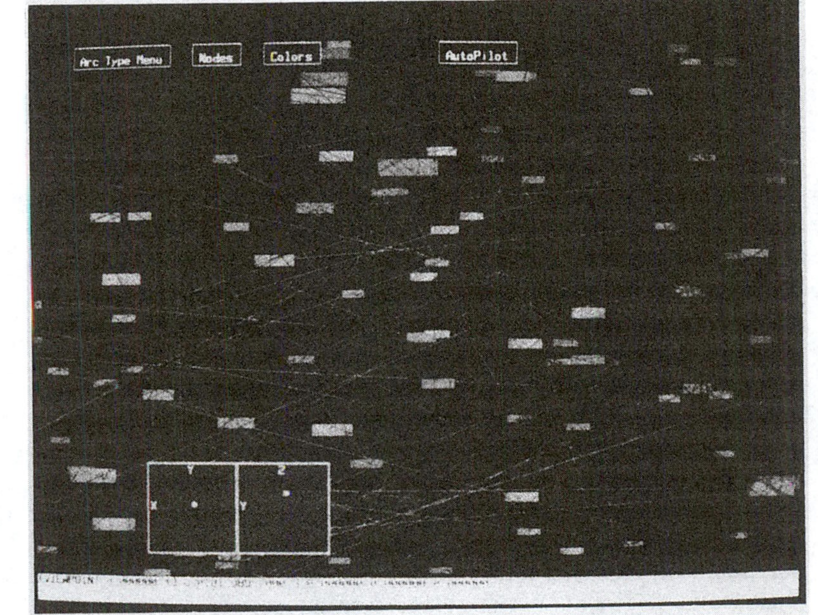

Figure 3-1: The complete knowledge base of Prolog modules with nodes assigned to random positions

Three potential sources of information for determining the positions of knowledge elements have been explored in SemNet. First, the positions of knowledge elements can be based on their properties through *mapping functions*, described below. Second, the connectivity between knowledge elements can be used to assign related elements to adjacent positions. Third, the user can assign knowledge elements to positions based on information that is not represented in the knowledge base.

3.1 Mapping Functions

In many cases, the elements of a knowledge base have properties that can be mapped to positions in three-dimensional space, establishing a spatial representation of the knowledge base organization. Suppose, for example, that SemNet was used to browse a semantic network describing the properties of all mammals. Rips, Shoben, and Smith (1973) found that people organize animals along three principal dimensions: size, predacity, and domesticity. If these three properties are defined in the knowledge base, or can be computed from other properties in the knowledge base, then these properties can be transformed into x, y, and z coordinates. The result should be a spatial representation of the knowledge base that closely corresponds to the user's conceptual representation. Hamsters and tigers would be assigned opposite values on all three dimensions of this space. In a large knowledge base there may be many dimensions that could be used to organize the knowledge base, depending on the user's task. In SemNet, the user may select the dimensions from a predefined list.

To use mapping functions in SemNet, the application knowledge base must contain a set of ordering functions, each of which produces an ordering of all knowledge elements. The names of these ordering functions are passed to the SemNet user-interface layer (see Section 2). When a user accesses the *MappingFunctions* tool, SemNet presents a list of the ordering functions. The user indicates which functions should correspond to each of the three display dimensions. SemNet sends these selections to the application, which returns normalized coordinates for each knowledge element.

3.2 Proximity Based Functions

In many knowledge-base applications, the relationships between knowledge elements may provide the key to understanding the knowledge-base organization. These relationships are easier to perceive if related knowledge elements are close together and unrelated knowledge elements are far apart. Several techniques have been explored in SemNet for determining knowledge element positions from the relationships between knowledge elements.

3.2.1 Multidimensional Scaling

One technique uses multidimensional scaling to assign positions to elements so that two elements directly connected by an arc are closer together than elements with no direct connections. (The chapter by McDonald and Schvaneveldt in this volume presents in detail proximity scaling techniques such as multidimensional scaling.) If two elements can be connected by more than one arc, the technique assigns positions so that the distance between two elements decreases as the number of arcs connecting them decreases. A test of this technique was conducted using a knowledge base of 53 elements that all had connections to other knowledge elements.

The first step in this technique is to construct a matrix summarizing the interconnections among the knowledge elements. The entry for row *i* and column *j* of the matrix is the number of slots in element *i* that point to element *j*. This matrix is made symmetric by summing across the diagonal (the element in row *i*, column *j* is added to the element in row *j*, column *i*). The symmetric matrix represents the number of interconnections between elements without regard to the direction of the connection.

The positions of the knowledge elements are defined by nonmetric multidimensional scaling applied to this symmetric matrix. This scaling technique yields a three-dimensional solution such that the distance between elements is monotonically related to the number of interconnections between the elements, to the extent that is possible. In our test, the KYST program (based on Kruskal, 1964a, 1964b, and described in Kruskal, Young, & Seery, 1973) with monotone regression and a Torsca starting procedure was used to perform this analysis. The choice of a starting procedure is important because the program iteratively adjusts the elements' positions and may reach a local optimum or saddle point from poor initial values. After 50 iterations the stress was 0.02, which indicates a good fit to the requirement of monotonicity, and changes in the position of elements were in the third decimal place. The final, three-dimensional solution was rotated to principal components.

To test the effectiveness of this technique, SemNet was initially given random positions for the 53 elements of the knowledge base. Qualitatively, this representation of the knowledge base was unaesthetic and confusing. Many of the arcs connecting the knowledge elements were long, and the arcs nearly obscured the knowledge elements. Then the elements were moved to the locations determined by the multidimensional scaling analysis. The results were striking. Not only were both ends of most arcs visible on a single screen, but since the arcs tended to be short, they were easier to trace, and even their two-dimensional projections had fewer crossings. It became apparent for the first time, for example, that our set of test nodes was in fact two disconnected subsets. There were further beneficial effects: Interesting subsets of interconnected nodes became visible, highly connected nodes took central positions, and more isolated nodes moved to the periphery.

Applying this multidimensional scaling technique to large knowledge bases poses some problems. Iterative nonmetric multidimensional scaling programs are slow, and therefore inappropriate for real-time analysis of very large knowledge bases. This problem may not be insurmountable, however. The analysis could be performed off-line (overnight, for example), and simple heuristics could be used to position new knowledge elements as they are defined. For example, an element connected to more than one other element could be positioned at the centroid of all the elements' positions.

3.2.2 Heuristics

Other techniques use heuristics to move related knowledge elements closer together. These heuristics require an initial position for every element, possibly a randomly chosen position, and a specified minimum distance between any two knowledge elements. This minimum distance ensures that nodes remain far enough apart to be discriminable. The heuristics define a new position for each element of the knowledge base, one at a time, and are applied iteratively until the knowledge elements no longer move noticeably.

The centroid heuristic defines the new position of a knowledge element as the weighted mean of the positions of all related knowledge elements, with each position weighted by the number of arcs that directly connect the elements. Because of these weights, a knowledge element moves closer to those knowledge elements with which it shares the most relationships. This heuristic could assign different weights to different kinds of relationships, accommodating differences in relationship importance. If the computed centroid is too close (less than the specified minimum distance) to any knowledge element, a new position is found along an arc between the original position and the centroid.

The centroid heuristic is fast and could readily be used in conjunction with the multidimensional scaling approach described above. The solution obtained is, however, strongly dependent on the initial positions. In tests we conducted with a large knowledge base, the centroid heuristic improved the original random positions significantly, but never untangled the complex web of interconnections.

An annealing heuristic was motivated by recent research on simulated annealing[1] (Kirkpatrick, Gelatt, & Vecchi, 1983). This technique is slower than the centroid heuristic but more successful at untangling the interconnections. A new position for each element is computed by adding a vector of random orientation and length to the current position. A scale factor controlled by the user determines the maximum length of the random vector. The element is moved to the new position if it is closer than the current position to the centroid, but not too close to any other element. By setting the scale factor high initially, knowledge elements can be moved large distances, potentially untangling the interconnections. When new positions are no longer found, the scale factor is gradually reduced until the changes in positions are acceptably small. Like the centroid heuristic, the annealing heuristic is sensitive to initial positions, but it yielded solutions that were judged substantially more effective than the solutions of the centroid heuristic. To illustrate the reduction of complexity that can be achieved by the annealing heuristic, Figures 3-1 and 3-2 show the same knowledge base with positions assigned randomly in Figure 3-1 and positions adjusted by the annealing heuristic in Figure 3-2. An organization of the knowledge base is clearly visible in Figure 3-2, making the knowledge base appear smaller and more comprehensible.

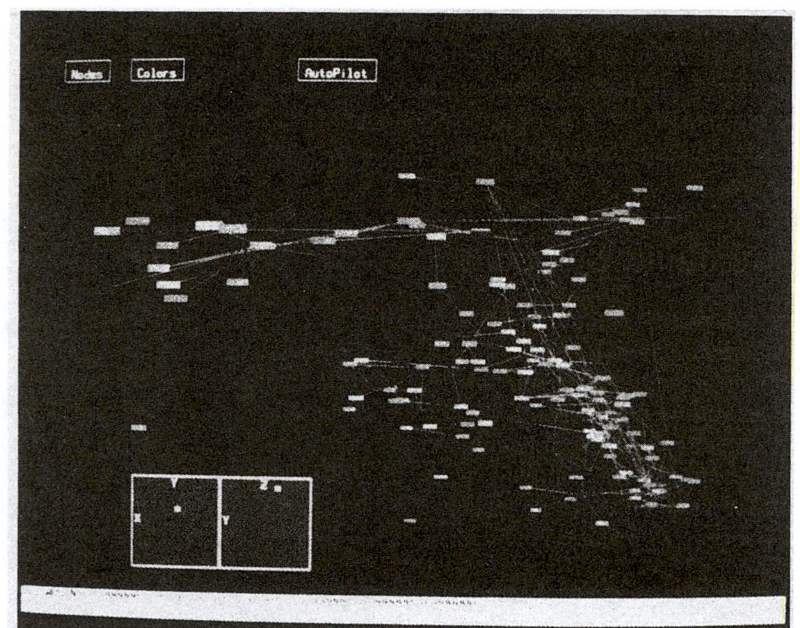

Figure 3-2: The complete knowledge base of Prolog modules with node positions determined by the annealing heuristic

3.3 Personalized Positioning

In some cases, the user may have information that is not in the knowledge base but should be considered when assigning positions to the knowledge elements. The user can simply move the knowledge elements to these positions and leave them there. This is the location method we use in our daily lives: We put things where we want and expect them to be there the next time we look for them. This method can be combined with other positioning techniques. For example, the user can fix the positions of certain knowledge elements, then let all others be adjusted by the annealing or centroid heuristic. These heuristics will treat the fixed positions as *anchors*, and all connected knowledge elements will be grouped around these anchors. For example, a linguist could fix one *verb* analysis node and one *noun* analysis node at opposite ends of the space. Then the annealing or centroid heuristic could be used to pull apart the remaining noun and verb nodes.

4. Coping with Large Knowledge Bases

Whatever strategies are used to organize the display of a graph, the number of nodes and arcs can eventually be overwhelming. Two limitations affect performance with large knowledge bases. First, the graphic hardware is limited in the speed with which it can compute and display information. As the number of objects to be displayed increases, the system's responsiveness decreases, degrading the real-time user interaction. Second, humans are limited in their ability to discriminate and attend to objects on the display.

Somehow, the total amount of information must be reduced. We addressed this issue in SemNet by inventing ways to find and display useful subsets of the knowledge base. The simplest methods involve selection by the user. More sophisticated methods were derived from Generalized Fisheye Views (Furnas, 1986).

When knowledge elements are of different types and not all types are of current interest, a simple subset-by-type strategy can be adopted. The user initiates this strategy by simply identifying which type of element should be displayed. For example, a user could specify that only mammals should be displayed in a knowledge base about animals. This capability has not been fully implemented in SemNet, but can be accomplished through interacting with the application program.

The underlying spatial metaphor of SemNet allows several strategies for dividing the knowledge base into subsets using spatial criteria. One strategy is a natural consequence of the three-dimensional graphics hardware, which shows only the part of the knowledge base within a restricted viewing angle when looking in a particular direction from the viewpoint. This allows the user to concentrate on the subset of nodes within this viewing angle. Moreover, the perspective view makes objects nearer the viewpoint appear larger, helping the user to examine local neighborhoods more effectively.

These local neighborhoods will be comprehensible only if related elements are within the same neighborhoods. In other words, proximity in euclidean space should correspond to proximity in the graph structure. In general, however, it is not mathematically possible to achieve perfect correspondence between proximity in arbitrary graph structures and proximity in three-dimensional euclidean space, so SemNet provides a *view_neighbors* tool that temporarily pulls all the nodes adjacent to any selected node into view. The *view_neighbors* tool is described in more detail in Section 5.2.4.

4.1 Fisheye Views

In addition to spatial subsets, SemNet's underlying spatial metaphor also supports more sophisticated information reduction strategies called Generalized Fisheye Views (Furnas, 1986). These strategies display details near a focal point and only more important landmarks further away. Such views attempt to give a useful balance of local details and surrounding context. Conceptually, these views are implemented by computing a degree-of-interest value for every object, then displaying only those objects that have a degree-of-interest value greater than a criterion. The degree-of-interest value for any object increases as the a priori importance of the object increases, and decreases as distance increases from the object to the point where the user is currently focused. The following sections discuss several generalized fisheye viewing strategies, two of which, one explicit and one implicit, are currently implemented in SemNet.

4.1.1 Fisheye Views from Clustering

Construction of a fisheye view requires that (1) interactions can be characterized as focused at a point in a reasonably static structure, (2) there be a notion of distance, and (3) there be a notion of differential a priori importance of objects. The first two prerequisites were readily satisfied in SemNet. The knowledge base is the stable structure, the focal point is a location in three-dimensional space, and distance can be defined as euclidean. Notions of differential importance, however, were more elusive. One might consider nodes with more incident arcs to be more important. Or perhaps the semantics of the domain might associate importance with some other feature of the network. For example, in a knowledge base, nodes higher in an *ISA*-sublattice might be considered more important. Or there might be purely non-structural application-specific importances (e.g., creation date). Any of these definitions of importance could be used in a standard fisheye strategy that eliminates less important nodes as distance increases. However, while all these definitions seem reasonable for particular applications, none seems sufficiently general.

The absence of satisfactory explicit notions of differential importance has led us to pursue new kinds of generalized fisheye views, all based on somehow identifying implicit notions of differential importance and making these notions explicit. For example, even though no individual knowledge-base element may be more important than others, *sets* of elements may exist that are more important than individual elements. If we could find a way to identify such sets, then an implicit structure could be made explicit by (1) introducing new *cluster-objects* that represent sets, and (2) assigning greater importance to these cluster-objects than to individual elements.

Consider the consequences that would emerge if we succeeded in finding ways to identify important sets of elements. Every element could be assigned to a unique set represented by a cluster-object, then every set could be assigned to a superset represented by another kind of cluster-object, and so on. The result would be a new hierarchical structure, with knowledge-base elements at the bottom and with successive layers of cluster-objects above the objects that they contain. In this metastructure, importance corresponds to height in the hierarchy even though no general definition of differential importance was available in the original structure. Furthermore, successively higher layers of the metastructure have fewer and fewer objects in them, allowing a fisheye strategy to be implemented by displaying knowledge elements near the focal point but only cluster-objects further from the focal point. As distance from the focal point increases, the displayed cluster-objects correspond to higher levels of the metastructure. The user can concentrate on knowledge elements in the neighborhood of the focal point in the global context of sets of elements represented by cluster-objects.

How should these cluster-objects be represented? They should probably be discriminable from individual knowledge elements, so that the user can understand the distortion or transformation of the view introduced by the fisheye process. For example, they may be represented by a special cluster icon carrying some identifying information. This information might indicate the level of the cluster and some sort of label. They might be labeled by an explicit cluster-name (if one is available), or labeled by example, that is, displayed with a short list of some knowledge elements inside the cluster, either randomly or systematically chosen (cf. Dumais & Landauer, 1984). Alternatively, one might try to make semantically appropriate pictographs for each individual pseudo-object, but this seems difficult to automate.

Recognizing the advantages of identifying important sets of elements, we have required a method for assigning the elements to these sets. In SemNet, euclidean neighborhoods have been used to assign elements to sets, which again emphasizes the importance of the positions assigned to elements. If semantic information is used to assign positions to the elements, then these euclidean neighborhoods may approximate meaningful subdivisions of the elements. Simple hierarchical clustering has been imposed on the nodes by dividing the space in half along the x, y, and z axes. Each of the resulting eight sub-regions has been itself similarly subdivided, and so on recursively down three levels. This successive octal subdivision yields a rooted 8-ary tree, with the SemNet objects partitioned among its leaves. The internal nodes of the tree are the cluster-objects.

Figure 4-1 shows the resulting SemNet display for one view of the same knowledge base depicted in Figures 3-1 and 3-2. The objects that are displayed in this fisheye view depend on the position of the viewpoint, which the user controls using the mouse. In the middle of the display, knowledge-base elements, such as *yesno* and *quantify*, are visible because these elements are in the same subdivision as the viewpoint. The large (green) rectangles, such as *pt* and *is*, are cluster-objects that represent the subdivisions adjacent to the subdivision containing the viewpoint. The (orange) rectangles, such as *terminal*, are cluster-objects representing sets of four subdivisions that are further away from the current subdivision. This fisheye technique of representing the more remote regions in correspondingly larger chunks essentially reduces the number of objects to be displayed on the screen logarithmically, yet preserves a balance of local detail and global context. A (blue) band at the bottom of each cluster-object represents the proportion of the knowledge base located within the volume represented by that icon. Each cluster-object is positioned at the center of the volume it covers and labeled with the name of its most highly connected node (a label-by-example heuristic).

Note that tree distance is used to determine the degree-of-interest value for all the objects. Cluster objects are interesting because they have high a priori importance, but knowledge-base elements in one subdivision are interesting because they are all equally close (in tree distance) to the viewpoint. Although the tree is based on a subdivision of euclidean space, tree distance is not identical to distance in euclidean space. Tree distance was chosen because the subdivision structure is static and easily computed, and the algorithms for what to display in any tree-structure fisheye are very fast. However, tree distance has several drawbacks. First, when the viewpoint is moved, the objects that are displayed change abruptly at (invisible) subdivision boundaries. This distracting effect is ameliorated by using euclidean distance to tell when a boundary is being approached, then highlighting the clusters that are about to change. For example, in Figure 4-1 the *is* and *pt* cluster objects have light green borders, indicating that the viewpoint is near the boundaries of those subdivisions. If the viewpoint moves much closer, the knowledge-base elements in one of those subdivisions will be exposed and the current subdivision will be represented by a cluster object. A second drawback of tree distance is that the subdivision structure is very heterogeneous with respect to the embedding euclidean space. As a result, a small motion crossing a low-level subdivision boundary has a much smaller effect than a similar motion crossing one of the highest level subdivisions (in which case everything changes). We were unable to fix this problem since, as far as we know, it can be remedied only by adopting some other metastructure (e.g., a non-hierarchical clustering model).

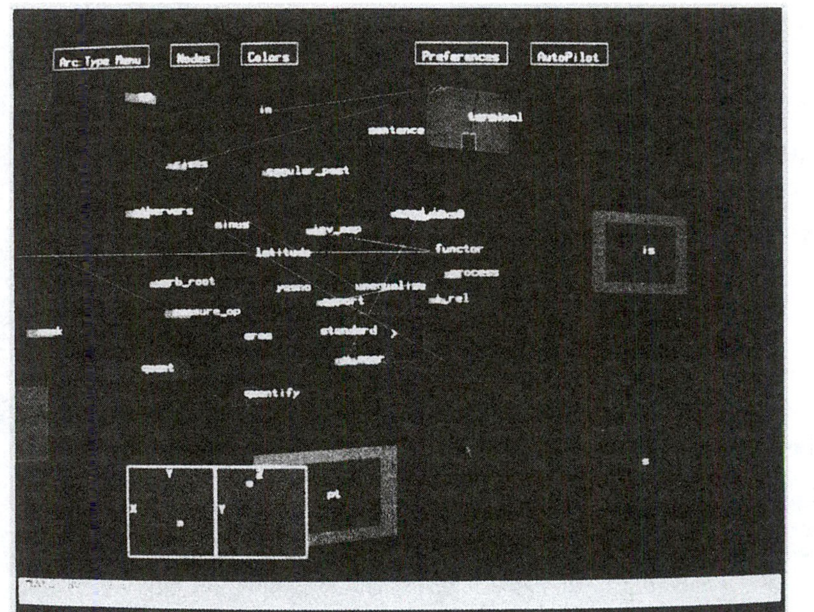

Figure 4-1: A fisheye view of the complete knowledge base of Prolog modules

We have already noted that the subdivision strategy for assigning knowledge-base elements to sets increases the importance of the positions assigned to the elements. In order for any spatial subdivisions to be meaningful, elements must first be placed in the space so that nearby elements are closely related. Otherwise the content of the spatially defined clusters will be essentially random, and the resulting metastructure will not have captured the implicit importance structure. The fisheye view would not make sense. Thus, either very meaningful mapping functions or proximity-based node placement techniques must be used. Furthermore, the octant subdivision strategy implicitly assumes that cuts perpendicular to the x, y, and z axes are the most appropriate. This may be defensible when coordinates come from mapping functions that make these axes meaningful. When object positions result from proximity-based techniques however, the final orientation of the cloud of points is typically arbitrary[2] , so the cuts will be similarly arbitrary. One possible solution would be to do the clustering more intelligently, based on the distribution of the nodes and not simply on nested, binary, orthogonal subdivisions.

4.1.2 Fisheye Views from Three-Dimensional Point Perspective

The SemNet interface contains another strategy for managing size. It comes naturally from the way three-dimensional graphics are used, and it exemplifies another generalized fisheye strategy for worlds that do not have explicit differential a priori importance. A balance of local detail and global context arises automatically from the geometry of point perspective in three dimensions: A few nearby points loom large and those further away appear smaller and smaller. We argue that this is not trivial -- an orthogonal projection of three-dimensional space would not achieve this fisheye-like balance, and would be correspondingly less useful. This ability of a movable perspective viewpoint in three-dimensional space to help deal with size and complexity through a combination of geometric subsets and fisheye views was the original motivation for its use in the SemNet interface.

It is useful to analyze this fisheye effect, not in terms of the geometry of projection, but in terms of a general metastructure strategy. This time, however, the metastructure is not a hierarchy of clusters. Instead, each

[2]Many proximity scaling packages, like KYST or MDS, rotate to some canonical orientation, such as principal components. While such orientations are well defined they are rarely semantically interpretable, so cuts based on halving the canonically oriented axes are also unlikely to be semantically sensible. The problem really is that the current subdivision scheme is blind; it is totally oblivious to the configuration of points, and any natural structure (e.g., natural clustering) they might have. That is, of course, why the technique can be so simple and so fast. An alternative is to use subdivision techniques, like agglomerative clustering, that more tediously (e.g., O(n#)) construct a hierarchy that reflects the detailed positions of points. The hope would be that it would thereby make semantically sensible clusters.

SemNet object is associated with a continuous set of graphic representations that differ only in size. These graphic representations are the same as those that result from perspective geometry. Combining these sets with the original knowledge-base structure yields a metastructure with a new size dimension orthogonal to the original structure. Now assume that the a priori importance of a graphic representation is inversely related to size: Smaller images of each object are more important than larger images. This assumption may seem counterintuitive, but reflects the intuition that it is more important that an object be represented, even if it is small, than not represented at all.

The fisheye view that results from this elaborated importance structure and euclidean distance is equivalent to the view that results from perspective geometry. Since the higher level graphic representations are smaller, the resulting views are reduced compared to a non-fisheye view (such as would result from an orthogonal projection). The geometric knowledge embedded in the three-dimensional graphics hardware selects the correct size for each object in the view quickly and automatically.

Theoretically, this fisheye conceptualization supports other transformations of the objects' representations. For example, the objects could change in form as well as size. The most detailed representation of an object (for use at close range) might be an icon containing the node's full English title and perhaps other useful information. Next might be a smaller box containing only the node's title, next only a small unlabeled box, and finally just a small point. The fisheye view would select the appropriate form and size for each knowledge-base element by first computing degree-of-interest values from distance and a priori importance, then displaying the representations with values closest to the criterion. At present, we simply make use of the IRIS hardware and the geometric fisheye; consequently, objects change only in size.

4.1.3 Fisheye Views from Sampling Density.

In addition to the two fisheye strategies currently implemented, there is at least one other strategy that we could have used that does not depend on explicit values of differential a priori importance. Consider a structure whose layout exhibits a kind of graded spatial autocorrelation between the objects: Only small changes happen from neighbor to neighbor in the space; major changes happen only gradually. In pictures, for example, local changes usually just delineate small details. In such a case, sampling density can be used to make explicit the distinction between major and minor features. In a picture, the image would be sampled very densely near the point of interest to give high resolution and detail. Regions successively further away would be sampled less and less densely, and only major changes in the image would be visible. This corresponds exactly to what the human retina does to achieve information compression. In SemNet a comparable strategy could be implemented since a proximity-based node layout should give the right kind of autocorrelational structure. Thus, one would sample the three-dimensional space densely near the current point of view, showing all objects. Further away, only a correspondingly smaller proportion of the objects would be permitted in the view -- only a coarse sampling to give the gist of the more remote regions.

4.2 The Display of Arcs

Two issues arise in the display of arcs. First, if not all nodes are visible, which arcs should be shown? In SemNet a simple strategy was adopted: Show a directed arc if and only if its origin node was explicitly visible.

A second problem, one we did not address, involves what to do when the number of arcs, not the number of nodes, is extremely large. This problem can be solved by following a similar approach. First, strategies for dividing the arcs into sets are needed. If, as in a knowledge base, the arcs are of different types (e.g., different semantic relations), those arcs corresponding to types that are not of current interest may be deleted. Fisheye strategies are also possible if arcs have differential importance; for example, in a knowledge base about animals, the user may determine that the ISA and EAT relationships are more important than the CREATOR-OF and DATE-OF-EXTINCTION relationships. Then less important arcs would be deleted as distance increased.

5. Navigation and Browsing

To explore graphical representations of large knowledge bases, such as those shown in Figures 3-1 and 3-2, the user must be able to move the viewpoint or move the entire knowledge base. Suppose, for example, a user needs to inspect a particular knowledge element and all its connections in Figure 3-2. This task could be accomplished by moving the viewpoint close to that element, restricting the view to the small set of elements in a local region. Although this technique provides a powerful method for coping with the size and complexity of the knowledge base, it raises a new set of problems associated with navigating in a virtual three-dimensional space. These problems can be decomposed into two aspects of navigation: recognizing locations and controlling locations.

5.1 Recognizing Locations

How does the user know where the current viewpoint is in a complex knowledge space? One solution is to provide navigation aids similar to those found in the real world. For example, when traveling in a foreign city, people use abstract scale models or maps to discover where places are in relation to each other and how to get to new places. Landmarks, both natural and man-made, often help to identify the current position. SemNet provides tools similar to maps that show the current position of the viewpoint in the x-y and the x-z planes. Structures similar to landmarks may occur naturally when knowledge elements form structures that, with experience, become recognizable.

When following a complex path in the real world, people sometimes leave marks so the path can be retraced later. This approach could be adopted in SemNet, allowing the user to place identifiable markers on each section of the knowledge; for example, an icon for an elephant could represent information about large African animals. In addition, SemNet could show the path that was followed to reach the current location and provide automatic means for retracing it. Path retracing could have the added benefit of helping to re-establish the context that led to the current position. These capabilities do not currently exist in SemNet.

From our experiences with navigating through a three-dimensional knowledge space, the single most important feature of the interface is to make the user experience a *real*, three-dimensional space. diSessa (1985) terms such a user a *naive realist* - that what the user sees and manipulates on the display screen is the knowledge itself, rather than simply an interface to actions that manipulate an invisible system. The same control movements the user already makes to control the real world should map directly into the virtual world. One important component of this is the quality of the three-dimensional imagery (Poltrock et al., 1986). Real-time movement of graphical objects, motion parallax, graphic depth cues, and stereopsis will enhance this display.

Many cues help a user to recognize the current static position of the viewpoint. The organization of the knowledge base and features of the graphical objects provide perceptual information about the viewpoint position. For example, objects near the viewpoint are larger than objects far from the viewpoint. Other ways that graphical objects communicate location were described in Section 4. A map of the space is provided by an *Absolute Positioning* tool (the (blue) rectangle at the lower left in Figures 1-1, 3-1, and 3-2) , which shows the current position of the viewpoint.

Because the space is three dimensional, the relative depth of objects is important too. When the viewpoint is stationary, however, the knowledge base looks flat because there are few effective cues to depth. Two methods were explored for enhancing the depth effects in a static display. One method is to vertically oscillate the viewpoint, creating the impression that the knowledge base is rocking around the x axis. Although this method improves perception of depth, linguists in MCC's Natural Language Project found it distracting. The second method is to make small random movements of the viewpoint. This method appears to be as effective as vertical oscillations and is more pleasant to watch.

5.2 Controlling Location

How should the user control the position of the viewpoint, thereby determining the portion of the knowledge base that is displayed? Five different methods have been explored for either moving the viewpoint in a complex three-dimensional knowledge space or moving the knowledge base itself.

5.2.1 Relative Movement

The first method implemented in SemNet evolved from past experience with real-time visual simulation systems for training pilots to fly helicopters. This method provides independent controls for three orthogonal rotations of the viewpoint and movement forward and backward along the line of sight. This movement method is accessed by selecting the helicopter flight option on SemNet's main system menu. A submenu allows the user to select roll, pitch, yaw, or forward and backward movement. Tools for adjusting the velocity of movement and rotation are also provided.

This relative movement method has proven difficult to use for several reasons. First, changes in orientation are confusing, perhaps because there are no visual cues such as the gauges provided in helicopters and airplanes to indicate the current orientation. Consequently, users quickly become lost and disoriented. To help users recover their orientation, functions were added to the flight menu that return the viewpoint to the center of the space and level off the orientation. Second, the relative movement method is slow and awkward to use. Users must often iteratively adjust one control after another to reach a location that is readily visible on the display. Characteristics of the available control devices (i.e., the mouse and keyboard) may be largely responsible for these problems. If the user had a joystick and accelerator that could be manipulated simultaneously, the helicopter model would probably be an effective method for controlling viewpoint. Some of the three-dimensional control devices that are becoming available commercially may provide acceptable substitutes for an accelerator and joystick.

5.2.2 Absolute Movement

With a map of the three-dimensional knowledge space, the user can point to the desired viewpoint location. One kind of map used in SemNet is shown in Figures 1-1, 3-1, and 3-2. Because the space is three dimensional, the map shown in the figures has two two-dimensional parts, one representing the x-y plane and the other representing the y-z plane. The position of the viewpoint in the three-dimensional knowledge space is represented by an asterisk in each plane of the map. The user manipulates the position of the viewpoint by moving the asterisk in one plane at a time using the mouse. A filter ensures that the viewpoint moves smoothly, retaining the experience of travel through a three-dimensional space.

This absolute movement method is quicker and easier to use than the relative movement method described above. It poses new problems however. First, viewpoint positioning is not very accurate; it is easy to move rapidly to an approximate position but difficult to adjust the viewpoint precisely. This problem could be solved by allowing the user to adjust the filter so the viewpoint moves more slowly. The second problem is that using two-dimensional maps of a three-dimensional space imposes an extra cognitive demand on the user, forcing the user to determine which map to use and which direction to move the mouse to cause desired movements. Moving the mouse up and down in the x-y plane or left and right in the y-z plane causes the viewpoint to move along the y axis. It is easy to confuse these motions and difficult to determine the correct mouse movements required to move the viewpoint toward a particular object. This unnaturalness may be solved when three-dimensional control and display devices are available, allowing a direct coupling of the user's actions and the display consequences.

Two different absolute movement tools have been implemented in SemNet to explore alternative ways of controlling three-dimensional movement in two-dimensional maps. One tool, shown in the figures, displays two maps; the other tool shows three maps corresponding to the x-y, y-z, and z-x planes. The third map is, of course, redundant; it provides no information that is not available in the other two maps. More importantly, users rarely used the z-x map, but restricted their attention to the other two maps.

The tool with three maps also presented a miniature version of the knowledge base, which was expected to help the user navigate. Any advantage of this information was overwhelmed, however, by the heavy processing load that it imposed on the computer. Movements were less smooth because of processing required to maintain the map images.

5.2.3 Teleportation

Teleportation, a movement method based on cache table principles, works nicely with other movement methods. Once the user has been to a location in the knowledge space, the chance of needing to go back to that same location increases dramatically. Typically, when entering new information into a knowledge-base, a user will find information that is similar to the piece to be entered, make a copy, and edit it. Teleportation allows the user to pick a recently visited knowledge element from a two-dimensional list (a menu) and instantly move to the location of the knowledge element. By selecting options from this menu, the user could pop to a location, make a copy of a knowledge element, then pop back to the original location to continue editing. This concept can easily be extended to create various types of bookkeeping lists that store concepts to be added, locations of interesting places, and concepts to be tested.

5.2.4 Hyperspace Movement

Browsing a knowledge base typically involves examining knowledge elements one at a time, observing which knowledge elements are related to the one under examination, then following a selected relationship to examine another knowledge element. The hyperspace movement method facilitates this kind of browsing. It is particularly useful in a large knowledge base in which the relationships among knowledge elements are not easily recognized and in situations in which a user is searching for an element similar to one that has been found. In a knowledge base about animals, a user could follow the *eats* relationship from *tiger* to *mongoose* to *snake* to *hamster*, thereby traveling from one end of the knowledge base to the other.

Hyperspace movement is accomplished by first selecting a function called *view_neighbors*. This function temporarily moves all the nodes connected to the selected knowledge element, positioning them around it. When this function is de-activated, or when a new node is selected, these nodes snap back to their original positions. If the next node selected is one of the moved nodes, the viewpoint follows this node back to its original position, the newly selected node is in the center of the display and all related nodes are distributed around it.

The hyperspace movement method is particularly useful when clustering methods are used to compress the information in the knowledge base (see Section 4). If an element is related to an element in another cluster, this method can be used to pull the connected element from the cluster. If the user decides this element is important, a single keystroke will move the viewpoint to this new element.

5.2.5 Moving the Space

All the movement methods described above involve moving the viewpoint through a static knowledge space. It is not clear that this is the best way to represent the movement task. Perhaps movement control would seem more natural to a user if it was conceptualized as manipulating the position of the knowledge base instead of manipulating the viewpoint. In support of this alternative, research has shown that when children are asked to describe how a structure would appear after some movement, they are more accurate if they are asked to imagine that the structure is rotated than if they imagine themselves moving to another viewpoint (Huttenlocher & Presson, 1979). Three SemNet tools allow the user to set the attitude or orientation of the knowledge space while keeping the viewpoint fixed. Initial findings suggest that this movement method is effective but it has not yet been systematically compared with the other methods.

6. Showing Dynamic Execution of a Knowledge Base

After a knowledge base has been entered, the user must test and debug it. Typically, the user makes a query or an assertion to the knowledge base, which processes this input and possibly makes internal changes to the data, usually returning a text string. To debug this process, the user needs a history of the nodes that were visited and the paths that were taken. In the past, this history was obtained by printing the current execution state as each node was visited. For complex knowledge bases this debugging trace may be hundreds of pages long, overloading the user.

The approach taken in SemNet is to show dynamically the changes that result from knowledge-base processing. During knowledge-base execution, when one node completes its processing and passes its result to another node, an object called a *sprite* travels down arcs between the nodes to show the progress of the execution. Attached to the sprite is a label showing the current value of the computation. In the Natural Language Project application, this label is the piece of the word the system is analyzing.

Since the knowledge base executes much faster than a human can follow, the speed of the sprite is under the user's control. To show the history of knowledge-base execution, both arcs and nodes have three color-coded states: background, active, and relaxed. Initially, all objects are set to the background color. When the sprite traverses an arc, the color of the arc and its connected nodes change to active. Both the nodes and the arc change to the relaxed color when the sprite has moved on to other arcs and nodes. By examining the color of the nodes and arcs, the user can determine which nodes have executed, which helps to localize errors.

When the user has determined that a particular region of the knowledge base is responsible for an error, extra debugging aids can be requested for the nodes in that region. When one of these nodes is encountered, a temporary fixed menu appears, which contains the rules that the node represents. Highlighting is used to show how each rule in the menu responded to the input.

7. Conclusion

As knowledge bases become larger, more powerful semantic and syntactic techniques will be required for exploring and manipulating the knowledge. SemNet offers a syntactic approach to solving this problem. SemNet's representation of a knowledge base is based entirely on the names and positions of the knowledge elements and the connections among them. SemNet demonstrates how major problems in knowledge-base management can be solved, or partially solved, with only this syntactic information. Of course, semantic information available to the application program could be used in conjunction with SemNet's syntactic techniques to achieve a more effective solution.

The positions of the knowledge elements greatly affect comprehension of the knowledge base structure. The application program assigns initial positions, allowing use of semantic information that is unavailable to SemNet. Alternatively, positions can be determined by heuristics designed to put knowledge elements close together spatially if they are neighbors in the graph structure formed by their interconnections. These methods for assigning positions become increasingly important and increasingly less effective as the knowledge base increases in size, pointing to the need for further research on this problem.

An important issue has been how, using only syntactic information, SemNet can reduce the displayed information by presenting less information about those knowledge elements unimportant to the user's immediate concern. To some extent, this information reduction is accomplished automatically by the three-dimensional graphic hardware if proximity-based positioning has been used. Objects near the viewpoint, which is assumed to represent the region of immediate interest, are displayed at full size. Object size diminishes as distance from the viewpoint increases, and objects outside the field of view are not displayed at all. The result is a fisheye view based on three-dimensional perspective. This method has been made more effective by combining it with a fisheye view based on clustering. All knowledge elements within local regions of euclidean space have been assigned to clusters, neighboring clusters have been assigned to higher level clusters, and so on. Only knowledge elements near the viewpoint are presented; further from the viewpoint, cluster-objects are displayed that represent all the knowledge elements in a region of the space. The combination of these two methods greatly reduces the displayed information while providing both local details and global context.

SemNet has been an exploratory project to investigate alternative solutions to problems endemic to large knowledge-base systems. SemNet was never intended to provide solutions to all knowledge-base problems. However, SemNet was intended to help users recognize and understand the structure or organization of a large knowledge base. To achieve this understanding, we hypothesize, the user must recognize the identities of knowledge-base elements, explicit relationships between elements, and the relative position of elements within the knowledge base. To expand an old aphorism, SemNet attempts to reveal the structure of the forest, not details about trees.

The details of the knowledge-base are de-emphasized and the structure is emphasized by representing the elements of the knowledge base as simple, labeled rectangles and the relationships between elements as color-coded arcs. Navigation tools enable a user to explore the structure, view different parts of it, and follow relationships from one element to another. Positioning heuristics and fisheye techniques are intended to ensure that the view presented to the user communicates the logical structure of the knowledge base.

Although SemNet has been an exploratory research project, an outcome of the project is a system that can be integrated with a wide range of applications. SemNet solves some but not all problems that are commonly encountered in knowledge-base applications. Indeed, a single system cannot address all knowledge-base problems because they depend on the application and the tasks that are to be performed. Consequently, SemNet is intended to be used in conjunction with an application program that would provide access to the contents of the knowledge-base elements. In the Prolog example shown in Figures 1-1 and Figures 3-1 to 4-1, SemNet shows the relationships among Prolog modules, while an application program would display the contents of these modules and support module construction and editing. The MCC Natural Language Project accomplished a tighter marriage of SemNet with the application program. When a linguist debugs a rule system using SemNet, the nodes represent collections of rules responsible for analyzing morphemes that visibly travel from one node to another. When an error is isolated to a node, the linguist can request a display of the rule collection, which SemNet obtains from the application program. Other potential applications of SemNet are: communicating the structure of large projects, debugging object-oriented programs, browsing through hypermedia documents, and representing connectionist models.

Acknowledgements

We would like to thank two of our colleagues, Jonathan Slocum and Jonathan Grudin for their intellectual support in the development of SemNet and the preparation of this paper. We also would like to acknowledge the contribution of Vernor Vinge, author of "True Names", for his visionary support of our work and other artificial realities.

References

diSessa, Andrea A. (1985). A principled design for an integrated computational environment. *Human-Computer Interaction, 1*, 1-47.

Dumais, S. T. & Landauer, T. K. (1984). Describing categories of objects for menu retrieval systems. *Research Methods, Instruments and Computers, 16*, 242-248.

Fairchild, K. M. (1985). *Construction of a semantic net virtual world metaphor* (Tech. Rep. No. HI-163-85). Austin, TX: Microelectronics and Computer Technology Corporation.

Fairchild, K. M., & Poltrock, S. E. (1986). *SemNet* [Videotape]. Presented at CHI'86 Human Factors in Computing Systems, Boston, 1986, and (Tech. Rep No HI-104-86), Austin, TX: Microelectronics and Computer Technology Corporation.

Fairchild, K. M., & Poltrock, S. E. (1987). *Soaring through knowledge space: SemNet 2.1* [Videotape]. Presented at CHI'87 Human Factors in Computing Systems, Toronto, 1987, and (Tech. Rep. No. HI-104-86, Rev. 1), Austin, TX: Microelectronics and Computer Technology Corporation.

Furnas, G. W. (1986). Generalized fisheye views. *Proceedings of CHI'86 Human Factors in Computing Systems*, 16-23. New York: ACM.

Huttenlocher, J., & Presson, C. C. (1979). The coding and transformation of spatial information. *Cognitive Psychology, 11*, 375-394.

Kirkpatrick, S., Gelatt, C. D., & Vecchi, M. P. (1983). Optimization by simulated annealing. *Science, 220*, 671-680.

Kruskal, J. B. (1964a). Multidimensional scaling by optimizing goodness of fit to a non-metric hypothesis. *Psychometrika, 29*, 1-27.

Kruskal, J. B. (1964b). Non-metric multidimensional scaling: A numerical method. *Psychometrika, 29*, 28-42.

Kruskal, J. B., Young, F. W., & Seery, J. B. (1973). *How to use KYST: A very flexible program to do multidimensional scaling* (Technical Memorandum). Murray Hill, NJ: Bell Laboratories.

Poltrock, S. E., Shook, R. E., Fairchild, K., Lovgren, J. E., Tarlton, P. N., Tarlton, M., & Hauser, M. (1986). *Three-dimensional interfaces: The promise and the problems* (Tech. Rep. No. HI-291-86). Austin, TX.: Microelectronics and Computer Technology Corporation.

Rips, L. J., Shoben, E. J., & Smith, E. E. (1973). Semantic distance and the verification of semantic relations. *Journal of Verbal Learning and Verbal Behavior, 12*, 1-20.

Shook, Robert E. (1986). *SemNet: A conceptual and interface evaluation* (Tech. Rep. No. HI-320-86-P). Austin, TX: Microelectronics and Computer Technology Corporation.

Slocum J., & Cohen, R. (1986). *NABU documentation, Natural Language Processing Project* (Tech. Rep. No. AI-228-86-Q). Austin, TX: Microelectronics and Computer Technology Corporation.

Vinge, V. (1981). *True names.* Dell Books.

Navigating Large Networks with Hierarchies

Stephen G. Eick and Graham J. Wills

AT&T Bell Laboratories

This paper is aimed at the exploratory visualization of networks where there is a strength or weight associated with each link, and makes use of any hierarchy present on the nodes to aid the investigation of large networks. It describes a method of placing nodes on the plane that gives meaning to their relative positions. The paper discusses how linking and interaction principles aid the user in the exploration. Two examples are given; one of electronic mail communication over eight months within a department, another concerned with changes to a large section of a computer program.

I. THE PROBLEM

It has almost become a cliché to start a paper with the observation that the amount of data in the world is growing rapidly, and that current efforts to extract useful information from data lag far behind the ability to create data. However the cliché is true, and no less so in the field of network analysis and visualization than in any other. In many areas, scientists are realizing that the tools they have been using are limited in utility when applied to large, information-rich networks. Not only are networks of interest large in terms of size (as measured by number of nodes or links between nodes), but also in terms of the data collected for each node or link. The ability to examine statistics on the nodes and relate them to the network is of crucial importance.

Examples of areas in which the analysis of large networks is important include:

i. *Trade flows*. The concern in this area is monitoring imports and exports of various products at several levels; international, interstate and local. Besides examining many types of trade goods, there is also strong interest in spotting temporal patterns.

ii. *Communication networks*. This is an important and wide category, covering not only telecommunication networks, but also electronic mail (email), financial transaction, ATM/bank data transferal and other data distribution networks.

iii. *Software Engineering*. Large software projects have a number of networks of interest associated with them. One such network is the *function call graph*, a network indicating which functions call which other functions. The network of inter-file dependencies states which files must be re-compiled when any file is altered. A good understanding of these networks allows efficient compilation strategies to be designed as well as aiding the planning of new additions to the system.

Previous research into network visualization includes Unwin, Sloan and Wills [12] which describes an exploratory analysis of oil imports/exports to and from European countries. The nodes are positioned on a map of the world at the center of their countries and a number of interactive methods, such as thresholding, are used to help analyze the data. Because there are relatively few countries in the world their methods work well, but even with the interactivety there would be problems applying this model to large data sets. Further, the use of geographic location is a limiting concept. Although it has the useful property of telling the user where the countries lie in relation to each other geographically, it provides no other information. Thus it devotes much space to showing well-known, unchanging facts.

Becker et al. [2] gives another method of interactively exploring network data. The paper examines telecommunications traffic, focusing on telephone traffic within the US during the October 17, 1989, earthquake. Geographic location is again used to position the 100 or so nodes, and the links are animated over time with their width and color changing to reflect various traffic statistics. The positioning is a major problem here as the focus of interest is California which is on the edge of the picture. Thus in all the displays we see many lines all crossing the US horizontally and becoming visually confused. The authors propose a number of techniques to alleviate this problem such as hiding small links, hiding nodes and drawing only parts of lines linking nodes. Although helpful, these do not really attack the core problem; the positioning of the nodes conveys too little information for both the screen 'real-estate' it uses and the clutter it creates.

In the next section we consider a section of the corporate email network and examine it with *HierNet*, a tool the authors have written for examining large hierarchical networks. Email is an interesting area of study, especially for large organizations, because dissemination of information and the synthesis that comes from good communication patterns is important for organizational efficiency. Understanding email networks has benefits when designing interfaces and electronic conferencing tools, allocating people to tasks, and investigating how people interact within a given domain. Figure 1 shows the communication patterns in our department at AT&T Bell Laboratories. In this snapshot of a screen display we have encoded information in several ways:

- The area of each node is proportional to the number of email messages sent or received by the individual (or machine id). The largest node, *MTS/Sys*, represents 1600 messages.
- The node color* shows the function; red for clerical, blue for technical staff, pink for technical staff from other departments, green for department heads (managers), yellow for machines.
- The links show email communication between individuals, where the common 'heat' scale has been used to code number of messages; blue for few, through green and yellow to red for many messages.

This display is appealing. We can see immediately that the departmental MTSs cluster at the center, surrounding the two main communication foci; the main secretary and the system administrator. (MTS/Sys). The departmental heads are well out from the center, with the other secretary. At the right are many external MTSs and at the lower left are a higher proportion of machines. One explanation for this last effect is that the departmental MTSs below and left of the MTS/Sys node do more applied work than those in the other areas, who are more theoretical in nature. The external MTSs generally tend also to be more theory-oriented, leading to the above pattern.

We characterize the domain we will investigate as that of *large* networks, with (possibly) *statistics* associated with each node and/or each edge. By large we mean ≥ 500 nodes, with millions of nodes not being an unreasonable amount. A *statistic* we take to mean some piece of information about the node or edge. This may be numeric, categorical, or simply a label. A further observation we can make is that the nodes of large networks often have a hierarchy imposed on them; for trade flow and travel networks we may take towns as a basic unit that we group into regions and similarly group regions into countries; communications networks are often constructed as hierarchical units with central servers or hubs. We will see that the existence of such a hierarchy allows us develop methods for the visualization of large networks.

Our approach to analyzing such data has three major lines of attack:

- *Node placement.* Instead of using a pre-defined (e.g., geographic) location, or using a layout made purely to reduce clutter, we use algorithms that position the nodes by considering the weighted links between the nodes. These methods place nodes that are strongly linked close together, giving meaning to relative locations. As a pleasant side effect, clutter is also reduced.
- *Interaction.* In both [2] and [12], interaction is used to let the user change viewing parameters such as node size, line width and length, etc. We use interaction for a similar purpose, but amplify its effect by combining it with linking.
- *Linking.* Scatterplot brushing [1] is the oldest method of linking data plots, but the idea has been generalized to linking many types of plot [13]. We provide several simple displays and allowing the user to interact with each to select a focus of interest. The other displays then update to reflect such a focus, allowing interesting features found in one plot to be related to other displays. This aids navigation of large networks by allowing the user to concentrate on interesting parts of the data set.

II. THE E-MAIL NETWORK

We now take a longer look at the email data set. We are interested in a number of questions such as

Q1. Do similar people send similar amounts of mail? To similar numbers of people?

Q2. Who talks with whom? Are there communities with similar interests?

Q3. How do these patterns change over time?

Mackay [8] provides a number of other interesting questions and hypotheses about email use. The data have been collected by instrumenting the UNIX mail program. The authors compiled a version of *mail* which logged each message as it was dealt with by the mail program; recording the sender and recipient and the date at which it was sent. A number of days of data were collected and have been aggregated into months for ease of processing.

* In the black and white figure, "color" is taken to mean gray level.

Figure 2 shows a view of the data as it is being analyzed using *HierNet*. *HierNet* is an X-windows application [9] with some Motif extras [4] which provides an environment in which we can visualize hierarchical networks. There are three windows displayed; the main window, which shows the network itself, a narrow window ('time') which shows the period under scrutiny, and a smoothed histogram of the number of messages each network link represents. The display represents the state of the network in the last month of the period studied (as shown by the position of the red box in the 'time' slider). The labels for the nodes are fictitious surnames, to preserve anonymity. Figure 1 shows the network at the previous month. The sizes of the nodes have been forced to be constant over all time periods to help the user spot patterns. Hence the three largest nodes are Friedman (MTS/Sys), Hardy (MTS) and Dreyfus (MTS). They are close together in both displays – an indication that they form a community with a common interest.

The 'link strengths' window shows the distribution of the number of messages per link, where the horizontal axis is mapped to the link strength and the vertical axis to the number of links with the given strength. This is smoothed using a *kernel density smooth* [10] to give a useful representation. This window can be interacted with in two ways. First, the degree of smoothing can be altered by moving the slider to the right of the window. The smoothed view is updated constantly and rapidly as the smoothing parameter is changed, allowing the user not only to choose a suitable value, but also to see different features. For example, consider Figure 3, in which we have shown four different levels of smooth. In the topmost display we have the highest level of smooth; the global features of the data are all that are visible. This shape conforms to a statistical distribution called the *Poisson* distribution – a plausible model for this kind of data [11]. This is an over-smoothed view, however, and as the degree of the smooth becomes less and less, it becomes clear that there are distinct clumps of link strengths, with the size of the clumps diminishing as they represent bigger and bigger links. Although a Poisson model could be considered as an initial model, a more realistic model would have to explain this phenomenon.

The other interaction method supported by this view is the ability to select sub-areas of the smoothed histogram and either show or hide them. Since this view is linked to the main view, the main view will show or hide links as this selection is made. In Figure 2 we have hidden all except the links with many messages. This gives a picture that shows the main communication pathways more clearly than Figure 1, but does not show any links for Wilde, the fourth largest node with over 600 messages to his credit in the month. Wilde has a different pattern of email usage to the other large nodes, sending few messages to many people rather than many messages to a few. He is also not part of the highly communicative group of Friedman, Dreyfus and Hardy.

This pattern is true for the last two time periods. Is it true for earlier time periods? Has the group of three always been together? We can use the time slider to move through the history of the network and observe the results, as follows. In Figure 4, the main view shows the earliest state of the process. The circle of nodes represents those email ids that have not yet 'entered the picture'. Only Friedman is in the department at this time. As we progress forward in time, we see the nodes begin to move in from the edges and Dreyfus (the next to move) moves immediately beside Friedman. At a later date, Hardy and Wilde both move into the picture. It takes them two time periods to reach the positions shown in the inset – close to where they end up in Figure 3. In fact the group of three stay together for the rest of the period, but Wilde moves around a lot. Generally, we observe that it takes about two months for most people to move to a reasonably stable position and that Friedman, Hardy and Dreyfus form a stable group whereas Wilde moves around a lot.

In summary, we have learnt that for this network:

A1. The amount of mail sent varies widely, but smoothly as shown by the node sizes in Figure 1. A smoothed histogram view of the node sizes confirms this. There is considerable variety in how the messages are sent, for example in the difference between Wilde and the other nodes. The view of link strengths shows that mail traffic between people is more clumped than might have been suspected.

A2. We have identified one community of three individuals. These are people with excellent computer and UNIX skills, who we may hypothesize regularly exchange email related to computer issues.

A3. This group formed as soon as the three settled into the organization and remained together from then on. Conversely, Wilde has no fixed communication patterns. By examining individuals as they join the department we can see that it takes about two months for most to establish communication patterns and settle in to their new position.

III. SOFTWARE ENGINEERING

A more complex example is shown in Figure 5. The data are based on a large software project, the 5ESS switch, the source files of which are allocated to various *modules*, and the modules themselves to subsystems. This forms a large hierarchy of files; the subsystem we investigate contains about a hundred modules with 6000 files. Displaying such a hierarchy alone is a formidable task. Tree displays become cluttered with a hundred nodes and even advanced techniques such as [5] have difficulty with over a thousand nodes. Figure 5 shows the modules and the links between them, calculated as explained below.

When a change to the program is required, an MR (*modification request*) is created, and every change to the source code required to implement the change is registered under that MR. Thus the MR database contains a history of modifications to source files. We generate links between files A and B equal to the sum of MRs which changed both files. Hence each link is a measure of 'co-change' and large links denote files that are changed together a lot. This method generates 8 million links. To manage this many links, we make use of the hierarchical information. Instead of looking at all file-file links, we form 3 smaller sets of links to summarize the important properties of the network:

- We retain all *file-file* links between files within a module. This gives us a model of how each module is changed internally.
- We sum all links between a file and files in another module to give a *file-module* link showing how files co-change with other modules.
- We sum all links between files in one module and files in another to give a *module-module* link denoting how changes in modules affect other modules.

Although we lose links between files and files in other modules, the file-module links capture the important aspect of those links; the 'breaking' of module independence, and we gain the informative module-module links. We reduce the number of links to about a quarter of a million, a manageable amount. In Figure 5 and 6 we retain only the strongest 1% of such links, reducing clutter. Note also that this hierarchical aggregation is scaleable. If we had many subsystems we can form module-subsystem and subsystem-subsystem links by taking the module-module links as a base and repeating the above method.

The interest in this data set lies in understanding what modules and files need to be changed at the same time. They are likely to form sets that have a similar function or which depend on common structures. Being able visually to indicate such classes and see how they interact is of importance in understanding how to divide modules among teams, form new modules that may interact with existing modules and re-organize the hierarchy for greater efficiency. Another important area is that of re-engineering; looking at the way the system has evolved and trying to model the process and re-implement it in better ways.

For Figure 5 we have used two statistics to code the nodes' size, shape and color. The number of files in the module gives the width of the node, and the number of changes made to files in the module is used to give the height. The node is colored to emphasize the aspect ratio of the resulting rectangle. Tall thin red nodes indicate modules with a large number of changes per file, whereas wide short green nodes indicate where the ratio of changes to files is low. All the links involving files are hidden in this Figure – we focus on comparing modules only.

There are several interesting features in this plot; we will indicate just two. The most immediate feature is the circular pattern to the lower right of center. There are about 25 small modules in a circle or inside a circle, and all are linked to all the others with the same weight. These links produce the blue spike in the smoothed histogram of link strengths. By dragging the mouse across the nodes it can be seen that each of the modules is named CC7sigv*??*, where '*??*' is a pair of numerals, and that each module contains exactly two files. Clearly there is an important association among these files. The authors consulted a developer who had worked in this area, who explained that all the modules had been created simultaneously and that they contained no executable code, but were simply descriptions of how certain data structures should be instantiated. These files are thus logically separate, since only one is used for each version, but are highly related in terms of function. The use of change history to spot this feature is in contrast to methods based on semantic analysis of the code, which could not have found such a relationship.

A second feature of interest is the group of six files at the far right, slightly above center. They are linked in a fairly strong way, but have only a weak connection to other modules. This shows a successful attempt at functional separation, resulting in a set of modules that does not need to change when other parts of the subsystem change. Investigation found that this part of the system dealt with ordinary telephone signaling, whereas the rest of the system dealt mainly with ISDN telephone communication.

One useful interactive technique that takes advantage of the hierarchy is the ability to expand and collapse levels of the hierarchy. After studying a module in terms of its links to other modules, we can replace it by its component files and see the file-file and file-module links for them. This can lead to some valuable insights. In Figure 6 the gray insets indicate where we have expanded a module into its component files. The large red module to the left has many files and its color indicates a high number of changes per file. When we expand it and zoom in, we see that there are few links shown; when changes are made to files, other files within the module are not affected. Furthermore, the absence of links leading out from the files to other modules means that changes do not necessitate many changes in other modules. This is an example of a module that should be reasonably easy to maintain.

In contrast, the other module we have expanded (the wide green one in the center of the right box) has a large number of files (562) and fewer changes per file. When we expand it, though, we do not even need to zoom to see that it is radically different. Many links come from the files of this module to other modules. This seems to be a contradiction. How can the individual files be linked strongly to other modules, but the module itself not strongly linked to other modules? The reason is that most of the files are linked to different modules, so that the average link from this module to another is actually small, since it depends only on links involving a few files. This module is not really a module at all. Its name 'hdr' gives a clue what function it performs. It is a collection of files describing the other modules, and hence its files change with those other modules.

For this data set we have:

- Used the hierarchy to reduce the size of the data set significantly without reducing the information content and allowed the user to interact with the hierarchy to see levels of information, hiding links and nodes to allow important features to be seen.
- Found a large group of modules that are practically identical. This information can be used to abstract the information in the modules further and produce smaller modules with greater independence.
- Located a group of modules performing a function independently of the others – useful information when allocating modules to developers; these should not be split up.
- Identified an anomalous module; one whose files are linked with most other modules.

IV. NODE PLACEMENT ALGORITHMS

In section I, we stated that we use algorithms that position nodes based on the weighted links between the nodes. In this section we outline ways of doing so and explain our preferred algorithm. A number of link-based placement algorithms exist. Many do not take the weights of links into account, being concerned only with connectivity [6], and others are aimed purely at creating as pleasant a layout as possible, for example by minimizing the number of links that cross each other. These methods are inappropriate in an interactive environment as the number of links displayed varies as the user desires. They also do not give any real meaning to the relative positions of nodes: What does a cluster of nodes mean when the positioning criterion is to minimize crossed links? One further drawback is that most of them have not been designed for use with large networks.

We therefore examine methods to position nodes such that the distance between nodes is related to strength of the link between them. Clearly such a relationship should be an inverse one, with nodes that have large links having short separation. The simplest form of such a relation is to require that the distance between two nodes be inversely proportional to the size of the link:

$$d_{ij} \propto \frac{1}{w_{ij}}$$

where d_{ij} is the displayed link length, w_{ij} is the size (weight) of the link.

The obvious candidate for such a placement algorithm is the statistical technique of *multidimensional scaling*, or MDS [7]. Given a matrix of dissimilarities, δ_{ij}, this method fits positions to the nodes that minimize $\Sigma(d_{ij} - \delta_{ij})^2$. Setting $\delta_{ij} = 1/w_{ij}$ would give a layout that should attempt to satisfy the above relationship.

Unfortunately this does work well for two reasons. The practical reason is that the method requires the inversion of the matrix of dissimilarities, which can be expensive for large systems such as we have explored. Another drawback can be seen by considering the quantity to be minimized:

$$\Sigma (d_{ij} - \delta_{ij})^2 = \Sigma (d_{ij} - \frac{1}{w_{ij}})^2 = \Sigma \frac{(d_{ij}w_{ij} - 1)^2}{w_{ij}^2}$$

The method tries to set $d_{ij}w_{ij}$ to be close to unity (as required), but the minimization is weighted by $1/w_{ij}^2$, with the result that small links have an inordinate importance relative to large ones – exactly the reverse of the situation we would like. For these reasons we cannot use MDS as a node placement algorithm.

Another method that has been used in a number of guises is that of directly minimizing an error function on the nodes. Using the function $\Sigma(d_{ij} - \delta_{ij})^2$, for example, gives a method equivalent to MDS. To implement minimization methods we start with some reasonable positioning of the nodes and use a method such as Newton's method or steepest descent to find a layout that minimizes the function (see [3] for details). Minimization methods are also known as *force-based* algorithms, as they are equivalent to releasing a set of nodes under a system of inter-node forces and letting them find an equilibrium layout. A common example of such an algorithm is to model the nodes as having springs attached between them, the strength of each spring being proportional to the size of the corresponding link. Some repulsive force between nodes is also required to prevent the nodes from coalescing.

Although widely used, the spring algorithm is not a perfect model. It certainly brings nodes closer together when the links are stronger, but it has a tendency simply to bring nodes which have a lot of strong links together, regardless of whether they have strong links to each other. It also tends to fill an area, since all nodes want to get as close to each other as the repulsive force will allow. Thus nodes will tend to fill in gaps. This behavior is useful in that it fits as many nodes as possible into an area, but it tends to hinder the ability to spot groups, as groups are always embedded in a sea of less important nodes that have drifted beside them.

We elect instead directly to minimize the function

$$\Sigma \left(w_{ij} - \frac{1}{d_{ij}}\right)^2 = \Sigma \frac{(d_{ij}w_{ij} - 1)^2}{d_{ij}^2}$$

This gives us the required relation, and also states that our interest lies most strongly in close nodes, where the weights are high. In contrast to the spring method, nodes with weak links are moved to positions well away from the other nodes, so that important groups are readily identified.

The hierarchy is also taken advantage of in the layout algorithm. Starting with the root node (which we place at some appropriate center, usually the origin), we consider the sub-network generated by its children and use our minimization algorithm to place them. We then re-center and re-scale to place the children at the parent's location and recursively use this algorithm on the child nodes. This gives us a layout algorithm that can deal with any depth of hierarchy, and which is comparatively fast as the slow part (the minimization routine) is only required to work on sub-networks.

V. CONCLUSIONS

We have demonstrated our approach on two real data sets; the email data set – with a small number of nodes and temporally indexed links, and a software engineering example – with a medium number of nodes and many links. For both we showed how the beginning of an exploration might start, drawing useful insights into how people communicate and how big programs are changed.

We have demonstrated a method of investigating large, hierarchical networks which is based on three lines of attack:

- Since the focus of the visualization is the layout of nodes and edges, a good *placement algorithm* is vital. We have described an algorithm that is fast, even for large networks, interpretable and which yields appealing and informative results.
- Because we are threatened with an excess of information, we use *linking* to allow us to focus on specific features of the data while retaining an overall context and providing ancillary information.
- We use *interaction* to allow the user to adjust parameters and edit the visualization, query for hidden information and directly manipulate the display.

With a good basic method and facilities for interaction, we are able to give the user the ability to navigate and explore large networks. The user can see small effects in the context of large trends and can see the evolution of networks over time and relate added information at the nodes and links to the overall display. We believe this approach to be a valuable method for the exploration of large, information-rich, hierarchical networks.

VI. REFERENCES

[1] Becker, R.A. and Cleveland, W.S. (1987). *Brushing Scatterplots*. Technometrics, Vol.29, No.2, pp. 127-142.

[2] Becker R.A., Eick, S.G., Miller, E.O. and Wilks, A.R. (1990). *Dynamic Graphics for Network Visualization*. Proceedings of IEEE Visualization Conference, 1990.

[3] Burden, R.L. and Faires, J.D. (1985). *Numerical analysis*. Duxbury Press, Boston, MA.

[4] Heller, D. (1991). *Motif Programming Manual*. O'Reilly and Associates, Sebastopol, CA.

[5] Johnson, B.J. and Shneiderman, B. (1991). *Tree-maps: A space-Filling Approach to the Visualization of Hierarchical Information Structures*. Proceedings of IEEE Visualization Conference, 1991.

[6] Koutsofias, E. and North, S.C. (1992). *Drawing Graphs with Dot*. Bell Laboratories technical report.

[7] Kruskal, J.B. and Wish, M. (1979). *Multidimensional Scaling*. Sage Publications, Newbury Park, CA.

[8] Mackay, W.E. (1988). *Diversity in the Use of Electronic Mail: A Preliminary Inquiry*. ACM Transactions on Office Information Systems, 6, 1988.

[9] Nye, A. (1991). *Xlib Programming Manual*. O'Reilly and Associates, Sebastopol, CA.

[10] Silverman, B.W. (1990). *Density Estimation for Statistics and data Analysis*. Chapman & Hall, New York.

[11] Taylor, H.M. and Karlin, S. (1984). *An Introduction to Stochastic Modeling*. Academic Press, London, UK.

[12] Unwin, A.R., Sloan, B. and Wills, G.J. (1992). *Interactive Graphical Methods for Trade Flows*. Proceedings of New Techniques and Technologies for Statistics, to appear.

[13] Velleman, P.F. (1988). *The DataDesk Handbook*. Odesta Corporation. Ithaca, NY.

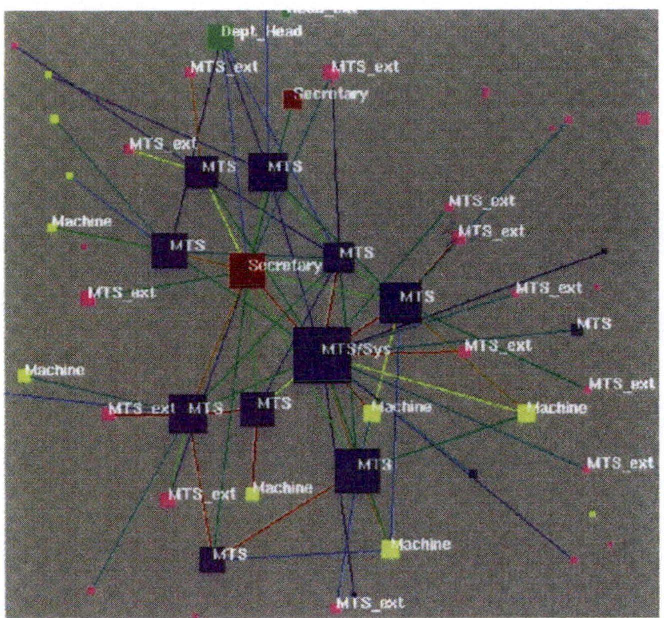

FIGURE **1**

Email network for a small department.

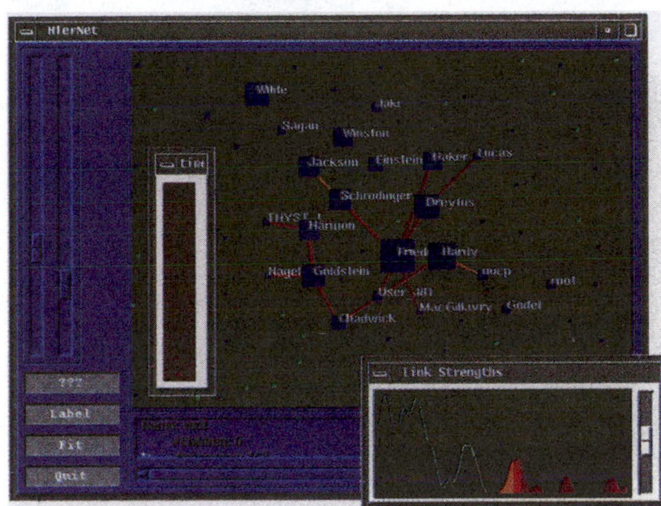

FIGURE **2**

The *HierNet* program being used to analyze the email data.

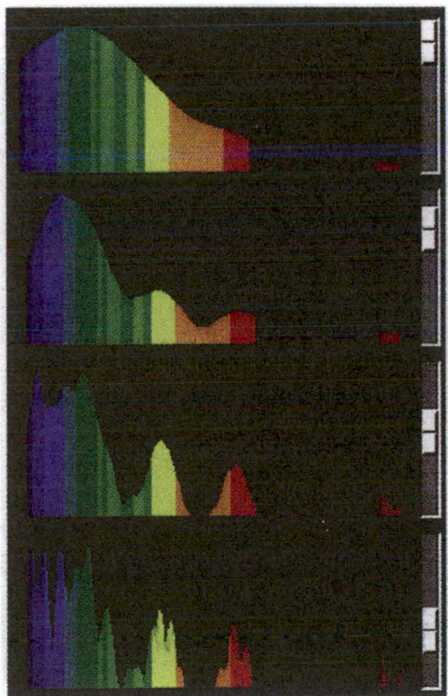

FIGURE **3**

Interactively smoothing a histrogram; four degrees of smoothing.

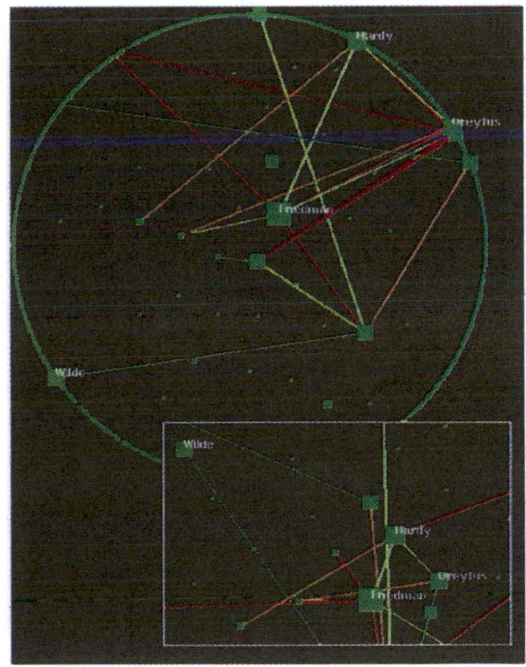

FIGURE **4**

Observing the behaviour of the email period of time.

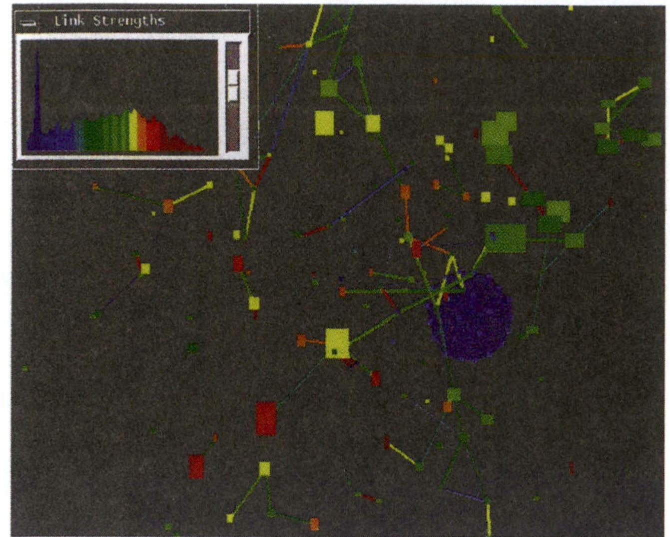

FIGURE **5**

Using *HierNet* to show groupings within a large software project.

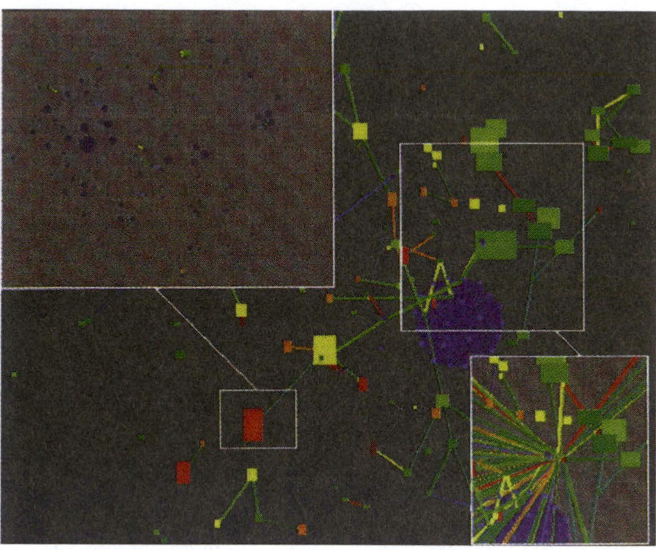

FIGURE **6**

Expanding and collapsing nodes within the hierarchy to see more or less detail.

Visualizing Network Data

Richard A. Becker, Stephen G. Eick†, and Allan R. Wilks

Abstract—**Networks are critical to modern society, and a thorough understanding of how they behave is crucial to their efficient operation. Fortunately, data on networks is plentiful; by visualizing this data, it is possible to greatly improve our understanding. Our focus is on visualizing the data associated with a network and not on simply visualizing the structure of the network itself. We begin with three static network displays; two of these use geographical relationships, while the third is a matrix arrangement that gives equal emphasis to all network links. Static displays can be swamped with large amounts of data; hence we introduce direct-manipulation techniques that permit the graphs to continue to reveal relationships in the context of much more data. In effect, the static displays are parameterized so that interesting views may easily be discovered interactively. The software to carry out this network visualization is called SeeNet.**

Index Terms—**Network visualization, parameter focusing, network data analysis, interactive graphics, data analysis, direct manipulation.**

I. Introduction

WE are currently in the midst of a networking revolution. Data communications networks such as the Internet now connect millions of computers, cellular phones have become commonplace, and personal communications networks are in the developmental stages. In parallel with the ever increasing network sizes has been a concomitant increase in the collection of network measurement data. Understanding this data is of crucial importance as we move to a modern, information-rich society.

Unfortunately, tools for analyzing network data have not kept pace with the data volumes. More network measurement data is available today than ever before, yet it is useless until it is understood. Traditional network analysis software and graphs cannot cope with the size of today's networks and their data collection capabilities.

We have developed some novel graphical tools for displaying network data, together with display manipulation techniques that can help extract meaningful insights from the masses of network data currently available. In addition, our tools scale to the even larger networks that are emerging.

A network consists of nodes, links, and possibly spatial information. Statistics, which may be raw data or data summaries and may vary over time, are associated with the nodes and the links. The link statistics may be directed, as in call flow of a circuit-switched network, or undirected, as in the network's capacity. The network may have a natural spatial layout as does a geographical trade-flow network, or may be abstract as in a personal communications network. Network data may be categorical, such as the type of node or link, or quantitative, such as a link's capacity. The data may be static, such as a network's capacity, or time varying, such as the network flow in several time periods.

Our focus is on visualizing network data and our motivating examples involve communications networks. Our goal is to understand the data and not the networks themselves. Thus the structure and connectivity of the graph are of secondary importance—data associated with the links and nodes is what we want to understand. For communications networks the important questions involve the sizes of the flows, the capacities of the links, link and node utilization, and variations through time.

A challenge in visualizing network data is coping with the data volumes—networks may have hundreds or thousands of nodes, thousands or tens of thousands of links, and data from many time periods. The three methods traditionally used to reduce the amount of network data to manageable size are:

- for large numbers of links or nodes, aggregation,
- for large numbers of time periods, averaging, and
- for detecting changes, thresholding and exception reporting.

Each of these data-reduction methods may obscure important information. Graphical displays, particularly network maps, have long been recognized as a crucial tool for analyzing network data. Graphical displays, however, even when running on powerful workstation-based systems, can become swamped and overly busy when faced with large networks and data volumes. We present techniques to address these display clutter problems.

We introduce three graphical tools, collectively named *SeeNet*[1], for visualizing network data. Our visualization techniques involve static displays, interactive controls, and animation. In Sections II, III, and IV we will illustrate these three techniques by using as an example the AT&T Long Distance Network—the national circuit-switched telecommunications network used by AT&T to carry long distance telephone calls. The example involves data from over 110 nodes (switches) that are (nearly) completely connected. Each node has a geographic location and there are statistics for each node, directed link statistics between every pair of nodes, and new data collected every five minutes. The challenge with this example involves the large number of links, over 12,000, and the time varying aspects of the data. Our data is from October 17, 1989, when an earthquake occurred in the San Francisco Bay area. In Section V, we will present our techniques using data from a

†Correspondence contact: AT&T Bell Laboratories - RM IHC 1G-351, 1000 E. Warrenville Road, Naperville, IL 60565 USA; e-mail: eick@research.att.com.

IEEECS Log Number V95003.

variety of networks, including Internet packet traffic and electronic mail messages within a research department. Section VI discusses SeeNet's uses within AT&T and describes its implementation, while Section VII places the work in the context of related research.

II. Static Network Displays

We now turn to a set of static techniques for displaying network data using telecommunications traffic among the 110 switches in the AT&T network on October 17, 1989, the day of the San Francisco earthquake. During a major network event such as an earthquake, interesting questions concern the network capacity and traffic flows:

- Where are the overloads?
- Which links are carrying the most traffic?
- Was there network damage?
- Are there any pockets of underutilized network capacity?
- Is the overload increasing or decreasing?
- Are calls into the affected area completing or are they being blocked elsewhere in the network?

The widely used techniques for statically displaying network link data involve displaying the data spatially on a map or representing the data as a matrix.

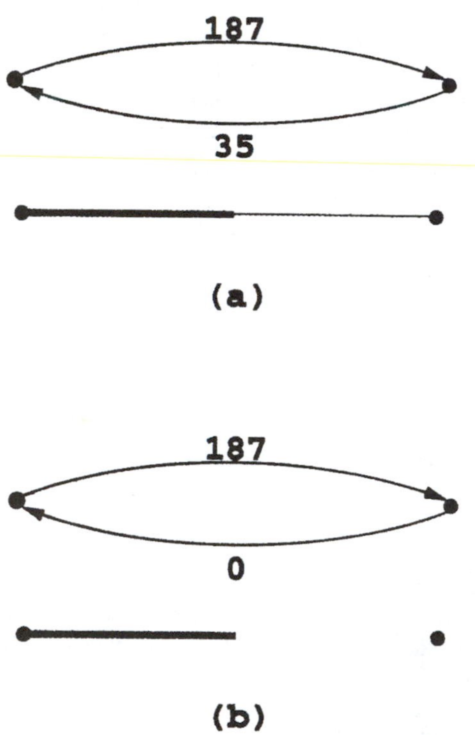

Fig. 1. Representing Link Data. In part (a), the upper illustration is a conventional arrow diagram with numbers to show link statistics; the lower illustration uses line thickness and color to convey the same information more compactly. Part (b) shows how half-lines represent statistics with value zero.

A. Link Maps

One way of displaying link data on a map is to draw line segments between each pair of nodes for which there is data. This pictures the connectivity of the network. To show the values of a link statistic, the segments may be colored, for example, or drawn with varying thicknesses. Since link data is often directional, it is possible to show data in both directions using arrows or by bisecting the segments and always using the half connected to a node to show the statistic with that node as the originating node.

Fig. 1 shows schematically how these segments are constructed. The upper half of part (a) shows that between the two nodes is a link with data for both directions; a compact form of this is represented in the lower half of part (a) by a pair of connecting line segments, with gray shade and thickness proportional to the data values. Part (b) of Fig. 1 illustrates a refinement that we often use to reduce clutter—if one of the data values is zero, the corresponding line segment is not drawn. A negative data value for a particular link can be shown using a dashed instead of a solid line.

Fig. 2 illustrates some of these ideas by showing a *linkmap* of the overload into and out of the Oakland node using only the bisected segments. The "island" on the map in the Atlantic Ocean is a blowup of the New York/New Jersey area, necessitated because of the larger density of nodes in that region. The message of this figure is clear; there is an overload into Oakland from every other node and out of Oakland to many of the nodes, particularly on the East Coast. The most heavily overloaded links are from Seattle, Denver, and some of the major cities on the West Coast.

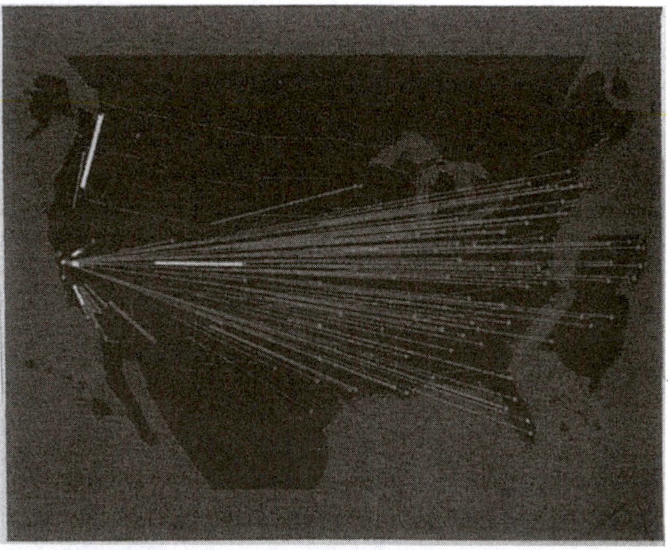

Fig. 2. Overload Into One Node. The overload into and out of the Oakland node. The half-lines between the nodes code the overload by direction.

The display in Fig. 2 works well because the lines encoding the link statistics do not overlap much. It is often the case, however, that these link-data displays have many overlapping lines and are therefore difficult to interpret. For example, look at Fig. 3, which shows the network-wide overload for the same time period as in Fig. 2. The plethora of lines makes the figure too complicated to understand easily. There is an overload focused on several of the nodes on the West Coast, but which of these nodes is most affected? Another difficulty is that the long transcontinental links cover the middle of the country and obscure potential problems underneath. A third problem is that it is hard to see where a half-line terminates if the other half is not displayed. Two simple techniques improve Fig. 3 by making the important links visually prominent. The important links (those with large overload) are drawn last so that they appear on top and are not obscured by the other links. The link thickness is used to encode the statistic redundantly, making the important links thicker and therefore more apparent.

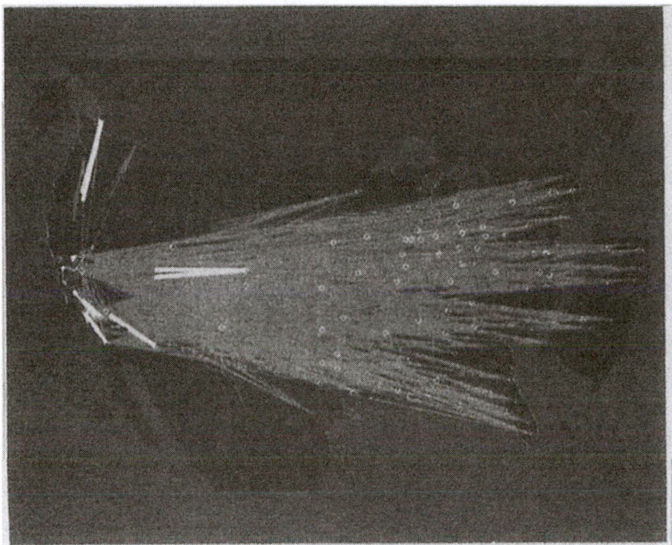

Fig. 3. Node-to-Node Network Overload. The network-wide overload after the earthquake for the same time period as Fig. 2. The display is ineffective because there are many long lines that obscure much of the country.

A different solution to the map-clutter problem caused by drawing too many lines involves aggregation at each node, with the resulting node data displayed using a node-based map or *nodemap*.

B. Nodemaps

The idea embodied in a nodemap is to display node-oriented data by showing a glyph or symbol such as a circle or square at each node on the map, with the visual characteristics such as size, shape, and color of the glyph coding the value of the statistic. More complex symbols can be used to represent more than one statistic simultaneously. For example, if "call attempts" is the statistic under consideration, there will typically be a count of inbound calls and of outbound calls at each node; these can be shown by using rectangles for the symbols, with the width and height proportional to the two statistics.

Fig. 4 shows the nodemap representation of the AT&T network-calling statistics for the same period as in Figs. 2 and 3. The data shown in Fig. 4 is the aggregate overload into and out of each node, shown on a square root scale. The tall, thin rectangles indicate an outbound overload, the short, fat rectangles indicate an inbound overload, and the square rectangles indicate a symmetric load. The area of the rectangle is approximately proportional to the total overload because of the square root scale. There are clear and obvious geographical patterns. The overload is from virtually every node in the country primarily into the northern California nodes and secondarily into southern California. The heaviest overload is in California, on the West Coast, and decreases gradually west to east.

Fig. 4. Overload Following Earthquake. Each rectangle shows the aggregate overload over all links; its horizontal dimension is proportional to the square root of the number of incoming calls in the preceding 5-minute period, and the vertical dimension encodes the outgoing calls.

A nodemap solves the display clutter problem in Fig. 3 nicely via aggregation. Unfortunately, however, it does this at the expense of detailed information about particular links. Another possible approach to the clutter problem is to omit information about geography.

C. Matrix Display

Like a linkmap, the matrix display concentrates on the links of a network. It tries to address two fundamental problems encountered by the geographic display of network links:

- undue visual prominence may be given to long lines and
- long (e.g., transcontinental) lines may overplot other lines.

As noted before, the linkmap partially addresses this problem by thickening the links in proportion to the statistic values and drawing the important links last.

Both problems may be solved simultaneously, however, by using a matrix display, which de-emphasizes the geography by displaying the network in a matrix form with each matrix element allocated to a link. Each node is assigned to one row and column with the (i, j) and (j, i) matrix elements associated with the j-to-i and i-to-j links. If the link data is not directed, both of these elements are assigned the same value. Fig. 5 demonstrates this technique with each of the small squares corresponding to one of the potential half-lines in Fig. 3, and the colored squares corresponding to the realized lines. The nodes are arranged in approximate geographical order with west-to-east along the horizontal axis and correspondingly along the vertical axis. The matrix representation shows that the earthquake overload is highly focused on five nodes experiencing major incoming blocking and on three others with some incoming blocking. There is one node with outgoing blocking to nearly every other node indicated by the vertical column. This result, obscured in the linkmap, is obvious with the matrix display.

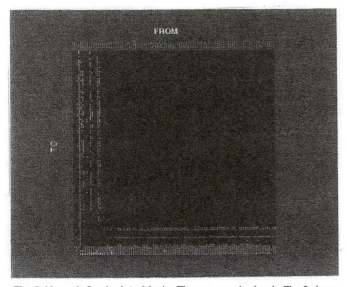

Fig. 5. Network Overload As Matrix. The same overload as in Fig. 3 shown using a matrix representation instead of a network map. The nodes are shown along the rows and columns in approximate west-to-east order in matrix form, with columns corresponding to "from" nodes and rows corresponding to "to" nodes. At the intersection of each row and column there is a square whose color codes the link statistic. The colored squares on the left and bottom correspond to the lines on Fig. 3. The nonsymmetry is due to the directed nature of the traffic.

It is clear the matrix display does well in comparison with the linkmap when there are many lines on the display. What it gives up for this is the information about geography, since the order of the nodes in the rows and columns is only slightly related to their geographic positions. Even if the nodes have no natural geographic layout, the inferences drawn from the matrix display are likely to be influenced by the order in which the nodes are assigned to rows and columns. This ambiguity of row and column order is the chief drawback of the matrix display—a display with one choice of orders may be clear, but the same display with rows and columns permuted may be hard to interpret.

III. Parameter Focusing

The static displays in Figs. 2 through 5 are natural and work well for many network data sets. The maps inherently show the spatial relationships between the nodes. The lines in Figs. 2 and 3 are ideal for showing link-related statistics while maintaining the geographic context. The glyphs in Fig. 4 show the nodal statistics, and the squares in Fig. 5 give each link the same visual prominence. But each of these displays must typically be constructed with great care to avoid visual overload. For example, if the network has too many links, say more than 10% of the $n^2/2$ possible links with n nodes, a linkmap may become cluttered and visually confusing. For a nodemap, as in Fig. 4, the glyphs must be carefully sized so that they overlap as little as possible. For network maps it may be necessary to modify the spatial layout if there are too many nodes too close together, as we did for the AT&T network map. The breakpoints used to assign colors for Fig. 5 must be carefully chosen to ensure that the colors in the squares convey meaning.

Each network display is determined by a group of display parameters as well as by the particular network data. The parameter values control the characteristics of the display, and we call the process of selecting these values *parameter focusing*. The idea is similar to adjusting parameters on a camera, e.g., focus, f-stop, exposure, before snapping a picture. Once the full set of parameters is determined, a static display can be produced because the set of parameters defines a particular map.

Of course, it takes talent, and sometimes luck, to select the proper parameter values. Just as a photographer brackets exposures to make sure that just the right amount of light is used for a photograph, a series of static displays can be made with a range of parameter values.

This tedious process, however, may be made more efficient through *dynamic* parameter adjustment. The analyst manipulates the display parameters dynamically while watching the display change; good parameter focusing is achieved when the display shows meaningful information about the data. This is akin to instant or video photography, and it makes it much easier to get the optimum image.

What parameter values are set in the focusing process? There are several broad classes:

Statistic: The choice of displayed statistic is the most important parameter. This parameter must be easy to select and to vary. For example, it may be informative to move back and forth between absolute overload and percentage overload. Transformations may also be needed: square roots, logarithms, and other computational tools should be readily available.

Levels: This parameter allows the analyst to decide which data to display or, conversely, which data to suppress. Our linkmap tool controls the levels parameter with a two-sided slider that restricts the display to any range of the displayed statistic. A generalization of this technique—brushing [1]—may be applied to the color scale. Our doubled-edged color slider is a special case of a more general slider enabling a user to select arbitrary, disconnected ranges on the scale [2].

Geography/Topology: This parameter allows display of an appropriate subset of the data, based upon network geography or topology. Geographic restriction can be accomplished by a general zoom operation that allows any rectangular subregion to be displayed. Control of network topology enables the analyst to deactivate (or reactivate) any nodes and associated links in the map. The operation is quick, making it possible to eliminate node pairs involving any particular location or group of locations, and thereby to concentrate on the other parts of the map. This operation also allows the analyst to focus on a particular location or set of locations by deactivating all locations and selectively reactivating the location or locations of interest.

Time: When the data at each node or link is varying through time, it is important to select the proper time point to display. In some cases, the proper time is known a priori; in others, it must be determined from a mass of available data. Our displays accommodate spatial time-series data, allowing the analyst to vary the displayed time point at will, and even automatically, providing snapshots at particular times or producing an animation. This enables the analyst to focus on the most interesting periods or to look for changes in network flows. Often, it is desirable to identify an interesting time period using one display and to investigate it in more detail with a different display.

Aggregation: This parameter is related to the displayed statistic parameter. It is important that the analyst have tools to aggregate statistics over geographical regions or logical subsets of a network. Although this is currently not a dynamic feature in our software, it is easy to use the underlying data management software to aggregate statistics over related locations or geographical regions.

Size: The size parameter controls the overall size of the symbols drawn on the map. Adjusting the size of the symbols allows the analyst to produce a map with symbols large enough to convey information yet small enough to avoid excessive interference with other symbols. This is a difficult problem to solve computationally, yet is simple when done interactively—human perception is a powerful tool for setting the size parameter appropriately. Our link map uses *line shortening* and *line width varying*, and our node map uses *symbol sizing*. With line shortening, the line connecting two locations is drawn only part-way from one location to the other. This helps to address the problem that lines running across the map can obscure what is happening in the middle of the map. The line width redundantly encodes the statistic along with color. Making the important lines thicker helps them stand out and be visually more prominent. With symbol sizing, the size of the rectangle around each location is adjustable. This prevents large rectangles from obscuring neighboring locations.

Color: We use color to encode the statistic values on our displays. By carefully choosing colors we can highlight the important data. On our linkmap and matrix displays the color is determined by the color slider. Adjusting the colors is a dynamic operation. The user may interactively move the boundaries between the colors and add or subtract individual colors. With many types of network data the distribution is skewed and so choosing colors naively is ineffective and will result in nearly all data items being represented by the same color. In nodemap we use color to encode differences in aspect ratios for rectangles and as a threshold for circles. The tall, thin rectangles are green, the short, fat rectangles are red, and the approximately square rectangles are white. Using a slider, the analyst controls how extreme the aspect ratio must be in order for the rectangle to be colored. This way color can be used to highlight important differences. Similarly, for circles the slider controls a threshold that determines how large the circle must be to be colored red.

We illustrate these techniques by continuing our analysis of the AT&T network data. Fig. 6 shows the same data as Fig. 3, except the half-lines are shortened. Fig. 6 also shows the sliders and other controls that allow dynamic parameter focusing. Shortening the lines reduces the visual clutter and neatly solves the line overplotting problem. In Fig. 3 the mass of transcontinental lines completely obscures the middle of the country, making it impossible to see network activity in the Midwest. In Fig. 6 the shortened line segments point east-west, showing that all of the network overflow was into and out of the West Coast. If there had been an overload in the middle of the country, then some of the nodes would have had circular fan-outs like the West Coast nodes.

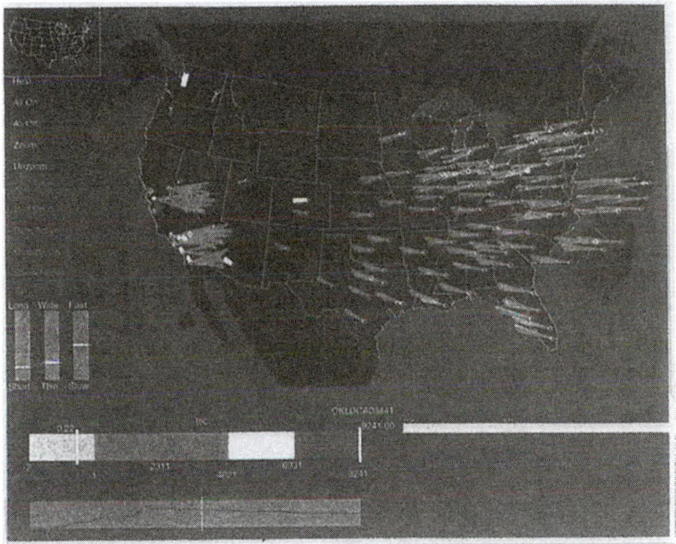

Fig. 6. Line Shortening. The figure shows the same data as Fig. 3, except the half-lines are drawn only part way between the nodes that they connect.

Network map displays often show exception statistics, like overload, that involve a small fraction of the links because otherwise they become overwhelmed by information (even on Fig. 3 less than 10% of the links are displayed). An interesting pervasive statistic (one involving most of the links between nodes) is the percentage of idle capacity of each link. Fig. 7 shows the percentage of idle capacity for links into and out of one node near Chicago. We use geographic restriction to focus on a particular location, thereby enabling us to display a pervasive statistic without the network map becoming too cluttered. To create Fig. 7 we have turned off all of the nodes and then momentarily turned on one of the nodes by touching it with the mouse.

There is idle capacity between Chicago and every other city, but the interesting aspect of this display involves the amount of idle capacity. At this time period, early evening in Chicago after the businesses have closed and before the evening residential traffic picks up, the thick colored lines indicate high percentages of idle capacity to nearly every other city except for the Bay Area and Southern California. Even to these areas where there was heavy blocking during this time period, there is a small amount of idle capacity. The reason for this involved network management controls. AT&T network managers directionalized the calling traffic, giving priority to traffic out of the disaster area while restricting the inbound traffic. The small amount of idle capacity ensured that calls out of the Bay Area could complete, but was not available for calls into the Bay Area.

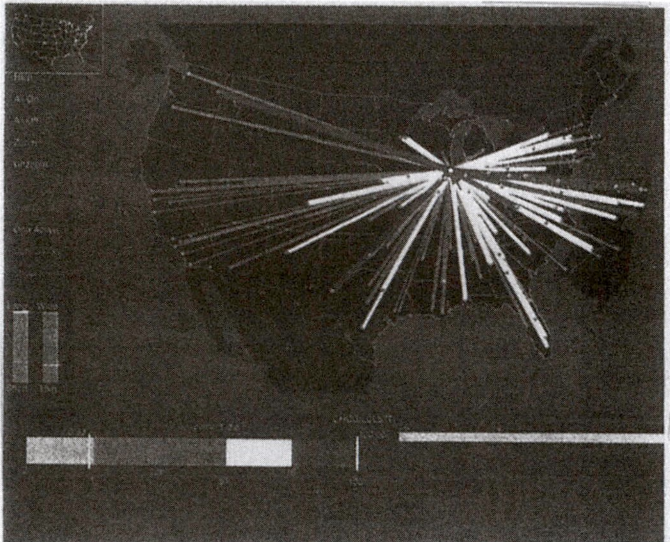

Fig. 7. Idle Network Capacity. The percentage of idle capacity on links into and out of a Chicago node. By turning off all nodes and interactively turning on selected nodes, we can study a pervasive network statistic.

There are several issues with parameter focusing. First, the space of all possible parameter values is large. Second, most combinations of the parameters do not lead to understandable displays. Third, the displays are sensitive to particular values of the parameters. To address these issues we have developed a network visualization system called SeeNet that provides interactive control over display parameters. The figures in this paper are SeeNet screen dumps.

In the next section we describe the ways in which the data analyst interacts with the displays described earlier, using SeeNet.

IV. Direct Manipulation

With parameter focusing there can be many different combinations of the parameters, most of which do not lead to interesting and interpretable displays. A solution to the problem of selecting the interesting parameter values involves direct manipulation [3]. SeeNet allows the analyst to modify the focusing parameters while continuously providing visual feedback, enabling the adjustment of the parameters to produce informative displays. The idea is, as with adjusting the focus on a camera, that the display should update smoothly, showing the results as the parameter controls are adjusted. For this to be effective, the computer response must be nearly instantaneous (less than 50 milliseconds).[2] When a parameter is being adjusted, every mouse movement causes a parameter to be modified. Manipulating a slider might involve hundreds of small, incremental mouse movements. Point and click user interfaces are less effective for parameter focusing because each adjustment requires a click. The effects of mouse movements are instantaneously reflected in the display, providing user feedback and determining whether or not the adjustment is making the display more informative. Using direct manipulation, the analyst may search a rich parameter space to focus on interesting displays.

A. Identification

SeeNet allows the interactive identification of nodes and links. The analyst identifies a node in SeeNet by touching the node with the mouse (no need to press a button), which causes the node to become active and turn a different color. In linkmap, identifying a node additionally causes its name to appear on the display; in nodemap, identifying a node shows its name and the data values for that node. This ability is crucial for an effective interactive display, where much information has been suppressed to make the display, making it possible to retrieve the suppressed information quickly.

A more complex form of identification is available in linkmap. Since two nodes determine a particular link, the analyst can first indicate an *anchor* node with a button press. Later node identifications then include information about the link between the identified node and the anchor node. In Fig. 6 the anchor node is `SKTNCA` and the current node is `OKLDCA`. The direct link statistics are displayed in the right-hand corner of the screen, `170` from `OKLDCA` to `SKTNCA` and `5827` in reverse. A time-series plot for the anchor-to-current link is displayed within the time slider.

Identification is also possible in the matrix display. In that case, identifying a link is easy, as the analyst can just point to the corresponding cell.

B. Linkmap Parameter Controls

There are three vertical sliders in linkmap to manipulate the line length between the links, the line thickness, and the animation speed (see Fig. 6). To obtain the pleasing result in Fig. 6 from Fig. 3, we manipulated the line length slider, moving it from `Long` toward `Short`. The line width slider sets the thickness of the maximum link and at the `Thin` end makes every line one pixel wide.

There are two horizontal controls, an interactive color legend and a time slider. The color legend functions as a double-edged slider with upper and lower thresholds. By manipulating the thresholds, the analyst may reduce the visual complexity of the display by eliminating those lines whose statistic values are not between the thresholds. A toggle determines whether the suppressed lines are inside (between) or outside the threshold bars. The double-edged slider enables an analyst to threshold from two directions, or using the toggle, to show simultaneously the lines with both high and low statistic values, while

[2] This corresponds to 20 frames per second and, in our and our users' experience, interactive network displays with significantly slower response time felt sluggish and were noticeably less satisfying.

ignoring those between. The time slider sets the current period and the area inside the slider is used to display a time-series for the active node or link.

C. Matrix Display Parameter Controls

The matrix display also uses linkmap's interactive color legend and time slider parameter controls. In addition, it has the capability to permute the rows and columns. As mentioned earlier, the orders of the rows and columns are an important design problem for the matrix layout. Careless ordering may make the display nearly impossible to interpret. Bertin [4] constructed mechanical systems for experimenting with different row and column orders and suggests a strategy for permuting the orders. In SeeNet, the analyst repositions a row or column using a *drag-and-drop* action. Depressing the left mouse button while touching a row or column label grabs it, and moving the mouse then drags it to a new position, where it is dropped into place when the mouse button is released.

D. Nodemap Parameter Controls

Three vertical sliders in nodemap manipulate the symbol size, animation speed, and color sensitivity level. Choosing an effective symbol size is a straightforward and intuitive operation for the person manipulating the slider.

There are two frequently used glyphs: a circle to code a single statistic and a rectangle to code two statistics (width and height). Other glyphs [5], encoding three or more variables, are possible, though we have had less success with them. By default the glyphs are white. Color is used to highlight the unusual glyphs: for circles the largest circles are colored red, and for rectangles color is tied to the aspect ratio. Short, fat rectangles are colored green, while tall, thin rectangles are colored red. The color sensitivity slider controls the cutoff values for color changes. We encode negative values using dashed instead of solid lines.

E. Animation

Animation is a useful technique to scan data from many time periods and is crucial for analyzing time-varying data from large networks with many time periods. If the data from each time period is correlated, the resulting animations show smooth evolutions. Unusual changes are then jarring and readily apparent. SeeNet's animation capability causes the computer to walk continuously over all of the time periods, with the `Fast-Slow` slider controlling the animation speed. Manual animation is possible by dragging the time bar forward or backward with the mouse, with the display updating continuously.

F. Zooming and Bird's-Eye

In SeeNet an analyst may zoom into any rectangular subregion by depressing the `Zoom` button and selecting a region. The selection action is accomplished by clicking on the center of the region and sweeping out. Center-to-edge sweeping differs from the traditional mechanism for sweeping out windows on workstations, which is to select a corner and sweep out to the other corner. We found this action difficult to use because it was hard to center the windows correctly when sweeping corner-to-corner. Our technique, center-to-edge, assures that the zoomed area will be centered appropriately and sized to cover the area of interest. Our zoom operation preserves the map aspect ratios. For the traffic matrix, the zooming operation is similar; selecting a rectangular subregion causes this region to expand to occupy the whole display.

A general problem with zooming in arbitrary abstract networks is maintaining global context—it is easy to get lost. SeeNet's bird's-eye view in the upper left-hand corner helps maintain the global context by showing the zoomed area on the original display. It is also possible to manipulate the zoomed area (in particular, to pan it) using the bird's-eye view.

We have also experimented with context-specific zooming to focus in on a particular region or state and also with continuous zooming. In our implementation of continuous, variable-gain zooming, the user selects the center of a sub-region and moves the mouse away to control the magnification. As with a variable zoom lens on an expensive camera, the zoomed region changes smoothly, tracking the mouse movements.

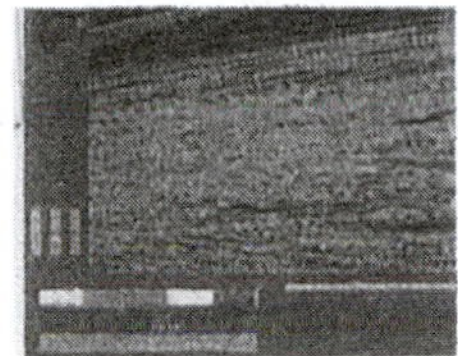
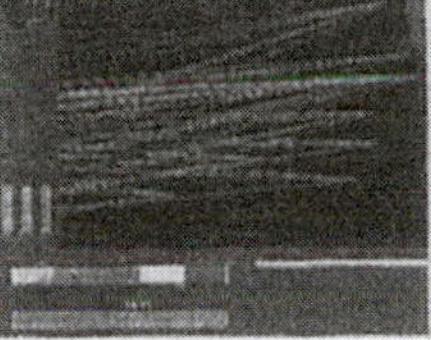
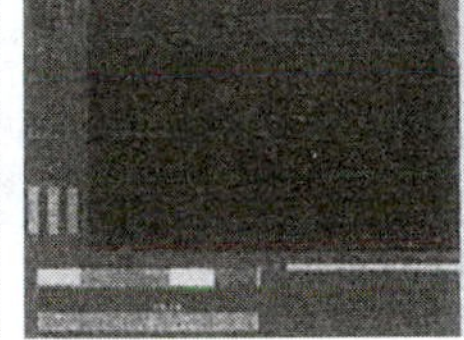

Fig. 8. Interaction Between Links And Zooming. The zoomed area is in the interior of the network shown in Fig. 3. The left pane shows all lines, the middle pane shows all lines terminating within the zoomed area, and the right pane shows all lines that both originate and terminate in the zoomed area.

In linkmap there is an interaction between the lines connecting the links and the zoomed view. There may be lines that: 1) pass through the zoomed area, but with both endpoints outside the zoomed area, 2) terminate on one node in the zoomed area, or 3) are completely inside of the zoomed area. The best choice for resolving this interaction depends on the application and the particular question of interest. Fig. 8 shows a zoomed view in the middle of the network from Fig. 3. The panes from left-to-right show the different interactions between the zooming and which lines are displayed. In the left pane, all line segments intersecting the display are drawn. Clearly, it is too busy to interpret. The middle pane contains any line segment with at least one endpoint in the display (that is, it excludes any segments both of whose endpoints lie outside the display). In the right pane, only lines that both begin and end inside the display are shown (in this case, none!). The middle and right panes show that there are many overloads between nodes inside the display and nodes outside, but none between nodes within the display. There are buttons on the display that determine which of these views to display, and the analyst is able to toggle quickly between them.

G. Conditioning

In many situations there are several related statistics for each link such as capacity, current utilization, and predicted utilization. Our approach to understanding multivariate link data involves conditioning. An analyst selects an interesting range for one or more background variables and sets the display to show a foreground variable. The conditioning operation filters out all links whose background variables are not within the selected ranges, visually showing the intersection between the sets.

Conditioning is a key technique for answering questions involving *and*. An important question, for example, might involve the overload on the larger links. The overload on the small links is less important because these links do not carry much traffic and is therefore less interesting. To show the large-link overload the analyst would use the double-edged slider to filter the smaller capacity links and set the display to show the overload. Conditioning and suppressing the links with smaller capacities visually focus the display on the large-link overloads.

H. Sound

In visualization systems, sound is another independent channel to the user for conveying information [6]. SeeNet uses sound in three ways:

- **Node State Changes**: When the analyst selects any node and either activates or deactivates it, SeeNet confirms the operation with an audible bell. There are different bells for activation and deactivation, and we find, in practice, the audible response to be an effective confirmation of the selection.
- **Conveying Slider Values**: As the sliders are manipulated, SeeNet plays a tone of varying pitch that tracks the slider bar's position. The pitch increases as the bar is moved up and decreases as the bar is moved down.
- **Animation Frame Changes**: During animations, SeeNet produces a "click" every time the current time period changes and a "bell-ringing" sound whenever the animation repeats. In practice, this is effective because the sound frees the viewer's attention from the time period slider. The audible clicks sound like a metronome keeping time, and the bell indicates that the animation is restarting. During our analysis of one particular dataset we discovered an error when, during the animation, we saw that the display changed only every three clicks. Data for each time period was erroneously repeated three times, but we had not noticed this until we simultaneously heard the clicks and watched the display.

V. Further Examples

The tools we have described are generic, and we have applied them to a variety of situations, some of which we wish to discuss in this section. We will use two examples: the CICNet packet-switched data network and an e-mail communications network.

A. CICNet

The CICNet network is one of the regional data networks of the U.S. portion of the Internet. It connects 13 universities and research facilities in the Great Lakes region. Fig. 9 shows large circles at each of the facilities. These large circles represent the packet routers. Lines are drawn between the routers to show which pairs of them are physically connected. The smaller circles represent local area networks attached to the routers. Each router counts the number of bytes it sends to and receives from each of the local area networks and the other routers to which it is connected. The nodes of Fig. 9 occur where line segments terminate at routers, and at each node we have drawn a rectangle, just as in Fig. 3. The size of the rectangle is determined by the number of incoming and outgoing bytes at that point over a 10-minute period.

Notice that unlike the AT&T example, the underlying map here is schematic, not geographic (though the layout of the routers is vaguely similar to the real geographic layout). The underlying map is actually a parameter to our nodemap tool, so that no change to the tool is needed to analyze this quite different situation.

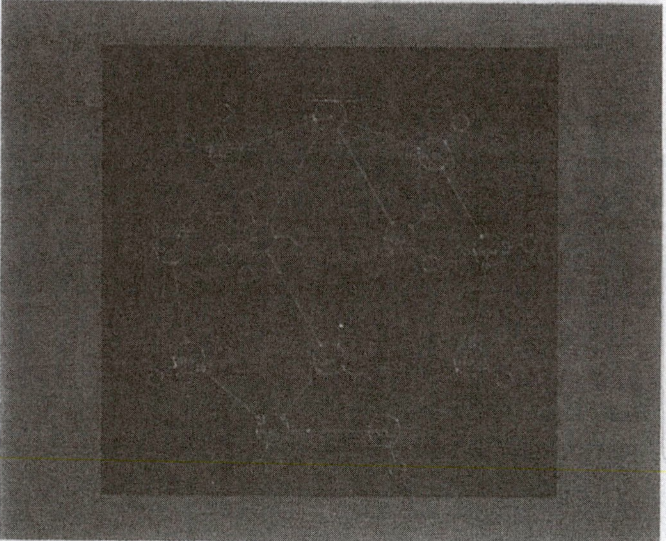

Fig. 9. Internet Network Packet Flows. A schematic representation of the CICNet regional network, showing routers (larger circles), local area networks (smaller circles), connections between them (line segments), and byte flows along the connections (rectangles where the line segments terminate on the router circles). A flow from the ARGON (Argonne National Labs) to the MINN (University of Minnesota) local area networks can clearly be discerned, in spite of the lack of explicit information about this pair.

Another difference between this example and the AT&T example is that the node statistics are not derived from an accumulation of link statistics. That is, thinking of the local area networks as the sources and sinks of the bytes flying around the network, we do not have direct information about the total traffic between arbitrary pairs of these sources and sinks. On the other hand, as Fig. 9 spectacularly demonstrates, it is immediately possible to infer such information—notice that there is a strong flow from Argonne to University of Minnesota in the 10-minute period shown here, as indicated by the sequence of red and green rectangles. Other, smaller flows are discernible as well.

Fig. 9 is one frame from a series of such frames representing all 10-minute periods for one month. Animating these, as described earlier, gives an excellent dynamic view of the network, and has led to some interesting insights [7].

B. E-mail Communications

Within the technical community, electronic mail is widely used for interpersonal communications. [8] In our location, members of the technical staff receive 30 to 40 messages per day. For nearly a year we logged the sender, receiver, message size, and time for every e-mail message sent or received by members of one of our departments at AT&T Bell Laboratories who volunteered for this study. This dataset is interesting because there is no natural geography or spatial layout associated with the network and there are no predetermined links.

In Fig. 10, each sender and receiver is represented as a node with the link statistics encoding the number of e-mail messages sent between the individuals in a time period (one month). During this period there were over 1500 different user IDs exchanging e-mail, and we have restricted the display using the slider to show only those links corresponding to 20 or more messages. We have aggregated the messages so that the link statistics are nondirectional.

Positioning nodes and links for drawing arbitrary graphs is a delicate operation involving subtle trade-offs [9]. There is a fundamental perceptual issue involving the node placement and the length of the links connecting them. Nodes that are close to each other are perceived to be related, and yet the link between them does not receive much visual real estate, making it hard to see. Conversely, distant nodes are not perceived to be related and yet are connected by a long, visually apparent link. Some of the best graph-drawing algorithms use this perceptual tension for conveying information related to particular applications.

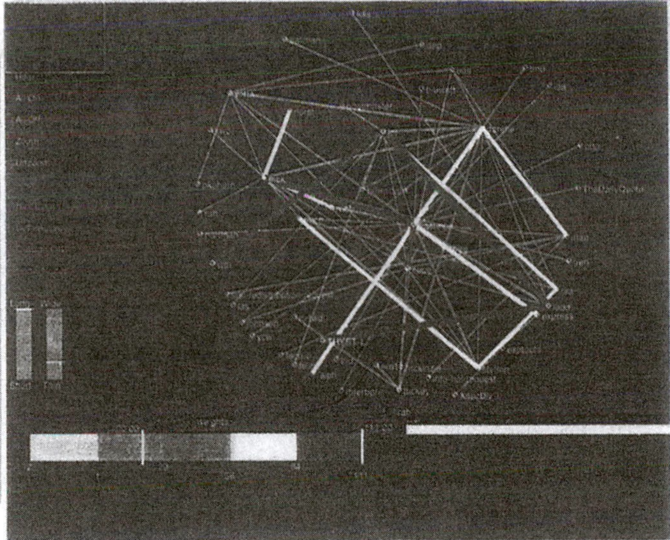

Fig. 10. Department E-mail Communication Patterns. Each node corresponds to a user, and the links encode the number of electronic mail messages sent between the users.

The node positioning in Fig. 10 uses a spring-tension model solved by synthetic annealing so that users exchanging large quantities of e-mail are close to each other. This results in a visually interesting and easily interpreted display [10]. User ID `hastings` is in the "e-mail center" of the department. `Hastings` is our resident computer expert, system administrator, and lead guru, and he communicates heavily with everyone else via e-mail. Other communications foci involve `eick`, `cope`, `jcr`, lead investigators, and `dorene`, our department secretary. Around the edge of the display are newer employees, members of other departments, and even automated e-mail response systems such as `TheDailyQuote`.

C. World Internet

In an example that covers a wider geographic region, we have used SeeNet to display statistics from the Internet. Fig. 11 shows country-to-country traffic across the NSFNET/ANSnet[3] backbone for the week of February 1-7, 1993. The colors and widths plotted are proportional to square root of the packet counts (square roots are often an appropriate transformation for counted data). To make the picture comprehensible, clutter was reduced by adjusting the lower threshold to display only those country-to-country links that carried more than one million packets that week. The data was displayed on a world map produced by S [11]. From the figure, the primary connections from the United States to other countries are visible (to many countries in Europe, Canada, the Far East, and Australia) as well as certain transit routes, for example from Australia to Europe. By deactivating the node for the United States, it is possible to focus on the transit traffic; similarly, with all the nodes deactivated, a mouse touch reactivates the current node and shows the packet counts to and from that country.

VI. The SeeNet System and Its Users

Originally we developed the SeeNet network visualization system for our research in network data analysis. Our objective and motivating example was to develop a system able to cope with the volumes of data generated by the AT&T long distance network traffic. Our static displays were modeled on existing network displays, and we invented the interactive techniques to overcome the display clutter problems associated with displaying large networks. SeeNet and the techniques embodied in it have evolved as the result of experience over the last several years in using it to visualize complex network data.

SeeNet has been used by many groups within AT&T to analyze network traffic, study overloads, engineer private line capacity changes, understand facility churn, display packet network traffic, and visualize network simulation output. It has also been embedded in the *PATTERNS* Network Operations Support System and is used daily by engineers for monitoring the performance of the FTS2000 Federal Telecommunications network.[4]

The original version of the SeeNet system ran on a Silicon Graphics IRIS workstation, although it has subsequently been ported to most X11-based Unix workstations, and there is also a limited version running under MS Windows. The current

[3] Thanks to Hans-Werner Braun at the San Diego Supercomputer Center and the NSFNET partnership for making the data available. It is in /pub/scsc/anr/data, available by anonymous ftp from ftp.sdsc.edu.

[4] This government network is currently the largest and most advanced private custom network in the world with well over a billion minutes of annual calling generated by over one million users at thousands of different locations.

version of SeeNet is written in C++ [12] using the Vz Visualization library. [13] Vz is an object-oriented, cross-platform library (X11, OpenGL, and MS Windows) that embodies linked views, direct manipulation, and data abstractions in a selective manner for building novel, production-quality visualization systems. In total SeeNet is about 6000 lines of code, divided into five views: the network map, the time slider, the interactive color scale, the bird's-eye, and the control panel. Each view is implemented as a Vz C++ class, is independent of the other views, and uses a publish and subscribe mechanism for coordinating responses to user actions.

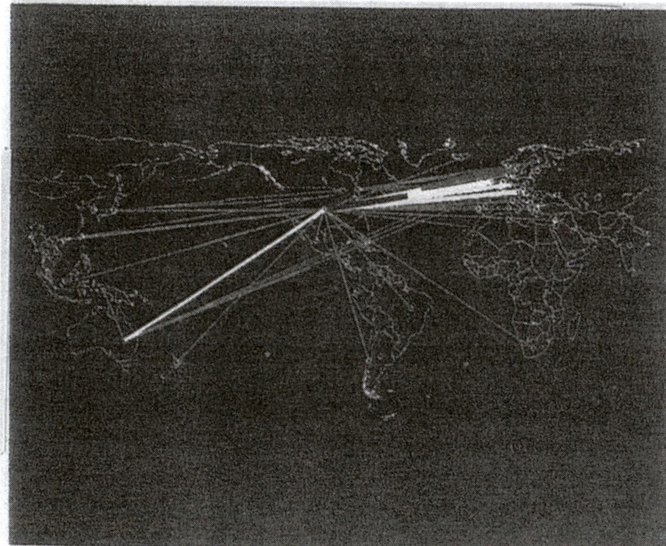

Fig. 11. Worldwide Internet Traffic. Traffic on the Internet, square root of packets transmitted from country to country across the NSFNET backbone during the first week of February 1993.

For a network with 100 nodes, for example, there are 9900 directioned node pairs and, for adequate performance with a pervasive network statistic, it is necessary to draw that many colored line segments several times per second. For SeeNet's parameter focusing to be most effective, the computer must respond continuously to control changes. To achieve sufficient performance on slower workstations and, in particular, on MS Windows personal computers, SeeNet uses several programming tricks. Each of the views is double buffered, either using hardware support if it is available or by rendering to an off-screen image. The node positions are stored in a quad-tree so that the identification operations are fast. To avoid redrawing the main display, the map is drawn in an underlay bitplane, and highlighting operations occur in an overlay bitplane so that they do not damage the main display. For systems without hardware overlay and underlay support, we simulate them using color map manipulation. At initialization time we precalculate as much as possible to avoid run-time overhead. For example, we sort the links in ascending order so the links are automatically drawn in the appropriate order.

The background maps, link statistics, node statistics, and colors are all input parameters to the program, making it easy to work with a variety of underlying maps and to explore different statistics. In early versions of SeeNet we used the S language [14] for data analysis. S provides data management, static graphics, computational analysis, and transformations in support of the dynamic operations. Using S, it is easy to investigate data transformations. Traffic flow statistics, for example, tend to be highly skewed with a few extreme values, so a logarithmic or square-root transformation can be used to ensure a more uniform distribution of the statistic. Map displays may have only a handful of red lines (the highest interval) out of thousands of links. A logarithmic or square-root transformation can be used to ensure a more equal distribution of colors. Other computations can be carried out prior to display. For example, given data for two adjacent time periods we might want to compute the change in the statistic from one period to the next. The resulting signed values can be displayed on the map to show where the flow is increasing or decreasing. Here the analyst would probably select a nonstandard color scale such as red for increasing, blue for decreasing. In addition, S can be programmed to provide a menu-driven user interface to select which data should be displayed in SeeNet.

VII. Discussion

In this section we briefly review some of the other work that has been done in this area, and then we compare and contrast our different techniques for displaying network data.

A. Related Research

Because of the importance of network data, there is a rich history in network visualization. Some fundamental early work is due to Bertin [4] who uses both node and link representations as well as matrix representations. Bertin also introduces the idea of interactively manipulating a network display using specially built, manual tools.

The data analysis setting we have described in this paper involves both a network and data on that network and concentrates on how to analyze the data. If we leave aside the data, we find much that has been written about displaying and attempting to interpret the structure of networks (or graphs, as they are usually called). For example, Fairchild, Poltrock, and Furnas [15] describe the SemNet system for displaying and manipulating a three-dimensional view of a possibly quite large network. One of the problems is how to create such a view, given the abstract structure of the network. Our earlier CICNet example presented a layout that we constructed by hand, but for a large network this is clearly impractical. This is a general problem—graph layout—about which much has been written in recent years, including several simple techniques in the paper under discussion.

Again focusing on the network rather than the network data, Sarkar and Brown [16] describe an innovative fisheye distortion for visualizing the structure of sparse networks. Their system, like ours, is dynamic and supports smooth transitions between the views. Their displays are engaging and interactive but do not address the fundamental problem in network data visualization: coping with the display clutter caused by too many link crossings.

Among other things, Paulisch [17] discusses both the problems of network layout and ways to focus on particular parts of the layout. One interesting idea involves what she calls "edge concentration," in which a local group of highly connected nodes is simplified by introducing a new pseudo-node with edges to each of the original nodes in the local group. We have thought of using this idea, but in a slightly different way, by collapsing such a group of highly connected nodes into a single node and showing only the collapsed node, with aggregated links to all nodes connected to any of the original nodes.

However, what is of more interest in comparing their work with ours is the means by which they have attempted to visually focus the large amount of displayed information: showing only a prenamed subset of the network, restricting the three-dimensional viewing angle, and using fisheye views. The last is a novel method of what could be called "gradual focusing," in which the piece of the network close to the focus of interest is displayed in complete detail, while only the more important features are shown for parts of the network further away. This technique can be introduced gradually, so that the level of detail varies with the distance from the point of interest.

Unwin, Sloan, and Wills [18] describe an exploratory analysis of oil imports and exports to and from European countries. The nodes, representing countries, are represented by symbols positioned on a map of the world in the center of their countries, and the links encode the oil imports and exports between the countries. This problem is simplified because there are not many European countries and, in particular, only a handful of oil-exporting countries. The authors use interactive methods, such as thresholding, for analyzing their oil data.

Eick and Wills [10] use aggregation, hierarchical information, node positioning, and linked displays for investigating large networks with hierarchies. They focus on abstract hierarchical networks with no natural spatial layouts. They represent networks using node and link diagrams, with shape, color, and other visual characteristics coding nodal information and with color and line thickness coding link information. They use node positioning and hierarchical aggregation to address the map clutter often present in large complex networks.

Researchers at NCSA [19] have added 3D graphics to their network maps. They display animations of Internet packet traffic with the network backbone raised above the network map. The links are color coded according to the size of the packet flows. Their techniques result in visually interesting displays of aggregate network traffic, especially with their creative use of 3D to overlay additional information.

Casner [20] describes an automated system for displaying airline traffic. His system is goal directed; it uses different graphical layouts depending on the particular question currently of interest. Although theoretically interesting, the system is not practical for large networks.

In other related work focusing on database visualization Consens et al. have developed a sophisticated interactive graph visualization system [21] for visualizing hygraphs. Hygraphs are a generalization of standard graphs containing nodes, links, labels, and container information. They have developed a sophisticated system called Hy^+ for browsing of hygraphs and applied it to visualize software structure [22] and network management data. [23] One of the most innovative aspects of their system is its foundation, a powerful programming language for manipulating hygraphs. Their focus is on extracting information from a complicated hygraph using interactive queries and displaying the results using their powerful browser.

Koike [24] describes a system called VOGUE, designed to display communication patterns in parallel processing computer systems. It is generally concerned with displaying networks, with nodes and links positioned in 3-space and rendered with various symbols, sizes, and colors. The system allows interactive selection of viewpoints. The author argues that 3D representations of data allow the user to "see two relations simultaneously and to focus on each single relation without changing mental models."

There are many possibilities for using sound to enhance data analysis, though we feel that efforts to date have not been notably successful. To see what others have tried, consider, for instance, Bly's work [25] or the paper by Mezrich, Frysinger and Slivjanovski [26]. More recently, Gaver investigated the use of sound in user interfaces [27], [28].

SeeNet's interactive user interface and parameter focusing techniques are motivated by statistical research in dynamic graphics [29], [30]. The essential idea involves the interactive controls for focusing the display. One special case of focusing, suppression, eliminates display clutter by interactively restricting what appears on the display. This technique is most efficient when it is dynamic as with our double-edged color slider [31], [32].

Recently, the Human-Computer Interface community has discovered the usefulness of interactive filtering techniques for building effective visualizations. Shneiderman describes three systems for visualizing real estate, the periodic table of elements, and movies that represent data spatially and uses double-edged sliders. [33] Ahlberg and Shneiderman also recognize that a nearly instantaneous response is critical for the effectiveness of the technique. [34]

B. Link Data

For link data, particularly for networks with geographic information, the spatial layout is visually more easily interpreted than the matrix representation. For small numbers of links, presenting the information on a map results in a more meaningful display because it preserves the network context. Maps present the spatial information clearly, and it is natural to layer the link information on top of the spatial layout.

The map representation breaks down when the number of links is large, because the display becomes too cluttered. This is particularly a problem when the links extend across a significant fraction of the display, as do the transcontinental lines in Fig. 3. This occurs, for example, when a pervasive statistic is displayed. There are three possible solutions to resolve the map-clutter problem:

- Reposition the nodes to minimize the number of long links (see Fig. 11 and Eick and Wills [10]). This can be done interactively.

- Apply interactive parameter manipulations such as thresholding and filtering to reduce the visual complexity.
- Use the matrix representation.

The matrix representation neatly solves the link overplotting problem in this example, because the links are represented by squares, tiled on the display. Since each square is assigned the same amount of visual real estate, the long links are not visually dominant. The resulting display is uncluttered since the squares cannot overplot each other, but loses the easy interpretation and context provided by the spatial map layout.

For ordering the rows and columns in matrix displays we have used geographic position, hierarchical clustering, and direct manipulation. None of these approaches is completely satisfactory, suggesting that more research in this area is needed. Some other approaches can be found in the paper by Friedman and Rafsky [35].

C. Node Data

The nodemap represents node data using variable-sized glyphs spatially positioned on the display. The size slider nicely solves the glyph overplotting problem by enabling the interactive selection of a size large enough to be visual, yet small enough not to cause excessive overlapping of the glyphs. Color is an effective visual cue, drawing attention to unusual glyphs, with the color sensitivity slider preventing overuse of the cue.

We have experimented with different types of glyphs for coding multiple statistics. For example, we tried crosses for two statistics and thermometers for three statistics. For a single statistic we prefer circles, for two statistics we prefer rectangles. For three or more statistics, more complex glyphs are possible, but we have had limited success. In the perception literature [36] researchers have found that humans visually decode area as a fractional power of the statistic that it encodes. This argues that rectangles may be a poor glyph choice. A possible solution to the visual glyph decoding problem is to transform the data, e.g., take square roots, so that area of the glyph is proportional to a meaningful statistic.

For our applications there are three reasons why we find rectangles so appealing. The first reason is that they overplot nicely. The second reason involves the aspect ratio. Rectangles with similar aspect ratios encode similar data patterns. By color coding according to the aspect ratio, red for the fat short ones, green for the tall thin ones, and white for the square ones, it is easy to identify the similarly shaped rectangles and therefore related nodes using our pre-attentive vision. [37] The color coding is made even more effective by linking the threshold to a slider. By manipulating the slider, the threshold can be set so that only rectangles with significantly different aspect ratios are colored, thereby focusing our attention on this important set. Finally, we have found that it is easy to compare the horizontal and vertical extents of similarly shaped rectangles by mentally juxtaposing them. This enables us to deduce quantitative results by observing that a designated rectangle may be twice or three times as large as another, for example.

VIII. Summary and Conclusions

This paper describes techniques for visualizing the data associated with large networks. Three static displays provide complementary views:

- a spatial layout with links between the nodes,
- a matrix layout with the links represented by cells, and
- a spatial layout with the nodes represented by glyphs.

For large networks displays produced using these well-known static techniques fail because the displays become cluttered and visually confusing.

To solve the display clutter problem, we invented a suite of parametric techniques embodied in a dynamic graphics software system called SeeNet that enable a user to focus the display and thereby reveal patterns in the network data. The dynamic parameters control:

- the data-based statistic that is displayed,
- which data values should be displayed (e.g., to omit low values),
- geographical or topographical regions that are displayed,
- which time interval is shown for time-based data,
- the level of aggregation of the statistic,
- the overall size of symbols.

Once these parameters are chosen, they completely determine a particular display. However, it is often difficult to choose these parameters numerically. To allow precise control over these parameters, SeeNet uses a direct-manipulation user interface containing sliders, buttons, and mouse-sensitive screen regions allowing the user to manipulate the parameters interactively. As the user modifies the controls, the network display smoothly updates. This parsimonious set of focusing parameters has been delicately chosen based on our experience visualizing a wide range of networks.

We have analyzed many different types of network data using SeeNet, and its features have evolved to meet our data analysis needs. SeeNet incorporates a small, carefully selected set of parameters that accommodate many kinds of network data.

Acknowledgments

We would like to acknowledge Larry Bernstein, Brian Johnson, Ron Kaufman, Eileen Miller, Carol Mummert, Eric Oberer, and Rich Wolf for ideas and encouragement during the formative stages of SeeNet and for careful proofreading of early drafts. Ken Cox implemented the Vz version of SeeNet.

References

[1] Richard A. Becker and William S. Cleveland, "Brushing Scatterplots," *Technometrics*, vol. 29, pp. 127-142, 1987.

[2] Stephen G. Eick, "Data Visualization Sliders," *UIST 94 Conference Proceedings*, Monterey, Calif., pp. 119-120, Nov. 1994.

[3] Ben Shneiderman, "Direct Manipulation: A Step Beyond Programming Languages," *IEEE Computer*, vol. 16, no. 8, pp. 57-68, 1983.

[4] Jacques Bertin, *Graphics and Graphic Information-Processing*, Berlin: Walter de Gruyter Co., 1981.

[5] Jeff Beddow, "Shape Coding of Multidimensional Data on a Micro-

computer Display," *Visualization 90 Conference Proceedings*, Los Alamitos, Calif., pp. 238-246, 1990.

[6] Mark Brown and John Hershberger, 'Color and Sound in Algorithm Animation," *IEEE Computer*, vol. 25, no. 12, pp. 52-63, 1991.

[7] Richard A. Becker and Allan R. Wilks, "Final Report: Network Traffic Analysis Project," *BBN Subcontract agreement #20510*, Feb. 1993.

[8] Michael F. Schwartz and David C.M. Wood, "Discovering Shared Interests Using Graph Analysis," *Communications of the ACM*, vol. 36, no. 8, pp. 78-89, 1993.

[9] Emden R. Gansner, Eleftherios E. Koutsofios, and Stephen C. North, "A Technique for Drawing Directed Graphs," *IEEE Trans. on Software Engineering*, vol. 19, no. 3, pp. 214-230, 1992.

[10] Stephen G. Eick and Graham J. Wills, "Navigating Large Networks with Hierarchies," *Visualization 93 Conference Proceedings*, San Jose, Calif., pp. 204-210, Oct. 1993.

[11] Richard A. Becker and Allan R. Wilks, "Maps in S," *AT&T Bell Laboratories Statistics Technical Report*, anonymous ftp at research.att.com:stat/doc/93-2, 1993.

[12] Bjarne Stroustrup, *The C++ Programming Language*, Reading, Mass.: Addison-Wesley, 1987.

[13] Visualization Group, *Vz Visualization Library: User's Guide Version 1.0*, AT&T Bell Laboratories, Jan. 1995.

[14] Richard A. Becker, John M. Chambers, and Allan R. Wilks, *The New S Language*, Pacific Grove, Calif.: Wadsworth & Brooks/Cole, 1988.

[15] Kim M. Fairchild, Steven E. Poltrock, George W. Furnas, "Three-dimensional Graphic Representations of Large Knowledge Bases," *Cognitive Science and Its Applications for Human Computer Interaction*, pp. 201-233, 1988.

[16] Manojit and Sarkar, and Marc H. Brown "Graphical Fisheye Views of Graphs," *Communications of the ACM*, vol. 37, no. 12, pp. 73-84, Dec. 1994.

[17] Frances Newbery Paulisch, *The Design of an Extendible Graph Editor*, Dissertation for the Department of Computer Science, University of Karlsruhe, Jan. 1992.

[18] Anthony R. Unwin, B. Sloan and Graham J. Wills, "Interactive Graphical Methods for Trade Flows," *Proceedings of New Techniques and Technologies for Statistics*, to appear.

[19] National Center for Supercomputing Applications, "A Visualization Study of Networking," video tape, Donna Cox and Robert Patterson, Co-Principal Investigators, University of Illinois, 1991.

[20] Stephen M. Casner, "A Task-Analytic Approach to the Automated Design of Graphics Presentations," *ACM Trans. on Graphics*, vol. 10, no. 2, pp. 111-151, 1991.

[21] M.P. Consens, F.Ch. Eigler, M.Z. Hasan, A.O. Mendelzon, E.G. Noik, A.G. Ryman, and D. Vista, "Architecture and Applications of the Hy^+ Visualization System," *IBM Systems J.*, vol. 33, no. 3, pp. 458-476, 1994.

[22] M.P. Consens, A.O. Mendelzon, and A.G. Ryman, "Visualizing and Querying Software Structures," *Proceedings 14th Int'l Conf. on Software Engin.*, pp. 138-156, 1992.

[23] M.P. Consens and M.Z. Hasan, "Supporting Network Management through Declaratively Specified Data Visualizations," *Proc. IEEE/IFIP Third Int'l Symp. on Integrated Network Management, III*, pp. 725-738, April 1993.

[24] Hideik Koike, "The Role of Another Spatial Dimension in Software Visualization," *ACM Trans. on Information Systems*, vol. 11, no. 3, pp. 266-286, 1993.

[25] Sara Bly, "Sound and Computer Information Presentation," *Lawrence Livermore Laboratory Technical Report UCRL-53282*, March 1982.

[26] J.J. Mezrich, S. Frysinger, and R. Slivjanovski, "Dynamic Representation of Multivariate Time Series Data," *J. of the Am. Statistical Assoc.*, vol. 79, pp. 34-40, 1984.

[27] William Gaver, "The SonicFinder: An Interface that Uses Auditory Icons," *Human-Computer Interaction*, vol. 4, pp. 67-94, 1989.

[28] William Gaver, "Synthesizing Auditory Icons," *CHI 93 Conf. Proceedings*, pp. 228-235, 1993.

[29] Richard A. Becker, William S. Cleveland, and Allan R. Wilks, "Dynamic Graphics For Data Analysis," *Statistical Science*, vol. 2, pp 355-395, 1987.

[30] Willian S. Cleveland and Marylyn E. McGill (eds.), *Dynamic Graphics for Statistics*, Pacific Grove, Calif.: Wadsworth & Brooks/Cole, 1988.

[31] Richard A. Becker, Stephen G. Eick, Eileen O. Miller, and Allan R. Wilks, "Dynamic Graphical Analysis of Maps—31 minute videotape," *Bell Laboratories ITV Facility*, Holdel, N.J., March 1989.

[32] Richard A. Becker, Stephen G. Eick, Eileen O. Miller, and Allan R. Wilks, "Network Visualization," *24th Int'l Symp. on Spatial Data Handling Proceedings*, Zurich, Switzerland, pp. 285-294, July 1990.

[33] Ben Shneiderman, "Dynamic Queries for Visual Information Seeking," *IEEE Software*, vol. 11, no. 6, pp. 70-77, Nov. 1994.

[34] Christopher Ahlberg and Ben Shneiderman, "Visual Information Seeking: Tight Coupling of Dynamic Query Filters with Starfield Displays," *CHI 94 Conf. Proceedings*, Boston, Mass., pp. 313-317, April 1994,

[35] Jerome H. Friedman and Lawrence C. Rafsky, "Fast algorithms for multivariate lining and planning," *Proc. of Computer Science and Statistics: 8th Annual Symp. on the Interface*, pp. 124-136, 1979.

[36] William S. Cleveland and Robert McGill, "The Visual Decoding of Quantitative Information on Graphical Displays of Data," *J. of the Royal Statistical Soc., Series A*, vol. 150, pp. 195-229, 1987.

[37] Robert Sekuler and Randolph Blake, *Perception*, Third ed., New York, N.Y.: McGraw-Hill, Inc, 1994.

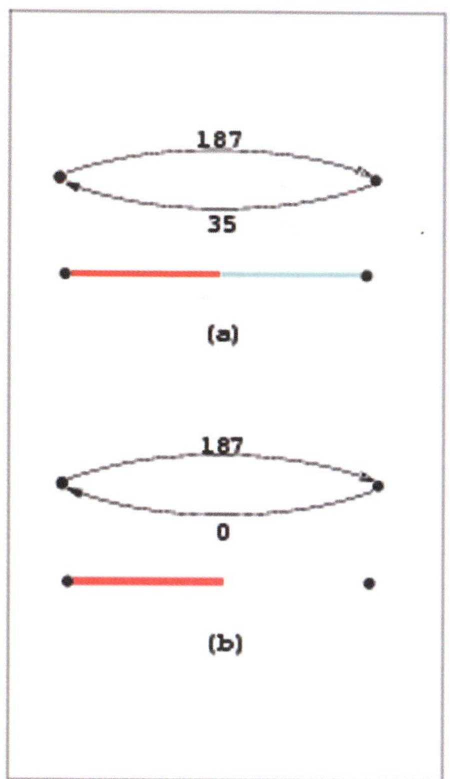

FIGURE 1

Represening Link Data. In part (a), the upper illustration is a conventional arrow diagram with numbers to show link statistics; the lower illustration uses line thickness and color to convey the same information more compactly. Part (b) shows how half-lines represent statistics with value zero.

FIGURE 2

Overload Into One Node. The overload into and out of the Oakland node. The half-lines between the nodes code the overload by direction.

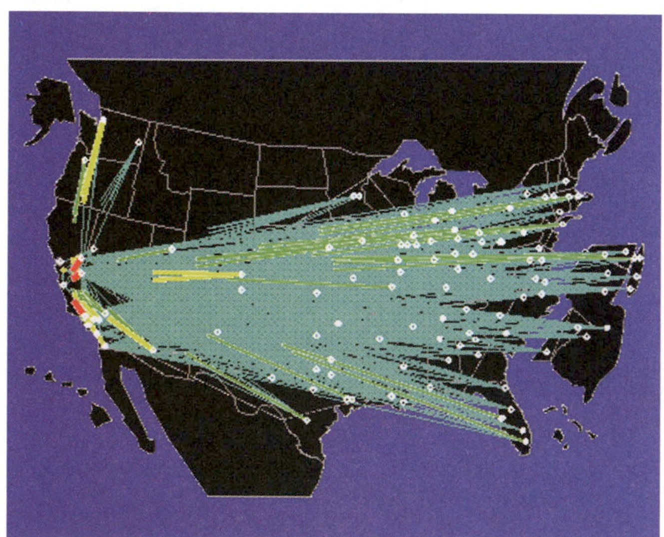

FIGURE 3

Node-to-Node Network Overload. The network-wide overload after the earthquake for the same time period as Fig. 2. The display is ineffective because there are many long lines that obscure much of the country.

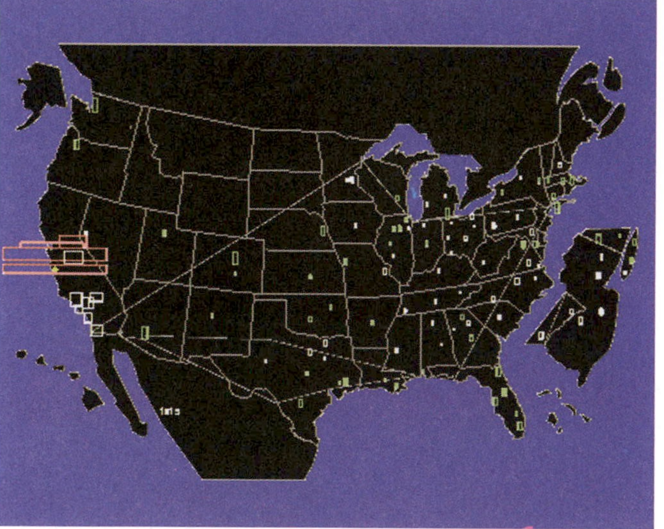

FIGURE 4

Overload Following Earthquake. Each rectangle shows the aggregate overload over all links; its horizontal dimension is proportional to the square root of the number of incoming calls in the preceding 5-minute period, and the vertical dimension encodes the outgoing calls.

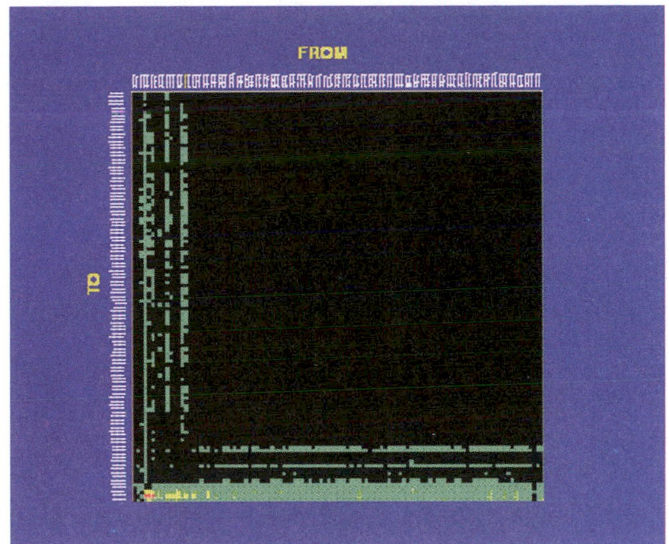

FIGURE **5**

Network Overload As Matrix. The same overload as in Fig. 3 shown using a matrix representation instead of a network map. The nodes are shown along the rows and columns in approximate west-to-east order in matrix form, with columns corresponding to "from" nodes and rows corresponding to "to" nodes. At the intersection of each row and column there is a square whose color codes the link statistic. The colored squares on the left and bottom correspond to the lines on Fig. 3. The nonsymmetry is due to the directed nature of the traffic.

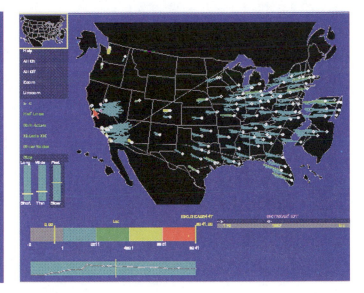

FIGURE **6**

Line Shortening. The figure shows the same date as Fig. 3, except the half-lines are drawn only part way between the nodes that they connect.

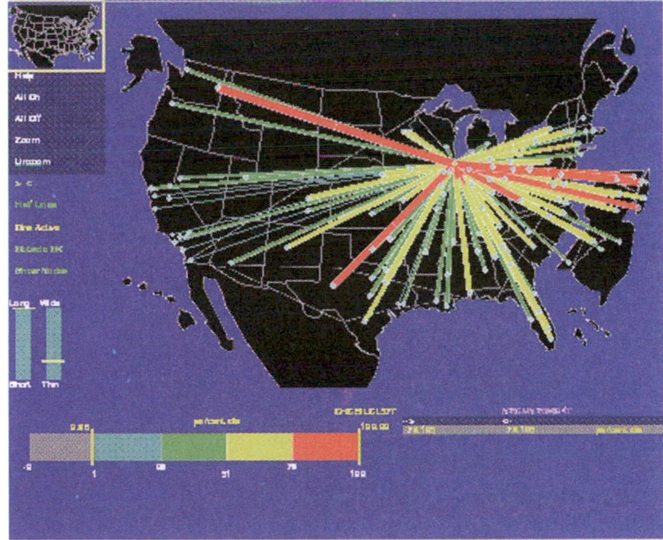

FIGURE **7**

Idle Network Capacity. The percentage of idle capacity on links into and out of a Chicage node. By turning off all nodes and interactively turning on selected nodes, we can study a pervasive network statistic.

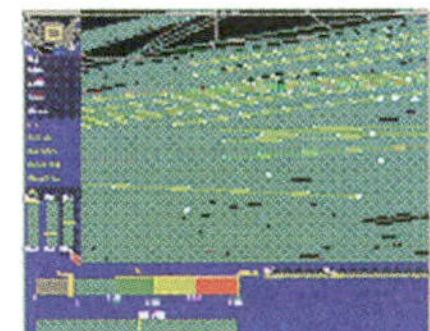

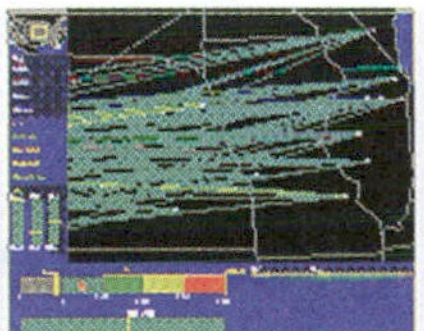

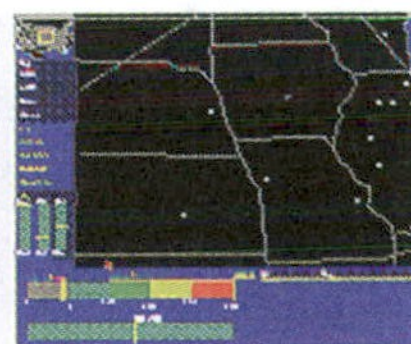

FIGURE **8**

Interaction Between Links And Zooming. The zoomed area is in the interior of the network shown in Fig. 3. The left pane shows all lines, the middle pane shows all lines termination within the zoomed area, and the right pane shows all lines that both originate and terminate in the zoomed area.

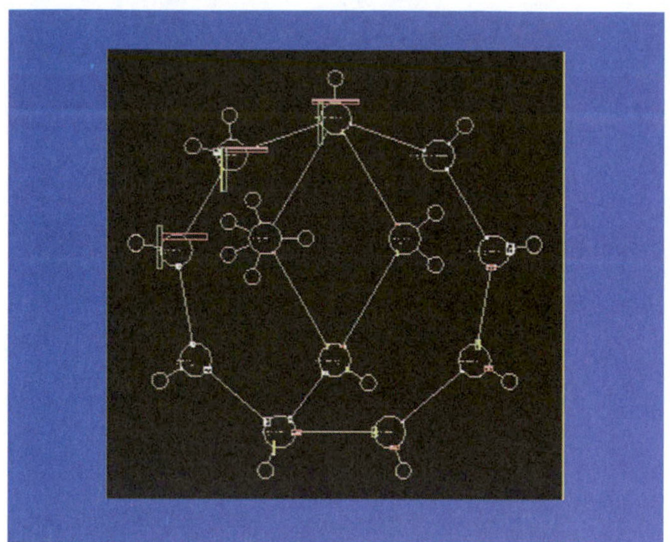

FIGURE **9**

Internet Network Packet Flows. A schematic representation of the CICNet regional network, showing routers (larger circles), local area networks (smaller circles), connections between them (line segments), and byte flows along the connections (rectangles where the line segments terminate on the router circles). A flow from the ARGON (Argonne National Labs) to the MINN (University of Minnesota) local area networks can clearly be discerned, in spite of the lack of explicit information about this pair.

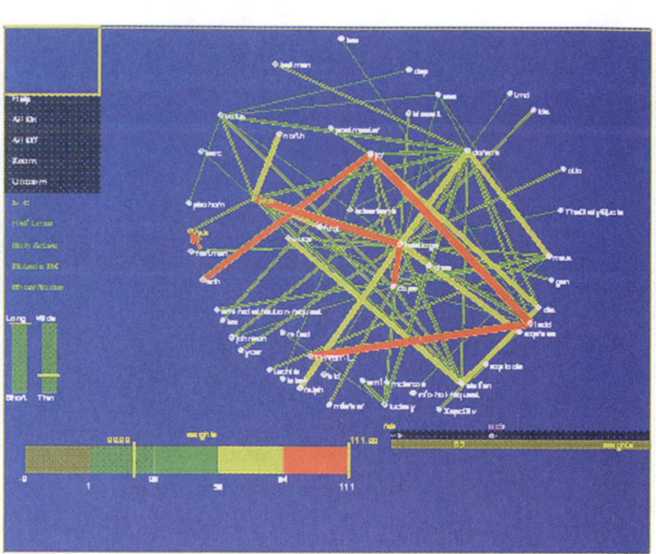

FIGURE **10**

Department E-mail Communication Patterns. Each node corresponds to a user, and the links encode the number of electronic mail messages sent between the users.

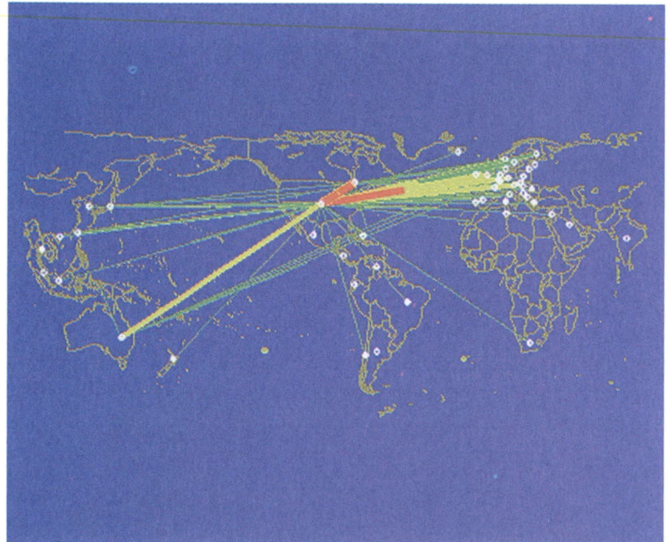

FIGURE **11**

Worldwide Internet Traffic. Traffic on the Internet, square root of packets transmitted from country to country across the NSFNET backbone during the first week of February 1993.

CHAPTER 3

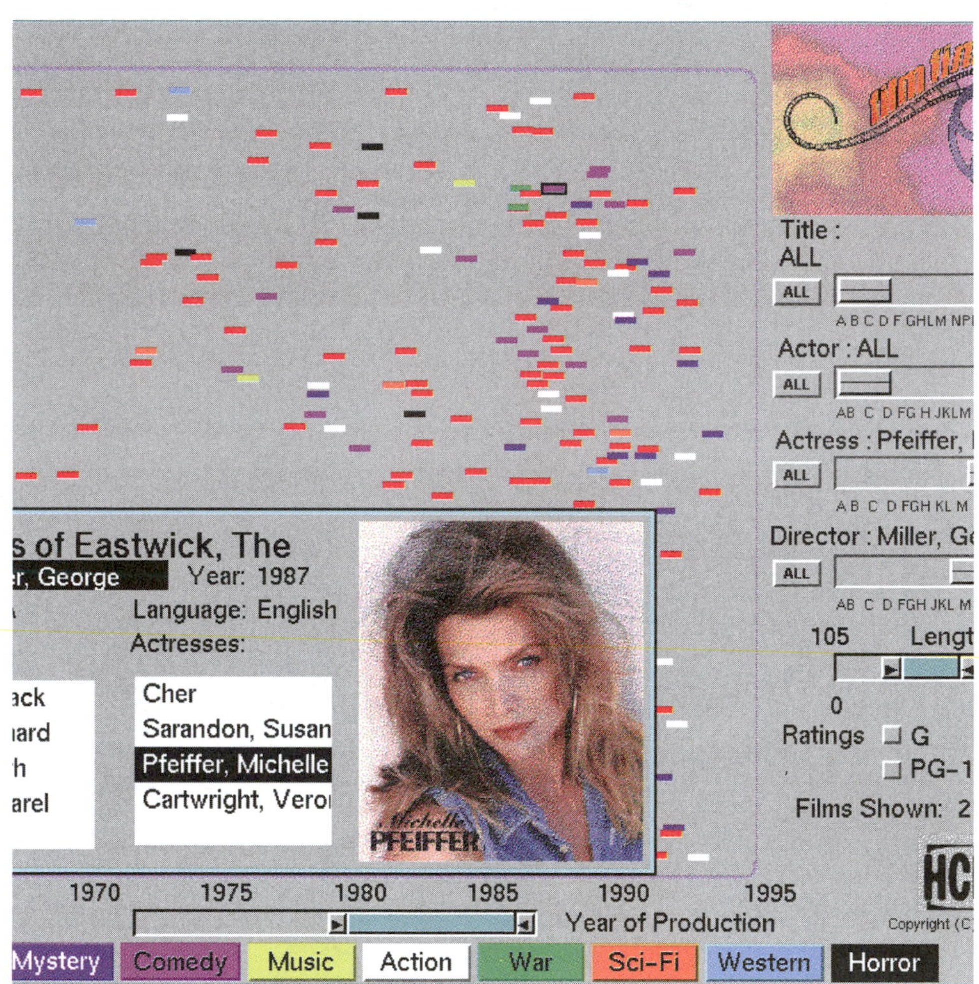

Action will remove the doubt that theory cannot solve.

– Tehyi Hsieh (1948)

Interaction

In the last chapter, we discussed the use of space for mapping data into different visual forms. Unlike visual artifacts created on paper, the computer allows visual artifacts to be created at the time of use and for large sets of data not previously seen by the visualization designer. In this chapter, we focus on another capability brought by the computer, the use of interaction. Rapid interaction fundamentally changes the process of understanding data. Rapid interaction, of course, allows the user to explore more possibilities in a given time, but it also allows the user to shift effort to the machine by watching what happens as the controls are modified.

TIME AND INTERACTION

How fast does interaction have to be? We can talk of three levels of interaction—at roughly 0.1 sec, 1 sec, and 10 sec. The finest level of interaction is at 0.1 second. This is the so-called *psychological moment* (Blumenthal, 1977; Card, Moran, and Newell, 1983). Stimuli within 0.1 second of each other fuse into a single percept. Two similar pictures seen within 0.1 second fuse into a perception of motion. Animation breaks down if longer than 0.1 sec/frame. If a sound and its echo arrive, say, within 0.04 sec of each other, the listener perceives a single sound, but with a changed quality, as though in a large room. An action and a stimulus event that occur within 0.1 second will seem to exhibit cause and effect. If a button changes color or moves within 0.1 second of being touched on the screen, the touch will seem to have caused the change. If data changes within 0.1 second of moving a slider, it will seem that the slider is directly changing the data. Slower sliders will cause control lag problems, where the user finds it difficult to set the control quickly.

The next higher level of interaction is at the 1-second level. This is the time of a minimal dialogue interaction component, the time of an *unprepared response,* part of what Newell (1990) called "immediate behavior." Events that happen in a little less than a second happen too quickly for the user to respond unless already prepared. An automobile driver requires a little less than a second (about 0.7 sec) to brake for an unexpected event. Control information in human dialogue has time constants in this region. If a speaker pauses for more than about a second, the listener feels compelled to say "uh-huh" or nod to assure the speaker the listener's end of the communication channel is intact. If the speaker cannot think of what to say for more than about a second, the speaker will say "ah" or otherwise indicate that his or her end of the channel is still working. This level of interaction can be exploited for smooth interaction with the user: animations that run in about a second can convey information without slowing the user down. Long operations can ensure that they have associated "thermometers" updating at least once a second.

The coarsest level of interactions, 10 seconds/cycle (by which we mean roughly 5 to 30 seconds/cycle), is the *unit task* (Card, Moran, and Newell, 1983). This is the typical pace of elementary interaction cycles in interactive systems, the pace of routine cognitive skill. An example is the time for a routine interaction with an interactive text editor. This would include the time for the user to select text on the screen and modify it, but not the time to compose difficult new text, since the latter would be problem solving (Card, Moran, and Newell, 1983). At the lower end of the range, 5 seconds/cycle is the speed of the fastest text editor (Engelbart's NLS system) or the time for a chess master to make a routine move. The unit task is the time to do the minimal unit of cognitive work.

Time is important in interaction, but the effect works differently at different parts of the interaction time scale. The response times of computer systems need to be tuned to these human time constants. Interaction can actually be slowed in some instances if the system goes too fast: simply showing the beginning and ending states without an animated transition may cause the user to misinterpret which objects were transformed into which other objects. Time has meaning. Interaction is a real-time process. The real-time nature of the process requires that a visualization system using interaction use some sort of scheduling mechanisms (Robertson, Card, and Mackinlay, 1989) to enforce animation and other time constants.

VISUALIZATION CONTROLS

What does interaction control? In information visualization, interaction involves the transformations that map data to visual form. In the reference model for information visualization developed in Chapter 1 (see Figure 3.1), the user manipulates *visualization controls* to change parameters in the chain of these transformations.

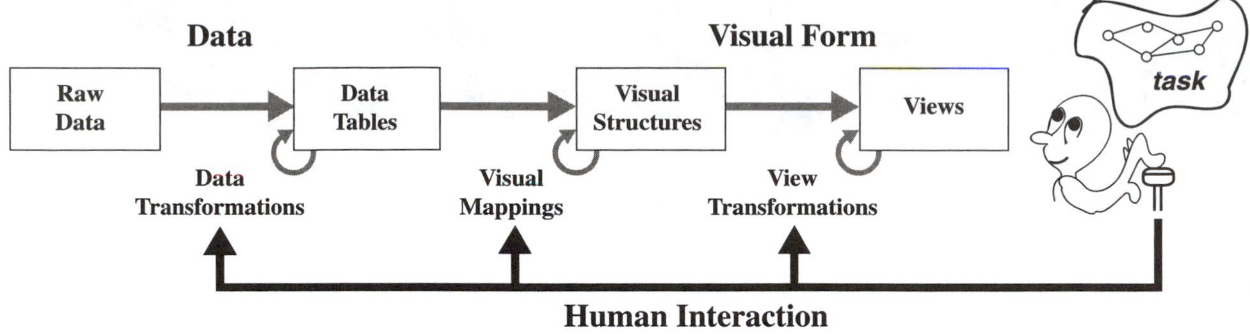

FIGURE **3.1**

Interactions change parameters of transformations.

These controls can be separate from the visualization or integrated into it. The FilmFinder (Ahlberg and Shneiderman, 1994c ●), which was used in Chapter 1 to introduce the reference model, has examples of both kinds of controls. Table 3.1 shows part of the Data Table for the FilmFinder augmented with additional information that describes its visualization controls. Writing the table this way allows us to see how some of the variables in the Data Table are mapped into the visualization and some are mapped into separate controls. The column titled "Visual Structure" shows that *FilmIDs* are mapped to points in a scattergraph, with the *Year* of the film mapped onto the X-axis and the *Popularity* of the film mapped onto the Y-axis. *FilmType* is mapped into the color of the points. The scattergraph also acts as a visualization control. The points in the scattergraph are buttons that generate a detail window about that specific film. The axes can be adjusted to clip the range of cases that are shown in the visualization.

The rest of the variables in Table 3.1 are mapped onto selector controls. These controls determine which of the objects in the Data Table are visible on the screen and which are hidden from view. *Length* of movie is mapped onto a two-sided slider. This slider allows the user to set the minimum and maximum length acceptable. *Title, Director, Actor,* and *Actress* are mapped onto a special "alphaslider" that allows the user to select the name from an alphabetical list. In

TABLE **3.1**

Visual Marks and Controls for FilmFinder.

Data								*Visual Form*			
Variable	**Type**	**Range**	**Case$_i$**	**Case$_j$**	**Case$_k$**	**...**		**Type**	**Visual Structure**	**Control**	**Transformation Affected**
FilmID	N	All-IDs	230	105	540	...	→	N	Points	Button	All (details)
Title	N	All-titles	Goldfinger	Ben Hur	Ben Hur	...	→sort	O		Alphaslider	Select cases
Director	N	All-directors	Hamilton	Wyler	Niblo	...	→sort	O		Alphaslider	Select cases
Actor	N	All-actors	Connery	Heston	Novarro	...	→sort	O		Alphaslider	Select cases
Actress	N	All-actresses	Blackman	Harareet	McAvoy	...	→sort	O		Alphaslider	Select cases
Year	Q	[1926, 1989]	1964	1959	1926	...	→	Q	X-axis	Axis	Clip range
Length	Q	[0, 450]	112	212	133		→	Q		Two-sided slider	Clip range
Popularity	Q	[1, 9]	7.7	8.2	7.4	...	→	Q	Y-axis	Axis	Clip range
Rating	O	{G, PG, PG-13, R}	PG	G	G	...	→	O		Radio buttons	Select cases
Film Type	N	{Drama, Mystery, Comedy, Music, Action, War, SF, Western, Horror}	Action	Action	Drama		→	N	Color	Radio buttons	Select cases

order to enable slider operation, the nominal types of these variables have been mapped into ordinal types, sorted alphabetically. Finally, *Rating* and *FilmType* have been mapped into radio buttons. Only one radio button in a set can be selected. Previously selected radio buttons from the set are automatically deselected.

When one of the controls is selected, the display is changed within 0.1 second, giving the user the direct experience of cause and effect. Changing the selection parameters immediately changes the movies displayed in the scattergraph. The FilmFinder shows how intimately interaction is related to visualization—only a third of the variables of the Data Table are mapped to visual outputs directly; the rest are controls. Furthermore, these controls depend for their effectiveness on their ability to be executed in 0.1 second.

INTERACTION TECHNIQUES

What sorts of interaction are there? Table 3.1 describes the *dynamic queries* technique. In Table 3.2 we list other techniques that have proved popular. Examples are given in this and other chapters. Many interaction techniques for information visualization are essentially a form of selection, selecting a subset of the objects in the Data Table. This allows them to be used to locate data, to reveal patterns in data, or to select the arguments of other transformations. Others allow for modification of data transformations.

Interacting with Data Transformations

Let us start with the interactions that modify data transformations, primarily by selecting which cases and variables will be visualized.

We have already discussed *dynamic queries* in connection with the FilmFinder. In particular, sliders or radio buttons are used to select value ranges for variables in the Data Table. The cases for which all the variables fall into the specified ranges are displayed. The other cases are hidden. Dynamic queries, then, are a visual means of specifying conjunctions, e.g., (Actor = "Clive Russell") AND (Actress = "Helena Bonham Carter") AND ((Length < 59 min) AND (Length < 276 min)) AND (Type = Action).

Direct walk proceeds by a set of linkages from case to case (Card, Pirolli, and Mackinlay, 1994; Furnas, 1997 ●). A Web browser, where the user links from page to page, is an example of direct walk. Through a series of clicks on visualizations, the user can search for information or modify it.

Details-on-demand expands a small set of objects to reveal more of their variables. It allows more of the variables of the case to be mapped to the visualization (because there is more space to show them).

In an *attribute walk,* the user selects some case and then searches for other cases with similar attributes. The technique was developed in a system called Rabbit for searching databases (Tou et al., 1982). The FilmFinder uses a similar technique where the details-on-demand window can be used to select cases with similar attributes.

TABLE **3.2**

Interaction techniques.

MODIFIES DATA TRANSFORMATION	MODIFIES VISUAL MAPPINGS	MODIFIES VIEW TRANSFORMATION
Dynamic queries	Dataflow	Direct selection
Direct walk	Pivot tables	Camera movement
Details-on-demand		Magic lens
Attribute walk		Overview + detail
Brushing		Zoom
Direct manipulation		

Brushing is used with multiple visualizations of the same objects (Cleveland and McGill, 1988; McDonald, 1990). Highlighting a case from the Data Table in one view selects the same case in the other views. Range sliders can be seen as an elementary form of brushing. The slider represents all the objects ordered by some variable (e.g., movie length). Selecting some range of these movies on the slider selects those same movies on the scattergraph.

Finally, *direct manipulation* can be used to modify transformations. For example, Hendon and Myer at Brown University (1994) have developed 3D widgets that can be embedded in visualizations, allowing multiple parameters to be adjusted.

Interacting with Visual Mappings

Interaction can also modify Visual Mappings, which represent the correspondence between data and visual forms.

Dataflow is a common technique used by commercial visualization systems to map data to visual form. The basic idea is to use an explicit representation such as node-link diagrams to represent the mapping. In ConMan, a research implementation by Haeberli (1988), visual mappings of computer graphics operations were specified by drawing links directly on top of the window system. The Advance–Visual Interface (AVI) by Upson et al. (1989) established the variant that is now used commercially, which is to have a separate window for the dataflow diagram.

Pivot tables is a technique found in modern spreadsheet programs that let the user rapidly manipulate the mapping of data to the rows and columns of a spreadsheet. They represent a domain-specific example of interacting with visual mappings.

Interacting with View Transformations

Finally, interaction can modify View Transformations.

Direct selection refers to the set of schemes that have evolved for selecting and highlighting objects and groups of objects. They enhance the appearance of a Visual Structure in some way, often to identify the set of objects that will be the arguments to some action.

Camera movement is the change of position of the observer, especially in 3D space. For example, information landscapes may sometimes benefit by allowing the user to view them from another angle, avoiding occlusions. Swinging the camera around could reveal parts of a visualization not otherwise visible.

Magic lenses select objects according to the X,Y position of their marks, and then apply further selection techniques, such as dynamic queries (Bier et al., 1994; Bier et al., 1993; Fishkin and Stone, 1995 ●). In addition, they can apply data or view transformations on the items selected. Because multiple lenses can be placed atop each other, they can be used to create more complex Boolean queries.

Overview + detail uses two or more levels of linked visualizations (Plaisant, Carr, and Shneiderman, 1995). One visualization displays either all of the objects or at least some visual framework that spans all of the objects, such as a map of the world or key nodes in a tree. Another window shows a more detailed view of the object. The nodes in the detail view are marked as a region that can be moved in the overview.

Zooming involves reducing the number of objects that are visible, but possibly increasing the number of variables per object that are shown. In addition, less compressed techniques may be used to view the objects. In the FilmFinder, individual films are represented by small rectangular areas. Zooming increases the size of these areas slightly (to enhance the perception of zooming), and when zooming reaches the point where there are fewer than 25 films, the *Title* attribute is displayed.

The papers in this chapter expand these ideas in more detail.

3.1 Dynamic Queries

The dynamic queries technique arose as a visual alternative to SQL for querying databases. For simple queries it is faster to use than SQL and requires little training. It is a natural method for requesting data when the output is going to have visual form. The first paper in this section, by Shneiderman (1994●), explains the rationale for dynamic queries and describes applications constructed with the technique. It also describes empirical evidence for the effectiveness of the dynamic queries. The second paper, Ahlberg and Shneiderman (1994c●), describes in more detail two applications, the HomeFinder and the FilmFinder, that we have used as a running example in Chapter 1. The simplicity of the applications makes them useful for understanding the technique.

Dynamic queries motivates the development of input controls that can specify variable values for rapid and simple search. The effectiveness of a control depends on the data type and on the cardinality of the values (the number of values that must be distinguished). At the simplest level are binary nominal variables. Buttons are natural for these. Slightly more complex are nominal variables with low cardinality, such as *FilmRating*. This variable can have four values: G, PG, PG-13, and R. Radio buttons (pushing in one button pushes out any other button in the set) are natural here. Simple sliders allow setting a single ordinal or quantitative variable value, such as maximum distance.

To handle more complex queries, more elaborate controls are required. Range sliders (Carr, Jog, and Kumar, 1994) allow the user to set an upper and lower bound. Essentially the control is two sliders, one for each end. A more difficult problem is how to select among nominal variables of high cardinality, such as the titles of movies. Alphasliders (Ahlberg and Shneiderman, 1994a) were invented for this purpose.

So far, the controls discussed are separate from the visualization. The controls use a considerable amount of space. Approximately half of the space for the FilmFinder, for example, is taken up by controls. More space can be made available for visualization by using the control itself as an auxiliary visualization. This is what Eick does (Eick, 1994a●) in the next paper. Eick shows four different designs. Some give detailed information about the distribution of objects along the variable of interest. Others expand the bunched-up parts of the distribution to make control more precise. In Eick's designs, it is possible to specify not only ranges but also discontinuous regions within the distribution. In user interface terms, these designs are an example of input on output (Draper, 1986), using the output of the system as a resource for input. Eick uses the visualization of variable distributions as part of another visualization control.

Another way of integrating the controls with the visualization is shown in Fishkin and Stone's paper (1995●) using magic lenses for dynamic queries. The magic lens see-through tools paradigm has been applied to a number of user interface tasks (Bier et al., 1994; Bier et al., 1993). In this paradigm, a see-through window is brought over some part of the display. Those elements in the Data Table with X,Y values in the range under the magic lens have the transformation of the lens applied to them. Lenses can be placed over lenses to specify chained transforms. Hence they can be carriers of any of the transforms of our reference model. Magic lenses allow queries that are more elaborate than dynamic queries alone. They allow types of Boolean queries that are difficult for sliders. Moreover, they allow data and view transformations to occur on the data in addition to selecting data. The Fishkin and Stone paper integrates magic lenses with dynamic queries.

FEATURE

DYNAMIC QUERIES FOR VISUAL INFORMATION SEEKING

Dynamic queries let users "fly through" databases by adjusting widgets and viewing the animated results. In studies, users reacted to this approach with an enthusiasm more commonly associated with video games. Adoption requires research into retrieval and display algorithms and user-interface design.

The purpose of computing is insight, not numbers. — Richard Hamming, 1962

BEN SHNEIDERMAN
University of Maryland
at College Park

Some innovations restructure the way people think and work. My experience with dynamic-query interfaces suggests that they are dramatically different from existing database-query methods. Dynamic queries continuously update search results — within 100 milliseconds — as users adjust sliders or select buttons to ask simple questions of fact or to find patterns or exceptions. To accomplish this, the dynamic-query approach applies the principles of direct manipulation to the database environment:[1]

- visual presentation of the query's components;
- visual presentation of results;
- rapid, incremental, and reversible control of the query;
- selection by pointing, not typing; and
- immediate and continuous feedback.

In short, a dynamic query involves the interactive control by a user of visual query parameters that generate a rapid (100 ms update), animated, visual display of database search results. (This use of the term "dynamic queries" is not the same as a dynamic query in Structured Query Language, which is posted at runtime instead of compile time.)

Although languages like SQL have become standard and form-based interfaces widespread, dynamic queries can empower users to perform far more complex searches by using visual search strategies. The enthusiasm users have for dynamic queries emanates from the sense of control they gain over the database. They can quickly perceive patterns in data, "fly through" data by adjusting sliders,[2] and rapidly generate new queries based on what they discover through incidental learning.

By contrast, typing a command in a keyword-oriented language usually generates a tabular list of tuples containing alphanumeric fields. This traditional approach is appropriate for many tasks, but formulating queries by direct manipulation and displaying the results graphically has many advantages, for both novices and experts.

For novices, learning to formulate queries in a command language may take several hours, and even then they will still likely generate many errors in syntax and semantics. In contrast, visual information-seeking methods can help novices formulate queries, and presenting graphical results in context, such as on a map,[3] can aid comprehension.

Experts may benefit even more from visual interfaces because they will be able to formulate more complex queries and interpret intricate results. Air-traffic control could hardly be imagined without a graphical display, for example. Visual displays also help users deal with the extreme complexity inherent in applications like network management. And statisticians, demographers, and sociologists, who deal with large multidimensional databases, can explore and discover relationships more easily using dynamic queries.[4,5]

EXAMPLES

An abundance of applications would benefit from this approach: Those with geographic aspects include travel agencies, hotels and resorts, and college selection; science or engineering applications include electronic circuits, networks, satellite coverage, and astronomy guides. Another likely candidate is a calendar or time-line application that shows events (concerts, meetings, conferences) selected by cost, priority rankings, or distance from home.

Geographic. Geographic applications are natural candidates for dynamic queries. Figure 1 shows the interface of a system that lets real estate brokers and their clients find homes by using a slider to adjust for things like price, number of bedrooms, and distance from work.[6] Each of 1,100 homes appears as a point of light on a map of Washington, DC. Users can explore the database to find neighborhoods with high or low prices by moving a slider and watching where the points of light appear. They can mark where they and their spouse work and adjust the sliders on a distance bar to generate intersecting circles of acceptable homes.

We conducted an empirical study of the HomeFinder using 18 psychology undergraduates to compare dynamic queries to natural-language queries (Symantec's Q&A) of the same database and to a 10-page paper listing of the same real estate data. We found that dynamic queries offered statistically significant speed advantages over either alternative for the three most difficult tasks, as Figure 2 shows. Subjective ratings of satisfaction dramatically favored dynamic queries. One subject using dynamic queries said, "I don't want to stop, this is fun!"

Another geographic application we built highlights entire US states that have cancer rates above a specified value, as shown in Figure 3.[7] Users can explore the database by selecting a year or by adjusting sliders for per capita income, college education, and smoking habits. The rapid change in

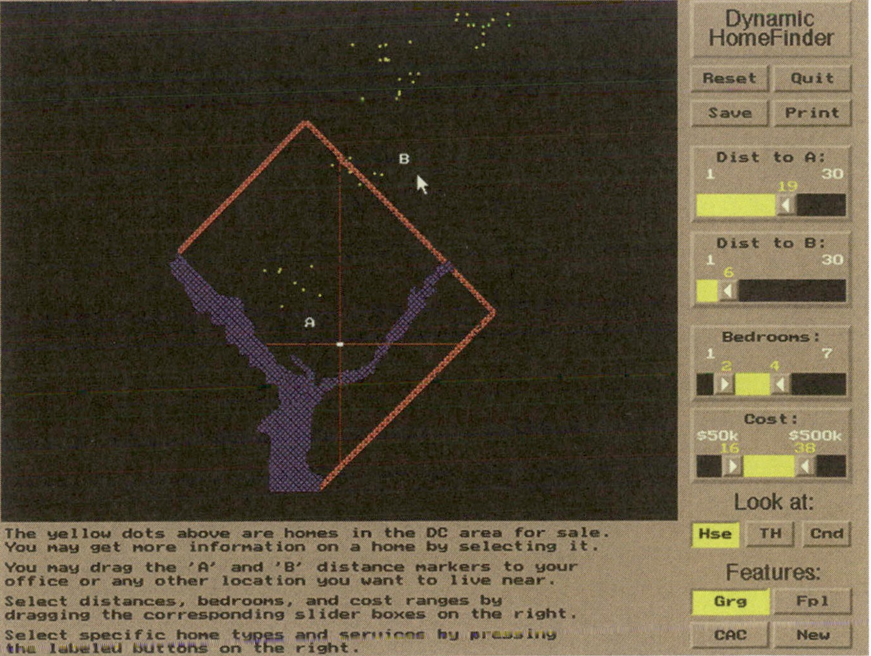
Dynamic HomeFinder
Reset
Quit
Save
Print
Dist to A:
1
30
19
Dist to B:
1
30
6
Bedrooms:
1
7
2
4
Cost:
$50k
$500k
16
38
Look at:
Hse
TH
Cnd
Features:
Grg
Fpl
CAC
New
B
A
The yellow dots above are homes in the DC area for sale.
You may get more information on a home by selecting it.
You may drag the 'A' and 'B' distance markers to your
office or any other location you want to live near.
Select distances, bedrooms, and cost ranges by
dragging the corresponding slider boxes on the right.
Select specific home types and services by pressing
the labeled buttons on the right.

Figure 1. The DC HomeFinder dynamic-query system lets users adjust the sliders for location, cost, number of bedrooms, home type (house, townhouse, or condominium), and features. The results are shown as points of light that can be selected to generate a detailed description at the bottom of the screen.

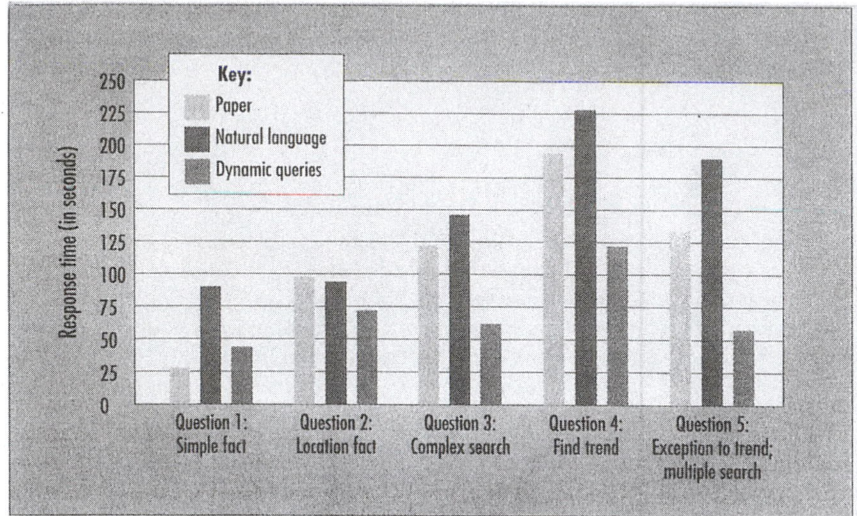

Figure 2. Means for response times of 18 subjects to five queries with paper, natural-language, and DC HomeFinder dynamic-queries interfaces. The results show an advantage for the dynamic-queries interface as query complexity increased.

colors, accomplished with color indexing on the palette, lets users detect changes in cancer rates over time and in correlation with demographic variables. The US National Center for Health Statistics is distributing an extended version of this system to its statisticians.

Education. One educational application is an element table, shown in Figure 4, that has sliders for atomic mass, atomic number, atomic radius, ionic radius, ionization energy, and electronegativity.[8] Students can refine their intuitions about the relationships among these properties and the atomic number or table position of the highlighted elements.

We evaluated this application against a form-based query interface with a graphical output and a form-based interface with a textual output. The results for several research tasks are shown in Figure 5. The 18 chemistry students achieved much faster performance using dynamic queries.

Alphanumeric. When there are no natural graphical displays for the output, dynamic queries can display result sets in a traditional alphanumeric tabular display. Figure 6 shows an example. In this application, the program creates the sliders and buttons semiautomatically, depending on the values in the imported ASCII database. As the users adjust the sliders with a mouse, the result bar on the bottom changes to indicate how many items remain in the result set, but the tabular display changes only when the user releases the mouse button. We adopted this policy to avoid the distraction of a frequently refreshed display.

Figure 7 shows another tabular display for a dynamic query system. This one lets users explore Unix directories.[9] Sliders for file size (in kilobytes) and age (in days) let users answer 10 questions, such as "How many files are younger than umcp_tai?" The results were displayed in standard long-directory display format.

We built three versions of the program and tested them on 18 users. The versions explored showing the results by

- highlighting matches with color,
- highlighting matches with asterisks on the same line, and
- displaying only the matching lines (that is, delete nonmatching files from the display).

The third approach, called expand/contract, was distracting if updates were made as the slider was being moved, so the displays were refreshed only when users stopped moving the sliders and released the mouse button. In five of the tasks there was a statistically significant speed advantage for the expand/contract interface. This result occurred only with medium-sized directories of

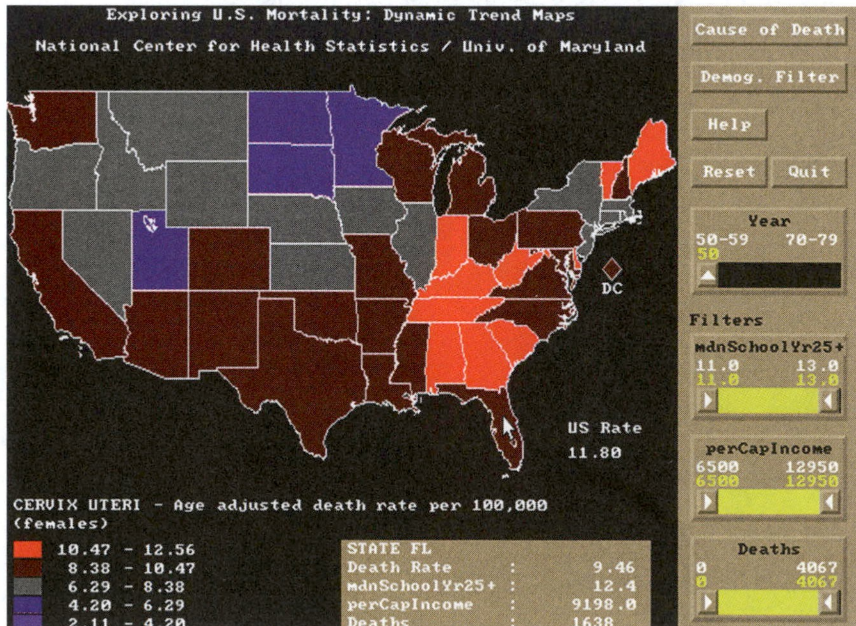

Figure 3. This dynamic query shows cervical cancer rates from 1950 to 1970 in each state. Adjustments can be made to the year and state demographic variables such as the percentage of college education, per capita income, and percent smokers.

approximately 60 entries (two screens), and not with smaller, one-screen directories. The benefits of expand/contract seem likely to grow as the directory size increases. These results help us develop guidelines and theories about how to design displays for dynamic queries.

ADVANTAGES

The dynamic query approach lets users rapidly, safely, and even playfully explore a database. They can quickly discover which sections of a multidimensional search space are densely populated and which are sparsely populated, where there are clusters, exceptions, gaps, or outliers, and what trends ordinal data reveal. Overviews like these, the ability to explore, and the capacity to rapidly specify known-item queries makes dynamic queries very appealing for certain problems.

For data in which there is a known relationship among variables, the dynamic queries interface is useful for training and education by exploration. For situations in which there are understood correlations, but their complexity makes it difficult for non-experts to follow, dynamic queries can allow a wider range of people to explore the interactions (among health and demographic variables, a table of elements, and economic or market data, for example). Finally, where there is so much data that even experts have not sorted out the correlations, dynamic queries may help users discover patterns, form and test hypotheses, identify ex-ceptions, segment data, or prepare figures for reports.

DISADVANTAGES

The dynamic query approach is poorly matched with current hardware and software systems. First, current database-management tools cannot easily satisfy these requirements for rapid searches, and rapid graphical display methods are not widely available. Therefore, we are exploring which data structures and algorithms can accommodate large data sets and permit rapid access.[10]

Second, application-specific programming is necessary to take best advantage of dynamic query methods. We have developed some tools, but they still require data conversion and possibly some programming. Standardized input and output plus software toolkits would make dynamic queries easier to integrate into existing database and information systems. Alternatively, dynamic queries could be generated by user-interface builders or user-interface management systems.

Third, current dynamic query approaches can implement only simple queries that are conjunctions of disjunctions, plus range queries on numeric values. Our filter/flow metaphor,[11] diagramed in Figure 8, offers one approach to providing full Boolean functionality. In Figure 8, users can select from the set of attributes and get an appropriate filter widget (type-in for interest areas, sliders for cost, and buttons for scholarships)

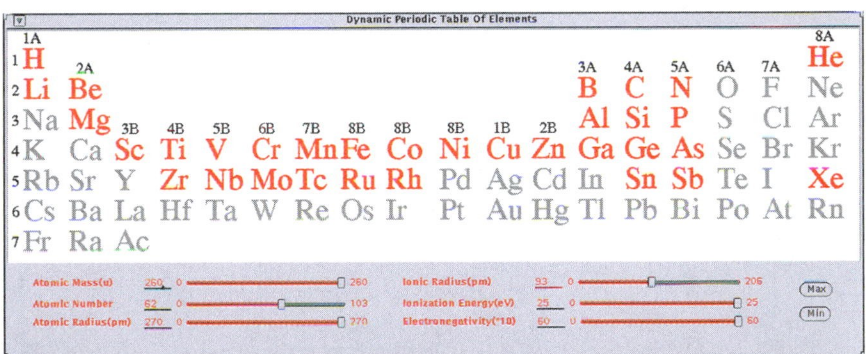

Figure 4. The chemical table of elements makes a natural visual display for information on chemical properties. Chemicals matching the query are shown in red. Runs and jumps are apparent.

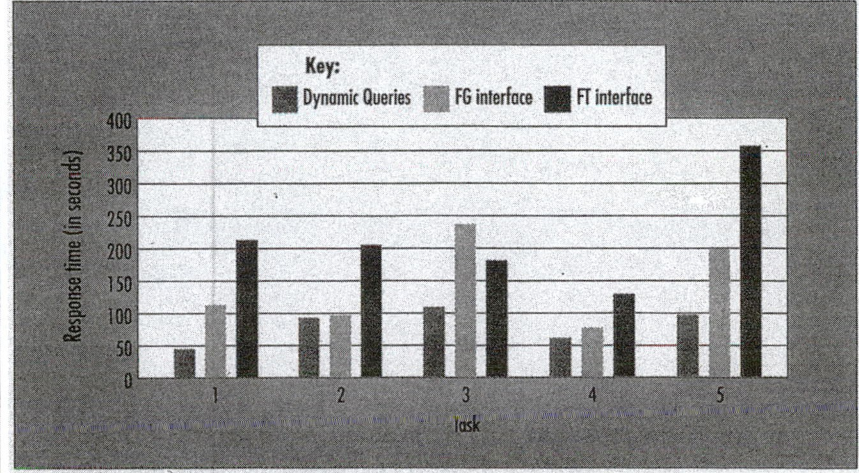

Figure 5. Mean response times for 18 subjects performing five tasks with the dynamic queries, form fill-in plus graphic output (FG), and form fill-in with tabular output (FT). The results strongly favor the dynamic-queries interface.

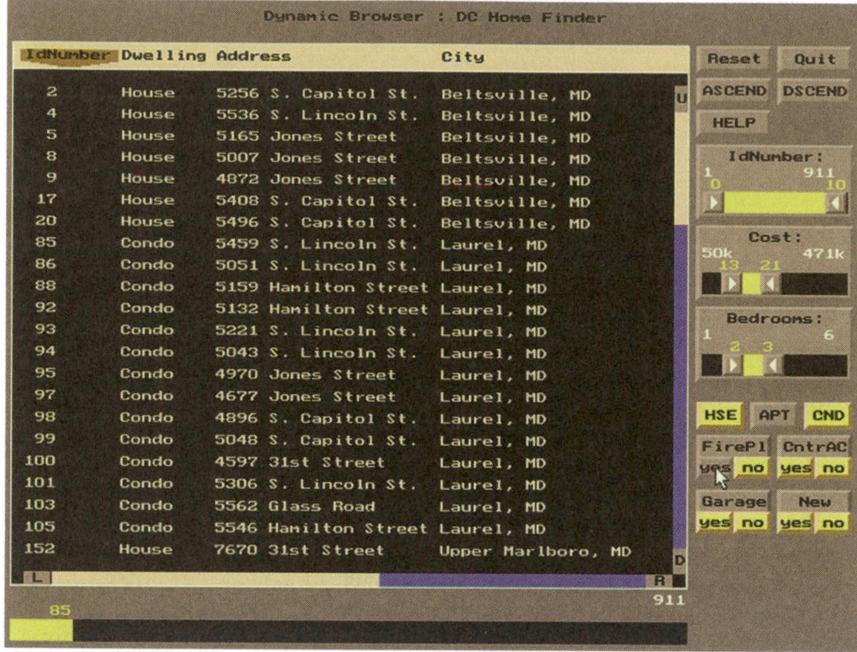

Figure 6. Even when there is no natural graphic framework for a dynamic query display, the method can be used with tabular alphanumeric output. As users adjust the sliders and buttons for the query, the result bar along the bottom indicates how many items match. When users stop moving the sliders and let go of the mouse button, the tabular display is rewritten.

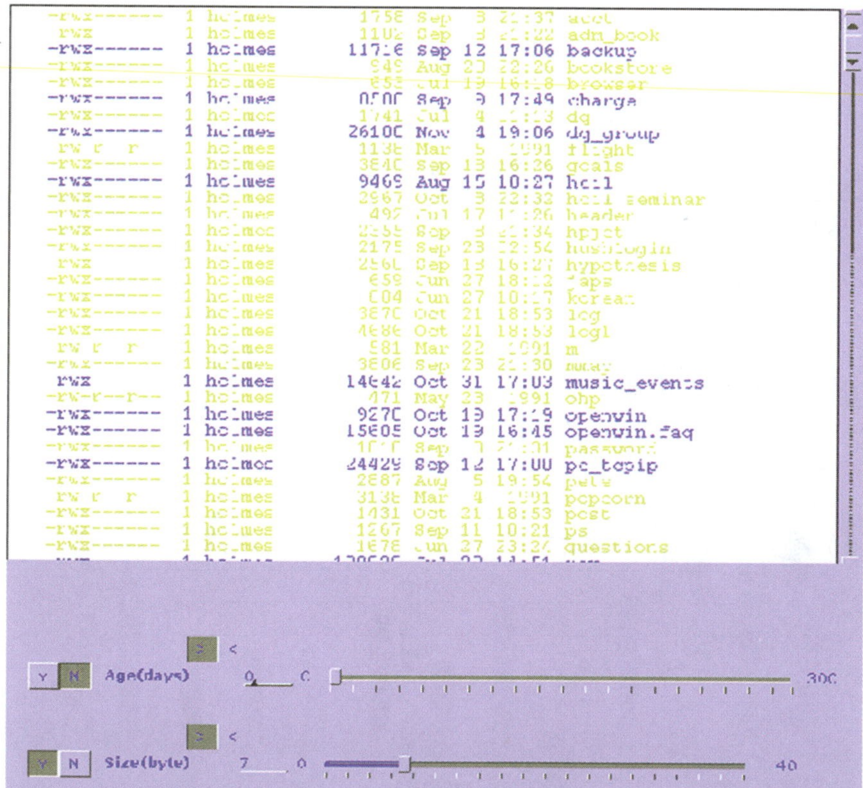

Figure 7. The standard long-format tabular display is the framework for Unix directory exploration. The sliders, built with Sun DevGuide, allow selections to be made on the age (in days) and size (in kilobytes) of files. We compare color highlighting and expand/contract methods of display in an exploratory study.

which is placed on the screen with flow lines showing Ands (sequential flow) and Ors (parallel flows). The *X* in each filter widget could be selected to negate the filter values. Clustering of one-in-one-out segments to form a new and saveable filter is possible. This approach was shown to be statistically significantly more effective than SQL for composing and comprehending queries, but the prototype must still be refined and implemented within a database-management system. More elaborate queries (group by, set matching, universal quantification, transitive closure, string matching) are still research-and-development problems.

Fourth, visually handicapped and blind users will have a more difficult time with our widgets and outputs, but we are exploring audio feedback to accommodate these users as well.

RESEARCH DIRECTIONS

Our initial implementations have generated enthusiasm, but we are more aware of challenges than successes. There are rich research opportunities in database and display algorithms and user-interface design.

Database and display algorithms. Because rapid display updates are essential, algorithms to store and retrieve multidimensional information need refinement. For small databases that fit in main memory, we have experimented with array indexing, grid structures, quad trees, and k-d trees. We found linear array structures with pointers to be effective with small databases, but their inefficient use of storage limited the size of the databases they could handle. Grid file structures are efficient with uniform distributions, while the quad and k-d trees became more attractive as the distributions became more skewed.[10]

For larger databases, alternatives include R-trees, grid files, multiple B-trees, and reduced combined indices.

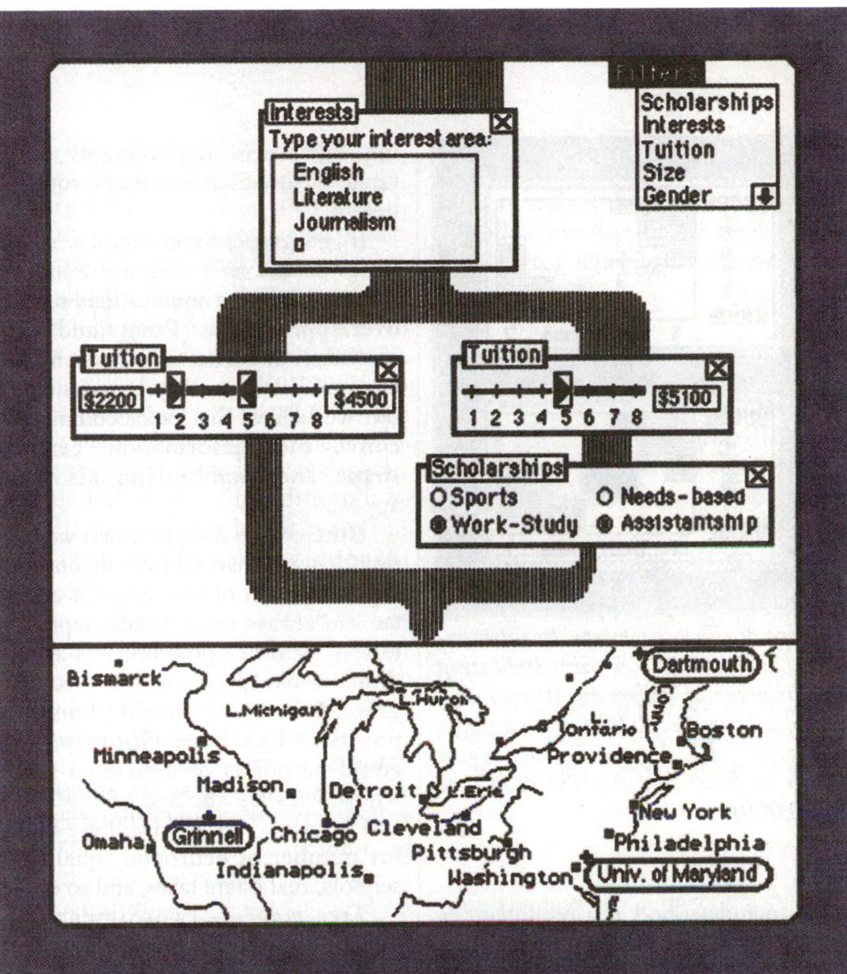

Figure 8. A mock-up of a filter/flow Boolean query ((Interests = English or literature or journalism) and ((tuition greater than or equal to $2,200 or less than or equal to $4,500) or ((tuition greater than or equal to $5,100) and (scholarships are available by work-Study or assistantship)))) combined with map output to show the result (Dartmouth, Grinnell, and the University of Maryland).

Treating inserts and deletes to stored information separately simplifies the design of efficient data structures.

The dynamic-query approach always displays the current query result. Each new query is a slightly enlarged or contracted version of the current query. In this case, special data structures kept largely in high-speed storage and algorithms might allow rapid updates. We believe an effective strategy is to organize data in "buckets" along each dimension. The size of the bucket is adjusted to the granularity of the slider mechanism. For example, if the slider has 100 positions for a field whose range is 1 to 50,000, the data should be organized into 100 buckets, each covering 500 points on the field. As the slider increases the selected set, buckets can be appended; as it decreases the selected set, buckets can be removed. With three dimensions of 100 buckets each, the database is conveniently broken into 1 million buckets, which can be stored and retrieved efficiently.

Also important are data-compression methods that will allow larger databases to fit in 32- Mbyte or smaller address spaces. Alternatively, dynamic queries could use parallel hardware and algorithms that search multiple storage spaces.

Screen-management algorithms also play an important role, and we expect that new algorithms will become an alternative to more expensive hardware. For example, it is often more effective to merely repaint the areas or points that have changed when a slider is moved or a button depressed, instead of repainting the entire display. Our early efforts suggest that in some cases manipulating the palette by color indexing may be an effective way to rapidly change irregularly shaped regions, even on popular personal computers.[7]

User-interface design. Humans can recognize the spatial configuration of elements in a picture and notice relationships among elements quickly. This highly developed visual system means people can grasp the content of a picture much faster than they can scan and understand text.

Interface designers can capitalize on this by shifting some of the cognitive load of information retrieval to the perceptual system. By appropriately coding properties by size, position, shape, and color, we can greatly reduce the need for explicit selection, sorting, and scanning operations. However, our understanding of when and how to apply these methods is poor; basic research is needed. Although our initial results are encouraging, there are many unanswered user-interface design questions. How can we

- design widgets to specify multiple ranges of values, such as 14 to 16 or 21 to 25?
- let users express Boolean combinations of slider settings?
- choose among highlighting by color, points of light, regions, and blinking?
- allow varying degrees of intensity in the visual feedback?
- cope with thousands of points or areas by zooming?
- weight criteria?
- select a set of sliders from a large set of attributes?
- provide "grand tours" to automatically view all dimensions?

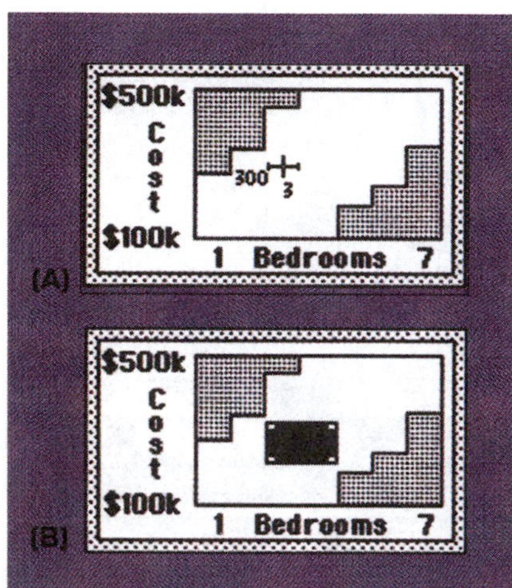

Figure 9. Two prototype two-dimensional widgets. (A) A point indicating the number of bedrooms (three) and cost of a home ($220,000) with a single selection. (B) A range of bedrooms (three to four) and cost ($130,000 to $260,000).

- include sound as a redundant or unique coding?
- support multidimensional input?

Display issues. We must reexamine basic research on color, sound, size, and shape coding in the context of dynamic queries. Of primary interest are the graphical display properties of color (hue, saturation, brightness), texture, shape, border, and blinking. Color is the most effective visual display property, and it can be an important aid to fast and accurate decision making.[12] Auditory properties may be useful in certain circumstances (for example, lower frequency sounds associated with large values; higher frequency with small values), especially as redundant reinforcement feedback.

We understand that rapid, smooth screen changes are essential for the perception of patterns, but we would like to develop more precise requirements to guide designers. In our experience, delays of more than two- to three-tenths of a second are distracting, but precise requirements with a range of situations and users would be helpful.

In geographic applications, sometimes points on a map are a natural choice, but other applications require overlapping areas. Points and areas can be on or off (in which case monochrome displays may be adequate), but we believe that color coding may convey more information. Texture, shape, and sound coding also have appeal.

Other issues emerge when we cannot identify a natural two-dimensional representation of the data. Of course we can always use a textual representation. Another possibility is a two-dimensional space, such as a scattergram. Instead of showing homes as points of light on a city map, they could be points of light on a graph whose axes are the age of the house and its price. We could still use sliders for number of bedrooms, quality of schools, real estate taxes, and so on.

Tree maps — two-dimensional mosaics of rectangular areas — are another way to visualize large amounts of hierarchical information. For example, we built a business application that visualized sales data for a complete product hierarchy, color-coded by profitability and size-coded by revenue.[13] Twelve professional users in our usability study could rapidly determine the state of financial affairs — large red regions indicate trouble and blue areas signal success. A slider let them observe quickly the changes to the tree map over time to spot trends or problems.

Input issues. Widget design is a central issue. Even in our early explorations we were surprised that none of the existing user-interface-management systems contained a double-boxed slider for the specification of a range (more than $70,000, less than $130,000). In creating such a slider we discovered how many design decisions and possibilities there were. In addition to dragging the boxes, we had to contend with jumps, limits, display of current values, what to do when the boxes were pushed against each other, choice of colors, possible use of sound, and so on.

We also came to realize that existing widgets are poorly matched with the needs of expert users, who are comfortable with multidimensional browsing. Two-dimensional input widgets to select two values at once are not part of any standard widget set that we have reviewed, so we created the one shown in Figure 9. Using a single widget means that only one selection is required to set two values and that correct selections can be guaranteed. In Figure 9, for example, the dotted areas indicate impossible selections (the cheapest seven-bedroom house is $310,000).

Input widgets that can handle three or more dimensions may facilitate the exploration of complex relationships. Current approaches for high-dimensional input and feedback are clumsy, but research with novel devices such as data gloves and a 3D mouse may uncover effective methods. With a 3D mouse, users lift the mouse off the desk and move it as a child moves a toy airplane.[14] The mouse system continuously outputs the six parameters (six degrees of freedom) that define its linear and angular position with respect to a fixed coordinate system in space.

Designers can decompose the rotation motion of the mouse into the combination of

- a rotation around the handle of the mouse and
- a change in the direction the handle is pointing.

When the mouse is held as a pointer, the rotation around the handle is created by a twist of the arm, and it may be natural to users to make the same twisting motion to increase the level of a database parameter as they would to increase the volume of a car radio. Changing the pointing direction of the mouse handle is done by the same wrist flexion that a lecturer would use to change the orientation of a laser pointer to point at another part of the conference screen. It may then also feel natural to users to imagine the planar space of two database parameters as vertical in front of them and point at specific parts by flexing their wrist up, down, and sideways.

For example, sophisticated users could perform a dynamic query of the periodic table of elements using the 3D mouse. They would find elements of larger atomic mass by translating the mouse upward; for larger atomic numbers they would move to the right; for larger ionization energies they would move toward the display; for larger atomic radius they would bend their wrist up; for larger ionic radius they would bend their wrist to the right; for larger electronegativity they would twist their arm clockwise. Sliders should probably still be present on the screen, but would move by themselves and give feedback on parameter values.

Another input issue is how to specify alphanumeric fields. Although a simple type-in dialog box is possible, more fluid ways of roaming through the range of values is helpful. To this end we developed an *alphaslider* to let users quickly sweep through a set of items like the days of the week or the 6,000 actor names in a movie database.[15]

Dynamic queries are a lively new direction for database querying. Many problems that are difficult to deal with using a keyword-oriented command language become tractable with dynamic queries. Computers are now fast enough to apply a direct-manipulation approach on modest-sized problems and still ensure an update time of under 100 ms. The challenge now is to broaden the spectrum of applications by improving user-interface design, search speed, and data compression. ◆

ACKNOWLEDGMENTS

I thank Christopher Ahlberg, Christopher Williamson, Holmes Liao, Boon-Teck Kuah, and Vinit Jain for implementing these ideas in a way that was even better than I anticipated. Kent Norman and Catherine Plaisant made important contributions to the work and this article. This research is supported by Johnson Controls, the National Center for Health Statistics, NCR Corporation, Sun Microsystems, and Toshiba.

REFERENCES

1. B. Shneiderman, "Direct Manipulation: A Step Beyond Programming Languages," *Computer*, Aug. 1983, pp. 57-69.
2. S. Eick, "Data Visualization Sliders," tech. report, AT&T Bell Laboratories, Napervillie, Ill., 1993.
3. M. Egenhofer, "Manipulating the Graphical Representation of Query Results in Geographic Information Systems," *Proc. IEEE Workshop on Visual Languages*, IEEE CS Press, Los Alamitos, Calif., 1990, pp. 119-124.
4. R.A. Becker and W.S. Cleveland, "Brushing Scatterplots," *Technometrics*, No. 2, 1987, pp. 127-142.
5. A. Buja et al., "Interactive Data Visualization Using Focusing and Linking," *Proc.* IEEE *Visualization*, IEEE Press, New York, 1991, pp. 156-163.
6. C. Williamson and B. Shneiderman, "The Dynamic HomeFinder: Evaluating Dynamic Queries in a Real-Estate Information Exploration System," *Proc. SIGIR Conf.*, ACM Press, New York, 1983, pp. 339-346.
7. C. Plaisant, "Dynamic Queries on a Health Statistics Map," *Proc. Conf. American Statistical Assoc.*, American Statistical Assoc., Alexandria, Va., 1993, pp. 18-23.
8. C. Ahlberg, C. Williamson, and B. Shneiderman, "Dynamic Queries for Information Exploration: An Implementation and Evaluation," *Proc. CHI Conf.*, ACM Press, New York, 1992, pp. 619-626.
9. H. Liao, M. Osada, and B. Shneiderman, "Browsing Unix Directories with Dynamic Queries: An Analytical and Experimental Evaluation," *Proc. Ninth Japanese Symp. Human Interface*, Society of Instrument and Control Engineers, Japan, 1993, pp. 95-98.
10. V. Jain and B. Shneiderman, "Data Structures for Dynamic Queries: An Analytical and Experimental Evaluation," *Proc. Advanced Visual Interfaces Conf.*, ACM Press, New York, 1994, to appear.
11. D. Young and B. Shneiderman, "A Graphical Filter/Flow Model for Boolean Queries: An Implementation and Experiment," *J. American Society for Information Science*, July 1993, pp. 327-339.
12. A. Marcus, *Graphic Design for Electronic Documents and User Interfaces*, ACM Press, New York, 1991.
13. B. Johnson and B. Shneiderman, "Tree-Maps: A Space-Filling Approach to the Visualization of Hierarchical Information Structures," *Proc. IEEE Visualization*, IEEE Press, New York, 1991, pp. 284-291.
14. S. Feiner and C. Beshers, "Worlds Within Worlds: Metaphors for Exploring N-Dimensional Virtual Worlds," *Proc. User Interface Software and Technology Conf.*, ACM Press, New York, 1990, pp. 76-83.
15. C. Ahlberg and B. Shneiderman, "Alphaslider: A Rapid and Compact Selector," *Proc. CHI Conf.*, ACM Press, New York, 1994.

Visual Information Seeking: Tight Coupling of Dynamic Query Filters with Starfield Displays

Christopher Ahlberg and Ben Shneiderman*
Department of Computer Science,
Human-Computer Interaction Laboratory & Institute for Systems Research
University of Maryland, College Park, MD 20742
email: ahlberg@cs.chalmers.se, ben @cs.umd.edu

ABSTRACT

This paper offers new principles for visual information seeking (VIS). A key concept is to support browsing, which is distinguished from familiar query composition and information retrieval because of its emphasis on rapid filtering to reduce result sets, progressive refinement of search parameters, continuous reformulation of goals, and visual scanning to identify results. VIS principles developed include: dynamic query filters (query parameters are rapidly adjusted with sliders, buttons, maps, etc.), starfield displays (two-dimensional scatterplots to structure result sets and zooming to reduce clutter), and tight coupling (interrelating query components to preserve display invariants and support progressive refinement combined with an emphasis on using search output to foster search input). A FilmFinder prototype using a movie database demonstrates these principles in a VIS environment.

KEYWORDS: database query, dynamic queries, information seeking, tight coupling, starfield displays

INTRODUCTION

In studying visual information seeking (VIS) systems for expert and first time users, we have found several user interface design principles that consistently lead to high levels of satisfaction. This paper defines these principles and presents a novel VIS system, the FilmFinder.

The exploration of large information spaces has remained a challenging task even as parallel hardware architectures, high-bandwidth network connections, large high-speed disks, and modern database management systems have proliferated. Indeed, these advances have left many users with the feeling that they are falling further behind and cannot cope with the flood of information [3, 18]. Now, the user interface design principles for VIS have the potential to reduce our anxiety about the flood, find needles in haystacks, support exploratory browsing to develop intuition, find patterns and exceptions, and even make browsing fun.

The key to these principles is understanding the enormous capacity for human visual information processing. By presenting information visually and allowing dynamic user control through direct manipulation principles, it is possible to traverse large information spaces and facilitate comprehension with reduced anxiety [14,16]. In a few tenths of a second, humans can recognize features in mega-pixel displays, recall related images, and identify anomalies. Current displays of textual and numeric information can be extended to incorporate spatial displays in which related information is clustered in 2-dimensional or higher spaces. This use of proximity coding, plus color coding, size coding, animated presentations, and user-controlled selections enable users to explore large information spaces rapidly and reliably.

KEY CONCEPTS

The principles of direct manipulation were a good starting point for design of visual information seeking applications [16]:

- visual representation of the world of action including both the objects and actions
- rapid, incremental and reversible actions
- selection by pointing (not typing)
- immediate and continuous display of results

However, when designing systems especially for information seeking tasks [11], additional principles are needed. A key VIS principle is to support browsing, which is distinguished from familiar concepts of query composition and information retrieval because of its emphasis on rapid filtering to reduce result sets, progressive refinement of search parameters, continuous reformulation of goals, and visual scanning to identify results. These goals are supported by the VIS designs developed in this paper:

dynamic query filters: query parameters are rapidly adjusted with sliders, buttons, etc.

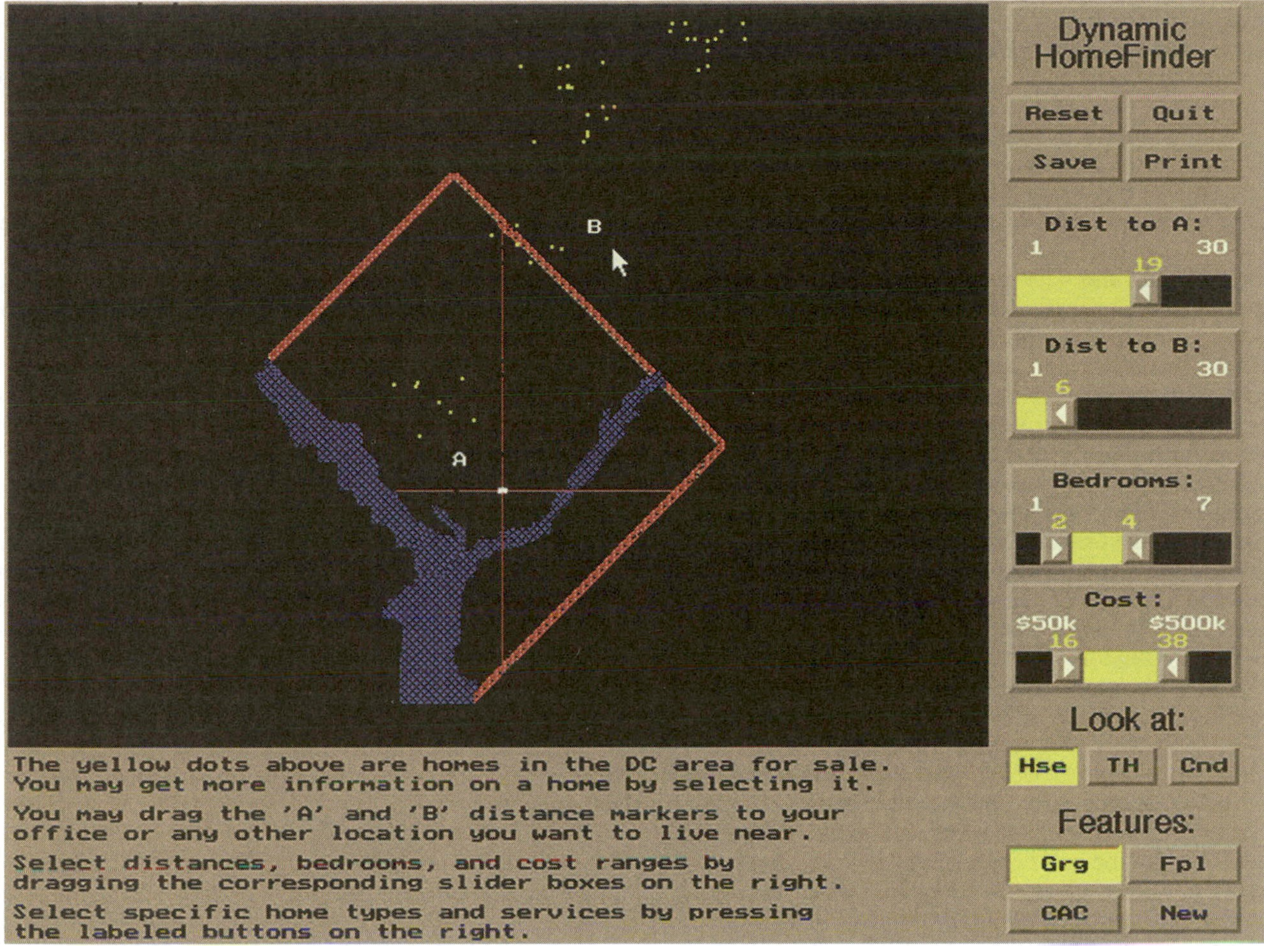
Dynamic HomeFinder
Reset
Quit
Save
Print
Dist to A:
1
30
19
Dist to B:
1
30
6
Bedrooms:
1
7
2
4
Cost:
$50k
$500k
16
38
Look at:
Hse
TH
Cnd
Features:
Grg
Fpl
CAC
New
B
A
The yellow dots above are homes in the DC area for sale.
You may get more information on a home by selecting it.
You may drag the 'A' and 'B' distance markers to your office or any other location you want to live near.
Select distances, bedrooms, and cost ranges by dragging the corresponding slider boxes on the right.
Select specific home types and services by pressing the labeled buttons on the right.

Figure 1: In the Dynamic HomeFinder query system each point satisfies the query described by the sliders for location, cost, number of bedrooms, home type (house, townhouse, or condominium), and buttons (Garage, Fireplace, Central Air Conditioning, or New construction). The points of light can be selected to generate a detailed description.

- starfield display: result sets are continuously available and support viewing of hundreds or thousands of items
- tight coupling: query components are interrelated in ways that preserve display invariants and support progressive refinement. Specifically, outputs of queries can be easily used as input to produce other queries.

Dynamic Query Filters

Our early work on dynamic queries [2, 6, 20] demonstrated dramatic performance improvements and high levels of user satisfaction. By allowing rapid, incremental and reversible changes to query parameters, often simply by dragging a slider, users were able to explore and gain feedback from displays in a few tenths of a second. For example, the Dynamic HomeFinder enabled users to adjust upper and lower bounds on home prices and see points of light on a map indicating available properties (Figure 1). This allowed users to immediately identify high or low cost communities, or find low cost homes in high-priced communities. Users could similarly adjust a slider to indicate number of bedrooms, and select toggles to indicate desire for garage, central air-conditioning, fireplace, etc.

Each of these query components (sliders, buttons, etc.) acted as a filter, reducing the number of items left in the result set. The effects were combined with simple AND logic, accounting for most naturally occurring queries. In situations where OR logic was required, users were usually quite satisfied, or actually preferred, generating a sequence of queries. This approach allowed users to see the size of the ORed components rather than merely the union of the result sets.

The work reported in this paper advances dynamic queries by demonstrating the efficacy of selection of items in alphanumeric lists with the Alphaslider [1, 12]. This query component allows users to select one item from a list of 10,000 or more, with a simple selection tool that takes little screen space, avoids use of the keyboard, and prevents typing errors.

Starfield Display

In our early work on dynamic queries the output was based on a naturally occurring spatial display. For example, the chemical table of elements was used with color highlighting of chemical names to indicate inclusion in the result set. In the Dynamic HomeFinder, points of light on a map of Washington, DC indicated properties that matched the query components. One step in the direction of generality was to build a version of the HomeFinder that had textual output as might be found in the tuples of a relational database display. As the query components were adjusted, the display remained stable, but when the user let go of the mouse button, the screen was refreshed with the correct result set.

To further support the widespread application of dynamic queries it seemed necessary to find other approaches to visual information display [4, 5, 7, 17]. Points of light are convenient because they are small yet highly visible, could be color coded, are selectable objects, and can be displayed rapidly. But if a natural map did not exist for an application, such as a set of documents, photos, songs, etc., could we create one that would be suitable? While we need to try further examples, our initial answer is affirmative. For many situations we have been able to create meaningful two-dimensional displays by selecting ordinal attributes of the items and use them as the axes. This starfield approach is a scatterplot with additional features to support selection and zooming. Our intuitions about what choices are most effective is still rough, but there is hope that we can formalize our decisions.

For example, in a database of documents, the year the document was written might be the horizontal axis while length in words might be the vertical axis. Large old documents might be at the upper left while short new documents might be at the lower right. Other attributes such as an author assigned importance value, number of co-authors, or number of references could also be used. In a database of people, the axes might be the age, number of years of education, salary, number of children, or other demographic variables.

Tight Coupling

The principle of tight coupling of interface components began to emerge in some direct manipulation graphic user interfaces. For example, if a user saves a document, the SAVE menu item becomes grayed out until a change is made. Tight coupling helps reveal the software state, and often constrains the user from making erroneous or useless actions.

A more complex example of tight coupling is the interrelationship between the text in a word processor, the position of the thumb in the scroll bar, and the page number displayed on the window border. Moving the thumb causes the text to scroll and the page number to be updated. We could write a logical proposition describing the relationship among these three display components. Such a statement would begin by indicating that when the top of the document is displayed, the thumb is at the top of the scroll bar and the page indicator is set at 1. Good program design would ensure the preservation of the display invariants. However, some word processors may fail to preserve this invariant when sections of the document are deleted or when the document is reformatted with a larger font. To compensate, some word processors may include a repaginate command, or update the thumb position only when it is moved. These errors violate the principle of tight coupling.

Tight coupling also applies to components of a query facility. In a well-designed facility, users should be able to see the impact of each selection while forming a query. For example, if a user specifies that they want films before 1935, then only certain actors or directors are selectable. This is to prevent users' from specifying null sets, e.g. films made before 1935 and directed by Francis Ford Coppola.

Another aspect of tight coupling is the linkage of *output-is-input* to support efficient use of screen space by eliminating the distinction between commands/queries/input and results/tables/output. In short, every output is also a candidate for input. This principle first emerged in our 1983 hypertext work [9] in which the notion of embedded menus replaced the earlier designs that had a paragraph of output followed by a menu to select further information. It seemed more logical to have highlighted words in the text and simply allow users to select those words with arrow keys, a mouse, or a touchscreen. The outputs-are-inputs principle reduced screen clutter by eliminating redundancy, and focused users' attention to a single location for gathering information and for applying an action to get more information.

This principle was applied in the chemical table of elements in which each element could be selected causing the sliders to be set to that element's values [2], in our health statistic map in which a state could be selected to retrieve its detailed data [13], and in the HomeFinder in which a point of light could be selected to retrieve detailed information or a photo, if it were available.

That database output can be used as input can be compared to functionality in spreadsheets where there is no such thing as input cells or output cells, or the Query by Example system [21] where input can be treated as output and vice versa. It has been referred to as a notion of Equal Opportunity [15]. In information retrieval systems this is useful as users can easily explore branches of a search and follow their associations as they come along -- associative database searching.

Tight coupling has several aspects:

- comprehensible and consistent affordances to guide users (highlighted words or areas, explicit handles, scrollbars, etc.).
- rapid, incremental, and reversible interactions among components.
- constraints on permissible operations to preserve *display invariants* (logical propositions relating the components, e.g. that the scroll bar thumb position constantly reflects the position in the document) and prevent errors.
- *continuous display* to always show the users some portion of the information space that they are

exploring. They begin by seeing a typical result set or item, which helps to orient them to what is possible in this information seeking environment. This seems more effective than starting with a blank screen or a form to fill in.

- *progressive refinement*, in which users can alter the parameters to get other results [18]. If the users see that there are too many items in the result set, they can reformulate their goal and seek a more restrictive value for one of the attributes.
- allow users to select *details on demand* [9]. This is the heart of hypermedia, but it applies to most designs. Instead of older query facilities which required alternation between query composition and result interpretation, our designs show results and invite further selections if details are needed. In the Dynamic HomeFinder, homes were shown as simple points of light until the user selected one of the points to get the details. This principle reduces clutter while the query is being shaped and allows users to get further information when they need it.

FILMFINDER DESIGN

To test these principles of visual information, we created a tool for exploring a film database, the FilmFinder. Watching a film is often a social activity so this tool was designed to encourage discussions and make the decision process easier for groups of viewers. Existing tools for learning about films include encyclopedias, such as *Leonard Maltin's Movie and Video Guide* [10]. They typically provide an alphabetic organization, with additional indexes, but these are difficult to use. Recently, computer-based encyclopedias such as Microsoft's Cinemania have appeared on the market. Although some of them employ novel approaches such as hypertext links they still do not provide users with an overview of the data. They employ a traditional approach to database queries with commands or form fill-in, and then provide a textual response in the form of scrolling lists. If the users are unhappy with the result, they compose a new query and wait for the new result. Progressive refinement can take dozens of steps and many minutes.

Before designing the tool, informal interviews were conducted with video store clerks and film aficionados. The FilmFinder [Color plate 1] tries to overcome search problems by applying dynamic queries, a starfield display, and tight coupling among components. Dynamic queries were applied by having a double box range selector to specify film length in minutes, by having buttons for ratings (G, PG, PG-13, R), large color coded buttons for film categories (drama, action, comedy, etc.), and our novel Alphasliders for film titles, actors, actresses, and directors.

The query result in the FilmFinder is continuously represented in a starfield display [Color plate 1]. The X-axis represents time and the Y-axis a measure of popularity. The FilmFinder allows users to zoom into a particular part of the time-popularity space [Color plate 2]. As users zoom in the colored spots representing films grow larger, giving the impression of flying in closer to the films. The labels on the axes are also automatically updated as zooming occurs. When fewer than 25 films are visible, their titles are automatically displayed.

To obtain more information about a particular element of the query results, users click on that element, getting desired details-on-demand [Color plate 3]. An information card which provides more information about attributes such as actors, actresses, director and language, is displayed. In a traditional retrieval system users would obtain more information by starting a new query. In the FilmFinder users can select highlighted attributes on the information card and thereby set the value of the corresponding Alphaslider to the value of that attribute. This forms the starting point for the next query and allows graceful and rapid exploration with no fear of error messages.

Tight coupling is strongly supported in the FilmFinder. When users select categories of movies using the category toggles, the starfield display and the query ranges of the Alphasliders are immediately updated [Color plate 2]. This effectively eliminates empty and invalid query results. The same is possible when users zoom into a particular part in the search space -- only those films that appear during that range of years and are in the particular popularity range will be part of the Alphaslider query range. The Alphasliders can even affect each other, selecting Ingmar Bergman on the Director slider would set the Actor slider to only operate over those actors who appear in Ingmar Bergman's movies. This interaction between the query widgets, and the possibility to use query results as input, creates a tightly coupled environment where information can be explored in a rapid, safe, and comprehensible manner.

FILMFINDER SCENARIO

Tools like the FilmFinder might be found in video stores, libraries, and homes - they might even come as a part of standard television sets. Imagine the Johnson family sitting down at their TV Saturday night to watch a movie that they all like. They turn on the TV and are presented with a FilmFinder's starfield visualization and a number of controls [Color plate 1]. All controls are operable by a wireless mouse and no keyboard is needed.

The family members don't have a specific film in mind, but they know that they want to see something popular and recent. After some discussion they agree on the categories for a search: drama, mystery, comedy, or an action film. To cut down the number of films further they select an actor that they all like, in this case Sean Connery. Observe in [Color plate 2] how the category toggles have been manipulated - and the Alphaslider indexes updated to contain appropriate values, the visualization has zoomed into the correct part of the information space, and Sean Connery has been selected with the Actor slider.

Now the number of films in the starfield has been cut down from about 2000 to 25 and the Johnsons decide to look further at *The Murder on the Orient Express*. They select it with their remote control and are presented with an information card [Color plate 3]. The description and image remind the Johnsons that they have already seen this film, so the information card can now become the tool to further refine their search.

Mr. Johnson sees Anthony Perkins' name and decides he wants to see a movie starring Anthony Perkins, while Mrs. Johnson wants to see a movie with Ingrid Bergman. To resolve the disagreement they select both actors in the information card, and the selection is reflected in the Alphaslider settings. When the information card is closed, the query result is updated and the Johnsons are presented with one movie with both Anthony Perkins and Ingrid Bergman which they decide to watch [Color plate 4].

FUTURE WORK

The dynamic queries approach has much to recommend it, but it must be extended to deal with larger databases, more varied kinds of information, and a greater range of query types. Current dynamic queries do not satisfy the demands of relational completeness, but they offer other features that depend on spatial output that are not available in existing relational databases. It appears productive to combine the strengths of both approaches.

When searching films - as well as for other information - it would be desirable to incorporate fuzzy searching to find similar films. To include such functionality in the FilmFinder would probably be desirable - but first algorithms must be devised and more importantly, the issue of to what extent the mechanisms should be user controlled must be examined.

When browsing the information space by zooming, it is important that this is done smoothly so users get a feeling of flying through the data. New algorithms and data structures are necessary to support the smooth flying through the data. A natural extension would be to add a third dimension so that some films would appear closer than others.

The tight coupling among query components in the FilmFinder was helpful - but there may be cases when such interrelationships not are desirable. Formal specification of the logical propositions for display invariants is a useful direction, because it could lead to proofs of correctness and advanced tools to build such interfaces rapidly.

REFERENCES

1. Ahlberg, C. and Shneiderman, B., 1993. The Alphaslider: A rapid and compact selector, *Proc. ACM CHI'94 Conference.*
2. Ahlberg, C., Williamson, C., and Shneiderman, B., 1992. Dynamic queries for information exploration: An implementation and evaluation, *Proc. ACM CHI'92 Conference*, 619-626.
3. Borgman, C. L., 1986. Why are online catalogs hard to use? Lessons learned from information-retrieval studies, *Journal of the American Society for Information Science 37*, 6, 387-400.
4. Buja, A., McDonald, J. A., Michalak, J., Stuetzle, W., 1991. Interactive data visualization using focusing and linking, *Proc. IEEE Visualization '91*, 156-163.
5. Egenhofer, M., 1990. Manipulating the graphical representation of query results in Geographic Information Systems, *1990 IEEE Workshop on Visual Languages*, IEEE Computer Society Press, Los Alamitos, CA, 119-124.
6. Eick, Steven, 1993. Data visualization sliders, AT&T Bell Laboratories Report, Napervillie, IL.
7. Feiner, S. and Beshers, C., 1990. Worlds within worlds: Metaphors for exploring n-dimensional virtual worlds, *Proc. User Interface Software and Technology '90*, ACM, New York, NY, 76-83.
8. Koved, L. and Shneiderman, B. 1986. Embedded menus: Selecting items in context, *Comm. of the ACM 29*, 4 (April 1986), 312-318.
9. Kreitzberg, Charles B., Details on Demand: Hypertext models for coping with information overload, in Dillon, Martin (Editor), *Interfaces for Information Retrieval and Online Systems,* Greenwood Press, New York, 1991, 169-176.
10. Maltin, L., 1993. *Leonard Maltin's Movie and Video Guide*, Penguin Books, New York.
11. Marchionini, G., 1993. *Information Seeking*, Cambridge Univ. Press, Cambridge, UK.
12. Osada, M., Liao, H., Shneiderman, B., Alphaslider: searching textual lists with sliders, *Proc. of the Ninth Annual Japanese Conf. on Human Interface*, Oct. 1993.
13. Plaisant, C., 1993. Dynamic queries on a health statistics atlas, Forthcoming Technical Report, Human-Computer Interaction Laboratory, University of Maryland, College Park, MD.
14. Robertson, G. G., Card, S. K., and Mackinlay, J. D., 1993. Information visualization using 3-D interactive animation, *Comm. of the ACM 36*, 4, 56-71.
15. Runciman, C. and Thimbleby, H., 1986. Equal opportunity interactive systems, *Int'l Journal of Man-Machine Studies 25* (4), 439-51.
16. Shneiderman, B., *Designing the User Interface: Strategies for Effective Human-Computer Interaction: Second Edition*, Addison-Wesley Publ. Co., Reading, MA (1992), 573 pages.
17. Singers, R., Endres, L., 1993, Metaphoric abstraction, the starfield and complex systems, in preparation, Johnson Controls, Milwaukee, WI.17. Welty, C., 1985. Correcting user errors in SQL, *Int'l Journal of Man-Machine Studies 22*, 463-477.
18. Welty, C., 1985. Correcting user errors in SQL, *Int' Journal of Man-Machine Studies 22*, 463-477.
19. Williams, M., 1984. What make RABBIT run? *Int'l Journal of Man-Machine Studies 21*, 333-352.
20. Williamson, C. and Shneiderman, B., 1992. The Dynamic HomeFinder: Evaluating dynamic queries in a real-estate information exploration system, *Proc. ACM SIGIR Conference*, 339-346.
21. Zloof M. Query-by-Example, *National Computer Conference*, AFIPS Press (1975), 431-437.

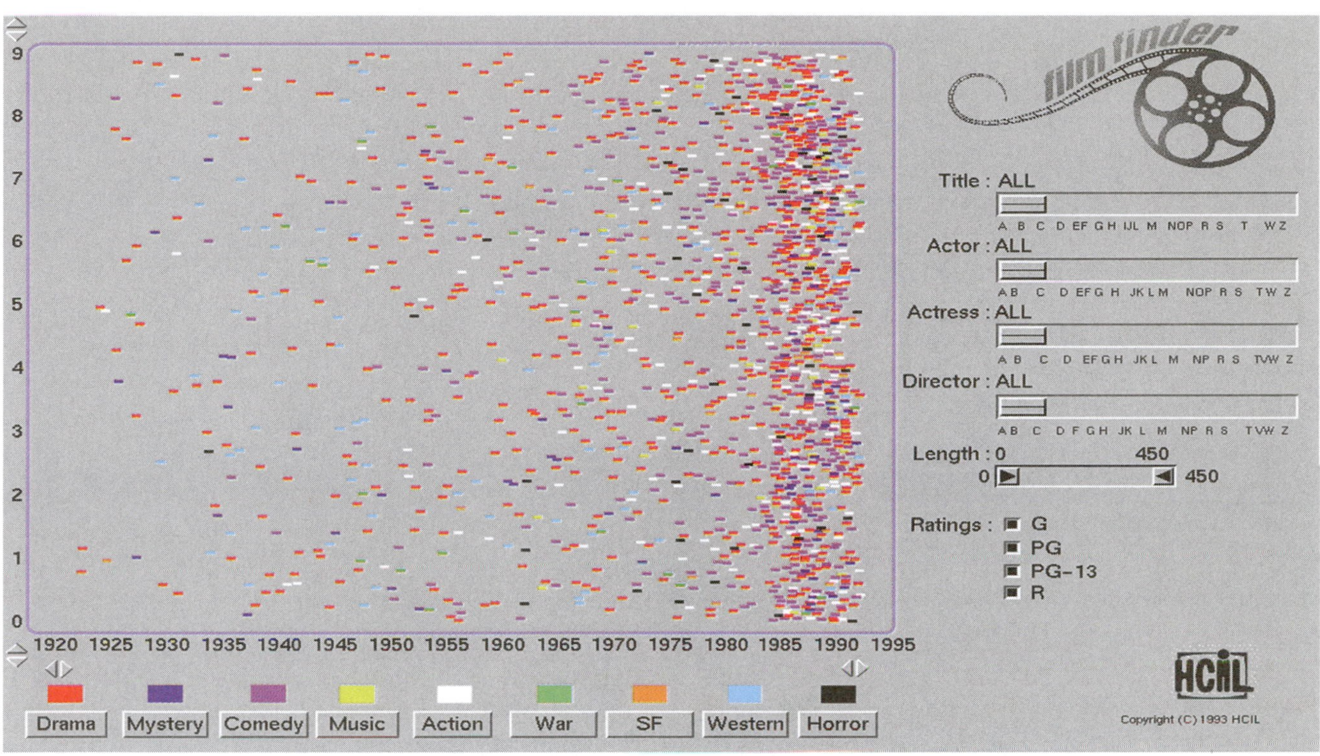

Ahlberg & Shneiderman, Color plate 1. The FilmFinder.

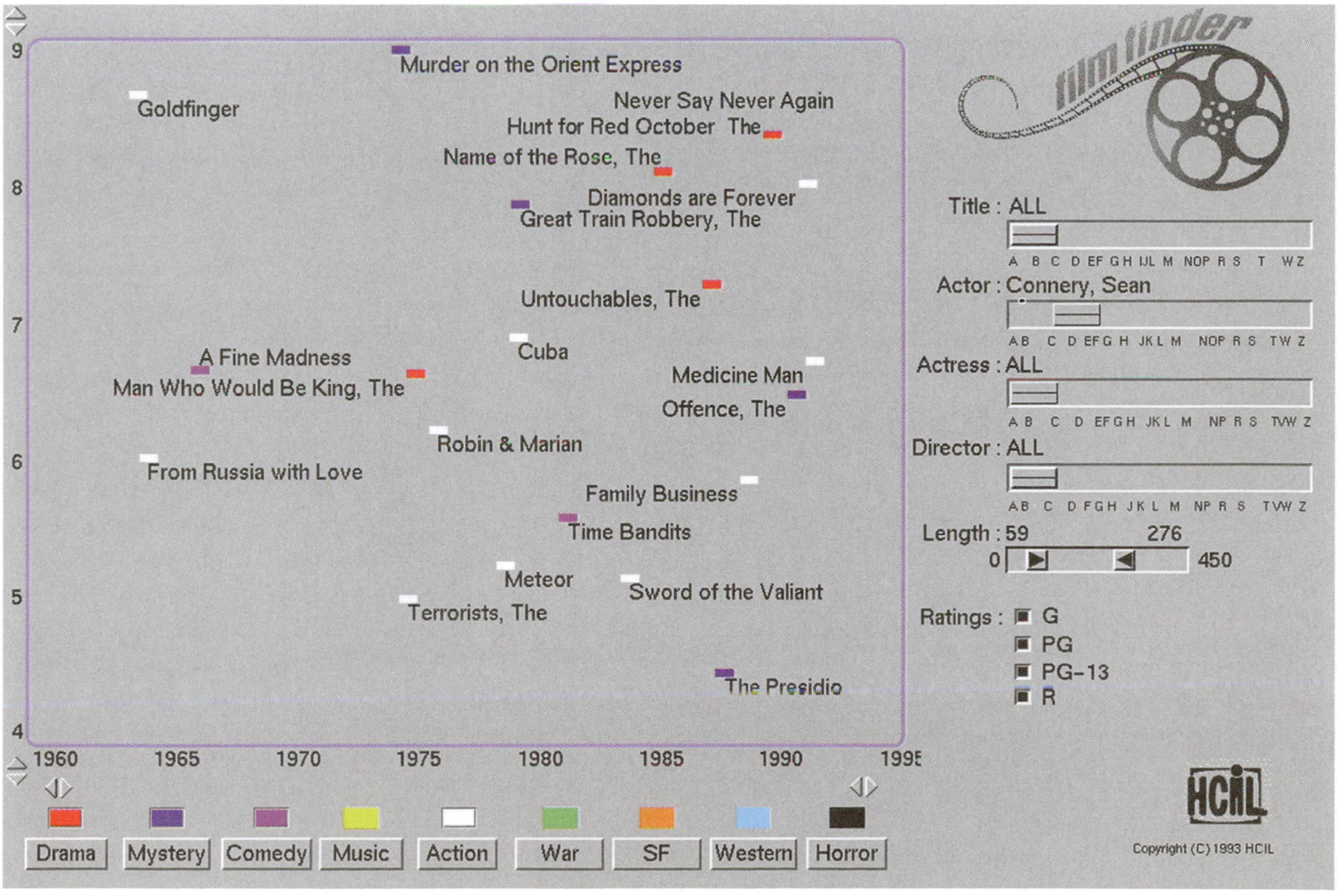

Murder on the Orient Express
Goldfinger
Never Say Never Again
Hunt for Red October The
Name of the Rose, The
Diamonds are Forever
Great Train Robbery, The
Untouchables, The
Cuba
Medicine Man
A Fine Madness
Man Who Would Be King, The
Offence, The
e Valiant
e Presidio

Murder on the Orient Express
Director: Lumet, Sidney
Year: 1974
Country: USA
Language: English
Actors:
Balsam, Martin
Cassel, Jean-Pierre
Perkins, Anthony
Connery, Sean
Gielgud, John
Actresses:
Bacall, Lauren
Bergman, Ingrid
Bisset, Jacquelin
Hiller, Wendy

film finder
Title : ALL
Actor : Perkins, Anthony
Actress : Bergman, Ingrid
Director : ALL
Length : 59 276
0 450
Ratings : G PG PG-13 R
9 8 7 6 5 4
1960 1965 1970 1975 1980 1985 1990 1995
Drama Mystery Comedy Music Action War SF Western Horror
HCIL
Copyright (C) 1993 HCIL

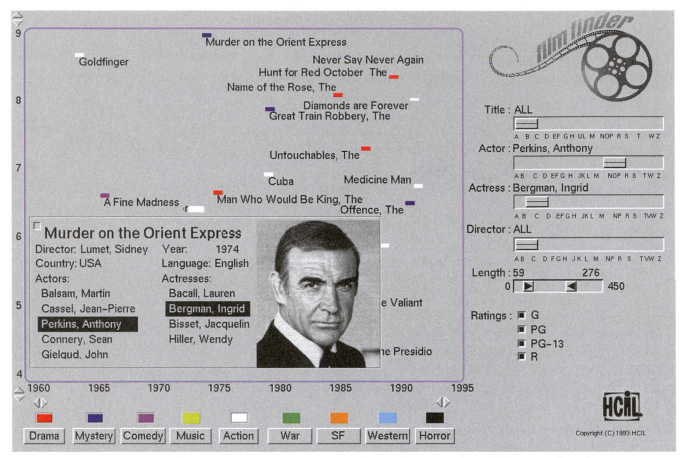

Ahlberg & Shneiderman, Color plate 3. Anthony Perkins and Ingrid Bergman has been selected in the information card - which is reflected in the Alphasliders.

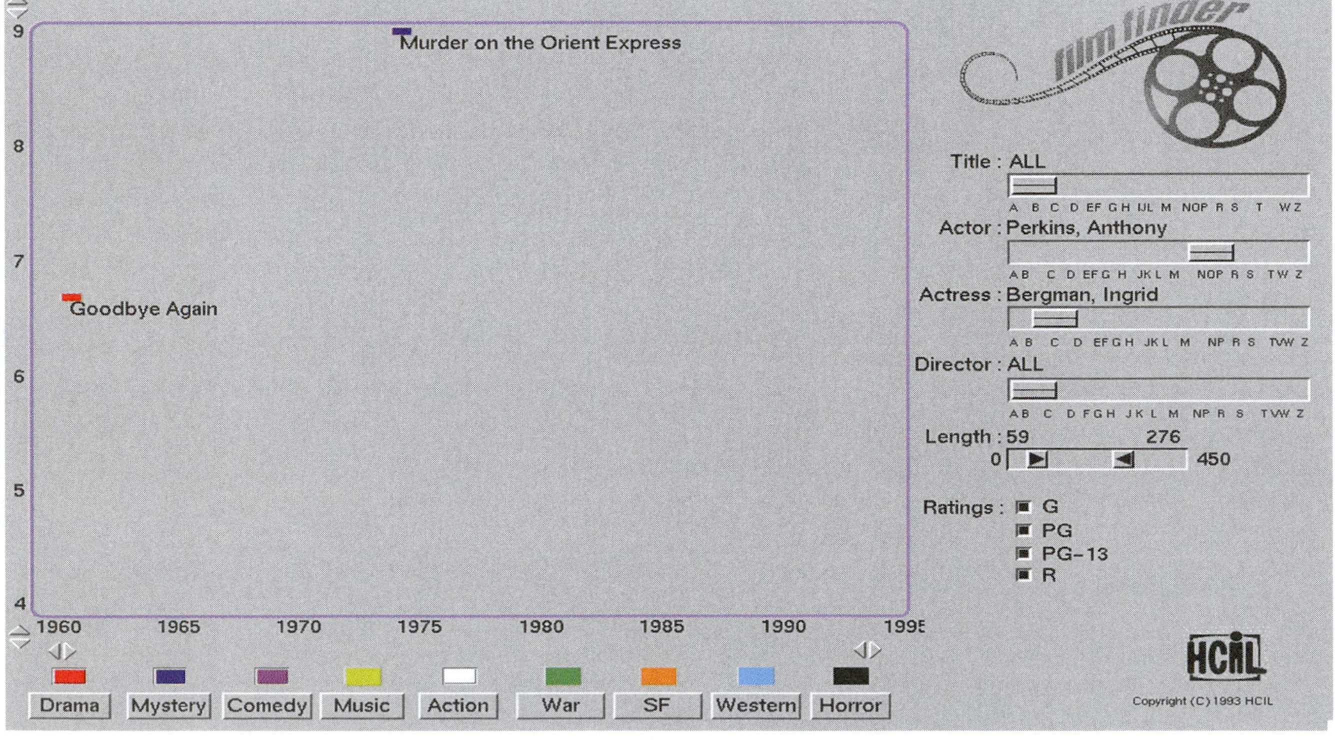

Data Visualization Sliders

Stephen G. Eick
AT&T Bell Laboratories - Room IHC 1G-351
1000 E. Warrenville Road
Naperville, Illinois 60566
eick@research.att.com

ABSTRACT

Computer sliders are a generic user input mechanism for specifying a numeric value from a range. For data visualization, the effectiveness of sliders may be increased by using the space inside the slider as

- an interactive color scale,
- a barplot for discrete data, and
- a density plot for continuous data.

The idea is to show the selected values in relation to the data and its distribution. Furthermore, the selection mechanism may be generalized using a painting metaphor to specify arbitrary, disconnected intervals while maintaining an intuitive user-interface.

KEYWORDS: high interaction, thresholding, information visualization, selection, dynamic graphics

INTRODUCTION

Sliders are a general-purpose user input mechanism enabling users to specify a single input value from a well-defined range. They are widely used in all graphical user-interface systems including Motif, Sun's OPEN LOOK, Apple's Macintosh, and Microsoft Windows. Sliders are easy to use, intuitive, and provide a sensitive mechanism for specifying values. Sliders have a threshold bar positioned within a scale that the user manipulates with a mouse to select a value. Graphical input tools with similar function include dials, bars, pointers, gauges, and potentiometers [6].

A common application of a slider in information visualization is to control a threshold filtering the entities shown on the display. For example, Becker et al. [3] use a double-edged slider with upper and lower thresholds on their network maps, Eick et al. [5] use a categorical slider on their software displays for selecting an arbitrary subset from hundreds of time-ordered software modifications, and Ahlberg et al. [1] describe their alpha-slider for selecting a single string from sorted list. Ahlberg and Shneiderman's FilmFinder [2] uses a suite of double-edged sliders.

The idea uniting these applications is filtering. In each case sliders are used to restrict the information portrayed on the screen, thereby pruning the visual clutter and enabling the analyst to see important underlying patterns. The pruning of visual clutter from data-rich displays by adjusting sliders is particularly effective in information visualization, and even more so when done dynamically.

Data Visualization Sliders

The data visualization slider in Figure 1 is tied to *frost*, the average number of frost free days in the state capitol [7] of the 48 continental states. The average number of frost free days ranges from 364.5 in California to 179 in North Dakota with an average of 264.

Figure 1 shows four instances of the slider that the user may toggle between with a pop-up menu. Slider versions A and B treat *frost* as continuous data within a range and versions C and D treat *frost* as categorical data with 50 discrete values, one for each state. The idea in A is to combine a visualization color[1] scale and a slider with interaction techniques. B extends this by showing the smoothed distribution of *frost*. C maps *frost* level to one color-coded bar, and is particularly interesting when there are enough distinct values so that each bar is one pixel wide [4]. D generalizes this idea to encode the *frost* in the bar's length.

This slider improves upon traditional sliders for data visualization in three ways:

- The space inside the slider is used as a color scale, thereby efficiently utilizing screen real estate, a limited and precious commodity. The color scale may have discrete values as in A and B or be a spectrum as in C and D.
- The data values are shown as tick marks in a "rug plot" [9] (p.135) along the edge in versions A and B and as the bar lengths in version D.
- The distribution of the data is shown as a density plot in version B and as the bar lengths in version D.

A user operates a traditional slider by depressing the left mouse button to engage the bar and then moves it to a new position. The slider in Figure 1 generalizes this intuitive user interface by enabling a user to select arbitrary regions. A user sweeps the mouse over the slider with the left button depressed to select a region or the middle mouse button depressed to de-select. The selected, or turned-on, regions are shown in their color and, the unselected, or turned-off,

[1] In the black and white version of this paper color has been mapped to gray level.

regions are shown in dark gray. This action is similar to operating a paint program, where the user paints-on or paints-off the intervals of interest. In A a portion of the bottom color is turned-off, in B the middle and top are turned-off, in C all bars are on, and in D only the top few bars are on. D is also interesting because the colors have been rescaled for finer fidelity within the top few bars.

Besides toggling between the versions, some other interesting pop-up menu options include:

- Color rescaling on C and D which re-allocates the color spectrum to the currently active bars, thereby providing increased color fidelity, and
- Range zooming for increased scale sensitivity,
- Animation for C and D which causes the computer to sequentially activate each bar in turn, and
- Labeling to print the statistic values next to the bars in C and D.

The density plot in B shows the smoothed distribution [8] of *frost*. By default, the color scale divisions in A and B are linear, but for skewed variables, linear spacing may be inefficient. The user may adjust the partitions interactively with the mouse to select a natural place for the division such as a low spot on the density curve.

Summary

The slider described here generalizes the generic functionality of traditions sliders along several orthogonal directions. The important ideas include:

- Enabling a user to specify an arbitrary number of disconnected intervals while preserving the intuitive slider interface.
- Using the space inside the slider as a color scale.
- Interactively rebinding the colors either to the active bars or adjusting the color divisions.
- Presenting the distribution of the data.
- Showing individual data values, either as tick marks or as bar lengths.
- Moving between the representations under user control, thereby enabling the users to explore from several perspectives.

Linking sliders to the data they control suggests many natural and obvious extensions.

REFERENCES

1. Christopher Ahlberg and Ben Shneiderman. The alphaslider: A compact and rapid selector. *CHI '94 Conference Proceedings*, pages 365–371, 1994.

2. Christopher Ahlberg and Ben Shneiderman. Visual information seeking: Tight coupling of dynamic query filters with starfield displays. *CHI '94 Conference Proceedings*, pages 313–317, 1994.

3. Richard A. Becker, Stephen G. Eick, Eileen O. Miller, and Allan R. Wilks. Dynamic graphical analysis of network data. In *ISI Conference Proceedings*, Paris, France, August 1989.

4. Stephen G. Eick. Graphically displaying text. *Journal of Computational and Graphical Statistics*, 3(2):127–142, June 1994.

5. Stephen G. Eick, Joseph L. Steffen, and Jr. Eric E. Sumner. Seesoft^{TM}—a tool for visualizing line oriented software statistics. *IEEE Transactions on Software Engineering*, 18(11):957–968, November 1992.

6. James D. Foley, Andries van Dam, Steven K. Feiner, and John f. Hughes. *Computer Graphics Principles And Practice*. Addison-Wesley, Reading, Massachusetts, 1990.

7. U.S. Bureau of the Census. *Statistical Abstract of the United States: 1992 (112th edition)*. U.S. Government Printing Office, Washington, DC, 1992.

8. B. W. Silverman, editor. *Density Estimation for Statistics and Data Analysis*. Chapman & Hall, 1986.

9. Edward R. Tufte. *The Visual Display of Quantitative Information*. Graphics Press, Cheshire, Connecticut, 1983.

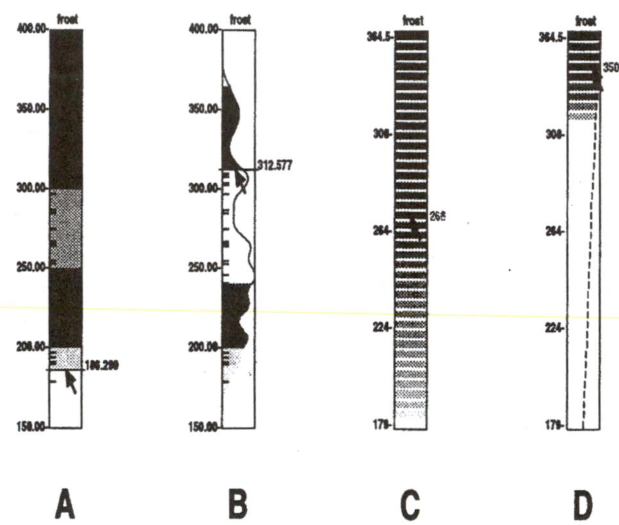

Figure 1: Four versions of a data visualization slider tied to *frost*, the average number of frost free days in the state capital. Sliders A and B treat *frost* as a continuous variable and C and D as a discrete variable. The space inside of the slider box functions as a color scale (A and B) and shows the distribution of the variable (B and D). Users operate the slider by turning or or off regions of interest using a painting metaphor (A, B and D), with the colored area on and gray area off, and may manipulate the color scale (D).

Enhanced Dynamic Queries via Movable Filters

Ken Fishkin, Maureen C. Stone
Xerox PARC, 3333 Coyote Hill Rd., Palo Alto CA 94304
E-mail: {fishkin, stone} @parc.xerox.com

ABSTRACT

Traditional database query systems allow users to construct complicated database queries from specialized database language primitives. While powerful and expressive, such systems are not easy to use, especially for browsing or exploring the data. Information visualization systems address this problem by providing graphical presentations of the data and direct manipulation tools for exploring the data. Recent work has reported the value of dynamic queries coupled with two-dimensional data representations for progressive refinement of user queries. However, the queries generated by these systems are limited to conjunctions of global ranges of parameter values. In this paper, we extend dynamic queries by encoding each operand of the query as a Magic Lens filter. Compound queries can be constructed by overlapping the lenses. Each lens includes a slider and a set of buttons to control the value of the filter function and to define the composition operation generated by overlapping the lenses. We demonstrate a system that supports multiple, simultaneous, general, real-valued queries on databases with incomplete data, while maintaining the simple visual interface of dynamic query systems.

Key Words: viewing filter, lens, database query, dynamic queries, magic lens, visualization

INTRODUCTION

Traditional database query systems require the user to construct a database query from language primitives [19]. Such systems are powerful and expressive, but not easy to use, especially when the user is unfamiliar with the database schema. Information visualization systems [15] provide graphical display of database values and direct manipulation tools for exploring relationships in the data. These systems have many advantages over language-based systems, including a visual representation that provides an intuitive feel for the scope of the data, immediate feedback, and incremental, reversible interactions. There is a tension in such systems, however, between providing expressive power and ease of use.

In this paper, we present a new direct manipulation technique for exploring a database displayed as a two dimensional set of points. With it, users can incrementally construct full boolean queries by layering queries encoded as Magic Lens™ filters [5,6,17]. Our work builds directly on two techniques for information visualization that were presented at CHI '94. The first, the *starfield display* [2], supports interactive filtering and zooming on scatterplot displays. The second, the *movable filter* [17], supports multiple simultaneous visual transformations and queries on underlying data. In this paper we combine the two techniques, enhancing the starfield display by augmenting it with the flexibility and functionality of the movable filter. The advantages include: a direct manipulation mechanism for creating general boolean queries, multiple simultaneous views, and a uniform mechanism for providing alternate views of the data. We also demonstrate how our query mechanism was extended to support general, real-valued queries on databases containing missing fields.

After describing related work, we describe using magic lens filters to generate boolean queries over graphically displayed data. We then discuss how they provide a uniform mechanism for generating multiple views of the data. We then extend our model to support real-valued queries over incomplete data, and present our conclusions and plans for future work. Concrete examples taken from an application for exploring US Census data are used throughout the paper.

RELATED WORK

Scatterplots or *thematic maps* are well-established techniques for displaying data as points in a 2-D field [4,18]. Such displays can encode large amounts of data and can provide an intuitive way to visualize groups of related data items. Transformations of the display produce patterns that are easy to interpret, even for high-dimensional datasets [14].

Dynamic queries [1] apply direct manipulation techniques to the problem of constructing database queries. A selector (e.g. a slider) or set of selectors is used to control the range of values required of a particular attribute or set of attributes. When combined with a graphical representation of the database such as a scatterplot, users can rapidly explore different subsets of the data by manipulating the selectors [2]. However, the number of attributes that can be controlled is limited by the number of selectors that can be easily applied to the data. The effect of combining slider filters is strictly conjunctive; disjunctive queries may only be performed by performing each sub-query sequentially. The effects of the selectors are global; there is no way to limit the scope to only a portion of the data except by zooming in on it. Finally, the number of selectors, and hence the number of possible queries, is fixed in advance.

The Aggregate Manipulator [11] as well as XSoft's Visual Recall™ [20] allow somewhat more powerful (but non-interactive) queries, supporting disjunctive and limited compound composition via textual, hierarchical, menu-driven interfaces. The conceptual prototype of Egenhofer [10] is a hybrid technique. Query operands are typed in using a database language, but those operands are visually composed, with modes that support disjunctive, conjunctive, and subtractive composition.

Magic lens filters [6,17] are a user interface tool that combine an arbitrarily-shaped region with an operator that changes the view of objects viewed through that region. The operator can be quite general, accessing the underlying data structures of the application and reformatting the data to generate a modified view. The filters are spatially bounded, may be parameterized, and are interactively positioned over on-screen applications. Filters may overlap, in which case they compose their effects in the overlap region.

Magic lens filters provide a number of advantages desirable for data visualization. Since they are spatially bounded, they can perform their operation within a restricted focus while maintaining global context. Since they can overlap, compositional semantics can be defined and controlled.

BOOLEAN QUERIES BY COMPOSITION

Given some mechanism for displaying data in scatterplot format, we can use a set of lenses to create dynamic queries on the data. Each lens acts as a filter that screens on some attribute of the data. A slider on the filter controls a threshold for numeric data. Buttons and other controls on the lens can control other functions. When the lenses overlap, their operations are combined. This provides a clean model for building up complex queries. This physical, rather than merely conceptual, composition of multiple sliders appeals to existing user intuitions that spatial overlaps imply a composition, as shown in Venn diagrams and color circles.

To create boolean queries by composing magic lens filters, we need to provide a way to specify how the filters are combined. To provide full boolean functionality, we need to provide a mechanism for the AND, OR, NOT and grouping or parenthesizing operations.

We define for each lens a filtering function and a composition mode that describes how the result of the filtering function is combined with the output of lenses underneath. More formally, a lens L=(F, M), where F is a filter and M is a boolean operator. The filter, F, describes the output calculation for the filter on some datum. The mode, M, describes how that output is combined with the output from lower filters. For example, given L1=(F1, OR) and L2=(F2, AND), the result of positioning L1 over L2 is (F1 OR F2). Conversely, the effect of positioning L2 over L1 is (F2 AND F1). We implement the composition mode as a button on the lens, making it easy to change the mode as needed.

The NOT operation can be encoded as a lens whose filter inverts the sense of the data coming in. Using the formalism of the previous paragraph, an inverting lens N = (NULL, NOT). That is, N applies a NOT to the output of lower filters, and has no intrinsic filter function. For example, consider the query (F1 OR NOT F2), where F1 and F2 filter for various attributes. To implement this query, the user would lay down filter F2, then the NOT filter N, then filter F1 with its composition mode set to OR.

To incorporate grouping, we need a mechanism for encapsulating the expression defined by a stack of lenses. To do this, we provide an operation that replaces a stack of lenses with a single *compound* lens that is semantically equivalent. The user creates such a compound lens by selecting a point on a stack of lenses through a click-through button, a partially transparent button on an overlaying lens [5]. All lenses beneath this point are combined to create a compound lens that generates the same query as the stack. The resulting lens also has a composition mode that defines how it is combined with other lenses. This new compound lens can be manipulated by the user just as any other lens, providing a simple way to encapsulate a complex query into a single conceptual unit.

To create the query (F1 AND F2) OR (F3 AND F4), for example, we create compound lenses for the values in parentheses: C1=(F1 AND F2) and C2=(F3 AND F4). By giving lens C1 a composition mode of OR, we can create the desired expression by positioning C1 over C2. Compound lenses may contain other compound lenses, allowing queries to grow to arbitrary complexity.

Since we can incorporate AND, OR, NOT, and grouping, we can represent any boolean query. Complex queries can be incrementally built up by direct manipulation of the lenses and their modes. Useful queries can be saved as compound lenses. The resulting lenses can then be used to build up more complex queries in a completely uniform manner. While we have implemented only three common boolean composition modes, this model supports any of the boolean operators.

EXAMPLES

To demonstrate these ideas we created an application to browse a database of US census data [7]. In this database, each row represents a city and the columns describe the city along various census metrics: population, crime rate, property tax rate, and so forth. We chose this database because it is publicly available, lends itself to fairly interesting queries, and the data elements have an intuitive mapping to the 2D plane, namely the physical location of the city on a map.

In this implementation, each lens is implemented as an X window [16]. A lens manager server extends the X window system to support magic lens functionality. Therefore, the lenses can be manipulated using the regular window manager interface. Lenses can display their output using the X graphics library, or, upon request, they can display it in PostScript® [3] form. Using this facility, the application can generate PostScript pictures describing its screen appearance. We used such generated PostScript for all the black and white figures in this paper. Choosing this form, instead of a screen snapshot, allows us to customize the presentation to fit the space and color limitations of the proceedings. The figures in the color plates are screen snapshots that show the screen appearance of the running application.

Color plate 1 shows a typical lens filter in action. Each city is displayed as a blue-rimmed white box at a point proportional to its latitude and longitude. The data attribute associated with the lens filter covering the center of the country, "1991 crime index," is displayed in the window header. Below that on the left is a slider used to control the threshold value for the query, and a label showing the current slider value (12158.5 in this example). The buttons to the right of the slider control whether the user is screening for data less than (<) or greater than (>) the slider value. Cities shown in red, rather than white, pass the filter. For example, in this case, cities in the center of the country with a crime rate greater than 12158.5 are shown in red. Buttons along the right edge of the application are used to spawn new lenses (13 different types are presently implemented), and for application housekeeping.

Figure 1 shows the effects of applying different composition modes to the composition of two filters. The composition mode for a lens is defined by a group of four radio buttons. The buttons labeled **AND** and **OR** set the composition mode accordingly. The **SELF** button causes the lens to display only the effect of its own filter, ignoring other lenses, and the **NOP** button sets the filtering function to NULL, disabling the effect of the lens. These two modes are useful when interpreting complex queries. In figure 1(a) we look for cities which have high annual salaries and low taxes. We can make the query less demanding by using the **OR** button to change the composition mode (figure 1(b)), to see cities which have either high salaries or low taxes. The **SELF** and **NOP** buttons can be used to examine these components separately, to determine which cities have high salaries and which have low taxes.

An alternative interface for setting the composition mode is to use a click-through tool. In this interface, a single button on the lens indicates the current mode. A click-through tool contains buttons that can be used to change the mode by clicking through them to the lens below. The advantage of this interface is that it supports a large set of composition modes without visual clutter The disadvantage is that it requires more steps to change the mode. Our application supports both interfaces; users can choose the interface they prefer. An example of a lens with a single mode button is shown in color plate 2.

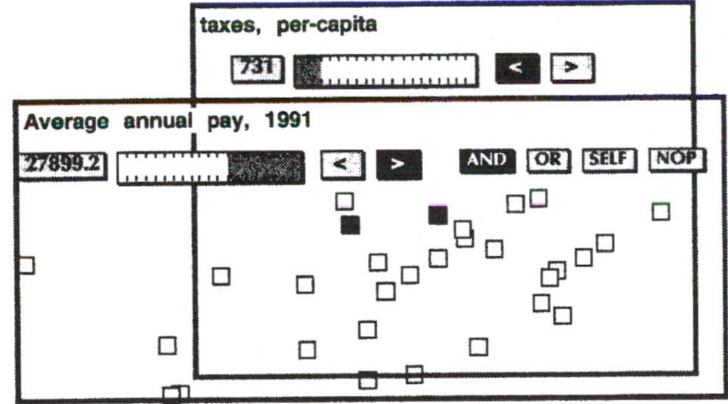

Figure 1(a) High salaries AND low taxes. Cities with partial data are shown in figure 1(b) but not in 1(a).

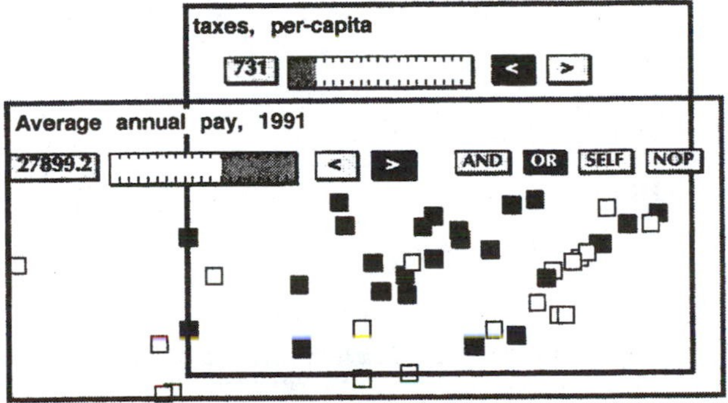

Figure 1(b) High salaries OR low taxes. Both conjunctive (AND) and disjunctive (OR) queries are incorporated in our system.

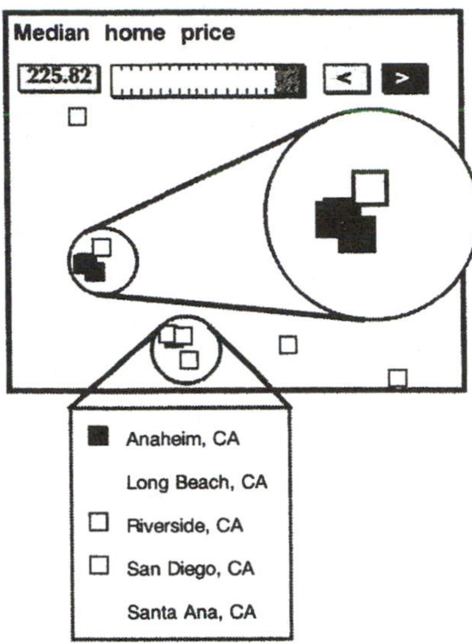

Figure 2. Semantic filters can be augmented with visual filters. Here, a magnifying lens and a call-out lens show clumped cities while maintaining context elsewhere.

MULTIPLE VIEWS

Simultaneous multiple queries can be performed by positioning different lenses over different parts of the display. Each lens, and hence each query, can be independently customized by manipulating the controls on the lens. We can also use lenses to generate alternate views of the data, such as magnifying lenses, callouts, sorted views, and other such transformations. The user interface of these visual transformations is identical to that of the semantic transformations (the filters).

For example, a scatterplot representation of the data will often have clumps, where some set of data points map to nearby points on the display or even overlap. Figure 2 shows two examples of this clumping, and uses multiple visual filters to aid in viewing the data. A small magnification lens is positioned over northern California, letting us see that there are four cities clumped into the bay area. Over southern California, a callout lens is placed. This lens displays the cities as a list, making it easy to separate them. The rest of the map is displayed in the usual manner. This allows easy identification of cities in the dense region while maintaining global context. The boxes next to the city names on the callout are active, so filters placed over them act exactly as if they were placed over the original map. Cities listed without boxes are missing the data selected by the filter, "Median home price."

In the star-field paradigm, a user manipulates a set of selectors, and observes their filtering effect on the data. By associating each selector with a single movable filter, we gain the ability to pose multiple simultaneous queries, each with its own set of parameters. For example, suppose we wish to determine which cities in each region of the country have relatively low housing prices. We have data available for the average housing price per city. However, the range of values for this attribute is wide, and varies geographically. For example, houses on the west coast are typically more expensive than houses in the midwest. Therefore, we need to filter on a higher threshold on the west coast than in the midwest. Figure 3 shows two filters with two different threshold values positioned over California and over Texas.

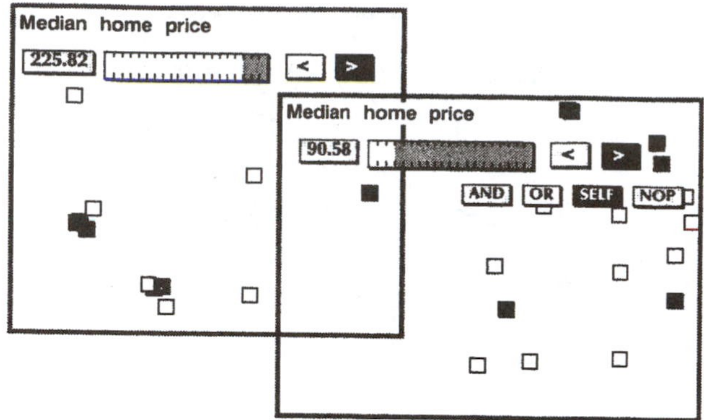

Figure 3. To find relatively high housing prices in California and Texas, two different filters are positioned simultaneously.

EXTENSIONS

In the previous section, we discussed how movable filters can be used to perform general boolean queries on scatterplot data. In this section, we discuss further extending the power of our filters such that they support real-valued queries and undefined data values.

Real-valued Queries

To support more powerful queries, we extended our system such that filters assign a real-valued score on the range [0...1] to each datum. Data with a score of 0 fails the filter entirely, data with a score of 1 succeeds entirely, and data with intermediate scores partially satisfy the filter. This provides more information about the value returned by the query. In general, the scoring function could be arbitrary—a filter might prefer data with extreme values, or assign a gaussian falloff to data with the highest score going to data of a certain value, or other similar metrics. Our implementation currently supports only linear and step scoring functions, but this is not due to any limitation imposed by the technique. We present the score visually by showing each datum as a partially filled-in square; the higher the score, the more of the square is filled in.

For example, in figure 4(a) a boolean filter is screening for crime rate, and both Dallas and Fort Worth are seen to have high crime rates. When we switch to real-valued filters (figure 4(b)) we see that Dallas has a lower crime rate than Fort Worth. The values displayed were computed as follows. As in the boolean case, the filter slider value defines a threshold. In figure 4, for example, the threshold is 12838. When screening for data greater than the threshold (>), data below the threshold is assigned a score of 0, as is the case for Arlington in Figure 4. The city in the database with the greatest value for the data (in the case of crime data, it happens to be Atlanta, GA, with a crime index of 18953) is assigned a score of 1.0. Cities with values between the threshold and the maximum are assigned a simple linear score equal to their value divided by the maximum value. When screening for values less than the threshold (<), values below the threshold are assigned non-zero scores in a similar manner.

Computations can be performed on the output of real-valued filters. For example, in figure 5 we have placed a sorting lens over a real-valued crime rate filter. Only the cities under the sorting lens are sorted. We can see that in Florida, Jacksonville has the lowest crime rate and Miami has the highest.

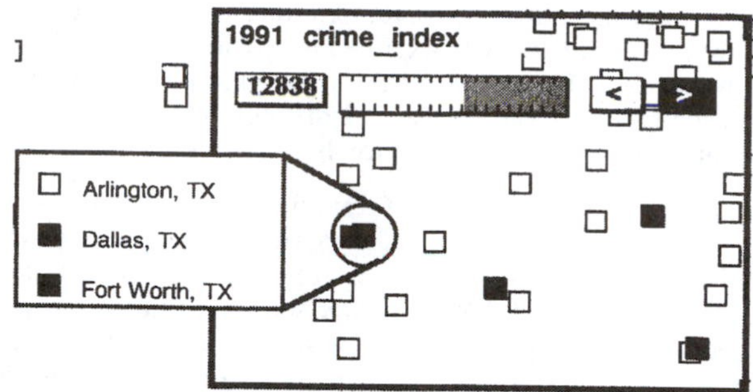

Figure 4(a) boolean query on crime rate for three cities in Texas.

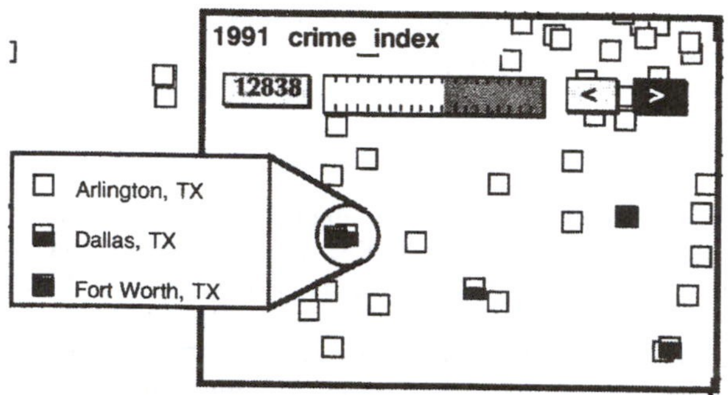

Figure 4(b) Real-valued query on crime rate for the same cities. Extending our filters from boolean-valued to real-valued allows distinctions to be maintained.

Real-valued filters require real-valued composition modes. The real-valued MIN and MAX composition modes correspond to the boolean AND and OR as in fuzzy logic [21]. That is, MIN and MAX work the same on 0.0 and 1.0 as AND and OR do on 0 (False) and 1 (True), but can also incorporate values in-between. A real-valued NOT filter returns 1.0 minus its input value.

Just as boolean filters can be composed with an arbitrary boolean operation, not just AND and OR, so too can real-valued filters be composed with an arbitrary numerical operation, not just MIN and MAX. These operations can be statistical transformations used to change the data distribution (sqrt, arcsin, etc.), fuzzy logic operators used to tune the query ("very," "somewhat," "more or less," etc.), or mathematical operators used for general manipulation (difference, log, etc.). Color

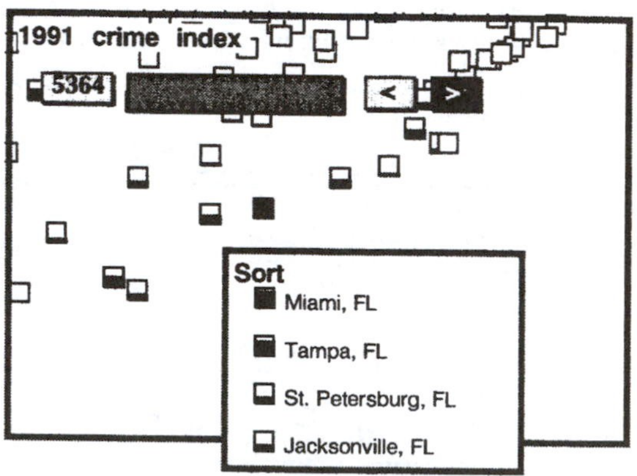

Figure 5. A sorting lens sorts cities by crime rate in Florida.

plate 2 shows some of these composition modes in use to visualize the correlation between poverty and crime rate. The DIFF composition mode is an example of a mathematical composition operator: it is defined as the absolute value of the difference between its two operands. The filter above that, the "Very" filter, is an example of an operator from fuzzy logic: Very(x) is defined as x squared [8]. By overlaying a real-valued NOT filter above that, we ask where crime rate and poverty rate are NOT VERY DIFFerent. The higher the score, the redder the city's box, the greater the correlation. We can see that poverty and crime rate are highly correlated in most cities.

Missing Data

Databases in general, and the US census database in particular, do not always have all data fully defined. In the case of the US census database, for example, some cities may have population figures included but not crime data, or vice versa. A robust information presentation system must address this problem to give an accurate view of the data. There are two issues: how such data is visually presented and how queries based on that data are performed.

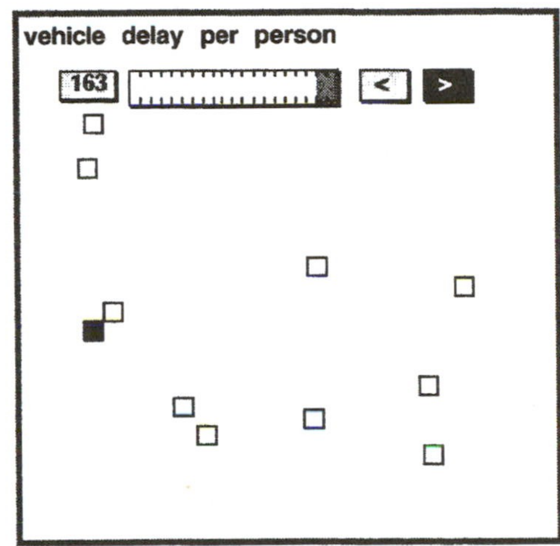

Figure 6(a). A filter finds only one city (San Francisco) with a high score.

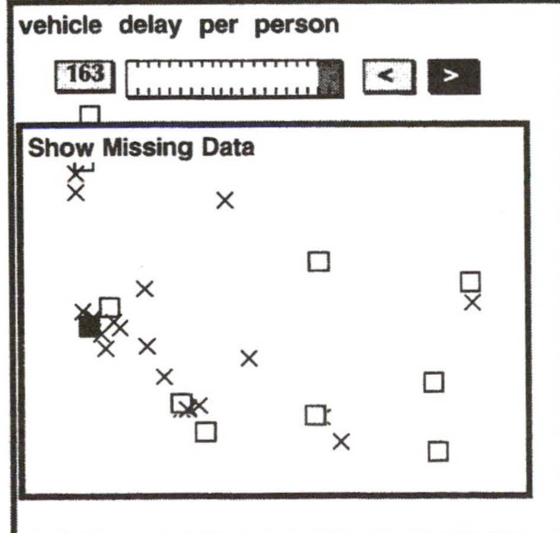

Figure 6(b). A missing data lens shows that attribute values are missing for many cities. Cities with missing data are marked with an 'X'.

We visualize missing data by use of a special lens. Normally, any city whose value as a result of a query is missing, or undefined, is simply not shown. The "Show Missing Data" lens makes these cities visible. For example, figure 6(a) shows a query, centered on the West Coast, filtering for cities with severe traffic delays. Only San Francisco is shown to have such delays. By adding a "Show Missing Data" lens, however, as shown in figure 6(b), we see that most of the other California communities don't have data for this category—perhaps San Francisco is not as unattractive as it first appeared.

We incorporated missing data into the semantics of composition by considering missing data to be analogous to the IEEE concept of a non-signaling Not-A-Number (NaN), a value that is defined to "afford retrospective diagnostic information inherited from invalid or unavailable data and results" [12]. In accordance with common practice [13], we then define:

OR(a,NaN) =a, MAX(a,NaN) = a

F(a,NaN) =NaN, for all other composition modes F.

Note that a city that is invisible because of missing data may re-appear when another filter is laid upon it, if that filter's composition mode is MAX or OR.

CONCLUSIONS

Applying magic lens filters to the problem of exploring and visualizing data creates a user model that is expressive yet easy to understand. Placing a lens over the data evokes the physical model of using a lens for filtering or enhancing the view of the data beneath it. Including a slider on the lens allows the user to dynamically vary the query by adjusting the filter threshold.

Overlapping the filters creates a natural metaphor for creating compound queries. By providing explicit composition modes and a mechanism for grouping expressions, the full power of a boolean query language can be expressed graphically. We have also demonstrated how this language can be expanded to include real-valued functions that gracefully handle missing values. Powerful queries can be built up incrementally, then preserved for future exploration. In this way, the lenses provide a mechanism for capturing the result of a data exploration session.

Magic lens filters provide a natural mechanism for visual transformations as well as semantic transformations of the data. We have shown examples of callout, magnification, missing data, and sorting lenses. Other possible functions include alternate representations of score such as color or size, and overlaying geographic information such as city or state boundaries.

In our application, magic lens filters have been combined with click-through tools to implement a wide range of user-interface operations. These can be used to manipulate the data, the filtering operations, or the tools themselves. For example, click-through tools are used to create compound lenses, generate figures, provide additional parameters for the filtering operations, and to change the layout of the buttons and sliders.

In summary, magic lens filters provide a uniform, powerful and extensible mechanism for data visualization and exploration applications.

FUTURE WORK

Within the particular application of analyzing city census data, we are working to include a wider variety of scoring functions, to explore other visual techniques (e.g. blurring and/or translucency as discussed in [9]) for expressing queries and their results, and to make the user interface smoother, faster and more sophisticated. This will enable us to perform user studies to help quantify the value of this technique.

We are also interested in extending this work to apply to other types of data and other forms of information visualization.

ACKNOWLEDGMENTS

We thank Jock Mackinlay for his enthusiasm, encouragement, and shared realization that magic lens filters could support disjunctive queries. We thank Eric Bier for his user-interface and illustration design expertise, and Ken Pier for his help in the preparation of the paper. Finally, we thank Xerox PARC for its continuing support.

REFERENCES

1. Christopher Ahlberg, Christopher Williamson, and Ben Shneiderman. Dynamic Queries for Information Exploration: an Implementation and Evaluation. *Proceedings of CHI '92,* 1992. pp. 619-626.
2. Christopher Ahlberg and Ben Shneiderman. Visual Information Seeking: Tight Coupling of Dynamic Query Filters with Starfield Displays. *Proceedings of CHI '94,* (Boston, MA, April 24-28) ACM, New York, (1994), pp. 313-317.
3. Adobe Systems Incorporated. *PostScript® Language Reference Manual, second edition.* Addison-Wesley, 1990.
4. Jacques Bertin. Semiology of Graphics. University of Wisconsin Press. 1983.
5. Eric A. Bier, Maureen C. Stone, Thomas Baudel, William Buxton, and Ken Fishkin. A Taxonomy of See-Through Tools. *Proceedings of CHI '94,* (Boston, MA, April 24-28) ACM, New York, (1994), pp. 358-364.
6. Eric A. Bier, Maureen C. Stone, Ken Pier, William Buxton, and Tony D. DeRose. Toolglass and Magic Lenses: The See-Through Interface. Proceedings of Siggraph '93 (Anaheim, CA, August), *Computer Graphics* Annual Conference Series, ACM, 1993, pp. 73-80.
7. Bureau of the Census. Statistical Abstract of the United States 1993. Washington DC, 1993.
8. C.L. Chang. Interpretation and Execution of Fuzzy Programs. In Fuzzy Sets and Their Applications to Cognitive and Decision Processes. Academic Press. New York. 1975. pp. 191-218.
9. Grace Colby and Laura Scholl. Transparency and Blur as Selective Curs for Complex Visual Information. Proceedings of SPIE '91 (San Jose, Feb). SPIE, 1991, pp. 114-125.
10. Max J. Egenhofer. Manipulating the Graphical Representation of Query Results in Geographic Information Systems. *Proceedings of the 1990 IEEE Workshop on Visual Languages.* IEEE Computer Society Press, Los Alamitos CA, 1990, pp. 119-124.
11. Jade Goldstein and Steven F. Roth. Using Aggregation and Dynamic Queries for Exploring Large Data Sets. *Proceedings of CHI '94,* (Boston, MA, April 24-28) ACM, New York, (1994), pp. 23-29.
12. IEEE. The IEEE Standard for Binary Floating-Point Arithmetic. IEEE, New York, 1985.
13. W. Kahan. How should Max and Min be defined? University of California, Berkeley. May 25, 1989.
14. Daniel A. Keim and Hans-Peter Kriegel. VisDB: Database Exploration Using Multidimensional Visualization. IEEE CG&A, **14**(5), September 1994. pp. 40-49.
15. George G. Robertson, Stuart K. Card, and Jock D. Mackinlay. Information Visualization Using 3D Interactive Animation. Communications of the ACM, **36**(4), April 1993. pp. 57-71.
16. Robert W. Scheifler, James Gettys, and Ron Newman. X Window System. Digital Press, Bedford MA, 1988.
17. Maureen C. Stone, Ken Fishkin, and Eric A. Bier. The Movable Filter as a User Interface Tool. *Proceedings of CHI '94,* (Boston, MA, April 24-28) ACM, New York, (1994), pp. 306-312.
18. Edward R. Tufte. The Visual Display of Quantitative Information. Graphics Press. 1983.
19. Jeffrey D. Ullman. Principles of Database Systems. Computer Science Press, 1980.
20. XSoft Corporation. Visual Recall for Windows. Xerox Corporation. Palo Alto, CA. 1994.
21. Lotfi Zadeh. Fuzzy Sets. Information Control, vol. 8, pp. 338-353. 1965.

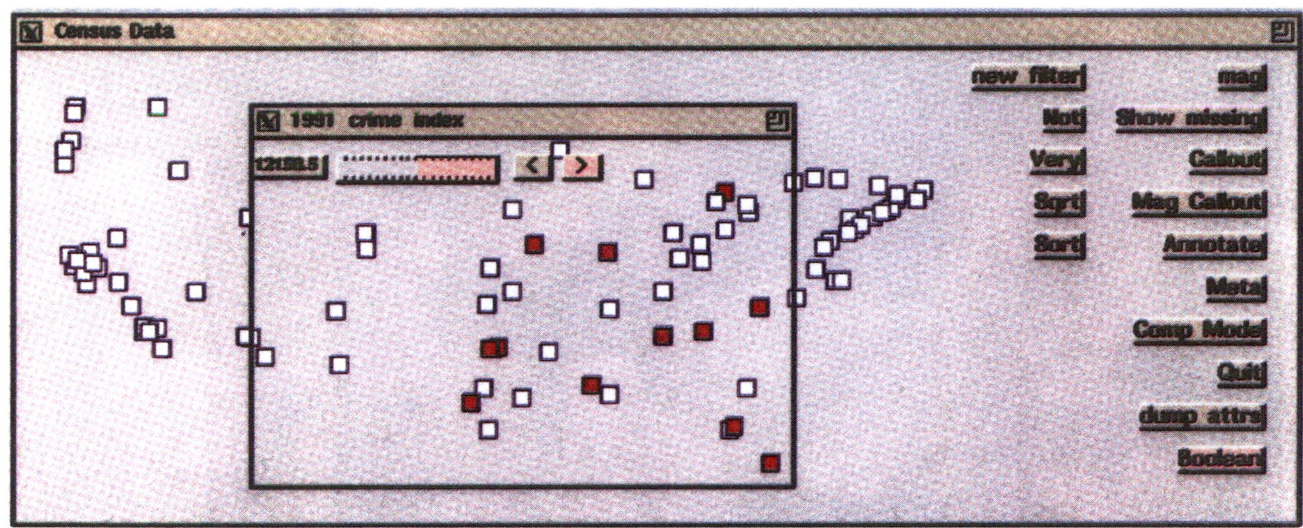

COLOR PLATE **1**

Displaying a database of US census data. Cities are displayed as boxes at a point proportional to their longitude and latitude. A filter screening for cities with a high crime rate is positioned over the central United States.

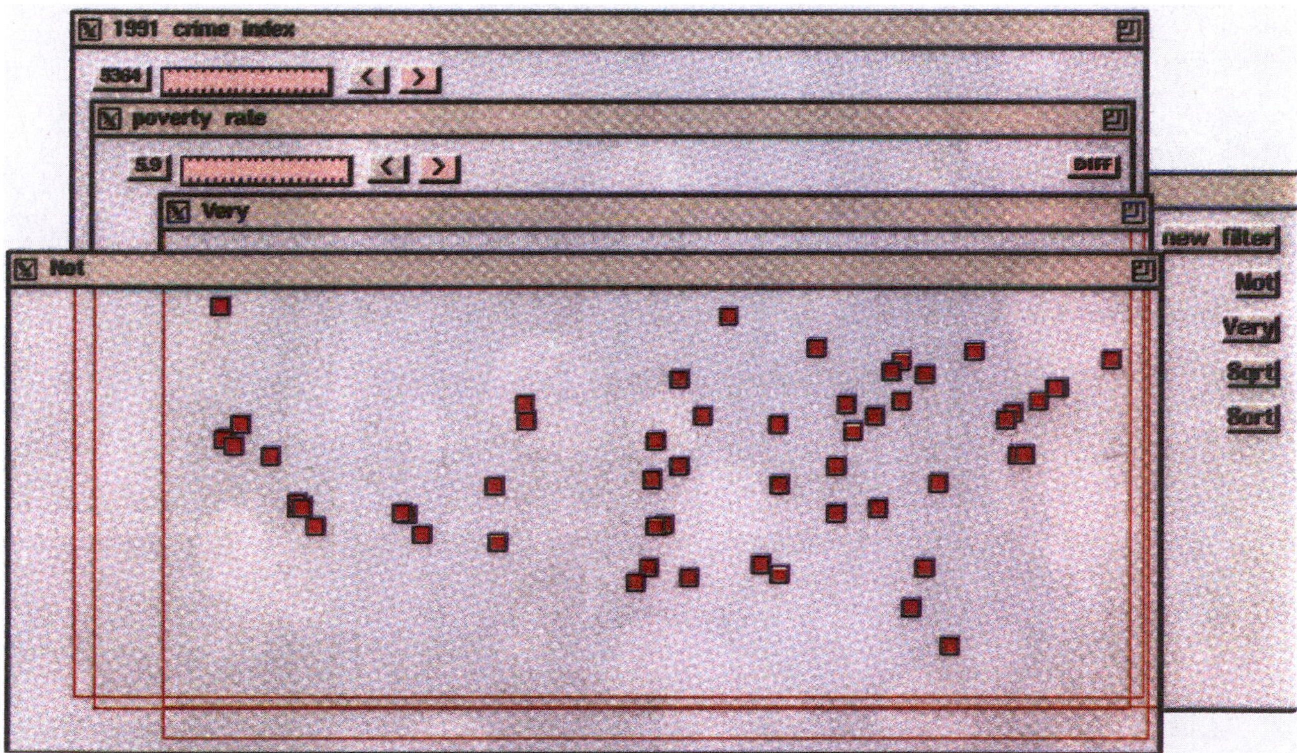

COLOR PLATE **2**

Real-valued filters support more powerful queries. The redder the city, the greater the extent to which poverty and crime rates are NOT VERY DIFFerent.

3.2 Interactive Analysis

As we saw in the last section, interaction can help find cases in a database and it can be used to reveal patterns. It can also be used to make comparisons and other analyses. The two papers in this section explore methods for performing such interactive visual analysis.

The first paper, Chuah et al. (1995b ●), concerns comparison in a 3D visualization. Approximate comparisons of large differences are easy, but more precise, quantitative comparison is not. Items to be compared must be brought together, yet their relationships to other data must somehow be preserved. Their scaling must be normalized. The distortions of 3D perspective must be overcome.

Chuah et al. lay data out on a 3D landscape with magnitudes mapped onto the length of bars. The visualization application is intended to help relief officials understand what resources are available in what part of the country. Both geography and data type (e.g., numbers of trucks at different locations) are important organizers. To allow for precise comparison of objects located in different places of the landscape, the paper provides means for defining a comparison set. Cases can be added to this set with the mouse. Several techniques can be used to visually highlight the cases in the set: making them brighter, exaggerating their width, or placing them on a grid. The comparison set can be moved together to a convenient place in the space, leaving behind a ghosted image to maintain the original spatial relationships. In this way, 3D occlusions can be overcome, comparison sets can be extracted from the environment, and their members can be visually normalized to help with comparison. For example, the items can be rescaled, and they can be reorganized into a 2D presentation with reference lines for more precise comparison.

In Tweedie et al. (1996 ●), visualization interaction is used to do complex trade-offs in the design of a product, such as a light bulb. There are three reasons why the design is complicated. First, the designer has certain input design parameters to work with, filament width, filament material, and so on. These lead to a set of output performance parameters such as cost, brightness, or lifetime. Requirements for the design are stated in terms of the output parameters. The design is based on the availability of simulations to predict outputs from inputs. The difficulty is that these do not have easy inverses, so the designer must proceed by some sort of hill climbing in the input design parameter space.

Second, the space is multivariable. The visualization proposed uses interaction over time to overcome the fact that the problem is too complex to depict by a simple visualization in space. Instead of seeing the space of outcomes, the user sees the outcome at a point and uses dynamic queries–style sliders to see the effect of moving one parameter a small step in some direction.

The third problem is that in the actual manufacturing of the product, input parameters will vary slightly from what was intended. Part of the design problem is to create designs with enough tolerance so that a high proportion of the final products is within the specifications.

The most successful visualization technique of the paper is to make a matrix of all the two-way scattergraphs of the output variables. Each point represents a design and is colored according to the figure of merit of the design. The figure of merit used is how many of the specifications the design matches. Another visualization technique is to associate a histogram with the slider for each input variable showing the figure of merit distribution associated with each possible value on the slider. Setting upper and lower bounds for the parameter on the slider changes the histogram in favorable or unfavorable ways.

The creation of the figure of merit scale is itself clever. Suppose the types and ranges of the output variables were

Cost	Q [0.20, 0.45]
Brightness	Q [800, 1175]
Lifetime	Q [750, 2200].

Given a set of specifications

Cost	Q [0.25, 0.35]
Brightness	Q [975, 1100]
Lifetime	Q [1175, 2200],

any given set of variables can be transformed into a string of binary variables recording whether the output variable was or was not within specification, for example,

$$\text{Cost} = .31 \rightarrow 1$$

(where 1 means it is in specification and 0 means it is not). The set of binary variables can then be added together to get a figure of merit based on the number of output variables within spec. A multivariable output has been reduced to a single scale. This reduction allows it to be mapped into a retinal variable.

SDM: Selective Dynamic Manipulation of Visualizations

Mei C. Chuah, Steven F. Roth, Joe Mattis, John Kolojejchick
School of Computer Science
Carnegie Mellon University
Pittsburgh, PA 15213, USA
Tel: +1-412-268-2145
E-mail: {mei+,roth}@cs.cmu.edu

ABSTRACT

In this paper we present a new set of interactive techniques for 2D and 3D visualizations. This set of techniques is called SDM (Selective Dynamic Manipulation). *Selective,* indicating our goal for providing a high degree of user control in selecting an object set, in selecting interactive techniques and the properties they affect, and in the degree to which a user action affects the visualization. *Dynamic,* indicating that the interactions all occur in real-time and that interactive animation is used to provide better contextual information to users in response to an action or operation. *Manipulation,* indicating the types of interactions we provide, where users can directly move objects and transform their appearance to perform different tasks. While many other approaches only provide interactive techniques in isolation, SDM supports a suite of techniques which users can combine to solve a wide variety of problems.

KEYWORDS: Interactive techniques, visualizations, direct manipulation.

INTRODUCTION

A well-designed visualization can be tremendously helpful in analyzing data. However, current static visualizations are limited in several important ways:

1. Users are not able to focus on different object sets in detail while still keeping them in context with the environment. This is especially important in large data sets that have too much information to be displayed in detail at once.
2. When the information space is dense, there will be a lot of clutter and object occlusion. Occlusion is a serious problem because data-points may be fully occluded and thus appear invisible to the user. In this way, occlusion may distort a user's perception of the data-space. In addition, clutter makes it difficult to perceive patterns in subsets of objects.

To appear in
Proceedings UIST'95
Symposium on User Interface
Software and Technology,
ACM, November 1995.

3. A data set may contain elements that have vastly different values. Thus, some objects may be dwarfed when shown in the scale used for the entire data set. In Figure 1, many of the objects (e.g., those in green) are dwarfed by the tall cylinder towards the right. With SDM we attempt to provide users with techniques that temporarily change the scale of a subset of objects, while keeping them in context with the environment. Figure 2 shows the same data set as Figure 1 except that the green objects have their heights scaled differently from the rest of the environment. The difference in height scales is shown by the ratio axes on the left of the visualization. Note that some of the bars that appeared to have the same height in Figure 1 actually have relatively large height differences when put on another scale.

Figure 1: Data visualization of a relief effort data set. Green bars are the currently selected objects.

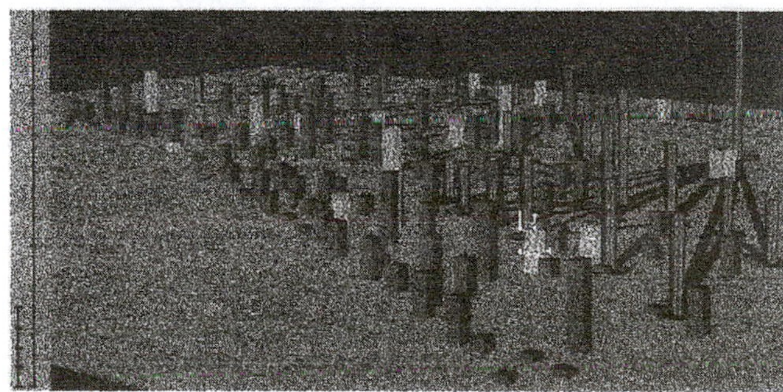

Figure 2: Visualization showing the same data set as Figure 1, except the heights of the green bars are scaled differently from the rest of the environment.

4. Many visualizations only allow users to view the underlying data. No tools are provided to classify sets of objects and save those classifications as new information is discovered. For example, after a user has identified several problematic/important data points, the user might want to save them as a set and change their color so that they are differentiated from the other objects.
5. It is difficult to compare quantities represented by graphical objects which are not spatially contiguous. For example, in Figure 3 it is difficult to compare which of the selected shelters (indicated by the green bars) has the most supplies (indicated by their heights) because they are not at the same distance from the user.

Figure 3: Selected objects that are at different distances from the user

In this paper we present a paradigm, Selective Dynamic Manipulation (SDM), which deals with all of the difficulties mentioned above. While some of the individual techniques that we discuss have been tried before, they have only been tried in isolation. Instead of isolated solutions, our approach is to provide a suite of interactive techniques that can be flexibly combined to solve a wide spectrum of problems. We believe that the unifying framework behind the techniques will make the system easy to learn, and the flexibility in using the methods will stimulate users to come up with multiple novel ways to solve tasks.

Our approach is different from many other interactive systems [4,9,15,18] because its selection and control methods are strongly centered on objects rather than on spaces. The goal of our approach is to provide a framework for solving a basic set of tasks and problems that are important when users are analyzing large, diverse data sets.

EXAMPLE DATA DOMAIN

The data domain for our examples is from a supply distribution network for a relief effort in a large-scale crisis. In Figure 1, supply centers are represented by cylinders, main routes between them by dark lines on the floor plane, and shelters where supplies are needed by rectangular bars. The heights of cylinders and bars indicate the quantities of material available at supply centers and needed by shelters. See [14] for color versions of figures.

Next, we outline the basic structure and approach of SDM and discuss how SDM can be used to address the five limitations mentioned previously.

SDM COMPONENTS

The structure of our SDM system is described based on the three primary components of interactive techniques: method of selection, interactive operations, and the feedback mechanisms and constraints placed on the behavior and appearance of objects.

1) Object-centered Selection

In object-centered selection the focus or selected set is made up of objects. Selection of these objects is done through their visualized representations or through data constraints.

Selection in SDM can be accomplished by clicking on objects and/or using sliders to place data constraints. The slider interface in SDM allows users to combine data constraints both conjunctive and disjunctively. In the future, we plan to generalize the selection facility so that there can be multiple linked displays. Selecting objects in a display will cause objects that have the same underlying data, in the other displays, to be selected as well.

After object sets are created, they may be named and saved. Users may save as many sets as they desire. Sets that are created will appear in a scrollable menu. Selecting a set in the menu causes it to be displayed. All the slider panels that form the set will also be shown. In this way users may switch between multiple self-defined sets easily. Note also that the object sets need not be made up of homogeneous types (e.g., a set may contain supply centers, shelters and routes).

2) Dynamic and Flexible Operations

Users may directly manipulate object set parameters through object handles. Direct manipulation refers to operating directly on objects instead of through menus or dialogues. The Document Lens [12] and Magic Lens [18] are examples of direct manipulation techniques that allow users to control their views of objects by operating on a lens. In contrast to manipulating an external object (such as a lens), SDM allows users to control an object set by directly controlling any element within that set through handles. Figure 4 shows the SDM handles used to manipulate objects. Our use of handles was motivated by related work on 3D widgets [7,17] and by 2D scaling handles in draw programs.

Attaching a handle to an object in a selected set and pulling or pushing its parts causes some or all objects in the selected set to change. The handles (Figure 4) were designed to look similar for different object types so that users need not remember the functions of many visually distinct handles. When handles are pulled or pushed, the objects contract, expand or move continuously. Using animation in this way helps users perceive the changes that have occurred or are occurring to an object set more easily.

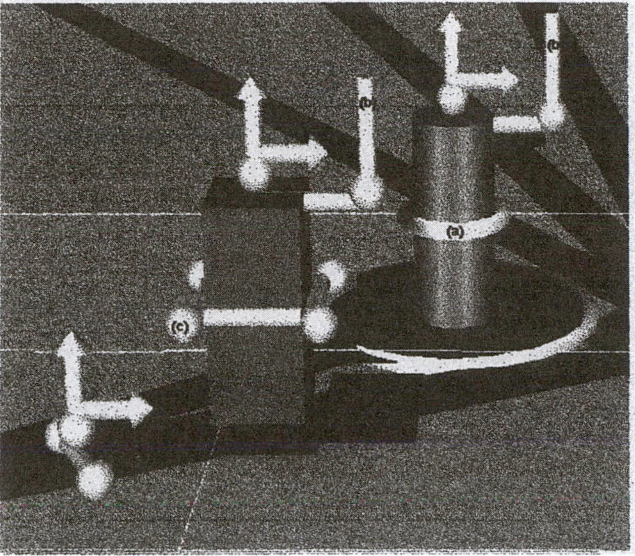

Figure 4: SDM handles

SDM operators can be applied flexibly. SDM allows users to control object parameters singly or alternatively to control multiple parameters simultaneously. The latter can be achieved by linking the object controls or by linking the parameters through formulas. This is in contrast to more constrained interactions offered by fisheye lenses [4] or stretching [15], which allow only a fixed technique for distortion.

Through handles, users may select which object parameters to change. For example, in Figure 4 part (a) controls the radius of the cylindrical object, part (b) controls the height of the object, and part (c) controls the width of the bar. The arrow handles on top of each object in Figure 4 enable users to shift the objects anywhere in the 3D space. Parameters can also be combined so that they can be manipulated through one handle.

3) Object Constraints and Feedback Techniques

SDM is an attempt at introducing a new physics of objects that supports great malleability and flexible control. In this new physics, an object may pass through other objects in the scene or have its position or appearance altered. For example, objects may be elevated (Figure 9) or translated on the floor plane (Figure 7). Objects may also have their widths (Figures 6,11, and 12) or heights (Figure 2) changed.

We believe that flexibility is key to the success of interactive techniques, but may lead users to lose context of the environment as well as misinterpret the data. Thus we have developed a small set of constraints and a suite of feedback techniques that we believe will help reduce confusion while still maintaining a high degree of flexibility.

Context persistence is one of the most important constraints in SDM. This is because many data analysis tasks require users to focus on or manipulate a select set of objects in the visualization, while still maintaining some relationship between the focus objects and the rest of the environment. For this reason we have constrained SDM operations to always maintain various degrees of context between the focus set and its environment. To this end we have also introduced feedback mechanisms that help users relate the focus set to other objects in the visualization without any confusion.

Another constraint in SDM is set-wide operations. All objects in the selected set are subject to the same forces applied to any object in the set. This is useful because it helps base SDM techniques on several real-world analogies. SDM move-shift operations are analogous to putting all objects in the selected set on a platform and then moving the platform. SDM width and height scaling operations are analogous to stretching a set of malleable objects from the top or side with the same force. All these operations maintain the relative position, width, and height of all objects in the selected set.

A defining feature of SDM is that changes are made to the objects and not to the view on the objects, as is done in [18]. Because of this, it is important to clearly indicate which objects have been altered, how they have been altered and how they can be returned to their home positions. To serve these purposes, SDM has a set of feedback mechanisms to reduce user confusion and increase system usability. These feedback mechanisms fulfill the following functions:

Clearly Identifies the Selected Set, and thus the Objects that will Change in Response to a User Action. This is done by painting the selected set differently from all other objects in the scene. In addition, a white grid may be drawn beneath all selected objects (as is shown in Figures 7 and 9) so that the approximate positions and spread of its elements can be easily identified.

Maintains Scene Context. When objects are displaced, users need to get feedback on the original object positions in order to maintain context with the rest of the environment. One way that SDM achieves this is by having multiple representations of an object. Each data object is represented by two graphical representations: the 'body' and the 'shell' graphical objects. Object shells are left behind in the home position when the object bodies are drawn out and displaced. Object shells always appear in the original object width and height. Figures 7, 9, and 13 show some examples of object sets which have been displaced and their shells, left behind at the original positions, widths and heights.

Maintains Temporal Continuity. Interactive animation is used to provide users with temporal continuity so that they can perceive, track and undo the effects of an operation on the scene. Animation helps users perceive changes to the scene without having to cognitively reassimilate relationships between the pre-action and post-action scenes [13].

This shift of cognitive load to the perceptual system allows the user to concentrate more on the results of an action rather than on the process of the action. It also provides additional feedback to the user as to which objects have changed and how they have changed relative to their previous states. Techniques such as fisheye lenses [4] do not have object continuity (interactive continuity). Focusing on one point causes a sudden magnification of that point and demagnification of other regions. Because of the abrupt change in the visualization it is easy for users to lose track of where they were before and how they got to the current state. User tests in [8] showed that insufficient temporal continuity caused poor user performance in some tasks.

Maintains the Relationships Between the Selected Set and the Environment. It is important to maintain the relationship between the selected set and other objects in the visualization so that elements within the selected set, which may have been altered, can be correctly interpreted with the rest of the environment. An example of such a feedback technique is the ratio axes technique (left of Figure 1 and 2). The ratio axes display the scale of the environment and the scale of the current selected set. By comparing the lengths of the axes, users can tell what the scale difference is between the selected set and its environment.

Allows Objects to be Easily Returned to Their Home Positions. Home mechanisms are available to return objects back to their home positions, as well as to their original width, height and color. In addition, we have implemented "object bumpers". It may be hard to manually move objects back to their home positions because such an action requires precise movement. With manual control, it is easy to accidentally overshoot the home point. For this reason, we provide object bumpers, where the initial object move indicates the direction of freedom, and from then on objects can only be moved back as far as their home positions.

APPLYING SDM TO VISUALIZATION PROBLEMS

We have discussed five useful operations in the data analysis process that are lacking in current static visualizations. Next we outline how SDM techniques can be used to fulfill those needs.

Focusing on a Select Set of Objects while Keeping Scene Context.

While navigating through an information space, it is often necessary for users to focus on certain parts of that space. However, during and after focusing, it is important for users to be able to tell where they are in the information space.

Figure 5: Painting focus objects

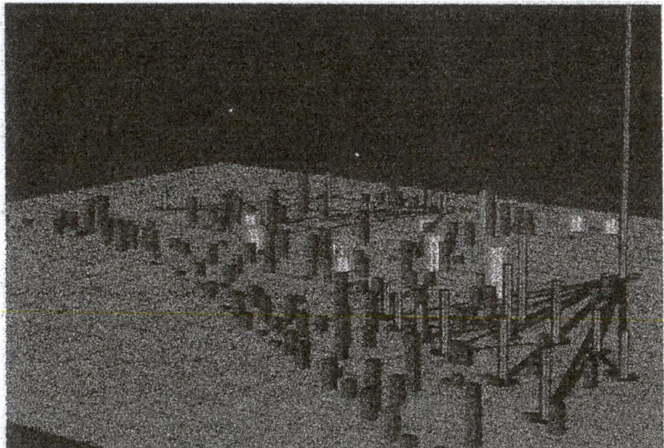

Figure 6: Expanding the selected set in place

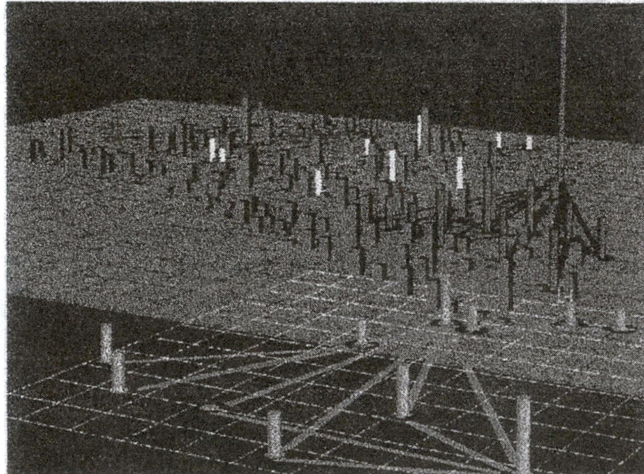

Figure 7: Pulling focus objects to the front

In SDM, focus can be achieved with several strategies. Objects may be painted so that they appear visually distinct from other elements of the environment. Objects can also be made more salient by increasing their widths. Figure 5 shows the original visualization and the selected object set (shown in green). Figure 6 shows the visualization after objects in the selected set have been expanded. Spatial context is maintained in these cases because the objects are not moved from their original positions. However, some context may be lost because expanding the selected objects may cause other objects in the scene to be occluded.

Alternatively, users may shift/move all focus objects to the front of the scene (shown in Figure 7). Context is still maintained because object shells (shown in white) are left behind. In addition, a user can move the focus set back and forth between its home position and its position at the front of the scene to achieve better scene context.

Viewing and Analyzing Occluded Objects.
Occlusion is closely related to the task of focusing while maintaining context. As was previously mentioned, expanding the selected objects may introduce occlusion, but this can be prevented by elevating the objects before expanding them.

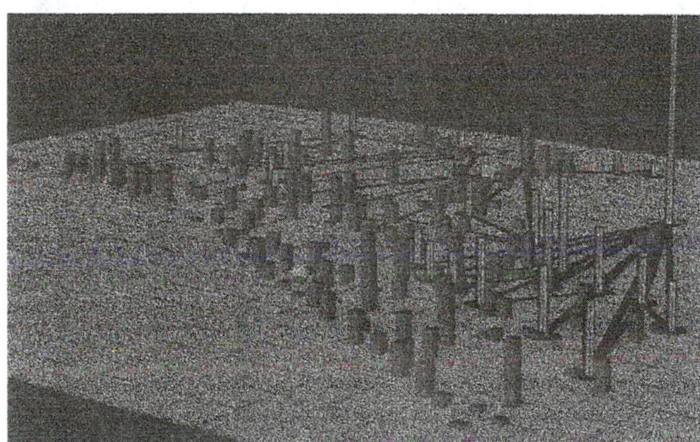

Figure 8: Initial view of occluded objects

Figure 9: Selected object set is elevated to solve occlusion problem

Figure 8 shows a dense information space with the interest objects (barely visible) shown in green. Many of the interest objects are partially if not fully occluded. After elevating the interest objects we can clearly see the pattern that they form (Figure 9). Another way to deal with occlusion is to make all objects, other than the interest set, invisible. This method, however, sacrifices scene context.

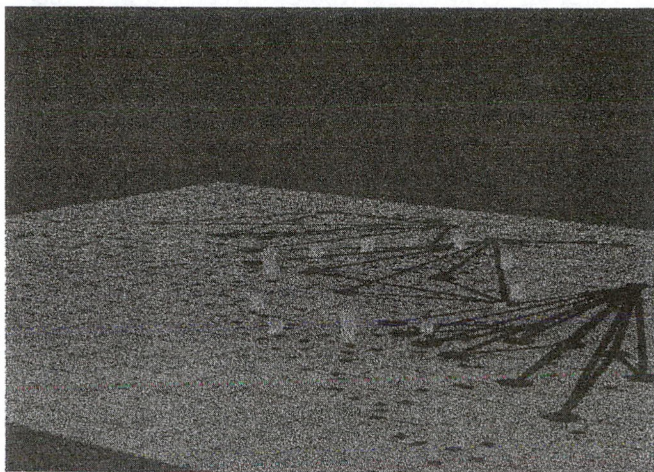

Figure 10: Objects other than the selected set are scaled to have zero height

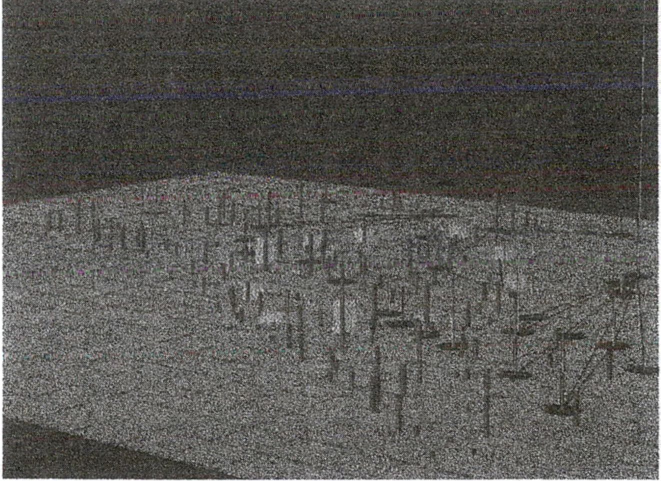

Figure 11: Objects other than the selected set are scaled to be very thin

The occlusion problem can also be solved by reducing to zero, the heights of objects that are not of interest (Figure 10). In this way, the spatial position of the other objects with respect to the interest objects is maintained. However, their height patterns are lost. Alternatively, users may make all objects, except the interest objects, very thin (Figure 11). This allows us to view the interest set clearly as well as use object heights to maintain information about the amount of supplies a center has or that a shelter needs. We are also exploring the use of transparency to deal with object occlusion.

Viewing Different Sets of Elements Based on Different Scales.

It is often the case, especially in large information spaces, that the widths and heights of objects are quite diverse. In these instances, the overall scale used may dwarf some objects, and it would be very difficult to observe width and height relationships among those dwarfed objects. This problem is worsened by the aggregation operation, which can create aggregate objects that show the total value of all its members. These objects will have much greater values associated with them compared to the other objects in the environment.

For these reasons it is important to provide ways to view different data sets at varying scales [6]. SDM allows users to do this. Suppose a user wants to compare a set of shelters (shown in Figure 1 in green) with low demand and see whether the demand distribution of those shelters are in any way related to the neighboring shelters, routes, and supply centers. To perform this task, the user can scale up the heights of the selected objects, so they can be compared more easily (Figure 2). The ratio axes on the left indicate that the selected objects are now eight times larger than the scale of the environment.

Interactively Augmenting the Visualization with New Classification Information.

It is often the case that a lot of new insights and information is revealed during data analysis. However, because this new information is not part of the underlying data, most visualization systems will not be able to visualize it until it is fully described in the database. This means that the newly discovered property will have to be fully characterized and values must be assigned for it to all elements. This is very cumbersome because it is often the case that users only have a partial characterization of the property and may only care about showing it for a subset of objects in the data set. It is therefore useful to be able to interactively classify subsets of objects in a visualization as new information is discovered about them.

Object classification is one of the main tasks in data analysis [16]. To support this task, SDM allows users to interactively change any property of an object or object set in the visualization so that they share some common properties that are not present in other objects in the environment. With this technique users can construct their own grouping/classification structure by making different subsets of objects distinguishable from each other and from objects in the environment. Note that the object sets may be changed and redefined at any time, so users are free to change the definitions of the classification structure any time throughout the data analysis process.

In Figure 12 the user has identified some important shelters. The user has chosen to increase the widths of these shelters as well as color them yellow, to differentiate them from the other shelters. The new features that have been added, width and color, only make sense to the user or group of users that are familiar with this convention. Nevertheless, this technique is useful because it offers a quick way to add information into the visualization, very much like the way we annotate printed text or paper maps.

Figure 12: Visualization augmented to show a new property, danger areas.

Comparing the Patterns, Widths, and Heights of Objects.

In the data analysis process, users frequently compare the various attributes of data objects. In a visualization, these attribute values are represented by graphical objects; thus this task reduces to comparing the different parameters of graphical objects. However, comparisons of object widths and heights are especially difficult to make in 3D visualizations. This is because it is difficult to compare the widths or heights of objects that are at different distances from the user (e.g., the green bars in Figure 3). The same problems are encountered in 2D visualizations when trying to compare the lengths of interval bars.

Figure 13: Two sets of objects made for height comparisons

SDM allows users to easily perform comparisons among objects of different depths by giving users the ability to draw a line of reference in the scene plane. Users can then move any set of objects to the reference line. By lining up objects in this way, their heights can be easily compared. Figure 3 shows the initial visualization and the selected objects (in green). Figure 13 shows the visualization after the selected objects have been pulled to the reference line. To maintain the relationship between objects and their shells, users may paint the objects which will cause their shells to also be painted. Users may also slide the objects back and forth between the reference line and their home points.

In addition to making comparisons within sets, users may also compare height trends among multiple sets. Figure 13 shows that the user has lined-up two different sets of objects. From the two lined up sets it is clear that one set (in green) has larger height variations than the other.

Another typical comparison operation is to find patterns formed by different object sets and then look for property differences among those patterns. In large data spaces, it is difficult enough to notice patterns among objects, much less compare them. This problem can be solved in SDM by separating out the subsets with the shift-move operator. The spatial shift operation maintains relative positions among elements within each subset; thus the patterns they form are preserved. The subsets may be further manipulated in their separate spaces to tease out any important differences or similarities.

In this section we have presented some techniques that can be used to aid users in exploring and analyzing large data sets. However, this set of techniques is by no means comprehensive. We envision that as users learn and get more comfortable with the system, they will start to combine the basic operations in new ways to fit their preferences in solving the task at hand.

IMPLEMENTATION

The current SDM implementation was developed in GL and C on a Silicon Graphics Indigo workstation. Figure 14 shows the general system architecture. The SDM architecture can be divided into three main sections: the data modeling section, the physicalization section and the manipulation section. We discuss each of these sections in greater detail below.

Data Modeling

The main component in the data modeling process is the *data set builder*. The data set builder takes *data objects* and groups them into data sets, based on the task being performed. A data set denotes a group of objects that will be visualized in a uniform manner, and as such can only contain homogeneous data object types (e.g., a data set of supply centers cannot also contain supply routes). However, a single data object can occur in multiple data sets. This allows, for example, a supply center to be grouped into both the "Critically Important" data set and the "Low on Supplies" data set.

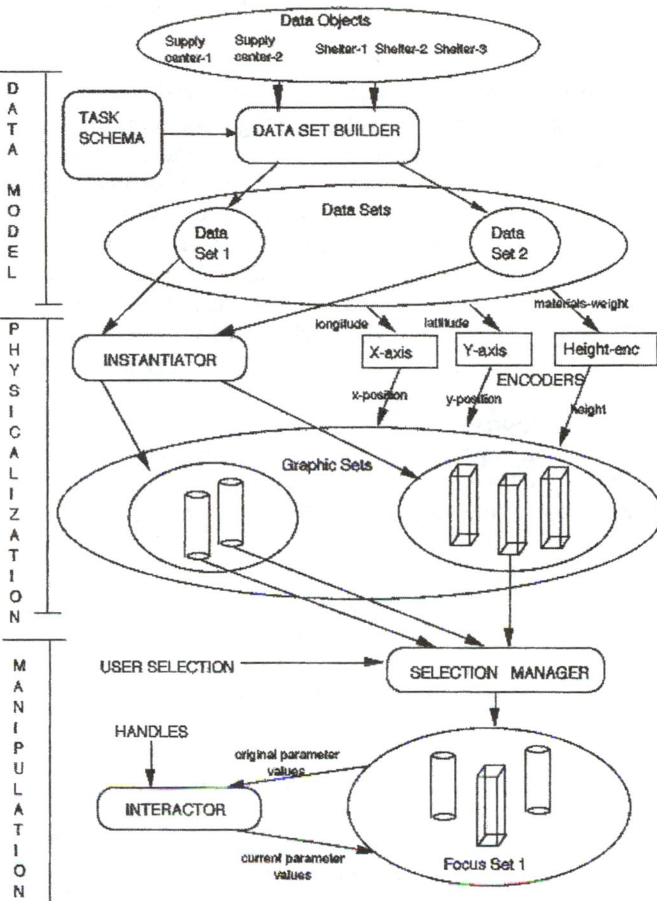

Figure 14: SDM system architecture and information flows

Physicalization

The physicalization process is based on the metaphor of creating "physical" objects in order to represent abstract data objects. The main component that performs this process is the *instantiator*, which has the responsibility of taking a selected data set and visualizing it as one or more *graphic sets*. Every object in a graphic set corresponds to a unique object in the data set that it represents.

Each object in a graphic set utilizes the same visual specifications. The specifications define the class of *graphic object* (e.g., cylinder, bar, sphere, etc.) that the graphic set will contain, along with the mapping between select attributes of the data objects and the various physical properties of the graphical objects. For example, a data set of supply centers might be visualized as a set of cylinders; where the "materials-weight" attribute is mapped to the *height* of the cylinder, and the "longitude" and "latitude" attributes are mapped to the x and y location of the cylinder.

Encoders perform the actual conversion of data-values (e.g., pounds of food) into graphical-values (e.g., height in inches). Some examples of encoders are x-axis encoders, y-axis encoders, and color-key encoders. Physical object properties that do not encode a data attribute are assigned a default value.

A single data set may be visualized as multiple independent graphic sets, in single or multiple data-graphics. Objects from the various graphic sets may encode different attributes of the data set, or may encode identical attributes of the data set multiple times. Allowing a data set to be multiply represented is useful in the case where a single graphical set is insufficient to effectively show all important attributes of the data set. It is also useful in those cases where we want to strengthen the effect of a data attribute by encoding it twice.

Manipulation

Once data objects have been "physicalized" as graphic objects, SDM gives users the ability to move and stretch the graphic objects, analogous to the manner in which users might manipulate physical models placed on a table. However, the "physics" provided by SDM is not limited to real-world manipulations; users can also elevate, compress, and perform other operations upon objects that wouldn't be possible with actual physical models. Thus, SDM exploits common physical metaphors so that users may quickly get comfortable with the system, and then extends these metaphors to take full advantage of the capabilities that real-time computer graphics provide.

There are two main components to the manipulation process: the selection manager and interactors. The *selection manager* enables users to group graphical objects into alternative focus sets. Users can group objects by selecting them with the mouse or by manipulating sliders and buttons, actions which the selection manager interprets to construct a focus set. Users can switch between focus sets in order to quickly locate objects that are relevant to the current task. Users may also save any focus set that might be relevant to a later task. This focus set will be present the next time the system is invoked.

The other major component of the manipulation is the set of *interactors*. Each focus set is associated with an interactor, which is responsible for changing the physical appearance of graphical objects in that set. Interactors are controllable through the handles that can be attached to objects in the visualization. Pushing or pulling on a handle causes the interactor to transform the values of select properties of graphical objects. Thus, encoders generate the original appearance of the graphical objects, based on the data that they represent, while interactors perform transformations on these properties to manipulate the objects as serves the user's purpose.

Values are only changed for those objects which have the properties that are being controlled. Because SDM allows for heterogeneous focus sets, it is possible that a set may contain bars, cylinders and lines. Operating on the radius property only affects the cylinders, since radius is not a property of bars or lines.

An interactor may be classified based on its two properties: cardinality and type. *Cardinality* indicates the number of properties that the interactor affects, and may be single or multiple. Single property interactors include those that change the height of an object, and those that move the x-position of an object. Multiple property interactors use constraints or evaluation functions to determine a "derived" property for an object, based on several of its basic properties. An example of a multiple property interactor is the alignment interactor, which transforms object positions in order to scale their perpendicular distance to a line on the object plane.

Type indicates the nature of the graphical transformation, and may be scale or shift. Shift interactors add constants to object properties. They are usually applied to graphical properties that are not relevant to the user's immediate task in order to make other properties more noticeable. An exception to this is position, since shifting objects to the front can make their relative positions more apparent. Scale interactors, on the other hand, proportionately transform property values so that they maintain their ratios relative to each other. They are typically used to enhance differences among the data values that are encoded.

PREVIOUS WORK

Previously, we discussed how SDM deals with the five limitations of current static visualizations. In this section we discuss how other interactive systems deal with these limitations. In doing this we highlight some of the major differences and the advantages and disadvantages of SDM compared to other systems.

Focusing on a Select Set of Objects while Keeping Scene Context.

Focus areas can be made larger in two ways: *object* magnification and *spatial* magnification. SDM uses object magnification, which only acts on the objects and not on the space between objects.

Magnification in other interactive techniques [3,4,15,18] is spatial because expanding the selected set causes the entire selected space to expand and not just the objects within it. Thus, the objects move out of their original positions and farther away from each other as their size increases. In [8], subjects found the change in distances between objects to be disorienting and jarring. In addition, because the between-object spaces have expanded, either some other space has contracted (as in [4] and [15]), or some objects are now occluded by the newly expanded region (as in a magnification magic lens [18]). Another disadvantage of spatial magnification is that is works well on tasks that are strongly based on object spatial position but fail when users want to focus on multiple object sets based on non-spatial properties.

Like some spatial magnification techniques, object magnification also faces the problem of occlusion. In object magnification many of the newly expanded objects may occlude or collide with other objects. This problem can be solved in SDM by elevating the expanded objects.

In contrast to spatial magnification, however, object magnification works for both spatially and non-spatially based tasks. For spatially based tasks users can simply collect all the data points in the desired space (either through their longitude and latitude or by selecting them from the visualization) and form a data set. Operating on that data set would effectively produce the effect of operating on the area that contains the data points. One disadvantage of object magnification, however, is that users cannot operate on parts of objects. For example, enlarging a particular road would mean that the whole road has to be enlarged and not just part of it. To solve this problem we are currently exploring techniques that combine spatial and object metaphors.

Some interactive techniques do not use magnification for focusing. Instead, they allow users to focus on certain data points (objects) by giving users the ability to change the appearance of object groups in real-time. Objects that are not in focus are either temporarily invisible [1] or uncolored [11] (i.e., they have a different appearance than the objects that are in focus). Users may easily regain context by making the invisible points reappear [1] or from the uncolored points [11].

Another important issue of focusing in context is the scope of the operation. Techniques such as fisheye lenses [4] and stretching [15] have unlimited scope because changes to the selected set causes changes to occur throughout the visualization. SDM and other techniques such as magic lenses [18] have limited scope in that operations affect only the selected space(s). Unlimited scope may be disconcerting to the user because a local action may affect objects in the entire visualization. A disadvantage of limited scope is that it may cause certain objects/regions to be occluded by the focus objects/regions.

Viewing and Analyzing Occluded Objects.
In dense information spaces, object occlusion is a major problem. Dynamic query sliders [1] solve this problem by providing users with the ability to flexibly change the visibility of objects. Other techniques deal with occlusion by only partially displaying the objects. For example in [2], when the telephone links are too dense, only sections of the links are shown to reduce occlusion. A problem with the approach in [2] is that the technique is limited to the length of the lines. In SDM, we propose more general techniques that apply to multiple object types.

Viewing Different Sets of Elements Based on Different Scales.
Under the stretching paradigm [15], this problem may be solved by pulling on the region surrounding each of the small objects in order to extend their heights. Care must be taken that the force applied to all objects is equal so that the object heights can be fairly compared. To solve this problem using fisheye lenses would be just as awkward because all dimensions of the objects would be magnified, not just its heights.

Another way to analyze objects that have widely differing widths and heights is to change the width and/or height scales to a logarithmic scale. In this way, width/height order is maintained. However, the linear relationships between the objects are lost. Therefore, it would be hard to compare the heights of two or more bars and determine approximately how much wider or taller one is than another.

Interactively Augmenting the Visualization with New Classification Information.
Painting is a way to classify object sets by using color. SDM allows users to classify objects not only by changing their color but also by changing any other parameter. In addition, current classification methods only have temporary effects, whereas SDM allows users to save objects sets to disk and restore them in future sessions.

Comparing the Patterns, Widths and Heights of Objects.
The calendar visualizer [10] solves the problem of width and height comparisons by using lighting to cast shadows on the back and side planes of the visualization (i.e., projecting an orthogonal image/shadow of the scene onto a flat plane). The main problem with this method is difficulty in identifying an object and its corresponding shadow. In addition, if the information space is dense, there will be too much overlap between shadows of the focus set and shadows of objects that are not relevant.

In general, the approach taken by SDM is different from other approaches because SDM provides a flexible set of methods that allow users to manipulate their information space in many different ways. Many other interactive techniques only allow users to distort the information space based on a fixed method. Fisheye lenses [4] and stretching [15] allow users to increase the area of the focus region by reducing the area of surrounding regions. Painting [11] allow users to focus on the selected set by changing its color.

An exception to this is the magic lens technique [18], which allows many different distortions depending on the lens that is being used. Like SDM, that research defines a unifying paradigm, derives a tool set from it, and provides composition of multiple operations. SDM operations, however, are designed to enable users to directly manipulate object appearance as they would in a draw program. Lenses, on the other hand, provide metaphors for viewing regions containing objects in different perspectives and can be general-purpose (e.g., to distinguish occluded objects) or application-specific (e.g., to view semantically related properties of objects). Unlike SDM, lenses do not address parameter manipulation per se.

CONCLUSION AND FUTURE WORK

We have presented a suite of techniques based on the SDM paradigm. These techniques enable users to:

- View selected objects in detail while keeping them in context with the rest of the environment.
- View occluded objects by elevating them or by reducing the widths and heights of surrounding objects.
- View different object sets in different scales.
- Add new information to the visualization that is not part of the underlying data.
- Compare the widths and heights of objects even when they are positioned far from each other.

Many current interactive techniques tend to examine and present solutions to isolated problems. The goal of SDM is to provide users with enough tools and flexibility that they can solve a wide spectrum of data analysis tasks. The flexibility provided also presents users with multiple alternative solutions for any given task. Although the examples presented in this paper use rectangular objects and cylinders, the same techniques apply just as well to other graphical objects.

In the future, we plan to integrate current SDM operations with other aggregation and interactive data manipulation interface techniques [5, 14]. We also intend to explore the possibility of using SDM to perform "what if" analyses, where changes to objects in the visualization actually propagate to the data objects that they represent.

ACKNOWLEDGMENTS

Funding for this project was provided by the Advanced Projects Agency (DAAA1593K0005) and the Army Research Laboratory.

REFERENCES

1. Ahlberg, C., Williamson, C., and Shneiderman, B. Dynamic queries for information exploration: An implementation and evaluation. *Proceedings CHI '92 Human Factors in Computing Systems,* ACM, May 1992, pp. 619-626.
2. Becker, R.A., Eicks S.G., and Wilks, A.R. Visualizing network data. *IEEE Transactions on Visualization and Graphics,* March 1995, pp. 619-626.
3. Bederson, B.B., and Hollan, J.D. PAD++: A zooming graphical interface for exploring alternate interface physics. *UIST '94*, November 1994, pp. 17-27.
4. Furnas, G.W. Generalized fisheye views. *Proceedings CHI '91 Human Factors in Computing Systems,* ACM, April 1991, pp. 16-23.
5. Goldstein, J., Roth, S.F., Kolojejchick, J., and Mattis, J. A Framework for knowledge-based interactive data exploration. *Journal of Visual Languages and Computing*, No. 5, 1994, pp. 339-363.
6. Herndon, K.P., van Dam, A., and Gleicher, M. Workshop report: The challenges of 3D interaction. *CHI '94 Human Factors in Computing Systems,* ACM, May 1994, pp. 469.
7. Herndon, K.P., and Meyer, T. 3D widgets for exploratory scientific visualization. *UIST '94*, November 1994, pp. 69-70.
8. Hollands, J.G., Carey, T.T., Matthews, M.L., and McCann, C.A. Presenting a graphical network: A comparison of performance using fisheye and scrolling views. *Designing and Using Human-Computer Interfaces and Knowledge Based Systems,* Elsevier Science B.V., Amsterdam, 1989, pp. 313-320.
9. Lamping, J., Rao, R., and Pirolli, P. A focus+context technique based on hyperbolic geometry for visualizing large hierarchies. *Proceedings CHI '95 Human Factors in Computing Systems,* ACM, May 1995, pp. 401-408.
10. Mackinlay, J.D., Robertson G.G., and DeLine, R. Developing calendar visualizers for the information visualizer. *UIST '94*, November 1994, pp. 109-119.
11. McDonald, J.A. Painting multiple views of complex objects. *ECOOP/OOPSLA '90 Proceedings*, October 1990, pp. 245-257.
12. Robertson, G.G., and Mackinlay J.D. The document lens. *UIST '93,* November 1993, pp. 101-108.
13. Robertson, G.G., Mackinlay, J.D., and Card, S.K. Cone trees: Animated 3D visualizations of hierarchical information. *Proceedings CHI '91 Human Factors in Computing Systems,* ACM, April 1991, pp. 173-179.
14. Roth, S.F. The SAGE Project. http://www.cs.cmu.edu/Web/Groups/sage/sage.html
15. Sarkar, M., Snibbe, S.S. Stretching the rubber sheet: A metaphor for viewing large layouts on small screens. *UIST '93,* November 1993, pp. 81-91.
16. Springmeyer, R.R., Blattner, M.M., and Max, N. L. A characterization of the scientific data analysis process. *Visualization '92*, October 1992, pp. 235-242.
17. Stevens, M.P., Zeleznik, R.C., and Hughs, J.F. An architecture for an extensible 3D interface toolkit. *UIST '94*, November 1994, pp. 59-67.
18. Stone, M.C., Fishkin, K., and Bier, E.A. The movable filter as a user interface tool. *Proceedings CHI '94 Human Factors in Computing Systems,* ACM, April 1994, pp. 306-312.

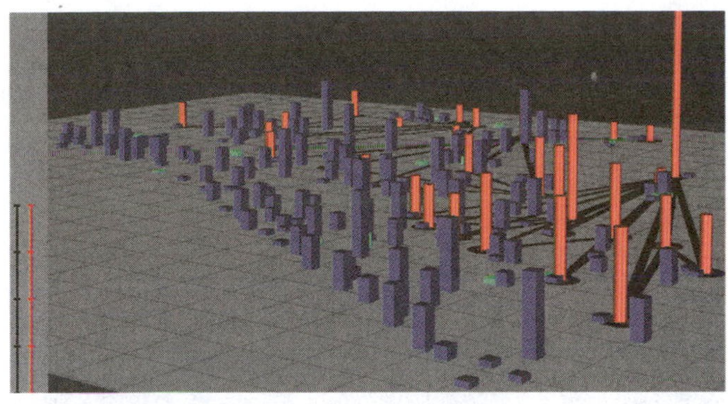

FIGURE **1**

Data visualization of a relief effort data set. Light gray bars are the currently selected objects.

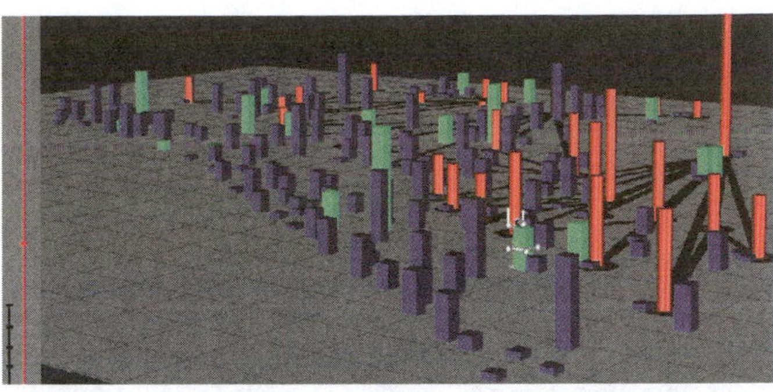

FIGURE **2**

Visualization showing the same data set as Figure 1, except the heights of the light gray bars are scaled differently from the rest of the environment.

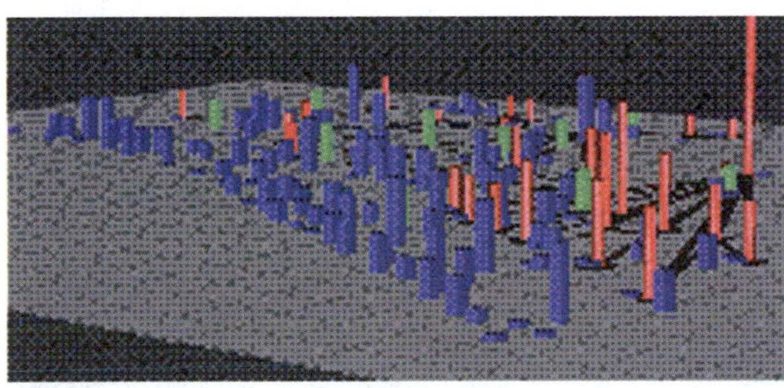

FIGURE **3**

Selected objects that are at different distances from the user.

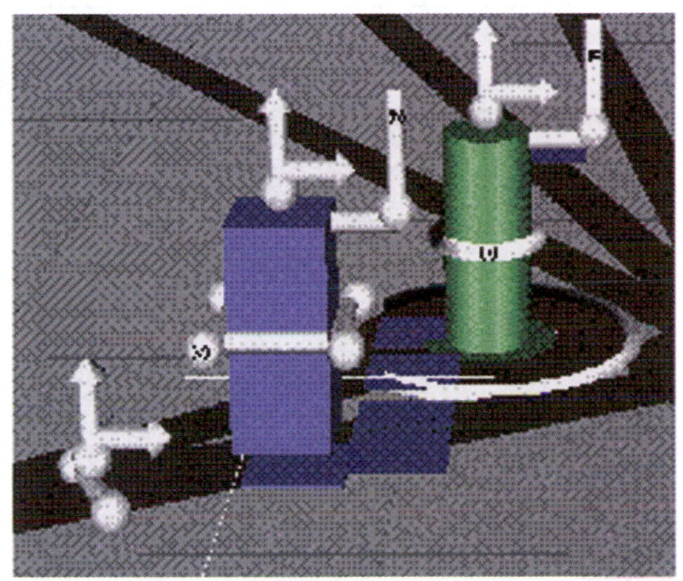

FIGURE **4**

SDM handles.

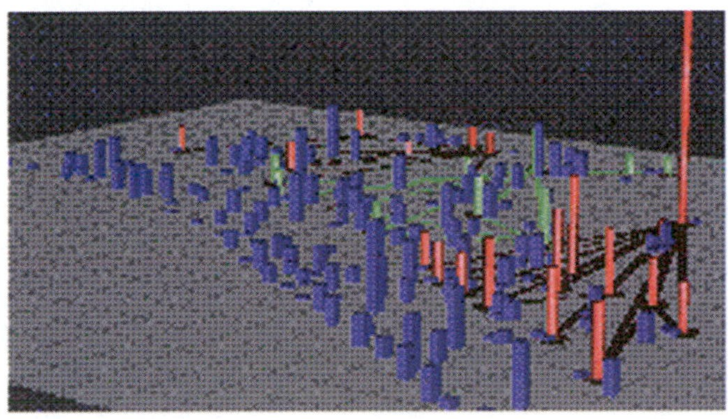

FIGURE **5**

Painting focus objects.

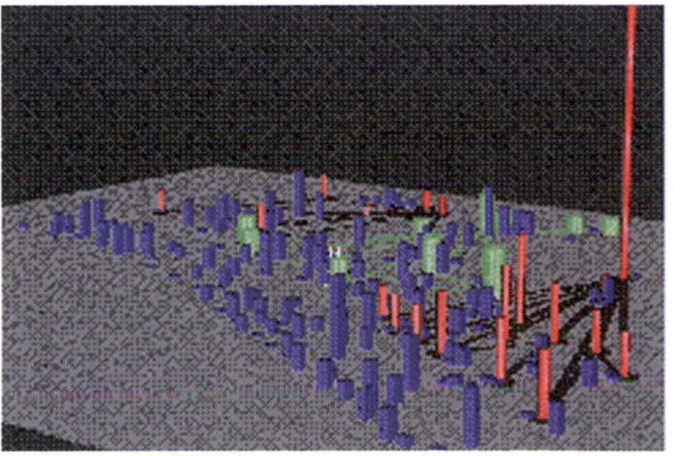

FIGURE **6**

Expanding the selected set in place.

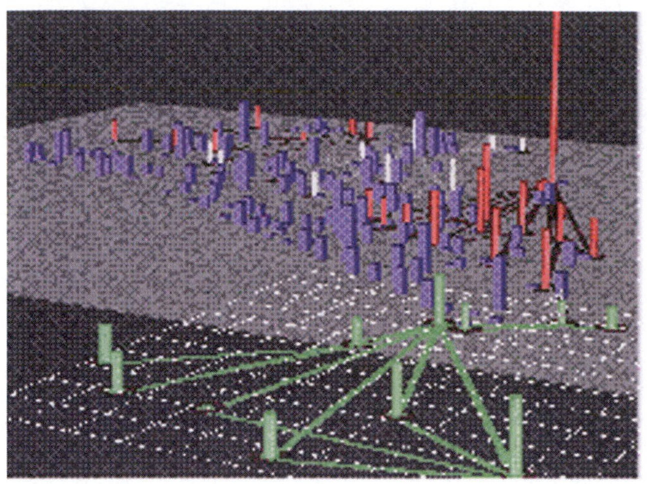

FIGURE **7**

Pulling focus objects to the front.

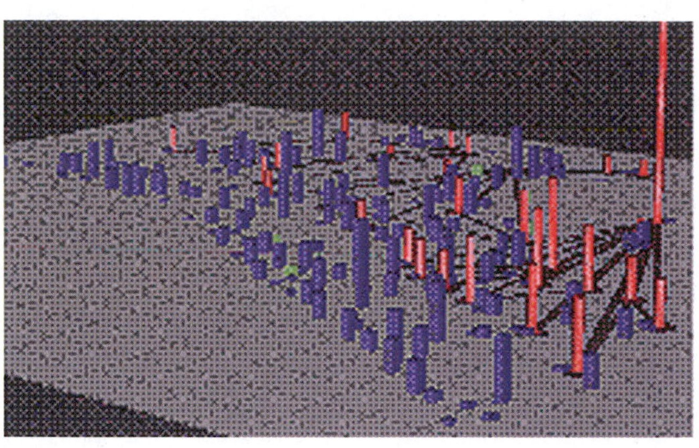

FIGURE **8**

Initial view of occluded objects.

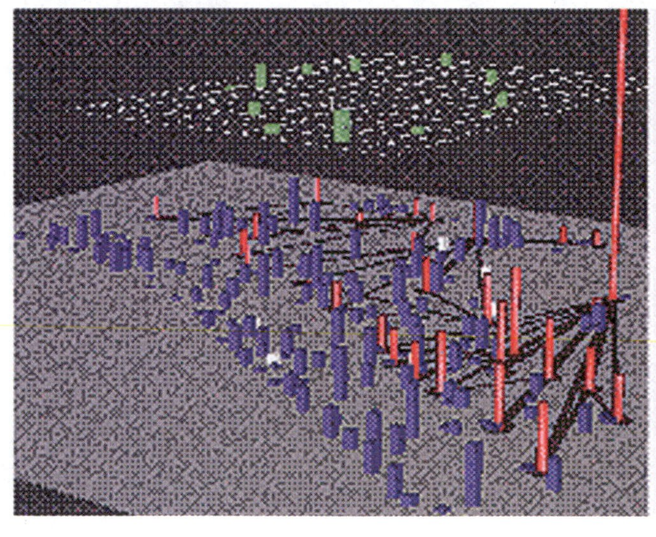

FIGURE **9**

Selected object set is elevated to solve occlusion problem.

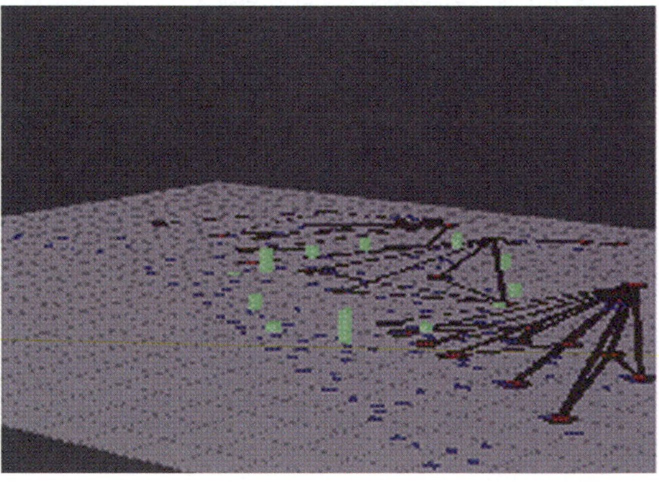

FIGURE **10**

Objects other than the selected set are scaled to have zero height.

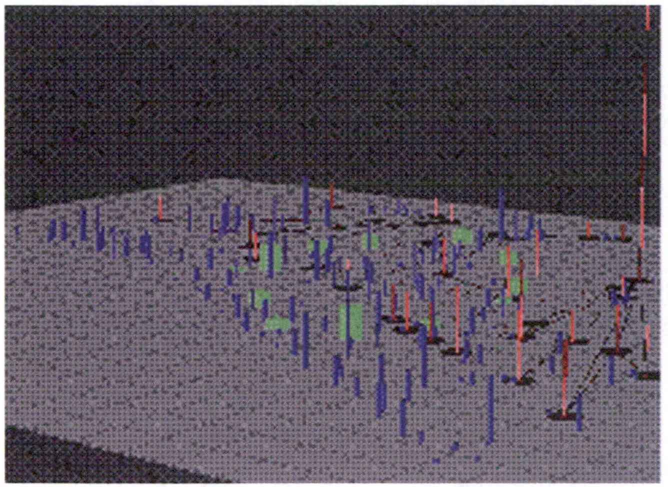

FIGURE **11**

Objects other than the selected set are scaled to be very thin.

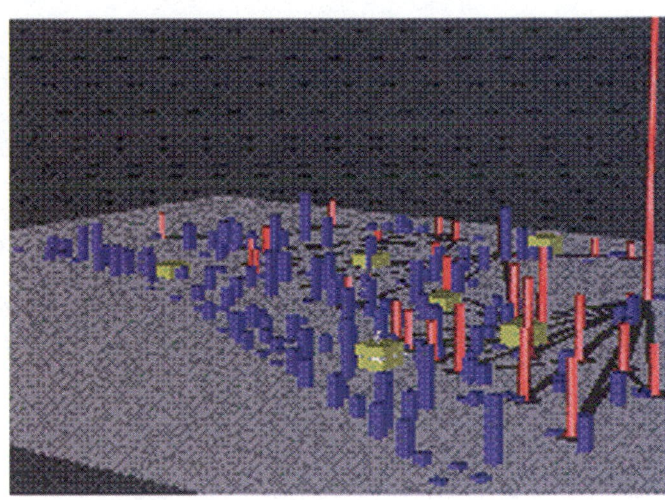

FIGURE **12**

Visualization augmented to show a new property, danger areas.

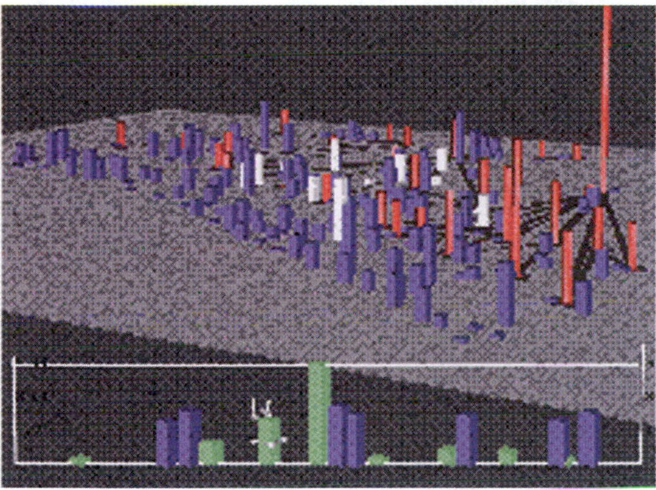

FIGURE **13**

Two sets of objects made for height comparisons.

Externalising Abstract Mathematical Models

Lisa Tweedie, Robert Spence, Huw Dawkes and Hua Su

Department of Electrical Engineering,
Imperial College of Science, Technology and Medicine
South Kensington , London, SW7 2BT
Tel: +44 171 594 6261
l.tweedie@ic.ac.uk

ABSTRACT

Abstract mathematical models play an important part in engineering design, economic decision making and other activities. Such models can be externalised in the form of Interactive Visualisation Artifacts (IVAs). These IVAs display the data generated by mathematical models in simple graphs which are interactively linked. Visual examination of these graphs enables users to acquire insight into the complex relations embodied in the model. In the engineering context this insight can be exploited to aid design. The paper describes two IVAs for engineering design: The Influence Explorer and The Prosection Matrix. Formative evaluation studies are briefly discussed.

KEYWORDS: Interactive Graphics, Visualization

INTRODUCTION

Many mathematical problems can benefit from being examined visually. Indeed most spreadsheets and statistical packages enable users to quickly create static representations of their data. These graphs have an accepted role as tools for mathematical problem solving. However the value of adding interactivity to such representations has yet to gain widespread recognition.

Responsive (i.e. rapid) interaction can facilitate active exploration of problems in a manner that is inconceivable with static displays. For example users can start to pose "What if" queries spontaneously as they work through a task. Such exploration can enormously facilitate the acquisition of qualitative insight into the nature of the task at hand, as well as revealing direct quantitative results.

In this paper we describe what we call Interactive Visualisation Artifacts (IVAs). These are environments developed to enable users to solve a particular task - in this case within the field of engineering design.

The IVAs we will discuss here differ from much existing work principally because we are not attempting to visualise raw data but, rather, data which is precalculated or generated on demand from mathematical models. We also exclude data which maps comfortably onto natural representations e.g. 3D volumetric models of flow through a pipe. Instead we focus on more *abstract* mathematical models which have no obvious representation.

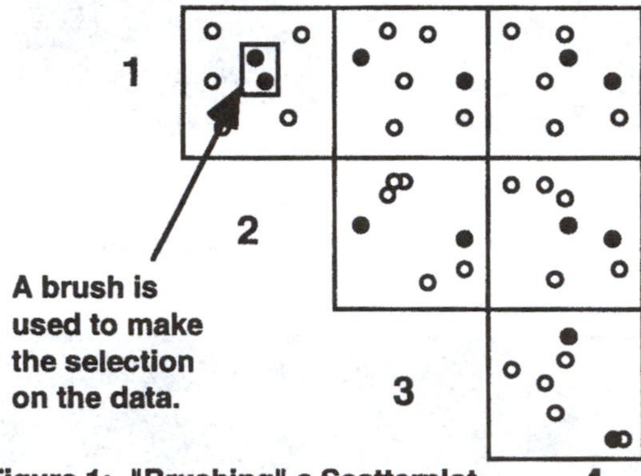
1
2
3
4
A brush is used to make the selection on the data.

Figure 1: "Brushing" a Scatterplot

We can take as an example the design of an engineering artifact. Mathematical models (equations) exist which relate the artifact's performance to the parameters that describe the physical nature of that artifact. Thus, for a bridge, performances such as traffic capacity and cost can be calculated from a knowledge of parameters such as cable diameters and foundation depth. A designer needs to explore the relationships between parameters and performances in order to elicit a useful design.

The development of IVAs for such applications requires the creation of new representations that externalise pertinent aspects of the model. The IVAs we describe in this paper show how such novel representations can be created by **interactively linking simple graphs in several ways**. On a simple level we can link many similar graphs, as Becker et al [3] did with their "brushed" scatterplots (Figure 1). We can also link different *types* of representations together. For example, by selecting a subset of data on a histogram and colour encoding the same subset on a scatterplot. These links can also perform different functions - for example the selected subset could be colour encoded or it could be hidden from view.

Two IVAs for engineering design are described in this paper: the Influence Explorer and the Prosection Matrix. They exhibit powerful and effective linking both within and between IVAs.

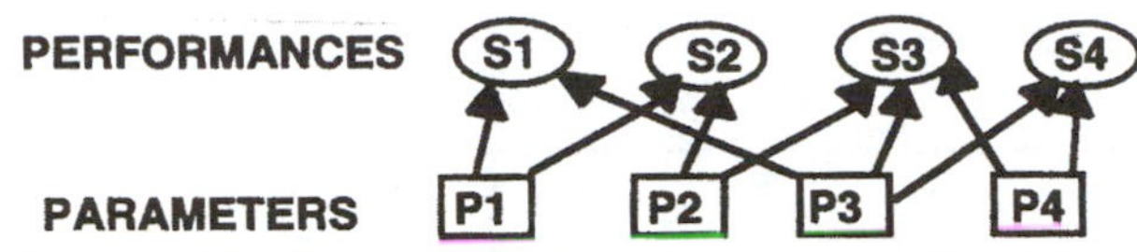

Figure 2: The Parameter->Performance relationship

Previous Work

The idea of linking graphical representations is not new. As early as 1978 Newton [12] was linking several scatterplots and colour encoding selections to discover trends in data. Many others have developed simple linking IVAs e.g. IVEE [1], Permutation Matrices [4], BEAD [5], SeeSoft ™[6], AutoVisual [7], VisDB [10], Nested Histograms [13], The Table Lens [14], Visulab [15], The InfoCrystal [17], The Attribute Explorer [18] and The Dynamic HouseFinder [20].

Most of these IVAs only use one type of representation to display data. However a combination of representations may also be beneficial, since the user is then able to consider the problem from several different perspectives. Schmid and Hinterberger [15] have called this "Comparative Multivariate Visualisation" and embodied the concept in their "Visulab" software. Here four different representations (Parallel Coordinates [9], Andrews Plots [2], Permutation Matrices [4] and Multiple Scatterplots [3]) can be linked in several ways : encoding with colour, hiding part of the data and reordering the data. The use of several different representations of data, and the manner of their linking, is a key issue in the development of IVAs.

Visual Design Issues

The design of any IVA should proceed with various characteristics of visual problem solving in mind (Tweedie [19]). As Nardi and Zarmer [11] point out, IVAs are external representations of the users problem which "*stimulate and initiate cognitive activity*". Zhang and Norman [21] identify that such external representations act as memory aids; provide information perceptually without need for interpretation; anchor and structure cognitive behaviour; and change the task.

Suchman [18] emphasises that "*it is frequently only on acting in a present situation that its possibilities become clear*". In other words users will often pick up information opportunistically from their environment. It is partly this tendency to stimulate opportunistic behaviour that makes IVAs interesting. Consequently, the visual cues provided must be designed to support this opportunistic process.

DESIGN FOR MANUFACTURABILITY

A typical task that has a mathematical model associated with it is that of engineering design. For a given product such as a light bulb, a model can be formed of the way the parameters (whose value is open to choice by the designer) influence performances (Figure 2). In the light bulb example, performances such as a bulb's brightness and its lifetime will partly be determined by parameters such as the number of coils in its filament and the thickness of that filament. The mathematical model is a set of equations, each relating a performance to a number of parameters.

The designer must choose numerical values for parameters in such a way that the performances they influence, usually in a very complex fashion, take on values acceptable to a customer. In other words, when designing a light bulb, the designer has to keep a specification in mind. If for example they are asked to design a light bulb that will be very bright and last for at least 6 months then they need to find the set of parameters values that will satisfy this specification.

The traditional design process

Given a set of parameters, an engineering artifact can be simulated to establish the corresponding performances. Unfortunately the reverse is not true: a designer cannot choose a performance value and calculate the parameters needed to achieve it. For this reason traditional design is characterised by a series of iterations in which the designer selects a set of parameters and then simulates the artifact to find out what the performances are. Design proceeds through the gradual adjustment of parameters until a satisfactory set of performance values is found. This design process is illustrated in figure 3a for an artifact defined by two parameters and influencing two performances. The design is represented by a single point moving in parameter and performance space. This "trial and error" approach can be tedious and time-consuming and is heavily dependent on a designer's expertise.

Precalculation

The design process can be immensely simplified if one has mathematical models of the relationship between parameters and performances. Figure 3b shows how such models can be used to create a precalculated exploration database. The designer selects a wide "Region of Exploration" in parameter space within which the final design might well be expected to lie. Within this region a large number of points (e.g. over 500) are generated randomly, each point representing a design. For each of these sets of parameter values the corresponding point in performance space is computed using the artifact's mathematical model. In our light bulb example, a dataset generated in this way would describe a variety of light bulbs each having randomly different parameter values and associated performances. The benefit of creating such a dataset is also illustrated in figure 3b. The designer can now readily select their desired performance values and "look up" which parameter sets give them those values.

Designing in the real world

Unfortunately the aim of engineering design is not simply that of finding a single set of parameter values that satisfies

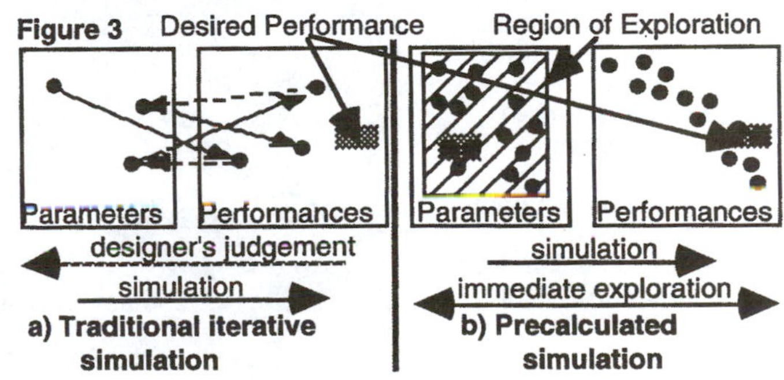

a specification. Inevitable fluctuations in manufacturing processes mean that parameter values can only be guaranteed to lie within a so-called tolerance *range*. For example the filament width of our light bulb might vary slightly during manufacture, and this variation could have a crucial effect on a performance. We therefore need to define exactly how much each parameter can vary. The combined set of parameter tolerance ranges defines a *tolerance region* in parameter space. These are the bulbs that will be manufactured.

Figure 4 shows the rectangular tolerance region for the simple case of two parameters. In the same space, an irregularly shaped "Region of Acceptability" defines the location of all the artifacts that satisfy the performance requirements. Achieving a good design is a matter of fitting these two regions to each other with maximum overlap

S2 - Lower Limit
S2 - Upper Limit
S1 Upper Limit
S1 Lower Limit
Parameter 2
Parameter 1
Tolerance Region (Manufactured Bulbs)

= Region of Acceptability
= Useful bulbs - overlap of the Tolerance Region and Region of Acceptability

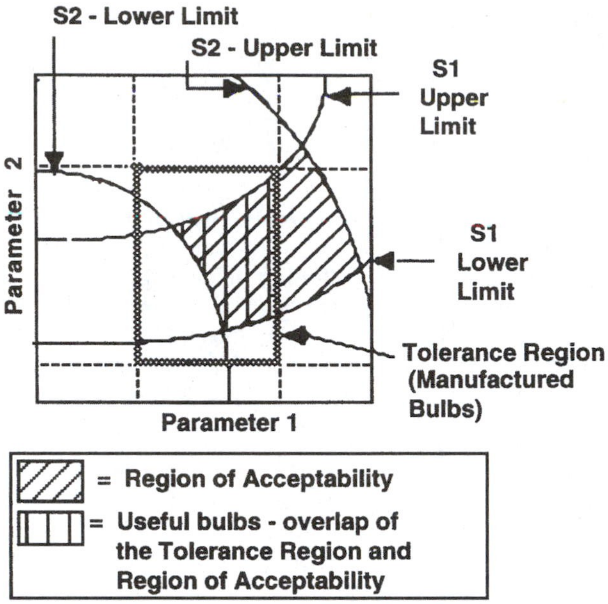

Figure 4: In 2-parameter space, two performances F1 and F2 define upper and lower limits for acceptable performance. Manufactured bulbs lie within the tolerance region.

Overall Design Objectives

As well as satisfying the customer's requirements on performance, it is usually the case that there is also some overall objective that must be achieved. One such objective is that of maximising the manufacturing yield, which is the percentage of mass-produced bulbs that satisfy the customer's requirements on performance. With reference to Figure 4, yield is that percentage of the tolerance region which lies within the region of acceptability.

Another such design objective might be the unit manufacturing cost of each bulb that is shipped to the customer. Usually the wider the tolerances are on the parameters the cheaper the bulb will be to manufacture.

THE INFLUENCE EXPLORER

Precalculation forms the backbone of the Influence Explorer. Once the data has been precalculated (as described earlier), it provides an exploration database on which to start an investigation. Figure 5 shows how the population of 600 precalculated designs is displayed in the form of histograms. All performance histograms are plotted horizontally to the left of the screen and the parameter histograms vertically to the right. An artifact is represented once on each plot in the appropriate bin. Each column in the histogram represents the number of designs that fall within that bin. In other words, the histograms are frequency plots.

Qualitative Exploration

In order to form an effective external representation of the task the Influence Explorer must allow the user to gradually build up a coherent picture of their problem, in other words the complexity must be introduced in stages.

In the initial stages of design the user will want to gain a *qualitative* understanding of the problem. The designer can place exploratory limits on parameters and performances, thereby defining ranges of those quantities. In Figure 5 a range of performance on S4 has been defined with a slider. This action leads to the colour linking (black) of those bulbs that lie within the selected range on the S4 histogram and all the other histograms, so that the selected subset can be viewed across all the histograms. The potential for exploring the inter-relation between parameters and performances is now apparent. Confidence in these perceived relations can be sought by interactively moving the selected range of S4 up and down its scale and observing the corresponding movement of the highlighted bulbs on the other scales. The power of such a dynamic action to generate insight is difficult to convey in static words and diagrams, but is *strikingly* obvious in actual use.

It is worth emphasising that the discovery of a "trade-off" relation between two performances is immensely important

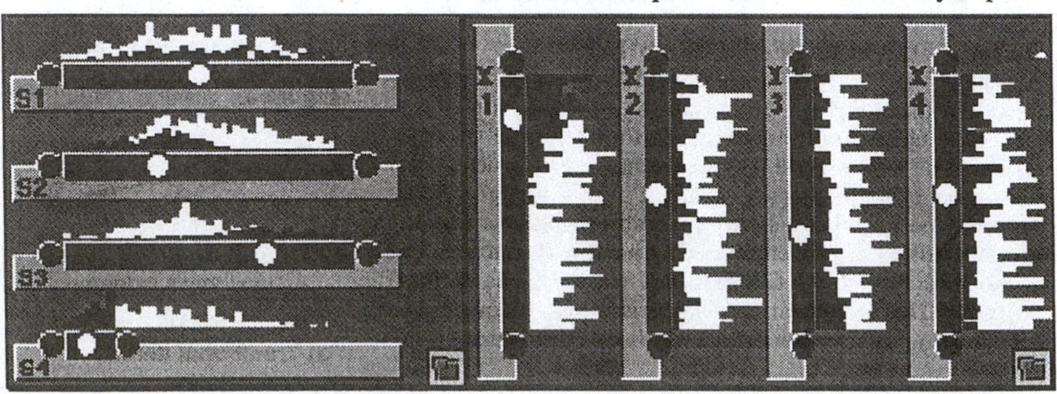

Figure 5: The performance (left) and parameter (right) histograms. A selection has been made on S4 and these same points are highlighted on each of the other histograms. Circles indicate the mean of the selected points.

in engineering design. In the Influence Explorer this discovery is virtually immediate, whereas in conventional design practice such a trade-off might be discovered only after tedious search or, at worst, not at all.

Additional tools enhance the functionality of the Influence Explorer. A mouse-click on a bulb in one histogram highlights that same bulb, and displays corresponding values, in all the other histograms. Another option connects these points with a line and allows the comparison of several different bulbs. These lines are known as "parallel coordinate" plots [9]. Yet another option places a circle on each of the histogram scales indicating the mean of the currently selected bulbs (see figure 5). This is useful when a range is being moved as it eases detection of trends.

Quantitative Design decisions

As well as indulging in *qualitative* exploration, the designer must at some stage take note of the *quantitative* detail associated with a customer's requirements on performance. To do so a "specification option" is selected (Figure 6 - colour plate).

The placement of upper and lower limits on the performance scales invokes another linking mechanism. Red colour coding identifies bulbs that lie within all the performance limits, those bulbs which fail one limit are colour coded black, while dark and light grey denotes two and three failed limits respectively. Such colour coding provides valuable sensitivity information. For example, it is immediately noticed (Figure 6 - colour plate) that a relaxation of the upper limit on S4 would turn some black bulbs into (acceptable) red bulbs, knowledge which might well lead to a discussion about the wisdom of that particular upper limit. Negotiations concerning performance specifications are common to engineering and could be considerably clarified using this information.

Design for Manufacture

As already explained, inevitable variations in the manufacturing process are such that, in the design of a *mass-produced* artifact such as a light bulb, the designer must be concerned with the selection of parameter *ranges* rather than specific values. It is the combination of all these selected parameter ranges that must satisfy the performance limits defined by the customer.

Parameter ranges are defined by the selection of upper and lower limits (Figure 7 - colour plate), in exactly the same manner as for the performances. Again, the selection of parameter limits invokes a linking mechanism, once more leading to additional colour encoding. Though at first sight complex, the coding is, we suggest, matched to an engineering designer's real needs and, given the motivation provided by a tool offering responsive exploration, is readily, even eagerly learned. Figure 8 (colour plate) is a replica of Figure 4 with the relevant colour codings shown. Figure 8 and the table attached to figure 7 may help clarify the rationale behind this coding:

- **Red** denotes bulbs that satisfy all limits. They lie within parameter limits (and are therefore manufactured) and they satisfy the customer's performance limits.
- **Black** denotes a bulb that satisfies all the performance limits but lies outside one parameter limit , and is therefore not manufactured. Thus it will turn red if one parameter limit is adjusted to include it.
- **Blue** bulbs are those which are manufactured (and hence lie within parameter limits) but fail one or more performances. These are the bulbs which cause a reduction in yield. Tightening a parameter limit to eliminate blue bulbs (for example raising the lower limit of X1 in Figure 7) will reduce the number of manufactured artifacts which violate a customer's requirements, hence raising the yield. The Blue bulbs are coded in two shades of blue - **Dark Blue** indicates those bulbs that are manufactured and only violate one performance limit; relaxation of that performance limit will turn those bulbs into red ones (e.g. in figure 7 expanding the lower limit on S1 will turn the dark blue bulbs red). **Light Blue** indicates those bulbs which are manufactured and violate more than one performance limit.
- **Grey** bulbs are those which fail one parameter range and one or more performance limits. They would therefore turn blue if they were to be enclosed within the tolerance region. Thus in Figure 7 if the upper limit on X2 is extended to turn the black bulbs into red ones, this gain in the number of (red) acceptable bulbs would be offset by the number of grey bulbs turning blue and, thereby, adding unsatisfactory bulbs to the manufacturing process.

The principal advantage of such colour coding is that it indicates how *altering* the parameter or performance limits will effect the overall usefulness of the design.

Yield Enhancement

To facilitate design for maximum yield the Influence Explorer continuously computes, and displays in numerical form, the value of the yield. The designer may well begin by attempting to select parameter ranges that maximise the yield, hopefully to a value of 100%. In order to achieve such a high yield the user needs to adjust the tolerances taking account of where the red and therefore "useful" points lie and trying to reduce the number of blue points. By keeping an eye on the yield the user can slowly optimise their solution until they have found an optimum yield.

100% yield can obviously be achieved by making the parameter ranges sufficiently small (Figure 14 - colour plate), but another overall objective - the minimisation of manufacturing cost - militates against such a solution. It is normally the case that the wider the parameter ranges, the lower the cost of the artifact. There is therefore a strong incentive to select parameter ranges that are as wide as possible commensurate with an acceptably high yield (see Figure 15 - colour plate).

Focused Sampling

Unfortunately when interacting with tolerances limits the precalculated data set becomes a constraining factor in the Influence Explorer. Since the requirements are now becoming specific, it is unlikely that many of the original 600 points will fall within *all* the performance and parameter requirements. This curse of dimensionality results in very few colour coded points. To overcome this problem the Influence Explorer is programmed to

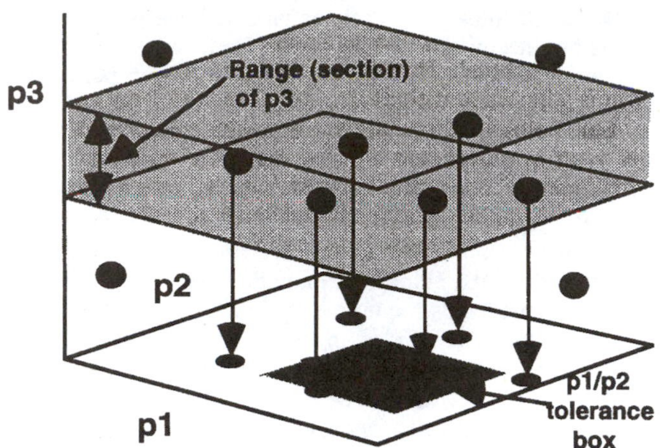

Figure 9: A section of p3 is projected onto a p1/p2 scatterplot

dynamically resample the model so that a number of points always fall within and close to the tolerance region. Evidence of this process can be seen in Figure 7 where the column heights within the tolerance limits are higher than column heights on the rest of each parameter histogram.

THE PROSECTION MATRIX

The Prosection Matrix provides an alternative perspective of the model. It is a set of scatterplots (Figure 10) arranged in a matrix, as suggested by Becker et al [3]. Each scatterplot corresponds to a different pair of parameters, and all possible parameter pairs are represented. Thus, for the bulb's four parameters there are six scatterplots.

The construction of each scatterplot is illustrated conceptually in Figure 9 for the simple case of a 3-parameter system. p1 and p2 are the scatterplot's two parameters. p3 is a third parameter on which a parameter range has been set. Only data that falls within p3's chosen parameter range is projected down onto the p1p2 plane. This is a **projection** of a **section** of parameter space, hence the name 'Prosection' (the term came from by a paper by Furnas and Buja [8]). This prosection process is repeated for every pair of parameters so that each scatterplot is displaying different data. The tolerance ranges for the scatterplots two parameters (p1 and p2 in figure 9) can also be projected on to the plot in the form of a tolerance box.

The Prosection Matrix shown in Figure 10 actually refers to a situation in which each parameter range is very small, leading to a small tolerance region (the small grey dot in the centre of each scatterplot). Because the parameter ranges are small, they define a very thin 'slice' through multi-dimensional parameter space, and therefore the resulting scatterplots show well-defined boundaries associated with the different performance limits of Figure 10. The colour coding used defines how well designs satisfy these performance limits. In Figure 10 designs that are acceptable are black, those that failed only one performance limit are dark grey and those that fail two are medium grey etc. One of the benefits of this colour coding is that the designer can explore the effect of moving the boundaries in the scatterplot. Thus, in Figure 11, the designer has moved the lower limit of performance S3 even lower. A comparison of Figure 10 and 11 reveals how the corresponding boundary has moved, increasing the area of the (here, black) acceptable region. Exploration of this kind allows a designer to form a strategy for combining and trading off different performance requirements.

Though Figure 9 provides a conceptual illustration of the formation of each scatterplot within the Prosection Matrix it is actually unsuitable for implementation because it would result in a very grainy representation. Instead, each scatterplot is filled using a matrix of small coloured squares. For example if we consider the (top left) X1X2 scatterplot in Figure 11 its area is divided in 44^2 squares, The Cartesian coordinates of each square's midpoint defines values of X1 and X2. Values of X3 and X4 are then

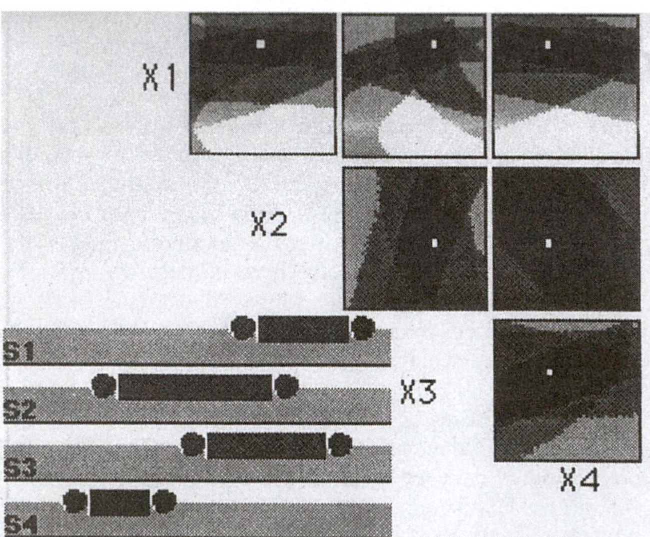

Figure 10: This Prosection Matrix represents 'slices' through parameter space. The grey scaling show how the data satisfies the performance requirements.

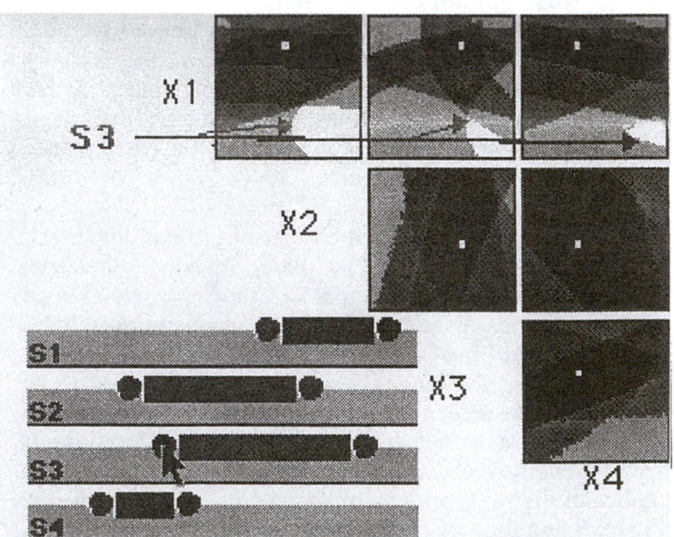

Figure 11: Adjusting a performance requirement and viewing how the related boundary moves in parameter space

selected randomly from within their tolerance range for each square. The corresponding values of the performances S1 to S4 are then computed from the model and compared with their respective limits. The square is then coloured according to the scheme already defined. For clarity, in the case of Figure 11 the X3 and X4 ranges are actually set to a single point so no randomisation occurs.

The existence of significant parameter *ranges* rather than single parameter values changes the detailed appearance of the Prosection Matrix but not its general character (Figure 12). Again consider the X1X2 scatterplot (top left). The original value of X1 has been replaced by a range of X1 as indicated by the yellow line. The immediate effect is that for all the scatterplots that don't have X1 as an axis, X1 is now randomly chosen within the selected *range* of X1 values rather than set at a single value. The increased fuzziness of these plots reflects this process. The rest of Figure 12 shows the effect of additionally assigning ranges to X2, X3 and X4.

Figure 13 (colour plate) shows how the Prosection Matrix looks when the performance and parameter limits are set as in Figure 7. The red regions now correspond to acceptable bulbs, whereas those that are manufactured lie within the yellow tolerance regions. The small percentage of red points within this region indicate a low yield (19%). In Figure 14 (colour plate) the user has set the tolerances to very narrow ranges to find a high yield (100%). Since wider tolerance ranges are normally associated with lower cost, the designer will endeavour to make the yellow -bounded tolerance region as large as possible, perhaps even trading off manufacturing yield against cost. Figure 15 (colour plate) shows how the user has adjusted the parameter ranges so that they just fit inside the red region, resulting in much wider tolerances (potentially cheaper components) whilst maintaining a reasonably high yield (96%)

FORMATIVE EVALUATION STUDIES

The design of IVAs is difficult - it is often hard to judge what users will find intuitive and how an IVA will support a particular task. We have therefore carried out a number of formative evaluation studies at different stages of the IVA's development. Ten pairs of subjects were tested. They were all graduate engineers/ scientists enrolled on PhD programs. The pairs worked together, first with the Influence Explorer, then the Prosection Matrix and finally both tools together. Reassuringly, each pair of subjects were able to complete a tolerance design task in about 30 minutes.

We learnt some very simple lessons from these evaluations:
a) *Maximise the directness of the interactivity.* For example one version of the Prosection Matrix forced users to map their interaction from the sliders. However users preferred to select and drag the tolerance box directly .
b) *Seek out the most crucial information and then represent it appropriately and simply.* The most obvious example of

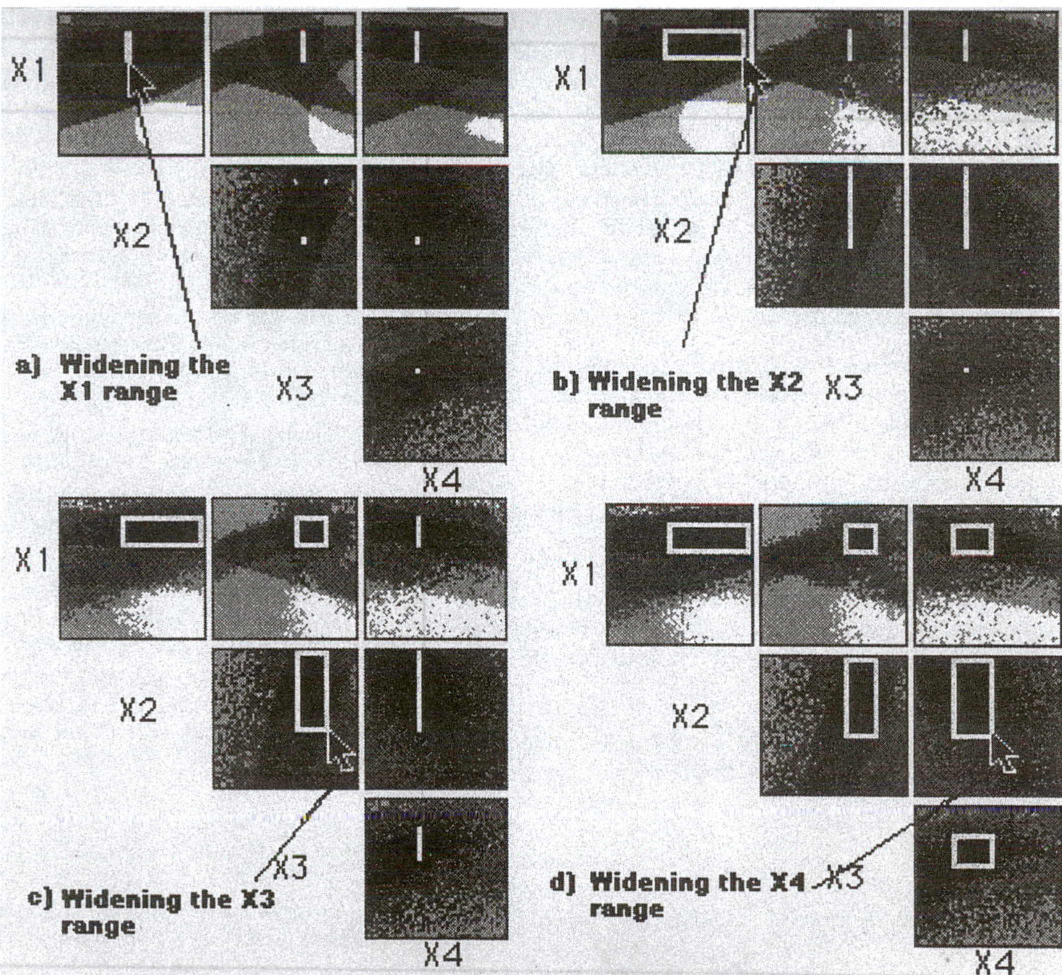

Figure 12: Gradually increasing the tolerance region so that sections of the data are projected. The boundaries become fuzzier as the ranges are adjusted.

this was the colour coding. Initially when considering the interface for setting up a performance specifications we attempted to colour code all the different variations of failure. Then we realised that this coding could be considerably simplified if we focused on encoding data that satisfied the performance limits and perhaps more importantly data that *almost* satisfied those limits. Colour coding the influence explorer for tolerance design was more difficult. The solution presented in this paper (Figure 8) has attempted to reduce the colour coded information to that which will provide immediate and useful information.
c) *There is a trade-off between the amount of information, simplicity and accuracy.* Ensuring that there is sufficient information to complete a task was an important issue. This emerged in the Influence Explorer when we tried adding tolerances with the original precalculated dataset. Using dynamic focused sampling overcame this problem.

CONCLUSIONS

The Influence Explorer and Prosection Matrix have now be utilised in a wide variety of industrial collaborations in electronic, structural and mechanotronic domains. The enthusiastic reaction of those who have observed and experimented with these IVAs suggests that the potential offered by immediately available and responsive interaction is considerable.

There are many reasons for this enthusiasm. One is the readiness with which opportunistic as well as planned exploration can be carried out. Another is the directness of external representations. Abstract Mathematical Models are difficult for the untrained user to interpret. However using these IVAs the problem holder can explore the model for themselves, and make use of their own considerable experience and knowledge to test the models validity in their own terms. A mathematical model is one thing, but an externalisation of that mathematical model that can be responsively explored is quite another. A third reason is that these tools transform a very difficult cognitive problem into a much easier perceptual task.

Many avenues of research and experimentation still need to be followed up. One concerns the enhancement of the designer's expertise by some of the automated tolerance design algorithms developed over the last two decades. One such algorithm was incorporated within the Influence Explorer and, when invoked, automatically and very rapidly (e.g. 10 seconds) adjusted the 'nominal value' of each parameter (the mid-point of the selected parameter range) to maximise the yield. Nevertheless, this automation needs to be complemented by an interface which will facilitate the human observation and guidance of automated design.

ACKNOWLEDGEMENTS

We thank Aarnout Brombacher (Philips, Eindhoven) and John Nelder. This work was implemented in C on a Macintosh by Huw Dawkes.

REFERENCES

[1] Ahlberg C. and Wistrand E., "IVEE: An Environment for Automatic Creation of Dynamic Queries Applications," CHI'95 Demonstrations, May 1995.

[2] Andrews D.F. "Plots of High-Dimensional Data" Biometrics, March 1972, pp 69-97

[3] Becker R.A., Huber P.J., Cleveland W.S. and Wilks A.R., "Dynamic Graphics for Data Analysis", Stat. Science 2, 1987.

[4] Bertin J., "Graphics and Graphic Information Processing", deGruyter Press, Berlin, 1977.

[5] Chalmers M., "Using a Landscape to represent a corpus of documents", Springer-Verlag Proceedings of COSIT '93, Elba, pp. 377-390, September 1993.

[6] Eick S.G., Steffen J.L. and Sumner E.E., " SeeSoft ™ - A Tool for Visualizing Line Oriented Software", IEEE Transactions on Software Engineering, pp. 11-18, 1992.

[7] Feiner S. and Beshers C."Worlds within Worlds: Metaphors for Exploring n-Dimensional Virtual Worlds", ACM Proceeings 1990 Conference on User Interface Software Design, pp 76-83

[8] Furnas G.W. and Buja A., "Prosection Views: Dimensional Inference through Sections and Projections", Journal of Computational and Graphic Statistics 3 (4), pp. 323-353, 1994.

[9] Inselberg A., "The plane with parallel co-ordinates", The Visual Computer 1, pp. 69-91, 1985.

[10] Keim D.A. and Kriegal H., "VisDB: Database Exploration using Multidimensional Visualization", IEEE Computer Graphics and Applications September, pp. 40-49, 1994.

[11] Nardi B.A. and Zarmer C.L., "Beyond Models and Metaphors: Visual Formalisms in User Interface Design", Journal of Visual Languages and Computing 4, pp. 5- 33, 1993.

[12] Newton C.M., " Graphics: from alpha to omega in data analysis", Graphical Representation of Multivariate Data, P.C.C. Wang (Ed) New York: Academic Press, pp. 59-92, 1978.

[13] Mihalisin T., Gawlinski E., Timlin J. and Schwegler J., "Visualizing Scalar Field on an N-dimensional Lattice", Proceedings of Visualization 90, IEEE CS Press, pp. 255-262, 1990.

[14] Rao R. and Card S.K., "The Table Lens: Merging Graphical and Symbolic Representations in an Interactive Focus + Context Visualization for Tabular Information", Proceedings of CHI'94, Boston, ACM Press, pp. 318-322, 1994.

[15] Schmid C. and Hinterberger H., "Comparative Multivariate Visualization Across Conceptually Different Graphic Displays", Proceedings of the SSDBM VII, IEEE Computer Society Press, September 1994.

[16] Spoerri A., "InfoCrystal: A visual tool for Information retrieval" Proceedings of Visualization '93 pp150-157.

[17] Suchman L.A., "Plans and Situated Actions - The Problem of Human-Machine Communication", Cambridge University Press, 1987.

[18] Tweedie L.A., Spence R., Bhoghal R. and Williams D., "The Attribute Explorer", ACM, Video Proceedings and Conference Companion, CHI'94, pp. 435-436, April 1994.

[19] Tweedie L.A., "Interactive Visualisation Artifacts: how can abstractions inform design?", People and Computers X : Proc. of HCI'95 Huddersfield, (Eds) Kirby M.A.R., Dix A.J. and Finlay J.E., Cambridge University Press, pp. 247-265, 1995.

[20] Williamson C. and Shneiderman B., "The Dynamic HomeFinder: Evaluating dynamic queries in a real estate information exploration system", ACM, Proceedings SIGIR'92, pp. 339-346, 1992.

[21] Zhang J. and Norman D.A., "Representations in Distributed Cognitive Tasks", Cognitive Science 18, pp. 87-122, 1994.

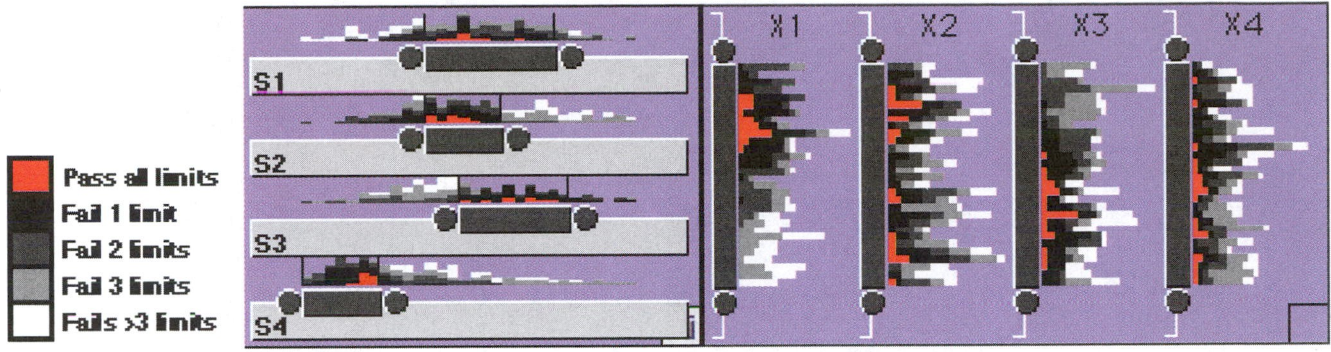

FIGURE **6**

Setting up limits on the performance histograms (left).

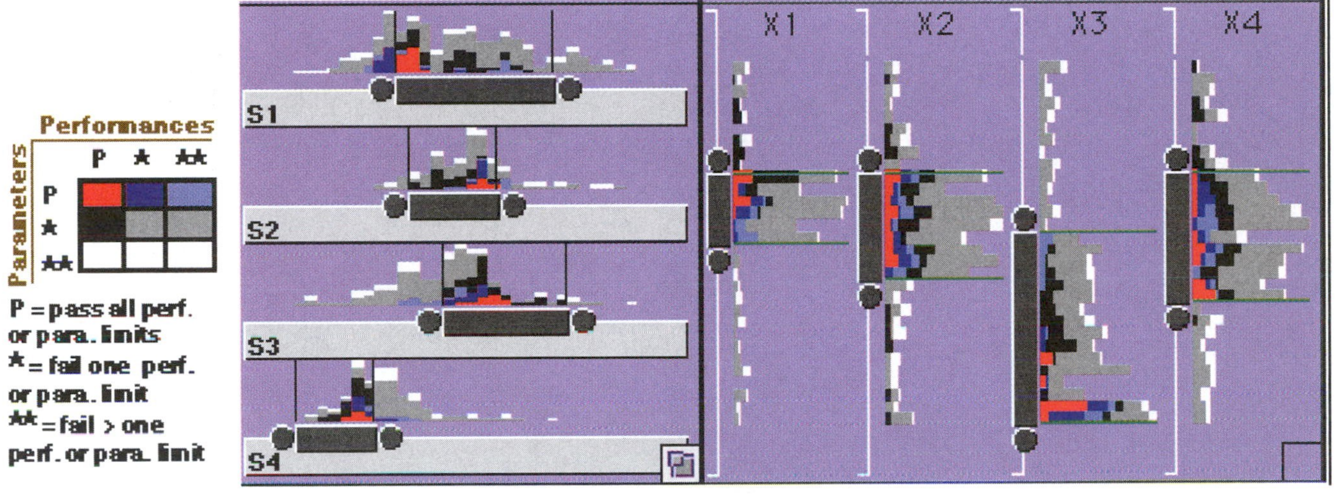

FIGURE **7**

Setting up ranges on the parameter histograms.

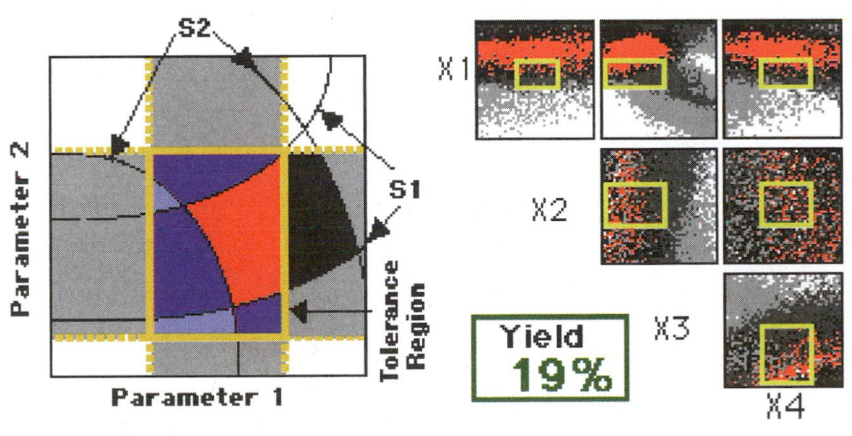

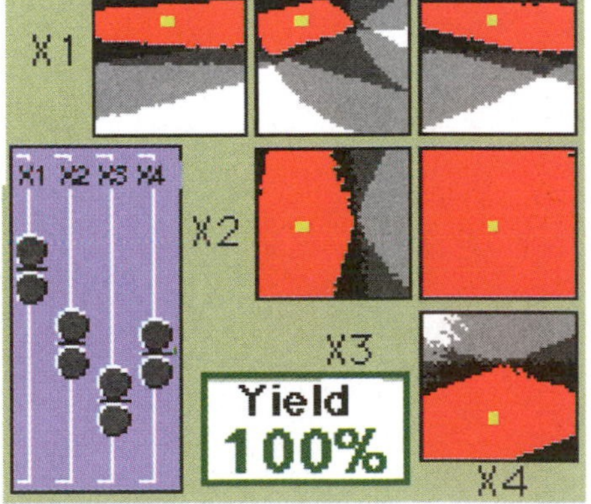

FIGURE **8**

The colour coding for the tolerance setting (Figure 7) shown in 2 parameter space.

FIGURE **13**

The Prosection Matrix for the settings from Figure 7.

FIGURE **14**

Here the parameter ranges are reduced to single values.

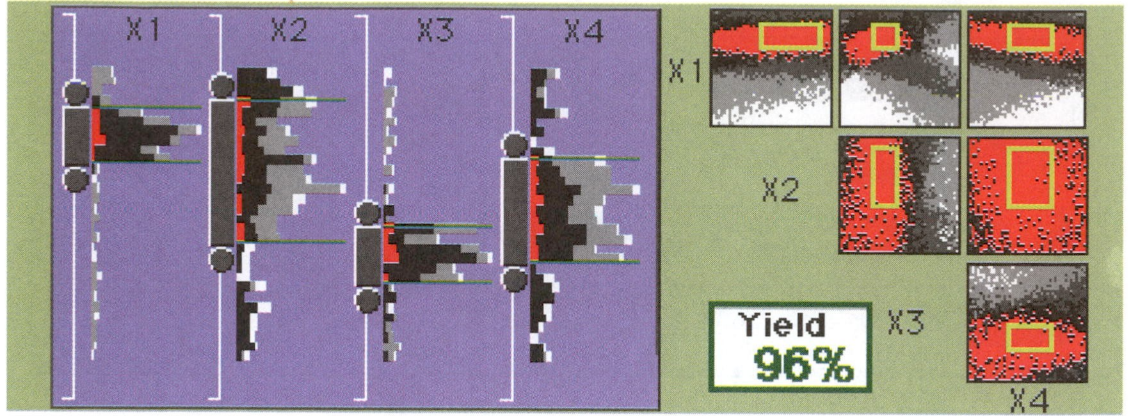

FIGURE **15**

Maximising the widths of the parameter ranges to get high yield and minimum cost. (the same specification is used as in Figure 6). Note how the rectangular tolerance region just fits inside the red region of acceptability.

3.3 Overview + Detail

The papers in this section concern the use of interaction to keep a view of the whole data available, while pursuing detailed analysis of a part of it. Information visualization often deals with large numbers of cases. Indeed, that is one of its virtues. A major user interface problem, therefore, is how to handle information on a large scale. In fact, scale is the major usability problem of current interfaces. A taxonomy developed by Plaisant, Carr, and Shneiderman (1995) describes techniques for browsing large images. Essentially, this is a version of the problem of the human visual system to which we referred in Chapter 1: how to partition limited bandwidth between the conflicting needs for both high spatial resolution and wide aperture in sensing the visual environment. Having an overview is very important. It reduces search, allows the detection of overall patterns, and aids the user in choosing the next move. A general heuristic of visualization design, therefore, is to start with an overview. But it is also necessary for the user to access details rapidly. One solution is overview + detail: to provide multiple views, an overview for orientation, and a detailed view for further work.

An early use of this technique for information was the Dataland system (Bolt, 1984), part of the Spatial Database Management System at MIT. The user sits in a room with a wall-sized display. On each side of the user's chair is a display. The display on the left is an overview; the display on the right holds a touch-sensitive visual control (e.g., a book control for flipping book pages). The overview display contains a movable "you are here" translucent rectangle showing which part of the overview is expanded on the wall. The overview is constant, but the user can zoom in on a portion, resulting in a smaller rectangle but a more detailed wall display. Moving or zooming the rectangle on the overview display, or changing the position on the large display—with a voice command, for example—results in an immediate update in the other display. Thus, the displays are "tightly coupled."

There is a limit of about 3 to 30 for an effective zoom factor (the ratio of sizes in the overview and detail displays) (Shneiderman, 1998). Beyond that ratio, intermediate views are needed. For example, consider the display in Figure 3.2. The detailed view contains lines of code, but not very many. In the overview, each line of code is reduced to a line one pixel high. This reduction is too extreme, so an intermediate view is used.

Overview + detail displays can be shown one at a time (time multiplexing), or they can be shown at the same time in different parts of the screen (space multiplexing), as in Figure 3.2. If they are shown at the same time, there is a trade-off for the amount of space to be devoted to each, which in turn affects the zoom factor. The design of overview + detail visualizations involves careful trade-offs in the use of space.

So far, we have been discussing spatial zooming, in which the detail view is just an enlarged version of the overview. But the appearance or even the content can change between overview and detail view. Text in the overview of Figure 3.2 is represented just by a single-pixel-wide line. But in the detail it is represented with letters. When the content is the same but the appearance changes, it is called *semantic zooming* (Bederson and Hollan, 1994 ●). Maps work this way. The line drawn on a map to represent a road is much thicker than the proportional width of the road, or it could not be

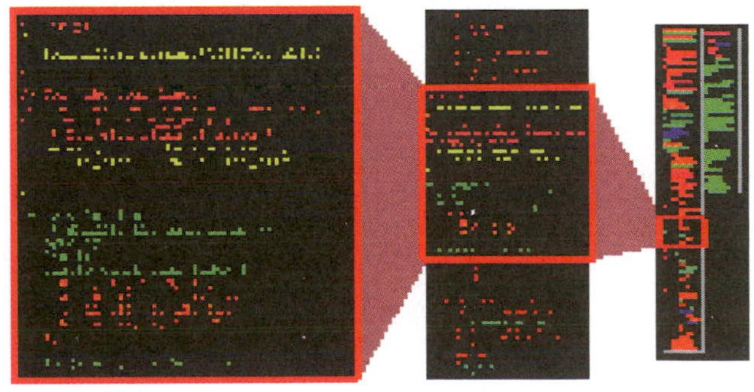

FIGURE **3.2**

Overview + detail technique, with intermediate view. From SeeSoft. Courtesy of Lucent Corporation.

seen. A school is represented symbolically on a road map (or it would be invisible), but its dimensions are represented literally on a plot map. In spatial zooming, the same variables appear in both overview and detail views. In semantic zooming, more of the variables in the Data Table might be revealed in the detailed view in addition to a change in mapping. Woodruff, Landay, and Stonebraker (1998) have recently developed an interface for controlling the parameters associated with semantic zooming.

One measure that is useful in comparing visualizations is the capacity to zoom in on an area of interest. Some systems allow users to click on a location and then replace it with a zoomed-in view. We call this *zoom-and-replace*. Some geographical information systems, such as CD-ROMs with all the streets in the United States, may have 15 levels of zooming. Smooth zooming, which allows continuous movement toward a point of interest, is computationally more demanding but cognitively more comprehensible, because it preserves the user's orientation. In overview + detail systems, typical zoom factors are in the range of 5 to 15. For greater zoom factors, often necessary with large maps, images, or microscope systems, an intermediate view is helpful in preserving orientation. For example, in Figure 3.2, the zoom factor between the most detailed view (the leftmost display in the figure) and the more comprehensive view (the rightmost display in the figure) is 13.7. This is broken into zoom factors of 2.3 and 6.

The first paper, Plaisant et al. (1996 ●), uses an overview with semantic zooming. Time is a good variable on which to base an overview, because it is a property of almost all documents and events. The first visualization discussed is for the caseload of the criminal justice system. Processes associated with the case can be plotted by their begin and end times. Linkages between the process are indicated by highlighting related processes when a process is clicked on. The visualization for medical records adds multiple detailed views. Clicking on the icons expands these in separate windows, displaying more properties. In this visualization, some of the overview is itself hierarchical. This shows that an overview need not be static, but can also be malleable.

The second paper, Kumar, Plaisant, and Shneiderman (1997 ●), visualizes a large hierarchy and uses dynamic queries sliders. The overview displays the entire tree. Sliders highlight those nodes on the tree meeting the filtering conditions set by the dynamic queries sliders. The user manually controls the level at which to display the tree, but the system automatically elides subnodes where there are no hits. Whereas dynamic queries were used in the FilmFinder to choose which cases in the Data Table to display and which variables to display for them, in this paper the cases to display propagate through the structuring of cases given in the Data Table itself. The paper therefore combines three types of interaction: dynamic queries, overview + detail, and automatic propagation.

Two empirical studies in the Kumar paper suggest that using the dynamic queries strategy with hierarchies is helpful. In the first study, in which users rated and critiqued features on both simple and complex tasks, dynamic queries and pruning were both popular. In the second study, users performed tasks with one of three versions of Kumar, Plaisant, and Shneiderman's system: a full tree, a partially pruned tree (unselected subtrees were elided), or a fully pruned tree (both unselected subtrees and unselected nodes were elided). The pruned trees were more than twice as fast to use as the full tree and were strongly preferred by users. Other results in the studies suggest that the usefulness of dynamic visualizations such as these can be strongly affected by the response time of the system.

LifeLines: Visualizing Personal Histories

Catherine Plaisant, Brett Milash*, Anne Rose, Seth Widoff, Ben Shneiderman*^
Human-Computer Interaction Laboratory
*Computer Science Dept., ^Institute for Systems Research
University of Maryland
A.V. Williams Bldg. College Park MD 20742
http://www.cs.umd.edu/projects/hcil
(301) 405-2768 - email: plaisant@cs.umd.edu

ABSTRACT

LifeLines provide a general visualization environment for personal histories that can be applied to medical and court records, professional histories and other types of biographical data. A one screen overview shows multiple facets of the records. Aspects, for example medical conditions or legal cases, are displayed as individual time lines, while icons indicate discrete events, such as physician consultations or legal reviews. Line color and thickness illustrate relationships or significance, rescaling tools and filters allow users to focus on part of the information. LifeLines reduce the chances of missing information, facilitate spotting anomalies and trends, streamline access to details, while remaining tailorable and easily transferable between applications. The paper describes the use of LifeLines for youth records of the Maryland Department of Juvenile Justice and also for medical records. User's feedback was collected using a Visual Basic prototype for the youth record.

Keywords

Visualization, history, timeline, personal record, justice, medical record, screen design, overview, screen management.

INTRODUCTION

Records of personal histories are needed in a variety of applications. Members of the medical and legal professions examine a record to garner information that will allow them to make an informed decision regarding their patient or case. Decision making critically depends on gleaning the complete story, spotting trends, noting critical incidents or cause-effect relationships and reviewing previous actions. Professional histories, in the form of résumés, help employers relate a prospect's skills and experiences to employment and education. Financial and retirement plans associate past and upcoming events to culminate in an expected result. In child and family social services, complex problems may require review of multiple related personal histories.

In most applications delays in gathering the information to elaborate a meaningful overview of the record can have deleterious effects. In a medical situation, a patient's treatment may be delayed while charts and lab results are assembled. In a social work situation, assistance to a youth in detention may be delayed for weeks while school and court records are brought together.

Once gathered in a single record, the information is often in the form of a puzzle and the reader has to browse the data in order to form the big picture of the record. The reader must pour through lengthy and diverse pages. Missing or overlooking a piece of the puzzle can have dramatic effects.

While more attention is now put on developing standards for gathering and exchanging personal records (especially in the medical field), we found that virtually no effort had been made to design appropriate visualization and navigation techniques to present and explore personal history records.

An intuitive approach to visualizing histories is to use graphical time scales. The flexible and natural ordering of the time scale in months, weeks, days and even minutes, gives the design an efficient and facile interpretation and the ability to divulge detail. The consistent linear time scale allows comparisons and relations between the quantities displayed. Most importantly, large data sets can be displayed along the time line to help relate a story [15].

We propose LifeLines as a general technique for visualizing summaries of personal histories. On a one screen overview multiple facets of the records are displayed. Aspects with varying status, such as medical conditions or legal cases, are displayed as horizontal lines, while icons indicate discrete events, such as physician consultations or legal reviews. Line color and thickness illustrate relationships or the significance of events. LifeLines always begin with a one screen overview of the record, and rescaling tools or filters allow users to focus on part of the record and see more details, providing a general visualization environment. Techniques to deal with complex records and issues of a standard personal record format are discussed.

This general visualization environment is not computationally demanding, requires only high level data descriptions, and can handle a variety of records. Those characteristics make LifeLines a practical example of a personal record format that could be rapidly exchanged or synchronized between multiple services.

THE CHALLENGE OF PERSONAL HISTORIES

In order to be a general tool LifeLines have to be able to present different facets of a person's life (medical, financial, education, work, hobbies, legal, etc.). A particular application might use LifeLines for only a subset of those facets. Each facet includes different stories or aspects. For example the medical facet of a person's history might include a 5 years story about their back pain. A famous artist's biography might include facets on painting, writing and influential personalities, its painting facet would then have different aspects such as style and themes. Each story or aspect includes events (e.g. an operation, a police arrest) and periods (e.g. two weeks of acute pain, the blue and pink period in Picasso's biography).

LifeLines present the personal history in a single screen, facets are shown as regions of the screens distinguished by alternating background colors, stories or aspects are lines, periods correspond to changes of size or color along the line, while discrete events are marked by icons.

Our work on the visualization of personal history started with a project with the Maryland Department of Juvenile Justice (DJJ), a Visual Basic prototype was developed to illustrate the principle of LifeLines (Figure 2 and 3), collect user feedback on the youth record design and explore the applicability of the LifeLines to other domains. Screen mockups have been prepared (Figure 4 and Color Plate 2) to discuss refined designs and particularly the use of LifeLines for medical records. .A video is also available in the CHI 96 Video [10].

RELATED WORK

Tufte [15] describes timelines as a frequent and powerful form of graphic design and presents many examples. An experiment in home automation showed that timelines could be quickly understood and used for data entry when scheduling devices in the home [10]. Novel techniques have been proposed to present calendars and timed information [9] and to analyze and search time scales [5] [14]. A design using timelines for medical records was proposed by Powsner and Tufte [13] who developed a graphical summary using a table of individual plots of test results and treatment data. In project management the Gantt chart [8] and PERT chart display the duration and type of tasks in a project. Many attributes of the tasks are stored but only synchronization and dependencies of tasks themselves are shown on the diagram. Software such as Microsoft Project uses these charts but the overviews do not provide the richness needed for personal histories, which are not carefully planned series of tasks but a mosaic of information that still need to be related to each other.

When navigating large spaces overviews have been found helpful [12] [2]. In the medical domain studies have shown the benefits of record summary. The Summary Time-Oriented Record, a pure text flowchart, was found to be helpful in an arthritis clinic [16]. Another text summary record uses scaled values to indicate the severity of a symptom and also notes the duration of the symptoms, allowing the timing of clinical events to become apparent [17]. Intensive care summary visualization software includes notions of filtering, severity scaling, and details on demand [4].

JUVENILE JUSTICE YOUTH RECORD

About 600 employees of the Maryland Department of Juvenile Justice are using an information system to process over 50,000 cases of delinquent youth behavior per year. In general a 'case' is opened when a complaint is filed against the youth (usually after a police intervention.) The success of a DJJ case worker's decisions relies greatly on knowledge of the youth's current status and previous case history. With the current system cryptic codes are used to access screens packed with lists of cases, placements or reviews, and to browse complex forms (Figure 1) while searching for detail information in dozens of screens. Important notes and decisions are often difficult to find in the deeply nested structure and more importantly it is very difficult to get an overview of the whole record. While attending a standard training session for the system we were told that the "trick is that you have to find the magic case", i.e. you have to be lucky and follow the right path to a case where a lot of information is available. The data entry is done over months or years, by clerical staff, field workers or detention facilities staff, geographically dispersed and with limited communication. Newly added or updated data may not be noticed, data entry errors are common and often remain unseen in the text screens. Delays are difficult to notice when browsing tables of dates.

```
DWJMIC03    ISYS - INFORMATION SYSTEM FOR YOUTH SERVICES   10/27/94   15:04
INQCASE               CASE DETAIL INQUIRY                  WJUM03
-----------------------------------------------------------------------------
YOUTH NUMBER: 000123456        CASE NO: 09/14/93  - 01
NAME:FRST XXXXXX          MID XXXXXXX          LST XXXXX                SUF
DOB: XX/XX/XX  VERIFIED(Y/N): N  RACE: X  SEX: X  COUNTY: 24
----  CASE  -----------------------------------------------------------------
RECEIVED:           DATE 09/14/93   SOURCE POLC   REASON DELQ   OFFICE 71610
INTAKE DECISION: DATE 09/14/93   CODE   CCAI   AGENCY REF TO
INTAKE REASON:
APPEALED:   / /      APPEAL DISP CODE:         APPEAL DISP DATE:   / /
LEGAL COUNSEL:                           JUDGE/MASTER:
COURT FINDING:         DISP DATE:   / /    DISP CODE:
TERM/COND: WARN
TERMINATION:  FIXED    / /    ACTUAL 09/19/93  LAST UPDT: 010/07/93  TEXT: N
CONSENT GIVEN(Y/N):   START DATE:   / /    EXPDT DATE:    / /    -----------
ALLEGED OFFENSE: 01 DATE 09/14/93 CODE RNWY  CTY 16  POL CMPLNT NO: 93045011
DESC/OFF RAN AWAY FROM MOM UPON RELEASE FROM CSC     ARREST DATE    09/14/93
LOCATION STREETS OF OXON HILL M.D.       ZIP 20745 0000     OTH INV(Y/N) Y
POLICE ID 1777              POLICE NAME NICODEMUS
ADJUDIC OFFENSE: 00 CODE        PETI              DISP CODE      DATE   / /
-----------------------------------------------------------------------------
NEXT REQUEST: INQCASE    NEXT KEY:
DC900004    NO MORE DATA
```

Figure 1: Sample screen from the existing DJJ system .

In response the LifeLines were designed to 1) present a youth record visual overview on a single screen, 2) provide direct access to all detail information from the overview with one or two clicks of the mouse, 3) promote critical information or alerts to the overview level.

Description of the interface

In this LifeLines design the facets of the youth records were chosen to be the cases, placements, case worker assignments and reviews (Color Plate 1 and Figure 2). Each facet is distinguished from the next by a switch of background color. The dates of the timeline legend shows that the youth Bart Simpson has been involved with DJJ for about a year. Thin vertical lines across the whole timeline mark each new year, giving a sense of scale to the diagram (e.g. compare Figure 2 and Figure 3). The first facet of the record shows the cases. There are 4 lines indicating four cases in Bart's record. Bart was first referred to DJJ for "breaking and entering" (B&E code). The case was handled informally and then closed after 3 months. He was referred again for the same offense, also handled informally and then for a more serious auto theft. That time the case was handled formally (i.e. went to court, i.e. to the States Attorney's Office - SAO) and Bart was adjudged delinquent DLNQ (i.e. was found guilty). The case was closed several months later. The right end of the timelines area shows today's status: we can see that there is only one case currently open, an attempted murder case for which a decision has not been made yet. Below the cases the placement facet shows that Bart is currently at Waxter (a detention center), in relation to the attempted murder case. We can see that last year Bart went to a drug abuse program for a while and later was placed at Cheltenham (a residential treatment center) when he was found guilty in the auto theft case. The assignment lines show who has been assigned to Bart over time. The currently assigned worker is Brown. The last facet in this record is the set of reviews. Reviews are discrete events where the youth's needs or progress are assessed. A click on Smith's name gives the worker's contact information. A click on a review icon brings the text of the review report on an overlapping window. Similarly details about cases or placement are obtained by clicking on the lines or labels.

Interrelationships between periods or events on the lines can be highlighted. For example one cannot tell by looking at the timelines if the drug abuse program was recorded as part of the auto theft case or the breaking and entering case, but clicking on the drug abuse program placement highlights the related case (i.e. in this instance the B&E case) and the social worker assigned to that case (Color Plate 1).

Line thickness and color are used to indicate the severity of the offense and the depth of penetration in the system (Color Plate 1). For example underage drinking would be a very thin line, but the alleged auto theft offense is a medium thickness line, which in the example of Color Plate 1 and Figure 2 is getting darker as the case progresses to court and darker again when Bart is found guilty (delinquent). On the other hand the recent case of alleged murder appears as a thick line but remains of light color because the case has not progressed yet. Severity levels are set following a policy.

At the top of the screen, next to the name, age and picture of the youth, a set of buttons gives access to the general contact information, aliases used, education, work and medical status screens but critical keywords from those screens always appear on the overview screen (e. g. suicide risk). Color coding could also be used for those buttons to suggest how recently the information was updated. A pale button can indicate 'out of date' data, a bright button recently modified information.

THE BENEFITS OF LIFELINES

LifeLines can:

1 - Reduce the chances of missing information. Because the data entry is performed over a long period of time by different people the LifeLines overview assists users in reviewing a disparate record. Yet unseen, or recently added and updated information can be revealed by highlighting.

2 - Facilitate the spotting of anomalies and trends. Intervals are easier to estimate on a timeline than in a table of dates. Repetitions of series of events result in visible patterns.

3 - Streamline the access to details. LifeLines act as large menus from which large numbers of detail screens can be accessed in a single step (about 35 from the record of Figure 2, and 100 in Figure 3)

4 - Remain simple and tailorable to various applications. The long term success of any record format depends on its sharability among collaborating services. LifeLines only uses high level data that can act as reference pointers to other services records.

DEALING WITH COMPLEX RECORDS

Keeping the overview

LifeLines begin with an overview of the entire record. Seeing this overview gives users a better sense of the type and volume of information available. Unfortunately, many youth records include so many cases that one page is not enough. Other applications such as medical records or biographies might require 50 or 100 lines. Screen size limits the number of lines which can be displayed, and the number of events and periods which can be identified on a line. Scroll bars are the common answer to pixel shortage but scrollbars are inadequate - if not harmful - when presenting overviews as users often forget to browse the complete image, or worse

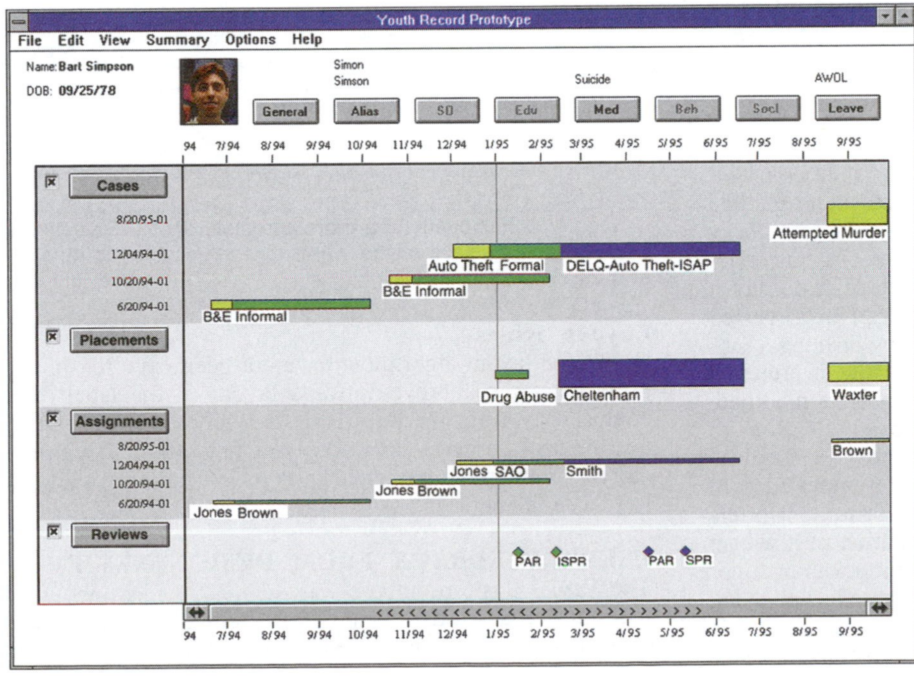

Figure 2:
A simple hypothetical youth record showing four cases, 3 placements, workers' assignments and review markers.

are even unaware that part of the image is hidden. To guarantee complete coverage of the overview, detail must be sacrificed for completeness in the first viewing of LifeLines. This raises two issues for the designer: how to represent all the information at the overview level , and how to reveal the next level of detail. Those problems are general to the design of image browsers for monitoring and decision making [12], and we propose a series of techniques tailored to LifeLines.

Silhouette and shadow

When all the lines and labels cannot be shown in the first screen the lines are brought closer to each other and the labels disappear (Figure 3a and 3b). It remains possible to see on this silhouette the number and importance of the cases, the type of placement and the number and date of reviews. Each line, period or event can still be selected individually. A background sensitive cursor can display the label of the underlying object (Figure 3a) and selecting a line or icon can display the labels of all associated events (i.e. the corresponding case, placements, assignments and reviews (Figure 3b)).

The natural next step for unusually large records is to remove all blank space and thickness coding, clumping all lines together to show a mere colored shadow of the record (which could then show hundreds of lines in one screen). Once the overview has been appreciated, semantic zooming can be used [18] as users expand desired facets to show thickness and labels again, zoom to a particular time period, or focus on a given case. Scrollable, resizable windows should only become necessary when the overview has been examined. Then filters can be offered to search, sort or hide items of a given type.

Facet hierarchy

LifeLines are organized by facets of the record. A complex record may require a hierarchy of facets containing the headings of the facets, stories and aspects. Displayed in the classic outline format (Color Plate 2), facets can be expanded and contracted to show increasing or decreasing levels of detail. Through direct manipulation, the user may rearrange the headings within any level of the tree. Sorting specified levels of the tree by importance, name, date or other factors becomes useful.

Rescaling

When the sheer density of periods and events on a time line requires intervals so small that they challenge the granularity of the time line a sub-time-line icon (or a special line style) can signify a section of the time line where the data density is too large. Details of that time period can be revealed progressively by rescaling (zooming in) or by opening a sub-time-line into a detail window. The term rescaling is preferred to zooming since only the horizontal dimension is modified. We were surprised by the diversity of design solutions to perform the time rescaling. Figure 2 shows a flexible-interval scroll bar, which is adjustable at both ends to represent the width of the desired interval of time, it offers adequate control, but requires the manipulation of a widget that is not altogether familiar. The screen mockup of Color Plate 2 shows compressed and stretched clock tools allowing the user to alternately compress or stretch the time scale centered on the last selected item. Another design is to separate the horizontal scroll bar from the selection of the time interval (e.g. week, month or year, which can be chosen in a menu or with a different slider). This is advantageous for reviewing specific fixed periods but requires users to focus their attention on the time period selection, rather than the data displayed. The 3D animation technique of the perspective wall [9] which folds the display in 3 panels could also be used but the facet hierarchy legend becomes an intrusion into the continuous scrolling. Lastly, the time scrollbar can be designed to allow multiple foci by dividing it into independent scrolling regions.

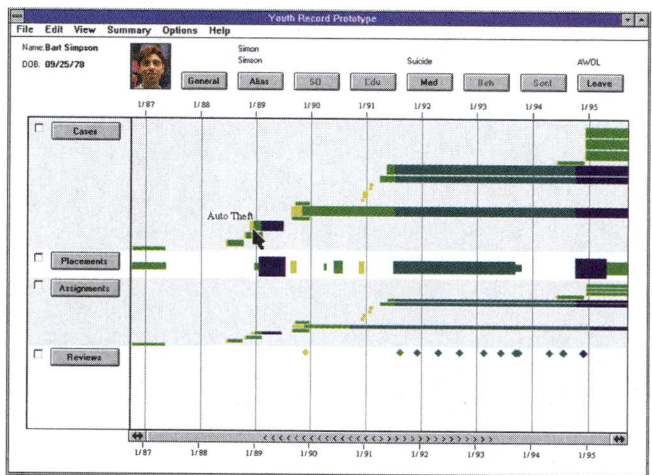

Figure 3a: Silhouette of a more complex record. Placing the cursor on a line displays the corresponding label.

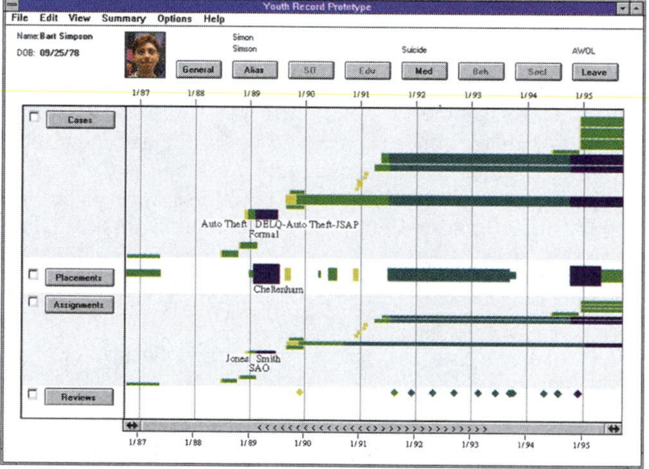

Figure 3b: Silhouette of a more complex record. Selecting a a line or icon displays all the labels for the corresponding case and associated events.

Layout issues

Optimized layout algorithms have not been explored in our project but the abbreviation and layout of the labels and compact layout of the lines is definitively a critical part of dealing with large records. We are not satisfied with the current prototype as too much space is left unused yielding a low "data-ink ratio" [15].

USER'S FEEDBACK FROM DESIGN REVIEW

The Visual Basic prototype was demonstrated to about 60 users during an all-day review. Small groups of 4 to 5 users were given a 20 minute demonstration of the LifeLines prototype. They were able to use the interface to explore a few record overviews that we had prepared based on real records. They were asked to comment on perceived advantages and problems, and to consider what additional data would be useful to display in the overview. Users were a representative group of social workers, supervisors and a few administrators of varying age, gender and computer experience recruited from field offices, detention facilities, program services and administrative services.

Most users were very enthusiastic about the interface. A few others appreciated the interface but expressed concerns about the possible bias associated with the color and thickness coding. Showing the offense severity brought to the surface underlying issues such as the data "quality" (possibility of errors or cases of uncertainty). The paradox might be that error prone data buried in a hard to navigate system seems less offensive than when the same data is made visible. The use of color and thickness coding is very powerful, and should be used carefully to avoid misleading overviews.

Positive comments were related to:

- the importance of the overview. Even if all the information is case based, the overview presents a youth record in one screen with more information than the current list of cases' screen .
- the ease of access to details. For example seeing the existence of the reviews and being able to read them by a single click - as opposed to a series of codes and screens- was highly appreciated.

Data entry errors were found in the records we used, which would have been difficult to locate in the multiple screens of the current text record. The long tables of dates used in the current system are difficult to review, while the timelines make more visible the fact that a case was left open by mistake, that reviews are overdue or that the court is taking too long to make a decision.

Many recommendations were made:

- the ability to show future events, e.g. to show the end of a placement or probation, a scheduled court hearing or review deadline.
- the need to be able to see exact dates, which can be done with a status bar or special cursor which could be moved from event to event to show dates and ordering of events.
- the marking of informal groups of related cases or events, e.g. stealing car radios from 10 cars can result in 10 individual cases that would be marked and seen as a group.
- the integration with data entry techniques.

Alternative layouts were proposed; additional data to be displayed was discussed. This suggests that control panels are necessary to let users or technical support staff modify the mapping of the data onto the LifeLines.

LIFELINES FOR MEDICAL RECORDS

Because our youth record Visual Basic prototype reads a simple format as input it was easy for us to explore other data sets such as our own personal resumes and sample medical records, which lead to new designs and layouts shown in the medical record screen mockups of Figure 4 and Color Plate 2.

An appropriate use of LifeLines

A patient's medical record is an important source of information for the physician. Medical records can be extremely complex, with data intervals ranging from seconds to decades. Clinical data lend themselves to a multimedia presentations, with sounds, such as patient interviews; images, such as X ray images or MRIs; quantitative data, e.g. lab test results or vital signs; and qualitative data, such as visual observations.

Certain characteristics make medical records specially suited for the LifeLines format:

- Clinical data can divide into scalable quantities and related free text [3]. For example, a quantitative blood pressure measurement may be classified as normal, elevated, or reduced, and may be linked to doctor's notes about a change in diet and exercise.
- Clinical data categorize neatly into sections on history, specimens, labs, reports, previous encounters and actions taken [17].
- Medical records use scaled values for simplicity of interpretation [13].
- Symptoms, treatments and assessments can easily by related graphically on the timeline where the temporal relation of clinical events becomes apparent.
- Events scheduled for the future can be viewed along with past events and current status.
- Medical records benefit from a concise summary. When summaries were introduced to cardiac, pulmonary and renal clinics, in the second year hospital stays were shorter by an average of one week. [13]

Scenario

In the sample medical record (Figure 4), we see that the patient is diabetic from medical alerts section at the top of the page and from the line in the manifestation facet. For treatment, he has regular, bimonthly consultations with an endocrinologist and administers insulin to control the symptoms. Early in May, this patient sprained his knee and visited an internist, his primary care physician, for suggestions. Dr. Wood referred him to an orthopedist, Dr. Jones, whom he visited for an opinion on his knee. The patient, however, desired a second opinion and visited Dr. Hansen who suggested arthroscopic surgery and prescribed acetaminophen to relieve the pain. Shortly after, the patient entered University Hospital where Dr. Hansen operated on the damaged ligament. Having received surgical treatment, the knee proceeded to heal and the severity of the tear, implied by the thickness of the line, decreased and the dosage of acetaminophen also decreased.

After leaving the hospital, the patient began physical therapy sessions with Dr. Carter. As the ligament continued to heal, sessions became farther apart, with two more scheduled appointments past the current date marked by the dashed red line in this example. Future events occur to the right of the current date line and appear gray. Meanwhile, the patient developed ear pain and returned to his internist. The internist saw in the medical alerts that the patient is allergic to penicillin and prescribed the antibiotic doxycycline for the diagnosed ear infection. The ear infection quickly healed and the patient finished off all of the antibiotic.

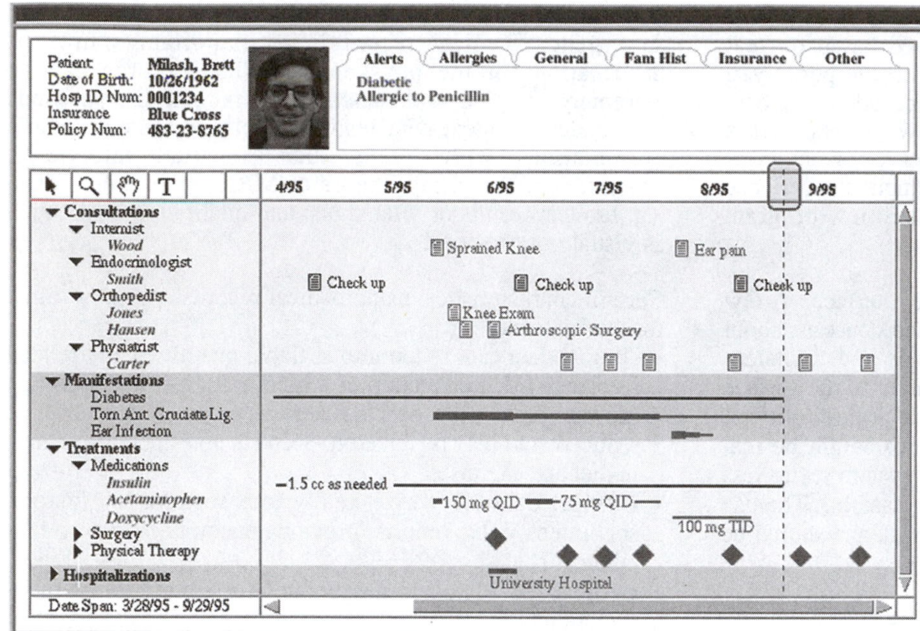

Figure 4 :
A medical record overview.
On the right of the dashed vertical line are shown the scheduled appointments (as seen around the end of August).

Encoding information

Labels for the consultation events in Figure 4 denote the chief complaints of the patient. They may, however, contain other information, such as the resulting diagnosis, or a suggested course of action, for example, a referral to a specialist. Other icons may be more indicative of the nature of the consultations: A clipboard or writing hand may represent a purely observational consultation, a flask means that lab results are available, an ambulance suggests an emergency situation and a syringe indicates that medications were administered (Color Plate 2).

Showing relationships

Quantities sharing a critical quality are grouped into similar facets but it may be important to view relationships between items outside of facet boundaries. Through the simple and consistent use of colors, groups can be identified. For example, color can be used to signify lines and events related to a diagnosis listed in the manifestations heading. In the example printed in Figure 4 all information related to the sprained knee was green and all information related to ear pain was magenta. This is a very telling scheme. However, it may be crucial to locate every consultation, illness and treatment related to Dr. Wood. Color Plate 2 shows how each physician can be assigned a color to mark his or her consultations, letters, prescriptions etc. The list of doctors serves as the color legend for the diagram.

OVERVIEW AND DETAILS - ELASTIC WINDOWS

Assuming that a large screen is available multiple windows can be used to see detailed reports while keeping the overview (Color Plate 2). By dragging an event icon to the region, space is allocated for a formatted report of all information associated with the icon. As more icons are placed on the region, the region divides into independently scrolling segments, with the new report placed in relation to the other reports with respect to where it was dropped on the screen [7].

When large records have been expanded in scrollable facets windows and multiple detail windows, new methods are needed to manipulate them beside the traditional vertical scroll bar assigned to each region, 1) the pump tool, available from the tool bar in the upper left corner of the time line region (Color Plate 2) is used to expand or contract the region from both ends, shrinking the adjacent regions [1], 2) the hook tool expands or contracts the region from one end and shrinks the adjacent region [1]. The master vertical scroll bar on the right hand side of the LifeLines allows the user to navigate across all the top-level facets.

TOWARD A PERSONAL HISTORY RECORD FORMAT

In order to develop a standard for the display of personal histories certain concessions are necessary to maximize the chances of their use. The use of pointers to other data sources offers an alternative to the unsuccessful attempts at all-inclusive, redundant records. The knowledge of the existence and type of an event is in some cases all that matters, and in all cases better that not having any record of the event at all because the information is in an incompatible format. Because of its simplicity and tailorability the overview of the LifeLines could act as a referencing tool to a complete physical record, with immediate access only to high level data. As more detail is needed, a system using LifeLines can establish a network connection with the appropriate system if possible or use contact instructions stored in the LifeLines to avoid an irking ϶data not found message.

LifeLines offer an effective visualization tool, but reality often thwarts complete and immaculate record keeping. Imprecise data should be acknowledged with adequate coding (e.g. an approximate date of birth should appear differently than a verified one). Confidentiality needs to be secured at least at the same degree as a paper record. The record owned by an individual would include a medical facet which can be copied when visiting a new doctor's office, providing basic summary data and pointers to other physician's records..But the patient would not authorize the doctors' office to copy bank account summaries or pointers to school records. Similarly social services could be authorized by the person or by the court to synchronize their records with court systems or school systems and speed up their required data gathering.

LIMITATIONS

For the designers, agreeing on an appropriate data encoding scheme is difficult. Icons, color and thickness codes have to be carefully designed to avoid biases. For the developers appropriate labeling of the timelines remains hard to optimize and smooth rescaling depends on efficient display algorithms, [6] [17].

Only the visualization aspect of the record has been discussed here and none of the data entry issues. Even if in many applications tedious data entry remains separated from the decision making task, it is clear that a complete implementation of the LifeLines will need some data entry mechanism to append or correct existing records. Our previous experience shows that constructing time lines by direct manipulation was an adequate solution in scheduling home automation devices [11].

CONCLUSION

Personal histories contain information that plays an important role in decision making. LifeLines are proposed as a simple and tailorable technique to represent a variety of personal history records. They provide a complete visualization environment offering overview, zooming, filtering and details on demand. Color coding, filtering and dynamic highlighting unveil relationships between events that may otherwise be difficult to see in paper records. Finally, techniques have been described to handle large records and to facilitate the associated window management, making LifeLines a useful starting point toward a standard personal history format.

ACKNOWLEDGMENT

This work was supported in part by the Maryland Department of Juvenile Justice and by the NSF grant NSF EEC 94-02384. We want to acknowledge Chris Cassatt from DJJ for his participation in this work, and Teresa Cronnell for her help with graphic design.

REFERENCES

1. Asahi T., Turo, D., Shneiderman, B. Using treemaps to visualize the analytic hierarchy process, to appear in *Information Systems Research*, (1996).

2. Beard, D., Walker II, J., Navigational techniques to improve the display of large two-dimensional spaces. *Behaviour and Information Technology 9* , 6 (1990), 451-466.

3. Boens, J., Borst, F., Scherrer, J., Organizing the clinical data in the medical record. *MD Computing* ; 9 (1992) 149-155.

4. Factor, M., Gelernter, D.H., Kolb, C.E., Miller, P.L., Sittig, D.F. Real-time dasta fusion in the intensive care unit. *IEEE Computer*, 24 (1991) 45-54.

5. Hibino, S., Rundensteiner, E. A., A visual query language for identifying temporal trends in video data, *Proceedings of the 1995 International Workshop on Multi-Media Database Management Systems.*, pp 74-81.

6. Jog, N., Shneiderman, B. Starfield information visualization with interactive smooth zooming. *Proc. of IFIP 2.6 Visual Databases Systems*. (Lausanne, Switzerland, March 27-29, 1995) 1-10.

7. Kandogan, E. , Shneiderman, B., Elastic windows: improved spacial layout and rapid multiple windows operations. Technical report CS-TR-3522, University of Maryland, (1995).

8. Lientz, B.P., Rea, K.P. *Project Management for the 21st Century*. Academic Press, San Diego, California, 1995.

9. Mackinlay, J.D., Robertson, G.G., Card, S.K. The Perspective Wall: detail and context smoothly integrated. In *Proceedings of SIGCHI '91* , (1991) 173-179, ACM, New York.

10. Milash, B., Plaisant, C., Rose. A., LifeLines: Visualizing Personal Histories, in CHI 96 Video Program, ACM, New York, (1996).

11. Plaisant, C., Shneiderman, B. Scheduling home control devices: design issues and usability evaluation of four touchscreen interfaces. *Int. J. Man-Machine Studies*, 36 (1992), 375-393.

12. Plaisant, C., Carr, D., Shneiderman, B., Image Browsers: Taxonomy, Guidelines, and Informal Specifications, *IEEE Software* , 12:2 (1995), 21-32.

13. Powsner, S.M., Tufte, E.R., Graphical summary of patient status. *The Lancet*, 344:8919 (August 6, 1994), 386-389.

14. Sanderson, P., Scott, J., Johnston, T., Mainzer, J., Watanabe, L., James, J., MacSHAPA and the enterprise of exploring sequential data analysis (ESDA), *Int. J Man-Machine Studies*, 41 (1992), 633-681.

15. Tufte, E.R., *The Visual Display of Quantitative Information*. Graphics Press, Cheshire, Connecticut, 1983.

16. Whiting-O'Keefe, Q.E., Simbork, D.W., Epstein, W.V., Warger, A. A Computerized summary medical record system can provide more information than the standard medical record. *JAMA*, 254:9 (1985), 1185-1192.

17. Wyatt J.C., Clinical data systems, Part 1: data and medical records. *The Lancet*, 344 (December 3, 1994), 1543-1547.

18. Bederson, B.B., Hollan, James D., Pad++: A Zooming Graphical Interface for Exploring Alternate Interface Physics, *Proceedings of UIST '94*, (Marina del Rey, California, November 2-4, 1994), 17-26, ACM, New York.

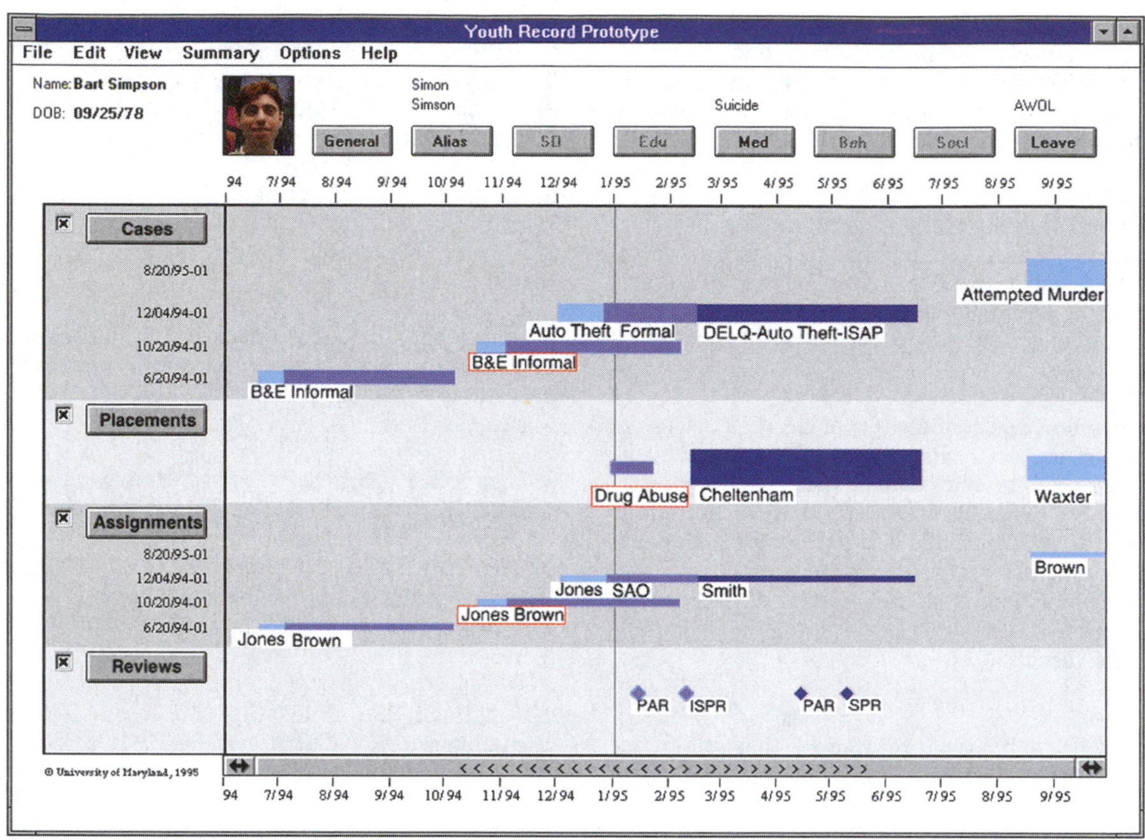

Plaisant, Color Plate 1 - Using LifeLines for Juvenile Justice records. This simple youth record shows cases, placements, assigned workers and available reviews. We can see a history of four cases, three already closed, one opened. A click on the "drug abuse" program highlights the labels of the associated breaking and entering case, and the workers who were assigned to the case (using red in this figure, but gray-out in the prototype).

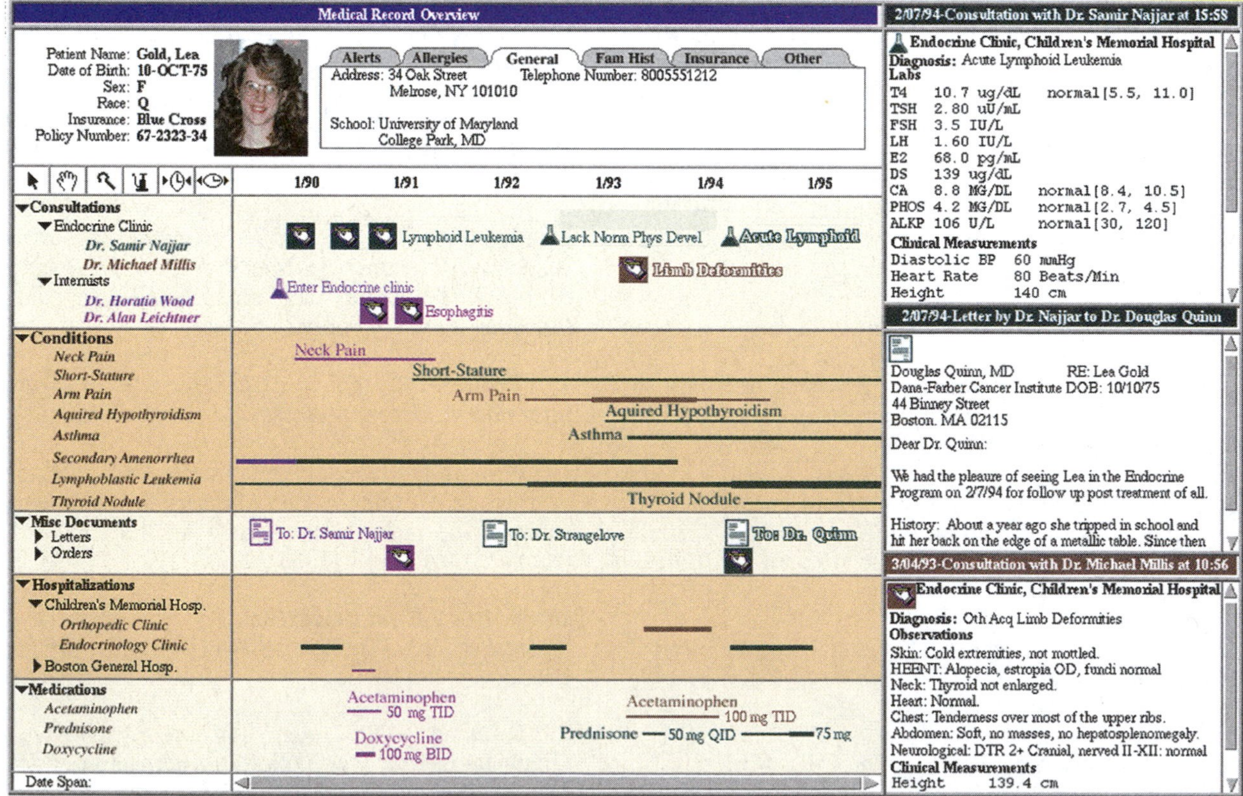

Plaisant, Color Plate 2 - Using LifeLines for medical records. Consultations, manifestations, documents, hospitalizations and treatments are shown in this record. Each doctor has a unique color. Line thickness shows severity and dosage. (Data partly based on a real case found in the literature.)

Browsing hierarchical data with multi-level dynamic queries and pruning

HARSHA P. KUMAR,* CATHERINE PLAISANT AND BEN SHNEIDERMAN

Human-Computer Interaction Laboratory, Department of Computer Science, Institute for Systems Research†, University of Maryland, College Park, MD20742-3255, USA. email:harsha@webizinc.com/plaisant@cs.umd.edu/ben@cs.umd.edu

(Received 6 November 1995 and accepted in revised form 3 September 1996)

Users often must browse hierarchies with thousands of nodes in search of those that best match their information needs. The *PDQ Tree-browser* (Pruning with Dynamic Queries) visualization tool was specified, designed and developed for this purpose. This tool presents trees in two tightly-coupled views, one a detailed view and the other an overview. Users can use dynamic queries, a method for rapidly filtering data, to filter nodes at each level of the tree. The dynamic query panels are user-customizable. Sub-trees of unselected nodes are pruned out, leading to compact views of relevant nodes. Usability testing of the PDQ Tree-browser, done with eight subjects, helped assess strengths and identify possible improvements. The PDQ Tree-browser was used in Network Management (600 nodes) and UniversityFinder (1100 nodes) applications. A controlled experiment, with 24 subjects, showed that pruning significantly improved performance speed and subjective user satisfaction. Future research directions are suggested.

1. Introduction

Decisions are an integral part of human life. Whether deciding what movie to see or choosing which universities to apply to, people are constantly faced with decisions. Many everyday decisions and in engineering applications require the selection of one or a few elements from many, possibly thousands of elements. In such cases, users often try to make a "good" choice by deciding first what they do *not* want, i.e. they first try to reduce the data set to a smaller, more manageable size. After some iterations, it is easier to make the final selection(s) from the reduced data set. This *iterative refinement* or *progressive querying* of data sets is sometimes known as hierarchical decision-making.

A hierarchical data set (HDS) (also called a "tree") organizes data points into a hierarchy. HDSs are common, e.g. sales & budget data, catalogs of products, library indices, computer file systems, etc. A HDS can be filtered (queried and reduced) effectively using a hierarchical-decision making process because the data is inherently hierarchical.

The original motivation for this work was our research on user interfaces for network management (Kumar, Plaisant, Teittinen & Shneiderman, 1994). While working on a user interface for satellite network configuration, we were faced with the task of choosing one leaf node from a large tree of thousands of nodes. Further, the task was such that the number of interesting leaf nodes could be reduced drastically based on selection criteria at various levels in the tree. This problem prompted us to design and implement the PDQ (Pruning with Dynamic Queries) Tree-browser.

2. PDQ Tree-browser requirements

Based on our task analyses in the network management scenario and other tree-browsing applications, we specified the requirements for the PDQ Tree-browser visualization tool as follows.

- Browse the entire tree and view it at different levels.
- Query nodes at all levels on the basis of attribute values. Querying mechanism should be easy, rapid, yet powerful.
- Hide uninteresting nodes and branches rapidly, and thus reduce the data set progressively. Iterate easily by revealing hidden nodes/branches.

3. Previous work

Information search is a vast topic (Marchionini, 1995), but previous work on hierarchical data is more limited. Early work emphasized aesthetic and easy-to-read tree and graph layouts (Battista, Eades, Tamassia & Tollis, 1989), and browsing/exploring/searching trees and graphs, but none of them provide a good solution to the attributes-based querying and browsing problem. Many visual browsers address two-dimensional-browsing, and some allow for manual pruning of uninteresting sub-trees/sub-graphs. Commonly used tree visualizations include two-dimensional node-link diagrams, space-filling treemaps, three-dimensional node-link diagrams and tables-of-contents or outliners.

An advantage of node-link visualizations of trees is that they are a familiar mapping of structured relationships and therefore easy to understand. They can also display attributes of links by color or size if required. However, node-link diagrams make inefficient use of screen space, and even trees of medium size need multiple screens to be completely displayed. This necessitates scrolling of the diagram and global context is lost, since only a part of the diagram is visible at any given time.

Beard and Walker (1990) used a *map window*—a miniature of the entire information space with a wire-frame box to aid users in remembering their location. The map window is better known as an *overview*, the entire information space shown in full size is the *detailed view* and the wire-frame box is the *field-of-view* or the *panner* (Plaisant, Carr & Shneiderman, 1995). The field-of-view can be dragged around in the overview to pan the detailed view. Similarly, scrolling the detailed view updates the position of the field-of-view in the overview. Hence, the overview and the detailed view are said to be *tightly-coupled*. Beard and Walker (1990) found that an overview significantly improves user performance, and the pan technique and the zoom and pan technique were significantly faster than the scroll technique.

Plaisant *et al.* (1995) provide a taxonomy and guidelines for image-browsers. This work attempts to standardize some of the terms being used by researchers today, e.g. detail view, field-of-view, etc. Different kinds of browsers such as "detail only", "one window with zoom and replace", and "tiled multilevel browser" are shown. The authors identify five classes of tasks that are accomplished with image browsers, e.g. open ended exploration, navigation, monitoring, etc.

The treemap visualization of tree structures uses a two-dimensional space-filling approach in which each node is a rectangle whose area is proportional to some attribute such as node size (Shneiderman, 1992). The treemap algorithm utilizes 100% of the designated space. Sections of the hierarchy containing more important information can be allocated more display space while portions of the hierarchy which are less important to the specific task at hand can be allocated less space. Treemaps have been used for file management, network management (Kumar *et al.*, 1994), budgets, sports data, etc.

Robertson, Mackinlay and Card (1991) and Chignell, Zubrec and Poblete (1993) used three-dimensional node-link diagrams in order to visualize tree structures. Robertson *et al.* (1991) in the Information Visualizer project at Xerox PARC, developed a tool called Cone Trees that allows for animation of three-dimensional trees. They contend that interactive animation can effectively shift cognitive processing load to the perceptual system. They describe *gardening operations* (Robertson *et al.*, 1991) where the user can manually prune and grow the view of the tree. Prune and grow operations are done either by menu or by gestures directed at a node. While these gardening operations do help in managing and understanding large, complex hierarchies, this manual mechanism of pruning or growing one subtree at a time, is clearly not sufficient nor very effective in specifying complex searches spanning several levels of the tree.

Chignell *et al.* (1993) built the Info-TV tool, which allows two styles of pruning as follows.

- The sub-branch(es) for which the chosen node is the root can be removed from the screen.
- The nodes and labels are removed, but the links remain.

The authors however, do not describe how the nodes whose sub-trees are to be pruned are specified by the user. It is assumed that the user makes these specifications manually by selecting these nodes.

Visualizations have also been used to browse graph structures. Examples of graph visualizations include hypertext graphs, finite-state diagrams, flow-charts, parse-trees, pert-charts, dataflow diagrams, wiring diagrams and hierarchical decompositions.

According to Henry and Hudson (1991) and Henry (1992), the "best layout" depends on the user's current region of interest. Consequently, a single layout algorithm cannot always produce the best results. Thus, the *ability of users to customize* the layout to meet their current needs and interests is essential. Therefore, users must be provided with *interactive tools* to *iteratively* dissect large graphs into manageable pieces. Henry and Hudson (1991) describe manual selection in which users select nodes and edges using simple direct manipulation techniques, and algorithmic selection in which users apply an algorithm to the graph. But by classifying manual selection into *only* individual selection or marquee selection, the authors are greatly restricting the range of interesting selection subsets that can be specified by the user. They conclude by identifying two primary future directions: using domain specific graph semantics to guide the layout and the selection, and creating a methodology that can be used to build *an interactive system for nonprogrammers to specify selection and layout algorithms*. Our work extends their strategies.

Gedye (1988) built a system that presents users with a list of all the objects. They can choose an object, and then upon choosing one particular relationship, a directed acyclic graph, tree, or an equivalence set is created in a new window. So, the tangled web that would have resulted by showing all the relationships is eliminated by using one window per relationship. Noting that both zooming and panning were inadequate for arbitrary graph structures, the authors implemented pruning in order to assist in the browsing. A sub-graph is selected that contains few enough nodes to comfortably fit in the window, and this sub-graph is displayed in its entirety. The sub-graph obtained by the pruning procedure is called the "display graph".

Schaffer, Zuo, Bartum, Dill, Dubs, Greenberg and Roseman (1996) found that users performed better using fisheye views of hierarchically-clustered graphs than using full-zoom views. Hollands, Carey, Matthews and McCann (1989), however found users getting somewhat disoriented while using fisheye views for complex tasks. None of the fisheye view implementations described above allow for attributes-based specification of the foci of interest. A novel alternative is the hyperbolic tree browser (Lamping, Rao & Pirolli, 1995).

The review of the literature pertaining to tree and graph browsers did not provide a good answer to the problem of specifying selection subsets on large connected data sets like trees and graphs. Those that do allow for uninteresting nodes/sub-trees/sub-graphs to be pruned out, require users to make subset specifications manually. We believe that dynamic queries can be used effectively for this purpose. Dynamic queries describes the interactive user control of visual query parameters that generates a rapid (100 ms update) animated visual display of database search results. Dynamic queries are an application of the direct manipulation principles in the database environment. They depend on presenting a visual overview, powerful filtering tools, continuous visual display of information, pointing rather than typing, and rapid, incremental, and reversible control of the query (Shneiderman, 1992). Dynamic queries have been applied to browse databases of houses, movies, chemical tables of elements, etc. These concepts of dynamic querying and tight-coupling are similar to those of Focusing and Linking (Buja, McDonald, Michalak & Stuetzle, 1991).

4. PDQ Tree-browser design

4.1. THEORY

Our PDQ Tree-browser design consists of the following features.

- Two tightly-coupled node-link views of the tree (Overview and Detailed View).
- Dynamic Query Environment for users to customize their dynamic query panels.
- Dynamic Queries at different levels of the tree.
- Pruning of sub-trees of uninteresting nodes to get more compact views.

4.1.1. Dynamic queries on hierarchical data sets

Dynamic queries have been applied to data sets consisting of independent data points (Ahlberg & Shneiderman, 1994). In such cases, whether a data point satisfies a given query or not does not affect the outcome for other data points. This is because there are no interrelationships between the data points. Thus, the data set can be thought of as "flat". Queries are merely queries on the attributes of individual data points. For example, in the FilmFinder, each movie is an independent data point. Similarly, in the HomeFinder (Shneiderman, 1994), each house is an independent data point.

In a "non-flat" data set, on the other hand, there are predefined interrelationships between data points. For example, in a HDS, some nodes are related to some others by the parent–child relationship (Kumar *et al.*, 1994). Therefore, whether a node matches a given query or not might affect some other nodes. Specifically, while searching a hierarchical data set in a top-down manner (i.e. parent first), it makes sense to prune out all descendant nodes of nodes that do not match the query. For example, if users are looking for departments in universities with low tuition, it makes sense to eliminate those departments whose universities have high tuition. When criteria (like low tuition, high average SAT scores, high placement indices, etc.) exist at all or most levels in the hierarchy, *stepwise refinement of the query* can be done to progressively reduce the initial (large) data set into a smaller set, from which good choices may be made.

4.1.2. Dynamic query environments

The HomeFinder and the FilmFinder are examples of systems that provide hard-coded graphical widgets for the user to manipulate in order to dynamically update the visual display. If the user wanted to find homes that were within 2 miles of any hospital, the current HomeFinder interface would have to be reprogrammed.

Therefore, a *Dynamic Query Environment*, first implemented in a browser for the National Center for Health Statistics (Shneiderman, 1994), should allow users to customize dynamic query control panels based on current interests. Users should be able to select what combination of attributes they wish to query on, and have the appropriate widgets created, at run-time. The method of selecting the attributes and creating widgets should be easy, and also allow for modifications/backtracking. Having the interface not be application-dependent would have the added advantage of reusability across applications.

4.2. DESCRIPTION OF THE INTERFACE

The PDQ Tree-browser interface consists of two main parts (Figure 1) as follows.

- **Data display:** the tree structure is visualized in two tightly-coupled views, a detailed view (on the right) and an overview (on the left). If the PDQ Tree-browser window is resized by the user, the field-of-view shape and size is updated automatically.

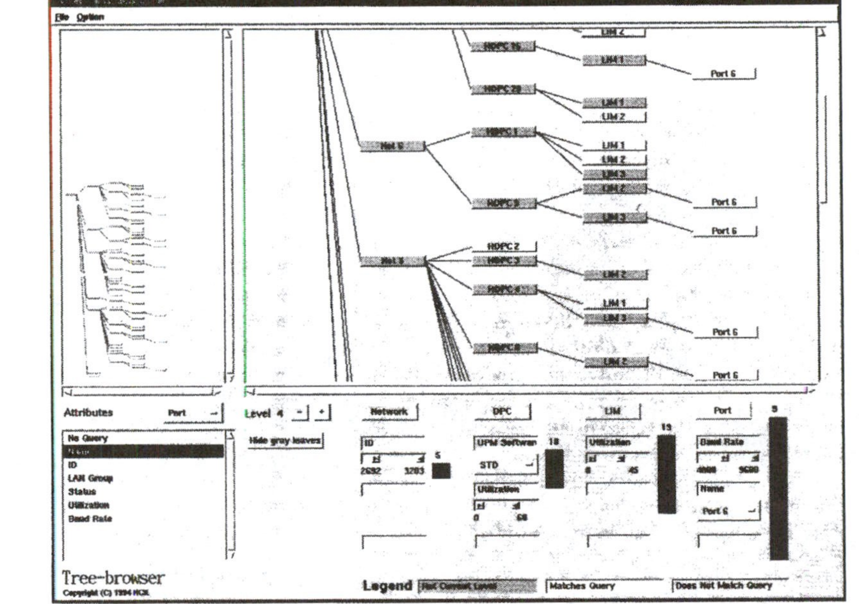

FIGURE 1. The PDQ Tree-browser interface.

- **Dynamic query panel:** this panel (below the Data Display) consists of two parts, the Attributes List on the left and the Widgets Panel on the right. Initially, there are no query widgets in the Widgets Panel. Users may select (by dragging-and-dropping) up to three attributes from the Attributes List for each level in the hierarchy (except the root level). This causes an appropriate widget (range-slider for numerical attributes and menu for textual attributes) to be created and initialized. Queries (on up to three attributes) at each level are AND-ed together. Users can replace an existing widget with another by dropping a new attribute name over the original widget's attribute name. Existing widgets can be deleted by dropping "No Query" onto the corresponding attribute name.

The Treeview and Range-slider widgets of the University of Maryland Widget Library™ (Carr, Jog, Kumar, Teittinen & Ahlberg, 1994) were used in the PDQ Tree-browser implementation.

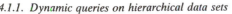

If users manipulate a widget at the current lowest level displayed, the nodes matching the query at that level are colored yellow, otherwise they are grey. These updates of the data display are real-time (within 100 ms of updates to the control widgets) in accordance with the principle of dynamic queries. Buffering was done in order to make the updates as smooth and flicker-free as possible.

If users manipulate a widget at a level other than the current lowest level, the tree visualization first "jumps" to that level, i.e. the level of the widget is made the tree's current lowest level. This is done so that the structure of the tree during direct manipulation of the widgets remains constant and only the colors of the nodes change. Then the nodes at the new lowest level are updated (by coloring yellow or grey) in real-time to show whether they match the query or not.

The tree structure changes *only* when the current lowest level of the tree is changed, which can be accomplished by users in three ways as follows.

- By clicking on the corresponding level button (i.e. the buttons labeled "Network", "DPC", "LIM" and "Port") just below the data display (Figure 1).
- By manipulating a widget at any level other than the current lowest level, as explained above.
- By clicking on the + or − buttons to either increase or decrease the levels displayed.

When the current lowest level is changed so as to show more levels, *pruning* of the tree is done so as to eliminate sub-trees of nodes that do not match the query at their own levels. For example, if the user manipulates the range slider for Network ID such that Nets 1 and 2 do not match the query (Figure 2), and then increases the lowest level displayed by 1, the children of nets 1 and 2 are not shown, while children of other nets are shown (Figure 3). Nets 1 and 2 now appear in grey, while all the other nets appear in orange, simply to show that those nodes did match the query at their own level. This feedback enables users to go back and change queries at higher levels, and thus iteratively refine the selection subset.

As explained above, nodes at the current lowest level are colored either yellow or grey, while nodes at higher levels are colored either orange or grey. Also, the level button corresponding to the current lowest level is colored yellow so as to focus the attention of the user to that level. Buttons at other levels are colored grey.

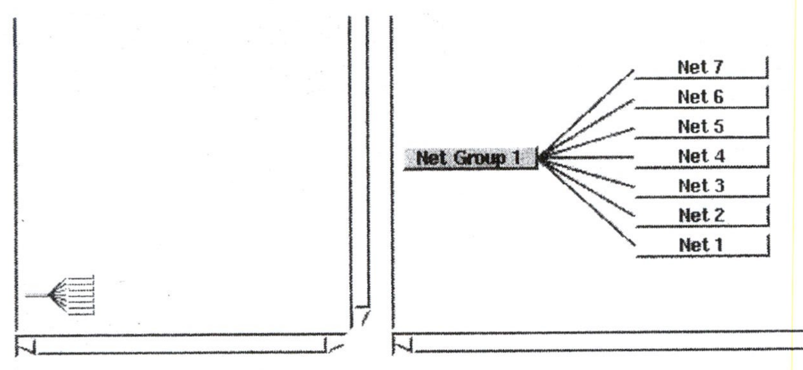

FIGURE 2. Nets 1 and 2 do not match query.

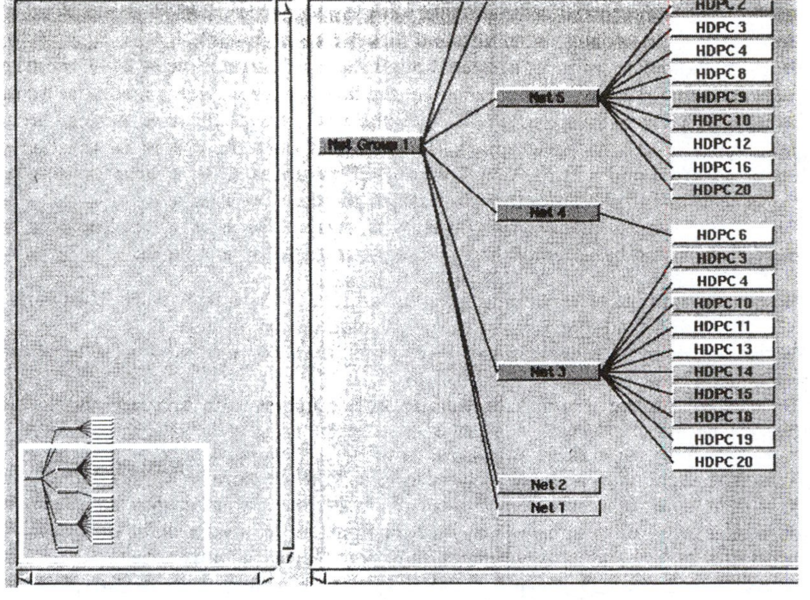

FIGURE 3. Sub-trees of Nets 1 and 2 are pruned out.

When the current lowest level is changed so as to show fewer levels, the tree is simply "folded" back to the new lowest level, and then the nodes at that level are colored either yellow or grey based on the query at that level. Thus, users can easily jump back and forth between levels in order to fine-tune their search.

The Attributes List on the left shows only the attributes corresponding to the current lowest level. Users can access names of attributes at other levels by choosing the appropriate level name (e.g. Network, DPC, etc.) from the attributes menu just above the Attributes List (Figure 1).

There are four feedback indicators, one corresponding to each level (other than the root level), that are updated in order to show the number and proportion of nodes that currently match the query (i.e. number of "hits"). The proportion of the feedback indicator that is colored yellow corresponds to the proportion of hits. This proportion is a percentage of the total number of nodes at that level, not of the number of nodes at that level currently displayed. The actual number of hits is also displayed at the top of each feedback indicator. Proportion indicators are displayed from level 1 down to the current lowest level only, those for deeper levels are hidden (greyed out). This is because calculating the number of nodes that *would* match the query at deeper levels is computationally intensive and would slow down the dynamic queries on nodes at the current level. At any time users can select the "Hide gray leaves" button to hide the greyed out nodes.

To summarize, the PDQ Tree-browser is a visualization tool for hierarchical data that makes use of dynamic queries and pruning. The PDQ Tree-browser uses two coordinated or tightly-coupled views of the same tree, one a detailed view and the other an overview. The user can select up to three attributes (numerical or textual) for dynamically querying nodes at each level in the hierarchy. Sub-trees of nodes that do not match the query at their own level are pruned out of the visualization. Thus, one can reduce a large data set (with thousands of nodes) to a much smaller set, from which good selections can be made.

4.3. EXAMPLE APPLICATION: THE UNIVERSITY FINDER

We applied the PDQ Tree-browser to two applications, Network Management and the UniversityFinder. The latter is described here. The database organizes universities hierarchically; we have regions of the world, followed by states, then universities, and finally, departments. The UniversityFinder demo is available on videotape (Kumar, 1995).

Let us say that I am a high-school senior looking for universities that best match my needs. The PDQ Tree-browser initially shows all the regions in the world. I ask to see the entire tree to get an idea of the size of the database. The feedback indicators show that there are 740 departments in 286 universities in 62 states in five regions of the world (Figure 4).

I realize that planning through this entire tree is not an easy task and return to the region level. Since I am only interested in regions where English is the primary language, I create a textual menu of primary languages by dragging-and-dropping the attribute Primary Language on to one of the empty slots under the Region level button. I select English from the menu and South America turns grey, while USA, Canada, Africa and Europe remain yellow.

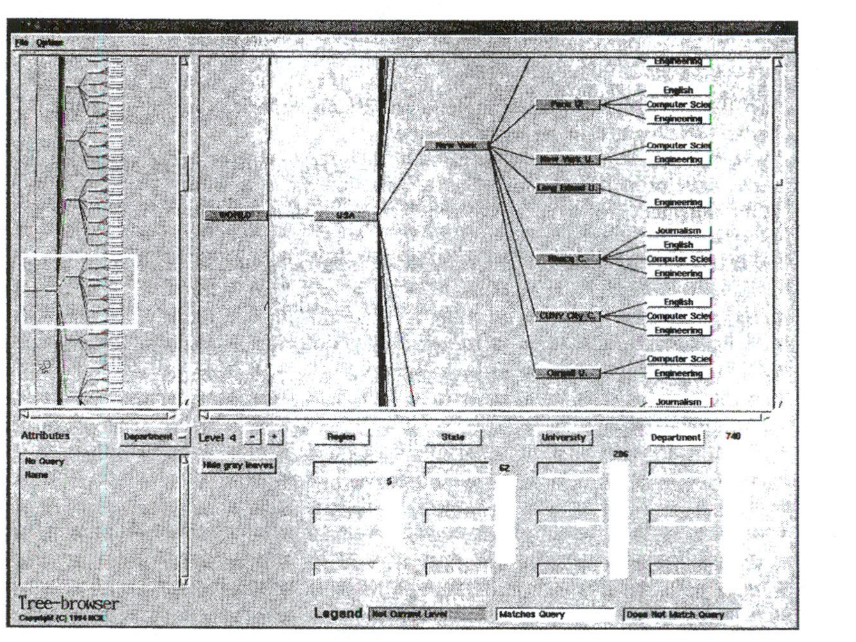

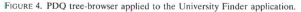

FIGURE 4. PDQ tree-browser applied to the University Finder application.

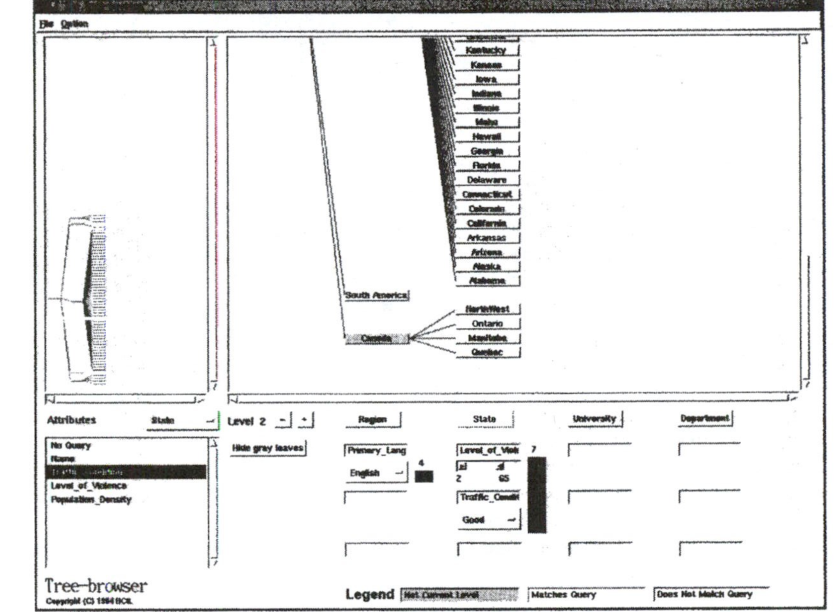

FIGURE 5. Querying for desirable states.

I now proceed to the state level. South America's sub-tree is not expanded. That sub-tree was pruned out since South America did not satisfy our criterion for primary language. However, South America is still shown in grey in order to provide context feedback.

I would really like to study in a state that is relatively safe, so I choose to query on the level of violence. I manipulate the range-slider to select only states with a violence index less than 65, leaving 37 states. I further reduce the number of interesting states by choosing only those with good traffic conditions. The number of states has now dropped to only seven (Figure 5).

Now, I can look at the universities, but first I recapture space occupied by uninteresting states by clicking on the "Hide gray leaves" button. This gives me a more compact view that often is visible on a single screen. When I now go to the university level, only the remaining seven states are expanded to show 25 universities.

I now reduce the number of universities by first eliminating those with high tuition and then setting the average SAT scores to closely match mine. I hide grey leaves once again and see that I am down to seven universities: a couple in Arkansas, a couple in Ontario, etc.

Satisfied with this set of universities, I proceed to the department level to closely

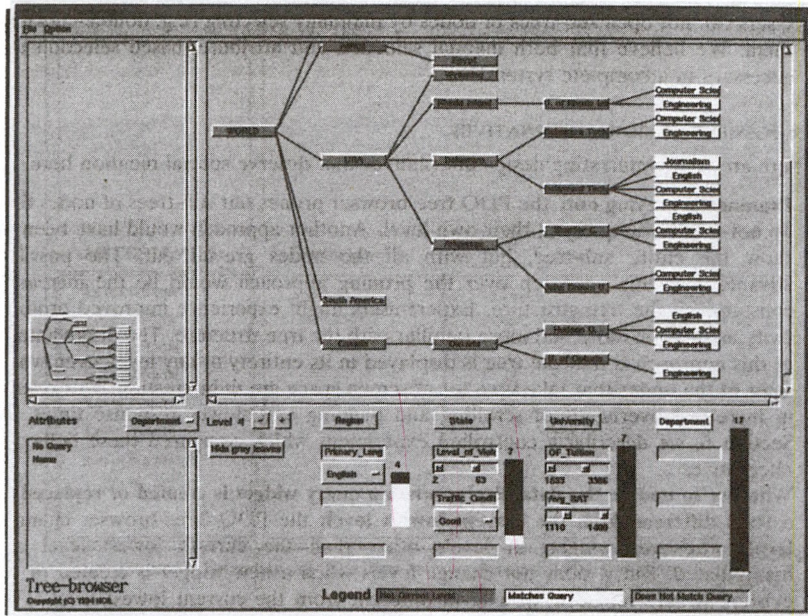

FIGURE 6. Final selection subset of 17 universities.

look at departments (Figure 6) that best match my interests and needs in terms of availability of financial aid, etc.

4.4. PDQ TREE-BROWSER LIMITATIONS

The UniversityFinder scenario demonstrates how the PDQ Tree-browser can be applied to everyday applications, in addition to complex applications like network management. The tool itself is general and can be used for any hierarchical data set with attributes for nodes at different levels of the hierarchy. However, the current implementation does have the following limitations:

- The PDQ Tree-browser interface has been "fine-tuned" for a tree of depth 5. The underlying tree data structure and node-link widgets place no constraints on the depth of the tree, but the current interface has been customized to look best for a tree of depth 5, e.g. the levels of the tree in the detailed view align nicely with the corresponding buttons and query widgets.
- Users can select only up to three attributes to query on at each level, and these queries can only be ANDed together. ORs and NOTs are not supported currently.
- Since the focus of this work was not on layout, the algorithm used produces an aesthetic tidy layout, but not the most compact one. Also, the implementation does not enforce the overview to always show the entire tree (so users might have to scroll the overview).
- Users can not open sub-trees of nodes by manually selecting (e.g. double-clicking) them. We believe that both manual selection and attributes-based selection are necessary in a complete system.

4.5. POSSIBLE DESIGN ALTERNATIVES

There are some interesting design alternatives that deserve special mention here.

- **Pruning vs. greying out:** the PDQ tree-browser prunes out sub-trees of nodes that do not match the query at their own level. Another approach would have been to show the entire sub-tree, but with all the nodes greyed out. The possible advantage of this approach over the pruning approach would be the increased constancy in the tree structure. Expert users might experience improved productivity as they get more and more familiar with the tree structure. The disadvantage of this approach is that the tree is displayed in its entirety at any level, even when most of the nodes that take up a lot of screen space are uninteresting. This results in increased overheads of scrolling and panning and slower response times. In Section 6, we describe a controlled experiment which compared these behavior alternatives.
- **Whether to update the data display when a query widget is created or replaced at a level different from the current lowest level:** the PDQ Tree-browser changes levels whenever widgets at levels other than the current lowest level are manipulated. But it does not change levels when a new widget is created or an existing widget replaced, at a level different from the current lowest level. This design decision was based on the assumption that users might create a number of widgets at different levels at the same time (e.g. at the beginning), and not want the level to change each time. The disadvantage of this approach is that the data display is potentially inaccurate till the next time users visit that level.

4.6. GENERALIZING THE DESIGN

This section attempts to generalize the PDQ tree-browser design so as to overcome some of its limitations and make it more generally applicable to trees of varying structures and sizes. Ideas on extending the query interface to allow specification of complex boolean queries are discussed. The PDQ Tree-browser illustrated the advantages of using dynamic queries and pruning while visualizing trees as two-dimensional node-link diagrams. The same advantages are there to be had by other tree visualizations as well, e.g. treemaps and Cone Trees. We illustrate this with examples for the treemap case.

4.6.1. Coping with varying structure and growing size

In this section, we examine some of the issues that need to be addressed in order for our design to be extensible to trees of varying structure and size.

- **Trees of arbitrary depth:** Figure 7 shows how one might extend the current PDQ Tree-browser interface to handle trees arbitrarily deep. Due to screen space constraints, it will not be possible to see all the query widgets at all levels in the hierarchy. In Figure 7, on the lower left corner, is a list of levels in the hierarchy, from which users select the current lowest level (level 2 in this case). The

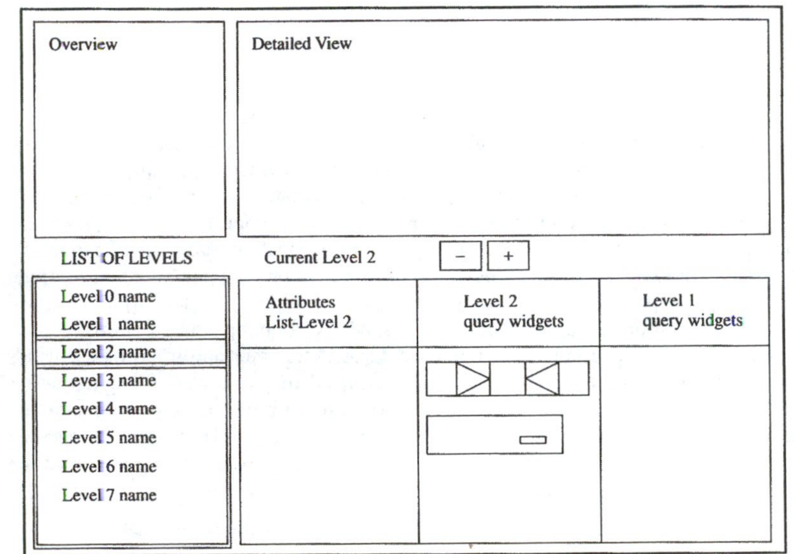

FIGURE 7. Extending the PDQ Tree-browser design to trees of arbitrary depth.

Attributes List then updates to show the list of attributes for level 2. The query widgets for the current lowest level and for the previous level visited (i.e. level 1 in this case) are shown in the query panel.

- **Trees of arbitrary size:** as the size of the tree to be visualized becomes larger, performance would tend to deteriorate and the browsing mechanism becomes inadequate. But there are approaches that can be taken to alleviate this problem as follows.

(1) *Performance issues.* Our node-link layout algorithm, in the worst case (i.e. when all nodes are to be shown), requires two complete traversals of the tree. Dynamically querying nodes at any level is more efficient in that it only requires traversal of each node at that level and not of the entire tree. Therefore, the system is likely to slow down appreciably as the size of the tree increases, especially for operations that require re-computation of the structure and layout.

More sophisticated data structures and algorithms would be necessary in order to minimize the performance deteriorations. For example, one might only traverse the nodes visible in the detailed view to evaluate dynamic queries. But this would mean that the overview would not be tightly-coupled with the detailed view. Algorithms for pruning could be improved so that only sub-trees that have been dynamically queried since the last structure change need to be traversed. There are several interesting challenges that remain to be solved, with respect to performance issues.

(2) *Interface issues.* Ideally, the overview would always show the entire data display in miniature, even if it means that no details are visible; and the overview provides only global context. However, when the size of the tree gets huge (say 50 000 nodes), there is no way that one overview would suffice. Plaisant, Carr and Hasegawa (1992) found that in some cases, it might even be useful to provide an intermediate view in addition to the overview and the detailed view, when the detail-to-overview zoom ratio is above 20.

Another feature that might be useful is to allow users to restrict the nodes to be displayed *before* displaying them. For example, if the user requests to see a new level with 20 000 nodes, the system should present the user with the option of restricting this set (feedback might be provided by displaying the number of matching nodes) before displaying it.

4.6.2. Specification of general boolean queries

The current PDQ Tree-browser implementation allows users to specify an AND of queries on zero to three attributes at each level. An improved interface would allow any number of ANDs, ORs and NOTs. But specifying complex boolean queries graphically is a challenge, as it may be difficult to interpret a set of graphical widgets, boolean operators and parentheses, even for experienced users.

The PDQ Tree-browser could accommodate complex boolean queries by using the Filter-Flow metaphor in which queries are shown as water streams flowing through sequential filters for ANDs, parallel filters for ORs, and inverted filters for NOTs (Young & Shneiderman, 1993). The decrease in the breadth of the water stream while passing through a filter represents the reduction in the data set due to the corresponding query.

4.6.3. Pruning applied to treemaps

It was in fact, a treemap of a network hub that first highlighted the need for some mechanism to hide subsets of nodes/prune sub-trees that were not interesting and recapture screen space. Uninteresting leaf nodes had taken up about 40 % of the total display space.

Figure 8 shows how pruning can help treemaps recapture screen space allocated to uninteresting sub-trees.

4.6.4. Dynamic queries and pruning applied to cone trees

Robertson *et al.* (1991) describe "gardening operations" where the user can manually prune and grow the view of the tree. Prune and grow operations are done either by menu or by gestures directed at a node. We believe that allowing users to make attributes-based subset specifications in addition to these manual subset specifications will help make Cone Trees more powerful and useful.

5. Usability testing

In order to assess and improve the PDQ Tree-browser, usability evaluations were performed, in which eight subjects were given training and asked to perform specified tasks using the PDQ Tree-browser. The UniversityFinder data was used in the testing.

FIGURE 8. Pruning applied to treemaps. (a) Level 1, (b) level 1 dynamically queried (c) level 2 without pruning, (d) level 2 with pruning.

5.1. METHODS

With each subject, the following procedures were followed.

- Introduction: the experiment was introduced to the subjects by explaining the UniversityFinder scenario (Section 4.3).
- Description of features: PDQ Tree-browser features were demonstrated one by one and subjects were given the opportunity to try each one.
- Tasks: subjects were asked to perform seven tasks. The initial tasks focused on specific features, while later tasks were designed to evaluate the tool as a whole (See Section 5.3 for details). Subjects were encouraged to think aloud while performing the tasks. Comments and suggestions were recorded as they were made. Interesting actions and sources of confusion were also recorded.
- Subjective evaluation: subjects were asked to rate specific features of the system (on a scale of 1 to 9), identify what they liked and disliked most about the PDQ Tree-browser and make suggestions for improvement.
- Analysis: finally, all comments and suggestions made by subjects were compiled into one list (Section 5.4). The mean and standard deviation were computed for each rating and some graphs were plotted.

5.2. SUBJECTS

Pilot testing was done with two graduate students, to try out the tasks and get preliminary reactions. The tasks were refined, a subjective evaluation questionnaire was designed, and the software was tested with six subjects. The subjects were familiar with tree structures and pruning, database querying, GUIs and direct manipulation widgets. The subjects ranged from graduate students and undergraduate seniors in Computer Science/Electrical Engineering to a faculty research assistant.

5.3. TASKS

The range of (seven) tasks included the following.
(1) **Feature-based testing:** testing the specific features of the PDQ Tree-browser.

- Tight-coupling of overview and detailed view: two-dimensional browsing of the node-link diagrams using panning, scrolling and changing levels features only.
- Dynamic Query Environments: building and modifying dynamic query panels using drags-and-drops. Directly manipulating the widgets to produce real-time color updates of the nodes.
- Tree Dynamics: tree pruning and associated structure and layout changes. Issues relating to getting familiar with the tree structure and disorientation due to structural changes. Ability to iteratively refine queries, by jumping back and forth between levels.

(2) **Task-based testing:** testing queries of varying complexity and type. This classification of queries is general and independent of this particular PDQ Tree-browser design and implementation.

- Simple "attributes-based" queries: for example, how many states have a level of violence index $<=60$ and good traffic conditions?
- Complex associative "structure-based" queries: for example, how many states satisfy all the following constraints: regions with standard of living $>=50$ but $<=95$, states with population density $<=72$ and good traffic conditions, public universities with out-of-state full-time tuition $<=\$3000$ per semester and average SAT scores of $>=$ 1100 and at least one department.

5.4. RESULTS

The subjective evaluations revealed which features were liked and which needed improvement as follows.

5.4.1. Most liked features

When asked what was the one thing they liked the most about the PDQ Tree-browser, subjects responses included the following.

- "Dynamic querying and pruning to get multiple views based on current interests."
- "Easy to learn, convenient and straight-forward to use."
- "The ability to locate interesting parts of large trees."
- "Easy to create complex multi-level queries."
- "I liked seeing the tree structure of the data, which would usually be tabular."

- "Shows adequate information."
- "Tightly-coupled overview and detailed view."

5.4.2 Subjective ratings

Users rated 22 aspects of the PDQ Tree-browser on scales of 1 to 9, where 1 was the worst rating and 9 the best rating. They also rated three possible features. For example, users gave a mean rating of 8.7 (S.D. = 0.5) to the usefulness of pruning, a mean rating of 8.2 (S.D. = 1.0) to the usefulness of dynamic queries, while the ease of range-slider manipulation got a mean rating of only 4.8 (S.D. = 2.4).

5.4.3 Suggestions for improvement

Subjects were also asked to make suggestions for improvement and possible new features. All the suggestions were tabulated, resulting in 19 possible enhancements to the system. Some of these are obvious ones that would be inexpensive to incorporate into the system, while others would require more effort as follows.

(1) Ability to manually add or remove one or more nodes to the selection subset resulting from the dynamic queries (by clicking, marquee, etc.). Thus, the ideal subset specification mechanism would allow both query-based specification as well as manual specification. Some issues relating to keeping track of these nodes and avoiding complications later in the query process need to be addressed.

(2) Pruning and the Hide Grey Leaves feature were clearly well liked by the subjects. Most of them used the latter frequently to recapture screen space from uninteresting grey nodes and focus the search. Removing nodes like this also made the system faster. Many subjects agreed that a Hide All Grey Nodes feature would be very useful. Some subjects also felt that the default behavior could be to hide grey nodes (when levels changed) and users could ask to see grey nodes (for context) if they were interested. This suggestion should help make the views even more compact. But the preferred default behavior depends on the structure of the tree (fan-out at each level) and also the type of tasks; therefore this requires more investigation. In fact, one subject liked seeing the grey nodes at higher levels and used the Hide Grey Leaves feature only once. He said the presence of the grey nodes at higher levels helped in visually separating disjoint groups of nodes.

(3) Subjects found the response time of some PDQ Tree-browser features to be slow, especially increasing levels when the number of nodes was high.

(4) It was observed that subjects get somewhat disoriented when the level of the tree was changed. This is because the layout algorithm generates a fresh layout whenever the tree structure changes, i.e. whenever more or less levels are requested to be seen. It is felt that this problem can be significantly alleviated by retaining the same current focus. For example, if the user asks to see the University level while the state Florida is near the center, the new view should be initialized to show universities within Florida.

(5) Panning the detailed view by dragging the field-of-view in the overview was found useful, but some improvements to the design are required. One subject emphasized the need to always fit the overview into one screen only, so that no scrolling of the overview is required. As mentioned before, this is what we had designed, but it was not enforced in this implementation. Another subject suggested that users should be able to click anywhere in the overview and have the field-of-view jump to that position. This would enable fast coarse navigation. Fine-tuning could then be accomplished by dragging the field-of-view.

(6) The catchiest quote received from one of the subjects was this: "Drag-and-drop becomes a drag for experienced users, so drop it!". Some other subjects also echoed the feeling that it might be easier and faster to just replace each drop area with a menu of attributes at that level. Some other subjects enjoyed the drag-and-drop mechanism to create and modify query panels.

(7) Ability to specify complex boolean queries involving ORs and NOTs, in addition to the ANDs allowed currently.

(8) One task (Task 6) required subjects to look for departments within three states, Wyoming, Wisconsin and Washington. This is basically restricting states to Wyoming OR Wisconsin OR Washington. The menu allows users to select 1-of-n textual values. A widget to select m-of-n textual values needs to be designed and implemented.

(9) One subject wished that there was a way to search upwards in the tree, i.e. to be able to query on universities and then see the states which contained the selected universities. Another subject made an interesting suggestion, that the PDQ Tree-browser should allow users to hide certain levels on demand. For example, if users are interested in looking at all universities in USA, and do not care about the states they are in, it should be possible to remove the State level totally and then get it back when desired.

6. A controlled experiment

With our guidance, three students, Robert Ross, Zhijun Zhang and Eun-Mi Choi, conducted a controlled experiment to compare three behavior alternatives for the PDQ Tree-browser. The UniversityFinder database was used in this experiment. These behavior alternatives related to pruning subtrees of nodes that did not match the query at their own levels. The three treatments were as follows (two of these were discussed in Section 4.5).

Full-tree: Sub-trees of unselected nodes are shown in their entirety, but are colored grey.

Partially-pruned: Sub-trees of unselected nodes are pruned out but the nodes themselves are shown in grey. (This is the behavior option that the PDQ tree-browser currently uses.)

Fully-pruned: Sub-trees of unselected nodes and the unselected nodes themselves are pruned out.

It was hypothesized that subjects using the full-tree interface would take longer than those using the partially or fully-pruned interfaces. Although the full-tree allows for a static display of the tree, its inclusion of all irrelevant nodes would probably slow down the response time, add too much useless information to the user's visual field, and create a need for excessive scrolling/panning of the displays to get to relevant nodes. Due to the longer task completion times and more difficult/complex searching required, users would also have lower subjective ratings for the full-tree interface than for the pruned interfaces. Further, the completion times and subjective ratings for the pruned interfaces would be approximately equal

TABLE 1
Mean task completion times (in s) with S.D.s in parentheses

Full-tree	Partially-pruned	Fully-pruned
1917 (609)	883 (121)	705 (139)

(differences would not be significant). It was postulated that the fully-pruned interface promised the most compact views, while the partially-pruned interface offered additional context feedback that might help in tasks requiring several iterations (to refine the query).

Twenty-four subjects were randomly assigned to use one (and only one) of these three treatments (between-groups experimental design). They performed a set of seven tasks. Afterwards, they filled out an electronic questionnaire (QUIS) to subjectively evaluate the treatment that they had used. The results (Tables 1 and 2) showed that the times to complete the set of seven tasks were significantly different at the 0.05 level with full-tree being slower than partially-pruned, which was slower than fully-pruned. In terms of subjective satisfaction, partially-pruned rated higher than fully-pruned, which was preferred to full-tree.

For total task completion time, an ANOVA gave $F(2, 21) = 25.2$ which was significant at the 0.01 level. Then, using pairwise t-tests, it was found that all results were significant at the 0.05 level. Therefore, in this controlled experiment, the fully-pruned interface was the fastest, while the full-tree interface was the slowest. The differences between the full-tree and the pruned interfaces were also significant at the 0.01 level, but the differences between the partially and fully-pruned interfaces were not. For subjective ratings also, the ANOVA produced an F that was significant at the 0.01 level. Also, all of the pairwise t-tests were significant at the 0.05 level. Users liked the partially-pruned interface the best and disliked the full-tree interface the most. Differences between the full-tree and the two pruned interfaces were also significant at the 0.01 level although differences between the partially and fully-pruned interfaces were not. In addition to the overall times for each interface, the times to complete each task were also compared.

The poor performance times of subjects using the full-tree interface might be partly due to poor system response times. Specifically, that interface had consistently (noticeably) slower response times, especially when expanding to the lower levels ("University" and "Department" levels).

TABLE 2
Mean subjective satisfaction ratings (normalized to 0–1, 1 being best) with S.D.s in parentheses

Full-tree	Partially-pruned	Fully-pruned
0.42 (0.12)	0.71 (0.08)	0.64 (0.07)

The differences between the two pruned interfaces were not as clear cut; task performance was faster with the fully-pruned interface but the partially-pruned interface got higher subjective ratings. The fan-out of the particular tree used probably increased the differences between these two interfaces. Specifically, the UniversityFinder tree has a large fan-out (50 states in USA) from the Region level to the State level, and this might help explain why the fully-pruned interface had faster performance times than the partially-pruned interface (a significant proportion of states were grey and thus took up a significant proportion of screen space). It would be interesting to repeat the experiment with trees of varying fan-out.

This controlled experiment clearly showed the advantages of pruning. The choice of whether nodes not matching the query should be greyed or removed is best provided via the interface to the users.

7. Conclusions

The PDQ Tree-browser visualization tool presents trees in two tightly-coupled views, one a detailed view and the other an overview. Users can use dynamic queries to filter nodes at each level of the tree. The dynamic query panels are user-customizable. Sub-trees of unselected nodes are pruned out, a feature that usability testing and a controlled experiment, showed to be very useful. Possible enhancements to the PDQ Tree-browser were identified.

The concepts of dynamic querying and pruning are general enough that they can be applied effectively to other existing tree visualizations like treemaps and Cone Trees. These concepts are also extensible to graph structures, but that would require careful thinking and design.

7.1. FUTURE DIRECTIONS

(1) PDQ Tree-browser refinements

- Implementing the improvements that were identified in the usability testing (Section 5.4.3).
- The PDQ Tree-browser interface has been "fine-tuned" for a tree of depth 5 (See Section 4.4 for details). The interface could be extended to cope with varying structure and growing size by following the suggestions in Section 4.6.1 or otherwise.
- Further study of which approach is better in terms of hiding vs. showing grey nodes (at higher levels) by default is needed (to extend the work of Ross *et al.*, 1994). This investigation should take into consideration different types of tasks, applications and tree structures (fan-out, depth, breadth, size) and attempt to identify when either approach will yield superior performance.

(2) General GUI extensions

Newer widgets need to be developed to enable users to specify multiple selections on textual attributes easily. Another useful widget would be an extension of the 2-box slider to a n-box slider.

(3) Extension to graph structures

The PDQ Tree-browser extended dynamic queries to one class of non-flat data sets, i.e. hierarchical data sets. The most general form of any data set, is the arbitrary graph. Graphs have nodes connected via an arbitrary number of links of different types. Each link represents a relationship between (among) the connected nodes. We believe that PDQ Tree-browser concepts of dynamic querying and pruning/selective growing can be extended to graph structures as well. Instead of distinct levels in the hierarchy, we would then think of distinct classes of nodes (and even links).

7.2. OTHER TREE-BROWSING RESEARCH ISSUES

(1) Semantics-based browsing
Generic two-dimensional browsers (Plaisant *et al.*, 1995) treat the information space being browsed as images only. We believe that browsing of trees can be facilitated by taking advantage of the underlying structure of the tree. Fast navigation between siblings, up to parents and grandparents, etc., without having to manually scroll and pan would be useful options. Traversal of the tree in preorder, postorder and inorder, and guided tours of nodes marked either manually or by a query are interesting topics for investigation.

(2) Layout issues
There is a clear need for layout guidelines for tightly-coupled overviews and detailed views, as the size and fan-out of trees vary. For example, if the tree is wider than deep (as was the case in the UniversityFinder scenario) then it makes sense to have the tree drawn from left-to-right (or right-to-left) and the overview to the left (or right) of the detailed view. On the other hand, if the tree is deeper than it is wide, then it might be better to have the tree drawn from top to bottom and the overview below the detailed view. If the tree structure changes frequently and has to be redrawn, then it might be a good strategy to utilize the overview optimally by making the remaining tree occupy the entire overview space. But this might lead to some disorientation, as the zoom ratio will keep varying.

We are thankful to Dr. Michael Ball for his insightful suggestions, to Robert Ross, Zhijun Zhang and Eun-Mi Choi for designing and running the controlled experiment that was described in this paper, and to all the usability testing subjects who provided us with invaluable feedback. Thanks also to Edward Johnson for suggesting the name "PDQ Trees" for our system.

This project was supported in part by Hughes Network Systems, Maryland Industrial Partnerships (MIPS), the Center for Satellite and Hybrid Communication Networks, and the National Science Foundation grants NSFD CD 8803012 and NSF-EEC 94-02384.

References

AHLBERG, C. & SHNEIDERMAN, B. (1994). Visual information seeking: tight coupling of dynamic queries with starfield displays. *Proceedings of the ACM Conference on Human Factors in Computing Systems*, pp. 313–317, New York: ACM.

BATTISTA, G. D., EADES, P., TAMASSIA, R. & TOLLIS, I. G. (1989). *Algorithms for drawing graphs: an annotated bibliography*. Technical Report, Brown University, Computer Science Department.

BEARD, D. V. & WALKER II, J. Q. (1990). Navigational techniques to improve the display of large two-dimensional spaces. *Behavior & Information Technology* **9**, 451–466.

BUJA, A., MCDONALD, J. A., MICHALAK, J. & STUETZLE, W. (1991). Interactive data visualization using focusing and linking. *Proceedings of the IEEE Visualization '91 Conference*, pp. 156–163. San Diego, CA: IEEE Computer Society Press.

CARR, D., JOG, N. K., KUMAR, H., TEITTINEN, M. & AHLBERG, C. (1994). *Using interaction object graphs to specify and develop graphical widgets*. Technical report CS-TR-3344, Department of Computer Science, University of Maryland, MD, U.S.A.

CHIGNELL, M. H., ZUBEREC, S. & POBLETE, F. (1993). An exploration in the design space of three dimensional hierarchies. *Proceedings of the Human Factors Society*, Santa Monica, CA.

GEDYE, D. (1988). *Browsing the tangled web*. Master's Thesis report, Division of Computer Science, University of California at Berkeley.

HENRY, T. (1992). *Interactive graph layout: the exploration of large graphs*. Ph.D. Thesis, University of Arizona, Tucson, AZ, U.S.A.

HENRY, T. R. & HUDSON, S. E. (1991). Interactive graph layout. In *Proceedings of the ACM SIGGRAPH Symposium on User Interface Software and Technology*, pp. 55–64, New York: ACM.

HOLLANDS, J. G., CAREY, T. T., MATTHEWS, M. L. & MCCANN, C. A. (1989). Presenting a graphical network: a comparison of performance using fisheye and scrolling views. In G. SALVENDY & M. J. SMITH, Eds. *Designing and Using Human–Computer Interfaces and Knowledge Based Systems*, pp. 313–320. Amsterdam: Elsevier Science.

KUMAR, H. (1995). Visualizing hierarchical data with dynamic queries and pruning—the Tree-browser. In C. PLAISANT, Ed. *HCIL Open House '95 Video*, Human–Computer Interaction Laboratory, University of Maryland, MD, U.S.A.

KUMAR, H., PLAISANT, C., TEITTINEN, M. & SHNEIDERMAN, B. (1994) *Visual information management for network configuration*. Technical Report CS-TR-3288, Department of Computer Science, University of Maryland, MD, U.S.A.

LAMPING, J., RAO, R. & PIROLLI, P. (1995). A focus and context technique based on hyperbolic geometry for visualizing large hierarchies. *Proceedings of the ACM CHI'95 Conference: Human Factors in Computing Systems*, pp. 401–408. New York: ACM.

MARCHIONINI, G. (1995). *Information Seeking in Electronic Environments*. Cambridge: Cambridge University Press.

PLAISANT, C., CARR, D. & HASEGAWA, H. (1992). *When an intermediate view matters—A 2D-browser experiment*. Technical Report CS-TR-2980, Department of Computer Science, University of Maryland MD, U.S.A.

PLAISANT, C., CARR, D. & SHNEIDERMAN, B. (1995). Image browser taxonomy and guidelines for designers. *IEEE Software* **12**, 21–32.

ROBERTSON, G. G., MACKINLAY, J. D. & CARD, S. K. (1991). Cone trees: animated 3d visualizations of hierarchical information. *Proceedings of the ACM Conference on Human Factors in Computing Systems*, pp. 189–194. New York: ACM.

SCHAFFER, D., ZUO, Z., BARTRUM, L., DILL, J., DUBS, S., GREENBERG, S. & ROSEMAN, M. (1996). Comparing fisheye and full-zoom techniques for navigation of hierarchically clustered networks. *ACM Transactions on Information Systems* **14**.

SHNEIDERMAN, B. (1992). Tree visualization with treemaps: 2-d space-filling approach. *ACM Transactions on Graphics*, **11**, 92–99.

SHNEIDERMAN, B. (1994). Dynamic queries for visual information seeking. *IEEE Software*, **11**, 70–77.

YOUNG, D. & SHNEIDERMAN, B. (1993). A graphical filter/flow representation of boolean queries: a prototype implementation and evaluation. *Journal of the American Society for Information Science*, **44**, 327–339.

CHAPTER 4

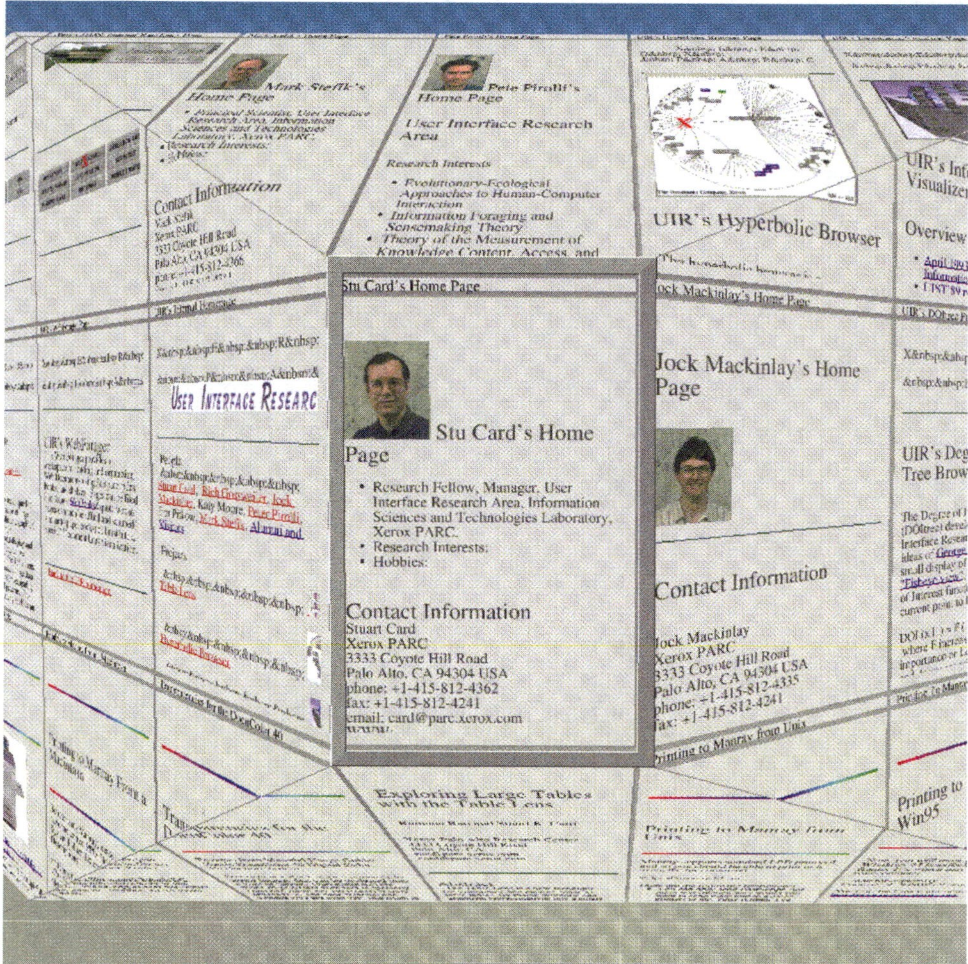

Always take flight to where there is a free view over the whole single great problem, even if this view is still not a clear one.

– Ludwig Wittgenstein,
Notebooks 1914–1916 *(entry for Nov. 1, 1914)*

Focus + Context

This chapter continues the theme of keeping "a view of the whole data available, while pursuing detailed analysis of a part of it." In Chapter 3, we saw one technique for accomplishing this purpose: overview + detail. Dedicated space is given to both the overview whole and to the detail part. Graphic indications relate the two.

The papers in this chapter develop another set of techniques, focus + context. These start from three premises: First, the user needs both overview (context) and detail information (focus) simultaneously. Second, information needed in the overview may be different than that needed in detail. Third, these two types of information can be combined within a single (dynamic) display, much as in human vision. One motivation for attempting an integrated display arises from the observation of designers (Bertin, 1977/1981) and students of graphical presentations (Larkin and Simon, 1987) that when information is broken into two displays (e.g., legends for a graph, or overview + detail), visual search and working memory consequences degrade performance. Another motivation, derived from Furnas's fisheye views and studies of attention (Furnas, 1981), is that the user's interest in detail seems to fall away from the object of attention in a systematic way and that display space might be proportioned to user attention. The working hypothesis of these papers is that it may be possible to create better cost structures of information by displaying more peripheral information at reduced detail in combination with the information in focus, dynamically varying the detail in parts of the display as the user's attention changes.

Furnas (1981 ●) was the first to articulate these ideas as fisheye views in the paper that begins this chapter. The notion of focus + context displays builds on fisheye views that emphasize there may be two distinct regions with different uses, possibly correlated with the use of automatic versus controlled processing. Focus + context visualization techniques are "attention-warped displays," meaning that they attempt to use more of the display resource to correspond to interest of the user's attention. We represent this in our reference model by saying that the user has a certain "degree of interest" (DOI) function associated with items in the Data Table, as proposed by Furnas. We want visual mappings and view transformations that result in an advantageous cost structure within the use of constrained display and attention resources. The limited resource for the user is attention—actually, attention over time. In terms of Chapter 1, attention implies controlled processing, which is largely serial. The limited resource for the computer display is space-time (the use of screen space over time) not screen space itself. The idea of focus + context displays is to use screen space-time so that more resource is available to the detailed processing, while at the same time more relevant context is also available, there is visual support for working memory, and the display gives evidence of where to go next. In other words, the idea is to improve the cost structure of the information space, thereby amplifying cognition.

The selective reduction of information for the peripheral, contextual area can be obtained by:

- Filtering
- Selective aggregation
- Micro-macro readings
- Highlighting
- Distortion

Filtering. Filtering is the selection of cases in the Data Table according to whether their variables are within specified ranges. The selection could be done manually, as in the dynamic queries technique, or it could be done automatically according to some model of degree of interest.

Selective aggregation. Selective aggregation creates new cases in the Data Table that are aggregates of other cases. In SemNet, data were aggregated when they were distant from the user's viewpoint. When the viewpoint got sufficiently close to an aggregate case, the aggregate dissolved into its component cases. Another example is Feiner and McKeown's (1991) control panels. Panel parts dynamically vary in detail as the user's interest in them changes.

Micro-macro readings. Micro-macro readings are graphics in which "detail cumulates into larger coherent structures" (Tufte, 1990). A good example is the illustration of sleep/wake for an infant (see Figure 1.8 in Chapter 1). Each of the approximately 3 million individual observations can be seen, but collectively they reveal the larger 25-hour and 24-hour circadian cycles, despite the irregularity of individual sleep times. This emergent larger structure allows individual observations to be kept in context.

Highlighting. Highlighting is a special kind of micro-macro reading. In highlighting, individual items are made visually distinctive in some way. The overall set of items provides a macro environment against which the micro reading of individual highlighted items can be interpreted.

Distortion. Most of the papers of this chapter are concerned with the last of these techniques, distortion, the relative changes in the number of pixels devoted to objects in the space. There are three main types of distortion: change in size of the objects representing cases, change in size due to perspective, or change in size of the space itself. These all have the effect of distributing more pixels to focus objects, but they differ in other respects. We can illustrate a few more subtle points about distortion by using cone trees (Robertson, Mackinlay, and Card, 1991).

1. Distortion can be achieved naturalistically by the use of perspective. In Figure 4.1, the user sees an undistorted 3D object; but actually items in front are larger and unoccluded, whereas those behind are smaller, dimmer, and may be partially obstructed. The effect is to allocate more pixels to cases with a higher degree of interest, but the user does not perceive this as a distortion.
2. Distortion can be combined with filtering. Figure 4.2 is a cone tree that appears in response to a search instruction. The overall structure of the cone tree appears, but those objects not passing the filter are elided. This reduces occlusions and allows the structure of the hits to be appreciated.

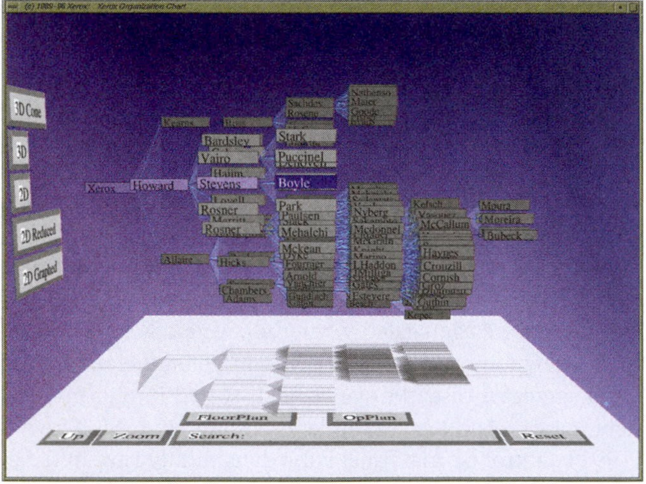

FIGURE **4.1**

Cone tree. Perspective generates the distortion. Items in the foreground form the focus; items in back of the tree form the context.

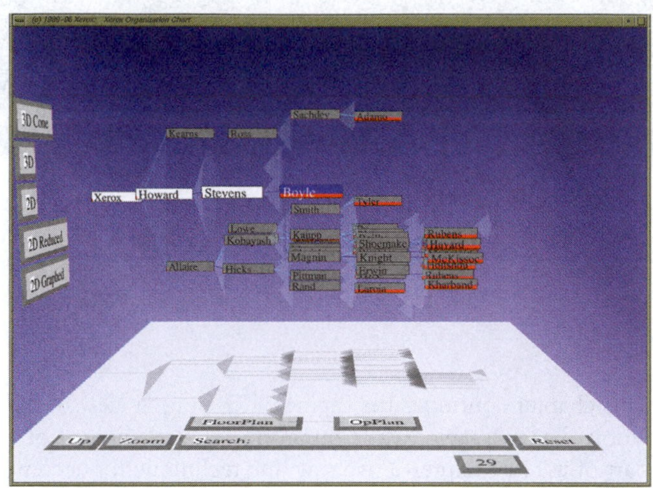

FIGURE **4.2**

Cone tree combining perspective distortion with filtering. Items matching a search are shown as focus. The structure of the other items is displayed as the context, but the items themselves are not displayed. If many items match, then perspective distortion prvides further focus + context separation.

3. Filtering can also be done dynamically using Furnas's algorithm for computing the degree of interest function for a tree given a node of interest. Figure 4.3(a) is a cone tree of a 10,000-node Web site. Figure 4.3(b) is the same tree in which the branches have been filtered according to the Furnas algorithm. Figure 4.3(c) shows the same tree in which the user has specified a different node as the node of interest. In this way, the usefulness of cone trees can be extended to much larger trees. For very large trees, Koike (1994) has shown that the dimensions of cone trees can be adjusted to have fractal properties.

For focus + context displays, the issue is where the user can "see through" deviations from a linear world (whether from selective deletions or from altering geometry) to an effective representation of the task. Think of the way a car driver "sees through" the left-to-right reversal of a rearview mirror, or whether these deviations disrupt performance. For overview + detail displays, the issue is whether the search and disruption of looking back and forth between the two displays reduces the performance. A point of controversy is how large of zoom factors can be tolerated by the two techniques. This is a more complicated question that involves the representation of the overview or context area. A related controversy is the efficiency of the techniques' use of space.

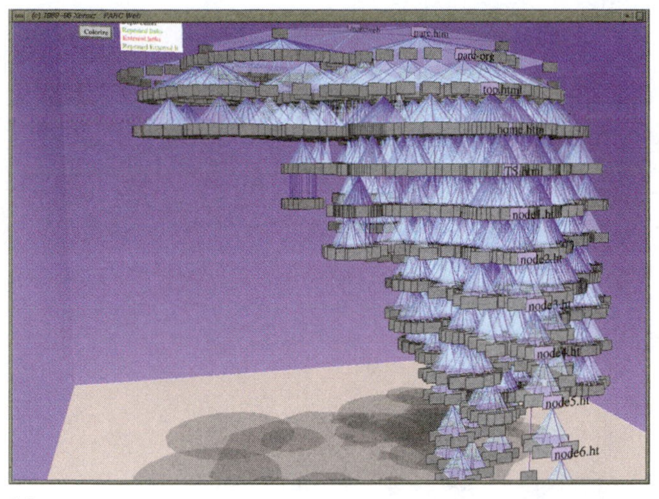

(a)

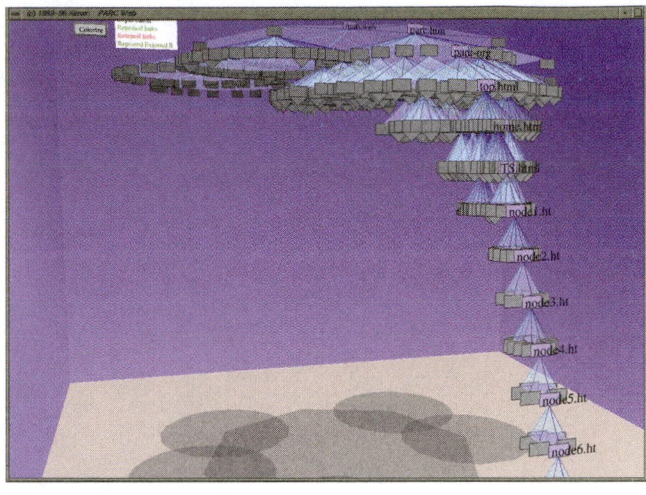

(b)

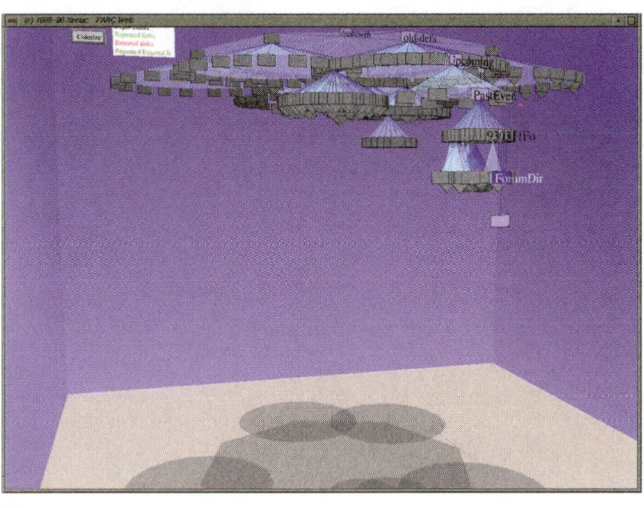

(c)

FIGURE **4.3**

(a) Cone tree of 10,000 PARC intranet nodes. (b) Same cone tree using Furnas's fisheye algorithm. (c) Same fisheye cone tree with different focal point. Developed by W. York at Xerox PARC.

4.1

Fisheye Views

One of the most seminal papers for focus + context displays is also one of the most obscure. In 1981, George Furnas wrote a technical report on "fisheye views." In the report, Furnas produced a simple mathematical analysis of a phenomenon that had appeared in art, in user interface designs, and even in the way people talk. It concerned how people leave out detail systematically when dealing with large structures. This analysis became well known, but because he did not publish it, his report entered the underground, invisible college. Copied, and the copies themselves copied, the report was passed around among the friends of Furnas, then the colleagues of the friends of Furnas, and then the students of the colleagues of the friends of Furnas. In seminars given by Furnas, presentations on fisheye views were accompanied by impressive data giving instance after instance where people behaved more or less according to the model. Finally, five years later (!), Furnas did publish a version of the report in the ACM CHI '86 conference proceedings (Furnas, 1986). This paper gave the essence of the analysis and included evidence for fisheye views compressed to a few sentences. The fuller data has never been published.

By now, almost all references in the literature are to the CHI '86 version, but we have chosen to publish for the first time the original 1981 report. The 1986 paper is farther from the moment of original insight than the original 1981 version, the connection to the systems of the day is muted, and some of the matters taken up in the original, but not the later version, are likely to be lost. In addition, mythology has grown up about the interpretation of the fisheye ideas that the original paper helps illuminate.

The fisheye idea starts with two observations. First, access to large structures has a bad cost structure (in our terms). Scrolling is slow and matters are even worse if it is necessary to use distant parts of the structure in connection with the current part. For example, in programming, it may be necessary to look at the variable declarations for a subroutine and at the for-loop beginning statement and at some local piece of code.

Second, intriguing examples can be found from everyday life, where a similar problem is solved by reducing detail for the parts distant from the immediate point of interest. The well-known Steinberg cartoon showing a New Yorker's view of the United States, in which locations not close to New York receive scant detail, is an amusing example. The fisheye camera lens is another. In addition, examining the Steinberg cartoon suggests that distance is not the only thing that matters. Important objects are less likely to be omitted than unimportant objects for the same distance.

Furnas proposes a *degree of interest* metric that is the sum of an a priori measure of importance (called LOD, "level of detail," in the report reprinted here) and distance from the point of interest. He then proceeds to work out a detailed set of examples for text trees (specifically, indented program listings) using a filtering function that elides lines with a low degree of interest. Level of detail is measured by how many nodes an item is from the tree's root. Distance is measured by the number of nodes from some designated point of interest node. The degree of interest function obtained by summing these two and thresholding produces a view of the tree as seen from the designated node. This picture more or less corresponds with the pictures people draw of hierarchies, such as organization charts or computer programs.

The clarity of the programming example in the report is, perhaps, why Furnas's concept has been so badly misunderstood. There is nothing in the general concept that restricts the application to trees or to filtering. In fact, at the end of the report, Furnas considers applications to euclidean space. Level of detail becomes some version of size, and distance becomes the usual geometrical notion of distance. The result is the classical, optical fisheye camera lens, hence the name. Geometrical level of detail could involve filtering or thresholding, or maybe only size reduction. Levels of detail might even involve an explicit decision by the designer of the appearance at each level. That is, level of detail might be what we called semantic scaling in Chapter 2.

The FISHEYE view: a new look at structured files

G. W. Furnas

Bell Laboratories
Murray Hill, New Jersey 07974

ABSTRACT

This paper introduces a new way to generate a small display of a large structure: in analogy to a very wide angle, or "fisheye lens." It is hypothesized that the most useful parts to show, the most "interesting" subset of a large structure, might be approximated by the contribution of two components. First is a component independent of the particulars of the current interaction, reflecting parts of the structure which are of a priori global importance. The second is meant to capture the contribution specific to the current focus of interaction, and is approximated by simple distance from the current focus -- more distant parts being intrinsically less interesting to the current interaction. By considering these two contributions, the "fisheye view" represents an effort to balance in an abbreviated view of a structure, the need for local detail against the need for global context: by showing full detail in the immediate neighborhood some place of current focus, but requiring increasing a priori importance as the distance from the focus increases.

The paper introduces fisheye views by way of general definitions, and then presents several special cases, most notably the fisheye treatment of hierarchical tree structures. An important subcase is considered at length: hierarchically structured sequential files, examples of which include structured programs, UNIX™ file structure listings, text heading/subheadings, and outlines. Various properties of fisheye views are mentioned, including the logarithmic compression that they provide. Ways to conceptualize fisheye views are also discussed for a number of other structures.

**** Bell Laboratories Technical Memorandum #81-11221-9, October 12, 1981 ****

™ UNIX is a trademark of Bell Laboratories

1. INTRODUCTION

As people come to use computers for working with larger and more complicated data bases there is a rapidly increasing interface problem. The essential difficulty is that while the size of the structures we work with on our computers grows the "windows" through which we look at those structures remain small. The windows are limited both by the technology of terminal screens and by the human visual processing capacity; we can examine only a small part of our external world at once.

The interface design problem amounts to deciding what parts of a large structure to show. This paper proposes one large class of possible solutions to this problem. In particular it will present a formal statement of the general class; a subsequent paper[1] will present a prototype program that implements a version of the general model.

Let us begin with the case of a large file that someone wants to work with, perhaps a program or text that is being edited. Current techniques generally involve a simple "flat window" view, showing consecutive lines of the file, with some mechanism for scrolling. In this arrangement, a small local piece of the structure is shown and the person has control over moving that locality over the structure.

The problem with this method is that often the meaning or importance of local information derives from its position in a larger context. It is important to stay oriented, i.e., to understand where in the global picture this locality fits. The purely local views provided by standard flat windowing do not support this.

Various partial solutions to the problem exist. A simple one is line numbering. In this way, at least relative, and sometimes even absolute, linear position in the file is made known as part of the local view. A related method, found in some text viewers (e.g., the BSD-UNIX *more*(1) command[2]), and screen editors (e.g., EMACS[3]), is to show some indication of what proportion of the way through the file the current view is. Such aids are important in keeping some track of where one is, but they provide minimal information. They reveal nothing about the global structure of the file, and where the current view fits.

A more sophisticated solution, used on a number of occasions and as early as 1968 in Englebart's Knowledge Augmentation Workshop[4], is the analog of a "zoom" lens. In files or structures that have what correspond to different levels of detail or resolution, one solution is to allow the user to flip between different views at different levels. In this way, one can start out at a global (very low detail) view, and then zoom in selectively on different local regions. This allows the user at any point to step back by zooming out and thereby see what part of the global structure the local area involved.

In such a zoom system local and global information are never available at once. Integration of such information must take place in human memory. Thus there remain difficulties in keeping oriented, particularly if the zooming facility is not fast and the user not adept.

In this regard, a more attractive approach is to offer two (or more) simultaneous windows, one with a detail view, another with a zoomed-out, higher level view. This has been implemented in a number of bit-mapped graphics environments, like Smalltalk[5], and some of the Lisp machines[6]. But this approach has problems, too, basically in understanding the correspondences between the two views. Where does the small view fit in the big picture and what visible features correspond?

A different proposal is offered here. Instead of using the analog of a zoom lens, we propose the analog of a "fisheye" lens. A very wide angle, or fisheye, lens used at close distance shows things near the center of view in high magnification and detail. At the same time, however, it shows the whole structure -- with decreasing magnification, less detail -- as one gets further away from the center of view.

There are several motivations for this approach. First, one typical reason people examine a structure is that they are interested in some particular detail. At the same time, they need context, i.e., some sense of global structure, and where within that structure their current focus resides. The idea is therefore to present detailed local regions, but to present selected important parts of the global structure as well.

Is there any reason to think that such a view is possible? Certainly, not all sorts of structures will support it, but a large number of familiar ones will, most notably hierarchical structures, such as are found in structured programs, file structures, manuscript chapter headings, menu access systems, biological taxonomies, and a myriad of other familiar contexts. The psychological feasibility remains to be explored, but there is suggestive evidence. For example, studies of editing patterns have shown that the likelihood that a person will look at or jump to some other region falls off gradually with how far away it is[7]. Seen in this light the idea is to match the display of the information to this behavior pattern and, since people have limited viewing capacity, give them access to nearby parts most easily, by showing them in full detail, and gradually less detail (only more global structure) at points further away.[1]

The principal purpose of this paper is to explore several aspects of the fisheye concept. First a general formulation will be given, followed by several different special case examples including fisheye views of general graph structures and of Euclidean space. The case to be most fully presented in this paper, however, is the definition of the fisheye for hierarchical tree structures, culminating in detailed discussion of a very common subcase -- hierarchically organized sequential files -- including structured program code, text outlines, file hierarchy listings, and headings and subheadings in papers. A number of interesting properties of the fisheye structures and definitions are pointed out along the way, to indicate some of the entailments of the new concepts presented here, particularly when there are implications for the utility of fisheye views or efficiency algorithms.

2. *GENERAL FORMULATION*

2.1 DOI Functions

In this section is presented a formal conception of the general fisheye lens. We begin by defining what will be called a "Degree Of Interest" (*DOI*) function over a file or structure. The idea is that during any given interaction, users are not equally interested in all parts of the file. Their interest may perhaps be thought to define a function over that file, telling for any given part of the file, say any given line of a text file, how interested they are in seeing that line, given their current purposes. A general interface strategy would be to show those parts of the file that are of greatest interest.

Now, in the UNIX[TM] environment there are a number of programs that can be considered degree of interest filters. The *grep*(1) command, for example, takes a file and filters it so as to end up printing out only those lines of the file that have a certain interesting property for the user, namely the lines containing substrings matching the user's target string. *Tail*(1) is another example, for use when the last portion of a file is of interest. Basically such filters are ways to cut out unwanted information, displaying only those parts that can be determined as sufficiently interesting on the basis of certain structural patterns within them.

1. In the late 60's and early 70's Doug Englebart, with his knowledge augmentation workshop at SRI, was working on ways of viewing hierarchically structured text[4]. (See also Nelson[8]). This included zooming, as mentioned above, and also ways to move about the structure, expanding various parts of the tree at will. Such a mechanism could easily implement a fisheye view. The point of this paper is to suggest that this case is of special interest, and to make it more formal, and generalizable.

TM UNIX is a trademark of Bell Laboratories

The importance of talking about a *DOI* function is to force a user-centered perspective. It asks the designer to project his program's output back into the head of the user, and in that way may encourage examination of the assumptions underlying the interaction. For example, a standard flat window view may be seen as a *DOI* filter. Its implicit *DOI* function says all lines within a half-screen width of the current line are of sufficient interest, and the rest not. Such a *DOI* function seems simplistic at best.

To replace this naive assumption, we wish to decompose a degree of interest function in a more psychologically motivated way, in particular into *a priori* and *a posteriori* components.

2.2 *Fisheye Components*

By the *a priori* component is meant that contribution to interest which largely transcends the particulars of a given interaction with the structure. It is instantiated here by any of various notions of global structural importance. Major, critical, or particularly informative pieces, are presumed to be of greater *a priori* interest than parts that might be considered only finer details. It is this variable that is most naturally manipulated in a zoom lens treatment. "Zoomed-out" views show only the major, critical features; one must "zoom-in" to see the details.

The *a posteriori* component is the contribution, to determining what parts are of most interest, that very specifically depends on the current interaction. In the fisheye view as elaborated here, this is approximated by a very simple model. In this model, interaction with the structure at any given moment is assumed to be focused at some point in the structure (this constraint is loosened a bit towards the end of the paper). The interaction-specific component of interest is then modeled simply by distance from this point. The assumption is that, to a first approximation, if all else were equal more distant parts of the structure would be of less interest than close neighbors. Clearly as interaction shifts the point of focus, this component shifts correspondingly.

Thus the fisheye requires a structure within which the following three properties can be sensibly defined:

1. focal point: '.'
2. distance from focus: $D(.,x)$ [$D(.,.)=0$]
3. level of detail, importance, resolution: $LOD(x)$

That is, first it requires that the structure, or more precisely the interaction with the structure, have a notion of a current point of focal interest (represented by '.', and called the "focal point" or just "focus").

Second there must be a notion of distance, $D(.,x)$ from this point of focus to any other place, x, in the structure. This may be as simple as linear distance in the file, or a more sophisticated, structurally-defined distance. [2]

Thirdly, there must be defined a notion of Level of Detail, $LOD(x)$, for every point in the structure. This is some measure of its intrinsic importance, particularly to the global structure: a notion of high versus low resolution, or degree of detail, or grossness of a feature, generality, etc. In this paper, level of detail will generally be associated with negative numbers, with the conventions that an increase in detail (decrease in generality) will be associated with a larger NEGATIVE number, e.g., $LOD(x)=0$ means x is at the most

2. While it is assumed, that the distance from the focal point to itself is zero, and that all other distances are positive, the distance need not be a true metric. Symmetry and the Triangle Inequality are not critical.

general level; -1, -2, etc. are successively more detailed.

Note that all these definitions assume units of a certain granularity to refer to the structure. For purposes of discussion, we will use the example of sequentially organized files, and will use as the units of discourse the lines of a file. That is '.' refers to the current line; $D(.,x)$ refers to the distance (in some suitable sense) from there to the line x; and $LOD(x)$ refers to the level of detail inherent in the line, x.

2.3 The Fisheye Definition

These components allow us to define a *DOI* function associated with a fisheye view, as follows. Adopting the convention that larger numbers mean higher interest, let us define the degree of interest function at a line, x, given the current point, to be

$$DOI(x \mid .) = F(\, LOD(x),\, D(.,x)\,)$$

where F is monotone increasing in the first argument, and decreasing in the second. That is, interest increases with global importance, and decreases with distance from the focus. One important class of examples is to let,

$$DOI(x \mid .) = f(\, g(LOD(x)) - h(D(.,x))\,)$$

where f, g and h are monotonically increasing. I.e., *DOI* is the difference of the level of detail and the distance from point (up to a positive monotone rescaling of any of these three quantities).

That is, global interest is assumed to decrease as detail gets finer, and as distance from the current focus increases. Thus, interest is assumed to be greatest for gross features, and things nearby.

Finally, to create the fish eye view, we display x if and only if its degree of interest, as just defined, is above some threshold k. [3]

3. A FISHEYE DEFINED FOR TREE STRUCTURES

An example will make this clearer. Consider the construction of a fisheye for tree structures.

3.1 The Underlying Fisheye Construction and its Properties

We begin by defining the tree distance, $d(x,y)$, between two points, x and y, to be the number of links intervening on the path connecting them in the tree. Then one natural definition of the necessary fisheye components is:

1. focal point: is some node of current interest in the tree
2. distance from focus:

$$D(.,x) = d(.,x)$$

3. Given the way quantities have been defined, *DOI* is usually negative, and in which case k would also be negative.

3. level of detail, importance, resolution:

$$LOD(x) = -d(r,x)$$

where r is the root of the tree.

That is, distance from point is simply the structural tree distance, and level of detail increases as distance from the root. Then the most straightfoward definition of a *DOI* function is,

$$DOI(x \mid .) = (LOD(x) - D(.,x))$$

$$= -(d(.,x) + d(r,x)).$$

That is, *DOI* at any node, x, is merely the (negative) sum of its distances from the root and from the focal point. To get the fish eye view, we simply apply some threshold, k, showing node x if and only if its *DOI* is greater than or equal to k.

Figure 1 illustrates the construction of the fisheye Degree of Interest Function. In 1(a), all nodes are labeled by their distance from the indicated point of focus, in 1(b), by their distance from the root. Figure 1(c) then shows the sum of these two numbers at corresponding nodes. The result is a diagram of the *DOI* function. The fisheye *DOI* function just defined has a number of interesting properties. Some are important to the utility of the fisheye, others to its efficient implementation, and still others simply offering alternate perspectives on the fisheye. In the spirit of enriching this introduction to the fisheye, we will now indulge in a few of these asides.

First notice that in general the *DOI* induces a family of fisheye views: one for each choice of threshold k. In the case of the tree structure *DOI* given here, a choice of $k=-3$ yields a view which consists of the current node and all its direct ancestors. We call this the zero-order fisheye view. The next possible choice of threshold, $k=-5$, yields what is then called the "first-order" fisheye view, in which all the immediate progeny of all direct ancestors are also included.[4] One could define a second-order fisheye, using the next threshold ($k=-7$), where all grandchildren of all ancestors would further be included.

Note also what sort of compression these fisheye views provide. To illustrate, let us consider a complete m-level tree with a branching factor, b, at each node. Such a tree has b^i nodes at level i (counting $i=0$ at the top, and $i=m$ at the bottom). Thus the whole tree has

$$\sum_{i=0}^{m} b^i$$

nodes. This sum is of order b^m.

The fisheye view of order-0 shows the root plus one node from each level, or $m+1$ nodes. The order-1 fisheye shows the root and b nodes at each level, for a total of $mb+1$ nodes. In general the order-K fisheye shows of order $m(b^K)$ nodes. Thus, the fisheye is essentially a logarithmic compressor, changing the displayed structure from being of size that is exponential in the depth of the tree to being linear with depth. The linear coefficient is b^K. This means the fisheye view is exponential in the fisheye-order (K) and polynomial in the branching factor (b). The important feature here is that, while the depth and branching factor of the tree may be beyond control, K is discretionary -- under designer or viewer control -- making substantial compression possible at will. The dependence on branching factor, b, is also very important. It implies that, for trees of a fixed total size, the fisheye is a considerably less effective compressor in trees with large branching factors. Certain abbreviation schemes for structures with large branching factors will

4. essentially equivalently: ancestors, and siblings of these.

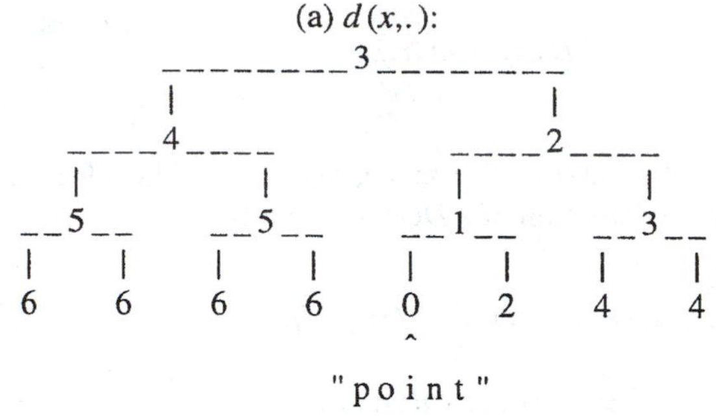

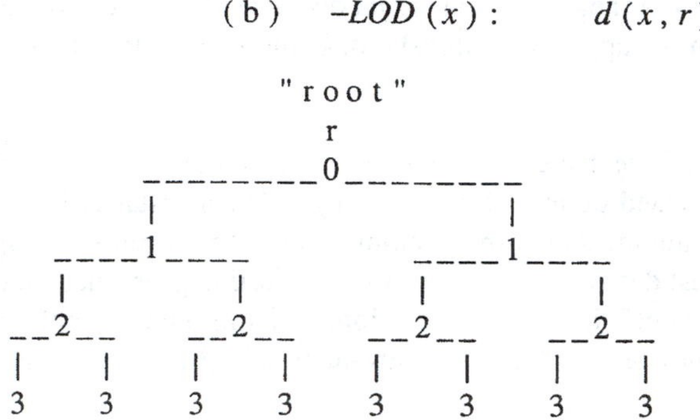

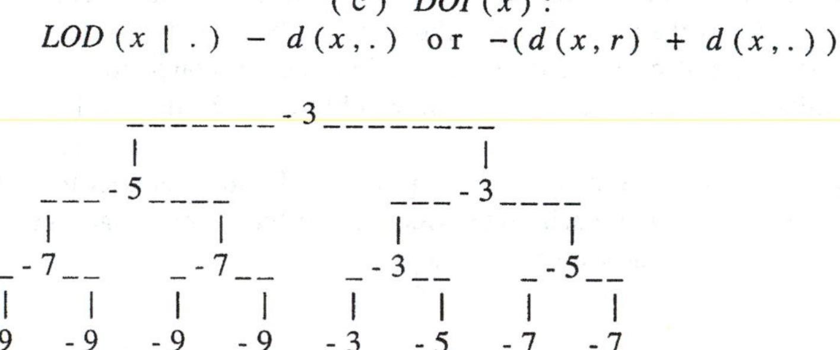

Figure 1. Construction of the Fisheye Degree of Interest (*DOI*) function.

be discussed briefly later.

Another interesting point involves the form of what might be called iso-interest contours, those points in the tree which share the same hypothetical level of interest, i.e., the same *DOI* value. Algebraically, as defined here for trees, any such contour is a locus of points such that the sum of its distances from two points (the focus and the root) is a constant. This is an analog to the definition of an ellipse in the Euclidean plane. The iso-interest contours are thus the tree analogs of a family of confocal "tree-ellipses." It is easy to see that the contours are convex and strictly nested, an observation with algorithmic implications to be discussed later. [5] The iso-interest contours may be pictured in a very simple way, made possible by the insensitivity of tree distances to graphical layout. Imagine the tree to be made of rigid rods, with loose joints at the nodes. Then imagine picking up the tree by the root and by the node of current focus, stretching the tree taut. This would leave all the remaining nodes to dangle below the straightened path connecting the root and focus, as in figure 2. In this form the successive *DOI* contours are lined up horizontally, descending from the direct path connecting the root and the focus.[6] Displaying the structure down to the *K*th level, corresponds to a *K*-order fisheye view (if top level is called "0").

3.2 Examples of the Tree Fisheye: Hierarchically Structured Sequential Files

In this section we consider the fisheye view as just defined for tree structures, applied to the instance of hierarchically structured sequential files. We begin with a specific case and subsequently generalize to a broader class of examples.

3.2.1 Indent Structured Files: Structured Programs, Outlines, etc. There are many examples where the hierarchical, or tree, structure of a file is manifest in the pattern of indent in the text. In this category fall text outlines (where structure is further indicated by Roman numerals, alphabetics, digits, etc.), and programs written in structured languages, like ALGOL, PASCAL, and C. In such files, increasing degree of indent typically indicates more detailed parts of the structure, i.e., parts at a greater distance from the root. Typically these files are more than just topological trees, in that there is an canonical ordering over the branches incident to each node. In an outline "I" precedes "II" and "III"; in most programs the ordering of statements makes a difference. Such structures are usually displayed with a depth-first traversal, and with the canonical ordering dictating the sequence of siblings. The substructure selected by the fisheye view can be displayed consistently with this ordering, by simply following the same rule, applied to the fisheye view's subtree. An example of the result follows.

Figure 3 figure presents several views of an outline of this paper. Shown in 3(a) is a view that would be shown in the usual flat window, centered on the line that corresponds to this part of the paper. The point to notice here is that a lot of detail is shown, but it is hard to tell from looking at this view, just where this fits in the big picture. Figure 3(b) shows the corresponding first order fisheye view centered on the same line. It is immediately clear what section of the outline is being examined.

The whole outline is shown in figure 3(c). In order to fit on the page, the print must be too small to read clearly, but the figure still aids comparison of the two preceding views. The box indicates the lines seen with the flat window. The underlined lines represent what the first order fisheye shows. Note that the local region around the focal line is shown in full detail, but adjacent information that would have been at the edge of the flat view is missing from the fisheye. It was replaced by more global contextual information -- in this case corresponding to higher level headings in the outline.

---

5. The analogy to Euclidean conic sections will be of further interest later, in a footnote on the application of fisheyes to Euclidean space.
6. This of course explains why the parity of the numbers is everywhere the same (odd in this example). Any node can be only an integer number of links off the main path, and that integer number of links must be added twice, once to each distance term, from the root and from the focus, thereby preserving parity.

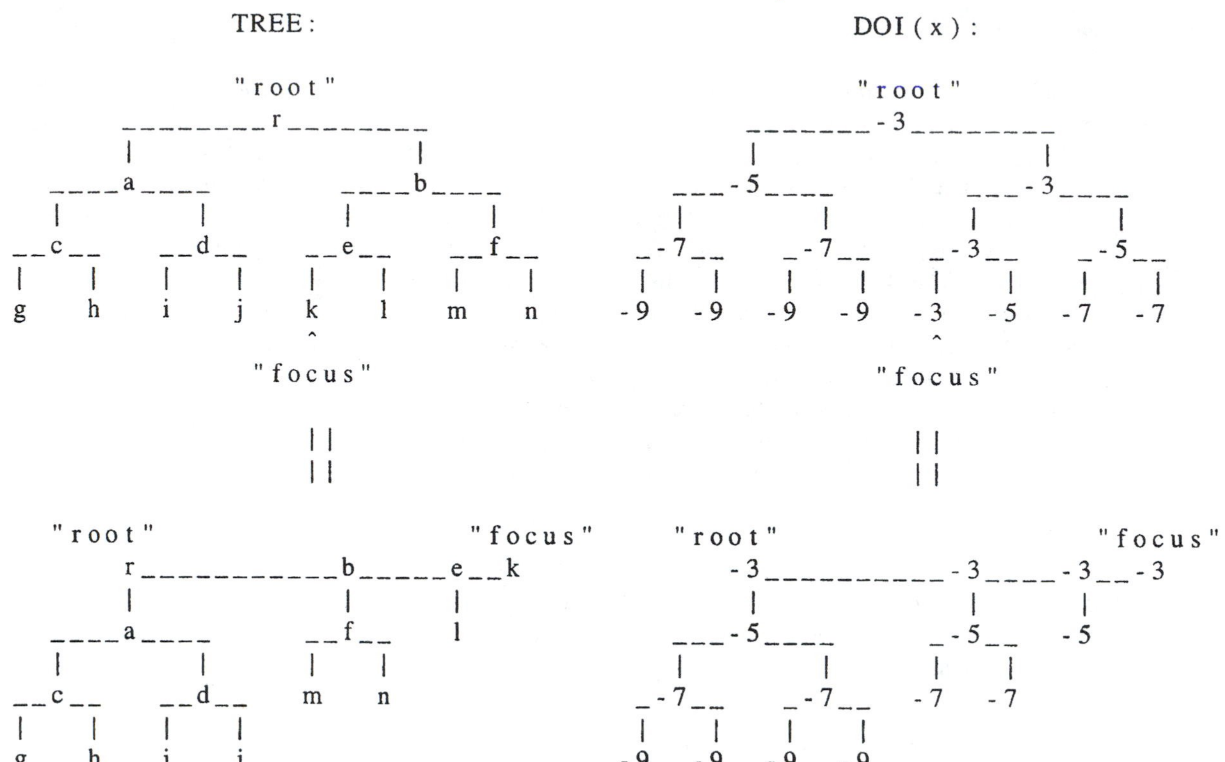

Figure 2. Horizontal Iso-*DOI* contours, formed by picking up tree at focus and root.

```
  70              ii. logarithmic compression, under user control
  71              iii. branching factor is critical
  72          c. Iso-DOI contours are ellipses
  73          e. The dangling tree
  74              Figure 2: shows the dangline DOI contours
  75          f. Changing focii -- lowest common ancestor
  76  B. Examples of Fisheye for Tree Structured Files
  77      1. Indent Structured Files: Structured Programs, Outlines, etc.
  78          a. Examples: Programs, Outlines, etc.
  79          b. Usually ordered - fisheye is compatible
  80          c. Specific example 1: paper outline
>>81              Figures 3,4,5: outline, regular and fisheye views
  82              i. some adjacent info missing
  83              ii. traded for global information
  84          d. Comment: standard window view = degenerate fisheye
  85          e. Specific example 2: C program code
  86              Figures 4:  C-program, regular and fisheye views
  87              i. What is shown
  88              ii. What is traded for what
  89          f. Other indent structures: biol. taxon., org. hierarch...
  90      2. Count-Until: A Simple Generalization of Indent Structure
  91          a. Other similar structures
  92              i. in addition to indent
```

Figure 3(a). A standard 'flat-window' view of the outline of this paper. Line numbers are in the left margin. ">>" marks the current line.

```
     1 The FISHEYE view: a new look at structured files
     2      I. ABSTRACT
     3      II. INTRODUCTION
 ...23      III. GENERAL FORMULATION
 ...51      IV. A FISHEYE DEFINED FOR TREE STRUCTURES
    52          A. The Underlying Fisheye Construction and its Properties
 ...76          B. Examples of Fisheye for Tree Structured Files
    77              1. Indent Structured Files: Structured Programs, Outlines, etc.
    78                  a. Examples: Programs, Outlines, etc.
    79                  b. Usually ordered - fisheye is compatible
    80                  c. Specific example 1: paper outline
  >>81                      Figure 3: outline, regular and fish views
    82                      i. some adjacent info missing
    83                      ii. traded for global information
    84                  d. Comment: standard window view = degenerate fisheye
    85                  e. Specific example 2: C program code
 ...89                  f. Other indent structures: biol. taxon., org. hierarch...
    90              2. Count-Until: A Simple Generalization of Indent Structure
...100              3. Examples of the Tree Fisheye: Other Hierarchical Structures
...106      V. FISHEYE VIEWS FOR OTHER TYPES OF STRUCTURES
...117      VI. A FEW COMMENTS ON ALGORITHMS
...140      VII. OTHER ISSUES
...162      VIII. CONCLUDING REMARKS AND SUMMARY
```

Figure 3(b). A fisheye view of the outline of this paper. Line numbers are in the left margin. "..." indicates missing lines. ">>" signals the current line.

```
  1 The FISHEYE view: a new look at structured files
  2     I. ABSTRACT
  3     II. INTRODUCTION
  4         A. The Problem - small window on large worlds
  5             1  Small screens
  6             2  Human vision capacity constraints
  7         B. Need for Context
  8             1. Partial solutions
  9                 a. line numbers, etc.
 10                 b. "zoom lens"
 11                 c  multiple windows
 12             2. Suggestion - "Fisheye lens"
 13         C. Fisheye Lens
 14             1  detail at focus, but also global contextual information
 15             2. feasibility:
 16                 a. there constraints on structures:
 17                     i  many common ones
 18                     ii. including trees
 19                 b. psychological:
 20                     i. emirical question
 21                     ii. suggestive: patterns editing [RBA study]
 22             3. cf. Englebart work.
 23     III. GENERAL FORMULATION
 24         A. Degree of Interest (DOI) Functions
 25             1. Intro
 26                 a. How interested in seeing given part of structure
 27                 b. General strategy: show  what is interesting
 28             2. Familiar UNIX examples: grep(1), tail(1)
 29             3. Major point
 30                 a. project view back to interest in subjects head
 31                 b. e.g., standard window
 32             4  Approach here -- decompose DOI into
 33                 a  distance
 34                 b. level of detail
 35         B  Fisheye Components
 36             1  Requires:
 37                 a. focal point: '.'
 38                 b  distance from focus: D(.,x)  [ D(.,.)=0 ]
 39                 c. level of detail, importance, resolution: LOD(x)
 40             2. Note on confusing sign conventions
 41         C  The Fisheye Definition
 42             1  Definition 1:
 43                 a. DOI(x|.) = F( LOD(x), D(.,x) )
 44                 b. F monotone increasing in first argument.
 45                 c. monotone decreasing in second
 46             2. Subclass Definition 2:
 47                 a. DOI(x|.) = f( g(LOD(x)) - h(D(.,x))  )
 48                 b. f, g and h are monotonically increasing.
 49             3. To get view -- apply a threshold, k.
 50             4. Interpretation.
 51     IV. A FISHEYE DEFINED FOR TREE STRUCTURES
 52         A. The Underlying Fisheye Construction and its Properties
 53             1. Definitions
 54                 a. points are nodes in a tree
 55                 b. Define d(x,y) = path length from x to y
 56                 c. Then,
 57                     i. focal point: node of current interest in the tree
 58                     ii. distance from focus: D(.,x) = d(.,x)
 59                     iii. level of detail, importance: LOD(x) = -d(r,x)
 60             2. Fisheye DOI Function
 61                 a. DOI(x|.) = -( d(.,x) + d(r,x) ).
 62                 b. Interpretation
 63             3. Apply threshold
 64             4. Figures illustrate DOI for a tree
 65                 Figure 1: figure showing this stuff
 66             5. Interesting points
 67                 a. Family of views
 68                 b. Compression
 69                     i. b^m --> m(b^K)
.............................................................................
|  70                     ii. logarithmic compression, under user control   |
|  71                     iii. branching factor is critical                  |
|  72                 c. Iso-DOI contours are ellipses                       |
|  73                 e. The dangling tree                                   |
|  74                     Figure 2: shows the dangline DOI contours          |
|  75                 f. Changing focii -- lowest common ancestor            |
|  76         B. Examples of Fisheye for Tree Structured Files               |
|  77             1. Indent Structured Files: Structured Programs, Outlines, etc. |
|  78                 a. Examples: Programs, Outlines, etc.                  |
|  79                 b. Usually ordered - fisheye is compatible             |
|  80                 c. Specific example 1: paper outline                   |
|>>81                     Figure 3: outline, regular and fish views          |
|  82                     i. some adjacent info missing                      |
|  83                     ii. traded for global information                  |
|  84                 d. Comment: standard window view = degenerate fisheye  |
|  85                 e. Specific example 2: C program code                  |
|  86                     Figures 4:  C-program, regular and fisheye views   |
|  87                     i. What is shown                                   |
|  88                     ii. What is traded for what                        |
|  89                 f. Other indent structures: biol. taxon., org. hierarch... |
|  90             2. Count-Until: A Simple Generalization of Indent Structure |
|  91                 a. Other similar structures                            |
|  92                     i. in addition to indent                           |
.............................................................................
 93                     ii. Point/Subpoint headings
 94                     iii. Unix file structure representation
 95                 b. All
 96                     i. have form
 97                         a) "count occurrances of RE1"
 98                         b) "until first occurrence of RE2"
 99                     ii. can thus be viewed with single facility
100             3. Examples of the Tree Fisheye: Other Hierarchical Structures
101                 a. linked trees
102                 b. E.g., Menu retrieval systems
103                     i. what they are
104                     ii. fisheye view of it
105                     iii. Reitman, et al.
106     V. FISHEYE VIEWS FOR OTHER TYPES OF STRUCTURES
107         A. Other Graph Structures
108             1. Need distance (graph distances)
109             2. Level of Detail:
110                 a. isa lattices
111                 b. road maps
112         B. Fisheye Views of Euclidean Space
113             1. LOD as Scale change
114                 a. footnote: fisheye with pixels
115                 b. footnote: fisheye with pyramids layers of maps
116             2. Non-geometric -- barrel distortion.
117     VI. A FEW COMMENTS ON ALGORITHMS
118         A. General Algorithm
119             1. Start at focus and move outward
120             2. Evaluate all DOI's and show if meet criterion
121             3. Versatile, but inefficient
122         B. Convexity and the Monotone Algorithm for Trees
123             1. Tree case is instructive
124                 a. monotone algorithm
125                 b. dismiss whole branches w/o consideration
126             2. concept behind it -- convexity
127                 a. definition:
128                     i. requires shortest path notion
129                     ii. subset convex iff
130                     iii. all points on shortest path connecting
131                     iv. are also in subset
132                 b. implies need only consider region near boundary
133                     i. explain
134             3. tree case example revisited
135                 a. implies all K-order fisheyes have good algorithm
136             4. footnote: general DOI convexity condition
137         C. Incremental changes
138             1. Other shortcut -- in interaction only parts will change
139             2. In tree -- does not change above first common ancestor
140     VII. OTHER ISSUES
141         A  Pruning Branches
142             1. Large branching factor means not much compression
143             2. Solution 1: ad hoc hack
144             3. Solution 2: fisheye
145                 a. motivation - siblings of higher interest if
146                     i. first or last (higher LOD)
147                     ii. closer to current point (smaller d(.,x))
148                 b. define DOI and Fisheye over siblings in this way
149                 c. implement as
150                     i. post filter
151                     ii. encorporate into original function
152         B. Multiple Focii
153             1. For comparison, cross reference
154             2. Analog of two windows
155             3. How:
156                 a. redefine fisheye concept to have multiple focii
157                 b. alter distance function - both focii 0 dist apart
158             4. Associated idea - automatic multiple focii
159                 a. variable's reference and its declaration
160                 b. show both automatically
161                 c. implement with looser graph and graph distance?
162     VIII. CONCLUDING REMARKS AND SUMMARY
163         A. General Motivation and Purpose -- show what people need to see
164         B. Decompose interest
165             1. Global, a priori
166             2. local, task specific
167         C. Actual programs and empirical work to follow
```

Figure 3(c). Full view of outline of this paper. Box shows lines in "flat" view. Underlines show lines in the fisheye view.

The fisheye ends up showing the current nearby neighborhood in complete indented detail just like a standard viewing window, but also spans the whole file, showing successively higher level information at more remote parts of the file. The hope is that the view thus keeps just the parts of greatest user interest. By discarding many detailed the parts of the tree structure, it achieves substantial compression, while it retains the skeleton of the global structure of the file.

Note that the standard flat window approach is actually a degenerate version of a fisheye, in which everything is given equal importance, ($LOD(x)$=0) and the distance, $d(.,x)$, is just the number of intervening lines. The threshold is then set to the halfsize of the window. Thus parts are displayed in full detail if they are within a half-window distance of the centering point of the window, and, beyond the edge of the window, no "detail" at all is shown. If a file has other than flat structure, and the structure is of semantic importance, the belief here is that more structurally defined fisheye functions accommodate the role of structure in determining interest. Thus both *LOD* and distance are based on structure: the connectivity patterns of the tree itself. The result is to discard some information that is physically adjacent but less structurally related in favor of the more physically remote, but structurally important things.

Indent level is used in many other sorts of files. Figure 4 presents an example for C program code. (This is a short calculator program which does RPN integer addition and subtraction, modulo 10^{40}.) The single flat window view of 4(a) shows lots of detail, some of which is not likely to be very useful when working on the indicated line (the arithmetic details of the previous case, intruding in the top of the picture, for example), and very little orienting information is available. On the other hand, the fisheye view, seen in figure 4(b), shows that the programmer is at a short "for" loop, within the 'e' case of a "switch" in which there are also four other cases '+', '-', 'q', and "default". This switch is in the "else" block of the indicated "if" statement, within a "while" loop, in program "main()" etc. It is conjectured that being able to see their work focus together with such contextual information will be of use to programmers working with structured code. In figure 4(c), the box again shows a standard window view, and the underlining shows how the fisheye trades some window space for remote higher level information.

A number of other domains are often shown with indent structuring, including biological taxonomies (kingdom, phylum, class, order, etc.), decision trees or classification keys ("simple or compound leaf"), and organizational hierarchies (e.g., BTL organizational phone book). The fisheye as sketched above is suitable for any of these.

3.2.2 Count-Until: A Simple Generalization of Indent Structure Indent is a familiar way to indicate hierarchical structure in a contiguously organized file, but there are several others in common use. One of these is the use of points and sub-points in heading numbers (as in "section 3.2.2"). These have wide use in some writing styles, like legal code books, and are available in many document formatting macro packages.[7] Hierarchical structure in the UNIX file system is indicated in yet another way. UNIX organizes its files into a tree of nested directories and subdirectories. Such hierarchical structure is indicated with slashes. Thus "/usr/gwf/fisheye.c" refers to the file "fisheye.c" in directory "gwf", which is a subdirectory of "/usr". (Note that in UNIX, the *pwd*(1) command, in printing the "full path name" of the current directory, gives its complete ancestral lineage, which amounts to a fisheye view of order 0).

In all three of these cases (indenting, subpoint notation, and UNIX file structure listings) level of detail is indicated by counting something in the initial portion of the associated line. The amount of white space before the first character gives indent level; the number of decimal points before a space gives the heading level; and the number of slashes before the end of the line gives the directory level. Thus a fisheye facility can easily embrace all these domains with a "count-until" strategy: i.e., by allowing its users to specify

7. Terry Gleason has written the READER[9]. programs which implement a first order fisheye view for text with headings produced by the UNIX memorandum macro package.

```
  28                      t[0] = (t[0] + 10000)
  29                          - x[0];
  30                      for(i=1;i<k;i++){
  31                          t[i] = (t[i] + 10000)
  32                              - x[i]
  33                              - (1 - t[i-1]/10000);
  34                          t[i-1] %= 10000;
  35                      }
  36                      t[k-1] %= 10000;
  37                      break;
  38                  case 'e':
>>39                      for(i=0;i<k;i++) t[i] = x[i];
  40                      break;
  41                  case 'q':
  42                      exit(0);
  43                  default:
  44                      noprint = 1;
  45                      break;
  46              }
  47              if(!noprint){
  48                  for(i=k - 1;t[i] <= 0 && i > 0;i--);
  49                  printf("%d",t[i]);
  50                  if(i > 0) {
```

Figure 4(a). Standard 'flat-window' view of a C program. Line numbers are in the left margin. ">>" signals the current line.

```
    1 #define DIG 40
    2 #include <stdio.h>
 ...4 main()
    5 {
    6         int c, i, x[DIG/4], t[DIG/4], k = DIG/4, noprint = 0;
 ...8         while((c=getchar()) != EOF){
    9             if(c >= '0' && c <= '9'){
...16             } else {
   17                 switch(c){
   18                     case '+':
...27                     case '-':
...38                     case 'e':
 >>39                         for(i=0;i<k;i++) t[i] = x[i];
   40                         break;
   41                     case 'q':
...43                     default:
...46                 }
   47                 if(!noprint){
...57                 }
   58             }
   59             noprint = 0;
   60         }
   61 }
```

Figure 4(b). A fisheye view of the C program. Line numbers are in the left margin. "..." indicates missing lines. ">>" signals the current line.

```
#define DIG 40
#include <stdio.h>

main()
{
        int c, i, x[DIG/4], t[DIG/4], k = DIG/4, noprint = 0;

        while((c=getchar()) != EOF){
                if(c >= '0' && c <= '9'){
                        x[0] = 10 * x[0] + (c-'0');
                        for(i=1;i<k;i++){
                                x[i] =  10 * x[i]
                                        + x[i-1]/10000;
                                x[i-1] %= 10000;
                        }
                } else {
                        switch(c){
                                case '+':
                                        t[0] = t[0] + x[0];
                                        for(i=1;i<k;i++){
                                                t[i] = t[i] + x[i]
                                                        + t[i-1]/10000;
                                                t[i-1] %= 10000;
                                        }
                                        t[k-1] %= 10000;
                                        break;
                                case '-':
                                        t[0] = (t[0] + 10000)
                                                - x[0];
                                        for(i=1;i<k;i++){
                                                t[i] = (t[i] + 10000)
                                                        - x[i]
                                                        - (1 - t[i-1]/10000);
                                                t[i-1] %= 10000;
                                        }
                                        t[k-1] %= 10000;
                                        break;
                                case 'e':
                                        for(i=0;i<k;i++) t[i] = x[i];
                                        break;
                                case 'q':
                                        exit(0);
                                default:
                                        noprint = 1;
                                        break;
                        }
                        if(!noprint){
                                for(i=k - 1;t[i] <= 0 && i > 0;i--);
                                printf("%d",t[i]);
                                if(i > 0) {
                                        for(i-- ; i >= 0; i--){
                                                printf("%04d",t[i]);
                                        }
                                }
                                putchar('\n');
                                for(i=0; i > k;i++) x[i] = 0;
                        }
                }
                noprint = 0;
        }
}
```

Figure 4(c). Full view of the C program. Box shows lines in "flat" view. Underlines show lines in the fisheye view.

some character to *count, until* the first occurrence of some other field separating character.

3.2.3 More Examples of the Tree Fisheye: Other Hierarchical Structures The focus in the previous examples has been on hierarchies implicitly represented in contiguous files. There are many file structures that are more truly hierarchical. Linked trees are the archetypical example. The fisheye in its purest tree formulation (section 3) can be immediately applied to such tree structures.

An interesting use would be in menu retrieval systems. Such systems present a screenful of alternatives (a "menu"), each choice from which would lead to yet another screenful of choices, and so on. Each screen can be thought of as a node, with the choices being arcs to other nodes. Typically the menus are arranged in tree structures, and users descend down the tree searching for information or services. Menu driven retrieval systems are often lauded for novice users of a system - since the user need not know much about the system's capabilities ahead of time. One problem noted with menu systems is that people get lost, lose track where they are in the structure, especially if it is large[10]. A suggestion sometimes made is to give people a list of where they have been, or to indicate the parent of the current node. Representing the structure with a fisheye, and allowing link traversal would amount to a menu access with global orienting information made available. J. S. Reitman, *et al.*[11] have in fact implemented what is essentially just such a system.

4. *FISHEYE VIEWS FOR OTHER TYPES OF STRUCTURES*

4.1 *Other Graph Structures*

There are graphs other than trees in the class of structures that can support a fisheye view. Such cases must allow a measure of distance and of level of detail. In general, graph distance may be difficult to define because there may be more than one path connecting two points, so choices must be made and justified: shortest path length vs. "resistor network equivalent" path length vs. transition network equivalent path, etc. Level of detail presents a more serious problem. Either the nodes or the arcs must have, or be representable at, varying levels of importance or detail.

One example of a case where nodes may have varying importance is the simple generalization of a conceptual hierarchy, known in Artificial Intelligence literature as an "ISA" network. Nodes are categories or concepts, and links are hierarchical (essentially set containment) relations between them. This becomes a directed graph (a DOG "isa" MAMMAL, and not vice versa) without cycles (nothing is its own superordinate). In such a structure, nodes higher in the hierarchy are more general, much as are nodes near the root of a tree. Thus the fisheye can be defined over such a structure.

The connectivity of roads on a map represent another example where both nodes and arcs my have varying importance. In a fisheye view, one could show all cities and roads near the focal point, but only increasingly larger cities and more substantial roads at more distant points. While this rule says what to display, it does not yet say how. For example, if the more distant regions are shown to scale, the map has been uncluttered in a perhaps useful way, but the view may remain unmanageably large. The reduction of actual view size is a problem of spatial distance, and not of graph connectivity. Problems of the fisheye view of space are dealt with in the next section.[8]

---

8. In discussion of fisheyes for graphs, there are also some issues of maintaining connectivity, when edges can be deleted from view. Such problems will not be dealt with here.

4.2 Fisheye Views of Euclidean Space

Fisheye views for examining dimensional structures (e.g., Euclidean space) present special challenges. A notion of distance may be readily available (e.g., Euclidean distance), but level of detail less so. Certain features of the structure may vary in importance, as in the road and cities case mentioned in the previous section, but as for the whole structure itself, we must think further. Returning to the zoom lens analogy, recall that the level of detail is often the variable manipulated by a zoom lens. In the case of spatial structure, this would typically correspond to a change of scale. A global view would be a small map of the entire region, a detail view would be an expanded version of a smaller region. There are several ways to use a scale parameter as the *LOD* for a fisheye view[9], but the net result, while more general and flexible, is essentially a return to the original wide angle lens optical analog with which we began. It deserves a few comments. The most important is that it is a non-geometric transformation; it introduces shape distortions. In a one dimensional case this is only a relative length distortion, that may be fairly innocuous (being essential to the view and perhaps fairly easy to compensate for mentally). In two- and higher dimensional cases, the distortion of shape is more complicated. It is the familiar barrel distortion of wide angle lenses, and is more severe at close range, when the difference in magnification between the center and edges is large. Only straight lines passing through the center remain straight, otherwise straight lines are curved, angles are distorted, and shapes are transformed in a way that varies with size and radius from the center. Whether humans can adjust to such a view is an open question, and no doubt depends on the degree to which their task requires complicated shape matching. (Truck drivers sometimes use fisheye mirrors as adjuncts to their usual sideview mirrors. Presumably this gives them a wider view of a world in which their task is to detect any large approaching object, with distortion being relatively unimportant.)

5. A FEW COMMENTS ON ALGORITHMS

The most general fisheye algorithm would make no use of the special character of the structure being viewed, nor of the particulars of the distance and Level of Detail functions. It would simply start at the focus and move away in all directions. At each distance therefrom the algorithm would display a point if and only if its level of detail caused the computed Degree of Interest to be sufficiently high. Such an algorithm would have the usual advantages and disadvantages associated with generality. It would allow very arbitrary and *ad hoc* definitions of the distance and detail functions, but would be very inefficient for many useful cases, since it would require a complete scan of the structure and the evaluation of the *DOI* for each point. Such inefficiencies can be substantial. The fisheye function, as defined in earlier sections for trees, provides a few useful examples of how large savings are possible.

---

9. One way to make a spatial fisheye is to break the whole detailed view into tiny picture elements (pixels). Then assign the level of detail j to every jth pixel (if any cell gets assigned multiple *LOD*'s, always use the highest). Then to implement the fisheye, get rid of all pixels that do not meet the threshold criterion -- effectively requiring a higher j as radius from the center increases. This keeps ever fewer pixels as the distance increases from the focal point. This specifies what elements will be shown but not how, achieving a reduction of information but not of view size. A view size compression is possible by drawing the remaining cells in radially towards the center until they repack densely. If the pixels are small enough, the result should mimic a wide angle lens view (except that many different shapes of fisheye functions are possible.)

   Another approach would layer the different scale views in a pyramid, with the most magnified view at the bottom, and the smaller ones stacked on top. In this case distance from the apex of the pyramid becomes the level of detail, quite analogously to the tree case. The fisheye *DOI* functions would cut curved surfaces through the pyramid, sweeping low near the center of focus, and rising back towards the apex away from the center. The simplest version, an additive combination function like the tree case above, would define the *DOI* in terms of the sum of the distances from two points: (1) the focal point and (2) some special point (the root of the tree and the apex of the pyramid), distance from which gives *LOD*. The result would therefore be elliptical iso-*DOI* surfaces. There is one difference from the tree case. Here we would only want to display points precisely at the threshold, and not everything above it. The chosen *DOI* surface could then be projected parallel to the altitude of the pyramid to yield a presentable flat form of the view.

5.1 Convexity and the Monotone Algorithm for Trees

As can be seen in the earlier figures 3(b) and 4(b), the application of a first-order fisheye criterion to the indented text version of an ordered tree has a very consistent visual form. Namely, from the center of focus, text indent regresses monotonically to the margin. (The regression is weakly monotone for a 1st-order and would have been strictly monotone for a 0-order fisheye.) This is because an "outdent" signifies a greater distance from the focus. The greater distance, by the fisheye concept, prohibits showing further detail, hence no further indents.

The monotonicity observation leads to a simple algorithm for implementing the fisheye for such files: Begin with the line of current focus and then move away in both directions up and down the file showing all and only lines that do not require indenting to a level greater than the previously displayed line.

A more general analysis of the monotone algorithm, used for the tree's first-order fisheye function, is instructive. Its efficiency derives from the fact that the *DOI* need never be evaluated for whole classes of nodes. All the descendents of nodes at a level higher than the focus can be dismissed without individual consideration. An implementation in terms of pointers from sibling to sibling can automatically provide such skipping of descendents, making for a very efficient algorithm.

The general principle behind this algorithm is based on the notion of convexity. The term "convexity" can only be applied to sets with a certain minimal kind of structure: there has to be a notion of a shortest path connecting any pairs of points. In Euclidean space, this path is the usual straight line between the points, in a tree, it is the connecting path through the tree. A subset is said to be convex if and only if all shortest paths between members of the subset contain only members of the subset.

Now we can describe the general convexity condition. If the subset of points in a view (i.e., that subset where the *DOI* is above threshold) is convex, then whole classes of points can be dismissed simply by examining the neighborhood of the boundary. The reasoning goes like this. Take a point on the boundary and move to a neighbor in some direction. If this neighbor has the same *DOI*, then it too is on the boundary, and so should be included. If on the other hand its *DOI* is less, then it is outside the region and convexity guarantees that no other points whose shortest path goes through the original boundary point and this neighbor will be in the subset of interest, so all points along such paths can be dismissed summarily. Finally, if the *DOI* is greater, then convexity guarantees that all points along shortest paths in this direction will be in the subset of interest, up to at most one other boundary point. The result is a tremendous reduction in the search. If there are systematic ways to generate the boundaries and neighbors and paths (e.g., sibling and descendent lists) then a very efficient algorithm results.

The *DOI* contours defined over the tree were convex for all thresholds and the preceding analysis applies. If a given node is in the view and its descendant is not, then none of the more remote descendants will be either, or there would be a violation of convexity. The use of a linked tree structure can take maximal advantage of this. One implication of this generalization is that a variation on the monotone strategy can be applied to general K-order fisheyes for trees. The more general algorithm would proceed from the point of focus to the margin, but would be less stringent about requiring monotonic progress. In particular, a K-order fisheye view would tolerate departures of up to K levels of detail from a a strict monotone decrease in *LOD*.

5.2 Incremental Changes

In interactive use still other savings are possible in some cases, owing to the fact that the fisheye view may not need to change much if the focus is moved to nearby points. In distance functions which are true metrics, parts of the structure far away from a point x will also be far from point y, if x and y are close to each other. As a result the fisheye *DOI* function will not change much at remote places.

The tree *DOI* functions provide a particularly nice example of this. The point is best made by returning to the "dangling tree" rendition of a tree's *DOI* function (see figure 2). Consider how the view changes when the point of focus is moved to a new node. Both the old and the new versions will have the path from the root to their respective focii at the top, with the rest dangling. The two dangling representations will differ only where these paths from the root begin to differ. This divergence begins at the lowest common ancestor of the old and new focii. Thus the corresponding *DOI* functions will differ only below this common ancestor. This observation leads to an efficient algorithm for interactive fisheye view generation: the view only need be recomputed below the lowest common ancestor. Note that this implies the *DOI* recomputation cost is smaller for the (behaviorally more frequent?) motions to nearby locations. In a hierarchically structured contiguous file, whose structure was a complete regular tree, this movement cost would be logarithmically related to the number of intervening lines in the file (as opposed to linearly related for a scrolling flat window).

6. *OTHER ISSUES*

Returning primary consideration to the case of trees, there are still a few other issues to discuss for a fisheye. One problem, mentioned in section 3.1, is that, for a given size structure, if the branching factor is too large, then not as much compression is achieved, and the view quickly gets too large to see easily. If it is believed that not all the branches at any given level are of equal interest, one can consider pruning these branches, decreasing the effective branching factor. There are a number of ways to do this. One is simply to get rid of unwanted branches with some *ad hoc* rule, aimed at some sort of abbreviation or ellipsis. Some principled approaches are possible, if for example the varied interest in branches can be conceived in a fisheye way. Suppose some subset of the siblings is considered of greater *a priori* importance, say the first few and last few in some natural ordering. Other siblings might be of special interest by virtue of being close to the center of focus (*aposteriori* component). Putting these two together we get a fisheye view of the ordered list of siblings: *LOD* increases from the ends towards the middle of the sibling order, and distance is absolute separation from the focus in the ordering. This would throw out all but the first few, last few and those right around the focus. Such pruning could be implemented as a second fisheye filter, working on the output of the first, or be incorporated directly into the original fisheye functions.

A second issue concerns the possibility of multiple simultaneous focii. There are times when one wishes to examine in detail more than one place at time, to make comparisons, or look at some distant part referenced from the current location. The restriction to a single focus would force such viewing to be done by alternation. Having both detailed regions available at the same time could be useful, and would require a fisheye with two (or more) focii. (A two focus fisheye view is a fisheye analog of two "flat" windows viewing different parts of the same file). This could be handled by directly redefining the fisheye to encompass two (or more) focii. A nearly equivalent formulation might redefine the distance function dynamically, where the two would-be focii are defined by fiat to be 0 distance apart, as though there were a shortcut bridge between them. Then distance to anything else becomes a shortest path distance from them, and the rest of the fisheye conception remains intact.

A related notion would be an automatic multifovea fisheye, where for certain purposes it would be assumed that secondary focii would automatically be of interest. For example, in editing a computer program, the lines where a variable is declared might be of interest any time one is examining a line where that variable is referenced. Implementing such a scheme would amount to dramatically redefining the distance function. The original tree structure with its distances might be augmented by a whole raft of cross reference links with some sort of graph distance. Any such viewer would probably have to be rather special purpose, but might be useful. The challenge would be to set up a system that could be easily and arbitrarily configured by the user, and still be efficient.

7. *CONCLUDING REMARKS AND SUMMARY*

This paper introduced the "fisheye lens" as a way to display large structures in which distance and level of detail can be defined. The general motivation was to give people a view of a structure that includes those parts they are most interested in seeing. The conjecture offered here is that such interest might usefully be decomposed into two components: first, the general, *a priori* or intrinsic importance of parts of the structure; second, a component dependent on the specific needs of the current examination of the structure -- here a simple notion of distance from the current point of focus. This combination, it is hoped, will provide a useful compromise, showing both detail at the place of central focus and global structure to maintain context.

How well this will actually work for humans, and in what contexts, remains to be seen. We have implemented an interactive version of a fisheye facility (first order fisheye, for the "count until" class of structured contiguous files, discussed in section 3.2.2, above) to explore how a fisheye might help people find things in familiar and unfamiliar text, and how it might help in learning of textual material. The program is described in detail in another paper.[1]

REFERENCES

1. Arias, J. P. and Furnas, G. W., FISHEYE: A program implementing "fisheye" viewing for hierarchically structured files. Internal Memorandum, Bell Laboratories, October, 1982.

2. *UNIX PROGRAMMER'S MANUAL, UNIX User's Manual 4.1 BSD,* Computer Sciences Division, Department of Electrical Engineering and Computer Science, University of California, Berkeley, CA. June, 1981.

3. Montgomery, W. A., An interactive screen editor for UNIX. BTL-TM80-5343-2, 1980.

4. Englebart, D. C., and W. K. English, A research center for augmenting human intellect. *AFIPS Conference Proceedings, Vol. 33, 1968,* 15 p. SRI-ARC Catalog item 3954.

5. L. Tesler, The Smalltalk environment, *Byte, 6, 1981,* pp. 90-147.

6. Weinreb, D. and Moon, D., *Lisp Machine Manual (Fourth Edition)* MIT Artificial Intelligence Laboratory Cambridge, Mass. 1981.

7. Allen, R. B., Patterns of Manuscript Revisions, *Behaviour and Information Technology, 1,* 1982, pp.177-184.

8. Nelson, T. H. *Computer Lib* Chicago: Hugo's Book Source 1974.

9. Gleason, T., READER: a program to assist with reading documents on terminals. Internal Memorandum, Bell Laboratories, April 1982.

10. Robertson, G., D. McCracken and A. Newell, The ZOG approach to man-machine communication, *Department of Computer Science Technical Report CMU-CS-97-148,* Carnegie Mellon University, Pittsburgh, PA, October, 1979.

11. Reitman, J. S., W. B. Whitten and T. W. Gruenenfelder, A general user interface for creating and displaying tree structures, hierarchies, decision trees, and nested menus. In Y. Vassiliou (ed) *Proceedings of the NYU Symposium on User Interfaces,* ABLEX publishers, in press.

4.2 Bifocal Lens

Spence and Apperley have a different starting point from Furnas, but come to a similar conclusion. The key problem for them is improving access for professionals to large information spaces. These information spaces are professional journals and normal office documents that would be found in an in-basket. They estimate that a professional needs access to about a million documents and a system to access them that requires little training. Their solution was influenced by the Spatial Data Management system at MIT (Bolt, 1984), which demonstrated how spatial display of data was an alternative to filing systems and binders. The Spatial Data Management system had a display wall, with which the user could interact by pointing and voice commands ("Put that there"), and two consoles near the user, one that displayed an overview of the data space and one that displayed detail. It also had the notion of a detail hierarchy. A user could zoom in on some particular object. As the zooming passed certain thresholds, the computer accessed more detailed maps for that smaller subregion and continued zooming on the map. Other elements in the data space would stay constant, making this an overview + detail sort of system, but the level of detail was variable.

Spence and Apperley's addition to the Spatial Data Management system idea is to define two levels of integrated display, an overview level and a detail level at the point of interest. Instead of two displays—an overview display with a "you are here" indication coordinated with a detailed view—they insert the detailed view into the overview. It is like moving a single object across the division in a *bifocal lens* pair of glasses. Whereas Furnas starts from the Data Table side (how important are different cases and how should this importance be mapped into a Visual Structure), Spence and Apperley start from the geometrical side (how can the Visual Structures that successfully work in a professional office be abstracted and amplified by computer). The notion of differential attention is central for each.

Like Furnas, Spence and Apperley posit that objects can be viewed at different levels of detail. In one example, they take a long wall of objects representing a user's in-basket. In order to fit this onto the screen of a CRT, they identify one place in the wall as the *point of interest*. A region around this point of interest is displayed at full size, but areas in the context region to both the left and right of it are drastically foreshortened in the X-direction. This works because the user mainly needs to identify items distant from the point of interest, not to read them. When the user selects an object in the context region, it moves to the center and is shown in detail. What was in the center moves to the context area and is reduced.

In this example, the objects are already assumed to have geometrical dimensions. There are two levels of detail. The distance of an object is the geometrical distance from the point of interest. We might consider that the user's degree of interest is reduced when the distance from the point of interest reaches a certain threshold. The interesting part is that in the area of lower degree of interest, the system applies a visual transfer function as a View Transformation. This visual transfer function determines how objects on the original wall X-axis will be mapped into the bifocal display. It says that items within a certain distance of the point of interest are in a focal area. They are mapped 1:1. Objects in the context area outside the focal area are compressed in X about 9.6:1. All items continue to be mapped 1:1 in Y.

A second example of a bifocal lens adds the feature of semantic zooming. Spence and Apperley divide part of the information space into a tree structure of journal volumes, issues, articles, and the higher-order entities to which these belong. Instead of defining the equivalent of Furnas's level of detail geometrically (as they did in the earlier example), they use this logical data structure at the Data Table level. As objects move from their full view into their compressed view, they change visual representation and aggregation. The table of contents of a journal becomes the spine of the journal for a given year, for example. The user can zoom this detailed view to different information levels.

Returning to our discussion of overview + detail versus focus + context displays, these displays are part of a more complex design space. They involve a trade-off among several design parameters, which in turn relate to characteristics of the application. The first parameter is the *zoom factor*, as previously mentioned. The zoom factor of Spence and Apperley's input tray bifocal lens example (Figure 4.4) is

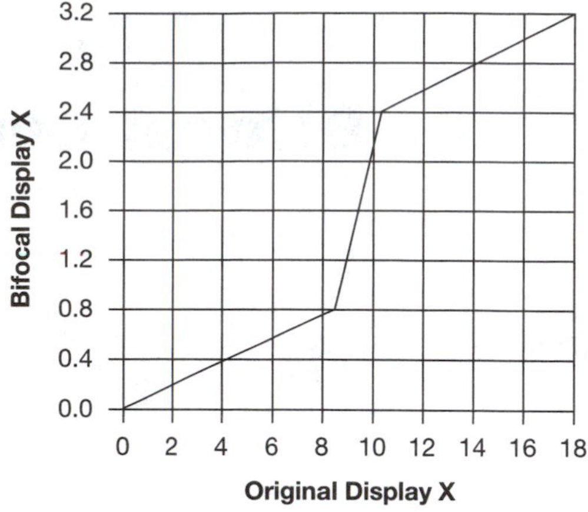

FIGURE **4.4**

Transfer function for Spence and Apperley's input tray (Spence and Apperley, 1982 ●, Figure 5).

9.6, while the zoom factor of Furnas's programming text in Figure 4.3(c) of his paper is 7.6; both are comparable to that in many overview + detail displays.

Another factor is the *focus/context space ratio,* that is, the ratio of the space devoted to focus as opposed to context display. The equivalent would be the *overview/detail space ratio.* In Figure 4.4, this ratio is 0.5—half of the display is devoted to context, half to focus. Varying this parameter might determine what zoom factors are tolerable. If the focal space has the requirement that it must hold a document of some fixed size and that size induces a large focus/context space ratio, there may not be enough space left to establish a context. An overview + detail display might be better because it collects all of the context display space together where it can be more effectively used. Overview + detail displays especially might be better if the representation of the overview is such that it can be small (e.g., a small overview map showing only major highways).

A third factor is whether the zoom factor is a step function or continuous function. (The zoom factor function is the first derivative of the visual transfer function in Figure 4.4). The bifocal lens uses a step function. The perspective wall (Mackinlay, Robertson, and Card, 1991), which is similar to the bifocal lens except with perspective distortion, uses a continuous-perspective zoom factor. Furnas's program text fisheye lens example uses a multiple step function. The great advantage of a continuous distortion is that it is like having many intermediate displays. Furnas's program view is like having perhaps five intermediate displays. The disadvantage is that the continuous nature of the function may induce distortions. Whether this is a problem depends on the visual transfer function and the task. Some transfer functions make straight lines curved. This is not so much of a problem in a fisheye rearview mirror of a car (except for misjudging distance), because the task is to determine whether another vehicle is alongside. The same distortion would be fatal for a task involving text. If a map were distorted, it would no longer be easy to estimate distances or to compare the length of two routes. Some continuous visual transfer functions leave straight lines straight (e.g., the perspective wall), but allow parallel lines to converge. This might be acceptable in the context region if it is paired with a rectilinear focus region. Other transfer functions leave parallel lines in both focus and context regions both straight and parallel. This is the case for the bifocal lens. There is also the question of whether the distortions undermine development of a stable mental model. Perspective transfer function can sometimes help here.

Another factor concerns whether the fisheye effect is obtained by geometrical distortion, elision, or semantic scaling. Even in a geometrical space, scaling can occur by deleting objects or details farther from the focus. This is what Steinberg's cartoon does and what Feiner and McKeown (1991) do for their control panels.

Both Furnas's and Spence and Apperley's papers use nonhomogeneous display techniques to handle large information spaces. SemNet, the Information Visualizer, and SeeNet, described elsewhere in the book, all designed to handle large information spaces, come to this position as well.

Data base navigation: an office environment for the professional

ROBERT SPENCE

Department of Electrical Engineering, Imperial College of Science and Technology, Exhibition Road, London SW7 2BT, England

and MARK APPERLEY†

University of Waikato, Hamilton, New Zealand

Abstract. The potential of the computer to assist in the everyday information handling activities of professional people has received little attention. This paper proposes a number of novel facilities to produce, for this purpose, an office environment in which a needed item of information can rapidly be sought and identified. It involves a new display technique which overcomes the classical "windowing" problem, and the use of natural dialogues utilizing simple actions such as pointing, gesturing, touching and spoken commands. The simple dialogue makes the scheme well suited to the professional person, who is most likely unwilling to learn complex command languages. Little disturbances to the appearance of the office need be involved.

1. Introduction

Professionals, such as lawyers, managers, company presidents and engineers, spend much of their working lives handling information. Items of information are accepted, examined, annotated, filed, shared, copied, assigned priority and eventually destroyed, to name only a few such activities. The potential of the computer and other electronic techniques to assist these information handling activities is immense, but curiously underexploited: few professionals have anything computationally more complex than a pocket calculator within their personal offices.

The slow emergence and acceptance of such computational assistance can be attributed to a number of factors, many of which are associated with human attitudes and behaviour rather than limitations set by technology. For example, constraints are imposed by the lack of enthusiasm of the typical professional to be trained in the use of complex command languages. Another impediment is the sensitivity of professionals to the appearance of their personal office, and particularly to the introduction of a keyboard (Manuel 1981). Also a major difficulty arises from the limitations set by human memory, which is such that a given item of information can often not be specified immediately, uniquely and without error: some preliminary searching or browsing is usually necessary and it is essential that this can be achieved with the most simple of commands.

With information handling it is useful to distinguish between two essentially different tasks. One is the specification of an item of information that is of interest—the other is the retrieval of that item from wherever it may be located. It is the former activity—specification—which is the subject of this paper, and for which we propose a novel scheme having many desirable features. By contrast with information retrieval, which is already the object of intensive research and where efficiency is dictated largely by hardware and software considerations, the human–computer interaction associated with information specification has received little attention.

The novel proposal presented in this paper is expressed in the form of a description of the Office of the Professional. It offers the significant benefit that very little skill is required of the user; only natural actions such as pointing, gesturing, speaking and touching are required. Nor is any radical change in the appearance of the professional's office involved. Furthermore, all components of the proposed scheme lie well within the capability of available technology, and the scheme is attractive from an economic point of view.

2. The office of the professional

Certain general characteristics of professional people have already been mentioned in order to demonstrate the problems that must be resolved if computers are to be used to simplify their information handling activities. These characteristics include a reluctance to be trained in the use of complex command languages, a dislike of keyboards and sensitivity to the appearance of their working environment, henceforth referred to as the 'Office of the Professional'. In addition, professional people frequently participate in discussions, are generally supported by a secretary, and may need to have access to an extremely large store of information.

The direct needs of these people just described are not entirely satisfied by the concepts and techniques normally associated with the term 'Office of the Future'. Considerable attention, supported by massive investment, has been directed towards this area. However, as popularly represented, such an environment is tailored rather to the needs of support staff having characteristics and job specifications very different from those of the professional. Secretaries or clerks can be given extensive training in such skills as typing and the operation of word processors; they are generally not required to have access to as much information as professionals, but they are often trained in, and adept at, the highly efficient organization of information. The information handled by such people is usually more structured and formal than that associated with the work of the professional.

In this paper, exclusive consideration is given to the information handling activities of the professional person. It is important to note, however, that many of the concepts and innovations described are equally relevant to other information handling activities, such as civil and military command and control and library search.

3. Information

The commodity most crucial to the activity of professionals, and which permeates their working environment, is information. While this commodity is often embodied in printed text, it can also include recorded speech and printed or projected pictures and diagrams. Individual items of information may vary in their extent, from a scribbled note to a lengthy legal document, and, as mentioned earlier, many different actions may be performed on a single item of information.

However, it is usually the sheer volume of information relevant to the professional's task that underlies the need for computer assistance. For this reason, in order to lay a basis for our scheme, it is convenient to select an illustrative example which will provide some understanding of the problem, introduce some of the concepts and establish necessary terminology.

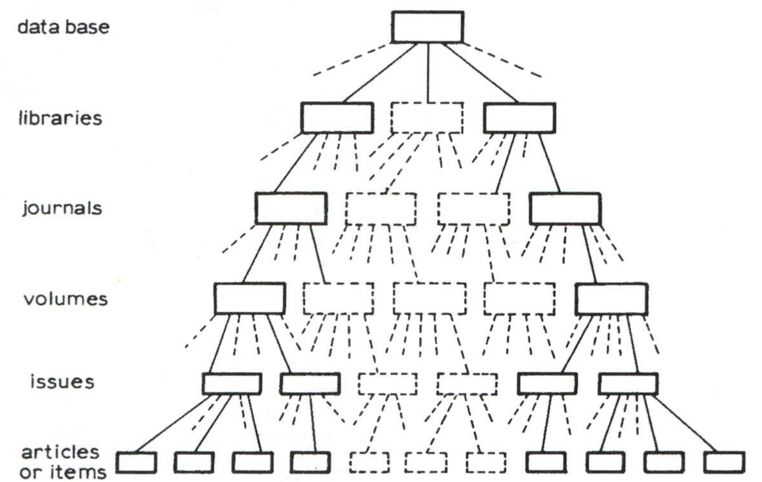

Figure 1. The terminology used to hierarchically classify the professional's data-base.

Assume that the information accessible to the professional is subdivided hierarchically into *libraries*, *journals*, *volumes*, *issues* and finally *articles* or *items*, as shown in figure 1. With a multiplication of ten at each level in the hierarchy, about 10^5 items might be involved, each of which may itself comprise several pages of text. The terminology used here is familiar for the example of a conventional scientific journal, with a total run of 20 years necessarily containing 20 volumes, hence 240 issues, and perhaps 5000 articles. For convenience, the same terminology is used in other contexts, as for example the professional's in-tray, which might also be classified as a journal. The contents of this in-tray, ranging from personal reminders and messages from colleagues to incomplete drafts of papers, will vary considerably from day to day.

From these examples it can be appreciated that the professional may require access to upwards of 10^6 conventional printed pages.

4. Location by visual scan

In order to retrieve an item of information in a conventional office, one must first locate, within the library (comprising perhaps a conventional library and/or collection of files in cabinets), the necessary book or file containing the item. In doing so, one most certainly relies upon memory of where the book was last located, as well as spatial and other clues ('behind the red book to the left on the top shelf') and symbolic or textual labels (e.g. book titles or coloured stickers) (Bolt 1979). This memory will be considerably enhanced if the available books can be *seen*, for it is then necessary only to follow the recall of the approximate location of a needed book by a rapid browsing or scanning action in order to locate it. If memory fails, a visual scan requiring not more than a few seconds will usually serve to find the book. Where books are visible throughout the working day, memory will be continually enhanced, albeit unconsciously, by constant awareness of their location.

As they have been developed to such a high degree of efficiency in the human being, spatial memory and search by visual scan should be exploited if possible in the Office of the Professional. For this reason, each journal in the proposed scheme is represented by an *icon* in full veiw of the user (i.e. the professional), and normally and conveniently affixed to the wall of the office. The icon might consist of a simple piece of coloured card, perhaps with a motif or label to assist identification, about the size of a large postcard (figure 2). Shape and colour can be utilized to aid rapid identification. Alternatively, for appearance's sake, and according to the taste of the individual, icons may appear like book spines. More bizarre but perfectly valid examples of icons would include the Picasso print hanging on the wall, or the plant decorating the alcove; the only requirement is that the icons be visible and fixed. For convenience, in later sections we shall refer to the surface on which the icons are located as the *wall*; in most cases it will be coincident with the conventional wall of the office.

5. Identification by pointing: the 'teletouch' facility

The required journal having been located by visual search, it must now be specifically identified and selected. Just as the ability to locate by visual scan is instinctive and highly developed in human beings, so is the identification of an artifact by pointing or touching. It is therefore proposed that journals, represented by icons as described above, be identified by a pointing action. Touching may at first appear preferable; however, to require all icons to be within arm's length might not only be inconvenient, but would also neglect the advantage, to human memory, of having the icons collectively occupying a wide field of view.

The location on the wall to which the user is pointing must clearly be sensed by some mechanism. As pointing is not an exact indication, the location sensed may not be precisely that which is intended, so confirmatory feedback (an illuminated spot on the wall) is essential in order that corrective action can be taken. There is much to be gained economically, as well as in flexibility, if the wall and associated icons are passive, the icons being constructed from inexpensive materials of the user's choice. Ideally, the user should not be required to wear any special equipment. If this requirement is not feasible, any encumbrance should be minimal; the equipment must obviously be light, unobtrosive and comfortable to wear.

These requirements can be adequately satisfied using presently available technology. The use of an electromagnetic sensing device on the user's arm, for example, has been demonstrated for this very application (Bolt 1980), but other effects (ultrasonic, capacitive, infra-red, etc.) offer a variety of alternative approaches. Indeed, the realization of a pointing-direction sensor is considerably eased by the comparatively low accuracy which can be tolerated (approximately $\pm 2°$) (E. Platt 1981, personal communication) given that confirmatory feedback (the "finger-print") allows errors to be corrected by a small movement of the hand. Similarly, a relatively simple mechanism, probably located on the office ceiling, will suffice to provide this 'fingerprint' by illuminating the wall position inferred from the pointing-position sensor. Many acceptable trade-offs within this scheme are possible. For example, although resulting in a less direct pointing action, the use of a touch-sensitive tablet, located on the desk surface, to manipulate the 'fingerprint' position, is an inexpensive alternative requiring no special attachments to be worn by the user. In certain situations, where very few journals are required, the icons themselves can of course be located on the desk.

As the identification of an icon essentially involves the action of touching, though at a distance, we refer to this means of icon identification as 'Teletouch', and the confirmatory illumination as the 'fingerprint' (figure 3).

In the preceding discussion, the actions involved in locating, identifying and selecting a journal of interest have been described. It is suggested that these actions are entirely natural to the human being, involve negligible or no training and that the maximum time that need typically elapse between the realization that a specific journal is needed and the subsequent selection of that journal is about 2 s. The importance of the user's constant but unconscious awareness of the icons located on the wall should not be underestimated.

6. Selection of the journal

Some action must now be taken to confirm that the icon to which the user is presently pointing is indeed the intended one, and that it is the associated journal that is of interest. As the eyes and one arm are fully occupied with the pointing action, this confirmation should preferably not involve any overt motor action on the part of the user; it is proposed that spoken-word recognition be employed. The recognition of isolated utterances in a single speaker environment has been extensively studied and applied (Bolt 1980), and presents few problems in terms of present-day technology (see, for example, VRM 1980)†. Although the successful recognition of a spoken command (e.g. "here") will usually be followed (see § 9) by the presentation of a new image on the desk display, it is suggested that an echo, in the form of a character display of the recognized word, be provided within an unobtrusive fixture on the desk (figure 4).

Figure 4. A general view of the office showing the public display (left), examples of icons on the wall (right), and the desk (front) containing the Bifocal Display, a writing tablet, and the voice response display (showing "HERE").

† A recently described system (Peckham 1981) claims to be able to recognize keywords within general conversation.

7. Extending the library of icons

Typically, because of limitations imposed by available office wall-space, and aesthetic or other reasons (e.g. poor eyesight), only 100–200 individual icons can be accommodated. This apparent limitation can be overcome by reserving part of the wall space as a dynamic icon area. This acts as a screen on to which can be projected one of a number of slides, each of which is an image of a collection or library of icons. Any of these icons can be selected in the manner already described. This library extension is provided quite simply by a computer-controlled slide projector. The index to the slides is a set of icons located in the permanent icon area, although this facility could be extended by using some of the slides as indexes to others, and is restricted only by the capacity of the projector cartridge.

8. Alternative selection procedures

It might be said of the Teletouch journal selection procedure (and of some of the other procedures yet to be described), that the operation could be more simply carried out if the user entered a code directly identifying the required journal. However, the motivating principles behind the Teletouch scheme must not be forgotten. This system requires no remembering of journal titles or codes, or conjuring up of appropriate keywords: the index is ever-present, with journals as familiar and as clearly identifiable as objects on one's desk. Alternatives would require the user to memorize codes or titles for up to 1000 journals, an unacceptable and, as has been shown, unnecessary burden. Consulting an index (requiring frequent updating) or a secretary are clearly unsuitable solutions, and implicitly neglect the potential offered by the computer.

In addition, such alternatives would require the relevant code to be entered, without error, possibly either by spoken utterance or via a keyboard. Speech input for journal identification would require a large vocabulary (up to 1000 utterances), taxing the performance of existing speech recognition units and involving the user in a lengthy training session. The time involved, and the probability of typing errors, would constitute significant disadvantages with an alphanumeric keyboard, and it is a recognized fact that many present-day professionals are reluctant to use keyboards or even to allow them to be seen on their desks. By comparison with these alternative approaches, the Teletouch facility, with its rapid 'browse-point-command' selection procedure, offers considerable advantages.

9. Data context

To illustrate the next task faced by the user, assume that the selected journal is the user's in-tray. This journal exhibits some interesting characteristics; at any instant, for example, the user will be uncertain as to its contents. Since the previous occasion on which this journal was accessed, additional items may have been added to it, by a secretary, by colleagues or automatically in response to some pre-ordained condition. Like a conventional in-tray, the data contained in it is essentially unstructured and, in this electronic form, the information can be in one, or a mixture, of many different forms including text, diagrams or pictures and possibly speech. Unlike archival material (e.g. a published scientific paper), an item within the in-tray may invite or even demand a response. These characteristics of the in-tray demonstrate the difficulty of conveniently examining its contents using conventional techniques.

The fundamental question is, "How can the user quickly become aware of the nature of the entire contents of the in-tray, and rapidly examine any individual item in detail?" To illustrate our solution to this problem, consider the in-tray to be represented by a number of conventional textual messages fixed to a long strip of paper (figure 5 (*a*)). A typical in-tray might contain say 20–50 such items. If a sampled message were to be presented in sufficient detail to allow it to be read then, at this level of detail, only three or four messages could be displayed simultaneously on a conventional VDU screen. Thus, if the conventional "windowing" approach to the examination of the in-tray is employed, all except three or four items will necessarily be masked (figure 5 (*b*)). This effect constitutes a serious problem: at a glance, the user has no idea of the extent or nature of the data contained in the in-tray; how many messages there are, whether any are urgent, or whether an expected message is present. The difficulty has much in common with that of trying to peruse a newspaper through a 2-column-inch sized keyhole ('How long is this article?', 'Where is the crossword?', 'What other headlines are there?', 'What page is this?'), or of attempting to locate a needed diagram or equation within a microfiched article.

A solution to this problem is to *focus* on the area of interest rather than use a window. This approach (figure 5 (*c*)), by dividing the VDU screen into three separate viewports, achieves two key objectives. First, it permits two or three items to be displayed in the central region with sufficient detail to be read in full. Second, at the same time the two outer 'demagnified' regions retain adequate detail of the entire remaining contents of the in-tray, in the form of colour, shape, tags, initial letters, etc., to indicate important attributes such as number, size, urgency, nature and origin of the individual items. Interaction with this 'bifocal' display, which is conveniently housed on the user's desk, is carried out using a touch-screen. The user is able to scroll the in-tray contents through the viewports by simply touching an item of interest in one of the outer regions and 'pulling' it into the central 'close-up' region for more detailed examination. By this action the whole strip of data representing the in-tray is moved across the screen†, preserving the spatial relationships between individual items, and retaining the overall view of the entire in-tray contents. Such a display can be implemented with available technology (Apperley and Spence 1981).

Certain aspects of the principle of this Bifocal Display deserve further comment. The effectiveness of the representations displayed in the outer 'demagnified' regions can be enhanced in a number of ways. In an initial search or browsing operation, humans usually perceive graphic representations more effectively than text. For this reason, and because of the effectively reduced resolution resulting from the horizontal contraction, attributes suitable for encoding items in the outer regions include colour, shape, size, tags, pulsed illumination and position. The use of alphanumerics will be restricted to possibly only a single character per item. A related consideration is distraction caused by detail irrelevant to the level of information search currently being conducted (Morse 1979). Thus, in most if not all cases, the representation of an item in the outer regions of the display should *not* merely be a demagnified version of its central region representation, but a representation more appropriate to the lower resolution of these regions (figure 5 (*c*)). A concept highly relevant to, and illustrative of, this technique of devising appropriate levels of detail, is that which Negroponte has termed "billboarding" (N. Negroponte 1979, personal communication)‡.

† Without wrap-around, although this technique might be relevant to certain activities.

‡ Negroponte shows two slides. One is a conventional view of a city street bordered by buildings having a variety of shapes and decorations. The other shows the same street, but with a box placed snugly around each building, each box being a different colour.

10. Movement of data through the bifocal display

The horizontal scrolling movement which appears to be suited to the in-tray example may not be appropriate for other journals. For example, with the user's personal diary, two scrolling modes are suggested. Suppose that when the diary icon is selected, the Bifocal Display shows the current week in the central region, with the rest of the current month, together with the adjacent months, in the outer regions (figure 6). As time is essentially infinite in its extent, it seems reasonable to display only a 12-month period within the three viewports of the display: as this portion is scrolled horizontally through the display, further months will appear on one side as others disappear from the opposite side. When browsing or searching through the immediate past or future with this display, it is convenient to undertake a vertical scroll, stepping through individual days with a window of 7 contiguous days. For a rapid jump of more than a few days, the most appropriate movement is a horizontal one, achieved by 'pulling' the desired period into the central region as previously described. Thus in the central region the diary can be considered to be a two-dimensional arrangement of 'pages' (figure 7), each representing 1 week, which can be scrolled through the central viewport both vertically (by days) and horizontally (by weeks) such that at a given time any 7 contiguous days can be seen in detail. If vertical scrolling leaves Tuesday at the top and Monday at the bottom, then subsequent horizontal scrolling will preserve this relationship.

It could easily be arranged for a flick of the finger (i.e. a rapid application-move-removal of the finger) to initiate a continuous movement of the volume through the central region of the display, such motion being terminated either by touching the display, or automatically when the edge of the volume reaches the edge of the central region.

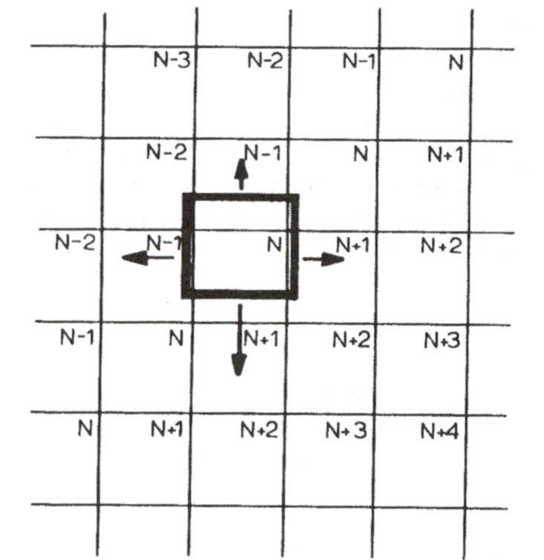

Figure 7. The conceptual two-dimensional arrangement of the diary pages, allowing horizontal scrolling of weeks and vertical scrolling of days.

11. Information levels

In order to describe additional beneficial attributes of the Bifocal Display, and at the same time provide a basis for estimating the amount of information that can be accessed within a library of reasonable size, it is useful to introduce the concept of *information levels*. Consider a different journal for illustration, for example the *I.E.E.E. Transactions on Circuits and Systems*. The wall constitutes the first level of information, where we locate and specify a simple icon (say the cover of a representative issue of this *Transaction*, see figure 3). The resulting image on the Bifocal Display might appear as shown in figure 8: the (annual) volumes displayed in the outer regions constitute the second level of information, whereas the individual monthly issues represented in the central region are at the third level. In this example, each monthly index (not yet shown) has been annotated by the user to provide iconic clues to items of special interest: at this level (level 3) these annotations take the form of coloured tags and the initial letters of the author's name.

For most items of interest, with exceptions such as short messages within an in-tray, the detail provided at information level 3 is insufficient. To obtain further detail, and still retain the advantages of the Bifocal Display, a 'zoom' action is carried out within the central region. First, a 'fingerprint' is placed upon the level 3 representation, in the central region, of the item of interest (the July issue, for example): it is assumed that a 'fingerprint' will always appear at the most recently touched position on the screen. Touching a 'zoom' control causes the fingerprinted item to increase in size until it fills the entire central region, at which time its image is replaced by a more detailed one, the information level 4 image which is more appropriate at this higher resolution. The displaced level 3 items from the central region are kept in view by slightly displacing the data in the outer regions to accommodate their level 2 images (figure 9).

For the in-tray, this level 4 representation would be adequate to enable most messages to be read. With the scientific periodical however, some vertical scrolling may be necessary in order to view the entire contents page of the monthly issue selected. The central region of the display will revert to level 3 when either an item in one of the outer regions is 'pulled' towards the centre, or the zoom is cancelled by touching the bistable zoom control a second time.

With the scientific periodicals, information level 4 still does not provide sufficient detail to enable an item (i.e an individual article) to be read. To obtain the required detail, which is contained in the information level 5 representation, a choice between two alternatives is suggested. First, a transition of the central region of the Bifocal Display to level 5 could be arranged in much the same manner as the transition from level 3 to level 4. Although such a hierarchical descent through a data space can result in one losing one's sense of location within the space, it must be remembered that, with the Bifocal Display, the entire data space remains visible within the information level 2 image in the outer regions of the display, so avoiding this problem. Alternatively, the need to be able to present information to colleagues gathered for discussion suggests the value of a 'public display', located within the office (figure 4), on which the level 5 image could be displayed.

As with the transition to level 4, the display of the level 5 representation of an item is initiated by fingerprinting the required item in the level 4 representation, and then touching the appropriate control. With the scientific periodical, a fingerprint would be placed on the title of an article in the issue's contents page displayed as the level 4 representation. The subsequent zoom or display action would lead to the display of the first page of the article. Movement through the article can be achieved by a page-turning action (e.g. using a joy-pad (Bolt 1980)) or by a vertical scrolling action. It is interesting to note that, with future publications, the concept of a page, imposed by the use of books and book-like binding of paper, may be lost. Certainly, scrolling has the advantage of retaining the maximum context around the area of interest.

The accessing of individual *items* at information level 5, within each *journal* appearing at level 1, is thus achieved by a three-level index comprising information levels 2, 3 and 4. At least 10 choices can be provided at each of these levels, allowing for more than 1000 items per journal.

12. Comment

The proposed scheme raises many questions which require a great deal of consideration, and which are not treated in this paper. We therefore comment briefly below on certain aspects of the scheme worthy of mention.

12.1. *Other information-handling activities*

Examples have been quoted of the many ways in which a professional handles information but, for the proposed scheme, details have been given only of the process of specifying the item required in a search procedure. The manner in which other activities such as journal creation, transmission of items, annotation, etc. might be achieved within the same system has been proposed, and to a limited extent evaluated, and some of these activities demonstrated in a videotape simulation of the system (Apperley and Spence 1980). However, further detailed study and evaluation of these activities is needed.

12.2. *Applications*

The paper basically describes a philosophy of human–computer interaction, and illustrates this philosophy in the important context of the Office of the Professional. The same philosophy would appear to offer considerable potential in other contexts, such as library search, civil and military command and control and in public and private viewdata systems.

12.3. *Data-bases*

The task of retrieving an item of information once it is specified has intentionally been ignored in this paper, as retrieval is a problem common to all information handling systems. Nevertheless, the manner in which specification is carried out may well influence the design of the data-base, as the previous discussion of information levels suggests (§ 11).

12.4. *Work profiles*

The final detailed form and extent of a scheme such as the one described will be strongly influenced by the nature of the professional's work, so that a necessary component in the gradual evolution and adoption of such schemes will be studies of typical work profiles. To be effective, such studies must do more than merely calculate the amount of text currently stored in an office: the location and nature of data-bases and the extent to which a person's information is shared with others, are important factors. Some work along these lines has already been carried out (Coulouris 1979).

12.5. *Information capacity*

Using the projected icon library facility (§ 7), the system described can easily provide for access to up to 1000 journals, and more than 1000 items can be accommodated within a single journal (§ 11). Thus, access to more than 1 000 000 items, each of which may itself consist of many pages, is well within the capabilities of the system.

12.6. *Technology*

Despite the claim (see also below) that the proposed scheme places no severe demands on available technology, certain clearly desirable improvements can be identified. Principal among these is a high definition but inexpensive display for the perusal of documents and images, although to some extent the format adopted for future documents may be influenced by available display technology.

12.7. *Human behaviour*

The formulation of the proposed scheme has illustrated the need to be wary of mimicking current conventional procedures. For example, unlike other workers (Kay 1977, Page and Walsby 1979), we do not attempt to reproduce the appearance of a conventional desk-top. Present-day procedures are constrained by available technology and past organizational decisions, and should not be retained if new technology offers better performance using alternative procedures. What *should* be mimicked and exploited are the highly developed and therefore instinctive human perceptual, cognitive and motor abilities that are at present constrained to operate within different technological and other limits.

12.8. *Claims*

Acknowledging the considerable amount of research and development that still remains to be carried out, we list the following key advantages for the proposed scheme:

(1) Very little specialized skill is demanded of the user. Only pointing, touching, gesturing and voiced commands are required. For annotation or short messages, hand printed character recognizers are readily available (Micropad 1979).

(2) The representation of journals by icons on a wall provides an inexpensive, extensive and flexible first-level of information, and permits extremely simple location and specification of a needed journal. Because of the ever-present nature of these icons, the user unconsciously becomes very familiar with their location and spatial interrelationships. Further, the icon capacity of the wall can be considerably extended if the technique of the projected icon library (§ 7) is exploited.

(3) The Bifocal Display presents a solution to the difficult problem of the blinkering effect of windowing, by providing an awareness, at a useful level of detail, of the entire context of an item of information while simultaneously providing a detailed view of that item.

(4) Apart from the obvious presence of the bifocal display on the desk surface, no radical change in the appearance of the office need be involved.

(5) As has been demonstrated in this paper, the scheme can provide access to relatively large volumes of information.

Acknowledgments

In arriving at our proposed scheme we have derived benefit from a knowledge of the work of others. However, we acknowledge a particular indebtedness to Professor Nicholas Negroponte and his colleagues at MIT, whose concepts, innovations and experiments show a thorough appreciation of the problems of human–computer interaction, and are also bold, imaginative and inspiring. Their work, and particularly their identification of the importance of spatiality, has been pivotal to our thinking.

We acknowledge valuable discussions with many other workers in the field of human–computer interaction, particularly Richard Jackson and his group at Philips Research Laboratories, England, and Ioannis Tzavaras of Imperial College.

References

APPERLEY, M. D., and SPENCE, R., 1980, *Focus on Information: The Office of the Professional* (videotape), Imperial College Television Studio, London, Production Number 1009; 1981 (to be published).

BOLT, R. A., 1979, *Spatial Data Management* (Architecture Machine Group, Massachusetts Institute of Technology, Cambridge, Massachusetts): 1980, "Put-that-there": voice and gesture at the graphics interface, *Computer Graphics*, **14**, 262.

COULOURIS, G., 1979, Personal computers in offices of the future, *Microprocessors and Microsystems*, **3**, 69.

KAY, A. C., 1977, Microelectronics and the personal computer, *Scientific American*, **237**, 231.

MANUEL, T., 1981, Automating offices from top to bottom, *Electronics*, **5**, 157.

MICROPAD, 1979, *Micropad Technical Summary*, Micropad Ltd., Ferndown, U.K.

MORSE, A., 1979, Some principles for the effective display of data, *Computer Graphics*, **13**, 94.

PAGE, I., and WALSBY, A., 1979, Highly dynamic text display system, *Microprocessors and Microsystems*, **3**, 73.

PECKHAM, J. B., 1981, Functional overview of an advanced speech recognition system, *The Computer Recognition of Speech*, I.E.E. Colloquium Digest No. 1981/46, pp. 6/1–6/5.

VRM, 1980, *Voice Recognition Module Reference Manual* (California: Interstate Electronics Corporation).

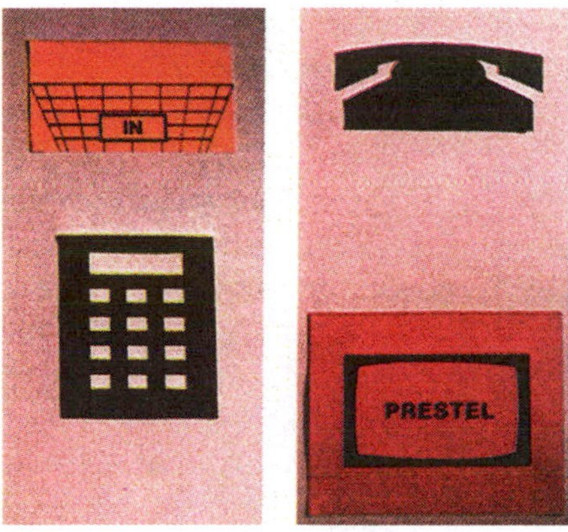

FIGURE **2**

Some examples of icons located on the wall, denoting (upper left) the user's in-tray, (lower left) a calculator facility, (upper right) a personal telephone directory and (lower right) access to the PRESTEL data-base.

FIGURE **3**

Icons representing journals in the user's library, showing the 'fingerprint' on the *I.E.E.E. Transactions on Circuits and Systems* journal.

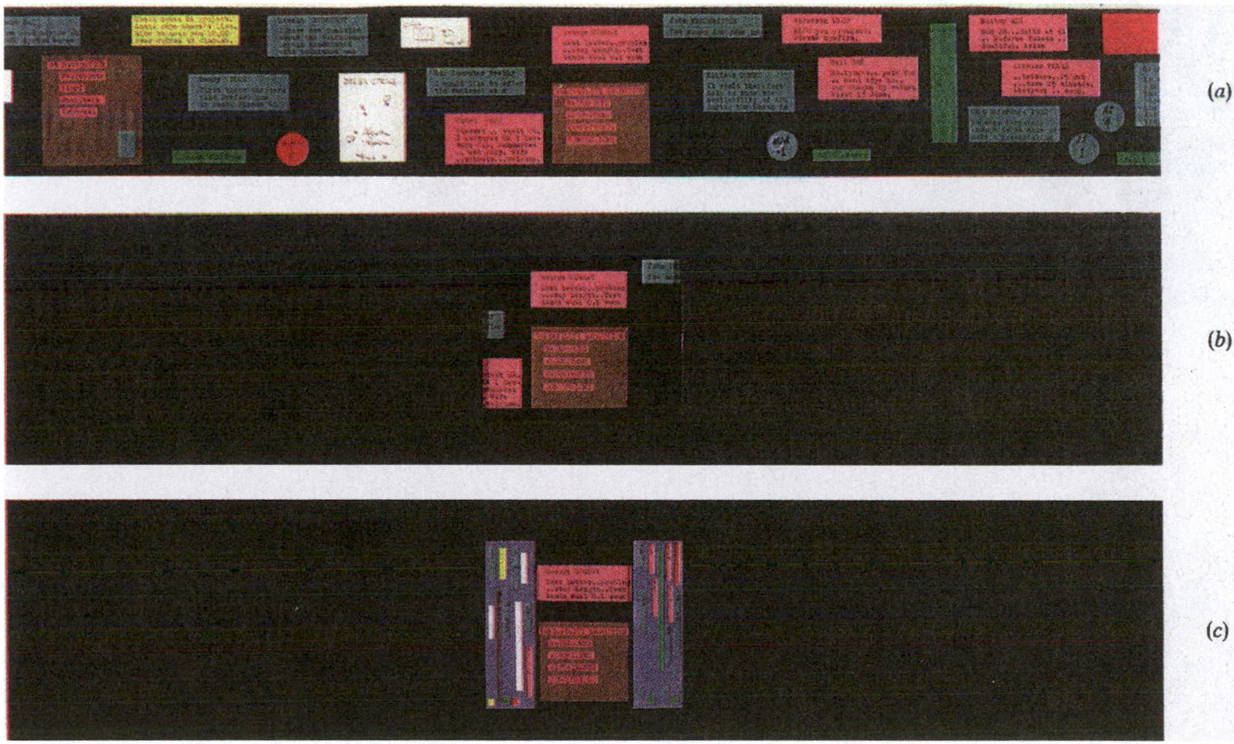

FIGURE **5**

(a) The data space representing the user's in-tray; (b) the same space seen throught a conventional viewing window; (c) the original data space seen through a 'bifocal' viewing system.

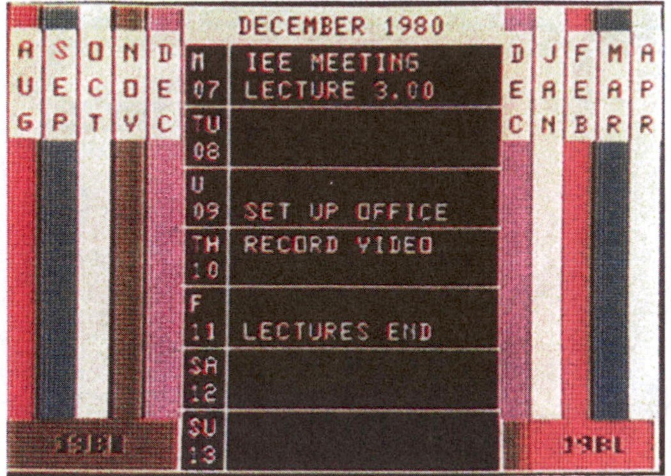

FIGURE **6**

The user's diary as it appears on the Bifocal Display, with the current week in the central region.

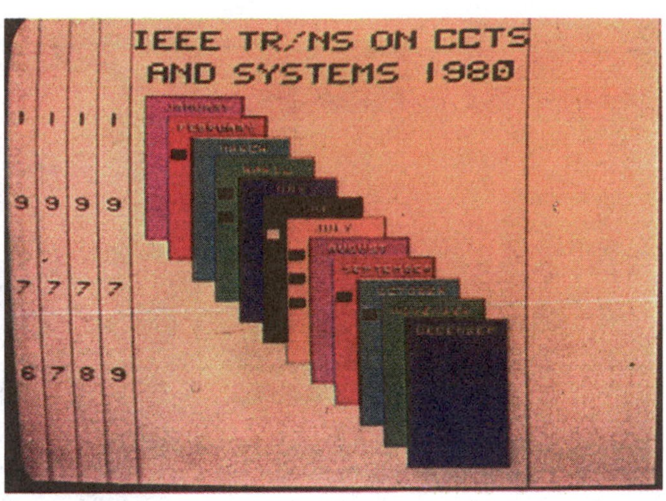

FIGURE **8**

The initial Bifocal representation of the *I.E.E.E. Transactions on Circuits and Systems* journal.

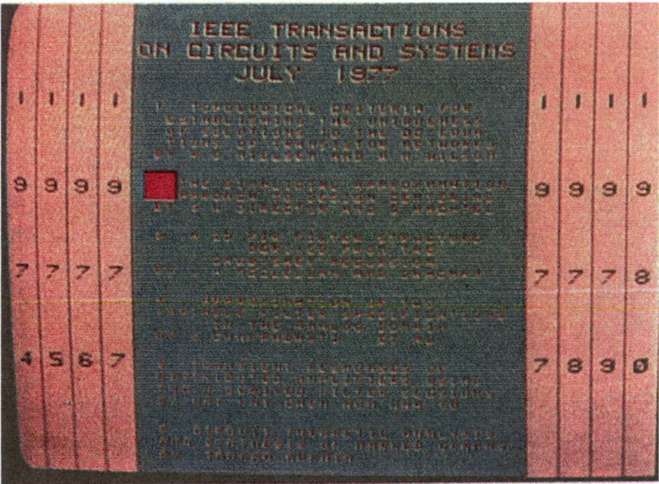

FIGURE **9**

Zooming in on one issue of the *Transactions* causes the displaced months to be represented in the outer regions (1977 on either side of the centre).

4.3

Visual Transfer Functions

The papers in this section explore various visual transfer functions (e.g., see Figure 4.4) as a means for achieving focus + context visualizations. These functions distort visualizations by stretching or compressing them as if they were on a rubber sheet, giving the portion of the visualization attended to more visual detail. The first study to discuss the use of visual transfer functions in this way was Farrand (1973), who used a visual transfer function to distort graphs. More recently, Sarkar and Brown (1992) have created distorted views of networks and maps.

The first paper in this section, on the table lens by Rao and Card (1994 ●), applies a visual transfer function to spreadsheet-like tables. The table lens can be thought of as a way of producing a large-scale spreadsheet, or as an updated version of Bertin's permutation matrix (Bertin, 1977/1981). The significance of this representation is that it is capable of effective visualizations for multidimensional data. In the table lens, a visual transfer function is used to create a sort of bifocal lens (or in some versions, a trifocal lens) independently in the X and Y directions. This effectively divides the display into focus and context areas. In the context areas, compact graphics replace numbers or text. The table lens adds focus + context techniques to the permutation matrix idea of Bertin, resulting in much larger permutation matrices than could previously be handled on a computer display. This makes it practical to analyze higher-dimensional data. The table lens can display on the screen spreadsheets up to 100 times larger than would usually fit. The significance of this capability of representing large tables in terms of knowledge crystallization is that the large tables can hold large schemata. The table lens is thus ideally suited for the exploratory data analysis by visual means of large sets of data, at least large compared to the sorts of data sets that could previously be seen with spreadsheets.

Leung and Apperley's paper (1994 ●) reviews and nicely organizes the different visual transfer functions that have been used. The bifocal lens and the table lens use step functions—values change discontinuously from one constant to another. Other systems, such as the polyfocal display (Kadmon and Shlomi, 1978) and the optical fisheye, use continuous transformation. Unlike the bifocal lens and the table lens, straight lines become curved. Leung and Apperley provide a classification of the techniques used.

Some additional distinctions are useful. One has to do with whether the Visual Transformations are visual transfer functions on a flat 2D surface or whether they are perspective transformations. Why is this interesting? The answer is because people have specialized perceptual abilities to process 3D perspective presentations. The contrast comes out in a comparison between the perspective wall and the bifocal lens. Both reduce the width of a long context area. In the bifocal lens, this is perceived as a discontinuity or distortion, but in the perspective wall, it is just perceived as the natural result of 3D distance. Perspective transformations are a method for obtaining the compression effects of distortion without the perception that there is a distortion. That is an interesting property for designing presentations. Of course, there are trade-offs in terms of unused display space (unless it is filled in with other information) and the fact that perspective distortion may make perspective displays more difficult to read text or make comparisons.

Another distinction is how display level is treated. As the degree of interest in some element of the display is changed, the representation of that element can change. Because the topic of Leung and Apperley's paper is rubber sheet visual transfer functions, smaller degree of interest translates into smaller dimensions. But as we saw, Spence and Apperley show how it is natural for objects in the context region to have a different representation: A journal in the focal region displays its table of contents, but a journal in the context region is represented like an annual bound journal volume with a spine—that is, semantic scaling. Focus + context can be achieved by using either data transformations (such as selection in the Data Table) or view transformations (such as visual transfer functions) or change of representation (such as semantic scaling). Level of detail in Furnas's paper corresponds to magnification in Leung and Apperley's context of rubber sheet transformations and, as we have seen, is not limited to just filtering.

The final paper by Carpendale, Cowperthwaite, and Fracchia (1997 ●) takes visual transfer functions two interesting additional steps. First, the functions are extended from 2D to 3D. Then, to overcome occlusions in 3D, they are applied to the line of sight between the user's viewpoint and the object of interest. Keahey (1997) has recently surveyed this area in a Ph.D. thesis. This is a very active area, and additional results can be found in Carpendale (1997), Gutwin and Greenberg (1997), Holmquist (1997), and Preimj, Raab, and Strothotte (1997).

The Table Lens: Merging Graphical and Symbolic Representations in an Interactive Focus+Context Visualization for Tabular Information

Ramana Rao and Stuart K. Card

Xerox Palo Alto Research Center
3333 Coyote Hill Road
Palo Alto, CA 94304
<rao,card>@parc.xerox.com

ABSTRACT

We present a new visualization, called the Table Lens, for visualizing and making sense of large tables. The visualization uses a focus+context (fisheye) technique that works effectively on tabular information because it allows display of crucial label information and multiple distal focal areas. In addition, a graphical mapping scheme for depicting table contents has been developed for the most widespread kind of tables, the cases-by-variables table. The Table Lens fuses symbolic and graphical representations into a single coherent view that can be fluidly adjusted by the user. This fusion and interactivity enables an extremely rich and natural style of direct manipulation exploratory data analysis.

KEYWORDS: Information Visualization, Exploratory Data Analysis, Graphical Representations, Focus+Context Technique, Fisheye Technique, Tables, Spreadsheets, Relational Tables.

INTRODUCTION

The size of information set which users can coherently bring together on the display of an interactive computer system limits the complexity of problems that can be addressed. In the last few years, we have been exploring the application of interactive graphics and animation technology to visualizing and making sense of larger information sets than would otherwise be practical by other means[3]. In this paper, we present a new visualization, the Table Lens, for manipulating large tables. Though elements of our design are broadly applicable, we have focused on the most widespread kind of table, variously called a cases-by-variable table, an object-attribute table, or loosely a relational table.

The Table Lens supports effective interaction with much larger tables than conventional spreadsheets do. A spreadsheet can display a maximum of 660 cells at once on a 19 inch display (at cell size of 100 by 15 pixels, 82dpi). The Table Lens can comfortably manage about 30 times as many cells and can display up to 100 times as many cells in support of many tasks. The scale advantage is obtained by using a so-called "focus+context" or "fisheye" technique. These techniques allow interaction with large information structures by dynamically distorting the spatial layout of the structure according to the varying interest levels of its parts. The design of the Table Lens technique has been guided by the particular properties and uses of tables.

A second contribution of our work is the merging of graphical representations directly into the process of table visualization and manipulation. Initially, graphical representations were incorporated because of their natural economy in showing cell values. However, a second, perhaps more important, advantage is the effectiveness with which humans are able to spot patterns and features in well-designed graphical renderings of collections of values. The combination of our focus+context technique and graphical mapping scheme, with a small set of interactive operators enables performing exploratory data analysis in a highly interactive and natural manner. After describing the focus+context technique, the graphical mapping scheme, and the Table Lens user interface, we illustrate this data exploration process with actual analysis scenarios.

TABLE LENS FOCUS+CONTEXT TECHNIQUE

Focus+Context techniques support visualizing an entire information structure at once as well as zooming in on specific items. This interplay between focus and context supports searching for patterns in the big picture and fluidly investigating interesting details without losing framing context. A number of such techniques have been developed in the last ten years including the Bifocal Display [7], Furnas's Fisheye techniques [1], the Perspective Wall [2], techniques for graphs and for direct manipulation of 2-D surfaces by Sarkar et al. [5, 6], and the Document Lens [4].

The Table Lens technique has been motivated by the particular nature of tables. The most salient feature of a table is the regularity of its content: information along rows or columns is interrelated, and can be interpreted on some reading as a coherent set, e.g. members of a group or attributes of an object. This is reflected in the fact that tables usually have labels at row and column edges that identify some portion

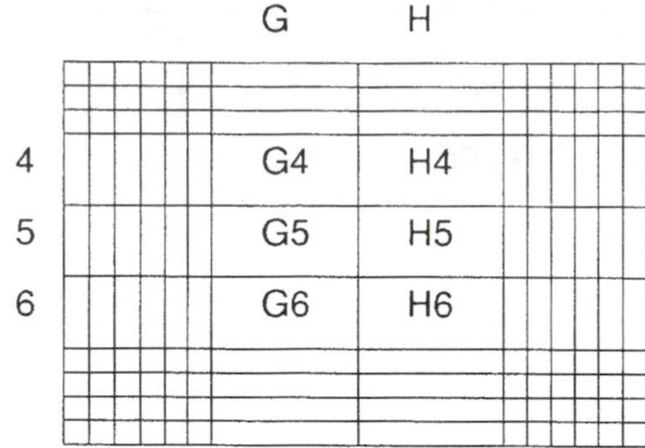

Figure 1: The Table Lens Focal Technique.

of the meaning of the items in the row or column. These observations indicated a need to preserve the coherence of rows and columns and their labels despite distortions to the table. Thus, the Table Lens mutates the layout of a table without bending any rows or columns. Cells in the focal area and the label row and column divide the total focus space of each dimension appropriately. Cells in the context divide the remaining space equally. Figure 1 shows a 10 by 14 table with a focus area of 3 by 2 cells.

The Table Lens technique is similar to that of Sarkar et al.[6]. Besides the difference in metaphor, the Table Lens distorts based on discrete cell boundaries as opposed to smaller pixel or continuous units. It is unlikely that providing support for partial inclusion of a cell in the focal area would be useful, but even then, a cell "detente" or "gravity" mechanism that aids "clicking" or "snapping" into cell borders is necessary. Our technique is further complicated by variable cell widths and heights. In particular, as the focus is moved around the table, it may have to change size to remain on cell boundaries.

An important property of the Table Lens technique is that distortion in each of the two dimensions is independent from the other. This means that rows and columns aren't bent by the distortion, and can thus be scanned entirely by a single horizontal or vertical eye motion. Furthermore, this enables label display, multiple focal areas, and multiple focal levels. Multiple focus areas are important for a number of reasons including comparing distal areas of the table and maintaining focus on summary rows or columns while investigating other portions of the table. Multiple focal levels allows dealing with larger tables and opens up a promising new design space (our current implementation has started this exploration by adding a third level). Below, for concreteness, we illustrate the case of two levels (i.e. focus and context), but point out issues arising with multiple focal levels.

As can be seen in Figure 1, though cells are allocated spaces along each dimension independently, there is an interaction in cell geometry. In fact, four types of cell regions are created by the distortions on the two axis: focal, row focal, column focal, and nonfocal. *Focal* cells are in the focus area along both axes, *row focal* and *column focal* are both half focal in that they are in the focal area of only one of the two axes, and *nonfocal* are in the context area along both axes. For cases with multiple focal levels, there are n by m types of areas, where n and m are the number of focal levels in each dimension (e.g. nine area types in our current implementation). As later described, each of the cell region types may require separate graphical treatment.

Distortion Function Framework

The distortions produced by many focus+context techniques can be described using a general framework starting from the notion of a degree of interest (DOI) function as introduced by Furnas [1]. A DOI function maps from an item to a value that indicates the level of interest in the item. The DOI function can be used to control how available space is allocated amongst items. The DOI function changes over time because of user interaction (e.g. the focus is moved) or system activity (e.g. search processes).

In the Table Lens, a DOI function maps from a cell address to an interest level, and each of the two dimensions has an independent DOI function. In particular, with one focal area, each dimension has a block pulse DOI (as in Figure 2, in which the contiguous focus area cells are at a higher level of interest than the context area cells. Multiple focal areas are characterized by a DOI function which contains multiple pulses. Multiple levels of focus are characterized by a DOI function with block pulses at different levels.

An additional framework concept is that of a transfer function that maps from uniformly distributed cell addresses to "interest-warped" physical locations. In fact, such a transfer function is the integral of the DOI function scaled appropriatedly to fit in the available space. Thus it essentially maps from an item to the total area that has been allocated to items of lesser cell address.

Figure 2 shows a DOI and an associated transfer function for one dimension and the effect of this distortion. The DOI function shown at the top of the figure is a square pulse that comes in three pieces at two different levels. The transfer function has three pieces at two different slopes, which map cells to the three areas of warping, the central focus area and the two flanking context pieces.

This framework allows contrasting Table Lens to other distortion techniques. The Table Lens distortion is equivalent to the distortion function of the Bifocal Display, except that it uses two independent distortions for each of the dimensions. The DOI/transfer functions of the Perspective Wall and the Document Lens are somewhat more complicated. In both cases, the interest level for context cells falls off with distance from the focus area, so the DOI is a flat-topped mountain with sloped regions falling off from the top. Also in both cases, the dimensions interact so the DOI function can not be decomposed into independent functions for each of the dimensions. Thus, their DOI/transfer curves are actually z-surfaces over an x-y plane.

Interactive Manipulation of Focus

The Table Lens supports a number of operations for controlling the focal area. These operations are analogous to ones on the Document Lens and Perspective Wall, though these techniques didn't originally support all the operations. In particular, there are three canonical manipulation operations:

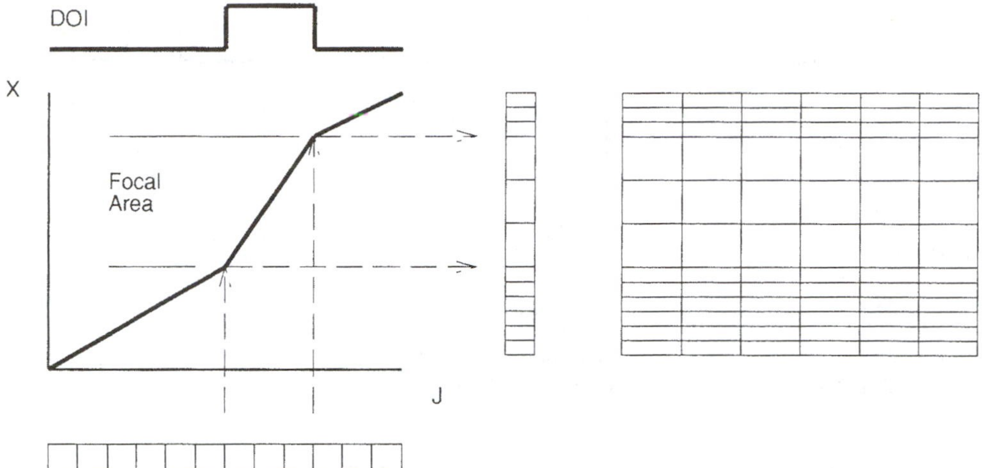

Figure 2: The DOI function maps from cell address to interest level, and the Transfer function maps from cell address to position along an axis. The Transfer function is the integral of the DOI function scaled to fit in the available space on the axis. Its effect can be visualized by the mapping of the cell array into a distorted cell array.

- *zoom* changes the amount of space allocated to the focal area without changing the number of cells contained in the focal area. It corresponds to pulling the lens closer to the viewpoint in the Document Lens and to increasing the width or height of the focus area of the Table Lens.
- *adjust* changes the amount of contents viewed within the focus area without changing the size of the focus area. It corresponds to stretching or shrinking the Perspective Wall, or pulling more or less of the table into the focus area.
- *slide* changes the location of the focus area within the context. It corresponds to sliding the Document Lens or Table Lens in its 2-d plane, or to panning to a different region on the Perspective Wall.

Each of these three operations can be understood visually as simple effects on the DOI and transfer functions as is illustrated in Figure 3. Zoom increases the slope of the focal area which also decreases the slope of the context pieces, since there is a fixed amount of available space. Adjust increases the number of cells in the focus area without changing the amount of space occupied by the focus area, thus the slope in the focal area must decrease. Finally, slide pushes the high slope area to a different spot on the axis.

Another important operation (motivated by actual use) is a coordinated adjust and zoom. A common need is to increase/decrease the number of cells in the focus without affecting their size. This requires doing an adjust plus enough of a zoom to add enough space to the focus to preserve the original cell sizes, an operation we call *adjust-zoom*.

If multiple focal areas are supported, then the various operations can be done on individual focal areas or on all of them as a set. If a single level of interest is desired then zoom must be applied across all the focal areas simultaneously, adjust behaves poorly and should be disallowed, and adjust-zoom can be performed on each of the focal areas independently. Multiple focal levels opens up a complex design space that needs further exploration.

GRAPHICAL MAPPING SCHEME

The Table Lens currently uses a graphical mapping scheme that is tailored for the most common type of table: the cases-by-variable array. In particular, this means that the underlying table represents a number of cases (the rows) for each of which values of various variables (the columns) are provided. For example, we use a table of baseball players performance/classification statistics for 1986 below.[1] In particular, this table contains 323 players by 23 variables, 17 quantitative (e.g. At bats, Hits, Home Runs, Salary '87) and 6 category (e.g. Team, Offensive Position, Team '87).

The Table Lens uses a number of different types of graphical representations, called presentation types, to display the contents of the table cells. In particular, presentation types utilize graphical vocabulary including text, color, shading, length, and position to represent underlying cell values. Six factors affect which presentation type and how in particular the type is used (examples given can be readily seen in the five color plates):

- *Value*. The cell value is depicted in some way by a presentation type. In a text representation, the cell's value is printed as a number or a string. In a bar representation, a quantity can be represented by the length of the bar.
- *Value Type*. The cell's value type determines which presentation type is used. In particular, a presentation type is chosen for each column of a cases-by-variables table. Quantitative variables are presented using a bar representation and category variables are presented using shaded, colored and/or positioned swatch representations.
- *Region Type*. Cells in focal, column focal, row focal, or non-focal region are treated differently. In particular, a focal cell uses a textual presentation as well as a graphical presentation so that the focal area is integrated into the graphical presentation of the context. A column that is focal uses a more

[1] The data, obtained from the CMU StatLib server, was collected by the American Statistical Association from Sports Illustrated and the 1987 Baseball Encyclopedia Update, Collier Books.

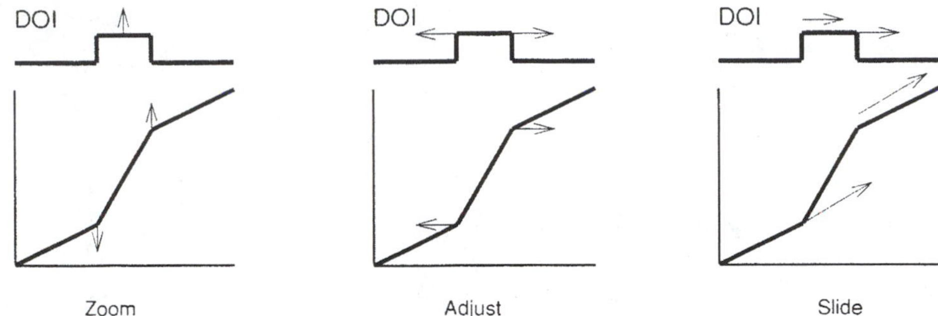

Figure 3: The three canonical focal manipulation operations are simple transformations on the DOI/transfer function. In each of the cases, the direction of the arrows can be reversed all at once.

colorful or detailed presentation type than nonfocal columns. The more focal the region is, the brighter the background shade (e.g. we currently use 3 gray levels).

- *Cell Size.* The cell size depends on the region type, but also depends on the amount of available space, and the size of the table. Presentation types may have a range of sizes in which they are usable and paint different amounts of ink depending on the space available.
- *User Choices.* A presentation type may provide a variety of options which can be directly set by users. For example, the bar presentation allows the user to choose how the bars are scaled to fit the available space including whether the left edge is zero or the minimum value. The category variable presentation allows the user to control the number of colors used and the mapping from category values.
- *Spotlighting.* Particular cells can be accented based on some criteria chosen by the user. For example, the user can spotlight quantity values that match some numerical predicate or special values like medians or quartiles or particular category values.

TABLE LENS USER INTERFACE

The screen interface for the current Table Lens system is shown in Color Plates 1 and 2. All plates are based on the baseball statistics data described above. Interaction is based on a small number of keyboard commands and pointer gestures. In particular, we use two mouse buttons: one for "touching" and another for "grasping." Pointer gestures are performed by pressing the touch button and drawing a stroke (e.g. "flicking" in various directions). Objects are dragged using the grasp button.

Focal Manipulation is supported using control points and pointer gestures. Grasping the control point at the upper-left corner cell is used to zoom all cells, and control points on each focus are used to adjust-zoom that focus. Touching any region in the context will slide the current focus to that location. Grasping any focus allows dragging (sliding) that focus to a new location. New foci are added by grasping a cell in the context which initiates a drag of a control point for adjust-zooming the new focus. Keyboard commands allow removing all focal spans on each dimension.

A number of operators are provided on columns. They can be moved between three levels of focus (hidden, non-focal, or focal) with "flick left" and "flick right" gestures (Color Plate 2 shows columns at each level of focus). Columns can be rearranged by grasping the column label and moving it to a new position in the table. Columns can be sorted in descending or ascending order with "flick down" or "flick up" gestures. All color plates show some column that has been sorted. Finally, new columns can be added and derived by a calculation over other columns, constants, and standard series. Color Plate 1 shows "Avg" and "Career Avg" columns that have been derived by dividing "Hits" by "At Bats."

Graphical mapping parameters and spotlights can be selected using column-specific or global dialog boxes. Controls include selection of applicable presentation types and presentation type parameters for the column (e.g. what value the left edge and right edges of the column represent in the bar presentation or how colors are assigned in the category swatch presentation). The user can also spotlight particular values in a column and focus on spotlighted rows. In Color Plate 2, the extremes, quartiles, and median in the "Hits" column and the right fielders in "Position" column are spotlighted. In addition, the focus has been set to the rows containing spotlighted values in the "Hits" columns with a keyboard command.

DATA ANALYSIS SCENARIOS

Color Plates 3, 4 and 5 illustrate various ways the Table Lens can be used to explore patterns in the data and investigate various explanatory models. Interestingly, every observation made below would be readily acknowledged by any baseball fan (of course, statistics-loving) as baseball-sensical.

In Color Plate 3, the quantitative variable "Career At Bats" is sorted. This reveals fairly clear correlation in the "Years in Major" and "Career Hits" Column. Inspecting the latter, the two values that stick out the most off the generally decaying "Career Hits" curve, are Wade Boggs and Don Mattingly. To confirm, what the eye sees, the "Career Average" column is derived by dividing "Career Hits" by "Career At Bats." This column confirms that the two have the highest two career averages, and furthermore reveals a reasonably flat pattern (the observed correlation) showing, as a statistician might quip, a regression to the average. (Also, note the increased noiseness with decreasing number of "Career At Bats.") This pattern remains prominent even when the column is non-focal and other sorts have been performed (as in other plates). Notice that both Boggs and Mattingly are, justifiably, paid relatively well for their topflight batting yields.

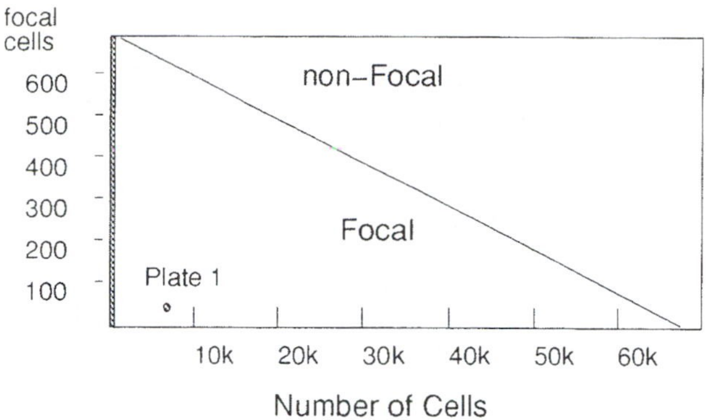

Figure 4: The gray strip indicates the region reachable using a spreadsheet. The Table Lens by trading full-sized cells for non-focal can show over 2 orders of magnitude more cells.

In Color Plate 4, a series of sorts on the category variables "Position," "Team," "Division," and "League" reveals the nesting of the last three variables, and the fact that every team carries a complete stable of player positions. The sporadic positions at the right of the column represent combination codes for players that divided their play significantly among more than one position. Also apparent by the patterns in the category variables "League '87" and "Team '87" (at the extreme right) is the relatively small amount of migration between years.

In Color Plate 5, quantitative performance based on category is explored. "Hits," and then "Position" are sorted. This shows the hits distributions within each position. The 2nd and 3rd batches from the bottom stand out somewhat; these are the right fielders and first basemen, reasonable positions in which to place strong hitters with less than stellar fielding skills. Confirming this, the right fielders are spotlighted (red bands) in Color Plate 2, and there is a clear bunching of the bands toward the top against the complete hits distribution. Also in Color Plate 5, on the offensive statistics, catchers and first basemen show the largest volume of "Put Outs" and the three infielders dominate in "Assists."

DISCUSSION

Interestingly, all of the observations made in the last section arose during demos to baseball fans who forgot about the demo and wanted to explore some particular relationship in the data. In addition, we have tested the Table Lens informally on a half dozen different datasets (Cars, Place Rated Almanac, Stock Market Data, Breakfast Cereal). In each of them, we were able to quickly find interesting correlations or patterns that made sense based on a basic understanding of the domain. For example, many relationships between car origin (American, European, or Japanese) and other properties, and changes to cars over time were observed. In several cases, we needed deeper domain knowledge to explain or confirm the validity of easily-observed patterns.

The baseball statistics table contains 323 rows by 23 columns for a total of 7429 cells. This is 11 times (an order of magnitude) more cells than our estimated maximum of 660 cells in a standard spreadsheet display. We calculate that the maximum size table the Table Lens can display on a 19 inch screen is about 68,400 cells more than two orders of magnitudes greater than a spreadsheet. Figure 4 depicts the advance in size of information sets achieved by our technique. The gray strip shows the displayable region of a typical spreadsheet program, where all cells are focal. The rest of the figure shows how a larger information set can be handled by progressively converting focal area into non-focal area.

Moreover, most of the patterns easily found using Table Lens would have been much harder or impossible to detect using a traditional spreadsheet. Most exploratory data analysis packages (e.g. S) require much greater overhead to learn and don't offer Table Lens's ease of interaction. Further work is necessary to systematically measure, compare, and explain the costs of extracting various information or performing various tasks using the Table Lens, spreadsheets, and exploratory data analysis packages.

CONCLUSION

Focusing on tables, we have gone beyond the usual design of a general focus+context mechanism to the complete design of end-user functionality. Perhaps the most interesting aspect of this work is the powerful way in which the Table Lens fuses graphical and symbolic representations into a coherent display. This fusion in combination with a small set of interactive operations (sorting and search) enables the user to navigate around and visualize a large data space easily isolating and investigating interesting features and patterns.

REFERENCES

1. George W. Furnas. Generalized fisheye views. In *Proceedings of the ACM SIGCHI Conference on Human Factors in Computing Systems*, pages 16–23. ACM, April 1986.

2. J. D. Mackinlay, G. G. Robertson, and S. K. Card. The perspective wall: Detail and context smoothly integrated. In *Proceedings of the ACM SIGCHI Conference on Human Factors in Computing Systems*, pages 173–179. ACM, April 1991.

3. G. G. Robertson, S. K. Card, and J. D. Mackinlay. Information visualization using 3d interactive animation. *Communications of the ACM*, 36(4), 1993.

4. George G. Robertson and J. D. Mackinlay. The document lens. In *Proceedings of the ACM Symposium on User Interface Software and Technology*. ACM Press, Nov 1993.

5. Manojit Sarkar and Marc H. Brown. Graphical fisheye views of graphs. In *Proceedings of the ACM SIGCHI Conference on Human Factors in Computing Systems*, pages 83–91. ACM, April 1992.

6. Manojit Sarkar, Scott Snibbe, and Steven Reiss. Stretching the rubber sheet: A metaphor for visualizing large structure on small screen. In *Proceedings of the ACM Symposium on User Interface Software and Technology*. ACM Press, Nov 1993.

7. Robert Spence and Mark Apperley. Database navigation: An office environment for the professional. *Behavior and Information Technology*, 1(1):43–54, 1982.

Table Lens: Baseball Player Statistics

Calculate: "Hits" / "At Bats" = "Avg"

	Avg	Career Avg	Team	Salary 87
Larry Herndon	0.24734983	0.27282876	Det.	225
Jesse Barfield	0.2886248	0.27268818	Tor.	1237.5
Jeffrey Leonar	0.27859238	0.27260458	S.F.	900
Donnie Hill	0.28318584	0.2725564	Oak.	275
Billy Sample	0.285	0.2718601	Atl.	NA
Howard Johnson	0.24545455	0.25232068	N.Y.	297.5
Andres Thomas	0.250774	0.2521994	Atl.	75
Billy Hatcher	0.25775656	0.25211507	Hou.	110
Omar Moreno	0.2339833	0.2518029	Atl.	NA
Darnell Coles	0.2725528	0.25153375	Det.	105

Row 304: Mike Lavalliere; Column 20: Put Outs Value: 468 810 -- 2163

Rao, Card, Color Plate 1

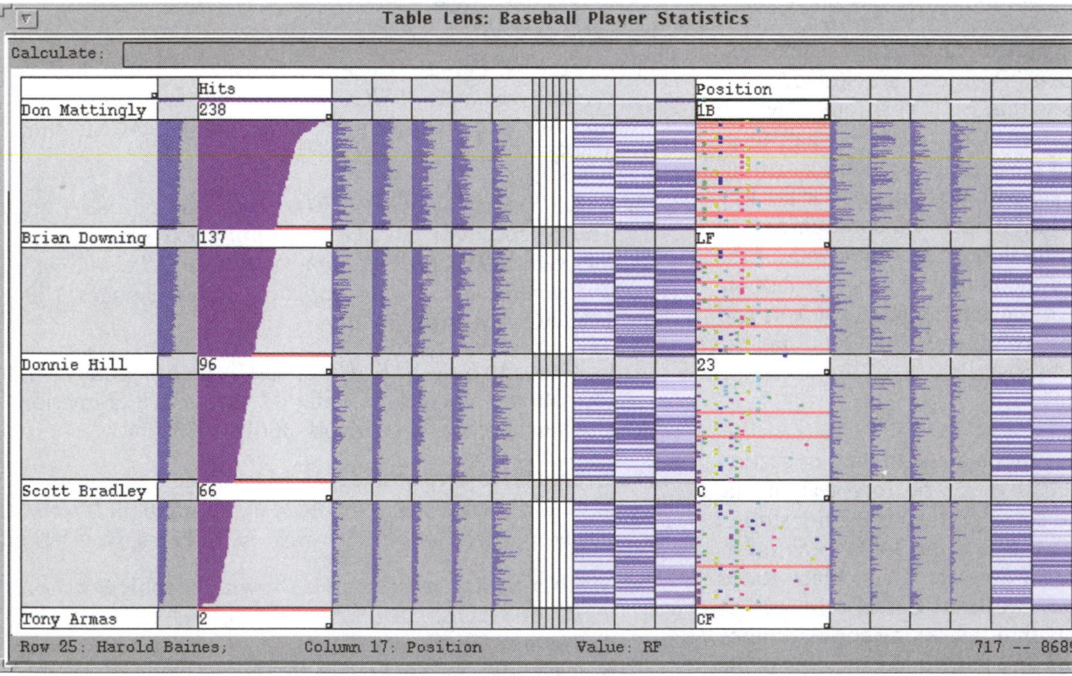

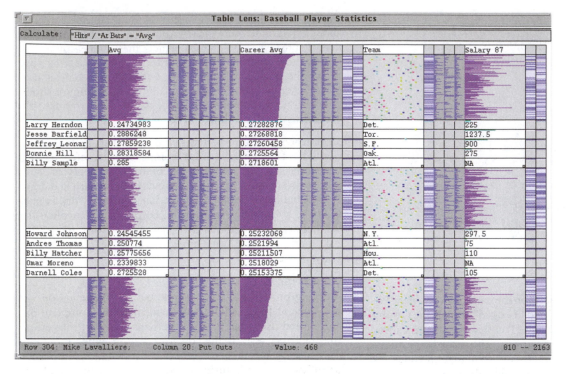

Rao, Card, Color Plate 2

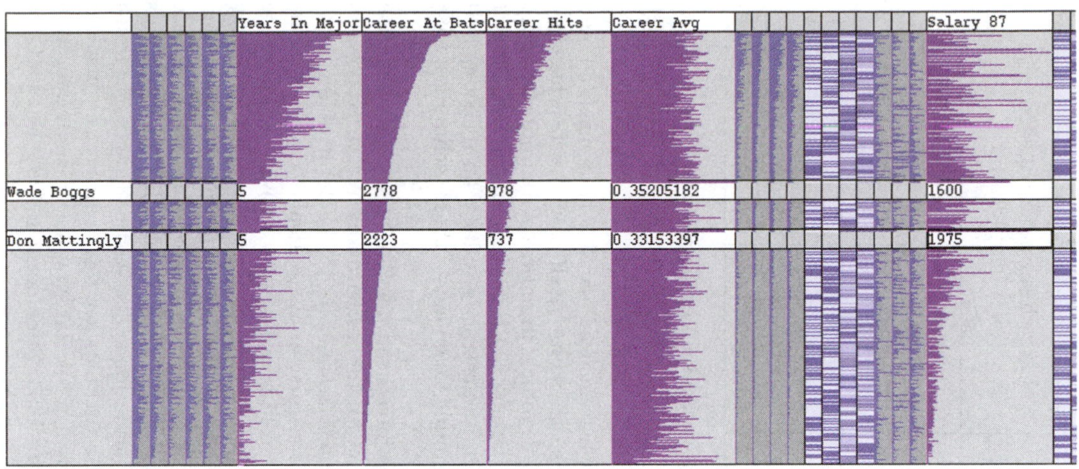

Rao, Card, Color Plate 3

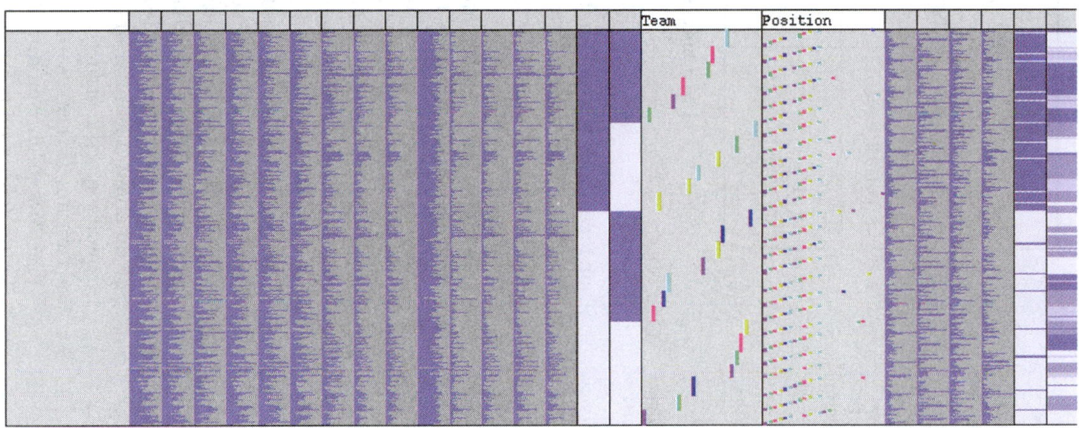

Rao, Card, Color Plate 4

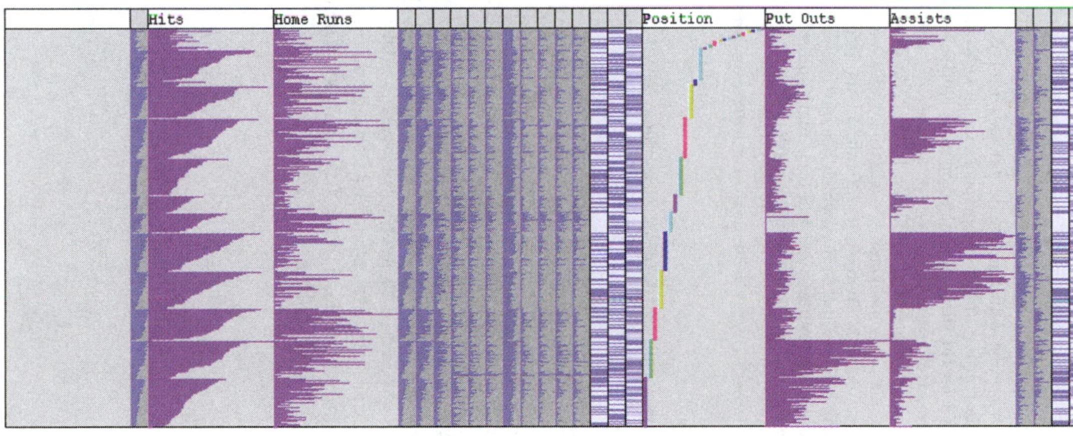

Rao, Card, Color Plate 5

A Review and Taxonomy of Distortion-Oriented Presentation Techniques

Y. K. LEUNG
Swinburne University of Technology
and
M. D. APPERLEY
Massey University

One of the common problems associated with large computer-based information systems is the relatively small window through which an information space can be viewed. Increasing interest in recent years has been focused on the development of distortion-oriented presentation techniques to address this problem. However, the growing number of new terminologies and techniques developed have caused considerable confusion to the graphical user interface designer, consequently making the comparison of these presentation techniques and generalization of empirical results of experiments with them very difficult, if not impossible. This article provides a taxonomy of distortion-oriented techniques which demonstrates clearly their underlying relationships. A unified theory is presented to reveal their roots and origins. Issues relating to the implementation and performance of these techniques are also discussed.

Categories and Subject Descriptors: H.5.2 [**Information Interfaces and Presentations**]: User Interfaces

General Terms: Human Factors

Additional Key Words and Phrases: Bifocal displays, distortion-oriented presentation, fisheye views, focus + context techniques, graphical interfaces, information visualization, Perspective Wall, presentation techniques

1. INTRODUCTION

One of the common problems associated with large computer-based information systems is the relatively small window through which an information space can be viewed. This gives rise to problems (i) in locating a given item of information (navigation), (ii) in interpreting an item, and (iii) in relating it to other items, if the item cannot be seen in its full context. Various techniques have evolved for accessing large volumes of data through a limited display surface, and these can be broadly categorized as distortion-oriented and nondistortion-oriented presentations. The data itself can also be classified according to whether it is inherently graphical in nature, with implicit spatial relationships, or whether it is nongraphical—although in many cases data of this latter type can be represented in an abstract graphical form [Leung and Apperley 1993b]. Figure 1 shows a simple taxonomy of these techniques, with examples of each of the four types.

Large Volumes of Data			
Inherently Graphical Data		Non-Graphical Data	
direct ↓	← graphical abstraction		direct ↓
Large Information Space (Graphical)		Large Information Space (Non-Graphical)	
Distorted View (Detail in context)	Non-Distorted View (Detail with little or no context)	Distorted View (Detail in context)	Non-Distorted View (Detail with little or no context)
encoding spatial transformation (geometric)	zooming windowing	data suppression (abstraction and thresholding)	paging clipping

Fig. 1. A taxonomy of presentation techniques for large graphical data spaces.

Nondistortion-oriented techniques have been used quite some time for the presentation of textual data [Monk et al. 1988; Beard and Walker 1990] and in a number of graphical applications [Donelson 1978; Herot et al. 1980; Leung 1989]. The most familiar approach is simply to display a portion of the information at a time, and to allow scrolling or paging to provide access to the remainder. An alternative, and one which does enhance the ability to find a specific item of information, is to divide the total information space into portions which can be displayed, and to provide hierarchical access to these "pages"; as one moves down the hierarchy then more detailed information is given about a smaller area of the information space. Another approach, which exploits specific structure in the data (in this case a tree structure), involves arranging or representing the data in a special way for presentation, as a Tree-Map [Johnson and Shneiderman 1991; Shneiderman 1992] or as a Cone Tree [Robertson et al. 1991].

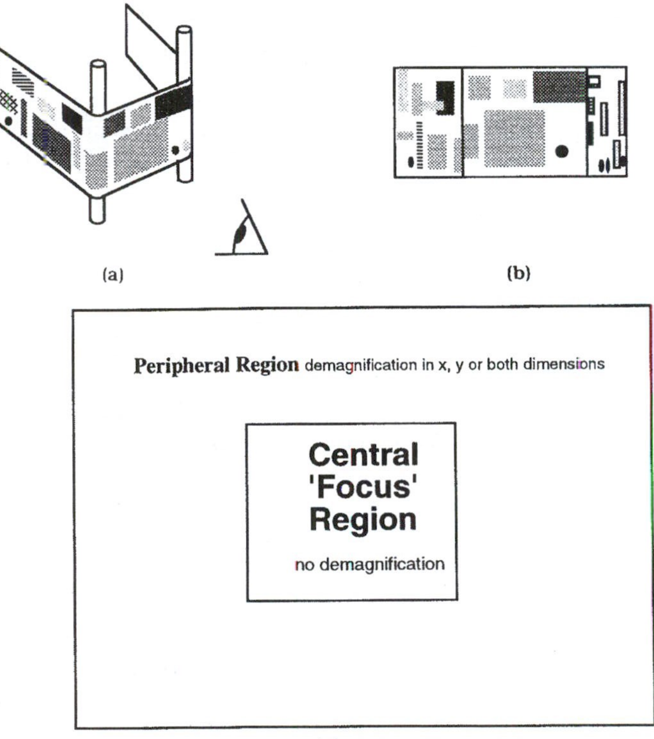

Fig. 2. (a) A mechanical model of a distortion-oriented presentation technique. This model characterizes both the Perspective Wall and the Bifocal Display; (b) the appearance of the data space transformed by a distortion-oriented presentation technique, in this case the Bifocal Display, obtained by viewing the model in (a) from infinity; (c) the presentation of a 2D distortion technique.

While nondistortion-oriented techniques may be adequate for small text-based applications, their main weakness is that generally they do not provide adequate context for the user to support navigation of large-scale information spaces. To overcome this shortcoming, distortion-oriented techniques have been developed and used, particularly in graphical applications. The main feature of these techniques is to allow the user to examine a local area in detail on a section of the screen, and at the same time, to present a global view of the space to provide an overall context to facilitate navigation (see Figure 2).

The growing interest in the application of distortion techniques in recent years [Leung 1989; Hollands et al. 1989; Mackinlay et al. 1991; Misue and Sugiyama 1991; Sarkar and Brown 1992; Robertson and Mackinlay 1993; Rao and Card 1994] can be attributed to the availability of low-cost and high-performance graphics workstations. Farrand [1973] provided an early discussion of computer-based application of distortion-oriented display techniques. He considered the graphical fisheye and designed his DECR (Detail Enhancing, Continuity Retaining) lens to address what he termed the DETAIL × SCOPE problem in information display. In the context of the noninteractive presentation of cartographic maps, Kadmon and Shlomi [1978] described the Polyfocal Display. Kadmon and Shlomi laid down the mathematical foundation for a variety of distortion techniques, and they also proposed the concept of a multifocal projection.

The Bifocal Display [Spence and Apperley 1982] was an early computer-based distortion-oriented display technique. The original illustration of the Bifocal Display was a one-dimensional representation of a data space whose area exceeded that of the screen; the example used was an "in-tray" coupled with an application for an office environment. The Bifocal Display was extended later to a two-dimensional form for the presentation of topological networks [Leung 1989]. A variant of the Bifocal Display in one-dimensional form was proposed later by Mackinlay et al. [1991] as the Perspective Wall.

Furnas' concept of a Fisheye View [Furnas 1986] was based on textual trees, and an implementation of this technique was illustrated in the presentation of program code in one-dimensional form and a calendar in two-dimensional form. No mathematics for the graphical application of this concept were provided. A number of Fisheye View-like applications have been developed [Hollands et al. 1989; Mitta 1990; Misue and Sugiyama 1991; Sarkar and Brown 1992; Schaffer et al. 1993] which differ not only in their application domains, but also in their form. While Sarkar and Brown [1992] attempted to formalize the mathematical foundation for the Fisheye View, their illustration of the technique applied to topological networks was based on a variation of the ideal Fisheye View.

The fast growing number of distortion-oriented techniques proposed by user interface designers calls for a taxonomy and a unified theory to relate and delineate these techniques for two main reasons. First, a taxonomy will help to clarify the confusion of terminologies and unravel the mystique of ever-increasing new presentation techniques confronting graphical user interface designers. Second, a well-defined classification will help to make the comparison and generalization of empirical results of experiments using these techniques a much easier task.

The main aims of this article are fourfold: (i) it reviews distortion-oriented presentation techniques reported in current literature and explains their fundamental concepts, (ii) it presents a taxonomy of these techniques clearly showing their underlying relationships, (iii) a unified theory of distortion-oriented techniques is presented to show their roots and origins, and (iv) issues relating to the implementation and performance of these techniques are discussed.

2. A REVIEW OF DISTORTION-ORIENTED PRESENTATION TECHNIQUES

The application of distortion-oriented techniques to computer-based graphical data presentation has a relatively short history, although the concept of distortion or deformation has been used over many centuries by cartographers in various map projections. Modern distorted displays can be found in familiar representations as the London Underground map and many subsequent subway systems and topological networks.

The essence of these techniques is the concurrent presentation of local detail together with global context at reduced magnification, in a format which allows dynamic interactive positioning of the local detail without severely compromising spatial relationships. Figures 2(a) and 2(b), show a mechanical analogy of a simple distortion technique (the Bifocal Display) applied in one dimension on a strip of graphical information. An illustration of a general two-dimensional distortion-oriented technique is shown in Figure 2(c). With these types of techniques there is usually a focus region where detailed information is displayed; in its surrounding regions, a demagnified view of the peripheral areas is presented.

A distorted view is created by applying a mathematical function, which is called a transformation function, to an undistorted image. The transformation function for a presentation technique defines how the original image is mapped to a distorted view. A magnification function, which is the derivative of a transformation function, on the other hand provides a profile of the magnification (or demagnification) factors associated with the entire area of the undistorted image under consideration. Figures 3(a) and 3(b) show the relationship of these two functions and illustrate how an elliptical object is transformed to its distorted form by applying the transformation function of a Bifocal Display in one dimension.

In a real-time system, the user may initiate a shift of the focus region to view an adjacent area in detail using an interaction device. Then the system will apply the transformation function to every entity contained in the repositioned image and update the display with a corresponding shift in the focus region and its contents; the peripheral regions are also updated at the same time. The system response time depends on three factors; the complexity of the mathematical transformations involved, the amount of information and detail to be presented, and the computational power and suitability of the system used for implementation.

The following subsections present a historical review of distortion-oriented techniques and their underlying concepts in chronological order. The general form of their respective transformation and magnification functions is illustrated and applied, both in one and two dimensions, to grids of squares (Figures 4(a) and 4(b)) to provide a better appreciation of the differences and similarities between these techniques. In order to simplify the comparison of these techniques, the grids are "normalized" to the same-sized display area before each distortion technique is applied. Further, system parameters are chosen so that similar magnification factors are applied in the central focus region.

2.1 Polyfocal Display [Kadmon and Shlomi]

Kadmon and Shlomi [1978] proposed a polyfocal projection for the presentation of statistical data on cartographic maps. Although their concept was applied in a noninteractive situation, they made a valuable contribution in laying down a solid mathematical foundation for many later distortion-oriented presentation techniques, although many of the later developments have been carried out without the knowledge of this work. Kadmon and Shlomi also proposed an implementation of a multifocal display. The graphical application of the Fisheye View [Sarkar and Brown 1992] could well be considered as a special case of the polyfocal projection.

The fundamental concept behind the polyfocal projection in its one-dimensional form can be illustrated by the transformation and magnification functions of Figures 5(a) and 5(b), where the highest peak (Figure 5(b)) is the focus of the display. (For a rigorous mathematical treatment of the polyfocal

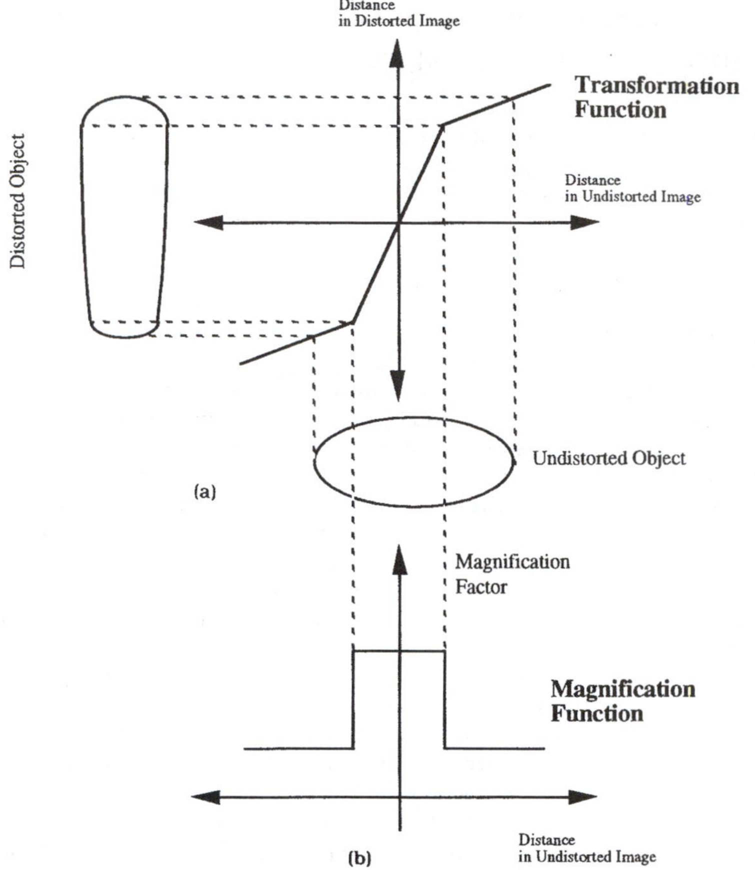

Fig. 3. (a) The transformation of an elliptic object by applying the transformation function of a Bifocal Display in one dimension; (b) the corresponding magnification function of the Bifocal Display.

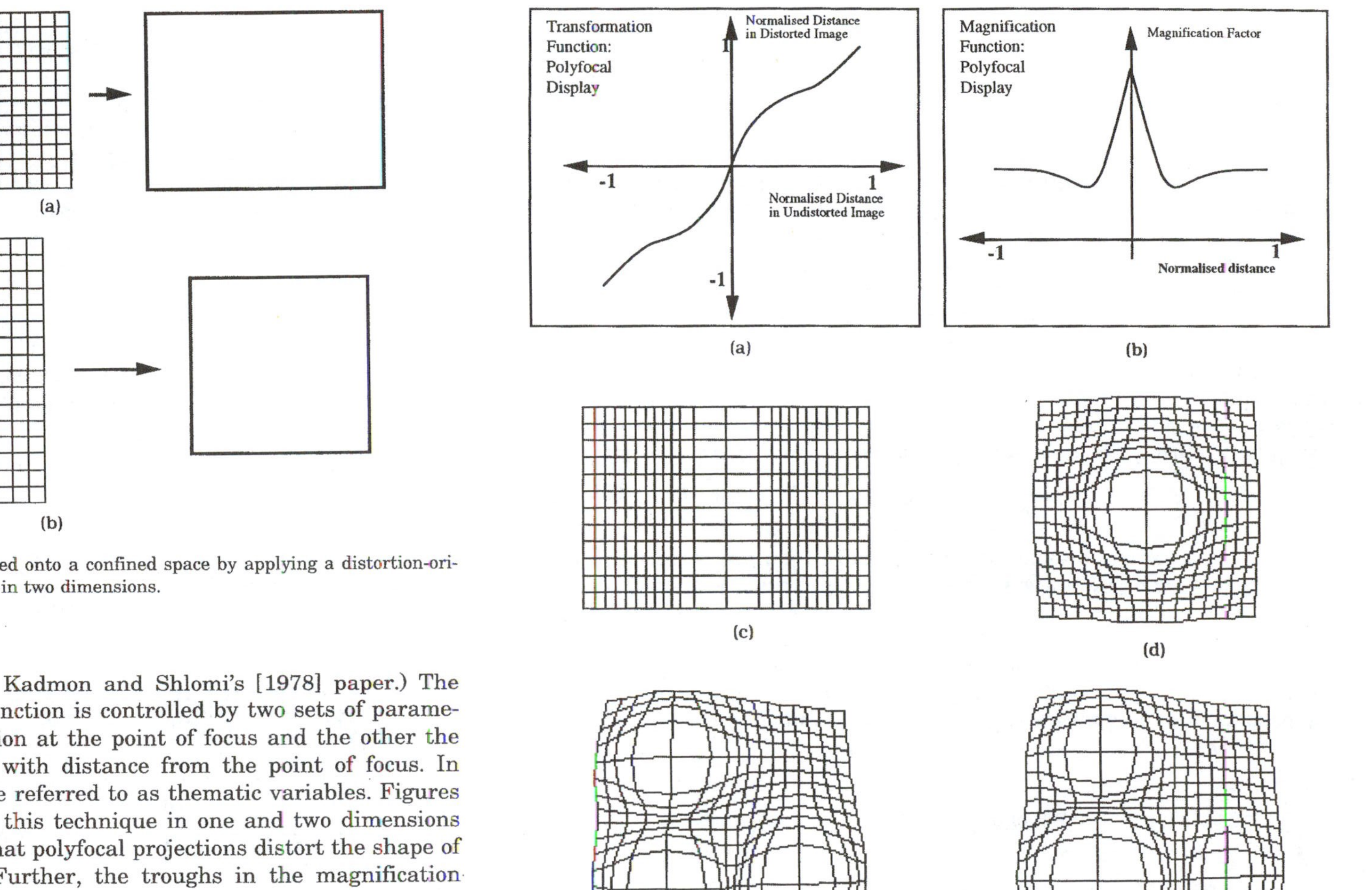

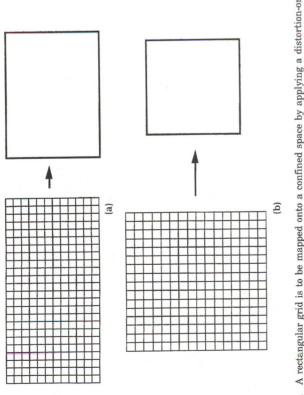

Fig. 4. A rectangular grid is to be mapped onto a confined space by applying a distortion-oriented technique; (a) in one dimension; (b) in two dimensions.

Fig. 5. The polyfocal projection: (a) a typical transformation function of a polyfocal projection; (b) the corresponding magnification function; (c) the application of the projection in one dimension; (d) the application of the projection in two dimensions; (e) a multiple-foci view of the projection using the same parameters for each focus point; (f) a multiple-foci view using different parameters.

display, readers should refer to Kadmon and Shlomi's [1978] paper.) The curvature of the magnification function is controlled by two sets of parameters; one controls the magnification at the point of focus and the other the rate of change of magnification with distance from the point of focus. In cartographic terminology they are referred to as thematic variables. Figures 5(c) and 5(d) show the effects of this technique in one and two dimensions respectively. It should be noted that polyfocal projections distort the shape of the boundaries of the display. Further, the troughs in the magnification function, which are inherent in polyfocal projections, serve to compensate for the high magnification factors in the area surrounding the point of focus.

In the case of a multifocal polyfocal projection, there will be multiple peaks in the magnification function, each contributing a certain amount of "pull" to the entire image. In theory there is no restriction on the number of these "peaks" in the magnification function; the only limitation is the computation time involved and the comprehensibility of the resulting distorted image. Figures 5(c) and 5(f) show two displays with multiple foci; the former with the same parameters applied to each focus and the latter with different sets of values for each focus. It should be noted that it is possible to have zero magnification where a section of the display is effectively shrunk to nothing, thus creating a "vanishing area." Negative magnification factors may also be possible, creating overlapping views.

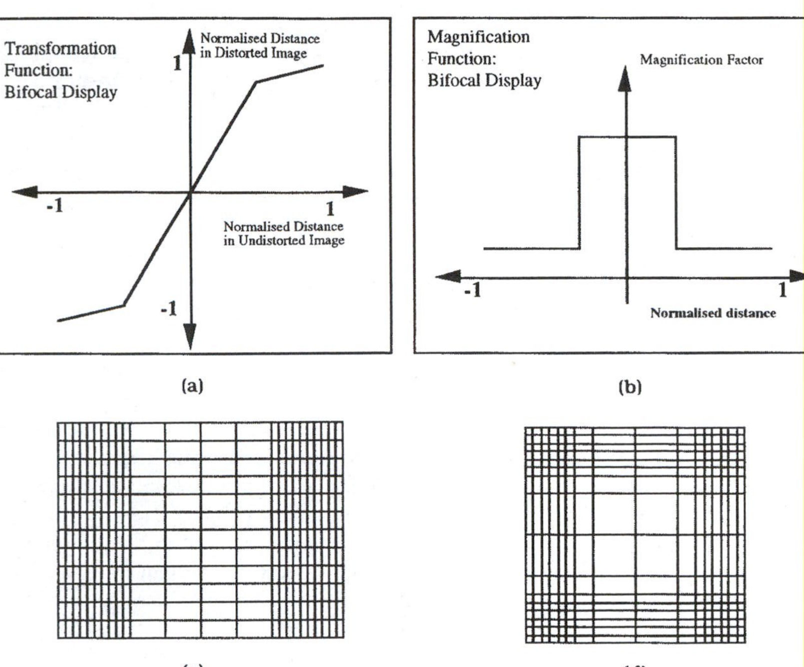

Fig. 6. The Bifocal Display: (a) a typical transformation function; (b) the corresponding magnification function; (c) the application of the display in one dimension; (d) the application of the display in two dimensions.

Demagnification in both X and Y dimensions	Demagnification in Y dimension	Demagnification in both X and Y dimensions
Demagnification in X dimension	**Central 'Focus' Region** no demagnification	Demagnification in X dimension
Demagnification in both X and Y dimensions	Demagnification in Y dimension	Demagnification in both X and Y dimensions

Fig. 7. Implementation of a 2D Bifocal Display.

2.2 Bifocal Display [Spence and Apperley]

The Bifocal Display [Spence and Apperley 1982] in a one-dimensional form involves a combination of a detailed view and two distorted sideviews, where items on either side of the detailed view are compressed uniformly in the horizontal direction. Spence and Apperley used the mechanical analogy already referred to in Figures 2(a) and 2(b) to describe the display. The transformation and magnification functions for this technique are shown in Figures 6(a) and 6(b). Figure 6(c) shows a one-dimensional Bifocal Display applied to a square grid. Although the Bifocal Display is relatively simple in terms of implementation and does provide spatial continuity between regions, it has the disadvantage of discontinuity of magnification at the boundary between the detailed view and the distorted view. An analysis of the implementation requirements of the Bifocal Display based on special-purpose memory management hardware has also been described [Apperley et al. 1982].

Leung [1989] extended the bifocal concept to a two-dimensional form in an implementation of the London Underground map. Figure 6(d) shows the effects of this technique in two dimensions. The visual area is subdivided into nine regions with a central focus region (see Figure 7), and other eight regions which are demagnified according to the physical position with respect to the central focus region; the same demagnification factor is used in both x and y directions in these regions. It should be noted that because the four corner regions are demagnified in both x and y directions using the same scale, these areas are not distorted. They are merely reduced in size.

2.3 Fisheye View [Furnas]

The Fisheye View concept was originally proposed by Furnas [1986] as a presentation strategy for information having a hierarchical structure. The essence of this technique is called *thresholding*. Each information element in a hierarchical structure is assigned a number based on its relevance (*a priori importance* or API) and a second number based on the distance between the information element under consideration and the point of focus in the structure. A threshold value is then selected and compared with a function of these two numbers to determine what information is to be presented or suppressed. Consequently, the more relevant information will be presented in great detail, and the less relevant information presented as an abstraction, based on a threshold value. Furnas' Fisheye View was illustrated by two text-based applications, one involving a large section of program code and the other a calendar. Koike [1994] considers the potential problem of this technique for presenting trees with different number of branches and offers an interesting refinement using fractal algorithms.

Mathematically the *degree of interest* (*DOI*) function, which determines for each point in the hierarchical information structure how interested the user

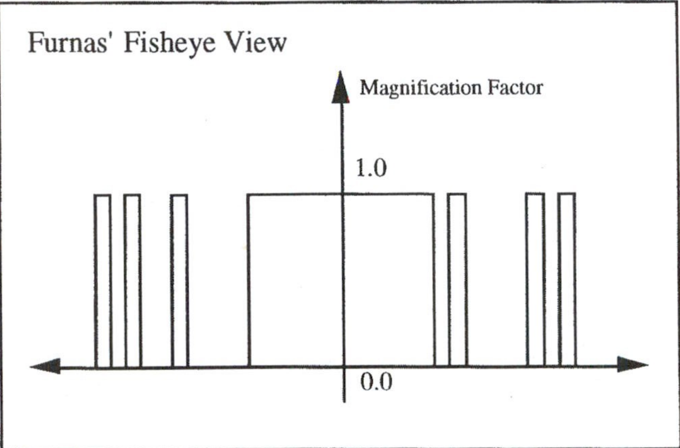

Fig. 8. A typical magnification function for Furnas' "Fisheye View."

is in seeing that point with respect to the current point of focus, is given by,

$$\mathbf{DOI}_{fisheye}(\mathbf{a}|. = \mathbf{b}) = \mathbf{API(a)} - \mathbf{D(a, b)},$$

where

(1) $\mathbf{DOI}_{fisheye}(\mathbf{a}|. = \mathbf{b})$ is the degree of interest in **a**, given that the current point of focus is **b**.

(2) **API(a)** is a static global value called *a priori importance* at point **a**; API values are preassigned to each point in the structure under consideration, and

(3) **D(a, b)** is the distance between point **a** and the point of focus **b**.

It is apparent that the **DOI** function of the Fisheye View is an information suppression function. The illustrations which Furnas used were text-based examples, and rather than involving demagnification per se, they involved the selective suppression and highlighting of components of the text depending on the prior degree of interest (DOI) values with respect to the object at the focus and a threshold value. The analogy with a traditional fisheye lens is cryptic. Furnas' technique can be described best by a magnification function, as shown in Figure 8.

A number of other implementations, all claiming to use this technique, have been reported and have created some confusion as to what a "fisheye view" really means. These implementations are not only different in their application domains, but also in their form, and they will be examined in detail in later sections.

2.4 Fisheye View [Hollands et al.]

Hollands et al. [1989] represented a fictitious subway network using both a Fisheye View and a simple scrolling view, and compared the users' performance with these two interfaces. Users performed three different tasks: a route task, a locate/route task, and an itinerary task. Although no details were provided of the implementation of the Fisheye View, the figures in their paper suggest that it is a graphical implementation of a much more general fisheye concept, which has more in common with the Bifocal Display than with Furnas' DOI functions. Furthermore, the station symbols displayed in the focus region of the Fisheye View were smaller than those in the scrolling view, apparently contradicting the fundamental concept of *degree of interest* [Furnas 1986]. The transformation and magnification functions used would appear to be similar to those of the Bifocal Display (Figures 6(a) and 6(b)).

2.5 Fisheye View [Mitta]

Mitta [1990] proposed a "fisheye" strategy for the presentation of aircraft maintenance data. The example used showed a solenoid assembly consisting of a number of components presented in different views. In each of these Fisheye Views certain components were suppressed so that users could focus their attention on the parts which were presented on the display screen. In the conclusion of the paper, Mitta wrote "Thus, future research efforts are to examine how information should be selected, in addition to what information should be presented" confirming that the technique used was an information suppression technique rather than the more conventional notion of a Fisheye View used by Hollands et al. [1989].

Mitta made reference to Furnas' work on Fisheye Views and extended a multiple-focus-point version of the same technique.

2.6 Perspective Wall [Mackinlay et al.]

The Perspective Wall [Mackinlay et al. 1991], a conceptual descendent of the Bifocal Display, is based on the notion of smoothly integrating detailed and contextual views to assist in the visualization of linear information.

The principle behind the Perspective Wall is illustrated in Figures 9(a) and 9(b). The two side panels, which show a distorted view of the out-of-focus regions, are demagnified directly proportional to their distance from the viewer; the corresponding transformation and magnification functions for this technique are shown in Figures 10(a) and 10(b). Although this technique is inherently two dimensional, for illustrative purposes its application to the two square grids in both one and two dimensions is shown in Figures 10(c) and 10(d). The main distinction between this technique and the Bifocal Display is that in the out-of-focus regions, the Perspective Wall demagnifies at an increasing rate in comparison with the Bifocal's constant demagnification (compare the magnification functions in Figures 6(b) and 10(b)). This rate of increase in the magnification function of the two side panels depends on the angle Θ; the greater this angle, the flatter the slope. There is a discontinuity in the magnification function at the points where the two side panels meet the middle panel; the bigger the angle Θ, the greater the discontinuity.

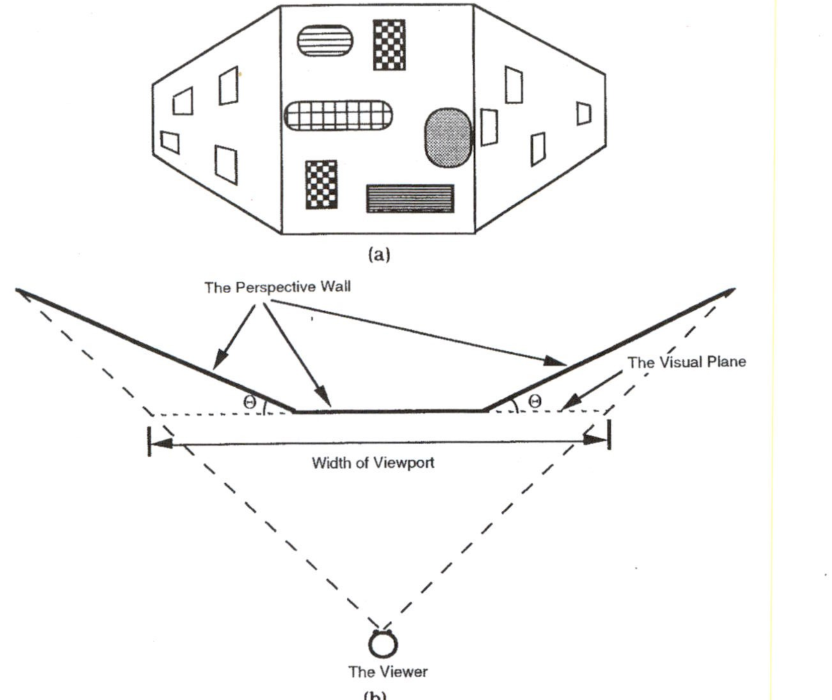

Fig. 9. With two side panels positioned at an angle the Perspective Wall provides a distorted view to the viewer; (b) a plan view of the Perspective Wall showing the relationships between the wall, the viewport, and the viewer.

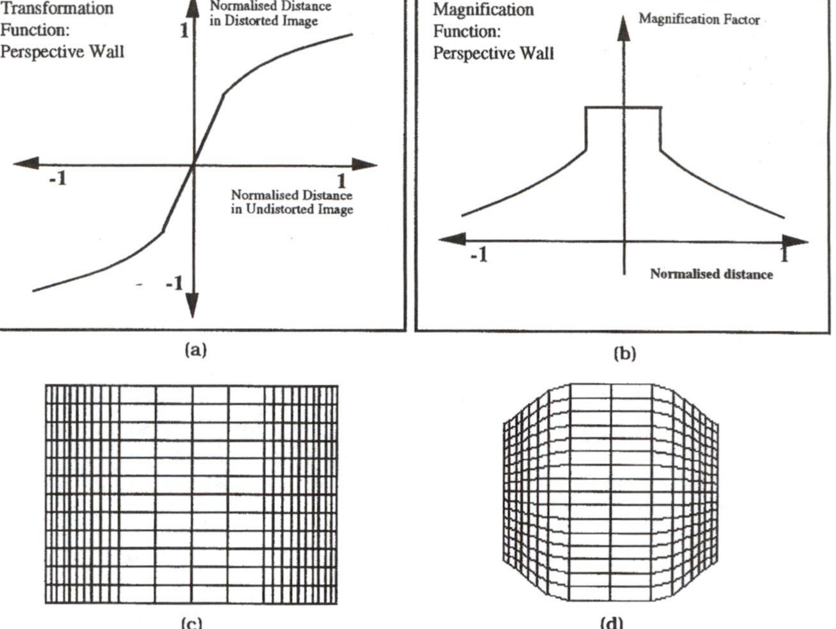

Fig. 10. The Perspective Wall: (a) a typical transformation function; (b) the corresponding magnification function; (c) the application of the wall in one dimension; (d) the application of the wall in two dimensions. Here the number of dimensions relates to the dimensions in which the perspective transformation is applied on the projection, not to the dimensionality of the model on which the projection is based.

The view generated by the Perspective Wall is dependent on a number of parameters: the length of the wall, the width of the viewport, the angle Θ, the size of the central region, etc. To get a better understanding of the Perspective Wall, consider the effect of increasing the angle Θ (Figure 9) while all other system parameters remain constant. As the angle Θ increases with the two side panels tilting backward (see Figure 9(b)), as a consequence, the viewer will have to be positioned further away from the wall because the width of the viewport is fixed. It should be noted that the position of the viewer determines the projection of the two side panels on the visual plane (see mathematical derivation of the transformation function in the Appendix). As the angle Θ is increased further, there is a position where the viewer is essentially positioned at infinity. At this point the demagnification in the peripheral regions will be constant, and it can be seen that the Bifocal Display is actually a special case of the Perspective Wall. This point can be seen also with the mechanical analogy of Figures 2(a) and 2(b); a close-up view would produce a Perspective Wall, and a view from infinity, a Bifocal Display.

The Perspective Wall does add a full 3D feel to the otherwise flat form of the Bifocal Display. However, this effect is produced at the cost of wasting expensive "real estate" in the corner areas of the screen, contrary to one of the prime objectives of distortion techniques to maximize the utilization of the available display area. This particular shortcoming of the Perspective Wall has been overcome more recently with the development of the Document Lens technique [Robertson and Mackinlay 1993].

2.7 Graphical Fisheye Views [Sarkar and Brown]

Sarkar and Brown [1992] extended Furnas' fisheye concept and laid down the mathematical formalism for graphical applications of this technique. They proposed two implementations, both of topological networks, one based on a Cartesian coordinate transformation system and the other on a polar system. Owing to the nature of polar transformation, in theory a straight line and

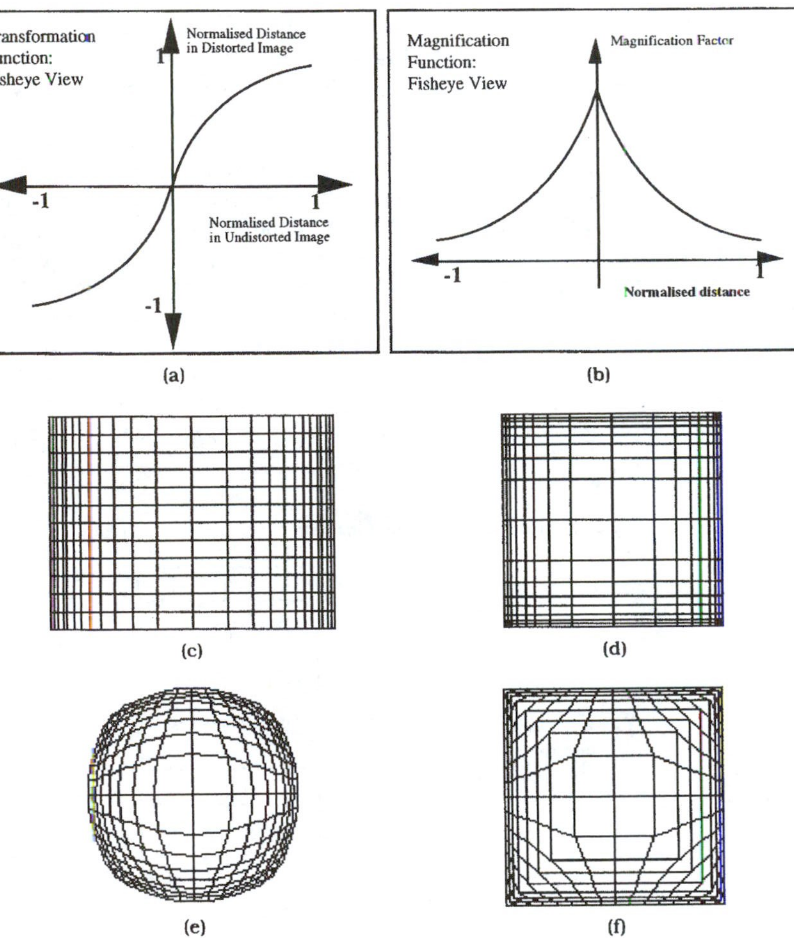

Fig. 11. The Fisheye View: (a) a typical transformation function; (b) the corresponding magnification function; (c) the application of the Fisheye View in one dimension; (d) a Cartesian Fisheye View in two dimensions; (e) a polar Fisheye View; (f) a normalized polar Fisheye View.

rectangle will normally be transformed into a curved line and a curvilinear rectangle respectively. To overcome this problem, the transformation was applied only to the nodes of the structure, and the nodes were then connected by straight lines. The transformation and magnification functions for the Fisheye View are respectively, (see Figures 11(a) and 11(b))

$$T(x) = \frac{(d+1)x}{(dx+1)} \quad \text{and} \quad M(x) = \frac{(d+1)}{(dx+1)^2},$$

where

—d is called the distortion factor; the larger this number is, the bigger the magnification and the amplitude of the peak in the magnification function; and,

—x is the normalized distance from a point under consideration to the point of focus. x can have a value $0 <= x <= 1$. If $x = 0$, the point under consideration is at the point of focus, and if $x = 1$, it is at a position furthest away from the point of focus on the boundary.

Figure 11(c) shows the application of this Fisheye View in one dimension. Figure 11(d) shows the two-dimensional Fisheye View with a Cartesian coordinate system, and Figure 11(e) with the transformation based on a polar coordinate system. It is interesting to note that the polar Fisheye View produces a rounded appearance which unfortunately does not provide a natural look when implemented on a rectangular screen. Sarkar and Brown proposed further that the rounded appearance of the Polar Fisheye View be remapped on a rectangular space; the result of this modified transformation is illustrated in Figure 11(f). Surprisingly, the appearance of Figure 11(f) bears some resemblance to that of a Perspective Wall (Figure 10(d)). As this perspective transformation is applied fully in two dimensions (the perspective transformation is not applied in the vertical direction in the middle panel for the Perspective Wall proposed by Mackinlay et al.), a more appropriate name for this technique would be Perspective Space [Leung and Apperley 1993a].

While these fisheye transformations provided the spatial distortion in two dimensions, Sarkar and Brown [1992] introduced a further information magnification in the third dimension based on the concept of *a priori importance* (API) proposed by Furnas. Their implementation of API was extended to three separate functions called $\text{Size}_{fisheye}$(S), Visual Worth (VW), and $\text{Details}_{fisheye}$(DTL). The purpose of these functions is twofold: first, they provide a flexible information suppression/enhancement mechanism to generate an effective Fisheye View, and second, the resulting display provides the viewer with a three-dimensional feel. This technique is potentially very powerful in displaying information which is multilayered and globally organized in a hierarchical tree or network structure.

Misue and Sugiyama [1991] described two transformation functions (polar and Cartesian versions) for graphical Fisheye Views which have some similar properties to those of Sarkar and Brown.

3. A TAXONOMY OF DISTORTION-ORIENTED PRESENTATION TECHNIQUES

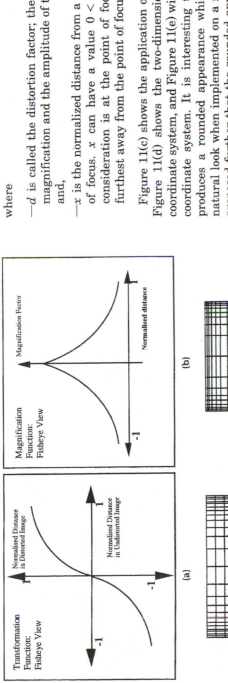

An examination of the transformation and magnification functions of the distortion-oriented presentation techniques described in the previous section (see Figure 12) reveals their underlying differences and similarities. These techniques can be classified conveniently in terms of their magnification functions: basically, there are two distinct classes. One class of these techniques has piecewise continuous magnification functions; the Bifocal Display

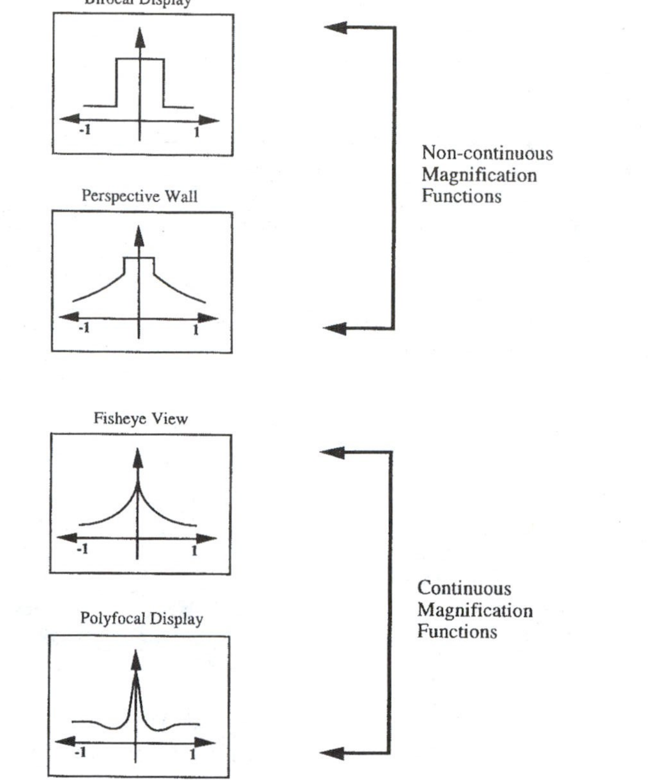

Fig. 12. A taxonomy of distortion-oriented presentation techniques.

and the Perspective Wall are typical examples. The other class has continuous magnification functions; the Fisheye View and the Polyfocal Projection belong to this second class.

Techniques with piecewise continuous functions can be classified further into those with constant or varying magnification functions; the Bifocal Display belongs to the former subclass and the Perspective Wall the latter. As explained in Section 2.6, the Bifocal Display is a special case of the Perspective Wall. A display which has multiple discrete levels of magnification in the magnification function could be generated; the limitation of extending the Bifocal Display concept to a higher level is imposed only by the system's resources. Further, the magnification factors used in these levels may be chosen in such a way that the function approximates to a continuous one. Figure 13 shows the general layout of a display with three magnification levels, and Figure 14 shows the magnification function for a display with four magnification levels which approximates that of a Fisheye View. Applications, and the complexity involved in the implementation, of these techniques are discussed in later sections.

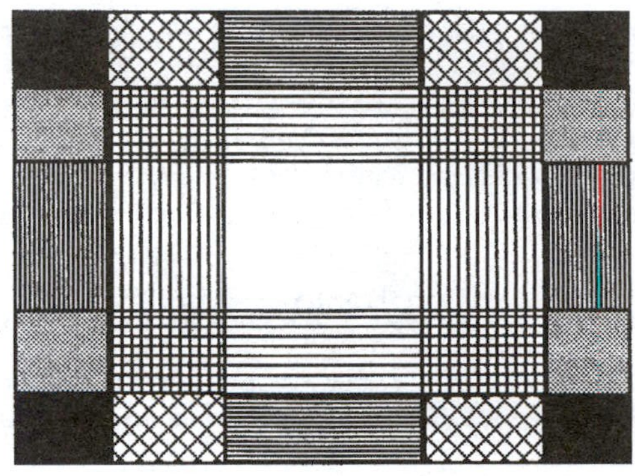

Fig. 13. The 25 regions that would be generated by extending a 2D Bifocal Display to incorporate three distinct magnification levels, rather than two.

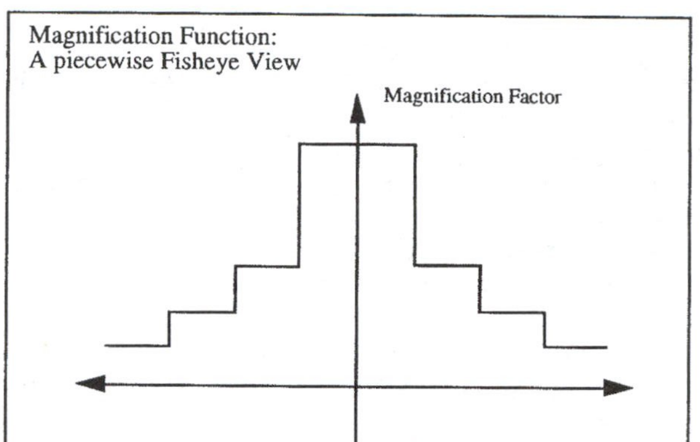

Fig. 14. The magnification function of a piecewise Fisheye View.

Techniques with continuous magnification functions have one undesirable attribute; they tend to distort the boundaries of the transformed image. The bigger the magnification factor at the focus is, the bigger this distortion at the boundaries will be. This is because these techniques are generally applied radially rather than independently in the x and y directions. Consequently, the corner areas are pulled in toward the point of focus. This problem can be overcome in two ways, as implemented by Sarkar and Brown [1992] in their Cartesian and Polar Fisheye Views. First, the transformation may be applied independently in the x and y directions as in the Cartesian Fisheye View (Figure 11(d)). Second, the distorted boundaries can be remapped onto a rectangular size of the display area as illustrated in Sarkar and Brown's

Polar Fisheye View (Figure 11(e)). It should be noted that because of the irregular shape of the boundaries in the Polyfocal Projection which is inherent in its transformation, more extensive calculation would be required in this case to perform the remapping operation.

A closer examination of the magnification functions for the Fisheye View and Polyfocal Projection (Figure 12) shows their strong similarities in their general profiles. One could consider the Fisheye View as a special case of Polyfocal Projection. The difference in these two functions is the dips in Polyfocal Projection's magnification function. It is the dips in the Polyfocal Projection's magnification function which make it possible for this technique to support a multiple-focus presentation as shown in Figures 5(e) and 5(f); techniques which do not have this property in their magnification function will not be able to provide a flexible multiple-focus system. This point is discussed further in a later section on implementation issues (Section 5.2).

4. A UNIFIED THEORY

While the taxonomy in the previous section gives a global view of distortion-oriented techniques, a unified theory is proposed here to provide a better insight and understanding of their underlying concept.

The simplest way of visualizing the working of a distortion-oriented presentation technique is to treat the displayed information as if it was printed on a stretchable rubber sheet mounted on a rigid frame.[1] This is an effective analogy which has been used by various researchers to describe distorted displays [Tobler 1973; Mackinlay et al. 1991; Sarkar et al. 1993]. The rubber sheet is densely populated with information to the extent that in its unstretched form, the viewer can see only the global context of the information structure and is not able to make out any detailed information from it. In order that a viewer can examine a particular section to access detailed information, the rubber sheet has to be stretched. Any stretching of the rubber sheet is analogous to applying magnification to a section of the screen. As the rubber sheet is mounted on a rigid frame, any stretching in one part of the sheet results in an equivalent amount of "shrinkage" in other areas. The consequence of this stretching and shrinking of the sheet is an overall distorted view. The amount of stretching or magnification and the manner in which it is applied on the sheet depend entirely on the magnification function of the distortion technique used.

To illustrate how this theory works, consider that the Bifocal Display technique is to be applied on a rubber sheet mounted on a rigid frame as shown in Figure 15(a). Three points, **a**, **b**, and **c** are marked on the sheet to show the effect of stretching. The dotted lines enclose an area in the middle to

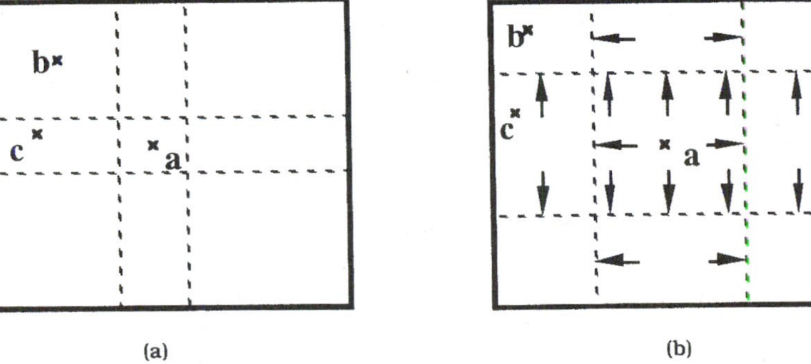

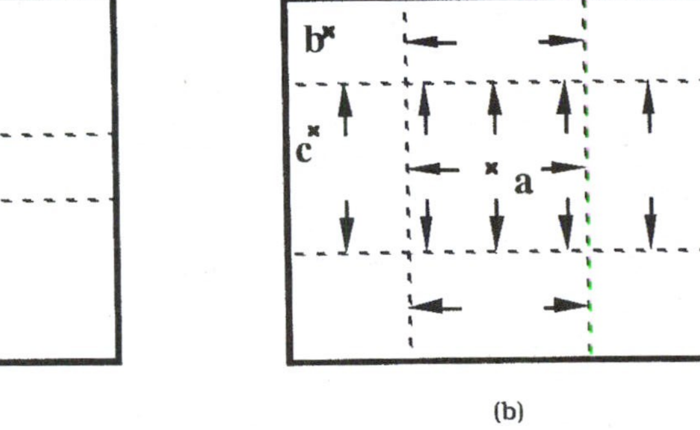

Fig. 15. (a) An unstretched rubber sheet mounted on a rigid frame and the positions on it of three points **a**, **b**, and **c**. Stretching is to be applied at the dotted lines; (b) the arrows indicate the directions of stretching applied to the sheet. Point **a** is not displaced since it is at the focus. Points **b** are **c** are both displaced.

be magnified in order that the viewer can examine its contents in detail; forces are applied along these lines to provide the magnification effect.

Figure 15(b) shows the sheet after stretching is applied in the directions of the arrows. As point **a** is located exactly at the point of focus and all the forces balance out, no displacement results at point **a**. Point **b** experiences two orthogonal forces as a consequence of the stretching applied near the top left-hand corner area. The stretching in these two directions causes **b** to be displaced in both directions toward the top left-hand corner. As a result, the four corner areas are being shrunk by an equivalent amount to accommodate the excess area caused by the stretching. Point **c** experiences three forces, two stretching forces applied vertically and a compressing force horizontally. If point **c** were situated at the midpoint between the two dotted lines, no vertical displacement would take place; in this case because **c** is situated above this midpoint, the resultant force displaces point **c** upward. At the same time, the compressing force that point **c** experiences causes shrinkage in the horizontal direction as indicated in Figure 15(b).

In the case of a multiple-focus view, the situation is similar. The only difference is that stretching or magnification will occur in a greater number of areas on the rubber sheet. The important fact is that the sum of all stretchings or magnifications must be equivalent to the total shrinkages or demagnifications. Otherwise, the rigid frame holding the rubber sheet would deform either because of insufficient surface to accommodate the "over-stretched" sheet or because of an oversupply of space to fit an "overshrunk" sheet. The former situation applies to the Polyfocal Projection (Figures 5(d)–5(f)) while the Polar Fisheye View (Figure 11(e)) and the Perspective Wall (Figure 10(d)) are examples of the latter. As explained in the previous section, techniques with continuous magnification functions by their mathematical nature deform the rectangular frame because of the radial influence

[1] It will be necessary for the edges of the sheet to be able to slide along the edges of the frame.

inherent in the transformation. "The unity gain at the periphery insures continuity retention in the interface to the real world" [Farrand 1973, p. 32].

5. DISCUSSION

5.1 Performance Issues

Although the techniques discussed in this article may be used to display static distorted images on the computer screen, in the context of human-computer interaction an input device will be used to support real-time interaction by users. To allow presentation and navigation of an information space, there are generally three basic interaction methods to effect a change of viewport using an input device: scrolling, pointing and selecting, and dragging.

With scrolling, as the user initiates a movement with the input device (e.g., moving a finger on a touch-sensitive screen or scrolling a mouse), the system detects the direction of the movement and updates the image on the display screen in real time; the amount of movement effected on the central focus area is directly proportional to the scrolling action on the input device made by the user. Depending on system response time, the implementation of scrolling usually involves the creation and the display of a number of intermediate images between the source image to the target image to provide a smooth, continuous visual transition as the focus region is repositioned. To improve performance, detail can be omitted from the nonfocus areas during interaction [Robertson and Mackinlay 1993].

With pointing and selecting, the user moves the central focus region to another location by first positioning the cursor using the input device, and then activating it to select the desired point of interest. The new display with a change of the focus region and its surrounding areas will be presented then.

Dragging incorporates features of both the previous methods. The user selects an item of interest and at the same time moves it (typically by a concurrent scrolling action) with an input device to a position desired by the user for detailed examination. To maintain context with this form of interaction, usually it will be necessary to have the central focus region fixed with respect to the display surface, with the data space appearing to move underneath. This will necessarily result in some regions of the display not being fully utilized if the point of interest is near a corner of the space, and in some areas of the space either not being shown, or being severely distorted.

Distortion-oriented techniques are inherently complicated in their implementation, and some require a significant amount of system time to generate a new image. While an excessively long system response time would render an interface "unusable," this problem may be overcome by using dedicated computer hardware and memory management systems to support the implementation of such techniques [Apperley et al. 1982; Card et al. 1991]. Further, as general-purpose graphics hardware becomes increasingly sophisticated and powerful, effective software solutions have become practicable [Robertson and Mackinlay 1993]. Also, it should be noted that a system response time that is too fast could be just as disconcerting to the user. The sudden shift of a distorted view or any fast scrolling movement on the display screen could cause visual discomfort to the viewer over prolonged, continuous use. This effect is similar to watching a home video taken by an amateur who panned the view jerkily at high speed.

Although there has been an increasing amount of research carried out on user performance in reading moving text on computer displays [Kang and Muter 1989; Chen and Chan 1990], little work has been done to investigate the effects of moving graphical images or to find out the optimum speed for scrolling graphical images on computer screens. Before empirical findings in this research area are available, systems with too short a response time will have to be slowed down by introducing delays during image updates on a trial-and-error basis. Fortunately, this problem relates only to high-performance computer systems, and generally it is easier to slow a system down than to speed it up.

5.2 Implementation Issues

The selection of an interface and its implementation are dictated often by the system hardware available, and its computational power. The complexity of a presentation technique will, therefore, have much influence on this decision. Although distortion-oriented techniques tend to be complex in their implementation, their complexities differ quite widely and depend primarily on the mathematical transformation functions used. Furthermore, very often, trade-offs between the computational power of the hardware and system memory can be made to yield optimum implementation. For example, distorted displays based on stepwise magnification functions may have their different views created and stored in memory in advance. The generation of a distorted view in real time will involve only the cutting and pasting of various sections of these bit maps stored in memory. Generally, systems with less computational power perform the operation of shifting graphic bit maps much faster than that of carrying out complicated mathematical calculations in real time. However, such systems do require adequate on-board memory to support the interface for satisfactory performance. In an implementation of the London Underground map using the Bifocal Display technique [Leung 1989], four separate bit maps, each with different magnifications applied in x and y directions, are stored in memory; altogether, the four bit maps take up six megabytes of system memory. As the user scrolls the mouse, the Bifocal Display is generated by cutting and pasting various sections of these bit maps in real time to generate the nine regions as shown in Figure 7. A similar technique has been applied in implementing the stepwise magnification function of the document lens, where the text is rendered for each of the five regions of a truncated pyramid in advance, and then clipped, scaled, and translated as appropriate during interaction [Robertson and Mackinlay 1993].

Display techniques using a continuous magnification function pose a problem for this implementation method. This is because of the continuum of magnification factors the system will have to cater to at every possible position of the point of focus on the image; the number of bit maps that have

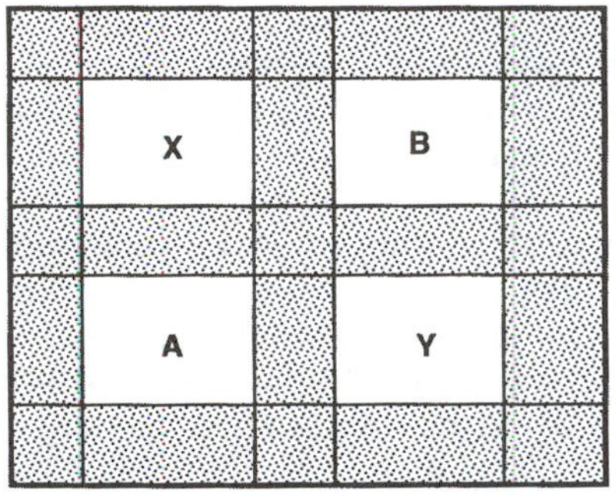

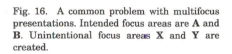

Fig. 16. A common problem with multifocus presentations. Intended focus areas are **A** and **B**. Unintentional focus areas **X** and **Y** are created.

to be stored will be too large to be practical for implementation. One way of overcoming this problem is to use a piecewise continuous magnification function to approximate a continuous function (see Figure 14). This method is an extension of the Bifocal Display to multiple magnification factors with a stepwise function.[2] It can be shown that if the number of distinct magnification levels is n, the number of bit maps the system will have to maintain is n^2. For example, Figure 13 shows a two-dimensional Bifocal Display extended to have three distinct levels of magnification; there are 25 regions on the screen and nine distinct mappings of the data to the display.

Interfaces with a scrolling-style interaction use this multiple-bitmap method typically to generate the distorted view and therefore require less computational power but demand greater system memory. In contrast, interfaces with dragging and pointing and selecting inputs will rely on the computational power of the system to generate the images by performing the mathematical transformation in real time. Dedicated hardware to support the interface may be considered for implementation if a piecewise approximation of the transformation function is not desirable. It is interesting to note that although the Perspective Wall has a piecewise continuous magnification function, the mathematical transformation for the two side panels involves fairly complicated calculations.

Multiple-focus views, which are akin to a multiple-window environment in some text-based and graphical systems, are often desirable. For example, if the user wishes to examine two entities that are located at the extremes of the display, a multiple-focus view would facilitate this application. However, there are some inherent conceptual limitations with the Cartesian (independent x and y) techniques in implementing multiple-focus views. To illustrate this point, consider the case where two focus views A and B are to be created on a Bifocal Display as shown in Figure 16. Because of the inflexibility in the transformation function, two unintended focus views are created at x and y as a side effect. The inflexibility applies typically to techniques whose magnification functions do not have a dip in them like that of the Polyfocal Projection (Figure 6(b)). One way of alleviating this problem is to facilitate a pop-up-window-type arrangement to support multiple views. However, this may create additional navigational problems for the user because of the discontinuity of the presentation in the detailed and demagnified views on the display.

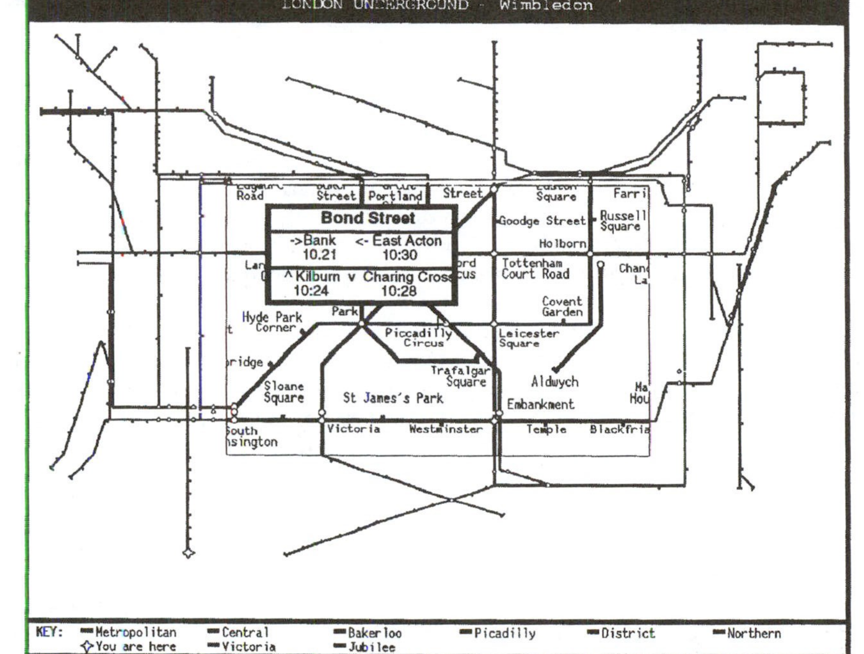

Fig. 17. An application of the combined spatial and information enhancement technique using a Bifocal Display. The train departure time information for Bond Street station, which is embedded in the station symbol, is revealed by user activation.

5.3 Hybrid Techniques and Application Domains

Although problems associated with presenting large volumes of data in a confined display screen area may be classified into spatial problems or information density problems, there are applications where both issues are relevant.

Consider a computer-based information system which provides information to the user about the time of arrival of the next train at any station on the London Underground map. Such a system entails two separate presentation problems. First, the London Underground map needs to be presented to the user to facilitate easy navigation. Second, the information about arrival times needs to be embedded in the map to avoid information clutter. Figure 17

[2] It would be tempting to refer to this as a trifocal, quadrafocal, etc. display. However, because of the use of the term polyfocal display to refer to a display with multiple foci, rather than multiple magnification factors, this terminology has been avoided.

illustrates an effective solution to this combined problem. In this example, the Bifocal Display technique has been used to tackle the spatial presentation problem; the user can navigate freely on the London Underground map, examining a small area in detail while maintaining global context of the map. When the user has located the station of interest, in this case Bond Street station, the embedded information is then revealed. This technique is potentially powerful, and greater research effort should be focused on exploring the application domains for such hybrid approaches.

Distortion-oriented techniques are very useful in solving the spatial problem. However, they should be used with some caution. Due consideration should be given to the type of information to be conveyed and how it will be perceived by the user. For example, in applications where the information to be presented is not well structured, these techniques may not have the desired effect. It should be pointed out that the Polyfocal Projection was originally intended for thematic cartography where maps are presented with a specific theme such as population density or temperature, rather than to show the absolute spatial distances between cities or countries. Leung and Apperley [1993b] discuss the relationship between these presentation techniques, the nature of the original data and its graphical representation, the physical characteristics of the display system (including resolution), the style of interaction, and the task being carried out.

6. CONCLUSION

Generally, there are two problems associated with the presentation of data in a confined space: a spatial problem and an information density problem. The Fisheye View concept that was first proposed by Furnas and later extended by Mitta is an information suppression technique aimed at solving the latter. In this context, the suppression of information creates an "information distortion." Such techniques are very different to those applied to spatial problems as discussed in this article.

This article has presented a taxonomy and a unified theory of graphical distortion-oriented presentation techniques for spatial problems. Depending on the problem domain, these techniques may be applied in both one or two dimensions. Based on their magnification functions, distortion-oriented techniques may be classified into two categories: those with continuous functions and those with noncontinuous functions. The Bifocal Display and the Perspective Wall belong to the former class, and the Polyfocal Projection and the Fisheye View to the latter. From an implementation viewpoint, multiple-focus regions are practical only with the Polyfocal Projection because other distortion-oriented techniques create extra unintended focus regions as a side effect.

The formalism put forward by Sarkar and Brown on the Fisheye View has laid down the ground work for graphical application of this technique for spatial problems. However, a number of variations of the implementation of this technique are possible.

The unified theory presented in this article has shown how magnification and demagnification work in tandem to create the desired distorted view. There is really no limitation on how these distorted views could be generated. A simple way of explaining these distortion techniques is to treat the display surface as a stretchable sheet of rubber mounted on a rigid rectangular frame. Magnification or "stretching" is carried out based on some mathematical transformation operating within that space. The basic law governing distortion-oriented techniques, which is a corollary of Newton's third law of motion, simply states that "where there is a magnification, there will be an equal amount of demagnification to compensate for the loss of display area in a confined space; otherwise the area of that confined space will change."

This article has aimed to demystify the complex mathematics and clarify the unnecessary confusion caused by different terminologies used in current literature. Research efforts should now be focused on a number of interrelated areas. First, a better understanding of these distortion techniques from the HCI perspective should be aimed at by gathering empirical evidence to evaluate the usability of these interfaces. Evaluation of graphical user interfaces is a highly complex task, and a multidimensional approach [Burger and Apperley 1991] is recommended because it provides a comprehensive view for effective interface evaluation. Second, with a better understanding of the usability of these techniques, optimum application domains can then be identified. Third, algorithms or specific hardware architectures should be developed to optimize system response time to enable these techniques to be applied in complex real-time situations. Finally, other nondistortion techniques, such as information suppression, should be investigated further since they are potentially powerful. They could be applied concurrently with the distortion-oriented techniques discussed in this article to complement their effectiveness.

APPENDIX

This section presents the mathematical derivation of the transformation and magnification functions for various distortion-oriented presentation techniques discussed in this article. (See Table A.I for variables and notations.) The transformation function of a distortion-oriented technique defines the way in which a point in the original object image is transformed to the distorted target image, and the magnification function describes the degree of distortion which has been applied to a particular point of interest. Mathematically these two functions are related; the magnification function is the first-order derivative of the transformation function.

Because of the symmetrical nature of two these functions, only the positive horizontal x dimension of the object image has been used for their derivation. For points on the negative horizontal axis, the following relationships apply:

$$\text{Transformation Functions} \quad T(-a) = -T(a)$$
$$\text{Magnification Functions} \quad M(-a) = M(a)$$

where a has a positive value.

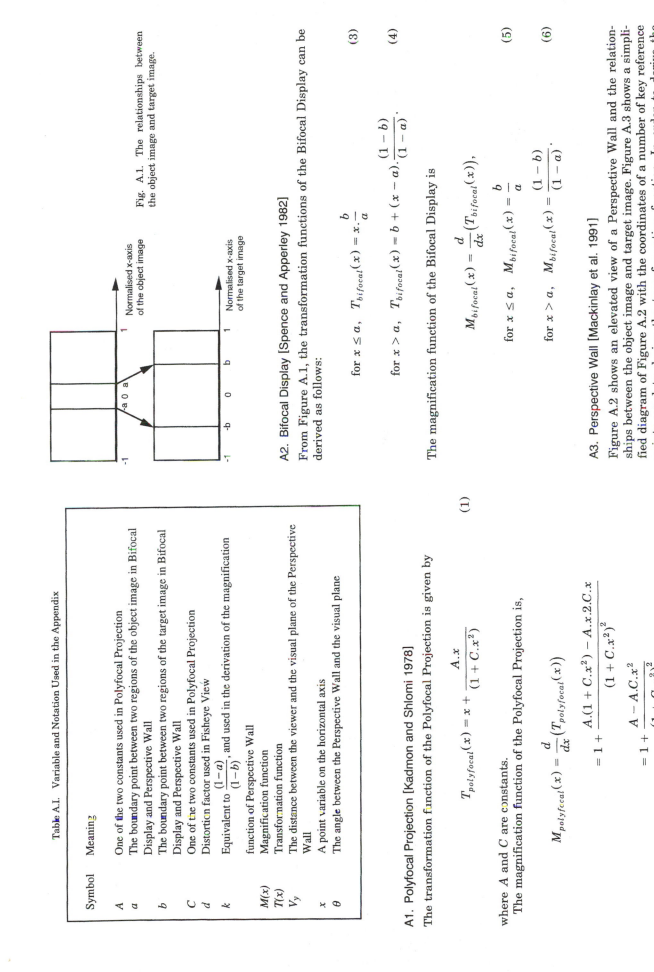

Table A.I. Variable and Notation Used in the Appendix

Symbol	Meaning
A	One of the two constants used in Polyfocal Projection
a	The boundary point between two regions of the object image in Bifocal Display and Perspective Wall
b	The boundary point between two regions of the target image in Bifocal Display and Perspective Wall
C	One of the two constants used in Polyfocal Projection
d	Distortion factor used in Fisheye View
k	Equivalent to $\frac{(1-a)}{(1-b)}$, and used in the derivation of the magnification function of Perspective Wall
$M(x)$	Magnification function
$T(x)$	Transformation function
V_y	The distance between the viewer and the visual plane of the Perspective Wall
x	A point variable on the horizontal axis
θ	The angle between the Perspective Wall and the visual plane

A1. Polyfocal Projection [Kadmon and Shlomi 1978]

The transformation function of the Polyfocal Projection is given by

$$T_{polyfocal}(x) = x + \frac{A.x}{(1 + C.x^2)} \tag{1}$$

where A and C are constants.

The magnification function of the Polyfocal Projection is,

$$M_{polyfocal}(x) = \frac{d}{dx}(T_{polyfocal}(x))$$

$$= 1 + \frac{A.(1 + C.x^2) - A.x.2.C.x}{(1 + C.x^2)^2}$$

$$= 1 + \frac{A - A.C.x^2}{(1 + C.x^2)^2}$$

$$M_{polyfocal}(x) = 1 + \frac{A.(1 - C.x^2)}{(1 + C.x^2)^2} \tag{2}$$

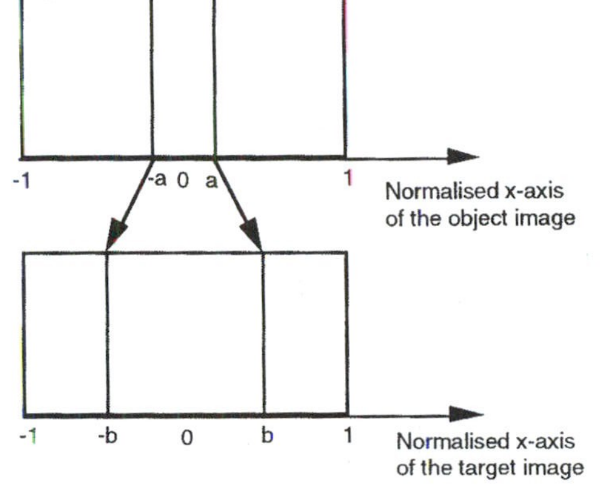

Fig. A.1. The relationships between the object image and target image.

A2. Bifocal Display [Spence and Apperley 1982]

From Figure A.1, the transformation functions of the Bifocal Display can be derived as follows:

$$\text{for } x \le a, \quad T_{bifocal}(x) = x.\frac{b}{a} \tag{3}$$

$$\text{for } x > a, \quad T_{bifocal}(x) = b + (x - a).\frac{(1 - b)}{(1 - a)}. \tag{4}$$

The magnification function of the Bifocal Display is

$$M_{bifocal}(x) = \frac{d}{dx}(T_{bifocal}(x)),$$

$$\text{for } x \le a, \quad M_{bifocal}(x) = \frac{b}{a} \tag{5}$$

$$\text{for } x > a, \quad M_{bifocal}(x) = \frac{(1 - b)}{(1 - a)}. \tag{6}$$

A3. Perspective Wall [Mackinlay et al. 1991]

Figure A.2 shows an elevated view of a Perspective Wall and the relationships between the object image and target image. Figure A.3 shows a simplified diagram of Figure A.2 with the coordinates of a number of key reference points used to derive the transformation function. In order to derive the transformation function of the Perspective Wall, the position of the viewers with respect to Wall will have to be determined first. The position of the viewer is dependent on the width of the viewport, the length of the side panel

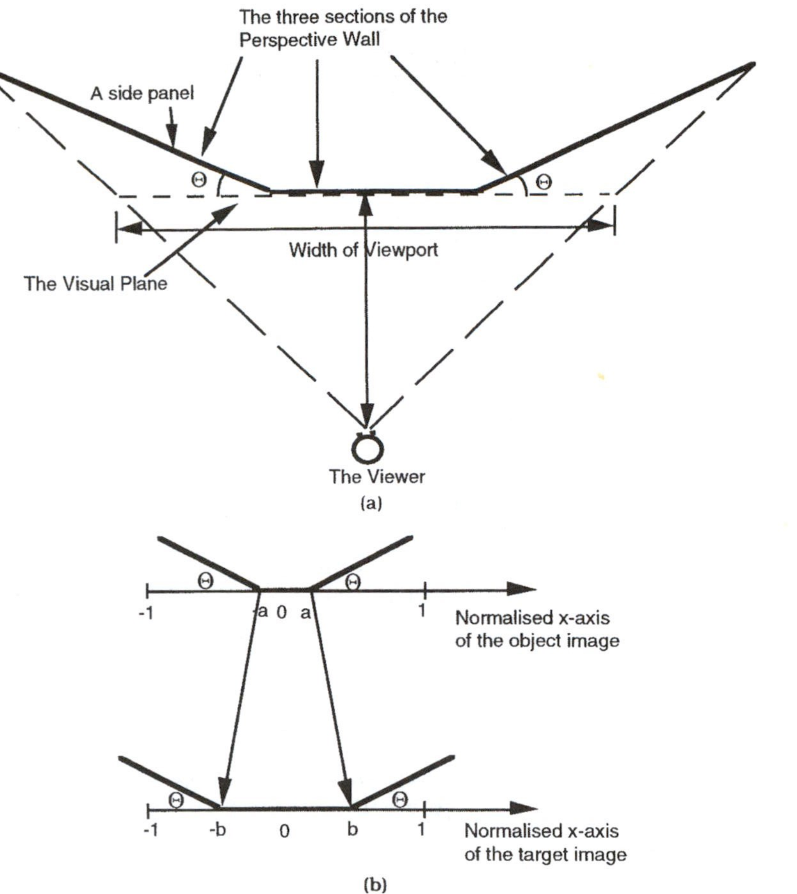

Fig. A.2. (a) The physical arrangement of the Perspective Wall; (b) the relationships between the object image and target image.

of the Perspective Wall, and θ, the angle between the side panel of the Perspective Wall and the visual plane (Figure A.2).

The position of V can be determined by equating the gradient of the two line segments: $\mathbf{V} - (\mathbf{1},\mathbf{0})$ and $(\mathbf{1},\mathbf{0}) - \mathbf{E}$ (see Figure A.3):

$$\frac{-V_y - 0}{0 - 1} = \frac{0 - (1 - a).\sin\theta}{1 - [b + (1 - a).\cos\theta]}$$

$$V_y = \frac{-(1 - a).\sin\theta}{1 - [b + (1 - a).\cos\theta]}. \tag{7}$$

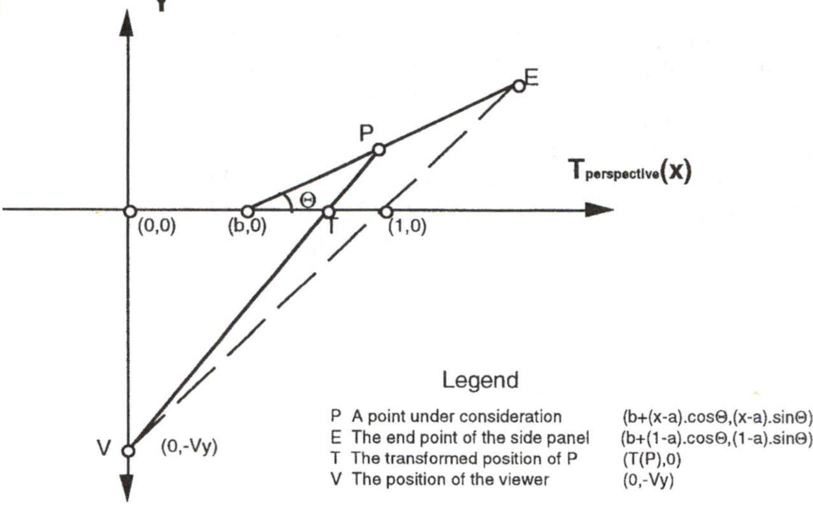

Fig. A.3. A simplified elevated view of the Perspective Wall.

Now, the transformed position of a point **P**, $\mathbf{T_X(P)}$, can be determined by equating the gradient of the two line segments: $\mathbf{T_X(P)} - \mathbf{V}$ **and** $\mathbf{P} - \mathbf{V}$,

$$\frac{T_x - 0}{0 - (-V_y)} = \frac{b + (x - a).\cos\theta - 0}{(x - a).\sin\theta - (-V_y)}$$

$$T_x = \frac{V_y[b + (x - a).\cos\theta]}{V_y + (x - a).\sin\theta}. \tag{8}$$

Substituting (7) in (8), we have

$$T_x = \frac{\dfrac{-(1 - a).\sin\theta}{1 - [b + (1 - a).\cos\theta]}.[b + (x - a).\cos\theta]}{\dfrac{-(1 - a).\sin\theta}{1 - [b + (1 - a).\cos\theta]} + (x - a).\sin\theta}$$

$$T_x = \frac{-(1 - a).\sin\theta.[b + (x - a).\cos\theta]}{-(1 - a).\sin\theta + (x - a).\sin\theta.\{1 - [b + (1 - a).\cos\theta]\}}. \tag{9}$$

Dividing the numerator and denominator of (9) by $\sin\theta$, we have

$$T_x = \frac{-(1 - a).[b + (x - a).\cos\theta]}{-(1 - a) + (x - a).\{1 - [b + (1 - a).\cos\theta]\}}. \tag{10}$$

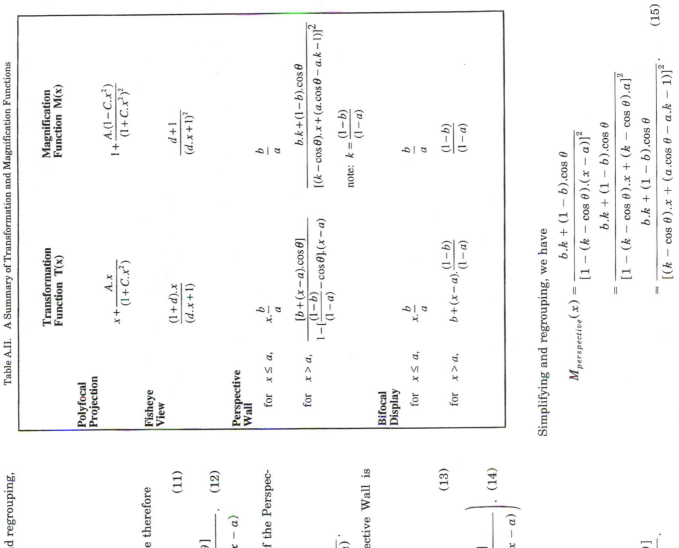

Dividing the numerator and denominator of (10) by $-(1-a)$ and regrouping, we have

$$T_x = \frac{-(1-a).[b+(x-a).\cos\theta]}{-(1-a)+[(1-b)-(1-a).\cos\theta].(x\text{-}a)}$$
$$= \frac{[b+(x-a).\cos\theta]}{1-\left[\dfrac{(1-b)}{(1-a)}-\cos\theta\right].(x-a)}.$$

The transformation functions for a general Perspective Wall are therefore

$$\text{for } x \le a. \quad T_{perspective}(x) = x.\frac{b}{a}, \tag{11}$$

$$\text{for } x > a, \quad T_{perspective}(x) = T_x = \frac{[b+(x-a).\cos\theta]}{1-\left[\dfrac{(1-b)}{(1-a)}\cos\theta\right].(x-a)}. \tag{12}$$

It should be noted that in Mackinlay et al.'s implementation of the Perspective Wall $a = b$, and hence (11) and (12) become

$$\text{for } x \le a, \quad T_{perspective}(x) = x,$$

$$\text{for } x > a, \quad T_{perspective}(x) = \frac{[a+(x-a).\cos\theta]}{1-[1-\cos\theta].(x-a)}.$$

By definition the magnification function of a general Perspective Wall is given by

$$M_{perspective}(x) = \frac{d}{dx}(T_{perspective}(x)),$$

$$\text{for } x \le a, \quad M_{perspective}(x) = \frac{b}{a} \tag{13}$$

$$\text{for } x > a, \quad M_{perspective}(x) = \frac{d}{dx}\left(\frac{[b+(x-a).\cos\theta]}{1-\left[\dfrac{(1-b)}{(1-a)}-\cos\theta\right].(x-a)}\right). \tag{14}$$

Let $k = (1-b)/(1-a)$, and simplifying (14), we have

$$M_{perspective}(x) = \frac{d}{dx}\left(\frac{[b+(x-a).\cos\theta]}{1-[k-\cos\theta].(x-a)}\right)$$
$$= \frac{\cos\theta}{[1-(k-\cos\theta).(x-a)]} + \frac{[b+(x-a).\cos\theta].[k-\cos\theta]}{[1-(k-\cos\theta).(x-a)]^2}.$$

Table A.II. A Summary of Transformation and Magnification Functions

	Transformation Function T(x)	Magnification Function M(x)
Polyfocal Projection	$x+\dfrac{A.x}{(1+C.x^2)}$	$1+\dfrac{A.(1-C.x^2)}{(1+C.x^2)^2}$
Fisheye View	$\dfrac{(1+d).x}{(d.x+1)}$	$\dfrac{d+1}{(d.x+1)^2}$
Perspective Wall		
for $x \le a$,	$x.\dfrac{b}{a}$	$\dfrac{b}{a}$
for $x > a$,	$\dfrac{[b+(x-a).\cos\theta]}{1-[\dfrac{(1-b)}{(1-a)}-\cos\theta].(x-a)}$	$\dfrac{b.k+(1-b).\cos\theta}{[(k-\cos\theta).x+(a.\cos\theta-a.k-1)]^2}$ note: $k=\dfrac{(1-b)}{(1-a)}$
Bifocal Display		
for $x \le a$,	$x.\dfrac{b}{a}$	$\dfrac{b}{a}$
for $x > a$,	$b+(x-a).\dfrac{(1-b)}{(1-a)}$	$\dfrac{(1-b)}{(1-a)}$

Simplifying and regrouping, we have

$$M_{perspective}(x) = \frac{b.k+(1-b).\cos\theta}{[1-(k-\cos\theta).(x-a)]^2}$$
$$= \frac{b.k+(1-b).\cos\theta}{[1-(k-\cos\theta).x+(k-\cos\theta).a]^2}$$
$$= \frac{b.k+(1-b).\cos\theta}{[(k-\cos\theta).x+(a.\cos\theta-a.k-1)]^2}. \tag{15}$$

With $a = b$, and therefore $k = 1$, the magnification functions of Mackinlay et al.'s implementation of the Perspective Wall become

$$\text{for } x \le a, \quad M_{perspective}(x) = 1$$

$$\text{for } x > a, \quad M_{perspective}(x) = \frac{a + (1 - a).\cos\theta}{[(1 - \cos\theta).x + (a.\cos\theta - a - 1)]^2}.$$

A4. Fisheye View [Sarkar and Brown 1992]

The transformation function of the Fisheye View is given by

$$T_{fisheye}(x) = \frac{1 + d}{\left(d + \dfrac{1}{x}\right)} = \frac{(1 + d).x}{(d.x + 1)} \tag{16}$$

where d is called the distortion factor. The magnification function of the Fisheye View is, therefore,

$$\begin{aligned} M_{fisheye}(x) &= \frac{d}{dx}\left(T_{fisheye}(x)\right) \\ &= \frac{(1 + d).(d.x + 1) - (1 + d).x.d}{(d.x + 1)^2} \\ &= \frac{(d.x + 1) + d^2.x + d - x.d - x.d^2}{(d.x + 1)^2} \\ &= \frac{d + 1}{(d.x + 1)^2}. \end{aligned} \tag{17}$$

A5. Summary

Table A.II summarizes the transformation and magnification functions of the distortion-oriented techniques derived earlier.

ACKNOWLEDGMENTS

The authors would like to thank Robert Spence for his valuable comments on an earlier draft. The assistance of Stuart Card in the reviewing process, and the very useful feedback from the reviewers, is also gratefully acknowledged.

REFERENCES

APPERLEY, M. D., TZAVARAS, I., AND SPENCE, R. 1982. A bifocal display technique for data presentation. In *Proceedings of Eurographics '82*. 27–43.

BOLT, R. A. 1979. *Spatial Data Management*. Architecture Machine Group, MIT, Cambridge, Mass.

BURGER, S. V., AND APPERLEY, M. D. 1991. A multi-dimensional approach to interface evaluation. In *Proceedings of the IFIP Conference on Human Jobs and Computer Interface-WG9.1*. IFIP, 205–222.

BEARD, D. V., AND WALKER J. Q., II. 1990. Navigational techniques to improve display of large two-dimensional spaces. *Behav. Inf. Tech. 9*, 451–466.

CARD, S. K., ROBERTSON, G. G., AND MACKINLAY, J. D. 1991. The information visualizer, an information workspace. In *Proceedings of CHI '91*. ACM, New York, 181–188.

CHEN, H. C., AND CHAN, K. T. 1990. Reading computer-displayed moving text with and without self-control over the display rate. *Behav. Inf. Tech. 9*, 467–477.

DONELSON, W. 1978. Spatial management of information. In *ACM SIGGRAPH '78 Proceedings*. ACM, New York, 203–209.

FARRAND, W. A. 1973. Information display in interactive design. Ph.D. dissertation, Dept. of Engineering, Univ. of California, Los Angeles, Calif.

FURNAS, G. W. 1986. Generalized fisheye views. In *Proceedings of CHI '86*. ACM, New York, 16–23.

HEROT, C. F., CARLING, R., FRIEDELL, M., AND FRAMLICH, D. 1980. A prototype spatial data management system. *Comput. Graph. 14*, 1, 63–70.

HOLLANDS, J. G., CAREY, T. T., MATTHEWS, M. L., AND MCCANN, C. A. 1989. Presenting a graphical network: A comparison of performance using fisheye and scrolling views. In *Designing and Using Human-Computer Interfaces and Knowledge Based Systems*, G. Salvendy and M. Smith, Eds. Elsevier, Amsterdam, 313–320.

JOHNSON, B., AND SHNEIDERMAN, B. 1991. Tree maps: A space-filling approach to the visualisation of hierarchical information structures. In *Proceedings of the 2nd International IEEE Visualisation Conference*. IEEE, New York, 284–291.

KADMON, N., AND SHLOMI, E. 1978. A polyfocal projection for statistical surfaces. *Cartograph. J. 15*, 1, 36–41.

KANG, T. J., AND MUTER, P. 1989. Reading dynamic displayed text. *Behav. Inf. Tech. 8*, 1, 33–42.

KOIKE, H. 1994. Fractal views: A fractal-based method for controlling information display. *ACM Trans. Inf. Syst.* To be published.

LEUNG, Y. K. 1989. Human-computer interaction techniques for map-based diagrams. In *Designing and Using Human-Computer Interfaces and Knowledge Based Systems*, G. Salvendy and M. Smith, Eds. Elsevier, Amsterdam, 361–368.

LEUNG, Y. K., AND APPERLEY, M. D. 1993a. Extending the Perspective Wall. In *Proceedings of OZCHI '93*. 110–120.

LEUNG, Y. K., AND APPERLEY, M. D. 1993b. E^3: Towards the metrication of graphical presentation techniques. In *Lecture Notes in Computer Science: Human-Computer Interaction*, Bass, L. J., Gornostaev, J. G., and Unger, C., Eds. Springer-Verlag, Heidelberg, 125–140.

MACKINLAY, J. D., ROBERTSON, G. G., AND CARD, S. K. 1991. The Perspective Wall: Detail and context smoothly integrated, In *Proceedings of CHI '91*. ACM, New York, 173–179.

MISUE, K., AND SUGIYAMA, K. 1991. Multi-viewpoint perspective display methods: Formulation and application to compound graphs. In *Human Aspects in Computing: Design and Use of Interactive Systems and Information Management*, H. J. Bullinger, Ed. Elsevier Science Publishers B. V., Amsterdam, 834–838.

MITTA, D. A. 1990. A fisheye presentation strategy: Aircraft maintenance data. In *Proceedings of Interact '90*. 875–885.

MONK, F. M., WALSH, P., AND DIX, A. J. 1988. A comparison of hypertext, scrolling and folding as mechanisms for program browsing. In *People and Computers*. Vol. 4, D. M. Jones and R. Winder, Eds. Cambridge University Press, Cambridge, Mass., 421–435.

RAO, R., AND CARD, S. K. 1994. The Table Lens: Merging graphical and symbolic representations in an interactive focus + context visualization for tabular information. In *Proceedings of CHI'94*. ACM, New York.

ROBERTSON, G. G., AND MACKINLAY, J. D. 1993. The Document Lens. In *Proceedings of the ACM Symposium on User Interface Software and Technology*. ACM, New York.

ROBERTSON, G. G., MACKINLAY, J. D., AND CARD, S. K. 1991. Cone Trees: Animated 3D visualizations of hierarchical information. In *Proceedings of CHI '91*. ACM, New York, 189–194.

SARKAR, M., AND BROWN, M. H. 1992. Graphical fisheye views of graphs. In *Proceedings of CHI'92*. ACM, New York, 83–91.

SARKAR, M., SNIBBE, S., AND REISS, S. 1993. Stretching rubber sheet: A metaphor for visualising large structure on small screen. In *Proceedings of the ACM Symposium on User Interface Software and Technology*. ACM, New York.

SCHAFFER, D., ZUO, Z., BARTRAM, L., DILL, J., DUBS, S., GREENBERG, S., AND ROSEMAN, M. 1993. Comparing fisheye and full-zoom techniques for navigation of hierarchically clustered networks. In *Proceedings of Graphics Interface '93*. Morgan-Kaufman, San Mateo, Calif.

SHNEIDERMAN, B. 1992. Tree visualization with Tree-Maps: 2-d space-filling approach. *ACM Trans. Comput. Graph. 11*, 1, 92–97.

SPENCE, R., AND APPERLEY, M. D. 1982. Database navigation: An office environment for the professional. *Behav. Inf. Tech. 1*, 1, 43–54.

TOBLER, W. R. 1973. A continuous transformation useful for districting. *Ann. New York Acad. Sci. 219*, 215–220.

Extending Distortion Viewing from 2D to 3D

M. Sheelagh T. Carpendale,
David J. Cowperthwaite, and F. David Fracchia
Simon Fraser University

Information does not equal knowledge. For information to become knowledge, we need to interpret and understand it. Visualization in general responds directly to this need. However, even after producing a visual representation, we must address issues involving exploration, navigation, and interpretation of the data. This article addresses visual exploration of 3D information layouts.

Comparing 2D and 3D information layout adjustment tools leads directly to a 3D visual access tool that clears a line of sight to any region of interest.

Several visual exploration techniques have been proposed for 2D information layouts. Many of these try to take advantage of humans' natural visual pattern-recognition abilities to understand global relationships while simultaneously integrating this knowledge with local details. This desire for detail-in-context views (also called fisheye, multiscale, and distortion views) has fueled considerable research in the development of distortion viewing tools. Generally, these tools provide space for magnification of local detail by compressing the rest of the image. In considering a possible detail-in-context view for 3D layouts, we first examine 2D distortion techniques, bearing in mind the particular 3D problem of occlusion.

While our technique can extend to any type of 3D information display, here we focus on graphs. Most previous distortion viewing work dealt only with discrete displays (principally graphs). Also, graphs are structures well suited to information display. A graph can display a set of objects or entities as nodes and relationships between these entities as edges. This basic entity-relationship structure parallels the basic subject-predicate structure of language. It also arises in cognitive science discussions about the distinction between knowledge as declarative or procedural. The same structure has been suggested as forming the basis for the mental models we use to store information internally. Its prevalence across such a variety of areas concerned with the way humans interact with knowledge or information indicates that related tools and techniques may eventually find quite diverse applications.

To preserve the representational power inherent in a graph, a distortion-based navigational tool should not disrupt certain properties or relationships in the graph. For example, an entity's spatial position and adjacency relationships may each carry specific meaning. They therefore should be minimally disturbed.

Partly because a graph's structure does not limit the size or complexity of the information it can represent, problems arise, such as a disparity between the information size and display size, and the number of information variables compared to the availability and length of display variables. Three-dimensional layouts offer the possibility of some increase in functional display space and an extra positional display variable.

Ware's studies[1] examined the amount of usable space in a 3D graph display. Discounting the two naive extremes of either an n-fold increase (3D = n^3 space or $n \times$ 2D space) or no increase from 2D space, since what is really seen is a 2D projection of the 3D space, Ware's results indicate approximately a three-fold increase in usable space in a 3D display. While encouraging because it seems to indicate that we gain something from our familiarity with 3D space, this result also shows that the fact that we can only see the 2D projection imposes a fundamental limitation. The amount of usable space relates much more closely to the 2D size of n^2 than to a full 3D space.

The fundamental problem remains, just as in the real world, that we cannot see through objects. Something between us and what we want to see blocks our view. While full rotation lets us view the 3D display from all angles, it does not eliminate the fact—inherent to working with 3D information—that some data will be buried within a structure, whether a solid model or a complicated 3D graph layout. Rotational ability definitely improves the situation and was tied closely to the three-fold increase in functional space Ware noted.[1]

For discrete information displays, information density can exacerbate occlusion. Given the considerable

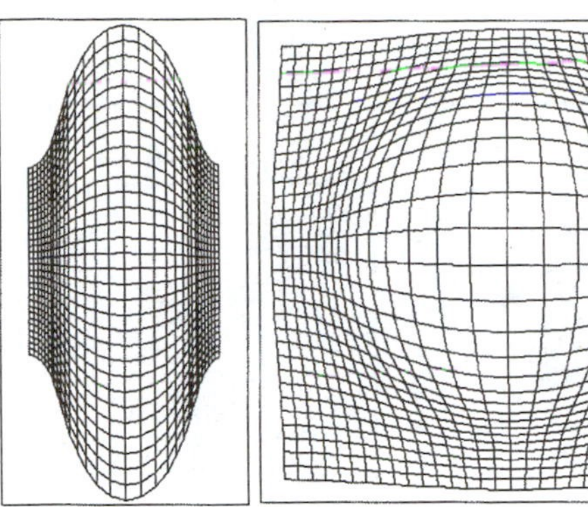
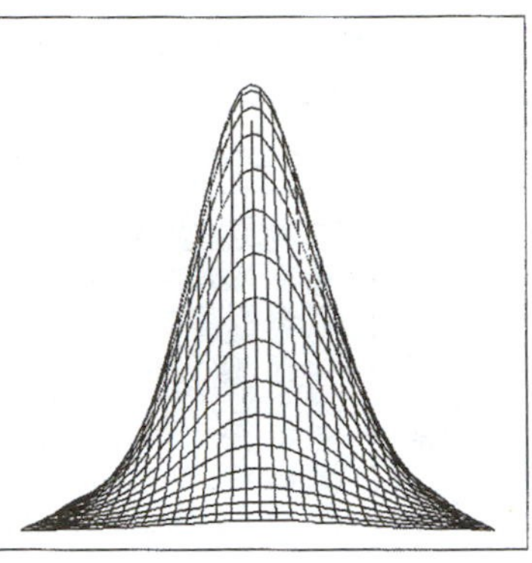

1 Distortion dimensionality showing a 3D distortion applied to a 2D surface. In projection 1D applied along the *x* axis (left); in projection 2D applied in both *x* and *y* (center); and side view of the 3D curve (right).

body of work addressing information density in 2D displays, those techniques might well apply to 3D displays. Specifically, can we apply distortion techniques to 3D in a manner that deals with occlusion and preserves context as in the 2D applications?

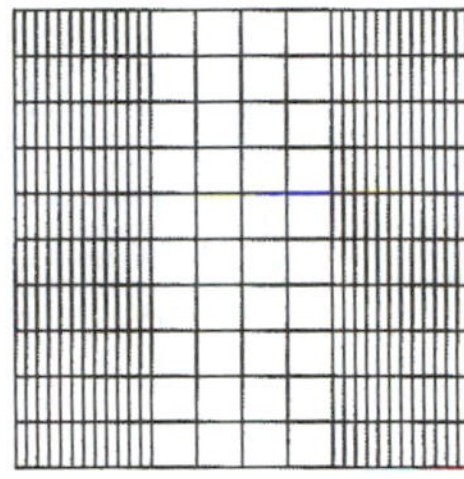
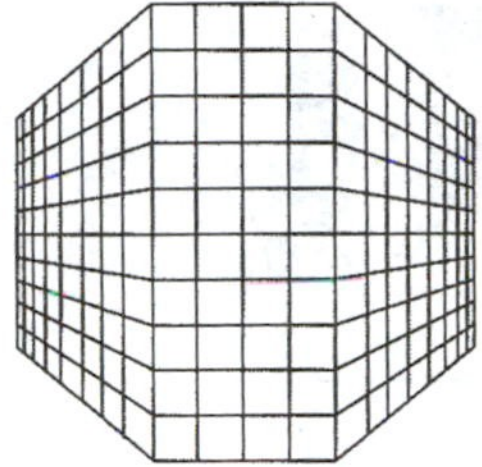
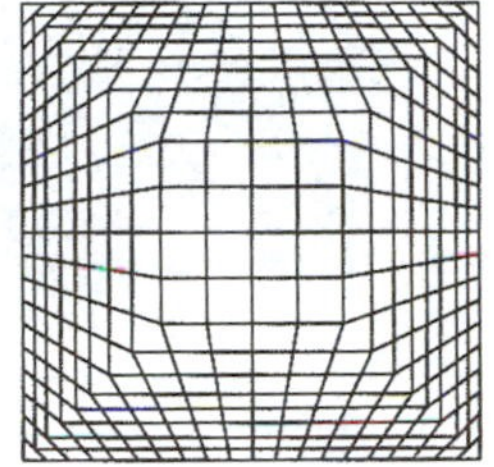

2 Distortion patterns found in Bifocal Display (left), Perspective Wall (center), and Document Lens (right).

We believe that studies supporting integrated detail-in-context viewing in 2D displays extrapolate to 3D. For instance, Furnas[2] indicated that humans store and recall information in great detail for areas of interest and gradually decreasing detail for the related context. This characteristic presumably applies for information in general regardless of the type of display. Certainly more general cognitive support for integrated displays—which permit use of our visual gestalt abilities and minimize cognitive load—applies to our ability to assimilate and interpret information, not to a particular style of display.

Information viewing and dimensionality

Researchers have used both filtering and distorting approaches to create detail-in-context views. Spence and Apperley[3] introduced distortion viewing with the Bifocal Display, and Furnas[2] introduced filtering with Generalized Fisheyes. Unlike filtering, most distortion techniques present all aspects of the image even if very compressed. Some techniques combine the two. For instance, Continuous Zoom[4] uses both filtering and distortion, and Graphical Fisheye[5] creates a graphic interpretation of Furnas's filtering method using compression as well as removal. We will discuss primarily spatial reorganization of an existing representation—thus, distortion.

One-, two-, and three-dimensional information representations are common, and a collection of viewing tools exists for each. A distortion can be applied along the *x*, *y*, or *z* dimensions of the computer display or in a combination thereof. Most current distortion techniques use a 2D distortion applied to a 2D information layout.

However, the dimensionality of the information representation and the dimensionality of the viewing technique do not have to match. Figure 1 shows a 3D distortion applied to a 2D surface from 3-Dimensional Pliable Surfaces (3DPS).[6] The distortion relies on perspective projection to create its reorganized views. The left and center images show the resulting projection. The right image shows the 3D curve from the side. In the leftmost image the distortion is applied along the *x* axis and not the *y* axis. In the center image it is applied in both the *x* and *y* directions.

Other examples of discrepancies between dimensionality of the representation and the distortion include Bifocal Display[3] (Figure 2, left image) and Perspective Wall[7] (Figure 2, center image). They apply, respectively, a 1D and a 3D distortion to a linear strip of information that can be thought of as 1D or, since it has width, 2D. Document Lens[8] (Figure 2, right image) offers a single rectangular focus through a 3D distortion of 2D text fields.

Viewing techniques for 3D data

Currently, the primary methods for accessing 3D space either adjust the viewing angle (rotation) or the viewing position (navigation). Combined, these two would seem to allow all possible views. However, the many problems identified include loss of context when flying through, loss of orientation, and the ever-present problem of occlusion. Nondistortion approaches to accessing the internal details of 3D structures use cutting planes, layer removal, and transparency. Cutting planes and layer removal provide visual access but remove context, while transparency requires some compromise between obtaining visibility and maintaining context.

Previous 3D detail-in-context approaches include Fairchild et al.'s Semnet[9] and Mitra's aircraft maintenance approach.[10] Semnet included three techniques. One, which uses semantics for positioning, creates an octree to display the focal region in full detail and more remote regions in progressively larger sections. This approach suffers from the sudden changes that occur between boundaries of regions of differing scales. A sec-

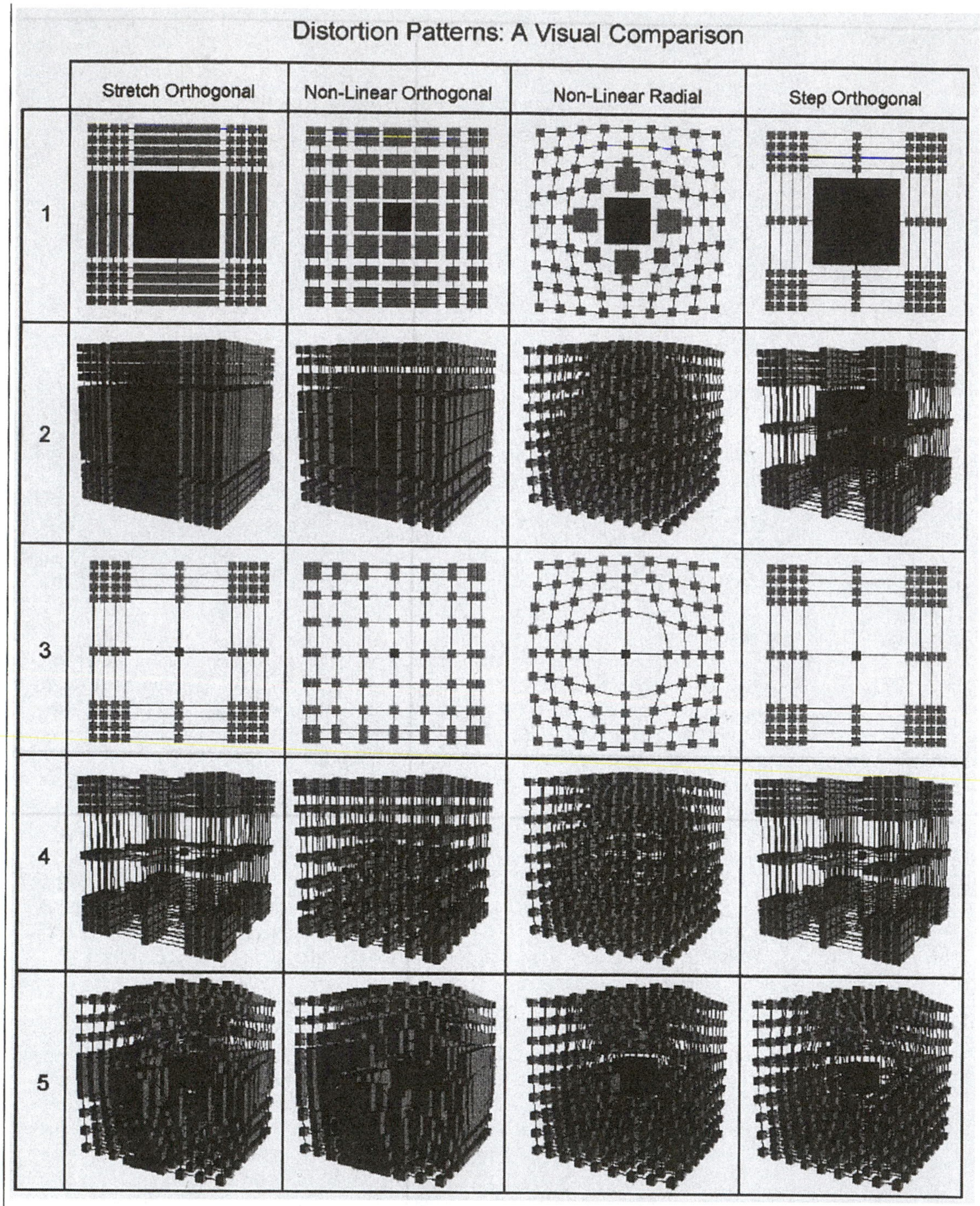

3 This chart presents visually the effect of different distortion techniques on spatial organization.

ond approach, based on density, samples more fully around the focus and less frequently as the distance from the focus increases. This approach would increase the congestion and therefore the occlusion problems in the focal region. Third, Fairchild noted the implicit fisheye provided by perspective in a 3D display. A natural single focal point exists for the information in the foreground.

Mitra[10] suggested using linear radial distortion with interactive filters for aircraft maintenance diagrams—3D exploded views of aircraft assembly parts. An adjustable threshold produces a filtered view based on the function of parts rather than proximity in the diagram. The user could adjust the threshold level to create views with more or less context. In this case exploding and filtering the view does create the space required to see into the structure, but doesn't ensure an unobstructed view. Moreover, progressive filtering removes much of the context, and the overall structure is not apparent in the overall exploded view.

While Fairchild and Mitra focused on providing detail-in-context views, the viewing techniques for 3D data largely concern various types of removal and filtering.

This is probably because in a 3D data display some parts of the display prevent you from seeing other parts—confirming the importance of addressing occlusion.

Examining the distortion viewing techniques developed for 2D data reveals possible extrapolations to 3D data. Rather than critique each technique's usefulness for 2D data, we observe the visual results of spatial reorganization patterns applied to 3D data.

Two-dimensional distortion patterns

Much of the considerable recent work on developing viewing tools for 2D information displays has focused on displaying sufficient detail within the global context. This prompted a general notion of distortion viewing or multiscale diagrams[11] where different sections of the information are displayed at different scales. These differing scales of magnified detail and compressed context can be integrated through various distortion functions.

Each approach produces characteristic distortion patterns. We examine displacement separately from magnification, one of several useful distinctions[12] when considering distortion viewing functions. The displacement function adjusts the display to accommodate the increased amount of space the magnified focus requires. Viewing tools generally apply displacement and magnification functions simultaneously. However, Leung and Apperley[13] introduced the possibility of a distinction between magnification and displacement. They discussed distortion viewing in terms of a transformation or displacement function with a derivative magnification function.

Since our purpose here is exploring what types of distortions might prove useful with 3D data, we examine the 2D distortion functions from the perspective of the resulting visual pattern. The top row in Figure 3 contains a sample of these 2D distortion patterns illustrated on a simple 2D grid graph. While not exhaustive, this set of techniques represents the types of distortion currently used in 2D. All four examples in row 1 show the characteristic patterns created by a traditional application of 2D distortion methods using displacement and magnification simultaneously: stretch orthogonal, nonlinear orthogonal, nonlinear radial, and step orthogonal techniques.

Many 2D techniques offer a choice of one or more of these distinctions. For example, Multi-Viewpoint Perspective,[14] Catgraph,[15] Rubber Sheet,[16] and Shrimp[17] all offer both orthogonal and radial approaches. As a result some of these techniques will appear under more than one of the following headings.

Stretch orthogonal

The first example (Figure 4 and row 1, column 1 in Figure 3) shows a simple orthogonal stretch formed by stretching all data on either of the two axes centered at the focus and compressing the remaining areas uniformly. Bifocal Display by Spence and Apperley[3] applied this distortion in one dimension and thus introduced the notion of distortion viewing to computational displays. They created a single-focus detail-in-context view for a personal information space displayed in a long strip. Leung extended this technique to use 2D stretch in 2D Bifocal Display.[18]

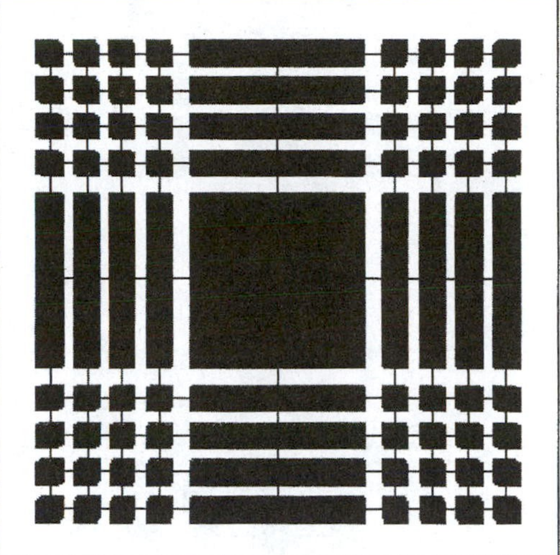

4 Orthogonal stretch applied to a 2D grid graph.

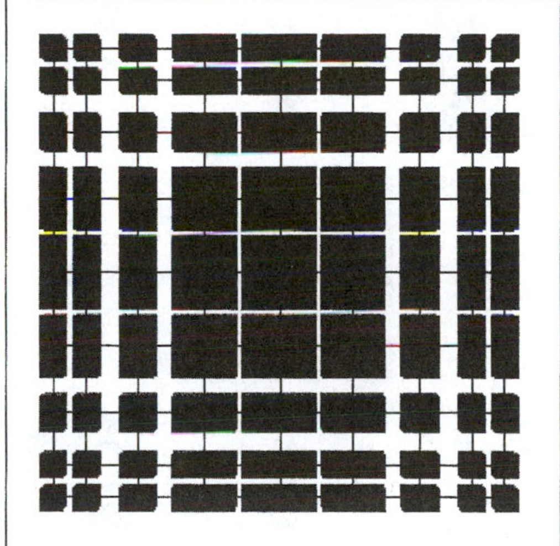

5 Nonlinear orthogonal distortion applied to a 2D grid graph.

The image in Figure 3, row 1, column 1 shows a 2D stretch with a single focal point. Subsequently, the orthogonal approach in Rubber Sheet[16] used this distortion to provide multiple focal points. The resulting distorted image uses available screen space well but has entire rows and columns of distorted data. In a multiple foci situation these stretched rows and columns create unrequested or "ghost" foci where they intersect.

Nonlinear orthogonal

The second example (Figure 5 and row 1, column 2 in Figure 3) shows a nonlinear orthogonal approach. Here the focus is magnified to the requested amount, and the magnification decreases according to some function of the orthogonal distance from the focus. This more gradual integration into the foci's immediate surroundings either limits the amount of magnification in the focal region or causes more extreme compression at the edges.

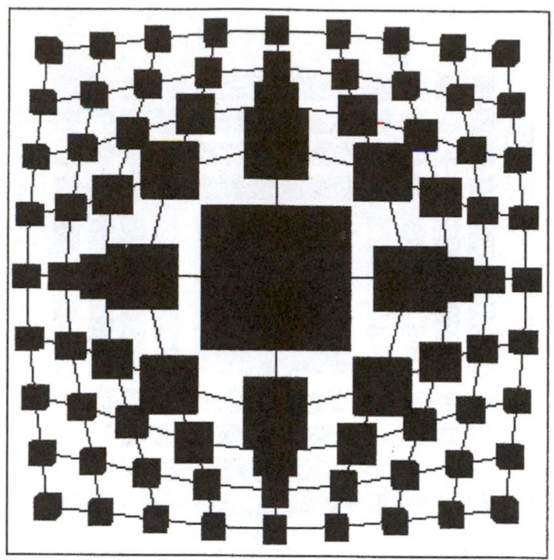

6 Nonlinear radial distortion applied to a 2D grid graph.

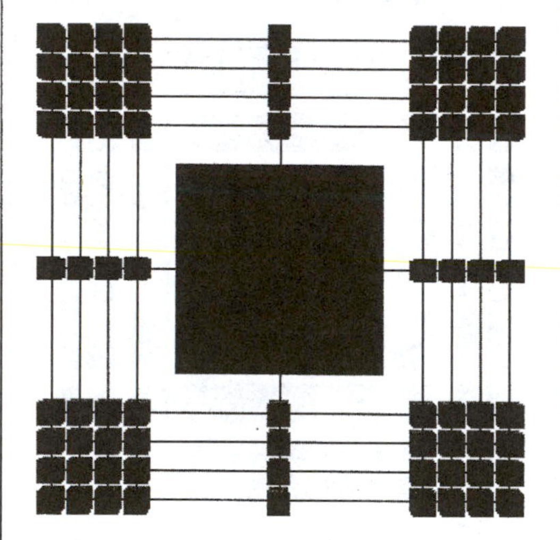

7 Step orthogonal distortion applied to 2D grid graph.

Various mathematical functions have been used with the nonlinear orthogonal approach, including arctan in Catgraph[15] and Multi-View Point Perspective,[14] and the hyperbola in Hyperbolic Space.[19] This figure's particular pattern is based on the sine curve.

The nonlinear orthogonal technique supports smooth integration of the focal area into its surrounding context. One problem noted with this approach is that the compression can become extreme at the edges if you allow much magnification in the focal and adjacent regions.

Nonlinear radial

The third example (Figure 6 and row 1, column 3 in Figure 3) is distinct from the first two because of the radial application of the magnification and distortion functions and because it is a constrained distortion. Note that the nonlinear function provides an effect of relative adjacent magnification similar to the image in column 2. However, the radial application causes adjacent edges to curve away from the focus. As a result items directly above and below or side by side shift slightly. This interferes with the orthogonal relationships in the original grid.

Misue et al.[20] asserted the importance of preserving orthogonality, proximity, and topology in creating distorted views that do not interfere with our mental map of the original image. As the other columns of Figure 3 illustrate, orthogonal distortions certainly respect orthogonality, but some have argued that radial distortions best preserve proximity.[12,17] This distortion pattern is constrained because its effects diminish towards the edge of the image. While the distortion in Figure 3, row 1, column 3 is minimally constrained, you can see that the outer rows of the grid are hardly affected. Most radial distortions suffer from extreme compression and distortion (the image having become virtually circular) at the edges. Constrained distortions were introduced in Pliable Surfaces[6] and subsequently used in nonlinear transformations.[21]

Creating a distorted view magnification in one place occurs at the expense of compression in another. Avoiding extreme compression at the edges of the image by constraining the distortion does not avoid the compression entirely. Pliable Surfaces[6] provides user control of both the location and relative rate of compression.

Step orthogonal

The fourth example (Figure 7 and row 1, column 4 in Figure 3) displays a step orthogonal approach. This performs the same distortion as the space filling orthogonal but leaves the data in the rows and columns aligned with the focus unstretched. This basic approach creates less data distortion but leaves more unused space. It also causes a marked grouping of the data not related to the information itself and could lead to misinterpretations. The Zoom family of viewing techniques[4,22] uses this method, as does the more recent Shrimp Views.[17]

Introducing distortion viewing to 3D

Certain problems arise when applying 2D distortion techniques to 3D displays. We intend to demonstrate the distinctive patterns of different types of distortion and show that while they offer considerable advantages in a 2D display, a naive application does little to improve access in 3D. Figure 3 serves as our reference for this discussion.

Figure 3 is organized as a chart. The top row displays four 2D distortion techniques, each used exclusively in the column it heads. We chose to use 2D and 3D grid graphs because these simple structures most clearly reveal the underlying patterns of the distortion functions. We chose a central focal point because we want to explore revealing obscured foci.

Figure 3, row 2

The second row shows a direct naive extrapolation of the 2D schemes to a 3D grid graph. Note that in the first two columns the distortion pattern propagates straight through to the surface. In fact, given focal points on the surface of a 3D structure, we achieve the same benefits that these distortion patterns obtain in 2D. This would continue to apply to any chosen focus visible in the 2D projection. However, simply applying these approaches to a 3D display does more to obscure a central focal

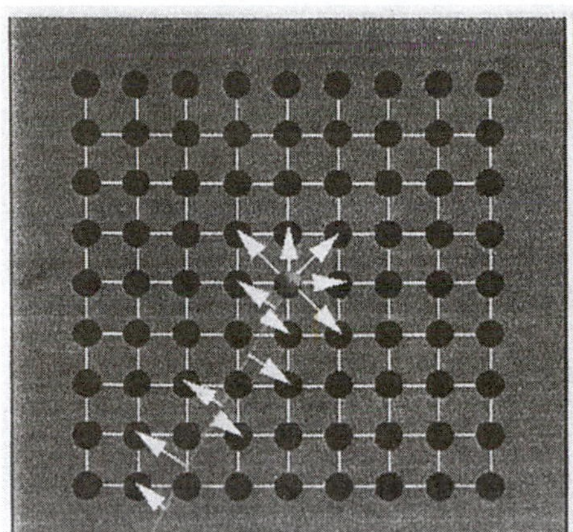
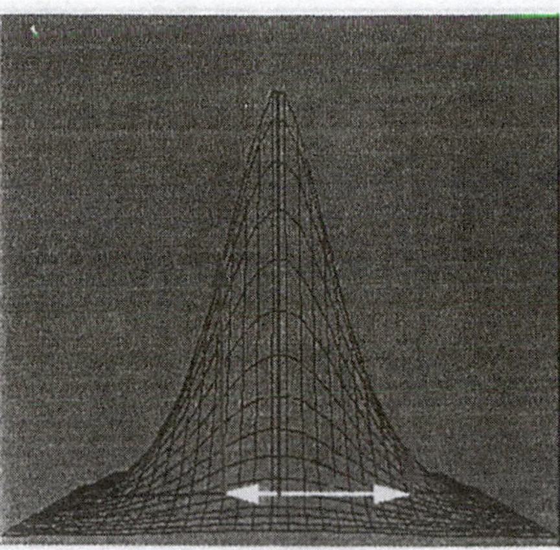
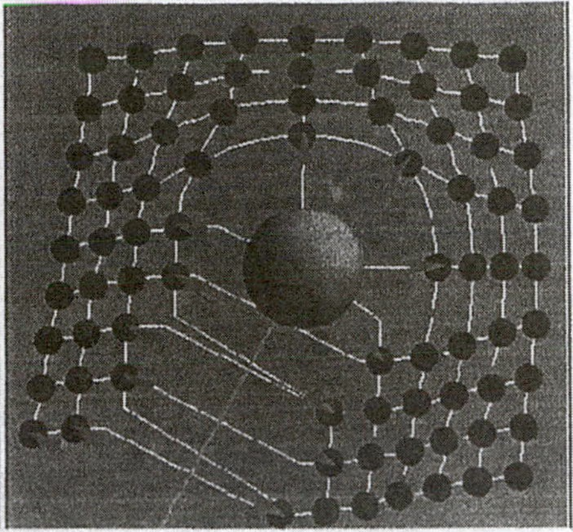

point than reveal it. In fact, the usual problem of some objects occluding others in 3D layouts is exacerbated in distortion approaches with space-filling aspects, notably columns 1 and 2.

Applying the radial Gaussian function in 3D best preserves the actual appearance of the 3D grid itself, as the function only minimally extends to the edges. However, the magnification/displacement appears as increased congestion in the center.

The amount of displacement at the edges of the orthogonal step function (row 2, column 4) does provide a view of the internal focal node. While this hints that displacement by itself might be useful, the resulting view is not entirely satisfactory—it still does not allow viewing from all angles, and the artificial groupings are pronounced.

For distortion to help us fully examine the internal aspects of 3D data, we need unrestricted visual access to the chosen focus. Furthermore, if we expect to provide context, it would be preferable to avoid radically reorganizing the data.

Figure 3, row 3

Following the insight provided by the naive application, the third row presents the same set of functions, revealing the displacement-only aspect on the 2D grid. Note that the stretch and step orthogonal (columns 1 and 4) resolve into the same pattern.

Figure 3, row 4

Row 4 applies this displacement-only distortion to the 3D grid. Despite eliminating the obscuring magnification, little improvement results from applying graduated and radial techniques (columns 2 and 3). Note that while the orthogonal approaches had seemed a less efficient use of space in two dimensions, in three dimensions the separation provides partial visual access. However, it creates artificial groupings that can still occlude the focus during rotation. The partial solution provided by the displacement-only patterns indicates the potential usefulness of using distortion to remove occluding objects.

Observations

At this point we have determined that a displacement-only function might best provide visual access. However, it appears that aligning this function with the data creates artificial groupings of apparent significance. Also, limiting the spread of the distortion produces a much more recognizable exterior, and the objects that concern us lie only between the focus and the viewer.

On the other hand, it seems that the magnification still aligns more appropriately with the data. For instance, the choice between relative local magnification or focal-only magnification depends on the task and information.

These observations led us to apply two techniques first developed in our 2D distortion method, 3DPS[6]—viewer-aligned distortion and constrainable distortions. In 2D we aligned focal regions with the viewer to keep more than one in sight and prevent the focal regions from occluding each other. In 3D we actually apply the displacement distortion radially along the line of sight, permitting interactive displacement of objects that obstruct the view. In 2D we constrained the distortion to maintain as much undisturbed context as possible and to give the user interactive choices on the compression's location and pattern. Applying the constrained distortion in 3D directly parallels this.

Visual access distortion

Visual access distortion[23] is a viewer-aligned, radially constrained, reversible distortion that clears the line of sight to chosen focal regions. We believe that effective 3D detail-in-context viewing requires

- controlling the magnification of a chosen focus or foci to display detail,
- viewing the focus as a 3D object with the usual advantage of rotation (examination from all angles),
- maintaining a clear visual path between the user and the focal point(s), and
- maintaining the surrounding context in a manner that respects the original layout.

Specifically, visual access distortion proceeds as follows. Select a focal point; in Figure 8 (left image) the central point has been selected. Then let L be a line segment extending from the focus to the viewpoint (the line of sight), indicated in the left image of Figure 8

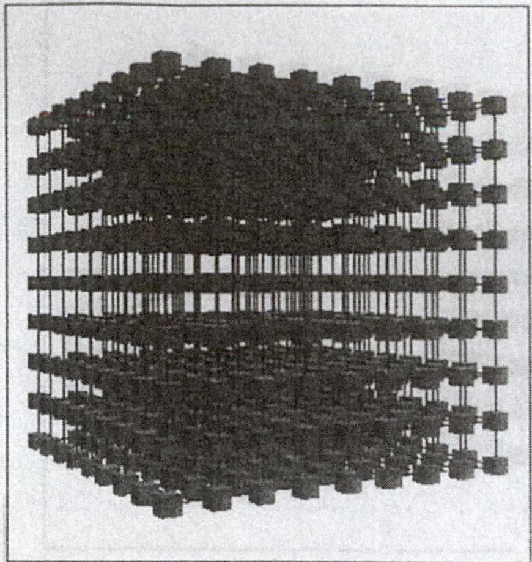
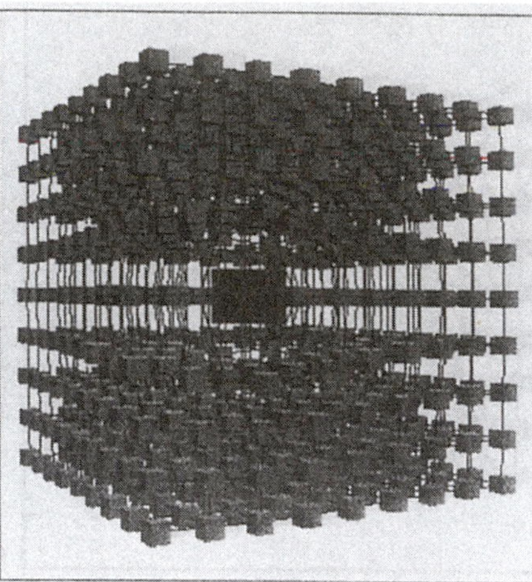
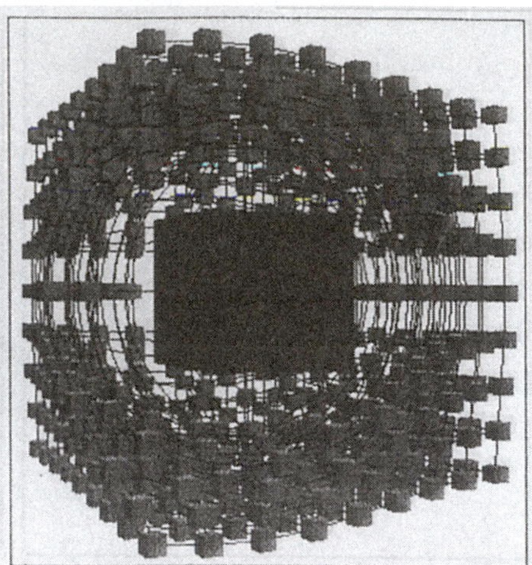

9 This series shows Gaussian visual access distortion applied progressively to the 3D grid.

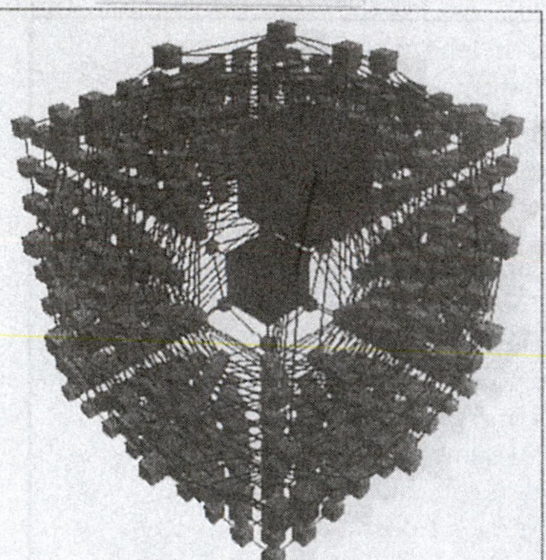
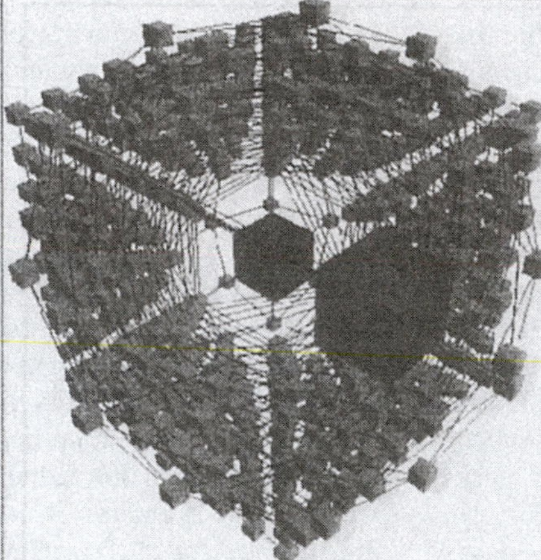
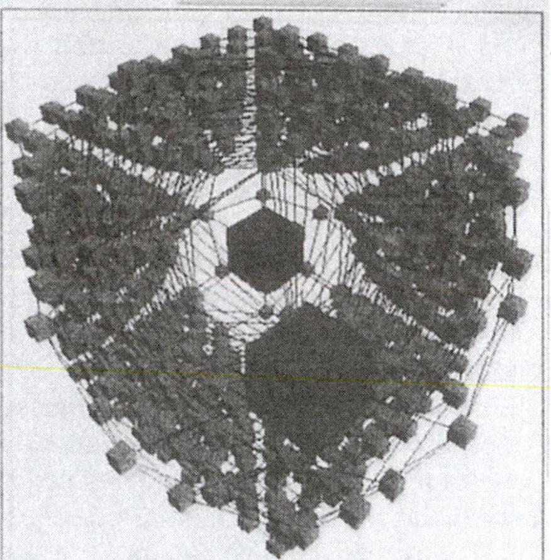

10 Even when the two foci are in line with the viewpoint, both remain visible because the distortion function from the furthest focus affects all occluding objects, including other foci.

extending from the focus. The vector **d** is the shortest vector from an object *O* in the display and a nearest point *P* on the line *L*. In Figure 8 (left image) yellow arrows reach from the focus and the line of sight to the adjacent points. The vector **d** defines the direction of the distortion at *O*, and its length |**d**| is used to determine the magnitude *M* of the distortion.

To achieve smooth integration back into the original data topology, use a Gaussian distribution to determine the displacement's magnitude. The profile of a Gaussian function (Figure 8, center) shows how the |**d**| (indicated in yellow) is used to calculate magnitude *M* of the distortion (indicated in green). For a given value of |**d**| you can determine the height of the Gaussian that gives the magnitude *M*. Figure 8 (right image) shows (in green) using the magnitude *M* along direction **d** to create the displacement. You can control the shape of the Gaussian function, and hence the distribution of the distortion, simply by adjusting the height and standard deviation of the curve. Since the viewing direction is along the line of sight, the distortions will appear to the viewer as radially symmetrical about the focus, though moderated by the effect of planar perspective projection.

The resulting distortion of the original data provides a clear visual path from the viewer to the focal node. The visibility of the focus persists under rotation of the data or motion of the viewpoint, smoothly deflecting nodes away from the line of sight as they approach it and returning them to their original positions as they move away (Figure 9). The creation of a clear visual path can now be combined with one of the magnification distortions described earlier to permit an unobstructed view of the magnified focus.

Multiple foci

Visual access distortion scales well to multiple focal points. Because each line of sight employs its own access distortion function, you can combine more than one focus in a single view.

In Figure 10 a simple average of the two functions at each point produces clear lines of sight to the two foci. The upper right focus is one layer deep into the $9 \times 9 \times$

9 cube. The lower left focus is eight layers deep, but still visible. As with a single focus, visual access persists during rotation. Figure 10 rotates the lattice (from left to right) until both foci are in line, one above the other, in the rightmost image. Figure 10 proceeds to continue rotating, but from top to bottom instead of left to right. In the left image the closer focal point comes down between the user and the further focal point. However, visual access distortion merely considers it another occluding object and shifts it to one side. The three images in Figure 10 show how close one focal point can come to occluding another as it crosses the line of sight.

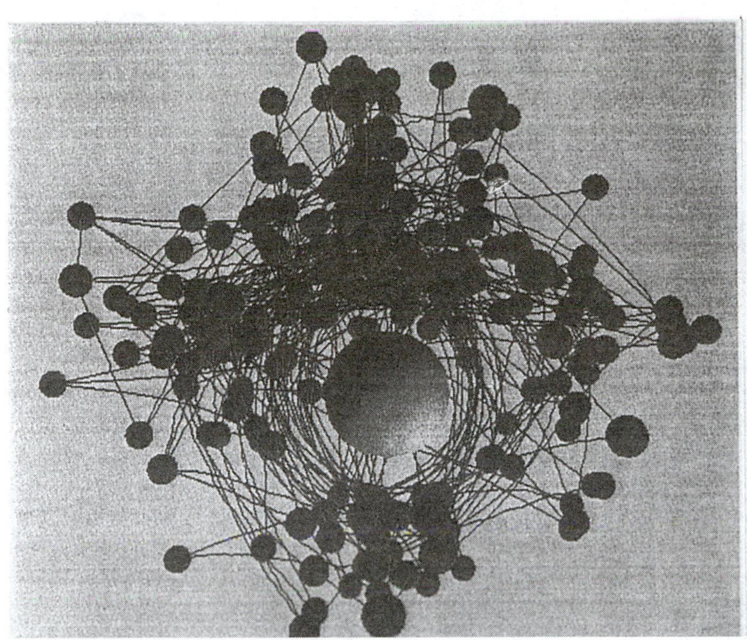

11 **Visual access distortion applied to a central node in a random graph. Note how the edges also curve away from the focal node.**

Arbitrary graphs

While we chose simple grid graphs to clearly reveal patterns in the distortion techniques, their effectiveness is not limited to this type of 3D grid layout. Figure 11 shows a polar graph layout that positions nodes by randomizing the magnitude of both the radius and angles. This image shows both access displacement and focal magnification. The displacement function applied to the nodes only can leave edges cutting across the focal node. In Figure 11 visual access distortion applied along the length of the edges curves them away from the line of sight, leaving a clear view of the focus.

Figure 3, row 5

The fifth and final row of the visual comparison chart (Figure 3) applies visual access distortion to the four 2D approaches, in each case successfully exposing the focus in context. Here the magnification component from each column's 2D distortion pattern is applied relative to the data, resulting in a range of node shapes and sizes. The displacement is then provided by visual access distortion applied relative to the viewer. Even in cases where the magnification has completely occluded the central focus node, applying the visual access distortion clears a line of sight to the focus.

In row 5, columns 1 and 2, the space-filling orthogonal approach and the graduated sine function had completely occluded the central focus node (see row 2, columns 1 and 2), virtually creating a solid. Similarly, with the radial Gaussian distortion (see row 2, column 3), the central focal node is practically obscured by its neighbors, since they also are magnified, though to a lesser degree. In all these cases visual access distortion provides visibility of the central focus.

In the case of the orthogonal step function, if you don't apply the distortion's displacement aspects, the artificial clusters are not generated (compare row 2, column 4 to row 5, column 4). The actual focus is magnified, while the entire context remains undisturbed. Here, applying visual access distortion achieves the desired focal visibility while minimally disturbing context.

Discussion

Distinguishing between data or viewer relative magnification or displacement patterns offers new flexibility in applying these techniques.

Browsing

In practice we most frequently use visual access distortion by itself—displacement only. If the focal node requires magnification, we use a simple step function, magnifying the chosen nodes only. By itself visual access distortion allows in-context browsing of a 3D display. With magnification it provides detail-in-context viewing.

A focal point can be either data objects or locations in space. When the focal point is an object, we apply visual access distortion from the viewpoint to the object's center. Browsing can involve sequential selection of objects or nodes. Alternatively, a location in space can set the end point of the line of sight cleared. The user can interactively control this line-segment-of-sight, creating a dynamic probe that moves fluidly through the space.

In browsing a 3D display, the user can select focal type and position as well as which distortion method to use for displacement, magnification, and access. During visual exploration each item is shifted out of the line of sight and then back into its original position. This motion provides effective visual feedback about the context and relative positions of the individual data items.

Other variations

Separating the magnification and displacement functions opens up possibilities for many new distortion viewing variations for 2D data as well. Figure 12 (next page) shows a sampling. The displacement function in the top row is nonlinear orthogonal, as in the second column of Figure 3. In Figure 12 the top row left uses radial Gaussian magnification, and the top row right uses step magnification. In the second row of Figure 12

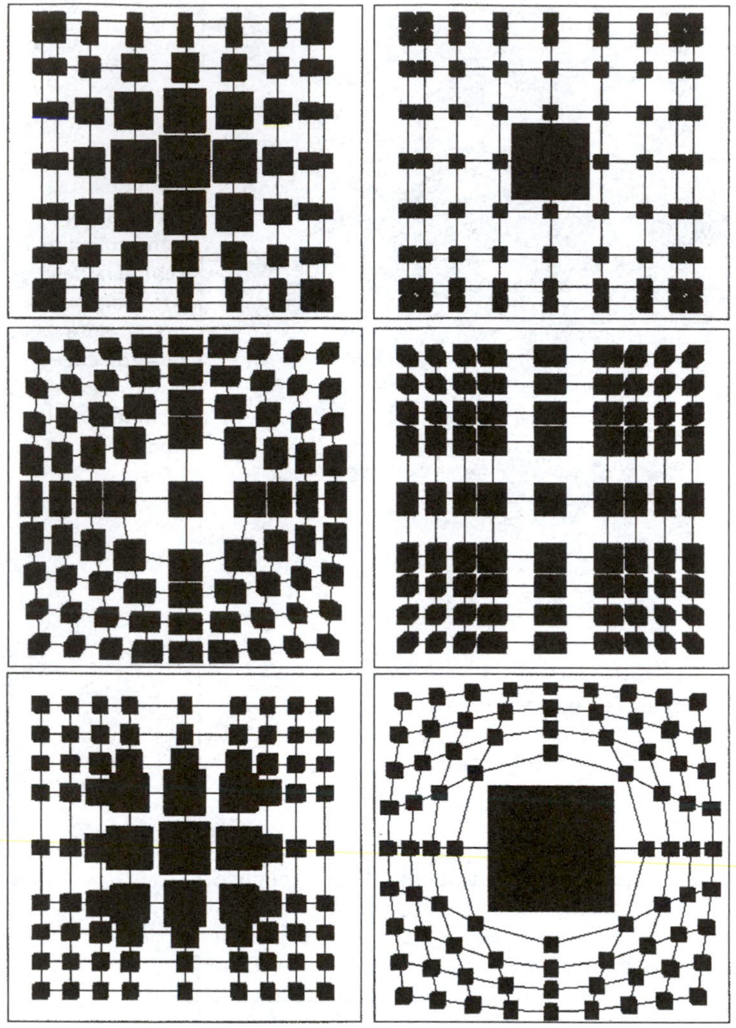

12 Additional distortion variations.

both images use a nonlinear (sine) magnification curve: radial Gaussian displacement on the left and orthogonal displacement on the right. The bottom row shows radial Gaussian magnification with orthogonal displacement on the left and step magnification with radial displacement on the right.

The last pattern (step-radial) in Figure 12 is currently used as part of Shrimp Views.[17] The others have not yet been explored in actual applications. Using distinct functions for magnification and distortion may improve finding a good match between a distortion viewing approach and the particular information and task at hand.

Conclusions

Future plans for visual access distortion include applying the ideas presented here to both general 3D graph structures and to solid 3D data. We also intend to investigate the potential of perceptual cues (3D grids, color and shading, stereo display) to reveal the nature of the distortions when applied to more general data sets.

Presumably, the availability of this type of access will allow fuller use of the third positional variable. While a 3D computational display will still resolve to its 2D projection when movement stops, being able to interactively shift objects to see behind them will make it possible to plan spatial organization with more freedom. ■

Acknowledgments

Thanks to the editors and reviewers for their comments and direction and to Anne Grbavec for recent help and encouragement. This research was supported by graduate scholarships and research and equipment grants from the Natural Sciences and Engineering Research Council of Canada, Forest Renewal British Columbia, and British Columbia Science Council. Thanks also to the Algorithms Lab, Graphics and Multimedia Research Lab, and School of Computing Science, Simon Fraser University.

References

1. C. Ware, D. Hui, and G. Franck, "Visualizing Object-Oriented Software in Three Dimensions," *Cascon 93 Proc.*, IBM's Center for Advanced Studies, Toronto, Canada, 1993, pp. 612-620.
2. G.W. Furnas, "Generalized Fisheye Views," *Human Factors in Computing Systems: CHI 86 Conf. Proc.*, ACM Press, New York, 1986, pp. 16-23.
3. R. Spence and M. Apperley, "Database Navigation: An Office Environment for the Professional," *Behavior and Information Tech.*, Vol. 1, No. 1, 1982, pp. 43-54.
4. L. Bartram et al., "The Continuous Zoom: A Constrained Fisheye Technique for Viewing and Navigating Large Information Spaces," *UIST 95: Proc. ACM Symp. on User Interface Software and Tech.*, ACM Press, New York, 1995, pp. 207-216.
5. M. Sarkar and M.H. Brown, "Graphical Fisheye Views," *Comm. ACM*, Vol. 37, No. 12, 1994, pp. 73-84.
6. M.S.T. Carpendale, D.J. Cowperthwaite, and F.D. Fracchia, "Three-Dimensional Pliable Surfaces: For Effective Presentation of Visual Information," *UIST: Proc. ACM Symp. on User Interface Software and Tech.*, ACM Press, New York, 1995, pp. 217-226.
7. J.D. Mackinlay, G.G. Robertson, and S.K. Card, "The Perspective Wall: Detail and Context Smoothly Integrated," *CHI 91 Conf. Proc.*, ACM Press, New York, 1991, pp. 173-180.
8. G. Robertson and J.D. Mackinlay, "The Document Lens," *UIST: Proc. ACM Symp. on User Interface Software and Tech.*, ACM Press, New York, 1993, pp. 101-108.
9. K.M. Fairchild et al., "Three-Dimensional Graphic Representations of Large Knowledge Bases," *Cognitive Science and its Applications for Human-Computer Interaction*, Lawerence Erlbaum Assoc., Hillsdale, N.J., 1988, pp. 201-234.
10. D.A. Mitra, "A Fisheye Presentation Strategy: Aircraft Maintenance Data," *Human-Computer Interaction: Interact 90*, Lawerence Erlbaum Associates, Hillsdale, N.J., 1990, pp. 875-880.
11. G.W. Furnas and B.B. Bederson, "Space-Scale Diagrams: Understanding Multiscale Interfaces," *CHI 95: Proc. ACM Conf. on Human-Computer Interaction*, ACM Press, New York, 1995, pp. 234-241.

12. M.S.T. Carpendale et al., *Exploring Distinct Aspects of the Distortion Viewing Paradigm,* Tech. Report TR 97-08, School of Computing Science, Simon Fraser University, Burnaby, B.C., Canada, March 1997.
13. Y.K. Leung and M.D. Apperley, "A Review and Taxonomy of Distortion-Oriented Presentation Techniques," *ACM Trans. on CHI*, Vol. 1, No. 2, 1994, pp. 126-160.
14. K. Misue and K. Sugiyama, "Multi-Viewpoint Perspective Display Methods: Formulation and Application to Compound Digraphs," *Human Aspects in Computing: Design and Use of Interactive Systems and Information Management*, Elsevier Science Publishers, Amsterdam, 1991, pp. 834-838.
15. K. Kaugers, J. Reinfelds, and A. Brazma, "A Simple Algorithm for Drawing Large Graphs on Small Screens," *Graph Drawing 94,* Lecture Notes in Computer Science, Springer-Verlag, Berlin, 1994, pp. 278-282.
16. M. Sarkar et al., "Stretching the Rubber Sheet: A Metaphor for Viewing Large Layouts on Small Screens," *UIST: Proc. ACM Symp. on User Interface Software and Tech.*, ACM Press, New York, 1993, pp. 81-91.
17. M.A. Storey and H.A. Muller, "Graph Layout Adjustment Strategies," *Graph Drawing 95*, Lecture Notes in Computer Science, Springer-Verlag, Berlin, 1995 pp. 487-499.
18. Y.K. Leung, "Human-Computer Interaction Techniques for Map-Based Diagrams," *Designing and Using Human-Computer Interfaces and Knowledge-Based Systems*, G. Salvendy and M. Smith, eds., Elsevier Science Publishers, Amsterdam, 1989, pp. 361-368.
19. J. Lamping, R. Rao, and P. Pirolli, "A Focus and Context Technique Based on Hyperbolic Geometry for Visualizing Large Hierarchies," *Proc. ACM Conf. Computer-Human Interaction* (CHI 95), ACM Press, New York, 1995, pp. 401-408.
20. K. Misue et al., "Layout Adjustment and the Mental Map," *J. Visual Languages and Computing*, Vol. 6, No. 2, 1995, pp. 183-210.
21. T. Keahey and E. Robertson, "Techniques for Nonlinear Magnification Transformations," *InfoVis 96: Proc. IEEE Conf. on Information Visualization*, IEEE Computer Soc. Press, Los Alamitos, Calif., 1996, pp. 38-45.
22. L. Bartram et al., "Contextual Assistance in User Interfaces to Complex, Time Critical Systems: The Intelligent Zoom," *Proc. Graphics Interface 94*, Canadian Information Processing Society, Toronto, Canada, 1994, pp. 216-224.
23. M.S.T. Carpendale, D.J. Cowperthwaite, and F.D. Fracchia, "Distortion Viewing Techniques for 3D Data," *InfoVis 96: Proc. IEEE Conf. on Information Visualization*, IEEE Computer Soc. Press, Los Alamitos, Calif., 1996, pp. 46-53.

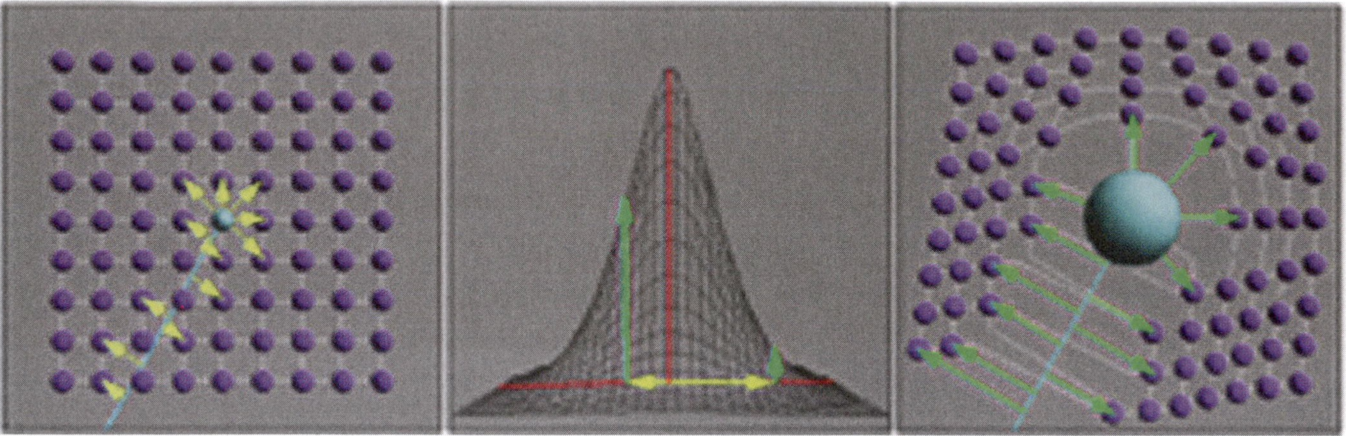

FIGURE 8

Cross-section views illustrate the visual access distortion algorithm: calculating the direction and distance from line of sight (left), calculating the displacement (center), and displacing the occluding objects (right).

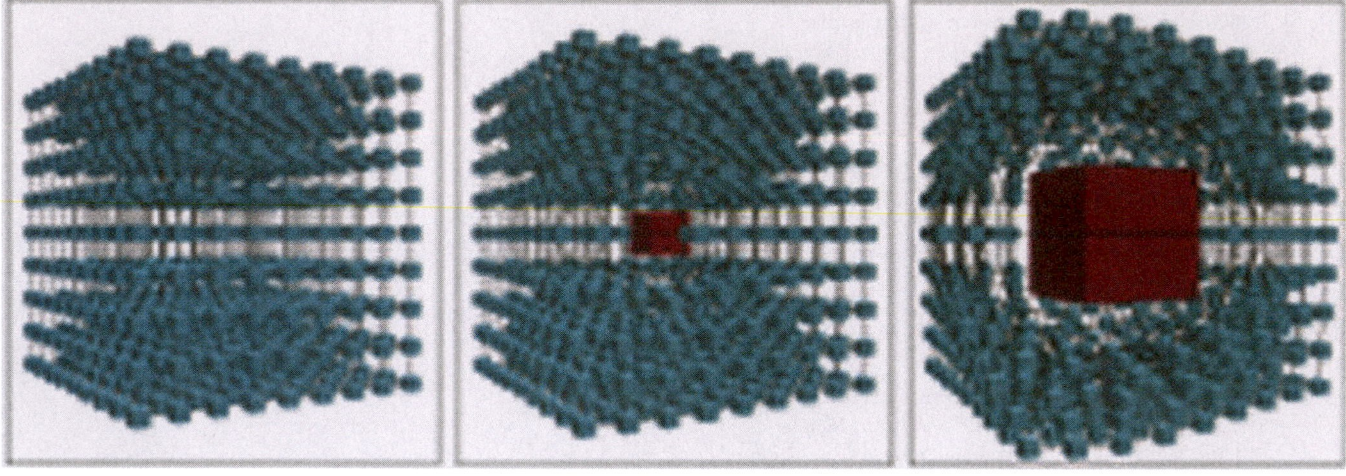

FIGURE 9

This series shows Gaussian visual access distortion applied progressively to the 3D grid.

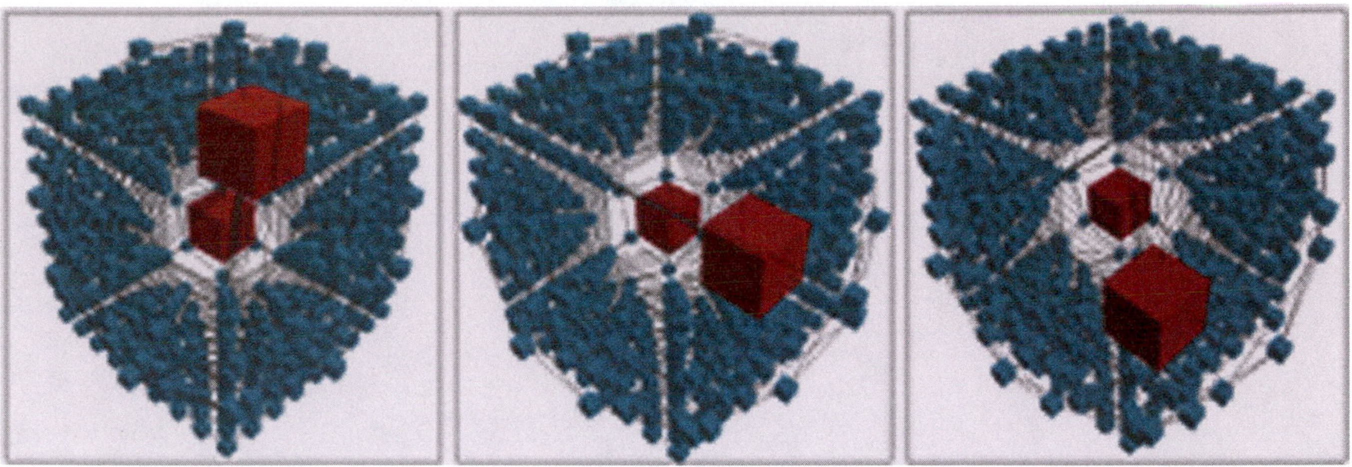

FIGURE **10**

Even when the two foci are in line with the viewpoint, both remain visible because the distortion function from the furthest focus affects all occluding objects, including other foci.

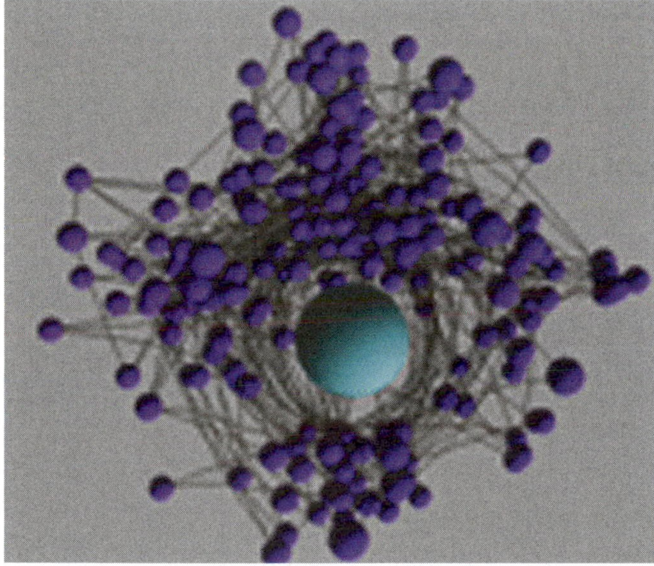

FIGURE **11**

Visual access distortion applied to a central node in a random graph. Note how the edges also curve away from the focal node.

4.4 Alternate Geometry

Previous papers in this chapter featured dynamic visualizations that present focus + context simultaneously. The paper in this section proposes that the space itself be distorted so as to have an intrinsic focus + context character by using a noneuclidean geometry. As the user moves around in the space, a virtual camera follows and constantly re-projects the view onto euclidean space on the screen. The differences between the geometries come out as stretching and squeezing as the user moves position or moves objects. We have already seen one method of achieving a similar effect—the use of 3D perspective to achieve focus + context. Lamping and Rao (1996 ●) use a projection of hyperbolic geometry into the 2D plane. In hyperbolic space, the space itself expands exponentially, so it is a good place to lay out trees, which also expand exponentially. Dragging part of a tree visualization to the center (or in one version, the left) of the display area gives it the maximum magnification. Parts of the visualization farther away from this point get progressively smaller (and at a rate much faster than ordinary perspective). Their system allows the user to browse quickly around large hierarchical structures.

Munzner and colleagues (1997; 1996) have created a 3D hyperbolic browser. The leaves of trees are projected onto the surface of a sphere (see Figure 4.5). Again, as users drag a part of the tree to the focal area, it gets much larger, and more distant parts of the tree appear on the sphere surface. Munzner claims to be able to explore trees up to 20,000 nodes.

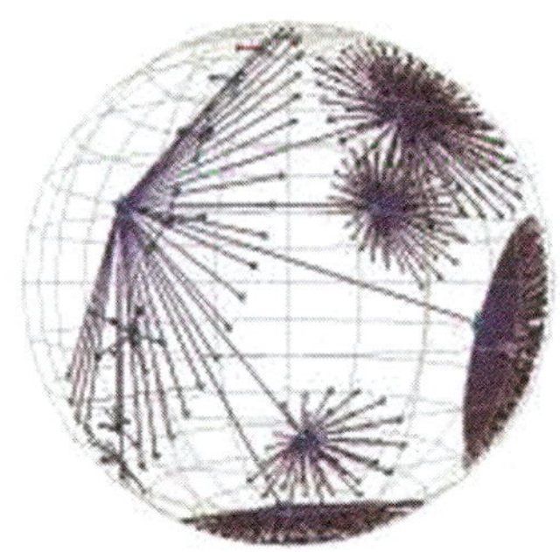
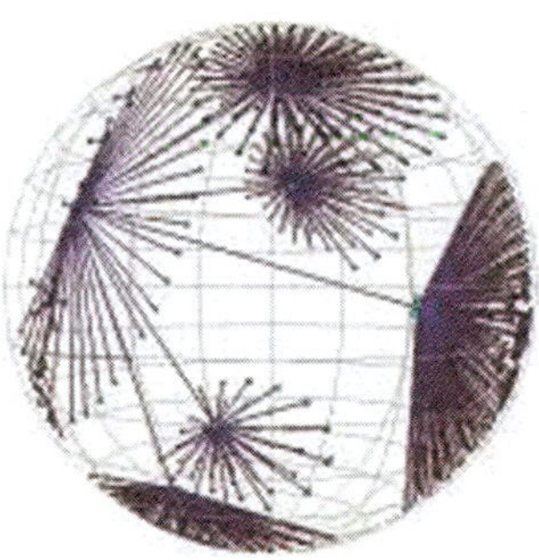
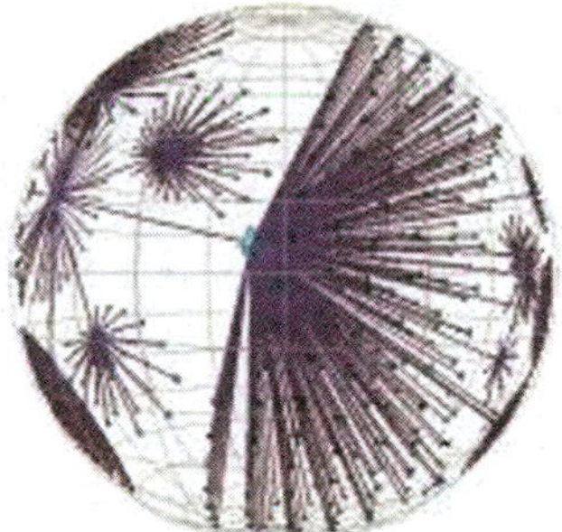
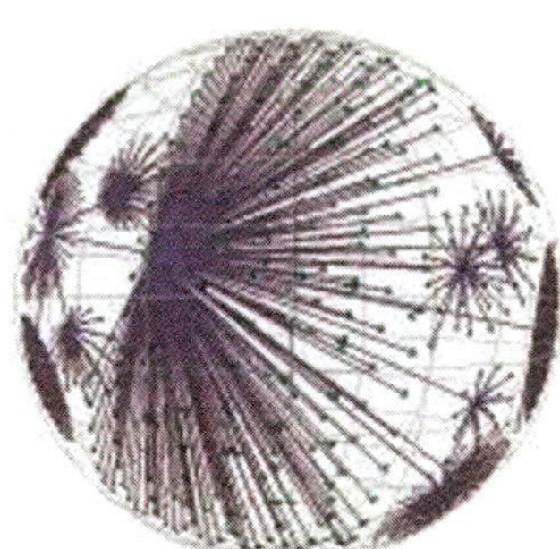

FIGURE **4.5**

Layout of a directed graph as a tree in 3D hyperbolic space. The sequence of images shows how more of the tree is revealed as the user moves to another part of the space. (Munzner, 1997, Figure 4).

The Hyperbolic Browser: A Focus+Context Technique for Visualizing Large Hierarchies.

John Lamping and Ramana Rao
Xerox Palo Alto Research Center
3333 Coyote Hill Road
Palo Alto, CA 94304
<lamping, rao>@parc.xerox.com

September 5, 1995

Abstract

We present a new focus+context technique based on hyperbolic geometry for visualizing and manipulating large hierarchies. Our technique assigns more display space to a portion of the hierarchy while still embedding it in the context of the entire hierarchy. We lay out the hierarchy in a uniform way on a hyperbolic plane and map this plane onto a display region. The chosen mapping provides a fisheye distortion that supports a smooth blending of focus and context. We have developed effective procedures for manipulating the focus using pointer clicks as well as interactive dragging and for smoothly animating transitions across such manipulation. Enhancements to the core mechanisms provide support for multiple foci, control of the tradeoff between node density and node display space, and for visualizing graphs by transforming them into trees.

KEYWORDS: Hierarchy Display, Information Visualization, Fisheye Display, Focus+Context Technique.

1 Introduction

In the last few years, Information Visualization research has explored the application of interactive graphics and animation technology to visualizing and making sense of larger information sets than would otherwise be practical [17]. An important aspect of this work has been the development of focus+context techniques for various classes of information structures, for example, hierarchical [18], chronological [11], calendar [12], and tabular information [15]. In these techniques, a detailed view of portion of an information set is blended with a view of the overall structure of the set typically using some kind of "fisheye" distortion of the entire structure. In addition, manipulation operations for controlling the mapping and navigating around

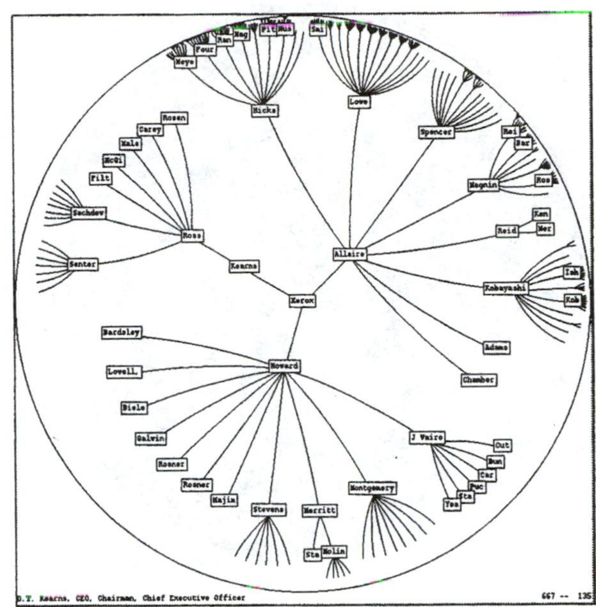

Figure 1: A partial organization chart of Xerox (circa 1988).

the structures are typically provided. In this paper, we present a new focus+context technique, called the hyperbolic browser for visualizing and manipulating large hierarchies.

The hyperbolic browser, illustrated in Figure 1, was originally inspired by the Escher woodcut shown in Figure 2. Two properties of the figures are salient: first, components diminish in size as they move outwards, and second, there is an exponential growth in the number of components with increasing radius. These properties—fisheye distortion and the ability to uniformly embed an exponentially growing structure—are the aspects of this construction (the Poincaré mapping of the hyperbolic plane) that originally attracted our attention.

The hyperbolic browser initially displays a tree with its root at the center, but the display can be smoothly transformed to bring other nodes into focus, as illustrated in Figure 3. In all cases, the amount of space available to a node falls off as a continuous function of its distance in the tree from the node in focus. Thus the context always includes several generations of parents, siblings, and children, making it easier for the user to explore the hierarchy without getting lost.

The hyperbolic browser supports effective interaction with much larger hierarchies than conventional hierarchy viewers and complements the strengths of other novel tree browsers. In a 600 pixel by 600 pixel window, a standard 2-d hierarchy browser can typically display 100 nodes (w/ 3 character text strings). The hyperbolic browser can display 1000 nodes of which about the 50 nearest the focus can show from 3 to dozens of characters of text. Thus the hyperbolic browser can display up to 10 times as many nodes while providing more effective navigation around the hierarchy. The scale advantage is obtained by the distortion of the

Figure 2: Original inspiration for the hyperbolic browser. Circle Limit IV (Heaven and Hell), 1960, (c) 1994 M.C. Escher / Cordon Art – Baarn – Holland. All rights reserved. Printed with permission.

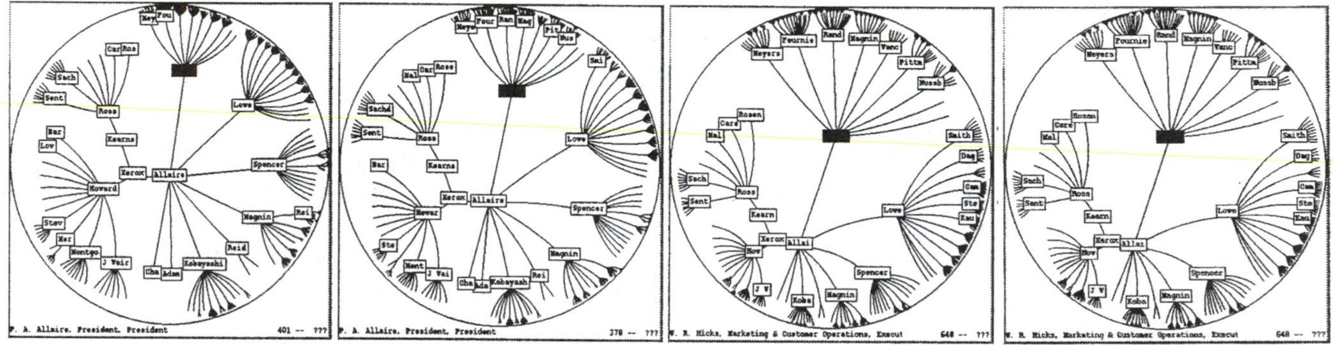

Figure 3: Clicking on the blackened node brings it into focus at the center.

elements of the tree display according to their distance from the focus, while easy navigation is obtained by interactive mechanisms for controlling the target area of focus.

Our approach is based on hyperbolic geometry [3, 13], though fortunately it doesn't require users to understand hyperbolic geometry. The essence of the approach is to lay out the hierarchy on the hyperbolic plane and map this plane onto a display region. On the hyperbolic plane (a construct of a non-Euclidean geometry), parallel lines diverge away from each other. This leads to the convenient property that the circumference of a circle grows exponentially with its radius, which means that exponentially more space is available with increasing distance. Thus hierarchies—which tend to expand exponentially with depth—can be laid out uniformly in hyperbolic space, such that the distance between parent and child and between siblings (as measured in the hyperbolic geometry) is approximately the same everywhere in the hierarchy.

While the hyperbolic plane is a mathematical abstraction, it can be mapped in a natural way onto the Euclidean unit disk, which provides a basis for display on conventional screens. The mapping focuses on one point on the hyperbolic plane by using more of the disk for portions of the plane near that point than on other portions of the plane; remote parts of the hyperbolic plane get miniscule amounts of space near the edge of the disk. Moving the focus point over the hyperbolic plane—equivalent to translating the hierarchy on the hyperbolic plane—provides a mechanism for controlling which portion of the structure receives the most space without compromising the illusion of viewing the entire hyperbolic plane. Other transformations of the mapping from the hyperbolic plane to the display can yield other effects including changing the relative amount of the display dedicated to the focus nodes and providing multiple foci.

Motion in the hyperbolic plane can yield unintuitive results, but these problems can be avoided by careful design. We have developed effective procedures for manipulating the focus using pointing and dragging and for smoothly animating transitions across such manipulation.

The performance requirements of the hyperbolic browser are relatively modest and can be achieved on today's median personal computer. In particular, this is true because our approach supports incremental layout and allows bounding the maximum cost of redisplay by truncating redisplay of nodes below a given resolution limit. Our original Commonlisp prototype runs adequately on low-end Unix workstations by using rendering degradation during animation. A portable C++ implementation (which supports Unix/X, Windows 3.1, and Windows NT) achieves frame rates of under 50 milliseconds for 1000 node tree on an Iris Indigo and a Pentium PC.

2 Problem And Related Work

Many hierarchies, such as organization charts or directory structures, are too large to display in their entirety on a computer screen. The conventional display approach maps all the hierarchy into a region that is larger than the display and then uses scrolling to move around the region. This approach has the problem that the user can't see the relationship of the visible portion of the tree to the entire structure (without auxiliary views). It would be useful to be able to see the entire hierarchy while focusing on any particular part so that the relationship of parts to the whole can be seen and so that focus can be moved to other parts in a smooth and continuous way.

A number of focus+context display techniques have been introduced in the last fifteen years to address the needs of many types of information structures [10, 21]. Many of these focus+context techniques, including the document lens [19], the perspective wall [11], and the work of Sarkar et al [20, 22], could be applied to browsing trees laid out using conventional

2-d layout techniques. The problem is that there is no satisfactory conventional 2-d layout of a large tree, because of its exponential growth. If leaf nodes are to be given adequate spacing, then nodes near the root must be placed very far apart, obscuring the high level tree structure, and leaving no nice way to display the context of the entire tree.

The Cone Tree[18] modifies the above approach by embedding the tree in a three dimensional space. This embedding of the tree has joints that can be rotated to bring different parts of the tree into focus. This requires currently expensive 3D animation support. Furthermore, trees with more than approximately 1000 nodes are difficult to manipulate. The hyperbolic browser is two dimensional and has relatively modest computational needs, making it potentially useful on a broad variety of platforms.

Another novel tree browsing technique is treemaps [7] which allocates the entire space of a display area to the nodes of the tree by dividing the space of a node among itself and its descendants according to properties of the node. The space allocated to each node is then filled according to the same or other properties of the node. This technique utilizes space efficiently and can be used to look for values and patterns amongst a large collection of values which agglomerate hierarchically, however it tends to obscure the hierarchical structure of the values and provides no way of focusing on one part of a hierarchy without losing the context.

Some conventional hierarchy browsers prune or filter the tree to allow selective display of portions of the tree that the user has indicated. This still has the problem that the context of the interesting portion of the tree is not displayed. Furnas [4] introduced a technique whereby nodes in the tree are assigned an interest level based on distance from a focus node (or its ancestors). Degree of interest can then be used to selectively display the nodes of interest and their local context. Though this technique is quite powerful, it still does not provide a solution to the problem of displaying the entire tree. In contrast, the hyperbolic browser is based on an underlying geometry that allows for smooth blending of focus and context and continuous repositioning of the focus.

Bertin[2] illustrates that a radial layout of the tree could be uniform by shrinking the size of the nodes with their distance from the root. The use of hyperbolic geometry provides an elegant way of doing this while addressing the problems of navigation. The fractal approach of Koike and Yoshihara [8] offers a similar technique for laying out trees. In particular, they have explored an implementation that combines fractal layout with Cone Tree-like technique. The hyperbolic browser has the benefit that focusing on a node shows more of the node's context in all directions (i.e. ancestors, siblings, and descendants). The fractal view has a more rigid layout (as with other multiscale interfaces) in which much of this context is lost as the viewpoint is moved to lower levels of the tree.

Hopkins' Pseudo Scientific Visualizer [6] also exploits radial layout and diminishing scale. A tree is laid out by laying out the children of a node at an equal distance in a circle around the node and recursing to each child with a smaller distance for its children. All graphical elements (e.g. fonts, glyphs) are scaled during the recursion. This technique can be extended to support interactive navigation by descending into any subtree and scaling it up to fill the window. However, further design work is needed to provide ancestral context during descent into the tree.

There have been a number of projects to visualize hyperbolic geometry, including an animated video of moving through hyperbolic space [5]. The emphasis of the hyperbolic browser

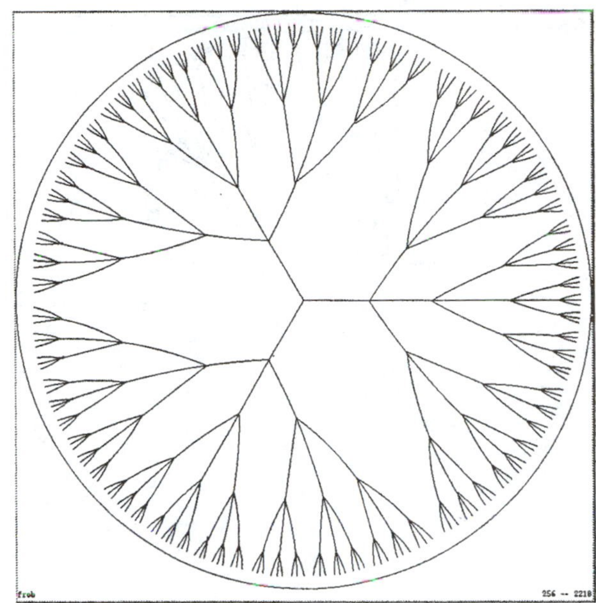

Figure 4: A uniform tree of depth 5 and branching factor 3 (364 nodes).

is a particular exploitation of hyperbolic space for information visualization. We don't expect the user to know or care about hyperbolic geometry.

3 Hyperbolic Browser Basics

The essential operations of the hyperbolic browser can be understood without detailed understanding of hyperbolic geometry. The mathematical details of the the implementation are deferred to a later section. The hyperbolic browser *lays out* a tree on the hyperbolic plane and then *maps* the structure to the Euclidean plane during the display operation. *Change of focus* is handled by changing the mapping from the hyperbolic plane to the Euclidean plane. Thus, node positions in the hyperbolic plane need not be altered during focus manipulation. Yet, the mapping is inexpensive. Further, it need be applied only to nodes currently visible at screen resolution. Thus display cost converges to a constant.[1] Space for displaying *node information* is also computed during layout and mapped through the mapping, again avoiding exhaustive update during change of focus.

[1] Our performance measurements using uniform trees on our portable C++ implementation shows a logarithm growth in display time up to several thousand nodes after which display time approaches a constant.

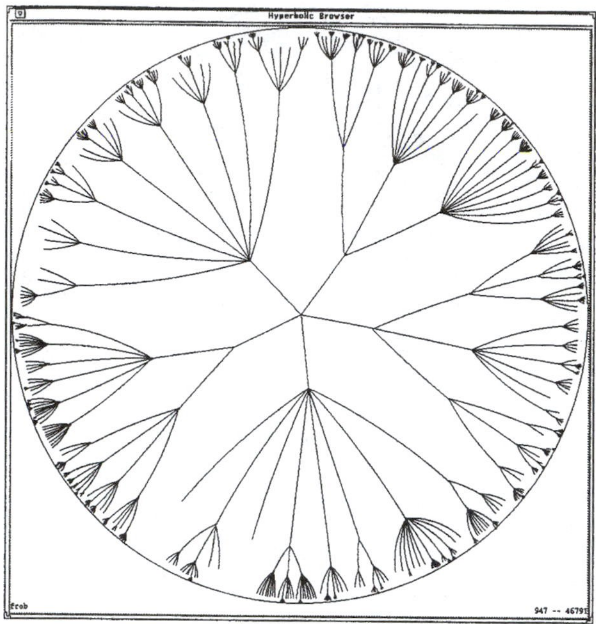

Figure 5: The initial layout of a tree with 1004 nodes using a Poisson distribution for number of children. The origin of the tree is in the center.

3.1 Layout

Laying a tree out in the hyperbolic plane is easier than on a euclidean plane, because the circumference and area of a circle grow exponentially with its radius. There is lots of room. Our recursive algorithm lays out each node based on local information. A node is allocated a wedge of the hyperbolic plane, angling out from itself, to put its descendants in. It places all its children along an arc in that wedge, at an equal distance from itself, and far enough out so that the children are some minimum distance apart from each other. Each of the children then gets a sub-wedge for its descendants. Because of the way parallel lines diverge in hyperbolic geometry, each child will typically get a wedge that spans about as big an angle as its parent's wedge, yet none of the children's wedges will overlap. To compute children's positions in terms of parent's positions, the layout routine navigates through the hyperbolic plane in terms of operations like moving some distance or turning through some angle. These operations are provided by the underlying implementation of the hyperbolic plane.

Figure 4 shows what the layout of a uniform tree looks like. Notice how the children of each node span about the same angle, except near the root, where a larger wedge was available initially. To get a more compact layout for non-uniform trees, we modify this simple algorithm slightly, so that siblings that themselves have lots of children get a larger wedge than siblings that don't (the wedge size grows logarithmically). This effect can be seen in Figure 5, where, for example, the five children of the root get different amounts of space. This tends to decrease

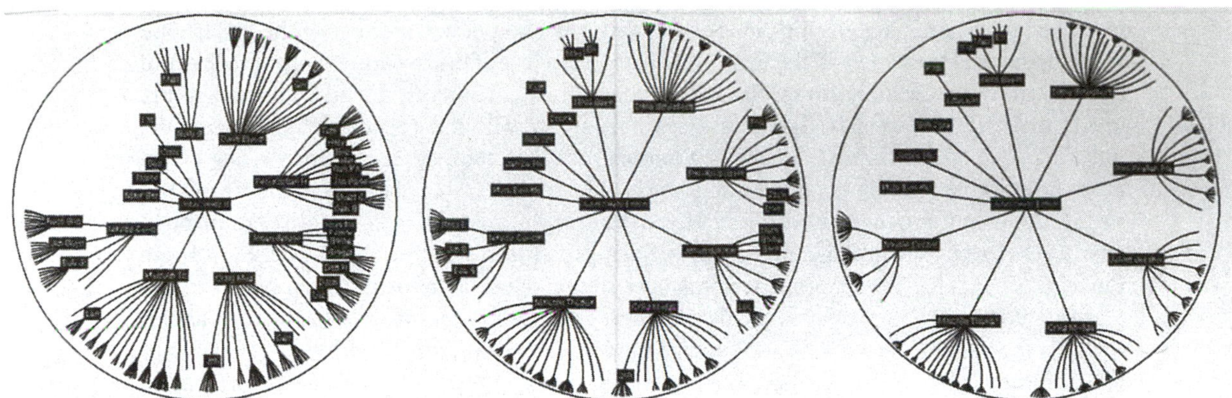

Figure 6: Layout using small, medium, and large values for minimum spacing between siblings.

the variation of the distances between grandchildren and their grandparent.

The layout routine has the convenient property that the layout of a node depends only on the layout of its parent and on the node structure of two (or maybe three) generations starting from the parent. In particular, there are no global considerations in the layout; the roominess of hyperbolic space renders that unnecessary. As a result, the layout need not be done all at once, but can be done incrementally. For example, if a user requests to browse a directory structure, there is no need to traverse the entire structure before displaying anything. Instead, the nodes nearest the root can be layed out and displayed, and then more nodes added as more of the structure is traversed. If the user adjusts the focus, the traversal can give priority to the part of the directory near the focus, so that the region in focus is always populated.

An important parameter to the layout routine is the minimum spacing (in the hyperbolic plane) between siblings. A small value for this parameter, as seen on the left side of Figure 6, results in nodes being relatively close to each other, and with the children of a node subtending a rather small angle. This also puts relatively more nodes in the focus region, but gives each less space. A large value has the opposite effect, as seen on right side of Figure 6. The preferred value depends, in part, on the tradeoff between showing overall tree structure vs. more information about nodes.

Another option in layout (in contrast to all examples so far illustrated) is to use less than the entire 360 degree circle for spreading out the children of the root node. With this option, children of the root could all be put in one direction, for example to the right or below, as in conventional layouts. An example of this option, discussed below, appears in Figure 10.

3.2 Mapping

Once the tree has been laid out on the hyperbolic plane, it must be mapped in some way to the ordinary Euclidean plane for display (we can barely imagine the hyperbolic plane, not to mention see it). There are two canonical ways of mapping the hyperbolic plane to the Euclidean plane. Both map the hyperbolic plane to the unit disk and put one vicinity of the hyperbolic plane in focus at the center of the disk while having the rest of the hyperbolic plane fade off in a perspective-like fashion toward the edge of the disk. One mapping, the projective mapping, or Klein model, preserves straightness: lines in the hyperbolic plane become chords across the unit disk. The other mapping, called the Poincaré model, is conformal: it preserves angles but maps lines in the hyperbolic space into arcs on the unit disk (as can be seen in the figures).

The Poincaré model worked more effectively for our purposes. Points that are mapped near to the edge by the Poincaré model get mapped almost right on the edge by the Klein model. As a result, nodes more than a link or two from the node in focus get almost no screen real-estate, thus limiting the context. Furthermore, the Klein mapping severely distorts angles towards the edge of the disk. The Poincaré model, in contrast, not only does a better job of dividing display space between focus and context, but also preserves angles and local shapes, so that structures throughout the display are easier to interpret and compare.

3.3 Change of Focus

The user can change focus either by clicking on any visible point to bring it into focus at the center, or by dragging any visible point interactively to any other position. In either case, the rest of the display transforms appropriately. Regions that approach the center become magnified, while regions that were in the center shrink as they move toward the edge. Figure 7 shows the same tree as Figure 5 with a different focus. The root has been shifted to the right, putting more focus on the nodes that were toward the left.

Changes of focus are implemented by adjusting the focus of the mapping from the hyperbolic plane to the Euclidean plane. We actually think of this in terms of rigidly moving the hyperbolic plane under the focus, rather than the equivalent motion of the focus over the hyperbolic plane. A change of focus to a new node, for example, is implemented by a translation in the hyperbolic plane that moves the selected node to the location that is mapped to the center of the disk. Thus, there is never a need to repeat the layout process. Rather the original node positions are rigidly transformed and mapped to the Euclidean plane during display.

To avoid loss of floating point precision across multiple transformations, we compose successive transformations into a single cumulative transformation, which we then apply to the positions determined in the original layout. Furthermore, since we only need the mapped positions of the nodes that will be displayed, the transformation is only computed for nodes whose display size will be at least a screen pixel. This yields a constant bound on redisplay computation, no matter how many nodes are in the tree. The implementation of translation can be fairly efficient, requiring about 20 floating point operations to translate a point and map it to the Euclidean plane, comparable to the cost of rendering a node on the screen.

3.4 Node Information

Another property of the Poincaré projection is that circles on the hyperbolic plane are mapped into circles on the Euclidean disk, though they will shrink in size the further they are from the origin. This can be used to identify screen space for displaying node information. We can compute a circle in the hyperbolic plane around each node that is guaranteed not to intersect

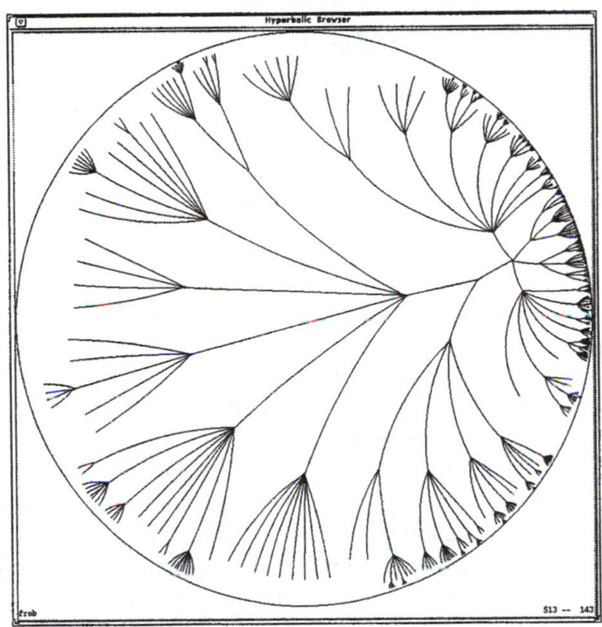

Figure 7: The same tree as in Figure 5 with focus on a node that was to the left and slightly below the origin.

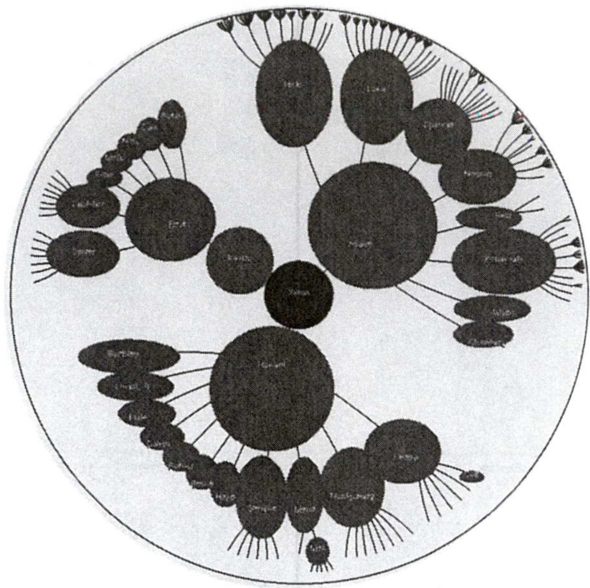

Figure 8: The regions available to nodes for displaying node information.

with the circle of any other node. When those circles are mapped onto the unit disk they provide a circular display region for each node of the tree in which to display a represenation of the node. The display regions can be used in conjunction with a facility that selects different representations for each node depending on the amount of space available. This could be used to implement a "zoom and bloom" space similar to that of the Pad systems [14, 1].

While the circle approach is very efficient, it does not make full use of the screen space, since significant parts of the display are not covered by any circle, especially when nodes have many children. A somewhat more expensive technique that does a better job of identifying screen space for displaying node information notes is based on calculating, during layout, the midway points in hyperbolic space between a node, its parent, its nearest siblings, and one of its children. These points are then mapped to the display space, and used to identify an elliptical display region for the node (shown in Figure 8). For convenience of the node display routines, the ellipses are always aligned with the axes, and given a slight horizontal bias. This computation is not exact, since it can lead to modest overlapping of display regions. However, it will typically be effective in practice, since it provides more node information without interfering with understanding of the structure.

Some applications can tolerate even greater amounts of overlap. For example, the browser supports a "long text" mode in which all nodes beyond an allocated space threshold disregard their boundaries and display up to some maximum number of characters. Despite the overlapping of the text, this leads to more text being visible and discernible on the screen at once (see Figure 9).

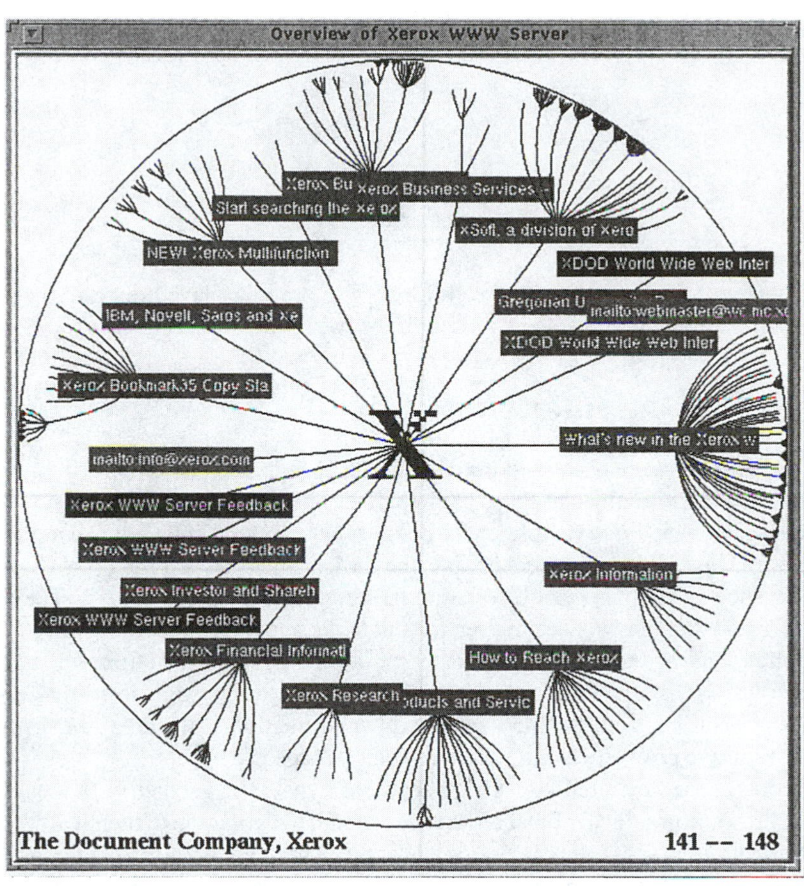

Figure 9: Long text mode with up to 25 characters displayed for each node that would normally display at least 2 characters.

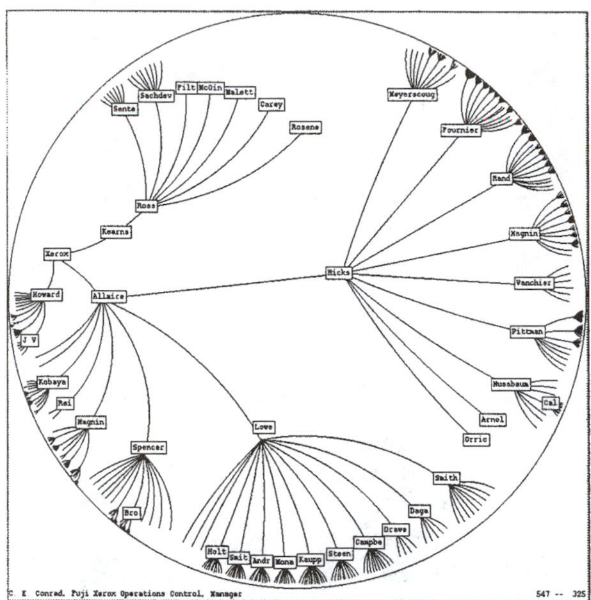

Figure 10: In right orientation mode, the children of the root are layed out only to its right, and the structure is rotated to display children of the focus node to its right.

4 Preserving Orientation

The use of hyperbolic space presented the challenging design problem of preserving a user's sense of orientation. Difficulties arise on the hyperbolic plane because objects tend to get rotated as they are moved. For example, most nodes rotate on the display during a pure translation. There is a line that doesn't rotate, but the farther nodes are on the display from that line, the more they rotate. This can be seen in the series of frames in Figure 3. The node labeled "Lowe", for example, whose children fan out to the upper right in the top frame ends up with its children fanning out to the right in the bottom frame. These rotations are reasonably intuitive for translations to or from the origin. But if drags near the edge of the disk are interpreted as translations between the the source and the destination of the drag, the display will do a counter-intuitive pirouette about the point being dragged.

This effect is caused by a fundamental property of hyperbolic geometry. In the usual Euclidean plane, if some graphical object is dragged around, but not rotated, then it always keeps its original orientation—not rotated. But this is *not* true in the hyperbolic plane. A series of translations forming a closed loop, each preserving the orientation along the line of translation, will, in general, cause a rotation. (In fact the amount of rotation is proportional to the area of the closed loop and is in the opposite direction to the direction the loop was traversed.) This leads to the counter-intuitive behavior that a user who moves the focus around the hierarchy can experience a different orientation each time they revisit some node, even though all they

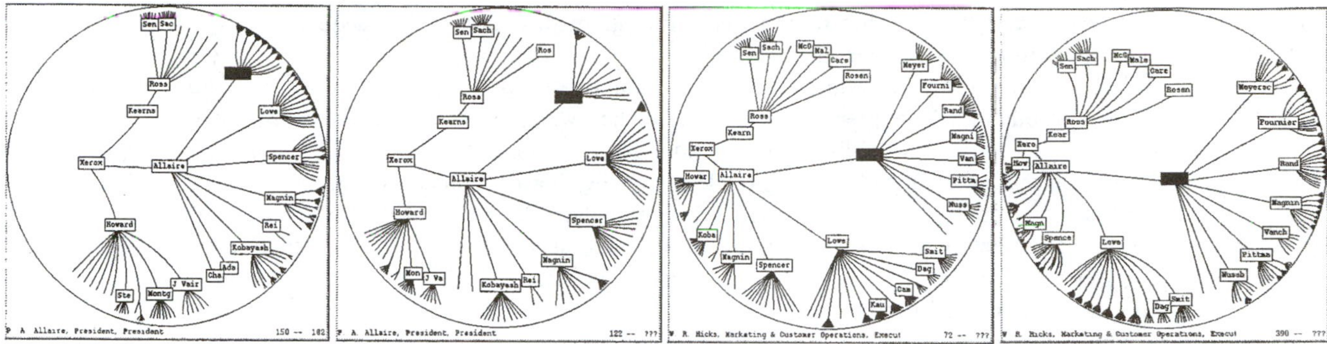

Figure 11: Animated transition with compromised rendering.

did was translations.

We address both of these problems by interpreting the user's manipulations as a combination of both the most direct translation between the points the user specifies and an additional rotation around the point moved, so that the manipulations and their cumulative effects are more intuitive. The key is to use the additional rotation to establish some property that the user can easily understand. From the user's perspective, drags and clicks move the point that the user is manipulating where they expect, while preserving some other intuitive property.

We have found two promising properties for guiding the added rotations. In one approach, rotations are added so that the original root node always keeps its original orientation on the display. In particular, the edges leaving it always leave in their original directions. Preserving the orientation of the root node also means that the node currently in focus also has the orientation it had in the original image. The transformation in Figure 3 works this way. It seems to give an intuitive behavior both for individual drags and for the cumulative effect of drags. In this approach, the user is typically not aware that rotation is being added.

The other approach doesn't attempt to preserve node orientation. Instead, when a node is brought to the focus, the display is rotated to have its children fan out in a canonical direction e.g. to the right. This is illustrated in Figure 10 and also in the animation sequence in Figure 11. This approach works best when the children of the root node are all laid out on one side, as also true in the two figures, so that the children of the root also fan out in the canonical direction when it is in focus.

5 Animated Transitions

Animated transitions between different views of a structure maintain object constancy and help the user assimilate the changes across views. The smooth continuous nature of the hyperbolic plane allows for performing smooth transitions of focus by rendering appropriate intermediate views.

Animation sequences are generated using the an "nth-root" of a transition transformation, i.e. the rigid transformation that applied n times will have the same effect as the original. Successive applications of the "nth-root" generate the intermediate frames. The sequences in Figure 3 and Figure 11 were generated this way.

Responsive display performance is crucial for animation and interactive dragging. This can be a problem for large hierarchies on standard hardware. We achieve quick redisplay by compromising on display quality during motion. These compromises provide options for use in a system that automatically adjusts rendering quality during animation, e.g. the Information Visualizer governor [16] or Pacers [23]. Fortunately, there are compromises that don't significantly affect the sense of motion. Figure 11 shows an animation sequence with the compromises active in the intermediate frames. Unless specifically looked for, the compromises typically go unnoticed during motion.

One compromise is to draw less of the fringe. Even the full quality display routine stops drawing the fringe once it gets below one pixel resolution. For animation, the pruning can be strengthened, so that descendants of nodes within some small border inside the edge of the disk are not drawn. This aggressively increases display performance, since the vast majority of nodes are very close to the edge. But it doesn't significantly degrade perceptual quality for a moving display, since those nodes occupy only a small fraction of the display, and not the part that the user is typically focusing on.

Another compromise is to draw lines, rather than arcs, which are expensive in the display environments we have been using. While arcs give a more pleasing and intuitive static display, they aren't as important during animation. This appears to be true for two reasons. The difference between arcs and lines isn't as apparent during motion. Furthermore, again particularly during motion, the user's attention tends to be focused near the center of the display, where the arcs are already almost straight.

One other possible compromise is to drop text during animation. We found this to be a significant distraction, however. And text display has not been a performance bottleneck.

6 Implementation

In this section, we present the details of the mathematics necessary to implement the hyperbolic browser. It is primarily of interest only to those interested in implementing our technique.

Representations Our implementation relies on representations for the hyperbolic plane, rigid transformations of the plane, and mappings from the plane to the unit disk. We represent a point in hyperbolic space by the corresponding point in the unit disk under the Poincaré mapping. Our representation thus directly encodes the mapping from the plane to the unit disk.[2] Points in the unit disk are represented as floating point complex numbers of magnitude less than 1.

[2] On graphics hardware that has fast support for 3×3 matrix multiplication, it might be faster to use the Klein model for the representation of the hyperbolic plane, as done in [5], because rigid transformations can then be expressed in terms of linear operations on homogeneous coordinates. Mapping to the display then requires computing the Poincaré mapping of points represented in the Klein model, which is just a matter of recomputing the distance from the origin according to $r_p = r_k/(1 + \sqrt{1 - r_k^2})$.

Rigid transformations of the hyperbolic plane are represented by circle preserving transformations of the unit disk. Any such transformation can be expressed as a complex function of z of the form

$$z_t = \frac{\theta z + P}{1 + \overline{P}\theta z}$$

Where P and θ are complex numbers, $|P| < 1$ and $|\theta| = 1$, and $\overline{P}$ is the complex conjugate of P. This transformation indicates a rotation by θ around the origin followed by moving the origin to P (and $-P$ to the origin).

Given a transformation, $< P, \theta >$ the inverse transformation (which is needed to map from display coordinates back into the hyperbolic plane) can be computed by:

$$P' = -\overline{\theta}P \qquad \theta' = \overline{\theta}$$

The composition of a transformation $< P_1, \theta_1 >$ followed by $< P_2, \theta_2 >$, is given by:

$$P = \frac{\theta_2 P_1 + P_2}{\theta_2 P_1 \overline{P_2} + 1} \qquad \theta = \frac{\theta_1 \theta_2 + \theta_1 \overline{P_1} P_2}{\theta_2 P_1 \overline{P_2} + 1}$$

Due to round-off error, the magnitude of the new θ may not be exactly 1. Accumulated errors in the magnitude of θ can lead to large errors when transforming points near the edge, so we always normalize the new θ to a magnitude of 1.

Layout The layout routine is structured as a recursion that takes a node and a wedge in which to lay out the node and its children. It places the node at the vertex of the wedge, computes a wedge for each child, and recursively calls itself on each child. The wedge is represented by the point at its vertex, the endpoint of its midline, and the angle from the midline to either edge of the wedge. The vertex and endpoint are represented by complex numbers. Since the endpoint is a point at infinity, its complex number has magnitude 1. For convenience of calculations, the endpoint is represented relative to the vertex, in the sense that the representation corresponds to where the endpoint would end up if the vertex were shifted to the origin.

The layout routine records the position of the vertex of the wedge as the position of the node. Then, if there are children, a simple procedure is to divide the angle of the wedge by the number of children, n, and subdivide the wedge into n equal sized wedges, each spanning that angle. The slightly more complicated procedure actually used in the figures gives different children different fractions of the wedge depending logarithmically on the number of children and grandchildren of each child

The children are placed in the middle of their subwedges at a distance computed by the formula

$$d = \sqrt{\left(\frac{(1-s^2)\sin(a)}{2s}\right)^2 + 1} - \frac{(1-s^2)\sin(a)}{2s}$$

where a is the angle between midline and edge of the subwedge and s is the desired distance between a child and the edge of its subwedge; we typically use a value of about 0.12 for s (the values used in Figure 6 are 0.06, 0.12, and 0.18 respectively). The result, d, is the necessary distance from parent to child. If the calculation of d results in a value less the s, we set d to s, to maintain a minimum spacing between parent and child. Both s and d are represented as the hyperbolic tangent of the distance in the hyperbolic plane. This form facilitates later operations in the Poincaré map, since it has the convenient property that a line segment on the unit disk with one end on the origin and extending the given amount represents a segment extending the represented distance in the hyperbolic plane.

Given a subwedge for a child, and the distance, d, to the child, the next step is to calculate a wedge inside the subwedge, with its vertex at the child, to use for the recursive call. Given the vertex, p, midline endpoint, m, and angle, a, of the subwedge, the corresponding parameters of the contained wedge that results from moving d into the subwedge can be calculated using the transformation apparatus:

$$\begin{aligned} p' &= \text{Trans}(dm, < p, 1 >) \\ m' &= \text{Trans}(\text{Trans}(m, < p, 1 >), < -p', 1 >) \\ a' &= \text{im}(\log(\text{Trans}(e^{ia}, < -d, 1 >))) \end{aligned}$$

where Trans is the transformation function described above, which takes a point and a transformation specification and returns the transformed point. The im(log(...)) in the formula for a' returns the angle corresponding to the complex number, doing the inverse of the conversion from angle to complex number done by the e^{ia} (these functions can be implemented using cos, sin, and arc tangent and complex number constructors and selector instead).

Display Node display involves recursing on the node structure. Starting from the root, the procedure draws a node's incoming link, recurses on its children, and finally draws the node. This procedure utilizes a "current transformation" which maps from the hyperbolic plane to the unit disk positions according to the current focus. The coordinates for drawing links and nodes are obtained by transforming the recorded positions and spacings of nodes by the current transformation and scaling the resulting unit disk coordinates to the actual display window size.

Links between nodes are drawn as arcs (corresponding to straight lines in the hyperbolic plane) to convey a sense of warping of the space and to preserve the angle near the node centers. The center of curvature of the arc that links two points represented by complex numbers a and b in the unit circle is given by

$$\begin{aligned} d &= \text{re}(a)\text{im}(b) - \text{re}(b)\text{im}(a) \\ c &= \frac{i}{2}\frac{(a(1+|b|^2) - b(1+|a|^2))}{d} \end{aligned}$$

In addition, if the quantity d is positive, then the arc from a to b goes clockwise around the circle. Otherwise it goes counterclockwise.

Interaction After layout, the recorded positions of the nodes are not changed, instead a current transformation is maintained for use during display. Initially, the current transformation is set to the identity transformation, $< 0, 1 >$. When the user clicks on a new position to be the focus, we compute a transformation that maps the indicated point on the hyperbolic plane to the origin. Similarly, when the user drags from one point to another, we compute a transformation that maps from the first indicated point to the second. In both cases, in orientation preserving mode, the orientation of the origin is preserved. The desired origin-preserving transformation can be calculated with:

$$\begin{aligned} a &= \text{Trans}(s, < -p, 1 >) \\ b &= \frac{\text{re}((e-a)(1+\overline{ae})) + \text{im}((e-a)(1-\overline{ae}))i}{1-|ae|^2} \\ T &= \text{Compose}(< -p, 1 >, < b, 1 >) \end{aligned}$$

where s is the starting point where the user first clicked, e is the ending point (either the origin or where the user ended their drag); and p is the point whose orientation is to be preserved (we use the image of the origin under the current transformation). Compose is transformation composition, defined earlier. T is the resulting transformation. This transformation is composed with the current transformation to get the new current transformation.

To provide a smooth animation between the current transformation and a new current transformation, a series of frames with transformations between the two are generated. Linear interpolation in disk coordinates can be used to compute the intermediate transformations, but we use a more sophisticated procedure involving calculation of the "nth root" of the transition transformation between the current and new transformations. The computation of the nth root of a transformation, $< P, \theta >$ is somewhat involved, with three cases. Different formulas apply in the different cases, but in addition some formulas are converted to equivalent forms to improve numerical stability. The procedure first computes:

$$d = 4|P|^2 - |\theta - 1|^2$$

Then depending on the value of d, one of following three intermediate computations is performed:

if $d > 0$

$$\begin{aligned} t &= \frac{\sqrt{d}}{|\theta+1|} \\ r &= \frac{\tanh\left(\frac{\text{argtanh}(t)}{n}\right)}{t} \\ a &= r^2 \frac{|\theta-1|^2}{|\theta+1|^2} \\ b &= r\sqrt{\frac{1+\frac{|\theta-1|^2}{|\theta+1|^2}}{1+a}} \end{aligned}$$

if $d = 0$

$$\begin{aligned} a &= \frac{1}{n^2}\frac{|\theta-1|^2}{|\theta+1|^2} \\ b &= \frac{1}{n}\sqrt{\frac{1+\frac{|\theta-1|^2}{|\theta+1|^2}}{1+a}} \end{aligned}$$

if $d < 0$

$$\begin{aligned} t &= \frac{\sqrt{-d}}{|\theta+1|} \\ a &= \frac{\tan^2\left(\frac{\arctan(t)}{n}\right)|\theta-1|^2}{-d} \\ b &= \frac{1}{|\theta-1|}\sqrt{\frac{4a}{(1+a)}} \end{aligned}$$

Finally, a transformation is calculated:

$$\begin{aligned} m &= \text{if im}(\theta) > 0 \text{ then } 1 \text{ else } -1 \\ \theta' &= \frac{1-a}{1+a} + \frac{2m\sqrt{a}}{1+a}i \\ P' &= Pb\sqrt{\theta'/\theta} \end{aligned}$$

7 Mappings for Dual Focus and Stretch Factor

While the Poincaré mapping is our basis for getting from the hyperbolic plane to the Euclidean plane, variations are sometimes useful. If we start with the Poincaré mapping to get to the Euclidean plane and then apply any conformal (angle preserving) mapping to the Euclidean plane, the composition will still have the advantages of being a conformal mapping from the hyperbolic plane to the Euclidean plane. But, it can have some properties that the Poincaré map lacks.

One useful mapping is a dual focus mapping, as shown in Figure 12, where there are two foci, one for each of two different points on the hyperbolic plane. We achieve this mapping by applying the transformation

$$z' = z\frac{a^2-1}{a^2z^2-1}$$

to the unit disk, represented as complex numbers. The result is that the points that would have mapped to a and $-a$ now become the two foci. If a is small, the display is elongated slightly, while if it is close to 1, the display looks more like a binocular view.

One use of the dual focus mapping is to put a node and one of its ancestors at the two foci, to better visualize their relationship, as done in Figure 12. This is done by first finding a

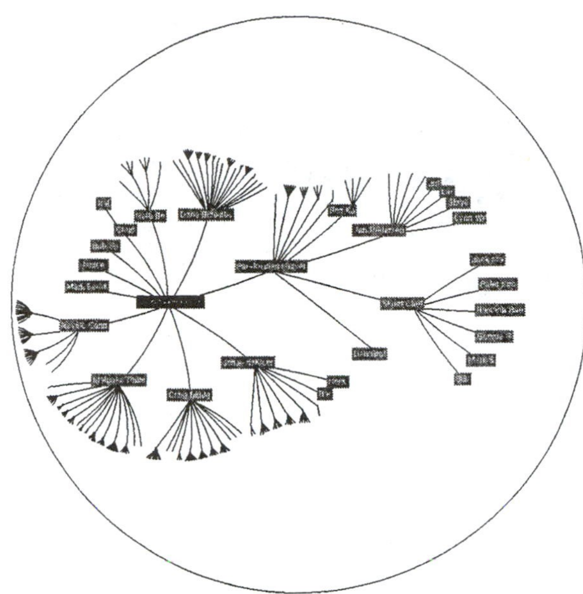

Figure 12: A dual focus mapping allows examining contexts of distant parts of the hierarchy.

circular mapping that puts those nodes an equal distance from the center, on either side, and then applying the dual focus mapping. A more prosaic use of the dual focus is to change the aspect ratio of the visualization (by up to about 50%) to better fit a window, while keeping a conformal mapping.

Another variant mapping is deliberately non-conformal. As mentioned above, there is a layout parameter for how close together to place sibling nodes (as shown in Figure 6). Often, a user might want to alter this parameter interactively so as to put more or fewer nodes in the focus region. Fortunately, a non-conformal circumference-reducing transformation can achieve almost the same effect without having to redo the layout. Figure 13 shows a side-by-side comparison of shrinking the sibling spacing in the layout by 50% and doing a 50% circumference reduction.

The idea is to move nodes radially further from or closer to the root node in the hyperbolic plane. The transformation we use adjusts the radial distance so that the circumference at that new distance is some ratio of the circumference at the original distance. If positions in the hyperbolic plane are represented by their Poincaré map, with the root centered, then the new radial distance, d' is related to the old radial distance, d by

$$s\frac{d}{d^2-1} = \frac{d'}{d'2-1}$$

where s is the scaling factor. This has approximately the same effect as a new layout with the spacing between siblings being adjusted by the same ratio.

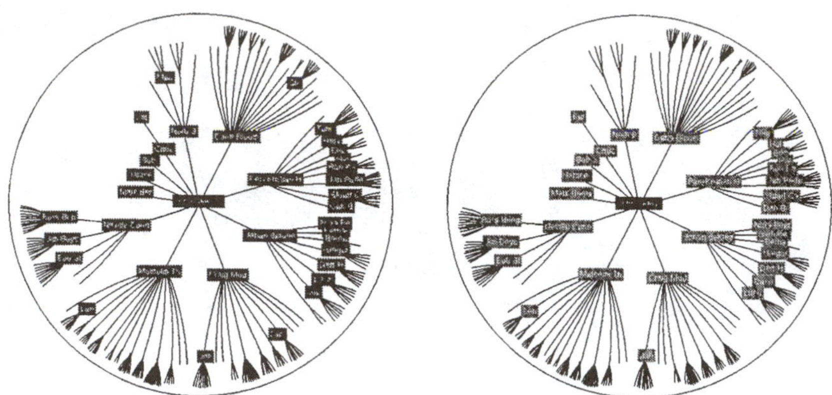

Figure 13: Using layout-time parameter for sibling spacing (left) vs. a display-time non-conformal circumference reduction mapping (right).

8 Visualizing Graphs

A natural question is whether the hyperbolic browser can be extended to visualize structures other than trees, for example, more general graph structures. The properties of the hyperbolic plane exploited for hierarchy layout apply similarly to laying out general graph structures: its spaciousness overcomes the metric problem of laying out structures in Euclidean space (i.e. the space is too confined). However, laying out general graph structures also presents a topological problem: dealing with crossing links. Since the hyperbolic plane has the same topological structure as the Euclidean plane, it doesn't overcome this problem.

The spaciousness of the hyperbolic plane, does, however, allow a finesse that would be more difficult using conventional layout techniques. This approach involves converting a graph with a tree, and then using the hyperbolic browser to visualize the resulting tree. This approach can be quite effective when the graphs are "almost" trees. For example, a directory structure may be a tree, except for some symbolic links that introduce non tree-like links. Similarly, the links in a World Wide Web structure are often mostly tree-like, with additional cross-references.

We convert a graph as a tree by making a copy of each graph node for each incoming edge, so that each edge goes to its own copy. Then one copy of a node is chosen as the main one, for example, the one (or the one of several) closest to the root. The children of a node are attached only to the main copy. This transformation is straightforwardly implemented using a breadth-first traversal of the graph. When the tree is displayed, the nodes that are copies can be visually distinguished. For example, the link structure of documents served by the Xerox WWW server starting from its root document is shown in this manner in Figure 14. The repeated nodes are shown with blue backgrounds.

This presents the problem of finding the children of repreated nodes. One solution is to maintain the original layout and provide a mechanism for automatically navigating to the main copy. So for example, when one of the repeated nodes is selected by the user, an animated

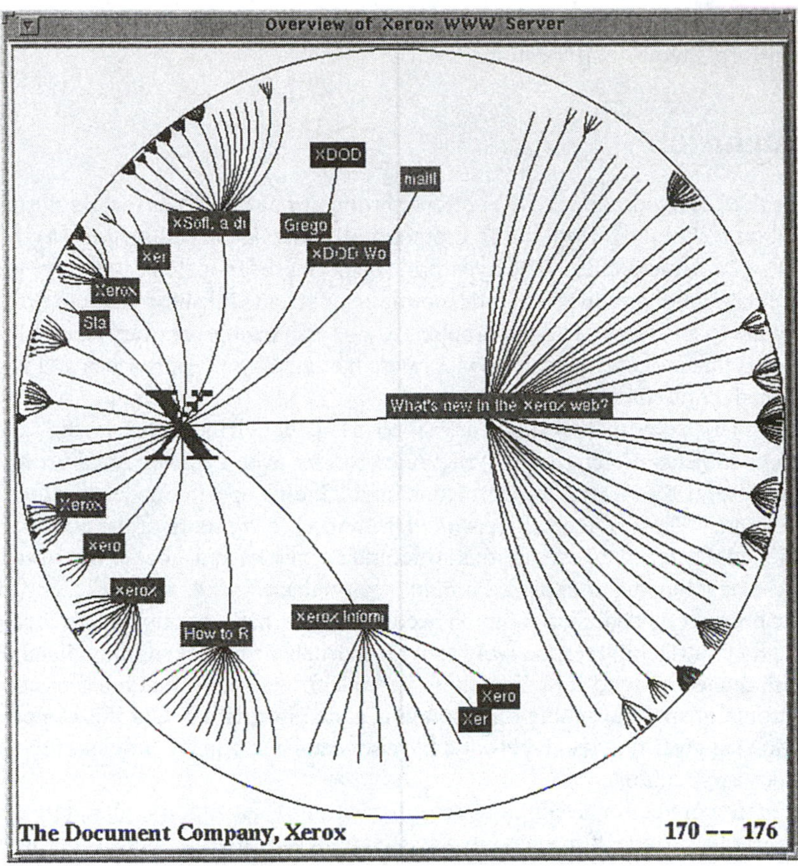

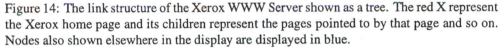

Figure 14: The link structure of the Xerox WWW Server shown as a tree. The red X represent the Xerox home page and its children represent the pages pointed to by that page and so on. Nodes also shown elsewhere in the display are displayed in blue.

transition can move the main copy of the node into focus, so that its descendants are visible. Understanding of the transition can be facilitated by using a path through the nearest common ancestor at a pace controlled by the length of the path.

An alternative approach for turning a graph into a tree gives all node repeats a copy of the descendent hierarchy, thus all node repeats are equally valid. This expands the graph out into a (possibly infinite) tree, with one tree node for each rooted path in the graph. Since layout can be done locally on the hyperbolic plane and thus incrementally, the entire logical structure need not be layed out initially. Rather only the part of the structure visible at pixel resolution needs to be layed out, with additional layout done as the user moves the focus. For efficiency, only one set of descendant hierarchy needs to be maintained since transformations can be calculated which map each unique descendant hierarchy (i.e. one per graph node) to each of its locations.

This is possible because of the roominess of the hyperbolic plane and the associated viability of using uniform layout at all locations.

9 Conclusion

We believe that the hyperbolic browser offers a promising new addition to the suite of available focus+context techniques. Hyperbolic geometry provides an elegant solution to the problem of visualizing large hierarchies. The hyperbolic plane has the room to lay out large hierarchies, and the Poincaré map provides a natural, continuously graded, fisheye mapping from the hyperbolic plane to a display. The hyperbolic browser can handle arbitrarily large hierarchies, with a context that includes as many nodes as are included by 3d approaches and with modest computational requirements.

A preliminary experimental study, described in [9], though inconclusive, did ascertain that all of its four subjects preferred the hyperbolic browser over a conventional browser in both "getting a sense of the overall tree structure" and "finding specific nodes by their titles," as well as "overall." Three of the subjects liked the ability to see more of the nodes at once and two mentioned the ability to see various structural properties and a better use of the space.

We have developed and explored a number of enhancements and variations of the core hyperbolic browser that address common needs. The alternative mappings for dual focus and interactive focus stretching respectively provide mechanisms for examining distal parts of hierarchy simultaneously and for controlling the tradeoff between the number of nodes visible and the amount of space available for displaying node information. Our initial work on graph visualization suggests that the hyperbolic browser can be applied to graphs of the kind common in many applications.

Many of the conventional techniques of information visualization would increase the value of the hyperbolic browser for navigating and learning hierarchies. For example, landmarks can be created in the space by utilizing color and other graphical elements (e.g. the prominent red X Xerox logo is an effective root marker). Other possibilities include providing a visual indication of where there are nodes that are invisible because of the resolution limit, using line thickness to convey depth or other information, and using a ladder of multiscale graphical representations in node display regions as done in "zoom and bloom" interfaces. The effective use of these types of variations are likely to be application or task dependent and so best explored in such a design context.

10 Acknowledgements

The focused work described here would not have ever materialized except for the rich context of information visualization work at PARC as initiated by Stuart Card, Jock Mackinlay, and George Robertson. A number of other colleagues have made valuable suggestions during the development of our prototypes. We would particularly like to thank Peter Pirolli for his collaboration on the experimental study described in a previous paper. We are also grateful for Barbara Gable's assistance in developing datasets and in obtaining copyright clearances for the Escher figure. The reviewers of this paper and its ancestors have steadily improved its quality. Xerox Corporation is seeking patent protection for technology described in this paper.

References

[1] B. B. Bederson and J. D. Hollan. Pad++: A zooming graphical interface for exploring alternate interface physics. In *Proceedings UIST'94*, pages 17–26. ACM Press, 1994.

[2] J Bertin. *Semiology of Graphics*. University of Wisconsin Press, 1983.

[3] H. S. M. Coxeter. *Non-Euclidean Geometry*. University of Toronto Press, 1965.

[4] George W. Furnas. Generalized fisheye views. In *Proceedings of the ACM SIGCHI Conference on Human Factors in Computing Systems*, pages 16–23. ACM, April 1986.

[5] C. Gunn. Visualizing hyperbolic space. In *Computer Graphics and Mathematics*, pages 299–311. Springer-Verlag, October 1991.

[6] Don Hopkins. The shape of psiber space. http://hello.kaleida.com/u/hopkins/psiber/psiber.html, 1989.

[7] B. Johnson and B. Shnedierman. Tree-maps: A space-filling approach to the visualization of hierarchical information. In *Visualization 1991*, pages 284–291. IEEE, 1991.

[8] Hideki Koike and Hirotaka Yoshihara. Fractal approaches for visualizing huge hierarchies. In *Proceedings of the 1993 IEEE Symposium on Visual Languages*. IEEE, 1993.

[9] John Lamping, Ramana Rao, and Peter Pirolli. A focus+context technique based on hyperbolic geometry for visualizing large hierarchies. In *Proceedings of the ACM SIGCHI Conference on Human Factors in Computing Systems*. ACM, May 1995.

[10] Y.K. Leung and M.D.Apperley. A review and taxonomy of distortion-oriented presentation techniques. *ACM Transactions on Computer-Human Interaction*, 1(2):126–160, June 1994.

[11] J. D. Mackinlay, G. G. Robertson, and S. K. Card. The perspective wall: Detail and context smoothly integrated. In *Proceedings of the ACM SIGCHI Conference on Human Factors in Computing Systems*, pages 173–179. ACM, April 1991.

[12] Jock Mackinlay, George Robertson, and Robert Deline. Developing calendar visualizers for the information visualizer. In *Proceedings of the ACM Symposium on User Interface Software and Technology*. ACM Press, Nov 1994.

[13] E. E. Moise. *Elementary Geometry from an Advanced Standpoint*. Addison-Wesley, 1974.

[14] K. Perlin and D. Fox. Pad: An alternaitve approach to the computer interface. In *Proceedings SIGGRAPH'93*, pages 57–64. ACM, 1993.

[15] R. Rao and S. K. Card. The table lens: Merging graphical and symbolic representations in an interactive focus+context visualization for tabular information. In *Proceedings of the ACM SIGCHI Conference on Human Factors in Computing Systems*. ACM, April 1994.

[16] G. G. Robertson, S. K. Card, and J. D. Mackinlay. The cognitive coprocessor architecture for interactive user interfaces. In *Proceedings of the ACM SIGGRAPH Symposium on User Interface Software and Technology*, pages 10–18. ACM Press, Nov 1989.

[17] G. G. Robertson, S. K. Card, and J. D. Mackinlay. Information visualization using 3d interactive animation. *Communications of the ACM*, 36(4), 1993.

[18] G. G. Robertson, J. D. Mackinlay, and S. K. Card. Cone trees: Animated 3d visualizations of hierarchical information. In *Proceedings of the ACM SIGCHI Conference on Human Factors in Computing Systems*, pages 189–194. ACM, April 1991.

[19] George G. Robertson and J. D. Mackinlay. The document lens. In *Proceedings of the ACM Symposium on User Interface Software and Technology*. ACM Press, Nov 1993.

[20] Manojit Sarkar and Marc H. Brown. Graphical fisheye views of graphs. In *Proceedings of the ACM SIGCHI Conference on Human Factors in Computing Systems*, pages 83–91. ACM, April 1992.

[21] Manojit Sarkar and Marc H. Brown. Graphical fisheye views. *Communications of the ACM*, 37(12):73–84, December 1994.

[22] Manojit Sarkar, Scott Snibbe, and Steven Reiss. Stretching the rubber sheet: A metaphor for visualizing large structure on small screen. In *Proceedings of the ACM Symposium on User Interface Software and Technology*. ACM Press, Nov 1993.

[23] Steven H. Tang and Mark A. Linton. Pacers: Time-elastic objects. In *Proceedings of the ACM Symposium on User Interface Software and Technology*. ACM Press, Nov 1993.

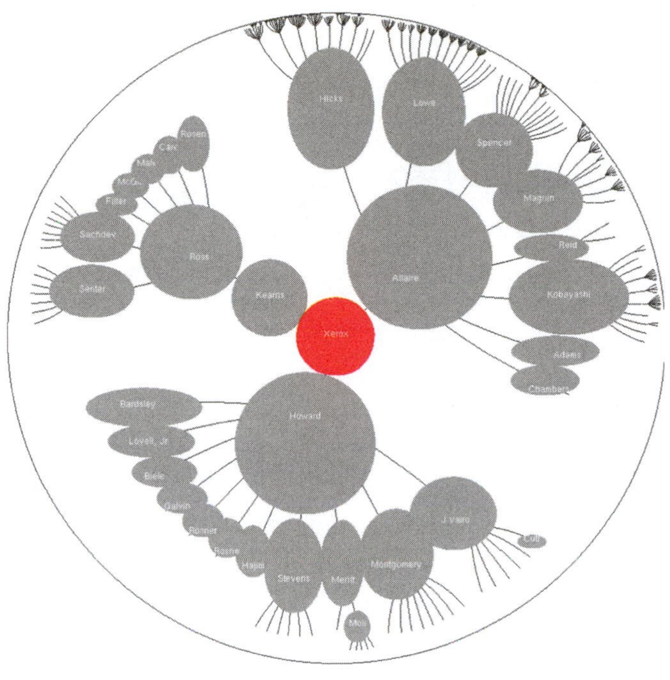

FIGURE **8**

The regions available to nodes for displaying node information.

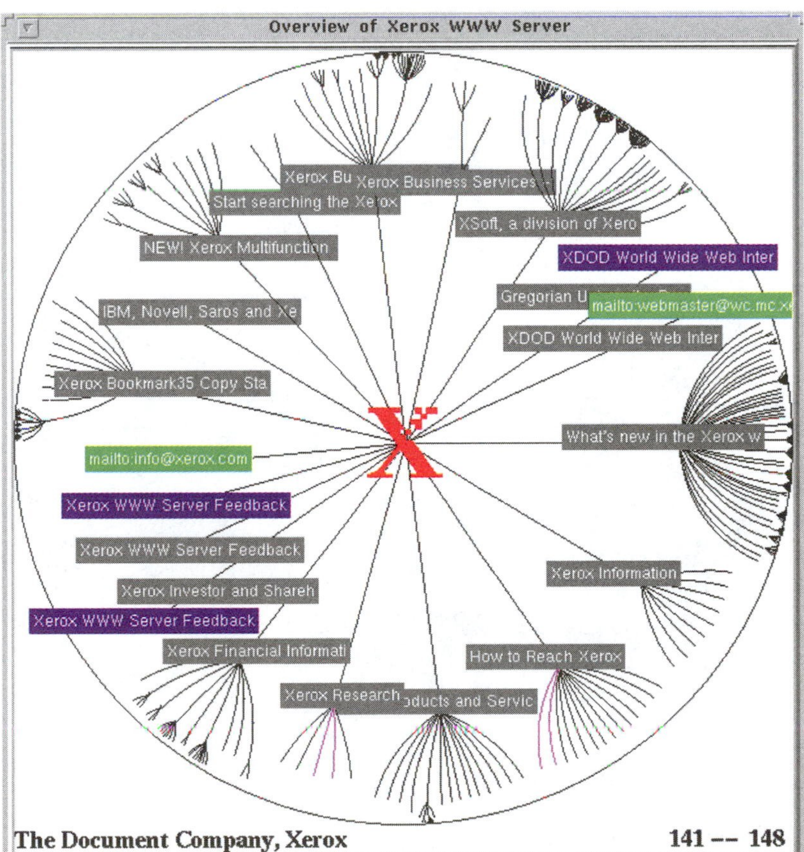

FIGURE **9**

Long text mode with up to 25 characters displayed for each node that would normally display at least 2 characters.

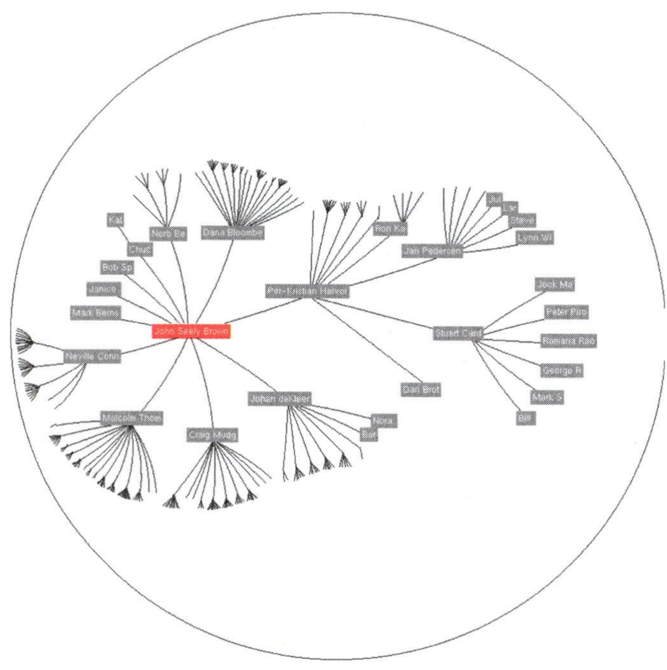

FIGURE **12**

A dual focus mapping allows examining contexts of distant parts of the hierarchy.

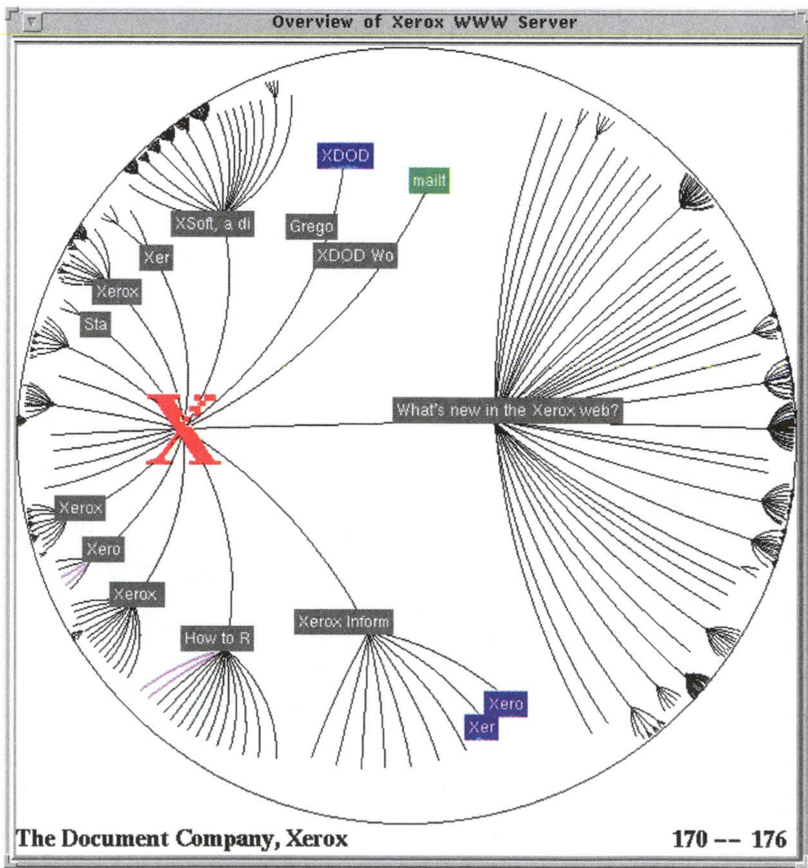

FIGURE **14**

The link structure of the Xerox WWW Server shown as a tree. The red X represent the Xerox home page and its children represent the pages pointed to by that page and so on. Nodes also shown elsewhere in the display are displayed in blue.

CHAPTER 5

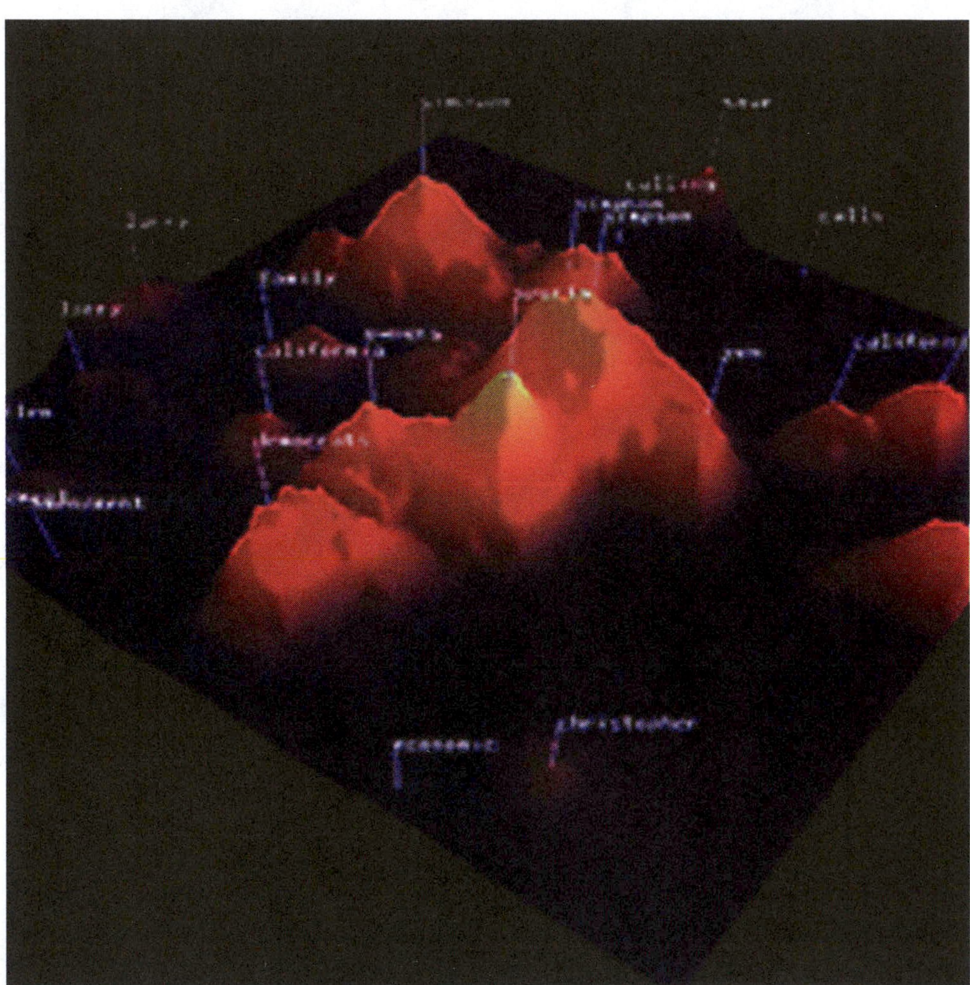

So much has already been written about everything that you can't find out anything about it.

– James Thurber (1961)

Data Mapping: Document Visualization

So far, we have discussed techniques for transforming abstract data as expressed in Data Tables into interactive visual forms. But some visualizations turn on the success of mapping between Raw Data and Data Tables. The visualization of text documents and document collections—*document visualization*—is an example of this, and we address these visualizations in this chapter.

There is another reason for concentrating on document visualization. Emerging technology trends imply that document visualization will be an important information visualization application for the future. Let us list several of these trends and restate them in simplified form:

	Trend	Interpretation
1.	*The World Wide Web*	Everything will be connected in a network, and there will only be *one* network.
2.	*Digital libraries*	*All* the world's knowledge will be on that network.
3.	*Communications advances*	Everything on the net will be virtually local.

These trends portend a vast information ecology in which information visualization could have a major role. We can already see dramatic harbingers of this ecology. Worldwide network capacity is currently growing at a thousand percent per year.[1] Our estimate is that the number of documents available at the desk of a seated user increased something like a factor of 10,000 in just four years from 1992 because of Internet growth and increased disk sizes. Personal computers used to be machines into which users *put* information and manipulated it (e.g., writing a paper, data analysis). Now they have become the primary portal through which users *get* information, whether from CD-ROM encyclopedias or Internet-based stock quotations. At the center of these trends are the Internet and the World Wide Web. But as the trends listed above should make plain, the Internet is just a component in the larger development of a new, universal, online information environment. Because it is important as both an application area and an area where data transformations from Raw Data to Data Table can occur, we devote these next two chapters to visualizations related to the World Wide Web and this larger information world. This chapter concentrates on visualization of text and documents; the next chapter explores how visualizations work together across multiple levels to form a larger visual information ecology.

Text documents are deeply bound with our work. We communicate with them. We treat them as extensions of our memories. We might be interested in the content of a single document or in discovering the relationships among documents of a large collection. The applications of text visualization seem endless and central to much of human work.

There are two separate arenas for visualization of text documents. One is the text document itself, which can be visualized in one, two, or three dimensions. The other is a collection of documents, which can also be visualized in one, two, or three dimensions. Although promising, visualization of a single text document is difficult. Even a single text page typically has typography that fills a 2D spatial substrate, leaving little room for additional visual enhancements. A 2D rendering of a page often requires carefully designed fonts to retain the document quality at the low resolutions of a computer display. A 3D rendering requires larger font sizes to achieve similar legibility, reducing the amount of text. A 3D rendering of a page, whether using vector fonts or texture maps, can strain the capacity of a computer for real-time performance because of the number of vectors or amount of texture memory required.

When pages are collected together into a document, there are additional challenges. Some documents, such as software programs, are very structured. Others, such as email, are less structured. Structured documents are easier to visualize because the structure can be mapped directly to a visual form with good odds that it will be meaningful. Unstructured documents require additional processing to be

[1]Estimate by John Sizemore, founder of the Internet provider UUNET, now a part of WorldCom. Quoted in a speech by Rick Tholman, president of Xerox, to the World Congress on Information Technology, June 22, 1998.

visualized. Text analysis algorithms are often complex, creating additional issues for making the resulting visual forms meaningful.

Visualization of document collections creates an additional layer of complexity. Even modest corpora have many thousands of documents. Internet pages number in the hundreds of millions. Careful design is required to ensure reasonable performance.

In this chapter, we consider methods for mapping single documents and document collections in 1D, 2D, 3D, and time-oriented Visual Structures.

5.1

Text in 1D

VECTOR SPACE ANALYSIS

How can text, which is purely nominal data, be mapped into spatial terms at all? We start with a paper by Salton et al. (1995 ●). This paper was selected because it gives a compact tutorial on the methods for mapping text from Raw Data into forms more amenable to visual presentation and because it uses these methods for a simple 1D circular visualization to obtain insight into large collections of text documents.

In the Salton et al. paper, text similarity is determined using vector space analysis, a technique invented by Salton and researched extensively by the information retrieval community over 30 years. Salton et al. are concerned with mapping the *semantics* of text documents into analytical forms. The basic idea is that a passage of text can be thought of as a vector in a high-dimensional space. The dimensions in the space are all the words that might have been used in the text (after removing certain common words, such as prepositions). Each dimension in the vector is weighted by the frequency of use of each of the words. Two passages of text are similar when their vectors point in the same general direction. This general similarity is augmented with a contextual measure that helps separate out different senses of a word. The information retrieval community uses vector space analysis to support free-form text queries rather than the Boolean queries found in traditional databases. Free-form text queries are somewhat easier for the user, and they allow texts themselves to be used as queries.

The paper maps document vectors into a Visual Structure based on a circle. Articles or parts of articles from an encyclopedia are arranged around the circle. Lines are drawn between parts of the circle with high similarity (see Figure 5.1). The resulting mapping of text to a 1D Visual Structure shows the rhetoric of a document such as the correspondence between introductory paragraphs and document sections.

The decomposition of a document into parts is an important aspect of this visualization. Text decomposition is useful for information retrieval because it supports the retrieval of

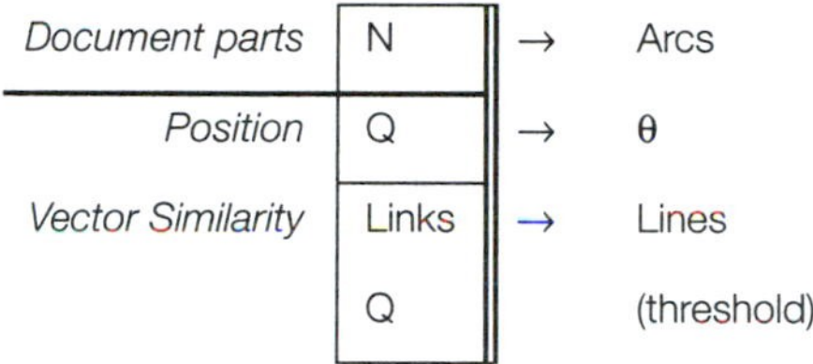

FIGURE **5.1**

Salton et al. (1995 ●) decomposes a document into a set of parts that map to arcs of a circle. Vector space analysis is used to calculate the similarity between these parts, which determines when lines are drawn between the arcs of the circle.

long documents that have parts with high similarity even though similarity measure for the full document may be low.

Salton was one of the founders of information retrieval, which has developed various techniques for analyzing text. This paper is an example of the combination of information retrieval and information visualization, an issue of growing interest in the information retrieval community (Hemmje, Kunkel, and Willett, 1994; Olsen et al., 1993).

REDUCED TEXT + INTERACTION

The second paper, by Eick, Steffen, and Sumner (1992 ●), describes the visualization in 1D of not a collection but a single document, which in this case is a computer program or a novel. Their tool SeeSoft reduces each text line to a pixel-width line (or in some versions, a pixel). Eick, Steffen, and Sumner are concerned with mapping the *form* of a text document into analytical visual form. The result is the visualization of a document as a narrow rectangle that fits on a computer display. A statistic associated with the text lines is mapped to a color ramp (see Figure 5.2). Dynamic queries are used to selectively light up lines in the visualization, for example, all of the lines in which a certain character of a story is mentioned. We include it as a 1D rather than a 2D

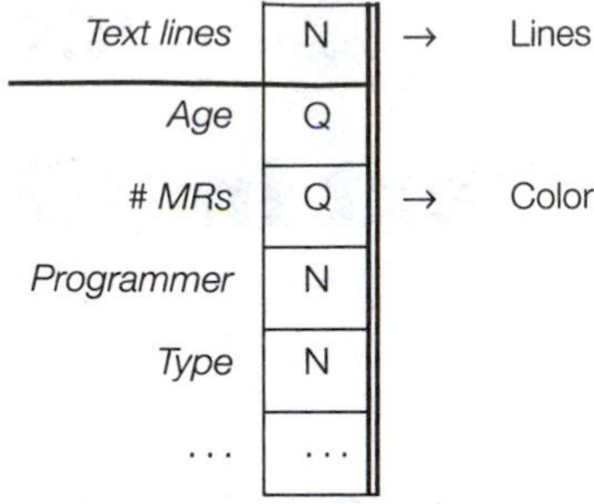

FIGURE 5.2

Description of SeeSoft (Eick, Steffen, and Sumner, 1992 ●), which maps text lines to pixel-width lines. The user could select a line-oriented statistic such as the number of modification requests (MR) to be mapped to the color of the line.

visualization because the second dimension is used for *folding* the basic 1D representation, first at the end of lines and second to get multiple text rectangles on the screen.

The SeeSoft paper was influential and historically important. This early information visualization includes interaction techniques that anticipated some of the work discussed in Chapter 3. It included an interactive color bar that supported dynamic query manipulations of the 1D text visualization. Brushing was also supported by the system. The paper also has compelling examples of these interactive techniques being used to solve realistic problems associated with visualizing software.

Automatic Analysis, Theme Generation, and Summarization of Machine-Readable Texts

Gerard Salton, James Allan, Chris Buckley, Amit Singhal

Vast amounts of text material are now available in machine-readable form for automatic processing. Here, approaches are outlined for manipulating and accessing texts in arbitrary subject areas in accordance with user needs. In particular, methods are given for determining text themes, traversing texts selectively, and extracting summary statements that reflect text content.

Many kinds of texts are currently available in machine-readable form and are amenable to automatic processing. Because the available databases are large and cover many different subject areas, automatic aids must be provided to users interested in accessing the data. It has been suggested that links be placed between related pieces of text, connecting, for example, particular text paragraphs to other paragraphs covering related subject matter. Such a linked text structure, often called hypertext, makes it possible for the reader to start with particular text passages and use the linked structure to find related text elements (*1*). Unfortunately, until now, viable methods for automatically building large hypertext structures and for using such structures in a sophisticated way have not been available. Here we give methods for constructing text relation maps and for using text relations to access and use text databases. In particular, we outline procedures for determining text themes, traversing texts selectively, and extracting summary statements that reflect text content.

Text Analysis and Retrieval: The Smart System

The Smart system is a sophisticated text retrieval tool, developed over the past 30 years, that is based on the vector space model of retrieval (*2*). In the vector space model, all information items—stored texts as well as information queries—are represented by sets, or vectors, of terms. A term is typically a word, a word stem, or a phrase associated with the text under consideration. In principle, the terms might be chosen from a controlled vocabulary list or a thesaurus, but because of the difficulties of constructing such controlled vocabularies for unrestricted topic areas, it is convenient to derive the terms directly from the texts under consideration. Collectively, the terms assigned to a particular text represent text content.

Because the terms are not equally useful for content representation, it is important to introduce a term-weighting system that assigns high weights to terms deemed important and lower weights to the less important terms. A powerful term-weighting system of this kind is the well-known equation $f_t \times 1/f_c$ (term frequency times inverse collection frequency), which favors terms with a high frequency (f_t) in particular documents but with a low frequency overall in the collection (f_c). Such terms distinguish the documents in which they occur from the remaining items.

When all texts or text queries are represented by weighted term vectors of the form $D_i = (d_{i1}, d_{i2}, \ldots, d_{it})$, where d_{ik} is the weight assigned to term k in document D_i, a similarity measure can be computed between pairs of vectors that reflects text similarity. Thus, given document D_i and query Q_j (or sample document D_j), a similarity computation of the form $sim(D_i, Q_j) = \Sigma_{k=1}^{t} d_{ik}d_{jk}$ can produce a ranked list of documents in decreasing order of similarity with a query (or with a sample document). When ranked retrieval output is provided for the user, it is easy to use relevance feedback procedures to build improved queries on the basis of the relevance of previously retrieved materials.

In the Smart system, the terms used to identify the text items are entities extracted from the document texts after elimination of common words and removal of word suffixes. When the document vocabulary itself forms the basis for text content representation, distinct documents with large overlapping vocabularies may be difficult to distinguish. For example, the vectors covering biographies of John Fitzgerald Kennedy and Anthony M. Kennedy, the current Supreme Court justice, will show many similarities because both Kennedys attended Harvard University, were high officials of the government, and had close relationships with U.S. presidents. The global vector similarity function described earlier cannot cope with ambiguities of this kind by itself. An additional step designed to verify that the matching vocabulary occurs locally in similar contexts must therefore be introduced as part of the retrieval algorithm. This is accomplished by insisting on certain locally matching substructures, such as text sentences or text paragraphs, in addition to the global vector match, before accepting two texts as legitimately similar (*3*).

Consider, as an example, a typical search conducted in the 29-volume Funk and Wagnalls encyclopedia, using as a query the text of article 9667, entitled "William Lloyd Garrison" (Garrison was the best known of the American abolitionists, who opposed slavery in the early part of the 19th century) (*4*). The upper portion of Table 1 shows the top 10 items retrieved in response to a global vector comparison. The top retrieved item is article 9667 itself, with a perfect query similarity of 1.00, followed by additional articles dealing with abolitionism and the slavery issue, retrieved with lower similarity values.

The upper portion of Table 1 consists of relevant items only, with the exception of article 9628, entitled "Gar," retrieved in position eight on the ranked list. Gar is a type of fish, obviously unrelated to the slavery issue but erroneously retrieved because truncated terms were used in the text vectors, and the truncated form of "Garrison" matches "Gar." (Removal of "-ison" as part of the stemming process first reduced "Garrison" to "Garr," as in "comparison" and "compar"; removal of the duplicated consonant then reduced "Garr" to the final

The authors are in the Department of Computer Science, Cornell University, Ithaca, NY 14853–7501, USA.

"Gar.") The lower portion of Table 1 shows the results obtained with an additional local text comparison that required at least one matching text sentence between the query article and each retrieved document. There are no matching sentences in documents 9667 ("Garrison") and 9628 ("Gar"), because gar, meaning fish, and "Gar" derived from the name Garrison are obviously not used in similar contexts. Hence the offending document 9628 was removed from the retrieved list. Most linguistic ambiguities are similarly resolvable by this global-local vector-matching process. The lower portion of Table 1 also differs from the upper in that certain text passages are retrieved (labeled "c" for section and "p" for paragraph) in addition to certain full document texts. The passage retrieval issue is examined in more detail in the next section.

Text Decomposition and Structure

Practical retrieval searches deal with text items that are heterogeneous in both subject matter and text length. Thus, in the same text environment it may be necessary to cope with short e-mail messages as well as long book-sized texts. In an encyclopedia, three-word articles representing cross-references from one subject to another occur routinely, in addition to many long treatments such as the 175-page article entitled "United States of America." In a vector-processing environment, long articles that deal with diverse subject matter are difficult to retrieve in response to short, more specific queries, because the overall vector similarity is likely to be small for such items. Thus, the full article "United States of America" is not retrieved in the top 10 items in response to the query about William Lloyd Garrison, even though certain sections in the article specifically deal with abolitionism.

Table 1. Text retrieval strategies. Query: article 9667, "William Lloyd Garrison." Section indicated by "c"; paragraph indicated by "p."

Document number	Query similarity	Title of retrieved item
	Global text comparison only	
9667	1.00	Garrison, William Lloyd
18173	0.53	Phillips, Wendell
76	0.48	Abolitionists
21325	0.40	Slavery
827	0.36	American Anti-Slavery Society
21326	0.35	Slave Trade
8097	0.35	Emancipation Proclamation
9628	0.30	Gar
2883	0.27	Birney, James Gillespie
5584	0.27	Clay, Cassius Marcellus
	Global-local text comparison and retrieval of text passages	
9667	1.00	Garrison, William Lloyd
18173	0.53	Phillips, Wendell
2974.c33*	0.50	Blacks in Americas
76	0.48	Abolitionists
21325.c8	0.42	Slavery
827	0.36	American Anti-Slavery Society
8097	0.35	Emancipation Proclamation
23173.c97*	0.31	United States of America
23545.p5*	0.29	Villard, Henry
5539.c28*	0.28	Civil War, American

*New article retrieved in restricted search.

The rejection of long articles can reduce retrieval performance in some cases. More generally, long articles are difficult for users to handle even when retrieval is possible, because long texts cannot easily be absorbed and processed. This suggests that long texts be broken down into smaller text passages and that access be provided to shorter text excerpts in addition to full texts. Various attempts have been made in the past to implement passage retrieval capabilities, but flexible systems capable of handling text excerpts do not currently exist (5).

The Smart system can deal with text segments of varying length, including text sections, paragraphs, groups of adjacent sentences, and individual sentences. The lower portion of Table 1 thus shows the results of a mixed search in which text sections and paragraphs are retrieved instead of full texts whenever the query similarity for a shorter text passage exceeds the similarity for the full article. A number of new items are promoted into the top 10 list when text passages are retrievable, including section 33 of document 2974, "Blacks in the Americas," and section 97 of "United States of America." The text of document 2974.c33 (section 33 of document 2974) covers the founding of the American Anti-Slavery Society by William Lloyd Garrison in 1833. The relevance of this text to abolitionism and William Lloyd Garrison explains its good retrieval rank and high similarity coefficient of 0.50.

The available evidence indicates that when searching an encyclopedia, the use of the combined global and local similarity computations improves retrieval effectiveness by about 10% over the use of global vector similarity measurements alone. An additional 10% improvement is obtainable by use of the passage retrieval capability that identifies document excerpts in addition to full texts (6). The results obtained by extensive testing in the TREC (Text Retrieval Evaluation Conference) environment indicate that the Smart system produces consistently superior retrieval performance (7). Furthermore, response times are comparable to those obtainable in commercial retrieval environments. A Smart search of the TREC collections (700,000 full-text documents, or 2.4 gigabytes of text) has typical response times of 3 s for a 10-term query or 6 s for a 20-term query.

When text passages are available for processing and similarity measurements are easily computed between texts and text excerpts, text relation maps can be generated that show text similarities that exceed a particular threshold value. Figure 1 shows a relation map for four encyclopedia articles related to William Lloyd Garrison ("Slavery," "U.S. Civil War," "Abolitionists,"

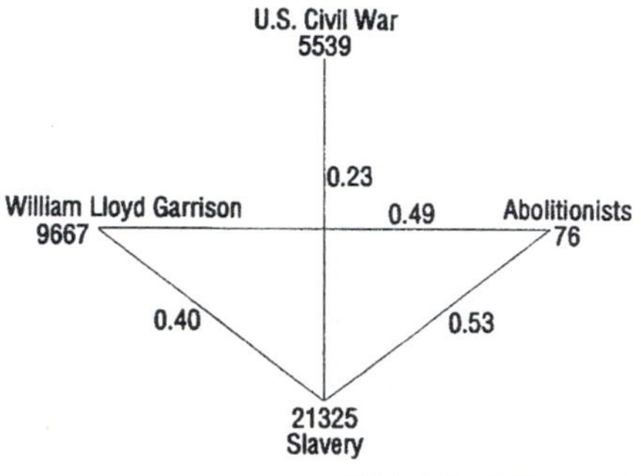

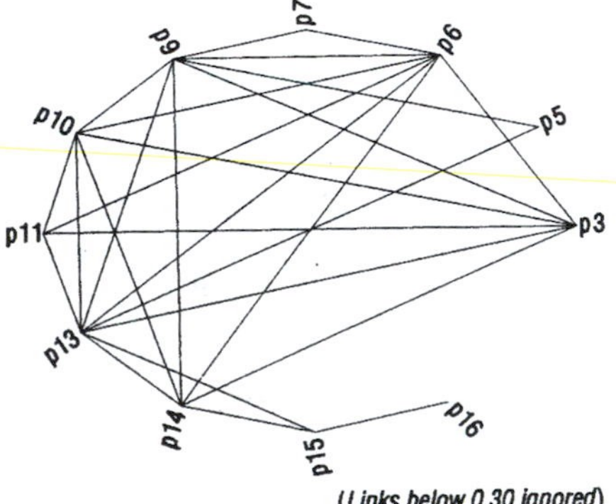

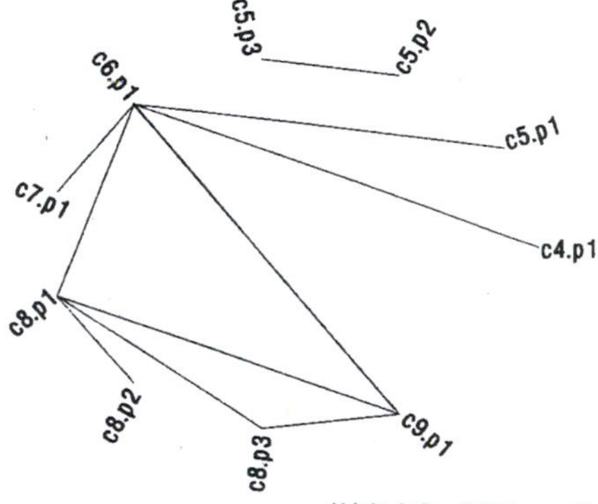

Fig. 1 (top). Basic text relation map. Vertices (nodes) represent texts; lines (links between nodes) represent text relations above a similarity threshold of 0.20. In all figures, "c" indicates section, "p" indicates paragraph. **Fig. 2 (middle).** Well-connected text relation map for paragraphs of article 21385, "Smoking." **Fig. 3 (bottom).** Poorly connected text relation map for paragraphs of article 21933, "Symphony."

and "Garrison"). The texts themselves are represented by nodes (vertices) of the map, and the pairwise text similarities are indicated by links (branches) between the corresponding node pairs. Figure 1 shows all similarities between full articles exceeding a similarity threshold of 0.20 (*8*). Text linking has been used in the past to build hypertext structures, but the links between related text pieces are normally assumed to be placed subjectively by individual text authors—a procedure manifestly impractical in environments where large masses of heterogeneous texts are stored for processing (*9*).

A study of various kinds of text relations between texts and text excerpts can reveal a good deal of information about the internal structure of individual texts, as well as the relations between different texts. Consider, as an example, the paragraph map for article 21385, "Smoking," shown in Fig. 2, which includes all pairwise paragraph similarities exceeding 0.30. In the corresponding graph, there are no disconnected components, and many similarities exist between adjacent paragraphs. The convex graph structure reflects a homogeneous treatment of the topic; in this case, the "Smoking" article emphasizes the health problems connected with smoking and the difficulties that arise when people attempt to quit smoking. For a homogeneous map such as this, it should be easy to determine the basic text content by looking at only a few carefully chosen paragraphs.

In contrast, consider the paragraph relation map in Fig. 3, which shows paragraph similarities for article 21933, "Symphony," and uses the same similarity threshold of 0.30. This map is much less dense; there are many outliers consisting of a single node only, and there is a disconnected component that includes paragraphs 2 and 3 of section 5. Clearly, the "Symphony" topic does not receive the same homogeneous treatment in the encyclopedia as "Smoking," and a determination of text content by selectively looking at particular text excerpts is much more problematic in this case. Attempts have been made in the past to relate certain manually linked hypertext structures to the corresponding text characteristics, but a detailed structural text analysis based on automatically linked structures at various levels of detail has not so far been undertaken (*10*).

In Figs. 1 to 3, the text nodes are equally spaced around the circumference of a circular structure. This makes it easy to recognize the links between individual text excerpts, but the actual link location in the running text is obscured. In particular, it is difficult to tell whether a link is placed at the beginning, in the middle, or at the end of a text. An alternative display format is shown in Fig. 4, in which the space assigned to each text along the circumference is proportional to the text length, and each text link is placed in its proper position within the texts. Figure 4 shows a paragraph map for four related articles ("Mohandas Gandhi," "Indira Gandhi," "Nehru," and "India") with the use of a similarity threshold of 0.30. It is obvious that the text of article 12017 ("India") is much longer than that of the other articles and that the coverage of Mohandas Gandhi (the Mahatma) is in turn more detailed than that of Indira Gandhi and Nehru.

Various kinds of topic relationships can be distinguished in Fig. 4, depending on the particular linking pattern between text elements. For example, when multiple links relate a particular (shorter) document such as "Indira Gandhi" (9619) and a subsection of a longer document such as "India" (12017), a narrower-broader text relation normally exists. Similarly, when a particular section of one document has multiple links to a particular section of another document, the two text items usually share a common subtopic. One can thus conclude that "Nehru" (16579) and the two "Gandhis" (9619 and 9620) represent subtopics of "India" (12017). Similarly, "Mohandas Gandhi" and "Nehru," and "Indira Gandhi" and "Nehru," are pairs of related documents that share common subtopics. Finally, the lives of the two Gandhis appear to be largely unrelated—a single linked paragraph pair exists that refers to unrest in India, a condition that plagued both politicians. The relation between Mohandas and Indira Gandhi is entirely through Nehru, who was a disciple of the Mahatma and also the father of Indira.

This type of analysis gives an objective view of the topic coverage in individual texts and of the information shared among sets of related texts. In the rest of this article, we examine three kinds of text analysis systems in more detail, which leads to the identification of text themes, the selective traversal of texts, and the summarization of text content by extraction of important text excerpts.

Text Theme Identification

A text theme can be defined as a specific subject that is discussed in some depth in a particular text or in a number of related texts. Themes represent centers of attention and cover subjects of principal interest to text authors and presumably also to text readers. The identification of text themes is useful for many purposes—for example, to obtain a snapshot of text content and as an aid in deciding whether actually to read a text.

Various approaches based on linguistic text analysis methods suggest themselves for the identification of text themes (*11*). In the present context, the text relation maps are used as inputs to a clustering process that is designed to identify groups of text excerpts that are closely related to each other but also relatively disconnected from the rest of the text (*12*). The following simple process leads to text theme identification: First, the triangles in the relation map are recognized (a triangle is a group of three text excerpts, each of which is related to the other two to a degree that is above the stated similarity threshold). A centroid vector is then constructed for each triangle, as the average vector for the group of three related items. Finally, triangles are merged into a common group (theme) whenever the corresponding centroids are sufficiently similar (that is, when the pairwise centroid similarity exceeds a stated threshold). Each theme may be represented by a global centroid vector that is constructed as the average vector of all text excerpts included in the theme.

Figure 5 shows the four themes derived by this method for the Gandhi-India subject area shown in Fig. 4. The following themes are apparent: (i) the single solid triangle consisting of paragraphs 9619.p5, 16579.p4, and 16579.p5 on the right-hand edge of Fig. 5 (main subject: Nehru); (ii) the single hashed triangle consisting of paragraphs 9619.p3, 12017.p219, and 12017.p220 (main subject: Sikhs, Punjab); (iii) the group of dark triangles consisting of paragraphs 9619.p7, 12017.p211, 12017.p216, 12017.p218, and 12017.p222 (main subject: Indira Gandhi); (iv) the group of light triangles consisting of paragraphs 9620.p3, 9620.p6, 9620.p8, 9620.p11, 9620.p14, 9620.p15, 9620.p18, 12017.p148, and 16579.p4 (main subject: Mohandas Gandhi). The clear separation between the two Gandhis already noted in the map of Fig. 4 is present also in the theme map of Fig. 5, in which no overlap exists between the dark and light triangle groupings.

An alternative, less onerous but also less refined theme generation method is to build a text relation map with the use of a high similarity threshold (where the number of linked text excerpts is small). Each disconnected component of the map, consisting of groups of highly related text excerpts, is then identified with a particular theme. The graph obtained by use of a text similarity threshold of 0.50 for the Gandhi-India subject area is shown in Fig. 6. The high similarity threshold reduces the similarity map to three areas, identified as Mohandas Gandhi (top theme), Indira Gandhi (middle), and Nehru (bottom). These themes duplicate those of Fig. 5, but the second theme in Fig. 5, which covers Indira Gandhi's problems with the Sikhs in Punjab, is no longer recognized as a separate subject.

When text relation maps are used as the main input, themes can be generated at various levels of detail. The larger the text excerpts used for text grouping purposes, the wider in general is the scope of the corresponding themes. Contrariwise, when sentences and other short excerpts are used in the grouping process, the theme coverage is normally narrow. Thus, when themes are derived from the texts of documents 9667 and 76 ("William Lloyd Garrison" and "Abolitionists," respectively), a theme derived from paragraph relations might cover the "beginnings of U.S. abolitionism"; a more detailed theme derived from sentence relations might cover the "founding of the newspaper *Liberator*," which was a milestone in the early years of the abolitionist movement. By suitable variation of the scope of the theme generation process, it is thus possible to derive a smaller number of broader themes or a larger number of narrower themes.

Selective Text Traversal

When large text collections are in use, flexible methods should be available that will skim the texts while concentrating on text passages that may be of immediate interest. Such a skimming operation can then be used both for selective text traversal, in which only text passages deemed of special importance are actually retrieved or read, and for text summarization, in which summaries are constructed by extraction of selected text excerpts.

In selective text traversal (*13*), starting with a text relation map and a particular text excerpt of special interest, a user may follow three different traversal strategies: (i) The path may cover many of the central nodes, which are defined as nodes with a large number of links to other nodes of the map. (ii) The path may use text excerpts located in strategic positions within the corresponding documents—for example, the first paragraphs in each text section or the first sentences in each paragraph. (iii) The path may use the link weight as the main path generation criterion by starting with the desired initial node and choosing as the next node the one with maximum similarity to the current node. This last strategy is known as a depth-first search.

When individual text excerpts are selected for path formation or summarization, a number of factors must receive special attention; among these are the coherence of the resulting text, that is, the ease with which the text can be read and understood; the exhaustivity of coverage of the final text, that is, the degree to which all the main subject areas are covered; the text chronology, that is, the accuracy with which timing factors are recognized; and finally, the amount of repetition in the selected text excerpts. Some of these factors are handled relatively easily; for example, text chronology is often maintained by the use of only forward-pointing paths and backtracking is not allowed (if a particular paragraph is included in a path, no other text excerpt appearing earlier in the same document can appear in the same path).

In the present context, text coherence is used as the main criterion, and forward depth-first paths are used in which each chosen text excerpt is linked to the most similar text excerpt not yet seen at this point. In a depth-first path, each chosen excerpt is closely related to the next one, and the chance of poor transitions between selected paragraphs is minimized. Consider, as an example, the paragraph map in Fig. 7, which is based on six documents related to the Greek god Zeus (article 24674). The assumption is that the path starts with the initial text paragraph of "Zeus" (24674.p3). A short depth-first path may be defined as a single-link path that includes only the initial text excerpt plus the next most similar excerpt. In Fig. 7, this defines path 24674.p3 to 17232.p4 (paragraph 4 of the

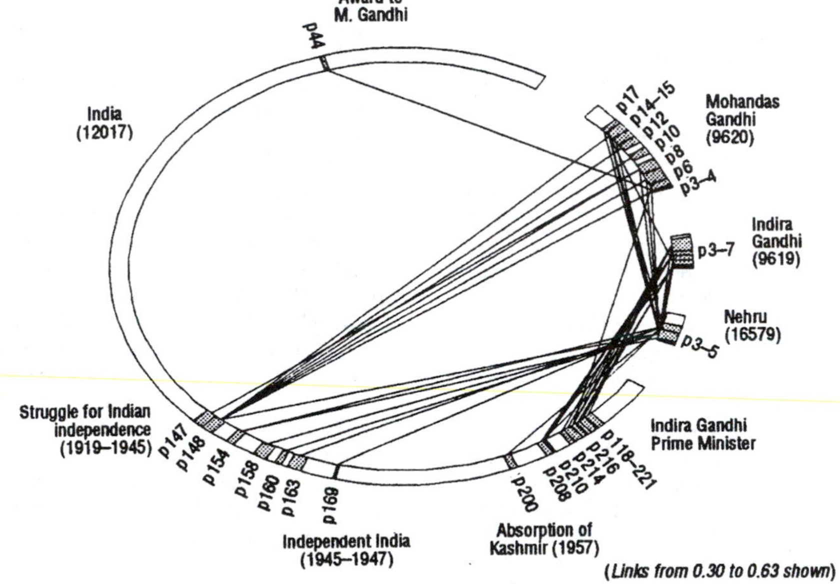

Fig. 4. Paragraph similarity map for articles related to "India" (12017). Length of curved segments is proportional to text length; links are placed in correct relative position within each text.

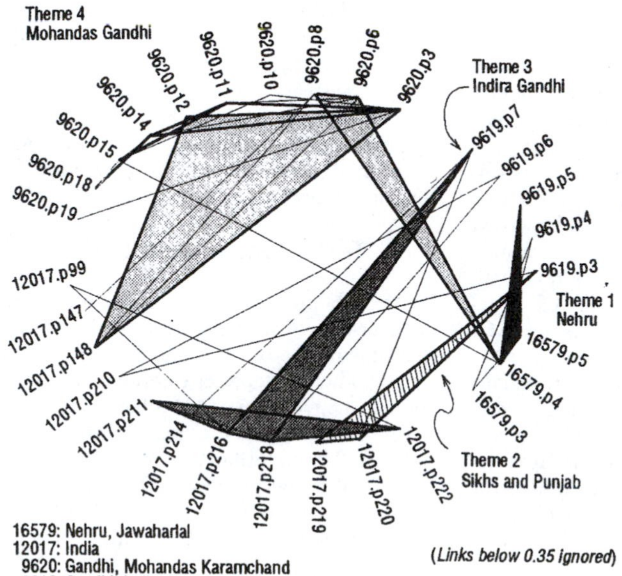

Fig. 5. Text themes derived by merging of triangles for four articles related to "India" (12017).

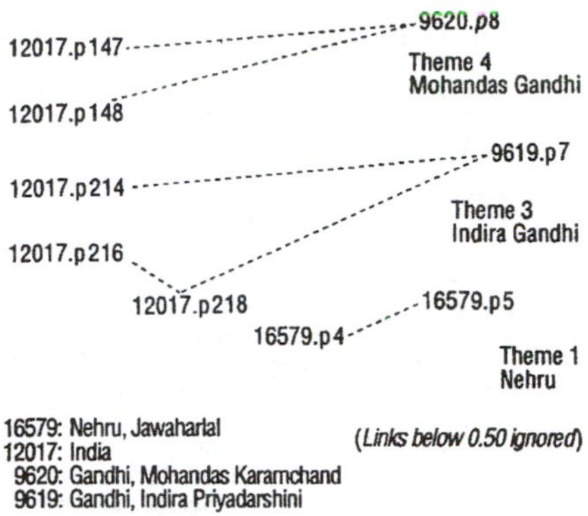

Fig. 6. Simplified text themes derived from high-threshold (disconnected) text relation map for articles related to "India" (12017).

article "Mount Olympus"). The corresponding paragraphs introduce Zeus as the god of the sky and the ruler of the Olympian gods and then proceed by identifying the 12 major Olympian deities, including Zeus, his wife Hera, and his siblings and children.

A more complete forward depth-first path proceeds from item 17232.p4 to include 10391.p6 (paragraph 6 of 10391, "Greek Religion and Mythology") and four additional paragraphs presented in detail in Fig. 7. The complete forward depth-first path includes information about Rhea, Zeus' mother; Cronus, Zeus' father; and the Titans, a race of giants that included Rhea and Cronus, among other gods.

Instead of initiating the text traversal at the beginning of a text, it is also possible for a searcher to use context-dependent text-traversal strategies that start with a special text excerpt of immediate interest. For example, someone interested in the foreign policy of President Nixon might locate paragraph 622 of article 23173 ("United States of America") by using a standard text search. A depth-first path starting at 23173.p622 can then be used to obtain further information. Such a path also includes paragraphs 9086.p13 (paragraph 13 of article 9086, "Gerald R. Ford") and 16855.p11 (paragraph 11 of 16855, "Richard M. Nixon"). The corresponding texts deal with the exchange of visits between President Nixon and Leonid Brezhnev; the continuation of detente between the United States and the Soviet Union that was pursued by President Ford and Secretary of State Kissinger; and finally, Nixon's approach to the People's Republic of China. A completely different topic will be covered by a depth-first path starting with paragraph 23173.p624, describing the Watergate break-in. The corresponding coverage includes Nixon's presumed implication in the Watergate burglary (23173.p624), Vice President Ford's staunch defense of Nixon during his term as vice president (9086.p8),

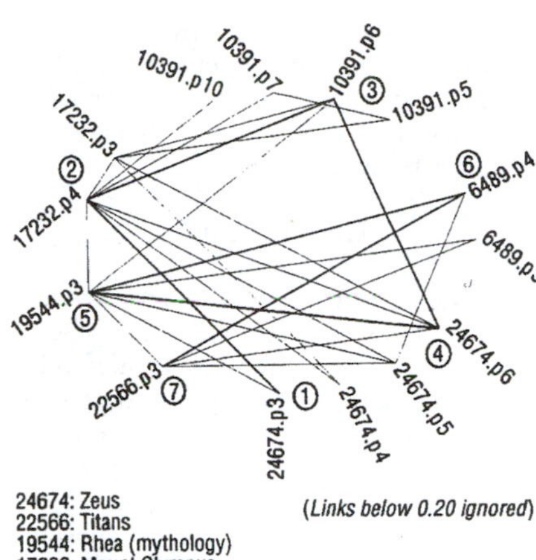

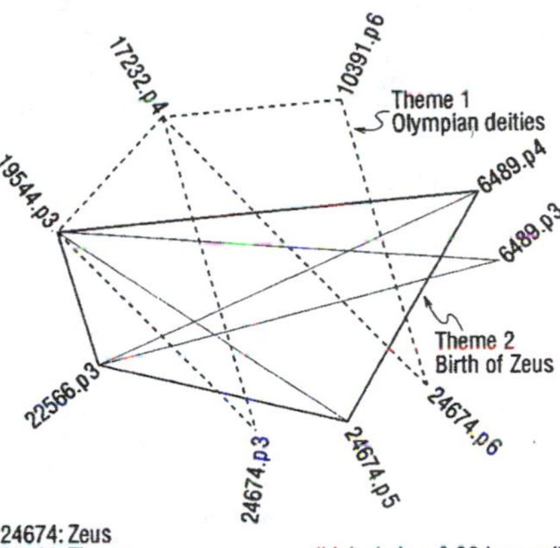

Fig. 7 (top). Depth-first paragraph-traversal order for six articles related to "Zeus" (24674). Path starts with initial paragraph of "Zeus" (24674.p3) and covers, in order, 17232.p4 ("Mount Olympus"), 10391.p6 ("Greek Religion and Mythology"), 24674.p6 ("Zeus"), 19544.p3 ("Rhea"), 6489.p4 ("Cronus"), and 22566.p3 ("Titans"). **Fig. 8 (bottom).** Two themes, "Olympian deities" (dashed triangles) and "birth of Zeus" (heavy lines), for articles related to "Zeus" (24674).

and finally, Nixon's resignation on 9 August 1974 and Ford's pardon (23848.p19).

Current experience indicates that a depth-first path provides a reasonably coherent body of information in practically every subject environment. The resulting paths may, however, be flawed in some ways. For example, there may be repetition of subject coverage in two or more excerpts in a given path; in the previous example, Nixon's resignation is mentioned in paragraphs 9086.p8 and 23848.p19. Repeated text passages may be eliminated by a sentence-sentence comparison, followed by the removal of duplicate occurrences of sufficiently similar sentences. Alternatively, a larger text excerpt in a path can sometimes be replaced by a shorter excerpt whose similarity to the previous text element is large. In the depth-first path of Fig. 7, the long paragraph 10391.p6 that deals with the divine hierarchy on Mount Olympus (node 3 in the figure) may be replaced by a group of three adjacent sentences (10391.g17) consisting of the first three sentences of the paragraph. Similarly, paragraph 22566.p13 is replaceable by sentence group 22566.g7, which includes only the last three sentences of the paragraph.

An alternative way of reducing the path size is to use theme generation methods to obtain text excerpts covering the desired subject area. Figure 8 shows a theme generation map obtained by triangle merging for the Zeus subject area used in Fig. 7. Two themes are distinguished, "Olympian deities" and "birth of Zeus." The two text excerpts that are most similar to the respective theme centroids are 17232.p4 ("The 12 major Olympian deities were Zeus and his wife Hera. . .") and 24674.p5 ("Zeus was the youngest son of the Titans Cronus and Rhea. . ."). An appropriate short path covering Zeus can then be obtained as 24674.p3 (the initial paragraph of the Zeus article), followed by 17232.p4 and 24674.p5, representing the most important paragraphs in the two themes, respectively.

Text Summarization

In the absence of deep linguistic analysis methods that are applicable to unrestricted subject areas, it is not possible to build intellectually satisfactory text summaries (*14*). However, by judicious text extraction methods, collections of text passages can be identified that provide adequate coverage of the subject areas of interest. For example, when homogeneous text relation maps are available, a good summary is normally obtainable by use of one of the longer text-traversal paths in chronological (forward) text order.

Consider, as an example, the paragraph map for document 16585 ("Horatio, Viscount Nelson") (Fig. 9). Two paths are shown that start with the initial text paragraph 16585.p3. The dashed path traverses all "bushy" nodes—that is, nodes in which the number of incident links is large (≥6). The path marked by a heavy line is a complex depth-first path—that is, a depth-first path obtained by starting at each of the bushy nodes, proceeding in depth first order, and assembling the resulting excerpts into a single path in forward text order. The shorter, dashed path covers the highlights of Nelson's life in paragraphs 16585.p3, p6, p9, and p11, which deal, respectively, with a summary of Nelson's achievements as a British naval commander, his role in the battle of Copenhagen in 1801 after he had

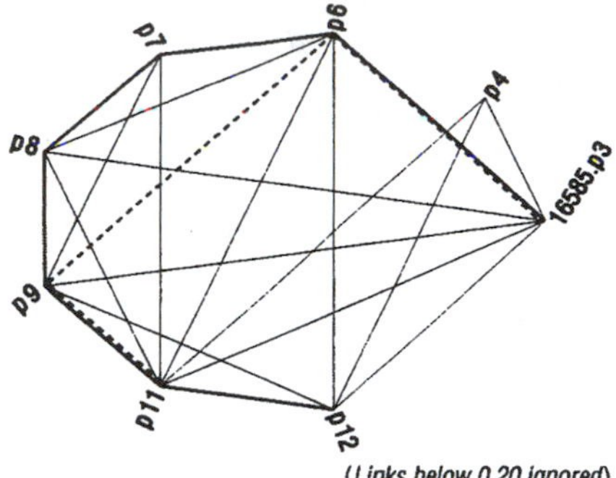

16585: Nelson, Horatio, Viscount Nelson

Fig. 9. Complex paths used for text summarization. Dashed path 16585.p3-p6-p9-p11 includes all bushy nodes; solid path 16585.p3-p6-p7-p8-p9-p11-p12 is a depth-first path.

become a vice admiral, and the crucial defeat of Napoleon during the battle of Trafalgar in 1805. The longer, solid path adds paragraphs p7, p8, and p12 of document 16585 to the paragraphs already present in the dashed path. This adds information about the battle of the Nile in 1798, plus a wrap-up paragraph covering Nelson's burial in St. Paul's Cathedral.

When the text relation map is substantially disconnected, the text-traversal process will not produce comprehensive summaries. In that case, adequate subject coverage is generally obtained by taking the initial paragraph of the main document under consideration, followed by the best paragraph for each text theme, as explained earlier. For the Zeus subject matter in Figs. 7 and 8, the resulting summary consists of paragraphs 24674.p3, 6489.p4, and 17232.p4. The corresponding summary introduces Zeus, the ruler of the Olympian Gods (24674.p3), mentions the story of the birth of Zeus as the sixth child of Cronus and Rhea (6489.p4), and terminates with an introduction to the 12 major Olympian deities (17232.p4).

When paths and themes are used for text summarization, longer summaries will be obtained when the text relation map is generated with low similarity thresholds. This produces denser maps with large numbers of text links. The themes may then partly overlap, and the summaries obtained by text extraction will be discursive. Contrariwise, when high similarity thresholds are used, the maps and themes tend to be disconnected and the summaries become sparser.

Conclusion

Formal evaluation data on the effectiveness of the methods introduced here are difficult to produce in the absence of detailed relevance information relating the content of many kinds of text excerpts to large numbers of subject queries. The experience accumulated with the wide-ranging subject matter in the Funk and Wagnalls encyclopedia indicates that useful output products are obtained in most cases. Because the approaches described here are robust and generally applicable to a wide variety of texts in many different environments, one may anticipate that such text-processing and knowledge-extraction capabilities will soon be widely used.

REFERENCES AND NOTES

1. M. Bernstein, J. D. Bolter, M. Joyce, E. Mylonas, in *Proceedings of Hypertext-91*, Association for Computing Machinery, San Antonio, TX, 15 to 18 December 1991 (ACM Press, Baltimore, MD), pp. 246–260; G. P. Landow, *Comput. Humanities* **23**, 173 (1989); J. D. Bolter, *Writing Space—The Computer, Hypertext, and the History of Writing* (Erlbaum, Hillsdale, NJ, 1991); P. Delaney and G. P. Landow, Eds., *Hypermedia and Literary Studies* (MIT Press, Cambridge, MA, 1991).
2. G. Salton, Ed., *The Smart Retrieval System—Experiments in Automatic Document Processing* (Prentice-Hall, Englewood Cliffs, NJ, 1971); ——, C. S. Yang, A. Wong, *Commun. ACM* **18**, 613 (1975); G. Salton, *Automatic Text Processing—The Transformation, Analysis, and Retrieval of Information by Computer* (Addison-Wesley, Reading, MA, 1989); *Science* **253**, 974 (1991).
3. G. Salton and C. Buckley, *Science* **253**, 1012 (1991); ——, in *Proceedings of SIGIR-91—Fourteenth International ACM-SIGIR Conference on Research and Development in Information Retrieval*, Chicago, IL, 13 to 16 October 1991, A. Bookstein, V. Chiaramella, G. Salton, V. V. Raghavan, Eds. (Association for Computing Machinery, New York, 1991), pp. 21–30.
4. An electronic version of the Funk and Wagnalls encyclopedia containing approximately 26,000 articles of text was used as a sample database in this study.
5. J. O'Connor, *Inf. Process. Manage.* 11, 155 (1975); *J. Am. Soc. Inf. Sci.* **32**, 227 (1980); S. Al-Hawamdeh and P. Willett, *Electron. Publ.* 2, 179 (1989).
6. G. Salton, C. Buckley, J. Allan, *Electron. Publ.* **5**, 1 (1992); G. Salton, J. Allan, C. Buckley, in *Proceedings of SIGIR-93—Sixteenth International ACM-SIGIR Conference on Research and Development in Information Retrieval*, Pittsburgh, PA, 27 June to 1 July 1993, R. Karfhage, E. Rasmussen, P. Willet, Eds. (Association for Computing Machinery, New York,1993), pp. 49–58.
7. C. Buckley, G. Salton, J. Allan, in *The First Text Retrieval Conference*, D. K. Harman, Ed. (NIST Special Publication 500-207, Government Printing Office, Washington, DC, 1993), pp. 59–72; C. Buckley, J. Allan, G. Salton, in *The Second Text Retrieval Conference*, D. K. Harman, Ed. (NIST Special Publication, Government Printing Office, Washington, DC, in press).
8. All text relation maps in this study are based on global text similarity as well as local context check restrictions. The similarity thresholds used to construct the text relation maps can be chosen so that the number of links does not greatly exceed the number of nodes appearing in the maps.
9. M. H. Anderson, J. Nielsen, H. Rasmussen, *Hypermedia* **1**, 255 (1989); M. Bernstein, in *Proceedings of the European Conference on Hypertext*, Versailles, France, November 1990, A. Rizk, N. Streitz, J. Andre, Eds. (Cambridge Univ. Press, New York, 1990), pp. 212–223; M. H. Chignell, B. Nordhausen, J. F. Valdez, J. A. Waterworth, *Hypermedia* **3**, 187 (1991); R. Furuta, C. Pleasant, B. Shneiderman, *ibid.* **1**, 179 (1989); P. Gloor, in *Proceedings of Hypertext-91—Third ACM Conference on Hypertext*, San Antonio, TX, 15 to 18 December 1991 (ACM Press, Baltimore, MD, 1991), pp. 107–121; T. C. Rearick, in *Hypertext/Hypermedia Handbook*, J. Devlin and E. Berk, Eds. (McGraw-Hill, New York, 1991), pp. 113–140.
10. R. A. Botafogo, E. Rivlin, B. Shneiderman, *ACM Trans. Inf. Sys.* **10**, 142 (1992); R. S. Gilyarevskii and M. M. Subbotin, *J. Am. Soc. Inf. Sci.* **44**, 185 (1993); C. Guinan and A. F. Smeaton, in *Proceedings of ECHT-92—ACM-ECHT Conference*, Milan, Italy, 30 November to 4 December 1992 (ACM Press, Baltimore, MD, 1992), pp. 122–130.
11. M. A. Hearst and C. Plaunt, in *Proceedings of SIGIR-93—Sixteenth International ACM-SIGIR Conference on Research and Development in Information Retrieval*, Pittsburgh, PA, 27 June to 1 July 1993, R. Korfhage, E. Rasmussen, P. Willet, Eds. (Association for Computing Machinery, New York, 1993), pp. 55–68.
12. F. Murtagh, *Comput. J.* **26**, 354 (1982); W. B. Croft, *J. Am. Soc. Inf. Sci.* **28**, 341 (1977); G. Salton and A. Wong, *ACM Trans. Database Syst.* **3**, 321 (1978).
13. G. de Jong, in *Strategies for Natural Language Processing*, W. G. Lehnert and M. H. Ringle, Eds. (Erlbaum, Hillsdale, NJ, 1982), pp. 149–176.
14. H. P. Luhn, *IBM J. Res. Dev.* **2**, 159 (1958); H. P. Edmundson and R. E. Wyllys, *Commun. ACM* **4**, 226 (1961); C. D. Paice, *Inf. Process. Manage.* **26**, 171 (1990); J. E. Rush, R. Salvador, A. Zamora, *J. Am. Soc. Inf. Sci.* **22**, 260 (1964).
15. The authors are grateful to the Microsoft Corporation for making the Funk and Wagnalls encyclopedia available in machine-readable form. Supported in part by NSF grant IRI 93-00124.

Seesoft—A Tool For Visualizing Line Oriented Software Statistics

Stephen G. Eick, *Member, IEEE,* Joseph L. Steffen, and Eric E. Sumner, Jr.

***Abstract*— The Seesoft® software visualization system allows one to analyze up to 50 000 lines of code simultaneously by mapping each line of code into a thin row. The color of each row indicates a statistic of interest, e.g., red rows are those most recently changed, and blue are those least recently changed. Seesoft displays data derived from a variety of sources, such as**

- **version control systems that track the age, programmer, and purpose of the code, e.g., control ISDN lamps, fix bug in call forwarding;**
- **static analyses, e.g., locations where functions are called; and**
- **dynamic analyses, e.g., profiling.**

By means of direct manipulation and high interaction graphics, the user can manipulate this reduced representation of the code in order to find interesting patterns. Further insight is obtained by using additional windows to display the actual code. Potential applications for Seesoft include discovery, project management, code tuning, and analysis of development methodologies.

***Index Terms*—Change management systems, code browsing, interactive graphics, line oriented statistics, scientific visualization.**

I. Introduction

A DIFFICULT problem in software engineering is understanding statistics collected at the source code line level of detail. This class of statistics includes information such as who wrote each line, when it was last changed, whether it fixes a bug or adds new functionality, how it is reached, how often it is executed, and so on. The problem is hard for large systems because of the volume of code. A moderately sized system may have thousands of lines of code and a large system may have millions of lines resulting in a large statistical data set. This paper describes a remarkable visualization technique to analyze line oriented data.

Line level data is available on all large software systems. It comes from version control systems, static analyzers, code profilers, and project management tools. This data, however, is underutilized because it is difficult to analyze. Version control systems such as the Revision Control System (RCS) [1], Source Code Control System (SCCS) [2], Change Management System (CMS) [3], Extended Change Management System (ECMS) [4], or SABLE [5] contain a complete history of the code. For each change to the software they typically capture information such as the affected lines, reason for the change, date, and responsible programmer. Static analyzers such as CIA [6] and cscope [7] capture the definitions of functions, types, macros, external variables, etc., and where they occur in the code. Profilers such as lcomp [8] perform basic block counting, indicating how often individual lines are executed.

Because of the volume of code it is difficult to gain insight from line oriented statistics or to get a perspective on the whole system. Statistical analysis techniques often involve aggregation. For many purposes, however, there is a need for finer grain detail. In addition, aggregation techniques discard the familiar and rich textual representation of the code. Code browsers, code formatting techniques [9], and version editors [10] are useful, but none of these generalizes to study arbitrary line oriented statistics.

Our approach to studying this class of data is to apply Scientific Visualization techniques [11]. We refer to this as *Software Visualization*. There is a distinguished history of visualization research starting with Tufte's seminal work [12]. Previous visualization work has involved traditional statistical data. Some notable examples include *MACSPIN* [13], scatter plot brushing [14], and dynamic graphical methods for analyzing network traffic [15]. Unfortunately, none of these methods is tailored for studying line oriented software data. We know of no techniques for studying this class of data that takes advantage of the underlying textual representation of software.

This paper describes a new technique for visualization and analysis of source code, and a software tool, Seesoft, embodying the technique. There are four key ideas: reduced representation, coloring by statistic, direct manipulation, and capability to read actual code. The reduced representation is achieved by displaying files as columns and lines of code as thin rows. The color of each row is determined by a statistic associated with the line of code that it represents. In several of our examples the statistic will be the date that the line was created. The visual impression is that of a miniaturized copy of the code with color depicting the age of the code. Then, using direct manipulation and high interaction graphics, a user manipulates the display to find interesting patterns. To display the actual code text the user opens up reading windows and positions virtual magnifying boxes over the reduced representation.

Fig. 1 shows a display of a directory containing 20 source code files containing 9 365 lines of code. The height of each column tells the user how large each file is. Files longer than one column are continued over to the next column. For the display, the line color[1] shows the age of each line using a rainbow color scale with the newest lines in red and the oldest

[1] In black and white versions of this paper color is to be interpreted as gray level. Red is equivalent to dark grey, green to medium gray, and blue to light gray.

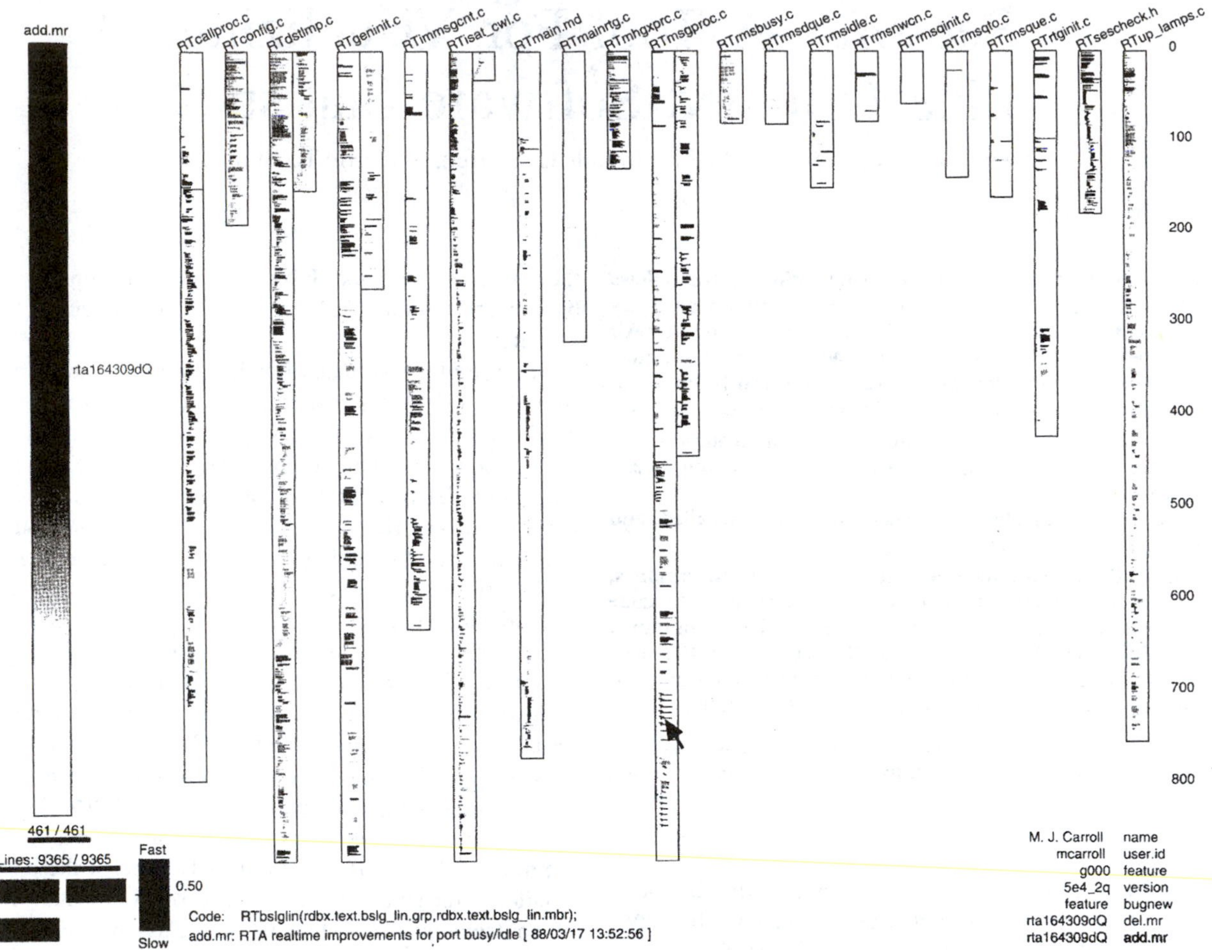

Fig. 1. Sample Seesoft display. A Seesoft display of a directory with 20 files and 9 365 lines of code. Each file is represented as a column and each line of code as a colored row. The files are either C code (.c), header (.h), or configuration management (.md) files. The color of each line is determined by the modification request (MR) that created the line. All MR's touching any of these files are shown on the left using a color scale with the oldest in blue and the newest in red.

in blue. On the left there is a scale showing the color for each of the 461 changes or modification requests (MR's) to this directory. The visual impression is that of a miniature picture of all of the source code with the indentation showing the usual C control structure and the color showing the age.

In the remainder of this paper we describe Seesoft and our visualization ideas in more detail. Section II describes the code display techniques and computer interaction methods used in Seesoft. Section III walks through a sample code analysis session to illustrate the types of insights that we have obtained while using Seesoft. Section IV discusses the general principles we use in our visualization techniques. These visualization techniques may be applied to the display of any ordered database. Section V discusses some software engineering applications. Section VI talks about our field experiences using Seesoft to solve some actual problems. Section VII describes how we implemented Seesoft, and Section VIII summarizes and concludes.

II. The Seesoft Software Visualization Tool

The Seesoft visualization tool displays line oriented source code statistics by reducing each file and line into a compact representation. The statistics are displayed with color. Then, using high-interaction graphics and direct manipulation techniques [16], the user manipulates the display to discover interesting patterns in the code and statistics.

For this approach to be effective the initial display must be informative and clear. With our display, programmers immediately recognize the files and lines of code because the display looks like a text listing viewed from a distance. The statistics are obvious from the row colors as is the spatial distribution of the statistic in the code. Next there must be easy and intuitive human interface techniques for the user to manipulate the display. We find that using direct manipulation techniques, in particular updating the screen in real-time in response to mouse actions, allows the user to manipulate Seesoft easily to find interesting patterns. Finally, there must be a technique to allow users to read the code. In our system users may open *code reading* windows that display the actual code corresponding to the rows underneath "magnifying" boxes that track mouse movement. This technique works well because it allows the user to have both an overview of the statistic and also read the interesting parts of the code. We now describe the Seesoft visualization tool in more detail.

Fig. 2. Example MR activation. As the user positions the mouse over an MR, the lines of code that MR created are activated.

2.1. Screen Description

The Seesoft screen layout consists of a file display, a mouse sensitive color scale, buttons, toggles, and a list of statistic names. Fig. 1 shows that the largest portion of the screen display consists of files shown as columns containing lines of code shown as colored rows. Using a 1280 × 1024 standard high-resolution monitor we can display about 900 lines of code per column. Files longer than 900 lines wrap and are displayed as multiple columns. For example, file `RTmsgproc.c` in the middle of Fig. 1 has 1 300 lines and is displayed in two columns. The name of each file is printed above it for easy identification. The row representation shows clearly the indentation and length of each line of code. The color of each line is tied to a line oriented statistic. This statistic is highlighted on the list of statistic names in the lower right-hand corner. The rows are just large enough so that block comments, functions, and control structures such as *case* and *if* statements are visible just by their indentation.

On the left side of the Seesoft display is a mouse sensitive color scale. Each color on the scale represents one value of the statistic associated with each line of code. The statistic might be age, programmer, feature, type of line, number of times the line was executed in a recent test, and so on. We often use the MR (modification request to a version control system) number for our statistic. The MR number is an interesting statistic because it comes in date order, is the smallest unit of program change, and is associated with programmers, developers, and features. The MR's are displayed sequentially with the newest at the top and oldest at the bottom. Underneath the scale, the number of activated statistic values and the total are shown, 461/461 in Fig. 1, as well as the number of activated code lines and total, 9365/9365. The color scale is a generalization of traditional sliders controlling thresholds. The user may select discontinuous threshold ranges, as well as the traditional continuous ranges that normal sliders may select.

At the bottom of the screen there is space for Seesoft to print the current code line and the statistic value. As the cursor is positioned over any color in the color scale the value of the statistic represented by the color is printed at the bottom of the Seesoft display. In Fig. 1 this is the MR number, abstract (a short description of the purpose of the MR), and date. If the cursor is over a row, Seesoft also prints the line of code associated with that row. We have additional methods of viewing that we describe below.

2.2. Linking Between the Color Bar and Code Lines

Each statistic value is linked to the lines of code having that value through a common color. When the user activates

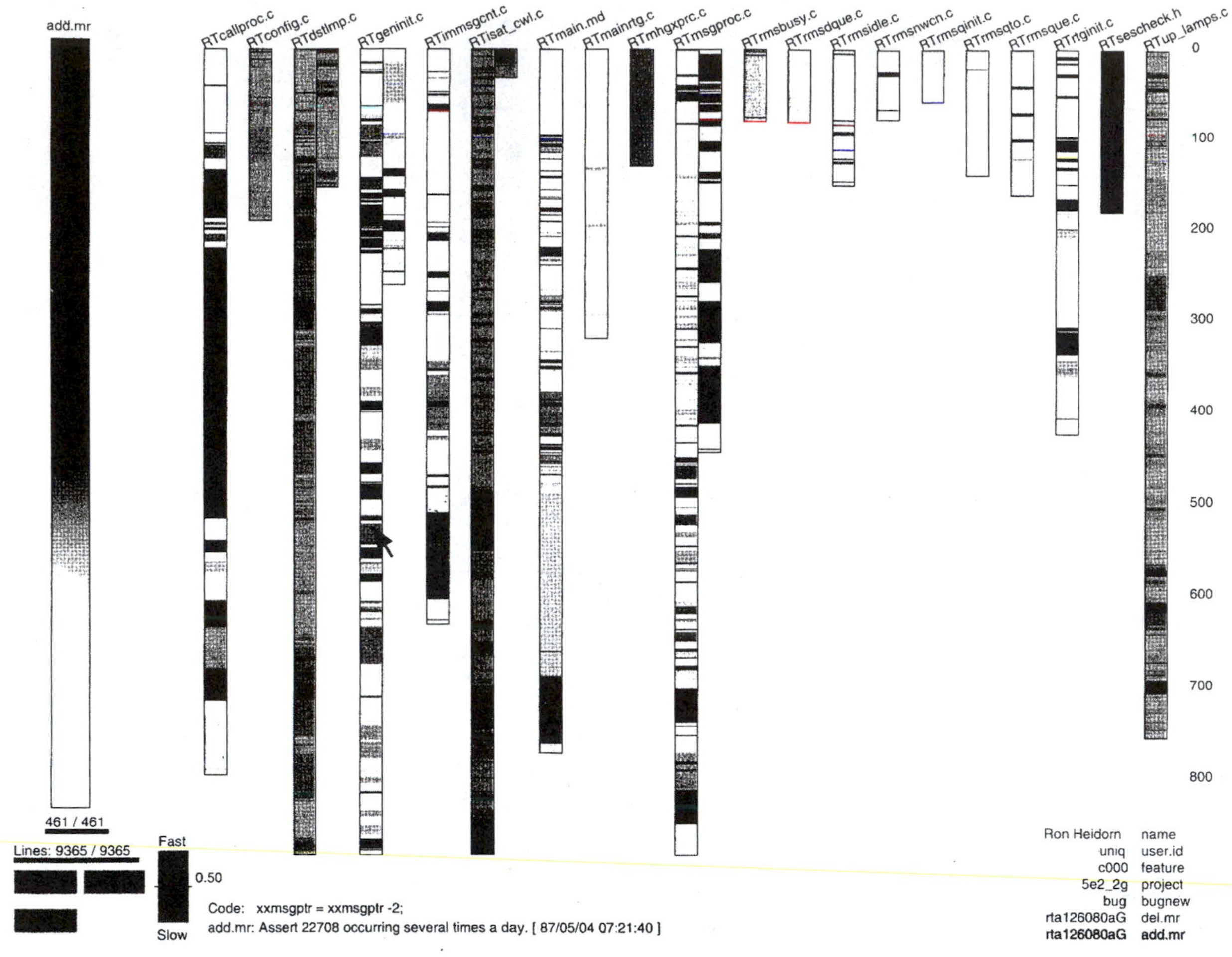

Fig. 3. Source code with no indentation. By turning off indentation it is easier to see the age of the code. The oldest lines are displayed in dark blue and the newest in red. The display shows the relative size of the files, age of the code, and how many times each file has been changed.

a value by positioning the cursor over it, the associated color is activated and the corresponding code lines are turned on. In Fig. 1 all MR's are activated and thus all code lines were visible. To obtain Fig. 2 from Fig. 1, first all MR's are deactivated and then the cursor is positioned over one MR in the scale. Activating a line of code activates its MR and thus any other lines of code created by that MR. Activating a file activates all of the lines in the file and thus all of the MR's used to create them.

2.3. Mouse Operations

The screen is mouse sensitive. As the user moves the mouse around the screen the entity under the mouse is automatically activated and the corresponding color and lines turned on. Activating MR's and code lines is described above. Activating a file name activates all lines within that file. When the mouse is moved away from an entity it is automatically deactivated. Depressing the left mouse button causes the activation to be permanent and the middle deactivates previously activated items. This style of user interaction is called brushing [17].

2.4. Buttons, Toggles, and Code Reading

At the bottom of the display there are mouse sensitive buttons and an animate slider. The user may turn off line indenting by clicking on the *Indent* button. This causes the rows to be drawn the full width of each column (see Figs. 3 and 4). The *Animate* button causes the computer to sequentially display all statistic values, one at a time.

Depressing the *Reading* window button causes two actions to occur. A window for displaying C code text is opened, and a small colored "magnifying" box is created. As the magnifying box is moved over the colored rows the actual code is displayed in the reading window (see Fig. 5). The size of the magnifying box is proportional to the amount of code that is displayed in the reading window. This enables the user to understand what fraction of the total code is visible in the code reading window. The border color on each reading window matches the color of its corresponding magnifying box.

III. Sample Code Analysis

This section describes a quick analysis of the change history in a sample directory using Seesoft. From the version control

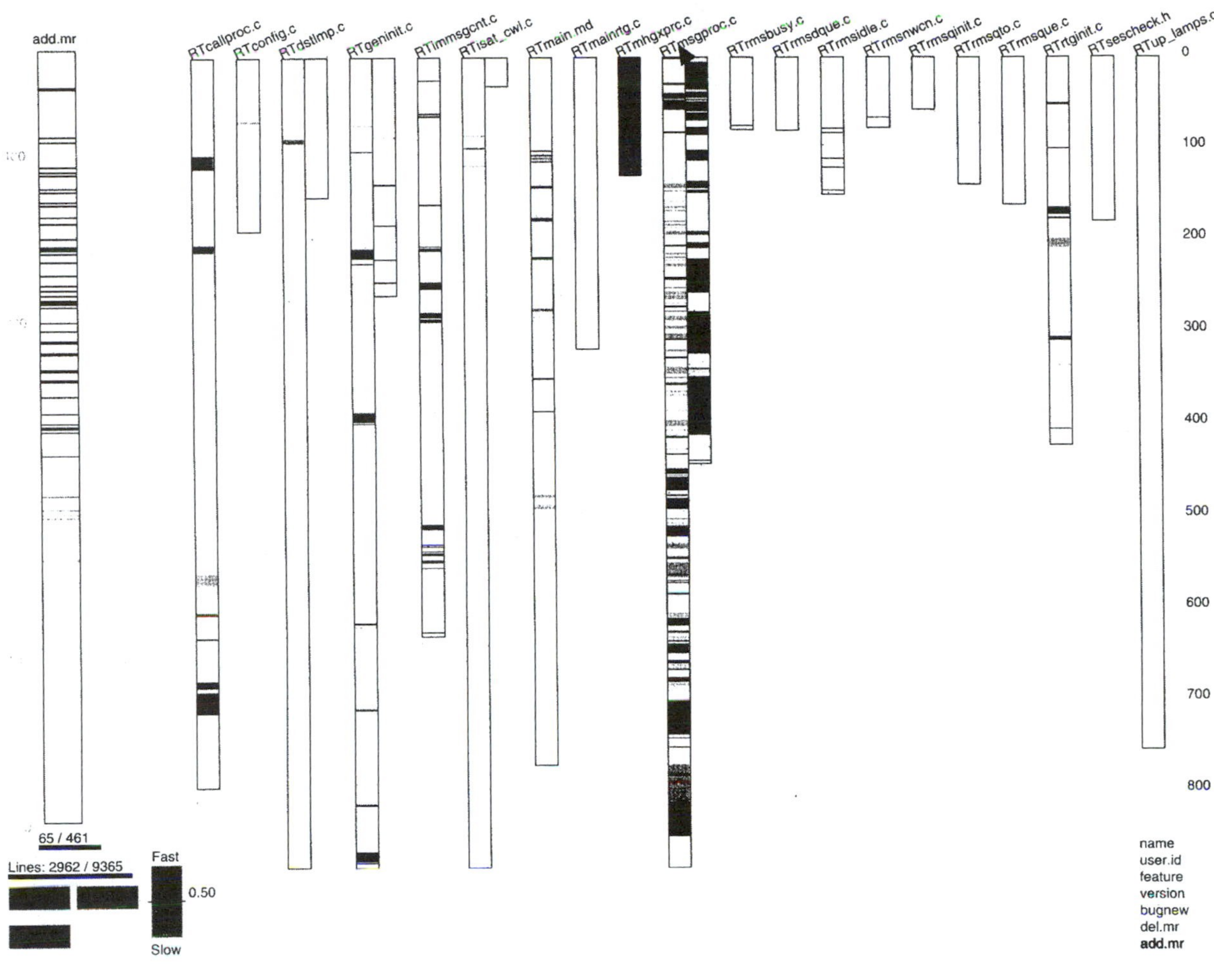

Fig. 4. A File With Many Changes. File `RTmsgproc.c` has been changed 65 times out of 461 total for this directory. The changes have occurred consistently over the last several years.

system for each line we obtain the adding MR, whether the change fixed a bug or added new functionality, the version, the feature number, the user id of the developer adding each line, and the developer's name. The directory has 20 source code files including a configuration management (.md) and an include (.h) file that were created by 461 MR's and 168 developers. In total there are 9 365 lines of code. Fig. 3 shows the code with indentation turned off, and the color of each line tied to the MR that created it. Turning off indentation makes it easier to see the age of the lines. The oldest code dates to 1984 and is shown in dark blue and the newest code from early in 1991 is shown in red. The age patterns of the files are striking. Much of the code in files `RTmsgpoc.c`, `RTcallproc.c`, `RTgeninit.c`, `RTmainrtg.c`, and `RTginit.c` is blue indicating that it dates to 1984. These files are interesting because along with the blue code they display many other colors indicating that they have been changed many times, including recently. There is a set of small light blue files (`RTrmsbusy.c`, `RTrmsdque.c`, `RTrmsidle.c`, `RTrmsnwcn.c`, `RTrmsqinit.c`, `RTrm-sqto.c`, and `RTrmsque.c`) dating to 1985, and a set of green files (`RTconfig.c`, `RTdstlmp.c`, `RTisat_cwl.c`, `RTmhgxprc.c`, and `RTup_lamps.c`) dating to 1987. The light blue and green files have been stable since few changes are shown.

In this directory there have been 461 changes. To find the files that have changed the most we turn off all lines and sequentially touch each of the file names. Fig. 4 shows that the file `RTmsgproc.c` has been changed 65 times, and the pattern of the changes on the MR color scale shows that changes have been occurring consistently since this file was created. We investigated the frequent changes and found that it is the main control flow for the directory. A common enhancement strategy has been to add a function call to this file and put the code for the new function definition in another file. Fig. 5 shows such an enhancement where a new function was added to fix a bug and a corresponding function call was inserted in `RTmsgproc.c`.

By activating files created by common MR's, there appear to be three different sets of files in this directory. Figs. 6, 7, and 8 show the groupings. Fig. 6 shows the set of green files that were added in 1987. These files were created for a major enhancement.[2] Fig. 7 shows the set of light blue files that have

[2] A 5ESS expert on this section of the code subsequently told us that these files were added to provide IDSN capability.

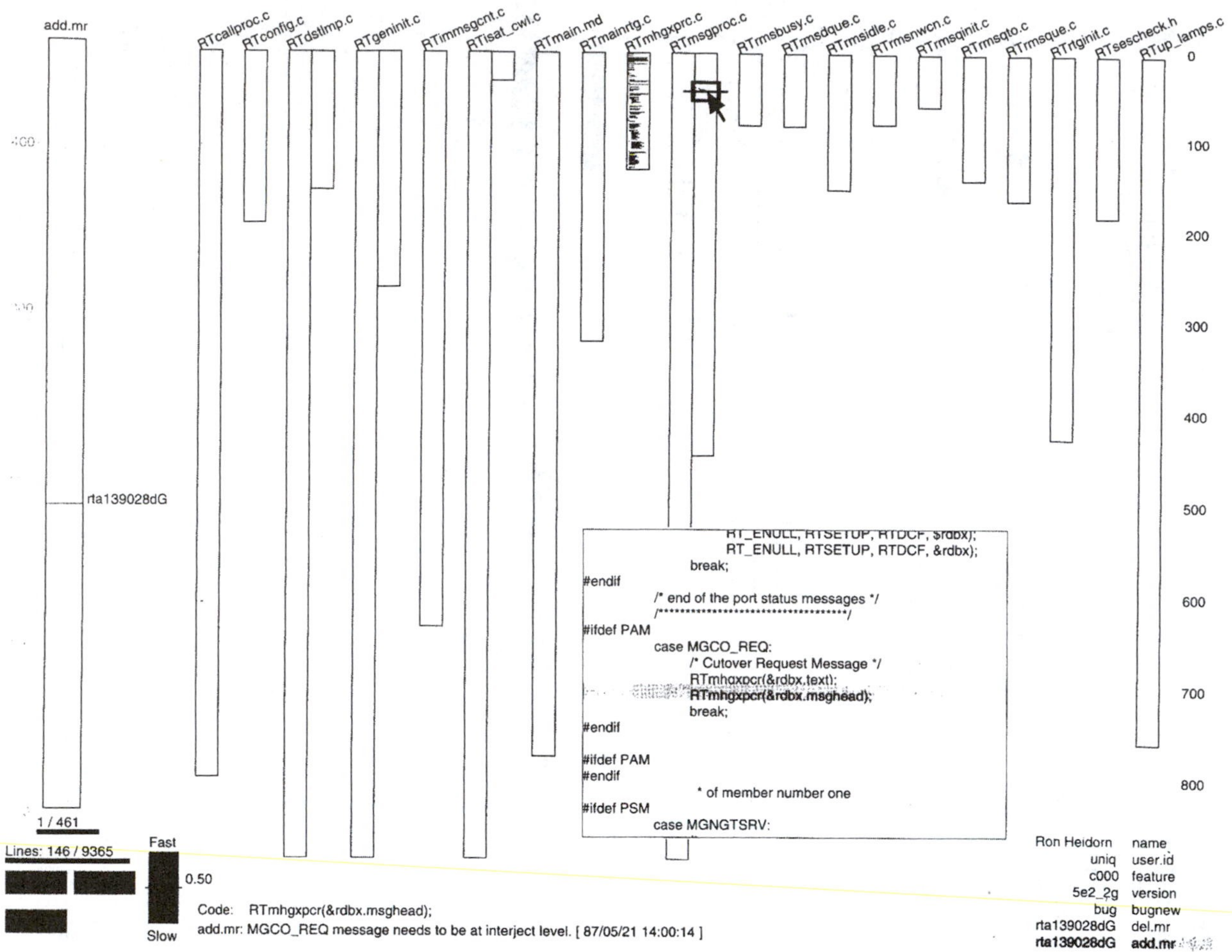

Fig. 5. Modular change. A bug is fixed by inserting a function call in `RTmsgproc.c`, shown in the *Code Reading* window, and putting the code for the function in a new file. The *Code Reading* window may be independently positioned.

been stable since 1985.[3] The heavily changed set of files in Fig. 8 are the control flow files in the program. In this directory there is a clear historical work pattern. New functionality is added by creating new functions and then inserting function calls in the main files. Through time there have been several major enhancements that created sets of files.

There are two types of MR's, new feature MR's and bug fixing MR's. Fig. 9 shows the display with the bug MR's in red. Certain files such as the green and light blue files have had few bug fixes. These files were created at one time with a small number of MR's. Other files have multiple bug fixes.

In Fig. 10 the line color is tied to the user id of the programmer writing each line. Files `RTconfig.c`, `RTdstlmp.c`, and `RTup_lamps.c` are written by one individual with a few changes by other people later to fix bugs. Some of the other files with lots of colors have been changed by many different developers. There is a relation between the locations of the bug fixes in Fig. 9 and the number of developers touching the files in Fig. 10. Files touched by many developers have more bug fixes.

[3] The expert was unaware that these files even existed.

What have we learned in this quick Seesoft session? We know which files are changed most often, the age of the code, and when each file was last changed. We also know that the files in this directory may be clustered into three groups, each group created by a different set of MR's. If it became necessary to divide this directory, files in each cluster could be kept together. We also know where code has been changed recently and that recent MR's have created fewer lines of code than earlier MR's. We also found that certain files have been changed continuously and that the bug fixing MR's are concentrated in these files. These files might be candidates to be restructured or rewritten to reduce maintenance costs.

IV. Visualization Techniques

Our approach to visualizing software is to think of source code files and lines as entities in an ordered database. In the preceding examples we display statistics associated with entities obtained from the version control system. For each entity we have a representation, columns, and rows, chosen so that we can view a large volume of data on a single screen. This allows us to gain insight into the overall structure of the database. Database queries are entered and answered visually.

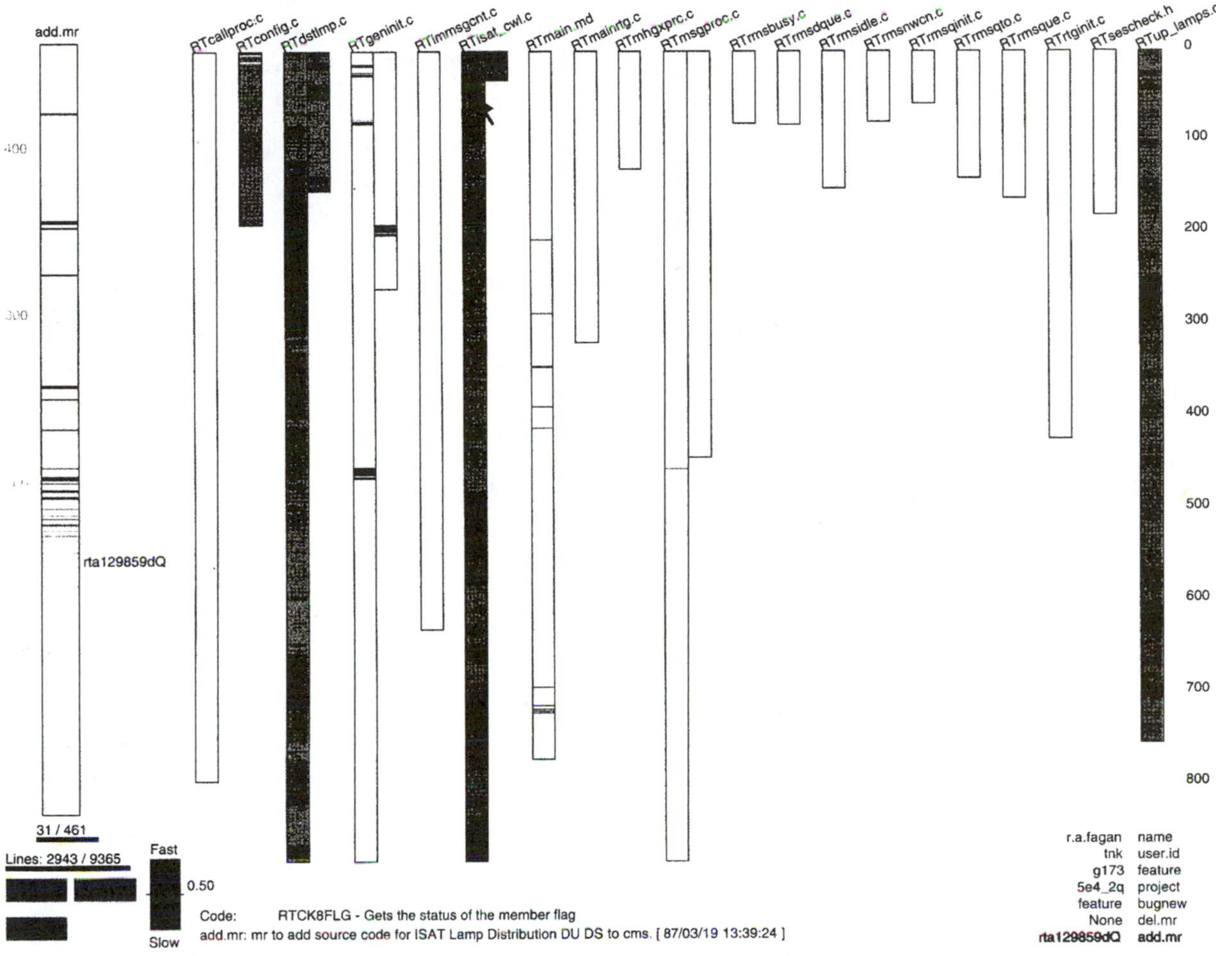

Fig. 6. Groupings of files—a significant new feature. A new feature was put into the code in 1987. This code is primarily in four files and has been stable.

As the user moves the cursor over mouse sensitive portions of the screen he or she is performing a series of database queries. Seesoft then activates the lines of code that resolve the database queries. This approach allows the user to probe the database by moving the mouse around the screen. When he or she discovers an interesting pattern, we provide a mechanism to view the database directly, the reading window in our case, in addition to the reduced representation.

We are currently in the process of obtaining some additional ordered databases. Our approach applies to databases where there is interest in understanding the overall structure and querying the database based on particular attributes. For example, one possible application would be to display a text corpus such as the Bible. Each book could be represented as a column and each verse as a row. A subject index or the age of each verse could be used to color the rows. Another application we are working on is to represent directories as columns and files as rows. This would allow us to visualize even more code on a single display.

The Seesoft user interface employs high interaction graphics and direct manipulation techniques. As the mouse is moved over the display screen entities are automatically activated and deactivated. Since there are no "point and click" delays and no waiting for screen refreshes, a different style of interaction is possible. Our style of interaction makes it easy for the user to experiment with different activations and to probe the display interactively. For example, with Seesoft it is possible to view each one of several hundred MR's by running the mouse over the color scale. Any unusual MR's will be visually obvious. This would be infeasible if the user were required to "click" on every MR.

V. Seesoft Applications

We envision Seesoft being used in several application areas including

- code discovery,
- new developer training,
- project management,
- quality assurance and system testing,
- software analysis and archeological studies,
- code coverage analysis, and
- code execution optimization.

The code discovery problem is faced by a programmer attempting to change an unfamiliar portion of the source code. Programmers, given requests for additional functionality, must

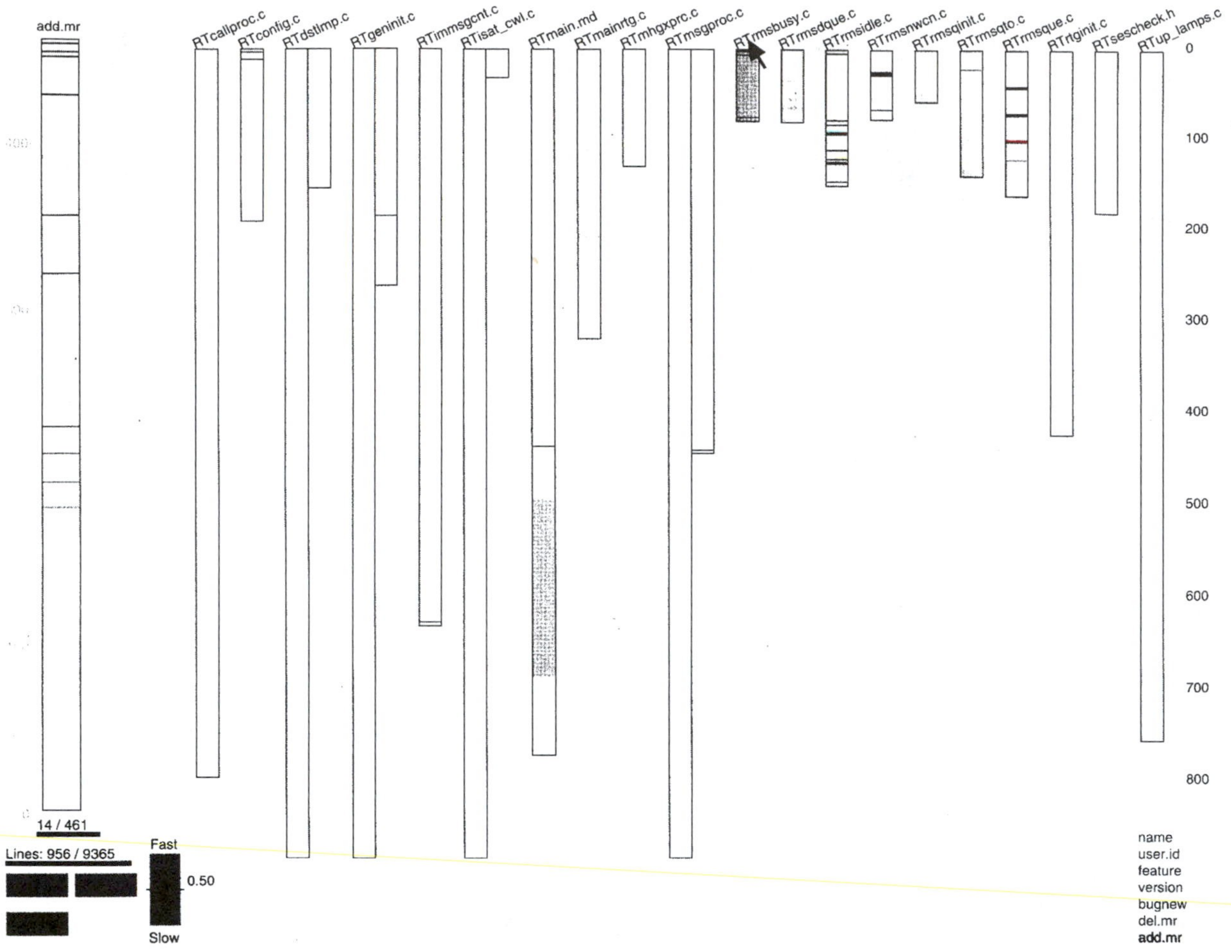

Fig. 7. Groupings of files—stable utility functions. By activating files created by common MR's, we find that there are three different sets of files in this directory. This set is a stable set of utility functions.

study the current code to determine which files contain the existing functionality and which lines to change within these files. This task is often difficult and time consuming. In fact it may take several weeks of detailed study to change a few lines with no unwanted side effects. On large, old projects a significant fraction of a programmer's time is devoted to code discovery. Using Seesoft a programmer can easily determine which lines were created to deliver an existing functionality, the programmers who created those lines, why they were created, and the purpose of nearby lines.

New programmer training is a problem faced by all large software projects. Multiyear projects with large development staffs have considerable staff turnover. Seesoft can ease the programmer training problem by providing new trainees with a global view of the source code. Since Seesoft displays tens of thousands of lines of code simultaneously, new programmers can form a mental picture of the code. Using Seesoft it is easy to answer questions such as:

- How are the files in my program organized?
- When were they last touched?
- Where is the code for this feature?
- What code was written by the person I am replacing?

A class of new programmers might be given Seesoft and access to a code expert. They would use Seesoft to view the code and could immediately ask the expert to explain the interesting things that they discovered.

Project managers monitor a development in order to ensure that the project is on schedule. Using Seesoft a project manager can visually track all source code changes done during the last week or month and can verify that recent changes are consistent with the schedule. In addition, he or she can identify potential trouble spots by the presence of a high level of churn or excessively complex code. A manager can check recent changes in order to trap quick fixes that are likely to cause long term difficulties. He or she can also use Seesoft to identify code that needs to be restructured or rewritten.

Quality assurance inspectors can use Seesoft to determine if new code meets coding specifications and is in the proper files. System testers can determine which regression tests to run by identifying the system functionality embodied in the files that are changed by recent MR's.

Analysts may use Seesoft to understand the effect of various software development environments and processes. For example, an analyst could compare code developed using C

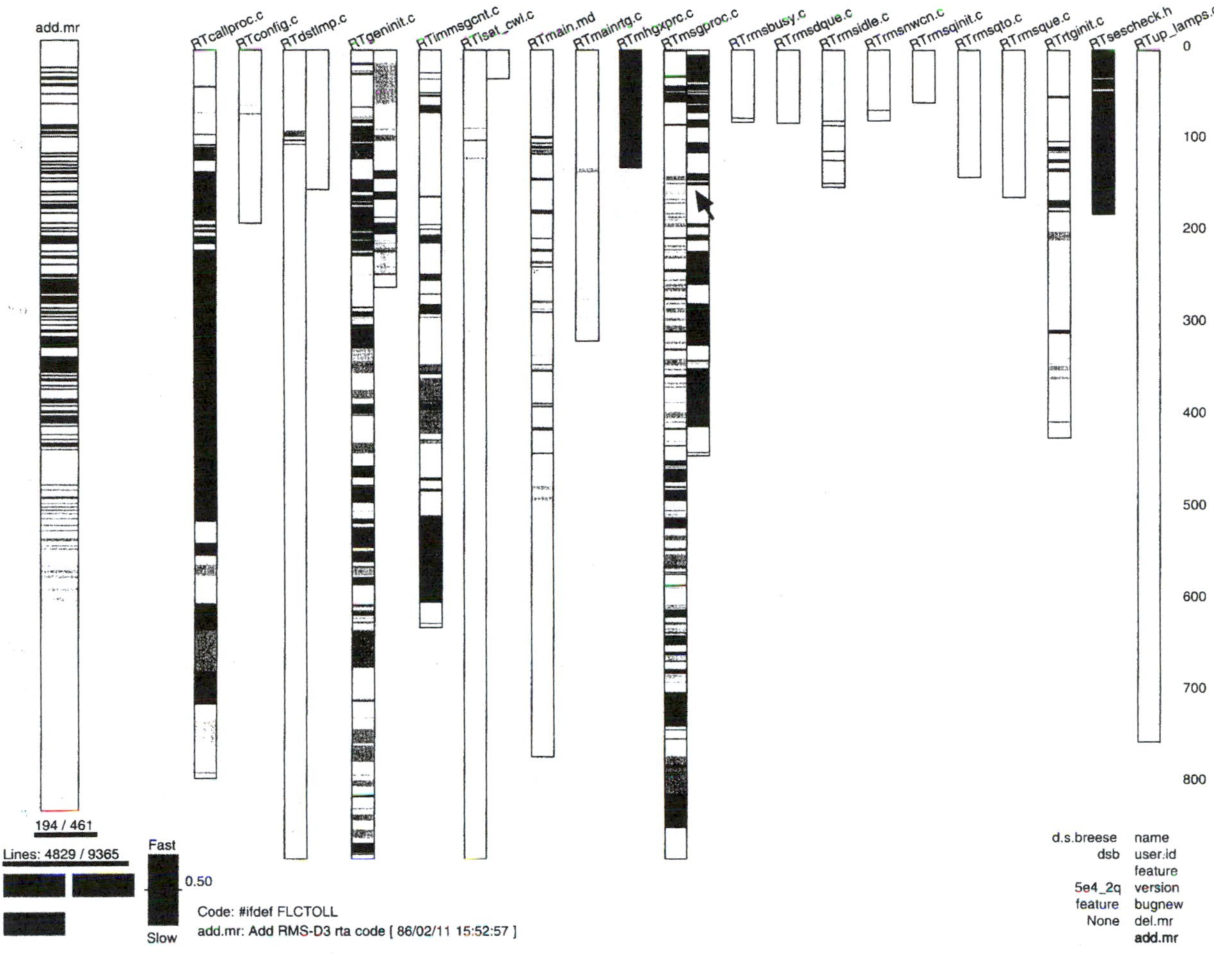

Fig. 8. Groupings of files—main process control flow. Activating files `RTmsgpoc.c`, `RTcallproc.c`, and `RTgeninit.c` creates this figure. These files control the flow in this directory. They have been changed many times, usually with small changes, as developers add hooks for new functionality. Many of the MR's are for bug fixes.

and C++ in order to determine if bug fixes in the C++ code were more localized. Analysis of multiple projects over time could be used to estimate the effects of project age and size on programmer efficiency.

Developers optimizing the performance of a program can use Seesoft to display execution frequency data for each line, identify hot spots, and then use data from static analyzers and version control systems to evaluate potential improvements.

VI. Seesoft Field Experiences

This section describes the experiences of some actual Seesoft users. The reaction of programmers and managers at all levels to Seesoft demonstrations has been enthusiastic. Many state that they wish that Seesoft had been available for some recent work. Another common scenario is that a department picks up responsibility for some unfamiliar code and would like to use Seesoft to help gain familiarity with the software. Since our visualization techniques are recent, our experiences to date with actual applications are limited, but preliminary results are promising.

The results in Figs. 9 and 10 suggest that files changed by many different developers have more bugs than files written by one or two developers. These and other results have led some projects to assign ownership of large sections of code to individuals who will have responsibility for all changes. To make the code assignments one developer used Seesoft to look at the change history of all of the code in her project. She divided the code into related areas using a clustering technique based upon the change history, and used Seesoft to review the results. She then used Seesoft to assess the activity level in each cluster, and assigned developers sets of clusters intended to balance the load.

Another Seesoft project involved object-oriented programming. A particular manager was interested in applying object-oriented programming to developing switching software. She used Seesoft as an archeological tool to determine which subsystems would benefit most. She found that in certain subsystems the embedded code rarely changed—new features involved adding new files. For these subsystems she concluded that the object-oriented approach would have limited value. For other subsystems, however, implementing new features involved making extensive changes to existing files, suggesting that using an object-oriented approach might be useful.

There have been several cases where developers were

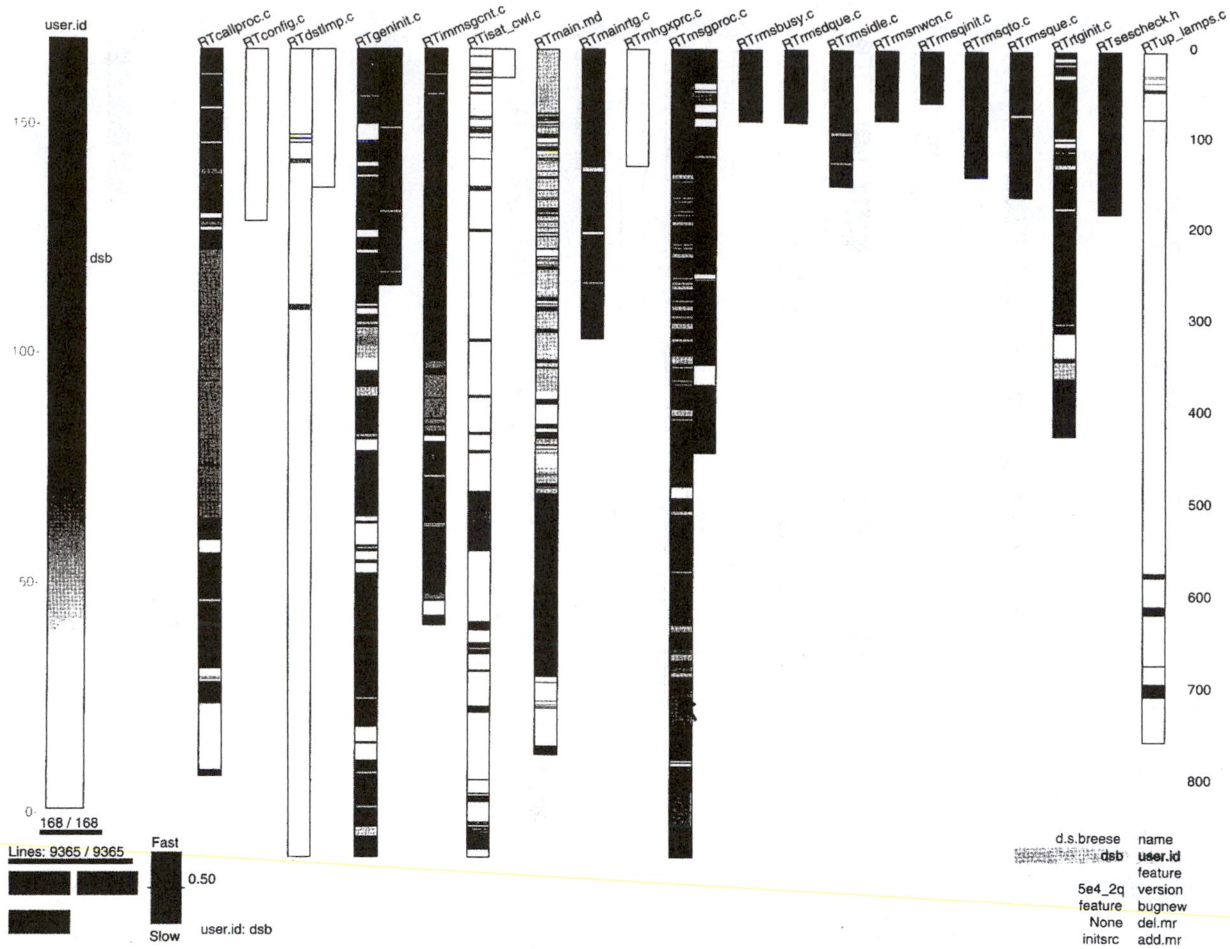

Fig. 9. Locations of bug fixes. MR's for fixing bugs are shown in red. Bug fixes are concentrated in a few of the files.

interested in looking at their own code. One particular expert looked at a recent port and discovered that he had made an error. He had copied a few files from another application and had intended to add a few lines of his own code to each file in order to complete the port. When he colored the copied code in blue, and his own in red, it was immediately obvious that he had failed to add code to one of the files.

VII. Implementation

Seesoft currently runs on Silicon Graphics Iris workstations, although we plan to port it to the X Window System [18]. Seesoft is written in C++ [19] and uses the Silicon Graphics GL graphics library. In total it is about 2 000 lines of C++ code. To deliver real-time user interaction we require the graphics capability to rapidly manipulate the displays, particularly the color map. Seesoft draws each statistic value and associated code lines in its own color. Activating and deactivating is done by manipulating the color map. The colors for the activated statistic values are turned on and for the deactivated values are turned off. Color map manipulation is fast on Iris workstations because it is done in hardware.

Our source code history data came from ECMS. We use the S language for data management and preliminary analysis [20]. To read this data we developed a series of shell scripts to strip unnecessary information and reformat the data for S input. S provides a computational environment, static graphics, and data management that support interactive manipulations. We link Seesoft into the S executive, perform all data manipulation in S, and then launch Seesoft from S.

Silicon Graphics Iris workstations come with 19-in color monitors. Using the column and row representation we find that we can easily understand 20 000 lines of code and can understand 50 000 if we are close to the monitor. In each column we can display about 900 lines and can comfortably fit 25 columns on a single monitor. With more than 50 000 lines displayed the columns become very narrow.

VIII. Discussion and Conclusion

This paper describes a new technique for visualizing line oriented statistics associated with source code and a software tool, Seesoft, embodying the technique. There are four key ideas: reduced representation, coloring by statistic, direct manipulation, and capability to read actual code. The reduced representation is achieved by displaying files as columns and lines of code as thin rows within the columns. The color of each row is determined by a statistic associated

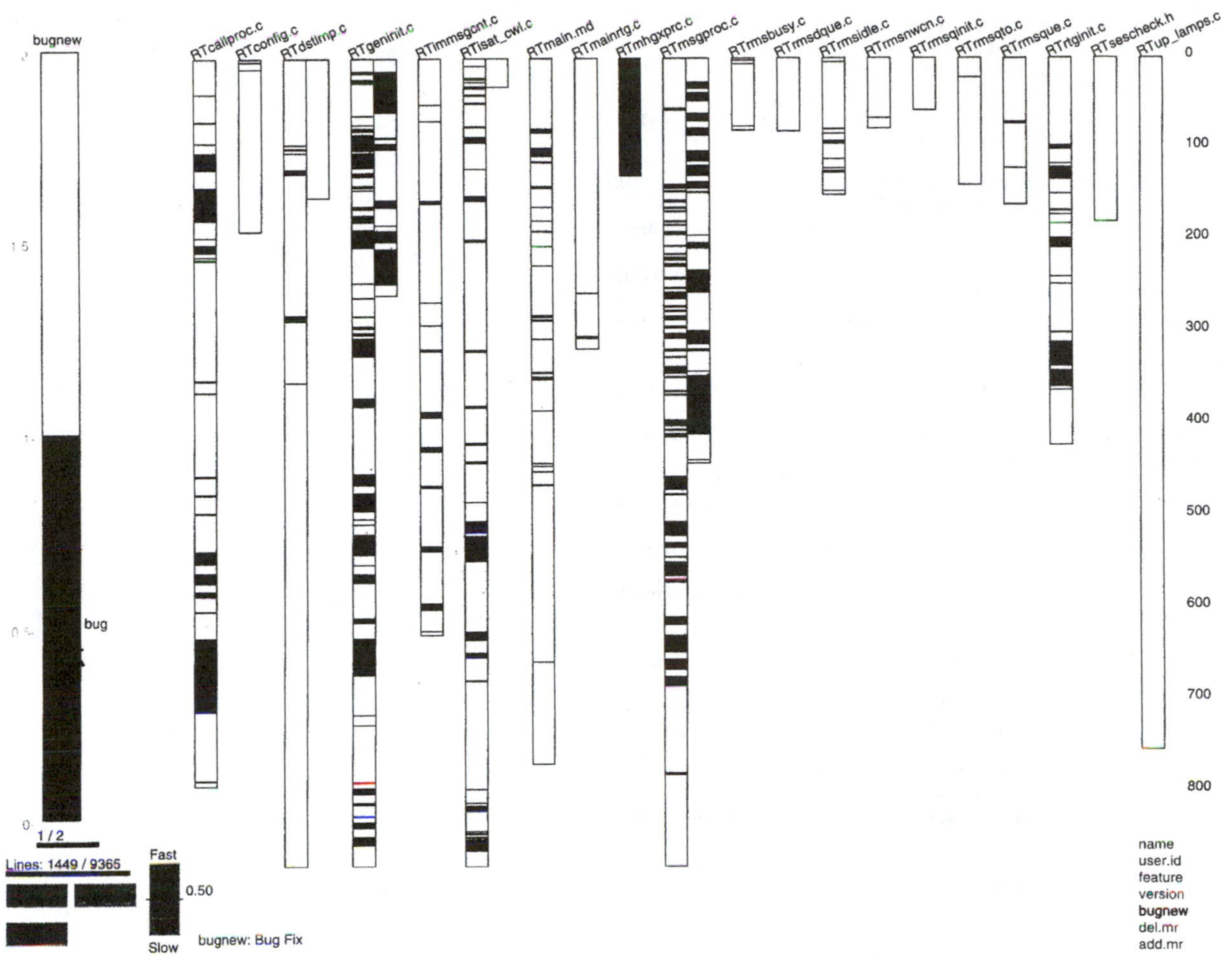

Fig. 10. The color shows the users making changes in this directory. Note that the files with lots of bug fixes are the same files that have been changed by many different developers.

with the line of code that it represents. In our examples we obtained the statistics from a version control system. The visual impression is that of a miniaturized copy of the code with color depicting the spatial distribution of a statistic. Then, using direct manipulation and high interaction graphics, a user manipulates the display to find interesting patterns. To display the actual code text the user opens up reading windows and positions magnifying boxes over the reduced representation.

Besides analyzing source code statistics, our technique has application to any ordered database. Examples include transaction databases, indexed text such as legal writings, a text corpus such as the Bible, and software documentation.

As with any method there are limitations. Our visualization technique provides a qualitative view of the distribution of a statistic in code. As with all graphical methods, the technique is useful for discovering patterns. After the patterns are discovered, hypotheses may be tested by means of standard statistical methods. Currently, Seesoft is unable to display more than 50 000 lines of code simultaneously; however, we are working on other techniques using different abstractions that scale beyond this limit. A key idea in Seesoft is its interactive use of direct manipulation techniques and use of color. It is difficult to describe these in a static monochrome medium such as this paper.

We developed Seesoft in conjunction with the 5ESS ®Telecommunications Switch Project, which includes millions of lines of code developed over 10 years. Because the initial results are so promising we are creating an 85-gigabyte optical disk based archive of the complete code history of 5ESS, including version control data, project management data, and cscope symbol databases derived from monthly snapshots of the code.

Acknowledgment

The authors would like to acknowledge helpful conversations with R. A. Becker, R. Drechsler, G. Nelson, and A. R. Wilks.

References

[1] W. F. Tichy, "RCS—A system for version control," *Software—Practice and Experience*, vol. 15, pp. 637–654, 1985.

[2] M. J. Rochkind, "The source code control system," *IEEE Trans. Software Engineering*, vol. SE-1, pp. 364–370, 1975.

[3] B. R. Rowland and R. J. Welsch, "Software development system," *Bell Syst. Tech. J.*, vol. 62, part 2, pp. 275–289, 1983.

[4] P. A. Tuscany, "Software development environment for large switching projects," in *Proc. Int. Switching Symp.*, pp. 199–214, 1987.

[5] S. Cichinski and G. S. Fowler, "Product administration through SABLE and NMAKE," *AT&T Tech. J.*, vol. 67, pp. 59–70, 1988.
[6] Y. F. Chen, "The C program database and Its applications," in *Proc. Summer USENIX Conf.*, 1989.
[7] J. L. Steffen, "Interactive examination of a C program with Cscope," in *USENIX Dallas 1985 Winter Conf. Proc.*, USENIX Association, pp. 170–175, 1985.
[8] P. J. Weinberger, "Cheap dynamic instruction counting," *AT&T Bell Laboratories Tech. J.*, vol. 63, pp. 1815–26, 1984.
[9] R. Baecker and A. Marcus, *Human Factors and Typography for More Readable Programs.* Reading, MA: Addison-Wesley, 1990.
[10] A. A. Pal and M. B. Thompson, "An advanced interface to a switching software version management system," in *Proc. 7th Int. Conf. Software Engineering for Telecommunications Switching Systems*, pp. 110–113, 1989.
[11] G. M. Nielson, B. Shriver, and L. J. Rosenblum, Eds., *Visualization in Scientific Computing.* Los Alamitos, CA: IEEE Computer Society Press, 1990.
[12] E. R. Tufte, *The Visual display of Quantitative Information.* Cheshire, CT: Graphics Press, 1983.
[13] A. W. Donoho, D. L. Donoho, and M. Gasko, *MACSPIN: A Tool for Dynamic Display of Multivariate Data.* Monterey, CA: Wadsworth & Brooks/Cole, 1986.
[14] R. A. Becker and W. S. Cleveland, "Brushing scatter plots," *Technometrics*, vol. 29, pp. 127–142, 1987.
[15] R. A. Becker, S. G. Eick, and A. R. Wilks, "Basics of network visualization," *IEEE Computer Graphics and Applications*, vol. 11, pp. 12–14, 1991.
[16] B. Shneiderman, "Direct manipulation: A step beyond programming languages," *IEEE Computer*, vol. 16, pp. 57–68, 1983.
[17] R. A. Becker, W. S. Cleveland, and G. Weil, "The use of brushing and rotation for data analysis," pp. 247–275 in *Dynamic Graphics for Statistics*, William S. Cleveland and McGill, Eds. Wadsworth, 1988.
[18] V. Quercia and T. O'Reilly, "X window system user's guide," O'Reilly & Associates, Inc., Sebastopol, CA, 1988.
[19] B. Stroustrup, *The C++ Programming Language.* Reading MA: Addison-Wesley, 1987.
[20] R. A. Becker, J. M. Chambers, and A. R. Wilks, The New S Language. Pacific Grove, CA: Wadsworth & Brooks/Cole, 1988.

5.2 Text in 2D

The obvious mapping of text to 2D is by tiling pages or generating composite pages. For example, tiled thumbnail images of pages are commonly used to represent collections of documents (e.g., Johnson et al., 1993b). This idea can be extended by focus + context techniques to show both the thumbnails and some detail (Robertson and Mackinlay, 1993 ●). An interesting example of composite pages is Golovchinsky (1997). Golovchinsky's system has a visualization that uses information retrieval techniques to create a newspaper view of a hypertext collection. Thumbnail images and composite pages are effective for relatively small collections of documents.

For larger collections, some attempts have been made to create a 2D semantic map of the document space. One way of doing this is to generate a 2D concept space from categorical axes, a kind of 2D Dewey decimal system or perhaps a map of a 1D Dewey decimal system versus year of publication. The problem is that the space may be sparsely populated or only roughly reflect the distinctions in a collection. Another way is to arrange a given collection of documents so that related ones are spatially near and form a map, a kind of conceptual grocery store (related things are mostly near and the space usage for each depends on the number of products actually present). This is what the Lin paper (1992b ●) does. Lin uses the idea of a self-organizing map from Kohonen (1989; 1990) to create a 2D visualization of a large text collection.

In Lin's system, documents from the collection are used to train the nodes in a 2D grid, creating neighborhoods of similar nodes according to topic. Documents in the Data Table are represented as vectors, where keywords are components of the vector. The Kohonen algorithm allows these vectors to adjust themselves iteratively ("training") until they converge on a 2D map. After training is complete, the documents in the collection are assigned to nodes, which allows the user to identify neighborhoods by sampling the documents associated with nodes. Boundaries are drawn separating the map into regions and the regions named.

In addition to interesting visualizations that lay out the space of concepts for some collection, the Kohonen maps can show other properties of the collection. For example, Lin's paper contains two figures showing the reading activity of an individual. The first map shows the location of the first 100 documents read by the person, and the second map shows the last 100 documents. Shifts in reading interests are clearly visible.

A Kohonen feature map has the obvious problem that it can be expensive to train. Lin avoids this problem by using small training sets and a supercomputer. Much of the research inspired by Lin's paper has explored other algorithms for the 2D layout of document collections (Chalmers, 1996; Hemmje, Kinkel, and Willett, 1994; Hendley et al., 1995; Ingram and Benford, 1995; Olsen et al., 1993; Wise et al., 1995 ●). The literature also includes the 2D layout of network nodes, briefly discussed in Section 2.5 (Eick and Wills, 1993 ●; Fairchild, Poltrock, and Furnas, 1988 ●). Generally, the algorithms involve some form of iterative optimization with subdivision strategies to improve performance. Chalmers (1996) compares various algorithms and describes an efficient algorithm he developed that uses stochastic techniques to improve performance. He uses his algorithm to create layout documents as a 2D landscape in a 3D space that allows the user to zoom into areas of interest.

Lin's 2D maps of document collections have regions with clear boundaries and succinct, descriptive labels. Unfortunately, it is not easy to automatically generate these boundaries and labels. Boundaries have to be drawn through territories that represent multiple topics. Subtle judgments may be required to make sure each of these topics is fairly represented. Labels must be derived from the contents of a region, which can have complex similarities and differences. The most effective labeling requires computational linguistic techniques, which is currently impracticable for large document collections.

Visualization for the Document Space

Xia Lin
Center for Computerized Legal Research
Pace University
White Plains, NY 10603
Bitnet: lin@pacevm

Abstract

Visualization for the document space is an important issue for future information retrieval systems. This article describes an information retrieval framework that promotes graphical displays which will make documents in the computer visualizable to the searcher. As examples of such graphical displays, two simulation results of using Kohonen's feature map to generate map displays for information retrieval are presented and discussed. The map displays are a mapping from a high-dimensional document space to a two- dimensional space. They show document relationships by various visual cues such as dots, links, clusters and areas as well as their measurement and spatial arrangement. Using the map displays as an interface for document retrieval systems, we will provide the user with richer visual information to support browsing and searching.

1. Introduction

Visual information plays an important role in human communication and recognition. In their day-to-day life, people are used to information on tangible media stored in visible locations. They employ a whole set of perception and association techniques, in addition to verbal communication techniques, to get information from the environment. However, when information is stored in a computer, it becomes invisible to people. All the clues for visual perception and associations disappear. Access to information in the computer relies on one's ability to generate a good query and the computer's capability to match the user's query to information stored in the database. At best, when interaction is involved, one can modify the query based on the retrieved results of the query. This is like searching for a book in a library without light. One can walk around from stack to stack. He can get a few books each time and walk out of the library to see if the book he is searching for is among them. If not, he has to walk in again to a location where he thinks the book would likely be, based on his knowledge about the library and the experience he has the last time. In this situation, success in finding the book greatly depends on user's ability to walk to the right place (generating a good query), and to adjust his locations until he gets to the right place (interactive query generation).

Could we turn the light on? Could we make information in the computer visualizable to the user? These are questions that researchers have been seeking for answers since early 1960s when the computer was first used for information retrieval. Doyle once proposed a semantic road map that could serve as "a view of the entire library at a glance"[1]. The view would help the searcher to "narrow his focus by recognition", and then to bring out more and more detail about relevant documents by "microscopes". However, the technology at that time prevented him from implementing and testing his idea further. Today, using advanced computer technology to revive Doyle's idea, we are in a much better position to build a map display that will make both document contents and relationships visualizable to the searcher.

This article proposes a map display for information retrieval based on Kohonen's feature map, a neural network's self-organizing learning algorithm. The map display is a mapping from a high-dimensional document space to a two-dimensional space. It shows document relationships by various visual cues such as dots, links, clusters and areas as well as their measurement and spatial arrangement. It 'abstracts" the underlying structure of a document space and displays it in a map form. Using the map display as an interface for document retrieval systems, we will provide the user with richer visual information to support browsing and searching. In the following sections, we first describe a framework that promotes graphical displays for information retrieval. Kohonen's feature map is then discussed, and two of its simulated results on visualizing document collections are presented. The final section discusses various types of graphical displays for information retrieval and different types of underlying engines for different types of graphical displays.

2. A framework of information retrieval

Fig. 1 shows two frameworks of information retrieval. The one on the left-hand side describes general characteristics of current retrieval systems. Given a query, typically a Boolean logic expression, the retrieval system searches through the whole database and returns those items that literally match the query. Then the retrieval system displays the search result to the user, usually in a linear form, such as a list of authors or a list of document titles. Within this framework, the "exact match" may be improved by some techniques, like "truncation match", "wild card match", or "proximity match", etc. In any of these cases, the retrieval system generally considers matching documents individually; no use is made of relationships among documents. The relationships of documents are sometimes reflected in the display. Even in such cases, because of its linearity, the display simplifies all relationships to a one-dimensional, linear order, either chronologically, alphabetically, or some kind of relevant (weighted) order between documents and the query.

To get around the framework of "exact match" and "linear display", we have the second framework. In this framework, the "exact match" is expanded to "fuzzy match"[1], and the "linear display" is replaced by "graphical display". "Fuzzy match" loosely covers retrieval methods using advanced statistics and probability theory, fuzzy logic, computational linguistics and various aspects of artificial intelligence. In these methods, measures ofdocument closeness are adopted and association of documents is considered at the time of matching and retrieving. To make these more effective, the framework emphasizes that the relationships of documents should also be considered during display. The display should be more than one dimensional in order to capture the complexity of document relationships. It should take advantage of graphical features to make information in the document set visible to the user; it should be constructed so that the capability of human perception can be utilized; and it should be able to intrigue the user to discover or recognize patterns that emerge from underlying data.

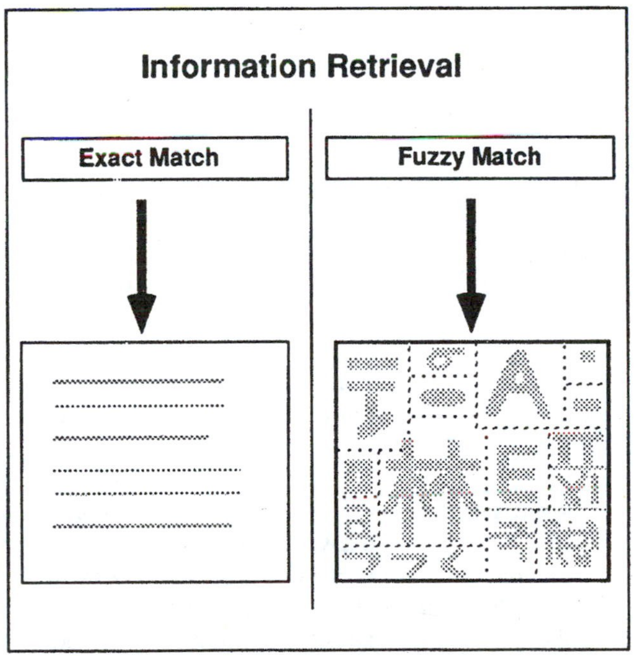

Fig.1 Two frameworks for information retrieval. The left hand side is the traditional "exact match — linear display" framework. The right hand side is the "fuzzy match — graphical display" framework. See text for discussions of the frameworks.

[1] "Fuzzy" should really be read as "not exact", as we use "fuzzy match" to refer all those that do notfall in the "exact match" category.

The frameworks simplify information retrieval into two steps: retrieval and display. For many years, research on information retrieval in fact was centered around these two steps. Traditional research focused more on retrieval than on display [2]. Current research has been making a great progress in terms of expanding "exact match" to "fuzzy match" [3]. It is unfortunate that results of "fuzzy match" are still most often displayed in linear forms. One may argue that the linear form could eventually be improved, such as displaying documents in orders relevant to the query. We strongly believe that, rather than improving the linear display, a two-dimensional display should couple better with the "fuzzy match". With appropriate construction, the two-dimensional graphical display will allow the screen to accommodate more documents, show relationships of documents, and reveal underlying structures and patterns. Combining these with human perception capabilities, the user will likely find it easier to do the most intelligent and subjective job in retrieval: making relevant judgments and selecting documents that satisfy his information needs.

Introducing two-dimensional graphical displays for information retrieval may provoke new thought on the matter of information retrieval. While the linear display seems to be a natural counterpart of the "exact match", we will show that the two-dimensional graphical display will serve better for results of "fuzzy match". As the "exact match" is expanded to "fuzzy match", the display is at least as important as retrieval. It is important to realize that query matching is inherently inaccurate [4]. While it is generally desirable to have high precision and high recall retrieval mechanisms, it is perhaps more practical to provide browsing aids so that the user can easily identify relevant information in a low precision/high recall situation. Graphical displays that let the user visualize document relationships and browse large amount of search results will likely relax the demands on matching mechanisms. Thus, our research is to construct and study graphical displays that can be integrated into various information retrieval systems to improve the functionality of the systems.

3. Kohonen's feature map algorithm

Kohonen's feature map algorithm is based on the understanding that "the representation of knowledge in a particular category of things in general might assume the form of a feature map that is geometrically organized over the corresponding piece of the brain" [5]. The algorithm takes a set of N-dimensional objects as input and maps them onto nodes of a two-dimensional grid, resulting an orderly feature map. Two main properties of such a feature map are:

- the feature map preserves the distance relationships between the input data as faithfully as possible. While some distortion is unavoidable, the mapping preserves the most important neighboring relationships between the input data, and makes such relationships geographically explicit.
- the feature map allocates different numbers of nodes to inputs based on their occurrence frequencies. The more frequent input patterns are mapped to larger domains at the expense of the less frequent ones [6].

Kohonen's feature map has been applied to many practical problems in various areas such as statistical pattern recognition, speech recognition, robot arms control, industrial process control, image compression, optimization problems and analysis of semantic information [7]. Early examples and applications of feature maps mostly demonstrated that the feature map could preserve metric relationships and the topology of input patterns. The application of the feature map to cognitive information processing particularly offers the possibility "to create in an unsupervised process topographical representations of semantic, nonmetric relationships implicit in linguistic data" ([6], p. 243).

In the following two sections, we present two simulation results of using Kohonen's feature map to generate map displays for the document space. The first is an example of how a set of documents retrieved by a query can be mapped to reveal major concepts and clusters of the document set. The second demonstrates how a personal collection can be mapped into a personal knowledge space to allow easy inspection of one's own personal collection.

4. A Map Display for documents on multilingual information retrieval

After conducting an extensive search on multilingual information retrieval on INSPEC database in DIALOG, we obtained a set consisting of 311 documents. From this set, we produced an inverted index of the 311 titles. After excluding some stop words, the most frequently occurring words and the least frequently occurring words (those appearing no more than 4 times), 40 words were retained. These words were used as the set of indexing words for this collection. These 40 words and 311 titles form a 40*311 matrix of documents vs. indexing words, where each row is a document vector and each column corresponds to a word. A document vector contains a "1" in a given column if the corresponding word occurs in the document title and a "0" otherwise.

The document vectors are used as input to train a feature map of 40 features and 140 nodes (140 nodes are chosen because the 10 by 14 rectangle seems to fit the screen best). Following the Kohonen's algorithm:

- each feature corresponds to a selected word;
- each document is an input vector;
- each node on the map is associated with a vector of weights which are assigned small random values at beginning of the training;
- during the training process, a document is randomly selected, the node closest to it in N-dimensional vector distance is chosen; and the weight of the node and weights of its neighboring nodes are adjusted accordingly;
- The training process proceeds iteratively for a certain number of training cycles. It stops when the map converges.
- When the training process is completed, each document is mapped to a grid node.

Fig. 2 is the semantic map of the documents obtained after 2500 training iterations. The map contains very rich information:

- The areas on the map can be seen as concept areas (more precisely, word areas). These areas, determined by mapping of unit vectors after the training is completed, visualize the general content of this collection. As we can see, multilingual information retrieval is represented by the map in roughly three parts, the languages such Chinese, Japanese, Arab and EUROTRA (the left part), the technologies such as software, interface, networks, speech (understanding), and expert (systems), (the middle part), and the tools such as (multilingual) dictionaries, thesaurus, bibliographies and libraries (the right part).

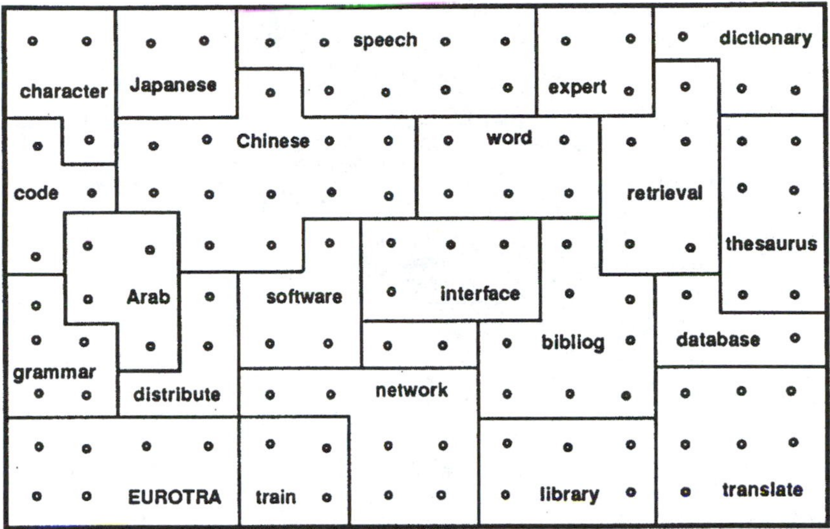

Fig.2 The map display for a document collection on multilingual information retrieval. The map shows the content of the collection roughly in three parts, the languages on the left, the technologies on the middle, and the tools on the right.

- The size of the areas corresponds to the frequencies of occurrence of the words appeared in the titles. Thus, that the area "Chinese" is larger than the area "Japanese" indicates that there are more documents on Chinese retrieval than documents on Japanese retrieval in this collection. Similarly, there are likely more discussions on distributed networks than on interface.
- The neighboring relationships of areas indicate frequencies of the co-occurrence of words represented by the areas. Areas of "character coding" is next to areas of "Japanese" and "Chinese" because they often co-occur in the documents. Thus, we may get the impression that a major issue for Asian languages retrieval is character coding. On the other hand, "EUROTRA" is next to "grammar", "distributed networks" and "training", so we know that EUROTRA (a major project on cross-retrieval on European languages) deals with more on grammars and distributed networks than on character coding. Without reading any documents, we have already seen a difference between Asian languages retrieval and European languages retrieval.

5.A map display for a personal collection

The second simulation was to apply Kohonen's feature map to a personal collection. A researcher's personal collection was collected in a HyperCard stack. The collection contained 660 documents, which were accumulated over many years as a by-product of the person's research activities. Each document in this collection contains a citation (author, title, source, etc.), an abstract and sometimes the first page of the article. We first did a preprocess that included the following four steps: 1) identification of unique words in the collection after necessary truncations, 2) exclusion of the stop words, 3) frequency counts of all the words identified, and 4) exclusion of the most and the least frequently occurring words. The preprocessing resulted in 1472 unique words which was then used to index the collection, creating 660 vectors of 1472 dimensions. After a normalization process, these vectors were used as input to train a 10 by 14 Kohonen's feature map. Figure 3 shows the result after 2500 learning iterations. The whole learning process took about 202 seconds in a Cray super-computer. As we see, the mapping of such a personal collection creates a personal knowledge space. The space shows the researcher's major research areas and the relationships of these areas. The size of areas, corresponding to the frequencies of the words, indicates relative importance of the areas to the researcher (the more often a word appears in the personal collection, the more likely the word will correspond to a large area in the space). The neighboring relationships, corresponding to the frequencies of co-occurring words, reflect associations of the areas resulting

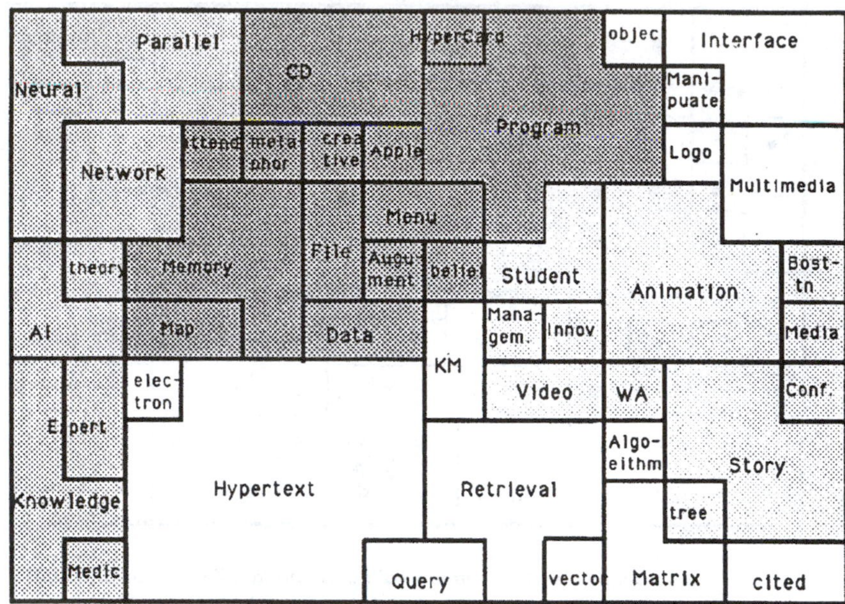

Fig.3. A map display for a personal collection. The display shows the person's major research areas and their relationships. The size of areas indicates relative importance of the areas to the searcher. The neighboring relationships reflect associations of the areas resulting from the activities of the researcher.

from the activities of the researcher. Some of these associations, such as the association of "query" with "retrieval", are clear to anyone in the field of research, other associations may need the interpretation of the researcher. For example, without knowing that the researcher was interested in animation for story-telling to students, we would not understand why "story" and "student" were represented as two major areas nearby the area marked "animation".

The space is organized in a hierarchical form. The colors (or the gray scales) indicate the four top levels of the hierarchy. Within each level there are subject areas organized by their inter-relationships. For example, within the first hierarchical level on the left, "traditional AI" and "neural networks" are located on different side of the area "AI". This indicates two different but associated approaches to artificial intelligence; while "parallel" is close to "neural networks", "expert (systems)" is close to "Knowledge (base)", and so on. When we looked further into the "neural networks" area (by analysis of mapping results not shown on the map), we could see that words mapped to this area were: connectionist, model, learning, process, unsupervised, net, error, and principle component analysis. (Evidently, the researcher is interested in comparing neural networks to principle component analysis.) Similarly, words mapped onto "hypertext" area included link, text, color, structure, browsing, and University of North Carolina at Chapel Hill (where the first hypertext conference was held).

Each document in the collection also has a unique position in the personal knowledge space. The document positions show the distribution of the personal collection over the personal knowledge space. This distribution may remind the researcher which areas he has more documents and in which areas he may need to have more documents. The distribution can also be used to show migration of the researcher's interest over time. Figure 4 gives the distributions of the first 100 documents and the last 100 documents in the collection. Since the documents are collected sequentially over time, we can see a clear migration of the researcher's interest from early more broad distribution over several areas, such as CD-ROMs, programming languages, and interfaces, to a more current concentration on neural networks, matrix (operations) and retrieval. The interpretation, of course, will make more sense to the researcher than to others. When the map was presented to the researcher, he confirmed that those areas and relationships shown on the map were "basically correct". He found that what we interpreted by the map sometimes even revealed interesting relationships he did not think about before. He thought that the map could be seen as a picture or a summary of his past six years research activities.

There are many other potentials for the personal knowledge space. One of the most important ones will be to incorporate such a space in a personal information system. A personal information system in the future will no longer limit to physical collection in his office or his

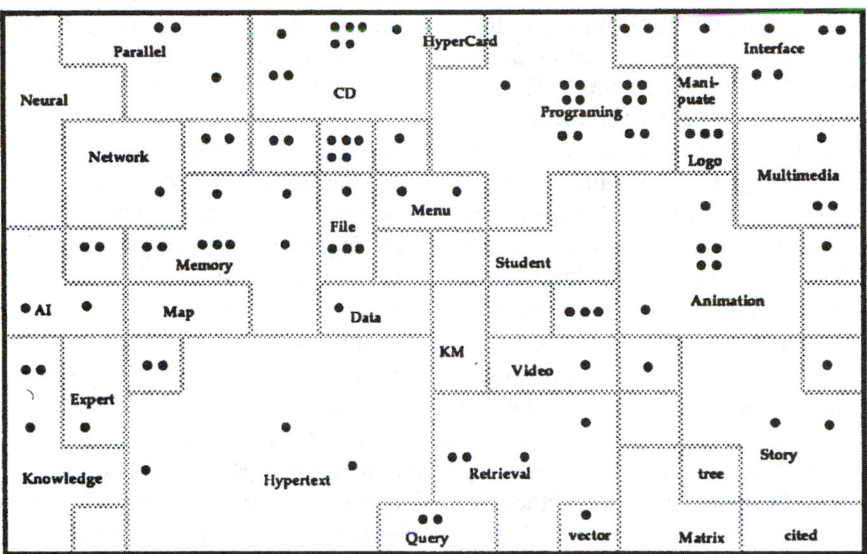

(a) Distribution of the first 100 documents in the personal collection

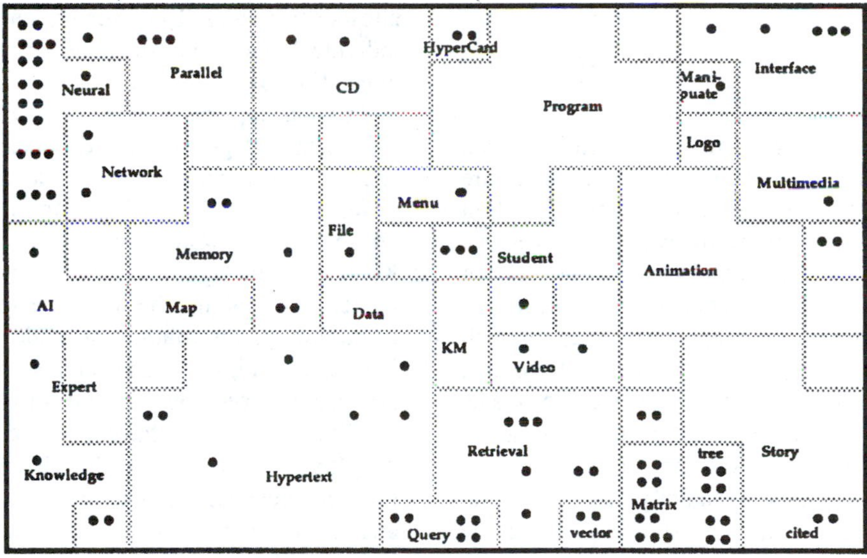

(b) Distribution of the latest 100 documents in the personal collection

Fig. 4. Document distribution on the personal knowledge space. The two different time periods of documents showed very different distributions, indicating the change of the personal research activities.

home. It will include those documents in many online fulltext databases that are reachable any time and that are constantly being added with more documents. Thus, a more important component of future personal information systems is a personal indexing and personal monitor. The indexing maintains an indexing to documents, both in-house and online, that he is interested in. A map of his personal interest will be drawn and undated as the indexing is updated. Based on the map, or the personal knowledge space, the monitor will routinely keep track of new documents in the online databases. Any documents that fall into the personal space will be shown on the space. All the indexing, updating, and monitoring may take place during the night. Thus, every morning, when a researcher come to his office, he will notice new documents by scanning through the map. Then he can decide if the new documents should be kept with his personal indexing or discarded. When documents are kept with the indexing, they will eventually change the map later through updating.

6. Discussions

Visualization for the document space is an important issue for future information retrieval systems. There are two fundamental questions related to this issue. The first is what kind of graphical displays that will better visualize the document space, and the second is which underlying engine will derive the graphical display that we select.

We would like to have the graphical display that will convey a great deal of information to the user so that effective use of the human visual capabilities can be made. The graphical display should help to reveal useful structure of the document space to assist the user in searching and browsing this space. It should eventually help the user to acquire new knowledge and understanding about the document space.

In the literature, there have been several types of graphical displays for information retrieval, mainly icon displays [8][9], hierarchical displays [10][11], network displays [12][13], and scatter displays [14][15]. The icon display takes advantage of a symbolization process to enhance the association between the graphical display and the underlying information. The hierarchical display imposes a rigid structure to obtain clusters and hierarchies from the underlying data. The network display explicitly makes links among items in order to support associations and visual inference. The scatter display emphasizes overall layout of a document space in an attempt to reveal the underlying structure as faithfully as possible. While the icon display is more individualized, the hierarchical display and the network display are more structuralized, and the scatter display is more spatialized (See [16]) for more discussion on these different forms of graphical displays).

In this paper, we proposed a map display that shows overall layout of a document space in a structuralized form. We argued that the map display may provide the right granularity and richer visual information, compared to other forms of graphical displays. The map display has a minimum-error mapping feature as does the scatter display. It shows implicit links through its neighboring relationships in order to avoid overly complex link structures as often found in many network displays. The map display lets the underlying structure "emerge" from the input data, rather than be "imposed" by programs or other artificial means, so it does not limit itself to a structure as rigid as the hierarchy, and clusters and groups can still come out naturally from the mapping. Spatial arrangement of visual cues on the map display also improves the association between documents and their major concepts.

The map display has many other potentials as well. It allows some naturally occurring ambiguities and lets each individual viewer impose his interpretations of the display, depending on his interests at the time of observation. With good implementation, the map display will be able to present multiple views of the same underlying structure, and let the user zoom in to display the views at a level of different details [17]. Furthermore, the map display can be generated automatically by its underlying engine, Kohonen's self-organizing feature map. As a dimensional reduction technique, the feature map has the properties of economic representation of underlying data and their interrelationships. As a visualization tool, the feature map produces rich geographic features for visual inferences.

Other engines that have been used to generate graphical displays often include hierarchical clusters, multidimensional scaling, principal component analysis, and various mathematical models such as graph theories, Lattices, PFnets, etc. It would be interesting to compare Kohonen's feature map with those of others within the context of generating graphical displays for information retrieval. When we used a data set, containing 900 patterns of 150 dimensions, to test several of these engines, we found that the hierarchical cluster program took more than 20 times longer than the Kohonen's feature map to produce a result. The principal component analysis just took about twice as much time as the feature map, and the multidimensional scaling was completely out of the race. While these comparisons need to be read with caution as they may be bias because of our particular implementations of these engines, our experience seems to suggest that Kohonen's feature map would be more feasible to implement on information systems than the other engines that we mentioned.

Acknowledgments. This article is based on the author's dissertation. The author wishes to thank his dissertation committee for their support and guidance. Partial of the work described in this article was conducted during my association with the Information Access Research Group at Apple, Summer, 1991. The author is particularly grateful to Tim Oren and Daniel Rose of the group for their help and fruitful discussions.

References

[1] Doyle, L. B. Indexing and abstracting by association. American Documentation, October, 1962, 378 - 390.

[2] Korfhage, R. R. To see, or not to see --- is that the query? Proceedings of the Fourteenth Annual International ACM/SIGIR Conference on Research and Development in Information Retrieval (Oct. 13-16, 1991; Chicago, Illinois). p. 134-141.

[3] Belkin, N. J. & Croft, W. B. Retrieval techniques. In Williams, M. Ed. Annual Review of Information Science and Technology, Vol.22, 109-145, 1987.

[4] Schatz, B.R.; & Caplinger, M.A. Searching in a hyperlibrary. Proceedings of the Fifth International Conference on Data Engineering (Feb. 6-10, 1989, Los Angeles, CA) p.188-97.

[5] Kohonen, T. Self-organization and associate memory. third ed. Berlin: Springer-Verlag, New York, 1989.

[6] Ritter, H. & Kohonen, T. Self-organizing semantic maps. Biological Cybernetics, Vol.61, 241-254, 1989.

[7] Kohonen, T. The self-organizing map. Proceeding of the IEEE. 78(9), 1464-1480, 1990.

[8] Herot, C. F. Spatial management of data. ACM Transactions on Database systems. 5(4), 493-514, 1980.

[9] Nielsen, J. Miniatures versus icons as a visual cache for videotex browsing. Behavior & Information Technology. 9(6), 441-449, 1990.

[10] Burgess, C.; & Swigger, K. A graphical database interface for casual naive users. Information Processing & Management, 22(6), 511-521, 1986.

[11] Rousseeuw, P. J. A visual display for hierarchical classification. Data Analysis and Informatics, IV. Proceedings of the Fourth International Symposium (Oct. 9-11, 1985, Versailles, France). p. 743-748.

[12] Fairchild, K. M.; Poltrock, S. E.; & Furnas, G. W. SemNet: Three-dimensional graphic representations of large knowledge bases. In: Cognitive Science and its applications for human-computer interaction (ed. by R. Guindon)., 201-233, 1988.

[13] Conklin, J.; & Begeman, M. gIBIS: a tool for all reasons. Journal of the Information Society for Information Science. 40(3), 200-213, 1989.

[14] Sammon, J. W. A nonlinear mapping for data structure analysis. IEEE Transactions on Computers. 18(5), 401-409, 1969.

[15] White, H.D., & Griffith, B. C. Author cocitation: A literature measure of intelligent structure. Journal of the American Society for Information Science, 32, 163-171, 1981.

[16] Lin, X. Self-organizing semantic maps for information retrieval. Doctoral Dissertation, University of Maryland at College Park, 1992.

[17] Lin, X.; Soergel, D; & Marchionini, G. A self-organizing semantic map for information retrieval. Proceedings of the Fourteenth Annual International ACM/SIGIR Conference on Research and Development in Information Retrieval (Oct. 13-16, 1991; Chicago, Illinois). p. 262-269.

5.3 Text in 3D

When we get to 3D, there are two common strategies for visualizing collections of text documents:

1. create a landscape using a 2D layout algorithm as discussed in the previous section, and
2. use a 3D variant of those layout algorithms to create a galaxy of points that show the clustering of documents in 3D.

Chalmers (1996) has also developed a system that generates 3D landscapes of a document collection. The SemNet paper (Fairchild, Poltrock, and Furnas, 1988 ●), included in Chapter 2, is an early example of the galaxy idea. Hendley et al. (1995 ●) have also developed a system called Narcissus that creates a 3D galaxy of documents. They also draw links between the points to show additional information.

The paper by Wise et al. (1995 ●), included in this section, has examples of both these strategies. Their 3D layout algorithm starts by clustering a document collection in a high-dimensional feature space. Centroids of the clusters become inputs to layout algorithms, either principal component analysis or multidimensional scaling. The documents are then scattered near their centroids to generate the visualizations. Clustering reduces the computational complexity of the layout but at the cost of making the layout less sensitive to the features of the individual documents.

The landscape visualization, called themescapes, conveys information about topics. Themescapes augment a 2D landscape of text with a height dimension showing the strength of a theme in a given region. Rather than the map metaphor used by Lin in the previous section, themescapes use a landscape metaphor. Borders are replaced with valleys, which separate topics naturally. It is easy to see areas that belong to multiple topics and make perceptual judgments of their relative influence on that part of the document collection. The two visualizations are intended to work together. The galaxy visualization provides an overview for the themescapes. The themescape and galaxy visualization on the surface seem to provide rapid answers to questions about what is in the database. But this may come at the expense of questions involving more detailed structure. The effectiveness of these visualizations compared to more conventional displays is not yet decided.

In addition to explorations of new visualizations, another contribution of this paper is a discussion of the process for mapping Raw Data document collections into visualizations. The focusing task is market or intelligence analysis, which involves a wide range of documents that must be processed to detect interesting patterns. The first step is to separate the text from the images and data. Algorithms are then applied to determine the features that are used by the clustering layout algorithm. Large collections require database technology to manage all the steps and keep the correspondence between the generated data and the raw text. Making effective visualizations for text implies having effective back-end algorithms for analyzing text structure and system infrastructure that can support the required scale of operations.

Visualizing the Non-Visual: Spatial analysis and interaction with information from text documents

James A. Wise, James J. Thomas, Kelly Pennock, David Lantrip, Marc Pottier, Anne Schur, Vern Crow
Pacific Northwest Laboratory
Richland, Washington

Abstract

This paper describes an approach to IV that involves spatializing text content for enhanced visual browsing and analysis. The application arena is large text document corpora such as digital libraries, regulations and procedures, archived reports, etc. The basic idea is that text content from these sources may be transformed to a spatial representation that preserves informational characteristics from the documents. The spatial representation may then be visually browsed and analyzed in ways that avoid language processing and that reduce the analysts' mental workload. The result is an interaction with text that more nearly resembles perception and action with the natural world than with the abstractions of written language.

1: Introduction

Information Visualization (IV), extends traditional scientific visualization of physical phenomena to diverse types of information (e.g.text, video, sound, or photos) from large heterogenous data sources. It offers significant capability to different kinds of analysts who must identify, explore, discover, and develop understandings of complex situations.

IV has been studied for many centuries, integrating techniques from art and science in its approach [7, 9]. The information analyst's perspective illustrates that their process involves more than envisioning information. [4] It is both the visual representations and the resultant interactions with it that entail the analyst's work.

Current visualization approaches demonstrate effective methods for visualizing mostly structured and/or hierarchical information such as organization charts, directories, entity-attribute relationships, etc. [3,9]. Free text visualizations have remained relatively unexamined.

The idea that open text fields themselves or raw prose might be candidates for information visualization is not obvious. Some research in information retrieval utilized graph theory or figural displays as 'visual query' tools on document bases [5,8], but the information returned is documents in their text form--which the user still must read to cognitively process. The need to read and assess large amounts of text that is retrieved through even the most efficient means puts a severe upper limit on the amount of text information that can be processed by any analyst for any purpose.

At the same time, "Open Source" digital information--the kind available freely or through subscription over the Internet--is increasing exponentially. Whether the purpose be market analysis, environmental assessment, law enforcement or intelligence for national security, the task is to peruse large amounts of text to detect and recognize informational 'patterns' and pattern irregularities across the various sources. But modern information technologies have made so much text available that it overwhelms the traditional reading methods of inspection, sift and synthesis.

2: Visualizing text

True text visualizations that would overcome these time and attentional constraints must represent textual content and meaning to the analyst without them having to read it in the manner that text normally requires. These visualizations would instead result from a content abstraction andspatialization of the original text document that transforms it into a new visual representation that communicates by image instead of prose. Then the image could be understood in much the way that we explore our worldly visual constructions.

It is thus reasonable to hypothesize that across the purposes for perusing text, some might be better satisfied by transforming the text information to a spatial representation which may then be accessed and explored by visual processes alone. For any reader, the rather slow serial process of mentally encoding a text document is the motivation for providing a way for them to instead use their primarily preattentive, parallel processing powers of visual perception.

The goal of text visualization, then, is to spatially transform text information into a new visual

Everything assumes parsing flat text. XML changes the problem.

representation that reveals thematic patterns and relationships between documents in a manner similar if not identical to the way the natural world is perceived. This is because the perceptual processes involved are the results of millions of years of selective mammalian and primate evolution, and have become biologically tuned to seeing in the natural world. The human eye has it's own contrast and wavelength sensitivity functions. It has prewired retinal "textons", or primitive form elements used to quickly build up components of complex visual images. Much of this processing takes place in parallel on the retinal level, and so is relatively effortless, exceptionally fast, and not additive to cognitive workload. Even at the visual cortex, perception appears to rely on spatially distributed parallel construction processes in a topography that corresponds to the real physical world. The central conjecture behind the approach to text visualization described here is that the same spatial perceptual mechanisms that operate on the real world will respond to a synthetic one, if analogous cues are present and suitably integrated. The bottleneck in the human processing and understanding of information in large amounts of text can be overcome if the text is spatialized in a manner that takes advantage of common powers of perception.

3. Visualization transformations: from text to pictures

Four important technical considerations need to be addressed in the creation of useful visualizations from raw text. First, there must be a clear definition of what comprises text and how it can be distinguished from other symbolic representations of information. Second, there must be a way to transform raw text into a different visual form that retains much of the high dimensional invariants of natural language, yet better enables visual exploration and analysis by the individual. Third, suitable mathematical procedures and analytical measures must be defined as the foundation for meaningful visualizations. Finally, a database management system must be designed to store and manage text and all of its derivative forms of information.

For the purpose of this paper, text is a written alphabetical form of natural language. Diagrams, tables, and other symbolic representations of language are not considered text. Text has statistical and semantic attributes such as the frequency and context of individual words, and the combinations of words into topics or themes. The differences between text's statistical and semantic compositions provide much of the opportunity for the text visualizations described in this paper. For example, reading a text document to extract it's semantic meaning is different from learning that a document is of a certain relative size, type, or authorship, with particular content themes. But both semantic and content knowledge can be valuable to an analyst. Identifying publishing activity on particular subjects from particular authors at certain places and times is useful, especially if one does not have to read all of the documents to determine that pattern.

In digital form,written text can be treated statistically to extract information about it's content and context, if not semantic meaning. While this does not necessarily entail natural language processing algorithms, it does require a set of special purpose processes to convert text to an alternative spatial form that can be displayed and utilized without needing to read it.

The first component of a software architecture to visualize text is the document database or corpora. Documents contained within such databases are derived from messages, news articles, regulations, etc., but contain primarily textual material. The next component is the text processing engine, which transforms natural language from the document database to spatial data. The output from the text engine is either stored directly in a visualization database, or projected onto a low dimensional, visual representation. Other components of the architecture are the Graphical User Interface (GUI), the display software (such as visualization packages), the Applications Interface (API), and auxiliary tools.

3.1: Processing text

The primary requirements of a text processing engine for information visualization are: 1) the identification and extraction of essential descriptors or text features, 2) the efficient and flexible representation of documents in terms of these text features, and 3) subsequent support for information retrieval and visualization.

Text features are typically one of three general types, though any number of variations and hybrids are possible. The first type is frequency-based measures on words, utilizing only first order statistics. The presence and count of unique words in a document identifies those words as a feature set. The second type of feature is based on higher order statistics taken on the words or letter strings. Here, the occurrence, frequency, and context of individual words are used to characterize a set of explicit or implicitly (e.g. associations defined by a neural network) defined word classes. The third type of text feature is semantic in nature. The association between words is not defined through analysis of the word corpus, as with statistical features, but is defined a priori using knowledge of the language. Semantic approaches may utilize natural or quasi-natural language understanding algorithms, so that the semantic relationships (i.e., higher-order information) are obtained.

Text features are a "shorthand" representation of the original document, satisfying the need of a text engine to be an efficient and flexible representation of textual information. Instead of a complex and unwieldy string of words, feature sets become the efficient basis of document representations and manipulations. The feature set information must be complete enough to permit flexible use of these alternatives. Text engines support both efficiency and flexibility, though these criteria are often in opposition.

The third requirement of the text engine is to support information retrieval and visualization. The text processing engine must provide easy, intuitive access to the information contained within the corpus of documents. Information retrieval implies a query mechanism to support it. This may include a basic Boolean search, a high level query language, or the visual manipulation of spatialized text objects in a display. To provide efficient retrieval, the text processing engine must pre-process documents and efficiently implement an indexing scheme for individual words or letter strings.

The more visual aspect of information retrieval is known as information browsing. The specificity of querying has a counterpoint in the generality of browsing. The text processing engine or subsidiary algorithms can support browsing by providing composite or global measures which produce an intuitive index into topics or themes contained within the text corpus. A set of measures which characterize the text in meaningful ways provide for multiple perspectives of documents and their relationships to one another. One example of such a measure is “similarity”. Based on the occurrence and the context of key words or other extracted features, measures of similarity can be computed which reflect the relatedness between documents. When similarity is represented as spatial proximity or congruity of form, it is easily visualized. A diversity of measures is essential, given that documents can be extraordinarily complex entities containing a large number of imprecise topics and subtopics. Clearly, no single visualizable snapshot of a document base can provide the whole picture.

3.2: Visualizing output from text processing

Composing a spatial representation from the output of the text analysis engine is the next step to visualizing textual information. Spatialization itself is composed of several stages. The first involves representing the document, typically as a vector in a high dimensional feature space. The vector representation is the initial spatial expression of the document, and a variety of comparisons, filters, and transformations can be made from it directly.

To represent each of these documents, an initial visualization may consist of a scatter plot of points (one for each document), collocated according to a measure of similarity based on vector representations. Since visualization of the textual information requires a low-dimensional representation of documents that inhabit a high-dimensional space, projection is necessary. Typically, linear or non-linear Principal Components Analysis or metric Multi-Dimensional Scaling (MDS) can be used to reduce dimensionality to a visualizable subspace. One serious concern with these techniques, is their exponential order of complexity, requiring that dimensionality reduction and scaling be considered simultaneously since a large corpus may contain 20,000 or more documents. For large document corpora, alternatives to the projection of each document point are necessary. In these cases, clustering can be performed in the high-dimensional feature space and the cluster centroids become the objects to be visualized. For a review of clustering and metric issues, see [11].

3.3: Managing the representation

There are two basic classes of data that must be managed. The first is the raw text files for each document. The text itself as well as a variety of header information fall into this category. This first class of data is static in nature, simple in structure, and therefore easy to manage. The second broad class of data is the visual forms of the text. This class of data is derived from the numerous algorithms designed to cluster, structure, and visually present information, and is both extensive and dynamic.

For the current text visualization endeavor, an object-oriented database was selected for managing text and its various visual forms. This paradigm was chosen for its flexibility of data representation, the power of inheritance, and the ease of data access where complexity of the data structures to be managed is great. The structures contain both high and low dimensional spaces, substructures such as clusters and super clusters, entities such as documents and cluster centroids, and a variety of other components. The class structure of the database also permits the common elements to be shared (inherited) through the hierarchy of data classes, while the differences between the structures can be specified at lower levels. The selected object-oriented database also implements database entities as persistent objects, where the access and manipulation of the data are one and the same, eliminating the need for a query mechanism as such.

3.4: Interface design for text visualization

To achieve direct engagement for text visualization [6], the interface must provide 1) a preconscious visual form for information 2) interactions which sustain and enrich the process of knowledge building, 3) a fluid environment for reflective cognition and higher-order thought, and 4) a framework for temporal knowledge building.

Three primary display types are made available to the analyst. Tools are arranged along the perimeter of the display monitor and can be used as operators on the representations. Conversely, the representations or selected areas in the representations can be dragged and dropped onto the tools to spawn the appropriate action. The analyst can work on the primary information views [1] in an area known as the backdrop, which serves as a central display resource for visual information; alternatively, she can move the views to the workshop or the chronicle. The workshop is a grid where selected views or parts of views can be placed for work and/or visual review. The grid has a number of resizable windows to hold multiple views. The chronicle is a space where representations of more enduring interest can be placed. Views placed in this area can be linked to form a sequenced visual story where decision points are highlighted. The workshop and the chronicle take advantage of the phenomena of visual momentum; the ability to extract information across a set of successively viewed displays [10] that can be a series of static or dynamic images. The characteristics of the backdrop, workshop, and chronicle, known collectively as storylining, provide the ability to capture and visually organize situations across the time-past, present, and future. This endows the analyst with the ability to summarize their experience of knowledge building [2].

4: Examples from the MVAB Project

The Multidimensional Visualization and Advanced Browsing project is currently exploring a number of representations for the visualization and analysis of textual information. These approaches have been showcased in SPIRE™, the Spatial Paradigm for Information Retrieval and Exploration, which was developed to facilitate the browsing and selection of documents from large corpora (20,000+ documents). Described below are the two major visualization approaches or views which were developed in the first year of this project: Galaxies and Themescapes.

Starfields and topographical maps were selected as display metaphors because they offer a rich variety of cognitive spatial affordances that naturally address the problems of text visualization. Starfields create point clusters which suggest patterns of interest. Maps offer topographies of peaks and valley that can be easily detected based on contour patterns. Both these spatial arrangements allow overview and detail without a change of view. Each view, however, offers a different perspective of the same information and serves as the organizing points for knowledge construction.

4.1: Galaxies

The Galaxies visualization displays cluster and document interrelatedness by reducing a high dimensional representation of documents and clusters to a 2D scatterplot of 'docupoints' that appear as do stars in the night sky. Although the resulting visualization is simple, it provides a critical first cut at sifting information and determining how the contents of a document base are related. The key measurement for understanding this visualization is the notion of document "similarity". The more similar that clusters and documents are to one another in terms of their context and content, the closer or more proximate they are located in the 2D space. By exploring and animating this visualization, analysts can quickly gain an understanding of patterns and trends that underlie the documents within a corpus. At the highest level of representation, Galaxies displays corpus clusters and the gisting terms which describe them. **(Figure 1)**

A simple glance at this spatial representation reveals the fundamental topics found within the corpus, and provides an avenue of exploration which can be followed by simply clicking on a cluster of interest to reveal the documents within. These documents can then be grouped, gisted, annotated, or retrieved for more detailed analysis. In addition to simple point and click exploration of the document base, a number of sophisticated tools exist to facilitate more in-depth analysis. An example of such a tool is the temporal slicer. Designed to help tie document spatial patterns with temporal ones, this tool utilizes document timestamps to partition the document base into temporal units. The granularity of these units can be defined by the user as years, months, days, hours or minutes. Slicing a database entails moving a "temporal window" through the documents, and watching the visualization populate itself with documents. **(Figure 2)**

The resulting emergence of clusters can indicate temporal links that relate topics. When viewed in terms of known historical events and trends, these growing cluster patterns can provide insight into external causal relationships mirrored in the corpus.

4.2: ThemeScapes

ThemeScapes are abstract, three-dimensional landscapes of information that are constructed from document corpora (Figure 3). The complex surfaces are intended to convey relevant information about opics or themes found within the corpus, without the cognitive load encountered in reading such content. A thematic terrain simultaneously communicates both the primary themes of an arbitrarily large collection of documents and a measure of their relative prevalence in the corpus. Spatial relationships exhibited in the landscape reveal the intricate interconnection of themes, the transformation of themes across the whole of the document corpus, and the existence of information gap, or "negative information."

The ThemeScapes' visual representation has several advantages. First, a ThemeScape displays much of the complex content of a document database. Elevation depicts theme strength, while other features of the terrain map such as valleys, peaks, cliffs, and ranges represent detailed interrelationships among documents and their composite themes. At a glance, it provides a visual thematic summary of the whole corpus. The second major advantage of thematic terrain is that it utilizes innate human abilities for

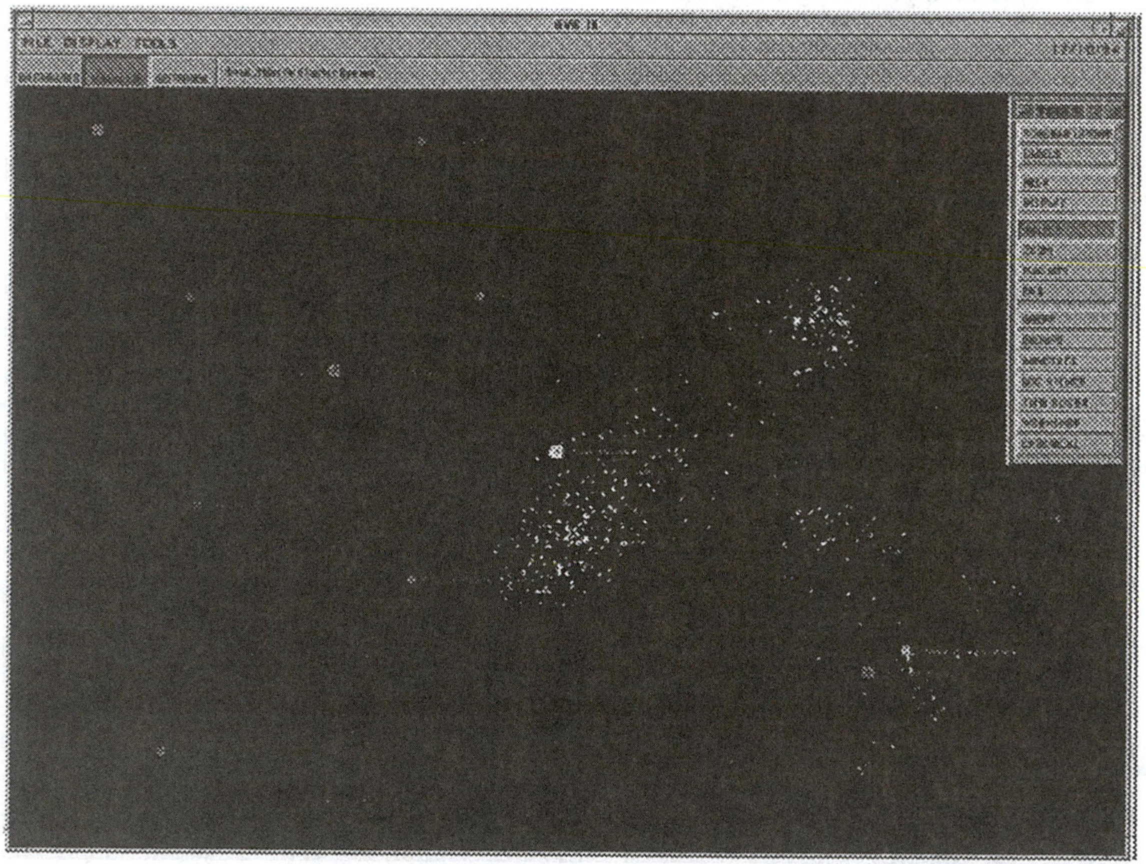

Figure 1: Galaxies visualization of documents and document clusters in a text database.

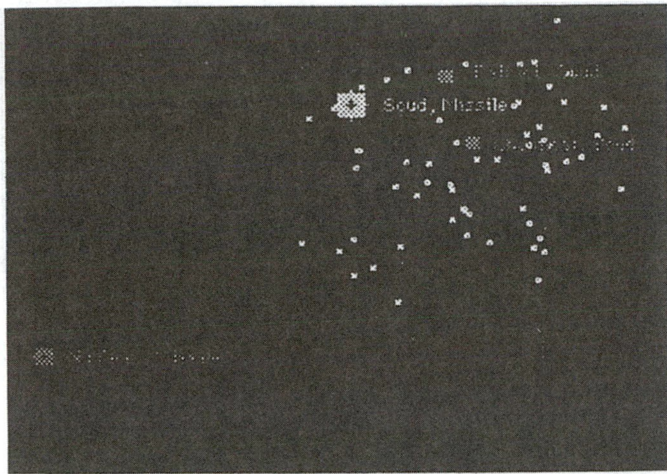

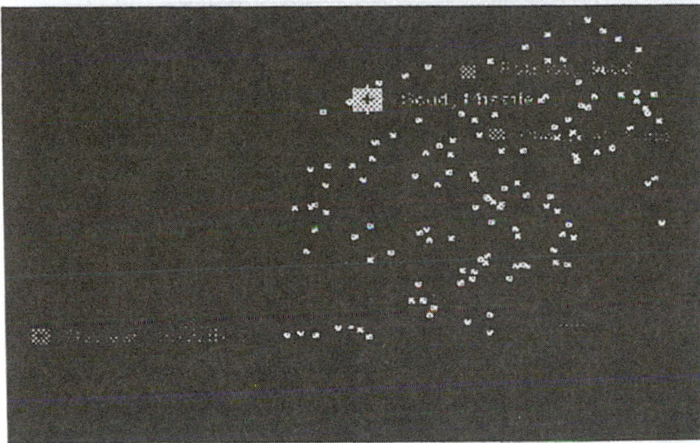

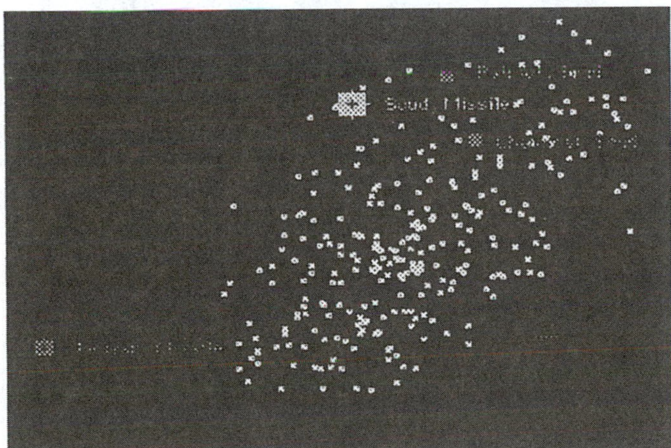

Figure 2a, b, c: Users can slice a corpus to relate document patterns with temporal ones.

pattern recognition and spatial reasoning. The complexity of the terrain is perceived and analyzed with parallel and preattentive processing which do not tax serial, attentional resources. This greatly expands the bandwidth of communication between the tool and the user. A third major advantage of the terrain implementation is its communicative invariance across levels of textual scale. An entire document corpus, a cluster of documents, individual documents, or even document components such as paragraphs or sentences can all be equally well visualized in a ThemeScape. This feature allows the ThemeScape to be used for automated document summarization as well as summarization of the whole document base, explicitly displaying the multitude of topics in a single image. Finally, ThemeScapes promote analysis by promoting exploration of the document space. Utilizing the metaphor of the landscape, associated tools allow the analyst to take 'core samples' and 'slices' through the thematic terrain to see its composition and to understand how thematic topics come to relate to one another in the underlying documents.

5: Conclusions and directions for future research and development

The MVAB project has started with a visualization (Galaxies) that provides a simplified universal view of the relationships among documents in an entire corpus. We have then proceeded to the Themescape visualization, which does the same for the thematic content expressed in those documents. In doing so, we have gone from a metaphor of points in space to one of a landscape. We are now pursuing development of a third visualization that would handle specific entity-attribute relationships found in the documents, such as treated by Link Analysis. This layering of informational detail and abstraction appears necessary for large document bases where investigating global structure is a primary concern yet relationships between individual objects are also important. It gives real meaning and form to the notion of 'data mining'.

So far, the R &D efforts on the MVAB project have shown that there appears to be substantial justification to the idea that text visualizations can overcome much of the user limitations that results from accessing and trying to read from large document bases. Even with the relatively simple first Galaxies visualization of documents as stars in a 2-D space, analysts have returned reports of enhanced insight and time savings such as "discovering in 35 minutes what would have taken two weeks otherwise." Analysts

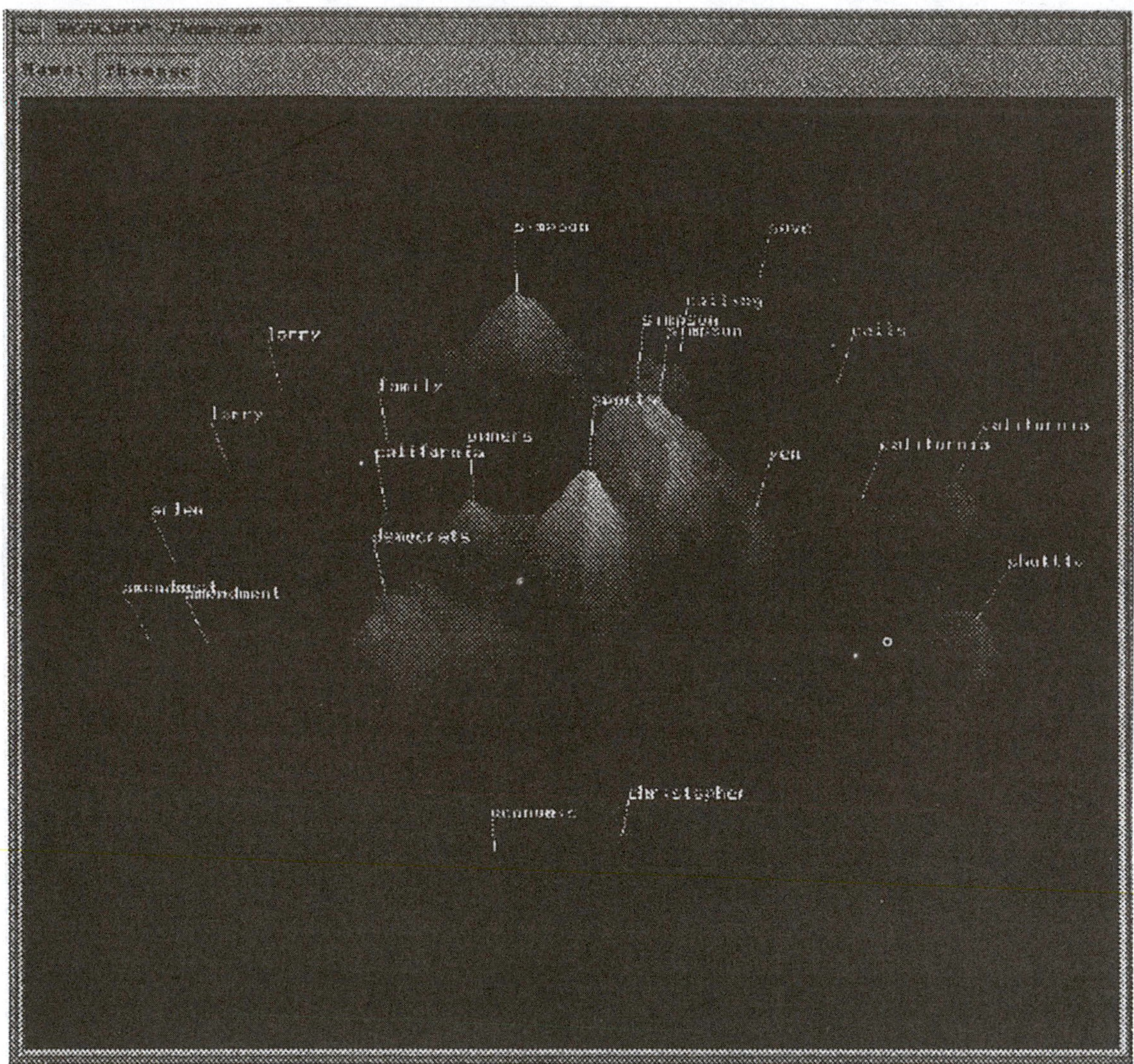

Figure 3: A ThemeScape of an entire week of CNN newstories comprising a document corpus

have also been quite creative with the tool, using the time slicer to do pattern recognition and comparison on evolving and historically documented situations. This kind of adaptation of what is essentially a visual browser has encouraged us to pursue analytical visualizations and to drop some distinctions among analysts' tasks that exist in the purely textual realm. For example, querying a document base by means of a Boolean text string is different from reading the documents returned from the query. However, the Themescape described above, although meant for visual analysis, also permits a different kind of visual querying than was ev er possible under the all-or-none choices of Boolean logic. Touching a Themescape can be a way to initiate a weighted query in terms of the themes that proportionally compose the elevation of the terrain. This allows the analyst to seek documents that talk about combinations of topics in a selected relative abundance based on the analyst's interests. Querying and analytical manipulation come together in a single visualization.

Users' experience also justifies the initial conviction that text visualizations will have to access and utilize the cognitive and visual processes that enable our spatial interactions with the natural world. This suggests visual metaphors that recapitulate experiences of viewing the night sky and traversing landscapes.

Another observation echoed in the growing popularity of Visual Data Analysis (VDA) programs is that perception and action are provocative complements to one another. An image must be acted on in some way, which in turn suggests new facets of its character that stimulate further visual inspection. Galaxies success with analysts is in no small part due to the abilities to pan, group and timeslice the docupoints in the display. The success of other text visualizations will likely be determined by whether the user can manipulate them along the lines of their analytical intuitions.

Future efforts will elaborate the visual metaphors described above, as well as new ones that effectively capture how concepts and decisions 'come into form'. Much of the analyst's world is a dynamic changing information terrain. Seeking coherance and patterns in this environment carries a high price in time and effort. Capturing the development of a story or the threads of a concept communicated in prose is a high order for text visualizations. But there appears to be no formal reason why at least some of these aspects cannot be captured as well in image as they can in words.

Other extensions of this research are suggested by the addition of sensory modalities like sound to the text visualization. If text content or connections can be captured in three dimensional solid forms, then those forms might also be given other properties, like density, that characterize their appearance and behavior in the real world. Through enhanced means of 'virtual interaction', these properties could reinforce and extend the impressions gained by visual inspection alone, and start to give much more of the affective content and tone that well written prose conveys.

It is evident that the potentials of text visualization are just beginning to be explored and realized. With them, the incredible diversity and volumes of written information available around the world may yet be made more accessible and comprehensible through this perceptual restructuring. And the limitations of an Information Age will not be set by the speed with which a human mind can read.

References

[1] Bannon, L. J., and Bodker, S., *Beyond the Interface: Encountering Artifacts in Use*. In Carroll J. M. (Ed.) Designing Interaction: Psychology at the Human Computer Interface pages 227-253. Cambridge, Cambridge University Press, 1991.

[2] Henniger, S., Belkin, N., *Interfaces Issues and Interation Stratigies for Information Retrieval Systems*. ACM Computer Interaction Tutorial Workbook #19, April 1994.

[3] Johnson, J. A., Nardi, B. A., Zarmer, C. L., and Miller, J. R., 1993. Information Visualization Using 3D Interactive Animation. *Communications of the ACM*, 36(4):40-56.

[4] Keller, P. R., and M. M. Keller. *Visual Cues: Practical Data Visualization*. IEEE Computer Society Press, Los Alamitos, California. 1993.

[5] Korfhage, Robert R. To See, or Not to See--Is That the Query? *Communications of the ACM*, 34, pages 134-141, 1991.

[6] Laurel, B. *Computers as Theatre*. Addison-Wesley, Reading, Massachusetts, 1993.

[7] Robertson, G. C., Card, S. K., and Mackinlay, J.D. 1993. Information Visualization Using 3D Interactive Animation. *Communications of the ACM*, 36(4):56-72

[8] Spoerri, Anselm. InfoCrystal: A visual tool for information retrieval. *Proceedings of Visualization '93*, pages 150-157. IEEE Computer Society Press, Los Alamitos, California, 1993.

[9] Tufte, E. R. *Envisioning Information*. Graphics Press, Cheshire, Connecticut, 1990.

[10] Woods, D. D., *Visual Momentum: a Concept to Improve Cognitive Coupling of Person and Computer*. International Journal of Man-Machine Studies 21: 229-244. 1984.

[11] York, J. and Bohn, S. *Clustering and Dimensionality Reduction in SPIRE*. Presented at the Automated Intelligence Processing and Analysis Symposium, Mar 28-30, 1995, Tysons Corner, VA.

FIGURE **1**

Galaxies visualization of documents and document clusters in a textual database.

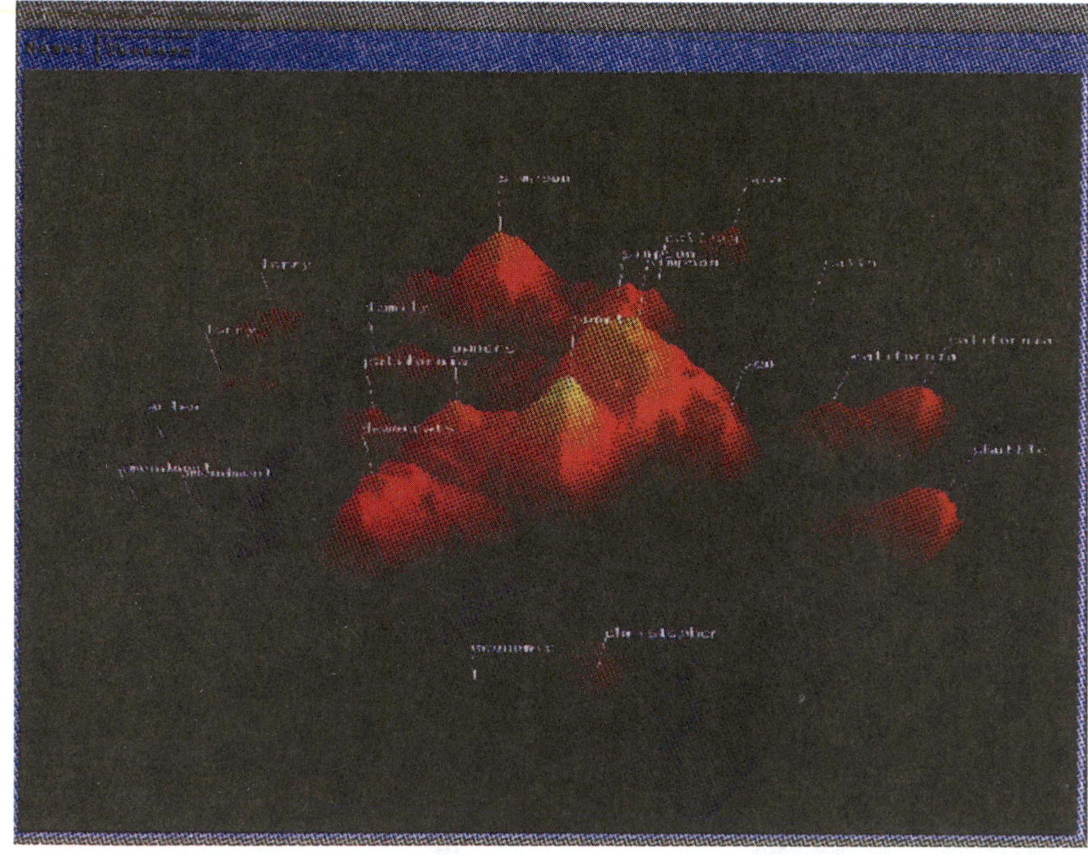

FIGURE **3**

A ThemeScape of an entire week of CNN newstories comprising a document corpus.

5.4

Text in 3D + Time

Previous sections of this chapter have described mappings of text to 1D, 2D, and 3D. This section extends this progression to include time. Rennison's paper (1994 ●), included in this section, describes Galaxy of News, a system that uses motion to augment a 3D galaxy of points. The focusing task is the visualization of news articles, similar to the task discussed by Wise at al. (1995 ●) in the previous section. The major difference is that Galaxy of News does not attempt to find a single position in space for the news articles. Instead, an associative relation network is generated that describes the relationship between each article and a set of topic categories. The visualization has the user starting at the top of a pyramid of topics. As the user zooms into subtopics, the corresponding articles move from their initial location into the user's view. Ultimately, these articles grow large enough that they can be read. The same article can be reached by more than one path in the tree if it is relevant to several topics. By using time, the Galaxy of News does not need to choose a single topic for an article and the user does not need to guess which topic was used to describe an article. The trade-off is that the article is located not at a certain place in space to which the user could return, but rather at the end of various paths.

This chapter has described a range of choices for mapping text documents and document collections to visual form, from a 1D Visual Structure representing a single linear text document to a 3D galaxy of points that represent a large document collection. Each choice has its advantages and disadvantages. When text is mapped directly to a visual form such as SeeSoft's reduced document, the resulting visualization is intuitive, but even the reduced text limits the amount of information that can be displayed on the one hand and on the other hinders the graphical encoding that can be used to show additional relationships in the text. When complex algorithms are used to generate a text visualization, subtle patterns in large text collections can be made visible, but the resulting mapping may be less intuitive. Not enough is presently known about how effective these techniques are and for which tasks. Perhaps a solution to this conflict can be found by noticing that Galaxy of News ultimately renders text in the visualization. Perhaps we can develop a workspace for text visualization that provides many different mappings for text as well as support for using them to think. The next chapter moves to this next level in visualization.

Galaxy of News
An Approach to Visualizing and Understanding Expansive News Landscapes

Earl Rennison
Visible Language Workshop
MIT Media Lab
20 Ames St.
Cambridge, MA 02139
E-mail: rennison@media.mit.edu

ABSTRACT

The Galaxy of News system embodies an approach to visualizing large quantities of independently authored pieces of information, in this case news stories. At the heart of this system is a powerful relationship construction engine that constructs an associative relation network to automatically build implicit links between related articles. To visualize these relationships, and hence the news information space, the Galaxy of News uses pyramidal structuring and visual presentation, semantic zooming and panning, animated visual cues that are dynamically constructed to illustrate relationships between articles, and fluid interaction in a three dimensional information space to browse and search through large databases of news articles. The result is a tool that allows people to quickly gain a broad understanding of a news base by providing an abstracted presentation that covers the entire information base, and through interaction, progressively refines the details of the information space. This research has been generalized into a model for news access and visualization to provide automatic construction of news information spaces and derivation of an interactive news experience.

KEYWORDS: Information visualization, abstracted information spaces, pyramidal information structures, 3D interactive graphics, information space design, information interaction design.

INTRODUCTION

As we enter the information age, concepts concerning news production, distribution, access and visualization are rapidly changing. Until recently, news was authored for relatively static media, such as print, audio/video tape. The information content was distributed in a one-way exchange via newspapers, radio, television, and so forth. And, in many ways existing computer systems and infrastructure are still directed toward these forms of distribution and management. Accessing and understanding news information in this structure is a secondary action and is most often left up to the readers, with little support by the information infrastructure.

To expound the problem, increasing news production resulting from the rise in connectivity has led to increasing complexity of news organization, management, and hence, understanding. As a result, authoring news articles and/or presentations that relate to other information (e.g. articles or presentations that are linked) will become increasingly more difficult to construct in a meaningful way so as to help the reader to understand the full nature of the news or information that is being presented. The current information infrastructure simply cannot handle the exploding scale of news information and its cross correlation. Hence, what is truly needed is an intelligent infrastructure that automatically builds the correlations and relationships between news articles, and automatically construct an environment, based on the information content, that allows readers to dynamically explore the expanding news base and allows them to gain an understanding that is deeper than what they would gain by looking at individual news articles.

To address this problem, we would ideally like to develop news systems that facilitate the following objectives:

- Allow people to explore and effectively browse through massively large news spaces
- Combine the effective aspects of both filtering and browsing and the ability to move between these modes of operation seamlessly with a single interface
- Facilitate ability to understand relationships between independently authored news items
    - To see how articles relate to each other
    - To find relationships between articles that where not previously known or obvious
- Organize disconnected articles into dynamically formed groups, based on the content of the articles, that allow

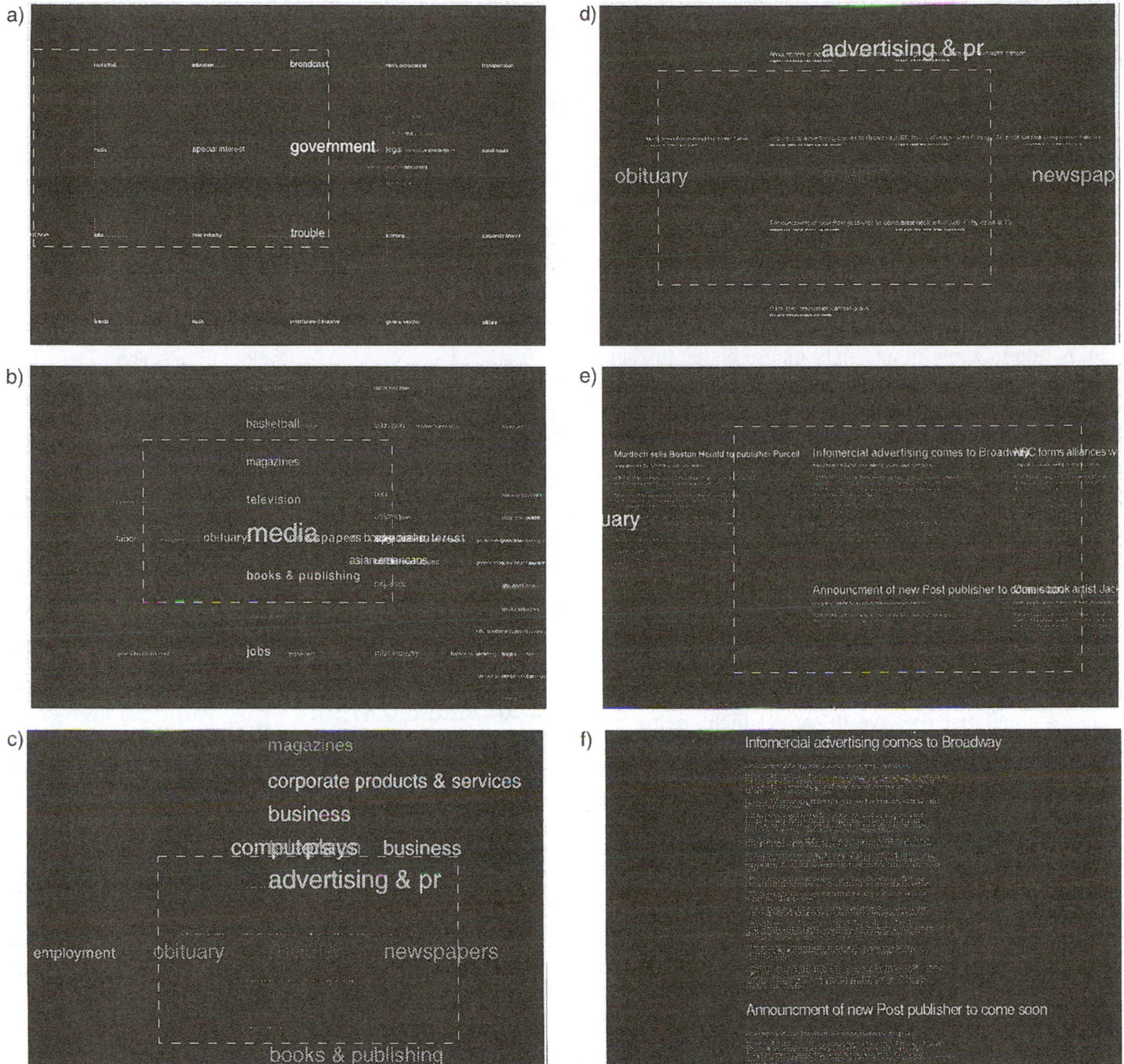

Figure 1: Screen Captures from a Progressive Zoom into a Sample News Information Space
a) Initial, wide-angle view of news space; b) area around Media cluster; c) zoom into Media cluster (headlines begining to show); d) headlines for Media cluster; e) article body beginning to drop in; f) full presentation of article headlines and body.
Dashed rectangles indicate the areas that are zoomed into and shown in the next screen capture.

quick access to related information and the ability to quickly understand the relationships

An infrastructure that supports these objectives would automatically build the correlations and relationships between the information elements (hence linking the elements together), and provide coupled mechanisms that dynamically constructs an environment that facilitates interactive navigation and intuitive access to related or correlated information. This is the approach explored with the Galaxy of News System.

EXAMPLE NEWS INFORMATION SPACE

To provide a better understanding of what the Galaxy of News system provides, let's consider an actual scenario currently used to demonstrate the system. In the Visible Language Workshop we receive news feeds from Clarinews. These news feeds are stored in a directory hierarchy specific to Clarinews. To initiate the visualization and access process, a user specifies all or a portion of the Clarinews database to be processed. The system then parses the content of articles and constructs relationships between the articles. These relationships are then stored in a relationship database. Once the process of creating these relationships is specified, the relationship database can be automatically updated daily.

After setting up the relationship construction process and building some relationships, the user starts a visualization front-end application, specifying what set of relationships to use (and hence, what portion of the database to visualize). When the front-end application starts up, it loads the appropriate relationships, and then constructs an information space that will help the user navigate through the information. Then, using the mouse and two keys (left mouse button to zoom in and right mouse button to zoom out), the user navigates through the information space and the system automatically presents information appropriate for the user's position in the space.

To give you an idea of what is presented to the user, the following example, shown in Figure 1, illustrates a sample path through an actual news space. The image in Figure 1.a. shows the initial view of the information space. In this view, root keywords of news clusters in an abstracted news hierarcy are shown. These root keywords provide an abstracted, representational view of the entire news database on a single screen. These root clusters are derived through an abstraction and generalization process described later in this paper. Also note that the space presented is non-linear and has a simulated fish-eye [9] effect highlighting the elements that are in the center of the space. In Figure 1.b., the user has zoomed toward the "Media" cluster. At this stage, the Galaxy of News application begins to expose the details of this cluster, as well as other clusters in the area. Note for reference that the structure of this cluster is illustrated in Figure 2.

As the user continues to zoom into the "Media" cluster, as shown in Figure 1.c., news articles previously located in other areas of the space are pulled into the background using animation. This process of animation maintains fluid consistency and helps the user understand what the system is doing. Note, at this point the typeface for the word "Media" begins to fade away, yet it is still visible. This gives the user a subtle clue that they have entered the "Media" subspace and helps maintain context as to where he or she is within the space without using a global navigation map.

Further zooming reveals the headlines of the articles relating to the media cluster, shown in Figure 1.c. It is hard to visualize in the screen shots provided, but subtle red lines illustrate to the user the associations of articles to keywords. As the user continues to zoom into the "Media" cluster, the red lines linking keywords and articles gradually fades away, and simultaneously, the bodies of the articles gradually drop in under the article headlines, as shown in Figure 1.e. These gradual changes of the keyword transparencey, red subject-article line transparency, and bodies of the articles provide for a very natural transition from the meta-space provided by the keywords and the detailed space of the news articles. If the user continues to zoom (Figure 1.f.), the full body of the articles is displayed so that it can be read.

An important aspect to point out with these images is that they convey only a limited view of what actually goes on when a user navigates through the space, though they do provide a general sense of the *experience*. A key part of the system is it's fluid movement and display of information, a feeling not conveyed in these images.

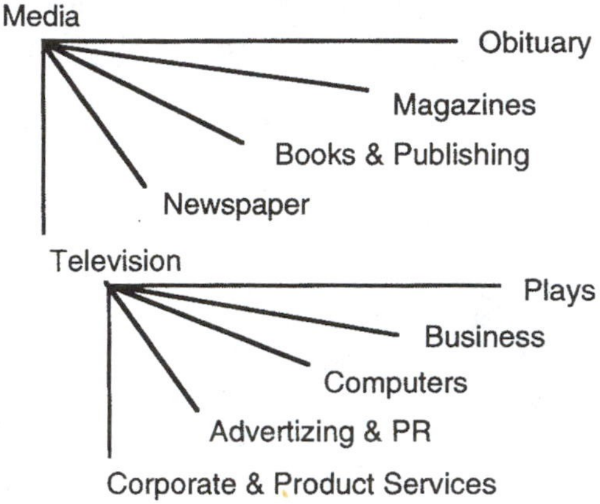

Figure 2: Example Derived Keyword Hierarchy

GALAXY OF NEWS MODEL FOR NEWS ACCESS AND VISUALIZATION

The Galaxy of News system explores a generalized model for news managing, accessing, and visualizing expansive news bases. This model (illustrated in Figure 3) strives to create a structured environment that accommodates automated integration of independently authored articles into self-constructing information spaces that allow users to visualize and access information in a fluid and interactive fashion. The key element of this model is the separation of news authoring, and information space and interaction design into two separate processes. In many ways, this is similar to the process of constructing a daily newspaper, except that the delivery environment is much more dynamic and accommodates direct user interaction.

The model defines three distinguishable perspectives or views: 1) the author's view, 2) the information space and interaction designer's view, and the 3) the reader's view. The author's sole purpose is creating content or information objects. Information space and interaction designers focus on specifying the process of constructing information spaces based on classes of information, as opposed to specific instances of information. And, the reader views the amalgamation of the information space constructed from news content. This approach breaks information production down into the creation of content, and the creation of ways to "experience" the content (i.e. the combination of visualization and interaction). This split predisposes this model to address information scale.

The model is comprised of four fundamental layers. At the base, or core, of the model is the news information base, and the other three are specifications of what information to visualize and how to visualize that information at each instance of interaction. A description of each of these layers follows.

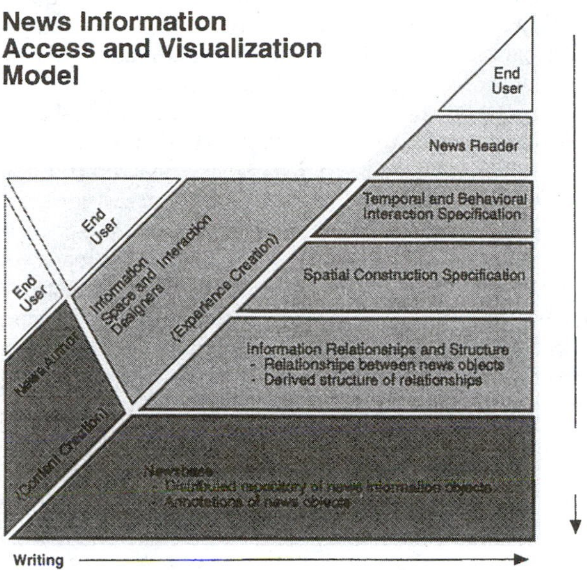

Figure 3: Galaxy of News Model for News Information Access and Visualization

News base

The news base consists of a set of information objects and their annotations. Example news information objects include text articles, photos and captions, graphs, graphic displays, video clips, sound clips, and so forth. In this model, the news base does not consist of raw data; rather only data that has been processed to represent some informational view of the data. Annotations consist of properties or symbolic descriptions of the information objects. They are either supplied by the author or automatically derived from the data, if feasible (e.g., a part of speech tagger can be applied to text articles to extract nouns/noun phrases and verbs [2; 3; 7). News articles provided by wire services provide annotations such as keywords, slugwords, location, time, subject, and so on. This information is used to build relationships between news articles.

Information Relationships

For a given set of information or classes of information, the relationships between instances of information objects can be defined. Examples include relationships between subjects, actions, and/or linguistic objects; between the time events occurred; between temporal ordering of events; and between combinations of these, as well as other properties.

Information relationships also consists of structures derived from other relationships. The model does not define specific techniques for deriving relationships structures, only that the relationships are constructed from the properties or symbolic descriptions extracted from the information objects. The Galaxy of News system defines one approach to constructing relationships and deriving a structure of the relationships (i.e. associative relations between subjects, described later in this paper); however, the model is not limited to that approach. Ultimately, it is the responsibility of the information space designer to specify the relationships, or the process of deriving the relationships, between information. The reason for this is that the spatial construction, and hence the visualization, process is intimately coupled with the information relationships.

Spatial Construction Specification

Using the information relationships described above, a spatial construction specification defines how information is presented graphically and spatially to users. The spaces can consist of two-dimensional, three-dimensional, or n-dimensional layouts, where dimensions above three can be modeled as micro worlds [8]. It is important to note that the information spaces are not defined for specific instances of information objects, rather for classes of information objects and the relationships between these classes. The actual information space constructed is derived from the collection of information objects, resulting in an emergent spatial structure. This is particularly relevant to news because the subjects change dynamically and a static space would not reflect these changes.

Temporal and Behavior Interaction Specification

This level defines the presentation and behavior of information objects during each instance of interaction with the user. The presentation of an appropriate level of detail at each view is fundamentally important. If only a limited subset of the information space can be presented at any moment or view, it is the responsibility of this layer to present the user with dynamic visual cues denoting the structure of the space and where the user is in the space. Temporal behavior can also be used to illustrate the underlying relationships between the information. For this purpose, the information space may be dynamically modified or reconstructed, using animation to illustrate changes [4]. It is the role of the "Information Interaction Designer" to specify these actions.

INFORMATION VISUALIZATION AND ACCESS IN THE GALAXY OF NEWS

One of the primary aspects of the Galaxy of News system is its approach to visualizing and accessing news information; hence the visualization aspects drive the architectural considerations of this system. The visualization approach presented in this paper is the result of extensive experimental research on visualization of multidimensional information conducted by the author and other members of the Visible Language Workshop at the Media Laboratory [5; 6; 10; 14]. The Galaxy of New system investigates several information access and visualization principles, including:

- Pyramidal encoding or presentation of news elements to provide progressive refinement of news information
- Visual clustering of news elements based on the content of news articles to provide structured information access

- Abstract three plus dimensional spaces that contain information objects
- Semantic zooming and panning, where zooming is synonymous with searching or filtering, and panning is synonymous with browsing
- Fluidity of interaction to understand and maintain the context of the information being presented
- Animation and motion to illustrate relationships between news elements
- Dynamic visual cues to aid in the navigation through an abstract news space
- Dynamic visual presentation of information to present the proper quantity of information at each instance of interaction and to eliminate distracting clutter

These principles define an outline for building a structured hierarchical representation of news, whereby the upper portions of the pyramid consist of general descriptions or abstractions of the lower levels which contain increasing levels of detail. Pyramidal representation offers news readers the ability to progress through a process of glancing, to investigating, to reading details in a fluid and selective manner, while maintaining context of where they are in the process (as illustrated in Figure 1). Hence, the information is structured such that news readers can gain a good understanding of the full range of news by looking at the top levels of the news information pyramid, and through fluid interaction, gain access to increasing levels of detail.

At first glance, these principles are similar to cone trees [13]; however, there are several significant differences. First, the hierarchical form is not explicitly presented to the user. The hierarchy is primarily used to present information to the user at the appropriate time. Second, not all the elements of the hierarchy are visible at a single glance. Rather, only elements that are relevant to the user's present view are shown. This is significant because it allows for an infinitely deep information hierarchy to be presented. Third, the user is able to navigate through the hierarchical space in an immersive fashion. As the user goes deeper into the hierarchy, the system reveals the substructures of the hierarchy.

The process of zooming in the information hierarchy is a form of interactive filtering. A similar approach was explored in the PAD system [12], which provides an infinite two dimensional information plane. One of the main limitations of the PAD approach is that once the space has been constructed, it is rigid as objects have fixed locations on the plane, and hence does not address the multiplicity of relationships between information objects. The Galaxy of News visualization and interaction approach addresses this by dynamically restructuring the space to pull in information relative to a given view. This process is animated to illustrate to the user what the system is doing. In effect, the approach is to construct information worlds within information worlds similar to [8], yet different in that the space is not tied to any dimensions -- the space is abstract.

An important and interesting aspect of the space constructed by the Galaxy of News system is that it is *not* based on any physical metaphors that we encounter on a daily basis such as windows, desks, folders, cabinets, rooms, buildings, streets, books, and so forth. Rather, it is based on abstract conceptual metaphors, e.g. galaxies and solar systems, which we understand, but only on a conceptual level since we do not experience these types of environments in our daily lives. As a result the space is freed from dimensional constraints, and hence, can represent many conceptual dimensions simultaneously. At first one might think that this would be very confusing to a user; however, usage of the system has shown that people have the ability to adapt to this abstract space given that appropriate visual cues are provided to the user.

Information Space and Interaction Design

The Galaxy of News system explores the separation of news information space design and the authoring of autonomous articles in a dynamic environment. To this end, the role of an information space and interaction designer is to specify 1) the types of relationships between news articles and the process of constructing these relationships; 2) rules for constructing a multidimensional spatial layout based on the relationships between news articles, and rules for building constraint networks to dynamically manage the spatial layout; and 3) actions the system takes when the user navigates through the space.

The iterative design process used in the development of the Galaxy of News information space resulted in the following features. The information space consists of three layers: 1) a hierarchy of keywords that go from general to more specific keywords, 2) headlines of articles, and 3) the body of articles. The keyword hierarchy is derived from the relationships between news articles. An example keyword hierarchy derived automatically from an actual news base is shown in Figure 2 above. Because this hierarchy was derived automatically, unlikely relationships were determined, e.g. the relationship between "Obituary" and "Media" which was derived from an article detailing the death of a comic book artist. Also, keywords may be duplicated in the keyword hierarchy, but there is only one copy of each article. An article is dynamically moved around the space depending upon where the user is within the space.

Since presentation of the space is non-linear, the system determines what information is to be displayed and how it is displayed at each instance the user moves through the space. As the user navigates through the space, the system controls the following parameters:

- Size of the keyword fonts
- Transparency of the keywords (as the user zooms past a keyword, it is kept in front of the user and is faded out over time, which helps with navigation)

- Location of articles within the space, animating the move between locations
- The color of articles as they move between keyword groups
- Line transparencies between
  - Parent and child keywords
  - Keywords and articles, indicating the relationship between the two
- Size of the article headline fonts
- How much of the article body to display, if any, and the transparency of the portion displayed (the body of the articles gradually drops in as the user zooms toward an article)

Also, some parameters are held fixed in the information space: the keyword locations in space are kept fixed to maintain a basic sense of structure, and the color of the keyword groups remain constant to indicate keyword clusters. These fixed parameters aid the user when navigating through the space by giving the user a sense of where they are within the space without having to provide something like a global map to aid in navigation. Further, the dynamic elements of the space–the size of the keyword fonts, the transparency and position of the keyword fonts as the user navigates into the region of a particular keyword, the lines emanating from keywords to articles becoming more transparent as the user navigates close to the articles–also provide implicit navigational aides. The combined effects of the fixed and dynamic parameters were carefully designed to assist the user in navigating through the space without using explicit navigational aides.

GALAXY OF NEWS SYSTEM

The architecture of the Galaxy of News system is illustrated in Figure 4. As shown in this illustration, the architecture

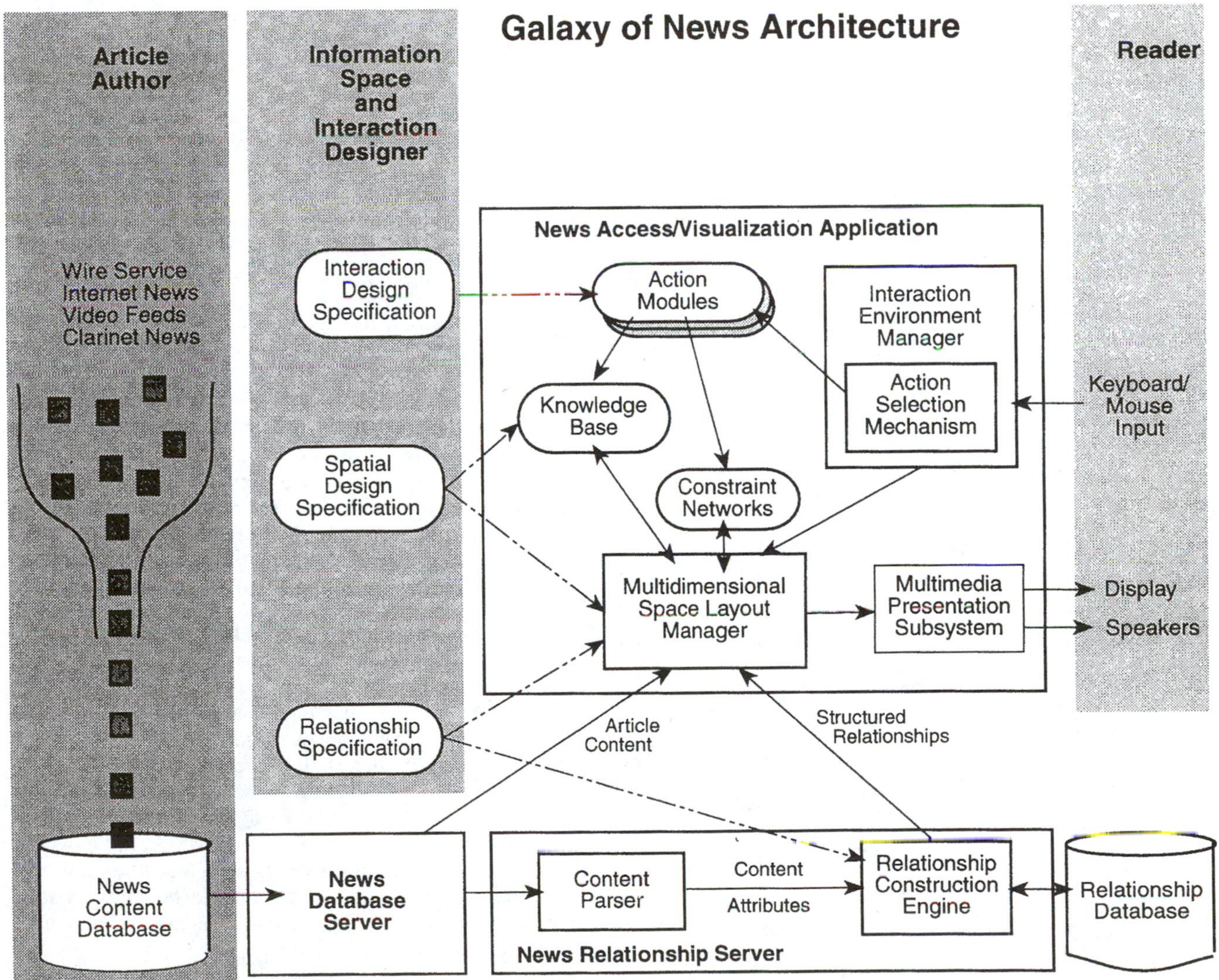

Figure 4: Architectural Overview of the Galaxy of News System

emphasizes three important aspects or views of the news production, management, access and visualization process: 1) authoring articles, 2) designing news information spaces for users to explore the news, and 3) reading or exploring the news. The architecture of the system supports the integration of these three views into a single environment.

Information Relationship and Structure Extraction Mechanisms

At the heart of the Galaxy of News system is a mechanism and representation for learning the relationships between news articles. The representation that maintains relationships between news articles is called an Associative Relation Network, or ARN. This representation and mechanisms that drive it use reinforcement techniques to capture the relationships between documents, and symbols extracted from those documents. The relationships between symbols contained in an ARN define the relationships between documents.

An ARN, illustrated in Figure 5, maintains weighted relationships between symbols contained in the network. An ARN is described as follows: For a given set of documents D , there exists a set of symbols S. The frequency of occurrence for symbol S_i, is defined as

$$c_i = \sum D_x : \{S_i, ...\}$$

where, $D_x : \{S_i, ...\}$ denotes a document containing S_i

The weighted relationship between S_i and S_j in a symmetric network is defined as

$$w_{i,j} = w_{j,i} = \sum D_x : \{S_i, S_j, ...\}$$

where, $D_x : \{S_i, S_j, ...\}$ denotes a document containing both S_i and S_j

With an ARN, the documents reinforce the associative weights between symbols that represent the relationships between documents. In effect, an ARN is used to learn about the structure of the news base. Hence, when the system starts, it has no previous knowledge about the symbols that are used to construct the network, and as it sweeps through the database, it learns the relationships between a set of symbols contained within the database.

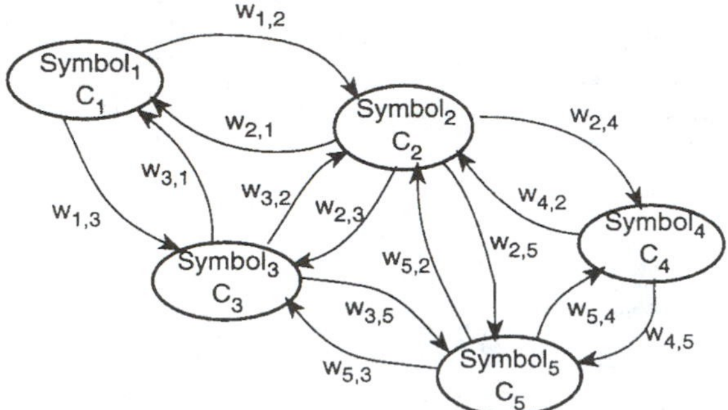

Figure 5: Simplified Associative Relation Network Representation

An ARN forms the basis for constructing an information space to allow people to explore the relationships between documents. Further, this representation is used to construct an abstracted information hierarchy. The information hierarchy is extracted from the ARN by using the following recursive process:

1. Search through the ARN and find all the statistically independent symbols
2. For each independent symbol, find all the symbols statistically dependent on the independent symbol
3. For each set of dependent symbols, find the independent symbols
4. Repeat steps 2 and 3 until all the dependent symbols are independent of one another.

The information hierarchy resulting from this process is used to progressively refine the presentation of information to the user, as described above.

News Information Space Construction

The current implementation uses the following approach to construct the news information space described above. First, news articles are parsed as they are received from their source, i.e. a Clarinet news feed. The parsing process extracts key information, such as keywords, locations, time event(s) occurred, subjects, actions, and so forth. After parsing, the original articles are stored in a database until referenced by the user.

Second, the key symbols are inserted into an ARN to construct relationships between articles. After parsing the articles and constructing the associative relation network, the system searches the network to extract the hierarchical relationships between the symbols, and hence, the articles. This process is described in the previous section.

After sorting the symbols into hierarchies, the peer elements in the hierarchy are sorted spatially so that symbols that are more closely related are placed next to one another. A relational distance between two symbols is determined by comparing the sets of associated symbols corresponding to the two symbols in question. This relational distance is used to perform a two dimensional sort. A third temporal sort is currently being developed.

Given the hierarchically structured and spatially sorted symbol set, a visual information space is constructed. The current implementation constructs a space that uses x- and y- dimensions to place the independent or root keyword symbols, and z- dimension to place keyword symbols of increasing levels of detail, followed by the articles. A recursive algorithm is used to place keywords within the space. First, the root keywords are placed using a constraint-based grid structure. Then, each set of keywords associated with the root keywords are placed behind their respective root keyword using separate constraint-based grids. The result of this process is a hierarchical grid structure containing the keywords.

During dynamic interaction with the user, the system employs both constraints and a set of heuristics to control the presentation of the hierarchical information to the user.

The constraints and heuristics used in the current implementation are described in the previous subsection.

System Architecture Components

The approach used to construct a news information space described in the previous subsection, is split into three main components: a news database server, a news relationship server, and an access and visualization application (illustrated in Figure 4). The relationship server is separated from the front-end application for speed and efficiency reasons. The separation between the news database and the news relationship server is presently a logistical solution, but in the future these two servers may be combined, especially to eliminate the potential problem of database inconsistencies.

The role of the news relationship server is to parse a set of news articles and build relationships between attributes contained in the articles. How these relationships are constructed is defined by a relationship specification (or procedure) defined by the information space designer. A relationship construction engine interprets the relationship specification, and uses it to build a structure representing the relationships between articles stored in a database. The relationship structures, such as the associative relation network described in the previous subsection, are derived by a server separate from the front-end application. These processes are separated because of the time required to build the relationships and allows the relationships to be used multiple times by multiple processes.

The system front-end application consists of two primary components: a multidimensional space layout manager, and an interaction environment manager. These two components are supported by a knowledge-base, constraint networks, and action modules. The knowledge-base is created by the information space designer and specifies rules for constructing a space based on the relationships between articles and meta-data that describes the articles, in this case keywords. The action modules are written by the information space and interaction designer, and define how the system responds to changing situations that are based on user interaction. To effect change in the display of information, the action modules can modify either the knowledge-base or the constraint networks.

Multidimensional Space Layout Manager. The Multidimensional Space Layout Manager constructs an abstracted information space based on the relationship structures specified by the information space designer. In addition, the layout manager controls what and how information is presented at each instance of interaction. Since the space the user navigates through is non-linear, the layout manager must compute a layout each time the user moves within the space. This continuous spatial regeneration creates a reactive environment. The layout manager utilizes a knowledge-base provided by the information space designer to perform this operation.

Interaction Environment Manager. The Interaction Environment Manager controls the systems response to user interaction. It performs this function by building a model of the user situated in an environment, in this case a three dimensional space. As the user moves within the environment an action selection mechanisms determines what actions, if any, the system should take to respond to the user. In the current implementation, the action selection mechanism uses a simple rule-based approach. When an action is selected and executed, it modifies the state of the knowledge-base and/or the constraint networks. These changes are subsequently interpreted by the layout manager to effect the layout and presentation of the space.

DISCUSSION

In developing the Galaxy of News system , we considered several alternative approaches. We considered using hypertext and hypermedia concepts and systems [11] to aid in accessing related articles or information in general. This technique has met with some success and has been employed by Mosaic[1] as an interface to World Wide Web documents. However, there are several inherent problems with the hypermedia approach, such as Mosaic. One of the most significant problems with hypermedia is its "hyper" aspect; the process of jumping to another location in an information space can easily confuse a user. This is primarily a result of the lack of a general, or known, structure of the information available to the user. Unless the author of the hypermedia document clearly presents the structure of the information, the user has no idea what other information is available other than the clues indicated by hot spots or hot text that link one node to another node. Hence, the utility of hypermedia systems are at the mercy of hypermedia content authors. Further, if all of the links between related news articles must be authored by hand, this problem will only expound with the growth of computer connectivity and the amount of news information available.

Another approach to this problem is to build news filters. In the past, we had a natural form of news filtering, known as editors, who selected what news we would read, or see (in the case of television). And, we had to either accept their filtering or choose another newspaper or channel. We had no choice but to trust what the newspapers, magazines, and newscasts were telling us. This choice was forced upon us because we had no other means to access information concerning events that happened in distant places and/or at different times. But, with the advent of the Internet and other related technologies, we will soon have direct access to ALL news articles. This clearly presents a dilemma. We cannot possibly read all the news available, and yet can we, or will we, trust news editors and other forms of news filters, such as intelligent autonomous agents. And, if we are aware that we have access to all news information, then trust concerning how information is filtered will be of primary importance. Hence, we took the approach to provide *access* to all the articles instead of using filtering or retrieval techniques.

FUTURE DIRECTIONS

The Galaxy of News system is currently targeted toward a fairly specific class of information–news articles. We are extending the system to handle other types of information objects, such as documents contained in the World Wide Web and images contained in a National Geographic archive. The Galaxy of News system shows promise in providing a tool for understanding the increasing size and complexity of information available via the WWW and other large information bases.

In addition, we are working on extending the system to support more sophisticated relationships between information objects. This work includes extending the system to support not only symbolic relationships, but also parametric relationships. Parametric relationships may be very useful in situations where it is not possible to derive symbolic descriptions of objects, such as with video, audio and images that have not been annotated. And, along with these more sophisticated relationships, we are working on ways to give readers the ability to control how the relationships effect the presentation of information, allowing users to explore deeper and more complex relationships between information objects. In effect, this would give users the ability to switch roles between reader and information space designer. Eventually, we can also see users moving back and forth between author, space designer and reader in a fluid fashion as they read and augment an expanding information space.

Because the space constructed by the current system is based entirely on the contents of a news base, the structure of the space will change along with the news base. This is effective when the user is primarily in an exploratory mode, the type of browsing the Galaxy of News system was originally targeted towards. However, if a user wants to conduct a more directed search with a specific type of information in mind, then it would be useful to have personalized views or structures to assist users with navigation. Hence, we are currently developing a learning algorithm that will monitor a user's interactions and provide the user with the ability to restructure the space so that the placement of information is more familiar to the user.

As noted earlier in this paper, we are developing a temporal extension to the associative relation network. This will allow us to learn event sequences and event sequence relationships. The temporal ARN can be applied to learn both implicit event sequences (i.e. sequences of events specified over disjoint documents) as well as explicit event sequences such as those found in videos. Once the temporal relationships are learned, they can be used to structure an information space and browse through temporal arrangements of information.

Finally, we are exploring methods for enhancing the action selection mechanism. As the relationships between the information objects grow more complex, the mechanisms for controlling what information is most appropriate to present in a given situation will need to be more sophisticated. We are exploring the utility of behavior-based artificial intelligence techniques to deal with these complexities. Further, we are exploring methods for providing guided tours through information spaces based on a user's previous history of interaction or information that is of interest to a local culture.

CONCLUSIONS

In this paper we have presented results of research conducted in developing the Galaxy of News prototype system. This system allows a news reader to gain a broad understanding of the contents of a news database, and as the user selectively zooms, the news reorganizes itself in relation to the focus of interest and progressively refines the details of the abstracted news information space. The information space is automatically constructed based on relationships derived from the contents of the news stories.

From the lessons learned in developing this system and its projected utility in managing, organizing, visualizing and accessing news information, we have defined a model for news information visualization and access. This model defines four layers that are used to construct an interactive news information space: 1) the news base, 2) derived relationships between the news information objects, 3) spatial construction specifications, and 4) temporal and behavior interaction specifications. The model also defines three different views onto the components used to construct the information space: 1) the reader's view, 2) the information space and interaction designer's view, and 3) the author's view. This model provides a structure for handling the rapidly expanding news base.

The experience of interacting in the abstract information spaces created by the Galaxy of News system clearly indicates the utility of abstracted multidimensional spaces for browsing through news bases. Galaxy of News represents a new approach to addressing problems of information scale and complexity that we will face in the midst of global interconnectivity. We believe the immersive techniques employed by the Galaxy of News system will significantly enhance information visualization, navigation and access.

ACKNOWLEDGMENTS

The author would like to acknowledge the continued support, advice and direction provided by Professor Muriel Cooper, Ron MacNeil, Dave Small and Suguru Ishizaki of the Visible Language Workshop. The author would also like to give a special thanks to Lisa Strausfeld for her insight and ideas which helped formulate and solidify the concepts explored in this research. A special thanks also goes to Maia Engeli, Robin Kullberg, Ishantha Lokuge, Rob Silvers, Jeffry Ventrell, Louis Weitzman, Yin Yin Wong, and Xiaoyang Yang for providing many critiques and suggestions. This work was sponsored by ARPA, JNIDS, NYNEX and Alenia.

REFERENCES

[1] Andreessen, Marc, NCSA Mosaic Technical Summary. 1993, National Center for Supercomputing Applications.

[2] Brill, Eric. A Simple Rule-Based Part of Speech Tagger. *Proceedings of Third Conference on Applied*

Natural Language Processing. 1992. Trento, Italy: ACL.

[3] Brill, Eric, *A Corpus-Based Approach to Language Learning*. 1993, University of Pennsylvania: PhD Thesis.

[4] Chang, Bay-Wei, and David Ungar. Animation: From Cartoons to the User Interface. *Proceedings of UIST*. 1993. Atlanta, Georgia:

[5] Colby, Grace, and Laura Scholl. Transparency and Blur as Selective Cues for Complex Information. *Proceedings of SPIE*. 1992.

[6] Cooper, Muriel, et.al. Information Landscapes. MIT Technical Note. April, 1994.

[7] Cutting, Doug, Julian Kupiec, Jan Pedersen, and Penelope Sibun. A Practical Part-of-Speech Tagger. *Proceedings of Third International Conference on Applied Natural Language Processing*. 1991.

[8] Feiner, Steven, and Clifford Beshers. Worlds within Worlds: Metaphors for Exploring n-Dimensional Virtual Worlds. *Proceedings of UIST*. 1990. Snowbird, Utah: ACM.

[9] Furnas, George. Generalized Fisheye Views. *Proceedings of Human Factors and Computer Systems, CHI*. 1989.

[10] Masuishi, Tetsuya, David Small, and Ronald L. MacNeil. 6,000x2,000 Display Prototype. *Proceedings of SPIE/IS&Ts Symposium on Electronic Imaging Science and Technology*. 1992.

[11] Nelson, Ted, *Literary Machines*. 1981, Swarthmore, PA.

[12] Perlin, Ken, and David Fox. Pad: An Alternative Approach to the Computer Interface. *Proceedings of Computer Graphics*. 1993.

[13] Robertson, George G., Jock D. Mackinlay, and Stuart K. Card. Cone Trees: Animated 3D Visualizations of Hierarchical Information. *Proceedings of UIST*. 1991. Hilton Head, South Carolina: ACM.

[14] Small, David, Suguru Ishizaki, and Muriel Cooper. Typographic Space. *Proceedings of CHI*. 1994. Boston, Massachusetts: ACM.

CHAPTER 6

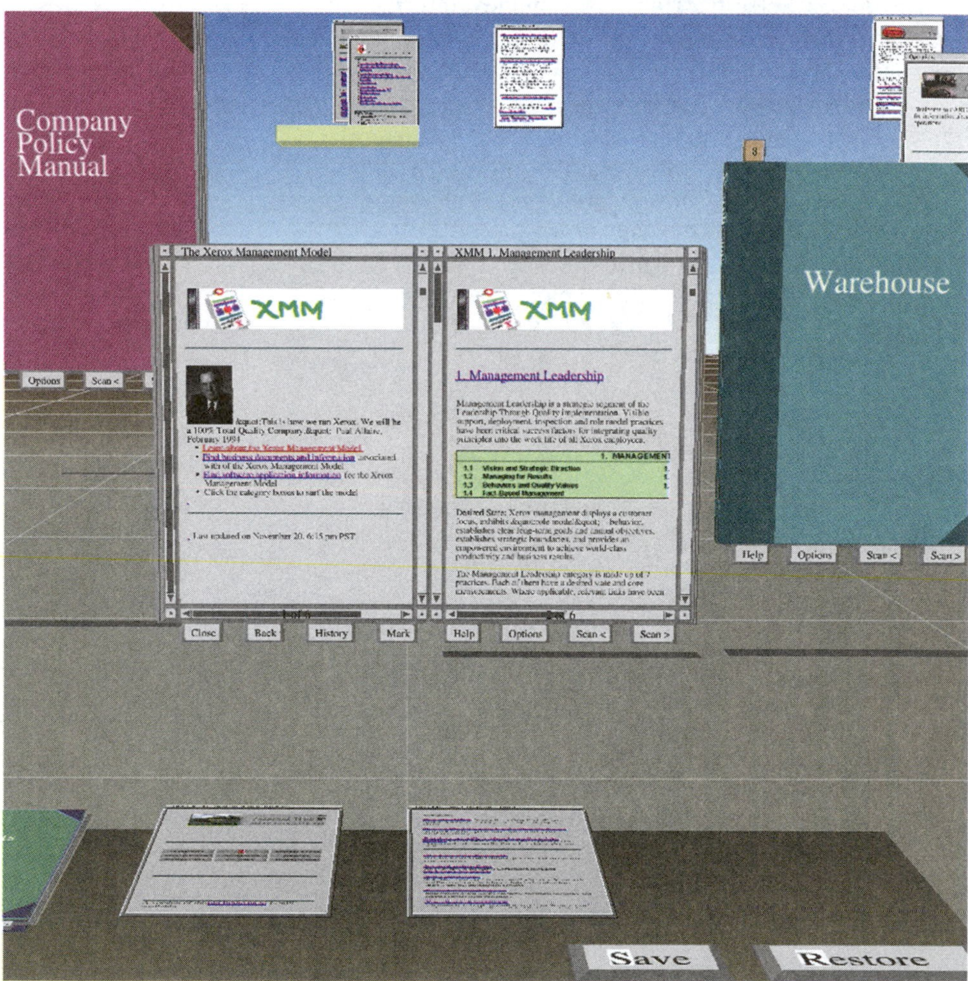

Vision is the art of seeing things invisible.

– Jonathan Swift (1711)

Infosphere, Workspace, Tools, Objects

So far, we have concentrated on the use of information visualization for understanding a particular set of data. In this chapter, we look beyond tools to other uses in the larger process of creating new knowledge. We said in Chapter 1 that the purpose of information visualization is to use perception for amplifying cognition—especially for knowledge crystallization, where a person gathers information for some purpose, makes sense of it, and then packages it into some form for communication or action (Figure 1.15). Information visualization techniques can be used as part of user interfaces for all of these activities.

It is useful to divide the application of information visualization into four levels (Figure 6.1). At the highest level is visualization to help users access information outside the immediate environment, such as information on the Internet or online databases on a server. This information collectively is sometimes called the *infosphere,* and we will adopt the term to mean all the information in the world outside the user's immediate grasp (neglecting in the interest of simplification important distinctions between whether the information is within or without the user's institution and whether it is part of a collection). Visualization can be applied to give the user a view into this world (e.g., Figure 6.2(a)).

At the next level, it is useful to define a second, intermediate level of application we will call an *information workspace* (e.g., Figure 6.2(b)). An information workspace, as a sort of cache, allows for improvement in the cost of information work (information in the workspace is visible and fast to access), and it is the staging area for integration of information from different sources. Information workspaces are oriented not around visualizations themselves, but around tasks. An information workspace might contain several visualizations related to one or several tasks. The analogy is to a desk or a workbench. On a desk, different tools can be brought into conjunction on an ad hoc basis. A telephone, a computer, and a notebook can all be used together, for example, although not formally integrated. The same desk can be used for multiple tasks. The purpose of information workspaces, like all workspaces, is to produce a more favorable cost structure for doing a task. Invention of the desktop metaphor workspace for personal computers was an important advance in user interfaces, and information visualization could play a significant role in advancing the techniques of workspaces that can handle information on a larger scale.

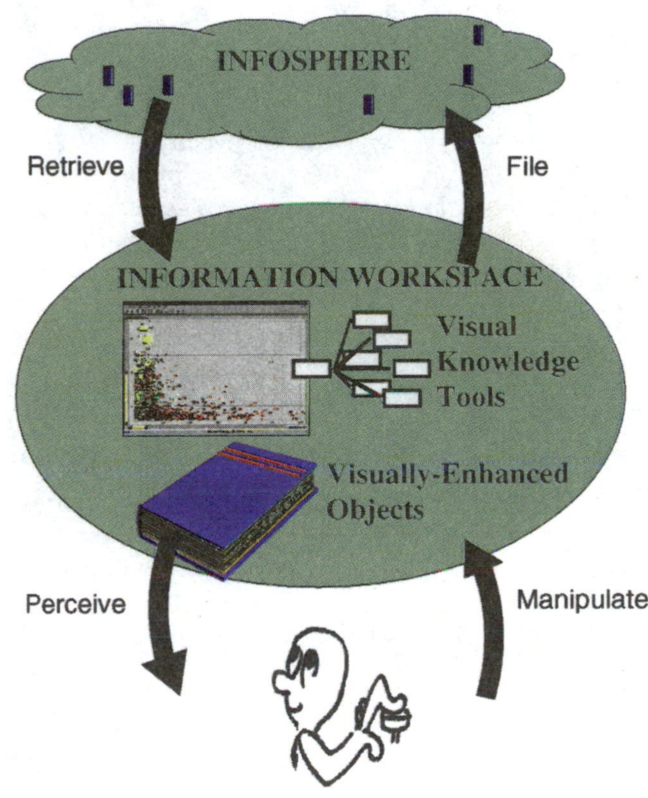

FIGURE **6.1**

Levels of application for information visualization.

At the third level are *visual knowledge tools* or "wide widgets" (e.g., Figure 6.2(c)). These are the sort of visualization tools described in many of the papers so far in this book. They contain a visual presentation of some data set and a set of controls for interacting with that presentation. The focus is on determining and extracting the relationships in a particular set of data.

At a fourth level are *visually enhanced objects,* coherent information objects enhanced by the addition of information visualization techniques. An example is Figure 6.2(d), in which voxel data of the brain have been enhanced through automatic surface rendition, coloring, slicing, and labeling. Abstract data structures representing neural projections and anatomical labels have been integrated into a display of the data. While it may sometimes not be easy to decide whether a particular visualization should be considered a visually enhanced object or a visual knowledge tool, the general distinction is still useful. Visually enhanced objects focus on revealing more information from some object of intrinsic visual form, whereas visual knowledge tools focus on creating new visual patterns as part of reducing the data to understanding. Visual knowledge tools sometimes provide containers for visually enhanced objects.

In the rest of this chapter, we examine three of these levels. We do not examine all four because visual knowledge tools are the content for most of the rest of the book. This chapter is focused on the others.

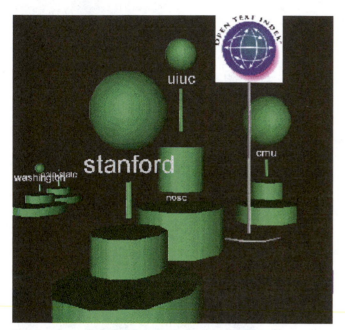

(a) Infosphere: Open text index visualization. See Bray (1996 ●, detail from Figure 11).

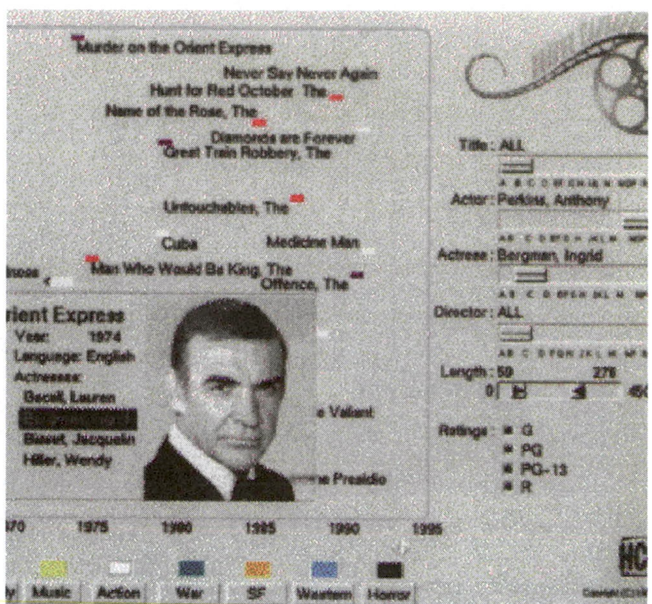

(c) Visual knowledge tool: FilmFinder. See Ahlberg and Shneiderman (1994 ●).

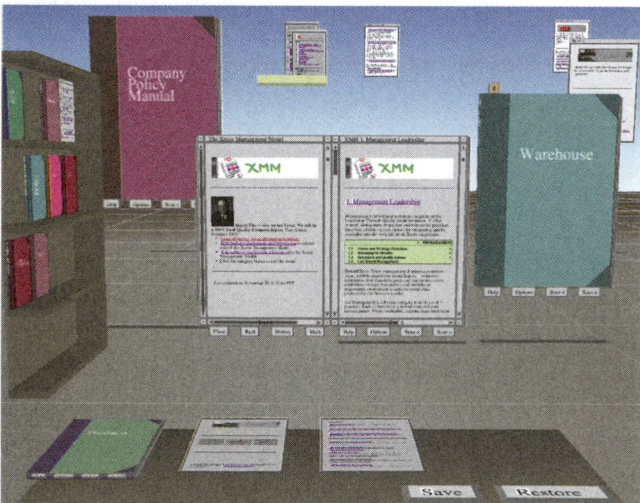

(b) Information workspace: Web forager. Courtesy of Xerox Corporation. See Card, Robertson, and York (1996 ●).

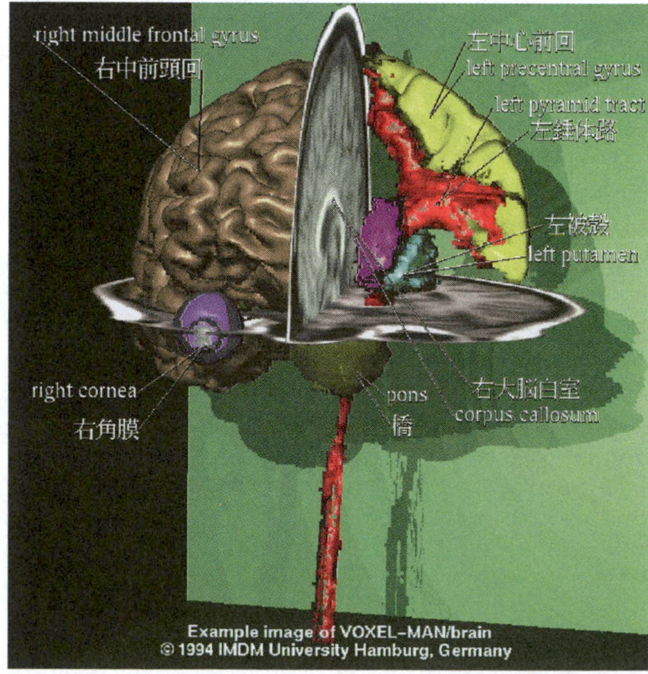

(d) Visually enhanced object: Voxel-Man. Courtesy of UMDM, University of Hamburg.

FIGURE **6.2**

Examples of information visualization techniques applied at different levels.

6.1

Internet and Infosphere

Current trends point to a future where vast online information sources are available to the seated user. Many people think of the World Wide Web, whatever its eventual form, as exemplifying this future. Currently the Web contains about 10 terabytes of information in about 200 million documents and is doubling every 12 months (Murphy, 1998). This is a vast and awesome number when we consider that the information is reachable by something like 50 million people (depending on how access is defined). Actually, the Web is a small fraction (3%) of the 300 pentabytes estimated to be on-line. The Web looks even smaller when we realize that it contains less than 1% of the amount of content in a single university library (the University of California at Berkeley) (Murphy, 1998). Hence, however large the Web is now, it has great potential to grow much larger in the future. Yet current methods of access leave much to be desired and do not adequately exploit this immense resource. Information visualization could play a substantial, even enabling, role here in helping users find information faster, understand the structure of the space, find patches of interesting information for greater examination, or make the space more learnable. This is an active area of information visualization research.

The Internet, by its nature, is abstract. People use metaphors to describe how to think about it. These metaphors in turn have some effect on the actual development of the Internet itself. When the Internet became public, Vice President Gore talked of creating an information superhighway, a virtual version of the national superhighway his father had helped create that knit together the nation for commerce and travel. Mark Stefik (1996) in our User Interface Research group at Xerox PARC has classified the metaphors for the Internet into four categories: (1) the digital library metaphor, (2) the electronic mail metaphor, (3) the electronic marketplace metaphor, and (4) the digital worlds metaphor. Each of these could provide a starting point for visualization. Take the digital worlds metaphor. Many researchers were inspired by the science fiction writer William Gibson, whose novel *Neuromancer* (Gibson, 1984) describes a visualization of a pure information space, the Matrix. Benedikt (1991) made an early attempt to lay out the principles for an "architecture" for such a place. In his conception, objects are defined by variables, as in our Data Table. Several of these variables are chosen to be the ones to map onto space (and time). These determine the location of the object in cyberspace; the rest are expressed as retinal variables or more complex articulations of the form that determines what is seen at that location. His Principle of Exclusion says that no two objects can be permitted to map onto the same exact point. His Principle of Maximal Exclusion says that we should map into spatial coordinates those variables in the Data Table that minimize potential overlap.

Figure 6.3 shows some other attempts to create visualizations of portions of the Web, either as a digital world or as a digital library or some combination. Figure 6.3(a) uses a Kohonen map to create a picture of entertainment resources on the Web. Figure 6.3(b) uses a VIBE-VR layout (Benford, Snowdon, and Mariani, 1995) that places objects according to their similarity to four concepts placed on the vertices of a tetrahedron. Figure 6.3(c) uses a curved timeline in 3D space to organize text and images (Small, Ishizki, and Cooper, 1994, MIT). The user can fly along the timeline. This project shows the impact of realistic images as part of an information space.

Whereas the visualizations in Figure 6.3 show a portion of the Web, the visualizations in Figure 6.4 are for specific collections, defined around the contents for a specific site. Figure 6.4(a) shows the Web site of the *Chicago Tribune*. The site is mapped onto a tree, and the tree is laid out circularly. Color indicates the type of information. Figure 6.4(b) shows the Web site of the *Encyclopedia Britannica*. This is a tree laid out on an information landscape. The nodes of the tree are stood up vertically, and the layout is packed in an unusual design that emphasizes central versus peripheral nodes. Figure 6.4(c) shows a dynamic representation of a Web site. As the user clicks on one of these nodes, related nodes appear dynamically allowing him or her to navigate to a position of interest.

Figure 6.5 goes the next step and shows a space-time visualization of the evolution of a Web site. The 7000 nodes of the Xerox Web site have been recast into a tree in such a way that there is a position in the tree for a node if it exists at any time during the time interval considered. Lines are colored and thickened depending on the amount of traffic to each node. In the visualization, each disk represents the site for a different week. From examination of the visualization it is possible to watch the addition and deletion of nodes (new nodes are yellow, deleted nodes are brown) and the changes in traffic (as a consequence of Xerox releasing its quarterly financial report).

The papers in this section sketch three additional ways for how the infosphere might be visualized. In order to visualize the Web in a useful way, it is necessary to understand something about its structure. The first paper, (Bray, 1996 ●), serves as a short tutorial on that structure. Of course, many statistics, such as the size of the Web, are instantly out of date. But the basic statistical structure is longer lasting. For example, sites are not strongly connected to each other; they are apparently much more strongly connected within. This suggests that the site is the proper unit of aggregate visualization. Some sites, however, are strongly connected, either being pointed to by many sites or themselves pointing to others. These sites form a natural backbone to the Web. From these basic facts about the Web, Bray invents a Web visualization as a landscape of sites. Sites are laid out on the 2D plane according to the strength of connections between them. Other properties of a site are mapped into the visual properties of the site icon. Sites with more pages are larger. Sites with many in-links are taller to make them more visible. Sites with many out-links are brighter. The color of the site reflects its domain.

The second paper by Andrews (1995 ●) also reflects knowledge of internal structure. He is part of a group that produced Hyper-G (Andrews, Kappe, and Maurer, 1995a, 1995b), a system that uses special servers to maintain both in- and out-links in accessible form. This allows the group to have more sophisticated hyperlink services than are possible with the one-way WWW links. Andrews gives examples of several mappings: (1) information mapped to predetermined virtual geographical landscapes, (2) information landscapes of 2D trees, and (3) dynamically unfolding localities in an information landscape.

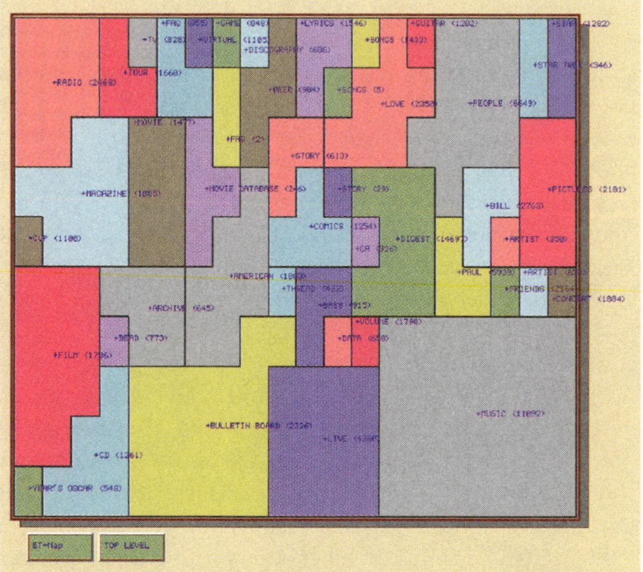

(a) ET-Map. Courtesy of AI Group, University of Arizona.

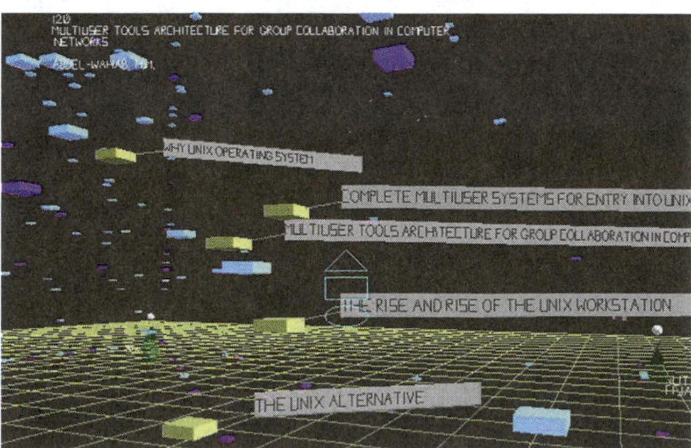

(b) Populated Information Terrains. Courtesy of Communications Research Group, University of Nottingham. See Benford, Snowdon, and Mariani (1995).

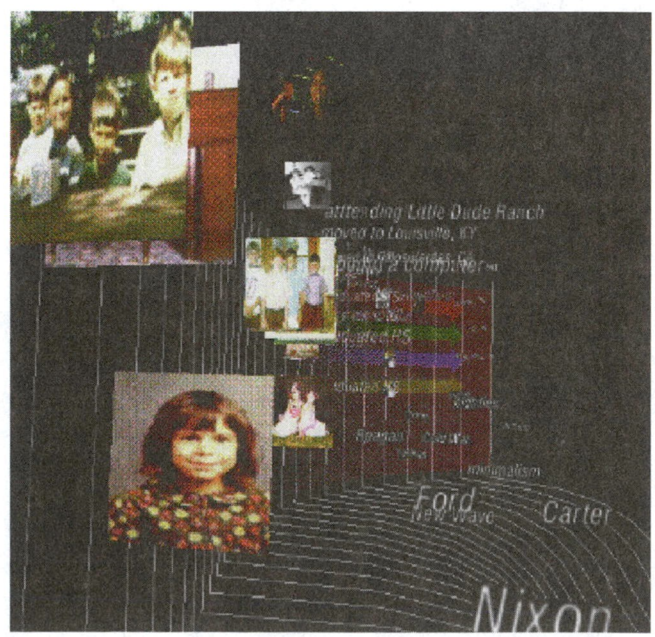

(c) Timeline. Courtesy of David Small, MIT Media Laboratory.

FIGURE **6.3**

Visualizations of regions of the World Wide Web.

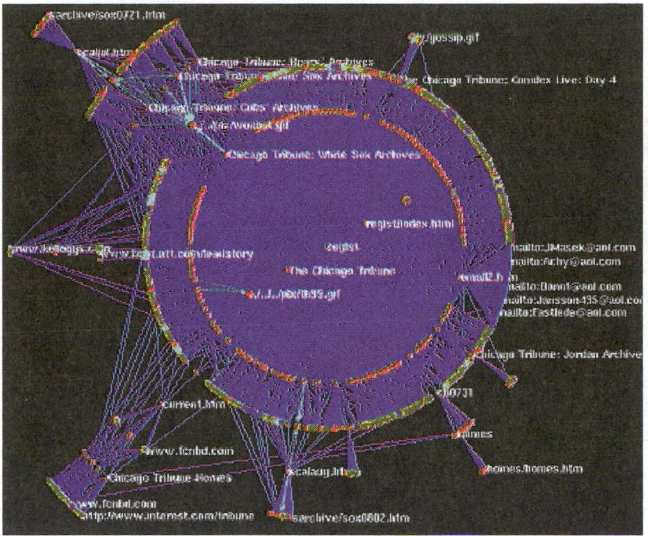

(a) NicheWorks. Courtesy of Lucent Technologies. See Wills (1997).

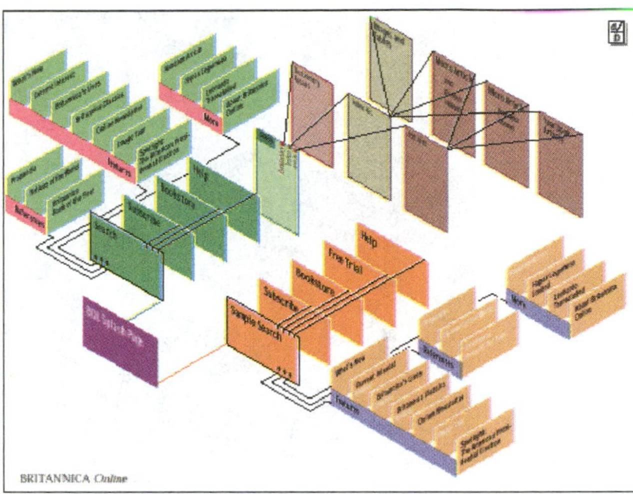

(b) Online Britannica screen. Courtesy of Dynamic Diagrams.

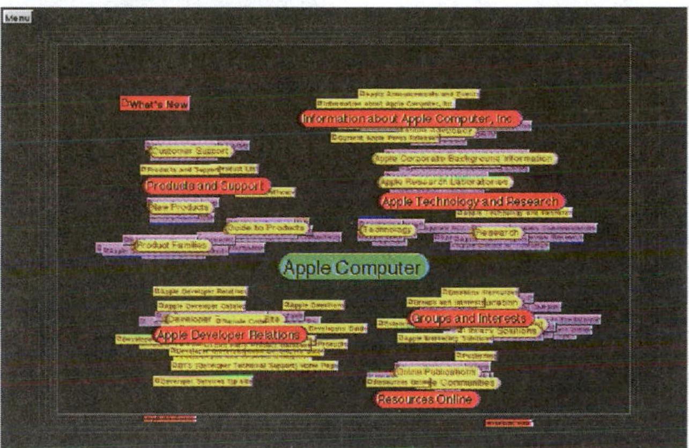

(c) Hotsauce. Courtesy of Apple Computer. See Apple Computer (1998).

FIGURE **6.4**

Visualizations of document collections or Web sites.

The last paper, by Hendley et al. (1995 ●), is an example of an attempt at a 3D information space. Web pages are represented by nodes in the space. Properties of Web pages are used to position the nodes in 3D space according to a force model. Some properties are also used to determine the appearance of a node. The nodes migrate from random initial positions into clusters and constellations. To keep the computational load reasonable, these asymptotic positions are static. In Hendley et al.'s vision, however, information nodes could be dynamically in orbit given adequate computing resources.

Each of these views is exploratory and dramatic. What remains is to demonstrate that such visualizations can make a difference in a practical system.

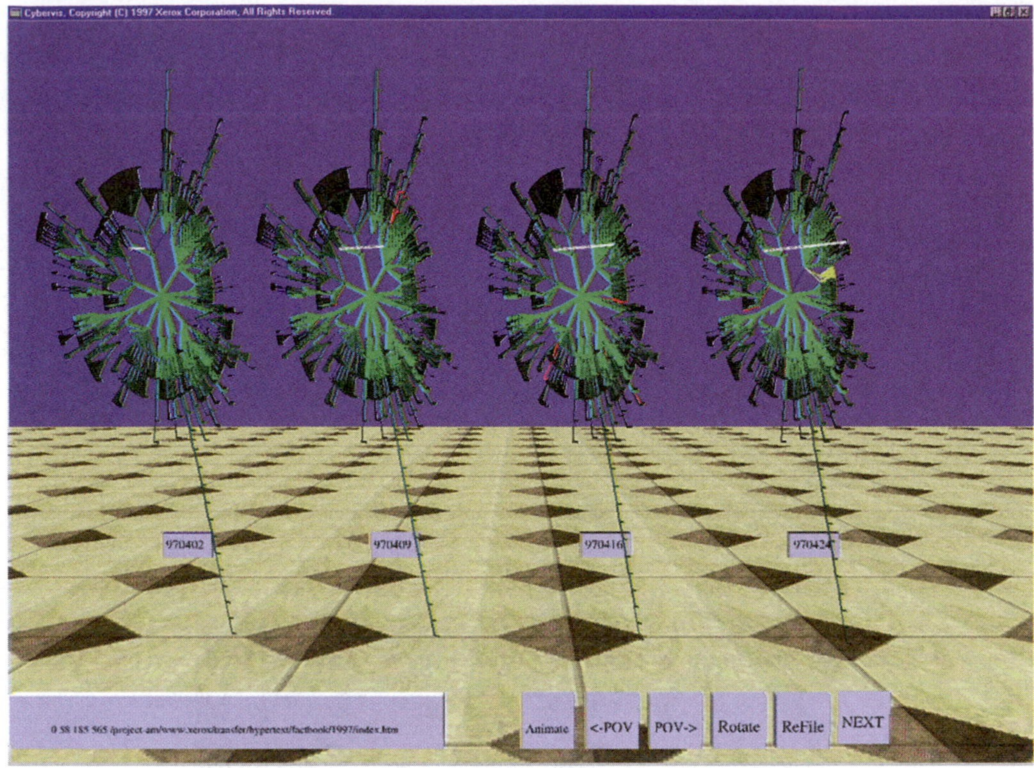

FIGURE **6.5**

Time tube. Xerox PARC (Chi et al., 1998, Figure 1).

Measuring the Web

Tim Bray *

Open Text Corporation [1], 101 – 1965 West Fourth Avenue, Vancouver, B.C., Canada V6J 1M8

Abstract

"When you can measure what you are speaking about, and express it in numbers, you know something about it; but when you cannot express it in numbers, your knowledge is of a meager and unsatisfactory kind; it may be the beginning of knowledge, but you have scarcely in your thoughts advanced to the state of science." – **Lord Kelvin** [2]

This paper presents some difficult qualitative questions concerning the Web, and attempts to provide some partial quantitative answers to them. It uses the numbers in these answers to drive some 3-D visualizations of localities in the Web.

Keywords: Robots; Indexing; Visualization; Statistics; Metrics

1. The questions

1.1. History

Since the **first robot was launched** [3] on Saint Valentine's Day 1995, the **Open Text Index** [4] software has examined millions of pages and maintained an ever-growing inventory of information about them.

This effort has been, from the outset, marketing-driven. Open Text is a long-time vendor of search and retrieval technology, and the WWW became, during the course of 1994, the world's largest and most visible retrieval problem. Failing to have attacked it would have been a vote of no confidence in our own technology.

As a business exercise, it has been successful. Open Text's **Livelink** [5] **Search** [6] and **Livelink** [7] **Spider** [8] are leaders in the fast-growing market for Web site indexers . Considered as an intellectual effort, it has been less than satisfying. We advertise our work as an Index of the WWW – and yet it covers much less than the whole. Our difficulty is similar to that of the **cartographers of centuries past** [9], struggling with the task of mapping territories which are still largely unknown. Observe, for example, the large *Terra Australis Incognita* in Fig. 1 [10].

1.2. Questions without answer

- How big is the Web?
- What is the "average page" like?
- How richly connected is it?
- What are the biggest and most visible sites?
- What data formats are being used?

* Email: tbray@opentext.com.

[1] http://www.opentext.com

[2] http://www-groups.dcs.st-and.ac.uk/~history/Mathematicians/Thomson.html

[3] http://www.opentext.com:8080/omw/f-progress.html

[4] http://www.opentext.com

[5] http://www.opentext.com/livelink

[6] http://www.opentext.com/livelink/otm_ll_ll.html

[7] http://www.opentext.com/livelink

[8] http://www.opentext.com/livelink/otm_ll_ll.html

[9] http://elvis.neep.wisc.edu/~cdean/index.html

[10] http://www.carto.com/

- What does the WWW look like?

This paper uses the resources of the Open Text Index to derive some approximations to the answers.

2. The answers

2.1. The sample

The information on which this report is based was extracted in November 1995, when the Open Text Index covered the content of about 1.5 million textual objects retrieved from the WWW. Today, the sample would be much larger. To keep things simple, we shall call these objects "pages". The pages were identified and retrieved as follows:

- *Initialization.* We started in late 1994 with a bootstrap list of some 40,000 URLs alleged to be those of "home pages" nobody can remember where this originally came from. We retrieved as many as possible of these (about 20,000) and formed the initial index.
- *Page Refresh.* For each indexed page, we maintain a time-stamp indicating the last time it was visited. Our initial page refresh strategy simply involved sorting the total inventory of pages oldest-first, and dedicating fixed periods of time to revisiting them in that order. Revisiting a page has three possible results: the page is gone, the page is there but has changed, or the page is unchanged.
  We have since become more sophisticated in our processes for selecting pages to revisit, but the possible outcomes are the same.
- *Enlargement.* Each time we copy in the contents of page, we extract from it all `http`, `gopher`, and `ftp` style anchors. Those that are not duplicates of already-indexed pages are queued for addition to the Index.
  Other sources of new pages are voluntary submissions to the Index and well-known Internet announcement venues.

Nobody can say how good a sample this is of the whole Web. However, the basic statistics presented

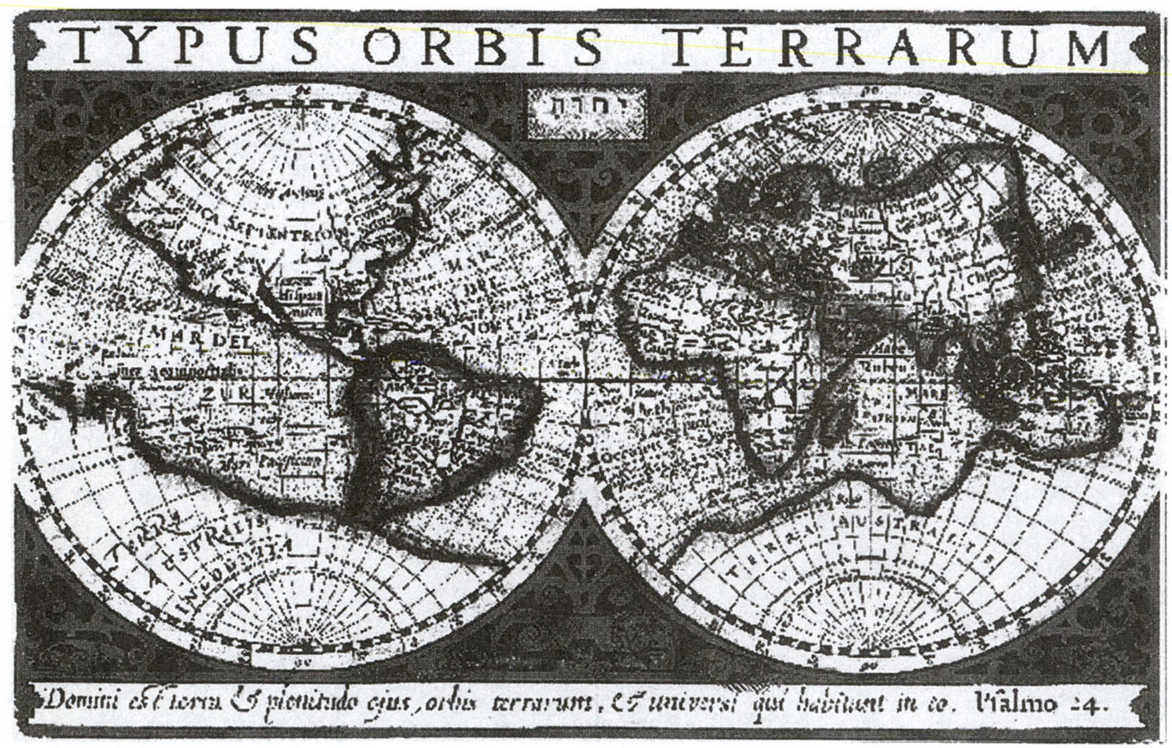

Fig. 1. 1601 Mercator-Hondius.

below about page size and contents have not changed much since we started measuring them, during which time the Index has grown by more than an order of magnitude. Thus, while there is probably systematic bias in these numbers, it does not seem a function of the sample size.

The following are personal intuitions about the sample, which should be taken as speculation rather than *ex cathedra* wisdom:

- "Home Pages" are over-represented (we acknowledge that there is no formal definition of this term).
- HTML pages are over-represented.
- Asian language pages are under-represented.
- "Good" pages are over-represented.
- Long-lived pages are over-represented.

2.2. How big is the Web?

Bear in mind, once again, that these numbers are the result of a snapshot taken in November 1995; recent estimates are in excess of 50 million.

Number of unique URLs: 11,366,121
Number of unique servers: 223,851

This includes only URLs that begin with `http`, `ftp`, or `gopher`. To find duplicates we apply the following heuristics:

- strip redundant port numbers (80 for http, 70 for gopher),
- convert hostnames to IP addresses,
- strip trailing slashes (this is sometimes [very rarely] wrong),
- remove Unix filesystem no-ops; for example both `/a/./b/./c` and `/a/d/../b/e/../c` are converted to `/a/b/c`.

The servers are counted simply by syntactic processing of URLs; there is no guarantee (or expectation) that all of them are actually valid.

2.3. What is a "site"?

Should the two terms "Web *site*" and "Web *server*" mean the same thing? Clearly, **www.berkeley.edu** [11] and **web.mit.edu** [12] are two different sites. But are Berkeley's Academic Achievement Division on server **www.aad.berkeley.edu** [13] and Academic Preparation and Articulation on **ub4.apa.berkeley.edu** [14] different? At Open Text, the **search engine** [15] and the **main corporate site** [16] have different webmasters, run on different computers, and exist to serve quite different purposes.

Formalizing the notion of a "site" causes some information loss, but allows us to develop some useful statistics. The current formalization (implemented in perl) may be summarized as:

- ⟨anything⟩(.edu or .com or .gov or .net)
- ⟨anything⟩(.co or .com).⟨country-digraph⟩
- ⟨anything⟩(.ac or .edu).⟨country-digraph⟩
- ⟨anything⟩(.army.mil, .af.mil or .navy.mil)
- ⟨anything-else⟩.mil
- ⟨anything⟩.⟨country-digraph⟩
- and a bunch of ad-hoc rules to help with the .k12, ⟨state-digraph⟩.us and ⟨province-digraph⟩.ca sites

Thus, `ucla.edu`, `ox.ac.uk`, `sun.com`, `cern.ch`, and `arl.army.mil` are all "sites".

These rules clearly underestimate the number of independently-operated "sites"; for example they make no distinction, at the "site" named UIUC, between the **University of Illinois Press** [17] and **NCSA** [18]. However, they also usefully conflate many superficially-different aliases, and capture something close enough to the human conception of a "site" to be useful, so we shall use them as the basis for quite a number of statistics.

Number of unique "sites": 89,271

2.4. What is the "average page" like?

The size of the average page has consistently been between 6K and 7k bytes during the entire lifetime

[11] http://www.berkeley.edu
[12] http://web.mit.edu
[13] http://www.aad.berkeley.edu
[14] http://ub4.apa.berkeley.edu
[15] http://www.opentext.com/omw/f-omw.html
[16] http://www.opentext.com
[17] http://www.uiuc.edu/providers/uipress/
[18] http://www.ncsa.uiuc.edu

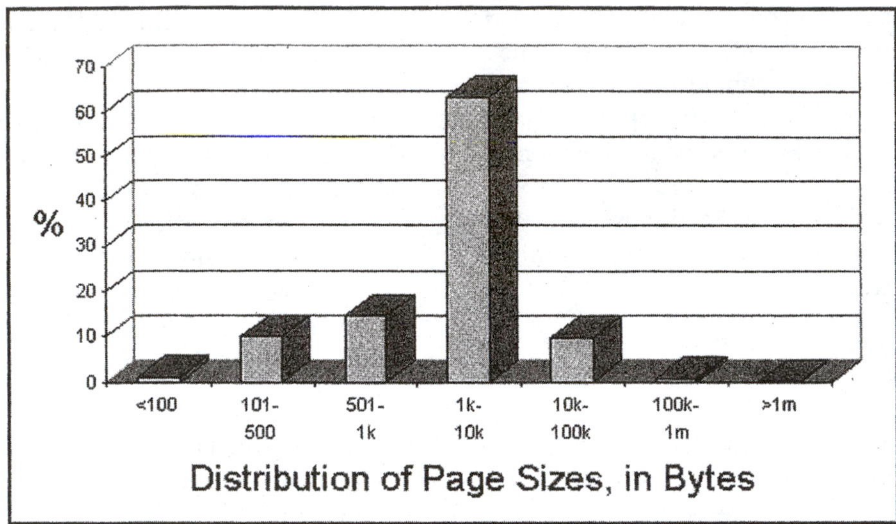

Fig. 2. Page size distribution.

of the Index. The size has fallen slightly as the sample size has grown, from just under 7000 to about 6500 at the time of writing. This amounts to about 1,050 ''words'', depending of course on how one defines a word – we use an indexable token beginning with an alphabetic character. Fig. 2 illustrates the clustering in this distribution, and the presence of a significant number of very large pages.

The page sizes are highly variable, as illustrated in the following table, which covers one snapshot of 1.524 million pages:

Mean	6518
Median	2021
Standard deviation	31678

The Web is quite graphically rich. Fig. 3 shows that just over 50% of all pages contain at least one image reference. It is interesting to note that about 15% of pages contain exactly one image. Quite likely, for many of the pages that contain large numbers of images, those images are in fact typographical marks of the ''reddot.gif'' variety.

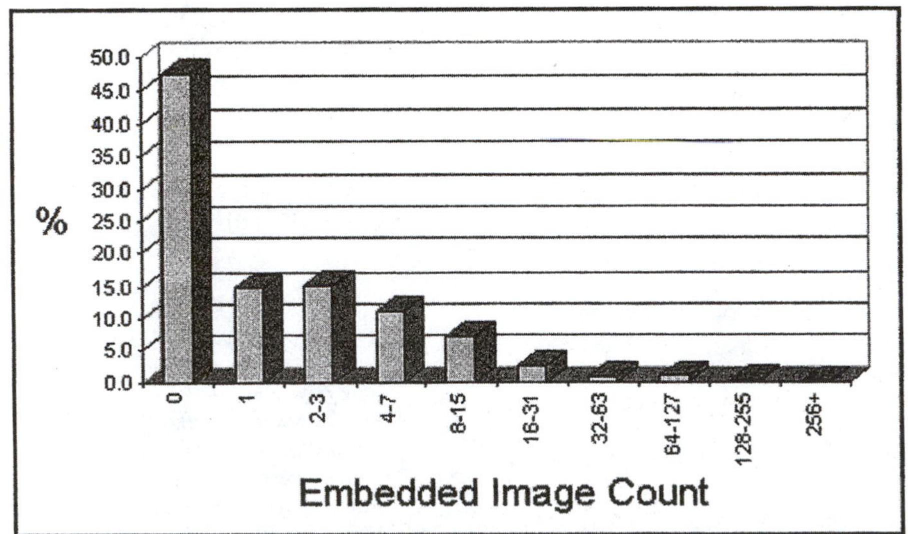

Fig. 3. Distribution of embedded image counts.

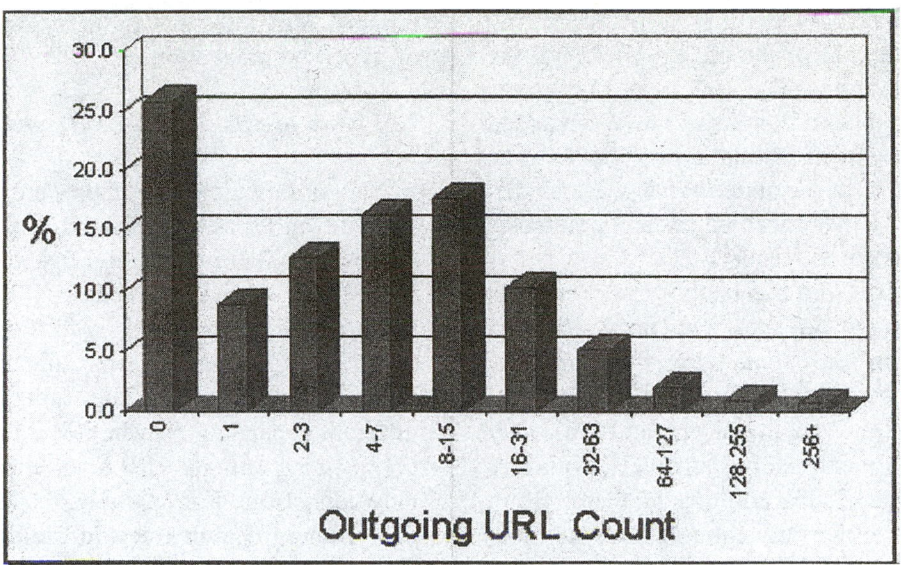

Fig. 4. Distribution of embedded URL counts.

2.5. How richly connected is it?

2.5.1. Outbound connections

As Fig. 4 shows, a large majority (just under 75%) of all pages contain at least one URL. Note that this includes local ("#"-prefixed) URLs; still, it is fair to conclude that pure "leaf" pages are in the minority. It is fairly uncommon (less than 10%) for a page to contain exactly one URL.

2.5.2. Inbound connections and off-site links

At one point in the history of the Open Text Index, we built a search function that would, for any URL, retrieve all pages that contained references to

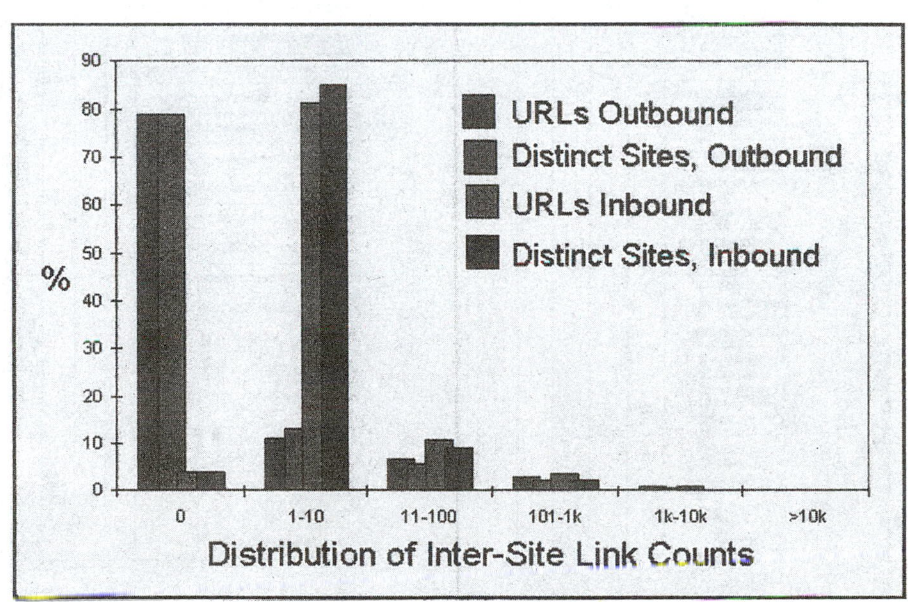

Fig. 5. Inter-site link count distribution.

that URL. This was easy to implement simply by doing a full-text search for the page's URL, but the results were disappointing. The vast majority of pages proved to have no incoming links at all. We realized quickly that the problem is that most WWW links are relative rather than absolute. What we had discovered, in fact, is that most pages are pointed-to only by other pages at the same site.

When we think of Web connectivity, we are more interested in inter-*site* linkages. Our analysis, summarized in Fig. 5, reveals some surprising facts.

First, a large majority of sites (over 80%) are pointed to by "a few" (between one and ten) other sites. Some sites are extremely "visible", with tens of thousands of other sites pointing to them. But a few (just less than 5%), oddly enough, have *no* other sites pointing to them. Presumably, these are sites that have been placed in the Index via the submission process, but are not, in one important sense, truly "connected" to the Web.

Second, web sites in general do a poor job of providing linkage to other web sites. Almost 80% of sites contain *no* off-site URLs. Clearly, a small proportion of web sites are carrying most of the load of hypertext navigation.

2.6. What are the biggest and most visible sites?

The observation that there are sites with thousands (even tens of thousands) of incoming URLs is interesting. These sites, highlighted in Fig. 6, must be deemed unusually "visible". They are, in some sense, at the centre of the Web. Perhaps not surprisingly, **UIUC** [19] leads the list, illustrated in the chart below, of such sites. The ordering is somewhat different depending on whether it is done by number of incoming off-site URLs, or the number of sites they come from. For example, the **European Molecular Biology Laboratory in Heidelberg** [20] and the **Geneva University Hospital** [21] both make the top-

[19] http://www.uiuc.edu

[20] http://www.embl-heidelberg.de/

[21] http://expasy.hcuge.ch/

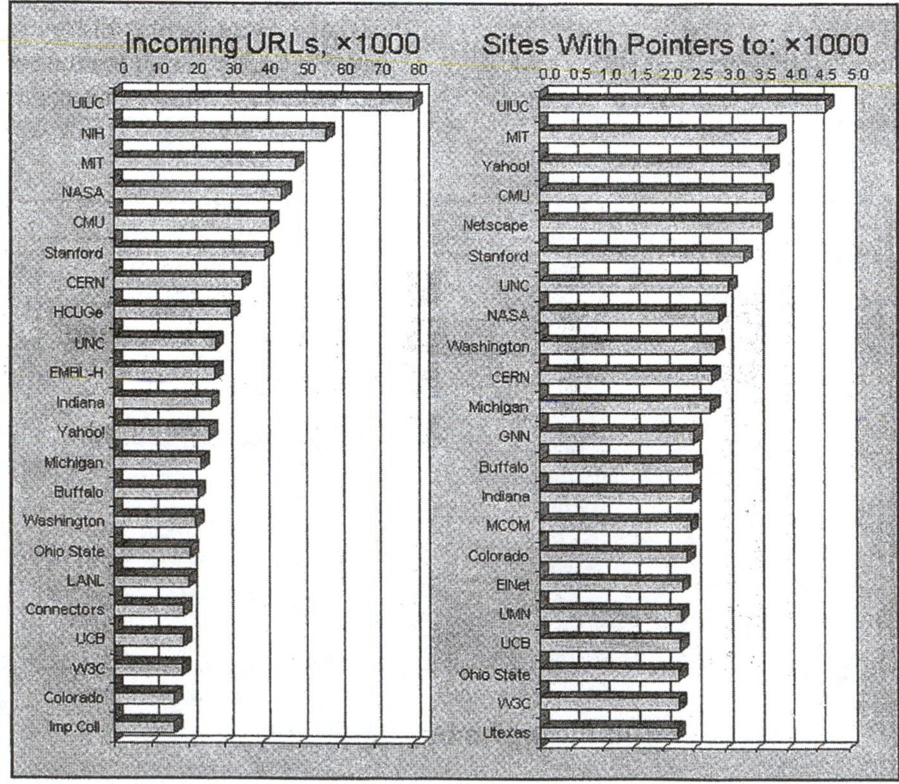

Fig. 6. Most visible sites.

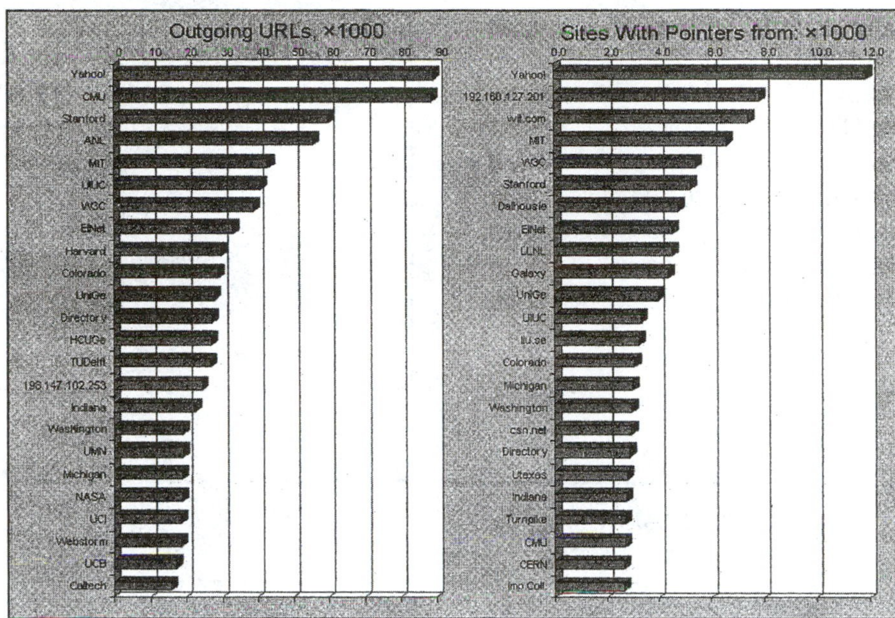

Fig. 7. Most lumous sites.

URL list by virtue of thousands of off-site pointers from sites such as **Argonne National Labs** [22].

With these exceptions, the top sites are a list of well-known universities, organizations (**CERN** [23] and the **World-Wide Web Consortium** [24]), and a few companies. The only commercial sites which make the top-10 list ranked by number of other sites are **Yahoo!** [25], number 3, and **Netscape** [26], number 5.

Reversing this statistic, we next rank Web sites by the number of *outgoing* URLs, and number of other sites they point to. At the top of the list are the relatively few sites who, as noted above, carry most of the Web's navigational workload. This statistic, illustrated in Fig. 7, is somewhat flawed. There are a small number of sites, not listed here, each of which contain more off-site pointers than all of these combined. These would be the Web indexers such as **Open Text** [27], **Lycos** [28], and **Infoseek** [29]. Not surprisingly, the list, whether ranked by URL count or number of sites pointed to, has **Yahoo!** [30] in position 1. There are a few other surprises here; but in general, we think that all the sites on this list deserve respect; they provide the silken strands that hold the Web together.

2.7. What formats are being used?

HTML is said to be the language of the Web. However, its most important underlying protocol, HTTP, can be used to transport anything. Unfortunately, the Open Text Index does not capture the MIME Content-Type that is associated with each page by its server. Thus, we can only use heuristics to approximate the measurements of data formats. The Open Text Index explicitly excludes data formats that are largely non-textual (graphics, PostScript, WP documents). Over the universe of textual pages on the Web, we think the following are fair:

- If it does not contain ⟨**TITLE**⟩ [31], it is not even trying to be HTML.

---

[22] http://www.anl.gov/
[23] http://www.cern.ch
[24] http://www.w3.org
[25] http://www.yahoo.com
[26] http://home.netscape.com
[27] http://www.opentext.com
[28] http://www.lycos.com
[29] http://www.infoseek.com/
[30] http://www.yahoo.com
[31] http://www.w3.org/pub/WWW/MarkUp/html-spec/html-spec_5.html#SEC5.2.1

- If it *does* contain ⟨TITLE⟩, it is making at least some effort to be HTML.
- If it contains ⟨**!DOCTYPE HTML** [32], it is really trying hard to be HTML.

Based on this heuristic, the analysis, summarized in Fig. 8, shows that a large majority of pages (over 87%) are making some effort to present themselves as HTML. A pleasing 5% have gone so far as to include an SGML declaration – of course this is no

[32] http://www.w3.org/pub/WWW/MarkUp/html-spec/html-spec_9.html

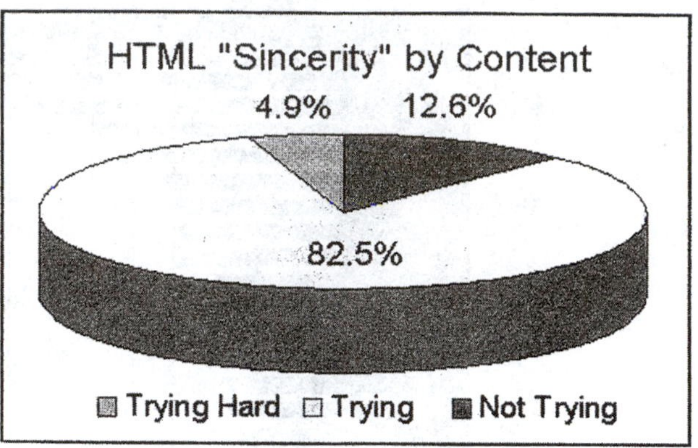

Fig. 8. HTML sincerity.

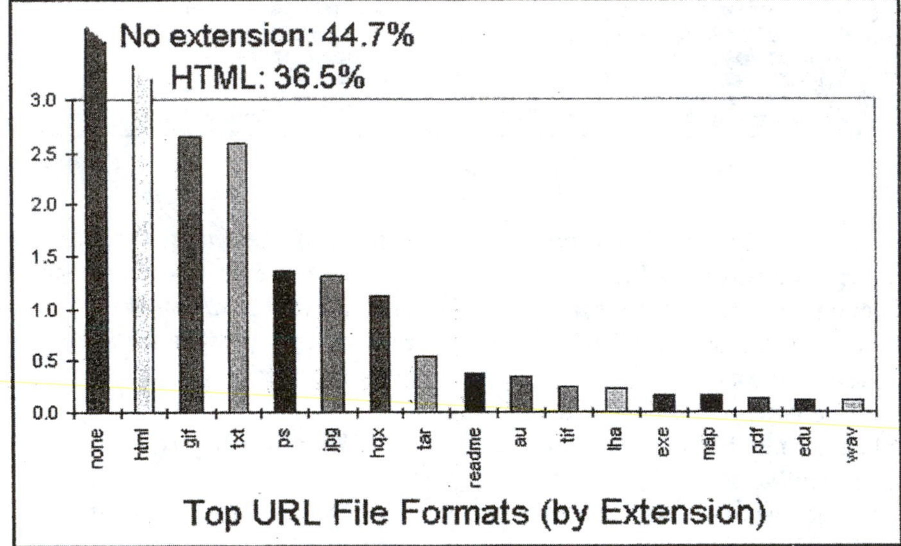

Fig. 9. Popular file formats, by extension.

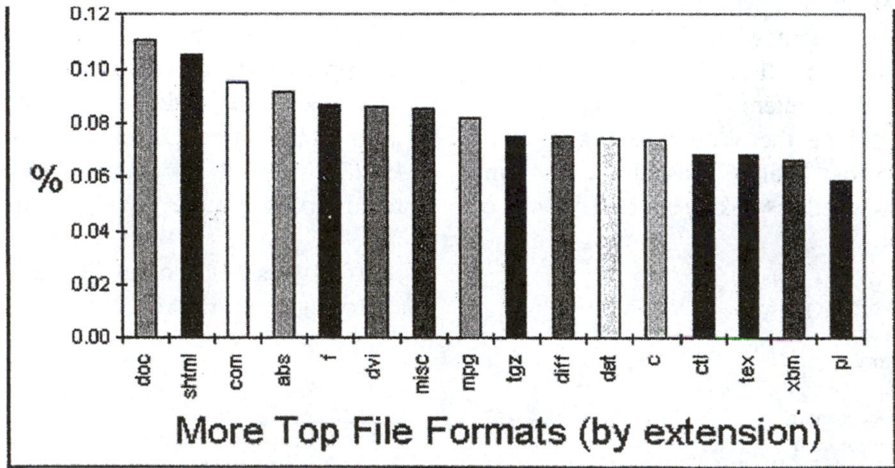

Fig. 10. More popular file formats, by extension.

guarantee that they are actually validated against any particular DTD. About one-eighth of all pages are either raw text or are making no effort whatsoever to be HTML.

There is one other source of information about data types: the file extension. Over 80% of all Web pages are likely HTML because they carry no file extension or are explicitly identified as such by extension. The 18% of files that are explicitly identified by extension as something other than HTML is, amusingly, larger than the proportion of pages that contain no tag.

Figs. 9 and 10 show which other file extensions most often appear in URLs. Not surprisingly, GIF graphics and Text files are the most popular, each at about 2.5%. PostScript, JPEG, and HQX files all hover just over 1%. All other formats are below 1%.

2.8. What does it look like?

The Web, when you are in it, feels like a place. It manifests, however, as a sequence of panels marching across your screen. This leads to an absence of perspective, of context, and finally, of comfort. Most of us who have worked with the Web, in particular those who have read **Gibson**[33] or **Stephenson**[34], want to see where we are. "Visualizing the Web" is **a perennial on the program**[35] of these conferences.

The database behind the Open Text Index, and behind the statistics in this paper, can be used to drive Web visualization. Some of the principles we adopt are:

- The "Site" is the appropriate unit of display.
- The appearance of a site should reflect its *visibility*, as measured by the number of other sites that have pointers to it.
- The appearance of a site should reflect its *size*, as measured by the number of pages it contains
- The appearance of a site should reflect its *luminosity*, as measured by the number of of pointers with which it casts navigational light off-site.
- The appearance of a site should reflect the information encoded in its Internet domain address.
- The appearance of a site should reflect any information about its subject category coverage that may be deduced heuristically from its textual content and from connectivity to other well-categorized sites.
- Sites should be distributed in space in a fashion that reflects the strength of their connectivity.

[33] http://www.unix-ag.uni-kl.de/ ~ kleinhen/gibson

[34] http://pathfinder.com/time/magazine/domestic/1995/special/special.fiction.html

[35] http://www.w3.org/pub/Conferences/Overview-WWW.html

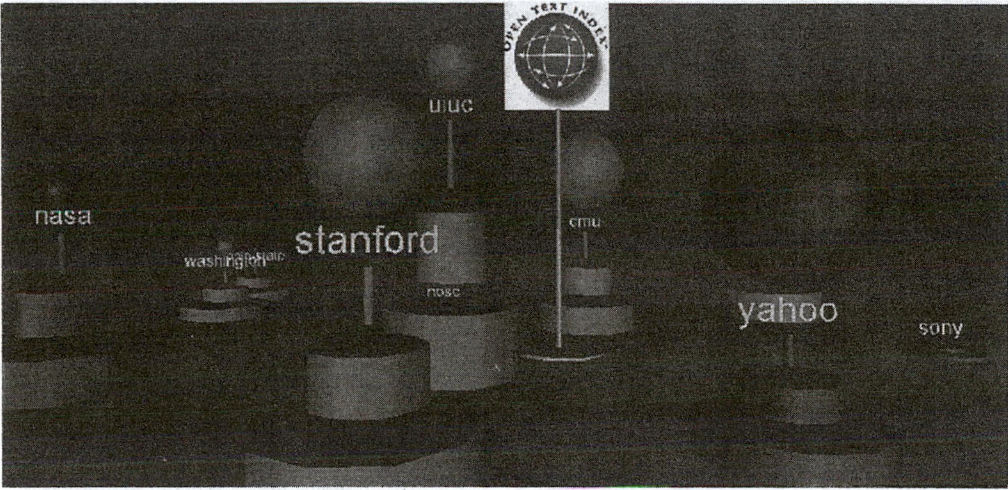

Fig. 11. Some well-known sites.

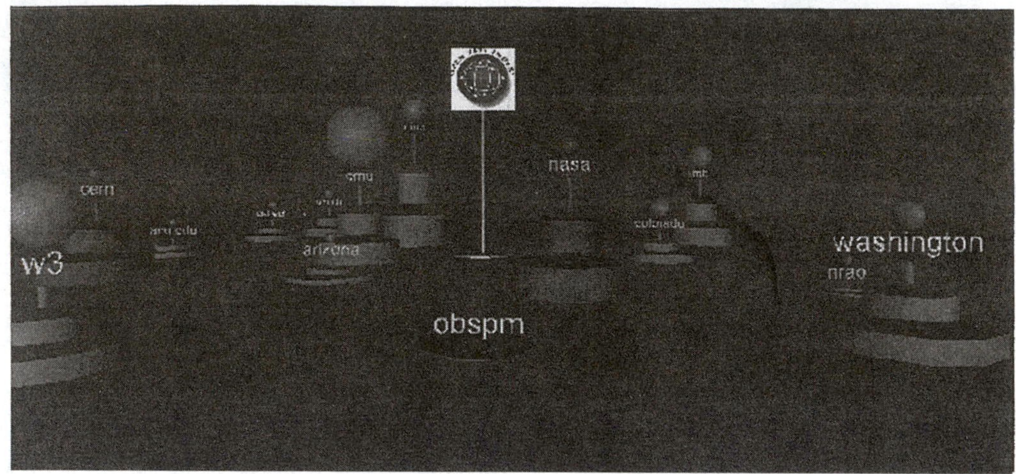

Fig. 12. NASA's neighborhood.

Fig. 13. At the very centre.

Let us examine some database-driven visualizations. The graphics are captured from **VRML** [36] representations generated dynamically from the Open Text Index database, viewed with **Paper Software** [37]'s WebFX plug-in (now appearing as **Netscape** [38]'s **Live3D** [39]). We represent sites as ziggurats crowned with globes: the diameter expresses the number of pages, the height the visibility, the size of a globe floating overhead the luminosity, and the colour the site's domain. We distribute sites in

[36] http://www.vrml.org/

[37] http://www.paperinc.com

[38] http://home.netscape.com

[39] http://home.netscape.com/comprod/products/navigator/live3d/index.html

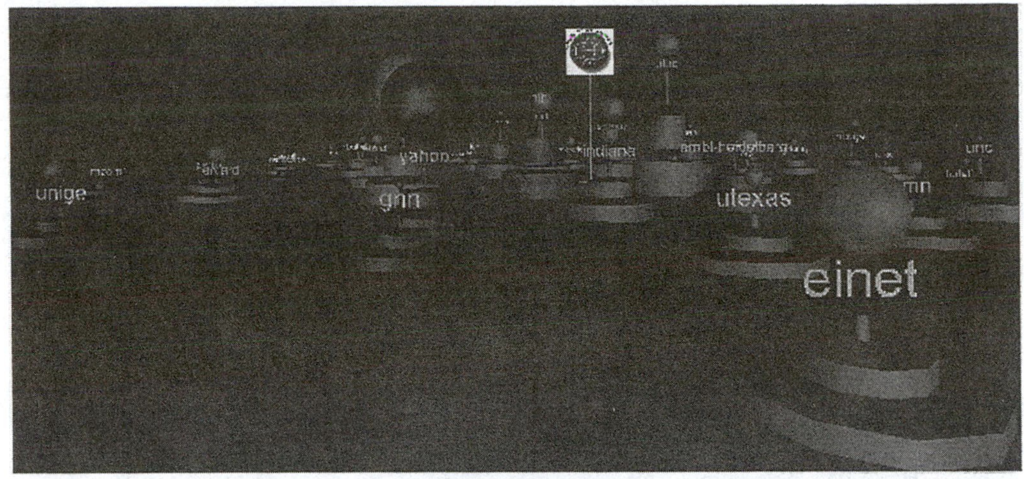

Fig. 14. A wider view.

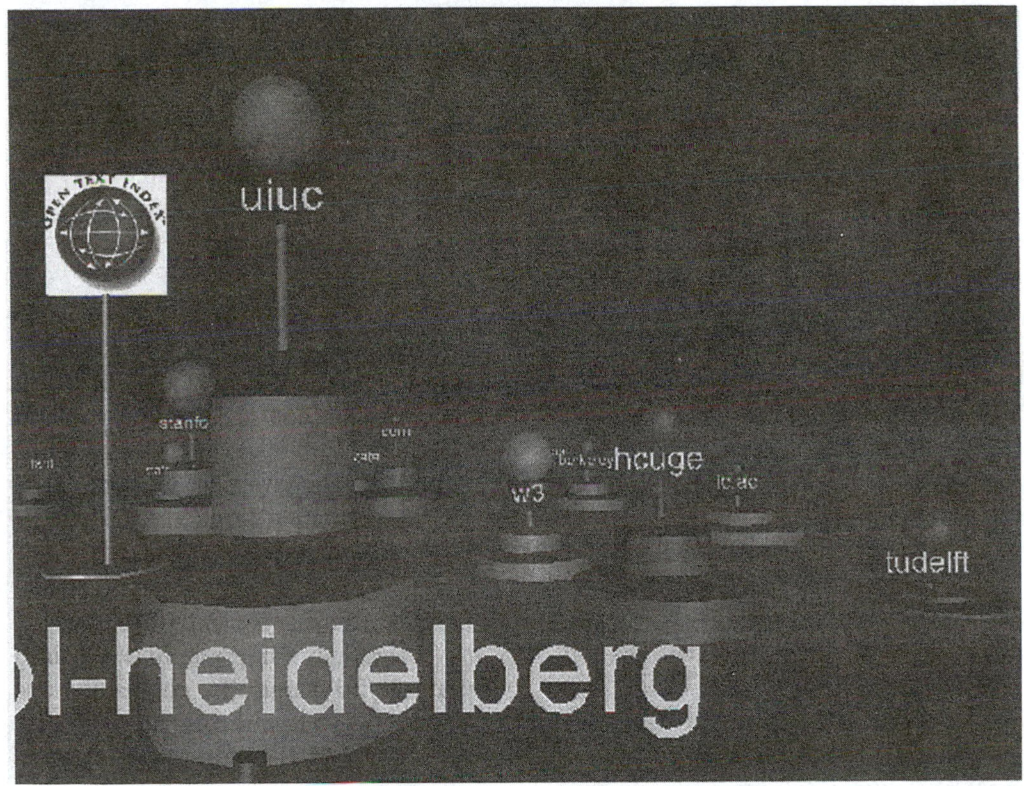

Fig. 15. The Web is world-wide, after all.

space based on the strength of the linkages between them.

Fig. 11 tells us that **UIUC** [40] (including **NCSA** [41], of course) is the Web's most visible site. Neither **Stanford** [42] nor **CMU** [43] is quite as visible, but both

[40] http://www.uiuc.edu

[41] http://www.ncsa.uiuc.edu

[42] http://www.stanford.edu

[43] http://www.cmu.edu

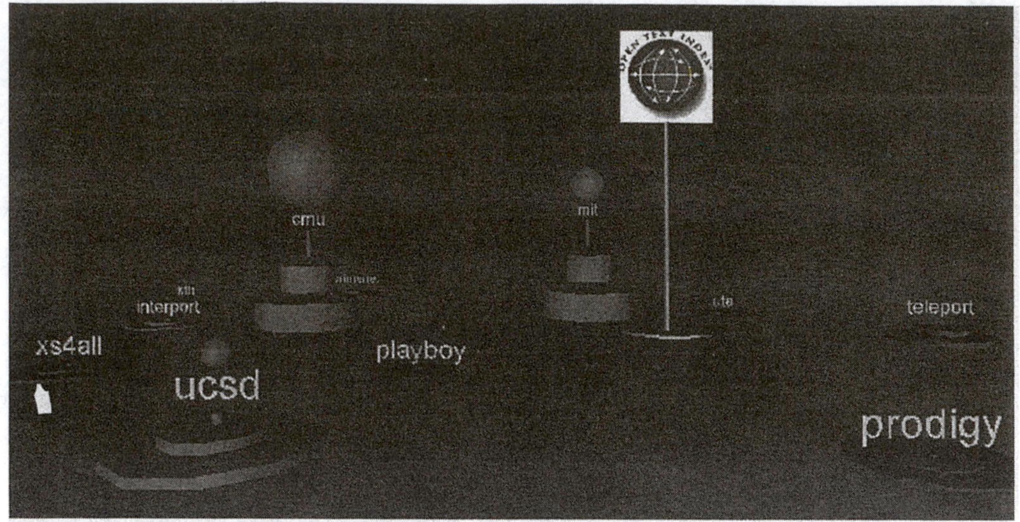

Fig. 16. Friends of Playboy.

cast more light on the Web. **Yahoo!** [44] is most luminous of all.

The sites most closely linked to NASA, shown in Fig. 12, are a mixed bag; Government sites are red, academic sites green and nonprofit organizations golden. CMU's navigational strength is obvious once again, as is the that of the Web Consortium site. NASA itself provides relatively little navigational help.

Fig. 13 shows the four most visible sites on the Web. The tiny red dot above the "i" in "nih" reveals **that very visible site** [45]'s poverty in outgoing links. UIUC's visibility and CMU's luminosity are obvious.

The scene in Fig. 14 starts to give a feeling for the Web's chaos. Commercial sites are rendered in blue, and network infastructure in cyan. The navigational strength of Yahoo! and **Einet** [46] are obvious.

Fig. 15's view, spiralling out from UIUC, has a European slant. Particularly interesting is the fact that the highly-illuminated **European Molecular Biology Laboratory** [47] in Heidelberg casts almost no light; the tiny dot representing its Web-luminosity may be visible in some viewers above and to the left of the "i" in "heidelberg".

The sites that are most closely linked to the **Playboy** [48] site, illustrated in Fig. 16, provide an interesting study in contrast. **CMU** [49], **MIT** [50], and **UCSD** [51] seem to have about the same number of pages. However, CMU leads MIT and then UCSD in both visibility and luminosity.

3. Conclusions

At the moment, we do not know very much about the Web. This statistical lore in this paper may be generated straightforwardly (at the cost of considerable computation) from a properly structured Web Index. We would like to devise a way to automate the generation of these statistics and, in particular, their graphical representations.

Techniques for presenting this information automatically, dynamically, compactly, and three-dimensionally are a significant subgoal of the larger campaign to build a working cyberspace. That in itself is a sufficient motivation for further work on the problem.

[44] http://www.yahoo.com
[45] http://www.nih.gov/
[46] http://www.einet.net/
[47] http://www.embl-heidelberg.de
[48] http://www.playboy.com
[49] http://www.cmu.edu
[50] http://web.mit.edu/
[51] http://www.ucsd.edu

Acknowledgements

None of this would have been possible without the data gathered via the superhuman efforts of the **Web Index team** [52]. Thanks are also due to **Tamara Munzner** [53] for provoking thought, and to **Lilly Buchwitz** [54] for polishing language. Thanks also to James Hess and the **Heritage Map Museum** [55] for the use of the "Typis Orbis Terrarum" map.

---

[52] http://search.opentext.com/team1.gif
[53] http://www-graphics.stanford.edu/~munzner/
[54] mailto:lillyb@opentext.com
[55] http://www.carto.com/

FIGURE 1

1601 Mercator-Hondius

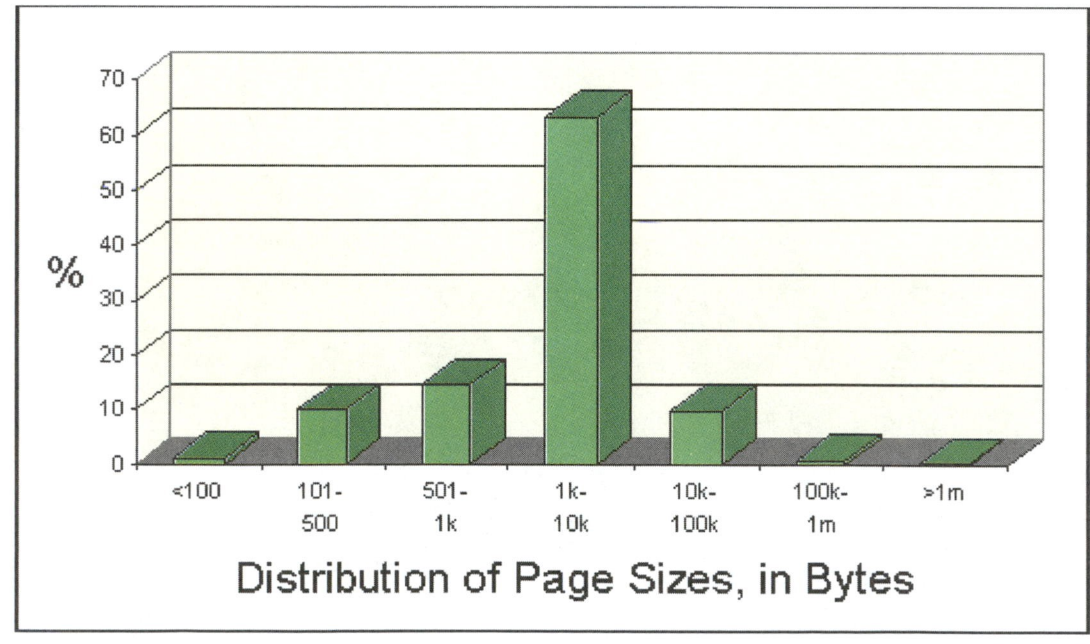

FIGURE 2

Page Size Distribution

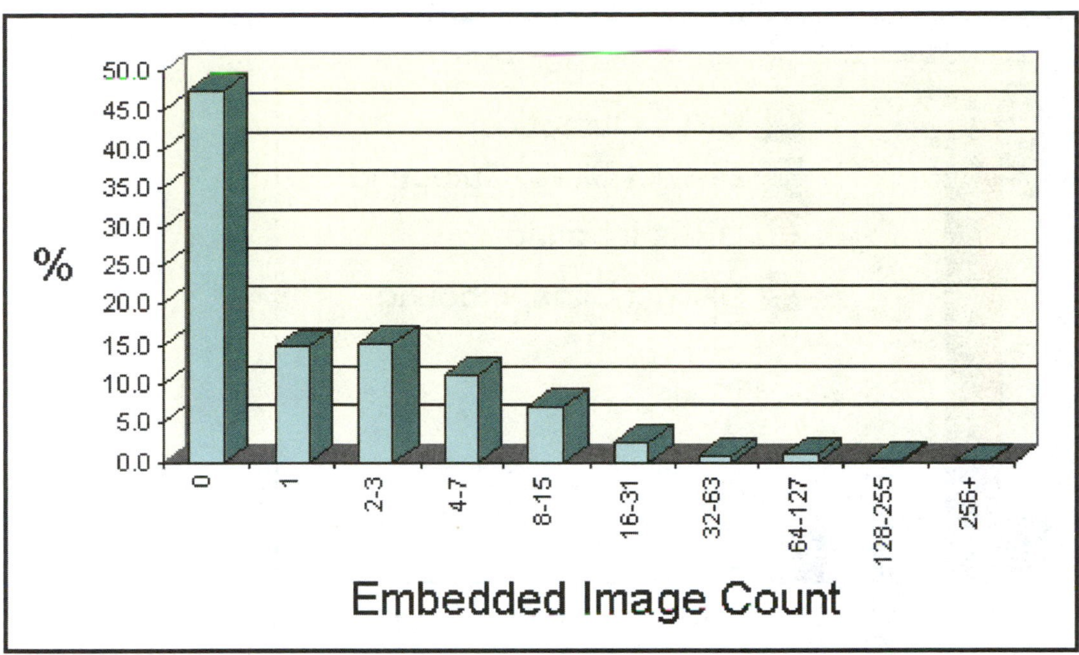

FIGURE 3

Distribution of Embedded Image Counts

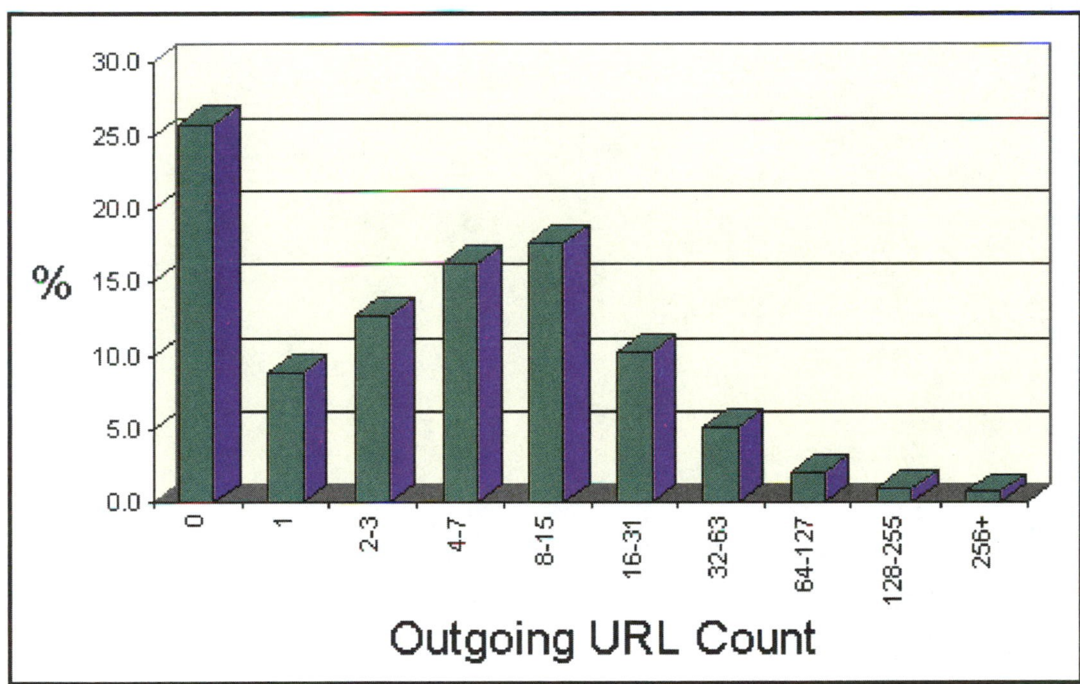

FIGURE 4

Distribution of Embedded URL Counts

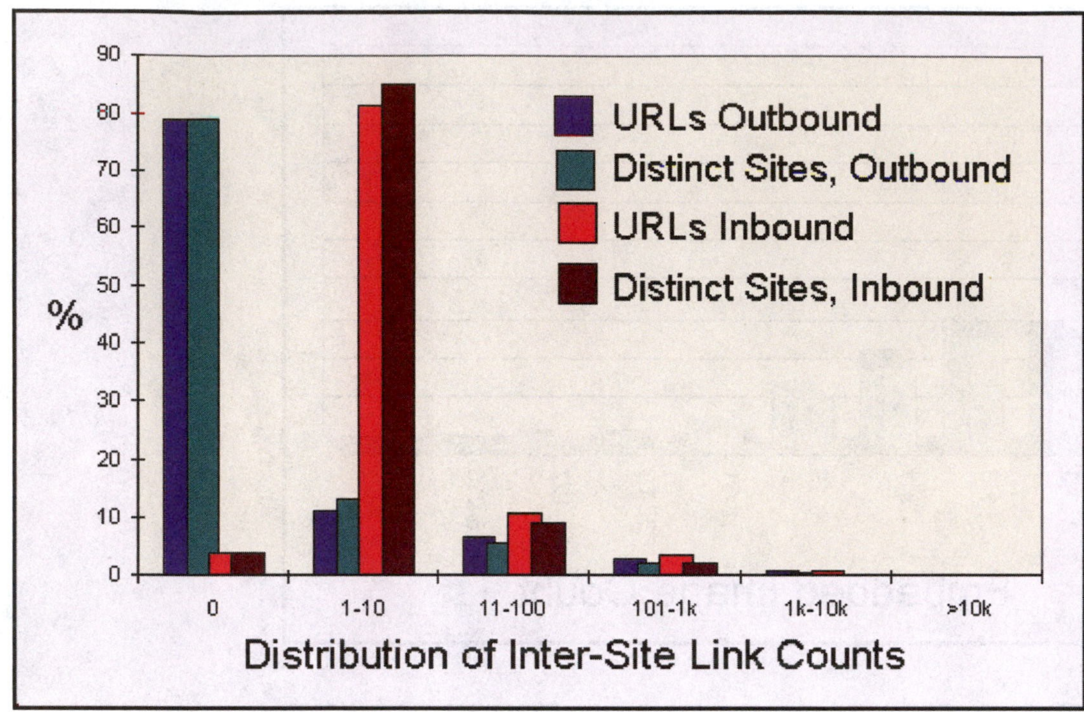

FIGURE **5**

Inter-Site Link Count Distribution

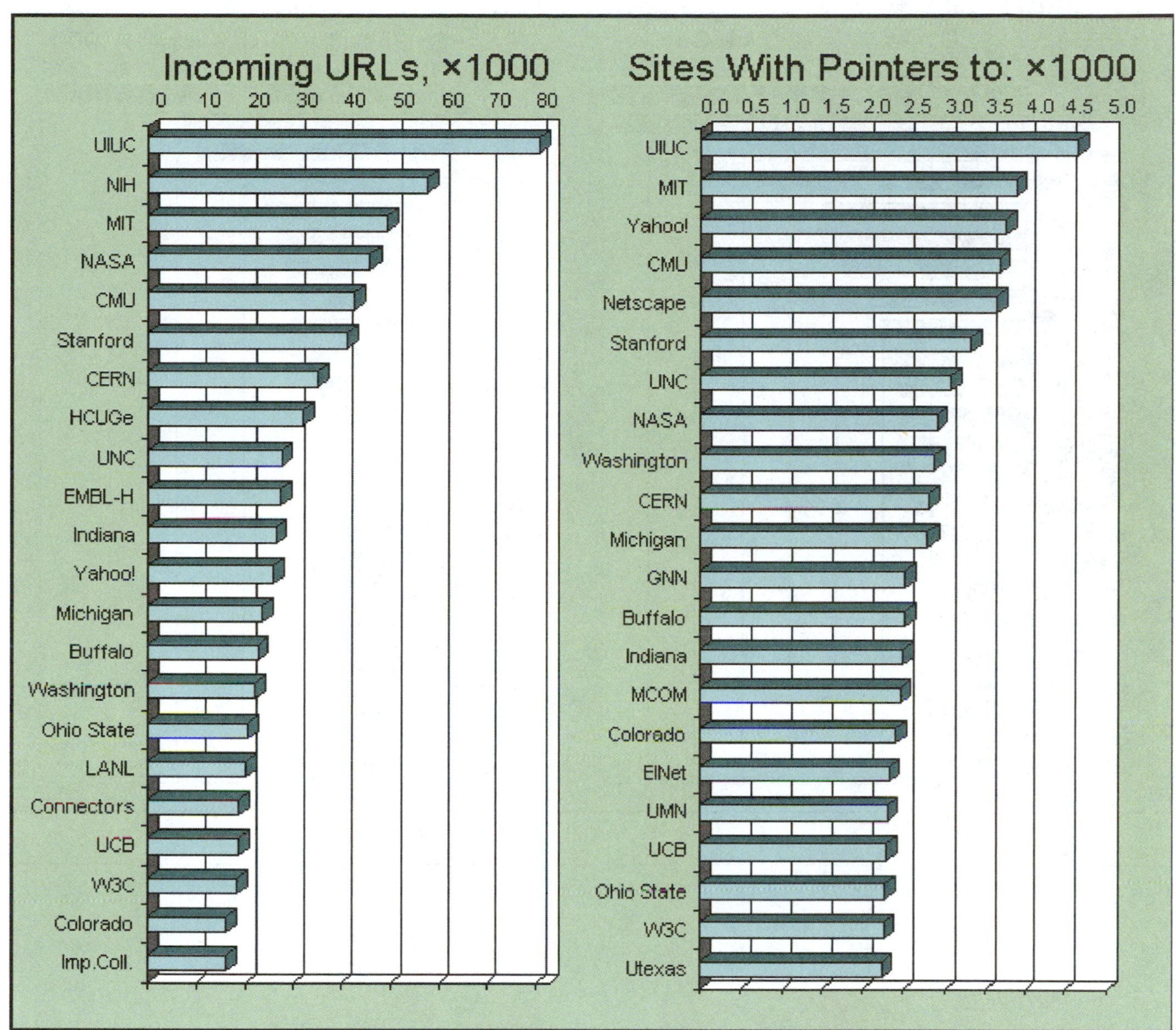

FIGURE 6

Most Visible Sites

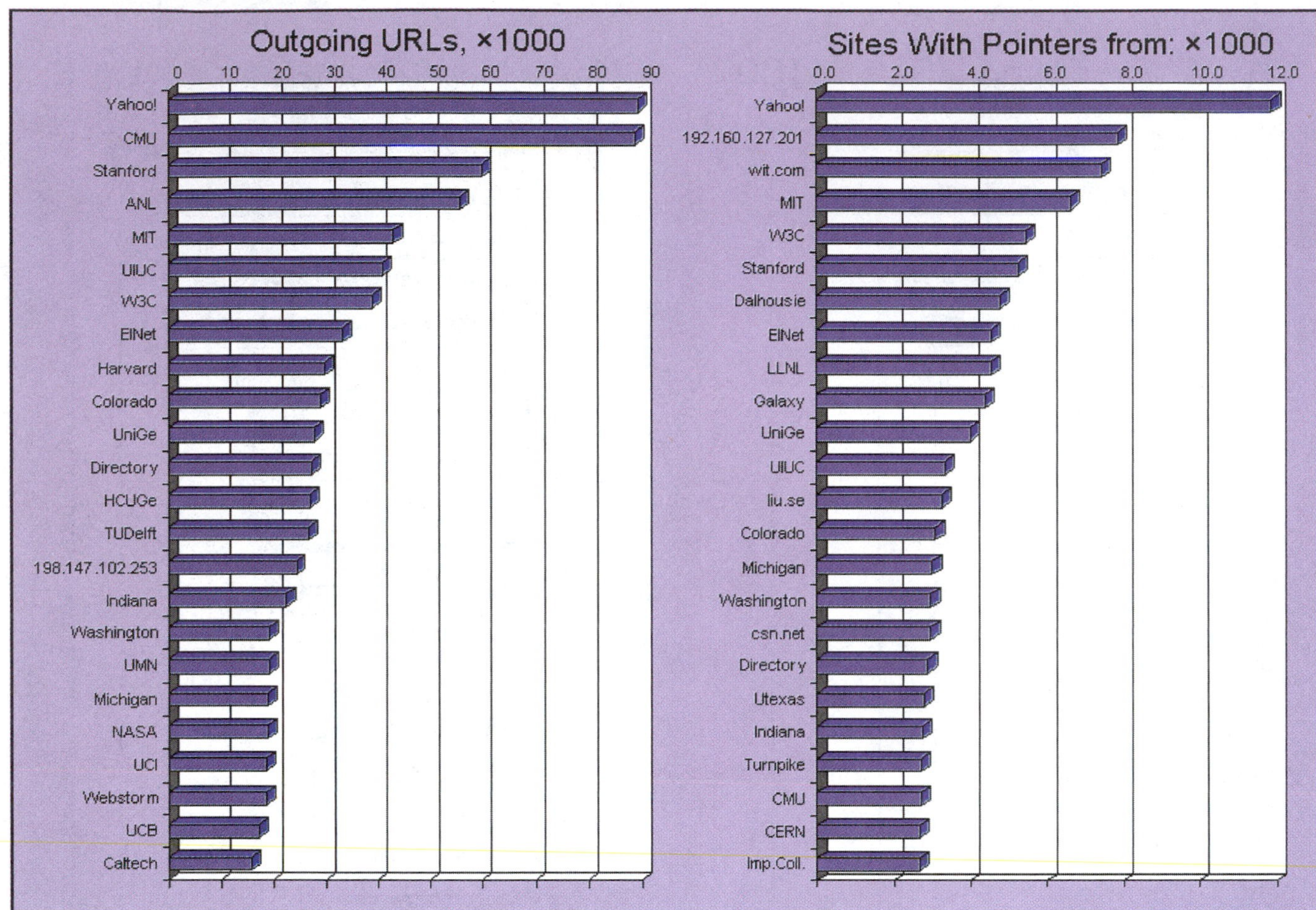

FIGURE **7**

Most Lumous Sites

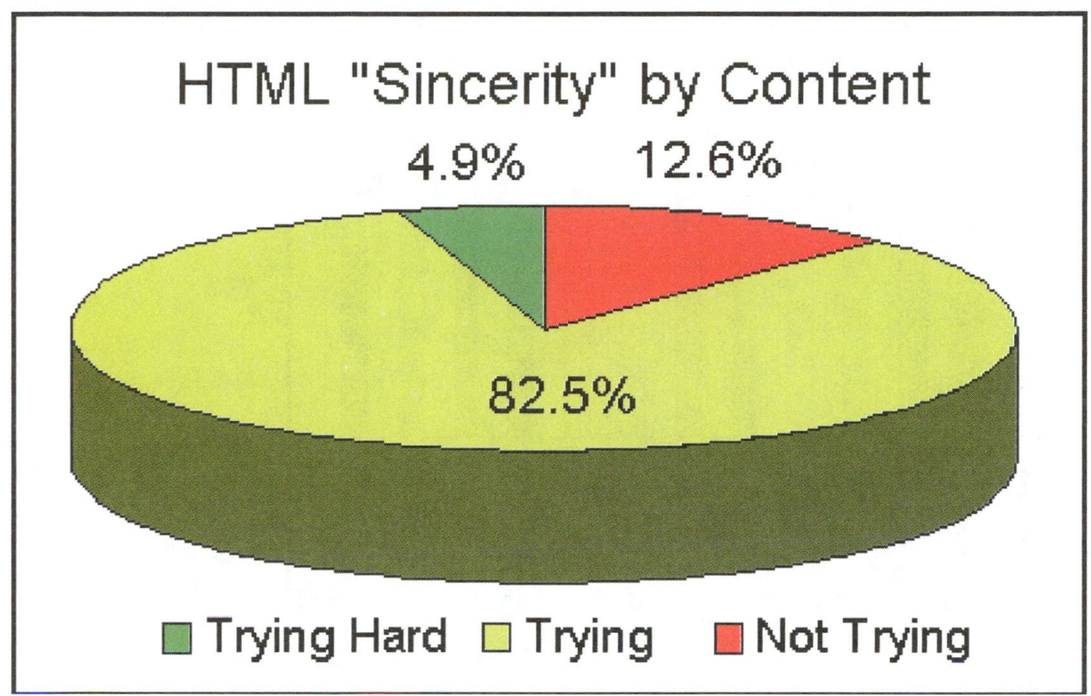

FIGURE 8

HTML Sincerity

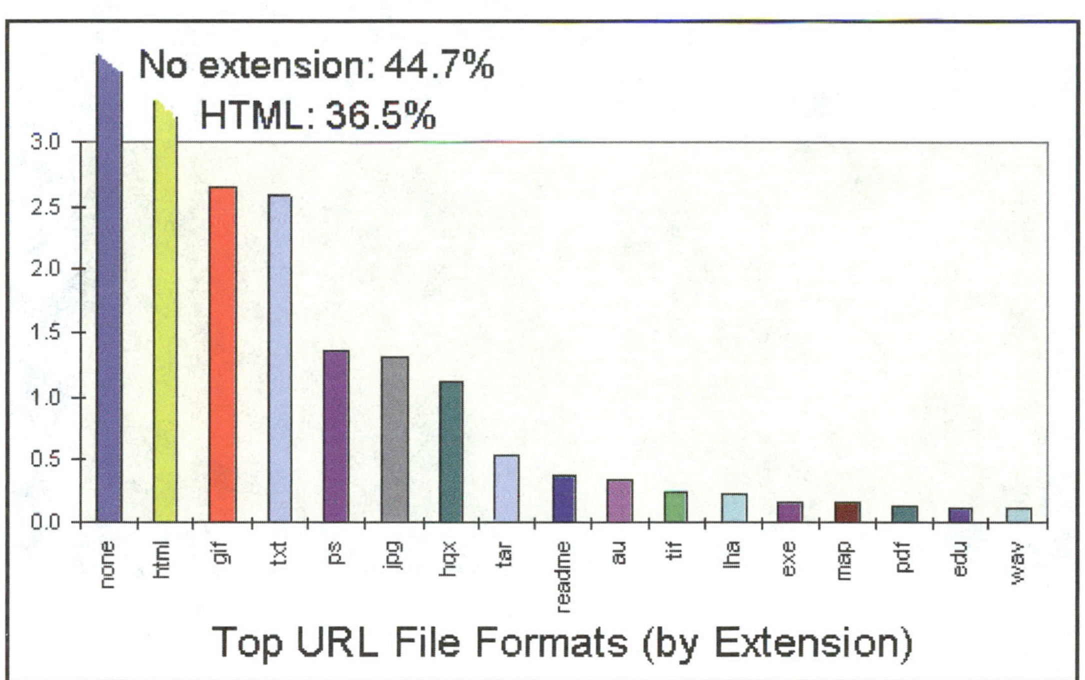

FIGURE 9

Popular File Formats, by Extension

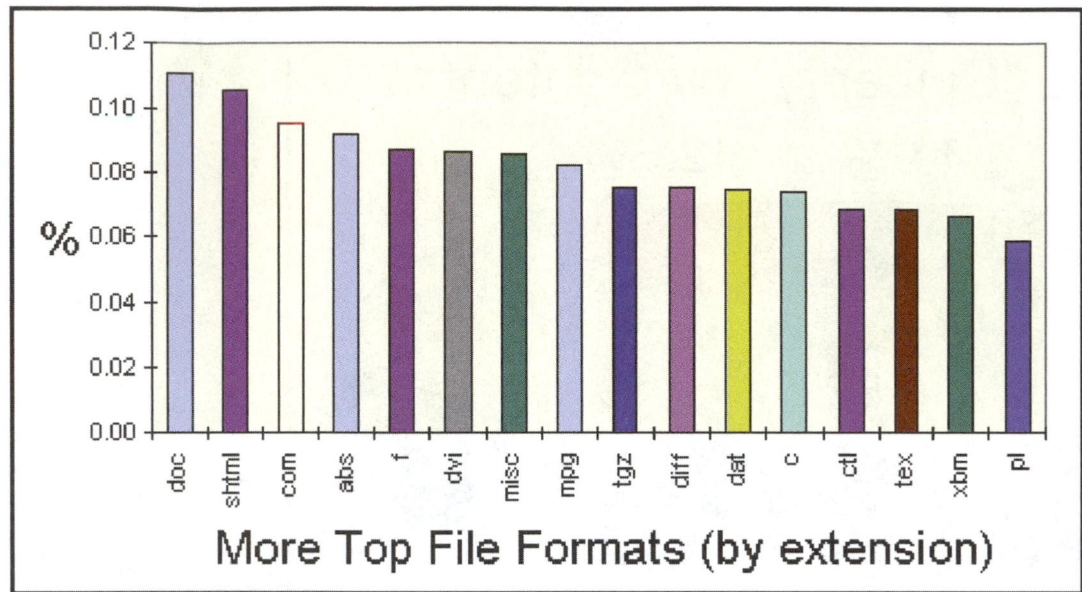

FIGURE **10**

More Popular File Formats, by Extension

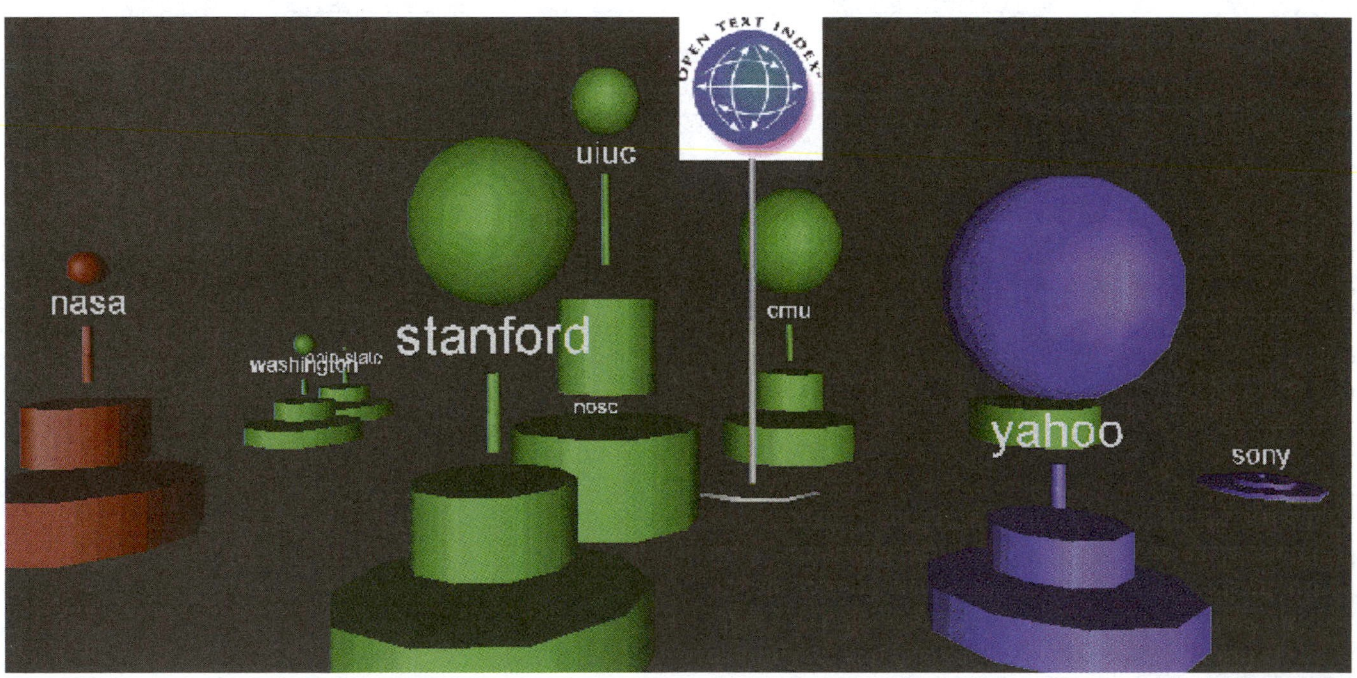

FIGURE **11**

Some Well-Known Sites

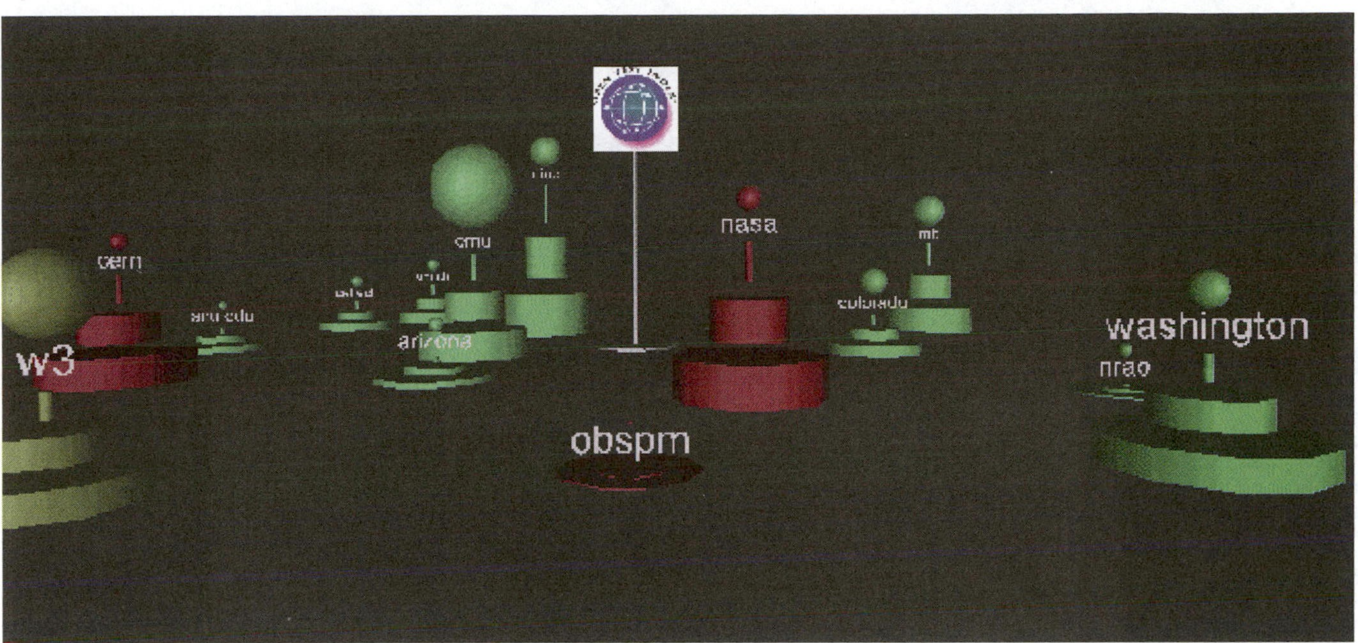

FIGURE **12**

NASA's Neighborhood

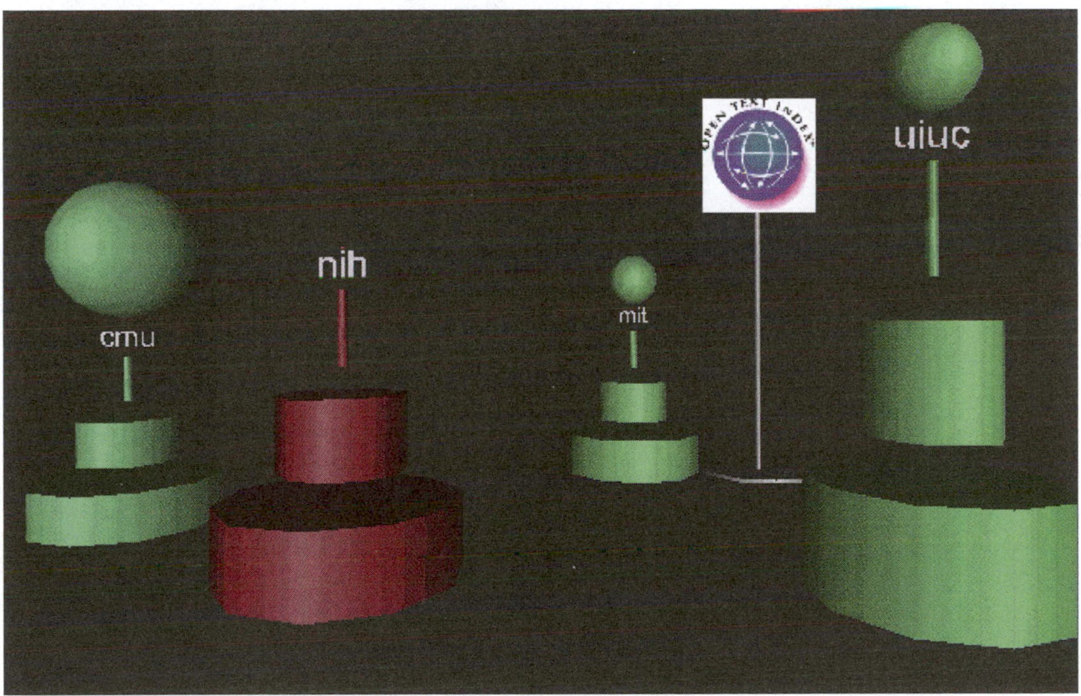

FIGURE **13**

At the Very Centre

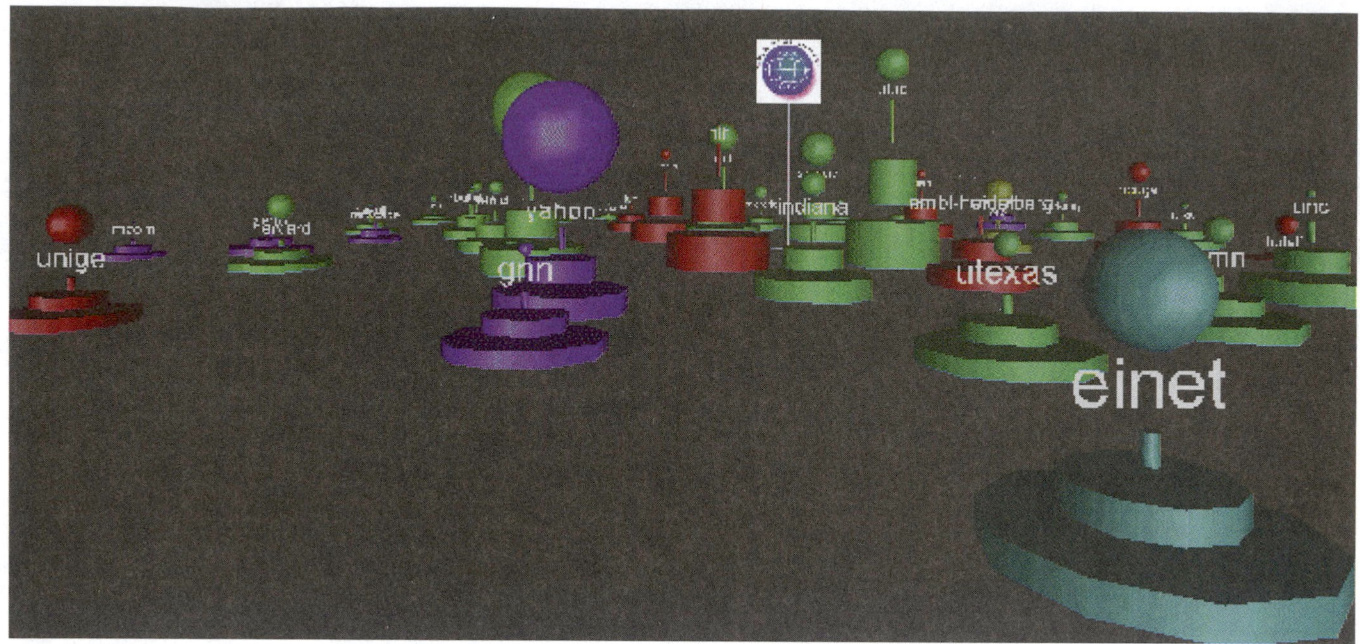

FIGURE **14**

A Wider View

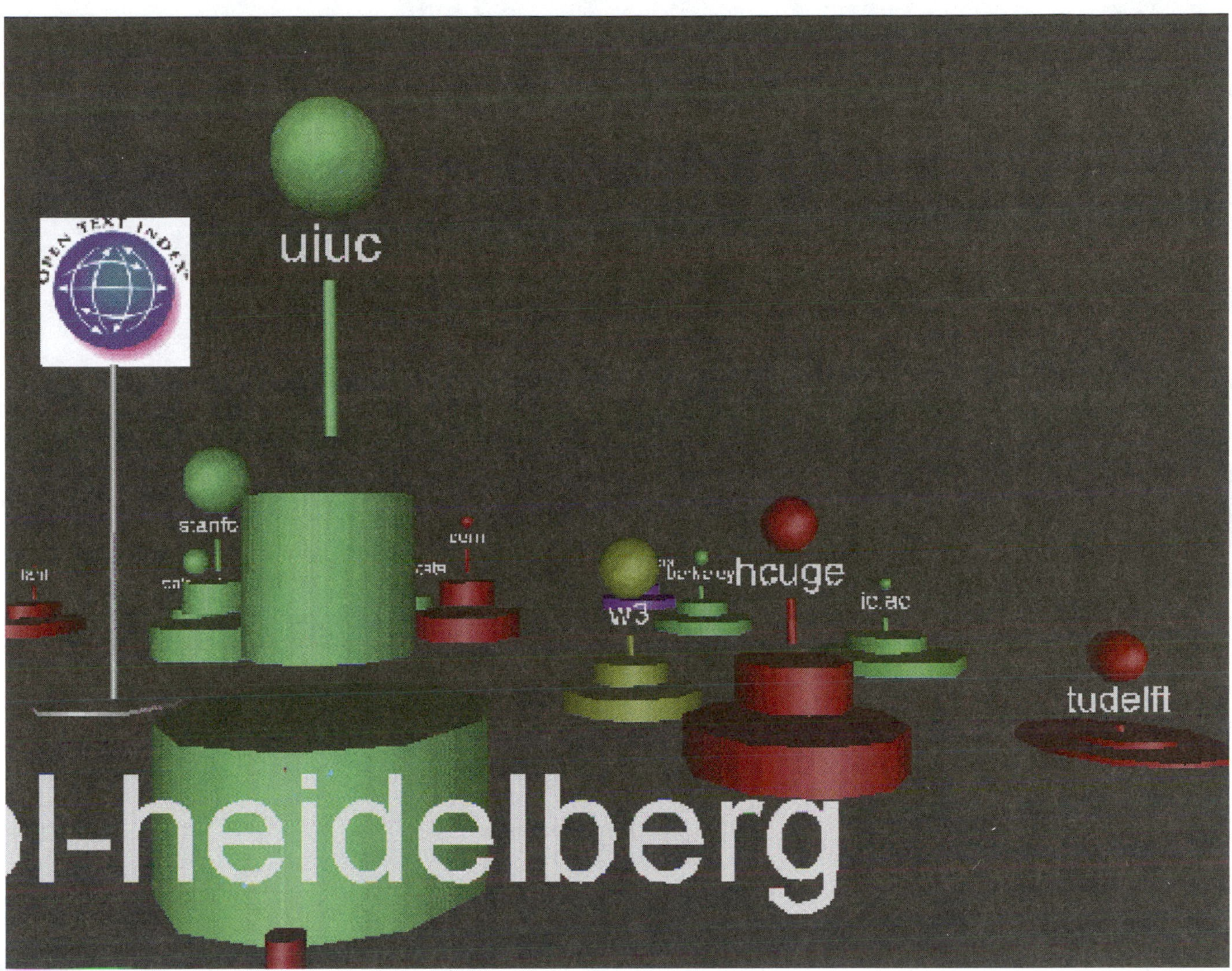

FIGURE **15**

The Web is World-Wide, After All

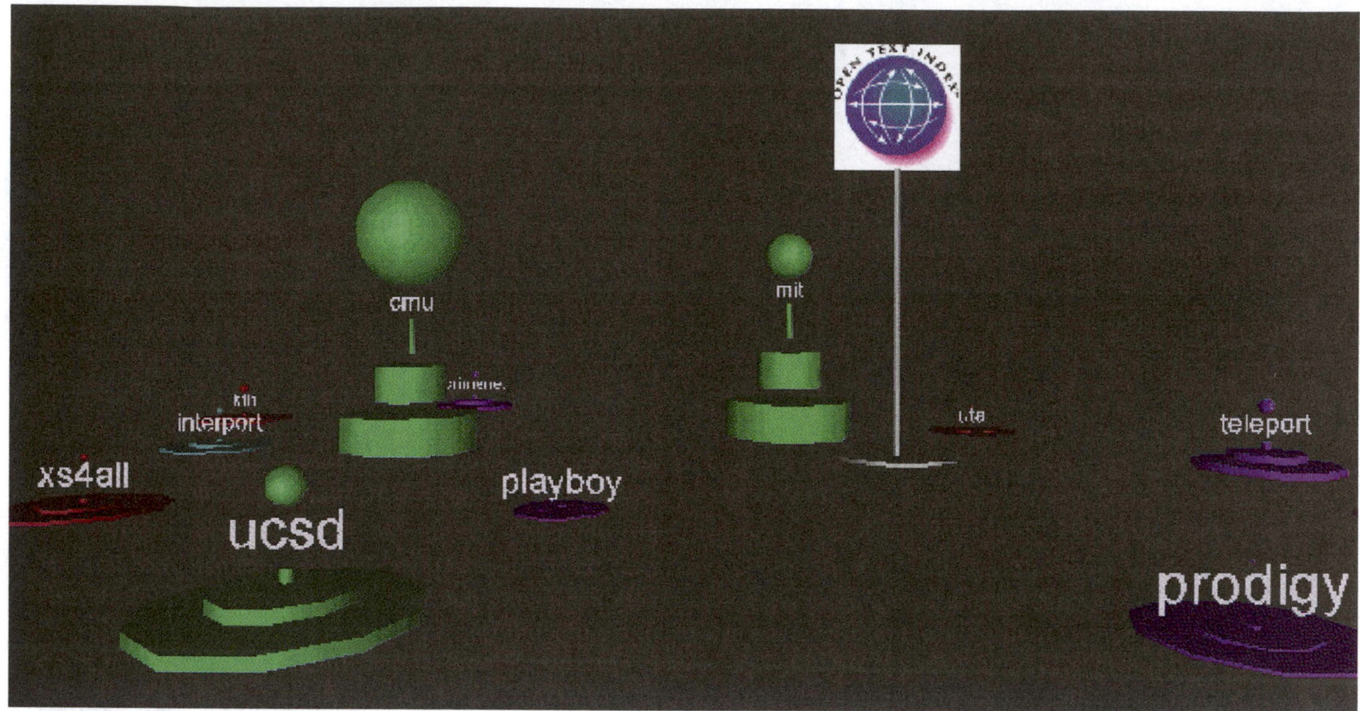

FIGURE **16**

Friends of Playboy

Case Study

Visualising Cyberspace: Information Visualisation in the Harmony Internet Browser

Keith Andrews

Institute for Information Processing and Computer Supported New Media (IICM)
Graz University of Technology,
A-8010 Graz, Austria.

kandrews@iicm.tu-graz.ac.at

Abstract

The explosive growth of information systems on the Internet has clearly demonstrated the need to organise, filter, and present information in ways which allow users to cope with the sheer quantities of information available.

The scope for visualisation of Gopher and WWW spaces is restricted by the limitations of their respective data models. The far richer data model supported by the Hyper-G Internet information system is exploited by its Harmony client to provide a number of tightly-coupled, two- and three-dimensional visualisation and navigational facilities, which help provide location feedback and alleviate user disorientation.

1 Introduction

There has been strong recent interest in the application of visualisation techniques to network information systems. The explosive growth of information systems on the Internet has clearly demonstrated the need to organise, filter, and present information in a way which allows users to cope with the sheer quantities of information available. More traditional (and arguably more functional) two-dimensional visualisations have been pushed into the sidelines as glamorous three-dimensional visualisations take the limelight. This paper presents the tightly-coupled, two and three-dimensional visualisations implemented in the Harmony client for the Hyper-G Internet information management system.

First let me distinguish between ***hand-crafted*** and ***automatically generated*** presentation of information. Hand-crafted presentation entails careful, prior construction of an information layout by a designer using appropriate tools. Such visualisations are generally designed for very specific applications and are often quite intricate in nature. Automatically generated visualisations are composed on-the-fly by the underlying system according to a set of pre-supplied layout rules and components. A neutral file format like the emerging Virtual Reality Modeling Language (VRML) [1] for 3D models, allows the distinction to be blurred somewhat at least as far as final presentation is concerned, since both hand-crafted and automatically generated VRML files can be displayed by one and the same viewer.

One issue affecting automatically generated visualisations is that of dynamic restructuring, for example to take into account changes in the database or in response to user queries or filters. In some cases this may be desirable, but in many cases an inherent advantage of spatial visualisations, that users can incrementally build a mental map of places and locations and navigate by visual memory, will be lost when the information space continually changes its form. At the very least, such changes should be made via smooth transitions as far as possible so as to take advantage human visual perception and object constancy [2].

Other issues include the choice of visual representations and navigational metaphors. What kind of visual representations are best? Two or three-dimensional icons of books for text documents, framed pictures for images, radios emitting audio clips, TV sets for video, etc. Should planar or truly 3D structure maps be used, indoor or outdoor scenes? In 3D visualisations, typical navigational metaphors include walking, flying, driving, teleportation, and magic carpets. However, why not bring the information to the user, rather than having the user navigate to the information? Indeed, the use of user-configurable home spaces, where users can place and organise frequently accessed information (or handles to it) might reduce the need for navigation in the first place. Whilst ideas abound and numerous techniques have been implemented, there has upto now been surprisingly little usability testing of information visualisation techniques.

2 Related Work

Two-dimensional visualisations of information structures are well covered in the literature. A good overview of 2D link maps in hypermedia systems can be found in [3], fisheye viewing techniques for graphs are detailed in [4]. Space-filling visualisations of hierarchically structured information using tree maps are described in [5], feature maps of arbitrary document spaces are described in [6], and hyperbolic visualisations of large trees in [7], to mention just a few techniques.

Perhaps the most well-known work in the area of three-dimensional information visualisation is that of Card et al [2, 8] at Xerox PARC on the Information Visualiser and 3D/Rooms. They allow users to interactively explore workspaces modeled as three-dimensional rooms. Particular data sets (nodes) are visualised in rooms of their own, and doors lead from one room to another in a manner similar to hypermedia links. The Information Visualizer provides three-dimensional representations for linear and hierarchically structured information: the perspective wall [9] and cone tree [10] respectively. Linear information, such as chronologically ordered information, is pasted on to a virtual wall from left to right. The wall has a large front section, and left and right sides which tail off into the background. Information can be slid along the wall to bring it into focus on the front section. The information can also be stretched or shrunk along the wall. Hierarchical information, such as part of a file system or a company hierarchy chart, is laid out as a uniform 3D cone. The tree can be rotated to bring interesting parts to the front and pruned to remove non-relevant information.

VizNet [11] also uses a cone tree representation for hierarchical information, but provides an additional spherical representation for associative relationships (local map). The current node is located (say) at the north pole, nodes similar to it are strung along lines of longitude. Lower level objects are displayed on lower level spheres (like peeling away layers of an onion).

SemNet [12] was an exploratory system which represented knowledge bases as directed graphs in 3D. Labeled rectangles (nodes) were connected by lines or arcs. The 3D layout has the advantage over 2D layouts that the nodes of an arbitrary graph can be positioned so that no arcs intersect. Several techniques for positioning nodes were explored: random, multidimensional scaling, heuristics, and manual editing. Clustering techniques and fisheye views were also implemented.

Serra et al [13] discuss the use of 3D object hierarchies with attached multimedia documents. Each component in the 3D object hierarchy (part-of relationships) may be combined into a *concept node* with text, image, and video documents. Links may be made from these text, image, and video documents to other concept nodes. However, there is no support for arbitrary links from (parts of) the 3D object as such, and the 3D object hierarchy itself forms the entire extent of the hyperstructure.

Smith and Wilson [14] describe a prototype system based on HyperCard and Virtus Walkthrough (a 3D visualisation system), in the context of an academic departmental information system. They enabled users to interactively explore a 3D model of the department: when they approached within a certain distance of a source anchor, it automatically triggered to display a corresponding text document.

The File System Navigator (FSN, or "Fusion") written by Joel Tesler and Steve Strasnick at Silicon Graphics [15] visualises a Unix file system as an information landscape. Directories are represented by blocks laid out on a plane, their height representing the cumulative size of the contained files. Smaller blocks atop the directory blocks represent files in the directory (their size also mapped to their height). Users can "fly" over the landscape, taking it in as a whole, or swoop down to a specific directory. Clicking on the arc to a subdirectory results in an invisible hand grabbing you and leading you through space to that subdirectory. Clicking on a file block brings a virtual spotlight to bear on that block, double-clicking opens the file for editing, etc.

The above systems are for the most part proof-of-concept prototypes for individual visualisation techniques. In Graz, we have integrated several tightly-coupled information visualisation techniques (including a two-dimensional graphical structure map generator, a three-dimensional document browser and a three-dimensional information landscape) into a real, day-to-day information tool running over the Internet: the Harmony client for the Hyper-G hypermedia information system [16, 17].

Visualisation techniques are being applied to other Internet information systems such as Gopher [18] and the World-Wide Web (WWW) [19]. GopherVR [20] is an experimental 3D spatial interface to the hierarchically structured information on a Gopher server. Visualisations of WWW spaces such as Webspace [21], the Navigational View Builder [22], and HyperSpace [23] have begun to appear. However, the scope for visualisation of Gopher and WWW spaces is severely restricted by the limitations of their respective data models: Gopher has only hierarchical structures and WWW has only forward hyperlinks. Hyper-G, on the other hand, has a much richer data model on which to base visualisations: a combination of hierarchical structure, (bidirectional) hyperlinks, and fully integrated search and retrieval facilities. The rest of this paper looks at the information visualisation facilities as currently implemented in the Harmony client for Hyper-G.

3 The Hyper-G Data Model

Information in Hyper-G may be structured both hierarchically into so-called *collections*, and by means of associative hyperlinks. A special kind of collection called a *cluster* groups logically related or multilingual versions of documents. Every document and collection must belong to at least one collection, but may belong to several. Navigation may be performed down through the collection hierarchy (the collection "hierarchy" is, strictly speaking, a directed acyclic graph), access rights assigned on a collection-by-collection basis, and the scope of searches restricted to particular sets of collections. Collections may span multiple Hyper-G servers, providing a unified view of distributed resources.

Links in Hyper-G are stored in a separate link database and are bidirectional (directed, but may be followed backwards): both the incoming *and* outgoing hyperlinks of a document are always known and available for visualisation. Furthermore, Hyper-G has fully integrated search facilities including full text search with relevance scores and some limited support for similarity measures between documents.

All in all, the richness of the Hyper-G data model provides plenty of scope upon which to base visualisations: hierarchical structure, (bidirectional) hyperlinks, and search and retrieval facilities. The Harmony client for Hyper-G exploits this richness to provide tightly-coupled two- and three-dimensional visualisation and navigational facilities help provide location feedback and alleviate user disorientation.

4 Dynamic 2D Structure Maps

The Harmony Session Manager (see Figure 1, top left) provides navigation through the collection structure, search facilities, and various general functions such as user identification and language selection. Collections may be opened and closed and clusters or individual documents activated within the graphical collection display by double-clicking. Central to the design of Harmony is the concept of *location feedback*. When a document or collection is visited, its location within the collection structure is automatically displayed in the Session Manager's collection browser (by opening up the path to it), regardless of whether the object was reached as the result of a search, by following a hyperlink, or via the local map. This simple technique is a powerful instrument in the fight against becoming "lost in hyperspace" – users can orient themselves with reference to a fixed structural framework. In the case of search results and the local map, mere selection of an object initiates location feedback, providing users with a sense of the context of an object, prior to any decision to view it (see Figure 1).

The Harmony Local Map facility provides a kind of short-range radar, generating on request (dynamically) a map of the hyperlink neighbourhood of a chosen document, similar to the local map of Intermedia [3]. However, Harmony's local map can also show other relationships, such as collection membership, annotations, inline images, and the textures applied to a 3D model, as can be seen in Figure 2. The number and type of incoming and outgoing relationships can be interactively configured in the Options panel. Single-clicking selects an object and activates location feedback, displaying the object's location in the collection structure. Users can navigate within the local map by generating a new map around any selected object; objects are accessed by double-clicking. One practical use of the Local Map is to check whether a particular inline image is used in multiple text documents before changing or deleting the image.

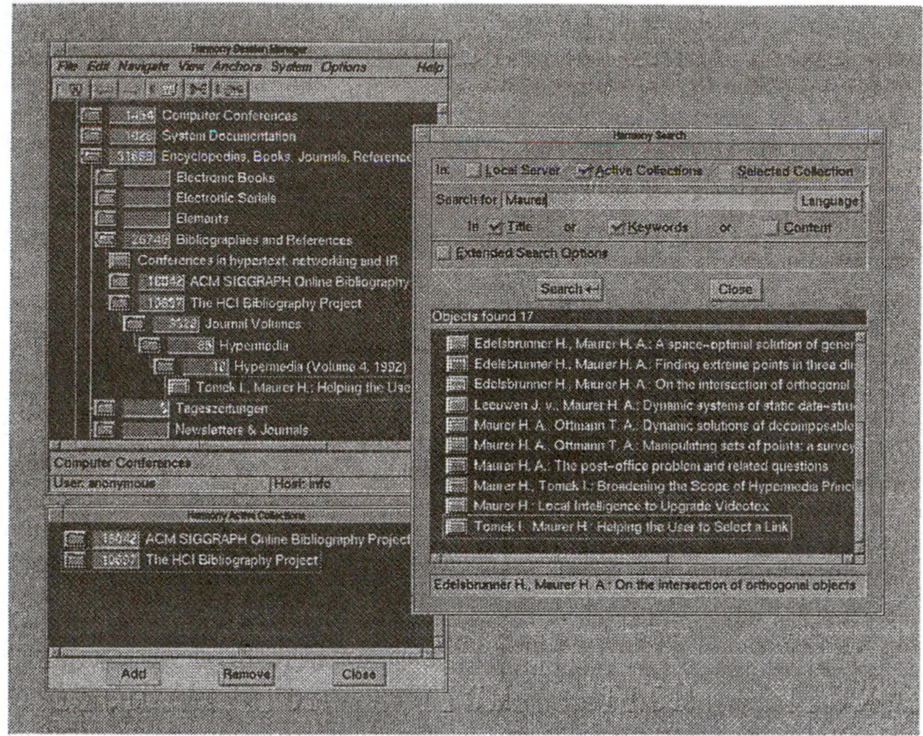

Figure 1: Location Feedback in Harmony

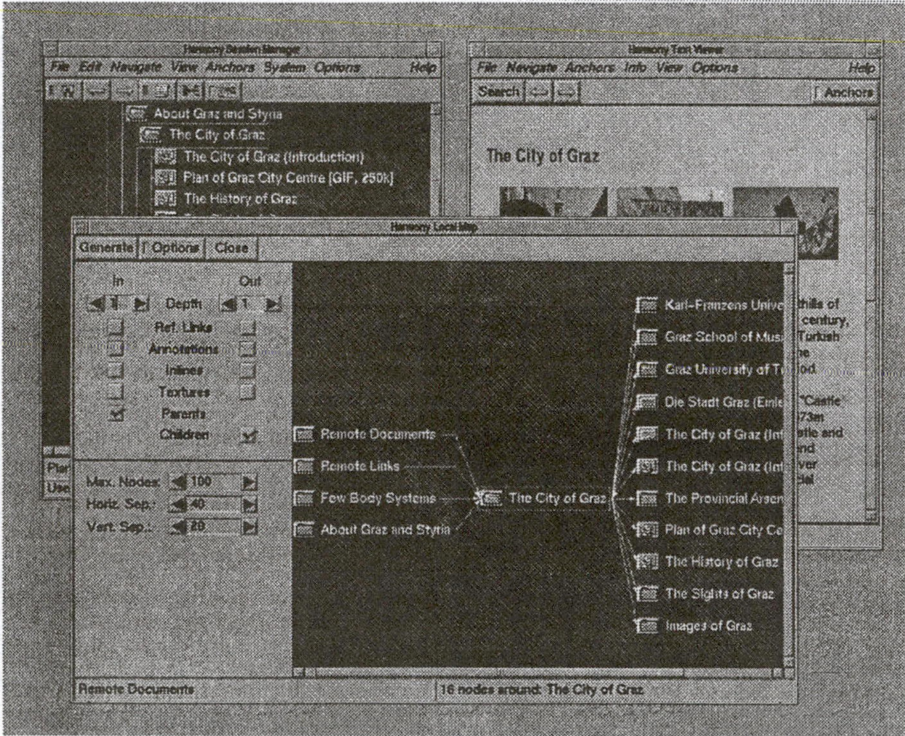

Figure 2: The Harmony Local Map

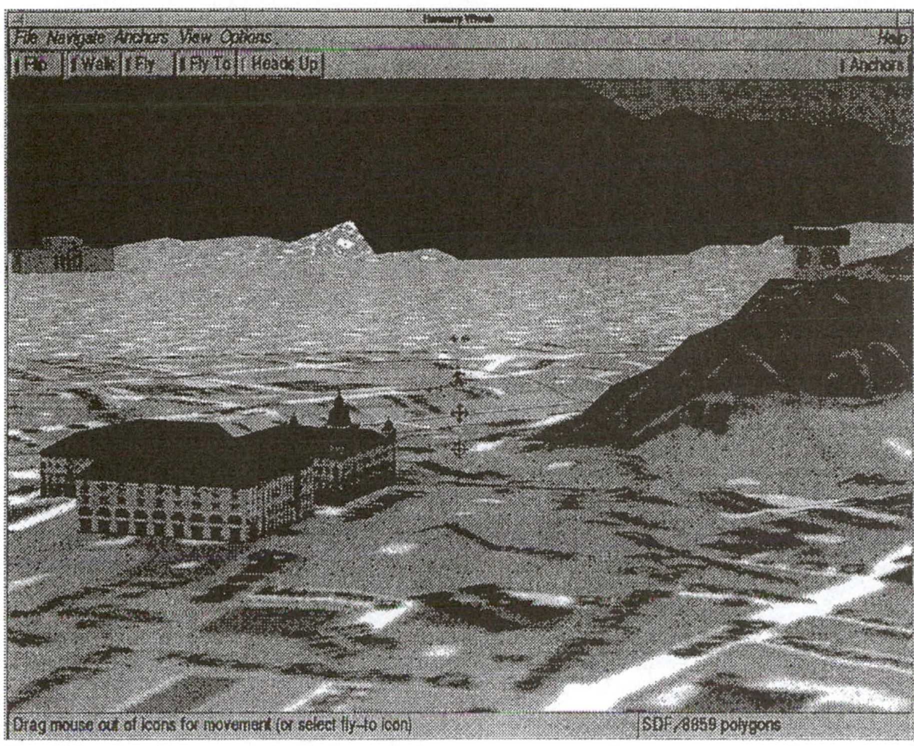

Figure 3: Harmony's VRweb 3D Viewer

5 3D Hyperdocuments

The Harmony VRweb 3D scene viewer displays model description files representing arbitrarily complex objects or scenes. The models may either be of the hand-crafted or of the automatically generated variety, depending upon the application. Both VRML and SDF, a file format derived from the Wavefront Advanced Visualizer, are supported. In Figure 3, a hand-crafted 3D plan of the centre of Graz features some of the sights of the city; embedded hyperlinks lead to further information about the various sights. Users typically explore a model of a scene by moving themselves (walk, fly, fly to, and heads-up navigation modes) and view a model of an object by moving the model (translate, rotate, zoom).

6 3D Structure Maps

Harmony's Information Landscape, shown in Figure 4, is an interactive, three-dimensional visualisation of the collection structure, tightly coupled to the Session Manager's two-dimensional collection browser display (changes in one are reflected in the other). The collection hierarchy is mapped out onto a plane, documents within a collection are arranged on top of the corresponding block; colour and height are currently used to encode document type and size respectively. Users can "fly" over the landscape looking for salient features, like flying over a file system directories with FSN [15]. A flat overview window (top right) provides a further aid to orientation. Whereas FSN reads in and lays out the entire directory hierarchy once at program start-up, Harmony's Information Landscape is constructed and laid out incrementally as users open and close collections and subcollections, access documents, and perform searches.

Work on the Information Landscape is still at an early stage. We are currently experimenting with the use of textured landscapes (as shown in Figure 5), and will introduce simple 3D icons to replace the basic blocks currently used. A default set of 3D icons will represent document type, with colouring used to represent document age and hence giving a rapid visual impression of where new information is located. The author of a collection will be able to specify an arbitrary model as its 3D icon: for example a model of the Eiffel Tower to represent a collection about Paris. A further innovation will be the superimposition of

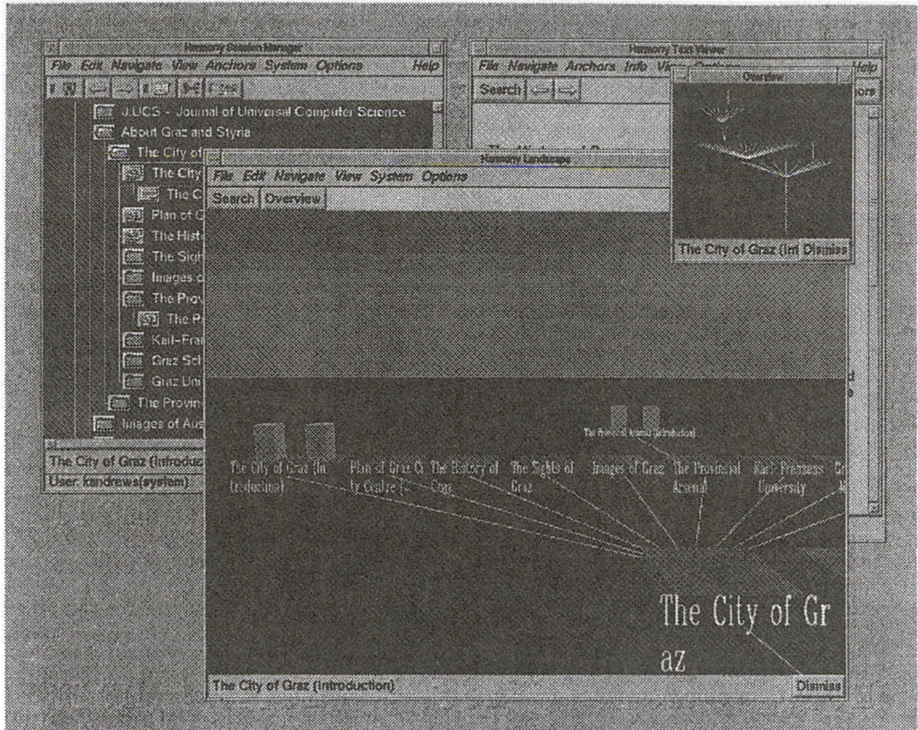

Figure 4: The Harmony Information Landscape

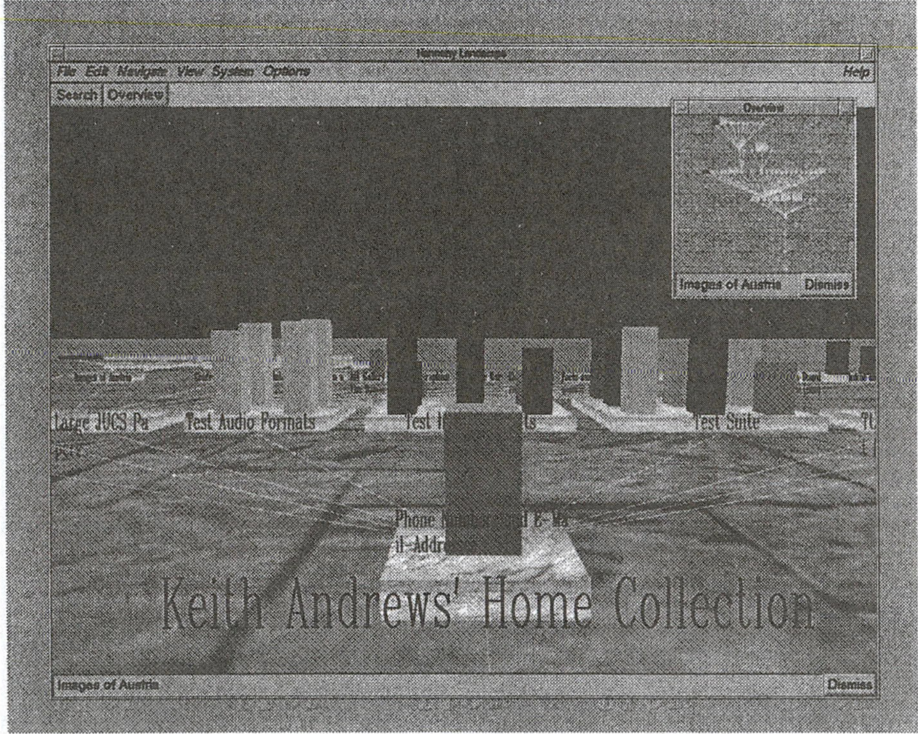

Figure 5: Textured Information Landscape

arced cables upon the landscape to represent the link relationships of a specific document. Through their ability to compactly display many thousands of objects, 3D visualisations are perhaps the only effective means of browsing in and judging the extent of large, dynamic information spaces.

7 Concluding Remarks

Following an overview of information visualisation techniques and current efforts to visualise Internet information spaces, I have presented in more detail the visualisation facilities currently available in the Harmony client for Hyper-G. Recent informal usability evaluations of Harmony (thinking aloud tests to provide design feedback) have shown in particular that the close coupling of several orthogonal visualisation and navigational facilities in Harmony helps provide location feedback and alleviate user disorientation.

In the near future, both hand-crafted and dynamically generated visualisations will start to abound, as modeling languages like VRML take hold and appropriate software becomes available for a wide variety of applications. The announcement of VRML browsers for Gopher, WWW, and Hyper-G can be expected to rapidly increase the number of visualisations of these information spaces.

Further information about Hyper-G and Harmony and installation details may be retrieved by anonymous ftp from `ftp.iicm.tu-graz.ac.at` in directory `/pub/Hyper-G` or from the IICM Information Server under `http://info.iicm.tu-graz.ac.at/` or `gopher://info.iicm.tu-graz.ac.at/`.

8 Acknowledgements

The financial support of Hyper-G by the Austrian Ministry of Science, JOANNEUM RESEARCH, and the European Space Agency is gratefully acknowledged. Current work on Virtual Information Spaces is partly financed by the Anniversary Fund of the Austrian National Bank, under project number 5334.

I am indebted to the members of my Harmony project team for their valuable input, hard work, and dedication.

References

[1] Gavin Bell, Anthony Parisi, and Mark Pesce. The Virtual Reality Modeling Language – Version 1.0 Specification. Available at `http://vrml.wired.com/vrml.tech/vrml10-3.html`.

[2] George G. Robertson, Stuart K. Card, and Jock D. Mackinlay. Information Visualization Using 3D Interactive Animation. *Communications of the ACM*, 36(4):56–71, April 1993.

[3] Kenneth Utting and Nicole Yankelovich. Context and Orientation in Hypermedia Networks. *ACM Transactions on Information Systems*, 7(1):58–84, January 1989.

[4] Manojit Sarkar and Marc H. Brown. Graphical Fisheye Views of Graphs. In *Proc. CHI'92*, pages 83–91, Monterey, May 1992. ACM.

[5] Brian Johnson and Ben Shneiderman. Tree-Maps: A Space-Filling Approach to the Visualization of Hierarchical Information Structures. In *Proc. IEEE Visualization '91, San Diego, CA*, pages 284–291, Los Alamitos, CA, October 1991. IEEE Computer Society Press.

[6] Xia Lin. Visualization for the Document Space. In *Proc. IEEE Visualization '92, Boston, MA*, pages 274–281, Los Alamitos, CA, October 1992. IEEE Computer Society Press.

[7] John Lamping and Ramana Rao. Laying out and Visualizing Large Trees Using a Hyperbolic Space. In *Proc. UIST'94, Marina del Rey, CA*, pages 13–14, New York, November 1994. ACM.

[8] Stuart K. Card, George G. Robertson, and Jock D. Mackinlay. The Information Visualiser, An Information Workspace. In *Proc. CHI '91: Human Factors in Computing Systems*, pages 181–188, New York, May 1991. ACM.

[9] Jock D. Mackinlay, George G. Robertson, and Stuart K. Card. The Perspective Wall: Detail and Context Smoothly Integrated. In *Proc. CHI'91, New Orleans, Louisiana*, pages 173–179, New York, May 1991. ACM.

[10] George G. Robertson, Jock D. Mackinlay, and Stuart K. Card. Cone Trees: Animated 3D Visualizations of Hierarchical Information. In *Proc. CHI'91, New Orleans, Louisiana*, pages 189–194, New York, May 1991. ACM.

[11] Kim Michael Fairchild, Luis Serra, Ng Hern, Lee Beng Hai, and Ang Tin Leong. Dynamic FishEye Information Visualizations. In Rae A. Earnshaw, Michael A. Gigante, and Huw Jones, editors, *Virtual Reality Systems*, pages 161–177. Academic Press, 1993.

[12] Kim Michael Fairchild, Steven E. Poltrock, and George W. Furnas. SemNet: Three-Dimensional Representations of Large Knowledge Bases. In Raymonde

Guindon, editor, *Cognitive Science and its Applications for Human-Computer Interaction*, pages 201–233. Lawrence Erlbaum, Hillsdale, NJ, 1988.

[13] Luis Serra, Tat-Seng Chua, and Wei-Shoong Teh. A Model for Integrating Multimedia Information Around 3D Graphics Hierarchies. *The Visual Computer*, 7(5-6):326–343, May/June 1991.

[14] Pauline A. Smith and John R. Wilson. Navigating in Hypertext Through Virtual Environments. *Applied Ergonomics*, 24(4):271–278, August 1993. Butterworth-Heinemann Ltd.

[15] Joel Tesler and Steve Strasnick. *FSN: The 3D File System Navigator*. Silicon Graphics, Inc., Mountain View, CA, 1992. Available by anonymous ftp from `sgi.sgi.com` in directory `sgi/fsn`.

[16] Keith Andrews, Frank Kappe, and Hermann Maurer. Hyper-G: Towards the Next Generation of Network Information Technology. *Journal of Universal Computer Science*, 1(4):206–220, April 1995. Special Issue: Selected Proceedings of the Workshop on Distributed Multimedia Systems, Graz, Austria, Nov. 1994. Available at `http://info.iicm.tu-graz.ac.at/Cjucs_root`.

[17] Keith Andrews, Frank Kappe, and Hermann Maurer. Serving Information to the Web with Hyper-G. *Computer Networks and ISDN Systems*, 27(6):919–926, April 1995. Proc. Third International World-Wide Web Conference, WWW'95, Darmstadt, Germany.

[18] Mark P. McCahill and Farhad X. Anklesaria. Evolution of Internet Gopher. *Journal of Universal Computer Science*, 1(4):235–246, April 1995. Selected Proceedings of the Workshop on Distributed Multimedia Systems, Graz, Austria, Nov. 1994. Available at `http://info.iicm.tu-graz.ac.at/Cjucs_root`.

[19] Tim Berners-Lee, Robert Cailliau, Ari Luotonen, Henrik Frystyk Nielsen, and Arthur Secret. The World-Wide Web. *Communications of the ACM*, 37(8):76–82, August 1994.

[20] Mark P. McCahill and Thomas Erickson. Design for a 3D Spatial User Interface for Internet Gopher. In *Proc. of ED-MEDIA 95*, pages 39–44, Graz, Austria, June 1995. AACE.

[21] Ed H. Chi. Webspace Visualization. Available at `http://www.geom.umn.edu/docs/weboogl/`, The Geometry Center, University of Minnesota.

[22] Sougata Mukherjea and James D. Foley. Visualizing the World-Wide Web with the Navigational View Builder. *Computer Networks and ISDN Systems*, 27(6):1075–1087, April 1995. Proc. Third International World-Wide Web Conference, WWW'95, Darmstadt, Germany.

[23] Andrew Wood, Nick Drew, Russell Beale, and Bob Hendley. HyperSpace: Web Browsing with Visualisation. Available at `http://www.cs.bham.ac.uk/amw/hyperspace/`. Poster/Demo at WWW'95, Darmstadt, Germany.

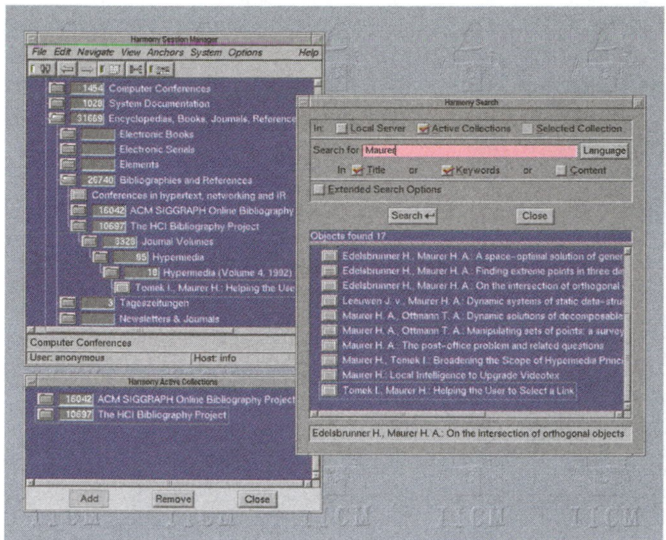

FIGURE **1**

Location Feedback in Harmony

FIGURE **2**

The Harmony Local Map

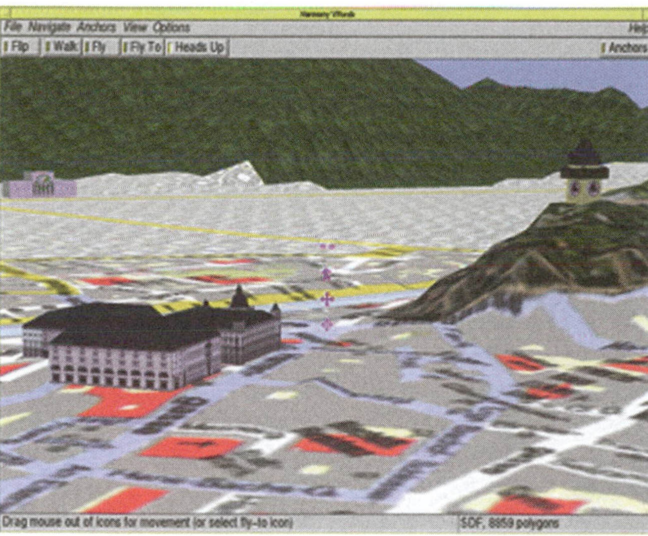

FIGURE **3**

Harmony's VRweb 3D Viewer

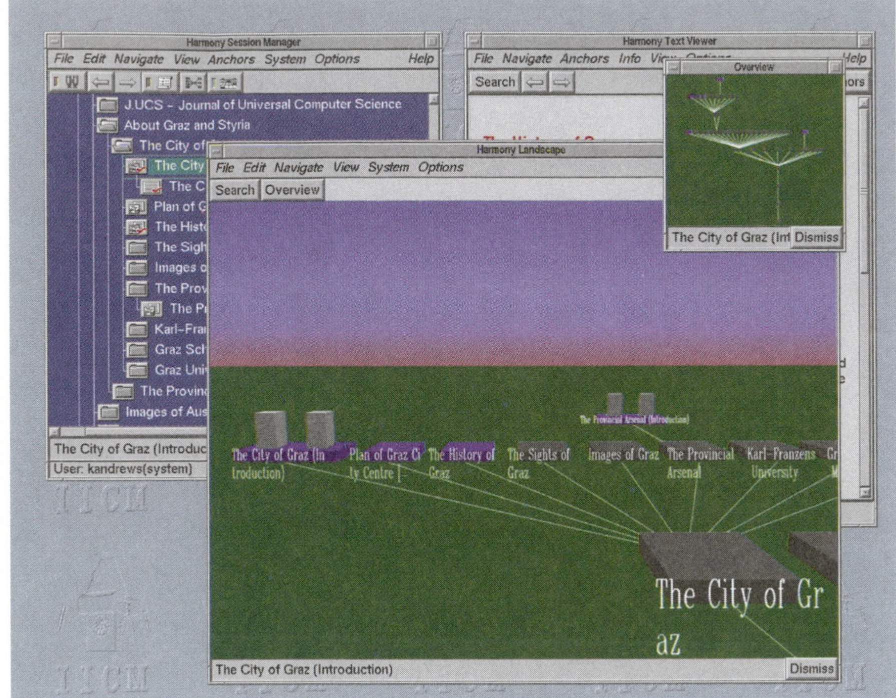

FIGURE 4

The Harmony Information Landscape

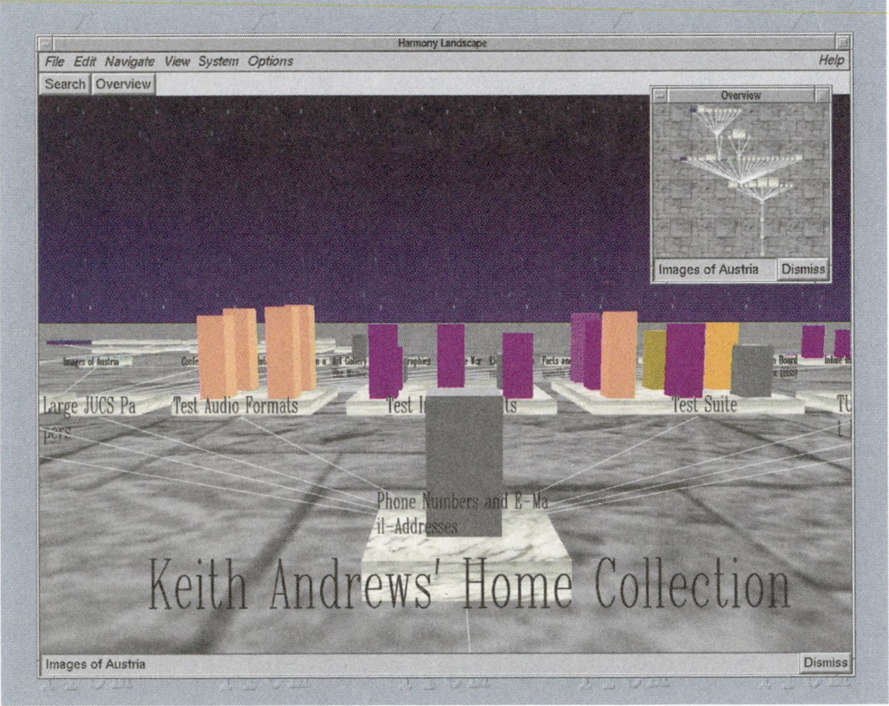

FIGURE 5

Textured Information Landscape

Case Study
Narcissus: Visualising Information

R.J.Hendley, N.S.Drew, A.M.Wood & R.Beale
School of Computer Science
University of Birmingham, B15 2TT, UK
{R.J.Hendley, N.S.Drew, A.M.Wood, R.Beale}@cs.bham.ac.uk

Abstract

It is becoming increasingly important that support is provided for users who are dealing with complex information spaces. The need is driven by the growing number of domains where there is a requirement for users to understand, navigate and manipulate large sets of computer based data; by the increasing size and complexity of this information and by the pressures to use this information efficiently. The paradigmatic example is the World Wide Web, but other domains include software systems, information systems and concurrent engineering.

One approach to providing this support is to provide sophisticated visualisation tools which will lead the users to form an intuitive understanding of the structure and behaviour of their domain and which will provide mechanisms which allow them to manipulate objects within their system.

This paper describes such a tool and a number of visualisation techniques that it implements.

1 Introduction

People are increasingly faced with the problem of filtering and interpreting enormous quantities of information. From this mass of data they need to extract knowledge which will allow them to make informed decisions. They need to organise and interpret the mass of detail in order that the information and knowledge that is required to support their tasks is accessible to them.

Although this is not a new problem, the rapid and accelerating increase in the quantity of information available and a growing need for more highly optimised solutions have both added to the pressure to make good and effective use of this information. There has also been an increased requirement for direct access to information by its end-user rather than indirect access through third parties (e.g. librarians or research assistants). Similarly, the increase in electronic access means that information which would previously have been implicitly filtered out through the high cost of identification and access is now available on the desk-top.

This paper reports on work which investigates the use of self organising systems and virtual reality techniques to provide an environment which reveals the structure of the system being explored and provides for the navigation through the system and manipulation of the objects. The system uses a KQML interface to communicate with (possibly several) host systems. Examples are presented from applications of the visualisation tool to the World Wide Web and to a program development environment.

2 Large information spaces

2.1 Problem domains

The problems of understanding, navigating through and manipulating complex information spaces are now being faced across a wide range of application areas and it is becoming increasingly important to provide tools which provide sophisticated support to users in these tasks.

Software Engineering is, in many respects, a classic example of the domains where these problems exist. The systems being constructed and manipulated can be very large and complex and will often have a large number of engineers working on them through their life. These engineers will need to construct and maintain an overall understanding of the structure, constraints and behaviour of the system with which they are working as well as having a very detailed knowledge of at least parts of that system. They will need to look at the system from several different perspectives. For instance, they may need to understand the control flow, data flow, class structure, profile information and so on. They will also have different information requirements depending upon the task which they are performing - e.g. whether they are constructing, debugging or maintaining the system. A large number of tools are available which support Software Engineers in some of their tasks (e.g. there are browsers, animators and so on), but these generally work at a relatively low level and are poor in providing support at the higher levels where it is often most important.

Concurrent Engineering, more generally, is an area where there is widespread support for users at the low level and yet where there is relatively little support for engineers in building an overall understanding of their systems. In these domains the overall complexity of the problem has traditionally been addressed through rigid compartmentalisation of the design and manufacturing processes with each sub-task operating within unnecessarily conservative constraints. This can lead to poor overall designs, since there is little chance for opportunistic optimisations across sub-components. Increasingly, economic and other factors are requiring that much more highly optimised designs should be produced and this is leading to many of the same problems that have been encountered within Software Engineering.

The World Wide Web (WWW) [1] is probably the best example of an information space where users need support. The structure of the web has evolved rather than been designed and the quantity of information is both very great and it is changing rapidly. Locating relevant information can be very difficult and although there are tools, such as search engines, which can help users to find information, the user is left without any overall *picture* of the information space. This is a particular problem since, often, a search will fail to locate the actual information required but *will* locate pages which are a small number of links away. A common strategy is to use a search engine to locate the potentially useful areas of the web and then to manually search outwards from these points. This manual search is often near blind since the user has virtually no information to guide them. Furthermore, in order to try to make the search as efficient as possible the user will frequently adopt a fairly complex strategy which places unreasonable memory requirements upon them - for instance, they will explore a branch and then backtrack, intending to resume the search from that point if they are unsuccessful elsewhere. This all leads to searches being much less reliable and efficient that they should be.

2.2 Information visualisation

One approach to these problems is to move more responsibility away from the user towards the machine. Routine tasks can be automated entirely and frameworks have been developed which can support the interaction between these tools and users. More sophisticated agents are also being developed which can locate, retrieve and filter information based upon the particular requirements of their users. These tools can reduce the quantity of detail that a user needs to contend with but, ultimately, the user still needs to process information in order to form an overall understanding of their system, if only to guide agents more effectively.

A complementary approach is to provide sophisticated visualisation tools which will present information to the user in a way in which the global, high-level structure is apparent and yet the low-level detail is still accessible. This will reduce the processing and memory requirements of the user and allow them to operate more effectively and efficiently. Some striking examples of the ways in which a good visual representation can unlock previously hidden structure and yet not obscure the detail are contained in Tufte [7].

Robertson [4] identifies four processes that need to be supported by appropriate visualisations:

- Sense making (building an overall understanding of the information).
- Design.
- Decision making (Building a decision and a rationale for that decision).
- Response tasks (finding information to respond to a query).

These processes usually impose different requirements on the visualisation since the information requirements of the different tasks vary and the mechanisms by which the information is accessed are different. Ideally though, a user should be able to work within one visualisation which is rich enough and sufficiently adaptable to support whatever task the user is performing.

2.3 The Narcissus system

Most visualisation systems rely upon a two dimensional representation and use a fixed layout algorithm. The use of a 3-dimensional representation through which users can navigate provides a much richer visualisation. This is partly because of the increased information density, but it is even more true when additional virtual reality techniques are employed to make the visualisation more sophisticated.

Similarly, by giving the objects that make up the information space behaviours that determine their movement through (and hence their position in) the 3-dimensional space (rather than using a global layout algorithm) we can generate much more effective views onto the objects and their inter-relationships.

The Narcissus system uses these techniques of self-organising systems and virtual reality to generate visualisations through which the users can navigate and manipulate objects in the visualisation. The system is implemented as a process which communicates with applications (e.g. web browsers and programming environments) using KQML [3]. This provides a degree of application independence and also allows the system to work concurrently with several, possibly heterogeneous, applications and also allows collaborative working between several users.

The results that have been produced confirm the intuition that these are powerful techniques. The emergent structure that can be revealed by the system is often remarkable. It is also clear that there are a large number of issues that still need to be explored and we are adapting the system to experiment with some potential techniques for addressing these problems.

3 Organising Objects

Many approaches have been used to produce useful spatial layout of objects (for instance, using a global layout algorithm or applying statistical techniques to produce clusters of related objects [6]). The approach that we have adopted is to give each of the objects in the information space a behaviour which determines its movement (and ultimately its position) in the 3-dimensional space. At present the rules which determine the behaviour are common to all of the *active* objects although, in the future, we will modify this so that the rules can vary between objects and between classes of objects. We also intend to experiment with agents that will wander through the information space and modify the rules and other attributes of the objects.

The current model is loosely based upon physical systems with rules defining forces that act between the objects. These forces cause the objects to move in space. There are two classes of force:

- All objects in the system exert a repulsive force on all of the other objects.
- Active relationships between objects lead to attractive forces being exerted between related objects.

By running the model, objects migrate through space so that they are spatial close to those objects with which they are semantically related. Normally, a steady state is reached within a relatively small number of steps through the model. Figure 1 shows the movement from a completely disorganised system towards one where the structure is becoming apparent.

The emergent structure can be striking and it appears that a set of visual clichés will emerge. For instance, Figure 2 shows a structure which is found quite often. In this example (which is from the application of Narcissus to a programming environment), the small objects inherit from the two larger ones. The central objects inherit multiply (e.g. from both of the large objects), while the peripheral ones inherit singly. This overall structure is very hard to interpret from the textual representation of the program and yet becomes immediately apparent from the visualisation.

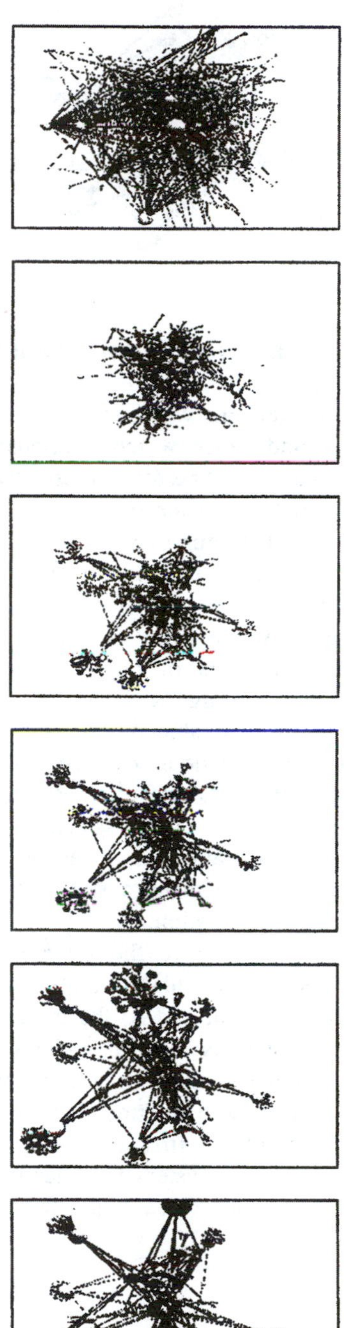

Figure 1: Moving from disorganised to organised structure

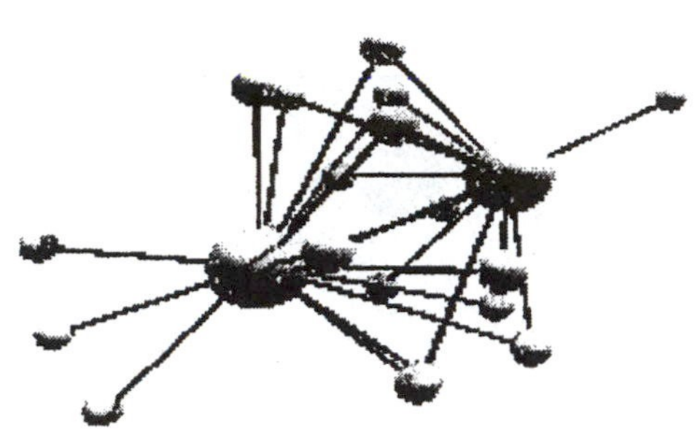

Figure 2: The barrel structure

The user can determine which relationships are active within the model and hence which relationships will be responsible for generating attractive forces between objects. The rules used to determine the forces are still subject to experimentation and it seems likely that there will be no single set of rules that are appropriate to all circumstances.

If the force is used to determine an object's acceleration, then a stable state can still include some motion with some clusters of objects pulsating whilst others may include orbiting satellites and so on. This motion can be a very valuable part of the visualisation since this dynamic behaviour can be useful for the recognition of individual clusters of objects and of similar structures. However, for the large systems at which this work is aimed, the computational cost can be very high and it can take a long time to reach a stable state when the force determines the acceleration.

An alternative is to have the force determine the velocity of an object. This leads to stable states in which there is no residual motion and so the model can be run until this quiescent state is reached and then turned off whilst the user navigates through and manipulates the system. Whilst this is a more practical solution, it does lose some of the richness of the first alternative and we will seek ways to optimise the system in order to leave some residual motion without incurring an unreasonable performance penalty.

4 The visualisation

4.1 The basic model

Providing a 3 dimensional virtual reality through which the user can move to explore and manipulate information is a potentially very powerful technique. The Narcissus system provides the user with a window onto their information space and allows the user to navigate through this space and to select and manipulate objects. The user is able to control some aspects of the behaviour of the objects and can select individual objects and classes of objects which should be visible. By default, the system draws arcs to represent the active relationships in the system although in some cases it is clearer when the user turns this off. Similarly, the system can label objects with their attributes (e.g. their URL) but this is often confusing and can obscure the structure. The user can either just display these attributes for selected objects or can set a distance threshold beyond which they are not displayed.

Figure 3 shows the representation of a collection of web pages. In this example, representing several hundred nodes, important structural information becomes obvious. For instance, the structure at the right of the visualisation is a collection of manual pages and examples. The large nodes are indexes into the pages, the ball-like structure represents the set of cross referenced manual pages and the structure below represents the examples.

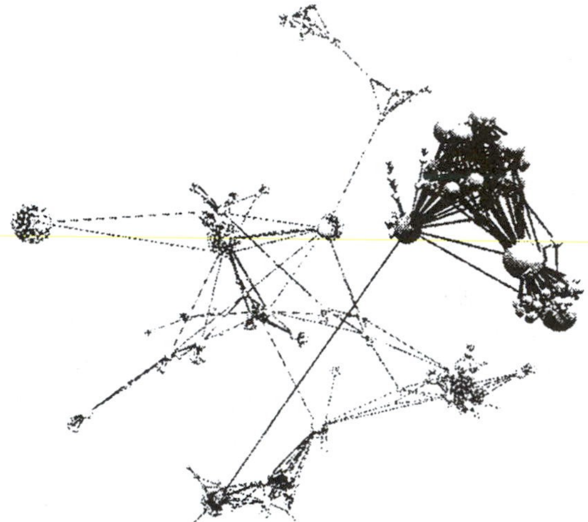

Figure 3: Representation of complex web structure

4.2 Extensions to the basic model

A number of other techniques have been developed to improve the visualisation of the system and the recognition of objects or clusters or classes of objects. Figure 4 shows an example where an icon has been used to render the surface of an object (In this case a world map has been used to represent a global object). In some cases this could be a useful and practical approach, for instance, in web browsing a user's image could be used to render the surface of their home page or a rendered image of a page could be projected onto the object which represents it. There are only pragmatic considerations which prevent this from being extended to movies, animations and so on. Empirical evaluations will be required to determine just how useful these techniques might be. Other alternatives include the use of 3 dimensional icons. Vion-Dury et al [8] report work where they have used a function of an object's name to generate a distinct polyhedral shape for the object. This is potentially useful, particularly when the name carries some semantic information which might lead to related objects having common physical features (In their domain of programming environments this is often the case).

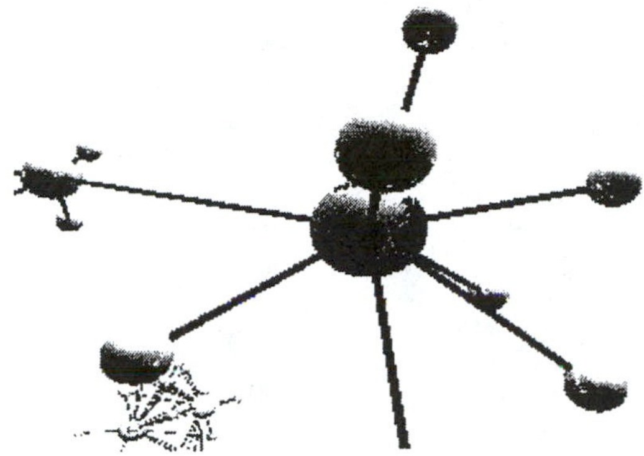

Figure 4: Icon rendered onto surface of an object

Figure 5 shows an example where the system has been used with a program development environment and colour has been used to overload additional information onto the visualisation. In this case, profile information has been used to colour objects according to the frequency with which they receive messages. This is a potentially useful technique in other domains, such as web browsing, where statistical information and other information is required as well as basic structural information.

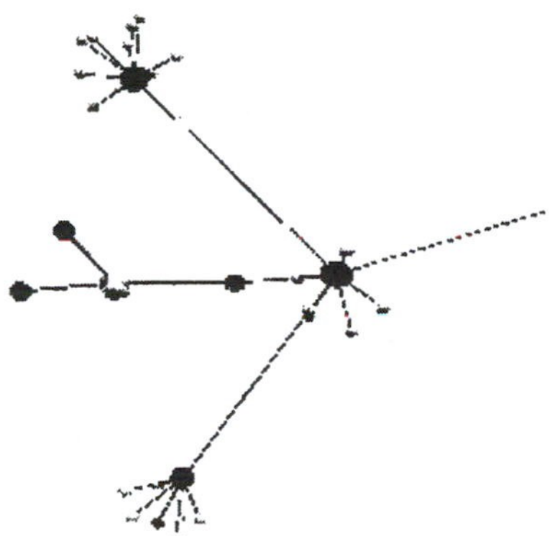

Figure 5: Visualising profile information

Another technique with which we are experimenting is to merge a cluster of individual objects into one compound object. This agglomeration removes some of the detail from the visual representation so that the overall structure is more clearly visible. These compound objects are formed by placing a translucent surface around the cluster so that from a distance it appears as one distinctive object but, as it is approached, the internal structure becomes more apparent and the user can smoothly move from a high-level view to one in which all the detail is available. Figure 6 shows such an agglomeration. These agglomerations might be given more than just a visual reality - it may be that it is more effective to jump to another space when the agglomeration is entered or to give the agglomeration some semantic significance which might, for instance, affect their behaviours.

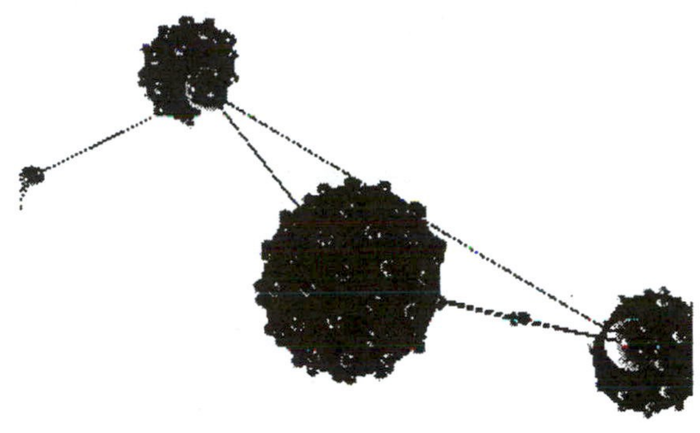

Figure 6: Clusters enclosed by translucent surface

5 The Narcissus system

5.1 Implementation

The first implementation of the Narcissus system was as a hard-wired visualisation for the SELF [5] programming environment. Since then it has been re-implemented as an independent system which communicates with other applications using KQML [3]. This implementation has been applied to web browsing and to program development. Narcissus itself is independent of the application(s) with which it is being used, although work is required to enable new applications to interact with the system. Figure 7 shows the system working with a modified version of xmosaic to provide visualisation support for web browsing.

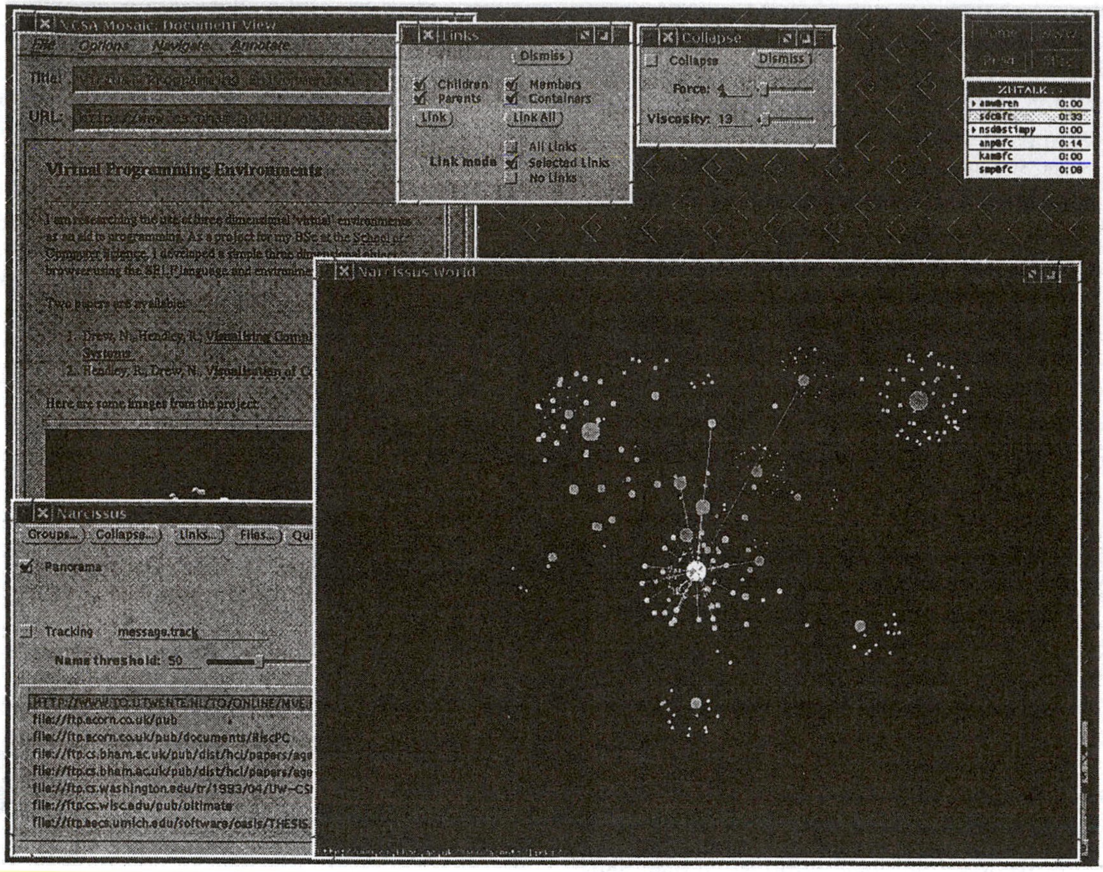

Figure 7: Narcissus applied to Web browsing

The use of KQML is useful not just because it provides application independence. Many of the domains in which visualisation is most important involve collaboration between multiple users and between multiple applications. Visualisation support in these domains should ideally integrate the work of these several users across all of their applications. At present this has only been validated across multiple instantiations of the modified xmosaic to provide a visualisation of concurrent web browsing.

The system allows the user to manipulate various parameters of the visualisation and of the forces acting on the objects. The user is able to move through the 3 dimensional representation of the world in order to change their view and to select objects (e.g. web pages) which are then manipulated using an appropriate tool (e.g. web pages are displayed and can be manipulated by a browser). An implementation is also presently being undertaken for an immersive VR system.

The performance of the system is dependent upon the size of the information space being manipulated, but with several hundred objects it provides acceptable interactive performance.

5.2 Evaluations

A formal empirical evaluation is presently being undertaken to assess the value of the visualisations provided by the system. Informal tests suggest that, for web browsing, the visual representations provided and the mechanisms for manipulating the objects and visualisation are useful.

6 Conclusions

The use of virtual reality and self organising systems is a powerful technique for information visualisation. The applications that we have built do show that important, high-level structure can become obvious using these techniques and that the low-level detail is still seamlessly accessible. It is also clear that navigating through the information space can be a relatively straightforward and natural task.

The approach appears to scale reasonably well to systems with many hundreds of nodes but with larger information spaces the techniques that we are evaluating for hiding low-level detail will become increasingly important.

One of the benefits of making abstract information structures more concrete is that it provides the user with the ability to recognise objects by their relative positions and by the distinctive shapes that clusters of objects form. Again, the formation of agglomerations of objects (either by forming surfaces around them or through attaching some iconic representation to them) will support this recognition. One problem that occurs with dynamic systems (that is systems where objects are being added, removed or have their relationships modified) is that a small change can cause the system to re-organise in a way which may significantly affect the visualisation. This may not be a major problem in practice and one virtue of the approach is that the user can at least watch the re-organisation taking place (e.g. when a new URL is added to the web visualiser, the user sees it moving into position and any other consequential changes taking place). One approach may be to freeze the system after an initial organisation and then to just allow local changes to the structure when modifications are made. The best solution will need to be determined empirically, but it is likely that incorporating other cues to recognition will, in any case, be valuable.

The behaviours of the objects are presently very simple and the rules which determine the behaviours are global to all objects. Extending this to provide a richer set of behaviours and allowing these to vary across the objects is part of our current work.

References

[1] Berners-Lee, T., Cailliau, R. Luotonen, A., Nielsen, H.F. & Secret, A. *The World Wide Web*. Communications of the ACM 37 (8), pp 87-96. 1994.

[2] Drew N.S.., Hendley R.J. *Visualising Complex Interacting Systems*. Proceedings of CHI95 (to appear) 1995.

[3] Finin T., Fritzon R., McKay D. et. al. *An Overview of KQML: A Knowledge query and manipulation language*. Technical Report, Department of Computer Science, University of Maryland. 1992.

[4] Robertson G., Card S., Mackinlay J. *Information visualisation using 3D interactive animation*. CACM Vol. 36, No. 4. 1993.

[5] Smith, R.B. & Ungar, D. *SELF, The power of simplicity*. in Proceedings of OOPSLA'87, published as SIGPLAN Notices 22 (12). 1987.

[6] Snowdon D., Benford S., Brown C., Ingram R., Knox I., Studley L. *Information visualisation, browsing and sharing in populated information terrains*. 1995.

[7] Tufte E. *Envisioning Information*. Graphics Press. 1990.

[8] Vion-Dury J., Suntan M. *Virtual images: Interactive visualisation of distributed object-oriented systems*. Proceedings of OOPSLA-94, ACM Press. 1994.

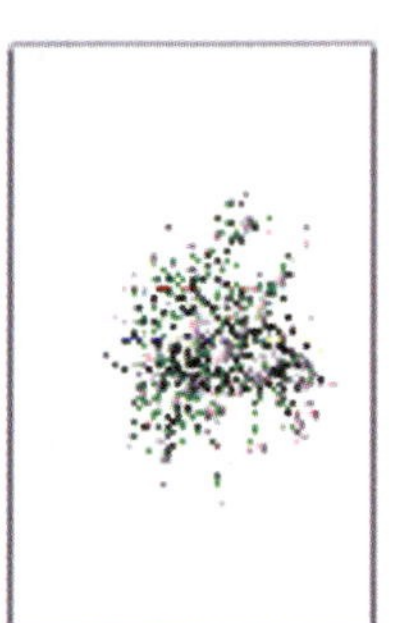

FIGURE **1**

Moving from disorganised to organised structure

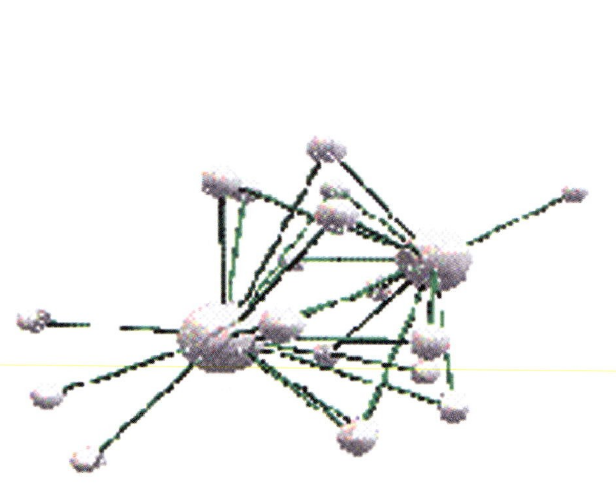

FIGURE **2**

The barrel structure

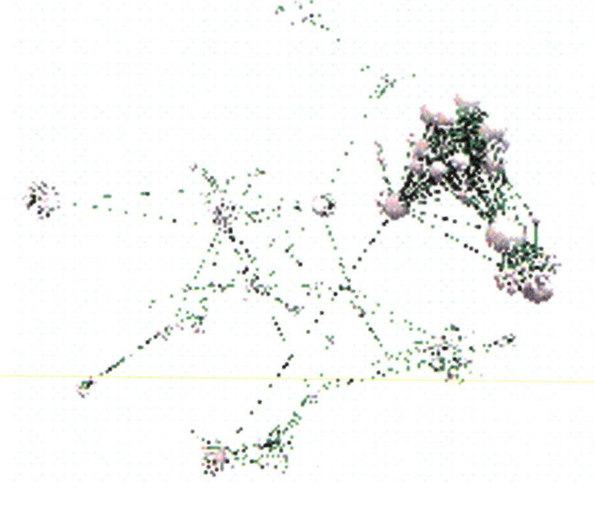

FIGURE **3**

Representation of complex web structure

FIGURE **4**

Icon rendered onto surface of an object

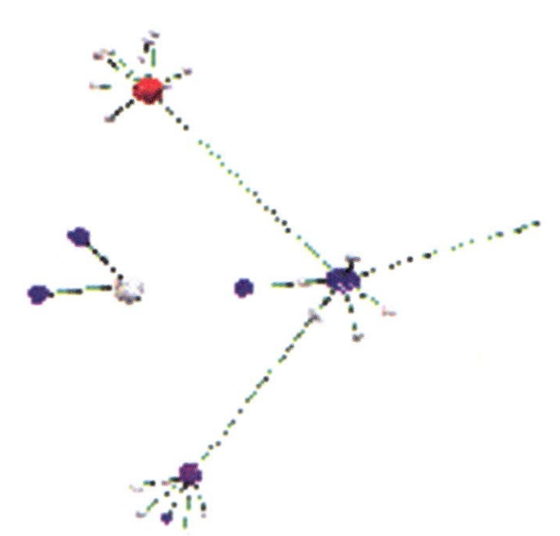

FIGURE **5**

Visualising profile information

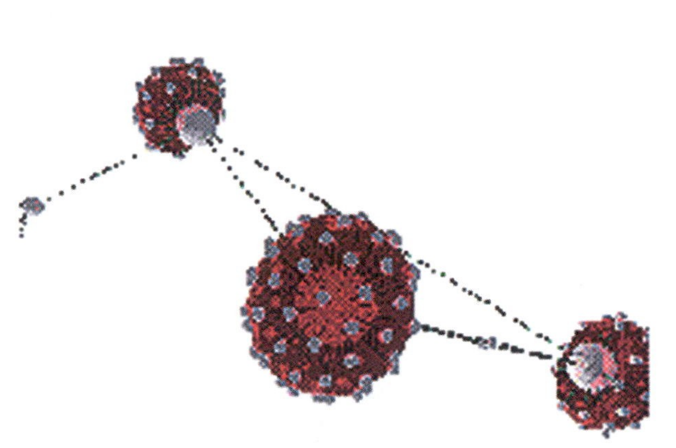

FIGURE **6**

Clusters enclosed by translucent surface

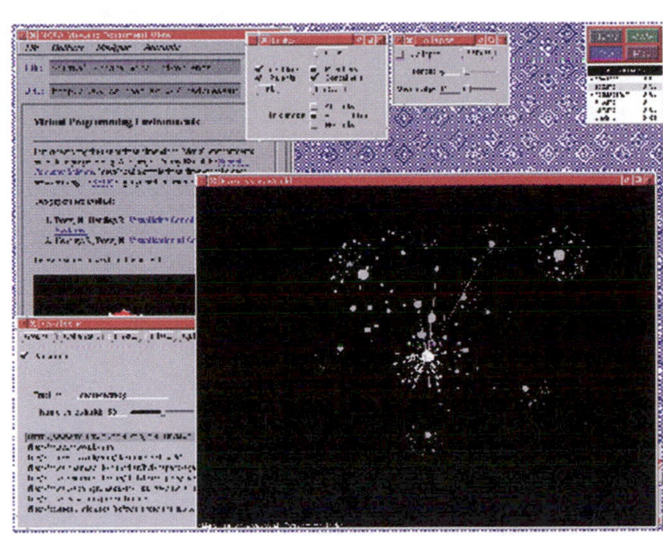

FIGURE **7**

Narcissus applied to Web browsing

6.2 Information Workspaces

In the previous section, we considered approaches to visualization of large information spaces, such as the World Wide Web and Web sites, that make up the infosphere. In this section, we consider proposals for information workspaces, environments in which the cost structure of needed information is tuned to the requirements of the work using it (Card and Henderson, 1987b; Card, Robertson, and Mackinlay, 1991). An information workspace is an intermediary place where selections from the infosphere can be brought together for fast access, for extraction of content pieces, and for embedding in visualization substrates. At the heart of the workspace notion is the fact that users exhibit locality of reference in the use of information (Henderson and Card, 1986). Clusters of information are used repeatedly. Hence, we can predict a degree of interest function over the information and can organize the cost structure so as to make quicker access to more likely used information.

The concept of an information workspace and how visualizations might improve it is the subject of the first paper by Robertson, Card, and Mackinlay (1993 ●). In their system, the information visualizer, they explore how data with different structure—long linear data, hierarchical data, geographically based data—can be put into active visualizations. Their workspace builds off the older idea of splitting a large workspace into multiple screen-sized workspaces (Henderson and Card, 1986), each of which holds information likely to be part of an information locality. To this concept, the information visualizer adds focus + context knowledge tools, zooming, and enforcement of real-time interaction rates. The multiple workspace mechanism allows the screen space to be virtually larger. The logarithmic zooming mechanism allows the space to be virtually denser. The focus + context visual knowledge tools allow more information to be packed into the same place. Each of these effects is worth something like 1 to 1.5 orders of magnitude (that is, a factor of around 10 to 30). Taking the lower number, collectively they allow in principle for an information workspace some orders of magnitude larger than a conventional interface.

The next paper, about Pad++ (Bederson and Hollan, 1994 ●), describes a 2D workspace that is infinitely zoomable. Perlin and Fox (1993) originated the system using a bitmapped display. Pad++ reimplemented and reengineered the system for smooth animation and large data spaces. Central to the idea of Pad++ is smooth zooming. Because the user can zoom in very far, it is possible to put an enormous amount of information in the same space. This requires careful management, however. Otherwise a user could make a mark at a high level and the mark could obliterate invisible information at the zoomed-in level. Conversely, information at the zoomed level could become invisible and lost at the higher level. When the user is zoomed in, the context disappears. To aid these problems, Bederson and Hollan use semantic zooming—as the user zooms out, the visual representation can change to something that can be read at the higher level. Data can be organized within bounding boxes. And portals from one part of the space can help with the lost context. The paper describes an application to visualization of a hierarchical directory system. As the user zooms away, larger-scale features of the director are visible and detail is replaced with other representations.

Card, Robertson, and York (1996 ●) describe an information workspace for the Web. It is directed at two severe problems of the current Web design. First, there is no real concept of workspace. Users cannot easily see multiple Web pages at the same time. For example, they cannot compare the content of two pages. Their only recourse is to start another copy of the browser and use the window desktop as the workspace. The solution explored in this paper is a 3D workspace. Ballay (1994) describes a previous 3D office workspace design. The Web forager adds structure to the 3D space and adds a very rapid interaction mechanism. Simple gestures allow the user to move documents or toss them back in 3D or allow the user to make simple movements in the space.

The second problem is that a Web page is too low a level of aggregation for information. It is as though the Library of Congress separately indexed every page of every book and the patrons had to check out each page separately from the stacks. The WebBook, in which Web pages are joined as pages in a book, is the solution proposed to this problem. The workspace provides a context in which Web pages can be combined by informal positioning or by grouping into piles or books. Books or piles can be changed into document lens renditions of an entire book. Visual knowledge tools could be combined in the same space.

In the final paper, Risch et al. (1997 ●) propose an information workspace that combines all parts of the knowledge crystallization task, from foraging for information in the infosphere, to sense making in the workspace with visual knowledge tools, to producing output products. The workspace is a 3D space in which 2D information maps are laid out on the floor and wall. This system does extensive analysis of text and databases, enabling "concept queries." Three-dimensional scattergraphs and a novel visualization that plots scattergraphs of objects on the surface of a transparent sphere are used to provide overviews of specific data sets. Additional analysis is provided by a "Link Net" visual knowledge tool, essentially a plot of parallel coordinates that uses a gridded array of points in 3D instead of a line.

George G. Robertson, Stuart K. Card, and Jock D. Mackinlay

INFORMATION VISUALIZATION USING 3D INTERACTIVE ANIMATION

I innovations are often driven by a combination of technology advances and application demands. On the technology side, advances in interactive computer graphics hardware, coupled with low-cost mass storage, have created new possibilities for information retrieval systems in which UIs could play a more central role. On the application side, increasing masses of information confronting a business or an individual have created a demand for information management applications. In the 1980s, text-editing forced the shaping of the desktop metaphor and the now standard GUI paradigm. In the 1990s, it is likely that information access will be a primary force in shaping the successor to the desktop metaphor.

This article presents an experimental system, the *Information Visualizer* (see Figure 1), which explores a UI paradigm that goes beyond the desktop metaphor to exploit the emerging generation of graphical personal computers and to support the emerging application demand to retrieve, store, manipulate, and understand large amounts of information. The basic problem is how to utilize advancing graphics technology to lower the cost of finding information and accessing it once found (the information's "cost structure").

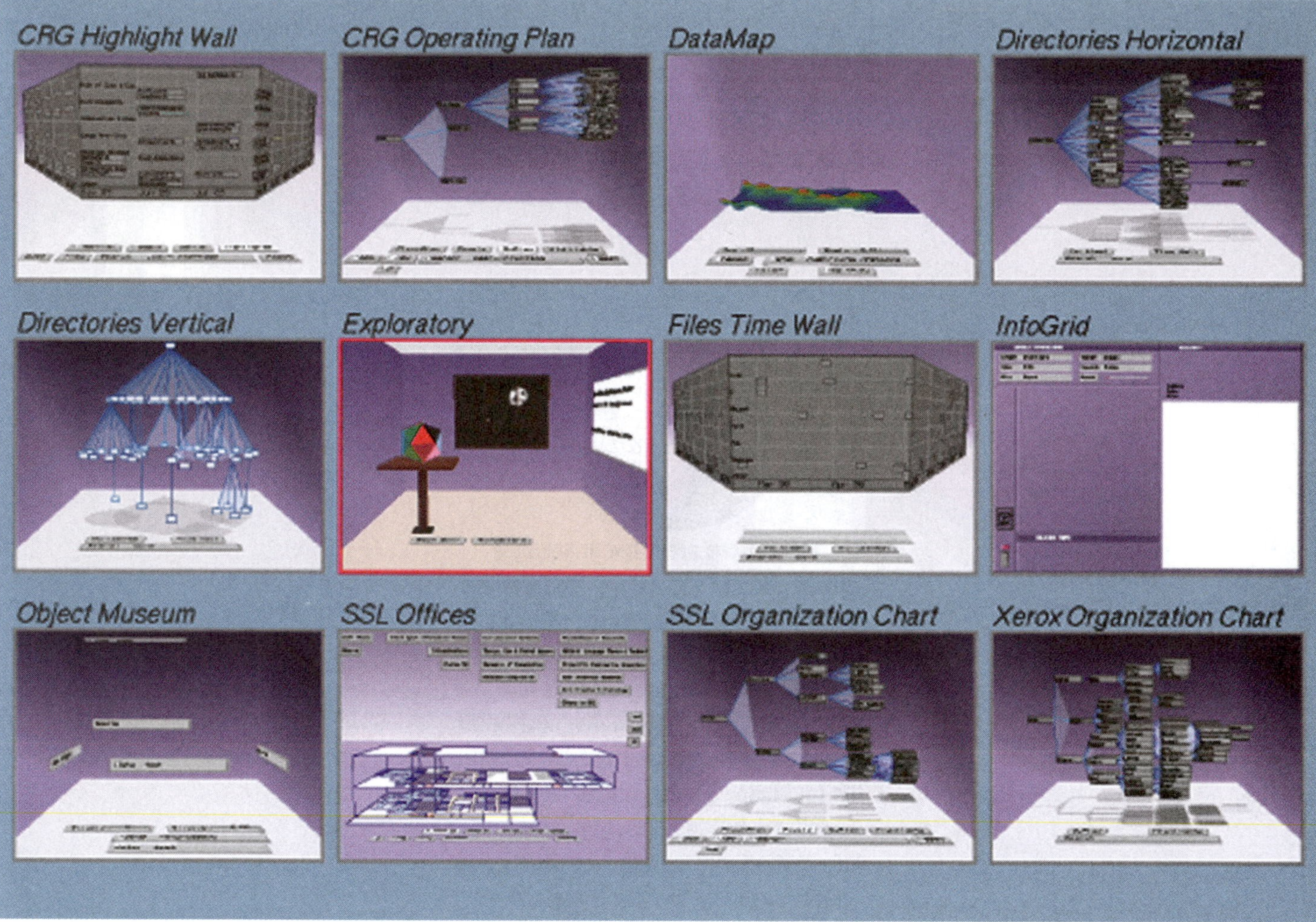

Figure 1.
Information Visualizer Overview

We take four broad strategies: making the user's immediate workspace larger, enabling user interaction with multiple agents, increasing the real-time interaction rate between user and system, and using visual abstraction to shift information to the perceptual system to speed information assimilation and retrieval.

Technology Advances

Since the early development of the standard GUI, hardware technology has continued to advance rapidly. Processor and memory technology have far greater performance at far lower cost. Specialized 3D graphics hardware has made it progressively faster and cheaper to do 3D transformations, hidden-surface removal, double-buffered animation, antialiasing, and lighting and surface models. At the same time, software support for real-time operating systems and emerging industry standard open graphics libraries (e.g., OpenGL and PEX) are simplifying the 3D programming task. The trend will bring these technologies to the mass market in the near future.

These technology advances have created many possibilities for user interface innovation. Yet the basic Windows-Icons-Menus-Pointing (WIMP) desktop metaphor has not changed much since its emergence in the Alto/Smalltalk work. Nonetheless, there is a great desire to explore new UI paradigms. Experiments with pen-based notebook metaphors, virtual reality, and ubiquitous computing are proceeding and may eventually influence the mass market. Brown University's Andy van Dam, in several recent conferences has exhorted us to break out of the desktop metaphor and escape flatland and a recent workshop focused on Software Architectures for Non-WIMP User Interfaces [9]. It is this kind of technology change that is driving our research in the Information Visualizer.

Information Access vs. Document Retrieval

Computer-aided access to information is often thought of in the context of methods for library automation. In particular, document retrieval [19] is usually defined more or less as follows: There exists a set of documents and a person who has an interest in the information in some of them. Those documents that contain information of interest are *relevant*, others not. The problem is to find all and only the relevant documents. There are two standard figures of merit for comparing and evaluating retrieval systems: *Recall* is the percentage of all the relevant documents found; and *precision* is the percentage of the documents found that are relevant. While this formulation has been useful for comparing different approaches, we propose extending the document retrieval formulation to take the larger context into account. From a user's point of view, document retrieval and other forms of information retrieval are almost always part of some larger process of information use [2]. Examples are *sensemaking* (building an interpretation of understanding of information), *design* (building an artifact), *decision making* (building a decision and its rationale), and *response tasks* (finding information to respond to a query).

In each of these cases:

1. Information is used to produce more information, or to act directly
2. The new information is usually at a higher level of organization relative to some purpose

If we represent the usual view of information retrieval as Figure 2(a), we can represent this extended view as Figure 2(b). Framing the problem in this way is suggestive: what the user needs is not so much information retrieval itself, but rather the amplification of information-based work processes. That is, in addition to concern with recall and precision, we also need to be concerned with reducing the time cost of information access and increasing the scale of information that a user can handle at one time.

Information Workspaces

From our observations about the problem of information access [2], we were led to develop UI paradigms oriented toward managing the cost structure of information-based work. This, in turn, led us to be concerned not just with the retrieval of information from a distant source, but also with the accessing of that information once it is retrieved and in use. The need for a low-cost, immediate storage for accessing objects in use is common to most kinds of work. The common solution is a *workspace*, whether it be a woodworking shop, a laboratory, or an office. A workspace is a special environment in which the cost structure of the needed materials is tuned to the requirements of the work process using them.

Computer screens provide a workspace for tasks done with the computer. However, typical computer displays provide limited working space. For real work, one often wants to use a much larger space, such as a dining room table. The Rooms system [10] was developed to extend the WIMP desktop to multiple workspaces that users could switch among, allowing more information to reside in the immediate work area. The added cost of switching and finding the right workspace was reduced by adding the ability to share the same information objects in different workspaces. Rooms also had an overview and other navigational aids as well as the ability to store and retrieve workspaces, all to remove the major disadvantages of multiple desktops.

The essence of our proposal is to evolve the Rooms multiple desktop metaphor into a workspace for information access—an *Information Workspace* [2]. Unlike the conventional information retrieval notion of simple access of information from some distal storage, an information workspace (1) treats the complete cost structure of information, integrating information access from distant, secondary or tertiary storage with information access from Immediate Storage for information in use, and (2) considers information access part of a larger work process. That is, instead of concentrating narrowly on the control of a search engine, the goal is to improve the cost structure of information access for user work.

With this system, we use four methods for improving the cost structure of information access:

1. *Large Workspace.* Make the Immediate Workspace virtually larger, so that the information can be held in low-cost storage
2. *Agents.* Delegate part of the workload to semiautonomous agents
3. *Real-Time Interaction.* Maximize interaction rates with the human user by tuning the displays and responses to real-time human action constants
4. *Visual Abstractions.* Use visual abstractions of the information to speed assimilation and pattern detection

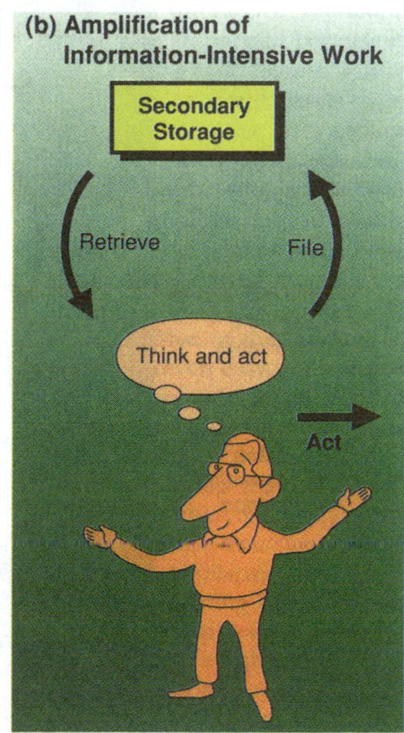

Figure 2. (a) Traditional information retrieval formulation and (b) reformulation with context of use

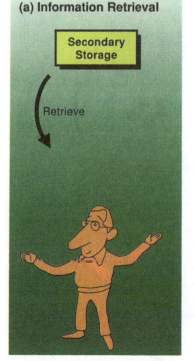

Table 1. Techniques used in the Information Visualizer to increase information access per unit cost

System Goal	Techniques
1. Large workspace to reduce access cost	More screen space → Rooms Denser screen space → Animation, 3D
2. Offload work to agents	search → search agents Organizing → clustering agents Interacting → Interactive Objects
3. Maximize real-time interaction rates	Rapid interaction, Tune to human constants → Cognitive Coprocessor Scheduler and Governor
4. Visual abstraction to speed pattern detection	Information Visualizations: Hierarchical structure → Cone Tree Linear structure → Perspective Wall Continuous data → Data Sculpture Spatial data → Office Floor Plan

Table 2. Information Visualizer solutions to basic UI problems.

Problem	Solution
1. Multiple Agent problem	Cognitive Coprocessor scheduler
2. Animation problem	Cognitive Coprocessor scheduler and governor
3. Interaction problem	Interactive Objects
4. Viewpoint Movement problem	Point of Interest Logarithmic Flier
5. Object Movement problem	Object of Interest Logarithmic Manipulator
6. Small Screen problem	3D/Rooms and 3D visualizations

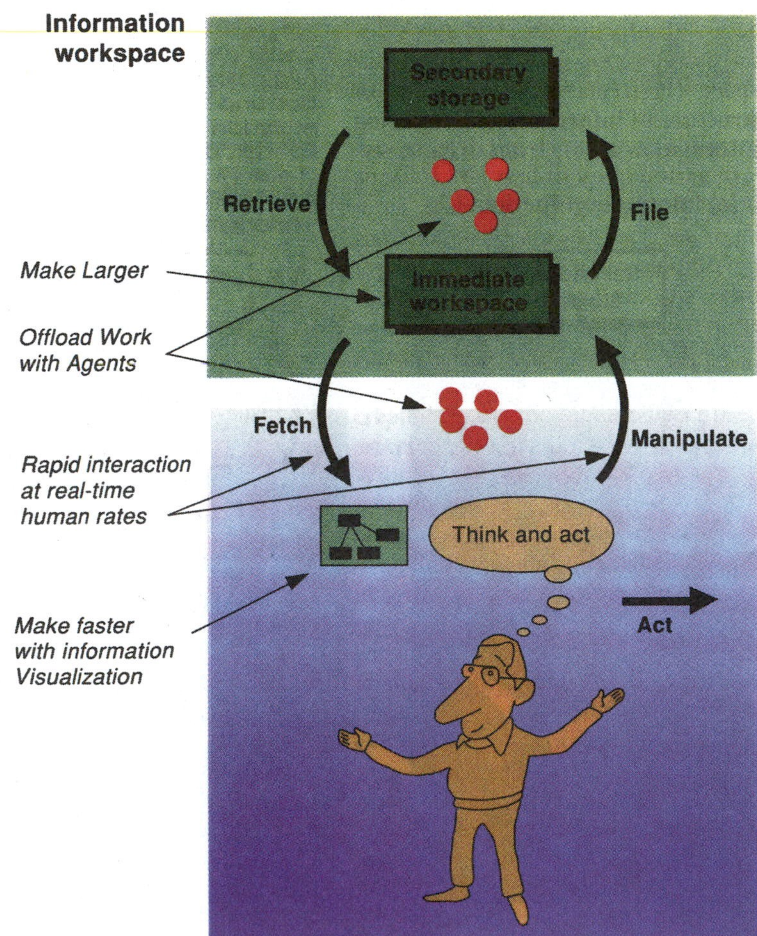

Figure 3. Improving the information cost structure in the information access model

These define the goals for our UI paradigm. Each of these is intended to decrease the costs for performing information-intensive tasks, or, alternatively, to increase the scope of information that can be utilized for the same cost. Figure 3 shows how these goals are applied to the reformulated information access problem shown in Figure 2(b).

The Information Visualizer system is our experimental embodiment of the Information Workspace concept with mechanisms for addressing each of these system goals (see Table 1): 1) [Large Workspace]. We use two methods to make the workspace larger: We add *more (virtual) screen space* to the Immediate Workspace by using a version of the Rooms system. We *increase the density of information* that can be held in the same screen space by using animation and 3D perspective. 2) [Agents]. To delegate part of the workload, we use agents to conduct searches, to organize information into clusters, or design presentations of information. We manage this by means of a scheduling architecture, called the Cognitive Coprocessor [17], that allows multiple display and application processes to run together. A kind of user interface agent, called Interactive Objects, is used to control and communicate with the system. 3) [Real-time Interaction]. To maximize human interaction rates, we use the properties of the scheduler to provide highly interactive animation and communication with the Interactive Objects. To tune the system to human action times, we require certain classes of actions to occur at set rates. To enforce these rates under varying computational load, we use a Governor mechanism in our scheduler loop. 4) [Visual Abstractions]. To speed the user's ability to assimilate information and find patterns in it, we use visualization of different abstract information structures, including linear structures, hierarchical structures, continuous data, and spatial data.

There have been many systems that have supported interactive animation-oriented UIs, starting with Ivan Sutherland's thesis [23] at the dawn of computer graphics. As with Sutherland's thesis, early examples required specialized and/or expensive computing machinery and were oriented toward specialized tasks. Cockpit simulation systems are a good example. The architectures for such systems share the animation-loop core with our system. The drop in cost for 3D animated systems and the increase in capability has accelerated experiments in using this technology as the basis of a new mass market user interface paradigm. One strategy has been to work up from building blocks. A. Van Dam's group at Brown has been working on an object-oriented framework for interactive animation, 3D widgets [3], and modeling time in 3D interactive animation systems. Silicon Graphics has recently introduced a high-level 3D toolkit, called Inventor. Another tack has been to drive the development by focusing on applications, for example, continuously running physical simulations. M. Green's group at the University of Alberta has developed a Decoupled Simulation Model for virtual reality systems [20]. Their architectural approach is similar to ours, but focuses more on continuously running simulations. D. Zeltzer and colleagues at MIT [25] have built a constraint-based system for interactive physical simulation. Our system, by contrast, is oriented toward the access and visualization of abstract nonphysical information of the form that knowledge workers would encounter.

UI Architecture

In order to achieve the goals set forth in Table 1 we have been led to a UI paradigm involving highly interactive animation, 3D, agents, and visualizations. This is one of the UI regimes now being made practical by current and predicted advances in hardware and software technology. There are several problems, however, which need to be addressed in order to realize such a UI paradigm:

1. *The Multiple Agent Problem.* How can the architecture provide a systematic way to manage the interactions of multiple asynchronous agents?
2. *The Animation Problem.* How can the architecture provide smooth interactive animation *and* solve the Multiple Agent problem?
3. *The Interaction Problem.* How can 3D widgets be designed and coupled to appropriate application behavior?
4. *The Viewpoint Movement Problem.* How can the user rapidly and simply move the point of view around in a 3D space?
5. *The Object Movement Problem.* How can objects be easily moved about in a 3D space?
6. *The Small Screen Space Problem.* How can the dynamic properties of the system be utilized to provide the user with an adequately large workspace?

Many of these problems are well known. The Multiple Agent and Animation problems are less obvious, and since they define the basic organization of the Information Visualizer, we describe them in more detail.

The Multiple Agent Problem. We want our architecture to support multiple agents to which the user can delegate tasks. In fact, we have previously argued [17] that T.B. Sheridan's analysis of the supervisory control of semiautonomous embedded systems [21] can be adapted to describe the behavior of an interactive system as the product of the interactions of (at least) three agents: a *user,* a *user discourse machine* (the UI), and a task machine or *application.* These agents operate with very different time constants. For example, a search process in an application and the graphical display of its results may be slow, while the user's perception of displayed results may be quite fast. The UI must provide a form of "impedance matching" (dealing with different time constants) between the various agents as well as translate between different languages of interaction. The application itself may be broken into various agents that supply services, some of which may run on distributed machines (e.g., an agent to filter and sort your mail). Even the UI may itself contain agents (e.g., presentation agents). These additional agents have their own time constants and languages of interaction that must be accommodated by the UI.

Impedance matching can be difficult to accomplish architecturally because all agents want rapid interaction with no forced waiting on other agents, and the user wants to be able to change his or her focus of attention rapidly as new information becomes available. For example, if a user initiates a long search that provides intermediate results as they become available, the user should be able to abort or redirect the search at any point (e.g., based on perception of the intermediate results), without waiting for a display or search process to complete. The UI architecture must provide a systematic way to manage the interactions of multiple asynchronous agents that can interrupt and redirect one another's work.

The Animation Problem. Over the last 65 years, animation has grown from a primitive art form to a very complex and effective discipline for communication. Interactive animation is particularly demanding architecturally, because of its extreme computational requirements.

Smooth interactive animation is particularly important because it can shift a user's task from cognitive to perceptual activity, freeing cognitive processing capacity for application tasks. For example, interactive animation supports object constancy. Consider an animation of a complex object that represents some complex relationships. When the user rotates this object, or moves around the object, animation of that motion makes it possible (even easy, since it is at the level of perception) for the user to retain the relationships of what is displayed. Without animation, the display would jump from one configuration to another, and the user would have to spend time (and cognitive effort) reassimilating the new display. By providing object constancy, animation significantly reduces the cognitive load on the user.

The Animation Problem arises when building a system that attempts to provide smooth interactive animation *and* solve the Multiple Agent problem. The difficulty is that smooth animation requires a fixed rate of guaranteed computational resource, while the highly interactive and redirectable support of multiple asynchronous agents with different time constants has widely varying computational requirements. The UI architecture must balance and protect these very different computational requirements.

In fact, the animation problem is one aspect of a broader Real-Time Interaction problem. Services need to be delivered under real-time deadline, under varying load, while simultaneously handling the Multiple Agent problem.

The Cognitive Coprocessor

Table 2 summarizes the Information Visualizer's solutions to each of the problems described earlier. The next few sections describe these solutions.

The heart of the Information Visualizer architecture is a controlled-resource scheduler, the Cognitive Coprocessor architecture, which serves as an animation loop and a scheduler for Sheridan's three agents and additional application and interface agents. It manages multiple asynchronous agents that operate with different time constants and need to interrupt and redirect one another's work. These agents range from trivial agents that update display state to continuous-running simulations and search agents. This architecture provides the basic solution to the Multiple Agent and Animation problems.

The Cognitive Coprocessor is an impedance matcher between the cognitive and perceptual information processing requirements of the user and the properties of these agents. In general, these agents operate on time constants different from those of the user. There are three sorts of time constants for the human that we want to tune the system to meet: perceptual processing (0.1 second) [1], immediate response (1 second) [15], and unit task (10 seconds) [15].

The perceptual processing time constant. The Cognitive Coprocessor is based on a continuously running scheduler loop and double-buffered graphics. In order to maintain the illusion of animation in the world, the screen must be repainted at least every 0.1 second [1]. The Cognitive Coprocessor therefore has a *Governor* mechanism that monitors the basic cycle time. When the cycle time becomes too high, cooperating rendering processes reduce the quality of rendering (e.g., leaving off most of the text during motion) so that the cycle speed is increased.

The immediate response time constant. A person can make an unprepared response to some stimulus within about a second [15]. If there is more than a second, then either the listening party makes a back-channel response to indicate that he is listening (e.g., "uh-huh") or the speaking party makes a response (e.g., "uh...") to indicate he is still thinking of the next speech. These serve to keep the parties of the interaction informed that they are still engaged in an interaction. In the Cognitive Coprocessor, we attempt to have agents provide status feedback at intervals no longer than this constant. Immediate response animations (e.g., swinging the branches of a 3D tree into view) are designed to take about a second. If the time were much shorter, then the user would lose object constancy and would have to reorient himself. If they were much longer, then the user would get bored waiting for the response.

The unit task time constant. Finally, a user should be able to complete some elementary task act within about 10 seconds (say, 5 to 30 seconds) [1, 15]. This is about the pacing of a point and click editor. Information agents may require considerable time to complete some complicated request, but the user, in this paradigm, always stays active. A user can begin the next request as soon as sufficient information has developed from the last request or even in parallel with it.

The basic control mechanism (inner loop) of the Cognitive Coprocessor is called the *Animation Loop* (see Figure 4). It maintains a *Task Queue*, a *Display Queue*, and a *Governor*. Built on top of the Animation Loop is an information workspace manager (and support for 3D simulated environments), called *3D/Rooms;* supports for navigating around 3D environments; and support for *Interactive Objects,* which provide basic input/output mechanisms for the UI. The task machine (which, for the Information Visualization application, is a collection of visualizers) couples with the Cognitive Copocessor in various ways. More details of this architecture can be found in [17].

Interactive Objects

The basic building block in the Information Visualizer, called *Interactive Objects,* forms the basis for coupling user interaction with application behavior and offloading work to an agent to handle user interaction. Interactive Objects are a generalization of Rooms Buttons [10]. They are used to build complex 3D widgets that represent information or information structure.

Rooms Buttons are used for a variety of purposes, such as movement, new interface building blocks, and task assistance. A Button has an appearance (typically, a bitmap) and a selection action (a procedure to execute when the Button is 'pressed'). The most typical Button in Rooms is a door—when selected, the user passes from one Room to another. Buttons are abstractions that can be passed from one Room to another, and from one user to another via email. Interactive Objects are similar to Buttons, but are extended to deal with gestures, animation, 2D or 3D appearance, manipulation, object-relative navigation, and an extensible set of types.

An Interactive Object can have any 2D or 3D appearance defined by a draw method. The notion of selection is generalized to allow mouse-based gestural input in addition to simple 'pressing'. Whenever a user gestures at an Interactive Object, a gesture parser is involved that interprets mouse movement and classifies it as one of a small set of easily differentiated gestures (e.g., press, rubout, check, and flick). Once a gesture has been identified, a gesture-specific method is called. These gesture methods are specified when the Interactive Object is created. The gesture parser can be easily extended to allow additional gestures and gesture methods, as long as the new gestures are easily differentiated from other gestures.

There are a number of types of Interactive Objects. In the current implementation, these include static text, editable text, date entry, number entry, set selection, checkmark, simple button, doors, sliders, and thermometers (for feedback and progress indicators). The basic set of 3D widgets supported for Interactive Objects can be easily extended.

Interactive Objects are generalized to the point that every visible entity in the simulated scene can be an Interactive Object (and should be, so that object-relative navigation is consistent across the scene). Thus, the surfaces of the 3D Room (the walls, floor, and ceiling) are Interactive Objects. All the controls (e.g., buttons, sliders, thermometers, text, and editable text) are Interactive Objects. And finally, the application-specific artifacts placed in the room are Interactive Objects.

Search Agents

Search agents are also used to offload user work. The Information Visualizer uses an indexing and search subsystem [5], which allows search for documents by keyword or by iterative "relevance feedback" (e.g., find the documents most like this document). Associative retrieval based on such linguistic searches can be used to highlight portions of an information visualization. Thus we can combine traditional associative searches with structural browsing.

In addition, clustering agents are used to organize information. Using a near-linear clustering algorithm [4], which allows interactive use of clustering, a structure can be induced on an unstructured (or partially structured) body of information. There are several ways this can be of use. For unstructured information, a user can induce a subject hierarchy, which can then be browsed with our hierarchy visualization tools. For information that already has a structure, the clustering results sometimes reveal problems with the existing structure. In general, if a

The heart of the Information Visualizer architecture is a controlled resource scheduler, the Cognitive Coprocessor architecture, *which serves as an animation loop and a scheduler for Sheridan's three agents and additional application and interface agents.*

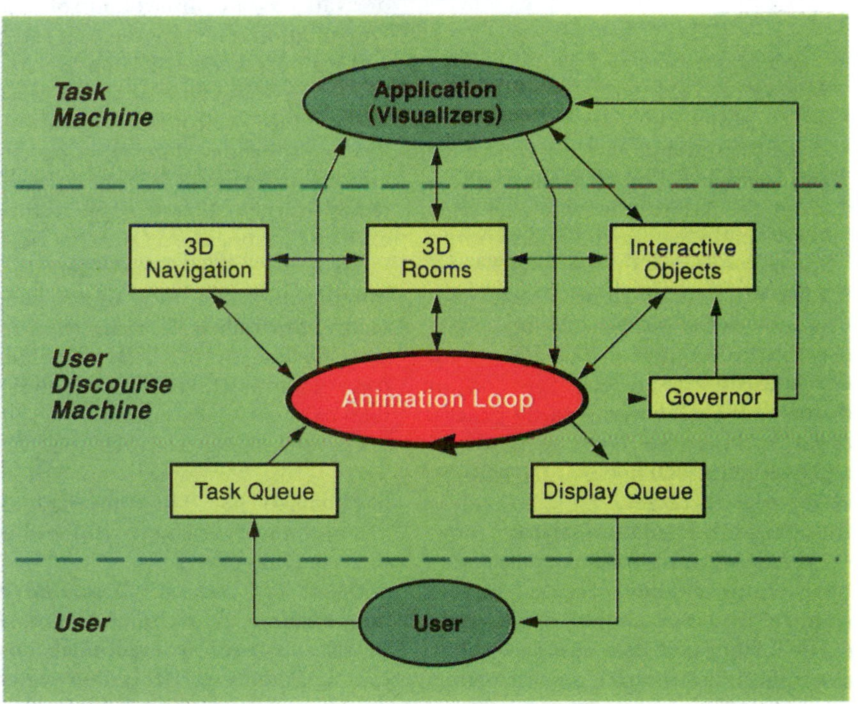

Figure 4. Cognitive Coprocessor Interaction architecture

user is unsure about the content of a corpus, and therefore unsure of what kinds of queries to make, clustering can provide an overview of the content of that corpus.

3D Navigation and Manipulation

In virtual 3D workspaces, techniques are required for moving the user (the viewpoint) and objects around the space. The Information Visualizer currently has five of these as building blocks, with others under development:

1. The Walking Metaphor
2. Point of Interest Logarithmic Flight
3. Object of Interest Logarithmic Manipulation
4. Doors
5. Overview

Walking Metaphor. The 'Walking Metaphor' [13] has virtual joystick controls superimposed as heads-up displays on the screen and controlled by the mouse. The controls are operators related to the way a human body might be moved (one control for body motion forward, backward, turn-left, or turn-right; a second for motion in the plane of the body: left, right, up, or down; and a third for rotating the head left, right, up, or down). This scheme is fairly general and works well for exploratory movement, which has no particular object as its target.

Large information spaces, however, involve numerous objects and/or highly detailed objects that require the user to move back and forth from global, orienting views to manipulate detailed information. Therefore, an important requirement for such systems is a movement technique that allows the user to move the viewpoint (1) rapidly through large distances, (2) with such control that the viewpoint can approach very close to a target without collision. We call this the problem of *rapid and controlled, targeted 3D movement* [12].

Point of Interest (POI) Logarithmic Flight. Our second navigation technique uses a point of interest logarithmic movement algorithm for very rapid, but precise movement relative to objects of interest [12]. Current techniques for moving the viewpoint [13] are not very satisfactory for targeted movement. They typically exhibit one or more of the following three problems: (1) inefficient interactions and movement trajectories, typically caused by 2D input devices; (2) difficulties controlling high velocities when the technique is based on flying or steering the viewpoint through the workspace; and (3) limits on human reach and precision when the technique is based on directly positioning the viewpoint.

Most viewpoint movement techniques focus on schemes for directly controlling the six degrees of freedom of viewpoint movement (3 position and 3 orientation) or their rate derivatives—a complex control task. Our solution is to have the user select a point of interest (POI) on the surface of an object and use the distance to this POI to calculate a logarithmic motion function. Two keys on the keyboard are used to indicate logarithmic motion along the ray toward and away from the POI. The viewpoint is automatically oriented during the flight to face the surface being approached by using the surface normal at the POI. Another control allows movement perpendicular to the surface normal. This allows for scrolling over extended objects (for example, a virtual blackboard) or circumnavigation around spherical objects (for example, a virtual globe.)

Object of Interest Logarithmic Manipulation. Logarithmic motion can also be used to manipulate objects with the same UI as POI viewpoint movement. The mouse cursor is used to control a ray that determines the lateral position of the object of interest (given the viewpoint coordinates) and the same keyboard keys are used to control the position of the object on the ray. However, the user must be able to control object position at a distance, where logarithmic motion is not effective. The solution is to use an acceleration motion clipped by a logarithmic motion. The object moves slowly at first (allowing control at a distance), then accelerates toward the viewpoint, and finally moves logarithmically slower for control near the viewpoint.

POI logarithmic flight and object of interest logarithmic manipulation both allow simple, rapid movement of the viewpoint and of objects in a 3D space over multiple degrees of freedom and scales of magnitude with only a mouse and two keyboard keys. We believe these techniques provide a mouse-based solution for the viewpoint movement and object movement problems that are as good or even better than those requiring special 3D devices. The chief advantage of a mouse-based solution is that mice are ubiquitous. Also, many users of information visualization (office workers, for example) are not likely to be willing to wear special equipment (such as gloves and helmets). Even so, the techniques could be adjusted to work with 3D devices such as the glove.

Doors. The 3D/Rooms system supports Doors that allow a user to move from one room (or workspace) through to a home position in another room. The Door is an Interactive Object that supports either manual control or scripted animation of opening and walking through to the other room.

Overview. As with Rooms, 3D/Rooms contains an *Overview* (see Figure 1) allowing the user to view all the 3D workspaces simultaneously. This is a navigation technique that lets the user view all the rooms and go to any room directly. In 3D/Rooms the user can also reach into the Rooms from the Overview, move about in them, and manipulate their objects.

3D/Rooms

3D/Rooms extends the logic of our Rooms system to three dimensions. In the classical desktop metaphor and the original Rooms system, the view of a Room is fixed. In 3D/Rooms, the user is given a position and orientation in the Room, and can move about the Room, zoom in to examine objects closely, look around, or even walk through doors into other Rooms. Thus 3D/Rooms is the same as Rooms, except that visualization artifacts (implemented as Interactive Objects) replace a collection of windows, and users can have arbitrary positions and orientations in the Rooms.

The effect of 3D/Rooms is to make the screen space for immediate storage of information effectively *larger* (in the sense that the user can get to a larger amount of ready-to-use information in a short time). The effect of rapid zooming, animation, and 3D is to make the screen space effectively *denser* (in the sense that the same amount of screen can hold more objects, which the user can zoom into or animate into view in a short time). By manipulating objects or moving in space, the user can disambiguate images, reveal hidden information, or zoom in for detail—rapidly accessing more information. Both the techniques for making the Immediate Storage space virtually larger and the techniques for making the space virtually denser should make its capacity larger, hence the average cost of accessing information lower, hence the cost of working on large information-intensive tasks lower.

Information Visualization

Recent work in scientific visualization shows how the computer can serve as an intermediary in the process of rapid assimilation of information. Large sets of data are reduced to graphic form in such a way that human perception can detect patterns revealing underlying structure in the data more readily than by a direct analysis of the numbers. Information in the form of documents also has structure. *Information visualization* attempts to display structural relationships and context that would be more difficult to detect by individual retrieval requests. Although much work has been done using 3D graphics to visualize physical objects or phenomena, only a few systems have exploited 3D visualization for visualizing more abstract data or information structure.

The SemNet [6] system is an early example of the exploitation of 3D visualization of information structures. The structures visualized in SemNet were mostly large knowledge bases, and were often arbitrary graphs. The results tended to be cluttered, and the cognitive task of understanding the structure was still quite difficult.

The *n*-Vision system [7] exploits 3D to visualize *n*-dimensional business data. Multivariate functions are displayed in nested coordinates systems, using a metaphor called worlds-within-worlds. Although *n*-Vision focuses on continuous multivariate functions, it does exploit the human 3D perceptual apparatus to visualize abstract data.

Silicon Graphics has recently released an unsupported system, called File System Navigator (FSN) [24], which explores what they call Information Landscapes. In this system the file system hierarchy is laid out on a landscape, with each directory represented by a pedestal which has boxes representing individual files on top of it. They effectively use the 3D space to present structure, while using box size to represent file size and color to represent age. FSN uses a technique called 'artificial perspective', a form of fisheye effect [8], to make more effective use of screen space.

In the Information Visualizer, we have explored 3D visualizations for some of the classical data organizations:

1. Hierarchical: The *Cone Tree* visualization [18] (see following description).
2. Linear: The *Perspective Wall* visualization [14] (see following description).
3. Spatial: The spatial structure of a building (see Figure 5) can be used as a structural browser for people. Selecting an organization will produce the names and pictures of its members and select their offices. Clicking on offices retrieves their inhabitants.
4. Continuous Data: In the Data Sculpture (see Figure 6), the user can walk around or zoom into this visualization containing over 65,000 sampling points as if it were a sculpture in a museum.
5. Unstructured: The Information Grid [16] is a 2D visualization for unstructured information.

These visualizations use interactive animation to explore dynamically changing views of the information structures. More visualizations are visible in the 3D/Rooms Overview of Figure 1. The visualizers attempt to present abstractions of large amounts of data tuned to the pattern detection properties of the human perceptual system. For example, they use color, lighting, shadow, transparency, hidden surface occlusion, continuous transformation, and motion cues to induce object constancy and 3D perspective.

Visualizing Hierarchical Structure: Cone Trees

Hierarchies are almost ubiquitous, appearing in many different applications, hence are good information structures to exploit. In some cases, arbitrary graphs can be transformed into hierarchies (with auxiliary links), so the utility of hierarchy visualization is further enhanced.

Cone Trees are hierarchies laid out uniformly in three dimensions. Figure 7 is a snapshot of a simple Cone Tree. Nodes are drawn as 3- × 5-inch index cards. The top of the hierarchy is placed near the ceiling of the room, and is the apex of a cone with its children placed evenly spaced along its base. The next layer of nodes is drawn below the first, with their children in cones. The aspect ratio of the tree is fixed to fit the room. Each layer has cones of the same height (the room height divided by the tree depth). Cone base diameters for each level are reduced in a progression so that the bottom layer fits in the width of the room. The body of each cone is shaded transparently, so that the cone is easily perceived yet does not block the view of cones behind it. The display of node text does not fit the aspect ratio of the cards very well, hence text is shown only for the selected path. Figure 8 shows an alternative layout, which is horizontally oriented and has text displayed for each node.

When a node is selected with the mouse, the Cone Tree rotates so that the selected node and each node in the path from the selected node up to the top are brought to the front and highlighted. The rotations of each substructure are done in parallel, following the shortest rotational path, and are animated so the user sees the transformation at a rate the

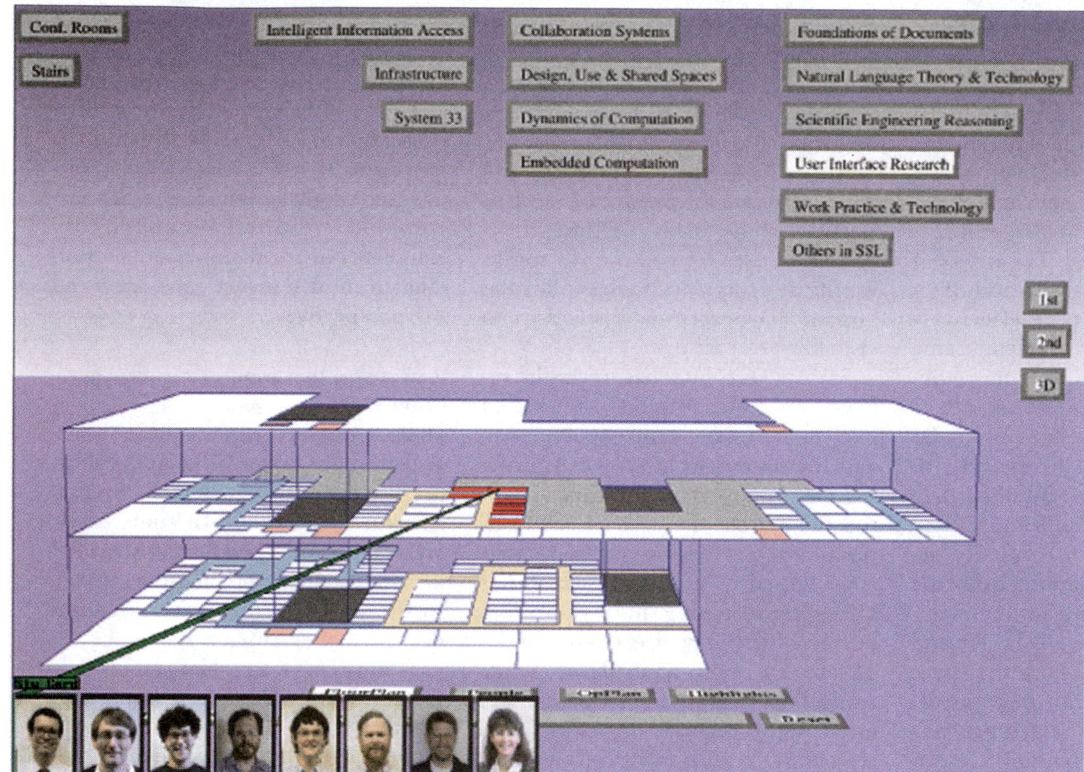

FIGURE 5

Visualization of partial floor plan of Xerox PARC

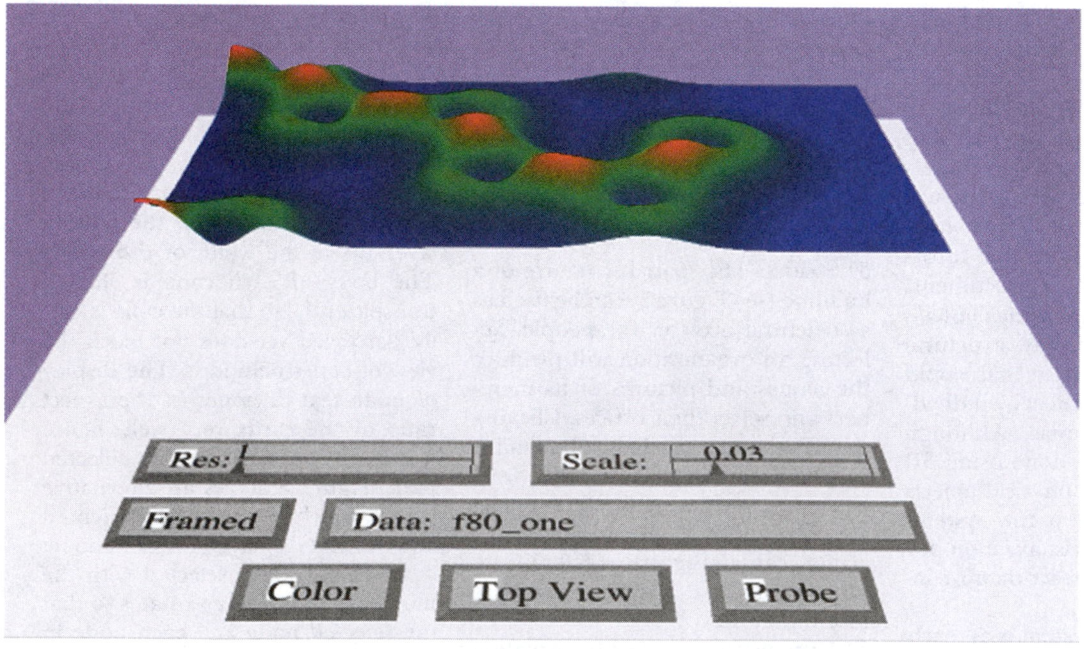

FIGURE 6

Data Sculpture visualization, showing a theoretical cross-section of a chain of silicon atoms

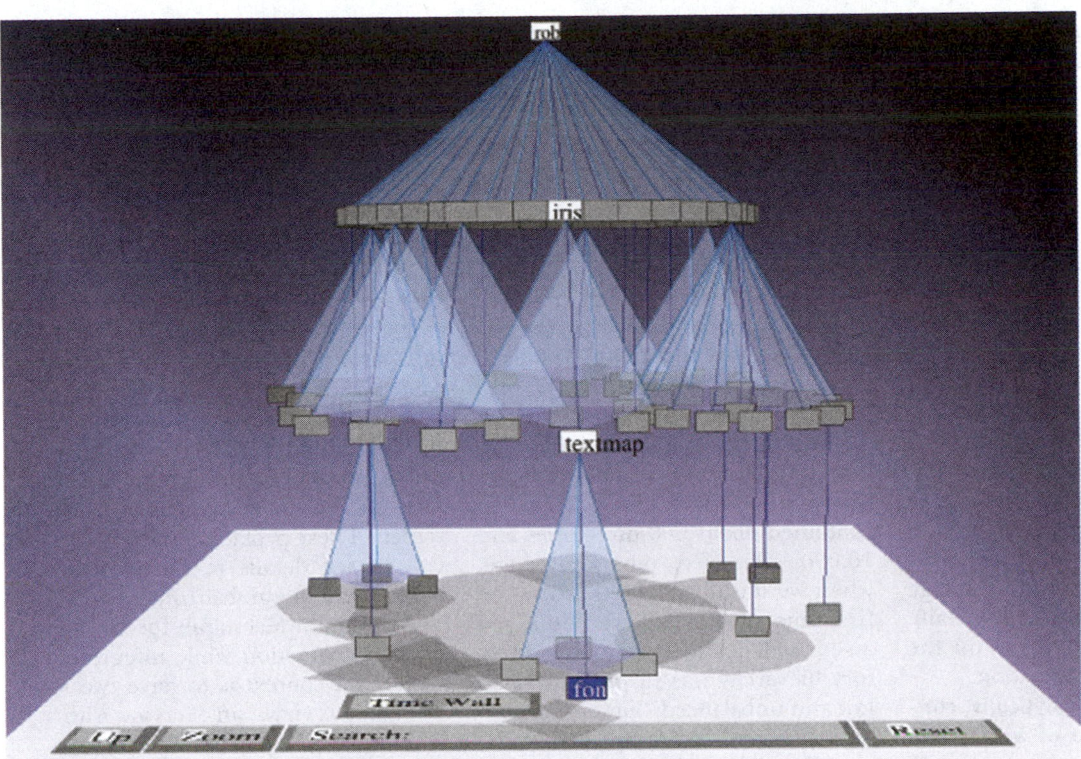

FIGURE 7

Cone Tree visualization of a directory hierarchy

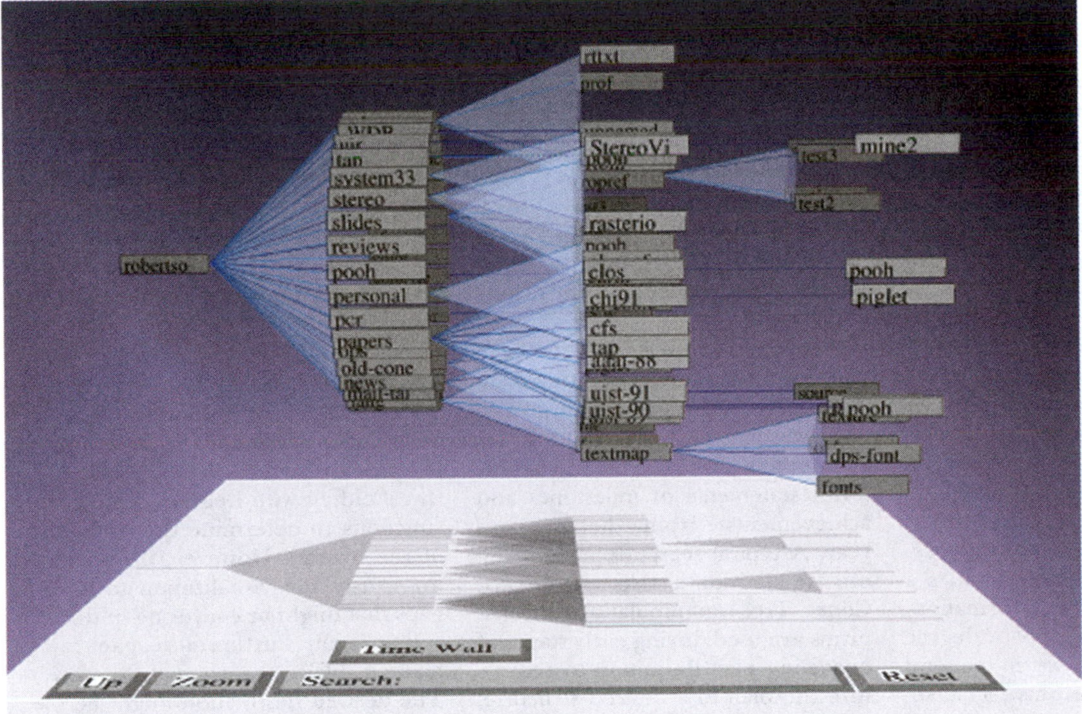

FIGURE 8

Horizontal Cone Tree visualization of a directory hierarchy

perceptual system can track. Typically, the entire transformation is done in about a second. The tree can also be rotated continuously to help the user understand substructure relationships.

The hierarchy is presented in 3D to maximize effective use of available screen space and enable visualization of the whole structure. A 2D layout of the same structure using conventional graph layout algorithms would not fit on the screen. The user would have to either scroll through the layout or use a size-reduced image of the structure. Most hierarchies encountered in real applications tend to be broad and shallow. This typical hierarchy aspect ratio is problematic for 2D layouts (a size-reduced image may look like a line with little detail). A 3D layout uses depth to fill the screen with more information.

To see this effect analytically, consider the aspect ratio of a 2D tree, ignoring the size of the nodes. If there are l levels and the branching factor is b, the width of the base is b^{l-1} and the aspect ratio is b^{l-1}/l. Aspect ratio for 2D trees increases nearly exponentially, and is much worse as the branching factor gets larger. Figure 9 shows what happens for small branching factors ($b = 2$ and $b = 3$). In contrast, the Cone Tree aspect ratio is fixed to fit the room by adjusting level height and cone diameters to fit. The line near the bottom of Figure 9 is a typical aspect ratio of four to three. Although fixing the aspect ratio introduces a limitation on the number of levels that can be effectively displayed (about 10), it makes Cone Trees independent of the number of nodes, branching factor, and number of levels (until the limit is reached).

In addition to perceptual effects already mentioned, the 3D perspective view of Cone Trees provides a fisheye view [8] of the information, without having to describe a degree of interest function, as in general fisheye view mechanisms. The selected path is brighter, closer, and larger than other paths, both because of the 3D perspective view and because of coloring and simulated lighting. SemNet [6] also reported a fisheye view effect from their use of 3D perspective. Our fisheye view effect is further enhanced by selection rotation, because the user can easily select a new object of interest and have the structure quickly reconfigure to highlight it.

Cone Tree: Examples

In Figures 7 and 8, Cone Trees are used for a file browser, showing one user's directory hierarchy, with each node representing a directory in a Unix file system. Information access is done on file names and file contents. We have also visualized an entire Unix directory hierarchy, which contained about 600 directories and 10,000 files. To our knowledge, when we did this in 1989, it was the first time anyone had ever visualized an entire Unix file system. The directory hierarchy was surprisingly shallow and unbalanced. Since then, both FSN [24] and TreeMaps [11] (a 2D visualization technique) have been used to visualize entire file systems.

Cone Trees have also been used as an organizational structure browser. Search is done in a database of facts about each person (e.g., title or office location) and a database of autobiographies. Users can search for other people with biographies similar to a selected person's biography. We have implemented several organization charts. The largest contained the top 650 Xerox Corporation executives. Since this requires 80 pages on paper, this is the first time the organization chart could be seen in one visualization.

We also have used Cone Trees to visualize a company's operating plan. Text narratives describe each portfolio, program, and project, and are augmented with project highlights (brief statements of milestones and achievements) from the previous year. A typical search finds all projects related to a selected project. Cone Tree manipulation mechanisms are used during early stages of operating plan definition to reorganize the plan to a desired structure.

Other potential applications include software module management, document management (library structure and book structure), object-oriented class browsers, and local area network browsers.

Visualizing Linear Structures: Perspective Wall

Case studies indicate that tasks often involve *spanning* properties (such as time) that structure information linearly [14]. This linear structure results in 2D layouts with wide aspect ratios that are difficult to accommodate in a single view. The principal obstacles to a visualization of linear information structures are (1) the large amount of information that must be displayed and (2) the difficulty of accommodating the extreme aspect ratio of the linear structure on the screen. These problems make it difficult to see details in the structure while retaining global context.

A common technique for viewing linear information while integrating detail and context is to have two simultaneous views: an overview with a scale-reduced version of a workspace, and a detailed view into the workspace where work can be accomplished. The overview typically contains an indication of the detailed view's location that can be manipulated for rapid movement through the workspace. However, a uniform scale reduction of the workspace causes it to appear very small. Furthermore, important contextual information, such as the neighborhood of the viewing region, is just as small as unimportant details. Finally, if the display space for the overview is increased to make the workspace appear larger, the space for the working view becomes too small.

Rather than a uniform overview of a workspace, an effective strategy is to distort the view so that details and context are integrated. Fisheye views [8] provide such distorted views by thresholding with Degree of Interest functions to determine the contents of the display. However, thresholding causes the visualization to have gaps that might be confusing or difficult to repair. Furthermore, gaps can make it difficult to change the view. The desired destination might be in one of the gaps, or the transition from one view to another might be confusing as familiar parts of the visualization suddenly disappear into gaps.

Spence and Apperley developed an early system called the Bifocal Display that integrates detail and context through another distorted view [22]. This 2D design is a conceptual ancestor of the Perspective Wall system. The Bifocal Display was designed for professional offices that contain information subdivided into a hierarchy of journals, volumes, issues and articles. Abstractly, the workspace consists of information items positioned in a horizontal strip. The display is a combination of a detailed view of the strip and two distorted views, where items on either side of the detailed view are distorted horizontally into narrow vertical strips. For example, the detailed view might contain a page from a journal and the distorted view might contain the years for various issues of the journal.

The *Perspective Wall* integrates detailed and contextual views to support the visualization of linearly structured information spaces, using interactive 3D animation to address the integration problems of the Bifocal Display. The Perspective Wall folds a 2D layout into a 3D wall that smoothly integrates a central region for viewing details with two perspective regions, one on each side, for viewing context (see Figure 10). This intuitive distortion of the layout provides efficient space utilization and allows smooth transitions of views. Space utilization analysis of the Perspective Wall technique indicates at least a three-fold improvement over simple 2D visualization (see [14] for details).

Perspective Wall: Implementation

The Perspective Wall's physical metaphor of folding is used to distort an arbitrary 2D layout into a 3D visualization (the wall), while automatically retaining any 2D task-specific features. More important, no special large- and small-scale versions of items must be designed (as in the Bifocal Display). The perspective panels are also shaded to enhance the perception of 3D. This intuitive visualization provides efficient space utilization for 2D layouts with wide aspect ratios. In addition, the vertical dimension of the wall can be used to

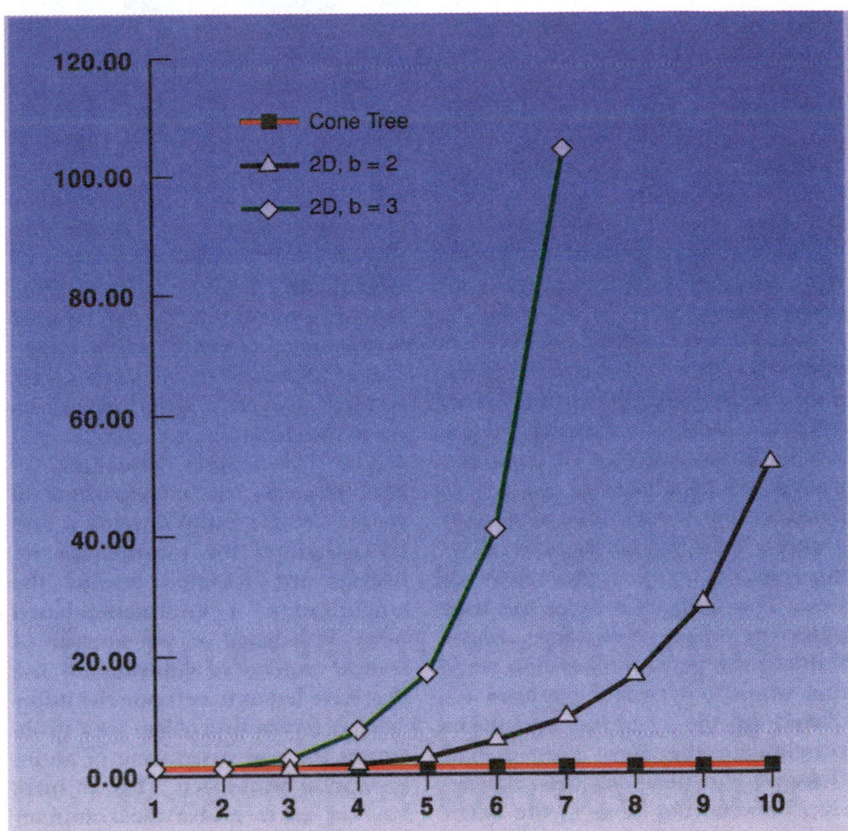

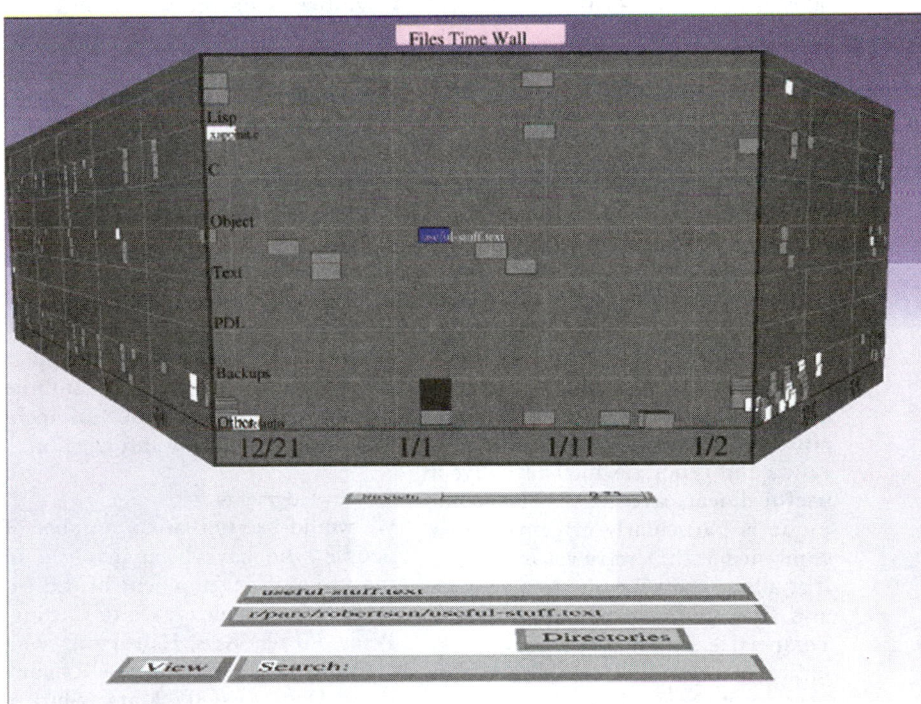

Figure 9. Aspect ratio of 2D and 3D trees

Figure 10. Perspective Wall visualization of files

visualize layering in an information space. The Perspective Wall in Figure 10 holds cards that represent files in a computer system that are structured by modification date (horizontally) and file type (vertically). The perspective view has the further advantage that it makes the neighborhood of the detailed view larger than more distant parts of the contextual view.

A major advantage of the Perspective Wall is that its intuitive 3D metaphor for distorting 2D layouts allows smooth transitions among views. When the user selects an item, the wall moves that item to the center panel with a smooth animation, as if it were a sheet in a player piano moving selected notes to the center of view. This animation helps the user perceive object constancy, which shifts to the perceptual system work that would otherwise have been required of the cognitive system to reassimilate the view after it had changed. Furthermore, the relationship between the items in the detail and context is obvious. Items even bend around the corner.

The Perspective Wall has the additional feature that the user can adjust the ratio of detail and context. This is quite important when the detailed view contains a lot of information. The metaphor is to stretch the wall like a sheet of rubber.

The Perspective Wall has been used to visualize various types of information. Figure 10 represents files in a file system that are classified by their modification date and file type. Vacations and other work patterns are clearly visible. The technique has also been used for corporate memoranda and reports, which also have a useful linear structure. The technique is particularly effective when combined with a retrieval technique that allows the user to select an item and find similar related items. The Perspective Wall makes it easy to visualize the results of such retrievals because it shows all similar items simultaneously and in context.

Summary

To summarize, we believe that the structure of information, the emerging technologies of 3D and interactive animation, and the human perceptual system can be effectively exploited to improve management of and access to large information spaces. There is a large class of applications for which these techniques work. It seems clear that interactive animation can effectively shift cognitive processing load to the perceptual system. And it seems plausible (but not yet proved) that 3D can be used to maximize effective use of screen space. Formal user studies are needed to verify and expand on these conclusions.

The Information Visualizer we have described is an experimental system being used to develop a new UI paradigm for information retrieval, one oriented toward the amplification of information-based work. It is based on our analysis of several aspects of information use that have led us to reframe the information retrieval problem as a problem in the cost structuring of an information workspace. This, in turn, has led us to evolve the computer desktop metaphor toward (1) the Cognitive Coprocessor interaction architecture (to support highly coupled iterative interaction with multiple agents), (2) 3D/Rooms (to manage information storage cost hierarchies), and (3) information visualization (to increase the level of information abstraction to the user). Collectively these techniques alter the cost of retrieving information from secondary storage and the cost of using it in workspace. Future work will focus on how these techniques aid in sensemaking, and will continue to explore the rich space of techniques for visualizing information.

Acknowledgments

We would like to thank a number of people who have been involved in the use and development of the Information Visualizer: Doug Cutting, Peter Pirolli, Kris Halverson, Walt Johnson, Jan Pedersen, Ramana Rao, Dan Russell, Mark Shirley, Mark Stefik, and Brian Williams.

References

1. Card, S.K., Moran, T.P. and Newell, A. *The Psychology of Human-Computer Interaction.* Erlbaum, Hillsdale, New Jersey, 1983.
2. Card, S.K., Robertson, G.G. and Mackinlay, J.D. The Information Visualizer: An information workspace. In *Proceedings of SIGCHI'91,* 1991, pp. 181–188.
3. Conner, D.B., Snibbe, S.S., Herndon, K.P., Robbins, D.C. and Zeleznik, R.C. Three-dimensional widgets. In *Proceedings of the 1992 Symposium on Interactive 3D Graphics,* 1992, pp. 183–188.
4. Cutting, D.R., Karger, D.R., Pedersen, J.O. and Tukey, J.W. Scatter/Gather: A cluster-based approach to browsing large document collections. In *Proceedings of SIGIR'92,* 1992, pp. 318–329.
5. Cutting, D.R., Pedersen, J.O. and Halvorsen, P.K. An object-oriented architecture for text retrieval. In *Proceedings of RIAO'91, Intelligent Text and Image Handling,* 1991, pp. 285–298.
6. Fairchild, K.M., Poltrock, S.E. and Furnas, G.W. Semnet: Three-dimensional graphic representations of large knowledge bases. In *Cognitive Science and its Applications for Human-Computer Interaction,* Guindon, R. Ed, Lawrence Erlbaum, 1988.
7. Feiner, S. and Beshers, C. Worlds within worlds: Metaphors for exploring *n*-dimensional virtual worlds. In *Proceedings of the UIST'90,* 1990, pp. 76–83.
8. Furnas, G. W. Generalized fisheye views. In *Proceedings of SIGCHI'86,* 1986, pp. 16–23.
9. Green, M. and Jacob, R. SIGGRAPH'90 Workshop Report: Software architectures and metaphors for non-WIMP user interfaces. *Comput. Graph. 25,* 3 (July 1991), 229–235.
10. Henderson, D.A. and Card, S.K. Rooms: The use of multiple virtual workspaces to reduce space contention in a window-based graphical user interface. *ACM Trans. Graph. 5, 3,* (July 1986), pp. 211–243.
11. Johnson, B. and Shneiderman, B. Space-filling approach to the visualization of hierarchical information structures. In *Proceedings IEEE Visualization '91,* 1991, pp. 284–291.
12. Mackinlay, J.D., Card, S.K. and Robertson, G.G. Rapid controlled movement through a virtual 3d workspace. In *Proceedings of SIGGRAPH '90,* 1990, pp. 171–176.
13. Mackinlay, J.D., Card, S.K. and Robertson, G.G. A semantic analysis of the design space of input devices. *Human-Computer Interaction, 5, 2–3,* 1990, pp. 145–190.
14. Mackinlay, J.D., Robertson, G.G. and Card, S.K. Perspective wall: Detail

and context smoothly integrated. In *Proceedings of SIGCHI'91*, 1991, pp. 173–179.

15. Newell, A. *Unified Theories of Cognition.* Harvard University Press, Cambridge, Mass., 1990.
16. Rao, R., Card, S.K., Jellinek, H.D., Mackinlay, J.D. and Robertson, G.G. The information grid: A framework for information retrieval and retrieval-centered applications. In *Proceedings of UIST'92*, 1992, pp. 23–32.
17. Robertson, G.G., Card, S.K. and Mackinlay, J.D. The Cognitive Coprocessor architecture for interactive user interfaces. In *Proceedings of UIST'89*, 1989, pp. 10–18.
18. Robertson, G.G., Mackinlay, J.D. and Card, S.K. Cone Trees: Animated 3D visualizations of hierarchical information. In *Proceedings of SIGCHI'91*, 1991, pp. 189–194.
19. Salton, G. and McGill, M.J. *Introduction to modern information retrieval.* McGraw-Hill, New York, 1983.
20. Shaw, C., Liang, J., Green, M. and Sun, Y. The decoupled simulation model for virtual reality systems. In *Proceedings of SIGCHI'92*, 1992, pp. 321–328.
21. Sheridan, T.B. Supervisory control of remote manipulators, vehicles and dynamic processes: Experiments in command and display aiding. *Advances in Man-Machine System Research 1*, 1984, JAI Press, 49–137.
22. Spence, R. and Apperley, M. Data base navigation: An office environment for the professional. *Behavior Inf. Tech. 1*, 1 (1982), 43–54.
23. Sutherland, I.E. Sketchpad: A man-machine graphical communication system. MIT Lincoln Laboratory Tech. Rep. 296, May 1965. Abridged version in SJCC 1963, Spartan Books, Baltimore, Md., 329.
24. Tesler, J. and Strasnick, S. FSN: 3D Information Landscapes. Man pages entry for an unsupported but publicly released system from Silicon Graphics, Inc. Mountain View, Calif. Apr. 1992.
25. Zeltzer, D., Pieper, S. and Sturman, D. An integrated graphical simulation platform. In *Proceedings of Graphics Interface '89*, 1989.

CR Categories and Subject Descriptors: H.3.3 [**Information Storage and Retrieval**]: Information Search and Retrieval—*retrieval models*; H.5.2 [**Information Interfaces and Presentation**]: User Interfaces—*interaction styles*; I.3.6 [**Computer Graphics**]: Methodology and Techniques—*interaction techniques*.

Additional Key Words and Phrases: Information visualization, information visualizer, information access, information cost structure

About the Authors:

GEORGE G. ROBERTSON is a principal scientist at Xerox Palo Alto Research Center.

STUART K. CARD is a research fellow and manager of the user interface research group at Xerox Palo Alto Research Center.

JOCK D. MACKINLAY is a member of the research staff at Xerox Palo Alto Research Center.

Authors' Present Address: Xerox PARC, 3333 Coyote Hill Road, Palo Alto, CA 94304; email: {robertson, card, mac kinlay} @parc.xerox.com

Pad++: A Zooming Graphical Interface for Exploring Alternate Interface Physics

*Benjamin B. Bederson**
Bell Communications Research
445 South Street - MRE 2D-336
Morristown, NJ 07960
(bederson@bellcore.com)

James D. Hollan
Computer Science Department
University of New Mexico
Albuquerque, NM 87131
(hollan@cs.unm.edu)

KEYWORDS
Interactive user interfaces, multiscale interfaces, zooming interfaces, authoring, information navigation, hypertext, information visualization, information physics.

ABSTRACT
We describe the current status of Pad++, a zooming graphical interface that we are exploring as an alternative to traditional window and icon-based approaches to interface design. We discuss the motivation for Pad++, describe the implementation, and present prototype applications. In addition, we introduce an informational physics strategy for interface design and briefly compare it with metaphor-based design strategies.

INTRODUCTION

If interface designers are to move beyond windows, icons, menus, and pointers to explore a larger space of interface possibilities, new interaction techniques must go beyond the desktop metaphor. While several groups are exploring virtual 3D worlds [4][8], we have developed a 2D interface based on zooming. With our system, Pad++, graphical data objects of any size can be created, and zooming is a fundamental interaction technique.

There are numerous benefits to metaphor-based approaches, but they also lead designers to employ computation primarily to mimic mechanisms of older media. While there are important cognitive, cultural, and engineering reasons to exploit earlier successful representations, this approach has the potential of underutilizing the mechanisms of new media.

For the last few years we have been exploring a different strategy for interface design to help focus on novel mechanisms enabled by computation rather than on mimicking mechanisms of older media. Informally the strategy consists of viewing interface design as the development of a physics of appearance and behavior for collections of informational objects.

For example, an effective informational physics might arrange for useful representations to be a natural product of normal activity. Consider how this is at times the case for the physics of the world. Some materials record their use and in doing so influence future use in positive ways. Used books crack open at often referenced places. Frequently consulted papers are at the top of piles on our desks. Use dog-ears the corners and stains the surface of index cards and catalogs. All these provide representational cues as a natural product of interaction but the physics of older media limit what can be recorded and the ways it can influence future use.

Following an informational physics strategy has lead us to explore history-enriched digital objects [11][12]. Recording on objects (e.g. reports, forms, source-code, manual pages, email, spreadsheets) the interaction events that comprise their use makes it possible on future occasions, when the objects are used again, to display graphical abstractions of the accrued histories as parts of the objects themselves. For example, we depict on source code its copy history so that a developer can see that a particular section of code has been copied and perhaps be led to correct a bug not only in the piece of code being viewed but also in the code from which it was derived.

This informational physics strategy has also lead us to explore new physics for interacting with graphical data. In collaboration with Ken Perlin, we have designed a successor to Pad [17] which is an graphical interface based on zooming. This system, Pad++, will be the basis for exploration of novel interfaces for information visualization and browsing in a number of complex information-intensive domains. The system is being designed to operate on platforms ranging from

---

* This author has moved to the University of New Mexico, Computer Science Department, Albuquereque, NM 87131, bederson@cs.unm.edu.

high-end graphics workstations to PDAs and Set-top boxes. Here we describe the motivation behind the Pad++ development, report the status of the current implementation, and present some prototype applications.

MOTIVATION

It is a truism of modern life that there is much more information available than we can readily and effectively access. The situation is further complicated by the fact that we are on the threshold of a vast increase in the availability of information because of new network and computational technologies. It is somewhat paradoxical that while we continuously process massive amounts of perceptual data as we experience the world, we have perceptual access to very little of the information that resides within our computing systems or that is reachable via network connections. In addition, this information, unlike the world around us, is rarely presented in ways that reflect either its rich structure or dynamic character.

We envision a much richer world of dynamic persistent informational entities that operate according to multiple physics specifically designed to provide cognitively facile access. The physics need to be designed to exploit semantic relationships explicit and implicit in information-intensive tasks and in our interaction with these new kinds of computationally-based work materials.

One physics central to Pad++ supports viewing information at different scales and attempts to tap into our natural spatial ways of thinking. The information presentation problem addressed is how to provide effective access to a large body of information on a much smaller display. Furnas [9] explored degree of interest functions to determine the information visible at various distances from a central focal area. There is much to recommend the general approach of providing a central focus area of detail surrounded by a periphery that places the detail in a larger context.

With Pad++ we have moved beyond the simple binary choice of presenting or eliding particular information. We can also determine the scale of the information and, perhaps most importantly, the details of how it is rendered can be based on various semantic and task considerations that we describe below. This provides semantic task-based filtering of information that is similar to the early work at MCC on HITS[13] and the recent work of moveable filters at Xerox [3][18].

The ability to make it easier and more intuitive to find specific information in large dataspaces is one of the central motivations for Pad++. The traditional approach is to filter or recommend a subset of the data, hopefully producing a small enough dataset for the user to effectively navigate. Two recent examples of work of this nature are latent semantic indexing [5] and a video recommender service based on shared ratings with other viewers [10].

Pad++ is complementary to these filtering approaches in that it is a useful substrate to *structure* information. In concert with recommending mechanisms, Pad++ could be used to layout the rated information in a way to make the most highly rated information largest and most obvious, while placing related but lower rated information nearby and smaller.

DESCRIPTION

Pad++ is a general-purpose substrate for exploring visualizations of graphical data with a zooming interface. While Pad++ is not an application itself, it directly supports creation and manipulation of multiscale graphical objects, and navigation through the object space. It is implemented as a widget for Tcl/Tk [16] (described in a later section) which provides a simple mechanism for creating zooming-based applications with an interpreted language. The standard objects that Pad++ supports are colored text, text files, hypertext, graphics, and images.

We have written a simple drawing application using Pad++ that supports interactive drawing and manipulation of objects as well loading of predefined or programmatically created objects. This application produced all the figures depicted in this paper.

The basic user interface for Pad++ uses a three button mouse. The left button is mode dependent. For the drawing application shown in this paper, the left button might select and move objects, draw graphical objects, specify where to enter text, etc. The middle button zooms in and the right button zooms out. Pad++ always zooms around the current cursor position - thus the user can control the zooming dynamically by moving the mouse while zooming. For systems with a two button mouse, we have experimented with various mechanisms for mapping zooming in and out to a single button. Typically, this involves having the first motion of the mouse after the button press determine the direction of the zooming.

Pad++ is a natural substrate for representing abstraction of objects using what we term *semantic zooming*. It is natural to see the details of an object when zoomed in and viewing it up close. When zoomed out, however, instead of simply seeing a scaled down version of the object, it is potentially more effective to see a different representation of it. Perlin [17] described a prototype zooming calendar with this notion. We foresee two ways to describe this type of object. The first is to have different objects, each of which is visible at different, non-overlapping, zooms. This method is supported with the *-minsize* and *-maxsize* options described in the Tcl/Tk Section. The second, and preferred method, is to describe a procedural object that renders itself differently depending on its viewing size or other characteristics. It is possible to prototype procedural objects with Tcl as described below.

RECENT ADVANCES

Our focus in the current implementation has been to provide smooth zooming in a system that works with very large graphical datasets. The nature of the Pad++ interface requires consistent high frame-rate interactions, even as the dataspace becomes large and the scene gets complicated. In many applications, speed is important, but not critical to functionality. In Pad++, however, the interface paradigm is inherently based on interaction. The searching strategy is to visually explore

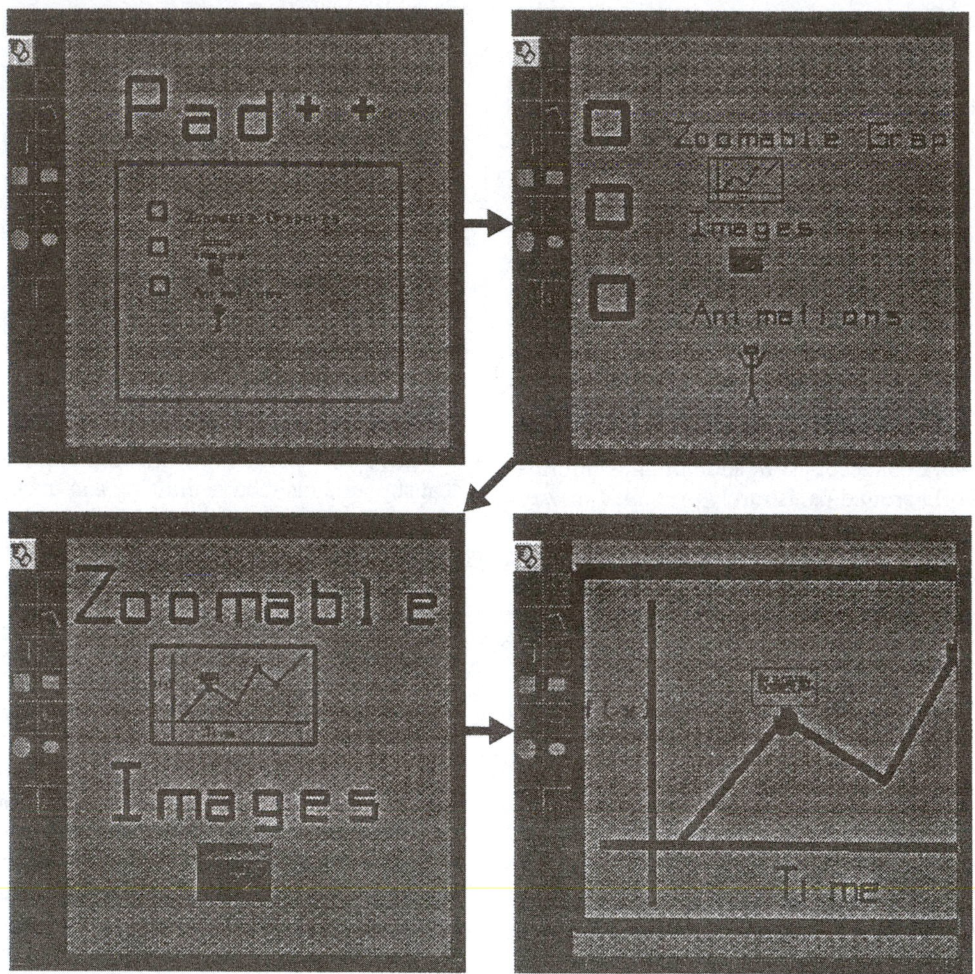

Figure 1: Sequence of snapshots (from left to right and top to bottom) as the view is zoomed in to a hand-drawn picture.

the dataspace, so it is essential that interactive frame rates be maintained.

IMPLEMENTATION

We implemented Pad++ in C++. It runs on either of two graphics systems: the Silicon Graphics computers graphics language facilities (GL); and standard X. The X version runs on SGI's, Suns, PC's running Linux, and should be trivially portable to other standard Unix[R] system. Pad++ is implemented as a widget for Tcl/Tk which allows applications to be written in the interpreted Tcl language. All Pad++ features are accessible through Tcl making it unnecessary to write any new C code.

EFFICIENCY

In order to keep the animation frame-rate up as the dataspace size and complexity increases, we implemented several standard efficiency methods, which taken together create a powerful system. We have successfully loaded over 600,000 objects and maintained interactive rates.

Briefly, the implemented efficiency methods include:

- **Spatial Indexing:** Create a hierarchy of objects based on bounding boxes to quickly index to visible objects.
- **Restructuring:** Automatically restructure the hierarchy of objects to maintain a balanced tree which is necessary for the fastest indexing.
- **Spatial Level-Of-Detail:** Render only the detail needed, do not render what can not be seen.
- **Clipping:** Only render the portions of objects that are actually visible.
- **Refinement:** Render fast with low resolution while navi-

[R]Unix is a registered trademark of Unix Systems Laboratories, Inc.

gating and refine the image when still.

- **Adaptive Render Scheduling:** Keep the zooming rate constant even as the frame rate changes.

One challenge in navigating through any large dataspace is maintaining a sense of relationship between what you are looking at and where it is with respect to the rest of the data (i.e., balancing local detail and global context). The rough animation or jumpy zooming as implemented in the original Pad [17] can be disorienting and thus not provide the most effective support for the cognitive and perceptual processing required for interactive information visualization and navigation.

An important interactive interface issue when accessing external information sources is how to give the user access to them without incurring substantial start-up costs while the database is parsed and loaded. In Pad++ this is accomplished with *parallel lazy loading*: only load the portion of the database that is visible in the current view. As the user navigates through the database and looks at new areas, those portions of the database are loaded. This lazy loading is accomplished in the background so the user can continue to interact with Pad++. When the loading is complete, items appear in the appropriate place.

An associated concept is that of ephemeral objects. Objects in Pad++ which are representations of data on disk can be labeled *ephemeral*. These objects are automatically deleted if they have not been viewed in several minutes, thus freeing system resources. When they are viewed again, they are loaded again in parallel as described above.

HYPERTEXT

In traditional window-based systems, there is no graphical depiction of the relationship among windows even when there is a strong semantic relationship. This problem typically comes up with hypertext. In many hypertext systems, clicking on a hyperlink brings up a new window (or alternatively replaces the contents of the existing window). While there is an important relationship between these windows (parent and child), this relationship is not represented.

We have begun experimenting with multiscale layouts of hypertext where we graphically represent the parent-child relationships between links. When a hyperlink is selected, the linked data is loaded to the side and made smaller, and the view is animated to center the new data.

The user interface for accessing hypertext in Pad++ is quite simple. The normal navigation techniques are available, and in addition, clicking on a hyperlink loads in the associated data as described above, and shift-clicking anywhere on a hypertext object animates the view back to that object's parent.

Pad++ can read in hypertext files written in the Hypertext Markup Language (HTML), the language used to describe objects in the well-known hypertext system, MOSAIC (from the NCSA at the University of Illinois). While we do not yet follow links across the network, we can effectively use Pad++ as an alternative viewer to MOSAIC within our file system. Figure 2 shows a snapshot with one of the author's home-page loaded and several links followed.

INTERFACE TO TCL/TK

Pad++ is built as a new widget for Tk which provides for simple access to all of its features through Tcl, an interpreted scripting language. Tcl and Tk [16] are an increasingly popular combination of scripting language and Motif-like library for creating graphical user interfaces and applications without writing any C code. The Tcl interface to Pad++ is designed to be very similar to the interface to the Tk Canvas widget - which provides a surface for drawing structured graphics.

While Pad++ does not implement everything in the Tk Canvas yet, it adds many extra features - notably those supporting multiscale objects and zooming. In addition, it supports images, text files, and hypertext, as well as several navigation tools including content-based search. As with the Canvas, Pad++ supports many different types of structured graphics, and new graphical widgets can be added by writing C code. Significantly, all interactions with Pad++ are available through Tcl.

Since Tcl is interpreted and thus slower than compiled code, it is important to understand what its role is in a real-time animation system such as Pad++. There are three classes of things that one can do with Pad++, and the importance of speed varies:

- **Create objects:** Slow - Tcl is fine
- **Handle events:** Medium - Small amount of Tcl is ok
- **Render scene:** Fast - C++ only

Because all rendering is done in C++, and typically only a few lines of Tcl are written to handle each event, Pad++ maintains interactive rates despite its link to Tcl. Tcl is quite good, however, for reading and parsing input files, and creating and laying out graphical multiscale objects.

The Tcl interface to Pad++ is, as previously mentioned, quite similar to that of the Tk canvas, and is summarized here to give a feel for what it is like to program Pad++. Every object is assigned a unique integer id. In addition, the user may associate an arbitrary list of text tags with each object. Every command can be directed to either a specific object id or to a tag, in which case it will apply to all objects that share that tag - implicitly grouping objects. Each Pad++ widget has its own name. All Pad++ commands start with the name of the widget, and in the examples that follow, the name of the widget is `.pad`.

Examples:

- A red rectangle with a black outline is created whose corners are at the points (0, 0) and (2, 1):

```
.pad create rectangle 0 0 2 1 -fill red
     -outline black
```

- Put item number 5 at the location (3, 3), make the object

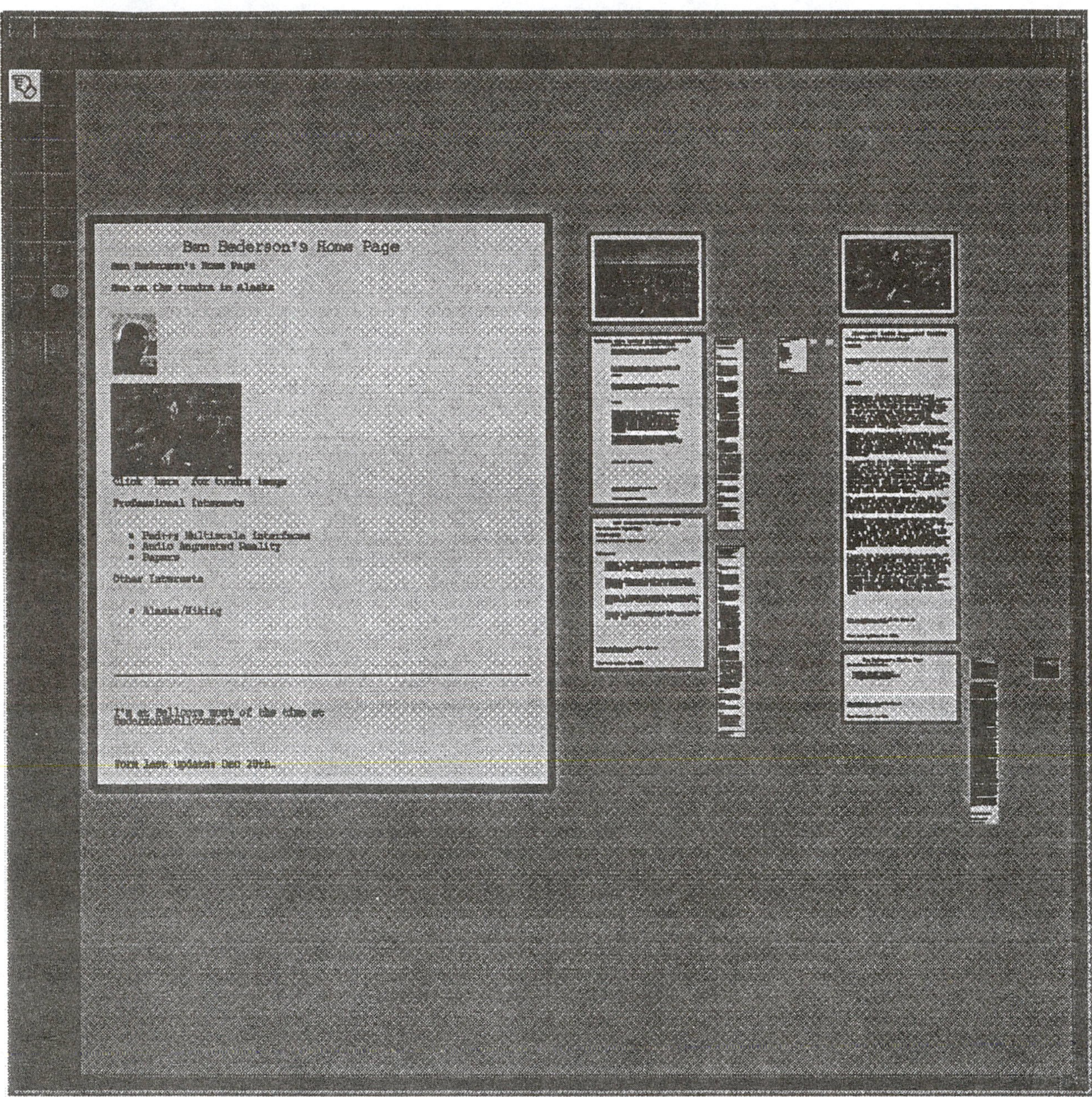

Figure 2: Hypertext. Links are followed and placed on the surface to the side, and made smaller.

twice as big, and make the object anchored at that point on its northwest corner:

```
.pad itemconfig 5 -anchor nw -place "3 3 2"
```

- Specify that item number 5 should only be visible when its largest dimension is greater than 20 pixels and less than 100 pixels.

```
.pad itemconfig 5 -minsize 20 -maxsize 100
```

- Make all items with tag `foo` turn blue when the left button of the mouse is pressed over any of those objects:

```
.pad bind foo <ButtonPress>
    {.pad itemconfig foo -fill blue}
```

As mentioned previously, Pad++ is a natural environment to represent abstraction through semantic zooming. Objects can be represented differently depending on their size by defining *procedural objects*. A procedural object is one that is rendered as a result of a special procedure (as opposed to predefined static objects such as lines or text). Pad++ supports Tcl procedural objects which are very useful for prototyping, but too slow for continued use. Tcl procedural objects work by specifying two Tcl scripts. One returns the bounding box of the object (necessary for efficiency), and the other renders the object (drawing routines are provided). A trivial example is shown here which draws "1993" in red when it is small, and "Jan Feb Mar" in black when it is a little bigger:

```
proc makeCalendar {} {
    .pad create tcl -script "cal" -bb "calBB"
}

proc cal {} {
    set view [.pad move_to]
    set size [lindex $view 2]
    if {$size < .1} {
        .pad set_color red
        .pad set_linewidth 2
        .pad draw_text " 1993" 0 0
    } else {
        .pad set_color black
        .pad set_linewidth 1
        .pad draw_text "Jan Feb Mar" 0 0
    }
}

proc calBB {} {
    return "0 0 11 1"
}
```

NAVIGATION

Finding information on the Pad++ surface is obviously very important as intuitive navigation through large dataspaces is one of its primary motivations. Pad++ support visual searching with zooming in addition to traditional mechanisms, such as content-based search.

Some basic navigation and searching mechanisms are provided at the Tcl interface for the application programmer. A few basic ones are:

- Smoothly go to the location (1, 0) at zoom of 5, and take 1000 milliseconds for the animation:

```
.pad move_to 1 0 5 1000
```

- Smoothly go to the location such that object #37 is centered, and fills three quarter's of the screen, and take 500 milliseconds for the animation:

```
.pad center 37 500
```

- Return the list of object ids that contain the text "foo"

```
.pad find withtext foo
```

Figure 3 shows a Tk interface based on these commands. Entering text in the top entry region returns a list of objects that contain that text. Double clicking on any of these objects smoothly animates the view to the specified object.

The smooth animations interpolate in pan and zoom to bring the view to the specified location. If the end point, however, is more than one screen width away from the starting point, the animation zooms out to a point midway between the starting and ending points, far enough out so that both points are visible. The animation then smoothly zooms in to the destination. This gives a sense of context to the viewer as well as speeding up the animation since most of the panning is performed when zoomed out which covers much more ground than panning while zoomed in.

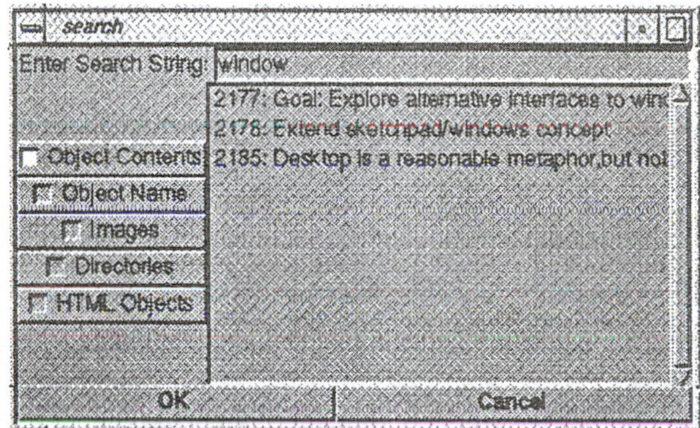

Figure 3: Content based search

VISUALIZATIONS

We built a Pad++ directory browser to explore how smooth zooming and the various efficiency mechanisms help in viewing a large hierarchical database, and to experiment with multi-scale layouts. The Pad++ directory browser provides a graphical interface for accessing the directory structure of a filesystem (see Figure 4). Each directory is represented by a square frame, and files are represented by solid squares colored by file type. Both directories and files show their filenames as labels when the user is sufficiently close to be able to read them. Each directory has all of its subdirectories and files organized alphabetically inside of it. Searching through the directory structure can be done by zooming in and out of the directory tree, or by using the content based search mechanisms described above. Zooming into a file automatically loads the text inside the colored square and it can then be edited and annotated.

We are able to load in a directory tree with over 600,000 objects, and maintain interactive animation rates of about 10 frames per second. Spatial indexing allows us to explore very

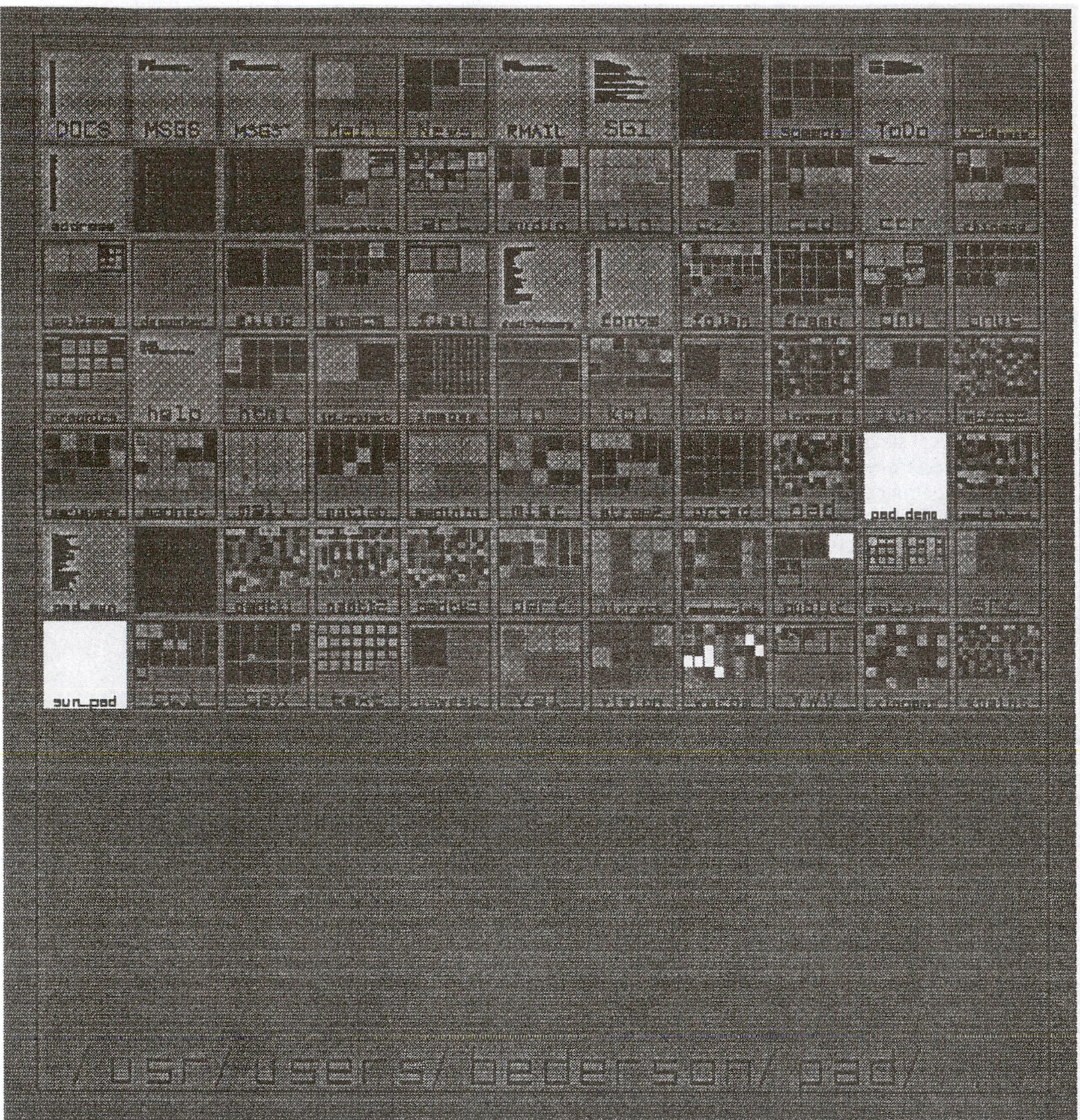

Figure 4: Directory browser snapshot

large databases while keeping the search time fast, since we render only the visible portion of the scene. While navigating with Pad++, very small objects are not drawn and larger ones are drawn with reduced resolution. The objects are then refined and drawn at high resolution when the user stops changing the view.

Another dataset we looked at with Pad++ is a timeline of interesting products, events, and papers in computer technology and user interfaces. History naturally lends itself to being looked back on at different scales. Figure 5 shows a sequence of snapshots as the view is zoomed into the current year. This visualization was created by a Tcl script which reads in a file with a simple format specifying starting and ending dates along with text or images.

PHYSICS AND METAPHOR

As we mentioned earlier, the exploration of Pad++ is part of the development of a more general strategy for interface design. Our goal is to move beyond mimicking the mechanisms of earlier media and start to more fully exploit the radical new mechanisms that computation provides. We think it provides an effective complement to the more traditional metaphor-based approaches. While an informational physics strategy for interface design may certainly involve metaphor, we think there is much that is distinctive about a physics-based perspective. As an interface strategy, it can be distinguished from a metaphor-based strategy in at least four ways.

First, metaphors necessarily pre-exist their use. Pre-Copernicans could never have used the metaphor of the solar system for describing the atom. In designing interfaces, one is limited to the metaphorical resources at hand. In addition, the metaphorical reference must be familiar to work. An unfamiliar interface metaphor is functionally no metaphor at all. One can never design metaphors the way one can design self-consistent physical descriptions of appearance and behavior. Thus, as an interface design strategy, physics offer designability and tailorability that metaphor does not.

Second, metaphors are temporary bridging concepts. When they become ubiquitous, they die. In the same way that linguistic metaphors lose their metaphorical impact (e.g., *foot of the mountain* or *leg of table*), successful metaphors also wind up as dead metaphors (e.g. file, menu, window, desktop). The familiarity provided by the metaphor during earlier stages of use gives way to a familiarity with the interface due to actual experience.

Thus, after awhile, even in the case of metaphor-based interfaces, it is the actual details of appearance and behavior (i.e. the physics) rather than any overarching metaphor that form much of the substantive knowledge of an experienced user. Any restrictions that are imposed on the behaviors of the entities of the interface to avoid violations of the initial metaphor are potential restrictions of functionality that may have been employed to better support the users' tasks and allow the interface to continue to evolve along with the users increasing competency.

The pervasiveness of dead metaphors such as files, menus, and windows may well restrict us from thinking about alternative organizations of computation. New conceptions of persistent objects and organizations of entities into units less monolithic than that of unstructured files are indeed in conflict with older metaphorical notions.

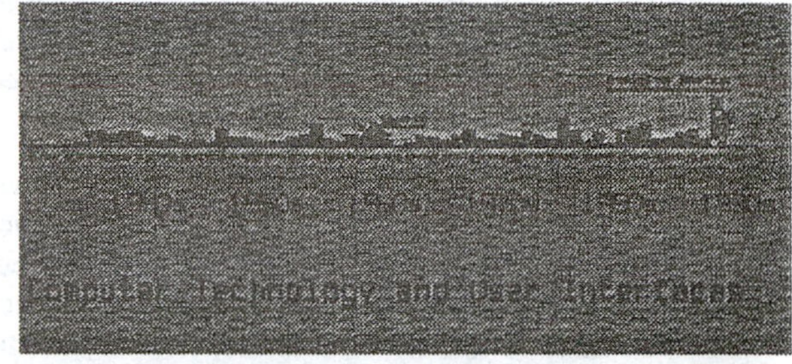

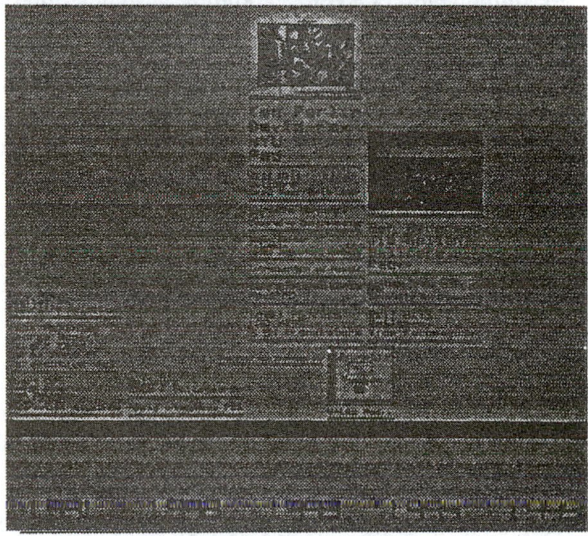

Figure 5: Timeline. Sequence of snapshots (from top to bottom) as the view is zoomed in.

Third, since the sheer amount and complexity of information with which we need to interact continues to grow, we require interface design strategies that *scale*. Metaphor is not such a scaling strategy. Physics is. Physics scales to organize greater and greater complexity by uniform application of sets of simple laws. In contrast, the greater the complexity of the metaphorical reference, the less likely it is that any particular structural correspondence between metaphorical target and reference will be useful.

Fourth, it is clear that metaphors can be harmful as well as helpful since they may well lead users to import knowledge not supported by the interface. There are certainly metaphorical aspects associated with a physics-based strategy. Our point is not that metaphors are not useful but that they may restrict the range of interfaces we consider.

There are, of course, also costs associated in following a physics-based design strategy. One cost is that designers can no longer rely on users' familiarity with the metaphorical reference and this has learnability consequences. However, the power of metaphor comes early in usage and is rapidly superceded by the power of actual experience. Furthermore, since empirical knowability naturally follows from a physics perspective, we can begin to question and quantify how much experimentation will be necessary to learn the designed-in principles, how many inductive steps will be required and of what kinds. Thus, one might want to focus on easily discoverable physics. As is the case with metaphors, all physics are not created equally discoverable or equally fitted to the requirements of human cognition.

CONCLUSION

We implemented Pad++, a zooming graphical interface substrate, focusing on efficiency and expandability. By implementing several efficiency mechanisms which act in concert, we are able to maintain high frame-rate interaction with very large databases. This development is part of an exploration of an informational physics perspective for interface design.

We are currently, in collaboration with NYU, continuing development of the Pad++ substrate as well as starting work in several application domains, such as history-enriched digital objects.

ACKNOWLEDGEMENTS

We would like to thank Ken Perlin and his students, David Fox and Matthew Fuchs, at NYU for enjoyable discussions and for seeding out interest in multiscale interfaces. We especially appreciate the support we have received from Craig Wier as part of ARPA's new HCI Initiative. This will allow us to continue our Pad++ research collaboration with Bellcore and NYU. We also would like to acknowledge other members of the Computer Graphics and Interactive Media Research Group at Bellcore for many discussions shared during our continuing search for the best cheeseburger.

REFERENCES

[1] Ronald M. Baecker, Human Factors and Typography for More Readable Programs, *ACM Press*, 1990.

[2] Benjamin B. Bederson, Larry Stead, and James D. Hollan, Pad++: Advances in Multiscale Interfaces, In *Proceedings of CHI'94 Human Factors in Computing Systems Conference Companion*, ACM/SIGCHI, 1994, pp. 315-316.

[3] Eric A. Bier, Maureen C. Stone, Ken Pier, William Buxton, and Tony D. DeRose. Toolglass and Magic Lenses: The See-Through Interface, In *Proceedings of 1993 ACM SIGGRAPH Conference*, pp. 73-80.

[4] Stuart K. Card, George G. Robertson, and Jock D. Mackinlay. The Information Visualizer, an Information Workspace, In *Proceedings of CHI'91 Human Factors in Computing Systems*, ACM/SIGCHI, 1991, pp. 181-188.

[5] Steve Deerwester, Sue T. Dumais, George W. Furnas, Tom K. Landauer, and Ray Harshman. Indexing by Latent Semantic Analysis. *Journal of American Society of Information Science*, 41, 1990, pp. 391-407.

[6] William C. Donelson. Spatial Management of Information, In Proceedings of *1978 ACM SIGGRAPH Conference*, pp. 203-209.

[7] Stephen G. Eick, Joseph L. Steffen, and Eric E. Sumner, Jr, Seesoft - A Tool for Visualizing Line-Oriented Software Statistics, *IEEE Transactions on Software Engineering*, Vol. 18 (11), pp. 957-968, November, 1992.

[8] Kim M. Fairchild, Steven E. Poltrock, and George W. Furnas. SemNet: Three-Dimensional Graphic Representations of Large Knowledge Bases, in *Cognitive Science and its Applications for Human-Computer Interaction*, Lawrence Erlbaum Associates, 1988.

[9] George W. Furnas, Generalized Fisheye Views, In *Proceedings of CHI'86 Human Factors in Computing Systems*, ACM/SIGCHI, 1986, pp. 16-23.

[10] William C. Hill, videos@bellcore.com: Recommending and evaluating items on the basis of communal history-of-use. *Bellcore Technical Report* #TM-ARH-023560, Morristown, NJ 07960, 1994.

[11] William C. Hill, James D. Hollan, David Wroblewski, and Tim McCandless, Edit Wear and Read Wear, In *Proceedings of CHI'92 Human Factors in Computing Systems*, ACM/SIGCHI, 1992, pp. 3-9.

[12] William C. Hill and James D. Hollan, History-Enriched Digital Objects, in press.

[13] James D. Hollan, Elaine Rich, William Hill, David Wroblewski, Wayne Wilner, Kent Wittenburg, Jonathan Grudin, and Members of the Human Interface Laboratory. An Introduction to HITS: Human Interface Tool Suite, in *Intelligent User Interfaces*, (Sullivan & Tyler, Eds), 1991, pp. 293-337.

[14] James D. Hollan and Scott Stornetta, Beyond Being There, In *Proceedings of CHI'92 Human Factors in Computing Systems*, ACM/SIGCHI, 1992, pp. 119-125. (also appeared as a chapter in Readings in *Groupware and Computer Supported Cooperative Work* (Becker, Ed.), 1993, pp. 842-848.

[15] George Lakoff and Mark Johnson, *Metaphors We Live By*. University of Chicago Press, 1980.

[16] John K. Ousterhout, *Tcl and the Tk Toolkit*, Addison Wesley, 1994.

[17] Ken Perlin and David Fox. Pad: An Alternative Approach to the Computer Interface, In *Proceedings of 1993 ACM SIGGRAPH Conference*, pp. 57-64.

[18] Maureen C. Stone, Ken Fishkin, and Eric A. Bier. The Movable Filter as a User Interface Tool, in *Proceedings of CHI'94 Human Factors in Computing Systems*, ACM/SIGCHI, 1994.

[19] Ivan E. Sutherland. Sketchpad: A man-machine graphical communications systems, In *Proceedings of the Spring Joint Computer Conference*, 1963, pp. 329-346, Baltimore, MD: Spartan Books.

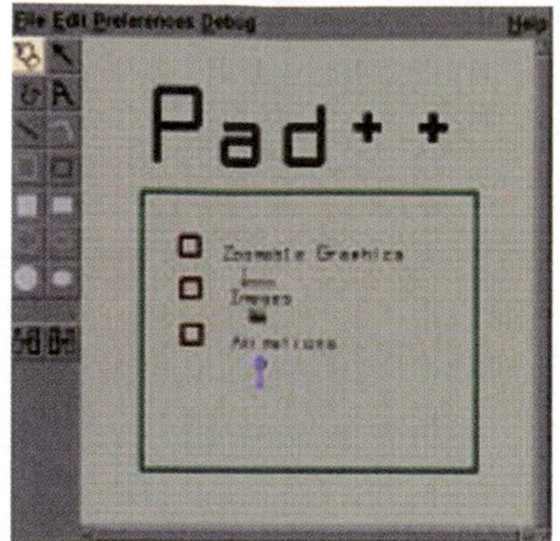

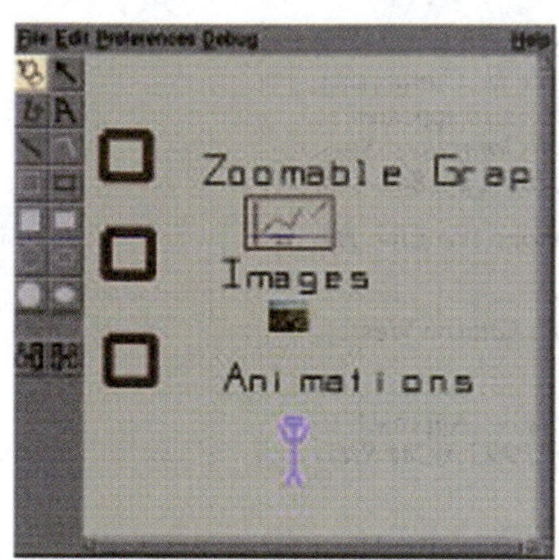

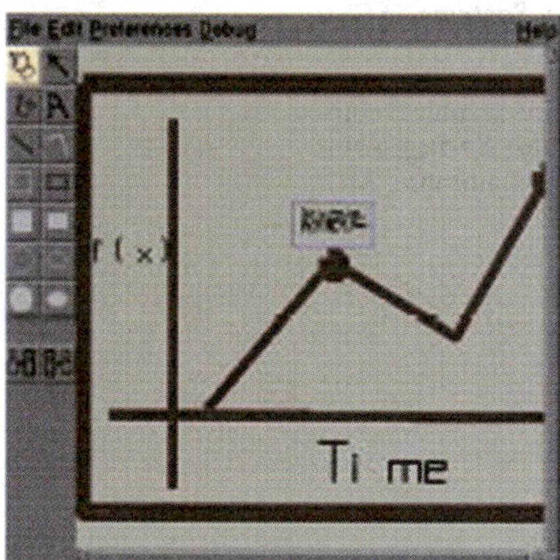

FIGURE **1**

Sequence of snapshots (from left to right and top to bottom) as the view is zoomed in to a hand-drawn picture.

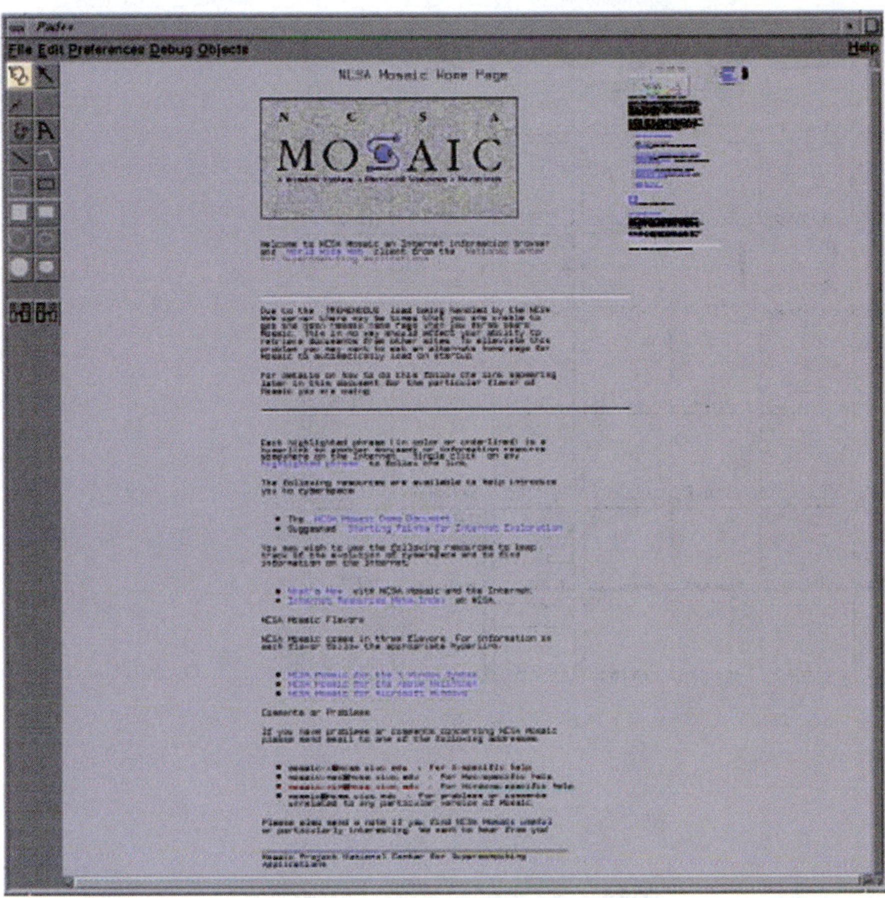

FIGURE 2

Hypertext. Links are followed and placed on the surface to the side, and made smaller.

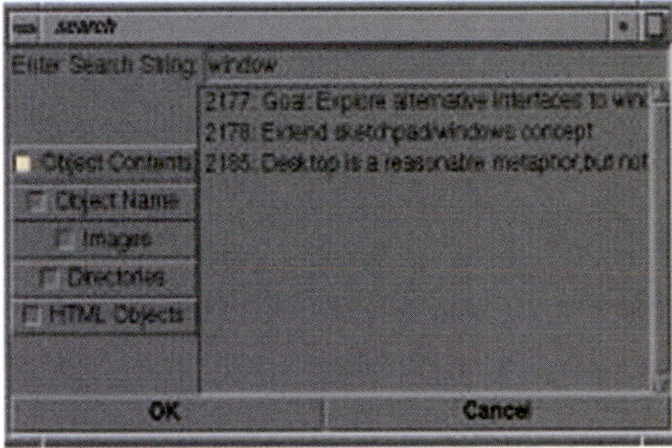

FIGURE 3

Content based search.

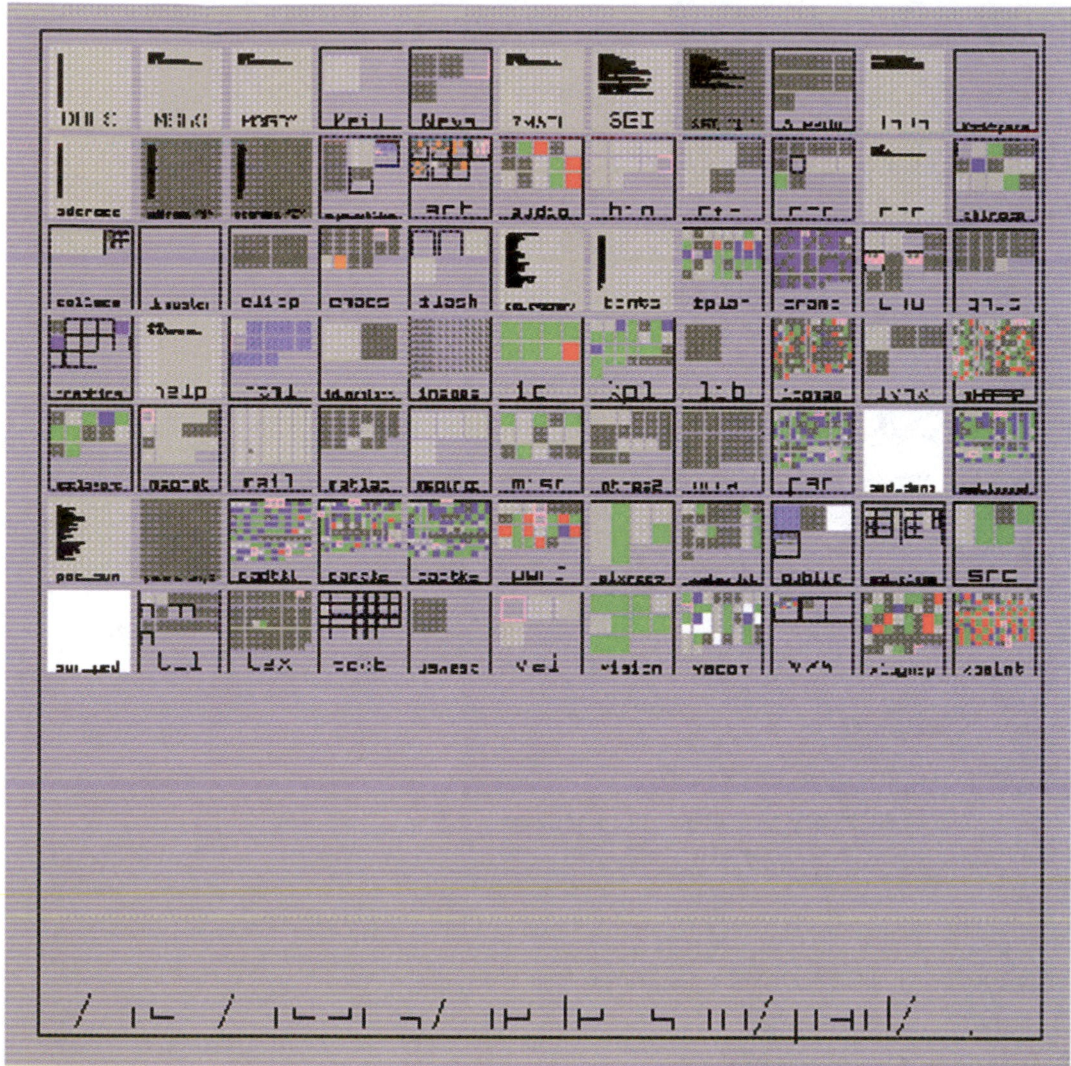

FIGURE 4

Directory browser snapshot.

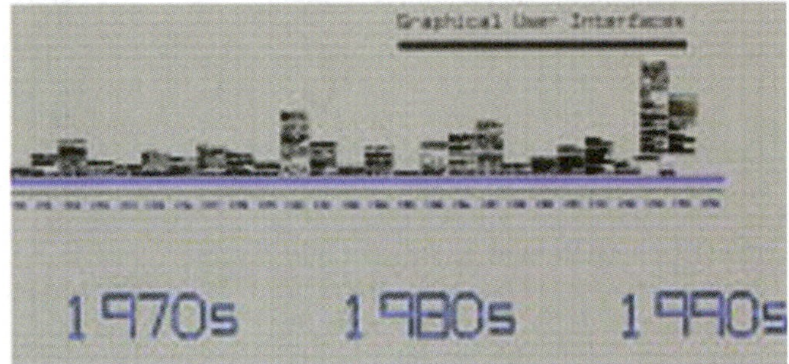

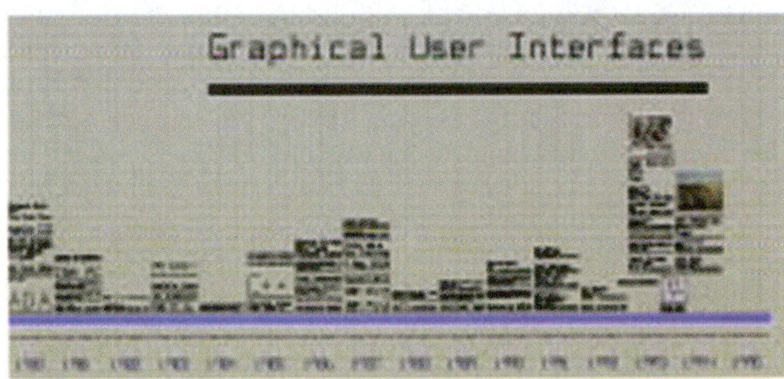

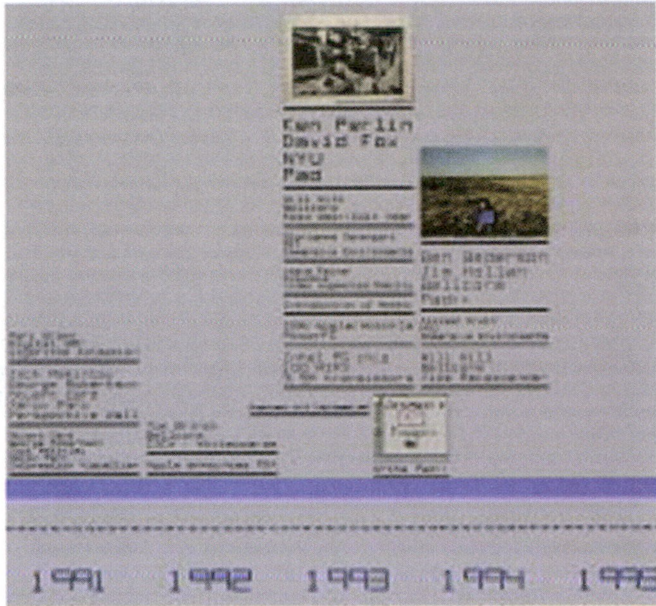

FIGURE 5

Timeline. Sequence of snapshots (from top to bottom) as the view is zoomed in.

The WebBook and the Web Forager: An Information Workspace for the World-Wide Web

Stuart K. Card, George G. Robertson, and William York
Xerox Palo Alto Research Center
3333 Coyote Hill Road
Palo Alto, California 94304
E-mail: {card | robertson | york}@parc.xerox.com

ABSTRACT
The World-Wide Web has achieved global connectivity stimulating the transition of computers from knowledge processors to knowledge sources. But the Web and its client software are seriously deficient for supporting users' interactive use of this information. This paper presents two related designs with which to evolve the Web and its clients. The first is the WebBook, a 3D interactive book of HTML pages. The WebBook allows rapid interaction with objects at a higher level of aggregation than pages. The second is the Web Forager, an application that embeds the WebBook and other objects in a hierarchical 3D workspace. Both designs are intended as exercises to play off against analytical studies of information workspaces.

Keywords
3D graphics, user interfaces, information access, World-Wide Web, information workspace, workspace.

INTRODUCTION

Whereas personal computers used to be viewed as knowledge processors—word processors or spreadsheet calculators, for instance, they are now becoming viewed as knowledge sources—portals to vast stores of information on-line or on CD-ROMs [1]. This is true because much work has become knowledge work and because the infrastructure for distributed knowledge access has been developing. The most dramatic development of this infrastructure has been the growth of the World Wide Web in the last couple of years. Uniform access protocols have enabled a person with a personal computer and a communications link access by button-click to millions of pages around the world.

Despite the exhilaration felt by many users at this achievement of wide-scale connectivity, there are problems that call for evolution of the medium: Pages are often hard to find, users get lost and have difficulty relocating previously-found pages, they have difficulty organizing things once found, difficulty doing knowledge processing on the found thing, and interacting with the Web is notoriously too slow to incorporate it gracefully into human activity. In this paper, we suggest a way of viewing the Web and its problems, then propose two related innovations, the WebBook and the Web Forager, to mitigate these problems.

INFORMATION FORAGING ON THE WEB

In an information-rich world, the limiting quantity for users isn't so much the information in the world as the user's own limited time. Just as animals forage for food and try to optimize their food rate of gain, users often seek strategies to optimize their information gain per unit time and in fact, we can make the analogy literal by thinking of the Web in terms of Information Foraging Theory [1], an analogue of foraging models from ecological biology [2].

In terms of this theory, the user stalks certain types of information. In a particular environment, this sort of information is encountered at a certain rate of λ relevant pages/hour, say. The Web is an evolving information ecology in which on the one hand users are trying to evolve methods to increase the encounter rates of relevant information and on the other hand information sources are trying to evolve their attractiveness to users. These result in a clumpy structure of patches of high λ. Three mechanisms in particular have evolved on the server side: First, indexes, such as Lycos [3] attempt to visit and form an inverted index of every page by following all the links. The user can formulate a keyword query and obtain a patch of possible links to forage. Creation of such a patch is a form of information enrichment.

A second sort of information enrichment is a table of contents lists such as Yahoo [4]. These systems provide typically a tree of categories with links of Web pages at their leaves. Again, this technique provides enriched patches for foraging. A third sort of enrichment are the home pages provided by many users, which collect together lists of related links. Again, these often provide patches with higher encounter rates. All three responses represent evolutionary adaptation (Lycos and Yahoo are successful enough that they have now been converted to businesses) and emergent self-organizing structure on the Web. Yet these innovations do not address the basic cost-structure problem of users using Web information as part of some activity.

THE COST STRUCTURE OF INFORMATION WORKSPACES

The Web maintains a uniform cost structure. The time per interaction is fast, compared to the time to, say, go to the library, but it is slow compared to interaction rates, say the time to interact with pieces of paper on a desk. Empirically, users tend to interact repeatedly with small clusters of information, a property known as locality of reference [5, 6]. As a result, information workspaces, that is, environments that are cost-tuned for doing information-based work, tend to exhibit a certain cost-structure of information: a small amount of information is organized to be available at very low cost, larger amounts are available at moderate costs, large amounts at high cost. By so doing, they capitalize on locality of reference and the activity is speeded considerably. A routine example would be a typical (ideal) office where a small amount of information is kept available on the desk; moderate amounts of information, moderately available in nearby files; and large amounts, slowly available are kept in a library down the hall. Users constantly rearrange their environments to *tune* the relative costs of the information, so as to make them efficient. And if they don't, they suffer accordingly. An important activity they do in such environments is to use them for *sensemaking* [7], that is, the restructuring, recoding, and analysis of information for purposes of insight.

But the Web does not exhibit the characteristics of a good information workspace. Users do not have the ability to create adequately tuned environments nor is sensemaking supported. The major effort to allow users to organize their workspaces has been the development of variants of the "hotlist" notion. Fig. 1 show a typical example from Netscape 1.1N. User actions are provided for adding or deleting an element to a hot list, arranging an element under a heading, changing it's position in the list, or searching for it. Because of the interface, these mechanisms are very slow to use and do not work well with more than a couple dozen entries. Even when the entry is found, the user must still wait for the slow access times before the page appears.

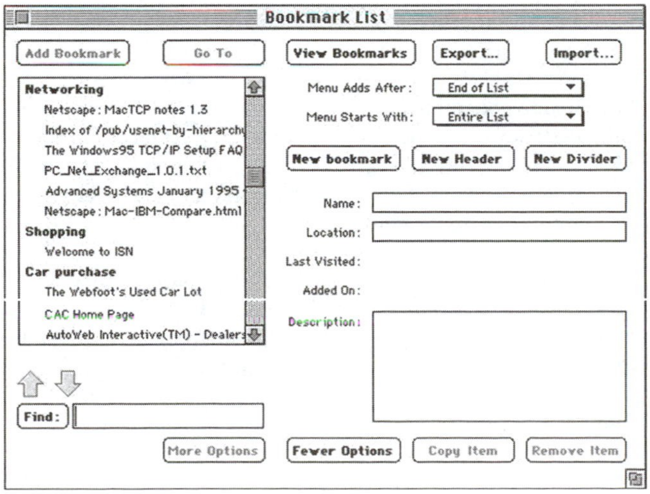

Fig. 1. Hotlist browser from Netscape.

Hence the space is not tunable to a reasonably cost-structured workspace. Multiple windows can be spawned for access to multiple pages, but these then slow the user down because they overlap. Finally, sensemaking is impeded. In the conventional Web browsers, users are always *at* a particular page. But the way a user works with information is to have multiple pages simultaneously available that can be juxtaposed, rapidly accessed, and structured, such as by grouping or other layout.

In order to make the use of the Web better able to support information work (or for that matter, entertainment), we propose in this paper two basic moves:

(1) A move from the single Web page as the unit of interaction to a higher, aggregate entity.

We call this entity a WebBook™, and it allows the user to group together related Web pages (an elementary form of sensemaking) and to manipulate these pages as a unit.

(2) A move from a work environment containing a single element to a workspace in which the page is contained with multiple other entities, including WebBooks.

We call this environment the Web Forager™. This information workspace allows for the intensive, rapid interaction among pages and allows for the assembly on the user side of hierarchical cost-structures of information necessary for the task tuning of the workspace.

Each of these has been implemented on a Silicon Graphics Iris computer using the Information Visualizer system [8]. Efforts are underway to reimplement them on a PC and to continue advancing the design.

THE WEBBOOK

Current Web servers and browsers focus attention at the link and page levels. These levels are too low to represent gracefully some higher-level structures, resulting in many more entities in the Web space than are necessary and

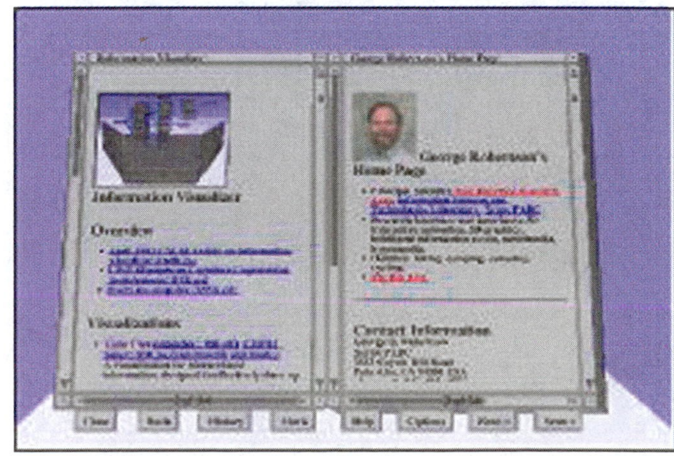

Fig. 2: Example of a WebBook (See Color Plate 2).

hence to orientation and sensemaking problems. We know from analysis of the web that there are structures that the user could take advantage of if the user were aware of their existence. For example, a typical home page on the web has a collection of related pages that can be reached with relative URLs (Uniform Resource Locators). It is very typical for the creator of such pages to use relative URLs instead of absolute URLs, so that the collection of pages can be physically moved easily. But current web browsers pay no attention to the distinction between relative and absolute URLs, and the user simply sees one page at a time, with no difference between a page "in the collection" and one outside the collection. Our proposal is to create a Web entity at a higher level of abstraction, a WebBook. A natural candidate structure to represent this abstraction is the book metaphor, which has been used by us [9] as well as others [10-18] previously.

Fig. 2 shows a picture of a WebBook. Given a collection of web pages, it preloads those pages and displays them as a collection using an augmented simulation of a physical book. 3D graphics and interactive animation are used to give the user a clear indication of the relationship between the pages of the book. Each page of the WebBook is a page from the web. Links are color coded so the user can easily tell the difference between a reference to another page in the book (red links) and a reference outside the book (blue links). Picking a red link will animate the flipping of pages to the desired page. Picking a blue link will close the current WebBook and look for the page elsewhere. If the page is in another WebBook stored on a bookshelf, that WebBook is opened to the desired page. If the page is in none of the WebBooks, then the Web Forager is used to display the individual page in the user's information workspace.

There are a number of features in the WebBook that make it intuitive to use. The user has several ways to flip through the pages of the book, all animated so the user can continue to see the text and images on pages while they turn. The simplest method is to click on a page (away from any link on that page); this will flip to the next or previous page

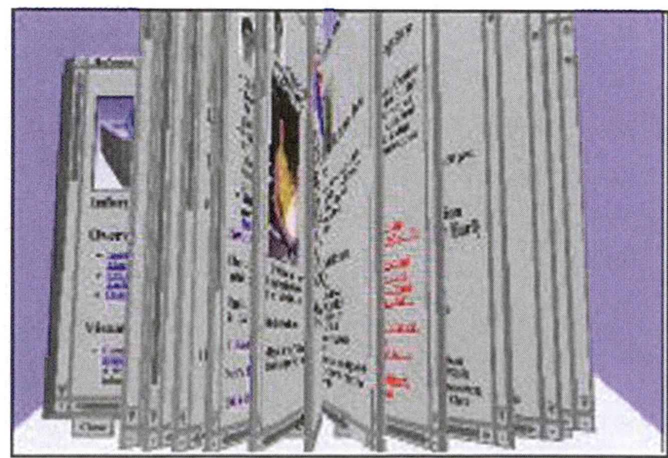

Fig. 3. Example of ruffling pages in a WebBook (See Color Plate 3)

depending on whether user clicked on the right or left page. The user can also click on the right or left edge of the book. The relative distance along that edge indicates how far to flip. The user can also scan the book with forward and backward scan controls (two of the buttons on the bottom of the book). The scan rate and pause time at each page is a user preference. When the user clicks on a page during a scan, the scan stops. Finally, the user can ruffle through the pages (Fig. 3) by clicking and holding the mouse button down. The ability to rapidly riffle through a set of pages has previously been a method of rapid scanning for information that could only be done with physical books.

In addition, the user can leave a bookmark on any page. When the book is closed, a bookmark is automatically left for the last page that was viewed. Also, there is a "Back" and "History" mechanism that follows the same convention as NetScape's versions of those commands. The WebBook can be stored on a bookshelf using a simple gesture. When it is removed from the bookshelf (by clicking on it), it reopens to the last page that was being viewed.

Each page in the WebBook has three scrollbars. Two of these are the familiar vertical and horizontal scrolling controls (left and bottom scrollbars). The third (on the right) is for scaling the font size, since the trade-off of font-size vs. amount of page viewed differs for individual pages. As the scale scrollbar is moved, images remain the same size but the text changes size and is refilled continuously. A menu command allows the user to apply a new font scale to all pages of the WebBook. The corners of each page of the WebBook are resize tabs, which the user can use to change the size of the book.

Books are compact but (except for bookmarks) sequential. Therefore we allow the user to explode the book out (in animation) so that all the pages are available simultaneously. The Document Lens [19] can then be used to inspect portions of interest. Fig. 4 shows the WebBook Document Lens view. The user is then able to pan and zoom over the entire set of pages, while retaining a focus plus context display of the book. When returning to the book view, the user sees an animation of the pages imploding into a book.

WebBook Applications

The WebBook can be used to view any collection of web pages. The principle difference is the method used to generate the URLs. The method used to collect URLs leads to a number of applications.

Relative-URL Books. One interesting choice of pages is based on recursively finding all relative URLs starting from a given page. These pages are intrinsically related because their creator wanted to be able to move them as a group. We have found this heuristic often produces coherent and interesting books.

Home-Page Books. Probably the simplest choice of pages is those pages referred to directly from a given page. Users throughout the net have strongly expressed their desire to make sense of the net by collecting sets of related URLs. The WebBook goes the next step and allows the collection of pages to be rapidly consulted without waiting for network delay speeds.

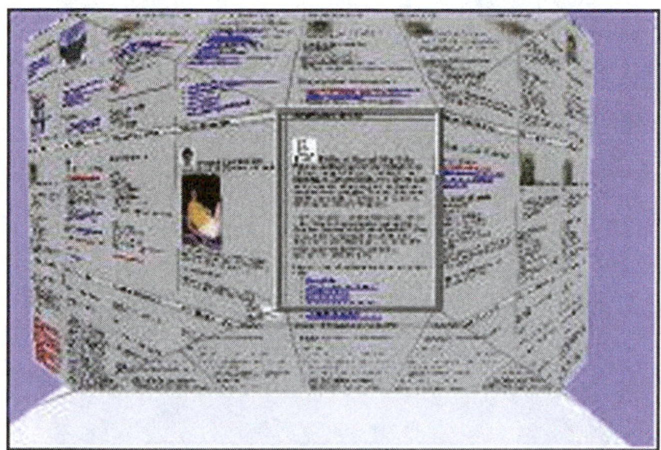

Fig. 4. WebBook viewed with a Document Lens.
(See Color Plate 4)

Topic Books. A variant is to make sets of books on interesting topics. For example, in our area houses for sale are published on the Web, usually one page per house and usually organized off the home pages of the real-estate brokers. But we have rearranged these ads into houses from a given city. It is then possible rapidly to look back an forth in order to make house comparisons.

Hot List Books. Another variant is hotlist pages. Our system can read any user's Netscape hotlist and automatically fashion it into a set of WebBooks. Although exactly the same URLs are involved, the transformation is dramatic because all the information on all the pages is readily available.

Search Reports. Since WebBooks can be created dynamically, they can be used to display the results of a content based search, either keyword based or relevance feedback (looking for pages similar to a given page). Later results from the search can still be retrieving pages while the user is examining the first pages of the book.

Book Books. A final example comes from observing how some people take multi-page documents and put them on the web. One way to do this is with a series of pages, with next and previous links between pages. When viewing one of these pages with a traditional web browser, there is no indication of how the pages are related. But, such a structure can be easily discovered, and a WebBook constructed from those pages, resulting in a collection of obviously related pages.

Related Work: The Book Metaphor

The book metaphor has been used in both 2D and 3D applications by a number of people for some time. What is new about the WebBook is the integration of an animated 3D book, used to show collections of web pages, with an information workspace manager (the Web Forager) and the application to Web problems.

A book metaphor was chosen after careful examination of a large number of web pages and page collections, and for several reasons: Informally, information on the Web tends to have non-homogeneous character, with closely related weblets situated in more loosely structured environments. An important subset of these have 'next' and 'previous' links, and thus are thus close operational analogues to books. Furthermore, books as an invention make very efficient use of display space. Starting with a book metaphor, it is easy to escape the serial nature of the physical form by having alternate forms into which the book is transformed, such as the Document Lens in this paper. A book metaphor makes it easy to put actual books on the Internet, something not so at present. We use the book metaphor not primarily because it is familiar, but because of the operational match to a corpus of interest and the efficient display characterization. As a bargain, its familiarity allows us to exploit irresistible affordances for low training costs.

Early experiments with giving users access to books, like Brown's Intermedia [10] system in 1985, had limited 3D graphics capabilities. Instead of a simulation of a physical book, Intermedia used 2D layouts of the pages, showing relationships between pages with the layout and with lines drawn between pages. In 1987, Card and Henderson reported the use of a 2D book simulation called "Catalogues" as part of the Rooms system [9], although page turning was not animated. The Xerox TabWorks system [16] was directly inspired by Catalogues. Also in 1987, the BellCore SuperBook Document Browser [13], was designed to transform existing electronic documents into hypertext documents with indexing and a fisheye table of contents, although SuperBook did not use a simulation of a physical book.

Use of a 2D physical book simulation, including page turning, was done in 1987 by Benest [17] for hypertext documents. Similar systems were reported by Miyazawa in 1990 [11] and Ichimura in 1993 [18]. Recently, PenPoint [14] and General Magic [15] have offered commercial products that use a book metaphor with bookshelves. These are actually 2D animations painted on a background that give the impression of a 3D environment. In 1993, Silicon Graphics introduced the SGI Demo Book [12] as a way of distributing collections of applications, documents, and games. Demo Book is a 3D book that simulates page flipping with animation. The pages hold a collection of icons, 4 rows by 5 columns on each page. The page flipping appears to have flexible pages (broken on the columns). The WebBook page flip currently uses rigid pages, but is displaying text and images instead of rows and columns of icons. Demo Book also has the notion of a bookshelf, although the book always opens to the first page rather than the last page viewed.

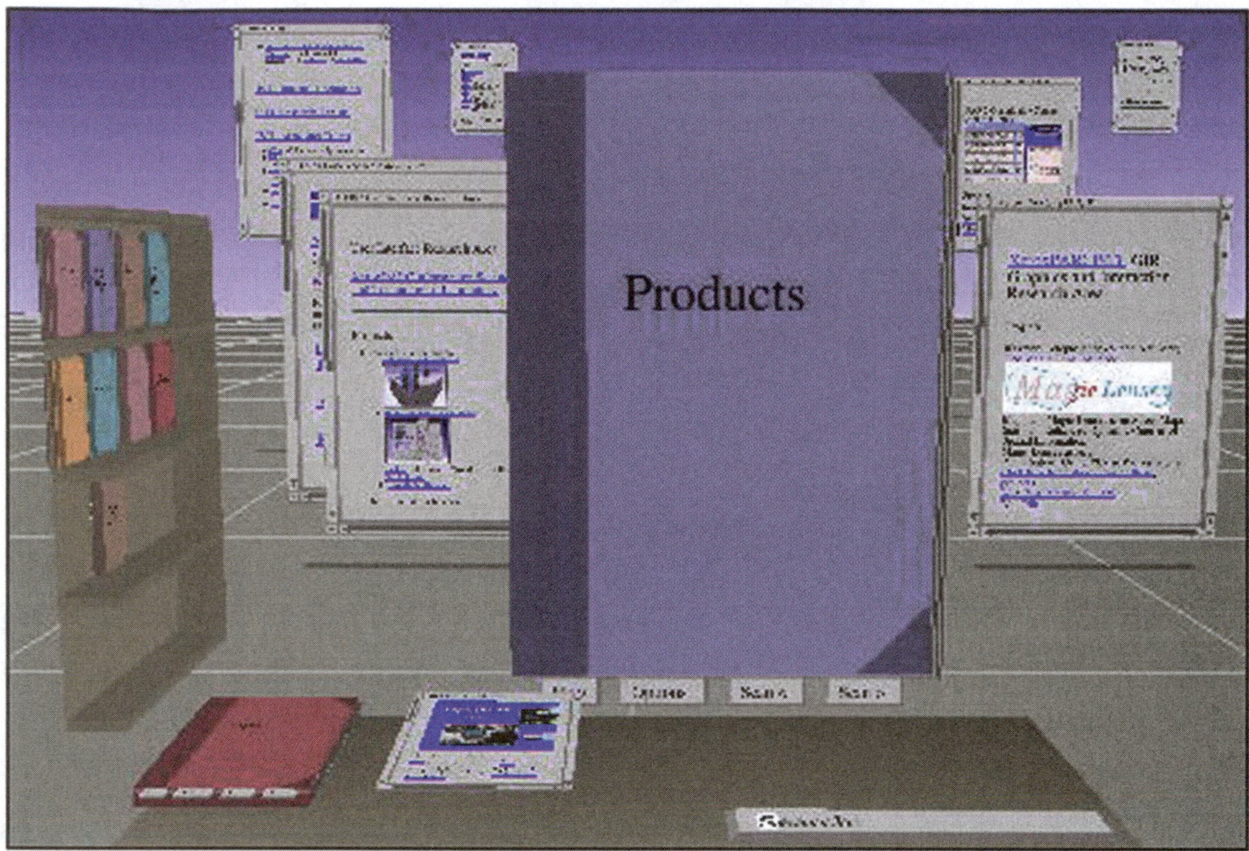

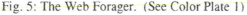

Fig. 5: The Web Forager. (See Color Plate 1)

In 1995, Brown described an experimental web browser, called DeckScape [20], that used a metaphor of decks of cards. Although not a book metaphor, it was an alternative way to solve the problem.

All these systems exploit the human perceptual and cognitive systems by using familiar objects, images and affordances. The page turning of a book conveys information about the relationship of pages, the direction you are moving in the book, the size of the book, and the contents of the book. The WebBook takes advantage of advances in graphics and processor power to get much closer to a realistic simulation of a book. At the same time, it goes beyond what is possible with a physical book.

THE WEB FORAGER

The WebBook provides a representation of a more aggregate Web entity above the page and allows rapid local interaction with it. The Web Forager allows interaction with multiples of such entities and allows for the necessary tradeoffs among fast access, number of entities, and screen space. The Web Forager is a proposal for a task-tunable information workspace [21] (see Fig. 5).

An individual Web page or a WebBook is presented in a 3D document space (see[22], [23]). Users can click on links in the usual way causing the new linked-to page to fly into the space. The HTML image on the new page develops at the slow Internet speeds (often 15~30 sec). Web pages entered into the space are stored locally and thence forward are available at user interface speeds (around 1~0.1 sec), permitting high interaction rates. These pages can also be grabbed and placed into WebBooks.

Our primary interest in this style of workspace is in exploring the potential for rapid interaction with large numbers of pages. We have previously explored the use of animation, scaling, and 3D-based distortions for building a workspace [21] as a way of handling large numbers of objects. Ark Interface, Inc. [24] produced a pseudo-3D workspace in which functions were associated with parts of a picture of a design studio. Staples [23] did a design mockup study for a 3D user interface. Her goal was to enrich the graphic vocabulary of the workspace by applying perspective, light, and transparency. Ballay [22] with co-workers at the MAYA Design Group implemented a 3D design for an office system. Their design is artistically striking and claimed to be able to handle hundreds of documents. We have sought to break new ground relative to their design on several fronts. First, we tried to increase the speed with which objects can be moved around the space by using gestures. Second, we focused on the Web. Third, the WebBook provides a higher-level object. Fourth, we have experimented with observer movement in the space. And Fifth, we have used a structured model for the generation of the design.

Hierarchical Workspace

The Web Forager workspace (see Fig. 5) is arranged hierarchically (in terms of interaction rates) into three main levels: (1) a Focus Place (the large book or page) showing a page, a book, or an open book at full size for direct interaction between user and content: (2) an Immediate Memory space (the air and the desk), where pages or books can be placed when they are in use, but not the immediate focus (like pages on a desk). A Tertiary Place (the bookcase) where many pages and books can be stored.

The Immediate Storage place has several tiers. Documents are arranged at several distinct z-distances in the 3D space. The user can move these documents back in space (the farther back, the smaller they become and the more documents that fit). Objects in the Immediate Storage place can be moved around in X and Y and moved forward and backward (that is, in Z) using a simple gesture language. A separate Intermediate Storage area is represented by objects on the desk. When the user moves around in the space, the desk, and hence objects on the desk, moves.

The Tertiary Storage area is the bookcase. In normal view, the bookcase is seen at an angle to reduce screen pixels consumed, while at the same time displaying enough information that recently-used books can be recognized. If the user touches one of the books or pages in the bookcase, it will fly up to the focus area (an object occupying that area will automatically fly back to an Immediate Storage position). But if the user wants to examine better the books before making a choice, then touching the bookcase will cause the user, desk and all, to fly to the bookcase (Fig. 6). Touching a book will then cause the user to fly back to the home position and the book to fly to the focus position.

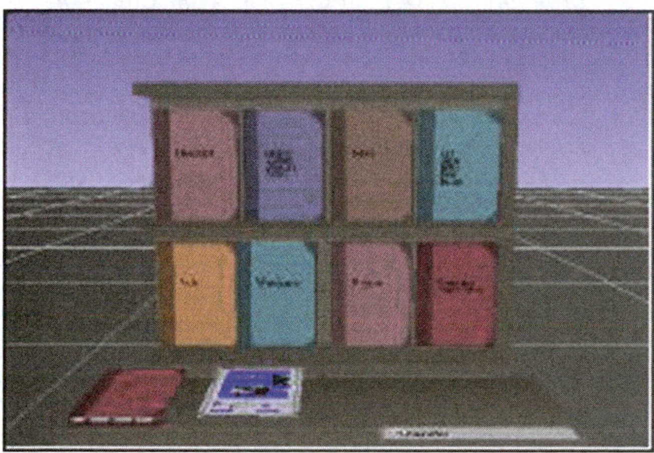

Fig. 6: User has flown to the bookcase where the titles of the books can be easily read. (See Color Plate 5)

The purpose of the workspace is to allow a number of objects to be displayed together (mitigating the limitations of the small screen space) in order to support information-intensive activities. The workspace sets up explicitly the capacity for speed/access-time tradeoff to allow tuning for such activities. The design aims to provide very rapid access to a small number of pages, smoothly integrated with the slower access to a large number. The Immediate

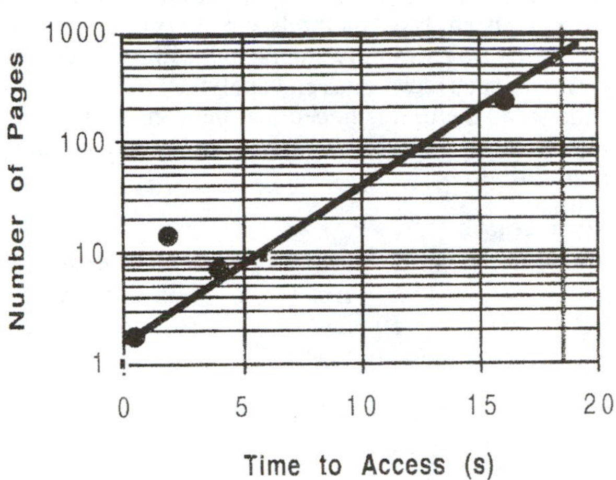

Fig. 7. Preliminary computation of Cost of Knowledge Characteristic Function for Web Forager.

Storage workspace can hold about 30 documents without occlusion, and over a hundred if occlusions are allowed (not counting book contents). Pages for ongoing activities migrate into the rapid access and manipulation region. In this way, repeated reference due to locality of reference statistics can result in faster interaction.

Cost of Knowledge Characteristic Function

In previous work [25], we have attempted to measure the access properties of a workspace by computing the Cost of Knowledge Characteristic Function, that is, a plot of how many objects can be accessed as a function of the time cost of accessing them. We surmise that a balanced workspace will exhibit an exponential relationship, most conveniently displayed as a straight line in semi-log coordinates. As a tool to use in refining our design, we have computed a preliminary version of this function. The computation assumes that there is a page in the Focus Position (hence the maximal occlusion), that the desk is full, and that one row of pages from each of the discrete Z-distances in the space shows (remember, the design of the space has been carefully set up to permit this).

The results are shown in Fig. 7. They are roughly in the expected relation, except that the images on the desk permit the fast part of the space to receive extra loading. An illustrative comparison with a conventional Web browser is shown as a gray line assuming a constant 18 sec per page retrieval. We hope to use this and related techniques to further refine the space in future research.

SUMMARY

The Web Forager workspace is intended to create patches from the Web where a high density of relevant pages can be combined with rapid access. In addition to multiple pages occurring simultaneously, the space contains groups of pages in the form of WebBooks, which can allow the user to express an elementary form of sensemaking by grouping and ordering. High density patches found around the net, whether created explicitly by searchers or discovered through Web analysis methods can be put into a form where they can be rapidly interacted with. Through the invention of such techniques and analytical methods to help us understand them, it is hoped that the connectivity of the Web, which has been so successful, can be evolved into yet more useful forms.

REFERENCES

1. Pirolli, P. and S. Card, *Information Foraging in Information Access Environments,* in *CHI '95, ACM Conference on Human Factors in Software.* 1995, ACM: New York. p. 51–58.

2. Stephens, DEW. and J. R. Krebs, Foraging theory. 1986, Princeton: Princeton University Press.

3. Mauldin, M.L. and J.R.R. Leavitt. *Web-agent related research at the CMT.* in *SIGNIDR.* 1994. McLean, Virginia:

4. Filo, D. and J. Yang, *Yahoo (Yet Another Hierarchical Officious Oracle).* 1994, Yahoo! Corp: Stanford, California.

5. D. A. Henderson, J. and S.K. Card, *Rooms: The use of multiple virtual workspaces to reduce space contention in a window-based graphical user interfaces.* ACM Transactions on Graphics, 1986. **5**(3 (July)): p. 211–241.

6. Card, S.K., M. Pavel, and J.E. Farrell, *Window-based computer dialogues.*, in *Human-Computer Interaction—INTERACT '84,* B. Shackel, Editor. 1984, Elsevier Science Publishers, B. V. (North-Holland): Amsterdam. p. 51–56.

7. Russell, D.M., *et al., The cost structure of sensemaking,* in *ACM/IFIPS InterCHI '3 Conference on Human Factors in Software.* 1993, ACM: New York. p. 269–276.

8. Robertson, G.G., S.K. Card, and J.D. Mackinlay, *Information visualization using 3D interactive animation.* Communications of the ACM, 1993. **36**(4 (April)): p. 57–71.

9. Card, S.K. and D.A. Henderson, *Catalogues: A Metaphor for Computer Application Delivery,* in *Human-Computer Interaction -- INTERACT'87.* 1987, Elsevier Science Publishers (North Holland): p. 959–963.

10. Yankelovich, N., N. Meyrowitz, and A. van Dam, *Reading and Writing the Electronic Book.* IEEE Computer, 1985. **18**(10 (October)): p. 15–30.

11. Miyazawa, M., *et al., An Electronic Book: APTBook,* in *Human-Computer Interaction -- INTERACT'90.* 1990, Elsevier Science Publishers (North Holland): Amsterdam. p. 513–519.

12. Silicon Graphics, *Demo Book.* 1993, Silicon Graphics: Mountain View, California.

13. Remde, J.R., L.M. Gomez, and T.K. Landauer, *Superbook: An Automatic Tool for Information Exploration,* in *ACM Hypertext '87 Proceedings.* 1987, p. 175–188.

14. Carr, R. and D. Shafer, *The Power of PenPoint.* 1992, New York: Addison-Wesley.

15. Sony Corporation, *Magic Link User's Guide, PIC-1000.* 1994, Tokyo: Sony Corporation. 203 pp.

16. Moll-Carrillo, H.J., *et al., Articulating a Metaphor Through User-Centered Design,* in *CHI '95, ACM Conference on Human Factors in Software.* 1995, ACM Press: New York. p. 566–572.

17. Benest, I.D., G. Morgan, and M.D. Smithurst, *A Humanized Interface to an Electronic Library,* in *Human-Computer Interaction -- INTERACT'87.* 1987, Elsevier Science Publishers (North Holland): Amsterdam. p. 905–910.

18. Ichimura, S. and Y., *Another Dimension to Hypermedia Access,* in *Hypertext '93.* 1993, ACM: New York. p. 63–72.

19. Robertson, G.G. and J.D. Mackinlay, *The Document Lens.* UST '93, ACM Conference on User Interface Software and Technology, 1993. : p. 101–108.

20. Brown, M.. and R. C. A. Shiner, *A New Paradigm for Browsing the Web,* in *CHI '95, ACM Conference on Human Factors in Software, Conference Companion.* 1995, ACM Press: New York. p. 320–321.

21. Card, S.K., J.D. Mackinlay, and G.G. Robertson. *The Information Visualizer: An information workspace,* in *CHI '91, ACM Conference on Human Factors in Computing Systems.* 1991.

22. Ballay, J.M. *Designing Workscape: An interdisciplinary experience.* in *ACM CHI '94, Human Factors in Computing Systems.* 1994. Boston: ACM.

23. Staples, L. *Representation in virtual space: Visual convention in the graphical user interface.* in *INTERCHI '93.* 1993. ACM.

24. Ark Interface Workspace *User's Guide.* 1990, Seattle, Washington: Ark Interface, Inc. 54.

25. Card, S.K., P. Pirolli, and J.D. Mackinlay, *The cost of knowledge characteristic function: Display evaluation for direct-walk dynamic information visualizations,* in *CHI '94, ACM Conference on Human Factors in Software.* 1994, ACM: New York. p. 238–244.

The *STARLIGHT* Information Visualization System

JS Risch, DB Rex, ST Dowson, TB Walters, RA May, BD Moon
Pacific Northwest National Laboratory
Richland, Washington USA
{js_risch, db_rex, st_dowson, tb_walters, ra_may, bd_moon}@pnl.gov

Abstract

STARLIGHT is an example of a new class of information system expressly designed around a visualization-oriented user-interface. Incorporating more traditional information storage and retrieval technologies into its design, the Starlight system also enables the integrated use of multiple, concurrent visualization techniques to support comparison of content and interrelationship information at several levels of abstraction simultaneously. This approach enables powerful new forms of information analysis, while at the same time easing cognitive workloads by providing a visual context for the information under study. Originally developed for intelligence analysis applications, the Starlight software is intended to support the rapid, concurrent analysis of complex multimedia information, including structured and unstructured text, geographic information, and digital imagery. The system uses novel 3-D visualization techniques that interactively generate easily understandable representations of explicit and implicit relationships contained in information collections of various types. This paper describes the general theory behind our approach, and the design and features of a Windows NT-based operational system.

1 Introduction and Problem Description

Like many information analysts, members of the U.S. Intelligence Community (IC) face the daunting task of making sense out of enormous quantities of multiformat, multimedia information. Unlike most other fields, however, intelligence analysts may also face the need to make life-or-death decisions under extreme time pressures that require them to perform these tasks quickly while maintaining exceptionally high quality standards. Unfortunately, conventional analysis tools and approaches are failing to keep pace with either the enhanced capabilities of modern information collection systems or the evolving analytical requirements of contemporary intelligence problems.

The intelligence analysis process is principally driven by the need to filter, distill, and correlate large quantities of structured and unstructured textual information. There is an increasing need, however, to correlate textual information with non-text information, such as data from relational databases, and with spatial information, such as maps, images, and schematic information. Another critical requirement is the need to automatically derive and clearly represent complex associations, including temporal interrelationships, among the elements of such multimedia information collections. Finally, the rapid tempo of contemporary intelligence analysis environments demands that information analysis systems preserve, as much as possible, the conceptual continuity of the analyst during analysis. We feel these requirements make the field of intelligence analysis a good candidate for the application of Information Visualization (IV) technologies.

2 Background

"Information Visualization" is the process of transforming abstract, typically non-numerical information (such as text) into more easily understandable, graphical forms. Information Visualization approaches typically involve converting non-numerical information into a numerical form prior to the application of statistical graphics or other visualization techniques commonly used by the scientific and business communities. In this way, inherently non-spatial information can be "spatialized," or converted to a spatial form, for easier analysis and assimilation.

Much previous IV research has concentrated on the development of visualization techniques individually applicable to relatively limited information domains (e.g., hierarchical data structures [1,2], semantic relationships [3], relative query results [4], relational data [5,6], many others). In contrast, Starlight represents an attempt to address the pressing problems of the U.S. IC by developing a visualization system that is capable of supporting the integrated analysis of a wide range of information types and structures. To accomplish this, Starlight incorporates multiple established and newly developed visualization techniques into its design, along with a comprehensive information preprocessing, storage and retrieval system.

The unique demands of intelligence analysis problems have driven our design of Starlight. The IC's heavy reliance on textual information required that an effective text visualization approach be a key component. The need to correlate text contents with information in relational databases led us to experiment with some of the approaches being developed by the data mining community. The requirement for integrating free- and structured-text information with map and image data led us to develop an approach for displaying this information concurrently with graphical representations of textual information. And the need to simultaneously depict complex interrelationships among elements of information collections led us to incorporate a system for dynamically constructing associative network diagrams into our design.

In addition to effective visual presentation capabilities, it was clear that a practical information analysis tool must also provide a complete *information system*, with the capability to ingest, store, and retrieve information dynamically during analysis. This was one of the key limitations of our earlier prototype [7]. Further, the realities of dynamic, often chaotic, intelligence analysis environments require that such systems employ flexible information structures that can rapidly accommodate new information and quickly generate the "view" of a particular data set appropriate to the immediate task. Finally, while high-end, dedicated graphics computers provide many powerful, advanced capabilities, their expense and complexity makes them impractical in most analysis domains. The current version of Starlight, hosted on a high-performance Intel platform operating under Windows NT, effectively addresses these requirements and represents one of the first attempts to bring emerging IV technologies to the desktops of intelligence analysts.

3 General Approach

Conceptually, we have divided the information analysis process into two main components and have organized the software to provide integrated support for both types. These two main components are *content* analysis and *interrelationship* analysis. By *content*, we mean both the semantic content ("meaning") of individual pieces of information, as well as their individual structure or form. An analysis of the occurrence and internal distribution of words in an individual document is an example of content analysis. By *interrelationships*, we mean the explicit and implicit associations present among information objects in a collection. Note that such associations can be considered at many different levels of abstraction. Examples of implicit interrelationships include general conceptual similarities among free-text documents. Examples of explicit interrelationships include direct references among documents (e.g., references in technical papers, URLs) or the co-occurance of important terms (e.g., person or place names).

Our approach, then, is to provide exploratory tools that will enable analysts to quickly develop and test hypotheses related to informational content and associative interrelationships. These tools take the form of a variety of text-based and graphical querying functions that operate on metadata about the information that are derived during a preprocessing phase. The results of these operations are presented in both graphical and textual forms.

To achieve our goals of accelerating and improving understanding of this information, we use a variety of proven and new 2-D and 3-D visualization methods in an integrated fashion. We integrate multimedia information, such as imagery and maps, with graphical representations of text collections to enable their concurrent analysis. This approach enables us to generate displays with very high information densities, providing users with the ability to compare information presented at several levels of abstraction simultaneously. Display complexity is managed through the application of proven visualization techniques such as layering, and through the employment of interactive information filtering tools. A variety of more traditional analysis tools provide support for Starlight's visual analysis tools. These include several integrated query engines and an automated mapping system.

Clearly, enabling the types of analyses discussed here requires the development of a comprehensive information system that includes components for information loading, storage, retrieval, and presentation, in addition to information analysis tools. Due to their visual orientation, we have termed such systems Visual Information Systems (VIS). In this sense, Geographic Information Systems (GIS) can be considered a type of VIS that deals specifically with the management, analysis, and display of geographic information.

4 Functional Design

Functionally, Starlight has two key components: 1) an information preprocessing and modeling system for characterizing information content, modeling associations among input data elements, and storing the modeled information for later retrieval and analysis, and 2) a visualization system/user interface used during exploratory analysis of the information model.

4.1 Information Preprocessing and Modeling

During the preprocessing phase, input text data is first reformatted to a standard form. During this process structured information (e.g., header information) is tagged and hierarchically related to emphasize semantic dependencies among the input information fields; special field types (e.g., date/time fields) are identified; and free-text portions of the data are flagged. Multimedia input data is handled similarly, through the use of text data descriptors that contain information pertaining to both the data as a whole (e.g., acquisition date, image file location) and specific features within the data (e.g., the locations and names of people in a photograph). Once reformatting has been completed, the text data is fed into a Starlight database construction utility. At this point, the structured and free-text components of the input data are separated and treated independently, however reciprocal references between them are maintained.

Free-text items are routed to a series of statistical and natural language processing utilities for both individual and group characterization. The first step in the statistical processing is the removal of words with low semantic content, along with words that occur so frequently within the text collection that they would serve as poor discriminators. At this point a clustering algorithm can be optionally applied to divide large input data sets into smaller, conceptually related subgroups. Finally, a variation of Latent Semantic Indexing (LSI) [8] is applied to the individual subsets. The results of this processing is a "semantic index" that is used to support "concept" queries in the analysis portion of the software. Additionally, the singular vectors resulting from the singular-value decomposition of the term-by-document matrix can be plotted to enable visualization of conceptual interrelationships among elements of the document sets.

In addition to the statistical processing, a variety of natural-language processing algorithms are applied to the free-text data to further characterize it. In particular, term-extraction algorithms are used to extract terms-of-interest from the data. These algorithms automatically identify and flag terms, such as the names of people, places, and organizations, found within the text. Place names extracted from the text are treated as a special case, and are run through a geo-referencing engine that associates the names with geographic coordinates for later use during the visualization and analysis process. All extracted terms are subsequently appended to the structured component of the original input data element.

Input and derived information is modeled in an object-oriented fashion, and is stored in two parallel, but interconnected, data structures: one for storing and retrieving the actual content of the input information, and the other for deriving, storing, and retrieving associative information developed from the structured components of the data.

Information content is stored in an object-oriented DBMS, along with the data indices developed during preprocessing. Currently Starlight includes three different content data stores, one for textual information, one for image information, and one for geographic information. Each of these data stores includes one or more dedicated data retrieval engines.

Structured information (both input and derived) is modeled using Leenstra, et. al.'s Contiguous Connection Model (CCM) [9], which is conceptually similar to the Semantic Database Model (SDM) of Hammer and McCleod [10]. With the CCM approach, a hierarchical schema is imposed on input (typically "flat") structured data in order to emphasize semantic dependencies among the input field values. Then, through an inversion process, an inverted index is constructed that relates multiple occurrences of the same field values in different records to one another. A query for information associated with a particular field/value pair returns a tree structure, called an Array Set, containing all information that is hierarchically related to the query.

The CCM supports dynamic data structuring and restructuring based on the particular "view" of the data required at any particular instant. For example, CCM-based modeling enables the object-attribute duality commonly found among real-world entities to be captured and effectively exploited. For example, an author "has-a" book, but the book also has an author. In the first case, a book title can be considered an attribute of the author, while in the second case, the author can be considered an attribute of the book. In reality, there is only one instance of a particular author and book title. In this case, queries against a CCM-based model of this relationship could be initiated from the point of view of the book or of the author, depending upon the current interest of the user. Further, through a capacity known as "role exchange," sets of attributes can be independently organized into logical groupings. For example, a person's role as an author may involve an entirely different set of attributes (publisher, publications, etc.) from that person's role as a researcher. The CCM enables attributes associated with different entity roles to be treated independently, or jointly, as required.

4.2 Information Visualization and Analysis

Databases generated by the data loading and preprocessing systems can be interactively explored using a variety of integrated visualization tools. Starlight's key visualization "venue" is a 3-D workspace that contains graphical representations of entire databases, along with ancillary information resources, such as maps and images [Fig. 1]. This workspace is intended to foster relatively high-level comparisons among elements of an information collection as a whole, providing a sense of the overall semantic "shape" of the collection. The workspace can be interactively navigated, providing users the ability to alternately examine large-scale patterns in the information from a distance, or move in to inspect local informational structures in detail. Additionally, multiple views of the workspace can be open at the same time, providing the capability to simultaneously monitor local and global informational patterns during analysis.

In the workspace, 3-D symbols represent individual database elements (e.g., documents). The 3-D spatial distribution of the symbols conveys information about their contents. Starlight currently uses two principal spatial distribution methods, one for collections of textual information, and another for representing collections of purely structured information.

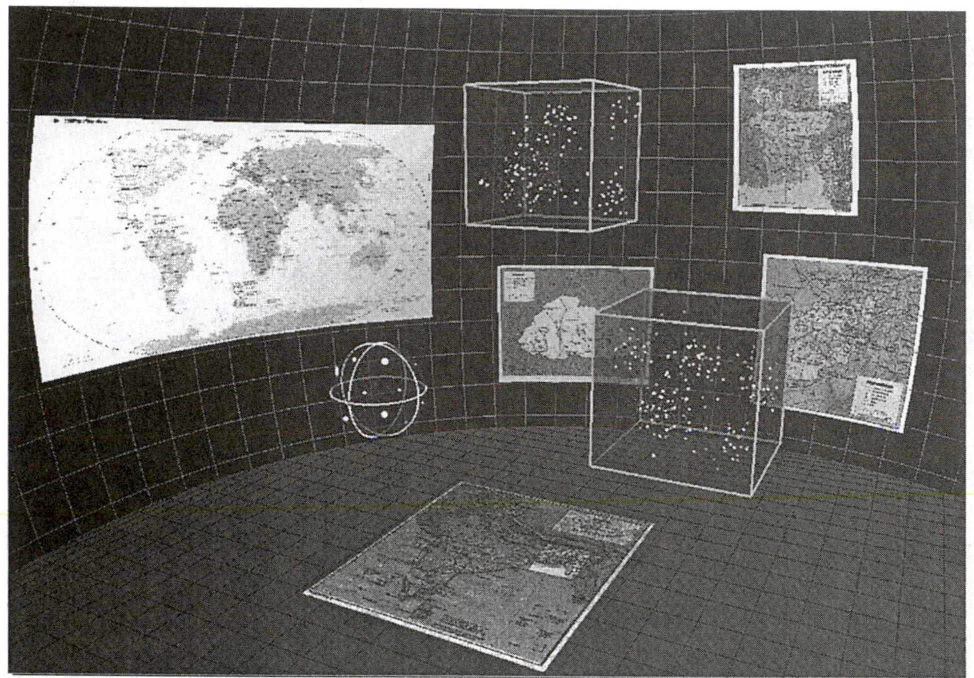

Figure 1. Synoptic view of a Starlight workspace, showing representations of two free-text data sets, a collection of structured information, and several supporting information resources.

In the case of collections of free-text documents, the results of the semantic analysis of the documents are used to generate a 3-D scatterplot that shows general conceptual or topical interrelationships among them. In this display, which we call a *Similarity Plot*, the proximity of any two symbols to one another is an indication of how conceptually similar they are to one another. Documents that are closely related to one another (i.e., that use the same words in similar combinations) will appear clustered close together, while less similar documents will appear distant from one another. This "starfield" display approach is similar to that used by several systems, including the *Bead* [11] and *SemNet* [3] systems. The goal of this approach is to provide a sort of automatically generated table-of-contents for the document collection.

For purely structured information, a different organizing principal must be used to generate meaningful spatial distributions of symbols. We are currently using the straightforward approach of enabling users to dynamically "sort the information into piles" distributed over the surface of a sphere (called a *Data Sphere*), based on the values associated with any given (categorical) field [Fig. 2]. For example, a user may elect to spatially redistribute a collection of personnel records based on the values in the "Employer" field. The system would first sort the records into groups based on the Employer field values, then evenly distribute the symbol groups over the surface of the sphere representing that collection. Note that free-text information also typically has a structured component to it. Consequently, users can chose to convert free-text Similarity Plot representations to Data Sphere representations, and back, should they wish to examine the structured attributes of the text using this method.

In addition to spatial distribution, symbol color and shape can be used to simultaneously convey additional dimensions of information. Users can elect to apply color and/or shape encodings to symbols based on values associated with particular fields of the structured data. In the case of categorical field types, either color or shape can be used to convey information about a particular data element's field value. Color alone can be used for ranged numerical field types. Note that symbol shape only becomes apparent when a workspace viewpoint is in close proximity to a symbol. Consequently, color is typically used for the most important fields, while shape encodings are reserved for fields of secondary or tertiary importance.

The combined use of meaningful spatial distributions of symbols, along with symbol color and shape encodings, provides three simultaneous visualization channels for conveying information about the elements of Starlight databases. A fourth channel is provided through the use of text displays of the contents of text fields associated with the data. Users can elect to display text in one of two ways: statically, in which an entire text field is displayed adjacent to an symbol, or via a novel 3-D text

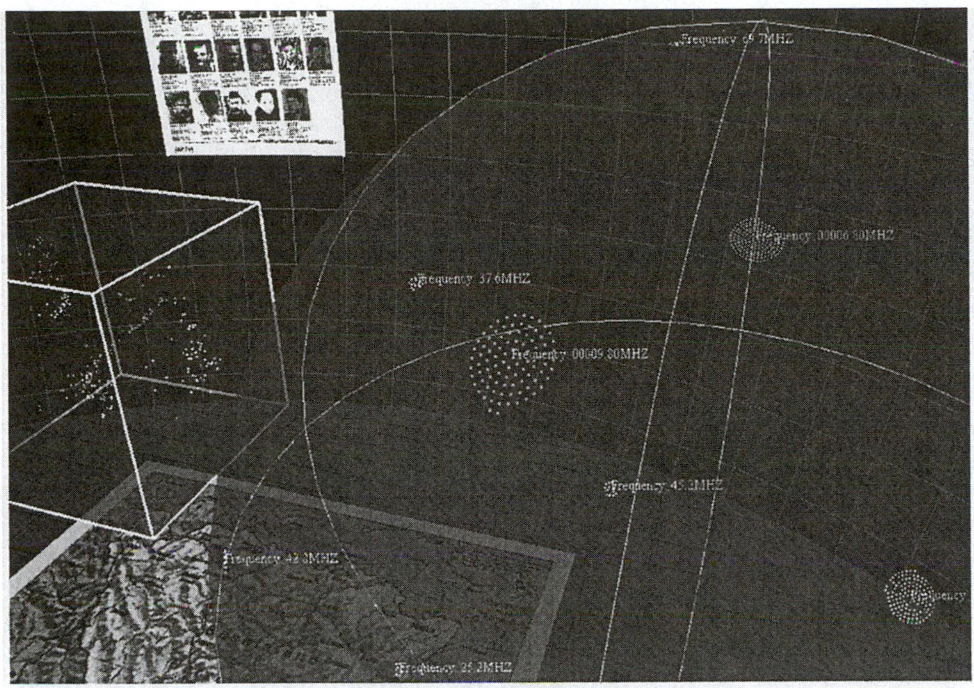

Figure 2. Close-up view of a *Data Sphere* showing structured data set elements grouped according to the values in a given field.

display technique that we call *text streaming*. With text streaming, individual words in a text field are consecutively displayed adjacent to their corresponding symbol, one word at a time. Users can adjust the rate of the text display to suit their preferred reading speed. Perhaps surprisingly, most users adapt readily to this method after a relatively short acclimation period. The advantage of this approach, of course, is that large amounts of textual information can be rapidly conveyed using only very small amount of screen real estate. In fact, an entire document can be streamed to a user in the screen space required for the display of only a single word. Multiple text fields associated with multiple database elements can be streamed simultaneously, providing users with the ability to quickly absorb and compare large quantities of textual information simply by shifting the focus of their gaze.

In addition to the interactive visualization techniques described above, a number of powerful data retrieval tools are available to Starlight users. Two general classes of query operations are possible, corresponding to the two general forms of analysis operations previously described. *Content Queries* operate on data element contents and return sets of elements that satisfy the query. *Association Queries* operate on the interrelationship model generated during preprocessing, and return maps of interrelationships among data element attributes. Association Queries enable a form of "link analysis" in which users can visualize and interactively navigate the complex network of associations that typically exists among the elements of any information collection.

Three types of Content Queries are possible: Boolean *Pattern Queries* for searching for occurrences of specific patterns of words or numbers, *Concept Queries*, for retrieving text describing concepts similar to those specified, and *Field Queries*, for searching the structured attribute information associated with database elements. The different types of content queries can be combined with one another in various ways, providing a powerful and highly flexible data retrieval capability. The results of a content query are presented to the user as a ranked list of the database elements that satisfy the query. Simultaneously, symbols representing database elements satisfying the query are automatically highlighted in the 3-D workspace view. This provides users with the ability to visually compare query results with other aspects of the data. These include overall conceptual relationships among the query results themselves, as well as their relationships to database elements that did not satisfy the query. Users can examine the full content of the information by selecting individual items from the results list for inspection, or by selecting highlighted symbols in the workspace display.

Association Queries provide the capability to visualize and interactively navigate the structure of connections between elements of a database developed during preprocessing. They generate a "snapshot" of the CCM database from a particular point of view. An Association Query returns a hierarchical data structure called an *Array Set* that describes the hierarchical interrelationships among database element attributes from the point of view of a particular attribute. For example, an Association Query for information related to a particular author might return an Array Set describing the dates of publication, publishers, titles, and abstracts, of all the publications by that author in the database. The hierarchical structure of the Array Set conveys the exact nature of the relationships among those attributes. Note that an Association Query for information related to a particular publisher would generate a completely different "view" of the associations model.

An Array Set resulting from an Association Query is presented to the user in a split view window [Fig. 3]. A tree representation of the Array Set is displayed in the left side of the window. The tree can be interactively explored by opening particular branches by clicking on them with the mouse cursor. The right side of the split view shows a 3-D graphical construct of the same information called a *Link Net*. The Link Net can be considered a hybrid visualization technique that incorporates features of the *cone tree* [1] and *parallel coordinates* [12] techniques. Like cone trees, Link Nets are representations of hierarchical information. The nodes in a Link Net correspond to particular field/value pairs. The query field/value pair used to generate an Array Set forms the root node of the tree, and is located at the top of the corresponding Link Net. Hierarchically related information is located beneath the root node on planes corresponding to the related fields. The planes are arrayed vertically on levels corresponding to the level in the Array Set hierarchy in which they occur. The planes are populated with symbols representing the unique values associated with that field that have been returned by the query. Direct hierarchical relationships between field/value pairs are shown by lines that connect related symbols. Note that associations described by Array Sets may include multiple, redundant occurrences of the same value for a particular field in separate branches of the tree. These occurrences are coalesced into a single symbol representation, simplifying the display considerably with no loss of information.

Clearly, the information content of an Array Set could be effectively communicated using a 2-D graphical approach. The use of the third dimension, however, provides an additional degree of spatial freedom with which to convey further information about the displayed interrelationships. For example, consider the values associated with a Link Net plane representing geographic coordinates. Symbols representing those coordinate values can be geographically positioned relative to one another to provide additional important information about the other attributes with which they are associated. Further, supporting information resources, in the form of maps and images, can be applied to the field planes to provide a visual context for the information presented in Link Nets. In the case of a geographic coordinate plane, links passing through coordinate value symbols will automatically be routed to the correct point on the map, providing a geographic context for the coordinates. In a similar fashion, an organizational chart might be applied to a plane containing organization names. Links will automatically pass through the appropriate points on the chart. Likewise, symbols representing temporal values can be positioned along a timeline to effectively convey temporal interrelationships.

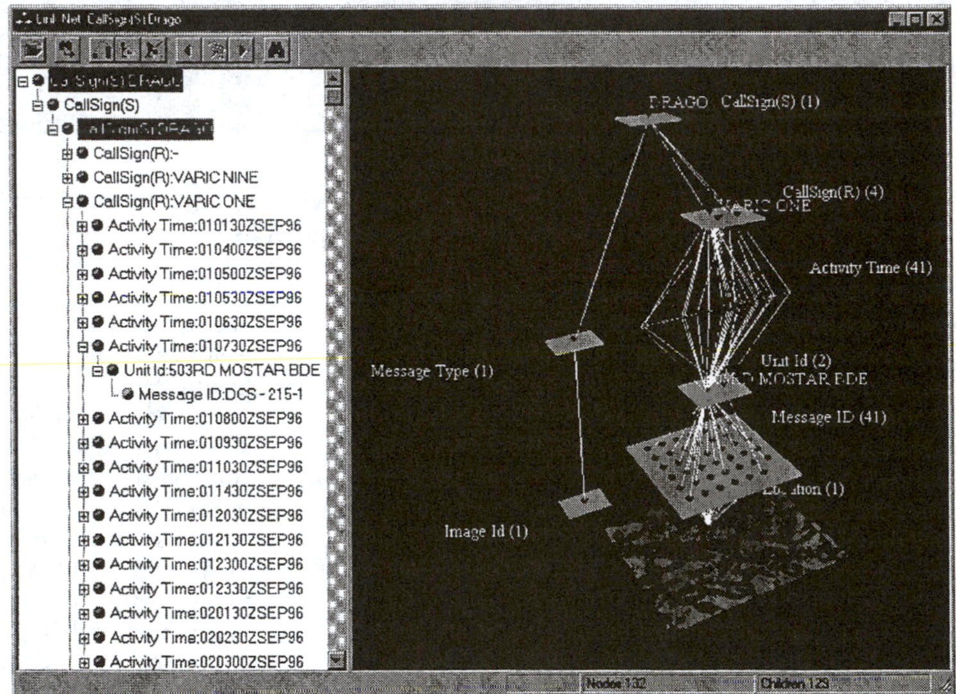

Figure 3. Array Set and corresponding Link Net visualization of information related to a particular transmitting call sign (DRAGO) from a simulated intelligence database. Note the temporal distribution of the transmissions to receiving call sign VARIC ONE, and the single geographic position of those transmissions.

The Link Net geometry provides a detailed, yet compact representation of the relationships described by its associated Array Set data structure. Note that Link Nets always have a plane containing symbols representing the data elements (e.g., documents) whose attributes are interrelated within the context of the Array Set. This provides fast access to the full detail of the original data at any time. Note also that color and/or shape encodings that have been applied to the data are reflected in the data element symbols shown in the Link Net display.

Link Nets can be graphically queried and interactively filtered to highlight single, or sets of, linkages among the attribute fields. Clicking on an individual symbol toggles the set of linkages associated with that particular field value. For example, clicking on a document symbol will display the attributes associated with that document; clicking on the root node will toggle on or off all the links in the Link Net. If a Link Net contains a temporal field, a slider can be used to interactively filter links by the time values they pass through. If a map has been applied to a plane, the links will be "geographically filtered;" only those links that pass through the geographic window described by the map will be displayed. These filtering techniques provide the user with a high degree of control over display complexity, helping ensure that the information presented can be easily assimilated.

A final important feature of the link analysis system is the ability of users to dynamically "hop" from the current Link Net display to one generated using any one of its field/value nodes. Performing the *hop* operation on a node results in the generation of a new Association Query using the selected field/value pair. The resulting Link Net is displayed in the same window, providing users with the ability to quickly navigate the complex network of associations among data elements.

At the same time that a new Link Net is generated, another, more abstract, representation of it is also constructed in the 3-D workspace [Fig. 4]. This graphical analogue of the Link Net is intended to provide users with the ability to compare multiple sets of associations with one another, at a higher, more abstract level, as well as with large-scale informational features displayed in the workspace. This feature takes the form of a single symbol representing the query field/value pair, called a *Tie-Node*. The Tie-Node is automatically located at the average 3-D coordinate of the data elements referenced in the Array Set, and is connected to them by rays. If an Ancillary Information Resource (AIR, e.g., a map) displayed in the 3-D Workspace has also been applied to one of the Link Net planes, then links connecting the Tie-Node to the appropriate locations on the AIR will also be displayed. Interactions with a Link Net that result in changes to its displayed links (e.g., filtering operations) are also reflected in the Tie-Node display. Tie-Nodes can be "expanded" as needed, generating direct connections between, for example, data element symbols and AIRs, or "collapsed" back to their symbolic form to simplify and better organize the display.

The associative Link Net and Tie-Node displays, in combination with the other visualization techniques employed by Starlight (spatial symbol distributions, color and shape encodings, text displays), enable the interactive generation of extremely rich information displays (Fig. 4). Such displays help convey, in an intelligible form, much more of the complexity inherent in multimedia information collections than is possible with traditional information analysis systems. Coupled with effective information preprocessing, storage, and retrieval systems, the visualization components of Starlight enable powerful forms of information analysis that hold the potential for greatly accelerating and improving the information analysis process.

5 Summary

Starlight is an example of a new class of information system, one that has been purpose-designed for the visual analysis of complex, multimedia information. The software couples a variety of established and novel visualization techniques with a comprehensive data storage and retrieval system, in effect extending and enhancing the capabilities of more traditional information retrieval systems. At the same time, Starlight enables new forms of information analysis by promoting visual comparisons of information presented at many levels of abstraction simultaneously. This includes the capability to concurrently analyze multimedia information, such as image and map information, along with textual information. If display complexity can be effectively managed, the very high information densities possible in Starlight displays are expected to accelerate the information analysis process while simultaneously reducing the stress levels of analysts. The effectiveness of this approach will be tested in the coming months in a number of intelligence and commercial information analysis domains.

6 Acknowledgements

The PNNL Starlight Project has benefited from the efforts of a great many talented people. We would especially like to recognize our colleagues in the Boeing Information and Support Services, Natural Language Processing Group, Andrew Booker, Mark Greaves, Fred Holt, Anne Kao, Dan Pierce, and Steve Poteet, for contributing the semantic text indexing and display components of Starlight, and our colleagues at Applied Technical Systems, Inc., Ed Marquardt, Lance Otis, and Tom Bougan, for the customization and use of their Contiguous Connection Model software. This work is supported by the U.S. Army under Contract 26970, and the U.S. Department of Energy under Contract DE-AC06-76RLO 1830. The Pacific Northwest National Laboratory is operated for the U.S. Department of Energy by the Battelle Memorial Institute.

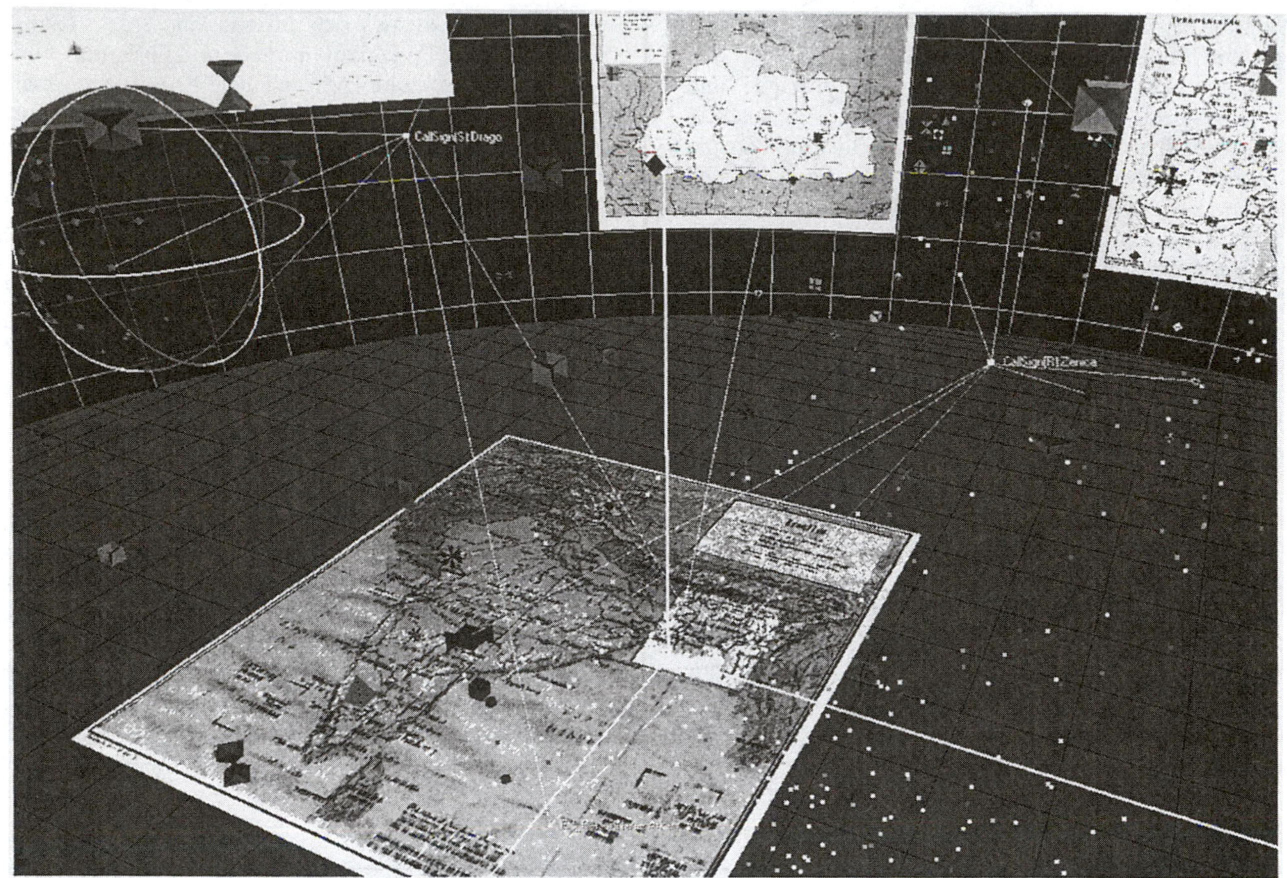

Figure 4. View of a complex Starlight workspace display showing multiple simultaneous visualization features, including a free-text similarity display, data element shape and color encodings, text labels, linkage Tie-Nodes, and linked ancillary information displays.

References

[1] Robertson, G.G., Card, S.K., and Mackinlay, J.D., 1991, "Cone Trees: Animated 3-D Visualizations of Hierarchical Information," In: *Proceedings of CHI '91*, pp. 189-194.

[2] Johnson, B., and Shneiderman, B., 1991, "Tree-Maps: A Space-Filling Approach to the Visualization of Hierarchical Information Structures," In: *Proceedings of the 2nd IEEE Visualization Conference*, pp. 284-291.

[3] Fairchild, K.M., Poltrock, S.E., and Furnas, G.W., 1988, "SemNet: Three-Dimensional Graphic Representations of Large Knowledge Bases," In: *Cognitive Science And Its Applications for Human-Computer Interaction*, Guindon, R. ed., Lawrence Erlbaum, pp. 201-233.

[4] Ahlberg, C., and Shneiderman, B., 1992, "Visual Information Seeking: Tight Coupling of Dynamic Query Filters with Starfield Displays," In: *Proceedings of CHI '92*, pp. 619-626.

[5] Ahlberg, C., and Wistrand, E., 1995, "IVEE: An Information Visualization and Exploration Environment," In: *Proceedings of Information Visualization '95*, pp. 66-73.

[6] Becker, B.G., 1997, "Using MineSet for Knowledge Discovery," *IEEE Computer Graphics and Applications*, v. 17, n. 4, pp. 75-78.

[7] Risch, J.S., May, R.A., Dowson, S.T., Thomas, J.J., 1996, "A Virtual Environment for Multimedia Intelligence Data Analysis," *IEEE Computer Graphics and Applications*, v. 16, n. 6, pp. 33-41.

[8] Dumais, S. T., Furnas, G. W., Landauer, T. K., and Deerwester, S., 1988, "Using Latent Semantic Analysis To Improve Information Retrieval," In: *Proceedings of CHI'88: Conference on Human Factors in Computing*, pp. 281-285.

[9] Leenstra, R.B., Wurden, E.H., Otis, L.N., and Wurden, F.L., 1996, "Data Management Systems and Methods Including Creation of Composite Views of Data," U.S. Patent 5,555,409, September 10, 1996.

[10] Hammer, M., and McLeod, D., 1981, "Database Description with SDM: A Semantic Database Model," *Transactions on Database Systems*, v. 6, n. 3, pp. 43-57.

[11] Chalmers, M., and Chitson, P., 1992, "Bead: Explorations in Information Visualization," In: *Proceedings of the 15th Ann. Int'l. SIGIR'92*, pp. 330-337.

[12] Inselberg, A., and Dimsdale, B., 1990, "Parallel Coordinates: A Tool For Visualizing Multi-Dimensional Geometry," In: *Proceedings of Visualization '90*, pp. 361 – 378.

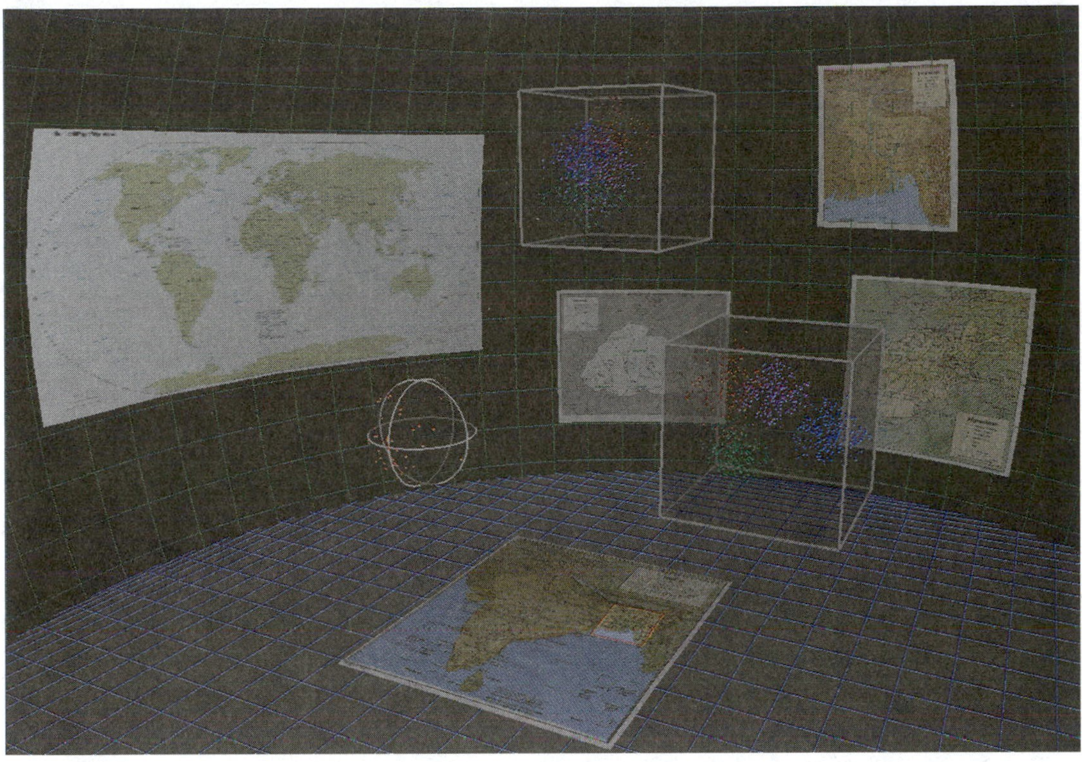

FIGURE 1

Synoptic view of a Starlight workspace, showing representations of two free-text data sets, a collection of structured information, and several supporting information resources.

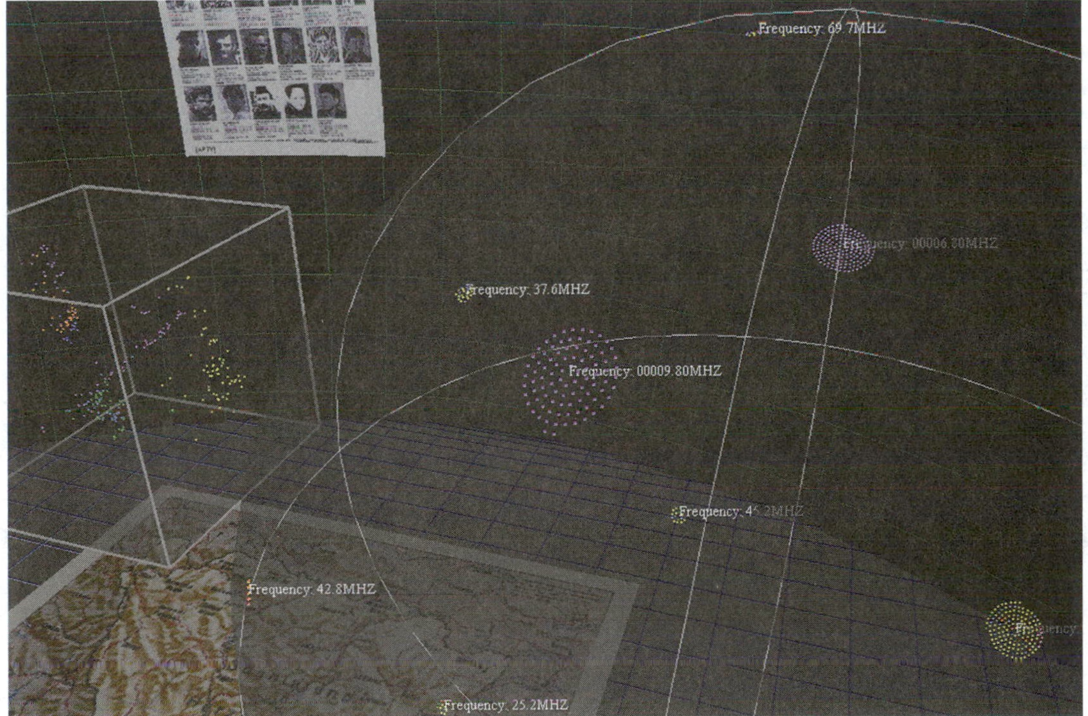

FIGURE 2

Close-up view of a *Data Sphere* showing structured data set elements grouped according to the values in a given field.

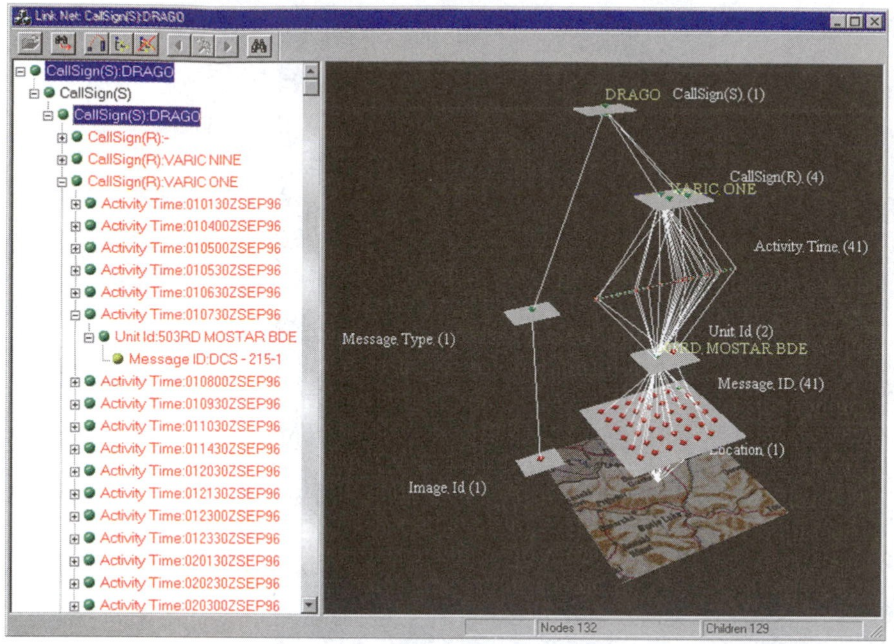

FIGURE 3

Array Set and corresponding Link Net visualization of information related to a particular transmitting call sign (DRAGO) from a simulated intelligence database. Note the temporal distribution of the transmissions to receiving call sign VARIC ONE, and the single geographic position of those transmissions.

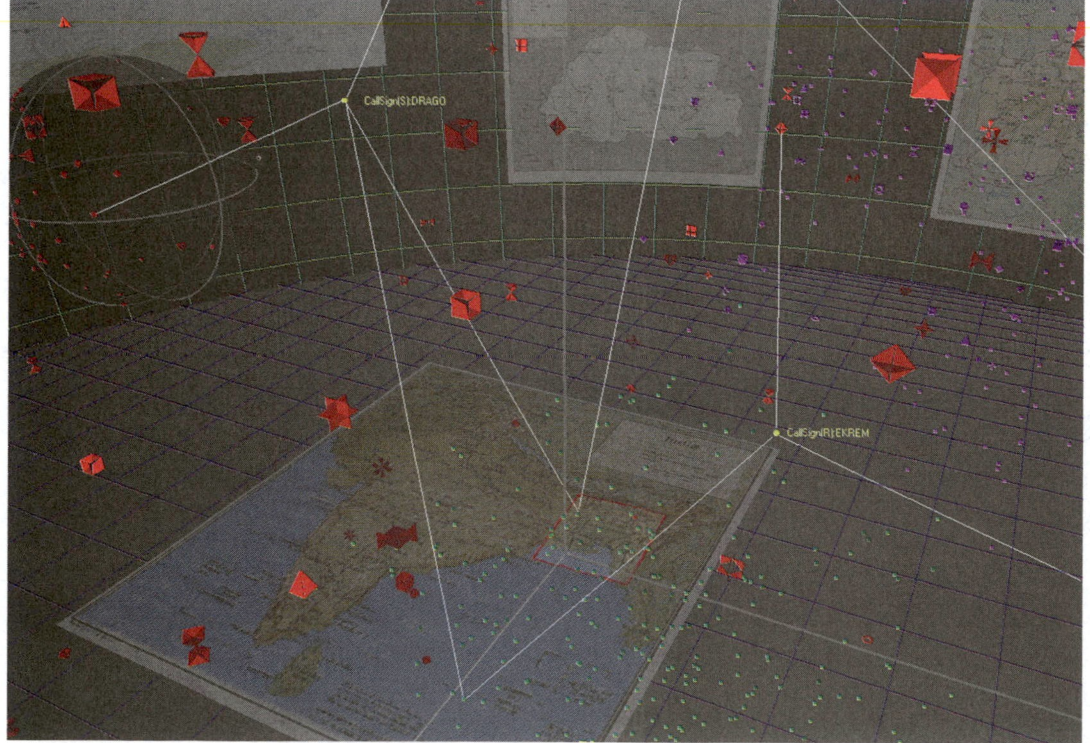

FIGURE 4

View of a complex Starlight workspace display showing multiple simultaneous visualization features, including a free-text similarity display, data element shape and color encodings, text labels, linkage Tie-Nodes, and linked ancillary information displays.

6.3

Visually Enhanced Objects

The papers in this section use visualization as part of a visually enhanced object. In these cases, the object itself is of interest. For example, an electronic medical textbook may be constructed using visualization components. In fact, this is exactly the case for the IMDM group at the University of Hamburg (Hohne et al., 1995). The situation is the inverse of that for information workspaces. Whereas information visualization was used as part of the user interface for a workspace that could contain various information objects, in this section we consider some visually enhanced objects that might be included in the workspace. Of course, we are talking about ideal conceptual types. Some particular design could blend the boundaries—a textbook, for example, that includes small internal workspaces.

The first paper in this section, by Robertson and Mackinlay (Robertson and Mackinlay, 1993 ●), is a proposal for an electronic document that allows the user both to see the entire document at once and to read any particular page. It does this using perspective focus + context techniques, pulling the focus part forward, leaving the other parts visible as the sides of a frustum. Search can be used to highlight parts of the document, and the distribution of these highlights shows the density of a topic in the context part of the document, thus suggesting places to examine.

The second paper, by North, Shneiderman, and Plaisant (1996 ●), explores building dynamic query and previewing techniques into a system for rendering a voxel image of a human. Here they have taken an object of interest, a particular specimen of human anatomy, and enhanced it with information visualization techniques. The technique is of interest not only because dynamic query techniques aid in the viewing, but also because they are able to solve the remote large data set problem. There are many applications (e.g., weather) where large, centrally curated data sets reside. They are too large for users to download the entire set for casual examination. North et al.'s system downloads a small sample, but one amenable to interactive examination using dynamic queries. Larger selections can then be downloaded according to the exact parts of interest.

Dix (1998) has made the point that most particular diagrams of interest can be made into information visualizations by adding interaction, such as dynamic queries or other information visualization techniques. For example, he took a cumulative bar chart and used interaction to line up different parts. In the same spirit, many visual objects or displays can be enhanced by adding visual interaction techniques to them—textbooks, catalogues, order forms.

THE DOCUMENT LENS

George G. Robertson and Jock D. Mackinlay

Xerox Palo Alto Research Center
3333 Coyote Hill Road
Palo Alto, CA 94304
415-812-4755, robertson@parc.xerox.com

ABSTRACT

This paper describes a general visualization technique based on a common strategy for understanding paper documents when their structure is not known, which is to lay the pages of a document in a rectangular array on a large table where the overall structure and distinguishing features can be seen. Given such a presentation, the user wants to quickly view parts of the presentation in detail while remaining in context. A fisheye view or a magnifying lens might be used for this, but they fail to adequately show the global context. The *Document Lens* is a 3D visualization for large rectangular presentations that allows the user to quickly focus on a part of a presentation while continuously remaining in context. The user grabs a rectangular lens and pulls it around to focus on the desired area at the desired magnification. The presentation outside the lens is stretched to provide a continuous display of the global context. This stretching is efficiently implemented with affine transformations, allowing text documents to be viewed as a whole with an interactive visualization.

KEYWORDS: User interface design issues, interface metaphors, graphic presentations, screen layout, 3D interaction techniques.

INTRODUCTION

In recent years, several efforts have been made to take advantage of the advances in 3D graphics hardware to visualize abstract information [3, 4, 7]. Our work on the Information Visualizer [7] has described a range of interaction techniques for understanding information and its structure. In particular, we have developed visualizations for hierarchical and linear structures, called the Cone Tree and the Perspective Wall. However, users often start with information with unknown structure. For example, a user may not know that a document is hierarchical such as a book that contains chapters and sections, or linear such as a visitor log. Therefore, we are also developing general visualization techniques that can be used for unfamiliar information.

Our basic goals remain the same as with our other work on the Information Visualizer. We want to use 3D to make more effective use of available screen space. We want to use interactive animation to shift cognitive load to the human perceptual system. We want a display that provides both a detailed working area and its global context (as in both the Cone Tree and Perspective Wall). We want to aid the user in perceiving patterns or texture in the information. The *Document Lens* is an experimental interaction technique implemented in the Information Visualizer to address this set of goals when information is placed in a rectangular presentation.

THE PROBLEM

If you lay the entire contents of a multi-page document out in two dimensions so it is all visible, the text will typically be much too small to read. Figure 1 shows a document laid out in this way. Yet, we would like to be able to do this so that patterns in the document can be easily perceived (especially when a search is done and the results are highlighted in a different color). Futhermore, we want the user to be able to quickly zoom into a desired part of the document so it can be read, *without* losing the global context.

We are particularly interested in revealing the texture or pattern of relationships between parts of a document. In Figure 1, a search has been done for the term "fish-

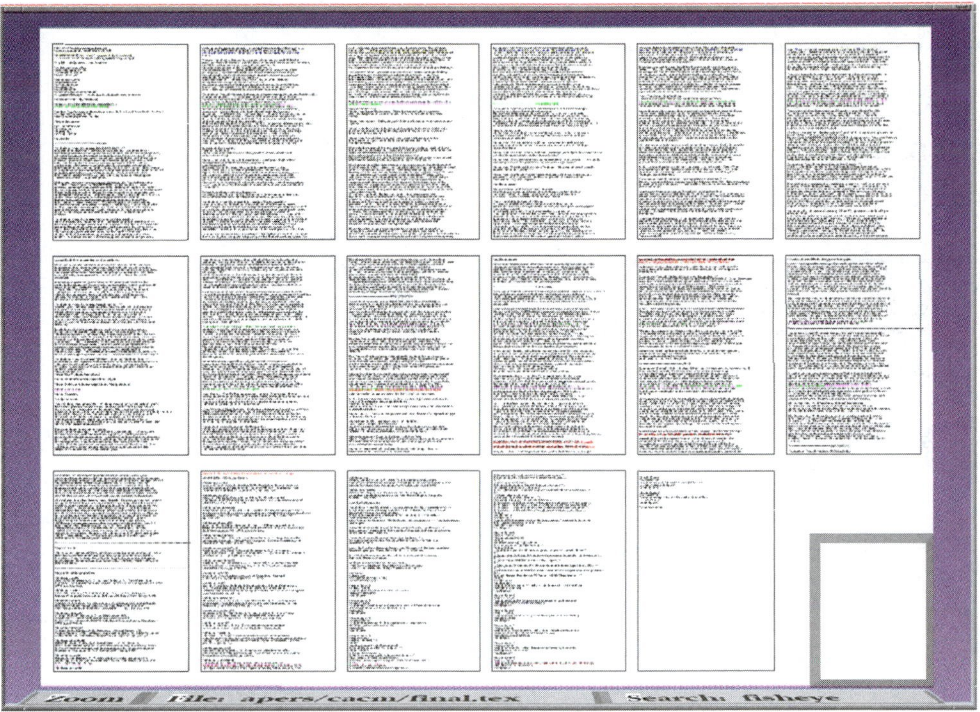

Figure 1: Document laid out on a 2D surface. Red highlights are the result of a search.

eye" in the document, which is the text from our recent CACM article [7]. If you look closely, you will see five places highlighted in red in the document that refer to the term, and most of these occurrences are close together. You can imagine that the sections of a structured document could be highlighted so that the pattern of references to a term can show how the sections relate to one another.

In order to focus on one part of a document while retaining the global context (so you can continue to see the interesting patterns), you need what we call a *Focus + Context Display*.

If you try to do this with a traditional magnifying lens (either a physical one or one implemented in software), you will necessarily obscure the parts of the document immediately next to the lens, thus losing the global context. Figure 2 illustrates this problem. Thus, a simple magnifying lens does not provide a focus + context display.

One possible solution is to use an optical fisheye lens (like looking at something through a glass sphere). Silicon Graphics has a demonstration that uses this technique on images. The problem is that the distortions that result from such a lens make reading text difficult even for the text in the middle of the lens.

Another strategy is to distort the view so that details and context are integrated. Furnas developed a general framework called *fisheye views* for generating distorted views [5]. Fisheye views are generated by Degree of Interest functions that are thresholded to determine the contents of the display. However, thresholding causes the visualization to have gaps that might be confusing or difficult to repair. Furthermore, gaps can make it difficult to change the view. The desired destination might be in one of the gaps, or the transition from one view to another might be confusing as familiar parts of the visualization suddenly disappear into gaps.

Sarkar and Brown developed a generalization of Furnas' fisheye views specifically for viewing graphs [8]. Their technique works in real time for relatively small graphs (on the order of 100 vertices and 100 horizontal or vertical edges). They acknowledge that the technique does not scale up to significantly larger graphs. The text in Figure 1 is from a relatively small document (16 pages). Even so, it requires approximately 400,000 vectors, or about 4000 times larger than the Sarkar and Brown technique can handle in real time.

Spence and Apperley developed an early system called the Bifocal Display that integrates detail and context through another distorted view [9]. The Bifocal Display was a combination of a detailed view and two distorted

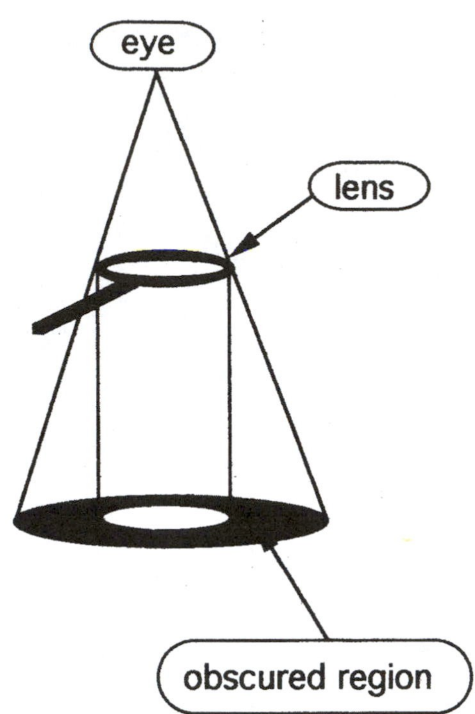

Figure 2: Illustration of the problem with a magnifier lens: parts of the image near the edges of the lens are obscured by the lens.

views, where items on either side of the detailed view are distorted horizontally into narrow vertical strips. For example, the detailed view might contain a page from a journal and the distorted view might contain the years for various issues of the journal. Because Bifocal Displays are two dimensional, they do not integrate detail and context completely smoothly. Two versions of an item are required, one for the detailed view and one for the distorted view. The relationship between these versions may not be obvious. As the focus moves, items suddenly expand or shrink, which may be confusing. Furthermore, the distorted view treats all contextual items identically, even those near the detailed view.

The Perspective Wall [7] is a technique for visualizing linear information by smoothly integrating detailed and contextual views. It folds wide 2D layouts into intuitive 3D visualizations that have a center panel for detail and two perspective panels for context. The Perspective Wall provides a fisheye effect without distortions by using the natural fisheye effects of 3D perspective. However, the Perspective Wall does not handle well 2D layouts that are large in both dimensions, such as a document laid out as pages in a rectangular array. Furthermore, it is unclear how to distort efficiently the corners of a 2D sheet when it is folded both horizontally and vertically. Hence a different approach is required.

THE DOCUMENT LENS

Assume that the document pages are laid out onto a large rectangular region. In general, what we need is a way of folding or stretching that region in 3D so that part of it is near you, but the rest is still visible (giving you the desired focus + context display). The 3D deformation should be continuous to avoid the discontinuities of fisheye views and the Bifocal Display and it should be possible to implement it efficiently on a wide class of graphics machines.

We propose a new kind of lens, called the *Document Lens*, which gives us the desired properties. The lens itself is rectangular, because we are mostly interested in text, which tends to come in rectangular groupings. The Document Lens is like a rectangular magnifying lens, except that the sides are elastic and pull the surrounding parts of the region toward the lens, producing a truncated pyramid. The sides of the pyramid contain all of the document not directly visible in the lens, stretched appropriately. This gives us the desired focus + context display; that is, the whole document is always visible, but the area we are focusing on is magnified. Figure 3 shows the lens moved near the center of the document and pulled toward the user. The resulting truncated pyramid makes the text in and near the lens readable. Notice that the highlighted regions are still visible, helping retain the global context. Also notice that the Document Lens makes effective use of most of the screen space.

In the current implementation, the lens size is fixed. It could obviously be made changeable by adding resize regions on the corners of the lens, similar to the familiar way of reshaping a window in many window systems.

The lens is moved using a technique similar to the general technique for moving objects in 3D described in [6], using only a mouse and keyboard. The mouse controls motion in the X-Y plane, and the Space and Alt keys move the lens forward and backward in the Z plane. Obviously, a 3D input device could be used as well, but we have found that the mouse and keyboard are sufficient. When the lens is moved, the movement is done with interactive animation, so that user always understands what is being displayed. This helps reduce cognitive load by exploiting the human perceptual system.

As we move the lens towards us, we are faced with two problems that must be solved to make this technique practical. First, we have a problem of fine control as the lens moves toward the eye. If you use a constant velocity, you will not have sufficient control near the eye. So, we use a logarithm approach function as we did in the general object movement technique [6].

Second, and more subtle, as the lens moves in the Z direction toward you, it moves out of view. In fact, up close, you can no longer even see the lens, and therefore cannot use it to examine anything except the center of the overall region is minute detail. Figure 4 illustrates this problem. Our solution is to couple movement of the lens with viewpoint movement, proportional to the distance the lens is from the eye. In other words, when the lens is far away, there is very little viewpoint movement; but, when the lens is near you, the viewpoint tracks the lens movement. Done properly, this can keep the lens in view and allow close examination of all parts of the whole document.

This method of display makes it quite easy to show search results. If you use the traditional technique of color highlighting the search results, then patterns in the whole document become evident, even when viewing part of the document up close. The simple search result shown in the figures is based on a simple string match, and is the only search currently implemented. More complicated searches could easily be added. In the Information Visualizer, we use relevance feedback search [1] and semantic clustering algorithms [2] to show relationships between documents. In a similar way, we could apply these to the elements of a document to show relationships between parts of a document. We could use relevance feedback search to select paragraphs and search for other paragraphs with similar content. Using the clustering algorithms, we could group paragraphs into semantically similar clusters. These search techniques enhance the richness of texture that we could make visible in documents.

Although we have focused on documents and text, the Document Lens can also be used to view anything laid on a 2D plane (e.g., images).

IMPLEMENTATION ISSUES

We have implemented a version of the Document Lens in the Information Visualizer. There are at least two ways to implement the truncated pyramid that results from moving the lens toward you, and get real time response. If you could produce a high resolution image of the 2D layout, you could use either software or hardware texture mapping to map the image onto the truncated pyramid. Currently, we know of no way to produce the required high resolution texture to make either of these approaches practical.

Conceptually, our approach involves rendering the text five times. Each of the five regions (the lens, top side, left side, bottom side, and right side) is translated, rotated, and scaled (in X or Y) to give the proper view of that side. For example, if the lower left corner of the lens is $(x1, y1, z1)$, then the left side is rotated $-\frac{180 \arctan(z1, x1)}{\pi}$ degrees about its left edge, and is stretched along the X axis by a factor of $\frac{\sqrt{x1^2+z1^2}}{x1}$. The top side is rotated about its top edge and stretched along the Y axis, and so on. Most graphics machines provide efficient implementations of these affine transformations. The next step is to clip the trapezoid parts to their neighbors' edges. This step can be implemented in software, but is relatively expensive. We do this step efficiently using the SGI graphics library user specified clipping planes. Finally, culling is done so that only the necessary pages of text need be rendered for each region. The result is that each page of text is rendered about two times on the average.

Another performance enhancement technique, shown in Figure 5, replaces text outside of the lens with thick lines. This is known as *greeking* the text. Greeking is used during all user interaction (e.g., during lens movement), so that interactive animation rates are maintained. Also, the user can choose to keep the text greeked at other times.

The limiting factor in this technique is the time it takes

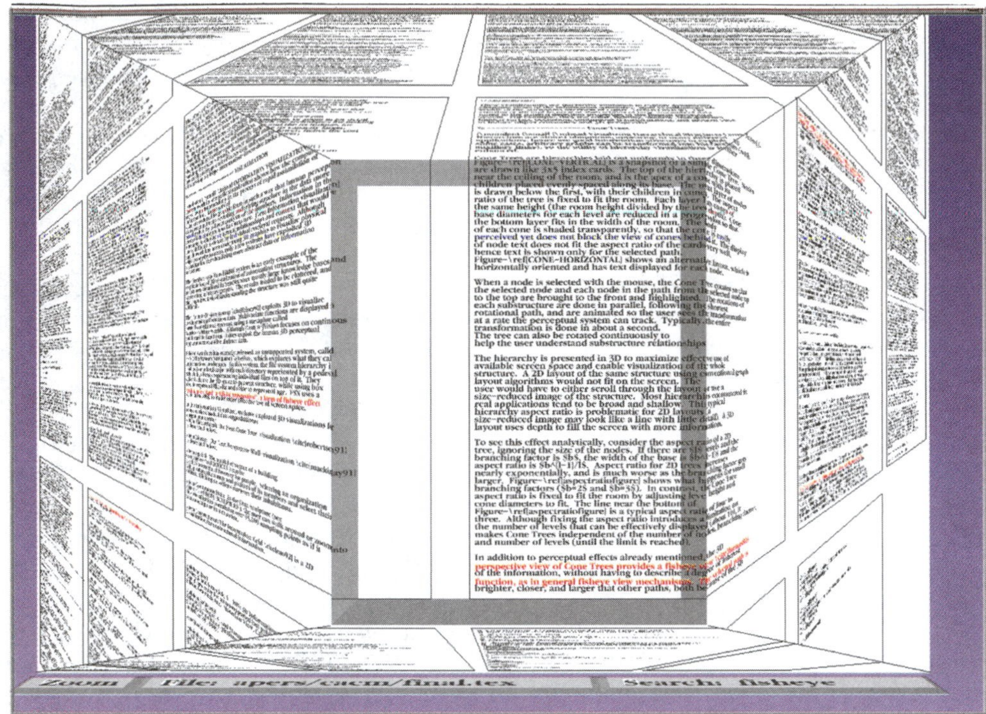

Figure 3: Document Lens with lens pulled toward the user. The resulting truncated pyramid makes text near the lens' edges readable.

to render text in 3D perspective. We use two methods, both shown in Figure 6. First, we have a simple vector font that has adequate performance, but whose appearance is less than ideal. The second method, due to Paul Haberli of Silicon Graphics, is the use of texture mapped fonts. With this method, a high quality bitmap font (actually any Adobe Type 1 outline font) is converted into an anti-aliased texture (i.e., every character appears somewhere in the texture map, as seen on the right side of Figure 6). When a character of text is laid down, the proper part of the texture map is mapped to the desired location in 3D. The texture mapped fonts have the desired appearance, but the performance is inadequate for large amounts of text, even on a high-end Silicon Graphics workstation. This application, and others like it that need large amounts of text displayed in 3D perspective, desperately need high performance, low cost texture mapping hardware. Fortunately, it appears that the 3D graphics vendors are all working on such hardware, although for other reasons.

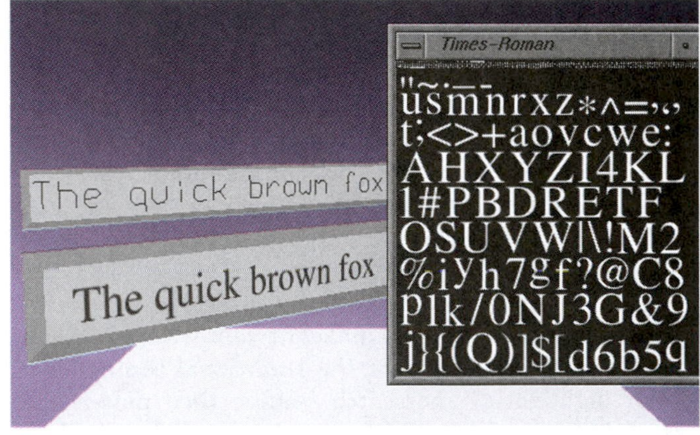

Figure 6: Vector font, texture-mapped font, and font texture map.

SUMMARY

The Document Lens is a promising solution to the problem of providing a focus + context display for visualizing an entire document. But, it is not without its problems. It does allow the user to see patterns and relationships in the information and stay in context most

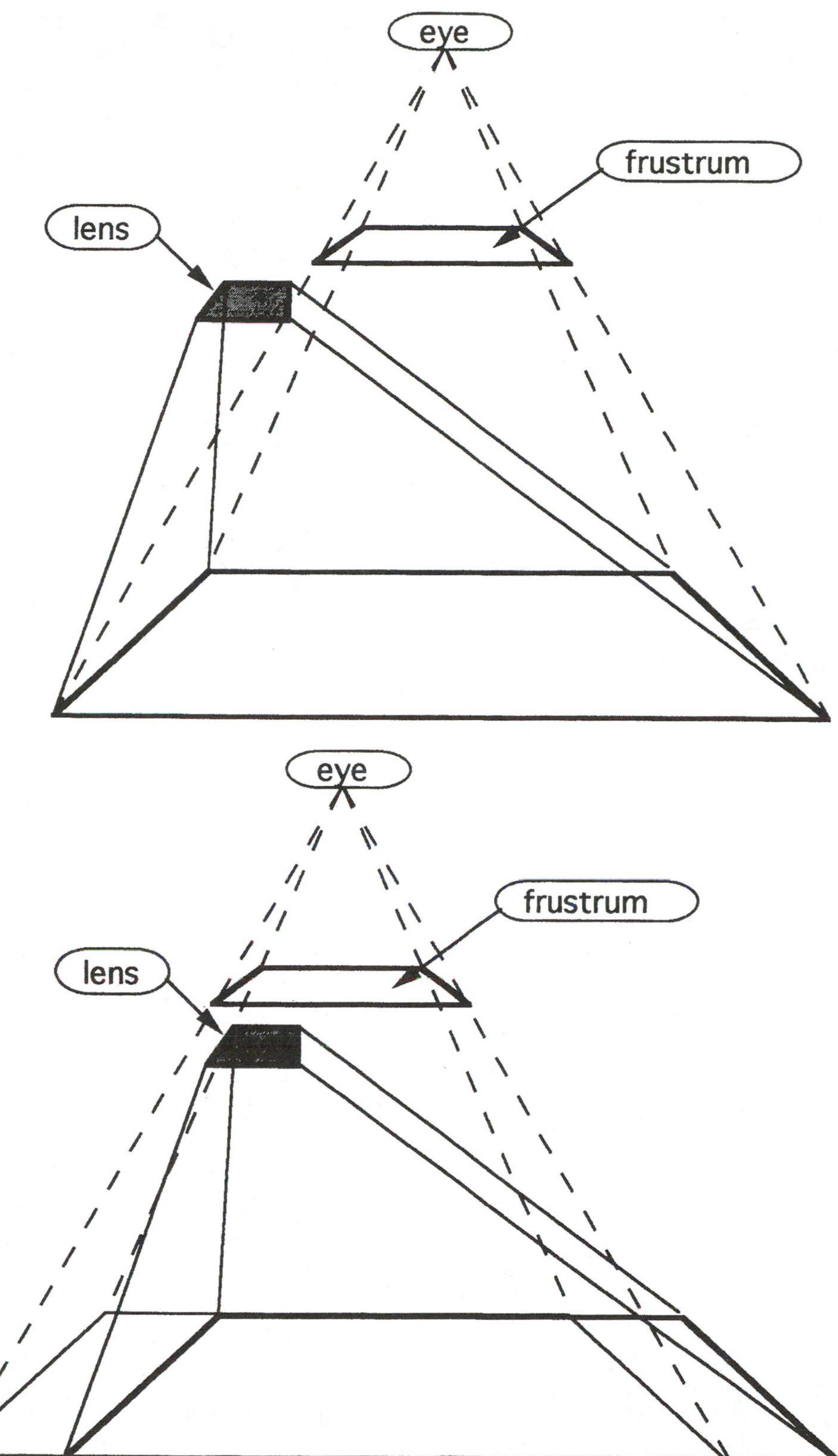

Figure 4: (a) Illustration of how the truncated pyramid may leave the viewing frustrum if lens movement is not coupled to viewpoint movement. (b) The frustrum after viewpoint movement.

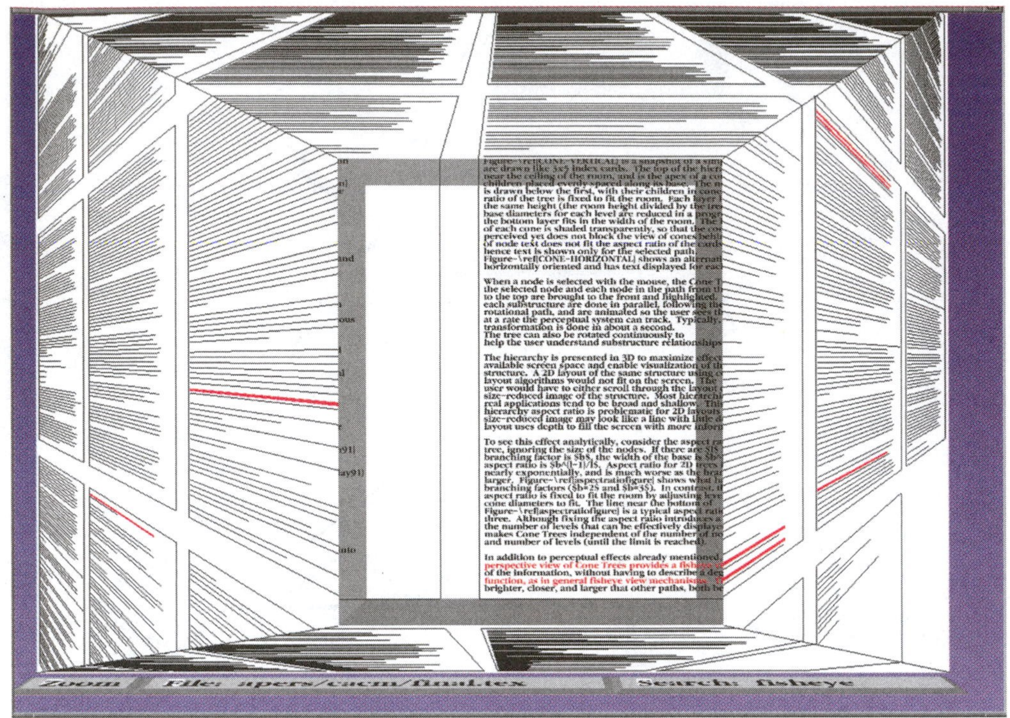

Figure 5: Document Lens with text on the sides greeked.

of the time. But, as the lens moves towards you, beyond a certain point the sides of the lens become unreadable or obscured, and you lose the context. This happens when the lens is close enough that it occupies most of the viewing frustrum. Sarkar and Brown observed the same problem for their distortion technique [8].

The coupling of lens movement with viewpoint movement is a critical part of this interaction technique. Without it, the Document Lens is useless. It may be that the obscuring problem of a close lens could be solved by coupling the size of the lens to its movement as well (making the close lens smaller).

The Document Lens has broader applicability that just viewing text documents. It could also be used to view any 2D graph (e.g., a map or diagram), providing a 3D perspective fisheye view. In that sense, it has some similarity to the Sarkar and Brown fisheye graph viewing technique [8]. However, generalized distortion is expensive. In contrast, the Document Lens works in real time for much larger graphs, efficiently doing a particular distortion using common affine transforms (3D perspective view, scaling, rotation), clipping, culling, and greeking.

There are some obvious additions that could be made to our current implementation, including adjustment to lens size and shape, and more elaborate search methods. But, these additions and usability testing have not been done because we need better hardware support for rendering large amounts of high quality text in 3D perspective. Fortunately, hardware trends (both in processor speed and 3D graphics hardware, particularly in texture mapping hardware) should make this a viable approach in the near future.

References

[1] Cutting, D. R., Pedersen, J. O. and Halvorsen, P.K. An Object-Oriented Architecture for Text Retrieval. In *Proceedings of RIAO'91, Intelligent Text and Image Handling,* 1991, pp. 285-298.

[2] Cutting, D. R., Karger, D. R., Pedersen, J. O. and Tukey, J. W. Scatter/Gather: A Cluster-based Approach to Browsing Large Document Collections. In *Proceedings of SIGIR'92,* 1992, pp. 318-329.

[3] Fairchild, K. M., Poltrock, S. E. and Furnas, G. W. Semnet: three-dimensional graphic representations of large knowledge bases. In *Cognitive science and its applications for human-computer interaction,* Guindon, R. (ed), Lawrence Erlbaum, 1988.

[4] Feiner, S. and Beshers, C. Worlds within worlds: metaphors for exploring n-dimensional virtual

worlds. In *Proceedings of the UIST'90,* 1990, pp. 76-83.

[5] Furnas, G. W. Generalized fisheye views. In *Proceedings of SIGCHI'86,* 1986, pp. 16-23.

[6] Mackinlay, J. D., Card, S. K., and Robertson, G. G. Rapid controlled movement through a virtual 3d workspace. In *Proceedings of SIGGRAPH '90,* 1990, pp. 171-176.

[7] Robertson, G., Card, S., & Mackinlay, J. (1993) Information visualization using 3D interactive animation. *Communications ACM, 36, 4,* April 1993, pp. 57-71.

[8] Sarkar, M. & Brown, M.H. (1992) Graphical fisheye views of graphs. In *Proceedings of SIGCHI'92,* 1992, pp. 83-91.

[9] Spence, R. and Apperley, M. Data base navigation: An office environment for the professional. *Behavior and Information Technology 1* (1), 1982, pp. 43-54.

User Controlled Overviews of an Image Library: A Case Study of the Visible Human

Chris North[†], *Ben Shneiderman*[†*], *and Catherine Plaisant*
Human-Computer Interaction Laboratory
[†]Department of Computer Science
[*]Institute for Systems Research
University of Maryland, College Park, MD 20742 USA
{north, ben, plaisant}@cs.umd.edu

ABSTRACT

This paper proposes a user interface for remote access of the National Library of Medicine's Visible Human digital image library. Users can visualize the library, browse contents, locate data of interest, and retrieve desired images. The interface presents a pair of tightly coupled views into the library data. The overview image provides a global view of the overall search space, and the preview image provides details about high resolution images available for retrieval. To explore, the user sweeps the views through the search space and receives smooth, rapid, visual feedback of contents. Desired images are automatically downloaded over the internet from the library. Library contents are indexed by meta-data consisting of automatically generated miniature visuals. The interface software is completely functional and freely available for public use, at: http://www.nlm.nih.gov/.

Keywords: Browsing, Digital Library, Image Database, Information Exploration, Information Retrieval, Internet, Medical Image, Remote Access, User Interface, Visualization, World-Wide Web.

INTRODUCTION

The Visible Human

The National Library of Medicine (NLM), for its Visible Human Project [NLM90], is in the process of creating a large digital library of anatomical images of the human body. It contains MRI and CT scans, as well as cryosection images (digital color photographs of cross-sections, Figure 1). Two cadavers, one male and one female, were carefully chosen as the subjects. The male dataset MRI and CT images were captured using the respective medical imaging scanners. The MRI images were captured at 4mm intervals throughout the body. Each is 256x256 pixels in resolution with 12-bit gray level encoding. The CT images were captured at 1mm intervals to correspond with the cryosections. Each is 512x512 pixels, also using 12-bit gray level. To capture the cryosection images, the cadaver was first frozen solid inside a large block of blue gel. Then, 1mm thick slices were successively cut away from an axial cross-section (planar cut perpendicular to the longitudinal axis of the body), and digital color images were taken of each newly exposed cross-section. A total of 1878 cryosection images were taken, spanning the body from head to toe. Each is 24-bit color and has a resolution of 2048x1216 pixels. The total result is a 15 Gigabyte image dataset of the male body. The female dataset will be captured at 1/3rd mm slices and, thus, is expected to require three times the storage space of the male dataset. In addition, 70mm film of cryosections may be scanned at higher resolutions for details of various anatomical structures.

The NLM provides public access to the Visible Human digital library via the internet. The entire dataset resides on a high capacity storage system with a high speed internet connection. A simple license agreement with NLM, intended for tracking data usage, allows any user with an internet capable computer to remotely access the full dataset. Each image is stored on the archive as a separate file with numerically indexed filenames ordered from head to toe. Using "ftp", a user remotely logs onto the archive machine with a special login ID and password provided with the license agreement, and downloads any number of image files by specifying the correct numerical filenames. The images can then be displayed locally using an appropriate image browsing software package. Also, several sample images are available to those without a license agreement on the Visible Human World Wide Web page at http://www.nlm.nih.gov/.

Because the library is available to the public, the user community is diverse. Users are of varying backgrounds and cover a wide range of expertise in human anatomy and computer skills. The most prominent user groups are medical professionals and students interested in using the images for education and modeling purposes, and computer science researchers and software developers creating medical imaging applications. Other users include elementary school teachers, curious internet surfers, and even martial arts experts! Some users wish to simply explore the dataset in an open-ended fashion, and download a sampling of images to browse. Other users, who desire a specific portion of the dataset, use a more directed search to locate and download images. Some desire only a single image or small set of images, perhaps to use as overheads while teaching an anatomy class. Others download an entire continuous block of images representing some portion of the body. In this case, the images are often used for 3D modeling of anatomical structures. For example, a medical expert might download all the cryosection images containing the heart, and load them into advanced software, such as Mayo Foundation's *ANALYZE*™, to visualize ventricle chambers. Very few attempt to download the entire library, since it would require weeks of continuous internet activity as well as overwhelming storage capacity.

Unfortunately, using the Visible Human digital library can be difficult. The ftp interface merely presents users with a long list of sequential image filenames. Browsing the data requires a trial-and-error process of guessing a file, downloading it (which could take several minutes), and displaying the image locally. A Web page interface that displays thumbnails of the library images would allow the user to visually browse the contents of the library, but would require paging through hundreds of thumbnails that must be downloaded for each access.

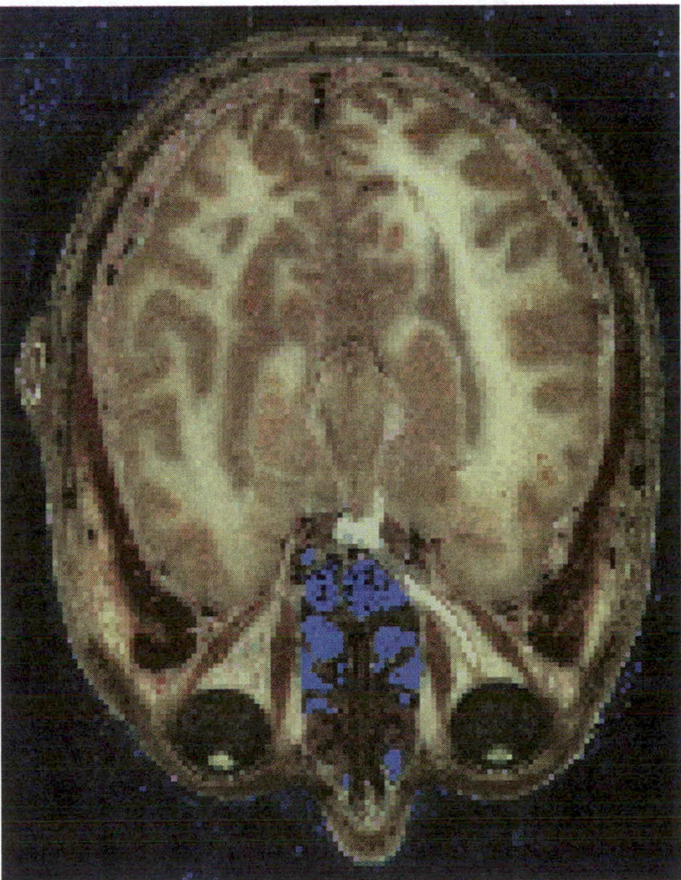

Figure 1: A Visible Human cryosection image of the male's head. Library cryosection images are full color and have 2048x1216 pixel resolution, larger than most CRTs.

Whether a user wants to simply browse the library or retrieve images for some other use, it is important to avoid unnecessary downloads. Because the dataset is extremely large and would take weeks to download, and it is desired that users with smaller computers with limited storage capacity have access, the ability to remotely explore a visual representation of the dataset and download only desired images is a requirement. Hence, there is a great need for an effective user interface to assist users in browsing the library and retrieving images.

Related Work

As digital libraries quickly increase in number, researchers are continually developing improved public access methods for the many different types of library information. The primary user interface approach, especially for libraries containing unstructured collections of heterogeneous documents, is the keyword query method. In this case, Information Retrieval systems preprocess documents in the library, usually using automated algorithms, to generate comprehensive indices (meta-data). Then, when a user enters a query, the system can quickly generate a list of matching documents. Since many of these libraries contain textual documents only, such as computer science technical reports [Van94], and use strictly textual queries, interfaces are often text-based for simple WWW or teletype access. More advanced GUI interfaces afford additional capability to manipulate and visualize the textual query [VN95,YS92]. Image libraries may also provide for query by image content [FBF94]. In this case, images are indexed by content features and, if available, textual annotations. These interfaces allow users to specify example images, interactively sketch objects, or use an image content description language to create a query. KMeD [CCT95] is an example of a multimedia library in the medical domain which combines both textual and medical image elements. Digital video libraries expand the query method further, using speech recognition on the audio tracks of videos for textual indexing [GAE94]. While the query method may be an effective means for retrieving documents based on keywords or image features, it does not provide the capability to "explore" or build a mental model of the contents of a library.

However, if the documents within a library are organized using some consistent, natural, comprehensible, orderly structuring method, then interfaces using a browsing approach are also applicable. Advanced user interface techniques for information exploration can be used to explore the library structure, usually specified by meta-data, and its contents. This gives users a way to learn about the library and locate interesting documents without relying on keyword search. Several common structuring methods exist [Lev95]. For example, Hypertext systems such as the WWW organize documents in a hierarchy or other graph representation. With an interface for browsing graph structured information (see [Kor95] for a review of several), users can utilize the links, perhaps representing relationships between documents, to discover related documents that might not be found using a keyword query. Implementations include utilizing the Dewey Classification hierarchy to browse a library catalogue [All94] and reference citations to browse articles [RPH95]. MeSHbrowse [KS95] is an interface for browsing a medical terminology hierarchy containing arbitrary inter-relationships (meta-data) as an index to a medical image digital library. Another structuring method organizes information by defined textual and numerical attributes. Doan applies dynamic query interface techniques to arbitrary distributed information of this form, allowing users to quickly learn overall contents, find trends, and locate documents of interest [DPS95]. Browsing computer science literature has been handled by attribute structure as well, using author names, publication dates and sizes, etc. [HHN95]. Some interfaces use the map motif to browse spatial information, in which case attributes represent geographical locations [KJ95, Pla93]. All of these systems are examples of how advanced information-exploration user interface techniques can capitalize on the structure of an organized library to add a new dimension, namely the capability to browse, to the user's tool set for the task of information retrieval.

The Visible Human digital library exemplifies another organizational method for structuring libraries. The medical imagery, although un-annotated, is concretely structured. That is, the images have a strict sequential ordering defined by the physical objects (the human body) represented. Hence, because of the previously described successes, we expect that a user interface, which utilizes this structure to provide a browsing environment, would be an effective means for users to retrieve desired images.

Guiding principles for designing a user interface for the Visible Human library come from related research of browsing techniques. Firstly, direct manipulation, with compelling success in many exploration interfaces, provides these principles: [Shn92]

- Visual representation of the search space;
- Rapid, incremental, reversible exploratory actions;
- Pointing and selecting, instead of typing; and
- Immediate, continuous, visual feedback of results.

Research in digital medical atlases has developed reconstruction and visualization techniques for annotated, segmented, 3D medical image data [HPR95]. Interface elements and strategies for browsing individual 2D images are thoroughly identified [PCS95]. In particular, a coordinated detail view and overview giving contextual feedback, as well as extraneous data download avoidance, are essential elements for remotely browsing very large images [CPH94]. Work on Query Previews [DPS95] shows the benefits of previewing downloadable data as a filtering process by issuing dynamic queries on meta-data. With this technique users drag sliders, click on options, and receive rapid visual feedback to identify desired data available for retrieval. With these principles as our motivation, we designed the interface described in the following section.

THE INTERFACE

We have developed a direct manipulation user interface, called the Visible Human Explorer (VHE), for remotely exploring the Visible Human digital library and retrieving images. It allows users to rapidly browse, on their own machine, a miniaturized version of the Visible Human dataset and, based on that exploration, download desired full resolution library images. The miniature dataset provides an overview of library content and acts as a preview mechanism for retrieval. The interface, along with the miniature dataset, is downloaded in advance and then used as an accessor to the archive. The payoff is quick, since downloading the VHE is equivalent to only about 3 image retrievals. With this paradigm, although implemented completely outside of any existing web browser, the interface can be thought of as an advanced, dynamic web-page application for browsing a medical image digital library.

The VHE direct manipulation interface (Figure 2) presents the user with a coordinated pair of orthogonal 2D cross-section views of the Visible Human body. The left view-window, or overview, displays a miniature coronal section, a front-view longitudinal cut of the body. It acts as an overview of the library, giving the user a general understanding of the contents of the body from head to toe. The images for this view were reconstructed directly from the cross-section images, taking advantage of the structural organization of the library, by sampling a single row of pixels from successive images to simulate a perpendicular cut. The resolution is decreased to approximately 150x470. The right view-window, or preview, displays a miniature axial section, the type of cut typically seen in medical atlas textbooks. The images for this view are reduced resolution thumbnail images (300x150) of the original library cross-sections and act as a preview of those higher resolution images. The magnification of this view is twice that of the overview, giving the user more detail of the library.

A horizontal indicator on the overview indicates the vertical position, on the body, of the axial section shown in the preview. The indicator is attached to a vertical slider widget spanning the height of the overview and can be dragged vertically across the body to sweep the cut, shown in the preview, through the body. As the user drags the indicator, the preview provides smooth, rapid feedback (<100msec) reflecting the axial cross-section at the sliding cut plane, resulting in a dynamic animated effect of motion through the body. This gives the user the ability to easily explore the contents of the entire body. Likewise, a sliding indicator in the preview controls the view shown in the overview. For example, the user can slide the overview to show a coronal section nearer to the front or back of the body. (See video report [NK96] for a demonstration of the dynamic interaction.)

While exploring, when the user locates an axial section in the preview for which high resolution data is desired, pressing the Full-Size Image button opens the Retrieval dialog box (Figure 3). This dialog handles the details of accessing the Visible Human library archive. After users

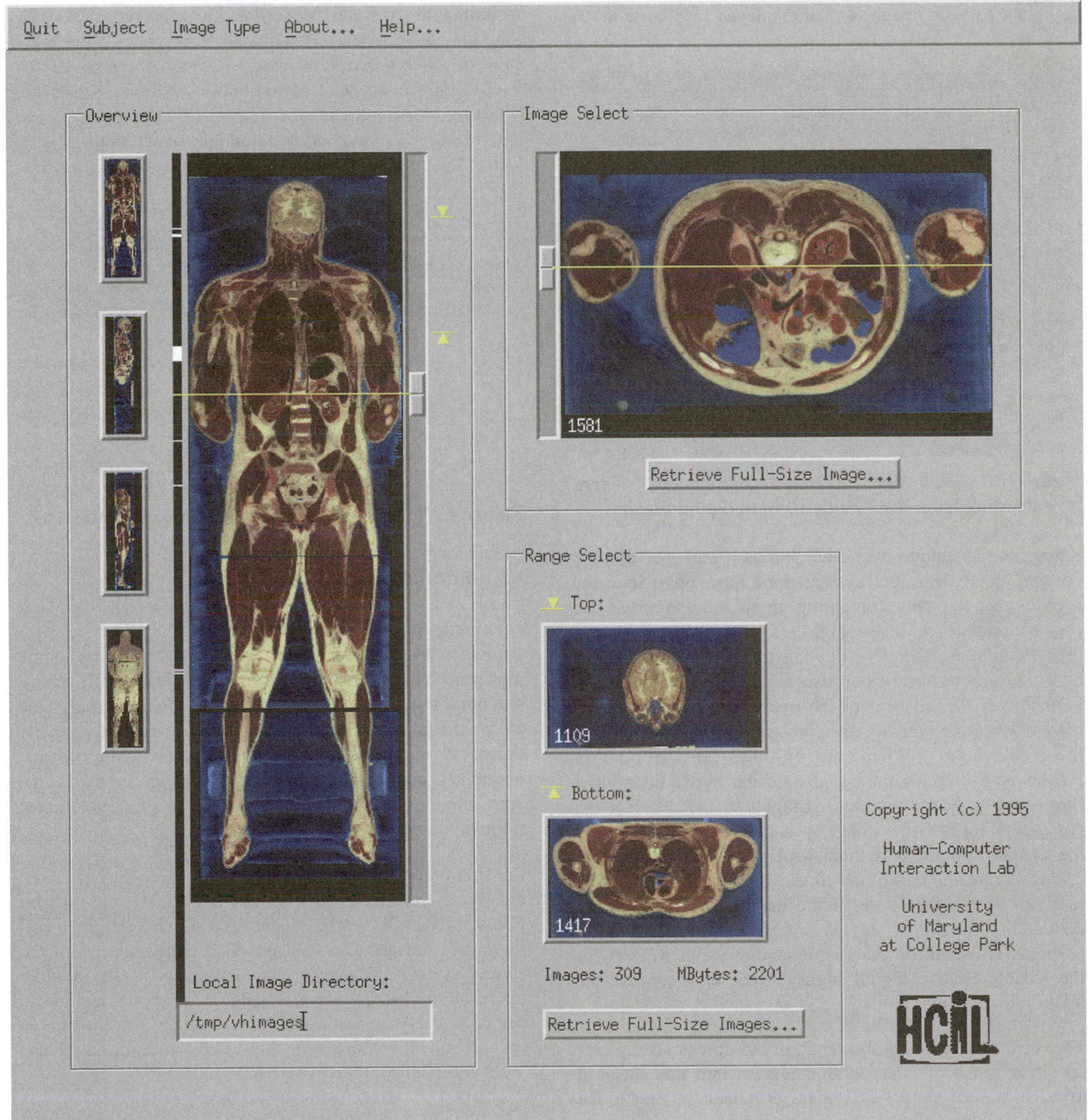

Figure 2: The Visible Human Explorer user interface, showing a reconstructed coronal section overview and an axial preview image of the upper abdominal region. Dragging sliders animates the cross-sections through the body.

type their Visible Human login ID and password into the corresponding textboxes and press the Retrieve button, the system begins to download the requested full resolution cryosection image from the NLM digital library over the internet to the user's computer. Since retrieval may take several minutes, depending on internet traffic, a status meter provides feedback on the progress of the retrieval. Users have the option to cancel the downloading at any time. Once the meter reaches 100%, the download is complete and the image is then displayed in a large detail view.

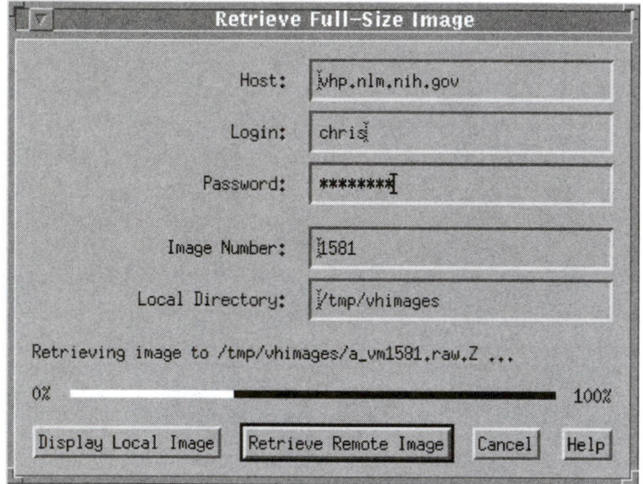

Figure 3: The VHE Retrieval dialog box meters downloading from the Visible Human digital library.

Since downloading over the internet can be a time consuming process, the system does have provisions for users with computers containing ample storage space. It can accumulate retrieved high resolution images on the user's computer, thereby allowing the user to browse not only the remote library but also a local cache as well. A vertical bar aligned next to the overview image shows tic marks indicating which axial cryosections are contained in the local cache. When one of these cross-sections is previewed by placing the cut plane slider over a tic mark, a flag in the preview window highlights to indicate that the corresponding full-size image is in the cache. Clicking on the Display button will then display the image from the cache, saving the download time. Below the overview, a text box shows the name of the user selectable directory containing the local image cache. This feature is particularly useful for users who acquire their own copy of the Visible Human digital library, since they can use the VHE to browse it as well.

The VHE also provides the capability to download any user specified range of cross-section images into this cache at once. The user simply places range indicators next to the overview slider, and selects a button to begin retrieval using the Retrieval dialog box. Two smaller axial cross-section views display images of the top and bottom slices of the user specified range. Feedback on the number of images within the range and the total size, in megabytes, of those library images is also provided. This feature is useful for retrieving commonly examined portions of the body a priori, or for obtaining a continuous block of images for use in 3D modeling applications.

Also, using the icon buttons adjacent to the overview, the user can select amongst different overview image types, including the coronal section, sagital section (side view longitudinal section), and a simple front view of the body (no cut). This gives the user a variety of views of the overall search space. Menu options (Figure 4) enable selecting between the male or female subjects, and between the MRI, CT, and cryosection medical image types. Currently, only the male cryosection meta-data is loadable.

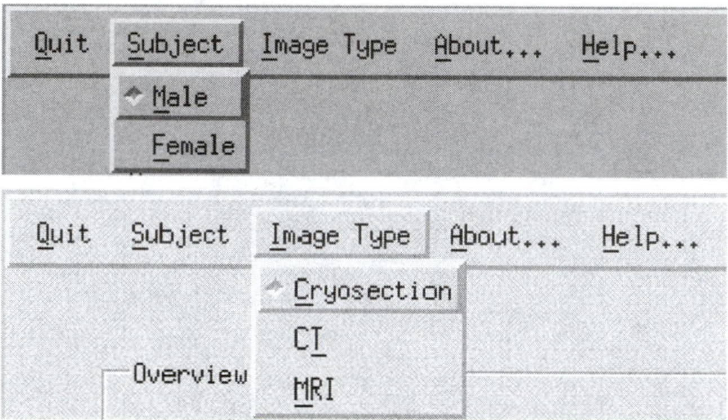

Figure 4: VHE menus for selecting amongst datasets.

Implementation and Performance

The VHE is implemented in the UNIX X/Motif environment on a Sun Sparcstation. The key to implementation is the use of meta-data, consisting of the miniature Visible Human thumbnail images, which acts as the library index. The benefit is two-fold: Firstly, the meta-data provides a manageable dataset for interactively browsing the library. Secondly, each axial section thumbnail provides a preview of and an index to the corresponding full size library image for automated retrieval purposes.

For optimal browsing performance, the meta-data is stored locally on the user's machine and is preformatted in 8 bit XImage [Nye90] format. Hence, as a slider is dragged, new thumbnail images can be moved directly from disk to screen using X Windows shared memory. On an older Sparcstation 1+, images are updated at approximately 20 per second. As a result, we expect that an implementation on a PC or Mac with reasonable I/O capabilities could also yield acceptable interactive performance.

The meta-data is pre-generated and comes packaged with the VHE software. To create the meta-data, we developed several tools to automatically generate it from the library images. The thumbnail meta-data preformatted for the axial preview window is cropped, spatially sampled, and color quantized directly from library images, and requires under 20 Megabytes of storage space. The overview meta-data formatted as coronal images is spatially sampled and reconstructed from the axial meta-data, and requires under 5 Megabytes of space. The total cryosection meta-data is 1/600th of the total size of the full resolution cryosection library data.

Benefits

The VHE interface design was chosen to be in harmony with user tasks. The tightly coupled 2D views of the dataset, combined with rapid, dynamic user control of movement through the third dimension, provides a highly interactive interface yet avoids unnecessary complexities. The result is an elegant interface affording convenient user exploration of the image data, for both novice and expert users. The need for learning time is essentially eliminated. Feedback is fast enough to engage the user. Users can quickly learn about the entire library by sweeping the views through the body, absorbing 20 MB of data in just a few seconds. Then, slower smaller movements to carefully examine interesting portions of the library help locate optimal images for downloading. Also, when dragging a slider, visualizing the resulting motion of the structural patterns in the cross-section thumbnails provides additional insight over, for example, simply viewing thumbnails side by side or in a click-and-wait incremental fashion.

As has been discovered in exploration interfaces for many other types of data, a visual overview of the data space is extremely helpful [Shn94]. When users search for specific data, the VHE overview quickly guides them to the desired location. It provides context for the axial preview thumbnails, some of which would otherwise be difficult to interpret exactly. It also promotes user exploration of the library, by eliminating the penalty of the possibility of getting lost or not being able to return to a desired location in a timely fashion. The preview allows users to select images, filtering out unwanted information, and download and zoom only on desired detailed data on demand.

DISCUSSION

Orthoviewer

While developing the VHE interface, we also implemented another prototype, dubbed the Orthoviewer (Figure 5), that generalizes the VHE motif. It presents the user with all three orthogonal views (sagital, coronal, and axial) of the Visible Human body simultaneously. Each view contains both a vertical and horizontal indicator line which reflects the position, with respect to the view, of the cut planes of the other two views. Each of these six indicators can be dragged, as in the VHE, to slide one of the views through the body. Pairs of corresponding indicators are tightly coupled. For example, dragging the vertical indicator in the sagital section animates the coronal view and also slides the horizontal indicator in the axial section, which reflects the position of the same cutting plane. Interestingly, we discovered that the Orthoviewer interface confuses many users. The addition of a third view and four indicators makes it difficult to decipher which indicator manipulates which view. Users typically resort to a trial-and-error process to find the appropriate indicator to operate. Also, since each indicator is tightly coupled to 2 other components, when dragging an indicator, the user is distracted by the additional motion. The interface simply provides too much dynamic information for many users to process. Users' cognition is consumed by the Orthoviewer interface instead of the data itself. As a result, we designed the VHE interface with a distinct overview-preview pair, as used in many successful browsing interfaces in other domains [KPS95].

User Feedback

In July 1995, we publicly released the VHE system on our Web site, enabling users to download and use it to access the Visible Human library. Our access logs indicate that over 300 users, from all over the world, have downloaded the software, after just 2 months. As a result, we received some informal feedback about the interface and its usage from actual users. We received 34 responses. Of those who indicated their occupation or field of study, users were evenly distributed between medicine and computer science, and between professional and student. Others were simply curious internet users. The medical users identified their use of the library information being primarily for learning and teaching gross anatomy and as a reference for radiology. The computer scientists identified their primary usage as test data for image processing and computer graphics algorithms research. All of whom gave in-depth

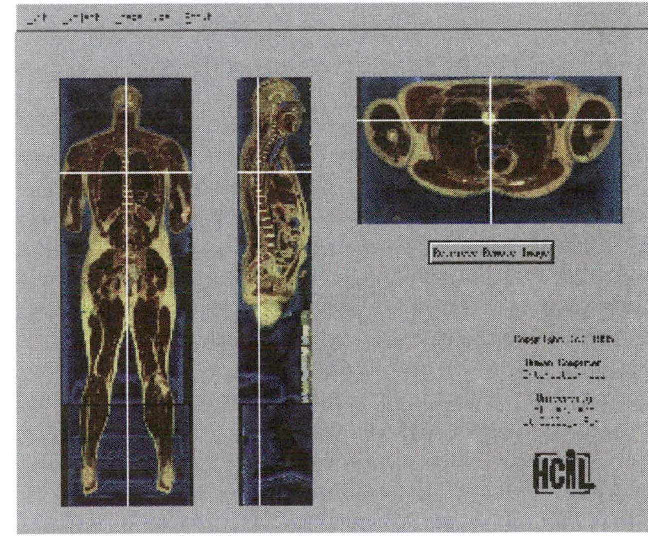

Figure 5: The Orthoviewer prototype interface shows three orthogonal views of the body. Dragging any of the six indicators animates corresponding views.

comments reported that the VHE interface was very helpful for visualizing the Visible Human library. One user stated: "Now I have a far better understanding of how the whole data-set looks." Users who need to download specific individual images were very pleased that, with the VHE interface, they were finally able to quickly locate and retrieve the proper library image. "Before using the VHE it was always a bit of a problem to get the right images." Short responses indicated the users' excitement with the interface's highly interactive nature, fast feedback, and quick learnability, trademarks of a direct manipulation interface. Also, some suggestions for improvement were offered. Multiple users suggested increasing the size of the preview image by a factor of 1.5 or 2, enabling visualization of most major organs. One user felt that simply displaying the existing preview images larger, without an increase in actual data resolution, would be sufficient. Several users were wary of the 25MB size of the meta-data. Another suggestion was to display MRI, CT, and cryosection previews simultaneously, enabling the user to browse all three portions of the library at once.

Generalizations and Limitations

The VHE interface demonstrates a browsing approach that could be generalized to other image sets in which images are sequenced in some meaningful progression. The Visible Human library contains spatially sequenced images, or volumetric data. While medical imaging is the most common form, the interface could be used to browse other cross-sectional or volumetric datasets, such as geological or atmospheric samplings, allowing users to visualize pattern changes in sedimentation layers or storm turbulence. Images could also be sequenced by time of capture, as in digital video. In this case, axial cross-sections would correspond to individual frames of the video sequence, and longitudinal sections would show motion patterns of video action across frames [ED94]. In fact, we originally encoded the VHE meta-data as an MPEG video, but opted for another representation for performance reasons. Also, the images themselves could be visual representations of more abstract scientific measurements. For example, astronomers could browse a library of spectrograms collected over a period of time to view changes in wave patterns. Applying the VHE interface to these different datasets would simply require creation of the miniature meta-data (we developed tools to automate this process for the Visible Human project), and alteration of interface dimensions to accommodate the appropriate image sizes.

Currently, the VHE interface approach is limited to libraries containing such sequenced images. For libraries containing heterogeneous collections of arbitrary, unrelated images or textual documents, the overview window would need to be redesigned to show a meaningful representation of the library. For example, chronological timelines or simple page numbers would provide additional understanding of library contents. In this case, the ability to quickly flip through many images or pages, like flipping through a book, would be very helpful when exploring large libraries.

Future Work

With respect to the VHE interface, improvements could be made, including those suggested in the User Feedback. Also, a helpful new capability might allow the user to browse higher resolution detailed data (retrieved from the Visible Human library) of a smaller portion of the body in the same fashion used to browse the initial miniature body. For example, if the user wishes to see the heart in higher detail, retrieving portions of all the library axial cross-sections containing the heart might be preferred over a single large axial image. A schema could allow the user to specify a small sub-region of the body to zoom on, then, after retrieval, the entire interface would be reused for exploring that sub-region in higher resolution. The overview and preview windows would display views of the zoomed sub-region, for example, a coronal and axial section (respectively) of the heart. Naturally, the user could return back to explore the initial miniature Visible Human body at any time. With this zooming method, users could browse high detailed data using the same interface techniques as described in this paper, instead of simply viewing high resolution data only as single large axial images.

In addition, investigation of other visual overview representation and browsing techniques for this type of digital library structure is needed. As computer hardware progresses, 3D representation techniques are becoming more tractable and attractive. Human factors research is required to determine usability measures of differences between 2D representations, of which the VHE is an example, and potential 3D representations.

In the broader picture, as the Visible Human digital library grows to include textual annotations, segmented images, attribute indexes, relationship graphs, video animations, and many other forms of information, additional user interface browsing techniques will apply. The graphical interface approach presented in this paper could be combined with Korn's textual browser intended for navigating a medical terminology hierarchy containing links to the Visible Human images [KS95]. If the two interfaces were tightly coupled, manipulating either the graphical or textual interface elements would immediately show effects in the other domain. Users could browse using a combined strategy, utilizing their knowledge of both medical terminology and visual appearance of human anatomy. We believe that integrating different interface approaches for various information types would provide a rich comprehensive browsing environment for an expanding Visible Human digital library.

ACKNOWLEDGMENTS

Chris North received a National Library of Medicine fellowship, administered by the Oak Ridge Institute for Science and Education. Additional funding was provided by a National Library of Medicine grant and National Science Foundation grant EEC 94-02384.

SOFTWARE

The VHE interface software is fully functional and freely available for public use. For more information, see http://www.cs.umd.edu/projects/hcil/Research/1995/vhe.html or anonymous ftp.cs.umd.edu in /pub/hcil/Demos/VHP.

REFERENCES

[All94] R. Allen. Navigating and Searching in Hierarchical Digital Library Catalogs. *Proc. Digital Libraries '94 Conf*, pg 95-100, 1994.

[CCT95] W. Chu, A. Cardenas, and R. Taira. KMeD: A Knowledge-Based Multimedia Medical Distributed Database System. *Information Systems*, vol 20, #2, pg 75-96, 1995.

[CPH94] D. Carr, C. Plaisant, and H. Hasegawa. The Design of a Telepathology Workstation: Exploring Remote Images. University of Maryland, Dept. of Computer Science Technical Report, CS-TR-3270, 1994.

[DPS95] K. Doan, C. Plaisant, and B. Shneiderman. Query Previews in Networked Information Systems. University of Maryland, Dept. of Computer Science Technical Report, 1995.

[ED94] E. Elliott and G. Davenport. Video Streamer. *Conf. Companion of Human Factors in Computing Systems Conf*, pg 65-66, 1994.

[FBF94] C. Faloutsos, R. Barber, M. Flickner, J. Hafner, W. Niblack, D. Petrovic, and W. Equitz. Efficient and Effective Querying by Image Content. *Journal of Intelligent Information Systems*, vol 3, pg 231-262, 1994.

[GAE94] S. Gauch, R. Aust, J. Evans, J. Gauch, G. Minden, D. Niehaus, and J. Roberts. The Digital Video Library System: Vision and Design. *Proc. Digital Libraries '94 Conf*, pg 47-52, 1994.

[HHN95] L. Heath, D. Hix, L. Nowell, W. Wake, G. Averboch, E. Labow, S. Guyer, D. Brueni, R. France, K. Dalal, and E. Fox. Envision: A User-Centered Database of Computer Science Literature. *Communications of the ACM*, vol 38, #4, pg 52-53, April 1995.

[HPR95] K. Hohne, A. Pommert, M. Riemer, T. Schiemann, R. Schubert, and U. Tiede. Medical Volume Visualization Based on "Intelligent Volumes". *Scientific Visualization: Advances and Challenges*, Academic Press, pg 21-35, 1995.

[KJ95] C. Kacmar and D. Jue. The Information Zone System. *Communications of the ACM*, vol 38, #4, pg 46-47, April 1995.

[Kor95] F. Korn. A Taxonomy of Browsing Methods: Approaches to the 'Lost in Concept Space' Problem. University of Maryland, Dept. of Computer Science Technical Report, 1995.

[KPS95] H. Kumar, C. Plaisant and B. Shneiderman. Browsing Hierarchical Data with Multi-Level Dynamic Queries and Pruning. University of Maryland, Dept. of Computer Science Technical Report, CS-TR-3474, 1995.

[KS95] F. Korn and B. Shneiderman. Navigating Terminology Hierarchies to Access a Digital Library of Medical Images. University of Maryland, Dept. of Computer Science Technical Report, 1995.

[Lev95] D. Levy. Cataloging in the Digital Order. *Proc. Digital Libraries '95 Conf*, 1995.

[NK96] C. North and F. Korn. Browsing Anatomical Image Databases: A Case Study of the Visible Human. *Conf. Companion of Human Factors in Computing Systems Conf*, 1996.

[NLM90] National Library of Medicine Long Range Plan: Electronic Imaging, *NIH Publication No. 90-2197*, U.S. Dept. of Health and Human Services, April 1990.

[Nye90] A. Nye. *Xlib Reference Manual*, O'Reilly & Associates Inc, 1990.

[PCS95] C. Plaisant, D. Carr, and B. Shneiderman. Image Browser Taxonomy and Guidelines for Designers. *IEEE Software*, vol 28, #3, pg 21-32, March 1995.

[Pla93] C. Plaisant. Facilitating data exploration: Dynamic Queries on a Health Statistics Map. *Proc. of the Government Statistics Section, Annual Meeting of the American Statistical Assoc. Conf. Proc*, pg 18-23, 1993.

[RPH95] R. Rao, J. Pedersen, M. Hearst, J. Mackinlay, S. Card, L. Masinter, P. Halvorsen, and G. Robertson. Rich Interaction in the Digital

Library. *Communications of the ACM*, vol 38, #4, pg 29-39, April 1995.

[Shn92] B. Shneiderman. *Designing the User Interface: Strategies for Effective Human-Computer Interaction: Second Edition*, Addison-Wesley Publ. Co, 1992.

[Shn94] B. Shneiderman. Dynamic Queries for Visual Information Seeking. *IEEE Software*, pg 70-77, Nov 1994.

[Van94] M. VanHeyningen. The Unified Computer Science Technical Report Index: Lessons in Indexing Diverse Resources. *Proc. 2nd Intl WWW '94: Mosaic and the Web*, pg 535-543, 1994.

[VN95] A. Veerasamy and S. Navathe. Querying, Navigating and Visualizing a Digital Library Catalog. *Proc. Digital Libraries '95 Conf*, 1995.

[YS92] D. Young and B. Shneiderman. A Graphical Filter/Flow Representation of Boolean Queries: A Prototype Implementation and evaluation. *JASIS*, vol 44, #6, pg 327-339, 1992.

CHAPTER **7**

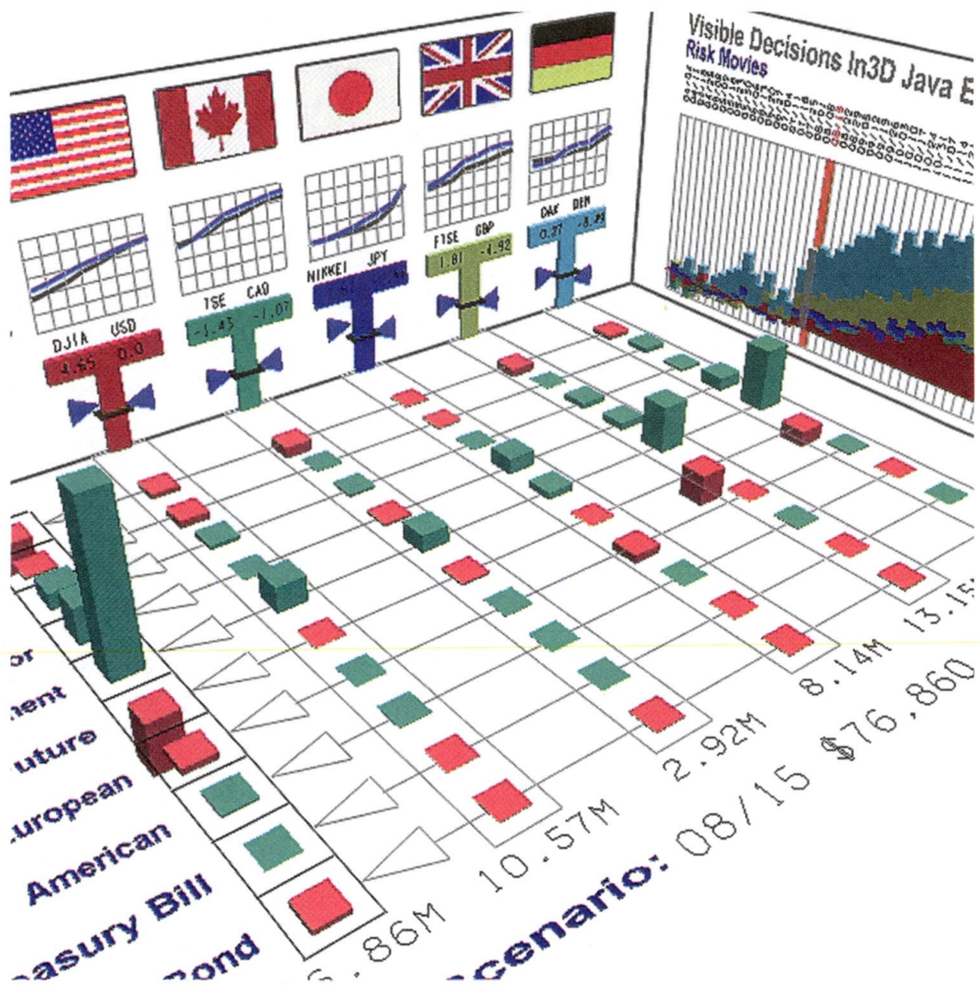

The eye obeys exactly the action of the mind.

– Ralph Waldo Emerson (1860)

Using Vision to Think

This chapter returns to the central topic of this book: using vision to think. In particular, the focus is on developing theoretical and engineering principles for the design of effective visualizations. Although much is known about the design of static presentations, visualization represents a new medium involving computer-based interactive visual representations that tap human skills not only in perception but in manipulation. Initially, the exploration for effective visualizations was primarily intuitive, informed by the principles developed for static presentations and resulting in a wide range of promising designs, including the ones collected in this volume. At this point, there is enough experience with this new medium to identify principles for the design of effective visualization. In this chapter we sample some attempts to develop these principles and analyses for information visualization.

We begin with the use of information visualization for crystallizing new knowledge as discussed in Chapter 1. This involves foraging for information, trying to make sense of it, and producing a result. What can be said about the use of information visualization for accessing information? A general principle governing the search for information is given by Information Foraging Theory (Pirolli and Card, 1995; Pirolli and Card, in press). This theory holds that in seeking information, people act adaptively, attempting to arrange their activities so as to increase the amount of information gained per unit cost consistent with the tools and information they have at hand (the "proximal mechanisms" available). Different actions people take have different costs and also result in different amounts of information gained. To make things more complex, the information seeker cannot actually know these in advance, but acts on beliefs or estimates, which may be based on experience with the statistics of the environment or on nearby clues about distant information. The first step in understanding the consequences of design decisions for information visualization systems is therefore an analysis of the cost-and-benefit structure of the space of actions available to the information seeker. This is what the first two papers seek to do.

The first paper, by Card, Pirolli, and Mackinlay (1994 ●), considers the situation where the user proceeds through an information space by "direct walk," a succession of direct manipulation actions such as clicking on successive World Wide Web pages. The paper proposes a metric for measuring the cost structure of such a situation, the "Cost-of-Knowledge Characteristic Function" (COKCF). This curve plots the amount of information that can be reached as a function of increasing cost (usually measured in time). The metric is motivated by, for example, a typical office with its progression from desktop to file drawer to filing cabinet to library. Smaller amounts of information (like what fits on the desktop) can be reached at less cost in time; larger amounts of information are accessible at higher time cost, resulting in a roughly exponential COKCF. The paper measures the COKCF for calendar visualization, from which it is determined that a conventional calendar program has a better cost structure for the most common requests, an undesired state of affairs. But using the metric, it is possible to diagnose the problem and compute the consequence of alternatives, implementing only the most promising. This allows a superior visualization to be created.

Furnas (1997 ●) analyzes the same basic situation, which he calls *view navigation,* but adds more considerations. He represents the objects in an information space as nodes together with all the possible navigation paths between them in a *view graph.* The user has a view of these nodes, which he moves along in the process of navigation. There is direct navigation among all the nodes that happen to appear together in the view, but Furnas is mainly interested in the case where the view is small with respect to the total information space. The view graph abstraction is an analytical tool for visualization design. For example, a minimal condition for effective visualization is that the view graph be *effective view traversable,* which means that it does not overwhelm the user with too many choices at any node and that the worst-case traversal of the view graph is short. An interesting implication of this principle is that view graphs can be augmented with additional links, typically a hierarchical structure, that can make a given graph more traversable. An important part of the paper is a discussion of an idealistic concept called *navigability,* requiring that every view compactly provide information (*scent* in information foraging terms) about the links to other views such that a user can find the shortest path to a goal. The dual of this concept is that every node has a *residue* at every other node so that the user can find it. Furnas derives order-of-magnitude estimates that characterize the cost of navigating through the several navigational structures he examines. Essentially, he derives Cost-of-Knowledge Characteristic Functions for different information visualization navigation structures analytically and shows with his scent/residue analysis how to raise the curve.

Moving from information foraging to sense making, we have Pirolli and Rao's paper (1996 ●). Sense making basically requires building a schema or description into which many pieces of information fit (Russell et al., 1993), that is, providing a compact description of some set of phenomena. Sense making also is sensitive to the cost structure of information. In this paper, Pirolli and Rao show analytically how by using information visualization in an exploratory data analysis (EDA) activity, they can make sense of multivariate data about as fast as skilled users of a specialized statistical system. In particular, the paper uses a GOMS-based (Goals, Operators, Methods, Selection Rules) problem space model (Card, Moran, and Newell, 1983) to compare table lens with Splus, a commercial data analysis application. The result is a calculation similar to the COKCF but not restricted to a direct walk task. This is one of the few papers to actually trace through in detail a benefit expected from information visualization and exactly how it comes about.

So far, we have talked about ways of analyzing the task users do with information visualization. We can also turn from the human and task side to the machine side, that is, to characterization of the architectures of information visualization systems. In this book we have used a simple reference model to organize the discussion. This reference model is really a version of the Smalltalk model-view-controller paradigm (Krasner and Pope, 1990). The model is the data transformations up to the Data Table; the view is the set of transformations up to the presentation; and the controller is the set of the controls for the parameters of these, except that controls can be of View Transformation parameters in addition to those for Data Transformations.

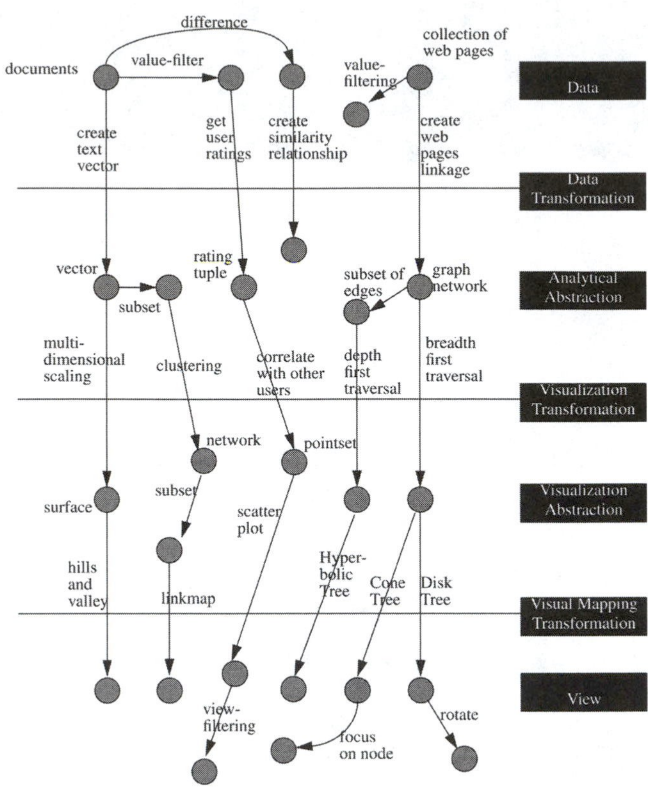

FIGURE **7.1**

Visualization operators (Chi and Riedl, 1998, Figure 3).

Chi and Riedl (1998) have extended this basic model as a way of categorizing the different operators that can be used in information visualization. Some of the operators they identified appear in Figure 7.1. They distinguish three classes of operator relationships. These are operators that are

- *operationally similar* (operators like rotate, whose implementations are the same across applications),
- *functionally similar* (operators like filtering that are semantically similar but require different implementations across applications), and
- *task dependent* (operators specially designed for a particular application domain).

There tend to be more operationally similar operators at the visual end of the reference model. Using the model to sort out operators in this way should help in the design of modular information visualization systems.

The fourth paper, by Tweedie (1997 ●), is the final reading in this book. We include it because it discusses a host of interesting ideas about using vision to think. The paper starts with the observation, also made here, that more attention should be paid to interactivity. The point of view is primarily cognitive, including the use of the term *externalization* rather than *visualization* to indicate the cognitive role of interactive visual representations. The paper develops a taxonomy of visualization and applies it to a range of visualizations. The first dimension, representation, divides data into value and structure. Visualizations often involve the derivation of new values and structure. The second dimension, interactivity, ranges from direct manipulation to indirect manipulation. This leads to the final axis of the taxonomy based on Draper's observation that input and output can reference each other. These input and output relations form the basis of a more detailed discussion of the various user actions that must be supported by a visualization.

The Cost-of-Knowledge Characteristic Function: Display Evaluation for Direct-Walk Dynamic Information Visualizations

Stuart K. Card, Peter Pirolli, and Jock D. Mackinlay

Xerox Palo Alto Research Center
3333 Coyote Hill Road
Palo Alto, California 94304
E-mail: card@parc.xerox.com, pirolli@parc.xerox.com, mackinlay@parc.xerox.com

ABSTRACT

In this paper we present a method, the Cost-of-Knowledge Characteristic Function, for characterizing information access from dynamic displays. The paper works out this method for a simple, but important, class of dynamic displays called direct-walk interactive information visualizations, in which information is accessed through a sequence of mouse selections and key selections. The method is used to characterize a simple calendar task for an application of the Information Visualizer, to compute the changes in characterization as the result of possible program variants, and to conduct empirical comparison between different systems with the same function.

KEYWORDS: Information visualization, dynamic displays, methodology, evaluation, 3D user interfaces, Information Visualizer.

INTRODUCTION

The personal computer is changing from a device into which information is mainly put for authoring or analysis (e.g., desktop publishing) to a device from which information is mainly accessed (e.g., CD-ROM encyclopedias and on-line data services). This trend can only increase as the national data superhighway comes into being and as local memory costs continue to drop. Tennant and Heilmeier [8] estimate, for example, that the amount of information available through one's computer by 1995 will be more than 10,000 times greater than the information available at the time of their writing, about 1991. A challenge of the 1990s is to develop ways of using emerging technologies to manage the complexity inherent in accessing and utilizing such vast quantities of information.

A key observation is that information in an information system has a cost structure, that is, a set of different costs for the information in different parts of the system [3]. Information retrieval and other information-handling systems reorganize this cost structure of information relative to some task. For example, retrieving paper documents from filing cabinets and placing them on a desk reduces the time costs substantially for a task in which the documents must be repeatedly referenced.

A goal in designing information access systems is to rearrange this cost structure in beneficial ways. In previous papers, we have reported the designs of experimental programming systems whose interfaces were designed for this purpose [3][4]. But methods are needed for conceptualizing and measuring the abilities of these and other systems to bring about the desired result.

In this paper we propose an abstraction, the *Cost-of-Knowledge Characteristic Function,* for characterizing the effect of the design of a dynamic display or human-computer dialogue on the cost structure of information. The purpose of the paper is to work out and measure empirically this abstraction for a simple case of information access, "direct-walk" information visualizations, by which we mean the use of the mouse to point to and gesture over displays of an information structure so as to navigate from one place in that structure to another.

THE COST-OF-KNOWLEDGE CHARACTERISTIC FUNCTION

We have argued that, at least in a world of abundant information, but scarce time, the fundamental information access task is not finding information, but the optimal use of a person's scarce time in gaining information [7]. That is, the important thing is to maximize information benefits per unit cost (The unit of cost considered in this article is primarily the user's time). To aid in doing this, we need to know how much additional information becomes available for each additional amount of time expended. We call the curve this notion defines the *Cost-of-Knowledge Characteristic Function.*

Fig. 1 shows a schematic plot of this function. Curve A shows a hypothetical office in which information is hierarchically arranged: Small amounts of information are placed on the low-cost access desktop, larger amounts of information are placed in the more expensive-to-access, but more capacious, desk file drawer, and large quantities of information are in the file cabinet. For simplicity, it is assumed that the average time to access the information within each of these categories is the same, and we have ignored the staircase function produced by the fact that the repositories are of discrete sizes.

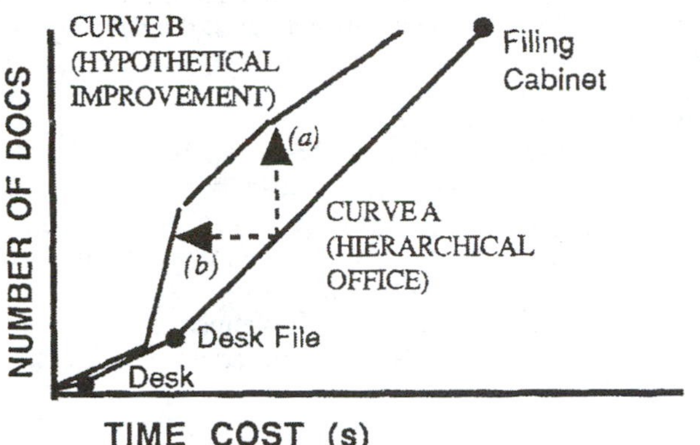

Fig. 1. Cost of Knowledge Characteristic Function

Now suppose that we were able to invent some device or procedure that improves information access. The Cost of Knowledge Characteristic Function should show that improvement by having at least some portion above the original curve (e.g., Curve B in Fig. 1). Notice that we can harvest this benefit in two ways, as shown by the arrows. If we keep the time cost the same, we could access more documents (arrow *a*). On the other hand, if we keep the number of documents the same, we can access them for a lower cost (arrow *b*). In this way, the Cost-of-Knowledge Characteristic Function is intended to help us reason through more complicated consequences of system improvements than just thinking that one system is better than another.

Direct Manipulation Walk of Information Structures

We now attempt to measure the function in Fig. 1 for an actual system. To keep the analysis simple, we investigate a basic, but important, information access task, which we dub a *direct walk of an information structure*.

> We define a *direct walk* to be a task in which a user navigates from a starting point to a goal point in an information structure by a series of mouse points or other direct-manipulation methods. Examples would be the series of mouse clicks and button choices required to operate the Macintosh hierarchical file system or a typical HyperCard stack or many help systems. The essence of a direct-walk is that an information structure is displayed and the user points to, flies to, or gestures over some part of this visible structure resulting in a new display at which time the cycle is repeated until the goal is found.

We do not believe the Cost of Knowledge Characteristic Function is limited to this class of dialogues. We simply choose these dialogues as a simple case on which to develop the methodology. In the remainder of this paper, we perform a series of analyses as exercises to establish the feasibility and utility of this concept. It should be noted that the emphasis is on the development of the methodology itself and that while useful information may be revealed about the systems we analyze (after all, that is the purpose!), our analyses do not constitute a complete evaluation of these systems, since that would require considering what other figures of merit might be relevant as well.

EMPIRICAL CHARACTERIZATION OF A SYSTEM

In our first analysis, we empirically measure the function of Fig. 1 for one particular task done by users of the Spiral Calendar, an application of the Information Visualizer [6] developed by Mackinlay and DeLine [5]. A user can access the schedule for various calendar dates by selecting objects that represent the appropriate period, then selecting the unit within that period, and so on. For example, to select June 4, 1982, the user would select the year 1982 within the Decade 1980-1989 object, this would cause the Year 1982 object to fly up and grow large. Then the user would select June from that Year object. This would cause the June Month object to fly up. The user would select 4 from the June month object causing the containing Week object to fly up. Finally, the user would select 4 from the week object, causing the daily schedule for that day to appear. There could be fewer selections or more selections depending on the condition of the display from which the user started.

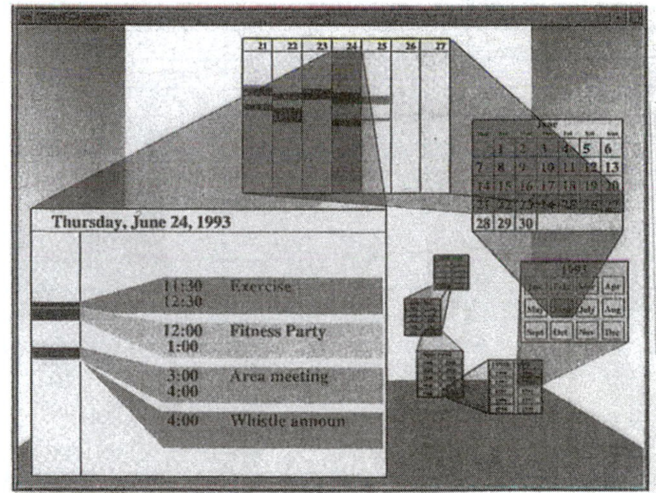

Fig. 2. The Spiral Calendar.

This system was measured using the following procedure:

Task

The general task measured can be described as follows:

> *A user is looking at the detailed hourly calendar for a certain day, and he or she wishes to view the daily calendar for another day. How long will it take to do this?*

Users had to position the calendar to a set of 11 different days related to the starting date (chosen to be September 7,

1993). These days were chosen to lie on a logarithmic scale: We specifically chose such a large range because we want to understand how the interaction scales with size.

Users

The measurement was done on four users, members of the professional staff of the lab. Users varied in their experience. Two had never used the Information Visualizer, one was one of the designers of the Spiral Calendar.

Procedures

As a warm-up, the user first performed a set of 11 accesses to dates different from, but similar to in time, those actually used in the experiment. These served to help the user assimilate the procedures of the experiment, to learn how to operate the Spiral Calendar, and to ask questions. As a limitation on the prototype, only data from 1993 was actually contained in the database and the calendars said 1993, regardless of the simulated year. Users were simply told of this limitation and that this data was being used to simulate a larger range of years.

The set of 11 tasks was randomized into a block of trials. Each user performed 5 of these blocks, each block separately randomized, for a total of 55 trials/user. Users were allowed to take a break between blocks if they wished. On each trial, the user flipped a page in a notebook asking him or her to navigate through the calendar to the day display of a specific date. The trials were videotaped and the time measured from when the user had turned from the notebook and was facing the display until the day page was done displaying.

Empirical Results

The results of the measurement are in Table 1, column (4). Plotting time to access a date as a function of number of days back (column 2) gives Fig. 3. As might be expected, the time required increases with the number of days back. This is obviously because there are more steps in the dialogue to reach distant dates. How much additional time can be understood by analyzing the predominant method users utilized.

Table 1. Computation of Cost of Knowledge Characteristic Function for Spiral Calendar.

(1) Task	(2) Days Back	(3) Date	(4) Access Time[a] Mean ±SD (s)	(5) Method	(6) No. Cycles	(7) Cost Method Time (s)	(8) Cost From Model[b] (s)	(9) Selection Branch Factor	(10) Access No. of Days Accessible
1	1	Sep. 6, 1993	5.6±0.97	Day	1	5.6±0.97	6.9	1	1
2	3	Sep. 4, 1993	11.1±1.80	Week	2	11.1±1.80	10.4	7	7
3	10	Aug. 28, 1993	14.3±0.49	Month	3	14.4±0.36	14.0	4.25	30
4	30	Aug. 8, 1993	14.6±0.77						
5	100	May 30, 1993	14.4±0.46						
6	300	Nov. 11, 1992	16.6±0.39	Year	4	17.2±0.35	17.5	12	365
7	1000	Dec. 12, 1990	17.8±0.35						
8	3000	Sep. 25, 1982	21.1±0.28	Decade	5	21.0±0.31	21.0	10	3,562
9	10,000	Apr. 22, 1966	21.2±0.69						
10	30,000	Jul. 20, 1911	20.7±0.46						
11	100,000	Nov. 23, 1719	24.3±1.40	Century	6	24.3±1.5	24.6	10	36,525
	300,000			Millennium	7		28.1	10	365,250
	1,000,000			Era	8		31.6	10	3,652,500

[a] Each mean is based on 4 users x 5 repetitions = 20 data points.
b Computed using $Time = 3.346 + 3.535 * NCycles$

Methods

The cost in time for accessing some date can be characterized in terms of the major methods available to users. Let us take the most extreme case, accessing the date November 23, 1719. A GOMS model [2] for this procedure would be

```
CENTURY-METHOD =
GOAL: DO-TASK
    GOAL: GET-DATE
        TURN-TO[MANUSCRIPT]
        GET-DATE
    GOAL: ACCESS-DAY-CALENDAR
        GET-YEAR    ••• If necessary
        GOAL: SELECT-CENTURY (1700's)
            POINT-TO (Century=1700-1790s))
                    ⇒ Century-display
        GET-YEAR    ••• If necessary
        GOAL: SELECT-DECADE (1710's)
            POINT-TO (1710-1719))
                    ⇒ Decade-display
        GET-YEAR    ••• If necessary
        GOAL: SELECT-YEAR: (1719)
            POINT-TO (1719))
                    ⇒ Year-display
        GET-MONTH ••• If necessary
        GOAL: SELECT-MONTH: (November)
            POINT-TO (November))
                    ⇒ Month-display
        GET-DAY     ••• If necessary
        GOAL: SELECT-WEEK: [??]
            POINT-TO [23]
                    ⇒ Week-display
        GET-DAY     ••• If necessary
        GOAL: SELECT-DAY: [23]
            POINT-TO (23))
                    ⇒ Day-display
```

Neglecting the initial part of this method that has to do with our experimental procedure, the method can be summarized in terms of seven cycles of pointing and display–one each for Century, Decade, Year, Month, Week, and Day. Other methods used in our measurement are the same, except that the larger units of time, such as the century, or the decade, or even the month, are eliminated if the date is close enough. To make the methods easy to talk about, we name them by the largest unit of time selected. The method for each task is listed in column (5) of Table 1.

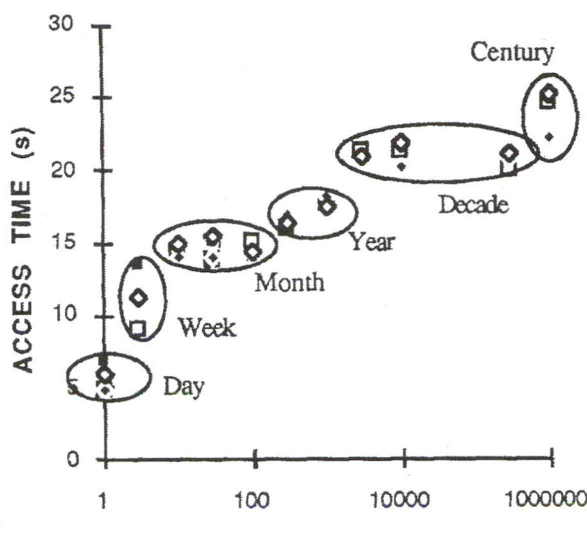

Fig. 3. Time as a function of number of days back.

Model for Access Time

On Fig. 3, we have circled those data points that are done with the same method and collapsed the data cells to one data point per method in Table 1, columns (5) and after. At this point, we can use our data to fit a simple model in order to characterize the direct walk time. To a first order of analysis, the time (in seconds) to select a date is just proportional to the number of cycles required (Fig. 4). By a regression analysis,

$$\textit{Time to Access} = 3.3 + 3.5 * \textit{NCycles}. \quad (1)$$

This model allows us to give a smoother characterization than the individual data points and we list the model times in Table 1, column (8).

Number of elements accessed

Finally, we compute the number of days that it is possible to reach in less than or equal to a certain amount of time. This is done by computing the number of days existing within the different periods serviced by the methods in Table 1. We list the result in Table 1, column (10). With the model, we can make reasonable estimates of what the data would be for other dates not actually measured (e.g., 1,000,000 days distant).

Cost-of-Knowledge Characteristic Function

We can now plot the Cost-of-Knowledge Characteristic Function of Fig. 1 by plotting the number of elements accessible (column 10) as a function of the cost in time (column 8) in Table 1. This is done in Fig. 5 (Curve A: Spiral Calendar). This graph, the first actual calculation of this concept we have been able to achieve, shows how, as would be expected in a reasonable system, the small amounts of knowledge can be accessed quickly, larger amounts of knowledge require longer times. For simplicity we have omitted the stair-case detail of the curve that would track abrupt representation shifts (e.g., from month to year). The metric is roughly linear, in semi-log coordinates, indicating that the items accessed increase exponentially. This linear shape of the curve may be a natural form for describing accessibility with cost for well-designed systems.

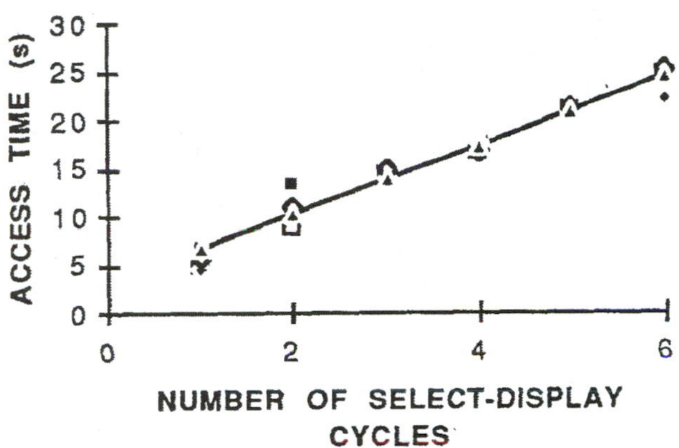

Fig. 4. Time as a function of the number of selection-display cycles.

COMPUTATIONAL CHARACTERIZATION OF DESIGN IMPROVEMENTS

With the Cost-of-Knowledge Characteristic Function conceptually in hand, we can now use it to help reason about and discover variants in the system design. Let us discuss briefly the effect of some design changes on the system measured in the last section.

One possibility is to speed up the system response. We notice (from Eq. 1) that the time per picking cycle is on the order of 3.5 s. This would seem to be relatively long. Assuming a mouse point of around 1 s [2] and a response animation time of 1 s [3] suggests that 2 s/cycle should be possible The discrepancy suggests re-examination of the animation algorithms. We now replot (as recalculated from Eq. 1) the Cost of Knowledge Characteristic Function that would have resulted from a faster 2 second user-action cycle (Curve B in Fig. 5). The curve is tilted upwards indicating an improvement in the system (if it can be achieved computationally and if some other phenomenon does not intervene). Notice that in this case we have plugged the results from previous models into our new model to cascade the speed with which we can think about design variants.

Another possibility is to eliminate the Week display (or probably better, to integrate it into the same display as the

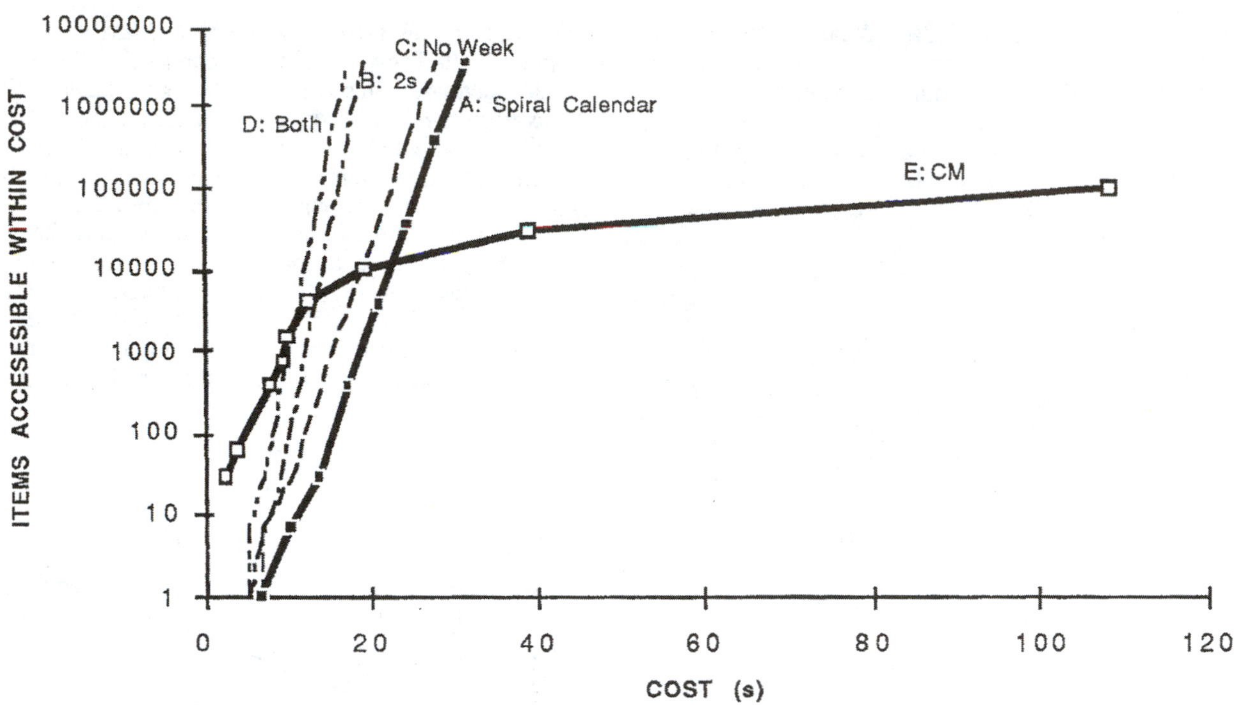

Fig. 5. Cost of Knowledge Characteristic Function for several variants of the Spiral Calendar and the CM calendar program.

Day) in order to reduce the number of action-display cycles required. If we were to do just this, then the Cost of Knowledge Characteristic Function Fig. 5 grows a bump at the bottom (Curve C), because of the larger branching factor at the Month level. In Curve D, we combine both variants.

Table 2. Computation of Cost of Knowledge Characteristic Function for Sun CM Calendar.

(1) TASK	(2) COST TASK TIME MEAN±SD (S)	(3) METHOD	(4) COST METHOD TIME MEAN±SD (S)	(5) COST FROM MODEL[b] (S)	(6) ACCESS NO. OF DAYS ACCESSIBLE
1	2.4±0.56	*Month*	2.3±0.34	2.8	30
2	2.2±0.25				
3	5.0±0.60	*Month2*	4.6±0.14	4.2	61
4	4.3±0.53				
5	9.0±0.90	*Year*	9.0±0.55	8.1	365
6	8.7±0.90	*Year2*	8.7±0.90	4.5	731
7	10.03±0.80	*Year4*	10.0±0.80	10.2	1461
8	12.8±0.70	*Year11*	12.8±0.70	12.8	4018

[a] Each mean is based on 4 users x 5 repetitions = 20 data points.
[b] *Time* = 1.340 + 3.889 **m** + 1.412 **P** + 0-.362 **B**.

With the Cost of Knowledge Characteristic Function, we are led to view variants in terms of their effect on the cost-structure of access rather than just on a single point.

EMPIRICAL COMPARISON AMONG SYSTEMS

In addition to using calculations to do paper comparisons among system variants before they are built, we can also use the Cost of Knowledge Characteristic Function to do comparisons between competing systems. As an example, we repeat our measurement and calculation, but this time for the Sun calendar program CM.

Procedure

The tasks and the procedure were exactly the same as for the Iris Spiral Calendar above. Four users participated in this measurement, two of these were users measured in the previous Spiral Calendar. The results are shown in Table 2, comparable to Table 1.

The GOMS analysis [2] of the methods is summarized in short-hand form in Table 3 column (4). In this analysis, there are three operators:

m	point, menu pull-down, and select
P	point and select
B	press a button (not including pointing)

These operators include the system response time of this particular system. They do not count the mental preparation time [2]. The time taken by the different methods is given in Table 3, which analyzes the predominant method used. (Remember, methods were restricted to be direct walk).

Table 3. Analysis of methods for CM calendar task.

METHOD	DISPLAY	ACTION	ANALYSIS
Month	Month display	Select Date	**P**
Month2	Month display	Select PREV button	2**P**
		Select Day	
Year	Month display	Select year on VIEW pulldown menu	**m** + 2**P**
	Year Month	Select Month Select Day	
Year(n)	Month display	Select year on VIEW pulldown menu	**m** + 3**P** + (n-2)**B**
	Year Year Month	Select PREV button (n-1) times Select Month Select Day	

In this case, we are not trying to predict method times, but to analyze them, so, as before we use regression analysis to assign numbers to the operators. The regression gives

$$Time = 1.3 + 3.9\ \mathbf{m} + 1.4\ \mathbf{P} + 0.36\ \mathbf{B}\ . \qquad (2)$$

This equation (the equivalent of Eq. 1 for CM) is used to determine a smoother version of the Cost of Knowledge Characteristic Function in Table 2, column (5). Finally, the number of days accessible within a given iso-cost contour is determined from an inspection of the program displays and summarized in Table 2, column (6). As before, we plot number of items accessible (column 6) against cost (column 5) in Curve E in Fig. 5.

A comparison between the Cost of Knowledge functions in Fig. 5 shows a rather dramatic contrast. The Spiral Calendar uses a uniform direct-walk method to access all dates and costs go up logarithmically. The CM program is at an advantage for lower numbers of items, but costs radically increase for numbers of items over about 10,000. (Remember, however, we are not characterizing the programs themselves, only certain methods. For example, we are not considering methods such as typing in the date directly that would be useful for larger numbers of items.)

The Spiral Calendar suffers because of its high cost intercept. Clearly there is payoff in concentrating effort at the low end of the curve to shift it to the left. The CM program suffers because users must shift through a more complex space of methods, changing methods for different regions of the space.

PROBABILITY DENSITY FUNCTION

Finally, it should be noted that whereas we have determined the Cost of Knowledge Function, we have not as yet weighted the items accessed by their value. There are several such weightings, but one of the most important is to weight items by a probability density function describing their frequency of use.

Anderson and Schooler [1] have shown that for many different kinds of information (e.g., news articles in the New York Times or messages in electronic mail) the probability an item D days old will be needed is given by

$$\Pr\{\text{needed}|D \text{ days ago}\} = A / (A + D^C), \text{ where}$$

where A and C are constants. For the case of electronic mail, $A = .34$ and $C = 0.83$, hence

$$\Pr\{\text{needed}|D \text{ days ago}\} = 0.34 / (0.34 + D^{0.83}).$$

If we multiply this function with the Cost of Knowledge Characteristic Functions in Fig. 5 to obtain a curve expressing the expected cost of accessing different numbers of items (see Fig. 6). In the case of the calendars, it expresses the fact that the user is likely to access recent dates much more frequently. The area under the curves is related to the total costs of using the two programs and the curve also shows in what area the costs are concentrated. Fig. 6 shows that the expected cost for the user is heavily contained in the in the most recent hundred days. For this reason, the Spiral Calendar prototype tested would be more expensive to use than CM (if only the direct walk feature were considered). On the other hand, if the task involved reference to historical dates, then a different probability density function would be appropriate.

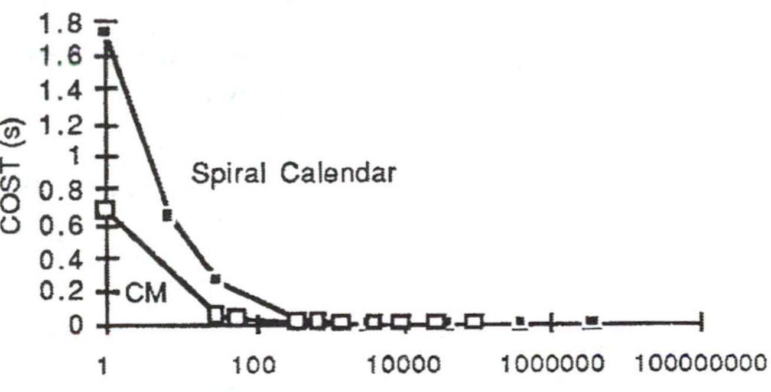

Fig. 6. Expected probability-weighted costs associated with retrievals.

CONCLUSION

This paper has introduced the Cost-of-Knowledge Characteristic Function as a method for analyzing interactive information visualizations. The metric was measured for direct-walk dialogue taken from two calendar programs. We have also done calculations showing the likely consequences for proposed variants of these systems in terms of the metric. Finally, we introduced the next step in the development of this analysis, taking into account the frequency of access for different items of information.

While we have explored direct-walk information access because of its simplicity, other more complex information access dialogues should be able to be analyzed with this basic method and it should be possible to elaborate the analysis for more insight.

The purpose of the paper was to move some of the qualitative reasoning behind the design of the Information Visualizer and other information access systems closer to a measurable, computable methodology. In this way, we hope to be able to understand more precisely the consequences of design decisions in this area. Indeed, in this case, we discovered the initial design of the Spiral Calendar, while good for handling very large time periods, was under-optimized for the frequent close-to-present dates. While obvious to the designers after the measurement, it was previously under-appreciated. A number of design suggestions have ensued, many couched in terms of what was required to move various pieces of the curves in Fig. 5.

It should be noted that individual differences, as indicated by the standard deviation in Tables 1 and 2, are relatively small, suggesting the results are not very sensitive to individual users. The method is therefore usable by an individual system builder with a stop watch, timing himself or herself. Indeed, a pilot of this experiment with one of the authors timing himself with a stopwatch while performing the role of the user yielded a very similar curve to that plotted in Fig. 5 (with 5 s/cycle instead of 3.5 s/cycle). This is a significant finding, because, while it is important to do formal user testing in building systems, it is also important to have inexpensive methods designers can use rapidly as they work to reduce the number of more expensive user tests required. This is similar to the way many experienced system builders now routinely perform system timings as they work.

Finally, according to Fig. 5, the number of information items accessible by these systems increases logarithmically with time cost, roughly at

$$\textit{Number of item accessible} = A\, e^{0.5\, t} \,,$$

where t is the cost of access in seconds. This is as expected, since the user has a succession of choices, each with a similar branching factor. But the cost structure for other information systems may also tend to arrange themselves logarithmically, when the user's shift among available access methods is taken into account. This would be interesting to know as well as knowing what are characteristic values for the exponents.

ACKNOWLEDGEMENTS

The Spiral Calendar was designed and implemented in the Information Visualizer by Robert DeLine (University of Virginia and Carnegie-Mellon University) as a summer project at Xerox PARC. An improved version has now been integrated into the standard Information Visualizer release by George Robertson (Xerox PARC).

REFERENCES

1. Anderson, J. R. and Schooler, L. J. Reflections of the environment in memory. *Psychological Science* 2(6 November), 1991: 396-408.

2. Card, S. K., Moran, T. P., and Newell, A. The Psychology of Human-Computer Interaction. Hillsdale, New Jersey: Erlbaum, 1983.

3. Card, S. K., Robertson, G. G., and Mackinlay, J. D. The Information Visualizer, an information workspace. In *Proceedings of CHI '91 ACM Conference on Human Factors in Computing Systems* (New Orleans, Louisiana, April 27–May 2, 1991). ACM, New York, 1991, pp. 181-188.

4. Henderson, D. A., Jr. and Card, S. K. Rooms: The use of multiple virtual workspaces to reduce space contention in a window-based graphical user interface. *ACM Transactions on Graphics 5* (3, July 1986)., 211-243.

5. Mackinlay, J. M. and DeLine, R. Designing calendar visualizes for the Information Visualizer. Research Report, Xerox PARC, Palo Alto.

6. Robertson, G. G., Card, S. K., and Mackinlay, J. D. Information visualization using 3D interactive animation. *Communications of the ACM*, 36 (4, April), 1993, 57-71.

7. Russell, D. M., Stefik, M. J., Pirolli, P., and Card, S. K. The cost structure of sensemaking. In *Proceedings of CHI '93, ACM Conference on Human Factors in Software* (April 24-29, Amsterdam). New York: ACM, 1993, pp. 269-276.

8. Tennant, H. and Heilmeier, G. H. Knowledge and equality: Harnessing the tides of information abundance. In Leebaert, D. (ed.), *Technology 2001: The Future of Computing and Communications*. Cambridge, Massachusetts: The MIT Press, 1991.

Effective View Navigation

George W. Furnas
School of Information
University of Michigan
(313) 763-0076
furnas@umich.edu

ABSTRACT

In *view navigation* a user moves about an information structure by selecting something in the current view of the structure. This paper explores the implications of rudimentary requirements for effective view navigation, namely that, despite the vastness of an information structure, the views must be small, moving around must not take too many steps and the route to any target be must be discoverable. The analyses help rationalize existing practice, give insight into the difficulties, and suggest strategies for design.

KEYWORDS: Information navigation, Direct Walk, large information structures, hypertext, searching, browsing

INTRODUCTION

When the World Wide Web (WWW) first gained popularity, those who used it were impressed by the richness of the content accessible simply by wandering around and clicking things seen on the screen. Soon after, struck by the near impossibility of finding anything specific, global navigation was largely abandoned in place of search engines. What went wrong with pure navigation?

This work presented here seeks theoretical insight into, in part, the problems with pure navigational access on the web. More generally, it explores some basic issues in moving around and finding things in various information structures, be they webs, trees, tables, or even simple lists. The focus is particularly on issues that arise as such structures get very large, where interaction is seriously limited by the available resources of space (e.g., screen real estate) and time (e.g., number of interactions required to get somewhere): How do these limits in turn puts constraints on what kinds of information structures and display strategies lead to effective navigation? How have these constraints affected practice, and how might we live with them in future design?

We will be considering systems with static structure[1] over which users must navigate to find things, e.g., lists, trees, planes, grids, graphs. The structure is assumed to contain elements of some sort (items in a list, nodes in a hypertext graph) organized in some logical structure. We assume that the interface given to the user is navigational, i.e., the user at any given time is "at" some node in the structure with a view specific to that node (e.g., of the local neighborhood), and has the ability to move next to anything in that current view. For example for a list the user might have window centered on a particular current item. A click on an item at the bottom of the window would cause that item to scroll up and become the new "current" item in the middle of the window. In a hypertext web, a user could follow one of the visible links in the current hypertext page.

In this paper we will first examine *view traversal*, the underlying iterative process of viewing, selecting something seen, and moving to it, to form a path through the structure.[2] Then we will look at the more complex *view navigation* where in addition the selections try to be informed and reasonable in the pursuit of a desired target. Thus view traversal ignores how to decide where to go next, for view navigation that is central.The goal throughout is to understand the implications of resource problems arising as structures get very large.

EFFICIENT VIEW TRAVERSIBILITY

What are the basic requirements for efficient view traversal? I.e., what are the minimal capabilities for moving around by viewing, selecting and moving which, if not met, will make large information structures, those encompassing thousands, even billions of items, impractical for navigation.

Definitions and Fundamental Requirements

We assume that the elements of the information structure (the items in a list, nodes in a hypertext graph, etc.) are organized in a logical structure that can be characterized by a *logical structure graph*, connecting elements to their logical neighbors as dictated by the semantics of the domain.[3] For an

1 We assume at least that the structure is relatively unchanging at least within the timeframe of a navigational interaction.

2 This is the style of interaction was called a *direct walk* by Card, et al [2]. We choose the terminology "view traversal" here to make explicit the view aspect, since we wish to study the use of spatial resources needed for viewing.

3 More complete definitions, and proofs of most of the material in this paper can be found in [3]

ordered list this would just be line graph, with each item connected to the items which proceed and follow it. For a hypertext the logical structure graph would be some sort of web. We will assume the logical graph is finite.

We capture a basic property of the interface to the information structure in terms of the notion of a viewing *graph* (actually a directed graph) defined as follows. It has a node for each node in the logical structure. A directed link goes from a node *i* to node *j* if the view from *i* includes *j* (and hence it is possible to view-traverse from *i* to *j*). Note that the viewing graph might be identical to the logical graph, but need not be. For example, it is permissible to include in the current view, points that are far away in the logical structure (e.g., variously, the root, home page, top of the list).

The conceptual introduction of the viewing graph allows us to translate many discussion of views and viewing strategies into discussions of the nature of the viewing graph. Here, in particular, we are interested in classes of viewing-graphs that allow the efficient use of space and time resources during view traversal, even as the structures get very large: Users have a comparatively small amount of screen real estate and a finite amount of time for their interactions. For view traversal these limitations translate correspondingly into two requirements on the viewing graph. First, if we assume the structure to be huge, and the screen comparatively small, then the user can only view a small subset of the structure from her current location. In terms of the viewing graph this means, in some reasonable sense,

> *Requirement EVT1 (small views).* The number of out-going links, or out-degree, of nodes in the viewing graph must be "small" compared to the size of the structure.

A second requirement reflects the interaction time limitation. Even though the structure is huge, we would like it to take only a reasonable number of steps to get from one place to another. Thus (again in some reasonable sense) we need,

> *Requirement EVT2 (short paths).* The distance (in number of links) between pairs of nodes in the viewing graph must be "small" compared to the size of the structure.

We will say that a viewing graph is Efficiently View Traversable (EVT) insofar as it meets both of these requirements. There are many "reasonable senses" one might consider for formalizing these requirements. For analysis here we will use a worst case characterization. The Maximal Out-Degree (MOD, or largest out-degree of any node) will characterize how well EVT1 is met (smaller values are better), and the Diameter (DIA, or longest connecting path required anywhere) will characterize how well EVT2 is met (again, smaller is better). Summarized as an ordered pair,

$$EVT(G) = (MOD(G), DIA(G)),$$

we can use them to compare the traversability of various classes of view-traversable information structures.

•• example 1: a scrolling list

Consider an ordered list, sketched in Figure 1(a). Its logical structure connects each item with the item just before

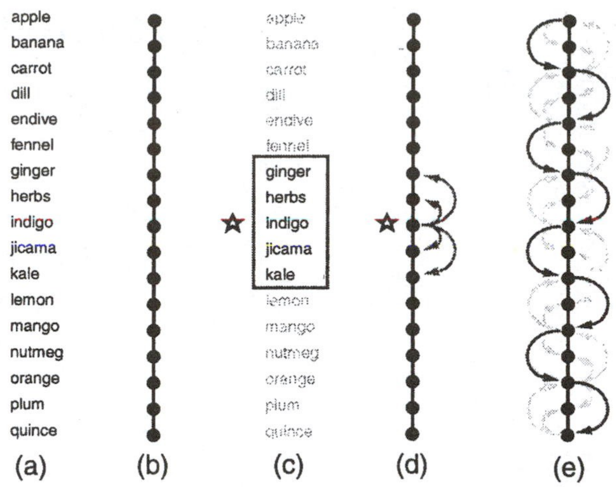

Figure 1. *(a) Schematic of an ordered list, (b) logical graph of the list, (c) local window view of the list, (d) associated part of viewing graph, showing that out degree is constant, (e) sequence of traversal steps showing the diameter of viewing graph is O(n).*

and just after it in the list. Thus the logical graph (b) is a line graph. A standard viewer for a long list is a simple scrolling window (c), which when centered on one line (marked by the star), shows a number of lines on either side. Thus a piece of the viewing graph, shown in (d), has links going from the starred node to all the nearby nodes that can be seen in the view as centered at that node. The complete viewing graph would have this replicated for all nodes in the logical graph.

This viewing graph satisfies the first requirement, EVT1, nicely: Regardless of the length of the list, the view size, and hence the out-degree of the viewing graph, is always the small fixed size of the viewing window. The diameter requirement of EVT2, however, is problematic. Pure view traversal for a scrolling list happens by clicking on an item in the viewing window, e.g., the bottom line. That item would then appear in the center of the screen, and repeated clicks could move all the way through the list. As seen in (e), moving from one end of the list to the other requires a number of steps linear in the size of the list. This means that overall

$$EVT(\text{ SCROLLING-LIST}_n) = (\ O(1),\ O(n)\ ),$$ [4]

and, because of the diameter term, a scrolling list is not very Effectively View Traversable. This formalizes the intuition that while individual views in a scrolling list interface are reasonable, unaided scrolling is a poor interaction technique for even moderate sized lists of a few hundred items (where scrollbars were a needed invention), and impossible for huge ones (e.g., billions, where even scroll bars will fail). ••

DESIGN FOR EVT

Fortunately from a design standpoint, things need not be so bad. There are simple viewing structures that are highly EVT, and there are ways to fix structures that are not.

---

4 $O(1)$ means basically "in the limit proportional to 1", i.e., constant -- an excellent score. $O(n)$ means "in the limit proportional to n"-- a pretty poor score. $O(\log n)$ would mean "in the limit proportional to $\log n$"-- quite respectable.

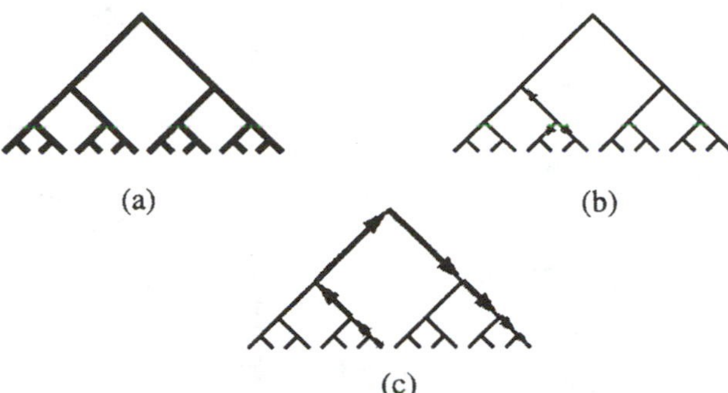

Figure 2. *An example of an Efficiently View Traversable Structure (a) logical graph of a balanced tree, (b) in gray, part of the viewing graph for giving local views of the tree showing the outdegree is constant, (c) a path showing the diameter to be O(log(n)).*

Some Efficiently View Traversable Structures

We begin by considering example structures that have good EVT performance, based on classes of graphs that have the proper degree and diameter properties.

•• *example 2: local viewing of a balanced tree.*

Trees are commonly used to represent information, from organizational hierarchies, to library classification systems, to menu systems. An idealized version (a balanced regular tree) appears in Figure 2(a). A typical tree viewing strategy makes visible from a given node its parent and its children (b), i.e., the viewing structure essentially mirrors the logical structure. Here, regardless of the total size, *n*, of the tree, the outdegree of each node in the viewing graph is a constant, one more than the branching factor, and we have nicely satisfied EVT1. The diameter of the balanced tree is also well behaved, being twice the depth of the tree, which is logarithmic in the size of the tree, and hence *O(log n)*. Thus,

$EVT(\text{BALANCED-REGULAR-TREE}_n) = (O(1), O(\log n))$ ••

•• *example 3: local viewing of a hypercube*

Consider next a *k*-dimensional hypercube (not pictured) that might be used to represent the structure of a factorially designed set of objects, where there are *k* binary factors (cf. a simple but complete relational database with *k* binary attributes), e.g., a set of objects that are either big or small, red or green, round or square, in all various combinations. A navigational interface to such a data structure could give, from a node corresponding to one combination of attributes, views simply showing its neighbors in the hypercube, i.e., combinations differing in only one attribute. Whether this would be a good interface for other reasons or not, a simple analysis reveals that at least it would have very reasonable EVT behavior:

$EVT(\text{HYPERCUBE}_n) = (O(\log n), O(\log n))$. ••

The conclusion of examples 2 and 3 is simply that, if one can coerce the domain into either a reasonably balanced and regular tree, or into a hypercube, view traversal will be quite efficient. Small views and short paths suffice even for very large structures. Knowing a large arsenal of highly EVT structures presumably will be increasingly useful as we have to deal with larger and larger information worlds.

Fixing Non-EVT Structures

What can one do with an information structure whose logical structure does not directly translate into a viewing graph that is EVT? The value of separating out the viewing graph from the logical graph is that while the domain semantics may dictate the logical graph, the interface designer can often craft the viewing graph. Thus we next consider a number of strategies for improving EVT behavior by the design of good viewing graphs. We illustrate by showing several ways to improve the view navigation of lists, then mentioning some general results and observations.

•• *example 4: fixing the list (version 1) - more dimensions*

One strategy for improving the View Traversability of a list is to fold it up into two dimensions, making a multi-column list (Figure 3).The logical graph is the same (a), but by folding as in (b) one can give views that show two dimensional local neighborhoods (c). These local neighborhoods are of constant size, regardless of the size of the list, so the outdegree of the viewing graph is still constant, but the diameter of the graph is now sublinear, being related to the square-root of the length of the list, so we have

$EVT(\text{MULTI-COLUMN-LIST}_n) = (O(1), O(sqrt(n)))$.

This square-root reduction in diameter presumably explains why it is common practice to lay out lists of moderate size in multiple columns (e.g., the "ls" command in UNIX or a page of the phone book). The advantage is presumably that the eye (or viewing window) has to move a much shorter distance to get from one part to another.[5] One way to think about what has happened is

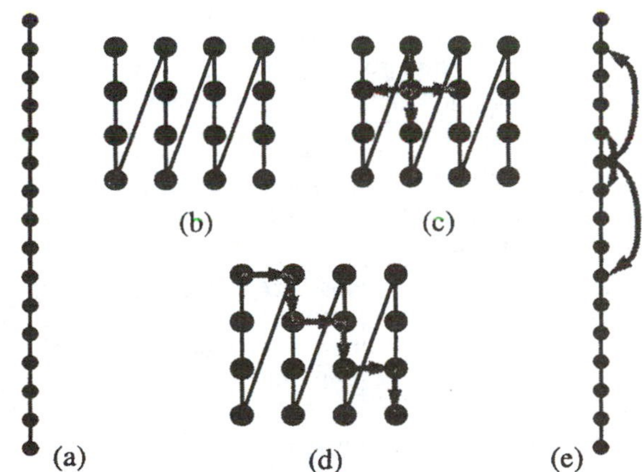

Figure 3. *Fixing the list viewer. (a) logical graph of the ordered list again, (b) the list is folded up in 2-D (c) part of the viewing graph showing the 2-D view-neighbors of Node6 in the list: out degree is O(1), (d) diameter of viewing graph is now reduced to O(sqrt(n)). (e) Unfolding the list, some view-neighbors of Node6 are far away, causing a decrease in diameter.*

5 Some really long lists, for example a metropolitan phone book, are folded up in 3-D: multiple columns per page, and pages stacked one upon another. We take this format for granted, but imagine how far one would have to move from the beginning to the end of the list if one only had 1D or 2D in which to place all those numbers! A similar analysis explains how Cone Trees [6] provide better traversability using 3-D.

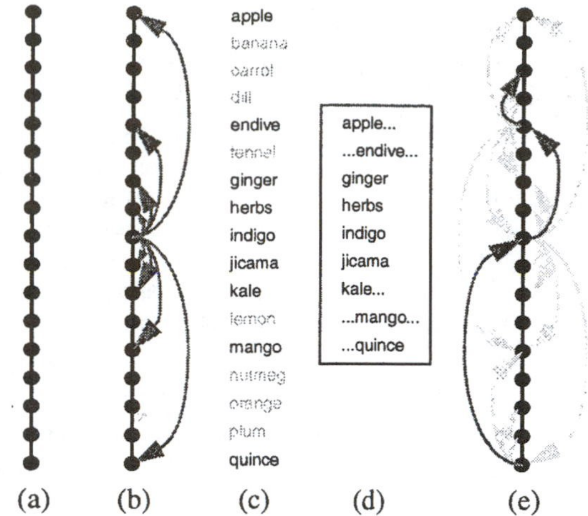

Figure 4. *Fixing the list viewer. (a) logical graph of the ordered list again, (b) part of viewing graph of fish-eye sampled list, showing that out degree is O(log(n)), (c) sample actually selected from list (d) view actually given, of size O(log(n)), (e) illustration of how diameter of viewing graph is now O(log(n)).*

illustrated in Figure 3 (e), where the part of the viewing graph in (c) is shown in the unfolded version of the list.••

The critical thing to note in the example is that some of the links of the viewing graph point to nodes that are not local in the logical structure of the graph. This is a very general class of strategies for decreasing the diameter of the viewing graph, further illustrated in the next example.

•• example 5: fixing the list (version 2) - fisheye sampling

It is possible to use non-local viewing links to improve even further the view-traversability of a list. Figure 3 shows a viewing strategy where the nodes included in a view are spaced in a geometric series. That is, from the current node, one can see the nodes that are at a distance 1, 2, 4, 8, 16,... away in the list. This sampling pattern might be called a kind of fisheye sampling, in that it shows the local part of the list in most detail, and further regions in successively less detail.

This strategy results in a view size that is logarithmic in the size of the list. Moving from one node to another ends up to be a process much like a binary search, and gives a diameter of the viewing graph that is also logarithmic. Thus

$$EVT(\text{ FISHEYE-SAMPLED-LIST}_n) = (O(\log n), O(\log n)).$$

Note that variations of this fisheye sampling strategy can yield good EVT performance for many other structures, including 2D and 3D grids. ••

The lesson from examples 4 and 5 is that even if the logical structure is not EVT, it is possible to make the viewing structure EVT by adding long-distance links.

•• example 6: fixing the list (version 3) - tree augmentation

In addition to just adding links, one can also adding nodes to the viewing graph that are not in the original logical structure. This allows various shortcut paths to share structure, and reduce the total number of links needed, and hence the general outdegree. For example, one can glue a structure known to be EVT onto a given non-EVT structure. In Figure 2 a tree is glued onto the side of the list and traversal is predominantly through the tree. Thus in Figure 2, new nodes are introduced (*O(n)*), and viewing links are introduced in the form of a tree. Since the outdegrees everywhere are of size ≤3, and logarithmic length paths now exist between the original nodes by going through the tree, we get

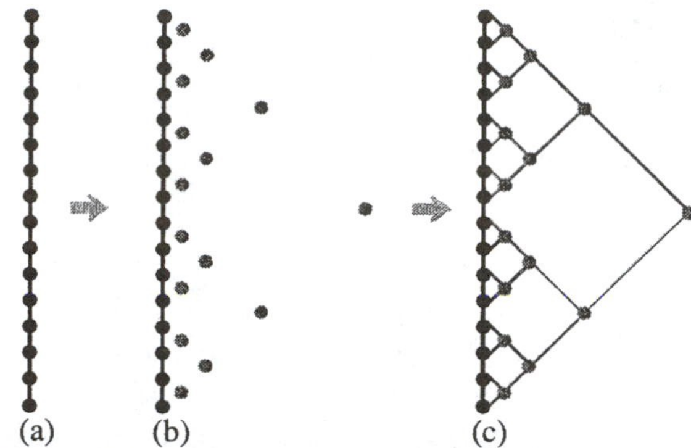

Figure 5. *Improving EVT of a list by adding a tree. The resulting structure has constant viewsize but logarithmic diameter*

$$EVT(\text{ TREE-AUGMENTED-LIST}_n) = (O(1), O(\log n)). \quad ••$$

Although there is not enough space here for details, we note in passing that an EVT analysis of zoomable interfaces is valuable in clarifying one of their dramatic advantages -- the diameter of the space is reduced from *O(sqrt(n))* to *O(log n)*. [3][4]

Remarks about Efficient View Traversability

Efficient View Traversability is a minimal essential condition for view navigation of very large information structures. In a straight forward way it helps to explain why simple list viewers do not scale, why phone books and cone-trees exploit 3D, why trees and fisheyes and zooms all help.

EVT analysis also suggests strategies for design. One can try to coerce an information world into a representation which naturally supports EVT1 and EVT2, e.g., the common practice of trying to represent things in trees. Alternatively one can fix a poor structure by adding long-distance links, or adding on another complete structure. Note that in general, the impact of selectively adding links can be much greater on decreasing diameter than on increasing view sizes, to net positive effect. One result of this simple insight is a general version of the tree augmentation strategy. In general terms, gluing any good EVT graph onto a bad one will make a new structure as good as the good graph in diameter, and not much worse than the worse of the two in outdegree. I.e., always remember the strategy of putting a traversable infrastructure on an otherwise unruly information structure!

Efficiently view traversable structures have an additional interesting property, *"jump and show"*: an arbitrary non-navigational jump (e.g., as the result of a query search) from one location to another has a corresponding view traversal version with a small rendering: a small number of steps each requiring a small view will suffice. Thus a short movie or small map will show the user how they could have done a direct walk from their old location to their new one. A similar concept was explored for continuous Pan&Zoom in [4].

NAVIGABILITY

Efficient view traversability is not enough: it does little good if a short traversal path to a destination exists but that path is unfindable. It must be possible somehow to read the structure to find good paths; the structure must be *view navigable.*

For analysis we imagine the simple case of some *navigator* process searching for a particular target, proceeding by comparing it to information associated with each outlink in its current view (*outlink-info,* e.g. a label). From this comparison, it decides which link to follow next.

In this paper we will explore an idealization, *strong navigability* , requiring that the structure and its outlink-info allow the navigator (1) to find the shortest path to the target (2) without error and (3) in a history-less fashion (meaning it can make the right choice at each step by looking only at what is visible in the current node). We examine this case because it is tractable, because it leads to suggestive results, and because, as a desirable fantasy, its limits are worth understanding.

To understand when strong view navigation is possible, a few definitions are needed. They are illustrated in Figure 6.

Consider a navigator at some node seeking the shortest path to a target. A given link is a defensible next step only for certain targets -- the link must be on a shortest path to those targets. We call this set of targets the *to-set* of the link, basically the targets the link efficiently "leads to". If the navigator's target is in the to-set of a link, it can follow that link.

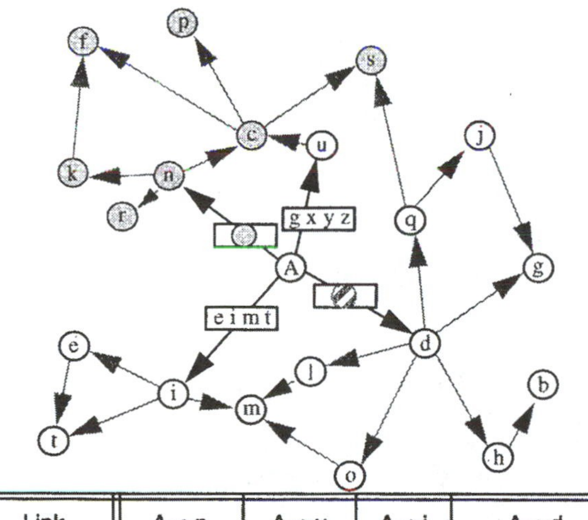

Link	A-->n	A-->u	A-->i	A-->d
to-set	c,f,k,n,p,r,s	c,f,p,s,u	e,i,m,t	b,d,g,h,j,l,o,q,s
outlink-info		g x y z	e i m t	
inferred to-set	c,f,k,n,p,r,s	g,x,y,z	e,i,m,t	?

Figure 6 *The outlink-info for link A-->i is an enumeration, and for A-->n is a feature (a shaded circle). These are both well matched. The link info for links to the right of A is not-well matched. The residue of f at A is the shaded-circle label. The residue of e at A is its appearance in the enumeration label. The node g has residue in the upper right enumeration label at A, but it is not good residue. The node h has no residue at A.*

We assume, however, that the navigator does not know the to-set of a link directly; it is a global property of the structure of the graph. The navigator only has access to the locally available outlink-info which it will match against its target to decide what link to take. We define the *inferred-to-set* of a link to be the set of all target nodes that the associated outlink-info would seem to indicate is down that link (the targets that would match the outlink-info), which could be a different set entirely.

In fact, we say that the outlink-info of a link is *not misleading with respect to a target* when the target being in the *inferred-to-set* implies it is in the true *to-set,* or in other words when the outlink-info does not mislead the navigator to take a step it should not take. (Note that the converse is not being required here; the outlink-info need not be complete, and may underspecify its *true-to-set.*)

Next we say that the outlink-info of node as a whole is said to be *well-matched with respect to a target* if none of its outlink-info is misleading with respect to that target, and if the target is in the inferred-to-set of at least one outlink. Further we say that the outlink information at a node is simply *well-matched* iff it is well-matched with respect to all possible targets.

We now state the following straightforward proposition:

> *Proposition (navigability):* The navigator is guaranteed to always find shortest paths to targets iff the outlink-info is everywhere well-matched.

Hence, the following requirement for a strongly navigable world:

> *Requirement VN1(navigability):* The outlink-info must be everywhere well matched.

The critical observation in all this for designing navigable information systems is that, to be navigable, the outlink-info of a link must in some sense describe not just the next node, but the whole to-set. This is a problem in many hypertext systems, including the WWW: Their link-labels indicate adjacent nodes and do not tell what else lies beyond, in the whole to-set. In a sense, for navigation purposes, "highway signage" might be a better metaphor for good outlink-info than "label". The information has to convey what is off in that direction, off along that route, rather than just where it will get to next. As we will see shortly, this is a difficult requirement in practice.

First, however, we turn the analysis on its head. The perspective so far has been in terms of how the world looks to a navigator that successively follows outlinks using outlink-info until it gets to its target: the navigator wants a world in which it can find its target. Now let us think about the situation from the other side -- how the world looks from the perspective of a target, with the assumption that targets want a world in which they can be found. This complementary perspective brings up the important notion of *residue* or *scent.*The residue or scent of a target is the remote indication of that target in outlink-info throughout the information structure. More precisely, a target has residue at a link if the associated outlink-info would lead the navigator to take that link in pursuit of the given target, i.e., to put the target in the inferred-to-set of the link. If the navigator was not being mislead, i.e, the outlink-info was well-matched for that target, then we say the residue was *good residue* for the target.(Refer back to the caption of Figure 6).

An alternate formulation of the Navigability proposition says that in order to be findable by navigation from anywhere in the structure, a target must have good residue at every node. I.e., in order to be able to find a target, the navigator must have some scent, some residue, of it, no matter where the navigator is, to begin chasing down its trail.

Furthermore, if every target is to be findable, we need the following requirement, really an alternate statement of VN1:

> *Requirement VN1a (residue distribution):* Every node must have good residue at every other node.

This is a daunting challenge. There are numerous examples of real world information structures without good residue distribution. Consider the WWW. You want to find some target from your current location, but do not have a clue of how to navigate there because your target has no good-residue here. There is no trace of it in the current view. This is a fundamental reason why the WWW is not navigable. For another example consider pan&zoom interfaces to information worlds, like PAD[5]. If you zoom out too far, your target can become unrecognizable, or disappear entirely leaving no residue, and you cannot navigate back to it. This has lead to a notion of *semantic zooming [1] [5],* where the appearance of an object changes as its size changes so that it stays visually comprehensible, or at least visible -- essentially a design move to preserve good residue.

The VN1 requirements are difficult basically because of the following scaling constraint.

> *Requirement VN2.* Outlink-info must be "small".

To understand this requirement and its impact, consider that one way to get perfect matching or equivalently perfect global residue distributions would be to have an exhaustive list, or enumeration, of the to-set as the outlink-info for each link (i.e., each link is labeled by listing the complete set of things it "leads to", as in the label of the lower left outlink from node *A*). Thus collectively between all the outlinks at each node there is a full listing of the structure, and such a complete union list must exist at each node. This "enumeration" strategy is presumably not feasible for view navigation since, being $O(n^2)$, it does not scale well. Thus, the outlink-info must somehow accurately specify the corresponding to-set in some way more efficient than enumeration, using more conceptually complex representations, requiring semantic notions like attributes (Red) and abstraction (LivingThings).

The issues underlying good residue, its representation and distribution, are intriguing and complex. Only a few modest observations will be listed here.

Remarks on View Navigability

Trees revisited. One of the most familiar navigable information structures is a rooted tree in the form of classification hierarchies like biological taxonomies or simple library classification schemes like the dewey decimal system. In the traversability section of this paper, balanced trees in their completely unlabeled form were hailed as having good traversal properties just as graphs. Here there is an entirely different point: a systematic labeling of a rooted tree as a hierarchy can make it in addition a reasonably navigable structure. Starting at the root of a biological taxonomy, one can take Cat as a target and decide in turn, is it an Animal or a Plant, is it a Vertebrate or Invertebrate, etc. and with enough knowledge enough about cats, have a reasonable (though not certain!) chance of navigating the way down to the Cat leaf node in the structure. This is so familiar it seems trivial, but it is not.

First let us understand why the hierarchy works in terms of the vocabulary of this paper. There is well matched out-link info at each node along the way: the Vertebrate label leads to the to-set of vertebrates, etc. and the navigator is not misled. Alternately, note that the Cat leaf-node has good residue everywhere. This is most explicit in the Animal, Vertebrate, Mammal,... nodes along the way from the root, but there is also implicit good residue throughout the structure. At the Maple node, in addition to the SugarMaple and NorwayMaple children, neither of which match Cat, there is the upward outlink returning towards the root, implicitly labeled "The Rest", which Cat does match, and which is good residue. This superficial explanation has beneath it a number of critical subtleties, general properties of the semantic labeling scheme that rely on the richness of the notion of cat, the use of large semantic categories, and the subtle web woven from of these categories. These subtleties, all implied by the theory of view navigation and efficient traversability not only help explain why hierarchies work when they do, but also give hints how other structures, like hypertext graphs of the world wide web, might be made navigable.

To understand the navigation challenge a bit, consider the how bad things could be.

The spectre of essential non-navigability. Consider that Requirement VN2 implies that typically the minimum description length of the to-sets must be small compared to the size of those sets. In information theory that is equivalent to requiring that the to-sets are not random. Thus,

- *example 7: non-navigable 1 - completely unrelated items.*

  A set of *n* completely unrelated things is intrinsically not navigable. To see this consider an abstract alphabet of size *n*. Any subset (e.g., a to-set) is information full, with no structure or redundancy, and an individual set cannot be specified except by enumeration. As a result it is not hard to show there is no structure for organizing these *n* things, whose outlinks can be labeled except with predominant use of enumeration[6], and so overall VN2 would be violated. ••

Such examples help in understanding navigability in the abstract, and raise the point that insofar as the real world is like such sets (is the web too random?), designing navigable systems is going to be hard. Having set two extremes, the reasonably navigable and the unnavigable, consider next a number of general deductions about view navigation.

Navigability requires representation of many sets. Every link has an associated toset that must be labeled. This means that the semantics of the domain must be quite rich to allow all these sets to have appropriate characterizations (like, RedThings, Cars, ThingsThatSleep). Similarly since a target must have residue at every node, each target must belong to n of these sets -- in stark contrast to the impoverished semantics of the purely random non-navigable example.

Navigability requires an interlocking web of set representations. Furthermore, these to-sets are richly interdependent. Consider the local part of some structure shown in Figure 7. Basically, the navigator should go to y to get to the

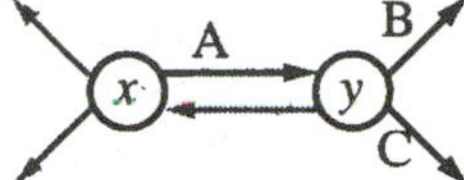

Figure 7. *Two adjacent nodes, x and y, in a structure. The to-sets associated with each outlink are labeled in upper case.*

targets available from y. In other words the to-set, A, out of x, is largely made up of the to-sets B and C out of neighboring y. (The exceptions, which are few in many structures, are those targets with essentially an equally good path from x and y.) This indicates that a highly constrained interlocking web of tosets and corresponding semantics and labels must be woven. In a hierarchy the to-sets moving from the root form successive partitions and view navigability is obtained by labeling those links with category labels that semantically carve up the sets correspondingly. Animals leads, not to "BrownThings" and "LargeThings" but to Vertebrates and Invertebrates -- a conceptual partition the navigator can decode mirroring an actual partition in the toset. Other structures do not often admit such nice partitioning semantics. It is unclear what other structures have to-sets and webs of semantic labelings that can be made to mirror each other.

Residue as a shared resource. Since ubiquitous enumeration is not feasible, each target does not get its own explicit listing in outlink-info everywhere. It follows that in some sense, targets must typically share residue. The few bits of outlink-info are a scarce resource whose global distribution must be carefully structured, and not left to grow willy-nilly. To see this consider putting a new page up on the web. In theory, for strong navigability, every other node in the net must suddenly have good residue for this new page! Note how cleverly this can be handled in a carefully crafted hierarchy. All the many vertebrates share the short Vertebrate label as residue. Global distribution is maintained by the careful placement of new items: put a new vertebrate in the right branch of the tree, and it shares the existing good residue. It is probably no accident that the emerging large navigable substructures over the web, e.g. Yahoo!, arise in a carefully crafted hierarchical overlay with careful administrative supervision attending to the global distribution of this scare residue resource.

Similarity-based navigation. One interesting class of navigable structures makes use of similarity both to organize the structure and run the navigator. Objects are at nodes, and there is some notion of similarity between objects. The outlink-info of a link simply indicates the object at other end of link. The navigator can compute the similarity between objects, and chooses the outlink whose associated object is most similar to its ultimate target, in this way hill-climbing up a similarity gradient until the target is reached. One might navigate through color space in this way, moving always towards the neighboring color that is most similar to the target. Or one might try to navigate through the WWW by choosing an adjacent page that seems most like what one is pursuing (this would be likely to fail in general).

Similarity based navigation requires that nodes for similar objects be pretty closely linked in the structure, but that is not sufficient. There can be sets of things which have differential similarity (not completely unrelated as in the non-navigable example 6), and which can be linked to reflect that similarity perfectly, but which are still fundamentally non-navigable, essentially because all similarity is purely local, and so there is no good-residue of things far away.

•• example 8: non-navigable set 2 - locally related structure.

This example concerns sets with arbitrary similarity structure but only local semantics, and that are hence non-navigable.Take any graph of interest, for example the line graph below. Take an alphabet as large as the number of links in the graph, and randomly assign the letters to the links. Now make "objects" at the nodes that are collections of the letters on the adjacent links:

Despite the fact that "similar" objects are adjacent in this organization, there is no way to know how to get from, say, LG to anything other than its immediate neighbors: There is no good-residue of things far away ••

This example might be a fair approximation to the WWW -- pages might indeed be similar, or at least closely related, to their neighbors, yet it is in general a matter of relatively small, purely local features, and cannot support navigation.

Weaker models of navigability. Suppose we were to relax strong navigability, for example abandoning the need for every target to have residue at the current node. Even then resource constraints dictate that it be possible to explore in a small amount of time and find appropriate good residue.This suggests that this relaxation will not dramatically alter the general conclusions. Imagine that you could sit at a node and send out a pack of seeing-eye bloodhounds looking for scent at each step. This really amounts to just changing the viewing

6 Technically, use of enumeration must dominate but need not be ubiquitous. Some equivalent of the short label "the rest" can be used for some links, but this can be shown not to rescue the situation.

graph, including the sphere that the bloodhounds can see (smell?) into the "viewed" neighbors. The constraints on how many hounds and how long they can explore basically remains a constraint on outdegree in the revised graph.

Combining EVT + VN = Effective View Navigability (EVN)

If we want an information structure that is both efficiently traversable, and is strongly view navigable, then both the mechanical constraints of EVT on diameter and outdegree and the residue constraints of VN must hold. In this section we make some informal observations about how the two sets of constraints interact.

Large scale semantics dominate. Since by assumption everything can be reached from a given node, the union of the to-sets at each node form the whole set of *n* items in the structure. If there are *v* links leaving the node, the average size of the to-set is *n/v*. If the structure satisfies EVT2, then *v* is small compared to *n*, so the average to-set is quite large.

The significance of this is that VN1 requires that outlink-info faithfully represent these large to-sets. If we assume the representations are related to the semantics of objects, and that representations of large sets are in some sense high level semantics, it follows that high level semantics play a dominant role in navigable structures. In a hierarchy this is seen in both the broad category labels like Animal and Plant, and in the curious "the rest" labels. The latter can be used in any structure, but are quite constrained (e.g., they can only be used for one outlink per node), so there is considerable stress on more meaningful coarse-grain semantics. So if for example the natural semantics of a domain mostly allow the specification of small sets, one might imagine intrinsic trouble for navigation. (Note that Example 8 has this problem.)

Carving up the world efficiently. Earlier it was noted that the to-sets of a structure form a kind of overlapping mosaic which, by VN1 must be mirrored in the outlink-info. Enforcing the diameter requirement of EVT2 means the neighboring to-sets have to differ more dramatically. Consider by contrast the to-sets of the line graph, a graph with bad diameter. There the to-sets change very slowly as one moves along, with only one item being eliminated at a time. It is possible to show (see [3]) that under EVT2 the overlap pattern of to-sets must be able to whittle down the space of alternatives in a small number of intersections. The efficiency of binary partitioning is what makes a balanced binary tree satisfy EVT2, but a very unbalanced one not. Correspondingly an efficiently view navigable hierarchy has semantics that partition into equal size sets, yielding navigation by fast binary search. More generally, whatever structure, the semantics of the domain must carve it up efficiently.

Summary and Discussion

The goal of the work presented here has been to gain understanding of view navigation, with the basic premise that scale issues are critical. The simple mechanics of traversal require design of the logical structure and its viewing strategy so as to make efficient uses of time and space, by coercing things into known EVT structures, adding long distance links, or gluing on navigational backbones. Navigation proper requires that all possible targets have good residue throughout the structure. Equivalently, labeling must reflect a link's to-set, not just the neighboring node. This requires the rich semantic representation of a web of interlocking sets, many of them large, that efficiently carve up the contents of the space.

Together these considerations help to understand reasons why some information navigation schemes are,

bad: the web in general (bad residue, diameter), simple scrolling lists (bad diameter)

mixed: geometric zoom (good diameter, poor residue),

good: semantic zoom (better residue), 3D(shorter paths), fisheyes (even shorter paths), balanced rooted trees (short paths and possible simple semantics)

The problem of global residue distribution is very difficult. The taxonomies implemented in rooted trees are about the best we have so far, but even they are hard to design and use for all purposes. New structures should be explored (e.g., hypercubes, DAG's, multitrees), but one might also consider hybrid strategies to overcome the limits of pure navigation, including synergies between query and navigation. For example, global navigability may not be achievable, but local navigability may be - e.g., structures where residue is distributed reasonably only within a limited radius of a target. Then if there is some other way to get to the right neighborhood (e.g., as the result of an query), it may be possible to navigate the rest of the way. The result is query initiated browsing, an emerging paradigm on the web. Alternatively, one might ease the residue problem by allowing dynamic outlink-info, for example relabeling outlinks by the result of an ad-hoc query of the structure.

Acknowledgments. This work was supported in part by ARPA grant N66001-94-C-6039. Many thanks to Maria Slowiaczek for helpful comments on drafts of this paper.

REFERENCES

1. Bederson, B. B. and Hollan, J. D., PAD^{++}: zooming graphical interface for exploring alternate interface physics. In *Proceedings of ACM UIST'94,* (Marina Del Ray, CA, 1994), ACM Press, pp 17-26.
2. Card, S. K., Pirolli, P., and Mackinlay, J. D., The cost-of-knowledge characteristic function: display evaluation for direct-walk dynamic information visualizations. In *Proceedings of CHI'94 Human Factors in Computing Systems* (Boston, MA, April 1994), ACM press, pp. 238-244.
3. Furnas, G.W., Effectively View-Navigable Structures. Paper presented at the 1995 Human Computer Interaction Consortium Workshop (HCIC95), Snow Mountain Ranch, Colorado Feb 17, 1995. Manuscript available at `http://http2.si.umich.edu/~furnas/POSTSCRIPTS/EVN.HCIC95.workshop.paper.ps`
4. Furnas, G. W., and Bederson, B., Space-Scale Diagrams: Understanding Multiscale Interfaces. In *Human Factors in Computing Systems, CHI'95 Conference Proceedings* (ACM), Denver, Colorado, May 8-11, 1995, 234-201.
5. Perlin, K. and Fox, D., Pad: An Alternative Approach to the Computer Interface. In *Proceedings of ACM SigGraph `93* (Anaheim, CA), 1993, pp. 57-64.
6. Robertson, G. G., Mackinlay, J.D., and Card, S.K., Cone trees: animated 3D visualizations of hierarchical information. *CHI'91 Proceedings,* 1991, 189-194.

Table Lens as a Tool for Making Sense of Data

Peter Pirolli and Ramana Rao

Xerox Palo Alto Research Center
3333 Coyote Hill Road
Palo Alto, CA 94304, USA
{pirolli, rao}@parc.xerox.com

ABSTRACT

The Table Lens is a visualization for searching for patterns and outliers in multivariate datasets. It supports a lightweight form of exploratory data analysis (EDA) by integrating a familiar organization, the table, with graphical representations and a small set of direct manipulation operators. We examine the EDA process as a special case of a generic process, which we call *sensemaking*. Using a GOMS methodology, we characterize a few central EDA tasks and compare performance of the Table Lens and one of the best of the more traditional graphical tools for EDA i.e. Splus. This analysis reveals that Table Lens is more or less on par with the power of Splus, while requiring the use of fewer specialized graphical representations. It essentially combines the graphical power of Splus with the direct manipulation and generic properties of spreadsheets and relational database front ends. We also propose a number of design refinements that are suggested by our task characterizations and analyses.

Keywords

Information visualization, multivariate visualization, database visualization, evaluation, GOMS, exploratory data analysis

INTRODUCTION

The Table Lens (Rao & Card, 1994, 1995) has been informally characterized as an effective tool for making sense of numerical and categorical data of the sort typically found in multivariate datasets. Here, we would like to refine the notion of "making sense" in a way that allows us to judge the effectiveness of tools such as the Table Lens. We would like to know if our tools maximize the support for necessary sensemaking functions while minimizing the costs of learning and use. Furthermore, we would like a characterization of the tool that exposes opportunities for design refinements and guidance in assessing them. Toward these ends, we will characterize a space of tasks for a particular instance of sensemaking, basic Exploratory Data Analysis (EDA). Our task characterization draws on concepts and methods from studies of sensemaking and discovery as problem-solving processes as well as from cognitive modeling techniques for human computer interaction.

In the words of Tukey, the field's founder, EDA includes a variety of techniques for "looking at data to see what it seems to say." For the purposes of this paper we focus on two typical EDA tasks involving multivariate datasets: (i) assessing a batch of data (i.e. the features of each single variable) and (ii) finding lawful relations among a set of observed variables. The first task is a kind data "browsing" which is typical of early stages of exploration when general insights are sought and the second task is perhaps the canonical task of EDA.

These two tasks can be accomplished with Table Lens as well as with its cousins in two categories: more broadly-purposed productivity applications (e.g. spreadsheets and relational databases) and more specialized exploratory data analysis packages (e.g. Splus, DataDesk). Table Lens, in some sense, integrates the virtues of both categories: the direct manipulation ease of use of the mainstream products with the tuned support for exploratory statistical processes.

Using the GOMS methodology (Card, Moran, & Newell, 1983; Olson & Olson, 1990), we characterize and analyze methods for accomplishing the two above mentioned EDA tasks using the Table Lens. This analysis provides basic time estimates for task (and constituent subtask) performance. Comparison with corresponding methods for performing these tasks using Splus and Excel reveals quantitative performances differences as well as qualitative understanding of the source of these differences. Perhaps the most important consequence of this kind of analysis is that it can provide insights which can fuel further design. In our case, we propose a number of refinements to the Table Lens which are clearly indicated by our analysis.

SENSEMAKING

Sensemaking refers to activities in which external representations such as texts, tables, or figures are interpreted into semantic content and represented in some other manner. Retrospective case studies of sensemaking in information work were presented in Russell, Stefik, Pirolli, and Card (1993) . A general recurring pattern of activity called a *learning loop complex* was observed. This loop involves component processes including: (a) a generation loop that involves a search for representations to capture important regularities in collected information, (b) a data coverage loop in which information is encoded into the representation forming encodons, and (c) a representation shift loop in which ill-fitting residue information triggers and guides search for a new representation, and (d) encodon consumption (formation) in which the representation drives the search for information. Here, *representations* refers collectively to internal cognitive structure as well as external resources such as tables, graphs, or hypermedia structures.

In cognitive science, the learning loop is consistent with process models of discovery that have been developed to address historical accounts of scientific breakthroughs (Langley, Simon, Bradshaw, & Zytkow, 1987) and protocol studies of people finding empirical laws (Qin & Simon, 1990) . In general, these accounts can be characterized as *search processes* operating in *problem spaces*.

The notion of problem solving as a process of search in problem spaces was developed in Newell and Simon's (1972) classic human information-processing theory. Basically, a human problem solver is viewed as an information-processing system with a problem. A *task environment* is the external environment, inclusive of the problem, in which the information processing system operates. For instance, a data analysis problem that required the use of the Table Lens would constitute a task environment. A *problem space* is a formalization of the structure of processing molded by the characteristics of the information-processing system, and more importantly, the task environment. A problem space is defined in terms of *states* of problem solving, *operators* that move the problem solving from one state to another, and *evaluation functions*. As a family, the discovery models can be characterized as *dual problem space search* models (Langley, et al., 1987) in which processing alternates between search in a problem space of possible representations and a search in a problem space that fits data to the representations.

In the case of Exploratory Data Analysis, one searches for models on one hand and searches to assess the fit of the models to the data on the other. In Tukey's (1977) classic characterization, data values can viewed as compositions of a fitted part and a residual part:

Data = Fit + Residual.

A typical goal in EDA might be, for example, to produce an equation that predicts the values of a dependent variable based on values of one or more independent variables. The predicted values would be the fitted part of the actual values. The differences between the predicted values and the actual values are the residual values (or residuals)--the residue of the sensemaking process in EDA. Typically, an evaluation function on the quality of the EDA modeling process involves assessing the total amount of residuals, and the guiding heuristic for the search process is to minimize that value, while also keeping the complexity of the model to a minimum (for instance one might prefer equations with fewer variables and lower-order polynomials).

REPRESENTATIVE EDA TASKS

EDA involves ferreting out regularities and irregularities as well as relationships in multivariate datasets (also variously called cases by variables array and multidimensional datasets and roughly the same as a relational table). Such datasets can be considered as multiple batches (i.e. the collected values of a single variable) or multiple cases (i.e. the values for all variables of single observation). For the purposes of this paper, we focus on two typical EDA tasks: (i) assessing the properties of a batch of data including central values, extremes, dispersion, and symmetry; and (ii) discovering lawful relationships among observed variables e.g. producing an equation that predicts the values of a dependent variable based on values of one or more independent variables.

The first task is a browsing task which involves browsing the batch of values for each variable. Typical EDA displays for supporting this task include Stem and Leaf Displays, Letter Value Displays, and Boxplots. The Letter Value Display is a textual summary of the batch that typically shows the median, quarters (the values half way between median and the extremes), and the extremes. The other displays more fully depict the batch as a whole and help with assessments like the following features:

- How nearly symmetric the batch is.
- How spread out the numbers are.
- Whether a few values are far removed from the rest.
- Whether there are concentrations of data.
- Whether there are gaps in the data.

The second task typically entails an iterative process, described above in terms of the concept of a dual problem space search. In data analysis terms, given a dependent variable that the analyst is interested in modeling with an equation involving a set of independent variables, the first step is to find a candidate variable that is highly correlated to the variable. This correlation may involve "re-expression" of the variable (i.e. transforming the values with a power function such as $1/x^2$, $1/x$, $\ln(x)$, x^2, x^3) to linearize the relationship between the two variables. With a selected independent variable in hand, the analyst would subtract the indicated fit (obtained from a regression) from the dependent variable to obtain a residual. That is: Residual = Data - Fit The process can then be repeated and additional independent variables can be consider to further explain the residual.

EDA TOOLS

The two EDA tasks---batch assessment and variable modeling---can be performed utilizing Table Lens, Splus, and Excel. Both Splus and Excel are much more richly featured than the Table Lens, and in general offer a greater variety of methods for performing these tasks. In our comparative analysis we focus on the best method offered by each tool.

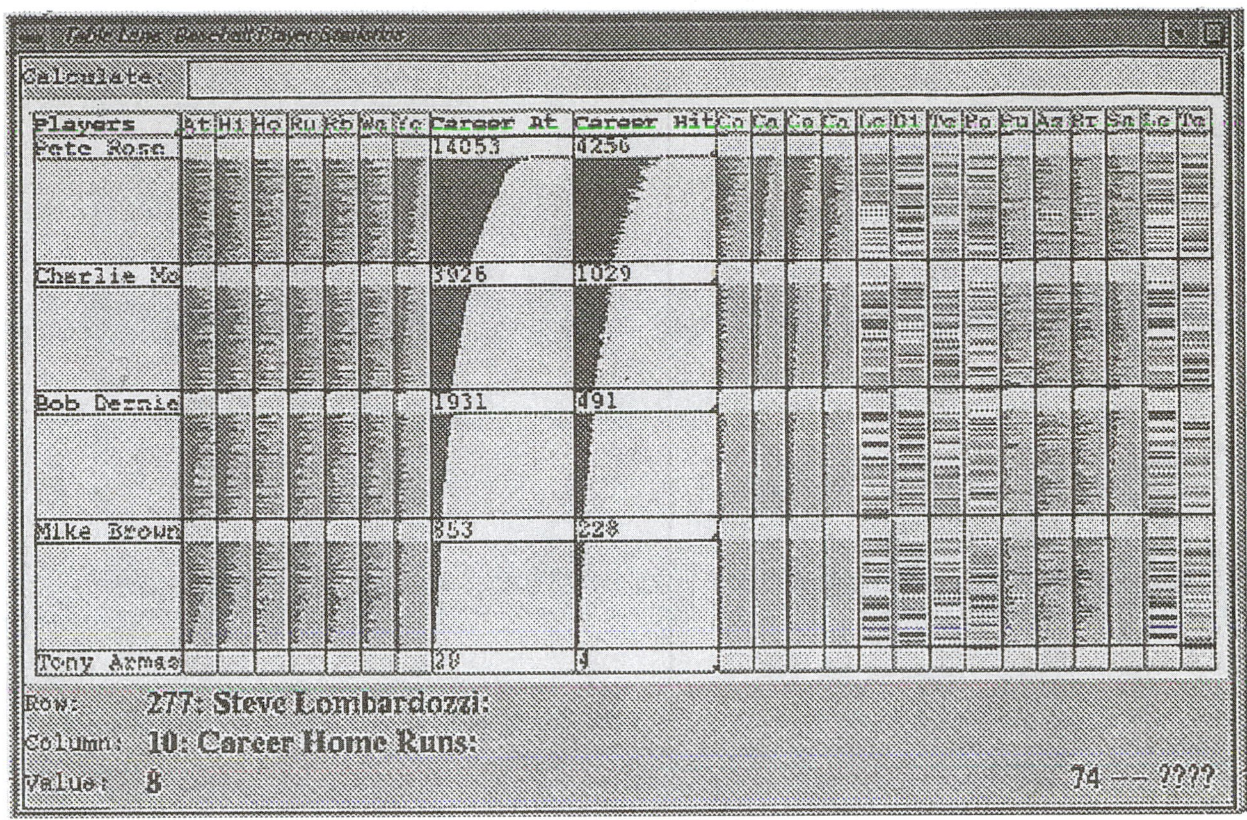

Figure 1. Table Lens visualizing a set of baseball statistics.

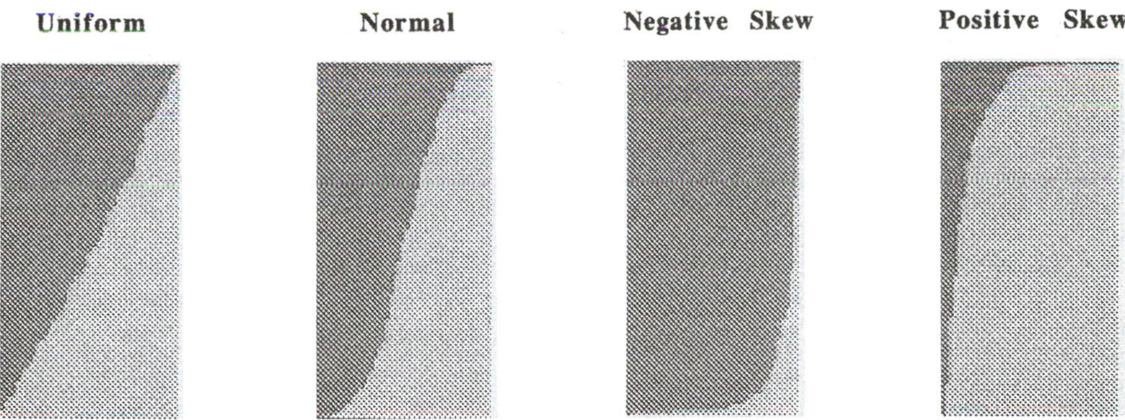

Figure 2. Prototypical distributions as they appear in the Table Lens.

Table Lens

The Table Lens (depicted in Figure 1) provides a structured graphical representation that supports browsing of the values for hundreds of cases and tens of variables on typical workstation display. Table Lens is essentially the graphical equivalent of a relational table or spreadsheet in which the rows represent cases and the columns represent variables. In addition, particular rows and columns can be assigned variable amounts of space, which allows "opening them up" to support direct incorporation of textual representations of values.

For quantitative variables, a graphical bar is used to represent the values. The bars within each variable's column align with its left edge which can indicate a minimum value, zero, or a lower "fence" (i.e. an outlier cutoff). The length of the bar is proportional to the relative size of the represented value. The use of graphical representations not

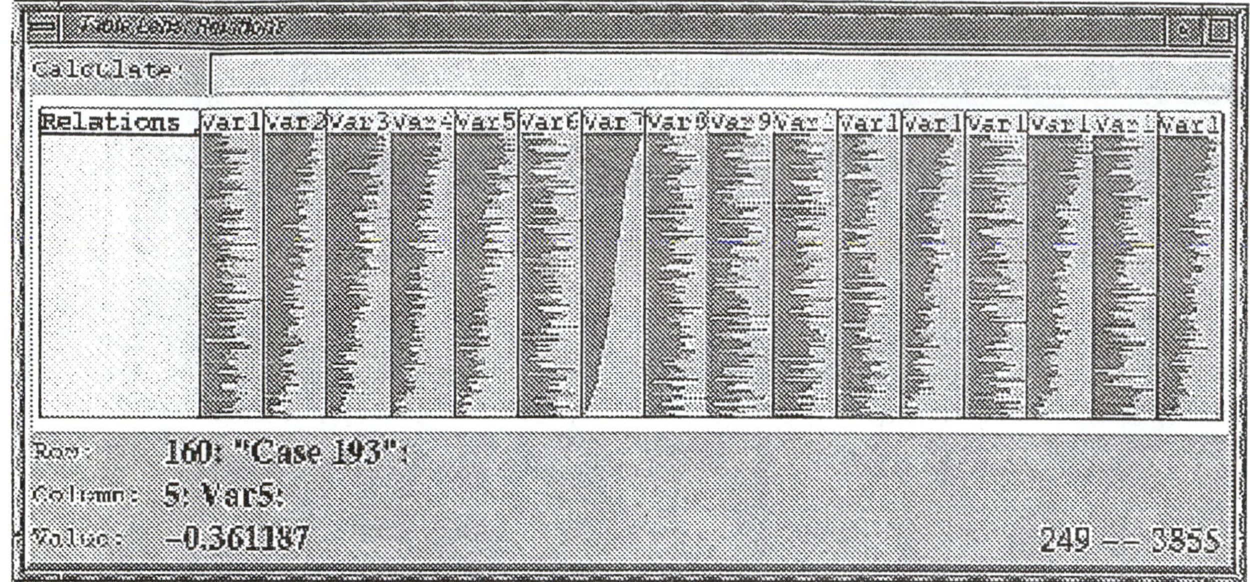

Figure 3. Correlations among column variables become apparent when one of the columns is sorted.

only provides a scale advantage---since the bars can be scaled to one pixel wide without perturbing relative comparisons---but also an exploration advantage, since large numbers of tiny bars can be scanned much more quickly than a bunch of textually represented numbers.

Besides controlling which rows and columns are "focused" (i.e. given space to display textual values), there are two other major operations necessary for performing the EDA tasks: sorting a column and creating a new column computed using a formula based on other columns. Performing a "down gesture" on a column (i.e. dragging the pointer down with mouse button held down in column and then releasing) causes the cases to be sorted by the values in that column. A formula can be entered by typing in an equation involving existing columns which can be "check" gestured during formula entry or else typed in by name. When the formula is committed by the user, a new column appears immediately to the right of the rightmost referenced column.

After a column is sorted, properties of the batch of values can be estimated by graphical perception and some amount of display manipulation. Central values can be viewed by focusing on values near the center of the column. Likewise, extremes can be read by focusing on the ends of the column. Assessing dispersion is a matter of comparing those extrema. Classifying the shape and the skew is a learnable skill, which is somewhat different for a curve of batch values than it is for a histogram. Figure 2 presents four common kinds of distributions that were used in our studies. Finally, a column can be re-expressed by invoking a formula based on that single column. Introducing a special operator facilitates many of these subtasks. This operator essentially incorporates the virtues of a five value summary (i.e. letter values) into the display by automatically focusing on the extremes, the median, and the quarters (see Figure 1). Besides revealing precisely the values for these locations, it also visually breaks up the table into quarters which aids shape and skew assessment.

Sorting is also the first step of looking for correlations among variables. After a first variable has been sorted, if another variable is correlated then its values will also appear to be sorted. For instance, Figure 3 shows a Table Lens display in which one of the columns--Column 7 from the left--has been sorted and positive correlations with variables in Columns 2, 3, 4, 5, 12, 14, and 16 are revealed. Thus looking for correlated variable is a matter of scanning across the columns to identify other columns which seem to exhibit a descending trend. New column computations can be used to fit a correlated variable to the sorted variable (or a re-expressed version of either or both of the variables) and in turn to display the residuals of that fit. The sorting and fitting process can then be iterated on the residual column.

Splus

Splus (Becker, Chambers, & Wilks, 1983) is a data analysis environment based on an interpretive programming environment model in which a variety of data manipulation and viewing techniques are integrated as a library of primitive operators. In particular, after having loaded and named a multivariate dataset in the interpreter's environment, a user can invoke a "brush tool," commonly known as a scatterplot matrix (Becker & Cleveland, 1984), which displays a matrix of all pairwise scatterplots. Optionally a histogram of each variable can be placed at the base of each column of scatterplots associated with that variable. Figure 4 shows a brush tool utilizing the histogram option. This view provides the strongest methods for performing both of our example tasks.

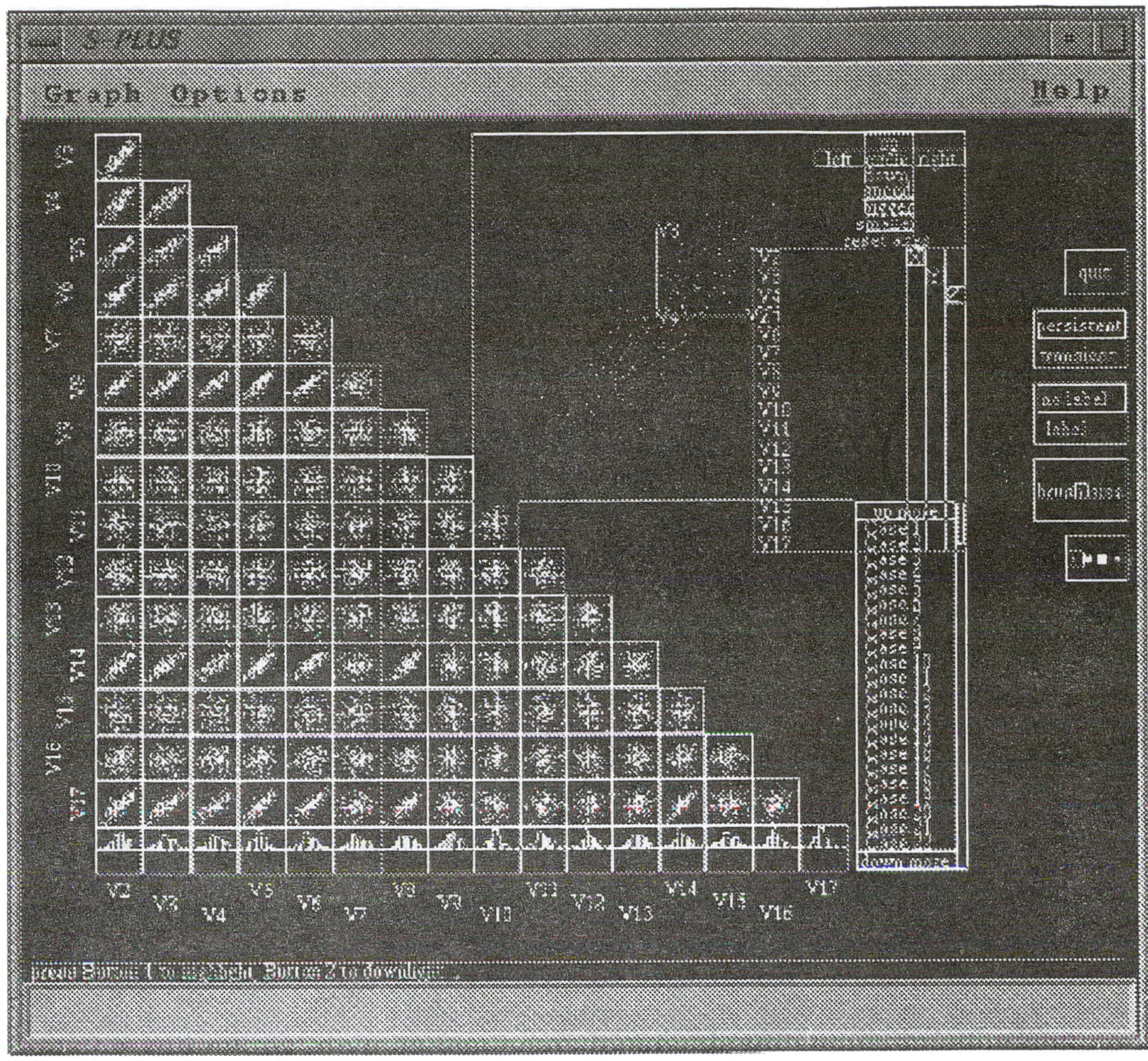

Figure 4. The Splus brush tool.

Batch assessment is performed by graphical perception of the histograms for the chosen variable displayed at the bottom of the column of matrices for that variable. Values have to be read by examining the histogram which for the case of many variables may be quite small (as in the Figure 4). An alternative method involves invoking a stem and leaf or boxplot display of the variable of interest by invoking the appropriate.command in the interpreter. Re-expression is performed by invoking a transform function on the batch of data.

Cross variable correlation involves scanning the row or column associated with a chosen variable and looking for scatterplots that reveal well formed lines. With training, one can learn whether the correlation is positive or negative depending on the angle of the line and also what re-expression may be indicated by curvatures in the relationships. One difficulty for inexperienced or occasional users is that interpretation is flipped depending on whether rows or columns are scanned.

Fitting variables (possibly re-expressed) and examining residuals involves a series of commands in the interpreter that amount to more or less the same operations as required in the Table Lens column computations, though there is more explicit datasets management involved (e.g. a command line style of naming etc.)

Excel

Excel is a broad spectrum productivity application that can be used to perform a variety of tasks, many which aren't even analytical in nature. The central representation is a textual table and additional mechanisms are provided for invoking computations and graphics, and tuning the tables purpose for handling multivariate data. After a multivariate table has been loaded into Excel, a user can draw on several separate mechanisms to perform EDA tasks. Some of the elements of the task can be performed by direct manipulation of the textual display, others require either the use of the embedded formula language or of the mechanism for generating graphical views of the data. So for example, some of batch assessment---extremes, medians, quarters--- can be performed by sorting by a particular column, however shape assessment is all but impossible without using a built-in statistical operator or by plotting the elements of the batch. All of the considered methods take a great deal of manipulation and knowledge to produce either summaries by computation or graphical views. Since in each case the best method involves generating one or another of the representations of Splus or Table Lens at a much greater initiation cost, we don't include Excel in our detailed analysis.

GOMS ANALYSIS OF EDA TOOLS

When faced with ill-defined sensemaking problems such as EDA we often want to explore the space of content and possible courses of actions available to us before exploiting them. In EDA one might, for instance, first identify which variables seem to be most strongly related to one another out of a large set of variables before investing time in refining exactly how those variables are related.

Here we present assessments of some EDA methods carried out with Table Lens and Splus. These assessments concern quantitative variables only, as these can be studied in simple ways with Table Lens.

Exploration: Assessing Properties of a Batch of Variables

One basic task in EDA is to understand important features of the distribution of values of a variable over the sample of cases that are under examination. An important set of such features are (a) the central tendency (e.g., the mean, mode, or median), (b) the dispersion (e.g., the range, standard deviation, or inter-quartile range), (c) the shape (e.g., normal, skewed, uniform), and (d) extreme values or outliers (e.g., the minimum and maximum values). We analyzed a representative task of finding such features using the Table Lens and Splus. The representative task involved finding the median, inter-quartile range (IQR), judging the shape (normal, uniform, positively skewed, or negatively skewed), and finding the maximum and minimum values.

In GOMS notation, the method for performing the variable characterization task is:

```
Goal: Characterize-variable
    Goal: Find-median
    Goal: Find-IQR
    Goal: Find-shape
    Goal: Find-min&max.
```

Table 1. Relevant perceptual, cognitive, and motor time-cost parameters from the HCI literature.

Parameter	Value	Source
Visual scan to target (1° arc ~ .25" @ 15" eye-screen distance)	4 msec/degree of visual arc	OO
Decode abbreviation	50~66 msec	OO
Mentally compare two words	47 msec	CMN
Point mouse at target of size S at distance D	$1030 + 960 \log_2(D/S + .5)$ msec	CMN
Read a word	300 msec	CMN
Mouse click	70 msec	CMN
Mouse gesture	70 msec	CMN
Keystroke	372 msec	CMN
Perceptual Judgement Time	92 msec	OO
Execute Mental Step	70 msec	OO
Retrieve from Memory	1200 msec	OO

Note: CMN = Card et al. (1983), OO = Olson and Olson (1990).

Table 2. GOMS analysis of methods to judge the shape of a distribution of the Nth column in a Table Lens display. Time estimates (in msec) are in bold.

```
METHOD: FIND-SHAPE =
Goal: Find-shape ; of the Nth column from left in Table Lens
   Goal: Find-and-sort-column                              [1893 + 101 N]
   Goal: Judge-distribution-shape                                   [93]
                                                                  ------
                                         Total (msec) = 1986 + 101 N

METHOD: FIND-AND-SORT-COLUMN =
Goal: Find-and-sort-column
   Goal: Match-column-variable-name ; first column
      Scan-to-column ; first column              [(3.5"/.25")•4  =  56]
      Decode-abbreviation[COLUMN-NAME]                              [50]
      Match[COLUMN-NAME, VARIABLE-NAME]                             [47]
                                                                  ------
                                                   Subtotal (msec) 153
   Goal: Match-column-variable-name ; If necessary, iterate N - 1 times
      Scan-to-column ; next column               [(.25"/.25")•4  =   4]
      Decode-abbreviation[COLUMN-NAME]                              [50]
      Match[COLUMN-NAME, VARIABLE-NAME]                             [47]
                                                                  ------
                                                   Subtotal (msec) 101

   Goal: Verify-column-match ; If there is a name match
      Mouse-Point [COLUMN-NAME]     [1030 + 96 log2(2"/.25" + .5) =1330]
      Scan-to-status-bar ; at lower left of window  [(6"/.25")•4 =  96]
      Read[STATUS BAR]                                             [300]
      Match[STATUS BAR, VARIABLE-NAME]                              [47]
                                                                  ------
                                                   Subtotal (msec) 1773

   Flick-Down ; If match found                                      [70]
                                                                  ------
     Total (msec) = 153 + (N - 1)101 + 1771 + 70 = 1893 + 101 N
```

Table 3. Summary of time costs for Table Lens methods for assessment of properties of a batch of variables. Estimates in msec.

Method	Literature-based Estimate + Average System Response	Empirical Estimate + Average System Response
Find-median (for N^{th} column)	$8325 + 101\,N$	$8470 + 64\,N$
Find-IQR (for N^{th} column)	$13811 + 101\,N$	$13710 + 64\,N$
Find-shape (for N^{th} column)	$1986 + 101\,N$	$2677 + 94\,N$
Find-max&min (for N^{th} column)	$8737 + 101\,N$	$8470 + 64\,N$
Random-variable-walk (for V variables)	$33061\,V + 202\,V^2$	$33741\,V + 144V^2$
Iterate-over-variables (for V variables)	$366 + 15034V$	$17710V$

Table Lens Analysis

To illustrate our method of analysis, we will expand the task analysis of one of these subgoals, `Find-shape`, down to basic operations involving the Table Lens, and show how we arrived at estimates of time costs from the human-computer interaction (HCI) literature. The goal of finding the shape of the distribution of a variable can be achieved in the Table Lens by (a) visually locating the column associated with the variable, (b) sorting the values in that column using a flick-down mouse gesture, and (c) making a perceptual judgment of the resulting shape. Table 1 contains relevant time parameters for perceptual, cognitive, and motor operations from a variety of literature sources. The `Find-shape` method is presented in Table 2, along with the submethod it uses to find and sort the desired column. Table 2 also presents an analysis of the time costs of the methods using the literature-based parameter estimates in Table 1.

As an empirical check, one of us performed self-timed speeded trials of finding and sorting variable columns in a 23 variable Table Lens dataset. Each variable was tested three times and the full sequence of trials was randomized. A regression (R^2 = .93) yielded empirical time cost estimates for the `Find-shape` method that are presented alongside the literature-based estimates in Table 3. The literature-based estimate of 101 msec per column scanned is about a 7% overestimate over the observed estimate of 94 msec per column scanned. The literature-based estimate of 1893 msec for the verification of the column match and the flick-down gesture is a 784 msec underestimate of the 2677 msec obtained empirically (about 30%). This empirical time includes, however, observer reaction time (trials were self-timed using a stop-watch).

Table 3 summarizes the literature-based and empirically estimated time costs for the Table Lens methods associated with the finding important features of a variable distribution. For each literature-based estimate, we constructed a GOMS task analysis like the examples in Table 2, and used relevant time-cost parameters from Table 1. The empirical estimates were produced from a number of small self-timed user experiments (by one of the authors). For each method or submethod, and at each parameter level (e.g., location of the target column), three to five replications were conducted. Similar mini-experiments were conducted to assess system response times--for example, to assess the time taken to sort a column. These system times were added, when appropriate, to the literature-based and empirical estimates of human performance times for the methods.

The `Find-median`, `Find-IQR`, `Find-shape`, and `Find-min&max` analyses assume that the user starts with a focus at a central location at the top of the Table Lens display, and must scan to some particular variable whose location is unknown. The last two rows of Table 3 present analyses for two methods that would iterate through all the variables in a dataset and characterize the median, IQR, shape, and extreme values. The `Random-variable-walk` simply assumes that the user randomly chooses a variable and a feature to characterize at random (without replacement), performs the method, and repeats the process until all variable features have been identified. Its time cost is just the sum of the time-costs for the `Find-median`, `Find-IQR`, `Find-shape`, and `Find-min&max` methods over *V* variables in a dataset. The Iterate-over-variables method, assumes that the user iterates through each variable, left-to-right, finding the median, IQR, shape, and extreme values. These two methods might be considered reasonable boundary cases at the highly inefficient and highly efficient ends of the spectrum of methods for finding the relevant distributional properties of variables in a dataset. The time costs for these two methods as a function of the number of variables in the data batch are presented in Figure 5.

Overall, the absolute differences between literature-based and empirically-based estimates range from about 2% to 50%, and in general there is good agreement between the two. For current purposes, this level of agreement seems satisfactory, so we have used literature-based estimates for the remaining analyses.

Splus

Table 4 presents literature-based time-cost estimates for Splus methods analogous to those analyzed for the Table lens. The methods for `Find-median`, `Find-IQR`, and `Find-max&min` largely involve cycles of typing in commands to the Splus intepreter and reading off the returned results. The `Find-shape` method involves typing in a command to plot a histogram and then judging the shape of the distribution.

At the bottom of Table 4 are methods for iterating through all the variables in the data set. Again, similar to the Table Lens method, the `random-variable-walk` method involves randomly choosing one of the first four methods and applying it to a randomly chosen variable (random choices are made without replacement). The iterate-over-variables method involves invoking the brush tool, making judgments of all the variable distribution shapes, then iteratively finding the median, IQR, and extreme values for each variable.

These two Splus methods are compared to the analogous Table Lens methods in Figure 6 (all estimates are literature-based). Figure 6 shows that time costs of the Table Lens methods bracket the time costs of the Splus methods. Most interesting is the suggestion that it is more efficient to iterate through a batch of variables in Table Lens extracting important features.

Exploration: Assessing Relations Among Variables

Another phase of EDA involves judging features about the relationships among variables. Here we examine the simple task of judging if two variables seem to be correlated. Later, we will discuss the tasks involved in determining more precisely how two variables are related.

Figure 5. Comparison of literature-based and empirically-based estimates for time-cost functions for Table Lens methods for finding important features of all variables V in a dataset.

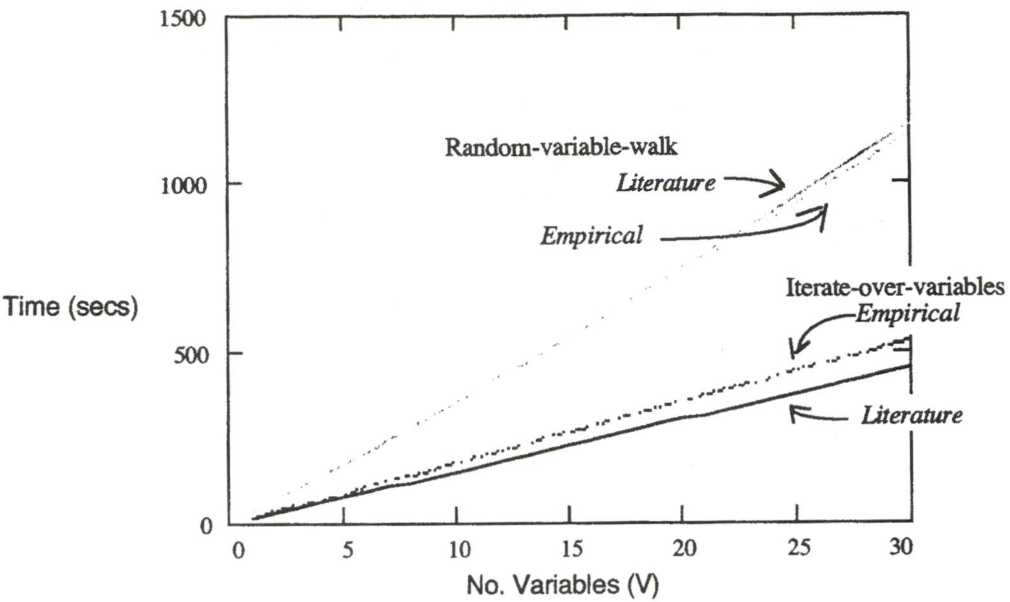

Figure 6. Comparison of time-cost functions for Table Lens and Splus methods for finding important properties of all variables V in a dataset. Time-costs are literature-based.

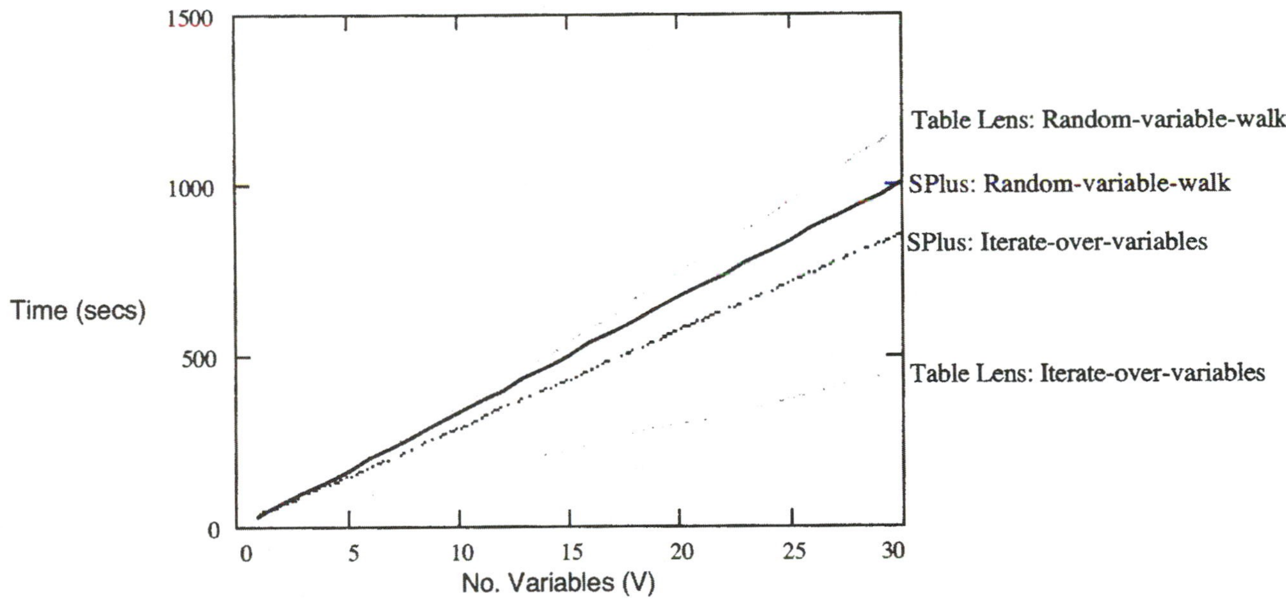

Table 4. Summary of time costs for Splus methods for assessment of properties of a batch of variable. Estimates in msec.

Method	Method Summary	Literature-based Estimate
`Find-median`	• Recall command and variable name • Execute mental steps and keystroke `median` command and arguments • Read result	5840
`Find-IQR`	• Recall commands and variable name • Execute mental steps and keystroke `quartile` command and arguments • Read upper and lower quartile results • Keystrokes to subtract results • Read result	11850
`Find-shape`	• Recall command and variable name • Execute mental steps and keystroke `hist` command and arguments • Scan to histogram display and judge shape	5344
`Find-max&min`	• Recall commands and variable name • Execute mental steps and keystroke `min` and `max` commands and arguments • Read results	10480
`Random-variable-walk (for V variables)`	• Randomly: try each method above on each variable	33514 V
`Iterate-over-variables (for V variables)`	• Recall brush command and dataset name • Execute mental steps and keystroke `brush` command and arguments • Iterate through histograms making shape judgments • Do `Find-median`, `Find-IQR`, `Find-min&max` for each variable	8086 + 28338 V

Table 5. Time cost functions for Table Lens and Splus for basic methods of judging the related variables in a dataset of V variables. Estimates in msec.

Method Summary	Literature-based Estimate
Table Lens For V variables, skipping C variables in "clusters". • Scan through each variable left-to-right • Sort the column (mouse-point and gesture) • Scan columns to the right, judging if they are correlated	$366 + 401\ V + 1156\ (V - C - 1) + 175\ V\ (V - C - 2)$
Splus For V variables, with R related variables • Scan through each pairwise scatterplot on each variable row of a brush display • For each related variable scan and read the variable names	$32\ V + 175\ V\ (V - 1) + 664\ R$

Table Lens

The basic method for finding relationships among variables in Table Lens involves sorting a variable column, and then scanning other columns to see which have shapes similar to (or perhaps inverted from) the shape of the sorted variable. When a cluster of several related variables is observed and remembered, the user can eliminate those from further consideration and concentrate on the remaining variables. This method and the literature-based time-cost estimate are presented in Table 5. As an empirical check, another set of self-timed speeded tasks was evaluated. Each evaluated dataset contained 16 variables. Three datasets (called 1-8 datasets) contained one cluster of eight related variables and eight unrelated variables. Three datasets (called 4-2 datasets) contained four clusters of two related variables and eight unrelated variables. For a cluster of related variables, the inter-variable correlations were $r = .9$. All variables contained 200 normally distributed values. Judging relations in 1-8 datasets took $M = 46.87$ secs and 4-2 datasets took $M = 57.17$ secs. The literature-based estimates are, 35.63 secs for $V = 16$ variables and $C = 7$ skipped cluster variables, 47.50 secs for $V = 16$ and $C = 4$, and 63.32 secs for $V = 16$ and $C = 0$.

Splus

In Splus, we assume that the main method for judging relations among a large batch of variables involves using the all-pairwise scatter plot in the Splus batch tool. Each pairwise scatter plot must be scanned and, when a relationship is detected, the variable names must be found and read. This method and its literature-based time-cost estimate are also presented in Table 5. Figure 7 presents a comparison of the Table Lens and Splus methods in Table 5. Again, it appears that the Table Lens methods have comparable time costs to Splus.

Exploitation: Search Through the Form of Relations

Our analyses so far have not have not focused on the tasks involved in finding the specific form of relation among sets of variables, once they have been identified. Typically this relies on the use of mathematical transformations and statistical techniques such as regression. In our design section we talk about some ways of incorporating direct interaction techniques for performing techniques that achieve these tasks.

Learning Costs

Our analyses suggest that the Table Lens achieves comparable performance with a well-established interface for EDA in the form of Splus. It does so, however, by relying on the use of only a few simple direct-manipulation commands such as column sorting. This suggests, that Table Lens is likely to be easier to learn.

DESIGN REFINEMENT

Considering the virtues of traditional EDA displays, the structure of the studied EDA tasks, and the costs for various methods suggests a number of refinements to Table Lens which would improve performance times for the tasks studied.

Boxplot Values.

One of the advantages of the Table Lens is that it can integrate a number of separate EDA graphical tools into a single representation which can be consistently interpreted. For example, the "quartering" operation described above opens focus on the values which represent the values shown in the EDA five value summary table i.e. the median, the two quarters, and the two extremes. Done in the context of the tabular form it is quite clear how those values fall in the overall distribution (see Figure 1).

Figure 7. Comparison of time-cost functions for finding related variables in a dataset using methods in Table Lens and Splus.

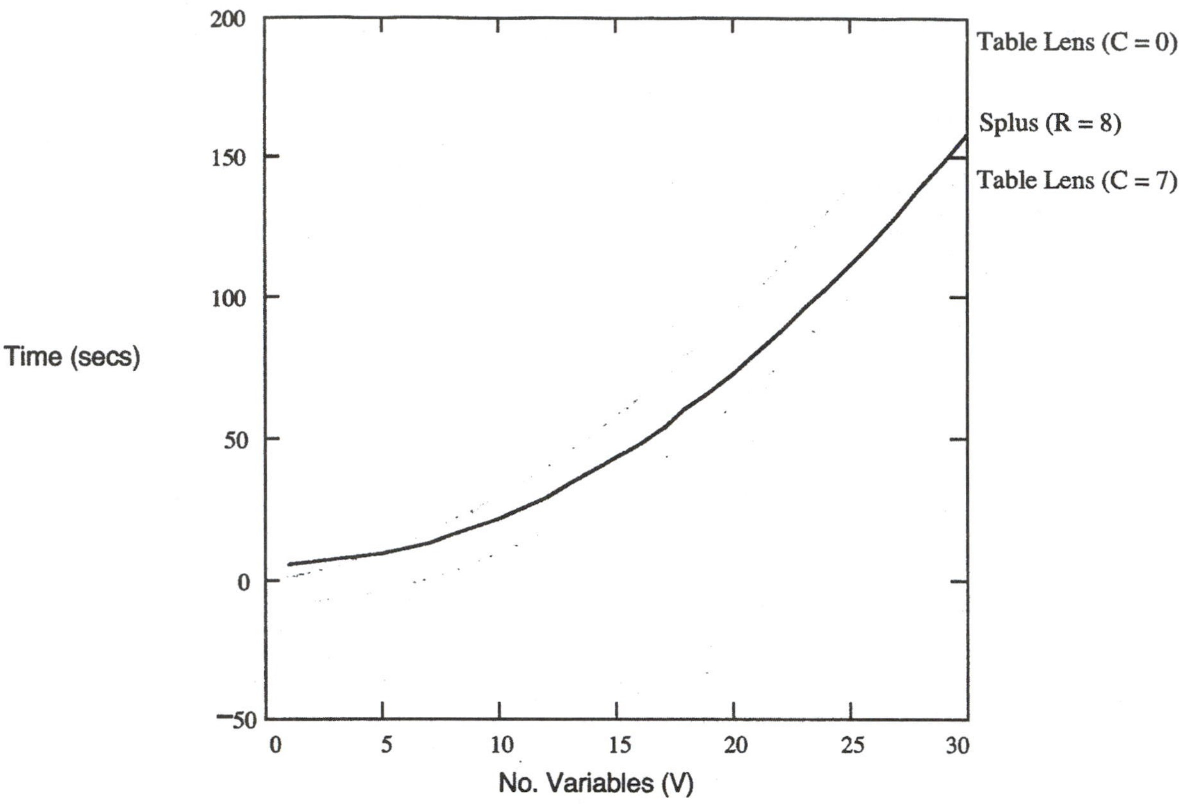

Another useful EDA graphical tool is the boxplot which graphically subsumes the letter values as well as others values. It conveys at a glance central values, skewness, tail length, and outliers. The box plot is a graphical structure that aligned with an axis representing the range of values in a batch and additional features are presented, including the median, quarters, outlier cutoffs, and outliers. Since the horizontal extent of a Table Lens column essentially represents a coordinate system for the range of values, the basic box plot can be shown superimposed on the base or the head of the column. Furthermore, rows representing extreme outliers, which lie outside the outer fence (typically defined as three-halves times the interquarter spread) can have their bars colored differently to set them apart.

Direct Manipulation Re-expression.

In both batch assessment and variable fitting task, a common need is to re-express a batch of data. A technique frequently used by expert analysts is to transform a data set using members of a "ladder of powers," which is a particular ordering of power transforms that distort the curve with increasing power to tame non-linearities and to variably treat one end or the other of the curve. Currently, Table Lens requires using a formula to generate a new column, and would thus require an iterative search of this set of transforms with the implied loads on activity, knowledge, and memory. This iteration can be removed by providing a direct manipulation interface that allows transforming the column in place.

One obvious thought is to put a slider on the column that allowed sliding through rungs of the ladder. An alternative, which perhaps reinforces the immediate feel of data manipulation, is to place "control points" on key locations of curve of sorted values. Then by pulling those control points in the right directions, the variables could be "pulled" up or down the ladder. This second approach is similar to the approach taken in SDM (Chuah, Roth, J. Mattis, & Kolojejchick, 1995) for transforming a selected set of data values, and is largely inspired by the Brown work on direct manipulation handles on graphical objects (Herdon & Meyer, Nov 1994; Zeleznik, Herndon, Robbins, Huang, Meyer, Parker, et al., 1993).

Another aspect of this process is that the analyst is attempting to make the batch confirm to the shape of some canonical distribution e.g. the normal distribution. Thus as the ladder of power is searched, the analyst is comparing the fit of the actual curve to an ideal curve. This process can be better supported by providing a reference curve superimposed on the actual curve. In addition, the total difference could be indicated in an output area. The reference curve itself could be manipulated to select different members of, what we might call, a ladder of distributions.

Variable Permutations.

Finding correlated variables involves sorting Table Lens and scanning all columns for related variables. As the prelude to the variable modeling task, this initiates a process of comparing correlated variables to select one for fitting. In a randomly organized table this may lead to many visual traversals of the table. An operator which permuted the variables so that more correlated variables on each side of the sorted variables were brought nearby would decrease the total amount of visual traversal distance necessary for this part of the task.

The value of ordering correlated variables in a best first order can be explained with a simple Information Foraging model analogously as for ordering operations in Scatter/Gather.(Pirolli & Card, 1995). Another way of seeing the value of variable ordering is that it allows column to be skipped (as in the C=7 case of Figure 5) thus improving performance.

This operation is analogous to the 2 way manual sorting operation of the "permutation matrix" described by Bertin (Bertin, 1983). It provides the general ability to group sets of variables that move as a group.

Fit Marks and Residual Curves

Once a correlated variable has been selected for fitting, the user of Table Lens must go through a cumbersome iterative process again using computed columns to perform re-expressions of both variables, line fitting, residual observation. The mechanisms for direct manipulation re-expression can be directly used here on both variables. The other 2 subtasks of fitting and residual monitoring can be supported in similar ways.

Given 2 variables, A and B, say A has been sorted and B is visibly correlated. When interest is focused on B, this can invoke a background fitting process which annotates the bars of B's column with "fit marks," say saliently colored points placed along each bar where the fitted line would indicate that case should be. As either variable is slid on the ladder of powers, the fit marks can be updated.

With this graphical aid, the user can quickly ascertain the deficit or excess between actual and fitted values of B. Again, an output area can be provided to display a computed measure of total difference. In this case, the user may also be interested in the shape of the residual, and in fact will ultimately want the residual as a separate column for further iteration using other variables. To support these tasks, the bases of the bars can be superimposed with bars that show the differences (perhaps in 2 colors for excess and deficits). This "residual curve" can be browsed and perhaps directly "dragged" apart into a separate column. Nominal variables, and nominal vs. quantitative variables.

SUMMARY

Table Lens supports quite well the studied EDA task, though there are a number of refinements suggested by the analysis that would increase its effectiveness. Though we haven't completed the analysis of learning costs, a quick analysis of the space of operators makes it clear that only a few operators are necessary to perform the tasks in the single Table Lens display, while a variety of displays are typically used in EDA tools and absolutely required by spreadsheets. The direct manipulation operators, the single familiar organization of the table, and the direct incorporation of graphics quite parsimoniously provide rich support for EDA tasks. We believe that with further improvements to the design, we can make accessible to a broad set of users the basic suite of EDA techniques.

REFERENCES

Becker, R. A., Chambers, J. M., & Wilks, A. R. (1983). *The New S Langugage*. University of Wisconsin Press.

Becker, R. A., & Cleveland, W. S. (1984). *Brushing a Scatterplot Matrix: High-Interaction Graphical Methods for Analyzing Multidimensional Data* (Tech. Rep). AT&T.

Bertin, J. (1983). *Semiology of Graphics*. University of Wisconsin Press.

Card, S. K., Moran, T. P., & Newell, A. (1983). *The psychology of human-computer interaction*. Hillsdale, NJ: Lawrence Erlbaum Associates.

Chuah, M. C., Roth, S. F., J. Mattis, & Kolojejchick, J. (1995). SDM: Malleable Information Graphics. In *Information Visualization 95* IEEE Computer Society Press.

Herdon, K. P., & Meyer, T. (Nov 1994). 3D Widgest for Exploratory Scientific Visualizations. In *Proceedings of the ACM Symposium on User Interface Software and Technology* ACM Press.

Langley, P., Simon, H. A., Bradshaw, G. L., & Zytkow, J. M. (1987). *Scientific discovery: Computational explorations of the creative processes*. Cambridge, MA: MIT Press.

Newell, A., & Simon, H. A. (1972). *Human problem solving*. Englewood Cliffs, NJ: Prentice Hall.

Olson, J. R., & Olson, G. M. (1990). The growth of cognitive modeling in human-computer interaction since GOMS. , *Human-Computer Interaction, 5*, 221-265.

Qin, Y., & Simon, H. A. (1990). Laboratory replication of scientific discovery processes. , *Cognitive Science, 14*, 281-312.

Pirolli, P. & Card, S. (1995). Information foraging in information access environments. In Proceedings of the

Conference on Human Factors in Computing Systems, CHI-95. Association for Computing Machinery

Rao, R., & Card, S. K. (1995). Exploring Large Tables with Table Lens. In *Video Proceedings of the ACM SIGCHI Conference on Human Factors in Computing Systems*

Rao, R., & Card, S. K. (April 1994). The Table Lens: Merging Graphical and Symbolic Representations in an Interactive Focus+Context Visualization for Tabular Information. In *Proceedings of the ACM SIGCHI Conference on Human Factors in Computing Systems*

Russell, D. M., Stefik, M. J., Pirolli, P., & Card, S. K. (1993). The cost structure of sensemaking. In *INTERCHI '93 Conference on Human Factors in Computing Systems*, (pp. 269-276). Amsterdam: Association for Computing Machinery`.

Tukey, J. W. (1977). *Exploratory data analysis*. Reading, MA: Addison-Wesley.

Zeleznik, R. C., Herndon, K. P., Robbins, D. C., Huang, N., Meyer, T., Parker, N., & Hughes, J. F. (1993). An Interactive 3D toolkit for constructing 3d widgets. In *Proceedings of SIGGRAPH'93* (pp. 81--84). ACM Press.

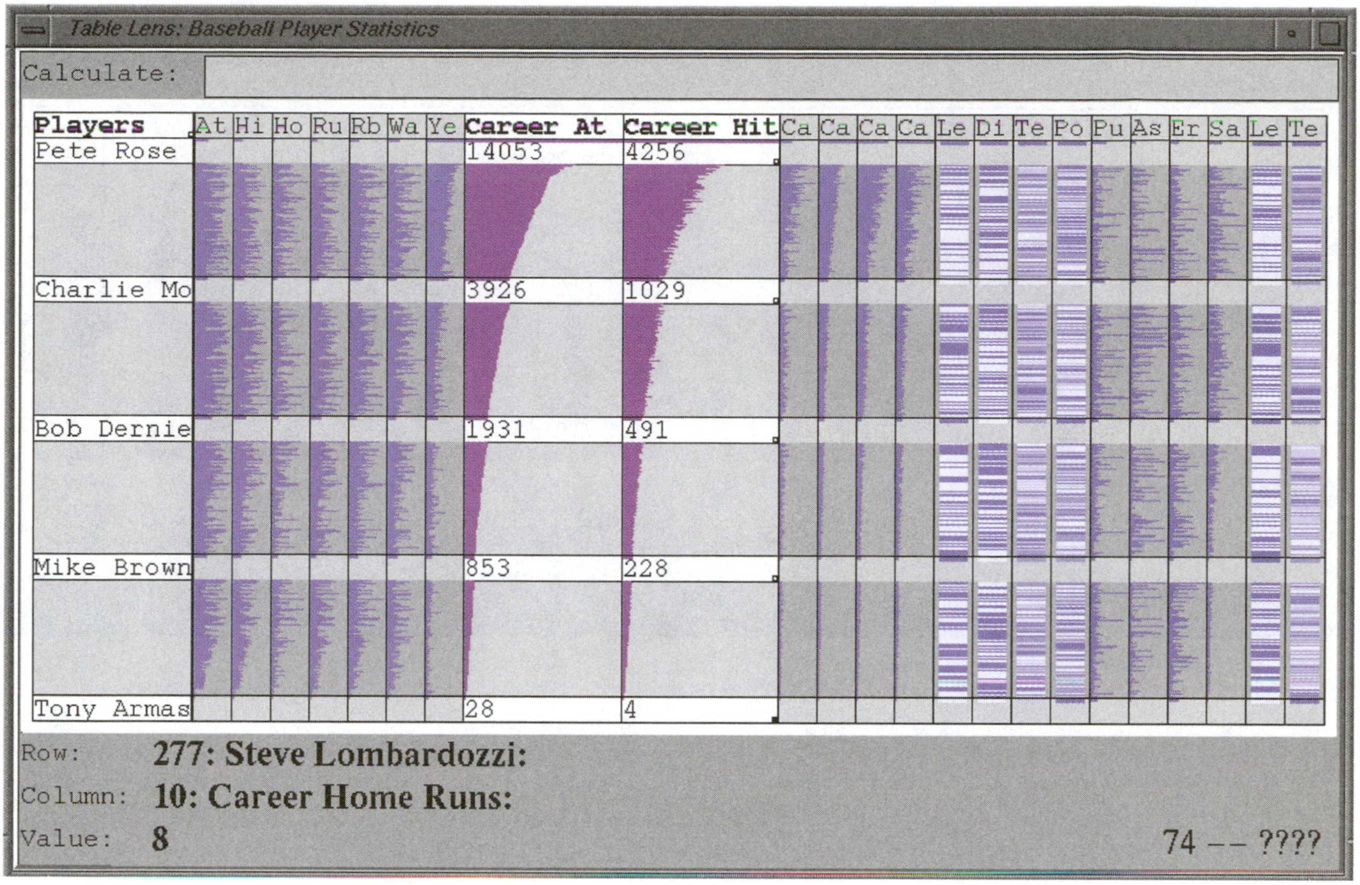

FIGURE **1**

Table Lens visualizing a set of baseball statistics.

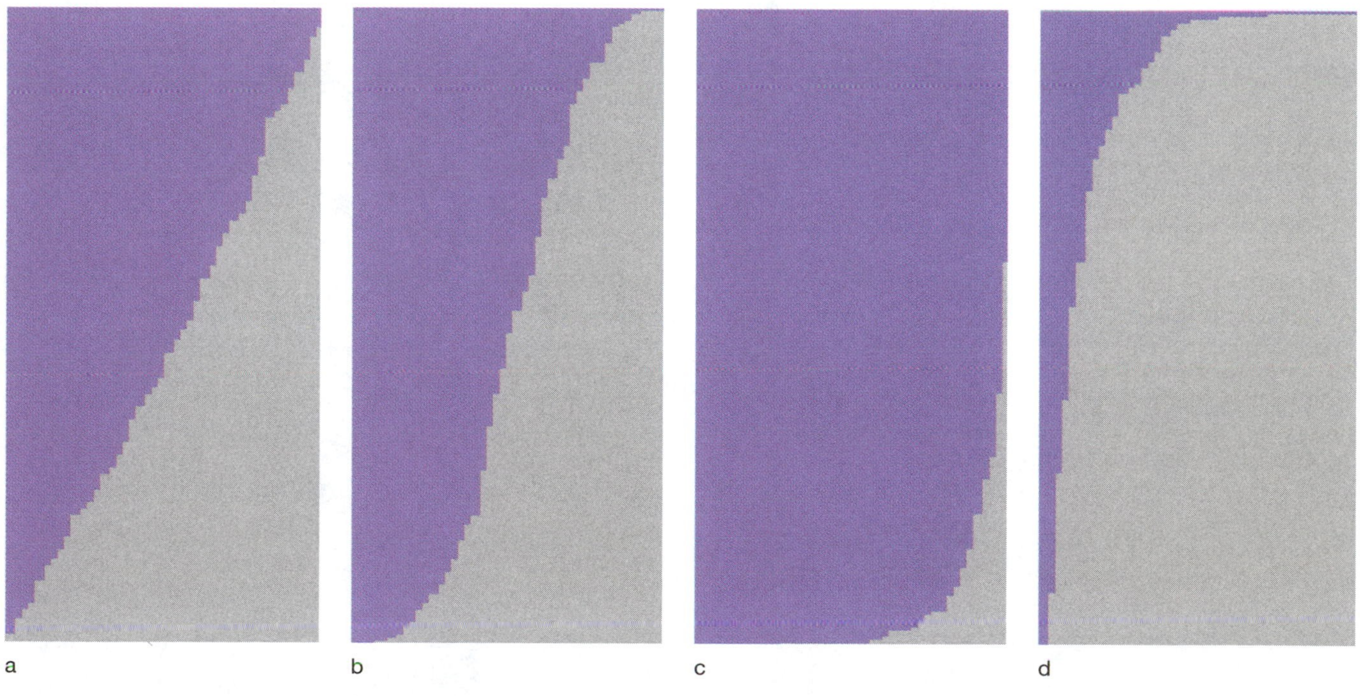

FIGURE **2**

Prototypical distributions as they appear in the Table Lens.

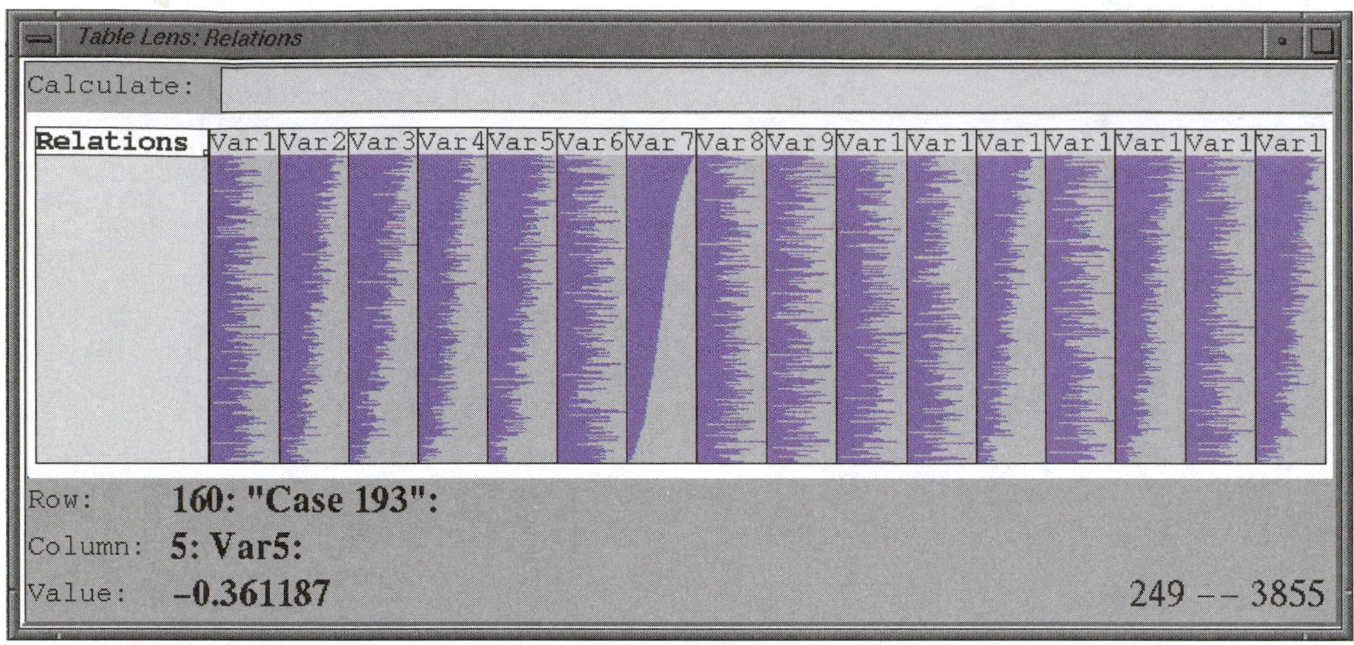

FIGURE 3

Correlations among column variables become apparent when one of the columns is sorted.

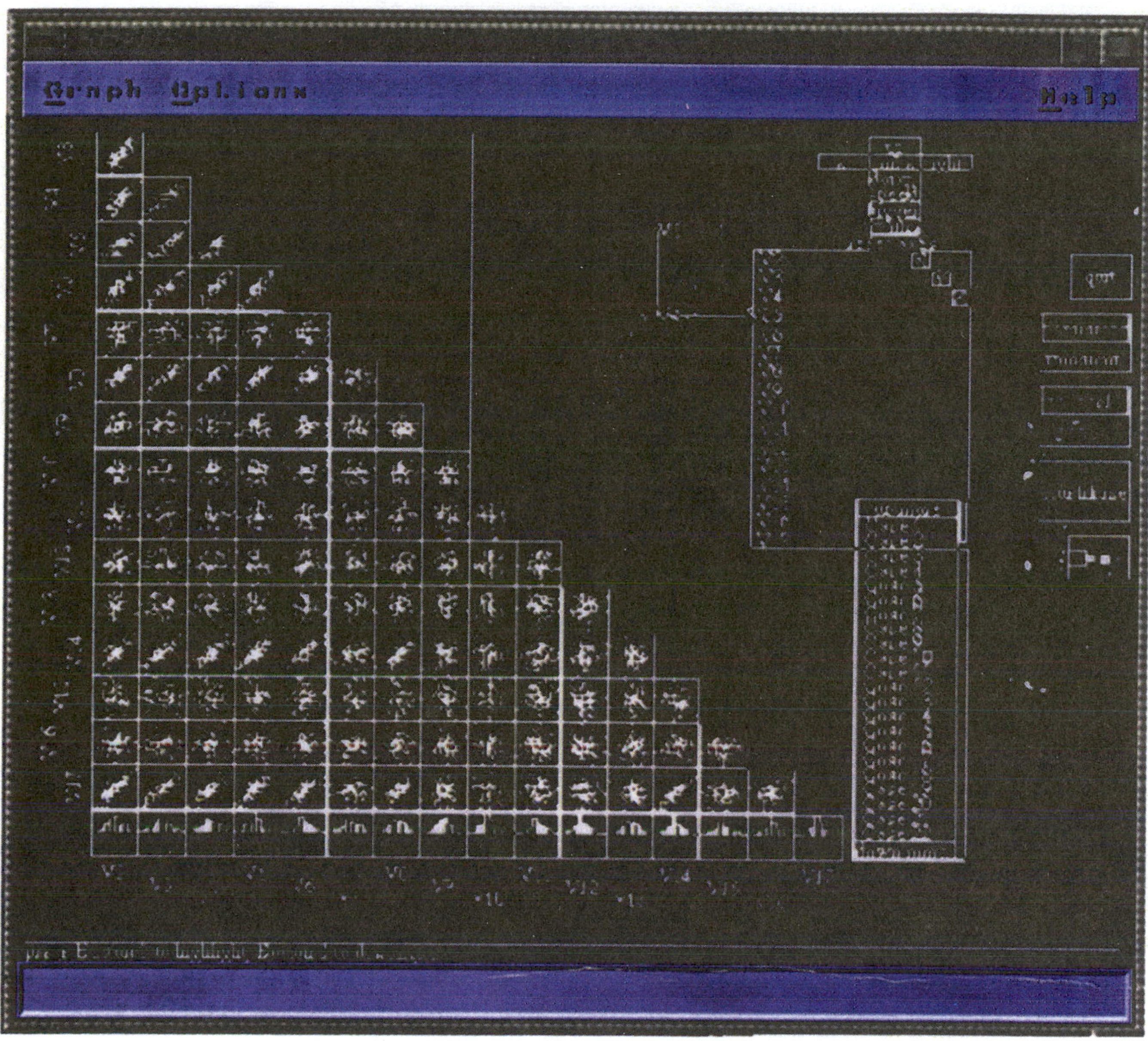

FIGURE **4**

The Splus brush tool.

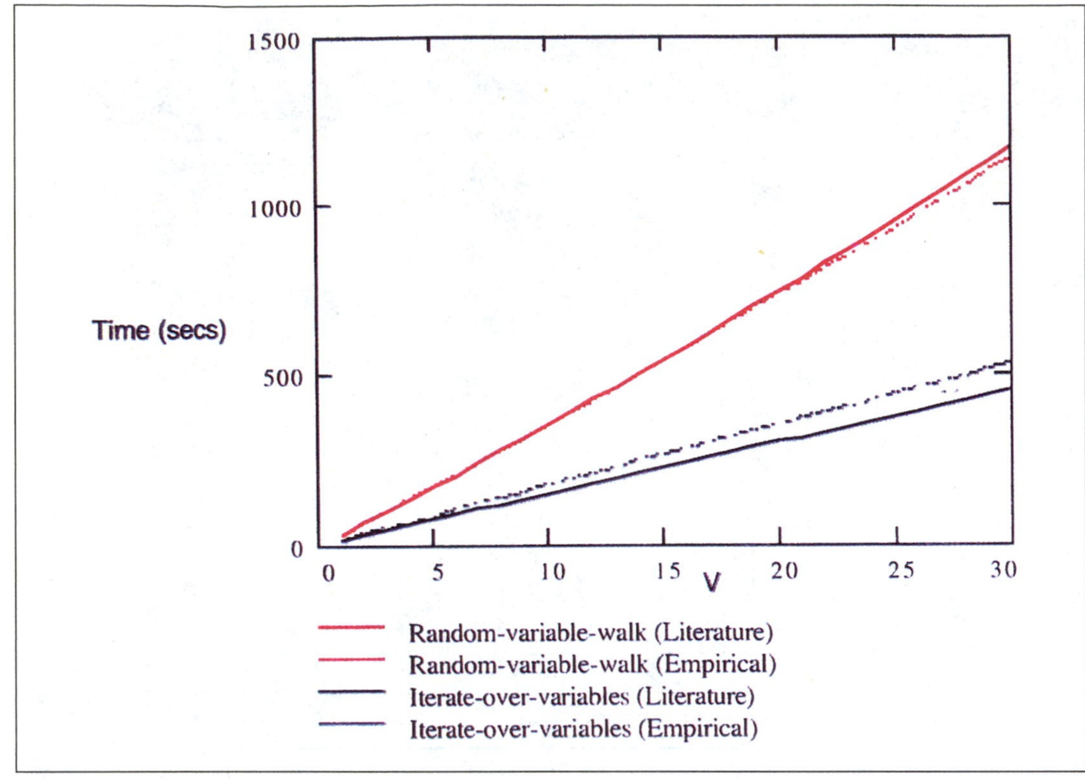

FIGURE **5**

Comparison of literature-based and empirically-based estimates for time-cost functions for Table Lens methods for finding important features of all variables V in a dataset.

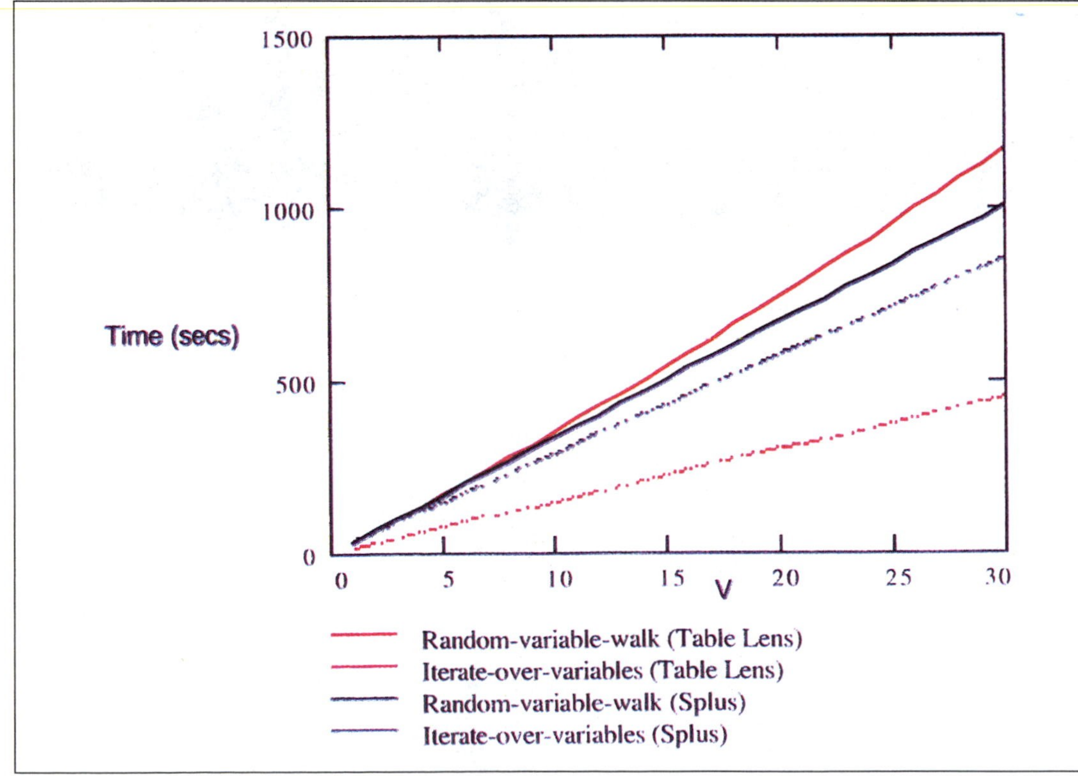

FIGURE **6**

Comparison of time-cost functions for Table Lens and Splus methods for finding important properties of all variables V in a dataset. Time-cost are literature-based.

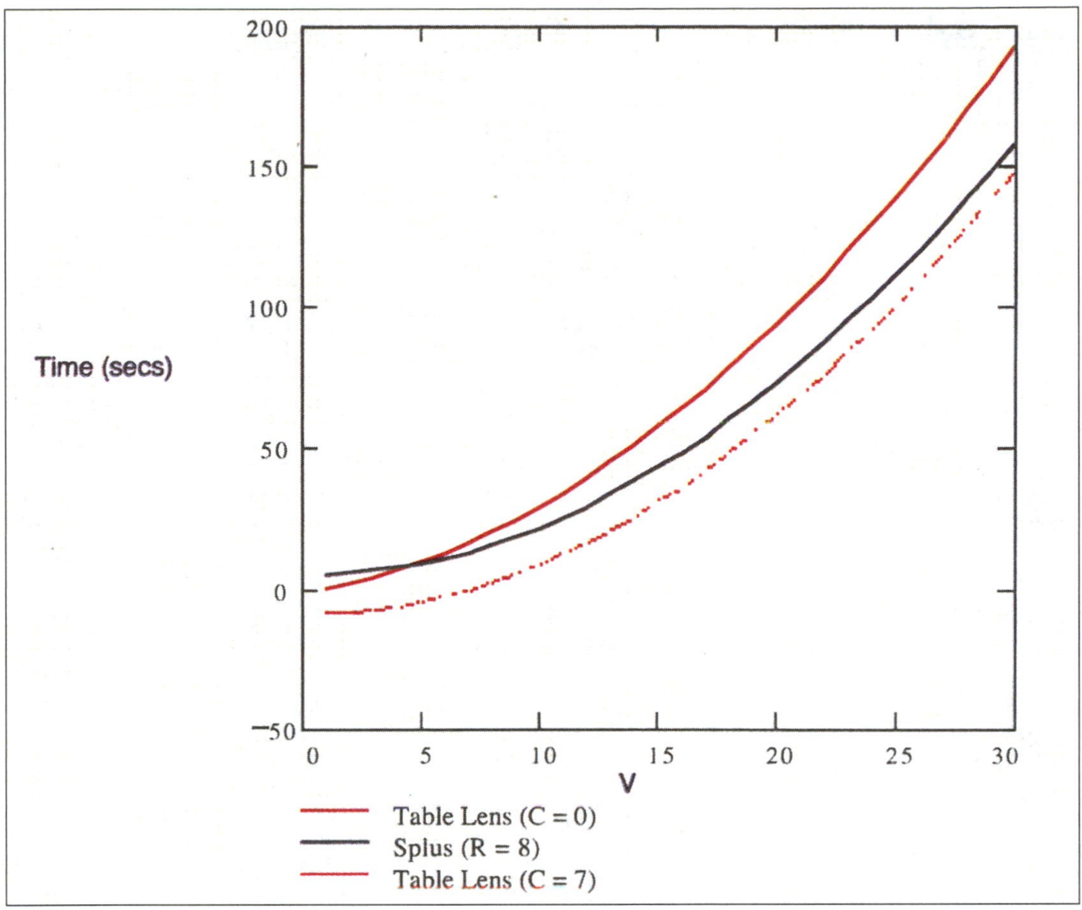

FIGURE 7

Comparison of time-cost functions for finding related variables in a dataset using methods in Table Lens and Splus.

Characterizing Interactive Externalizations

Lisa Tweedie
Department of Electrical Engineering,
Imperial College of Science, Technology and Medicine
South Kensington , London, SW7 2BT
Tel: +44 171 594 6261
l.tweedie@ic.ac.uk *

ABSTRACT

This paper seeks to characterize the space of techniques that exist for interactive externalisations (visualisations). A selection of visualisations are classified with respect to: the types of data represented, the nature of the visible feedback displayed and the forms of interactivity used. Such characterization provides a method for evaluating potential designs and comparing different tools.

KEYWORDS

Visualization, Interactive Graphics, Taxonomy

CHARACTERIZATION

The recent interest in Information Visualization is based on the fairly valid assumption that externalising problems can support problem-solving [30,51]. However we do not have a clear understanding of what features enhance this process, or how such representations best map to tasks. In particular, little attention has been paid to the value that **interactivity** brings to these externalisations.

In the late sixties, Simon [37] noted that *"An early step towards understanding any set of phenomena is ... to develop a taxonomy. This step has not yet been taken with respect to representations. We only have a sketchy and incomplete knowledge of the different ways in which problems can be represented and much less knowledge of the significance of the differences".*

Taxonomies of static representations have now been developed [6, 36, 50]. On the input side, Card et al [9] have also classified the design space of input devices. Ahlberg and Truve [1] have extended this work to outline the design space of query devices. The value of such abstractions is that they discard *"irrelevant details while isolating and emphasizing those properties of artifacts and situations that are most significant for design"* [8].

This paper is a first step in the characterization of **interactive** externalizations. It considers three aspects of externalisations: Firstly the underlying data used to create the representation, secondly the forms of interactivity available to the user and thirdly the input and output information that is explicitly represented by the externalisation. Fourteen examples of interactive visualizations are examined in relation to these aspects. Two of these visualizations are then described in more detail from a data-centric perspective. Taken as a whole these characterization methods enable potential designs to be evaluated and different techniques compared.

REPRESENTATIONS AND INTERACTIVITY

Larkin and Simon [26] suggest that part of the value of diagrams is that they group information together, thereby enabling users to make full use of the patterns perceived. Such grouping is facilitated by visualization tools in two ways, through the **representation** itself and through the **interactive** mechanisms that act on that representation.

Casner [11] identifies that *"Different presentations of the same information best support different tasks"*. In other words, each question that a user wants to ask requires an entirely different presentation. Whilst this limitation applies to static presentations, it is not relevant when interactivity allows different features of the data to be made salient as and when required. Here, the underlying representation becomes a medium through which different features of the data are made explicit. A single representation can now be used to answer many different questions.

REPRESENTATIONS

Bertin [6] suggests that the form of representation used is dependent on the type of data to be displayed. He argues that there are two forms of data that can be represented for any problem: the data **values** and the data **structure** (Figure 1 a and d). Values are associated with the different numerical or categorical attributes relevant to a problem. The structure comprises the relations (e.g. links, mathematical equations, constraints) that characterize the data as a whole. These two forms of information have also been called low level (data driven) and high level (conceptual) views of a problem [23]. Different graphical techniques display different forms of data. Histograms, for instance, represent attribute values, whereas a tree diagram represents structural relationships within a whole data set.

What Bertin neglected in his taxonomy is that as well as having "raw" value and structural data, we can also transform this "raw" data into meta-data (data about data). One type of transformation keeps the data in its original form (values → derived values: Figure 1b, structure → derived structure: Figure 1e). This will be called

* http://www.ee.ic.ac.uk/research/information/www/lisat.html

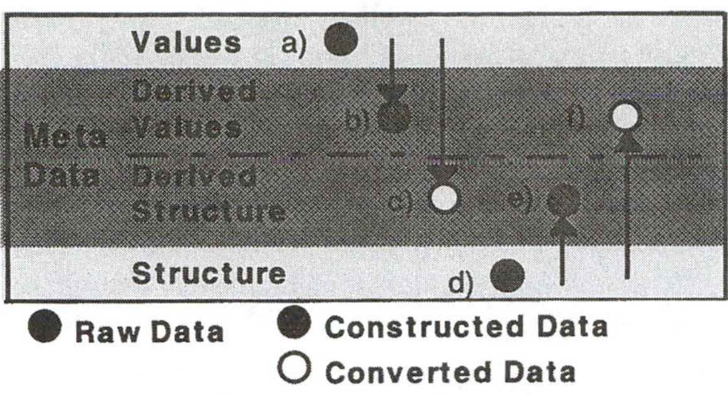

Figure 1: Types of Information Represented

constructed data. Another converts data into a different form (data → derived structure: Figure 1c , structure → derived values: Figure 1f). This will be called **converted data**. These additional forms of data provide a valuable extension of the design space.

Representations of Data Values

Representations of data values show the relations between subsets of the data. Such representations tend to map different attributes to axes. For instance, a scatterplot shows the relations between two attributes. A matrix of scatterplots shows the relationships between attributes of multivariate data set. The viewing of structure in these plots can be enhanced using interactivity. A histogram simply represents the quantity of values in a particular bin however when interactivity is added relationships between different can also be seen [31, 43, 44, 45]. Parallel Co-ordinate plots [24] also show relational information between attributes. Both Scatterplots and Parallel Co-ordinate plots loose detailed value information when there is too much data (due to overplotting).

Representations of Data Structure

Representations of data structure are representations of the relations within a single set. Bertin [6] has identified five different forms of structural representation: rectilinear, circular, ordered patterns, unordered patterns and stereograms (Figure 2). **Rectilinear** (meaning "straight line") representations are in the form of lists. These representations are useful for relating order to some other feature of the data [17]. NetMap [14] is an example of a **Circular** representation. Here the different entities (e.g. banks, people, telephone numbers) are placed around the circumference of a circle. Connections between entities (e.g. between two people) are represented by lines. **Ordered patterns** are representations that form a pattern in which one direction is ordered. Trees are a good example. **Unordered patterns** are all the other two dimensional structural representations in which no order is present. Two of the best known representations of this type are networks and Venn diagrams. Finally **Stereograms** are representations where the structure suggests a volume.

Representations of Constructed Data

As well as 'raw' data values and inherent data structure, users are often interested in looking at summary statistics. For instance a user may be interested in looking at the mean of a set of data (a derived value). Tukey's [41] Box plots and Mihalisin's [28] Nested Histograms are both examples of representations which use such derived values. Wilkinson [46], has enhanced Scatterplot Matrices by placing summary statistics at the edges of the scatterplots. Equally, combining information about how one structure relates to another can provide valuable insights. For instance Furnas and Zacks [20] describe multi-trees that link two different trees (sets of structured data) resulting in a new derived structure. Eisenberg [19] uses algorithms to create 3D "constructed" structures (Example L).

Representations of Converted Data

In other situations we may need to convert the information type in order to discover useful information.

For instance we may have a data set but not know the structural relations within it. **Derived structure** about a set of data values can be obtained from calculations across the whole data set. This has been particularly popular in the field of information retrieval where the structure of a set of documents is often not well understood (e.g. Bead [12] described in example E).

We may have a good understanding of the structural relations within our problem e.g. a full set of mathematical equations (a model). However such models are often not very easy to understand in algebraic form. Instantiating such models with a set of data values and calculating the resulting outputs can create **derived values** which can be visualized [27, 44, 49].

INTERACTIVITY: DIRECT/INDIRECT MANIPULATION

The interactive tools provided to act on a visualization can be described in terms of the **balance of control** between the user and computer. For instance Norman [31] describes two modes of activity: first person "do-it-yourself" activity and third person "command mode" activity. In fact these form two extremes of a continuum. Lunzer [27] characterizes the intervening forms of manipulation as: manual (e.g. physically dragging a mouse in order to drag an on screen object), mechanized (e.g. making a selection with a tool such as a slider), instructable (e.g. using formula's in a spreadsheet), steerable (e.g. directing an algorithm to perform in a certain way) and automatic (e.g. using an algorithm that performs automatically).

Much of the interactivity in the visualization tools developed to over the last decade can be described as making use of **direct manipulation** (DM). In other words a literal replication of physical behavior in the real world. This can be direct in the sense of manually moving an object (Figure 3) or based on a tool metaphor (mechanized). However the key is that it is "literal" so that users can easily understand how it should behave based on their knowledge of the real world.

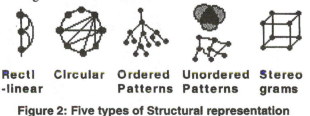

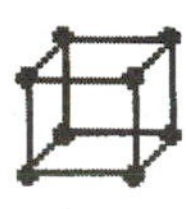

Figure 2: Five types of Structural representation

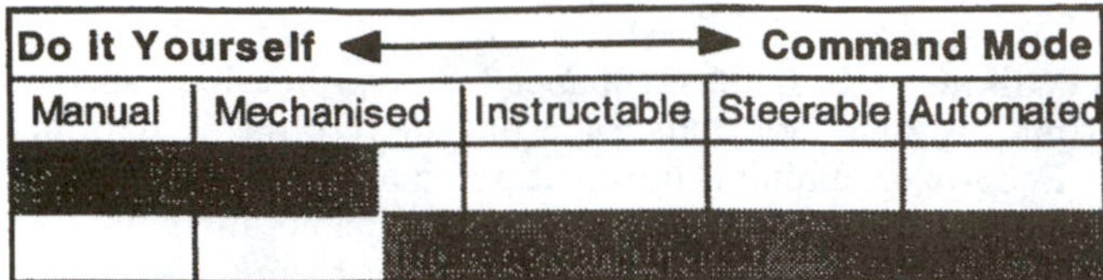

Do It Yourself
Command Mode
Manual
Mechanised
Instructable
Steerable
Automated

Figure 3: Balance of Control at the Interface [32, 27]

However, as Smith [39] has identified the computer provides many opportunities to add more "magical" functionality which does not rely on direct physical metaphors. More recent information visualizations have started to make use of this **Indirect manipulation** (IM). For instance, Smets et al [38] provide designers with "magical" tools that stretch and deform an object in a virtual reality environment. The tools *"do not merely mimic everyday ones; instead they offer new behaviors to designers"*. The examples that follow will attempt to clarify the value of indirect manipulation further.

INPUT/OUPUT RELATIONS ACROSS TIME

If we are to make use of indirect manipulation then the **visible feedback** provided becomes a key issue. One way to enhance such feedback is to explicitly represent the user's input, tightly coupled to a visualization of output. In this way the rules governing the interaction are externalized and users can observe and learn the effects of their actions.

The importance of mutual reference between input and output information was outlined by Draper [15] who identifies four classes of relationship:

- input→input (e.g. relate two handed input [7])
- input→output (e.g. relate a slider and histogram)
- output→input (e.g. link an error message with its cause)
- output→output (e.g. link two output displays [30])

Draper argues that all four of these relations provide vital information in natural language and are central in creating a dialogue between the user and computer. These classes will be used here to identify the different forms of visible feedback present in a particular externalization.

An important aspect of mutual reference is the passage of time. Most visualizations represent the current state, however, it is often important for a user to compare the results of a current query with a previous query (historical: input↔output). Linking representations of past input and output mean that all the historical input/output relations can be explored directly. Such historical information can be crucial. For instance Data Desk [45] is an application that allows a sequence of Boolean queries to be made graphically using brushing on histograms and scatterplots. However users are not provided with any explicit representation of their ongoing query, so they can easily forget what their query is.

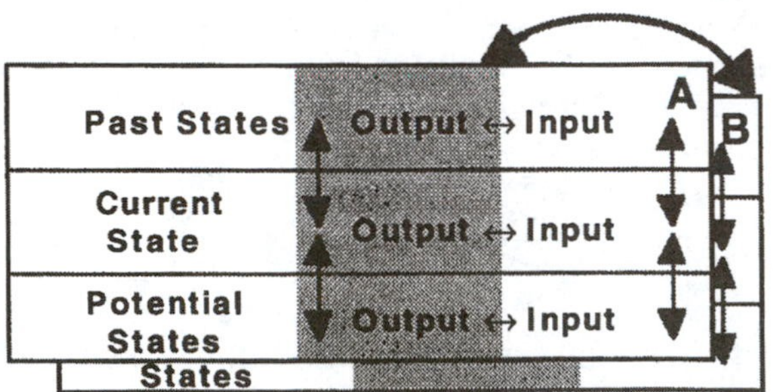

Figure 4: The possible visible feedback relationships for two externalizations A & B

Another time related issue is the consideration of potential states e.g. where in the space have I not searched? Visualizations that encode sensitivity to change are providing such information (Example G).

Figure 4 shows the visible feedback characteristics for a representation "A". A second representation "B" may be tightly coupled to "A" resulting in inter-representation reference. By explicitly representing the past, present and potential input/output information, we can provide the user with many opportunities to refer to and learn from their own activity.

ILLUSTRATIVE EXAMPLES

A) Parallel Coordinates [24] (Figure 5b)
Purpose: View relations in multivariate data:
Data type: Values
Representation: Attributes are represented as axes and data items are represented as lines between the axes.
Interactivity: a) Data can be hidden by selecting subgroups with sliders on the axes. The first filter hides the data (mechanized DM). However subsequent filters become more complex to interpret (mechanized IM).
b) A few selections can be colour coded (mechanized DM).
c) Axes can be reordered(manual DM)
I-O Representation: Input → Output is represented

B) Dynamic Queries [2] (Figure 10)
Purpose: Find useful sets in multivariate data
Data type: Values
Representation: A scatterplot is used to display two of the attributes, the remainder are represented as sliders.
Interactivity : Data is hidden (mechanized DM) or filtered (mechanized IM) by selecting ranges on sliders.
I-O Representation: Input→Output is represented

C) NetMap [14] (Figure 2)
Purpose: View relations in multivariate data
Data type: Structure
Representation: Attributes are placed around the edges of a circle. Relationships between attributes are represented as lines going between the attributes.
Interactivity: a) Colour encoding of attribute values (mechanized DM)
b) A number of filtering operations are available e.g. "Entities connected > 3 times". This is set up by filling in a form (instructable IM).
I-O Representation: Only the output is represented

D) Filter Flow [48] (Figure 5f)
Purpose: Construct Database Queries
Data type: Values
Representation: Attributes are shown as slider blocks. Data is shown as a stream of varying thickness (depending on the number of data items that satisfy the query at each point).
Interactivity: Users can add in various AND or OR gates. (instructable IM).
I-O Representation: input → quantity of output

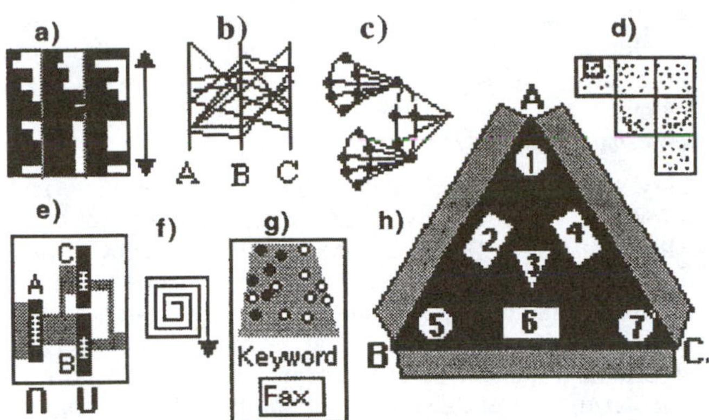

Figure 5: a) The Table Lens b) Parallel Co-ordinates c) Cone Trees d) The Scatterplot Matrix e) Filter Flow f) spiral ordering in VisDB g) Bead h) The Info-Crystal

E) Bead [12] (Figure 5g)
Purpose: document retrieval
Data type: Derived structure (a network - converted from values) and Derived values (constructed usage information)
Representation: Bead calculates a "distance" (based on the number of common keywords) between each pair of documents in a corpus. The resulting network is then flattened onto a plane, using a complex algorithm, so that similar documents are close together. In this way users can view clusters of closely related documents. This is an example of derived structure. The display also dynamically updates usage circles which indicate how often a particular document has been accessed by the whole community.
Interactivity: a) Encoding: A query can be made using a particular keyword. All the documents with that keyword are highlighted. In this way colour serves to group the documents on the landscape (mechanized DM).
b) Navigation: movement over the plane (manual DM)
I-O Representation: Input (keyword) → Output

F) Scatterplot Matrix [3] (Figure 5d)
Purpose: View relations in Multivariate Data
Data type: Value data
Representation: A Matrix of scatterplots
Interactivity: Brushing to encode/hide data (manual DM)
I-O Representation: Input (Brush) → Output

G) The Attribute [43] and Influence Explorers [44]
Purpose: Find useful sets in multivariate data
Data type: Attribute Explorer : Values, Influence Explorer : Derived Values
Representation: Histograms represent each attribute.
Interactivity: a) Users can select a single item by selecting any data point (Figure 7). In this way that data point is highlighted on each of the other histograms (manual DM)
b) Users can select limits on a histogram with a slider (Figure 7). Once more than one slider limit is selected, additive encoding is employed. This encodes the data satisfying all the slider limits in black. The data that fails one set of limits is encoded dark grey. This allows users to see data that satisfies a query and data that just fails it. This encoding overcomes the common problem in database querying of choosing all or none of the data. Additive encoding allows the user to view the attributes affecting the query and make appropriate adjustments (mechanized IM).
I-O Representation: Input→Output information is encoded. The colour coding provides visible information about how to adjust a query to improve the hit rate (potential: output→ input).

H) The InfoCrystal [40] (Figure 5h)
Purpose: formulating a query for document retrieval
Data type: Values
Representation: The query is encoded in the form of a shape with one corner for each query term. In figure 5h three query terms are shown. The shapes in the centre represent the hits for each of the Boolean combinations.
Interactivity: The user can build up various by combining shapes (instructable IM).
I-O Representation: Input→Output information is shown. However the user has to read the Output values they are not presented graphically.

I) Cone Trees [35] (Figure 5c)
Purpose: Displaying File hierarchies
Data type: Structure
Representation. This representation uses 3D "cone" trees of information to represent file hierarchies.
Interactivity: Users can rotate the trees and bring the relevant part into focus (manual DM)
I-O Representation: Input (current focus)→Output

J) Pad++ [4]
Purpose: Substrate for presenting information
Data type: Any
Representation: Users are able to navigate through "multi-scale" space using panning and zoom. Views at different scales are linked using windows called "portals"
Interactivity: Multi-scale zooming (mechanized IM)
I-O Representation: Input→Output is represented.

K) VisDB [25]
Purpose: view relations in multivariate data
Data type: Value data
Representation: A user assigns weights to several slider selections. The computer then performs an algorithm to order the data points. Finally the data is represented in a window as a spiral list (see figure 5f). This facilitates the identification of clusters in the data.
Interactivity: Placing of weights (steered IM).
I-O Representation: Input → Output is represented.

L) Hypergami [19]
Purpose: Create an optimum layout for origami shapes
Data type: Derived Structure (Constructed)
Representation: Users build a 3D shape and then interact with various algorithms to work out the best origami layout
Interactivity: Users can observe algorithms work, and adjust variables as the algorithms execute. They can also make post-algorithmic adjustments (steered IM)
I-O Representation: Only Output is represented

M) Permutation Matrices [6] /Table Lens [34]
Purpose: view relations in multivariate data
Data type: Values
Representation: This is essentially a graphical spreadsheet (value in each cell is encoded as height)
Interactivity: Reorder the cells (mechanized DM)
I-O Representation: Only output is represented

	Direct	Indirect
Meta Data	Bead [12], Enhanced Scatterplot Matrices [46] Spreadplots [49].	Hypergami [19] Influence Explorer [44] Pad++ [4].
Raw Data	Scatterplot Matrix [3] Table Lens [34], Cone Trees [35].	Dynamic Queries [2], Filter Flow [48], Visdb [25], Pad++ [4], InfoCrystal [40], Attribute Explorer [43], NetMap [14], Parallel Coordinates [24].

Interactivity

Figure 6: Defining Characteristics of Externalizations

O) Spreadplots [49]

Purpose: view principle component factors
Data type: derived Values (Converted)
Representation: 3D Scatterplot
Interactivity: Can rotate (manual DM)
I-O Representation: Only output is represented

SKETCHING THE SPACE OF THE POSSIBLE

From the fourteen examples given in the previous section five types of interactivity can be identified: hiding/filtering, labeling/Boolean encoding, animated navigation, reordering and algorithmic transformation. Both Parallel Coordinates and Dynamic Queries allow hiding (DM) and more complex filtering (IM). Bead simply allows labeling (DM) whereas the Attribute and Influence explorers allow more complex encoding (IM). Both Bead and ConeTrees allow direct navigation around the representation (DM) whereas Pad++ provides more "magical" navigation (IM). Parallel Coordinates and the Table Lens allow direct reordering (DM) whereas VisDB uses an algorithmic method to reorder the data points (IM). All algorithmic transformations provide indirect manipulation. However in many software packages algorithms are solely used as automatic tools. Hypergami and VisDB both allow steered interaction with algorithms. Eisenberg [19] stresses the importance of providing control to the user. As he points out *"We might find in practice, that an algorithm rich in interactive capabilities actually outperforms (in the quality of solutions) a more time efficient "black box algorithm"*

Figure 6 shows how the examples given in the previous section were classified in terms of: raw/meta data and direct/indirect manipulation. Although many of the visualizations have explored combining direct and indirect manipulation, this is mainly on sets of raw data. Visualizations of meta data are more uncommon. In a sense meta data and indirect manipulation are both visualizations of algorithms. Indirect manipulation can demonstrate an algorithm on the fly, whereas meta data can represent algorithm in pre-calculated form, both need to be exploited.

Most of visualizations reviewed explicitly represented Input→Output relations. A special case of input→ouput representation is the "object symbol" [32] where both input and output are represented as a single entity [e.g. 4, 7, 17, 43, 44]. This proximity emphasizes the relationship between the two and so encourages use of visible feedback.

A number of visualization tool-kits are now being developed that allow users to perform colour linking on more than one representation of output. This allows Output→Output relations to be compared across representations (13, 25).

Very little use seems to have been made of historical information in the visualizations developed to date. Although Bead [12] presents an interesting concept when it represents the history of a communities selections. In the examples examined here "potential" Information has been visualized in two ways. First, when visualizing an algorithm a number of different alternatives can be pre-calculated. This enables potential solutions to be explored (27,44). Secondly the Additive encoding described in example G can provides users with information about which attribute to interact with next.

Different representations have different strengths, so for instance it may be valuable to experiment with combining a representation of structure with one of values, or a representation of raw data with one of meta data. The space of possible designs discussed in this paper could be used as a starting point to consider the many alternatives available.

DETAILED DESCRIPTIONS OF USE

Up to this point, the characterizations developed have described the information that externalization's make explicit and the interactivity they use, in general terms. However, it is worth considering a couple of examples in more detail to try and understand how this information is actually used.

Norman [32] identified that there are two gulfs that a user must overcome if they are to utilize any computer artifact: The Gulf of Execution (how do I specify the question I want to ask?) and the Gulf of Evaluation (how do I interpret what is displayed?). These are the action rules (syntax) and interpretation rules (semantics) of the interface. If one could describe these action and interpretation rules then one would be close to describing how the information is used.

Benyon [5] suggested that taking a "data-centric" perspective may prove valuable. As he puts it *"data is probably the only thing people have in common with computers"*, it can therefore form a common ground on which to base descriptions.

Green and Benyon [22] have used a version of entity relationship diagrams (a technique used in data base design) to describe information artifacts. They are called ERMIA diagrams and describe information artifacts in terms of the entities and relations from which they are constructed. In other words they develop a structural (high level) description of the artifact. These form a useful notation for identifying the rules that a user might need to know to interpret a particular artifact.

The next section will outline DIVA [42] another "data centric" method which attempts to describe the action rules of an externalization. The users actions are described in terms of the selections that they can make on the data. The consequence of each selection is then described in terms of the how the computer acts on the data. Finally the perceptual comparisons facilitated by these consequences are described in terms of which subsets of the data can now be compared. This approach produces a "data driven" (low level) description of the artifact.

Zhang and Norman [51] have made a distinction between the external rules (that can be checked perceptually by interaction with the environment) and internal rules (those that must be checked mentally). DIVA focuses on the former whereas ERMIA diagrams tend to describe internal rules.

DIVA: DESCRIBING ACTIONS

Bertin [6] argued that any data set can be seen as a matrix of objects against attributes. Questions can be asked of this data at three different levels i.e. about: a single item, a set of items, or the whole set. These questions can relate to objects or attributes.

The combination of three possible levels and two different types of question (object or attribute) provides six possible questions a user might ask i.e. questions about: a single object or attribute, a set of objects or attributes or all of the objects or attributes (denoted as **o, a, [o], [a], O, A**) . These six classes of questions can be used as a notation to describe users selections and the consequent groupings that are available for comparison in the display.

There are two types of perceptual comparison. Firstly there is comparison of different groupings within a static display (Static Comparison). Secondly the user has the power to interact with the visualization and make changes. In this way they can compare two discrete. It can be useful to further distinguish comparison within an attribute and comparison between attributes as these often involve different operations.

Description 1: The Attribute Explorer

As an illustration we will first describe the Attribute Explorer [43]. The domain is the search for a house amongst a database of houses. Each attribute is represented as a histogram with a slider attached. There are two basic interactions that can be performed by the user: the selection of a single object and a set of attribute bins (Figure 7). The initial salient structure shows a set of houses (objects) grouped by their attributes.

The central column of figure 8 shows how the user can select a single object (o^1 - a house). The consequence of this is that o^1's attribute values are highlighted on each of the histograms.

When the display is static, the user can compare the selected house (o^1) with the whole set (O) within a particular histogram. Between histograms the user can compare the different values of the selected house (i.e. o^1 with o^1). Dynamically the user can select one house (o^1) and then another (o^2) sequentially. This facilitates comparisons of these two houses both within a histogram and between histograms (o^1 with o^2).

The right column of figure 8 describes how a user can select attribute bins($[a^1]$) with a slider. Initially a set of

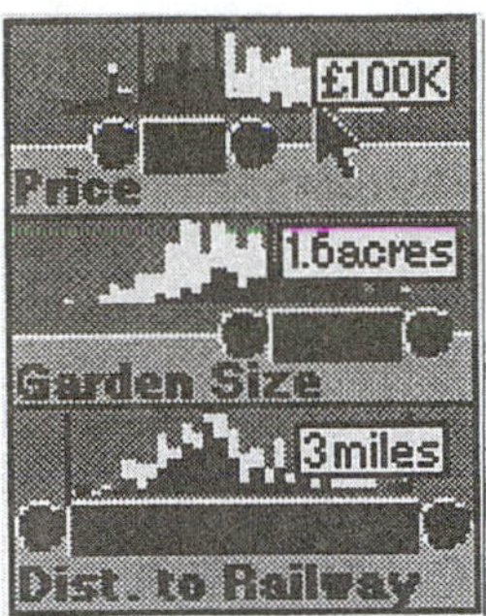

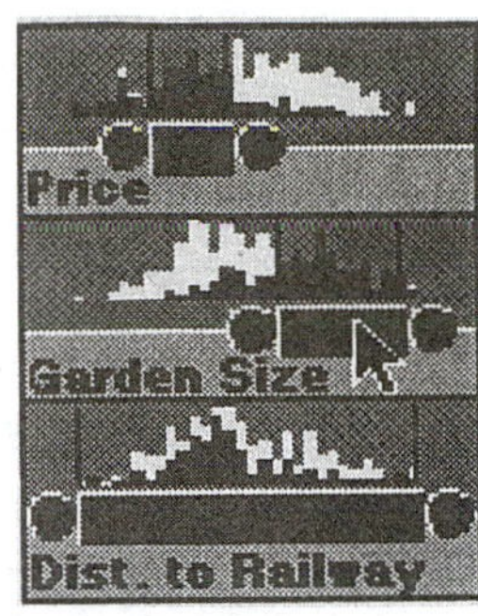

Figure 7: Selection of a single house (by clicking on a data point) and a set of houses (slider)

attribute bins are selected. The consequence of this selection is the black and dark grey additive encoding described in example G earlier.

Whilst the display is static the user can compare the black objects $[o^{b1}]$, the dark grey objects $[o^{dg1}]$ and full set of objects O with each other, within a histogram. Between histograms the black objects distribution on each scale can be compared ($[o^{b1}]$ with $[o^{b1}]$) and in the same way the dark grey objects distribution on each scale can be compared ($[o^{dg1}]$ with $[o^{dg1}]$). If the user adjusts the display dynamically then the user can compare the original black set of objects with the new set of black objects ($[o^{b1}]$ with $[o^{b2}]$). The same goes for the dark grey objects ($[o^{dg1}]$ with $[o^{dg2}]$). This occurs both within and between histograms.

The description allows the identification of the possible comparisons on the display and encourages speculation about additional comparisons that might improve the tool.

Description 2: Dynamic Queries

The same database of houses could be explored with the "Dynamic Queries" [2] interface. As described earlier this allows a user to combine a number of different filters in a simple fashion. These selections can be made using both sliders and buttons (see Figure 9)

The initial salient structure of this display is that the data is grouped by its longitude and latitude attributes (i.e. it is displayed on a map). The user interacts with the system by selecting a set of attribute bins [a] with a slider. The consequence of this selection is that it is added as an extra filter on the data. The resulting data set is displayed as a scatterplot (Figure 9). This means that as the user moves the sliders the data displayed changes.

Initial Salient Structure: Objects grouped by two attributes		
Selection	o^1 (House)	$[a]^1$ (attribute bin)
Consequence	**label o^1**	**additive $[a]^1$**
Static Comparison Within attribute	**o^1 with O**	**$[o]^{b1}/[o]^{dg1}/O$**
Between attributes	**o^1 with o^1**	**$[o]^{b1}/[o]^{b1}$ and $[o]^{dg1}/[o]^{dg1}$**
Dynamic Comparison Within attribute	**o^1 with o^2**	**$[o]^{b1}/[o]^{b2}$ and**
Between attributes	**o^1 with o^2**	**$[o]^{dg1}/[o]^{dg1}$**

Figure 8: A description of the Attribute Explorer

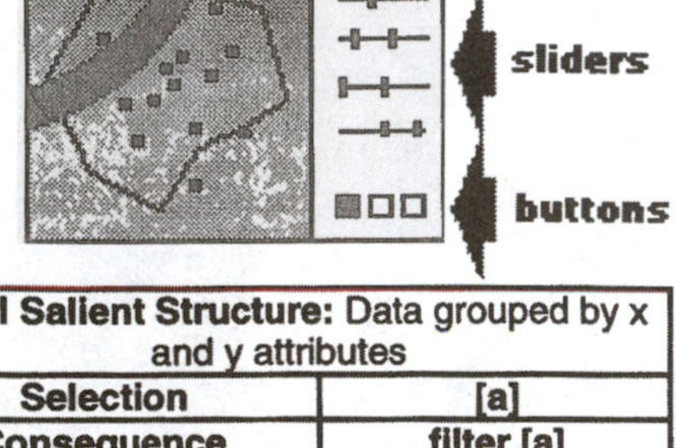

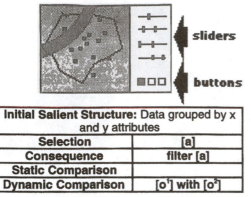

Initial Salient Structure: Data grouped by x and y attributes	
Selection	[a]
Consequence	filter [a]
Static Comparison	
Dynamic Comparison	[o1] with [o2]

Figure 9: The Dynamic Home Finder

The table in Figure 9 shows that the the interactive filtering does not facilitate any more perceptual comparison in the static display than the initial salient structure. However when a slider is moved (or a button pressed) the user can compare the effect of the current query result with the previous query ([o^1] with [o^2]).

LEARNING FROM DIVA DESCRIPTIONS

The cost of knowledge [10] in a display is likely to affect the use of a visualization. As Simon [37] reminds us, humans often satisfice i.e. they will expend the minimum effort to achieve a satisfactory answer. DIVA descriptions can be used to assess the cost of knowledge of a particular comparison.

If the comparison that a user wants to make is part of the initial salient structure of a visualization the comparison can be immediately seen and requires little work. However if the comparison requires work to be seen (i.e. the user must make a selection) then work is added to the cost. If the comparison requires dynamic rather than static comparisons to be performed then this requires a further cost. Thus the order of cost of knowledge is: Initial Salient Structure < Static Comparison < Dynamic Comparison.

The Dynamic Queries Interface described provides little static information to the user (although more recent implementations do provide more static information). However if one were to add additive encoding to the scatter plot display (and/or the sliders), so that data points that were close to satisfying the user's query were encoded, then this would reduce the cost of knowledge for searching for useful houses.

OVERVIEW

This paper has suggested a number of fairly simple ways to characterize interactive externalizations. These suggest a number of recommendations for design:

a) It is important to explicitly represent Input and Output relations. This provides an externalization of the current state of the interaction. This is important if the user is to engage in a dialogue with the visualization.

b) One should also consider these Input/Output relations over time. Both historical and potential information can be invaluable ways to keep up a dialogue with the user. Such representations have not yet been fully exploited

c) Another useful distinction might be between interaction performed by the user and that performed by a community. Chalmers et al [12] has just started exploring the visualization of such data. The growth of the World Wide Web, and the large amounts of communal information it can provide means that such meta data is becoming both available and useful.

d) The importance of exploiting novel forms of interactivity and data was also identified. We can form many rich displays using both indirect manipulation and meta data. I believe we still only have a very limeted understanding of the possibilities available to us.

e) This paper has very much ignored contextual information. Other frameworks might be useful for providing this perspective. For instance, Activity Theory might provide a valuable starting point for describing a visualization in its context of use [29].

This paper has attempted to provide an overview of a new and exciting area. It's main purposes are to encourage others *"to explore the space of the possible"* [16] and to stimulate discussion. As Green [21] has identified, HCI needs new vocabulary and concepts in order to raise the level of discussion about interfaces. Hopefully some of the descriptions presented here can help with that process.

ACKNOWLEDGMENTS

I am grateful to Bob Spence for many valuable discussions. Thanks also to the participants of AVI'96 & FADIVA (Gubbio) for stimulating conversations that contributed to the ideas expressed here.

REFERENCES

1. Ahlberg C. and Truve S. "Exploring Terra Incognita in the Design Space of Query Devices" Proceedings Engineering for Human Computer Interaction, EHCI'95, North Holland.

2. Ahlberg C., Williamson C. and Shneiderman, B. "Dynamic Queries for Information Exploration: An Implementation and Evaluation" Proceedings of CHI'92 pp. 619-626 ACM Press.

3. Becker R.A., Huber P.J., Cleveland W.S. and Wilks A.R. "Dynamic Graphics for Data Analysis", Stat. Science 2, 1987.

4. Bederson B., Hollan J.D., Perlin K., Meyer J., Bacon D. and Furnas G. " Pad++: A Zoomable Graphical Sketchpad for exploring Alternate Interface Physics" Journal of Visual Languages and Computing (1996) 7, pp. 3-31.

5. Benyon D. (1992) "Task analysis and sytem design: the discipline of data" Interacting with Computers 4 (1) 246-249

6. Bertin J. "Graphics and Graphic Information Processing" deGruyter Press, Berlin, 1977.

7. Bier E.A., Stone M.C., Fishkin K., Buxton W., Baudel T. "A Taxonomy of See-Through Tools" in Proceedings of CHI'94 pp. 358-364, ACM Press

8. Brooks, R. "Comparative Task Analysis: An Alternative Direction for Human-Computer Interaction Science" pp. 50-59, in "Designing Interaction" John M. Carroll (Ed), Cambridge University Press (1991)

9. Card S.K., Mackinlay J.D. and Robertson G.G " The Design Space of Input Devices" Proceedings of CHI'90, pp. 117-124 ACM Press.

10. Card S.K., Pirolli P. and Mackinlay J.D. "The Cost of Knowledge Characteristic Function: Display Evaluation for Direct-walk Dynamic Information Visualizations" Proceedings of CHI'94 ACM Press

11. Casner S. "A Task-Analytic Approach to the Automated Design of Graphic Presentations" ACM Transactions on Graphics 10, (2) pp. 111-151

12. Chalmers M., Ingram R. and Pfranger C. (1996) "Adding Imageability feature to Information Displays" Proceedings of UIST'96 pp

13. Dawkes H., Tweedie L.A. and Spence B. (1996) "VICKI-The Visualisation Construction Kit" in the Proceedings of Advanced Visual Interfaces '96, Gubbio, Italy.

14. Davidson C. "What your database hides away" New Scientist 9th January 1993

15. Draper S. "Display Managers as the Basis for User-Machine Communication" in (Eds) D. Norman and S. Draper *User Centered System Design* Lawrence Erlbaum Associates

16. Draper, S. "Critical Notice: Activity theory: the new direction for HCI?" IDIOMS (1993) pp. 812-821

17. Eick S.G. "Data Visualization Sliders" UIST'94 November pp. 119-120, ACM Press

18. Eick S.G., Steffen J.L. and Sumner E.E. "SeeSoft ™ - A Tool for Visualizing Line Oriented Software", IEEE Transactions on Software Engineering, pp. 11-18, 1992.

19. Eisenberg M. "The Thin Glass Line: Designing Interfaces to Algorithms" in Proceedings of CHI'96, ACM Press.

20. Furnas G.W. and Zacks J. "Multitrees: Enriching and Reusing Hierarchical Structure" In Proceedings of CHI'94, ACM Press

21. Green T.R.G. "Cognitive Dimensions of Notations" in A.Sutcliffe and L. Macaulay "People and Computers VI: Proceedings of HCI'89" Nottingham, pp 443-460, Cambridge University Press.

22. Green T.R.G. and Benyon D.R. "The skull beneath the skin: entity-relationship models of information artifacts" Int. J. Human Computer Studies (1996) 44 pp. 801-828

23. Howe D. "Data Analysis for Database Design", Edward Arnold 1983.

24. Inselberg A. "The plane with parallel coordinates", The Visual Computer 1, pp. 69-91, 1985.

25. Keim D.A. and Kriegal H. "VisDB: Database Exploration using Multidimensional Visualization", IEEE Computer Graphics and Applications September, pp. 40-49, 1994.

26. Larkin J.H. and Simon H. A. "Why a Diagram is (Sometimes) worth Ten Thousand Words" Cognitive Science 11 (1987) pp. 65-99

27. Lunzer A. `Reconnaissance: a widely applicable approach encouraging well-informed choices in computer-based tasks. Ph.D. thesis. TR-1996-4, Department of Computing Science, University of Glasgow, February 1996. 266pp.

28. Mihalisin T., Gawlinski E., Timlin J. and Schwegler J. "Visualizing Scalar Field on an N-dimensional Lattice", Proc. of Visualization 90, IEEE CS Press, pp. 255-262, 1990.

29. Nardi B.A. " Context and Consciousness" MIT Press 1996.

30. Nardi B.A. and Zarmer C.L. "Beyond Models and Metaphors: Visual Formalisms in User Interface Design", Journal of Visual Languages and Computing 4, pp. 5- 33, 1993.

31. Newton C.M. "Graphics: from alpha to omega in data analysis", in Graphical Representation of Multivariate Data, P.C.C. Wang (Ed) Academic Press, pp. 59-92, 1978.

32. Norman D. "The Psychology of Everyday Things" 1988, Basic Books.

33. Norman D.A. "Cognitive Artifacts" pp. 17-38 in "Designing Interaction" John Carroll (Ed), Cambridge Uni. Press (1991)

34.. Rao R. and Card S.K. "The Table Lens", Proceedings of CHI'94, Boston, ACM Press, pp. 318-322, 1994.

35. Robertson, G., Mackinlay J. and Card S.K. "Cone Trees: Animated 3D Visualizations of Hierarchical Information" Proceedings of CHI'91 pp. 189-194 ACM Press

36. Robertson, P.K. "A Methodology for choosing Data Representations" IEEE Computer Graphics and Applications May 1991 pp. 56-67.

37. Simon H.A. "The Sciences of the Artificial" MIT Press 1969

38. Smets G, Gaver W.W., Overbeeke C.J. and Stappers P.J. "Designing in Virtual Reality: Perception-Action Coupling and Form Semantics" Adjunct Proceedings INTERCHI'93.

39. Smith R. "Experiences with the Alternate Reality Kit: An Example of the Tension between Literalism and Magic" in the Proceedings of CHI and GI '87, ACM Press.

40. Spoerri A. "InfoCrystal: A visual tool for Information retrieval" Proceedings of Visualization '93 pp. 150-157.

41. Tukey J. "Exploratory Data Analysis" Reading, MA: Addison Wesley

42. Tweedie L.A. "Interactive Visualization Artifacts: how can abstractions inform design?", People and Computers X : Proc. of HCI'95 Huddersfield, (Eds) Kirby M.A.R., Dix A.J. and Finlay J.E., Cambridge University Press, pp. 247-265, 1995.

43. Tweedie L.A., Spence R., Bhoghal R. and Williams D. "The Attribute Explorer", ACM, Video Proceedings and Conference Companion, CHI'94, pp. 435-436, April 1994.

44. Tweedie L.A., Spence R., Dawkes H. and Su H. "Externalizing Abstract Mathematical Models" Proceedings of CHI'96 pp. 406-412 ACM Press

45. Vellman P. "The DataDesk Manual" Data Description Inc. Ithaca N.Y. 1985

46. Wilkinson L. "Enhancing Scatterplot Matrices" in Survey and Statistical Computing A.Westlake(Ed) Elsevier Science, 1992.

47. Williamson C. and Shneiderman B. "The Dynamic HomeFinder: Evaluating dynamic queries in a real estate information exploration system", ACM, Proceedings SIGIR'92, pp. 339-346, 1992.

48. Young D. and Shneiderman B. "A graphical filter/flow model for Boolean queries: An implementation and experiment" J. of the American Soc. for Information Science 44 (4) pp. 327-339

49. Young F.W, Faldowski R.A. and McFarlane M.M. "Multivariate Statistical Visualization" in C.R. Rao (Ed) Handbook of Statistics Vol. 9, Elsevier Science (1993)

50. Zhang J. "A representational analysis of relational information displays" International Journal of Human Computer Studies, 1996, 45, pp59-74

51. Zhang J. and Norman D.A. "Representations in Distributed Cognitive Tasks", Cognitive Science 18, pp. 87-122, 1994.

CHAPTER 8

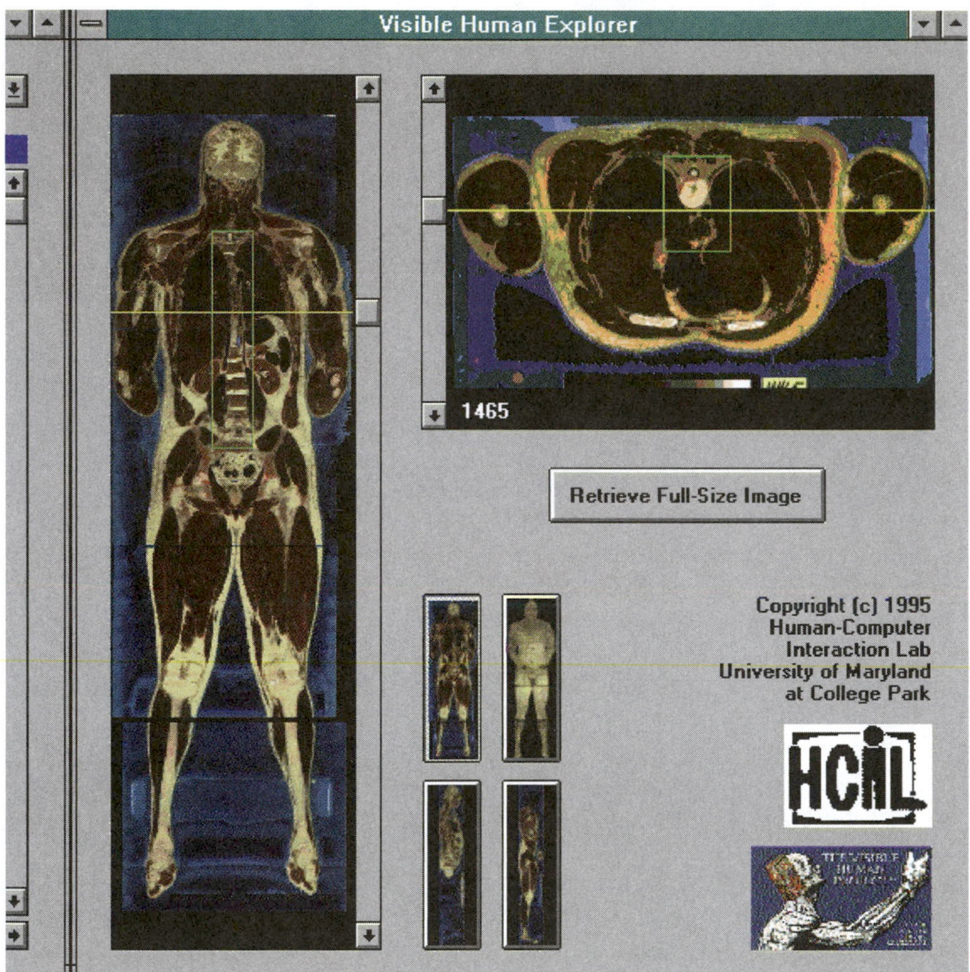

When there is no vision,
the people perish.

– Proverbs 29:18

Applications and Implications

INTRODUCTION

Galileo's telescopes and Leeuwenhoek's microscopes generated new opportunities for scientists that led to refined understandings of our world. Their innovative ways of seeing the physical world also opened numerous commercial possibilities. Similarly, the x-ray machine, computer-assisted tomography (CAT) scan, and magnetic resonance imagery (MRI) changed medical practice while aerial photography and then satellite-based remote imaging revolutionized military strategy, community planning, and crop management. Now the infoscopes and cyberscopes of information visualization are beginning to produce new understandings of the world around us and to create scientific and commercial possibilities.

Better scientific visualizations, models, and animations of physical worlds and 3D objects are important, as are multilayered maps of the geophysical world. We have much to learn from designers of scientific visualizations, computer-assisted design and manufacturing (CAD/CAM), and Geographic Information Systems (GIS). However, this book concentrates on visualizations of novel information worlds. These abstract information worlds include the directories and files on the hard disk of your computer, your medical history growing in folders at your doctor's office, and the collections of information spreading across the World Wide Web. In each case a visual presentation might give you an overview to know what is available and what is not. Then, with direct manipulation actions, you can navigate around the regions, zooming in or selecting when you want in more detail. An effective user interface would also allow you to filter out what you don't want, or mark and annotate objects for later study.

This basic process occurs in so many applications that it might be a visual information-seeking mantra for designers:

> Overview first, zoom and filter, then details-on-demand
> Overview first, zoom and filter, then details-on-demand
> Overview first, zoom and filter, then details-on-demand
> Overview first, zoom and filter, then details-on-demand
> Overview first, zoom and filter, then details-on-demand

The mantra is a useful starting point for design, but other tasks need support as well. Users need to explore relationships among objects, such as links that join Web pages or references that point to scientific articles. At least two further common tasks need support: extraction of objects for further examination or consultation with others, and history keeping to record the user's actions and results.

Other graphical user interface principles, such as "output becomes input," help designers remember that displays of information can also be an environment for input of new values. A graphical display of books on a library shelf can be used to click to get details on a book, drag to remove a book from circulation, shift-click to change the title of a book, or click on a new book template to add a book.

Some of these ideas are new, but there are many lessons to be learned from existing applications. Designers of air traffic control systems understood the necessity of a visual presentation for the demanding tasks of enforcing safe separation while supporting on-time arrivals. Their basic strategy was to provide a stable, high-resolution, plan-view display (overhead or god's-eye view) of aircraft locations coupled with indicators for aircraft headings and text for flight numbers and altitude. The work of air traffic controllers and pilots is stressful, making comprehensible, predictable, and controllable interfaces essential.

Many applications designers still have much to learn from the thoroughly researched and well-tested air traffic control system. It has much in common with GIS and scientific data visualization, but there are also lessons for designers of information visualizations, which is the focus of this book. Information visualization applications include statistical and categorical data, digital libraries, personal services, and other data (see Table 8.1 for a more thorough list).

APPLICATIONS

The definition of information visualization stressed three goals: discovery, decision making, and explanation. Powerful visual tools can support discovery; Galileo's telescope enabled him to discover the moons of Jupiter, and microscopes revealed the structure of cells. Now, information visualization tools are supporting drug discovery by pharmaceutical researchers and credit card fraud detection by financial analysts. Visual data mining complements the algorithmic approaches for exploring data warehouses. Surprising patterns that appear in data sets can sometimes be found by

TABLE **8.1**

Applications of information visualization.

Statistical and Categorical Data
Census, health, labor, economic, and other demographic data
Stocks, bonds, bank accounts, currency trading
Sales by region, product, salesperson, customer
Manufacturing process supervision
Drug, chemical, material attributes
Digital Libraries
Books, films, videos, photos, maps, manuscripts, audio recordings
Patents, scientific journal articles, legal citations and statutes
Newspaper and magazine articles
Scientific and social science data sets
World Wide Web pages
Personal Services
Travel info on airlines, trains, hotels, restaurants
Classified ads for homes, real estate, jobs
Consumer comparisons of cars, TVs
Sports statistics
Entertainment events
Complex Documents
Biography, resume, annual report
Book, film, video, manuscript, audio recording
Patent, scientific article, treaty, contract
Software module, data structure
Histories
Medical patient histories
Student, sales client, legal case, employment histories
Economic trends, stocks
Project management, Gantt charts, PERT-CPM
Classifications
Library subject headings, animal species, patent listings
Tables of contents, organization charts, family trees
Hard disk data directories
Budgets, sales
Networks
Telecommunications connections and usage
Highways, pipelines, electronic circuits
Scientific articles or legal citations
Social structures, organizational relationships

algorithms, but visual presentations can lead to deeper understanding and novel hypotheses. These in turn can be checked with algorithmic processes such as cluster analysis, factor analysis, hierarchical decomposition, or multidimensional scaling.

More common applications of information visualization are for decision making. These might be for personal tasks such as finding a videotape or choosing a travel itinerary, or for business decisions such as finding a stock or locating a new sales office. Many of these tasks are repetitive, but new requirements and availability of products guarantee that the decision-making process is a creative challenge.

Information visualization also serves to explain processes in ways that may lead to better predictions or to provocative insights, which can become the basis for action. Views of pollution data across a region may explain how a power plant's emissions are tied to daily or seasonal cycles. Visualizations of data access patterns on the World Wide Web may explain why congestion occurs in the early afternoon at a given server.

The breadth of applications for information visualization is large and growing. As creative users push the limits of current tools, designers will be pressed to provide ever greater functionality. This snapshot and taxonomy of applications will change in the coming years, but it is meant to portray some of the possibilities.

Statistical and Categorical Data

Information visualization provides significant advantages that complement spreadsheets, statistical packages, and data mining tools (Cleveland, 1993, 1994; Wainer, 1997). Starting with tabular information is convenient because each object is neatly represented as one row of the table and each attribute becomes a column. This simplifies movement of data across software packages and leads to natural representations such as tables (Rao and Card, 1994 ●), 2D or 3D scatterplots (Ahlberg and Wistrand, 1995a; Buja, Cook, and Swayne, 1996) (Figure 8.1), multidimensional spaces (Feiner and Beshers, 1990b ●; Keim and Kriegal, 1994 ●; Tweedie et al., 1996 ●), innovative representations such as parallel coordinates (Inselberg, 1997 ●) (Figure 8.2), or combinations (Berkin and Orton, 1994; Roth et al., 1996; Livny et al., 1997).

Users of statistical and categorical data are often seeking to discover specific objects that best match their requirements, such as scientists who are looking for drugs, chemicals, or materials with high solubility, low melting point, and low toxicity. Financial analysts may be trying to find the best stocks to buy based on high dividends, low price/earnings ratios, and low volatility (Figure 8.3). Sales managers may be trying to find products that are selling well to high-income, youthful consumers in suburban regions.

However, users with statistical and categorical data may also be seeking to understand patterns, for example, clinical researchers who are studying decreased white blood cell counts in patients with varying dosages of medication. Manufacturing supervisors may be looking for low yields in chip manufacturing in relation to temperature variations, and economists may be hunting for changes in unemployment as a function of inflation indicators.

Digital Libraries

Information visualization enhances browsing by presenting more choices in a compact and meaningful overview, and complements searching by helping users understand the distribution of search results (Pirolli et al., 1996 ●; Plaisant et al., 1997; Rao et al., 1995). General libraries might contain books, films, videos, photos, maps, manuscripts, or audio

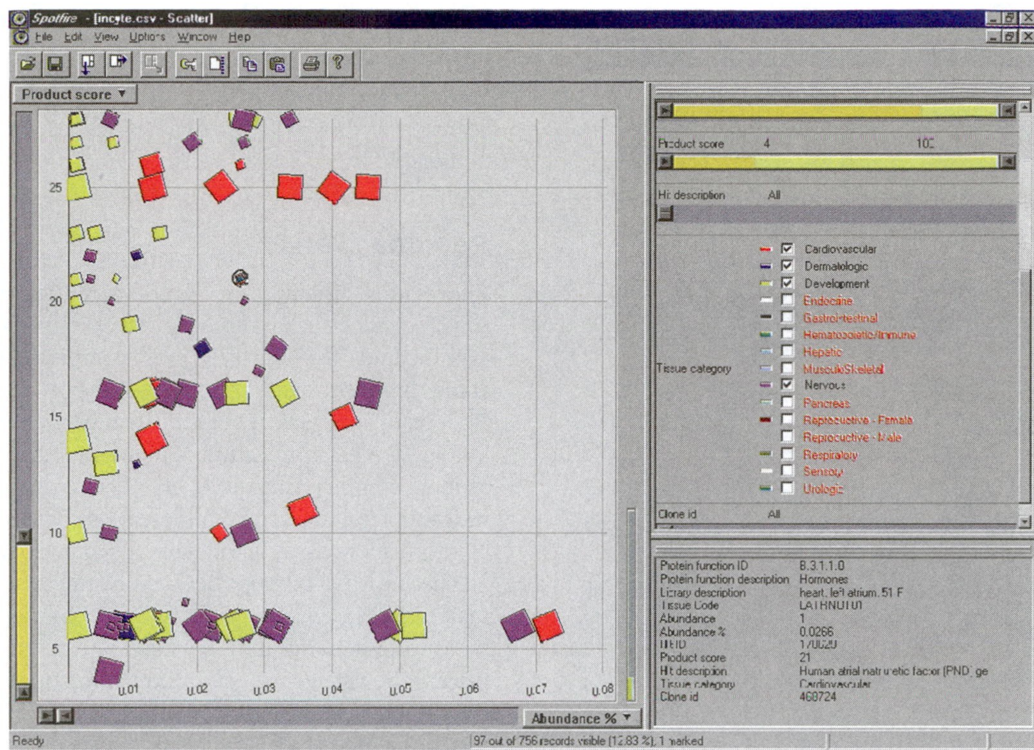

FIGURE **8.1**

Visualization of human genome samples with Spotfire (http://www.spotfire.com). The user wants to identify strong contenders for doing biological testing in drug discovery. Location, color, size, and rotation have been used to code five variables while additional variables are manipulated by sliders and buttons on the right.

recordings, and specialized libraries might focus on patents, scientific journal articles, and legal citations and statutes. Other popular libraries might contain collections of newspaper or magazine articles or personal collections such as in Presidential libraries. Important applications that are often listed under the digital library concept are scientific databases and archives such as NASA's remote-sensing environmental data sets.

Showing all the items in a library with millions of objects at one time is not feasible with today's displays. However, even larger libraries can be accommodated with interactive techniques such as representing hundreds of collections first, and then zooming in or jumping to a display of the contents of a selected collection.

Users of digital libraries may be interested to browse it just to find out what is available, but more often they are seeking one or more objects to satisfy an information need. Browsing questions ("What's available about European immigrants to the U.S. in the 1890s?") are vaguer while known-item searches have specific answers ("Find the author of *The Name of the Rose*"). Browsing questions are often best answered by exploration, while known-item searches often can be answered with a typed query.

Searches by keywords are attractive if users are familiar with the terms and know what they are after. However, often users submit queries and get a zero-hit or a mega-hit result set with little guidance as to how to proceed. To cope with this problem, query previews can indicate the cardinality of the result set (Doan, Plaisant, and Shneiderman, 1996; Tanin, Beigel, and Shneiderman, 1997). Query previews are especially appealing when presented as an information visualization technique in which attribute values are shown with an accompanying bar whose length indicates the size of the result set (Figure 8.4). For example, in a NASA environmental data library, users can select from 13 time ranges, 17 geographic regions, and 13 parameter values. The bars next to each attribute value change as selections are made, to show, for example, that there are no Radiance data sets for South America before 1970. At the bottom a preview bar is used to show the size of the result set for the current query. When the result set is an acceptable size, the user can move on to the query refinement phase.

Previews are nicely complemented by overviews that are constructed by representing each object in the collection in a 2D display. It then might show time along the X-axis and a meaningful variable such as size, quality, or cost along the Y-axis. The early FilmFinder (Ahlberg and Shneiderman, 1994c ●) used year of production along the X-axis and popularity (measured by video store rentals) or length in minutes along the Y-axis. Another strategy is to show relevance along one or both axes. For example, news articles might be organized by relevance to sports along the X-axis and relevance to

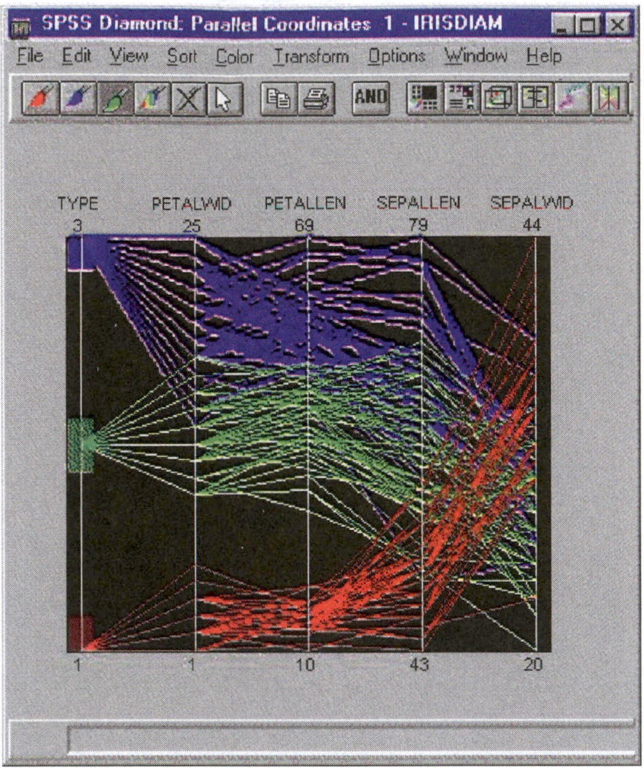

FIGURE **8.2**

Fisher's Iris data were first used by Ronald Fisher in an article motivating the statistical technique of discriminant analysis. This parallel coordinates display in SPSS Diamond shows four discriminating variables—petal and sepal length and petal and sepal width—and three species of iris.

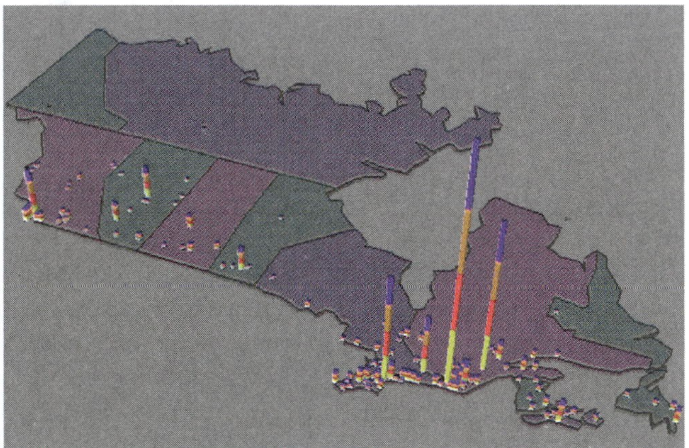

FIGURE **8.3**

This visualization from Visible Decisions (http://www.vdi.com) uses a combination of 3D graphics and interactive queries and filtering to permit users to view performance across Canada (or any other geographic region for that matter) in an intuitive manner.

business along the Y-axis. Then stories about sales of a team would appear along the diagonal.

Sophisticated mathematical techniques for mapping a multidimensional document space into two or three dimensions have been used by many researchers, but critics complain that these displays mislead users since similar items may or may not be close to one another (Chalmers and Chitson, 1992; Hemmje, Kunkel, and Willett, 1994; Kim and Korfhage, 1994; Lin, 1995 ●; Olsen et al., 1993; Wise et al., 1995 ●).

Personal Services

Information visualization has the potential to facilitate personal services such as finding travel information, scanning classified ads for homes or jobs, comparing offers for consumer products, exploring sports statistics, and browsing collections of entertainment events (Ahlberg and Shneiderman, 1994c ●). This application is likely to expand dramatically as more commercial services are offered on the Internet. The next Yahoo! or amazon.com is likely to come from application of information visualization methods to personal services.

This task is complex because of the many criteria that may form the basis for a query. For example, users' priority in finding a home may be location, neighborhood, size, price, schools, age, or condition (Williamson and Shneiderman, 1992). Flexible search strategies are helpful and easy relaxation of queries is usually appreciated to see if there is a slightly more expensive house in a nearby neighborhood that would satisfy the users. Another challenge is that many of the users are first-time users of this application, and they may have less than average computing experience. However, users are often very motivated to carry out their searches since they directly benefit from the results.

Airline reservations seem like a good candidate for visualization because the complex criteria or geography, time, and cost are conveniently represented in visualizations (Casner, 1991). A map could be used to pick departure and arrival cities and a calendar for the date. Then alternative flight times and the cost could be shown visually by bars of varying length for time and thickness or color for cost.

Complex Documents

While visualization has often been applied for collections of similar objects, it can also be effective in collections of disparate objects that may occur in complex documents. For example, a biography may contain a textual report, quotations, lists of dates and accomplishments, maps with residences, photos, audio recordings, and more. Similarly a film may contain hundreds of segments with different content and meaning. Some documents such as patents have a required structure that can support effective searching and browsing.

The tasks associated with complex documents are varied, but lawyers studying a contract or a scientist reviewing an article often begin by trying to gain an overview of what is included and its size to determine if further browsing is warranted (Robertson and Mackinlay, 1993; Hearst, 1995). Readers often begin by viewing previews such as abstracts or tables of contents (Egan et al., 1989; Chimera and Shneiderman, 1994) and then jump into sections. They may page through quickly, use keyword searches to find specific items,

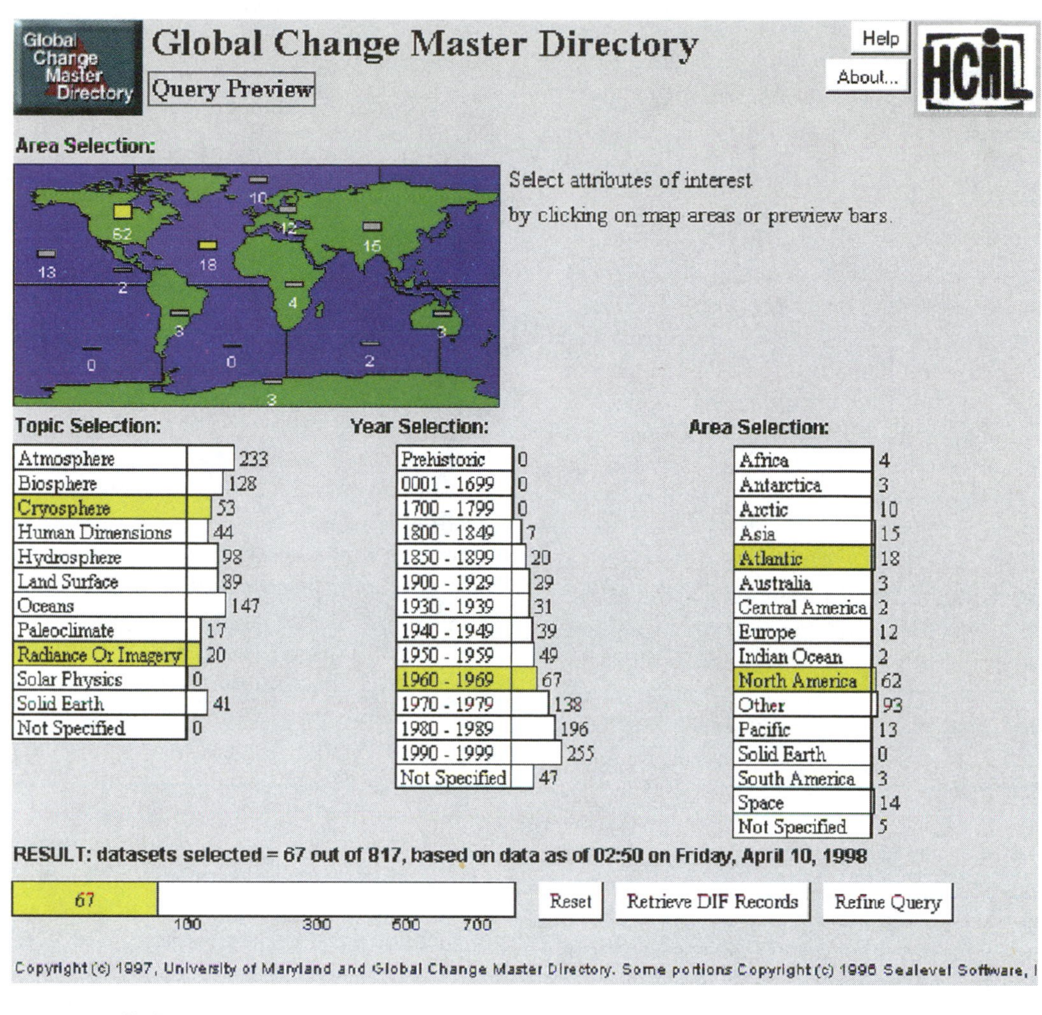

FIGURE **8.4**

NASA's Global Change Master Directory applies query previews to showing users which data sets are available according to topics, years, and areas. In this example, (Radiance OR Imagery OR Cryosphere) AND (North America OR Atlantic) AND 1960–1969 would yield 67 data sets.

extract sections for later study, or compare the contents of a section to other documents. Annotations and bookmarks are valuable in returning to previously found material.

A special case of complex documents is software. Programmers often need to review large programs written by others in order to make modifications or repair bugs. This intellectually challenging task can be facilitated by having overviews of an entire system (Eick, Steffen, and Sumner, 1992) with adjustable color coding to reveal features of the code, data, comments, or execution history. A related task is browsing data structures, which could be input data streams, stored databases, or dynamic data structures. Sometimes animated displays have been helpful for professionals and students, but these must be tediously programmed for each situation.

Histories

The lessons of the past are so important that it is natural to expect that information visualizations would facilitate exploration of historical data. For example, medical patient histories may capture 10,000 events in a 100-year life span, ranging from long-term chronic problems such as arthritis or obesity, to accidents, surgeries, or vaccinations (Plaisant et al., 1996; Lindwarm et al., 1998). The data is complex because it includes doctors' notes, prescriptions, blood test results, x-rays, sonograms, electrocardiograms, and so on. Physicians are usually interested in recent events, but information about earlier surgeries, vaccinations, or blood pressure history often influences treatment decisions. Getting an overview and then zooming in on objects of interest to get details-on-demand is a common process.

Similar scenarios could be envisioned with personal history overviews of student performance, legal cases, or employment. Overviews of temporal data are already common in economics or stock performance analysis to spot trends, identify cyclic patterns, and forecast future activity (Hibino and Rundensteiner, 1997; Mackinlay, Robertson, and Card, 1991; Sanderson et al., 1992).

Another category of temporal data presentation is with project management. Current software enables users to explore thousands of interrelated steps in the construction of a large building. A key task is to see which tasks are on the critical path; that is, a delay in these tasks would cause a delay in completion of the project.

Classifications

Classifications are ubiquitous because they help organize complex information in a way that hierarchically differentiates objects and reduce the amount of information that users need to cope with at any time. Classification hierarchies for biological species go back to the Swedish botanist Linnaeus, whose *Systema Naturae* was published in 1735. Modern hierarchies can be complex: the U.S. Library of Congress subject headings fill 24 volumes and the Library of Medicine Medical Subject Headings (MeSH) contain more than 14,000 terms at seven levels.

Tree-structured classifications are common in tables of contents of books, organization charts, and family trees. Users often start at the root and browse through the tree, trying to grasp the overall structure, while noting highlights or scanning and marking specific objects.

Tree-structured organizations for computer directories and files (or folders and documents) with tens of thousands of nodes have become common, but browsing strategies are usually limited to 40–80 nodes at a time. Getting an overview that enables users to find large old files or spot duplicates could be accomplished with appropriate information visualization tools. Among the many proposals are node-link diagrams that spread out in a planar presentation (Kumar, Plaisant, and Shneiderman, 1997 ●); cone trees that use circular presentations in a 3D space (Robertson, Mackinlay, and Card, 1991; Carrière and Kazman, 1995); treemaps that use space-filling 2D presentations (Shneiderman, 1992b; Johnson and Shneiderman, 1991 ●; Asahi, Turo, and Shneiderman, 1995); hyperbolic trees (Lamping and Rao, 1996 ●); and CHEOPS, a pyramid of overlapping triangles (Beaudoin, Parent, and Vroomen, 1996).

Classifications vary greatly in size (total number of nodes, number of levels, fan-out at each level) and complexity (fixed-level balanced binary trees with similar nodes throughout to arbitrary depth and fan-out and distinct node types at every level). Flexible visualization tools are needed to accommodate this diversity in structure and the tasks that users have. Tasks can deal with

topology only

How many nodes?

What is the highest fan-out of any node?

How far is the deepest node from the root?

Which level has the most nodes?

Which subtree of the root has the most nodes?

nodes with names

What are the names of all the nodes from the root to node x?

What are the names of all nodes at level three?

What are the names of all leaf nodes?

What are the names of all children of node z?

nodes with names and attributes

Which node has the largest size?

Find all nodes whose age is older than 90 days.

Which region of a sales hierarchy has the greatest volume?

Are there any nodes that have identical attributes?

Networks

Networks become necessary when a tree structure is inadequate to capture the complex relationships among objects. Each node in a rooted tree structure has only one parent, except the root node, which has no parents. Each node in a network can be linked to multiple nodes, and there is rarely a single root. Nodes and links can have multiple attributes, and there may even be multiple links between pairs of nodes and a direction for flow along each link. More complex situations may be represented by networks of trees, or trees of networks (Becker, Eick, and Wilks, 1995 ●; Eick and Wills, 1993).

Networks can represent social structures among a dozen people or vast telecommunications systems with millions of nodes. Highway systems, pipelines, or electronic circuits are common network structures for which flows along links are more important than attributes of nodes. Interesting questions that are computationally difficult include shortest paths between pairs of nodes, maximum flow possible between pairs of nodes, or most efficient path to traverse all nodes (traveling salesman problem).

Another family of network problems include scientific article references or legal citations (Mackinlay, Rao, and Card, 1995) (Figure 8.5). Scientists may want to trace back from a given article to see the articles it references, and repeat this procedure to find the sources of an idea. They may want to go forward to see who references the given article and what work it has influenced. Similarly lawyers must search back in time to find precedents for a decision and look forward to see if the decision was overturned or confirmed.

A major application of network visualization is to hypertexts (Brown, 1989; Utting and Yankelovich, 1989) and the World Wide Web (Andrews, 1995 ●; Mukherjea, Foley, and Hudson, 1995; Card, Robertson, and York, 1996; Kandogan and Shneiderman, 1997; Nation et al., 1997) (Figure 8.6). Some projects attempt to visualize the entire Web, just one Web site, the results of a search, the neighborhood around the current Web page, or the set of pages visited by a user. Relationships among Web pages may be strong or weak, based on common themes or explicit links, and a common project is to show the frequency of traversals over a day or month period.

Information visualization of networks is a major challenge because of the elaborate topology, the large numbers

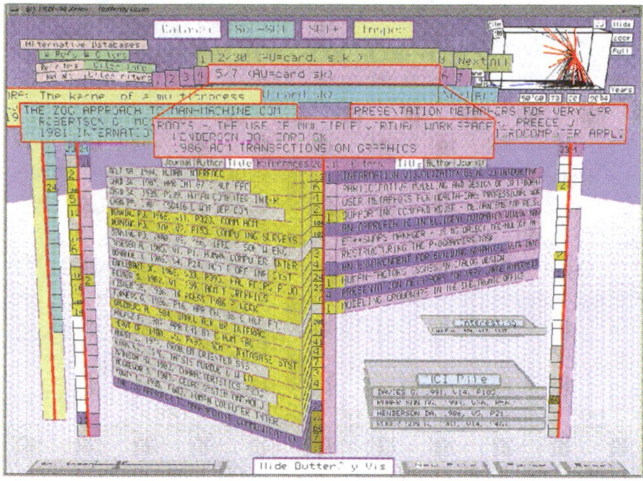

FIGURE **8.5**

This snapshot shows the Butterfly visualizer application for searching citation links. Link-generating queries support automatic creation of asynchronous query processes that grow a visualization of the search space. Metaphorically, the Butterfly visualization is like an informtion landscape that can be watched and pruned by the user to grow the search in fruitful directions (Mackinlay, Rao, and Card, 1995, Plate 1).

of nodes, and the complexity of the tasks. Even with small numbers of nodes (less than 100), the layout may become cluttered and the relationships hidden. Planar layouts are desirable but not always realizable. Three-dimensional visualizations are appealing at first glance, but the complexity of navigation may lead to disorientation, which interferes with successful task completion. Nodes and links may be so numerous that they occlude relevant information. User control to limit the number of nodes displayed seems an essential part of an effective user interface. Nodes or links could be restricted to only those connected to a given node or those whose attributes satisfy certain criteria. Major challenges exist for information visualization researchers who wish to make browsing of networks convenient.

LIMITATIONS AND CAUTIONS

Information visualization is a major development that is already having substantial influence. It will open possibilities for many people, but it has limitations that need to be addressed.

By its name and definition, information visualization is for sighted people. Those with no or limited vision will not be able to use these powerful tools. However, there is a parallel movement on the theme of *sonification* or *audiolization*

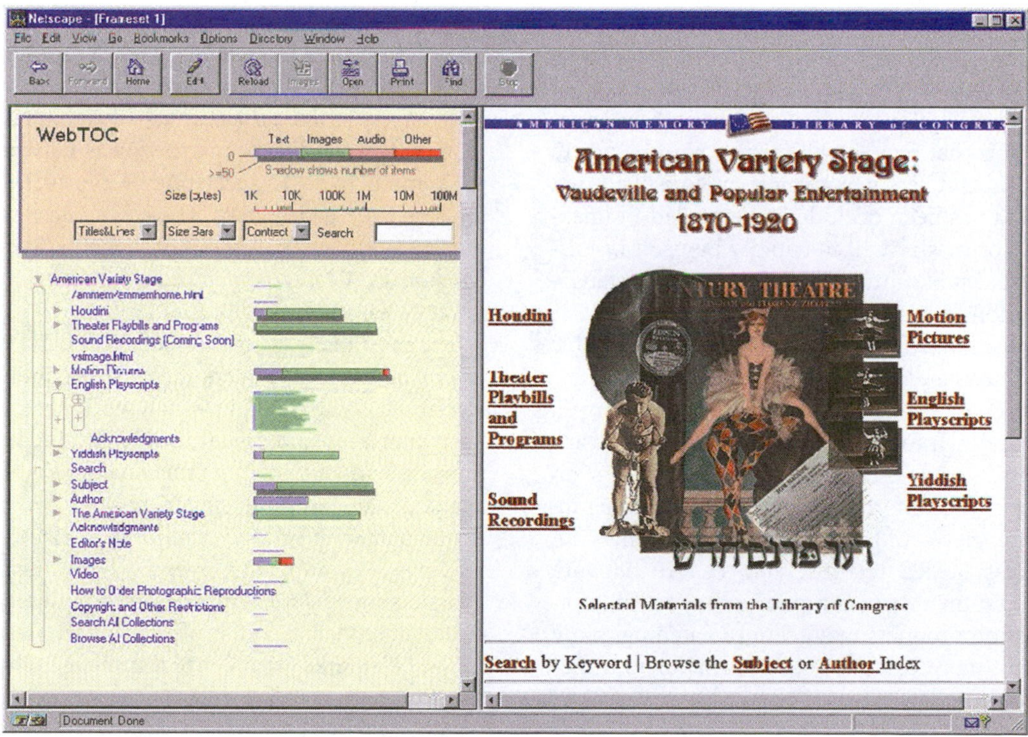

FIGURE **8.6**

WebTOC occupies the frame to the left of the home page it represents: the American Memory collection entitled "American Variety Stage: Vaudeville and Popular Entertainment 1870–1920." The top portion is a legend and control panel for WebTOC. Links are listed with a bar that represents the volume of information available when following that link. Users can then expand the hierarchy (e.g., here "English Playscripts" has been expanded and the labels removed to compare file sizes).

that seeks to create auditory equivalents of visualization tools. In fact, some argue that our auditory capabilities have unique features that may complement human visual abilities. The capacity to pick up outliers, akin to the missed note in a symphony performance, may be greater in sonic environments. Second, auditory information is omnidirectional and therefore easily heard even when the users' attention is not focused on it. Audiolizations may be effective for long-term monitoring tasks and for attention getting when anomalies appear. One medical lab worker described a system that played the sound of lab results through a speaker, allowing the staff to move about freely. When they heard an anomaly, they would come over and examine the sample in greater detail. A third advantage of audiolizations may be their use in telephone-based systems. Users might be able to listen to a symphony of sounds representing the stock market or their portfolio, and they could recognize significant patterns that required further attention.

Another concern about information visualization is that many users may not be visually oriented. They may prefer textual or numerical data formats in scrolling lists rather than visual presentations. This matches user preferences for textual instructions rather than a map. Preferences do not always align with performance, and some users do better with visual presentations, even if they have a low preference for them. High-density displays, richly packed with useful information, may make some users anxious, giving them feelings of information overload. Many users will need training in and accommodation to the user interfaces for information visualization, just as they did for graphical user interfaces.

As with any new technique, a great danger with information visualization is that people will misuse it and come to incorrect conclusions. Users may misinterpret displays, not realizing that data has been occluded or encoded in unexpected ways. Color or size will inevitably be used in misleading ways, just as it has throughout the history of statistical data presentation.

Likely but preventable frustrations will be incompatible formats for data, nonstandard widgets, and inconsistent terminology. A successful industry is more likely to emerge if designers of competing products can agree soon about using common formats, widgets, and terminology. Open standards have proven to be enormously successful in other information technologies—for example, Unix file formats, Library of Congress MARC records, and TCP/IP network protocols. Cooperation among competing vendors of information visualization products may seem threatening, but it is likely to benefit more companies and consumers if they can agree on some standards.

IMPLICATIONS

It is hard to predict the future, but some guesses may help shape decisions about research directions and applications. The continuing shift from textual to graphical user interfaces enables more people to accomplish more ambitious tasks. Students will have remarkable access to databases and libraries that will enable them to explore data and access the literature in ways that were only possible for advanced researchers just a few decades ago. Census data that was only available to specialists will be accessible to students, teachers, journalists, and curious citizens. Primary sources such as Presidential libraries, national archives, photographic databases, and commercial records will be searchable from homes, schools, and businesses.

Scientific and information visualizations are likely to expand from complex applications for a few specialists to popular tools for most computer users. While air traffic control or drug discovery are specialist tasks, spin-off technologies should enable people to plan car trips, get personalized weather forecasts, search for consumer products, and find a new home.

Personal services are likely to be the largest area of commercial applications. Today, schedule information is relayed to most travelers by agents using telephones to give departure and arrival times with flight numbers and prices. Most users are given limited choices, but soon improved visual presentations are likely to enable more customers to make their own reservations. Instead of typing in dates and times, users should be able to smoothly select a range and immediately see the possibilities with the costs. Similarly, home buyers may bypass real estate agents and find it more convenient to mark their geographic choices, drag for a price range, and mark house sizes to generate a set of candidate houses on a map. Then a click would produce pictures and a house tour. The process of *disintermediation*—the elimination of middlemen or agents—has been growing as networks spread, but the trend is likely to accelerate as information visualization tools become widespread. The economic efficiency of direct buying is substantial, yielding benefits for producers and consumers. Closer contact can improve information flow, lower costs, and provide better feedback.

The most likely profession for substantial change is medicine. Current record keeping is just beginning to move into electronic databases, but much work needs to be done on user interfaces and visualizations for presenting information. Individual patient histories will be more conveniently available, enabling physicians to see a complete history of major surgeries on one screen and select blood pressure readings for comparison over a 70-year life span. Allergies, genetic abnormalities, injuries, and preferences will all become more visible to the physician, whose treatment plan might be entered with a visual language. Physician and organizational records could become more visible, enabling patients, medical evaluators, or accountants to do comparisons or find outstanding (or poor) performers. Clinical research across tens of thousands of patients will become feasible, allowing flu epidemics or food poisonings to be spotted earlier and permitting research to be done on outcomes of treatments on selected populations.

Legal research is already quite computerized and sophisticated, but information visualization is likely to provide more thorough and appropriate sets of precedents and statutes. Following the rich network of citations from a known case back in time to find related precedents or forward in time to see if the case was overthrown may improve the quality of legal arguments. Visual overviews of cases may help lawyers and judges follow complex proceedings, crime sequences, and defendant histories.

Financial analysts are also heavy computer users, but their search tools generally yield textual lists or the occasional retrospective chart of stock prices or interest rates. Newspapers and financial reports, largely designed for printing on paper, stress compact coded numerical data, but the dynamics of the screen favor more visual displays. Dynamic queries to filter out unwanted data and show groups of candidate stocks, bonds, or currency trades might produce even more competitive markets and more investor participation.

Scientific users are likely to become even more sophisticated in their approaches to research. So much data will be available that many scientists will be able to work only by reprocessing or exploring previously collected data. Conducting experiments to find new drugs will still be necessary, but drug discovery will shift more and more to the computer. Chemical compounds will be more easily searchable from vast databases of known molecular structures and their physical properties (solubility, melting point, acidity, etc.). Drug effects will be evaluated in every patient who uses it, leading to earlier detection of negative side effects and positive spin-offs. Environmental databases are likely to be a major technical challenge. The huge amounts of data available to researchers is inviting, but the difficulty of detecting complex phenomena on a global basis is daunting. Can the impact of increasing atmospheric carbon dioxide on mean temperatures or ocean levels be detected in the turbulence of daily and seasonal changes?

The tools of information visualization are likely to become common as components of word processors and spreadsheets. While early tools are independent applications, the future is likely to favor integration into existing applications. Word-processor designers will add visualization tools for complex documents, and spreadsheet designers will add starfields, parallel coordinates, or glyphs to help show data patterns. Sales management or survey analysis packages will also weave in appropriate visualizations in graceful and evolutionary ways. Patent lawyers or labor negotiators will find that their software becomes more visual. Problems will remain, but more users will have better visual tools for coping.

CHALLENGES

The proliferation of designs indicates a lively field, but many designs are poor. Evaluations by users, field tests within companies, usability tests of new products, and controlled experimentation will all contribute to the refinement of information visualizations. This section describes several issues that influence many information visualization situations.

Two- vs. Three-Dimensional Presentations

One of the popular debates in information visualization circles is about 2D versus 3D presentations (Robertson, Card, and Mackinlay, 1993 ●; Tufte, 1983, 1990, 1997). Proponents of 2D presentations point out that the screen is two dimensional and our visual perceptions are based on seeing only a 2D projection of the 3D world. They make two technology arguments: users are familiar with paper presentations, and 2D presentations can be faster on computers. They also make cognitive and perceptual arguments: 2D presentations are simpler, and occlusion is less of a problem.

Promoters of 3D presentations point out that the real world is three dimensional and that our experience is based on movement in three dimensions. They argue that the technology will soon make realistic 3D displays available on every computer, complete with lighting models, shadows, texture, and real-time animation. They claim that 3D pointing devices and better control widgets will enable smooth navigation without disorientation. On the cognitive and perceptual issues, they claim that there is more space available on the screen when it represents 3D objects, thereby permitting more information to be displayed.

Argumentative debaters see a winner-take-all contest, while compromisers argue that there is room for both, and that users should be allowed to choose based on their preferences or the task. A more productive path might be to identify the components or features of 2D or 3D designs that promote comprehensibility, predictability, and control and support problem solution.

A more detailed analysis might separate out the wide range of 3D applications that have been proposed:

- Immersive Virtual Environment
  - with head-mounted stereo display, body and head tracking, glove control for flying
  - applied to virtual wind tunnel, electrostatic charge fields, gas molecules
- Semi-immersive Virtual Environment
  - with special glasses to see onscreen stereo display, handheld 3D navigation device
  - or large-screen projections on one or more walls
  - applied to storm simulations, crystal growth, bone structure
- Desktop 3D for 3D worlds
  - with 3D objects on a 2D display, handheld 3D navigation device
  - applied to medical, architecture, manufacturing design
- Desktop 3D for artificial worlds
  - with familiar 3D worlds to represent information
  - applied to library shelves, file cabinets, shopping malls

- Desktop 3D for novel information spaces
  with cone/cam trees, perspective wall, WebBook, 3D scatterplot
  applied to cityscapes, landscapes, themescapes, walls, rooms
- Chartjunk 3D (dimensional puffery)
  eye-catching and appealing but slows users with distracting pixels
  applied to bar charts, pie charts, histograms, icons

A deeper understanding is beginning to emerge from empirical studies. User preference for some 3D displays of bar charts or other business graphics was found, but performance speed and accuracy may degrade (Spence, 1990; Carswell, Frankenberger, and Bernhard, 1991; Levy et al., 1996). Network data structures were found to be more effective in 3D rather than 2D versions (Ware and Franck, 1996), but tree structures were found to be more useful in 2D versions (Poblete, 1995). A study of a three-level menu hierarchy with 121 items found no benefit for 3D over 2D versions, but both visual forms were better recalled than textual lists (Sutcliffe and Patel, 1996). As more studies are done, appropriate independent and dependent variables will be found.

Overview + Detail vs. Focus + Context

A second popular debate in information visualization is about strategies for dealing with large information spaces such as in maps, large networks or trees, and lengthy timelines. One approach is to zoom in on a selected point by jumping to the next level of detail, or preferably by moving smoothly with an animated transition (Bederson and Hollan, 1994 ●). Zooming is simple for users to understand, but users lose the overview after they have zoomed in and the mechanism for zooming out is not always apparent.

Strategies that allow users to maintain an overview and simultaneously examine details are strongly preferred. The *overview + detail* strategy is to keep an overview in one window and show a detail view in a second view. The overview window contains a field-of-view box that indicates what is shown in the detail view, and acts as a widget, enabling users to change the contents of the detail view (Plaisant, Carr, and Shneiderman, 1995; Eick, Steffen, and Sumner, 1992; Jerding and Stasko, 1995a, 1995b). Users like the stable overview, but critics suggest that integrating the two views is cognitively difficult for some viewers.

A second family of strategies, *focus + context,* is to show details at a focus point that is kept in the context of the overview. The bifocal view (Spence and Apperley, 1982 ●) proposed a magnified area, leaving the remainder with a lower level of detail, and led to applications such as the perspective wall (Robertson, Card, and Mackinlay, 1993 ●). An alternate conception, the fisheye view, had varying levels of magnification around a focal point with a degree of interest function (DOI) controlling how much is elided as the distance grows from the focal point (Furnas, 1986; Sarkar and Brown, 1994). Using a hyperbolic DOI function, large hierarchies could be explored in a fixed circular screen space (Lamping and Rao, 1996 ●). These magnification or distortion strategies are appealing visually, but critics complain about the greater potential for disorientation.

Refinements of these strategies are emerging in new applications, and some empirical investigations are sharpening our understanding of the benefits (Schaffer et al., 1996). A deeper understanding of task sequences and frequencies will also help designers. An important metric is the zoom factor, the ratio of length of the diagonal (in pixels) in the detail view to the length of the diagonal in the field-of-view box. In the focus + context strategy, the zoom factor is the ratio of an object's diagonal in the focus area to the object's diagonal in the context area. Typical zoom factors in papers on overview + detail strategies are 5–15, while in focus + context papers it is 2–5, although the hyperbolic tree supports higher zoom factors.

The scalability of these techniques is also in question. Overview + detail strategy can be applied repeatedly to support zoom factors of 100 or 1000. Combinations of these strategies are also possible, and refinements are still needed to create landmarks, follow paths, return to previous viewpoints, annotate objects, and automate common action sequences.

Reengineering the Desktop

Information visualization is likely to contribute to dramatic changes to the desktop. The independent overlapping windows strategy has been the commercial mainstay since 1984 when the Apple Macintosh was introduced. As screens have grown larger and tasks more complex, new possibilities are being explored. The capacity to manage groups of windows was addressed by the Rooms strategy in which users could move among many clusters of independent overlapping windows (Henderson and Card, 1986). Variations of this theme have been implemented in commercial systems under the term "workspaces" or "virtual desktops." Hierarchical nesting of window clusters and a tiled approach were implemented in Elastic Windows (Kandogan and Shneiderman, 1998). For complex tasks with many windows, the Elastic Windows strategy offers multiple-window open/close, resize, and move. In a study of programming tasks, 12 knowledgeable users had significantly faster performance, especially as task complexity grew.

Three-dimensional worlds of action have been tried in some commercial systems and in the WebBook and Web forager research prototype (Card, Robertson, and York, 1996). WebBook users can flip pages in the book, place a book on the desk or bookshelf, and bring related books nearby. In theory, users are familiar with 3D worlds and should be able to navigate easily. A second argument is that three dimensions offers more space to place objects, so more of them can be close at hand. Critics complain that navigation is still not easy in three dimensions, and that occlusion is a serious problem.

Another increasingly popular strategy is to make zooming a primary mechanism for navigation. These so-called multiscale interfaces, such as Perspecta and Pad++ (Bederson and Hollan, 1994 ●), enable users to zoom into a text grouping and see expanding detailed presentations of related materials. This approach could be used to replace the overlapped windows design by placing all user files and folders on the desktop. As the user zooms in on a folder, it gets larger and then reveals the objects it contains. This process can be repeated to arbitrary depths. Smooth zooming is an appealing strategy, but variable-sized objects may be disorienting.

Other desktop strategies emerge from choosing an organization based on usage. The Personal Role Management strategy (Shneiderman and Plaisant, 1994; Plaisant and Shneiderman, 1995) organizes the desktop according to the many roles that an individual has in an organization. Each role has a schedule, a hierarchy of tasks, a set of people, a vision statement, and a set of documents and folders. For example, lawyers may have a role for each case in which they are participating. Each role has a schedule of hearings or meetings, a hierarchy of research and preparation tasks, and pictures of the participants, such as other lawyers, the judge, witnesses, and the defendant. The window management strategy could be any of those mentioned above, but they would all allow operations such as dragging an evidence document to a judge picture to submit it or consulting a schedule to see if there were conflicts on a proposed hearing date.

Coping with Multiple-Valued Attributes

In relational database design, attributes that have multiple values (for example, multiple authors of a book or multiple geographic regions for a satellite image) are not permitted in a normalized relation. Designers must create a separate relation, and users must perform a join to retrieve multiple values. Similar problems emerge in visualizing data sets in which attributes have multiple values. A multiple-valued attribute could be represented as multiple items on a display, but this leads to extra clutter and some confusion. Links between pairs of displays mimic the join operation, but seeing patterns across displays is more difficult.

Understanding Human Perception

While there is a rich research literature on human perceptual abilities, many studies need to be redone in the context of information visualization. Studies of color perception with pairs of colors or clusters of less than a dozen items need to be scaled up to deal with the thousands of items in many information visualization displays. How can size and color coding be used to avoid misleading interpretations? How can relationships among nonadjacent objects be shown most effectively? When might blink coding be used? How can zooming and other animations be made smooth and user controlled?

CONCLUSIONS

We cannot predict the range of applications of information visualization, but as hardware/software improvements enable larger/faster displays and more powerful user controls, designers will take advantage of these possibilities. Scientific researchers and financial analysts are among the early adopters, but the commercial applications users are likely to follow soon after. As with graphical user interfaces in the early 1980s, there will be resistance from some sources, but the power of information visualization will be compelling for most users and applications.

CHAPTER 9

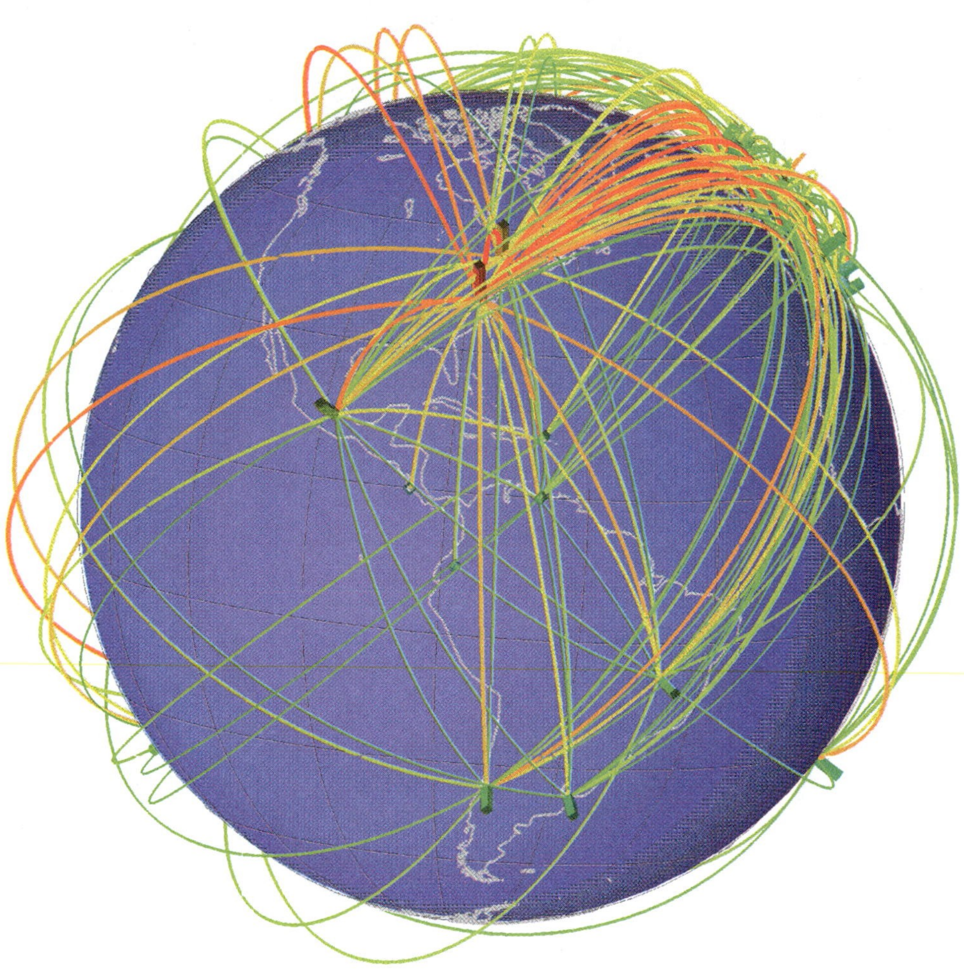

And those who have insight will shine brightly like the brightness of the expanse of Heaven.

– Daniel 12:3

Conclusion

Work on a new technology typically goes through several phases. The first phase is exploratory. Systems are constructed as existence proofs that such a system can be made, inventing new techniques in the process. Next is an abstraction phase. From examining the exploratory systems, patterns begin to emerge from which a characterization of the design space can be worked out. In later phases, there are demonstrations that the abstractions are sufficiently powerful to reliably build a promised system with specified properties. Finally, engineering knowledge is codified into handbooks and texts. Information visualization is at the end of its first exploratory stage. The papers in this book are mostly explorations that develop new techniques and interesting systems. From examining these, we can abstract several patterns and principles. Let us summarize our conclusions.

Information visualization is the use of computer-supported interactive visual representations of abstract data to amplify cognition. Its purpose is not the pictures themselves, but insight (or rapid information assimilation or monitoring large amounts of data). Information visualization is a part of the new media made possible by the development of the real-time visual computer. This medium has promise for five reasons:

1. It brings increased resources to the human in the form of perceptual processing and expanded working memory.
2. It can reduce the search for information.
3. It can enhance the recognition of patterns.
4. It enables the use of perceptual inference and perceptual monitoring.
5. The medium itself is manipulable and interactive.

We organized the discussion around a reference model for information visualization that followed data along a set of transformations in a modifiable visualization pipeline from Raw Data to a standard Data Table form to Visual Structures and finally to a View seen by the user. The user can interact with any of these transformations by controlling parameters. Techniques for information visualization can be understood in terms of transformations possible at different points in this model.

The ultimate transformation—from machine display to human eye—sets limits and possibilities on both sides. On the human side, human perception has certain important characteristics. The problem of the perceptual system is to partition limited bandwidth between the conflicting needs for both high spatial resolution and wide aperture in sensing the visual environment. This it does with a hierarchical, dynamic focus + periphery design. Automatic parallel processing of peripheral information is combined with controlled processing of focused information.

On the display side, geometric and semiotic constraints provide a graphical vocabulary from which most visualizations are constructed. The most powerful graphical resource for coding information is spatial extent. Just as data can be distinguished by whether it is nominal, ordinal, or quantitative (we even distinguished subcategories such as spatial), so the spatial axes can be similarly distinguished according to whether they are unstructured (unlabeled), nominal (labeled), ordinal (have an ordinal quantity associated with them), or quantitative (e.g., weighted links). The graphic space is defined by composing together spatial axes to form a substrate into which the rest of the visual representation is poured. Which data variables are associated with the axes of the space is the most potent representational decision. Only two or at most three variables can be encoded into graphical axes; additional variables must be encoded using other graphical properties. The graphic properties of connection and containment allow additional ways to use space in coding. In addition, variables can be associated with what type of mark is placed upon the graphical substrate and these marks can be modified by retinal properties, such as size, orientation, grayscale, color, texture, and shape.

SPACE

The most basic decision in designing an information visualization is how to use these spatial axes. Information visualizations can be made from a single dimension. This is common when the visualization is part of a control (e.g., a slider whose background is a 1D visualization) or when data has very long linear extent (in which case the visualization is often folded to get more on the screen). Two-dimensional visualizations can be made from sets of points or filled-in topographies. Three-dimensional visualizations get more interesting. Visualizations can be made from sets of points in

3-space or solid 3D objects. But probably the most flexible is 2D information landscapes (or 2D posters) set in a 3-space world. Often the landscapes have parts that project into the third dimension. To gain more flexibility, visualizations often "cheat" by folding displays or overloading (using the same space for more than one presentation).

It is possible to produce displays in higher dimensions than 3D (in fact, multivariable data sets are actually the norm) by composing the spatial axes to be parallel rather than orthogonal to each other. This is done by permutation matrices, orthogonal coordinates, and the table lens. More exotic alternatives are possible techniques such as having one variable iterate faster than the others or ordering the relevance of results and mapping them onto a folded 1D display. The properties of connection and containment can also be brought to bear. Either technique is especially good for visualizing trees. Trees are much easier to lay out than general graphs. In fact, it is often worthwhile seeing if a graph problem can be encoded into a tree problem without doing too much violence. Networks are important structures, but creating successful visualizations with them involves finding

1. a good way to position the nodes,
2. a means to keep the links from becoming a visually impenetrable tangled mess,
3. a technique to handle large scale, and
4. finding a technique for navigation without becoming lost.

TIME AND INTERACTION

The use of time and interaction is the property that computers make possible beyond previous generations of information displays. Interaction, to be effective, has to occur within certain time constraints characteristic of humans. Animations and cause-effect relationships (e.g., pushing a button and confirming it has been pushed) need to happen within 0.1 sec. Dialogue needs to have a back and forth within about 1 sec, and cognitive actions need to proceed on a scale of around 5 to 30 seconds. Interaction in information visualization implies controlling the parameters of the visualization transformations. One method for doing this is dynamic queries using sliders to control interactive filtering with responses in less than 0.1 sec.

Interactive systems allow for visualizations and the solution of visualization problems too difficult to solve by clever static presentations alone. For example, separate items scattered across a perspective 3D information landscape can be temporarily grouped together, normalized, and compared. For another example, complex interactions of some variables on others can be explored by fiddling sliders and watching a summary display.

One particularly useful interaction technique for handling large information spaces is to coordinate two displays, one giving an overview, the other giving detail. Typically, by adjusting a view port on the overview, the user can select a portion on the detail display, panning or zooming in to locate information of interest. This works for a zoom factor of between around 5 and 30. Higher zoom factors required intermediate views. A related technique is details-on-demand, where a detailed display pops up within a main overview display only when requested.

FOCUS + CONTEXT

An interesting variant of the overview + detail idea is the notion of focus + context. Essentially, the detail area is embedded in the overview. This produces a two-level focus + context display, such as the bifocal lens. A visual transfer function can be used to specify more complex variations in magnification across the display, some of which produce distorted displays. One interesting subset of these are perspective transforms, which have the effect of compressing the display in the contextual regions, but without the user experiencing this compression as a distortion. According to the shape of the transfer function, parallel straight lines can become curved, become straight but not parallel, or remain both straight and parallel. In the fisheye lens and its variants, a formal degree of interest function is defined that models the user's interest in some information object as the sum of an intrinsic interest value and a value decreasing with distance from the focus. Change in magnification by means of a transfer function is not the only way to compress the context area. Items with low degree of interest can also be elided or aggregated, or their representations can change. In general, information objects can be given multiple levels of representation that vary in detail and size of bounding box. This permits "semantic zooming," in which zooming for detail does not result in just a strict enlargement.

DOCUMENT VISUALIZATION

In addition to visual transformations, visualization also depends on data transformations. This is especially the case for text. By using vector representations of words and combining these to get vector representations of entire articles, it is possible to compute approximately the semantic similarity of text. Multidimensional scaling and other techniques can be used to map matrices of similarities into geometrical coordinates. From that position, text documents and document collections can be represented graphically in 1D, 2D, or 3D visualizations. In 1D, the fact that text is intrinsically linear can be used to lay text out in order. Using retinal properties to encode other aspects of the text, such as age or fictional character, gives rise to interesting patterns. In 2D, we can map tiles of pages, present scattergraph pointsets, or make topographical renderings like Kohonen maps. In 3D, we can present 3D pointsets or information landscapes. In 3D + time, it is possible to have a representation in which the points representing topics and text documents are not in single, fixed positions. The user steers in the space toward ever more refined sets of topics until finally finding articles of interest.

INFOSPHERE, INFORMATION WORKSPACES, VISUAL KNOWLEDGE TOOLS, AND VISUALLY ENHANCED OBJECTS

We can use information visualization at different levels of interaction: the infosphere (the set of external sources of information), information workspaces, visual knowledge tools, and visually enhanced objects. Currently, the greatest challenge for visualizing the infosphere is visualization of the Internet. Web sites are natural units of visualization because of their modularity—most sites have much more connectivity within the site than between sites. Several techniques have been popular for visualizing the Internet: 2D topographies of topics, information landscapes (2D topographies in a 3D world), or 3D pointsets with or without links. Another interesting technique is to hang information of simulations of geographical referents. More work has been done on the visualization of single sites. Here trees (possibly with folding) have been popular, since node connections may have a rough tree character and trees are easier to lay out. Time has been used as part of a dynamic layout in which nodes change as the user steers toward a topic of interest. And time as a property of node creation, deletion, and movement has been used as part of a visualization of the dynamic changes of Web sites through time.

USING VISUALIZATION TO THINK

It is possible to study analytically how information visualization works for the task of knowledge crystallization. One technique for navigation of large information spaces involves a succession of information linkages. The user clicks on a link and gets a new presentation, which itself has links. The navigation through such visualizations can be characterized in terms of a "Cost-of-Knowledge Characteristic Function," which plots the expansion of possible information sites as a function of interaction time. Similarly, different navigation methods can be characterized by their view navigability, the average number of moves to get to some piece of information. These characterizations can be strongly altered by adding "scent" or "residue" of distant nodes to local nodes such that the user has a higher probability of proceeding in the direction of the goal. It is also possible to analyze the expected cost of using an information visualization for making sense of a data set. This involves characterizing the sense-making goal, the methods available for achieving it, and their costs. Finally, progress is starting to be made on the structure of the design space of information visualization systems.

APPLICATIONS

The breadth of applications for information visualization is large and growing. One of the first applications was for statistical analysis. Visualization is especially helpful for multivariate data and for large data sets. A newer use is for searching and browsing digital libraries. By coupling overviews of the library with queries that highlight some search, a patron can get a sense of what is available as well as learn about relationships in the collection, thereby enabling more complex searches. Information visualization has the potential to facilitate search for personal services, such as airline reservations, homes, or classified ads. These tasks can be complex because of the many criteria that may form the basis for a query. Another potential use of information visualization is in complex documents, such as scientific papers, technical manuals, film scripts, or computer programs. In each of these, readers often try to get a sense of the whole or to cross-reference one part from another. A particular type of document for which visualization is especially applicable is histories, such as medical patient histories, employment histories, or project histories. These need to be assimilated quickly, but are complex. Timelines are applicable, as are a number of other techniques. Classifications, such as library subject categories, animal species, or computer disk directories, are a somewhat related classification area. There is the problem of both getting an overview to see related categories and getting detail about a subset of categories. Tree visualizations could be useful here as well as those based on spatialization of similarity. Finally, networks of documents, social relationships, or pipelines are another application area that could receive additional work. Although the application areas have very different content, it is interesting how widely applicable is the technique of overview first, zoom and filter, then details-on-demand. Other techniques, such as using output for input, also transfer across many applications.

FUTURE TRENDS

Several trends seem likely for information visualization.

1. *Entering the mainstream.* Information visualization will enter the mainstream. It is currently possible to do interesting studies and applications of information visualization with a high-end PC and a $175 graphics adapter card. This compares to the $30,000 to $100,000 required just a few years ago. Hardware continues to improve rapidly in cost performance, and there is a trend to integrating it more closely with the PC, including location on the motherboard and using special buses. Information visualization has potentially far more users than scientific visualization, and those users have more mainstream uses. Information visualization companies are entering the marketplace.
2. *Moving toward applications.* From initial studies that explored the visualization technology, there is a movement toward using existing techniques and creating new techniques in connection with some particular application. Enough technology exists that it forms a reusable bag of tools. Focusing on applications helps fill in the gaps and is a way of establishing the value of the techniques.

3. *Integrated packages.* Groups of individual visualizations are being put together to form integrated packages. This is really part of moving toward applications, but for applications in which information visualization is the main purpose. Packages and applications enable delivery to a wider user base.
4. *Networks.* Networks are emerging as an important delivery means. Some visualizations can be done across the network. Others use the network for their data. Still others are visualizations of a piece of the network itself.
5. *Educational infrastructure.* Information visualization is starting to emerge as a topic for courses. Books, videotapes, and other educational material are starting to become available.

UNSOLVED PROBLEMS

Several key issues remain for future research in information visualization. Here is our list:

1. *New metaphors/new visualizations.* The stock of visualizations is still not large and they are not easy to invent. We feel there are still a number of important visualizations waiting to be discovered.
2. *Bringing science to the craft.* We have discussed several pieces of work that attempt to analyze or characterize the use of visualization for some task.
3. *The visualization of cyberspace.* As we argued earlier, it now looks like cyberspace may evolve into the one net where most information resides. It will be overwhelmingly large. Information visualization could play a crucial role in taming this space.
4. *Collaborative visualizations.* People often work on problems together. While some systems have begun to explore shared visualizations, there is much more that can be learned.
5. *A characterization of information visualization down to the operator level.* We organized our discussion around gross characterizations of transformations and their place in the cycle of transformations from Raw Data to View. The next step would be an analysis of the types of operators and how this analysis could be used to construct a modular system.
6. *The perceptual analysis of dynamic information displays.* Much work remains to be done to understand dynamic displays and how they work perpetually.
7. *Advances in the science of dynamic spatial cognition.* There is currently a growing literature in spatial cognition. This literature needs to be connected to information visualization and the spatial cognition of dynamic display explored.
8. *A theory of knowledge crystallization.* The process of knowledge crystallization needs to be studied empirically, integrating information visualization into its larger context.

Information visualization is a set of technologies that use visual computing to amplify human cognition. Perhaps the most interesting future of this new field will be coevolving this technology with the uses to which it can be put: how to use visual machines to amplify scholarship, to simplify management of complex activities, to enable large numbers of people to control and understand complexity in their lives. In fact, a prime question to ask is, "What new things could we now do with this technology that were previously unthinkable?" It is as important to understand the nature of information-intensive tasks as it is to understand the details of information visualization technology. Otherwise, the field will evolve into a set of techniques for making pretty pictures looking for a use. At this point, it is a deep understanding of how particular activities could be amplified—or a deep understanding of the interaction between external cognition, information, and human cognition—that could open up the next big advances. In a world that is a massive network of documents and devices, information visualization will be a core part of the new technology for human interfaces. Information visualization has the promise of using vision to increase the scale of what we can think about. A picture is worth ten thousand nodes.

APPENDIX **A**

Relevant Videos

VIDEOS FROM ACM SIGCHI

Listed below are archival videos from the ACM SIGCHI conference on video programs showing the segments relevant to information visualization. Copies may be ordered from

ACM Member Services Department
1515 Broadway, New York, NY 10036 USA
Tel.: +1 212 626 0500, email: acmhelp@acm.org
www.acm.org/sigchi

CHI'98

Viewing Web Sites Using a Hierarchical Table of Contents Browser: WebTOC
David Nation

CHI'97

Query Previews in Networked Information Systems: The Case of EOSDIS
C. Plaisant, T. Bruns, B. Shneiderman, and K. Doan, University of Maryland

CHI'96

Dynamic Timelines: Visualizing the History of Photography
R. L. Kullberg, MIT

Visualizing Large Trees Using the Hyperbolic Browser
J. Lamping and R. Rao, Xerox PARC

The Influence Explorer—A Tool for Design
L. Tweedie, B. Spence, H. Dawkes, and H Su, Imperial College, England

LifeLines: Visualizing Personal Histories
B. Milash, C. Plaisant, and A. Rose, University of Maryland

Visualizing Information Retrieval Results: A Demonstration of the TileBar Interface
M. A. Hearst and J. O. Pedersen, Xerox PARC

Exploring Information with Visage
P. Lucas, MAYA Design Group; and S. F. Roth, CMU

Temporal Typography: A Proposal to Enrich Written Expression
Y. Y. Wong, MIT

Lifestreams: An Alternative to the Desktop Metaphor
S. Fertig, E. Freeman, and D. Gelernter, Yale University

Browsing Anatomical Image Databases: A Case Study of the Visible Human
C. North and F. Korn, University of Maryland

The Information Forager
S. K. Card, G. G. Robertson, and W. York, Xerox PARC

CHI'95

Exploring Large Tables with the Table Lens
Ramana Rao and Stuart K. Card, Xerox PARC

Visual Decision-Making: Using Treemaps for the Analytic Hierarchy Process
Toshiyuki Asahi, David Turo, and Ben Shneiderman, University of Maryland

The DragMag Image Magnifier
Colin Ware, University of New Brunswick; and Marlon Lewis, SatLantic, Inc.

SageTools: An Intelligent Environment for Sketching, Browsing, and Customizing Data-Graphics
Steven Roth, John Kolojejchick, Joe Mattis, and Mei C. Chuah, Carnegie Mellon University

A Taxonomy of See-Through Tools: The Video
Eric A. Bier, Ken Fishkin, Ken Pier, and Maureen C. Stone, Xerox PARC

The Movable Filter as an Interface Tool: The Video
Eric A. Bier, Ken Fishkin, Ken Pier, and Maureen C. Stone, Xerox PARC

Lyberworld: A 3D Graphical User Interface for Fulltext Retrieval
Matthias Hemmje, German National Research Centre for Computer Science

Organization Overviews and Role Management: Inspiration for Future Desktop Environments
Catherine Plaisant and Ben Shneiderman, University of Maryland

CHI'94

Visual Information Seeking Using the FilmFinder
Christopher Ahlberg and Ben Shneiderman, University of Maryland

The Attribute Explorer
Lisa Tweedie, Bob Spence, David Williams, and Ravinder Baghel, Imperial College

Typographic Space
David Small, Suguru Ishizaki, and Muriel Cooper, Massachusetts Institute of Technology

Dynamaps: Dynamic Queries on a Health Statistics Atlas
Catherine Plaisant and Vinit Jain, University of Maryland

Analysing NBA Statistics
David Turo, University of Maryland

Toolglass and Magic Lenses: The See-Through Interface
Eric A. Bier, Maureen C. Stone, Ken Pier, Ken Fishkin, Thomas Baudel, and Matt Conway, Xerox PARC; William Buxton, University of Toronto; and Tony DeRose, University of Washington

CHI'93

The Human Guidance of Automated Design
Lynn Colgan, British Aerospace; Robert Spence, Imperial College; and Paul Rankin, Philips Labs

Browsing Graphs Using a Fisheye View
Marc H. Brown, James R. Meehan, DEC Systems Research Center; and Manojit Sarkar, Brown University

High Interaction Data Visualization Using SeeSoft to Visualize Program Change History
Joseph L. Steffen and Stephen G. Eick, AT&T Bell Laboratories

Exploring Remote Images: A Telepathology Workstation
Catherine Plaisant, David A. Carr, and Hiroaki Hasegawa, University of Maryland

QOC in Action: Using Design Rationale to Support Design
Diane McKerlie and Allan MacLean, Rank Xerox Cambridge EuroPARC

CHI'92

Dynamic Queries: Database Searching by Direct Manipulation
Ben Shneiderman, Christopher Williamson, and Christopher Ahlberg, University of Maryland

An Introduction to Zeus
Marc H. Brown, DEC SRC

Pointing and Visualization
William C. Hill and James D. Hollan, Bellcore

VIDEOS FROM THE UNIVERSITY OF MARYLAND

Listed below are selections from the University of Maryland Human-Computer Interaction Laboratory, Technical Video Series. The HCIL video series (1991–1998) includes video reports and demonstrations from HCIL projects. The series is edited by Catherine Plaisant (plaisant@cs.umd.edu).

The list of video segments is related to information visualization. Several of these video reports were subsequently reprinted or re-edited for the ACM SIGCHI video program. Those videos are marked with an asterisk (*). Requests for the tapes (VHS or PAL) may be sent to

Human-Computer Interacton Laboratory
UMIACS, A.V. Williams Building
University of Maryland
College Park, MD 20742
(301) 405-2769
hcil-info@cs.umd.edu

Abstracts and prices are available online at *http://www.cs.umd.edu/hcil/Research/video-reports.html.*

1998 HCIL Video Reports

LifeLines: Enhancing Navigation and Analysis of Patient Records
Catherine Plaisant and Jia Li

Pad++: A Zooming Interface
Ben Bederson

Query Previews for NASA EOSDIS, An Update
Ben Shneiderman and Catherine Plaisant

Genex: A Medical Scenario
Ben Shneiderman

1997 Video Reports

Bringing Treasures to the Surface: Previews and Overviews in a Prototype for the Library of Congress National Digital Library
Catherine Plaisant, Anita Komlodi, Gary Marchionini, Ara Shirinian, David Nation, Steve Karasik, Teresa Cronnell, and Ben Shneiderman

Viewing Web Sites Using a Hierarchical Table of Contents Browser: WebTOC
David Nation

Using Multimedia Learning Resources for the Baltimore Learning Community
Becky Bishop and Josephus Beale

Visual Data Mining Using Spotfire
Ben Shneiderman

Query Previews in Networked Information Systems: The Case of EOSDIS
Catherine Plaisant, Tom Bruns, Ben Shneiderman, and Khoa Doan

1996 Video Reports

Elastic Windows for Rapid Multiple Window Management
Eser Kandogan

LifeLines: Visualizing Personal Histories (revised version)*
Brett Milash, Catherine Plaisant, and Anne Rose

Designing Interfaces for Youth Services Information Management
Jason Ellis, Anne Rose, and Catherine Plaisant

Query Previews in Networked Information Systems: The Case of EOSDIS*
Catherine Plaisant, Tom Bruns, Ben Shneiderman, and Khoa Doan

Baltimore Learning Communities
Gary Marchionini, Allison Gordon, Tracy Vitek, Horatio Jabari-Kitwala, and Victor Nolet

Visual Information Seeking Using the FilmFinder* (Extract from the HCIL1994 Video Report)
Christopher Ahlberg and Ben Shneiderman

1995 Video Reports

Introduction (Including a Revised Version of the FilmFinder)
Ben Shneiderman

Using Dynamic Queries for Youth Services Information
Anne Rose and Ajit Vanniamparampil

LifeLines: Visualizing Personal Histories
Brett Milash, Catherine Plaisant, and Anne Rose

Dynamic Queries and Pruning for Large Tree Structures
Harsha Kumar

Browsing Anatomical Image Databases: The Visible Human*
Flip Korn and Chris North

BizView: Managing Business and Network Alarms
Catherine Plaisant, Rina Levy, and Wei Zhao

WinSurfer: Treemaps for Replacing the Windows File Manager
Marko Teittinen

1994 Video Reports

Visual Information Seeking Using the FilmFinder*
Christopher Ahlberg and Ben Shneiderman

Organization Overviews and Role Management: Inspiration for Future Desktop Environments*
Catherine Plaisant and Ben Shneiderman

Visual Decision-Making: Using Treemaps for the Analytic Hierarchy Process
Toshiyuki Asahi, Ben Shneiderman, and David Turo

Visual Information Management for Satellite Network Configuration
Catherine Plaisant, Harsha Kumar, and Marko Teittinen

Dynamic Queries Demos: Revised HomeFinder and Text Version Plus Health Statistics Atlas
Ben Shneiderman

1993 Video Reports

Dynamaps: Dynamic Queries on a Health Statistics Atlas
Catherine Plaisant and Vinit Jain

Hierarchical Visualization with Treemaps: Making Sense of Pro Basketball Data*
Dave Turo

TreeViz: File Directory Browsing
Brian Johnson

1992 Video Reports

Dynamic Queries: Database Searching by Direct Manipulation*
Ben Shneiderman, Chris Williamson, and Christopher Ahlberg

Treemaps for Visualizing Hierarchical Information
Ben Shneiderman, Brian Johnson, and Dave Turo

Three Strategies for Directory Browsing
Rick Chimera

Filter-Flow Metaphor for Boolean Queries
Degi Young and Ben Shneiderman

Remote Direct Manipulation: A Telepathology Workstation*
Catherine Plaisant and Dave Carr

1991 Video Reports

Scheduling Home Control Devices*
Catherine Plaisant and Ben Shneiderman

Pie Menus
Don Hopkins

Three Interfaces for Browsing Tables of Contents
Rick Chimera

Bibliography

The boldface numbers to the right of each reference indicate the pages in the book on which the reference is cited.

Adobe Systems Incorporated. (1990). *PostScript Language Reference Manual.* 2nd ed. Reading, MA: Addison-Wesley. **254**

Ahlberg, C., and Shneiderman, B. (1994a). The Alphaslider: A Compact and Rapid Selector. *Proceedings of CHI'94, ACM Conference on Human Factors in Computing Systems.* 365–371. **235, 243, 245, 251**

Ahlberg, C., and Shneiderman, B. (1994b). Visual Information Seeking Using the FilmFinder. *Conference Companion of CHI'94, ACM Conference on Human Factors in Computing Systems.* 433. . . . . . **31**

Ahlberg, C., and Shneiderman, B. (1994c ●). Visual Information Seeking: Tight Coupling of Dynamic Query Filters with Starfield Displays. *Proceedings of CHI'94, ACM Conference on Human Factors in Computing Systems,* New York. 313–317. . . . **26, 225, 232, 235, 251, 253, 297, 464, 551, 627, 628**

Ahlberg, C., and Truve, S. (1995). Exploring Terra Incognita in the Design Space of Query Devices. *Proceedings of EHCI'95, Engineering for Human-Computer Interaction.* Amsterdam: North-Holland. **618, 620, 621**

Ahlberg, C., and Wistrand, E. (1995a). IVEE: An Information Visualization and Exploration Environment. *Proceedings of InfoVis'95, IEEE Symposium on Information Visualization,* New York. 66–73. . . . . **59, 551, 626**

Ahlberg, C., and Wistrand, E. (1995b). IVEE: An Environment for Automatic Creation of Dynamic Queries Applications. *Conference Companion of CHI'95, ACM Conference on Human Factors in Computing Systems.* 15–16. . . . . **277**

Ahlberg, C., Williamson, C., and Shneiderman, B. (1992). Dynamic Queries for Information Exploration: An Implementation and Evaluation. *Proceedings of CHI'92, ACM Conference on Human Factors in Computing Systems,* New York. 619–626. . . . . . **8, 238, 245, 246, 253, 271, 622**

Ahlberg, C. *See* Holmquist and Ahlberg (1997).

Al-Hawamdeh, S., and Willett, P. (1988). Paragraph-Based Searching in Full-Text Documents. *Electronic Publishing, 2*(4), 179–192. . . . . **414**

Allan, J. *See* Salton, Allan, and Buckley (1993); Salton, Allan, Buckley, and Singhal (1995); Salton, Buckley, and Allan (1992).

Allen, R. B. (1982). Patterns of Manuscript Revisions. *Behavior and Information Technology, 1*(2), 177–184. . . . . **314**

Allen, R. B. (1994). Navigating and Searching in Hierarchical Digital Library Catalogs. *Proceedings of DL'94, ACM Conference on Digital Libraries.* 95–100. . . . . **572**

Alvey, B. *See* Anick, Brennan, Flynn, Hanssen, Alvey, and Robbins (1990).

Anderson, J. R., and Schooler, L. J. (1991). Reflections of the Environment in Memory. *Psychological Science, 2*(6), 396–408. . . **587**

Anderson, M. H., Nielsen, J., and Rasmussen, H. (1989). A Similarity-Based Hypertext Browser for Reading the Unix Network News. *Hypermedia, 1*(3), 255–265. . . . . **415**

Andreessen, M. (1993). *NCSA Mosaic Technical Summary.* National Center for Supercomputing Applications. **459**

Andrews, D. F. (1972). Plots of High Dimensional Data. *Biometrics.* **277**

Andrews, K. (1995 ●). Visualizing Cyberspace: Information Visualization in the Harmony Internet Browser. *Proceedings of InfoVis'95, IEEE Symposium on Information Visualization,* New York. 97–104, color plates 147–148. . . . . **466, 630**

Andrews, K., Kappe, F., and Maurer, H. (1995a). Serving Information to the Web with Hyper-G. *Computer Networks and ISDN Systems, 27*(6), 919–926. . . . . **466, 495**

Andrews, K., Kappe, F., and Maurer, H. (1995b). Hyper-G: Towards the Next Generation of Network Information Technology. *Journal of Universal Computer Science, 1*(4), 206–220. . . . **495**

Anick, P., Brennan, J., Flynn, R., Hanssen, D., Alvey, B., and Robbins, J. (1990). A Direct Manipulation Interface for Boolean Information Retrieval via Natural Language Query. *Proceedings of SIGIR'90, ACM Conference on Research and Development in Information Retrieval.* 135–150. . . . . **147**

Anklesaria, F. X. *See* McCahill and Anklesaria (1994).

Apperley, M. D., and Spence, R. (1980). *Focus on Information: The Office of the Professional.* Video. London: Imperial College Television Studio. **336**

Apperley, M. D., Tzavaras, I., and Spence, R. (1982). A Bifocal Display Technique for Data Presentation. *Proceedings of Eurographics'82, Conference of the European Association for Computer Graphics.* 27–43.. . . . . **354, 360**

Apperley, M. D. *See* Burger and Apperley (1991); Leung and Apperley (1993a, 1993b, 1994); Spence and Apperley (1982).

Apple Computer. (1998). *Welcome to HotSauce MCF: Fly through the Internet with HotSauce.* **467**

Arias, J. P., and Furnas, G. W. (1982). *FISHEYE: A Program Implementing "Fisheye" Viewing for Hierarchically Structured Files.* Internal Memorandum, AT&T Bell Laboratories. **313, 320**

Ark Interface. (1990). *Workspace User's Guide.* Seattle: Ark Interface, Inc. **548**

Asahi, T., Turo, D., and Shneiderman, B. (1995). Using Treemaps to Visualize the Analytic Hierarchy Process. *Information Systems Research, 6*(4), 357–375. . . . . **292, 630**

Asimov, D. (1985). The Grand Tour: A Tool for Viewing Multidimensional Data. *SIAM Journal on Scientific and Statistical Computing, 6*(1), 128–143. . . . . **95**

Atkinson, R. C., Herrnstein, R. J., Lindzey, G., and Luce, R. D. (1988). *Stevens' Handbook of Experimental Psychology.* Vol. 1, 2nd ed. New York: John Wiley & Sons. **24**

Aust, R. *See* Gauch, Aust, Evans, Gauch, Minden, Niehaus, and Roberts (1994).

Averboch, G. *See* Heath, Hix, Nowell, Wake, Averboch, Labow, Guyer, Brueni, France, Dalal, and Fox (1995).

Avitzur, R., Robins, G., and Newman, S. (1994). *Apple Graphing Computer.* Cupertino, CA: Apple Computer. **3**

Bacon, D. *See* Bederson, Hollan, Perlin, Meyer, Bacon, and Furnas (1996).

Badre, A. *See* Gray, Badre, and Guzdial (1996).

Baecker, R. M., and Marcus, A. (1988). *Human Factors and Typography for More Readable Programs.* Reading, MA: Addison-Wesley. **160, 419, 538**

Baecker, R. M. *See* Price, Baecker, and Small (1993).

Baker, M. J., and Eick, S. G. (1995●). Space-Filling Software Visualization. *Journal of Visual Languages and Computing, 6,* 119–133. . . . . **150**

Ballay, J. M. (1994). Designing Workscape: An Interdisciplinary Experience. *Proceedings of CHI'94, ACM Conference on Human Factors in Computing Systems,* Boston. 10–15. . . . . **514, 548**

Banchoff, T. (1978). Computer Animation and the Geometry of Surfaces in 3- and 4-Space. *Proceedings of ICM'78, International Congress of Mathematicians.* 1005–1013. . . . . **97**

Banchoff, T. *See* Feiner, Salesin, and Banchoff (1982).

Banks, D. C. *See* Jin and Banks (1997).

Bannon, L. J., and Bødker, S. (1991). Beyond the Interface: Encountering Artifacts in Use. In J. M. Carroll (ed.), *Designing Interaction: Psychology at the Human Computer Interface.* Cambridge, UK: Cambridge University Press. 227–253. . . . . **445**

Barber, R. *See* Faloutsos, Barber, Flickner, Hafner, Niblack, Petrovic, and Equitz (1994).

Bartram, L. (1994). Contextual Assistance in User Interfaces to Complex, Time Critical Systems: The Intelligent Zoom. *Proceedings of Graphics Interface'94,* Toronto. 216–224. . . . . **372**

Bartram, L., Ho, A., Dill, J., and Henigman, F. (1995). The Continuous Zoom: A Constrained Fisheye Technique for Viewing and Navigating Large Information Spaces. *Proceedings of UIST'95, ACM Symposium on User Interface Software and Technology,* New York. 207–216. . . . . **189, 369, 372**

Bartram, L. *See* Schaffer, Zuo, Bartram, Dill, Dubes, Greenberg, and Roseman (1993, 1996).

Bassett, E. W. (1995). IBM's IBM Fix. *Industrial Computing, 14*(41), 23–25. . . . . **112**

Battista, G. D., Eades, P., Tamassia, R., and Tollis, I. G. (1994). Annotated Bibliography on Graph Drawing. *Computational Geometry: Theory and Applications,* 4(5), 235–282. . . . . **188, 295**

Baudel, T. *See* Bier, Stone, Baudel, Buxton, and Fishkin (1994).

Beach, R. J. (1985). *Setting Tables and Illustrations with Styles.* Unpublished Ph.D. Thesis, University of Waterloo, Waterloo, Ontario, Canada. **67**

Beach, R. J., and Stone, M. C. (1983). Graphical Style—Towards High Quality Illustrations. *Proceedings of SIGGRAPH'83, ACM Conference on Computer Graphics.* 127–135. . . . . **67**

Beale, R. *See* Hendley, Drew, Wood, and Beale (1995).

Beard, D. (1990). A Visual Calendar for Scheduling Group Meetings. *Proceedings of CSCW'90, ACM Conference on Computer Supported Cooperative Work,* New York. 279–290. . . . . **183**

Beard, D., and Walker, II, J. Q. (1990). Navigational Techniques to Improve the Display of Large Two-Dimensional Spaces. *Behavior and Information Technology,* 9(6), 451–466. . . **153, 288, 295, 350**

Beard, D. *See* Ouh-Young, Beard, and Brooks (1989).

Beatty, J. C. *See* Ware and Beatty (1985).

Beaudoin, L., Parent, M.-A., and Vroomen, L. C. (1996). Cheops: A Compact Explorer for Complex Hierarchies. *Proceedings of IEEE Visualization'96 Conference.* 87–100. . . . . **630**

Becker, B. G. (1997). Using MineSet for Knowledge Discovery. *IEEE Computer Graphics and Applications, 17*(4), 75–78. . . . **551**

Becker, R. A., and Cleveland, W. S. (1984). *Brushing a Scatterplot Matrix: High-Interaction Graphical Methods for Analyzing Multidimensional Data.* Technical Report. AT&T Bell Laboratories. . **600**

Becker, R. A., and Cleveland, W. S. (1987). Brushing Scatterplots. *Technometrics, 29*(2), 127–142. . . . . **95, 208, 218, 237, 419**

Becker, R. A., and Wilks, A. R. (1993a). *Final Report: Network Traffic Analysis Project* (BBN Subcontract Agreement 20510). . . . **222**

Becker, R. A., and Wilks, A. R. (1993b). *Maps in S.* Statistics Technical Report. AT&T Bell Laboratories. **223**

Becker, R. A., Chambers, J. M., and Wilks, A. R. (1988a). *The New S Language.* Pacific Grove, CA: Wadsworth and Brooks/Cole. **224, 428, 600**

Becker, R. A., Cleveland, W. S., and Weil, G. (1988b). The Use of Brushing and Rotation for Data Analysis. In W. S. Cleveland and M. E. McGill (eds.), *Dynamic Graphics for Statistics.* Belmont, CA: Wadsworth. 247–275. . . . . **419**

Becker, R. A., Cleveland, W. S., and Wilks, A. R. (1987). Dynamic Graphics for Data Analysis. *Statistical Science, 2,* 355–395. . . . . **225, 276, 277, 280, 619, 620**

Becker, R. A., Cleveland, W. S., and Wilks, A. R. (1988c). In W. S. Cleveland and M. E. McGill (eds.), *Dynamic Graphics for Statistics.* Belmont, CA: Wadsworth. 1–12. . . . . **115**

Becker, R. A., Eick, S. G., and Miller, E. O. (1989a). Dynamic Graphical Analysis of Network Data. *Proceedings of ISI'89,* Paris. **251**

Becker, R. A., Eick, S. G., and Wilks, A. R. (1991). Basics of Network Visualization. *IEEE Computer Graphics and Applications, 11*(3), 12–14. . . . . **419**

Becker, R. A., Eick, S. G., and Wilks, A. R. (1995). Visualizing Network Data. *IEEE Transactions on Visualization and Computer Graphics, 1*(1 March), 16–28. . . . . **187, 188, 189, 271, 630**

Becker, R. A., Eick, S. G., Miller, E. O., and Wilks, A. R. (1989b). *Dynamic Graphics Analysis of Maps.* Holdel, NJ: Bell Laboratories ITV Facility. **225**

Becker, R. A., Eick, S. G., Miller, E. O., and Wilks, A. R. (1990a). Dynamic Graphics for Network Visualization. *Proceedings of IEEE Visualization'90 Conference,* San Francisco. 93–95. . . . **8, 207, 208**

Becker, R. A., Eick, S. G., Miller, E. O., and Wilks, A. R. (1990b). Network Visualization. *Proceedings of 24th International Symposium on Spatial Data Handling,* Zurich. 285–294. . . . . **225**

Beddow, J. (1990). Shape Coding of Multidimensional Data on a Microcomputer Display. *Proceedings of IEEE Visualization'90 Conference,* San Francisco. 238–246. . . . . **115, 127, 221**

Bederson, B. B. (1994). Pad++: Advances in Multiscale Interfaces. *Proceedings of CHI'94, ACM Conference on Human Factors in Computing Systems,* New York. 315–316. . . . . **285, 538**

Bederson, B. B., and Hollan, J. D. (1994●). Pad++: A Zooming Graphical Interface for Exploring Alternate Interface Physics. *Proceedings of UIST'94, ACM Symposium on User Interface Software and Technology,* Marina del Rey, CA. 17–26. . . . **28, 31, 270, 290, 392, 513, 594, 634, 635**

Bederson, B. B., Hollan, J. D., Perlin, K., Meyer, J., Bacon, D., and Furnas, G. W. (1996). Pad++: A Zoomable Graphical Sketchpad for Exploring Alternate Interface Physics. *Journal of Visual Languages and Computing,* 7(1), 3–31. . . . . **619, 620**

Bederson, B. B. *See* Furnas and Bederson (1995).

Begeman, M. *See* Conklin and Begeman (1989).

Beigel, R. *See* Tanin, Beigel, and Shneiderman (1997).

Belkin, N. J., and Croft, W. B. (1987). Retrieval Techniques. *Annual Review of Information Science and Technology, 22,* 109–145. . . **433**

Belkin, N., and Croft, B. (1992). Information Filtering and Information Retrieval: Two Sides of the Same Coin. *Communications of the ACM, 35*(12 Dec.), 29–38. . . . . **144, 146**

Belkin, N. *See* Henniger and Belkin (1994).

Benedikt, M. (1991). Cyberspace: Some Proposals. In M. Benedikt (ed.), *Cyberspace: First Steps.* Cambridge, MA: MIT Press. 119–224. . . . . **465**

Benest, I. D., Morgan, G., and Smithurst, M. D. (1987). A Humanised Interface to an Electronic Library. *Proceedings of INTERACT'87,* Amsterdam. 905–910. . . . . **546, 547**

Benford, S., Snowdon, D., and Mariani, J. (1995). Populated Information Terrains: First Steps. In R. A. Earnshaw, J. A. Vince, and H. Jones (eds.), *Virtual Reality Applications.* London: Academic Press. 27–39. . . . . **466**

Benford, S., Snowdon, D., Greenhalgh, C., Ingram, R., Knox, I., and Brown, G. (1995). VR-VIBE: A Virtual Environment for Co-operative Information Retrieval. *Proceedings of Eurographics'95, Conference of the European Association for Computer Graphics,* Maastricht, The Netherlands. 349–360. . . . . **465**

Benford, S. *See* Ingram and Benford (1995); Snowdon, Benford, Brown, Ingram, Knox, and Studley (1995).

Bentley, J. L., and Friedman, J. H. (1979). Data Structures for Range Searching. *ACM Computing Surveys, 11*(4 Dec), 397–409. . . . . **183**

Benyon, D. (1992). Task Analysis and System Design: The Discipline of Data. *Interacting with Computers, 4*(1), 246–249. . . . **620**

Benyon, D. R. *See* Green and Benyon (1996).

Berger, M., and Bokhari, S. (1987). A Partitioning Strategy for Nonuniform Problems on Multiprocessors. *IEEE Transactions on Computers,* C-365, 570–580. . . . . **183**

Bergeron, R. D., and Grinstein, G. G. (1989). A Reference Model for the Visualization of Multidimensional Data. *Proceedings of Eurographics'89, Conference of the European Association for Computer Graphics.* Amsterdam: North-Holland. 393–399. . . . . **115**

Bergeron, R. D., Keim, D. A., and Pickett, R. M. (1994). Test Datasets for Evaluating Data Visualization Techniques. In G. G. Grinstein and H. Levkowitz (eds.), *Perceptual Issues in Visualization.* Heidelberg: Springer-Verlag. **133**

Bergeron, R. D., Meeker, L. D., and Sparr, T. M. (1992). Visualization-Based Model for a Scientific Database System. In H. Hagen, M. Miller, and G. Nielson (eds.), *Focus on Scientific Visualization.* Berlin: Springer-Verlag. 103–121. . . . . **127**

Bergeron, R. D. *See* Wong, Crabb, and Bergeron (1996).

Berkin, A. L., and Orton, M. N. (1994). LinkWinds: Interactive Scientific Data Analysis and Visualization. *Communications of the ACM, 37*(4), 42–52. . . . . **626**

Berners-Lee, T., Calliliau, R., Luotonem, A., Nielsen, H. F., and Secret, A. (1994). The World-Wide Web. *Communications of the ACM, 37*(8), 76–82. . . . . **495, 504**

Bernhard, D. *See* Carswell, Frankenberger, and Bernhard (1991).

Bernstein, M. (1990). An Apprentice that Discovers Hypertext Links. *Proceedings of ECHT'90, ACM European Conference on Hypermedia Technology.* 212–223. . . . . **415**

Bernstein, M., Bolter, J. D., Joyce, M., and Mylonas, E. (1991). Architectures for Volatile Hypertext. *Proceedings of ACM Hypertext'91 Conference,* San Antonio, TX. 246–260. . . . . **413**

Bertin, J. (1967/1983). *Semiology of Graphics: Diagrams, Networks, Maps* (W. J. Berg, Trans.). Madison, WI: University of Wisconsin Press. **7, 29, 70, 74, 253, 386, 609**

Bertin, J. (1977/1981●). *Graphics and Graphic Information Processing.* Berlin: De Gruyter. 24–31. . . . . **1, 7, 12, 16, 18, 21, 26, 30, 35, 57, 93, 127, 221, 224, 277, 307, 341, 616, 617, 619, 621**

Beshers, C., and Feiner, S. K. (1988). Real-Time 4D Animation on a 3D Graphics Workstation. *Proceedings of Graphics Interface'88,* Edmonton, Canada. 1–7. . . . . **97**

Beshers, C., and Feiner, S. K. (1989). Scope: Automated Generation of Graphical Interfaces. *Proceedings of UIST'89, ACM Symposium on User Interface Software and Technology,* Williamsburg, VA. 76–85. . . . . **99, 102**

Beshers, C. *See* Feiner and Beshers (1990a, 1990b, 1993).

Beyer, K. *See* Livny, Ramakrishnan, Beyer, Chen, Donjerkovic, Lawande, Myllymaki, and Wenger (1997).

Bhogal, R. *See* Tweedie, Spence, Williams, and Bhogal (1994).

Bier, E. A., Stone, M. C., Baudel, T., Buxton, W., and Fishkin, K. (1994). A Taxonomy of See-Through Tools. *Proceedings of CHI'94, ACM Conference on Human Factors in Computing Systems,* Boston. 358–364. . . . . **234, 235, 253, 254, 618, 620**

Bier, E. A., Stone, M. C., Pier, K., Buxton, W., and DeRose, T. (1993). Toolglass and Magic Lenses: The See-Through Interface. *Proceedings of SIGGRAPH'93, ACM Conference on Computer Graphics,* Anaheim, CA. 73–80. . . **183, 234, 235, 253, 254, 531**

Bier, E. A. *See* Stone, Fishkin, and Bier (1994).

Blake, R. *See* Sekular and Blake (1994).

Blanchard, C. *See* Zimmerman, Lanier, Blanchard, Bryson, and Harvill (1987).

Blattner, M. M. *See* Springmeyer, Blattner, and Max (1992).

Blum, H. *See* Lee, Slagle, and Blum (1977).

Blumenthal, A. L. (1977). *The Process of Cognition.* Englewood Cliffs, NJ: Prentice Hall. **231**

Bly, S. (1982a). Presenting Information in Sound. *Proceedings of CHI'82, ACM Conference on Human Factors in Computing Systems.* 371–375. . . . . **97**

Bly, S. (1982b). *Sound and Computer Information Presentation.* Lawrence Livermore Laboratory Technical Report UCRL-53282. . **225**

Bødker, S. *See* Bannon and Bødker (1991).

Boens, J., Borst, F., and Scherrer, J. (1992). Organizing the Clinical Data in the Medical Record. *MD Computing, 9,* 149–155. . . **291**

Boff, K. R., Kaufman, L., and Thomas, J. P. (1986). *Handbook of Perception and Human Performance.* New York: John Wiley & Sons. **24**

Bohn, S. *See* York and Bohn (1995).

Bokhari, S. *See* Berger and Bokhari (1987).

Bolt, R. A. (1979a). *Spatial Data Management.* Cambridge MA: MIT, Architecture Machine Group. **334, 335, 337**

Bolt, R. A. (1979b). Spatial Data Management 1980, "Put-that-There" Voice and Gesture at the Graphics Interface. *Computer Graphics, 14*(3), 262. . . . . **334, 366**

Bolt, R. A. (1984). *The Human Interface—Where People and Computers Meet.* Belmont, CA: Lifetime Learning Publications. . **285, 331**

Bolter, J. D. (1991). *Writing Space—The Computer, Hypertext, and the History of Writing.* Hillsdale, NJ: Lawrence Erlbaum Associates. **413**

Bolter, J. D. *See* Bernstein, Bolter, Joyce, and Mylonas (1991).

Booth, K. S. *See* Healey, Booth, and Enns (1995).

Borgman, C. L. (1986). Why are Online Catalogs Hard to Use? Lessons Learned from Information-Retrieval Studies. *Journal of* the American Society for Information Science, 37(6), 387–400. . . . . **244**

Borst, F. *See* Boens, Borst, and Scherrer (1992).

Botafogo, R. A., Rivlin, E., and Shneiderman, B. (1992). Structural Analysis of Hypertexts: Identifying Hierarchies and Useful Metrics. *ACM Transactions on Information Systems, 10*(2), 142–180. . . . . **415**

Bowman, W. J. (1968). *Graphic Communication.* New York: John Wiley & Sons. **74**

Bradshaw, G. L. *See* Langley, Simon, Bradshaw, and Zytkow (1987).

Bray, T. (1996●). Measuring the Web. *Computer Networks and ISDN Systems, 28*(7–11-May), 992.. . . . . **13, 464, 466**

Brazma, A. *See* Kaugers, Reinfelds, and Brazma (1994).

Brennan, J. *See* Anick, Brennan, Flynn, Hanssen, Alvey, and Robbins (1990).

Brill, E. (1992). A Simple Rule-Based Part of Speech Tagger. *Proceedings of Third Conference on Applied Natural Language,* Trento, Italy. 152–155. . . . . **455**

Brill, E. (1993). *A Corpus-Based Approach to Language Learning.* Unpublished Ph.D. Thesis, University of Pennsylvania. **455**

Brooks, F. (1988). Grasping Reality through Illusion—Interactive Graphics Serving Science. *Proceedings of CHI'88, ACM Conference on Human Factors in Computing Systems,* Washington, DC. 1–12. . . . . **102**

Brooks, F. *See* Ouh-Young, Beard, and Brooks (1989).

Brooks, R. (1991). Comparative Task Analysis: An Alternate Direction for Human-Computer Interaction Science. In J. M. Carroll (ed.), *Designing Interaction.* New York: Cambridge University Press. 50–59. . . . . **616**

Brown, C. *See* Snowdon, Benford, Brown, Ingram, Knox, and Studley (1995).

Brown, G. *See* Benford, Snowdon, Greenhalgh, Ingram, Knox, and Brown (1995).

Brown, M. D., and Krogh, M. (1988). Imcomp—An Image Compression and Conversion Algorithm for the Efficient Transmission, Storage, and Display of Color Images. *NCSA Data Link,* 2(3), 11–24. . . . . **42**

Brown, M. D. *See* DeFanti and Brown (1988, 1989a, 1989b); DeFanti, Brown, and McCormick (1989).

Brown, M. H., and Hershberger, J. (1992). Color and Sound in Algorithm Animation. *IEEE Computer, 25*(12), 52–63. . . **160, 222**

Brown, M. H., and Shillner, R. A. (1995). A New Paradigm for Browsing the Web. *Proceedings of CHI'95, ACM Conference on Human Factors in Computing Systems,* New York. 320–321. . **547**

Brown, M. H. *See* Sarkar and Brown (1992, 1994).

Brown, P. (1989). Do We Need Maps to Navigate Round Hypertext Documents? *Electronic Publishing, 2*(2). **630**

Brueni, D. *See* Heath, Hix, Nowell, Wake, Averboch, Labow, Guyer, Brueni, France, Dalal, and Fox (1995).

Bruggeman-Klein, A., and Wood, D. (1989). Drawing Trees Nicely with Tex. *Electronic Publishing,* 2(2 July), 101–115. . . . . **153**

Bruin, J. D. *See* Engelhardt, Bruin, Janssen, and Scha (1996).

Bruns, T. *See* Plaisant, Marchionini, Bruns, Komlodi, and Campbell (1997).

Bryson, S. *See* Zimmerman, Lanier, Blanchard, Bryson, and Harvill (1987).

Buckley, C. *See* Salton and Buckley (1991); Salton, Allan, and Buckley (1993); Salton, Allan, Buckley, and Singhal (1995); Salton, Buckley, and Allan (1992).

Buja, A., Cook, D., and Swayne, D. F. (1996). Interactive High-Dimensional Data Visualization. *Journal of Computational and Graphical Statistics, 5*(1), 78–99.. . . . . **95, 626**

Buja, A., McDonald, J. A., Michalak, J., and Stuetzle, W. (1991). Interactive Data Visualization Using Focusing and Linking. *Proceedings of IEEE Visualization'91 Conference,* New York. 156–163. . . . . **237, 246, 296**

Buja, A. *See* Cook and Buja (1997); Furnas and Buja (1994).

Burden, R. L., and Faires, J. D. (1985). *Numerical Analysis.* Boston: Duxbury Press.. . . . . **211**

Bureau of the Census. (1993). *Statistical Abstract of the United States.* Washington, DC. **254**

Burger, S. V., and Apperley, M. D. (1991). A Multi-Dimensional Approach to Interface Evaluation. *Proceedings of IFIP Conference on Human Jobs and Computer Interface'91.* 205–222. . . . . . . **362**

Burgess, C., and Swigger, K. (1986). A Graphical Database Interface for Casual Naive Users. *Information Processing and Management,* 22(6), 511–521. . . . . **438**

Burks, M. B. *See* Roth, Lucas, Senm, Gomberg, Burks, Stroffolino, and Kolojejchick (1996).

Buxton, W. *See* Bier, Stone, Baudel, Buxton, and Fishkin (1994); Bier, Stone, Pier, Buxton, and DeRose (1993).

Calliliau, R. *See* Berners-Lee, Calliliau, Luotonem, Nielsen, and Secret (1994).

Campbell, G., DeFanti, T. A., Frederiksen, J., Joyce, S. A., Leske, L. A., Lindberg, J. A., and Sandin, D. J. (1986). Two-Bit/Pixel Full Color Encoding. *Proceedings of SIGGRAPH'86, ACM Conference on Computer Graphics.* 215–223. . . . . **42, 50**

Campbell, L. *See* Plaisant, Marchionini, Bruns, Komlodi, and Campbell (1997).

Caplinger, M. A. *See* Schatz and Caplinger (1989).

Card, S. K. (1996). Visualizing Retrieved Information: A Survey. *IEEE Computer Graphics and Applications, 16*(2), 63–67. . . . . **12**

Card, S. K., and Henderson, D. A. (1987a). Catalogues: A Metaphor for Computer Application Delivery. *Proceedings of INTERACT'87.* 959–963. . . . . **546, 547**

Card, S. K., and Henderson, D. A., Jr. (1987b). A Multiple, Virtual-Workspace Interface to Support User Task Switching. *Proceedings of CHI+GI'87, ACM Conference on Human Factors in Computing Systems and Graphics Interface,* Toronto. 53–59. . . . . **513**

Card, S. K., and Mackinlay, J. D. (1997). The Structure of the Information Visualization Design Space. *Proceedings of InfoVis'97, IEEE Symposium on Information Visualization,* Phoenix. 92–99. . . **17, 26**

Card, S. K., Mackinlay, J. D., and Robertson, G. G. (1990). The Design Space of Input Devices. *Proceedings of CHI'90, ACM Conference on Human Factors in Computing Systems.* 117–124. . . . . **616**

Card, S. K., Moran, T. P., and Newell, A. (1983). *The Psychology of Human-Computer Interaction.* Hillsdale, NJ: Lawrence Erlbaum Associates. **231, 520, 580, 583, 584, 585, 587, 597, 602**

Card, S. K., Pavel, M., and Farrell, J. E. (1984). Window-Based Computer Dialogues. *Proceedings of INTERACT'84,* Amsterdam. 51–56. . . . . **545**

Card, S. K., Pirolli, P., and Mackinlay, J. D. (1994●). The Cost-of-Knowledge Characteristic Function: Display Evaluation for Direct-Walk Information Visualizations. *Proceedings of CHI'94, ACM Conference on Human Factors in Computing Systems,* Boston. 238–244. . . . . **14, 15, 233, 549, 580, 589, 622**

Card, S. K., Robertson, G. G., and Mackinlay, J. D. (1991). The Information Visualizer: An Information Workspace. *Proceedings of CHI'91, ACM Conference on Human Factors in Computing Sys-*

tems, New Orleans. 181–188. . . . . . **7, 8, 14, 16, 140, 159, 360, 494, 513, 517, 530, 548, 582, 585**

Card, S. K., Robertson, G. G., and York, W. (1996●). The WebBook and the Web Forager: An Information Workspace for the World-Wide Web. *Proceedings of CHI'96, ACM Conference on Human Factors in Computing Systems*, New York. 111–117. . . . . . **13, 464, 513, 630, 634**

Card, S. K. *See* Chi, Pitkow, Mackinlay, Pirolli, Gossweiler, and Card (1998); Elkind, Card, Hochberg, and Huey (1990); Henderson and Card (1986); Johnson, Jellinek, Klotz, Rao, and Card (1993); Mackinlay, Card, and Robertson (1990a, 1990b); Mackinlay, Rao, and Card (1995); Mackinlay, Robertson, and Card (1991); Pirolli and Card (1995, in press); Rao and Card (1994, 1995); Rao, Card, Jellinek, Mackinlay, and Robertson (1992); Rao, Pedersen, Hearst, Mackinlay, Card, Masinter, Halvorsen, and Robertson (1995); Robertson, Card, and Mackinlay (1989, 1993); Robertson, Mackinlay, and Card (1991); Russell, Stefik, Pirolli, and Card (1993).

Cardenas, A. *See* Chu, Cardenas, and Taira (1995).

Carey, T. T. *See* Hollands, Carey, Matthews, and McCann (1989).

Carling, R. *See* Herot, Carling, Friedell, and Framilch (1980).

Carpendale, M. S. T. (1997). *Exploring Distinct Aspects of the Distortion Viewing Paradigm*. Technical Report TR 97-08. Burnaby, B.C., Canada: School of Computing Science, Simon Fraser University. **342, 371, 372**

Carpendale, M. S. T., Cowperthwaite, D. J., and Fracchia, F. D. (1995). Three-Dimensional Pliable Surfaces: For Effective Presentation of Visual Information. *Proceedings of UIST'95, ACM Symposium on User Interface Software and Technology*, New York. 217–226. . . . . **32, 342**

Carpendale, M. S. T., Cowperthwaite, D. J., and Fracchia, F. D. (1996). Distortion Viewing Techniques for 3D Data. *Proceedings of InfoVis'96, IEEE Symposium on Information Visualization*, Los Alamitos, CA. 46–53, color plate 119. . . . . **369, 372, 373**

Carpendale, M. S. T., Cowperthwaite, D. J., and Fracchia, F. D. (1997). Extending Distortion Viewing from 2D to 3D. *IEEE Computer Graphics and Applications*, July/Aug., 42–51 . . . . . **373**

Carpenter, L. *See* Drebin, Carpenter, and Hanrahan (1988).

Carr, D. A., Jog, N., and Kumar, H. P. (1994). *Using Interaction Object Graphs to Specify and Develop Graphical Widgets*. Technical Report CS-TR-3344. University of Maryland. **235, 297**

Carr, D. A., Plaisant, C., and Hasegawa, H. (1994). *The Design of a Telepathology Workstation: Exploring Remote Images*. Technical Report CS-TR-3270. University of Maryland, Department of Computer Science. **572**

Carr, D. A. *See* Plaisant, Carr, and Hasegawa (1992); Plaisant, Carr, and Shneiderman (1995).

Carr, R., and Shafer, D. (1992). *The Power of PenPoint*. New York: Addison-Wesley. **546**

Carrière, J., and Kazman, R. (1995). Interacting the Huge Hierarchies: Beyond Cone Trees. *Proceedings of InfoVis'95, IEEE Symposium on Information Visualization*, New York. 74–81. . . . . **630**

Carswell, C. M., Frankenberger, S., and Bernhard, D. (1991). Graphing in Depth: Perspectives on the Use of Three-Dimensional Graphs to Represent Lower-Dimensional Data. *Behavior and Information Technology, 10*(6), 459–474. . . . . **634**

Casner, S. (1991). Task-Analytic Approach to the Automated Design of Graphic Presentations. *ACM Transactions on Graphics, 10*(2, April), 111–151. . . . . **8, 225, 616, 628**

Chalmers, M. (1993). Using a Landscape Metaphor to Represent a Corpus of Documents. In A. U. Frank and I. Campari (eds.), *Spatial Information Theory: A Theoretical Basis for GIS*. New York: Springer-Verlag. 377–390. . . . . **277**

Chalmers, M. (1996). A Linear Iteration Time Layout Algorithm for Visualizing High-Dimensional Data. *Proceedings of IEEE Visualization'96 Conference*. 127–132. . . . . **431, 441**

Chalmers, M., and Chitson, P. (1992). BEAD: Exploration in Information Visualization. *Proceedings of SIGIR'92, ACM Conference on Research and Development in Information Retrieval*. 330–337. . . . . **147, 554, 628**

Chalmers, M., Ingram, R., and Pfranger, C. (1996). Adding Imageability Feature to Information Displays. *Proceedings of UIST'96, ACM Symposium on User Interface Software and Technology*. 33–39. . . . . **617, 619, 620, 622**

Chambers, J. M. *See* Becker, Chambers, and Wilks (1988a).

Chan, K. T. *See* Chen and Chan (1990).

Chang, B.-W., and Ungar, D. (1993). Animation: From Cartoons to the User Interface. *Proceedings of UIST'93, ACM Symposium on User Interface Software and Technology*, Atlanta. 45–55. . . . . **455**

Chang, C. L. (1975). Interpretation and Execution of Fuzzy Programs. In *Fuzzy Sets and Their Applications to Cognitive and Decision Processes*. New York: Academic Press. 191–218. . . . . **257**

Chen, G. *See* Livny, Ramakrishnan, Beyer, Chen, Donjerkovic, Lawande, Myllymaki, and Wenger (1997).

Chen, H. C., and Chan, K. T. (1990). Reading Computer-Displayed Moving Text with and without Self-Control over the Display Rate. *Behavior and Information Technology, 9*(6), 467–477. . . . **360**

Chen, Y. F. (1989). The C Program Database and Its Applications. *Proceedings of USENIX'89*. **419**

Chi, E. H., and Riedl, J. T. (1998). An Operator Interaction Framework for Visualization Spreadsheets. *Proceedings of InfoVis'98, IEEE Symposium on Information Visualization*. **580**

Chi, E. H., Pitkow, J., Mackinlay, J., Pirolli, P., Gossweiler, R., and Card, S. K. (1998). Visualizing the Evolution of Web Ecologies. *Proceedings of CHI'98, ACM Conference on Human Factors in Computing Systems*. 400–407. . . . . **468**

Chignell, M. H., Nordhausen, B., Valdez, J. F., and Waterworth, J. A. (1991). The HEFTI Model of Text to Hypertext Conversion. *Hypermedia, 3*(3), 187–205. . . . . **418**

Chignell, M. H., Zuberec, S., and Poblete, F. (1993). An Exploration in the Design Space of Three Dimensional Hierarchies. *Proceedings of Human Factors Society'93*, Santa Monica, CA. 333–337. . . . . **296**

Chimera, R. (1992). Value Bars: An Information Visualization and Navigation Tool for Multi-Attribute Listings. *Proceedings of CHI'92, ACM Conference on Human Factors in Computing Systems*. 293–294. . . . . **58**

Chimera, R., and Shneiderman, B. (1994). An Exploratory Evaluation of Three Interfaces for Browsing Large Hierarchical Tables of Contents. *ACM Transactions on Information Systems, 12*(4 October). 383–406. . . . . **628**

Chimera, R., Wolman, K., Mark, S., and Shneiderman, B. (1991). *Evaluation of Three Interfaces for Browsing Hierarchical Tables of Contents*. Technical Report CAR-TR-539CS-TR-2620. University of Maryland. **153**

Chitson, P. *See* Chalmers and Chitson (1992).

Choi, E. *See* Ross, Zhang, and Choi (1994).

Chomut, T. (1987). *Exploratory Data Analysis in Parallel Coordinates*. Unpublished M.Sc. Thesis, UCLA. **108**

Chu, W., Cardenas, A., and Taira, R. (1995). KMeD: A Knowledge-Based Multimedia Medical Distributed Database System. *Information Systems, 20*(2), 75–96. . . . . **571**

Chua, T.-S. *See* Serra, Chua, and Teh (1991).

Chuah, M. C., Roth, S. F., Mattis, J., and Kolojejchick, J. A. (1995a). SDM: Malleable Information Graphics. *Proceedings of InfoVis'95, IEEE Symposium on Information Visualization,* New York. 36–42. . . . . **13, 261, 608**

Chuah, M. C., Roth, S. F., Mattis, J., and Kolojejchick, J. A. (1995b●). SDM: Selective Dynamic Manipulation of Visualizations. *Proceedings of UIST'95, ACM Symposium on User Interface Software and Technology,* Pittsburgh. 61–70. . . . . . . **261**

Cichinski, S., and Fowler, G. S. (1988). Product Administration through SABLE and NMAKE. *AT&T Technical Journal, 67*(4), 59–70. . . . . . . **419**

Cleveland, W. S. (1980). *The Elements of Graphing Data.* Belmont, CA: Wadsworth. **72, 74**

Cleveland, W. S. (1993). *Visualizing Data.* Summit, NJ: Hobart Press. **626**

Cleveland, W. S. (1994). *The Elements of Graphing Data.* Rev. ed. Murray Hill, NJ: AT&T Bell Laboratories. **626**

Cleveland, W. S., and McGill, M. E. (1988). *Dynamic Graphics for Statistics.* Pacific Grove, CA: Wadsworth and Brooks/Cole. **7, 84, 95, 161, 226, 233**

Cleveland, W. S., and McGill, R. (1984). Graphical Perception: Theory, Experimentation and Application to the Development of Graphical Methods. *Journal of the American Statistical Association, 79*(387), 531–554. . . . . . . **73**

Cleveland, W. S., and McGill, R. (1987). The Visual Decoding of Quantitative Information on Graphical Displays of Data. *Journal of the Royal Statistics Society Series A, 150,* 195–229. . . . . . . **225**

Cleveland, W. S. *See* Becker and Cleveland (1984); Becker and Cleveland (1987); Becker, Cleveland, and Weil (1988b); Becker, Cleveland, and Wilks (1987, 1988c).

Cohen, R. *See* Slocum and Cohen (1986).

Colby, G., and Scholl, L. (1991). Transparency and Blur as Selective Cues for Complex Visual Information. *Proceedings of SPIE'91,* San Jose. 114–125. . . . . . . **258, 455**

Conklin, J., and Begeman, M. (1989). gIBIS: A Tool for All Reasons. *Information Society for Information Science, 40*(3), 200–213. . **438**

Conner, D. B., Snibbe, S. S., Herndon, K. P., and Zeleznik, R. C. (1992). Three-Dimensional Widgets. *Proceedings of Symposium on Interactive 3D Graphics.* 183–188. . . . . . . **519**

Consens, M. P., and Hasan, M. Z. (1993). Supporting Network Management through Declaratively Specified Data Visualizations. *Proceedings of IFIP'93, Conference of International Federation for Information Processing.* 725–738. . . . . . . **225**

Consens, M. P., Eigler, F. C., Hasan, M. Z., Mendelzon, A. O., Noik, E. G., Ryman, A. G., and Vista, D. (1994). Architecture and Applications of the Hy+ Visualization Systems. *IBM Systems Journal, 33*(3), 458–476. . . . . . . **225**

Consens, M. P., Mendelzon, A. O., and Ryan, A. G. (1992). Visualization and Querying Software Structures. *Proceedings of 14th International Conference on Software Engineering.* 135–156. . **225**

Cook, D., and Buja, A. (1997). Manual Controls for High-Dimensional Data Projections. *Journal of Computational and Graphical Statistics, 6*(4), 464–480. . . . . . . **95**

Cook, D. *See* Buja, Cook, and Swayne (1996).

Cooper, M. (1994). *Information Landscapes.* MIT Technical Note. **455**

Cooper, M. *See* Small, Ishizki, and Cooper (1994).

Coulouris, G. (1979). Personal Computers in Offices of the Future. *Microprocessors and Microsystems, 3,* 69. . . . . . . **338**

Cowperthwaite, D. J. *See* Carpendale, Cowperthwaite, and Fracchia (1995, 1996, 1997).

Cox, D. J. (1990). The Art of Scientific Visualization. *Academic Computing, 20.* **159**

Cox, D., and Patterson, R. (1991). *National Center for Supercomputing Applications, A Visualization Study of Networking.* Video. . **225**

Cox, K. C., Eick, S. G., and Wills, G. J. (1997). Visual Data Mining: Recognizing Telephone Calling Fraud. *Journal of Data Mining and Knowledge Discovery, 1*(2), 225–231. . . . . . . **9**

Cox, K. C. *See* Eick and Cox (1995); Roman, Cox, Wilcox, and Plun (1992).

Coxeter, H. S. M. (1965). *Non-Euclidean Geometry.* Toronto: University of Toronto Press. **384**

Crabb, A. H. *See* Wong, Crabb, and Bergeron (1996).

Croft, B. *See* Belkin and Croft (1992).

Croft, W. B. *See* Belkin and Croft (1987).

Cruz, I. F., and Tamassia, R. (1998). Graph Drawing Tutorial. *http://www.cs.brown.edu/people/rt/papers/gd-tutorial/gd-constraints.pdf.* **188**

Cutler, A., and McShane, R. (1960). *The Tractenberg Speed Systems of Basic Mathematics.* Garden City, NY: Doubleday. **2**

Cutting, D. R., Karger, D. R., Pedersen, J. O., and Tukey, J. W. (1992a). Scatter/Gather: A Cluster-Based Approach to Browsing Large Document Collections. *Proceedings of SIGIR'92, ACM Conference on Research and Development in Information Retrieval.* 318–329. . . . . . . **521, 567**

Cutting, D. R., Kupiec, J., Pedersen, J. O., and Sibun, P. (1992b). A Practical Part-of-Speech Tagger. *Proceedings of Third Conference on Applied Natural Language.* 133–140. . . . . . . **455**

Cutting, D. R., Pederson, J. O., and Halvorsen, P. K. (1991). An Object Oriented Architecture for Text Retrieval. *Proceedings of RIAO'91.* 285–298. . . . . . . **521, 567**

Dalal, K. *See* Heath, Hix, Nowell, Wake, Averboch, Labow, Guyer, Brueni, France, Dalal, and Fox (1995).

Davenport, G. *See* Elliott and Davenport (1994).

Davidson, C. (1993). What Your Database Hides Away. *New Scientist, 9th January.* **617, 618, 620**

Dawkes, H., Tweedie, L. A., and Spence, R. (1996). VICKI—The Visualisation Construction Kit. *Proceedings of AVI'96, Workshop on Advanced Visual Interfaces,* Gubbio, Italy. 257–259. . . . . . **620**

Dawkes, H. *See* Tweedie, Spence, Dawkes, and Su (1996).

Deerwester, S., Dumais, S. T., Furnas, G. W., Landauer, T. K., and Harshman, R. (1990). Indexing by Latent Semantic Analysis. *Journal of the American Society for Information Science, 41*(6), 391–407. . . . . . . **531**

Deerwester, S. *See* Dumais, Furnas, Landauer, and Deerwester (1988).

DeFanti, T. A., and Sandin, D. J. (1987). The Usable Intersection of PC Graphics and NTSC Video Recording. *IEEE Computer Graphics and Applications,* October, 50–58. . . . . . . **42**

DeFanti, T. A., and Brown, M. D. (1988). Scientific Animation Workstations. *SuperComputing,* Fall, 10–13. . . . . . . **43**

DeFanti, T. A., and Brown, M. D. (1989a). Insight through Images. *Unix Review,* March, 42–50. . . . . . . **42**

DeFanti, T. A., and Brown, M. D. (1989b). Scientific Animation Workstations: Creating an Environment for Remote Research, Education, and Communication. *Academic Computing,* Feb., 10–12, 55–57. . . . . . . **42**

DeFanti, T. A., Brown, M. D., and McCormick, B. H. (1989●). Visualization—Expanding Scientific and Engineering Research Opportunities. *IEEE Computer, 22*(8), 12–25. . . . . **31, 37, 59**

DeFanti, T. A. *See* Campbell, DeFanti, Frederiksen, Joyce, Leske, Lindberg, and Sandin (1986); McCormick and DeFanti (1987).

deJong, G. (1982). An Overview of the FRUMP System. In W. G. Lehnet and M. H. Ringle (eds.), *Strategies for Natural Language Processing.* Mahwah, NJ: Lawrence Erlbaum Associates. 149–176. . . . . **416**

Delaney, P., and Landow, G. P. (eds.). (1991). *Hypermedia and Literary Studies.* Cambridge, MA: MIT Press. **413**

DeLine, R. *See* Mackinlay, Robertson, and DeLine (1994).

DeRose, T. *See* Bier, Stone, Pier, Buxton, and DeRose (1993).

Diehl, C. *See* Pirolli, Schank, Hearst, and Diehl (1996).

Dill, J. *See* Bartram, Ho, Dill, and Henigman (1995); Schaffer, Zuo, Bartram, Dill, Dubes, Greenberg, and Roseman (1993, 1996).

Dimsdale, B. *See* Inselberg and Dimsdale (1990).

Ding, C., and Mateti, P. (1990). A Framework for the Automated Drawing of Data Structure Diagrams. *IEEE Transactions on Software Engineering, 16*(5), 543–557. . . . . **157**

diSessa, A. A. (1985). A Principled Design for an Integrated Computational Environment. *Human-Computer Interaction, 1*(1), 1–47. . . . . **201**

Dix, A. J., and Ellis, G. (1998). Starting Simple—Adding Value to Static Visualization through Simple Interaction. *Proceedings of AVI'98, Workshop on Advanced Visual Interfaces,* L'Aquila, Italy. 124–134. . . . . **561**

Dix, A. J. *See* Monk, Walsh, and Dix (1988).

Doan, K., Plaisant, C., and Shneiderman, B. (1996). Query Previews in Networked Information Systems. *Proceedings of ADL'96, Advances in Digital Libraries.* 120–129. . . . . **572, 627**

Doan, K. *See* Plaisant, Doan, and Shneiderman (1995).

Donelson, W. (1978). Spatial Management of Information. *Proceedings of SIGGRAPH'78, ACM Conference on Computer Graphics.* 203–209. . . . . **99, 350, 538**

Donjerkovic, D. *See* Livny, Ramakrishnan, Beyer, Chen, Donjerkovic, Lawande, Myllymaki, and Wenger (1997).

Donobo, A. W., Donobo, D. L., and Gasko, M. (1986). *MACSPIN: A Tool for Dynamic Display of Multivariate Data.* Monterey, CA: Wadsworth and Brooks/Cole. **419**

Donobo, D. L. *See* Donobo, Donobo, and Gasko (1986).

Dowson, S. T. *See* Risch, May, Dowson, and Thomas (1996); Risch, Rex, Dowson, Walters, May, and Moon (1997).

Doyle, L. B. (1962). Indexing and Abstracting by Association. *American Documentation,* October, 378–390. . . . . **432**

Draper, S. W. (1986). Display Managers as the Basis for User-Machine Communications. In S. W. Draper (ed.), *User Centered System Design.* Hillsdale, NJ: Lawrence Erlbaum Associates. 339–352. . . . . **235, 618**

Draper, S. W. (1993). Critical Notice: Activity Theory: The New Direction for HCL? *IDIOMS,* 812–821. . . . . **622**

Drebin, R. A., Carpenter, L., and Hanrahan, P. (1988). Volume Rendering. *Proceedings of SIGGRAPH'88, ACM Conference on Computer Graphics.* 65–74. . . . . **49**

Drew, N. S., and Hendley, R. J. (1995). Visualizing Complex Interacting Systems. *Conference Companion of CHI'95, ACM Conference on Human Factors in Computing Systems.* 204–205. . . . . **509**

Drew, N. S. *See* Hendley, Drew, Wood, and Beale (1995).

Dubes, S. *See* Schaffer, Zuo, Bartram, Dill, Dubes, Greenberg, and Roseman (1993, 1996).

Dumais, S. T., and Landauer, T. K. (1984). Describing Categories of Objects for Menu Retrieval Systems. *Research Methods, Instruments and Computers, 16,* 242–248. . . . . **198**

Dumais, S. T., Furnas, G. W., Landauer, T. K., and Deerwester, S. (1988). Using Latent Semantic Analysis to Improve Information Retrieval. *Proceedings of CHI'88, ACM Conference on Human Factors in Computing Systems.* 281–285. . . . . **553**

Dumais, S. T. *See* Deerwester, Dumais, Furnas, Landauer, and Harshman (1990).

Eades, P. *See* Battista, Eades, Tamassia, and Tollis (1994); Misue, Eadest, and Lai (1995).

Earnshaw, R. A. *See* Rosenblum, Earnshaw, Encarnação, Hagen, Kaufman, Klimenko, Nielson, Post, and Thalmann (1994).

Eberhardt, J. *See* Egan, Remde, Gomez, Landauer, Eberhardt, and Lochbaum (1989).

Ebert, C. (1992). Visualization Techniques for Analyzing and Evaluating Software Measures. *IEEE Transactions on Software Engineering, 18*(11), 1029–1034. . . . . **160**

Edmundson, H. P., and Wyllys, R. E. (1961). Automatic Abstracting and Indexing, Survey and Recommendations. *Communications of the ACM, 4*(5), 226–234. . . . . **417**

Egan, D. E., Remde, J. R., Gomez, L. M., Landauer, T. K., Eberhardt, J., and Lochbaum, C. C. (1989). Formative Design Evaluation of Superbook. *ACM Transactions on Office Information Systems, 7*(1), 30–42. . . . . **628**

Egenhofer, M. J. (1990). Manipulating the Graphical Representation of Query Results in Geographic Information Systems. *Proceedings of IEEE Workshop on Visual Languages'90,* Los Alamitos, CA. 119–124. . . . . **237, 246, 254**

Eick, S. G. (1993). *Data Visualization Sliders.* Technical Report. Naperville, IL.: AT&T Bell Laboratories. **243,248**

Eick, S. G. (1994a●). Data Visualization Sliders. *Proceedings of UIST'94, ACM Symposium on User Interface Software and Technology,* Marina del Rey, CA. 119–120. . . . . **58, 218, 235, 237, 245, 617, 620**

Eick, S. G. (1994b). A Graphical Technique to Display Ordered Text. *Journal of Computational and Graphical Statistics, 3,* 127–142. . **161**

Eick, S. G. (1994c). Graphically Displaying Text. *Journal of Computational and Graphical Statistics, 3*(2), 127–142. . . . . **251**

Eick, S. G., and Cox, K. C. (1995). Case Study: 3D Displays of Internet Traffic. *Proceedings of InfoVis'95, IEEE Symposium on Information Visualization,* Atlanta. 129–131. . . . . **188**

Eick, S. G., and Wills, G. J. (1993). Navigating Large Networks with Hierarchies. *Proceedings of IEEE Visualization'93 Conference,* San Jose. 204–210. . . . . . **25, 187, 188, 189, 223, 225, 431, 630**

Eick, S. G., Steffen, J. L., and Sumner, E. E. (1992●). Seesoft—A Tool for Visualizing Line Oriented Software Statistics. *IEEE Transactions on Software Engineering, 18*(11-Nov.), 957–968. . . . . **8, 27, 58, 161, 251, 277, 411, 412, 538, 623, 629, 634**

Eick, S. G. *See* Baker and Eick (1995); Becker, Eick, and Miller (1989a); Becker, Eick, and Wilks (1991, 1995); Becker, Eick, Miller, and Wilks (1989b, 1990a, 1990b); Cox, Eick, and Wills (1997).

Eigler, F. C. *See* Consens, Eigler, Hasan, Mendelzon, Noik, Ryman, and Vista (1994).

Eisenberg, M. (1996). The Thin Glass Line: Designing Interfaces to Algorithms. *Proceedings of CHI'96, ACM Conference on Human Factors in Computing Systems.* 181–188. . . . . **617, 619, 620**

Elkind, J. I., Card, S. K., Hochberg, J., and Huey, B. M. (1990). *Human Performance Models for Computer-Aided Engineering.* Boston: Academic Press. **24**

Elliott, E., and Davenport, G. (1994). Video Streamer. *Proceedings of CHI'94, ACM Conference on Human Factors in Computing Systems.* 65–66. . . . . **576**

Ellis, G. *See* Dix and Ellis (1998).

Ellson, R. (1990). Visualization at Work. *Academic Computing, 26.* **157**

Encarnação, J. *See* Rosenblum, Earnshaw, Encarnação, Hagen, Kaufman, Klimenko, Nielson, Post, and Thalmann (1994).

Enderton, H. B. (1972). *A Mathematical Introduction to Logic.* Orlando, FL: Academic Press. **71**

Endres, L. *See* Singers and Endres (1993).

Engelbart, D. C., and English, W. K. (1968). A Research Center for Augmenting Human Intellect. *Proceedings of AFIPS'68.* 15. . **313**

Engelhardt, Y., Bruin, J. D., Janssen, T., and Scha, R. (1996). The Visual Grammar of Information Graphics. In S. University (ed.), *Artificial Intelligence in Design Workshop Notes.* 24–27. . **26**

English, W. K. *See* Engelbart and English (1968).

Enns, J. T. *See* Healey, Booth, and Enns (1995).

Epstein, W. V. *See* Whiting-O'Keefe, Simbork, Epstein, and Warger (1985).

Equitz, W. *See* Faloutsos, Barber, Flickner, Hafner, Niblack, Petrovic, and Equitz (1994).

Erickson, T. *See* McCahill and Erickson (1995).

Evans, J. *See* Gauch, Aust, Evans, Gauch, Minden, Niehaus, and Roberts (1994).

Factor, M., Gelernter, D. H., Kolb, C. E., Miller, P. L., and Sittig, D. F. (1991). Real-Time Data Fusion in the Intensive Care Unit. *IEEE Computer, 24*(11), 45–54.. . . . **288**

Fairchild, K. M. (1985). *Construction of a Semantic Net Virtual World Metaphor.* Technical Report HI-163-85. Austin, TX: Microelectronics and Computer Technology Corporation. **190**

Fairchild, K. M., and Poltrock, S. E. (1986). *SemNet.* Video. Boston. **190**

Fairchild, K. M., and Poltrock, S. E. (1987). *Soaring through Knowledge Space: SemNet 2.1.* Video. Toronto. **205**

Fairchild, K. M., Poltrock, S. E., and Furnas, G. W. (1988●). SemNet: Three-Dimensional Representations of Large Knowledge Bases. In R. Guindon (ed.), *Cognitive Science and Its Applications for Human-Computer Interaction.* Hillsdale, NJ: Lawrence Erlbaum Associates. 201–233. . . . . **187, 188, 189, 224, 369, 431, 438, 441, 494, 526, 530, 551, 554, 562**

Fairchild, K. M., Serra, L., Hern, N., Hai, L. B., and Leong, A. T. (1993). Dynamic FishEye Information Visualizations. In A. Earnshaw, M. A. Gigante, and H. Jones (eds.), *Virtual Reality Systems.* San Diego: Academic Press. 161–177. . . . . **494**

Fairchild, K. M. *See* Poltrock, Shook, Fairchild, Lovgren, Tarlton, Tarlton, and Hauser (1986).

Faires, J. D. *See* Burden and Faires (1985).

Faldowski, R. A. *See* Young, Faldowski, and McFarlane (1993).

Faloutsos, C., Barber, R., Flickner, M., Hafner, J., Niblack, W., Petrovic, D., and Equitz, W. (1994). Efficient and Effective Querying by Image Content. *Journal of Intelligent Information Systems, 3,* 231–262. . . . . **571**

Farrand, W. A. (1973). *Information Display in Interactive Design.* Unpublished Ph.D. Thesis, USC, Los Angeles. . . . **341, 351, 360**

Farrel, E. J. (1987). Visual Interpretation of Complex Data. *IBM Systems Journal, 26*(2), 174–200. . . . . **115**

Farrell, J. E. *See* Card, Pavel, and Farrell (1984).

Faulhabel Jr., T. *See* Upson, Faulhabel Jr., Kamins, Laidlaw, Schegel, Vroom, Gurwitz, and van Dam (1989).

Feiner, S. K. (1985). APEX: An Experiment in the Automated Creation of Pictorial Explanations. *IEEE Computer Graphics and Applications, 5*(11), 29–37. . . . . **67**

Feiner, S. K. (1988). Seeing the Forest for the Trees: Hierarchical Display of Hypertext Structures. *Proceedings of COIS'88,* Palo Alto, CA. 205–212. . . . . **159**

Feiner, S. K., and Beshers, C. (1990a). Visualizing *n*-Dimensional Virtual Worlds with *n*-Vision. *Computer Graphics, 24*(2), 37–38. . . . . **115, 127**

Feiner, S. K., and Beshers, C. (1990b●). Worlds within Worlds: Metaphors for Exploring *n*-Dimensional Virtual Worlds. *Proceedings of UIST'90, ACM Symposium on User Interface Software and Technology.* 76–83. . . . . **8, 84, 93, 94, 242, 246, 277, 455, 456, 523, 562, 626**

Feiner, S. K., and Beshers, C. (1993). AutoVisual: Rule-Based Design of Interactive Multivariate Visualizations. *IEEE Computer Graphics and Applications, 13*(4), 41–49. . . . . **28**

Feiner, S. K., and McKeown, K. (1991). Automating the Generation of Coordinated Multimedia Explanations. *IEEE Computer, 24*(10), 33–41. . . . . **307, 332**

Feiner, S. K., Salesin, D., and Banchoff, T. (1982). DIAL: A Diagrammatic Animation Language. *IEEE Computer Graphics and Applications, September,* 43–54. . . . . **97**

Feiner, S. K. *See* Beshers and Feiner (1988, 1989); Foley, van Dam, Feiner, and Hughes (1990).

Fenner, B. *See* Munzner, Fenner, and Hoffman (1996).

Ferrari, L. D. *See* Robertson and Ferrari (1994).

Fertig, S. *See* Freeman and Fertig (1995).

Feynman, R. P., and Hutchins, E. (eds.) (1986). *Surely You're Joking, Mr. Feynman! Adventures of a Curious Character, As told to R. Leighton.* New York: Bantam Books. 236–253. . . . . **44**

Fikes, R. *See* Tou, Williams, Fikes, A. Henderson, and Malone (1982).

Filo, D., and Yang, J. (1994). *Yahoo (Yet Another Hierarchical Officious Oracle).* Stanford, CA: Yahoo! Corp. **544**

Finger, J. J., and Genesereth, M. R. (1985). *RESIDUE: A Deductive Approach to Design Synthesis.* Technical Report KSL-85-1. Stanford, CA: Stanford University. **79**

Finin, T., Fritzon, R., and McKay, D. (1992). *An Overview of KQML, A Knowledge Query and Manipulation Language.* Technical Report. University of Maryland, Department of Computer Science. **505, 507**

Finsterwalder, R. (1991). *A Parallel Coordinate Editor as a Visual Decision Aid in Multi-Objective Concurrent Control Engineering Environment.* Swansea, UK.. . . . **108**

Fishkin, K., and Stone, M. C. (1995●). Enhanced Dynamic Queries via Movable Filters. *Proceedings of CHI'95, ACM Conference on Human Factors in Computing Systems.* 415–420. . . . **31, 234, 235**

Fishkin, K. *See* Bier, Stone, Baudel, Buxton, and Fishkin (1994); Stone, Fishkin, and Bier (1994).

Flickner, M. *See* Faloutsos, Barber, Flickner, Hafner, Niblack, Petrovic, and Equitz (1994).

Flynn, R. *See* Anick, Brennan, Flynn, Hanssen, Alvey, and Robbins (1990).

Foley, J. D., van Dam, A., Feiner, S. K., and Hughes, J. F. (1990). *Computer Graphics Principles and Practice.* Reading, MA: Addison-Wesley.. . . . **251**

Foley, J. D. *See* Mukherjea and Foley (1995); Mukherjea, Foley, and Hudson (1995).

Fowler, G. S. *See* Cichinski and Fowler (1988).

Fox, D. *See* Perlin and Fox (1993).

Fox, E. *See* Heath, Hix, Nowell, Wake, Averboch, Labow, Guyer, Brueni, France, Dalal, and Fox (1995).

Fracchia, F. D. *See* Carpendale, Cowperthwaite, and Fracchia (1995, 1996, 1997).

Framilch, D. *See* Herot, Carling, Friedell, and Framilch (1980).

France, R. *See* Heath, Hix, Nowell, Wake, Averboch, Labow, Guyer, Brueni, France, Dalal, and Fox (1995).

Franck, G. *See* Ware and Franck (1996); Ware, Hui, and Franck (1993).

Frankenberger, S. *See* Carswell, Frankenberger, and Bernhard (1991).

Frederiksen, J. *See* Campbell, DeFanti, Frederiksen, Joyce, Leske, Lindberg, and Sandin (1986).

Freeman, E., and Fertig, S. (1995). Lifestreams: Organizing Your Electronic Life. *Proceedings of AAAI Fall Symposium on AI Applications in Knowledge Navigation*. **58**

Friedell, M. (1983). *Automatic Graphics Environment Synthesis*. Cleveland, OH: Case Western Reserve University. **67**

Friedell, M. *See* Herot, Carling, Friedell, and Framilch (1980).

Friedman, J. H., and Rafsky, L. C. (1979). Fast Algorithms for Multivariate Lining and Planning. *Proceedings of Computer Science and Statistics: 8th Annual Symposium on the Interface*. 124–136. . . . **226**

Friedman, J. H. *See* Bentley and Friedman (1979).

Fritzon, R. *See* Finin, Fritzon, and McKay (1992).

Furnas, G. W. (1981 ●). *The FISHEYE View: A New Look at Structured Files*. Murray Hill, NJ: AT&T Bell Laboratories. . . **187, 307**

Furnas, G. W. (1986). Generalized Fisheye Views, Human Factors in Computing Systems. *Proceedings of CHI'86, ACM Conference on Human Factors in Computing Systems*, New York. 16–23. . . . **152, 156, 184, 196, 197, 265, 266, 270, 271, 311, 344, 351, 354, 355, 369, 386, 454, 526, 531, 563, 634**

Furnas, G. W. (1997 ●). Effective View Navigation. *Proceedings of CHI'97, ACM Conference on Human Factors in Computing Systems*, Atlanta. 367–374. . . . . **233, 580, 592, 593**

Furnas, G. W., and Bederson, B. B. (1995). Space-Scale Diagrams: Understanding Multiscale Interfaces. *Proceedings of CHI'95, ACM Conference on Human Factors in Computing Systems*. 234–241. . . . . **371, 589, 592, 596**

Furnas, G. W., and Buja, A. (1994). Prosection Views: Dimensional Inference through Sections and Projections. *Journal of Computational and Graphical Statistics*, *3*(4), 323–353. . . . . **280**

Furnas, G. W., and Zacks, J. (1994). Multitrees: Enriching and Reusing Hierarchical Structure. *Proceedings of CHI'94, ACM Conference on Human Factors in Computing Systems*, Boston. 330–336. . . . . **617**

Furnas, G. W. *See* Arias and Furnas (1982); Bederson, Hollan, Perlin, Meyer, Bacon, and Furnas (1996); Deerwester, Dumais, Furnas, Landauer, and Harshman (1990); Dumais, Furnas, Landauer, and Deerwester (1988); Fairchild, Poltrock, and Furnas (1988).

Furuta, R., Plaisant, C., and Shneiderman, B. (1989). A Spectrum of Automatic Hypertext Construction. *Hypermedia*, *1*(2), 179–195. . . . . **415**

Gallop, J. (1994). Underlying Data Models and Structures for Visualization. In L. Rosenblum, R. A. Earnshaw, J. Encarnação, H. Hagen, A. Kaufman, S. Klimenko, G. Nielson, F. Post, and D. Thalmann (eds.), *Scientific Visualization: Advances and Challenges*. San Diego: Academic Press. 237–250. . . . . **17, 20**

Ganapathy, S. *See* Weimer and Ganapathy (1989).

Gansner, E. R., Koutsofios, E. E., North, S. C., and Vo, K. P. (1993). A Technique for Drawing Directed Graphs. *IEEE Transactions on Software Engineering*, *19*(3), 214–230. . . . . . . **160, 223**

Gasko, M. *See* Donobo, Donobo, and Gasko (1986).

Gauch, J. *See* Gauch, Aust, Evans, Gauch, Minden, Niehaus, and Roberts (1994).

Gauch, S., Aust, R., Evans, J., Gauch, J., Minden, G., Niehaus, D., and Roberts, J. (1994). The Digital Video Library System: Vision and Design. *Proceedings of DL'94, ACM Conference on Digital Libraries*. 47–52. . . . . **571**

Gaver, W. W. (1989). The SonicFinder: An Interface that Uses Auditory Icons. *Human-Computer Interaction*, *4*(1), 67–94. . . . **225**

Gaver, W. W. (1993). Synthesizing Auditory Icons. *Proceedings of CHI'93, ACM Conference on Human Factors in Computing Systems*. 228–235. . . . . **225**

Gaver, W. W. *See* Smets, Gaver, Overbeeke, and Stappers (1993).

Gedye, D. (1988). *Browsing the Tangled Web*. Unpublished Master's Thesis, University of California, Berkeley. **296**

Gelatt, C. D. *See* Kirkpatrick, Gelatt, and Vecchi (1983).

Gelernter, D. H. *See* Factor, Gelernter, Kolb, Miller, and Sittig (1991).

Gell-Mann, M. (1994). *The Quark and the Jaguar: Adventures in the Simple and the Complex*. New York: W. H. Freeman and Company. **11**

Genesereth, M. R. *See* Finger and Genesereth (1985); Mackinlay and Genesereth (1985).

Gettys, J. *See* Scheifler, Gettys, and Newman (1988).

Gibson, W. (1984). *Neuromancer*. New York: Ace Books. **465**

Gilyarevskii, R. S., and Subbotin, M. M. (1993). Russian Experience in Hypertext: Automatic Compiling of Coherent Texts. *Journal of the American Statistical Association*, *44*(4), 195–193. . . . . **415**

Gleason, T. (1982). *Reader: A Program to Assist with Reading Documents on Terminals*. AT&T Bell Laboratories. **323**

Gleicher, M. *See* Herndon, van Dam, and Gleicher (1994).

Gnanamgari, S. (1981). *Information Presentation through Default Displays*. Philadelphia: The Wharton School, University of Pennsylvania. **67**

Goldstein, J., and Roth, S. F. (1994). Using Aggregation and Dynamic Queries for Exploring Large Data Sets. *Proceedings of CHI'94, ACM Conference on Human Factors in Computing Systems*, New York. 23–29. . . . . **254**

Goldstein, J., Roth, S. F., Kolojejchick, J. A., and Mattis, J. (1994). A Framework for Knowledge-Based Interactive Data Exploration. *Journal of Visual Languages and Computing*, *5*(4), 339–363. . . . . **272**

Golovchinsky, G. (1997). Queries? Links? Is There a Difference? *Proceedings of CHI'97, ACM Conference on Human Factors in Computing Systems*, Atlanta. 407–414. . . . . **431**

Gomberg, C. C. *See* Roth, Lucas, Senm, Gomberg, Burks, Strofolino, and Kolojejchick (1996).

Gomez, L. M. *See* Egan, Remde, Gomez, Landauer, Eberhardt, and Lochbaum (1989); Remde, Gomez, and Landauer (1987).

Gossweiler, R. *See* Chi, Pitkow, Mackinlay, Pirolli, Gossweiler, and Card (1998).

Gray, M., Badre, A., and Guzdial, M. (1996). Visualizing Usability Log Data. *Proceedings of InfoVis'96, IEEE Symposium on Information Visualization*. 93–98. . . . . **58**

Green, M., and Jacob, R. (1991). SIGGRAPH'90 Workshop Report: Software Architectures and Metaphors for Non-WIMP User Interfaces. *Computer Graphics*, *25*(3), 229–235. . . . . **516**

Green, M. *See* Shaw, Liang, Green, and Sun (1992).

Green, T. R. G. (1989). Cognitive Dimensions of Notations. *Proceedings of HCI'89*, Nottingham. 443–460. . . . . **622**

Green, T. R. G., and Benyon, D. R. (1996). The Skull Beneath the Skin: Entity-Relationship Models of Information Artifacts. *International Journal of Human-Computer Studies, 44*(6), 801–828. . . . . **620**

Greenberg, S. *See* Gutwin and Greenberg (1997); Schaffer, Zuo, Bartram, Dill, Dubes, Greenberg, and Roseman (1993, 1996).

Greenfeld, N. R. *See* Zdybel, Greenfeld, and Yonke (1981).

Greenhalgh, C. *See* Benford, Snowdon, Greenhalgh, Ingram, Knox, and Brown (1995).

Griffith, B. C. *See* White and Griffith (1981).

Grinstein, G. G. *See* Bergeron and Grinstein (1989); Pickett and Grinstein (1988).

Grudin, J. *See* Hollan, Rich, Hill, Wroblewski, Wilner, Wittenburg, and Grudin (1991).

Gruenenfelder, T. W. *See* Reitman, Whitten, and Gruenenfelder (1984).

Guinan, C., and Smeaton, A. F. (1992). Information Retrieval from Hypertext Using Dynamically Planned Guided Tours. *Proceedings of ECHT'92, ACM European Conference on Hypermedia Technology*. 122–130. . . . . **415**

Gunn, C. (1991). *Visualizing Hyperbolic Space, Computer Graphics and Mathematics*. Berlin: Springer-Verlag. 299–331. . . . **385, 396**

Gurwitz, R. *See* Upson, Faulhabel Jr., Kamins, Laidlaw, Schegel, Vroom, Gurwitz, and van Dam (1989).

Gutwin, C., and Greenberg, S. (1997). *Interactive Fisheye Views for Groupware*. Calgary, Canada: Department of Computer Science, University of Calgary. **342**

Guyer, S. *See* Heath, Hix, Nowell, Wake, Averboch, Labow, Guyer, Brueni, France, Dalal, and Fox (1995).

Guzdial, M. *See* Gray, Badre, and Guzdial (1996).

Haeberli, P. E. (1988). ConMan: A Visual Programming Language for Interactive Graphics. *Proceedings of SIGGRAPH'88, ACM Conference on Computer Graphics*. 103–111. . . . . **233**

Hafner, J. *See* Faloutsos, Barber, Flickner, Hafner, Niblack, Petrovic, and Equitz (1994).

Hagen, H. *See* Nielson, Hagen, and Muller (1997); Rosenblum, Earnshaw, Encarnação, Hagen, Kaufman, Klimenko, Nielson, Post, and Thalmann (1994).

Hai, L. B. *See* Fairchild, Serra, Hern, Hai, and Leong (1993).

Halstead, M. H. (1977). *Elements of Software Science*. New York: Elsevier. **169**

Halvorsen, P. K. *See* Cutting, Pederson, and Halvorsen (1991); Rao, Pedersen, Hearst, Mackinlay, Card, Masinter, Halvorsen, and Robertson (1995).

Hammer, M., and McLeod, D. (1981). Database Description with SDM: A Semantic Database Model. *Transactions on Database Systems, 6*(3), 43–57. . . . . **553**

Hamming, R. W. (1973). *Numerical Analysis for Scientists and Engineers*. New York: McGraw-Hill. **6**

Hanrahan, P. (1997). Information Visualization-1: Lecture Slides for Thursday, October 10. *http://graphics.stanford.edu/courses/cs348c-96-fall/infovis1/slides*. **37**

Hanrahan, P. *See* Drebin, Carpenter, and Hanrahan (1988).

Hanssen, D. *See* Anick, Brennan, Flynn, Hanssen, Alvey, and Robbins (1990).

Harshman, R. *See* Deerwester, Dumais, Furnas, Landauer, and Harshman (1990).

Hart, J. C., Sandin, D. J., and Kauffman, L. H. (1989). Ray Tracing Deterministic 3D Fractals. *Proceedings of SIGGRAPH'89, ACM Conference on Computer Graphics*. 289–296. . . . . **45**

Harvill, Y. *See* Zimmerman, Lanier, Blanchard, Bryson, and Harvill (1987).

Hasan, M. Z. *See* Consens and Hasan (1993); Consens, Eigler, Hasan, Mendelzon, Noik, Ryman, and Vista (1994).

Hasegawa, H. *See* Carr, Plaisant, and Hasegawa (1994); Plaisant, Carr, and Hasegawa (1992).

Hauser, M. *See* Poltrock, Shook, Fairchild, Lovgren, Tarlton, Tarlton, and Hauser (1986).

Hayes, B. C. *See* Vincente, Hayes, and Williges (1987).

Healey, C. G., Booth, K. S., and Enns, J. T. (1995). High-Speed Visual Estimation Using Preattentive Processing. *ACM Transactions on Computer-Human Interaction, 3*(2), 107–135. . . . . **30**

Hearst, M. A. (1995). TileBars: Visualization of Term Distribution Information in Full Text Information Access. *Proceedings of CHI'95, ACM Conference on Human Factors in Computing Systems*. 59–66. . . . . **58, 628**

Hearst, M. A., and Plaunt, C. (1993). Subtopic Structuring for Full-Length Document Access. *Proceedings of SIGIR'93, ACM Conference on Research and Development in Information Retrieval*. 59–68. . . . . **415**

Hearst, M. A. *See* Pirolli, Schank, Hearst, and Diehl (1996); Rao, Pedersen, Hearst, Mackinlay, Card, Masinter, Halvorsen, and Robertson (1995).

Heath, L., Hix, D., Nowell, L. T., Wake, W., Averboch, G., Labow, E., Guyer, S., Brueni, D., France, R., Dalal, K., and Fox, E. (1995). Envision: A User Centered Database of Computer Science Literature. *Communications of the ACM, 38*(4), 52–53. . **572**

Heilmeier, G. H. *See* Tennant and Heilmeier (1991).

Heller, D. (1991). Motif Programming Manual. Sebastopol, CA: O'Reilly and Associates. **209**

Hemmje, M., Kunkel, C., and Willett, A. (1994). LyberWorld—A Visualization User Interface Supporting Fulltext Retrieval. *Proceedings of SIGIR'94, ACM Conference on Research and Development in Information Retrieval*, Dublin, Ireland. 149–259. . . . . **411, 431, 628**

Henderson, D. A. Jr. *See* Tou, Williams, Fikes, A. Henderson, and Malone (1982).

Henderson, D. A., Jr., and Card, S. K. (1986). Rooms: The Use of Multiple Virtual Workspaces to Reduce Space Contention in a Window-Based Graphical User Interface. *ACM Transactions on Graphics, 5*(3 July), 211–243. . . . . **513, 517, 520, 545, 583, 634**

Hendley, R. J., Drew, N. S., Wood, A. M., and Beale, R. (1995●). Narcissus: Visualising Information. *Proceedings of InfoVis'95, IEEE Symposium on Information Visualization*, New York. 90–96, color plate 146. . . . . **60, 431, 441, 467**

Hendley, R. J. *See* Drew and Hendley (1995).

Hendon, K. P., and Meyer, T. (1994). 3D Widgets for Exploratory Scientific Visualization. *Proceedings of UIST'94, ACM Symposium on User Interface Software and Technology*. 69–70. . . . . **233**

Henigman, F. *See* Bartram, Ho, Dill, and Henigman (1995).

Henik, A. *See* Kahneman and Henik (1981).

Henniger, S., and Belkin, N. (1994). *Interfaces Issues and Interaction Strategies for Information Retrieval Systems*. New York: ACM. . **445**

Henry, T. R. (1992). *Interactive Graph Layout: The Exploration of Large Graphs*. Unpublished Ph.D. Thesis, University of Arizona, Tucson. **296**

Henry, T. R., and Hudson, S. E. (1990). *Viewing Large Graphs.* Technical Report 90-13. University of Arizona. **152, 153**

Henry, T. R., and Hudson, S. E. (1991). Interactive Graph Layout. *Proceedings of UIST'91, ACM Symposium on User Interface Software and Technology,* New York. 55–64. . . . . **296**

Herman, G. T. *See* Levkowitz and Herman (1992).

Hern, N. *See* Fairchild, Serra, Hern, Hai, and Leong (1993).

Herndon, K. P., and Meyer, T. (1994). 3D Widgets for Scientific Visualization. *Proceedings of UIST'94, ACM Symposium on User Interface Software and Technology.* 69–70. . . . . **264, 608**

Herndon, K. P., van Dam, A., and Gleicher, M. (1994). The Challenges of 3-D Interaction. *Proceedings of CHI'94, ACM Conference on Human Factors in Computing Systems.* 469. . . . . **268**

Herndon, K. P. *See* Conner, Snibbe, Herndon, and Zeleznik (1992); Zeleznik, Herndon, Robbins, Huang, Meyer, Parker, and Hughes (1993).

Herot, C. F. (1980). Spatial Management of Data. *ACM Transactions on Database Systems, 5*(4), 493–514. . . . . **438**

Herot, C. F., Carling, R., Friedell, M., and Framlich, D. (1980). A Prototype Spatial Data Management System. *Computer Graphics, 14*(1), 63–70. . . . . **350**

Herrnstein, R. J. *See* Atkinson, Herrnstein, Lindzey, and Luce (1988).

Hershberger, J. *See* Brown and Hershberger (1992).

Hesselink, L. *See* Lavin, Levy, and Hesselink (1997).

Hibino, S., and Rundensteiner, E. A. (1995). A Visual Query Language for Identifying Temporal Trends in Video Data. *Proceedings of International Workshop on Multi-Media Database Management Systems.* 74–81. . . . . **288**

Hibino, S., and Rundensteiner, E. A. (1997). User Interface Evaluation of a Direct Manipulation Temporal Visual Query Language. *Proceedings of ACM Multimedia'97 Conference.* 99–107. . . . . **629**

Hill, W. C. (1994). *Videos@bellcore.com: Recommending and Evaluating Items on the Basis of Communal History-of-Use.* Bellcore Technical Report TM-ARH-023560. . . . . **530**

Hill, W. C., and Hollan, J. D. (1994). History-Enriched Digital Objects. *The Information Society, 10*(2). **531**

Hill, W. C., Hollan, J. D., Wroblewski, D., and McCandless, T. (1992). Edit Wear and Read Wear: Their Theory and Generalization. *Proceedings of CHI'92, ACM Conference on Human Factors in Computing Systems.* 3–9. **58, 530**

Hill, W. *See* Hollan, Rich, Hill, Wroblewski, Wilner, Wittenburg, and Grudin (1991).

Hinterberger, H. *See* Schmid and Hinterberger (1994).

Hix, D. *See* Heath, Hix, Nowell, Wake, Averboch, Labow, Guyer, Brueni, France, Dalal, and Fox (1995).

Ho, A. *See* Bartram, Ho, Dill, and Henigman (1995).

Hoadley, E. D. (1990). Investigating the Effects of Color. *Communications of the ACM, 33*(2), 120–139. . . . . **157**

Hochberg, J. *See* Elkind, Card, Hochberg, and Huey (1990).

Hoffman, E. *See* Munzner, Fenner, and Hoffman (1996).

Hohne, K., Pommert, A., Riemer, M., Schiemann, T., Schubert, R., and Tiede, U. (1995). Medical Volume Visualization Based on "Intelligent Volumes." In *Scientific Visualization: Advances and Challenges.* San Diego: Academic Press. 21–35. . . . . . . **561, 572**

Hollan, J. D., and Stornetta, S. (1992). Beyond Being There. *Proceedings of CHI'92, ACM Conference on Human Factors in Computing Systems.* 119–125 (also appeared as a chapter in R. M. Baecker (ed.) (1993). *Readings in Groupware and Computer-Supported Cooperative Work.* San Francisco: Morgan Kaufmann, 842–848.) **539**

Hollan, J. D., Rich, E., Hill, W., Wroblewski, D., Wilner, W., Wittenburg, K., and Grudin, J. (1991). An Introduction to HITS: Human Interface Tool Suite. In J. W. Sullivan and S. W. Tyler (eds.), *Intelligent User Interfaces.* New York: ACM Press. 293–337. . . . . **531**

Hollan, J. D. *See* Bederson and Hollan (1994); Bederson, Hollan, Perlin, Meyer, Bacon, and Furnas (1996); Hill and Hollan (1994); Hill, Hollan, Wroblewski, and McCandless (1992).

Hollands, J. H., Carey, T. T., Matthews, M. L., and McCann, C. A. (1989). Presenting a Graphical Network: A Comparison of Performance Using Fisheye and Scrolling Views. In *Designing and Using Human-Computer Interfaces and Knowledge Based Systems.* Amsterdam: Elsevier Science B. V. 313–320. . . . . **266, 270, 296, 351, 355**

Holmquist, L. E., and Ahlberg, C. (1997). *The Zoom Browser: Providing a Focus + Context View of Web Pages.* Technical Report SSKKII. Gothenburg University. **342**

Holub, R. A. *See* Levkowitz, Holub, Meyer, and Robertson (1992).

Hopkins, D. (1989). The Shape of Psiber Space, *http://hello.kaleida.com/u/hopkins/psiber/psiber:html.* **386**

Howe, D. (1983). *Data Analysis for Database Design.* Edward Arnold. **616**

Huang, N. *See* Zeleznik, Herndon, Robbins, Huang, Meyer, Parker, and Hughes (1993).

Hudson, S. E. *See* Henry and Hudson (1990, 1991); Mukherjea, Foley, and Hudson (1995); Veerasamy, Hudson, and Navathe (1995).

Huey, B. M. *See* Elkind, Card, Hochberg, and Huey (1990).

Hughes, J. F. *See* Foley, van Dam, Feiner, and Hughes (1990); Stevens, Zeleznik, and Hughes (1994); Zeleznik, Herndon, Robbins, Huang, Meyer, Parker, and Hughes (1993).

Hui, D. *See* Ware, Hui, and Franck (1993).

Hull, J. (1989). *Options, Futures, and Other Derivative Securities.* Englewood Cliffs, NJ: Prentice Hall. **97**

Hutchins, E. (1996). *Cognition in the Wild.* Cambridge, MA: MIT Press. **3, 16**

Huttenlocher, J., and Presson, C. C. (1979). The Coding and Transformation of Spatial Information. *Cognitive Psychology, 11*(7), 375–394. . . . . **203**

Ichimura, S., and Matsushita, Y. (1993). Another Dimension to Hypermedia Access. *Proceedings of ACM Hypertext'93 Conference,* New York. 63–72. . . . . **546, 547**

IEEE. (1985). *The IEEE Standard for Binary Floating-Point Arithmetic.* New York: IEEE.. . . . . **257**

Ingram, R., and Benford, S. (1995). Legibility Enhancement for Information Visualisation. *Proceedings of IEEE Visualization'95 Conference,* Atlanta. 209–216. . . . . **431**

Ingram, R. *See* Benford, Snowdon, Greenhalgh, Ingram, Knox, and Brown (1995); Chalmers, Ingram, and Pfranger (1996); Snowdon, Benford, Brown, Ingram, Knox, and Studley (1995).

Inselberg, A. (1981). *N-Dimensional Graphics, Part I—Lines and Hyperplanes.* In IBM LASC, Technical Report G320-2711, IBM LA Scientific Center. **107**

Inselberg, A. (1985). The Plane with Parallel Co-ordinates. *The Visual Computer, 1*(2), 69–91. . . . . **94, 277, 279, 617, 618, 620**

Inselberg, A. (1996). Parallel Coordinates: A Guide for the Perplexed. In *Hot Topics Proc. Proceedings of IEEE Visualization'96 Conference.* 35–38. . . . . **107**

Inselberg, A. (1997●). Multidimensional Detective. *Proceedings of InfoVis'97, IEEE Symposium on Information Visualization, IEEE Information Visualization.* 100–107. . . . . **94, 626**

Inselberg, A., and Dimsdale, B. (1990). Parallel Coordinates: A Tool for Visualizing Multi-Dimensional Geometry. *Proceedings of IEEE Visualization'90 Conference,* Los Alamitos, CA. 361–375. . . . . **7, 107, 115, 127, 556**

Ishizki, S. *See* Small, Ishizki, and Cooper (1994).

Jacob, R. *See* Green and Jacob (1991).

Jain, V., and Shneiderman, B. (1994). Data Structures for Dynamic Queries: An Analytical and Experimental Evaluation. *Proceedings of AVI'94, Workshop on Advanced Visual Interfaces,* New York. 1–11. . . . . **239, 240**

James, J. *See* Sanderson, Scott, Johnston, Mainzer, Watanabe, and James (1992).

Janssen, T. *See* Engelhardt, Bruin, Janssen, and Scha (1996).

Jellinek, H. D. *See* Johnson, Jellinek, Klotz, Rao, and Card (1993); Rao, Card, Jellinek, Mackinlay, and Robertson (1992).

Jerding, D. F., and Stasko, J. T. (1995a). The Information Mural: A Technique for Displaying and Navigating Large Information Spaces. *Proceedings of InfoVis'95, IEEE Symposium on Information Visualization,* New York. 43–50. . . . . **31, 32**

Jerding, D. F., and Stasko, J. T. (1995b). Using Information Murals in Visualization Applications. *Proceedings of UIST'95, ACM Symposium on User Interface Software and Technology,* Pittsburgh. 73 and 74. . . . . **634**

Jin, L., and Banks, D. C. (1997●). TennisViewer: A Browser for Competition Trees. *IEEE Computer Graphics and Applications,* July/August, 63–65. . . . . **151**

Jog, N., and Shneiderman, B. (1995). Information Visualization with Smooth Zooming on a Starfield Display. *Proceedings of IFIP Conference on Visual Databases,* London. 1–10. . . . . **293**

Jog, N. *See* Carr, Jog, and Kumar (1994).

Johnson, B. (1993). *Treemaps: Visualizing Hierarchical and Categorical Data.* Unpublished Ph.D. Thesis, University of Maryland. **151**

Johnson, B., and Shneiderman, B. (1991●). Tree-maps: A Space-Filling Approach to the Visualization of Hierarchical Information Structures. *Proceedings of IEEE Visualization'91 Conference,* San Diego. 284–291. . . . . **29, 149, 150, 161, 183, 210, 242, 366, 386, 494, 526, 551, 630**

Johnson, J. A., Nardi, B. A., Zarmer, C. L., and Miller, J. R. (1993a). Information Visualization Using 3D Interactive Animation. *Communications of the ACM, 36*(4), 40–56. . . . . **442**

Johnson, M. *See* Lakoff and Johnson (1980).

Johnson, W., Jellinek, H. D., Klotz, L., Rao, R., and Card, S. K. (1993b). Bridging the Paper and Electronic Worlds: The Paper User Interface. *Proceedings of INTERCHI'93, ACM Conference on Human Factors in Computing Systems,* New York. 507–512. . . **431**

Johnston, T. *See* Sanderson, Scott, Johnston, Mainzer, Watanabe, and James (1992).

Joshi, A. K., Kaplan, S. J., and Lee, R. M. (1977). Approximate Responses from a Data Base Query System: Applications of Inferring in Natural Language. *Proceedings of AAAI'77.* 211–212. **126**

Joyce, M. *See* Bernstein, Bolter, Joyce, and Mylonas (1991).

Joyce, S. A. *See* Campbell, DeFanti, Frederiksen, Joyce, Leske, Lindberg, and Sandin (1986).

Jue, D. *See* Kacmar and Jue (1995).

Kacmar, C., and Jue, D. (1995). The Information Zone System. *Communications of the ACM, 38*(4), 46–47. . . . . **578**

Kadmon, N., and Shlomi, E. (1978). A Polyfocal Projection for Statistical Surfaces. *Cartograph Journal, 15*(1), 36–41. . . . **341, 351, 352, 353, 363**

Kahan, W. (1989). *How Should Max and Min Be Defined?* Technical Report. University of California, Berkeley. **257**

Kahn, K. M. (1979). *Creation of Computer Animation from Story Descriptions.* Unpublished Ph.D. Thesis, MIT, Cambridge, MA. . **67**

Kahn, P. (1998). *Mapping Web Sites: Planning Diagrams to Site Maps.* Web page, seminar. Dynamic Diagrams. **467**

Kahneman, D., and Henik, A. (1981). Perceptual Organization and Attention. In M. Kubovy and J. Pomerantz (eds.), *In Perceptual Organization.* Hillsdale, NJ: Lawrence Erlbaum Associates. 181–211. . . . . **66**

Kamada, T. (1988). *On Visualization of Abstract Objects and Relations.* Unpublished Ph.D. Thesis, University of Tokyo, 7-3-1 Bunkyo-ku, Tokyo 113 Japan. **152, 153**

Kamins, D. *See* Upson, Faulhabel Jr., Kamins, Laidlaw, Schegel, Vroom, Gurwitz, and van Dam (1989).

Kandogan, E., and Shneiderman, B. (1995). *Elastic Windows: Improved Spatial Layout and Rapid Multiple Windows Operations.* Technical Report CS-TR-3522. University of Maryland. . . . **292**

Kandogan, E., and Shneiderman, B. (1997). Elastic Windows World Wide Web Browser. *Proceedings of UIST'97, ACM Symposium on User Interface Software and Technology.* 169–177. . . . **630**

Kandogan, E., and Shneiderman, B. (1998). Elastic Windows: Design, Implementation, and Evaluation of Multi-Window Operations. *Software Practice and Experience, 28.* **634**

Kang, T. J., and Muter, P. (1989). Reading Dynamic Displayed Text. *Behavior and Information Technology, 8*(1), 33–42. . . . . **360**

Kaplan, S. J. (1982). Cooperative Responses from a Portable Natural Language Query System. *Artificial Intelligence, 19*(2), 165–187. . . . . **126**

Kaplan, S. J. *See* Joshi, Kaplan, and Lee (1977).

Kappe, F. *See* Andrews, Kappe, and Maurer (1995a, 1995b).

Karger, D. R. *See* Cutting, Karger, Pedersen, and Tukey (1992a, 1992b).

Karlin, S. *See* Taylor and Karlin (1984).

Kauffman, L. H. *See* Hart, Sandin, and Kauffman (1989).

Kaufman, A. *See* Rosenblum, Earnshaw, Encarnação, Hagen, Kaufman, Klimenko, Nielson, Post, and Thalmann (1994).

Kaufman, L. *See* Boff, Kaufman, and Thomas (1986).

Kaugers, K., Reinfelds, J., and Brazma, A. (1994). A Simple Algorithm for Drawing Large Graphs on Small Screens. In *Graph Drawing 94, Lecture Notes in Computer Science.* Berlin: Springer-Verlag. 278–282. . . . . **371, 372**

Kay, A. C. (1977). Microelectronics and the Personal Computer. *Scientific American, 237*(3), 231. . . . . **338**

Kazman, R. *See* Carrière and Kazman (1995).

Keahey, T. A. (1997). *Nonlinear Magnification.* Unpublished Ph.D. Thesis, Department of Computer Science, Indiana University, Bloomington. **342**

Keahey, T. A., and Robertson, E. L. (1996). Techniques for Non-Linear Magnification Transformations. *Proceedings of InfoVis'96, IEEE Symposium on Information Visualization,* Los Alamitos, CA. 38–45. . . . . **372**

Keeler, M. *See* Upson and Keeler (1988).

Keim, D. A., and Kriegel, H.-P. (1994). VisDB: Database Exploration Using Multidimensional Visualization. *IEEE Computer Graphics and Applications,* Sept, 1994, 40–49. . . . . . **94, 95, 253, 277, 619, 620, 626**

Keim, D. A., and Kriegel, H.-P. (1996). Visualization Techniques for Mining Large Databases: A Comparison. *Transaction on Knowledge and Data Engineering, 8*(6), 923–938. . . . . **108**

Keim, D. A., and Lum, V. (1992). Gradi: A Graphical Database Interface for a Multimedia DBMS. *Proceedings of International Workshop on Interfaces to Database Systems'92,* London. 95–112. . . . . **126**

Keim, D. A., Kriegel, H.-P., and Seidl, T. (1994). Supporting Data Mining of Large Databases by Visual Feedback Queries. *Proceedings of IEEE Conference on Data Engineering'94,* Los Alamitos, CA. 302–313. . . . . **134**

Keim, D. A. *See* Bergeron, Keim, and Pickett (1994).

Keller, M. M. *See* Keller and Keller (1993).

Keller, P. R., and Keller, M. M. (1993). *Visual Cues: Practical Data Visualization.* Los Alamitos, CA: IEEE Press. **442**

Kellogg, W. A. *See* Rogowitz, Ling, and Kellogg (1992).

Kilpatrick, P. J. (1976). *The Use of a Kinesthetic Supplement in an Interactive Graphics System.* Unpublished Ph.D. Thesis, University of North Carolina, Chapel Hill. **96**

Kim, H., and Korfhage, R. R. (1994). BIRD: Browsing Interface for the Retrieval of Documents. *Proceedings of IEEE Symposium on Visual Languages'94.* 176–177. . . . . **628**

Kinoshita, K. *See* Miyazawa, Kinoshita, Kobayashi, Yokoyama, and Matsushita (1990).

Kirkpatrick, S., Gelatt, C. D., and Vecchi, M. P. (1983). Optimization by Simulated Annealing. *Science, 220*(4598), 671–680. . . . . . **195**

Klimenko, S. *See* Rosenblum, Earnshaw, Encarnação, Hagen, Kaufman, Klimenko, Nielson, Post, and Thalmann (1994).

Klotz, L. *See* Johnson, Jellinek, Klotz, Rao, and Card (1993b).

Knox, I. *See* Benford, Snowdon, Greenhalgh, Ingram, Knox, and Brown (1995); Snowdon, Benford, Brown, Ingram, Knox, and Studley (1995).

Knuth, D. E. (1973a). *The Art of Computer Programming.* Vol. 1. Reading, MA: Addison-Wesley. **69**

Knuth, D. E. (1973b). *Fundamental Algorithms.* Vol. 1, 2nd ed. Reading MA: Addison-Wesley. **153**

Kobayashi, M. *See* Miyazawa, Kinoshita, Kobayashi, Yokoyama, and Matsushita (1990).

Kohonen, T. (1989). *Self-Organization and Associate Memory.* New York: Springer-Verlag. **431, 434**

Kohonen, T. (1990). The Self-Organizing Map. *Proceedings of the IEEE, 78*(9), 1464–1480. . . . . **431, 434**

Kohonen, T. *See* Ritter and Kohonen (1989).

Koike, H. (1993). The Role of Another Spatial Dimension in Software Visualization. *ACM Transactions on Information Systems, 11*(3), 266–286. . . . . **225**

Koike, H. (1994). Fractal Views: A Fractal-Based Method for Controlling Information Display. *ACM Transactions on Information Systems, 13*(3 July), 305–323. . . . . **308, 354**

Kolate, G. (1982). Computer Graphics Comes to Statistics. *Science, 217*(Sept.), 919–920. . . . . **115**

Kolb, C. E. *See* Factor, Gelernter, Kolb, Miller, and Sittig (1991).

Kolojejchick, J. A. *See* Chuah, Roth, Mattis, and Kolojejchick (1995a, 1995b); Goldstein, Roth, Kolojejchick, and Mattis (1994); Roth, Lucas, Senm, Gomberg, Burks, Stroffolino, and Kolojejchick (1996).

Komlodi, A. *See* Nation, Plaisant, Marchionini, and Komlodi (1997); Plaisant, Marchionini, Bruns, Komlodi, and Campbell (1997).

Korfhage, R. R. (1991). To See or Not to See—Is that the Query? *Proceedings of SIGIR'91, ACM Conference on Research and Development.* **433, 442**

Korfhage, R. R., and Olson, K. (1991). Information Display: Control of Visual Representations. *Proceedings of IEEE Workshop on Visual Languages'91.* **147**

Korfhage, R. R. *See* Kim and Korfhage (1994).

Korhage, R. R. *See* Olsen, Korhage, Sochats, Spring, and Williams (1993).

Korn, F. (1995). *A Taxonomy of Browsing Methods: Approaches to the "Lost in Concept Space" Problem.* Technical Report. University of Maryland, Department of Computer Science. **572**

Korn, F., and Shneiderman, B. (1995). *Navigating Terminology Hierarchies to Access a Digital Library of Medical Images.* Technical Report 96-01. University of Maryland, Department of Computer Science. **572, 576**

Korn, F. *See* North and Korn (1996).

Kosslyn, S. M. (1994). *Image and Brain: The Resolution of the Imagery Debate.* Cambridge, MA: MIT Press. **24, 25, 30**

Koutsofios, E. E., and North, S. C. (1992). *Drawing Graphs with Dot.* Technical Report 910904-59113-08TM. AT&T Bell Laboratories. **211**

Koutsofios, E. E. *See* Gansner, Koutsofios, North, and Vo (1993).

Koved, L., and Shneiderman, B. (1986). Embedded Menus: Selecting Items in Context. *Communications of the ACM, 29*(4), 312–318. . . . . **248**

Kraemer, E., and Stasko, J. T. (1993). The Visualization of Parallel Systems: An Overview. *Journal of Parallel and Distributed Computing, 18*(2), 105–117. . . . . **160**

Krasner, G. E., and Pope, S. T. (1990). A Cookbook for Using the Model-View-Controller User Interface Paradigm in Smalltalk80. *Journal of Object-Oriented Programming, August,* 26–48. . . . . **580**

Krebs, J. R. *See* Stephens and Krebs (1986).

Kreitzberg, C. B. (1991). Details on Demand: Hypertext Models for Coping with Information Overload. In M. Dillon (ed.), *Interfaces for Information Retrieval and Online Systems.* New York: Greenwood Press. 169–176. . . . . **246**

Kriegel, H.-P. *See* Keim and Kriegel (1994, 1996); Keim, Kriegel, and Seidl (1994).

Krogh, M. *See* Brown and Krogh (1988).

Kruskal, J. B. (1964a). Multidimensional Scaling by Optimizing Goodness of Fit to a Non-Metric Hypothesis. *Psychometrika, 29,* 1–27. . . . . **194**

Kruskal, J. B. (1964b). Non-Metric Multidimensional Scaling: A Numerical Method. *Psychometrika, 29,* 28–42. . . . . **194**

Kruskal, J. B., and Wish, M. (1979). *Multidimensional Scaling.* Newbury Park, CA: Sage Publications. **211**

Kruskal, J. B., Young, F. W., and Seery, J. B. (1973). *How to Use KYST: A Very Flexible Program to Do Multidimensional Scaling.* Technical Memorandum. Murray Hill, NJ: AT&T Bell Laboratories. . . . **194**

Kuhn, W. (1990). Editing Spatial Relations. *Proceedings of 4th International Symposium on Spatial Data Handling,* Zurich. 423–432. . . . . **157**

Kumar, H. P. (1995). *Visualizing Hierarchical Data with Dynamic Queries and Pruning.* HCIL Open House '95 Video. Human Computer Interaction Laboratory. **299**

Kumar, H. P., Plaisant, C., and Shneiderman, B. (1997●). Browsing Hierarchical Data with Multi-Level Dynamic Queries and Pruning. *International Journal of Human-Computer Studies, 46*(1), 103–124. . . . . **150, 286, 575, 630**

Kumar, H. P., Plaisant, C., Teittinen, M., and Shneiderman, B. (1994). *Visual Information Management for Network Configuration.* Technical Report CS-TR-3288. University of Maryland, Department of Computer Science. **295, 296, 297**

Kumar, H. P. *See* Carr, Jog, and Kumar (1994).

Kunkel, C. *See* Hemmje, Kunkel, and Willett (1994).

Labow, E. *See* Heath, Hix, Nowell, Wake, Averboch, Labow, Guyer, Brueni, France, Dalal, and Fox (1995).

Lai, W. *See* Misue, Eadest, and Lai (1995).

Laidlaw, D. *See* Upson, Faulhabel Jr., Kamins, Laidlaw, Schegel, Vroom, Gurwitz, and van Dam (1989).

Lakoff, G., and Johnson, M. (1980). *Metaphors We Live By.* Chicago: University of Chicago Press. **539**

Lamping, J., and Rao, R. (1994). Laying Out and Visualizing Large Trees Using a Hyperbolic Space. *Proceedings of UIST'94, ACM Symposium on User Interface Software and Technology.* 13–14. . **494**

Lamping, J., and Rao, R. (1996●). The Hyperbolic Browser: A Focus + Context Technique for Visualizing Large Hierarchies. *Journal of Visual Languages and Computing, 7*(1), 33–55. . . . . **28, 29, 32, 381**

Lamping, J., Rao, R., and Pirolli, P. (1995). A Focus + Context Technique Based on Hyperbolic Geometry for Visualizing Large Hierarchies. *Proceedings of CHI'95, ACM Conference on Human Factors in Computing Systems,* New York. 401–408. . . . **272, 296, 372, 404, 630, 634**

Landauer, T. K. *See* Deerwester, Dumais, Furnas, Landauer, and Harshman (1990); Dumais and Landauer (1984); Dumais, Furnas, Landauer, and Deerwester (1988); Egan, Remde, Gomez, Landauer, Eberhardt, and Lochbaum (1989); Remde, Gomez, and Landauer (1987).

Landay, J. *See* Woodruff, Landay, and Stonebraker (1998).

Landow, G. P. (1989). Hypertext in Literary Education, Criticism, and Scholarship. *Computers and the Humanities, 23,* 173–198. . . . . **413**

Landow, G. P. *See* Delaney and Landow (1991).

Langley, P., Simon, H. A., Bradshaw, G. L., and Zytkow, J. M. (1987). *Scientific Discovery: Computational Explorations of the Creative Processes.* Cambridge, MA: MIT Press. **598**

Lanier, J. *See* Zimmerman, Lanier, Blanchard, Bryson, and Harvill (1987).

Lantrip, D. *See* Wise, Thomas, Pennock, Lantrip, Pottier, Schur, and Crow (1995).

Larkin, J., and Simon, H. A. (1987). Why a Diagram is (Sometimes) Worth Ten Thousand Words. *Cognitive Science, 11*(1), 65–99. . . . . **15, 16, 307, 616**

Laurel, B. (1993). *Computers as Theatre.* Reading, MA: Addison-Wesley. **449**

Lavin, Y., Levy, Y., and Hesselink, L. (1997). Singularities in Nonuniform Tensor Fields. *Proceedings of IEEE Visualization'97 Conference,* Phoenix. 585. . . . . **7**

Lawande, S. *See* Livny, Ramakrishnan, Beyer, Chen, Donjerkovic, Lawande, Myllymaki, and Wenger (1997).

Leavitt, J. R. R. *See* Mauldin and Leavitt (1994).

LeBlanc, J., Ward, M. O., and Wittels, N. (1990). Exploring N-Dimensional Databases. *Proceedings of IEEE Visualization'90 Conference,* San Francisco. 230–234. . . . . **122, 127**

Leckie, J., Masters, G., Whitehouse, H., and Young, L. (1975). *Other Homes and Garbage: Designs for Self-sufficient Living.* San Francisco: Sierra Club Books. **3**

Lee, R. C. T., Slagle, J. R., and Blum, H. (1977). Triangulation Method for the Sequence Mapping of Points from *n*-Space to Two-Space. *IEEE Transactions on Computers, C-26*(3), 288–292. . . . . **115**

Lee, R. M. *See* Joshi, Kaplan, and Lee (1977).

Leenstra, R. B., Wurden, E. H., Otis, L. N., and Wurden, F. L. (1996). Data Management Systems and Methods Including Creation of Composite Views of Data, *U.S. Patent 5,555,409.* **553**

Leeuw, W. C. d., and Wijk, J. J. v. (1993). A Probe for Local Flow Field Visualization. *Proceedings of IEEE Visualization'93 Conference,* San Jose. 39–45. . . . . **38**

Leong, A. T. *See* Fairchild, Serra, Hern, Hai, and Leong (1993).

Leske, L. A. *See* Campbell, DeFanti, Frederiksen, Joyce, Leske, Lindberg, and Sandin (1986).

Leung, Y. K. (1989). Human-Computer Interaction Techniques for Map-Based Diagrams. In G. Salvendy and M. Smith (eds.), *Designing and Using Human-Computer Interfaces and Knowledge Based Systems.* Amsterdam: Elsevier. 361–368. . . **350, 351, 354, 360, 371**

Leung, Y. K., and Apperley, M. D. (1993a). E(3): Towards the Metrication of Graphical Presentation Techniques. In L. J. Bass, J. G. Gornostaev, and C. Unger (eds.), *Lecture Notes in Computer Science: Human-Computer Interaction.* Heidelberg: Springer-Verlag. 125–140. . . . . **350**

Leung, Y. K., and Apperley, M. D. (1993b). Extending the Perspective Wall. *Proceedings of OZCHI'93, CHISIG Annual Conference on Human-Computer Interaction.* 110–120. . . . . **357**

Leung, Y. K., and Apperley, M. D. (1994●). A Review and Taxonomy of Distortion-Orientation Presentation Techniques. *ACM Transactions on Computer-Human Interaction, 1*(2, June), 126–160. . . . . **341, 371, 385**

Levkowitz, H., and Herman, G. T. (1992). Color Scales for Image Data. *IEEE Computer Graphics and Applications, 12,* 78–80. . **173**

Levkowitz, H., Holub, R. A., Meyer, G. W., and Robertson, A. K. (1992). Color vs Black and White in Visualization. *IEEE Computer Graphics and Applications, 12*(14), 20–22. . . . . **173**

Levy, D. (1995). Cataloging in the Digital Order. *Proceedings of DL'95, ACM Conference on Digital Libraries.* **572**

Levy, E., Zacks, J., Tversky, B., and Schiano, D. (1996). Gratuitous Graphics? Putting Preferences in Perspective. *Proceedings of CHI'96, ACM Conference on Human Factors in Computing Systems.* 42–49. . . . . **634**

Levy, Y. *See* Lavin, Levy, and Hesselink (1997).

Liang, J. *See* Shaw, Liang, Green, and Sun (1992).

Liao, H., Osada, M., and Shneiderman, B. (1993). Browsing Unix Directories with Dynamic Queries: An Analytical and Experimental Evaluation. *Proceedings of Ninth Annual Japanese Conference on Human Interface'93.* 95–98. . . . . **238**

Liao, H. *See* Osada, Liao, and Shneiderman (1993).

Lientz, B. P., and Rea, K. P. (1995). *Project Management for the 21st Century.* San Diego: Academic Press. **288**

Lin, X. (1992a). *Self-Organizing Semantic Maps for Information Retrieval.* Unpublished Ph.D. Thesis, University of Maryland.. **438**

Lin, X. (1992b●). Visualization for the Document Space. *Proceedings of IEEE Visualization'92 Conference,* Boston. 274–281. . . . . **59, 431, 494**

Lin, X. (1995). Visual Displays of SIGIR Documents. *Proceedings of SIGIR'95, ACM Conference on Research and Development in Information Retrieval.* 364. . . . . **628**

Lin, X. (1996). Graphical Table of Contents. *Proceedings of DL'96, ACM Conference on Digital Libraries.* 45–53. . . . . **59**

Lin, X., Soergel, D., and Marchionini, G. (1991). A Self-Organizing Semantic Map for Information Retrieval. *Proceedings of SIGIR'91, ACM Conference on Research and Development in Information Retrieval,* Chicago. 262–269. . . . . **147, 438**

Lindberg, J. A. *See* Campbell, DeFanti, Frederiksen, Joyce, Leske, Lindberg, and Sandin (1986).

Lindwarm, D., Rose, A., Plaisant, C., and Norman, K. (1998). Viewing Personal History Records: A Comparison of Tabular Format and Graphical Presentation Using LifeLines. *Behavior and Information Technology.* *17*(5), 249–262. . . . . **629**

Lindzey, G. *See* Atkinson, Herrnstein, Lindzey, and Luce (1988).

Ling, D. T. *See* Rogowitz, Ling, and Kellogg (1992).

Linton, M. A. *See* Tang and Linton (1993).

Livny, M., Ramakrishnan, R., Beyer, K., Chen, G., Donjerkovic, D., Lawande, S., Myllymaki, J., and Wenger, K. (1997). DEVise: Integrated Querying and Visual Exploration of Large Datasets. *Proceedings of ACM SIGMOD Conference.* 301–312. . . . . **626**

Lochbaum, C. C. *See* Egan, Remde, Gomez, Landauer, Eberhardt, and Lochbaum (1989).

Lockwood, A. (1969). *Diagrams: A Visual Survey of Graphs, Maps, Charts and Diagrams for the Graphic Designer.* New York: Watson-Guptill.. . . . . **74**

Lovgren, J. E. *See* Poltrock, Shook, Fairchild, Lovgren, Tarlton, Tarlton, and Hauser (1986).

Lucas, P. *See* Roth, Lucas, Senm, Gomberg, Burks, Stroffolino, and Kolojejchick (1996).

Luce, R. D. *See* Atkinson, Herrnstein, Lindzey, and Luce (1988).

Lum, V. *See* Keim and Lum (1992).

Lunzer, A. (1996). *Reconnaissance: A Widely Applicable Approach Encouraging Well-Informed Choices in Computer-Based Tasks.* Unpublished Ph.D. Thesis, University of Glasgow. . . **617, 618, 620**

Luotonem, A. *See* Berners-Lee, Calliliau, Luotonem, Nielsen, and Secret (1994).

MacDonald, L. W. (1990). Using Colour Effectively in Displays for Computer-Human Interface. *Displays,* 129–142. . . . . **157**

MacEachren, A. M. (1995). *How Maps Work.* New York: The Guilford Press.. . . . . **26, 30**

Mackay, W. E. (1988). Diversity in the Use of Electronic Mail: A Preliminary Inquiry. *ACM Transactions on Office Information Systems,* *6*(4 Jan), 380–397. . . . . **208**

Mackinlay, J. D. (1986a). *Automatic Design of Graphical Presentations.* Unpublished Ph.D. Thesis, Stanford University.. . . **57, 70, 73, 75, 77**

Mackinlay, J. D. (1986b ●). Automating the Design of Graphical Presentations of Relational Information. *ACM Transactions on Graphics,* *5*(2), 110–141. . . . . . **8, 17, 23, 26, 27, 29, 32, 57, 150**

Mackinlay, J. D., and Genesereth, M. R. (1985). Expressiveness and Language Choice. *Data Knowledge Engineering,* *1*(1), 17–29. . **70**

Mackinlay, J. D., Card, S. K., and Robertson, G. G. (1990a). Rapid Controlled Movement through a Virtual 3D Workspace. *Proceedings of SIGGRAPH'90, ACM Conference on Computer Graphics.* 171–176. . . . . **522, 565**

Mackinlay, J. D., Card, S. K., and Robertson, G. G. (1990b). A Semantic Analysis of the Design Space of Input Devices. *Human-Computer Interaction,* *5*(2–3), 145–190. . . . . **17, 522**

Mackinlay, J. D., Rao, R., and Card, S. K. (1995). An Organic User Interface for Searching Citation Links. *Proceedings of CHI'95, ACM Conference on Human Factors in Computing Systems,* New York. 67–73. . . . . **15, 630, 631**

Mackinlay, J. D., Robertson, G. G., and Card, S. K. (1991). The Perspective Wall: Detail and Context Smoothly Integrated. *Proceedings of CHI'91, ACM Conference on Human Factors in Computing Systems,* New York. 173–180. . . . . . . **8, 32, 84, 288, 290, 332, 343, 355, 363, 369, 382, 385, 494, 523, 526, 527, 629**

Mackinlay, J. D., Robertson, G. G., and DeLine, R. (1994). Developing Calendar Visualizers for the Information Visualizer. *Proceedings of UIST'94, ACM Symposium on User Interface Software and Technology,* Marina del Rey, CA. 109–118. . . . **271, 382, 583**

Mackinlay, J. D. *See* Chi, Pitkow, Mackinlay, Pirolli, Gossweiler, and Card (1998); Card and Mackinlay (1997); Card, Mackinlay, and Robertson (1990); Card, Pirolli, and Mackinlay (1994); Card, Robertson, and Mackinlay (1991); Rao, Card, Jellinek, Mackinlay, and Robertson (1992); Rao, Pedersen, Hearst, Mackinlay, Card, Masinter, Halvorsen, and Robertson (1995); Robertson and Mackinlay (1993); Robertson, Card, and Mackinlay (1989, 1993); Robertson, Mackinlay, and Card (1991).

MacNeil, R. L. *See* Masuishi, Small, and MacNeil (1992).

Mainzer, J. *See* Sanderson, Scott, Johnston, Mainzer, Watanabe, and James (1992).

Malone, T. W. *See* Tou, Williams, Fikes, A. Henderson, and Malone (1982).

Maltin, L. (1993). *Leonard Maltin's Movie and Video Guide.* New York: Penguin Books. **247**

Mandler, R., Salomon, G., and Wong, Y. Y. (1992). A 'Pile' Metaphor for Supporting Casual Organization of Information. *Proceedings of CHI'92, ACM Conference on Human Factors in Computing Systems,* Monterey, CA. 627–634. . . . . **58**

Manuel, T. (1981). Automating Offices from Top to Bottom. *Electronics, 157*. **333**

Marchak, F., and Zulager, D. (1992). Effectiveness of Dynamic Graphics in Revealing Structure in Multivariate Data. *Behavior, Research Methods, Instruments and Computers,* *24*(2), 253–257. . . . . **127**

Marchionini, G. (1995). *Information Seeking in Electronic Environments.* Cambridge, UK: Cambridge University Press. . . **248, 295**

Marchionini, G. *See* Lin, Soergel, and Marchionini. (1991); Nation, Plaisant, Marchionini, and Komlodi (1997); Plaisant, Marchionini, Bruns, Komlodi, and Campbell (1997).

Marcus, A. (1991a). *Graphic Design for Electronic Documents and User Interfaces.* New York: ACM Press. **242**

Marcus, A. *See* Baecker and Marcus (1988).

Marcus, R. (1991b). Computer and Human Understanding in Intelligent Retrieval Assistance. *Journal of the American Society for Information Science, 28*. **147**

Mariani, J. *See* Benford, Snowdon, and Mariani (1995).

Mark, S. *See* Chimera, Wolman, Mark, and Shneiderman (1991).

Masinter, L. *See* Rao, Pedersen, Hearst, Mackinlay, Card, Masinter, Halvorsen, and Robertson (1995).

Masters, G. *See* Leckie, Masters, Whitehouse, and Young (1975).

Masuishi, T., Small, D., and MacNeil, R. L. (1992). 6,000 x 2,000 Display Prototype. *Proceedings of SPIE/IS&Ts'92.* **455**

Mateti, P. *See* Ding and Mateti (1990).

Matsushita, Y. *See* Ichimura and Matsushita (1993); Miyazawa, Kinoshita, Kobayashi, Yokoyama, and Matsushita (1990).

Matthews, M. L. *See* Hollands, Carey, Matthews, and McCann (1989).

Mattis, J. *See* Chuah, Roth, Mattis, and Kolojejchick (1995a, 1995b); Goldstein, Roth, Kolojejchick, and Mattis (1994); Roth and Mattis (1990).

Mauldin, M. L., and Leavitt, J. R. R. (1994). Web-Agent Related Research at the CMT. *Proceedings of SIGNIDR'94,* McLean, VA. . **544**

Maurer, H. *See* Andrews, Kappe, and Maurer (1995a, 1995b).

Max, N. L. *See* Springmeyer, Blattner, and Max (1992).

May, R. A. *See* Risch, May, Dowson, and Thomas (1996); Risch, Rex, Dowson, Walters, May, and Moon (1997).

McCabe, T. J. (1970). A Complexity Measure. *IEEE Transactions on Software Engineering, 1,* 312–327. . . . . **169**

McCahill, M. P., and Anklesaria, F. X. (1994). Evolution of The Internet Gopher. *Journal of Universal Computer Science, 1*(4), 235–246. . . . . **495**

McCahill, M. P., and Erickson, T. (1995). Design for a 3D Spatial User Interface for Internet Gopher. *Proceedings of ED-MEDIA'95, Conference on Educational Multimedia and Hypermedia.* 39–44. . . . . **495**

McCandless, T. *See* Hill, Hollan, Wroblewski, and McCandless (1992).

McCann, C. A. *See* Hollands, Carey, Matthews, and McCann (1989).

McCormick, B. H., and DeFanti, T. A. (1987). Visualization is Scientific Computing. *Computer Graphics, 21*(6 November). . . **6, 8, 37, 40, 42**

McCormick, B. H. *See* DeFanti, Brown, and McCormick (1989).

McCracken, D. *See* Robertson, McCracken, and Newell (1979).

McDonald, J. A. (1990). Painting Multiple Views of Complex Objects. *Proceedings of ECOOP/OOPLSLA'90.* 245–257. . **31, 233, 271**

McDonald, J. A. *See* Buja, McDonald, Michalak, and Stuetzle (1991).

McFarlane, M. M. *See* Young, Faldowski, and McFarlane (1993).

McGill, M. J. *See* Salton and McGill (1983).

McGill, R. *See* Cleveland and McGill (1984, 1987, 1988).

McKay, D. *See* Finin, Fritzon, and McKay (1992).

McKeown, K. *See* Feiner and McKeown (1991).

McLeod, D. *See* Hammer and McLeod (1981).

McShane, R. *See* Cutler and McShane (1960).

Meeker, L. D. *See* Bergeron, Meeker, and Sparr (1992).

Mendelzon, A. O. *See* Consens, Eigler, Hasan, Mendelzon, Noik, Ryman, and Vista (1994); Consens, Mendelzon, and Ryan (1992).

Meyer, G. W. *See* Levkowitz, Holub, Meyer, and Robertson (1992).

Meyer, J. *See* Bederson, Hollan, Perlin, Meyer, Bacon, and Furnas (1996).

Meyer, T. *See* Herndon and Meyer (1994); Herndon and Meyer (1994); Zeleznik, Herndon, Robbins, Huang, Meyer, Parker, and Hughes (1993).

Meyrowitz, N. *See* Yankelovich, Meyrowitz, and van Dam (1985).

Mezrich, J. J., Frysinger, S, F., and Slivjanovski, R. (1984). Dynamic Representation of Multivariate Time Series Data. *Journal of the American Statistical Association, 79*(385), 34–40. . . . . **225**

Michalak, J. *See* Buja, McDonald, Michalak, and Stuetzle (1991).

Michard, A. (1982). Graphical Presentation of Boolean Expressions in a Database Query Language: Design Notes and an Ergonomic Evaluation. *Behavior and Information Technology, 1*(3), 279–289. . . . . **147**

Micropad. (1979). *Micropad Technical Summary.* Ferndown, UK: Micropad Ltd. **338**

Mihalisin, T. (1990a). Graphing in Multiple Dimensions with MGTS. *Suntech Journal, 3*(1), 25–31. . . . . **122**

Mihalisin, T. (1990b). Visualizing Scalar Field on an N-Dimensional Lattice. *Proceedings of IEEE Visualization'90 Conference,* Los Alamitos, CA. 255–262. . . . . **127, 277, 617**

Mihalisin, T., Timlin, J., and Schwegler, J. (1991 ●). Visualizing Multivariate Functions, Data, and Distributions. *IEEE Computer Graphics and Applications, 11*(13), 28–35. . . . . **8, 94**

Milash, B., Plaisant, C., and Rose, A. (1996). LifeLines: Visualizing Personal Histories. Video. *Conference Companion of CHI'96, ACM Conference on Human Factors in Computing Systems.* 392–393. **288**

Milash, B. *See* Plaisant, Milash, Rose, Widoff, and Shneiderman (1996).

Miller, E. O. *See* Becker, Eick, and Miller (1989a); Becker, Eick, Miller, and Wilks (1989b, 1990a, 1990b).

Miller, J. R. *See* Johnson, Nardi, Zarmer, and Miller (1993a).

Miller, P. L. *See* Factor, Gelernter, Kolb, Miller, and Sittig (1991).

Minden, G. *See* Gauch, Aust, Evans, Gauch, Minden, Niehaus, and Roberts (1994).

Misue, K., and Sugiyama, K. (1991). Multi-Viewpoint Perspective Display Methods: Formulation and Application to Compound Graphs. In H. J. Bullinger (ed.), *In Human Aspects in Computing: Design and Use of Interactive Systems and Information Management.* Amsterdam. 834–838. . . . . **351, 357, 371, 372**

Misue, K., Eadest, P., and Lai, W. (1995). Layout Adjustment and the Mental Map. *Journal of Visual Languages and Computing, 6*(2), 183–210. . . . . **372**

Mitta, D. A. (1990). A Fisheye Presentation Strategy: Aircraft Maintenance Data. *Proceedings of INTERACT'90.* 875–885. . . . . . **351, 355, 369, 370**

Miyazawa, M., Kinoshita, K., Kobayashi, M., Yokoyama, T., and Matsushita, Y. (1990). An Electronic Book: APTBook. *Proceedings of INTERACT'90,* Amsterdam. 513–519. . . . . **546, 547**

Moise, E. E. (1974). *Elementary Geometry from an Advanced Standpoint.* New York: Addison-Wesley. **384**

Moll-Carrillo, H. J. (1995). Articulating a Metaphor through User-Centered Design. *Proceedings of CHI'95, ACM Conference on Human Factors in Computing Systems,* New York. 566–572. . . . . **546, 547**

Monk, F. M., Walsh, P., and Dix, A. J. (1988). A Comparison of Hypertext, Scrolling and Folding as Mechanisms for Program Browsing. In D. M. Jones and R. Winder (eds.), *People and Computers.* Vol. 4. Cambridge, MA: Cambridge University Press. 421–435. . . . . **350**

Montgomery, W. A. (1980). *An Interactive Screen Editor for UNIX.* Technical Report BTL-TM80-5343-2. . . . . **313**

Moon, B. D. *See* Risch, Rex, Dowson, Walters, May, and Moon (1997).

Moon, D. *See* Weinreb and Moon (1981).

Moore, W. J. (1962). *Physical Chemistry.* Englewood Cliffs, NJ: Prentice Hall. **8**

Moran, T. P. *See* Card, Moran, and Newell (1983).

Morgan, G. *See* Benest, Morgan, and Smithurst (1987).

Morse, A. (1979). Some Principles for the Effective Display of Data. *Proceedings of SIGGRAPH'79, ACM Conference on Computer Graphics and Interaction, 13*(2), 94–101. . . . . **336**

Motro, A. (1990). Flex: A Tolerant and Cooperative User Interface to Databases. *IEEE Transactions on Knowledge and Data Engineering, 2*(2), 231–246. . . . . **126**

Mukherjea, S., and Foley, J. D. (1995). Visualizing the World-Wide Web with the Navigational View Builder. *Computer Networks and ISDN Systems, 27*(6), 1075–1087. . . . . **495, 630**

Mukherjea, S., Foley, J. D., and Hudson, S. E. (1995). Visualizing Complex Hypermedia Networks through Multiple Hierarchical Views. *Proceedings of CHI'95, ACM Conference on Human Factors in Computing Systems,* Denver. 331–337. . . . . **189**

Muller, H. A. *See* Storey and Muller (1995).

Muller, H. *See* Nielson, Hagen, and Muller (1997).

Munzner, T. (1997). H3: Laying out Large Directed Graphs in 3D Hyperbolic Space. *Proceedings of InfoVis'97, IEEE Symposium on Information Visualization,* Phoenix. 2–10. . . . . **381**

Munzner, T., Fenner, B., and Hoffman, E. (1996). Visualizing the Global Topology of MBone. *Proceedings of InfoVis'96, IEEE Symposium on Information Visualization.* 85–91. . . . . **188, 381**

Murphy, J. (1998). It's Not the Size that Counts, but How You Measure It. *New York Times.* July 5, 1998.. . . . . **465**

Murtagh, F. (1983). A Survey of Recent Advances in Hierarchical Clustering Algorithms. *The Computer Journal, 26*(4), 354–359. . . . . **415**

Muter, P. *See* Kang and Muter (1989).

Myllymaki, J. *See* Livny, Ramakrishnan, Beyer, Chen, Donjerkovic, Lawande, Myllymaki, and Wenger (1997).

Mylonas, E. *See* Bernstein, Bolter, Joyce, and Mylonas (1991).

Nardi, B. A. (1996). *Context and Consciousness.* Cambridge, MA: MIT Press. **622**

Nardi, B. A., and Zarmer, C. L. (1993). Beyond Models and Metaphors: Visual Formalisms in User Interface Design. *Journal of Visual Languages and Computing, 4,* 5–33. . . . . . **277, 616, 618**

Nardi, B. A. *See* Johnson, Nardi, Zarmer, and Miller (1993a).

Nation, D. A., Plaisant, C., Marchionini, G., and Komlodi, A. (1997). Visualizing Websites Using a Hierarchical Table of Contents Browser: WebTOC. *Proceedings of 3rd Conference on Human Factors and the Web.* **150, 630**

Navathe, S. *See* Veerasamy, Hudson, and Navathe (1995).

Naylor, B. F. *See* Thibault and Naylor (1987).

NCSA. (1990). *Smog—Visualizing the Components.* Video. University of Illinois at Urbana/Champaign, Visualization Services and Development Group. **84**

Nelson, T. H. (1974). *Computer Lib.* Chicago: Hugo's Book Source. **316**

Nelson, T. H. (1981). *Literary Machines.* Swarthmore, PA: Mindful Press. **459**

Newell, A. (1990). *Unified Theories of Cognition.* Cambridge, MA: Harvard University Press. **231, 520**

Newell, A., and Simon, H. A. (1972). *Human Problem Solving.* Englewood Cliffs, NJ: Prentice Hall. **598**

Newell, A. *See* Card, Moran, and Newell (1983); Robertson, McCracken, and Newell (1979).

Newman, R. *See* Scheifler, Gettys, and Newman (1988).

Newman, S. *See* Avitzur, Robins, and Newman (1994).

Newton, C. M. (1978). Graphics: From Alpha to Omega in Data Analysis. In P. C. C. Wang (ed.), *Graphical Representation of Multivariate Data.* San Diego: Academic Press. 59–92. . . . . **277, 617**

Niblack, W. *See* Faloutsos, Barber, Flickner, Hafner, Niblack, Petrovic, and Equitz (1994).

Niehaus, D. *See* Gauch, Aust, Evans, Gauch, Minden, Niehaus, and Roberts (1994).

Nielsen, H. F. *See* Berners-Lee, Calliliau, Luotonem, Nielsen, and Secret (1994).

Nielsen, J. (1990). The Visual Presentation of Information: Miniatures versus Icons as a Visual Cache for Videotex Browsing. *Behavior and Information Technology, 9*(6), 441–449. . . . . **438**

Nielsen, J. *See* Anderson, Nielsen, and Rasmussen (1989).

Nielson, G. M., Hagen, H., and Muller, H. (eds.). (1997). *Scientific Visualization: Overviews, Methodologies, and Techniques.* Los Alamitos, CA: IEEE Computer Society Press. **4, 38**

Nielson, G. M., Shriver, B., and Rosenblum, L. J. (1990). *Visualization in Scientific Computing.* Los Alamitos, CA: IEEE Computer Society Press. **419**

Nielson, G. M. *See* Rosenblum, Earnshaw, Encarnação, Hagen, Kaufman, Klimenko, Nielson, Post, and Thalmann (1994).

NIH (1990). *National Library of Medicine Long Range Plan: Electronic Imaging.* NIH Publication 902197. Department of Health and Human Services. **570**

Noik, E. G. *See* Consens, Eigler, Hasan, Mendelzon, Noik, Ryman, and Vista (1994).

Noll, M. (1967). A Computer Technique for Displaying *n*-Dimensional Hyperobjects. *Communications of the ACM, August,* 469–473. . . . . **97**

Nordhausen, B. *See* Chignell, Nordhausen, Valdez, and Waterworth (1991).

Norman, D. A. (1988). *The Psychology of Everyday Things.* New York: Basic Books. **618, 620**

Norman, D. A. (1991). Cognitive Artifacts. In J. Carroll (ed.), *Designing Interaction.* New York: Cambridge University Press. . **623**

Norman, D. A. (1993). *Things that Make Us Smart.* Reading, MA: Addison-Wesley. **1, 16, 34**

Norman, D. A. *See* Zhang and Norman (1994).

Norman, K. *See* Lindwarm, Rose, Plaisant, and Norman (1998).

Norman, M. L. *See* Winkler and Norman (1986).

North, C., and Korn, F. (1996). Browsing Anatomical Image Databases: A Case Study of the Visible Human. *Conference Companion of CHI'96, ACM Conference on Human Factors in Computing Systems.* 414–415. . . . . **573**

North, C., Shneiderman, B., and Plaisant, C. (1996●). User Controlled Overviews of an Image Library: A Case Study of the Visible Human. *Proceedings of DL'96, ACM Conference on Digital Libraries.* 74–82. . . . . **13, 561**

North, S. C. *See* Gansner, Koutsofios, North, and Vo (1993).

North, S. C. *See* Koutsofios and North (1992).

Nowell, L. T. *See* Heath, Hix, Nowell, Wake, Averboch, Labow, Guyer, Brueni, France, Dalal, and Fox (1995).

Nye, A. (1990). *Xlib Reference Manual.* Sebastopol, CA: O'Reilly & Associates. **209, 574**

Olsen, K. A., Korhage, R. R., Sochats, K. M., Spring, M. B., and Williams, J. (1993). Visualization of a Document Collection: The VIBE System. *Information Processing and Management, 29*(1), 69–81. . . . . **411, 431, 628**

Olson, G. M. *See* Olson and Olson (1990).

Olson, J. R., and Olson, G. M. (1990). The Growth of Cognitive Modeling in Human Computer Interaction since GOMS. *Human-Computer Interaction, 5*(2–3), 221–265. . . . . . . **597, 602**

Olson, K. *See* Korfhage and Olson (1991).

OpenGl Architecture Review Board. (1992). *OpenGl Reference Manual.* Reading, MA: Addison-Wesley. **174**

O'Reilly, T. *See* Quercia and O'Reilly (1988).

Orton, M. N. *See* Berkin and Orton (1994).

Osada, M., Liao, H., and Shneiderman, B. (1993). Alphaslider: Searching Textual Lists with Sliders. *Proceedings of Ninth Annual Japanese Conference on Human Interface'93.* **246**

Osada, M. *See* Liao, Osada, and Shneiderman (1993).

Otis, L. N. *See* Leenstra, Wurden, Otis, and Wurden (1996).

Ouh-Young, M., Beard, D., and Brooks, F. (1989). Force Display Performs Better than Visual Display in a Simple 6-D Docking Task. *Proceedings of EEERAC'89*. 1462–1466. . . . . **97**

Ousterhout, J. K. (1994). *TCL and TK Toolkit*. Reading, MA: Addison-Wesley. **531, 533**

Overbeeke, C. J. *See* Smets, Gaver, Overbeeke, and Stappers (1993).

Page, I., and Walsby, A. (1979). Highly Dynamic Text Display System. *Microprocessors and Microsystems, 3*(2), 73–76. . . . . **338**

Pal, A. A., and Thompson, M. B. (1989). An Advanced Interface to a Switching Software Version Management System. *Proceedings of SETSS'89*. 110–113. . . . . **419**

Parent, M.-A. *See* Beaudoin, Parent, and Vroomen (1996).

Parker, N. *See* Zeleznik, Herndon, Robbins, Huang, Meyer, Parker, and Hughes (1993).

Patel, U. *See* Sutcliffe and Patel (1996).

Patterson, R. *See* Cox and Patterson (1991).

Paulisch, F. N. (1993). *The Design of Extendable Graph Editor*. Unpublished Ph.D. Thesis, University of Karlsruhe. **224**

Pavel, M. *See* Card, Pavel, and Farrell (1984).

PCSSCA. (1986). *Presidential Commission on the Space Shuttle* Challenger *Accident*. Committee on Science and Technology, House of Representatives. **5**

Peckham, J. B. (1981). *Functional Overview of an Advanced Speech Recognition System*. I.E.E Colloquium Digest No. 1981/46. . **335**

Pedersen, J. O. *See* Cutting, Karger, Pedersen, and Tukey (1992a); Cutting, Kupiec, Pedersen, and Sibun (1992b); Cutting, Pederson, and Halvorsen (1991); Rao, Pedersen, Hearst, Mackinlay, Card, Masinter, Halvorsen, and Robertson (1995).

Pennock, K. *See* Wise, Thomas, Pennock, Lantrip, Pottier, and Schur (1995).

Perlin, K., and Fox, D. (1993). Pad: An Alternative Approach to the Computer Interface. *Proceedings of SIGGRAPH'93, ACM Conference on Computer Graphics*. 57–64. . . . . **31, 392, 456, 513, 530, 531, 533, 594**

Perlin, K. *See* Bederson, Hollan, Perlin, Meyer, Bacon, and Furnas (1996).

Petrovic, D. *See* Faloutsos, Barber, Flickner, Hafner, Niblack, Petrovic, and Equitz (1994).

Pfranger, C. *See* Chalmers, Ingram, and Pfranger (1996).

Pickett, R. M., and Grinstein, G. G. (1988). Iconographic Displays for Visualizing Multidimensional Data. *Proceedings of IEEE Conference on Systems, Man and Cybernetics'88*, Piscataway, NJ. 361–370. . . . . **127**

Pickett, R. M. *See* Bergeron, Keim, and Pickett (1994).

Pieper, S. *See* Sturman, Zeltzer, and Pieper (1989); Zeltzer, Pieper, and Sturman (1989).

Pier, K. *See* Bier, Stone, Pier, Buxton, and DeRose (1993).

Pirolli, P., and Card, S. K. (1995). Information Foraging in Information Access Environments. *Proceedings of CHI'95, ACM Conference on Human Factors in Computing Systems*, New York. 51–58. . . . . **544, 580, 609**

Pirolli, P., and Card, S. K. (1999). Information Foraging. *Psychological Review*, forthcoming. **580**

Pirolli, P., and Rao, R. (1996●). Table Lens as a Tool for Making Sense of Data. *Proceedings of AVI'96, Workshop on Advanced Visual Interfaces*, Gubbio, Italy. 67–80. . . . . **14, 580**

Pirolli, P., Schank, P., Hearst, M. A., and Diehl, C. (1996). Scatter/Gather Browsing Communicates the Topic Structure of a Very Large Text Collection. *Proceedings of CHI'96, ACM Conference on Human Factors in Computing Systems*. 213–220. . . . . **626**

Pirolli, P. *See* Card, Pirolli, and Mackinlay (1994); Chi, Pitkow, Mackinlay, Pirolli, Gossweiler, and Card (1998); Lamping, Rao, and Pirolli (1995); Russell, Stefik, Pirolli, and CarD (1993).

Pitkow, J. *See* Chi, Pitkow, Mackinlay, Pirolli, Gossweiler, and Card (1998).

Plaisant, C. (1993). Facilitating Data Exploration. Dynamic Queries on a Health Statistics Map. *Proceedings of American Statistical Association'93*, Alexandria, VA. 18–23. . . . . **237, 241, 246, 578**

Plaisant, C., and Shneiderman, B. (1992). Scheduling Home Control Devices: Design Issues and Usability Evaluation of Four Touchscreen Interfaces. *International Journal of Man-Machine Studies, 36*(3), 375–393. . . . . **293**

Plaisant, C., and Shneiderman, B. (1995). Organization Overviews and Role Management: Inspiration for Future Desktop Environments. *Proceedings of IEEE 4th Workshop on Enabling Technologies: Infrastructure for Collaborative Enterprises*, Los Alamitos, CA. 14–22. . . . . **635**

Plaisant, C., Carr, D. A., and Hasegawa, H. (1992). *When an Intermediate View Matters—A 2D-Browser Experiment*. Technical Report CS-TR-2980. University of Maryland, Department of Computer Science. **301**

Plaisant, C., Carr, D. A., and Shneiderman, B. (1995). Image Browsers: Taxonomy and Design Guidelines. *IEEE Software, 12*(2 (March)), 21–32. . . **234, 285, 288, 290, 295, 296, 305, 572, 634**

Plaisant, C., Doan, K., and Shneiderman, B. (1995). *Query Previews in Networked Information Systems*. College Park, MD: Institute for Systems Research. **31**

Plaisant, C., Marchionini, G., Bruns, T., Komlodi, A., and Campbell, L. (1997). Bringing Treasures to the Surface: Iterative Design for the Library of Congress National Digital Library Program. *Proceedings of CHI'97, ACM Conference on Human Factors in Computing Systems*. 518–525. . . . . **626**

Plaisant, C., Milash, B., Rose, A., Widoff, S., and Shneiderman, B. (1996●). LifeLines: Visualizing Personal Histories. *Proceedings of CHI'96, ACM Conference on Human Factors in Computing Systems*, New York. 221–227. . . . . **286, 629**

Plaisant, C. *See* Carr, Plaisant, and Hasegawa (1994); Doan, Plaisant, and Shneiderman (1996); Furuta, Plaisant, and Shneiderman (1989); Kumar, Plaisant, and Shneiderman (1997); Kumar, Plaisant, Teittinen, and Shneiderman (1994); Lindwarm, Rose, Plaisant, and Norman (1998); Milash, Plaisant, and Rose (1996); Nation, Plaisant, Marchionini, and Komlodi (1997); North, Shneiderman, and Plaisant (1996); Shneiderman and Plaisant (1994).

Plaunt, C. *See* Hearst and Plaunt (1993).

Playfair, W. (1786). *The Commercial and Political Atlas*. London. . . **7**

Plun, J. Y. *See* Roman, Cox, Wilcox, and Plun (1992).

Poblete, F. (1995). *Assessing the Effects of Interacting with Two-Dimensional and 3D Computer Visualizations on the Learning of Information Structure*. Unpublished Ph.D. Thesis, University of Toronto. **634**

Poblete, F. *See* Chignell, Zuberec, and Poblete (1993).

Poltrock, S. E., Shook, R. E., Fairchild, K. M., Lovgren, J. E., Tarlton, P. N., Tarlton, M., and Hauser, M. (1986). *Three-Dimensional Interfaces: The Promise and the Problems*. Technical Report HI-291-86. Austin, TX: Microelectronics and Computer Technology Corporation. **201**

Poltrock, S. E. *See* Fairchild and Poltrock (1986, 1987); Fairchild, Poltrock, and Furnas (1988).

Pommert, A. *See* Hohne, Pommert, Riemer, Schiemann, Schubert, and Tiede (1995).

Pope, S. T. *See* Krasner and Pope (1990).

Post, F. *See* Rosenblum, Earnshaw, Encarnação, Hagen, Kaufman, Klimenko, Nielson, Post, and Thalmann (1994).

Pottier, M. *See* Wise, Thomas, Pennock, Lantrip, Pottier, Schur, and Crow (1995).

Powsner, S. M., and Tufte, E. R. (1994). Graphical Summary of Patient Status. *The Lancet, 344*(August 6), 386–389. . . . . **291**

Preimj, B., Raab, A., and Strothotte, T. (1997). Coherent Zooming of Illustrations with 3D-Graphics and Text. *Proceedings of Graphics Interface'97,* 105–113. . . . . **342**

Presson, C. C. *See* Huttenlocher and Presson (1979).

Price, B. A., Baecker, R. M., and Small, I. S. (1993). A Principled Taxonomy of Software Visualization. *Journal of Visual Languages and Computing, 4*(2), 211–266. . . . . **160**

Qin, Y., and Simon, H. A. (1990). Laboratory Replication of Scientific Discovery Processes. *Cognitive Science, 14,* 281–312. . . **598**

Quercia, V., and O'Reilly, T. (1988). *X Window System User's Guide.* Sebastopol, CA: O'Reilly & Associates, Inc. **428**

Raab, A. *See* Preimj, Raab, and Strothotte (1997).

Rafsky, L. C. *See* Friedman and Rafsky (1979).

Ramakrishnan, R. *See* Livny, Ramakrishnan, Beyer, Chen, Donjerkovic, Lawande, Myllymaki, and Wenger (1997).

Rao, R., and Card, S. K. (1994●). The Table Lens: Merging Graphical and Symbolic Representations in an Interactive Focus + Context Visualization for Tabular Information. *Proceedings of CHI'94, ACM Conference on Human Factors in Computing Systems,* New York. 318–322 and 481–482. . . . . **13, 32, 93, 184, 277, 341, 351, 382, 597, 619, 620, 626**

Rao, R., and Card, S. K. (1995). Exploring Large Tables with the Table Lens. *Conference Companion of CHI'95, ACM Conference on Human Factors in Computing Systems,* New York. 403–404. . **597**

Rao, R., Card, S. K., Jellinek, H. D., Mackinlay, J. D., and Robertson, G. G. (1992). The Information Grid: A Framework for Information Retrieval and Retrieval-Centered Applications. *Proceedings of UIST'92, ACM Symposium on User Interface Software and Technology,* 23–32. . . . . **523**

Rao, R., Pedersen, J. O., Hearst, M. A., Mackinlay, J. D., Card, S. K., Masinter, L., Halvorsen, P. K., and Robertson, G. G. (1995). Rich Interaction in the Digital Library. *Communications of the ACM, 38*(4), 29–39. . . . . **572, 626**

Rao, R. *See* Johnson, Jellinek, Klotz, Rao, and Card (1993b); Lamping and Rao (1994, 1996); Lamping, Rao, and Pirolli (1995); Mackinlay, Rao, and Card. (1995); Pirolli and Rao (1996).

Rasmussen, H. *See* Anderson, Nielsen, and Rasmussen (1989).

Rea, K. P. *See* Lientz and Rea (1995).

Rearick, T. C. (1991). Automating the Conversion of Text into Hypertext. In J. Devlin and E. Berk (eds.), *Hypertext/Hypermedia Handbook.* New York: McGraw-Hill. 113–140. . . . . **415**

Reinfelds, J. *See* Kaugers, Reinfelds, and Brazma (1994).

Reitman, J. S., Whitten, W. B., and Gruenenfelder, T. W. (1984). A General User Interface for Creating and Displaying Tree Structures, Hierarchies, Decision Trees, and Nested Menus. *Proceedings of NYU Symposium on User Interfaces.* **330**

Remde, J. R., Gomez, L. M., and Landauer, T. K. (1987). Superbook: An Automatic Tool for Information Exploration. *Proceedings of ACM Hypertext'87 Conference.* 175–188. . . . . . . **546, 547**

Remde, J. R. *See* Egan, Remde, Gomez, Landauer, Eberhardt, and Lochbaum (1989).

Rennison, E. (1994●). Galaxy of News: An Approach to Visualizing and Understanding Expansive News Landscapes. *Proceedings of UIST'94, ACM Symposium on User Interface Software and Technology,* New York. 3–12. . . . . **60, 451**

Resnikoff, H. L. (1987). *The Illusion of Reality.* New York: Springer-Verlag. **11, 16, 24, 25**

Rex, D. B. *See* Risch, Rex, Dowson, Walters, May, and Moon (1997).

Rice, J. R. (1991). Ten Rules for Color Coding. *Information Display, 7*(3), 12–14. . . . . **157**

Rich, E. *See* Hollan, Rich, Hill, Wroblewski, Wilner, Wittenburg, and Grudin (1991).

Riedl, J. T. *See* Chi and Riedl (1998).

Riemer, M. *See* Hohne, Pommert, Riemer, Schiemann, Schubert, and Tiede (1995).

Rips, L. J., Shoben, E. J., and Smith, E. E. (1973). Semantic Distance and the Verification of Semantic Relations. *Journal of Verbal Learning and Verbal Behavior, 12,* 1–20. . . . . **194**

Risch, J. S., May, R. A., Dowson, S. T., and Thomas, J. J. (1996). A Virtual Environment for Multimedia Intelligence Data Analysis. *IEEE Computer Graphics and Applications, 16*(6), 33–41. . . . **552**

Risch, J. S., Rex, D. B., Dowson, S. T., Walters, T. B., May, R. A., and Moon, B. D. (1997●). The STARLIGHT Information Visualization System. *Proceedings of IEEE International Conference on Information Visualization,* London. 42–49. . . . . **13, 514**

Ritter, H., and Kohonen, T. (1989). Self-Organizing Semantic Maps. *Biological Cybernetics, 61*(4), 241–254. . . . . **434**

Rivlin, E. *See* Botafogo, Rivlin, and Shneiderman (1992).

Robbins, D. C. *See* Zeleznik, Herndon, Robbins, Huang, Meyer, Parker, and Hughes (1993).

Robbins, J. *See* Anick, Brennan, Flynn, Hanssen, Alvey, and Robbins (1990).

Roberts, J. *See* Gauch, Aust, Evans, Gauch, Minden, Niehaus, and Roberts (1994).

Robertson, A. K. *See* Levkowitz, Holub, Meyer, and Robertson (1992).

Robertson, E. L. *See* Keahey and Robertson (1996).

Robertson, G. G., and Mackinlay, J. D. (1993●). The Document Lens. *Proceedings of UIST'93, ACM Symposium on User Interface Software and Technology.* 101–108. . . . . . **35, 184, 264, 343, 351, 356, 360, 369, 385, 431, 546, 561, 628**

Robertson, G. G., Card, S. K., and Mackinlay, J. D. (1989). The Cognitive Co-processor for Interactive User Interfaces. *Proceedings of UIST'89, ACM Symposium on User Interface Software and Technology.* 10–18. . . . . **8, 231, 396, 518, 519, 520**

Robertson, G. G., Card, S. K., and Mackinlay, J. D. (1993●). Information Visualization Using 3D Interactive Animation. *Communications of the ACM, 36*(4), 57–71. . . . . **84, 150, 244, 253, 343, 382, 442, 493, 494, 504, 513, 545, 562, 563, 564, 583, 633, 634**

Robertson, G. G., Mackinlay, J. D., and Card, S. K. (1991). Cone Trees: Animated 3D Visualizations of Hierarchical Information. *Proceedings of CHI'91, ACM Conference on Human Factors in Computing Systems,* New York. 189–194. . . . . . **8, 150, 153, 266, 296, 301, 308, 350, 351, 359, 382, 385, 456, 494, 523, 551, 556, 591, 619, 620**

Robertson, G. G., McCracken, D., and Newell, A. (1979). *The ZOG Approach to Man-Machine Communication.* Department of Computer Science Technical Report CMU-CS-97-148. Pittsburgh: Carnegie Mellon University. **330**

Robertson, G. G. *See* Card, Mackinlay, and Robertson (1990); Card, Robertson, and Mackinlay (1991); Card, Robertson, and York (1996); Mackinlay, Card, and Robertson (1990a, 1990b); Mackinlay, Robertson, and Card (1991); Mackinlay, Robertson, and DeLine (1994); Rao, Card, Jellinek, Mackinlay, and

Robertson (1992); Rao, Pedersen, Hearst, Mackinlay, Card, Masinter, Halvorsen, and Robertson (1995).

Robertson, P. K. (1991). A Methodology for Choosing Data Representations. *IEEE Computer Graphics and Applications,* May, 56–67. . . . . **616**

Robertson, P. K., and Ferrari, L. D. (1994). Systematic Approaches to Visualization: Is a Reference Model Needed? In L. J. Rosenblum, R. A. Earnshaw, J. Encarnação, H. Hagen, A. Kaufman, S. Klimienko, G. M. Nielson, F. Post, and D. Thalman, (eds.), *Scientific Visualization.* London: Academic Press. **17**

Robin, H. (1992). *The Scientific Image: From Cave to Computer.* New York: H. N. Abrams, Inc. **37**

Robins, G. *See* Avitzur, Robins, and Newman (1994).

Rochkind, M. J. (1975). The Source Code Control System. *IEEE Transactions Software Engineering, SE-1*(4), 364–370. . . . . . . **419**

Rogers, Y. *See* Scaife and Rogers (1996).

Rogowitz, B. E., Ling, D. T., and Kellogg, W. A. (1992). Task Dependence, Verticality, and Preattentive Vision: Taking Advantage of Perceptually-Rich Computer Environments. *Human Vision, Visual Processing and Digital Display III, SPIR Vol. 1666.* . . **85**

Roman, G. C., Cox, K. C., Wilcox, C. D., and Plun, J. Y. (1992). Pavane: A System for Declarative Visualization of Concurrent Computations. *Journal of Visual Languages and Computing, 3*(2), 161–193. . . . . **160**

Rose, A. *See* Lindwarm, Rose, Plaisant, and Norman (1998).

Rose, A. *See* Milash, Plaisant, and Rose (1996); Plaisant, Milash, Rose, Widoff, and Shneiderman (1996).

Roseman, M. *See* Schaffer, Zuo, Bartram, Dill, Dubes, Greenberg, and Roseman (1993, 1996).

Rosenblum, L. J., Earnshaw, R. A., Encarnação, J., Hagen, H., Kaufman, A., Klimenko, S., Nielson, G. M., Post, F., and Thalmann, D. (eds.). (1994). *Scientific Visualization: Advances and Challenges.* London: Academic Press. **38**

Rosenblum, L. J. *See* Nielson, Shriver, and Rosenblum (1990).

Ross, R., Zhang, Z., and Choi, E. (1994). *Using the Tree-Browser to Visualize Information for Database Queries.* Unpublished Report. University of Maryland, Department of Computer Science.. **304**

Roth, S. F. (1994). The SAGE Project, *www.cs.cmu.edu/Web/Groups/sage/sage.html.* **264, 272**

Roth, S. F., and Mattis, J. (1990). Data Characterization for Intelligent Graphics Presentation. *Proceedings of CHI'90, ACM Conference on Human Factors in Computing Systems,* New York. 193–200. . . . . **8**

Roth, S. F., Lucas, P., Senm, J. A., Gomberg, C. C., Burks, M. B., Stroffolino, P. J., and Kolojejchick, J. A. (1996). Visage: A User Interface Environment for Exploring Information. *Proceedings of InfoVis'96, IEEE Symposium on Information Visualization.* 3–10. . . . . **626**

Roth, S. F. *See* Chuah, Roth, Mattis, and Kolojejchick (1995a, 1995b); Goldstein and Roth (1994); Goldstein, Roth, Kolojejchick, and Mattis (1994).

Rousseeuw, P. J. (1985). A Visual Display for Hierarchical Classification. *Proceedings of Data Analysis and Informatics.* 743–748. . . . . **438**

Rowland, B. R., and Welsch, R. J. (1983). *Software Development System. Bell System Technical Journal, 62*(1), 275–289. . . . . . **419**

Rubin, S. M., and Whitted, T. (1980). A 3-Dimensional Representation for Fast Rendering of Complex Scenes. *Proceedings of SIGGRAPH'80, ACM Conference on Computer Graphics.* 110–116. . . . . **100**

Runciman, C., and Thimbleby, H. (1986). Equal Opportunity Interactive Systems. *International Journal of Man-Machine Studies, 25*(4), 439–451. . . . . **246**

Rundensteiner, E. A. *See* Hibino and Rundensteiner (1995, 1997).

Russell, D. M., Stefik, M. J., Pirolli, P., and Card, S. K. (1993). The Cost Structure of Sensemaking. *Proceedings of INTERCHI'93, ACM Conference on Human Factors in Computing Systems,* Amsterdam. 269–276. . . . . **10, 545, 580, 582, 597**

Russell, S. (1985). *The Complete Guide to MRS.* Technical Report KSL-85-12. Stanford, CA: Stanford University. **79**

Ryan, A. G. *See* Consens, Mendelzon, and Ryan (1992).

Ryman, A. G. *See* Consens, Eigler, Hasan, Mendelzon, Noik, Ryman, and Vista (1994).

Salesin, D. *See* Feiner, Salesin, and Banchoff (1982).

Salomon, G. *See* Mandler, Salomon, and Wong (1992).

Salton, G. (1988). A Simple Blueprint for Automatic Boolean Query Processing. *Information Processing and Management, 24*(3). . . **146**

Salton, G. (1989). *Automatic Text Processing—The Transformation Analysis, and Retrieval of Information by Computer.* Reading, MA: Addison-Wesley. **413**

Salton, G. (ed.). (1971). *The Smart Retrieval System—Experiments in Automatic Document Processing.* Englewood Cliffs, NJ: Prentice Hall. **413**

Salton, G., Allan, J., and Buckley, C. (1993). Approaches to Passage Retrieval in Full Text Information Systems. *Proceedings of SIGIR'93, ACM Conference on Research and Development in Information Retrieval.* 49–58. . . . . **413**

Salton, G., Allan, J., Buckley, C., and Singhal, A. (1995●). Automatic Analysis, Theme Generation, and Summarization of Machine-Readable Text. *Science, 264*(3 June), 1421–1426. . . . . . **59, 411**

Salton, G., and Buckley, C. (1991). Automatic Text Structuring and Retrieval—Experiments in Automatic Encyclopedia Searching. *Proceedings of SIGIR'91, ACM Conference on Research and Development in Information Retrieval.* 21–30. . . . . **413**

Salton, G., Buckley, C., and Allan, J. (1992). Automatic Structuring of Text Files. *Electronic Publishing, 5*(1), 1–17. . . . . **414**

Salton, G., and McGill, M. J. (1983). *Introduction to Modern Information Retrieval.* New York: McGraw-Hill. **126, 516**

Salton, G., and Wong, A. (1978). Generation and Search of Clustered Files. *Transactions on Database Systems, 3*(4), 321–346.. **413**

Salton, G., Yang, C. S., and Wong, A. (1975). A Vector Space Model for Automatic Indexing. *Communications of the ACM, 18*(11), 613–620. . . . . **413**

Samet, H. (1989). *Design and Analysis of Spatial Data Structures.* Reading, MA: Addison- Wesley. **156**

Sammon, J. W. (1969). A Nonlinear Mapping for Data Structure Analysis. *IEEE Transactions on Computers, 18*(5), 401–409. . **438**

Sanderson, P., Scott, J., Johnston, T., Mainzer, J., Watanabe, L., and James, J. (1992). MacSHAPA and the Enterprise of Exploring Sequential Data Analysis (ESDA). *International Journal of Man-Machine Studies, 41*(5), 633–681. . . . . **288, 629**

Sandin, D. J. *See* Campbell, DeFanti, Frederiksen, Joyce, Leske, Lindberg, and Sandin (1986); DeFanti and Sandin (1987); Hart, Sandin, and Kauffman (1989).

Santana, M. *See* Vion-Dury and Santana (1994).

Sarkar, M. (1993). Stretching the Rubber Sheet, A Metaphor for Viewing Large Layouts on Small Screens, *UIST'93, Conference on User Interface Technology.* New York: ACM Press. 81–91. . . . **371**

Sarkar, M., and Brown, M. H. (1992). Graphical Fisheye Views of Graphs. *Proceedings of CHI'92, ACM Conference on Human Factors in Computing Systems,* New York. 83–91 . . . . **341, 343, 351, 352, 356, 357, 358, 385, 494, 563**

Sarkar, M., and Brown, M. H. (1994). Graphical Fisheye Views. *Communications of the ACM, 37*(12), 73–84. . **224, 369, 385, 634**

Sarkar, M., and Snibbe, S. S. (1993). Stretching the Rubber Sheets: A Metaphor for Viewing Large Layouts on Small Screens. *Proceedings of UIST'93, ACM Symposium on User Interface Software and Technology.* 81–92. . . . . . . **265, 270, 271, 343, 344, 359, 385**

Scaife, M., and Rogers, Y. (1996). External Cognition: How Do Graphical Representations Work? *International Journal of Human-Computer Studies, 45*(2), 185–213. . . . . **1**

Scha, R. *See* Engelhardt, Bruin, Janssen, and Scha (1996).

Schaffer, D., Zuo, Z., Bartram, L., Dill, J., Dubes, S., Greenberg, S., and Roseman, M. (1993). Comparing Fisheye and Full-Zoom Techniques for Navigation of Hierarchically Clustered Networks. *Proceedings of Graphics Interface'93,* San Mateo, CA. . **351**

Schaffer, D., Zuo, Z., Bartram, L., Dill, J., Dubs, S., Greenberg, S., and Roseman, M. (1996). Navigating Hierarchically Clustered Networks through Fisheye and Full-Zoom Methods. *ACM Transactions on Computer-Human Interaction, 3*(2), 162–188. . . . . **296, 634**

Schall, M. (1994). Diamond and Ice: Visual Exploratory Data Analysis Tools. *Perspective, Journal of OAC at UCLA, 18*(2), 15–24. . . . . **108**

Schank, P. *See* Pirolli, Schank, Hearst, and Diehl (1996).

Schatz, B. R., and Caplinger, M. A. (1989). Searching in a Hyperlibrary. *Proceedings of Fifth International Conference on Data Engineering'89,* Los Angeles. 188–197. **433**

Schegel, D. *See* Upson, Faulhabel Jr., Kamins, Laidlaw, Schegel, Vroom, Gurwitz, and van Dam (1989).

Scheifler, R. W., Gettys, J., and Newman, R. (1988). *X Window System C Library and Protocol Reference.* Bedford, MA: Digital Press. **100, 254**

Scherrer, J. *See* Boens, Borst, and Scherrer (1992).

Schiano, D. *See* Levy, Zacks, Tversky, and Schiano (1996).

Schiemann, T. *See* Hohne, Pommert, Riemer, Schiemann, Schubert, and Tiede (1995).

Schmid, C. F. (1983). *Statistical Graphics: Design Principles and Practices.* New York: John Wiley & Sons. **108, 277**

Schmid, C., and Hinterberger, H. (1994). Comparative Multivariate Visualization Across Conceptually Different Graphic Displays. *Proceedings of SSDBM'94,* Los Alamitos, CA.. . . . . **74**

Scholl, L. *See* Colby and Scholl (1991).

Schooler, L. J. *See* Anderson and Schooler (1991).

Schubert, R. *See* Hohne, Pommert, Riemer, Schiemann, Schubert, and Tiede (1995).

Schur, A. *See* Wise, Thomas, Pennock, Lantrip, Pottier, Schur, and Crow (1995).

Schwartz, M. F., and Wood, D. C. M. (1993). Discovering Shared Interests Using Graph Analysis. *Communications of the ACM, 36*(8), 78–89. . . . . **227**

Schwegler, J. *See* Mihalisin, Timlin, and Schwegler (1991).

Scott, J. *See* Sanderson, Scott, Johnston, Mainzer, Watanabe, and James (1992).

Sears, A., and Shneiderman, B. (1991). High Precision Touchscreens: Design Strategies and Comparisons with a Mouse. *International Journal of Man-Machine Studies, 34*(4), 593–613. . . . **157**

Secret, A. *See* Berners-Lee, Calliliau, Luotonem, Nielsen, and Secret (1994).

Seery, J. B. *See* Kruskal, Young, and Seery (1973).

Seidl, T. *See* Keim, Kriegel, and Seidl (1994).

Sekular, R., and Blake, R. (1994). *Perception.* 3rd ed. New York: McGraw-Hill. **226**

Senm, J. A. *See* Roth, Lucas, Senm, Gomberg, Burks, Stroffolino, and Kolojejchick (1996).

Serra, L., Chua, T.-S., and Teh, W.-S. (1991). A Model for Integrating Multimedia Information Around 3D Graphics Hierarchies. *The Visual Computer, 7*(5-6)(May/June), 326–343. . . . . **494**

Serra, L. *See* Fairchild, Serra, Hern, Hai, and Leong (1993).

Shafer, D. *See* Carr and Shafer (1992).

Shaw, C., Liang, J., Green, M., and Sun, Y. (1992). The Decoupled Simulation Model for Virtual Reality Systems. *Proceedings of CHI'92, ACM Conference on Human Factors in Computing Systems.* 321–328. . . . . **519**

Sheridan, T. B. (1984). Supervisory Control of Remote Manipulators, Vehicles and Dynamic Processes: Experiments in Command and Display Aiding. *Advances in Man-Machine System Research, 1,* 49–137. . . . . **519**

Shiffrin, R. M. (1988). Attention. In R. C. Atkinson, R. J. Herrnstein, G. Lindzey, and R. D. Luce (eds.), *Stevens' Handbook of Experimental Psychology.* Vol. 2. New York: John Wiley & Sons. 739–811. . . . . **25**

Shillner, R. A. *See* Brown and Shillner (1995).

Shlomi, E. *See* Kadmon and Shlomi (1978).

Shneiderman, B. (1983). Direct Manipulation: A Step Beyond Programming Languages. *IEEE Computer, 16*(8), 57–68. . . . . **220, 236, 420**

Shneiderman, B. (1992a). *Designing the User Interface: Strategies for Effective Human-Computer Interaction.* 2nd ed. Reading, MA: Addison-Wesley. **244, 285, 572**

Shneiderman, B. (1992b). Tree Visualization with Tree-Maps: A 2-Dimensional Space Filling Approach. *ACM Transactions on Graphics, 11*(1), 92–99. . . . . **8, 152, 296, 367, 630**

Shneiderman, B. (1994●). Dynamic Queries for Visual Information Seeking. *IEEE Software, 11*(6), 70–77. . . . . . **127, 225, 235, 297, 575**

Shneiderman, B. (1996). The Eyes Have It: A Task by Data Type Taxonomy for Information Visualization. *Proceedings of IEEE Workshop on Visual Languages'96.* 336–343. . . . . **31, 35**

Shneiderman, B. (1998). *Designing the User Interface: Strategies for Effective Human-Computer Interaction.* 3rd ed. Reading, MA: Addison-Wesley.. . . . . **31**

Shneiderman, B., and Plaisant, C. (1994). The Future of Graphic User Interfaces: Personal Role Managers. *Proceedings of People and Computers IX: The Ninth Conference of the British Computer Society Human-Computer Interaction Specialist Group.* 3–8. . . **635**

Shneiderman, B. *See* Ahlberg and Shneiderman (1994a, 1994b, 1994c); Ahlberg, Williamson, and Shneiderman (1992); Asahi, Turo, and Shneiderman (1995); Botafogo, Rivlin, and Shneiderman (1992); Chimera and Shneiderman (1994); Chimera, Wolman, Mark, and Shneiderman (1991); Doan, Plaisant, and Shneiderman (1996); Furuta, Plaisant, and Shneiderman (1989); Jain and Shneiderman (1994); Jog and Shneiderman (1995); Johnson and Shneiderman (1991); Kandogan and Shneiderman (1995, 1997, 1998); Korn and Shneiderman (1995); Koved and Shneiderman (1986); Kumar, Plaisant, and Shneiderman (1997); Kumar, Plaisant, Teittinen, and Shneiderman (1994); Liao, Osada, and Shneiderman (1993); North, Shneiderman, and Plaisant (1996); Osada, Liao, and Shneiderman (1993); Plaisant and Shneiderman (1992, 1995); Plaisant, Carr, and Shneiderman. (1995); Plaisant, Doan, and

Shneiderman (1995); Plaisant, Milash, Rose, Widoff, and Shneiderman (1996); Sears and Shneiderman (1991); Tanin, Beigel, and Shneiderman (1997); Williamson and Shneiderman (1992); Young and Shneiderman (1993).

Shoben, E. J. *See* Rips, Shoben, and Smith (1973).

Shook, R. E. (1986). *SemNet: A Conceptual and Interface Evaluation.* Technical Report HI-320-86-P. Austin, TX: Microelectronics and Computer Technology Corporation. **192**

Shook, R. E. *See* Poltrock, Shook, Fairchild, Lovgren, Tarlton, Tarlton, and Hauser (1986).

Shriver, B. *See* Nielson, Shriver, and Rosenblum (1990).

Silicon Graphics. (1993). *Demo Book* (Computer Program). Mountain View, CA: Silicon Graphics. **546, 547**

Silverman, B. W. (ed.). (1990). *Density Estimation for Statistics and Data Analysis.* New York: Chapman & Hall. **209, 252**

Simbork, D. W. *See* Whiting-O'Keefe, Simbork, Epstein, and Warger (1985).

Simon, H. A. (1969). *The Sciences of the Artificial.* Cambridge, MA: MIT Press. **616, 622**

Simon, H. A. *See* Langley, Simon, Bradshaw, and Zytkow (1987); Larkin and Simon (1987); Newell and Simon (1972); Qin and Simon (1990).

Singers, R., and Endres, L. (1993). Metaphoric Abstraction, the Starfield and Complex Systems. *International Journal of Man-Machine Studies, 22,* 463–477. . . . . **246**

Singhal, A. *See* Salton, Allan, Buckley, and Singhal (1995).

Sittig, D. F. *See* Factor, Gelernter, Kolb, Miller, and Sittig (1991).

Slagle, J. R. *See* Lee, Slagle, and Blum (1977).

Slivjanovski, R. *See* Mezrich, Frysinger, and Slivjanovski (1984).

Sloan, B. *See* Unwin, Sloan, and Wills (1992).

Slocum, J., and Cohen, R. (1986). *NABU Documentation, Natural Language Processing Project.* Technical Report AI-228-86-Q. Austin, TX: Microelectronics and Computer Technology Corporation.. . . . . **192**

Small, D., Ishizki, S., and Cooper, M. (1994). Typographic Space. *Proceedings of CHI'94, ACM Conference on Human Factors in Computing Systems,* Boston. 437–438. . . . . **455**

Small, D. *See* Masuishi, Small, and MacNeil (1992).

Small, I. S. *See* Price, Baecker, and Small (1993).

Smeaton, A. F. *See* Guinan and Smeaton (1992).

Smets, G., Gaver, W. W., Overbeeke, C. J., and Stappers, P. J. (1993). Designing in Virtual Reality: Perception-Action Coupling and Form Semantics. *Conference Companion of INTERCHI'93, ACM Conference on Human Factors in Computing Systems.* 11–12. . . . . **618**

Smith, E. E. *See* Rips, Shoben, and Smith (1973).

Smith, P. A., and Wilson, J. R. (1993). Navigating in Hypertext through Virtual Environments. *Applied Ergonomics, 24*(4), 271–278. . . . . **494**

Smith, R. (1987). Experiences with the Alternate Reality Kit: An Example of the Tension between Literalism and Magic. *Proceedings of CHI+GI'87, ACM Conference on Human Factors in Computing Systems and Graphics Interface.* 61–67. . . . . **618**

Smith, R. B., and Ungar, D. (1987). The Power of Simplicity. *Proceedings of OOPSLA'87.* 227–242. . . . . **507**

Smithurst, M. D. *See* Benest, Morgan, and Smithurst (1987).

Snibbe, S. S. *See* Conner, Snibbe, Herndon, and Zeleznik (1992); Sarkar and Snibbe (1993).

Snowdon, D., Benford, S., Brown, C., Ingram, R., Knox, L., and Studley, L. (1995). *Information Visualisation, Browsing and Sharing in Populated Information Terrains.* **505**

Snowdon, D. *See* Benford, Snowdon, and Mariani (1995); Benford, Snowdon, Greenhalgh, Ingram, Knox, and Brown (1995).

Sochats, K. M. *See* Olsen, Korhage, Sochats, Spring, and Williams (1993).

Soergel, D. *See* Lin, Soergel, and Marchionini (1991).

Sony Corporation. (1994). *Magic Link User's Guide.* Technical Report PIC 1000. Tokyo: Sony Corporation. **546, 547**

Sparr, T. M. *See* Bergeron, Meeker, and Sparr (1992).

Spence, I. (1990). Visual Psychophysics of Simple Graphical Elements. *Journal of Experimental Psychology: Human Perception and Performance, 16,* 683–692. . . . . **634**

Spence, R., and Apperley, M. D. (1982 ●). Data Base Navigation: An Office Environment for the Professional. *Behavior and Information Technology, 1*(1), 43–54. . . . . **31, 332, 343, 351, 354, 363, 369, 371, 527, 563, 634**

Spence, R. *See* Apperley and Spence (1980); Apperley, Tzavaras, and Spence (1982); Dawkes, Tweedie, and Spence (1996); Tweedie, Spence, Dawkes, and Su (1996); Tweedie, Spence, Williams, and Bhogal (1994).

Spoerri, A. (1993a ●). InfoCrystal: A Visual Tool for Information Retrieval. *Proceedings of IEEE Visualization'93 Conference,* Los Alamitos, CA. 150–157. . . . . **94, 95, 141, 142, 146, 283, 442, 619, 620**

Spoerri, A. (1993b). Visual Tools for Information Retrieval. *Proceedings of IEEE Workshop on Visual Languages'93.* 160–168. . . . . **146**

Spring, M. B. *See* Olsen, Korhage, Sochats, Spring, and Williams (1993).

Springmeyer, R. R., Blattner, M. M., and Max, N. L. (1992). A Characterization of the Scientific Data Analysis Process. *Proceedings of IEEE Visualization'92 Conference.* 235–242. . . . . . **268**

Staples, L. (1993). Representation in Virtual Space: Visual Convention in the Graphical User Interface. *Proceedings of INTERCHI'93, ACM Conference on Human Factors in Computing Systems.* 348–354. . . . . **548**

Stappers, P. J. *See* Smets, Gaver, Overbeeke, and Stappers (1993).

Stasko, J. T. *See* Jerding and Stasko (1995a, 1995b); Kraemer and Stasko (1993).

Steffen, J. L. (1985). Interactive Examination of a C Program with Cscope. *Proceedings of USENIX'85.* 170–175. . . . . **419**

Steffen, J. L. *See* Eick, Steffen, and Sumner (1992).

Stefik, M. J. (1996). *Internet Dreams: Archetypes, Myths, and Metaphors.* Cambridge, MA: MIT Press. **465**

Stefik, M. J. *See* Russell, Stefik, Pirolli, and Card (1993).

Stephens, D., and Krebs, J. R. (1986). *Foraging Theory.* Princeton, NJ: Princeton University Press. **544**

StereoGraphics. (1989). *Crystal Eyes Product Literature.* San Rafael, CA: StereoGraphics Corp. **96**

Stevens, M. P., Zeleznik, R. C., and Hughes, J. F. (1994). An Architecture for an Extensible 3D Interface Toolkit. *Proceedings of UIST'94, ACM Symposium on User Interface Software and Technology.* 59–67. . . . . **264**

Stevens, S. S. (1946). On the Theory of Scales of Measurement. *Science, 103*(2684), 677–680. . . . . **69**

Stometta, S. *See* Hollan and Stometta (1992).

Stone, M. C., Fishkin, K., and Bier, E. A. (1994). The Movable Filter as a User Interface Tool. *Proceedings of CHI'94, ACM Conference on Human Factors in Computing Systems,* New York. 306–312. . . . . **253, 254, 264, 265, 270, 271, 531**

Stone, M. C. *See* Beach and Stone (1983); Bier, Stone, Baudel, Buxton, and Fishkin (1994); Bier, Stone, Pier, Buxton, and DeRose (1993); Fishkin and Stone (1995).

Stonebraker, M. *See* Woodruff, Landay, and Stonebraker (1998).

Storey, M. A., and Muller, H. A. (1995). Graph Layout Adjustment Strategies, *Graph Drawing 95, Lecture Notes in Computer Science.* Berlin: Springer-Verlag. 487–499. . . . . **371, 372, 376**

Strasnick, S. *See* Tesler and Strasnick (1992).

Stroffolino, P. J. *See* Roth, Lucas, Senm, Gomberg, Burks, Stroffolino, and Kolojejchick (1996).

Strothotte, T. *See* Preimj, Raab, and Strothotte (1997).

Stroustrup, B. (1985). *The C++ Programming Language.* Reading, MA: Addison-Wesley. **227, 428**

Studley, L. *See* Snowdon, Benford, Brown, Ingram, Knox, and Studley (1995).

Stuetzle, W. *See* Buja, McDonald, Michalak, and Stuetzle (1991).

Sturman, D., Zeltzer, D., and Pieper, S. (1989). Hands-On Interaction with Virtual Environments. *Proceedings of SIGGRAPH'89, ACM Conference on Computer Graphics,* Williamsburg, VA. 19–24. . . . . **99, 101**

Sturman, D. *See* Zeltzer, Pieper, and Sturman (1989).

Su, H. *See* Tweedie, Spence, Dawkes, and Su (1996).

Subbotin, M. M. *See* Gilyarevskii and Subbotin (1993).

Suchman, L. A. (1987). *Plans and Situated Action.* New York: Cambridge University Press. **277**

Sugiyama, K. *See* Misue and Sugiyama (1991).

Sumner, E. E. *See* Eick, Steffen, and Sumner (1992).

Sun, Y. *See* Shaw, Liang, Green, and Sun (1992).

Sutcliffe, A., and Patel, U. (1996). 3D or Not 3D: Is It Nobler in the Mind? *Proceedings of 1996 British HCI Conference.* 79–94.. . . **634**

Sutherland, I. E. (1963). Sketchpad: A Man-Machine Graphical Communications Systems. *Proceedings of Spring Joint Computer Conference,* Baltimore. 329–346. . . . . **539**

Sutherland, I. E. (1965a). *Sketchpad: A Man-Machine Graphical Communication System.* Technical Report 296. Cambridge, MA: MIT Lincoln Laboratory.. . . . . **519**

Sutherland, I. E. (1965b). The Ultimate Display. *Proceedings of IFIP'65, Conference of International Federation for Information Processing.* 506–508.. . . . . **96**

Swayne, D. F. *See* Buja, Cook, and Swayne (1996).

Swigger, K. *See* Burgess and Swigger (1986).

Taira, R. *See* Chu, Cardenas, and Taira (1995).

Tamassia, R. (1996). Strategic Directions in Computational Geometry Working Group Report. *ACM Computing Surveys, 28*(4 December), 591–606.. . . . . **188**

Tamassia, R. *See* Battista, Eades, Tamassia, and Tollis (1994); Cruz and Tamassia (1998).

Tang, S. H., and Linton, M. A. (1993). Pacers: Time-Elastic Objects. *Proceedings of UIST'93, ACM Symposium on User Interface Software and Technology,* New York. 35–44. . . . . **396**

Tanin, E., Beigel, R., and Shneiderman, B. (1997). Design and Evaluation of Incremental Data Structures and Algorithms for Dynamic Query Interfaces. *Proceedings of InfoVis'97, IEEE Symposium on Information Visualization.* 81–86. . . . . **627**

Tarlton, M. *See* Poltrock, Shook, Fairchild, Lovgren, Tarlton, Tarlton, and Hauser (1986).

Tarlton, P. N. *See* Poltrock, Shook, Fairchild, Lovgren, Tarlton, Tarlton, and Hauser (1986).

Taylor, H. M., and Karlin, S. (1984). *An Introduction to Stochastic Modeling.* London: Academic Press. **209**

Teh, W.-S. *See* Serra, Chua, and Teh (1991).

Teittinen, M. *See* Kumar, Plaisant, Teittinen, and Shneiderman (1994).

Tektronix. (1987). *3D Stereoscopic Color Graphics Workstation.* TEK 4126 Product Literature. Beaverton, OR. **96**

Tennant, H., and Heilmeier, G. H. (1991). Knowledge and Equality: Harnessing the Tides of Information Abundance. In D. Leebaert (ed.), *Technology 2001: The Future of Computing and Communications.* Cambridge, MA: MIT Press. 117–149. . . . . **582**

Tesler, J., and Strasnick, S. (1992). *FSN: The 3D File System Navigator.* Mountain View, CA: Silicon Graphics. . . **494, 495, 523, 526**

Tesler, L. (1981). The Smalltalk Environment. *Byte, 6*(8), 90–147. . . . . **313**

Thalmann, D. *See* Rosenblum, Earnshaw, Encarnação, Hagen, Kaufman, Klimenko, Nielson, Post, and Thalmann (1994).

Thibault, W. C., and Naylor, B. F. (1987). Set Operations on Polyhedra Using Binary Space Partitioning Trees. *Proceedings of SIGGRAPH'87, ACM Conference on Computer Graphics.* 153–162. . . . . **102**

Thimbleby, H. *See* Runciman and Thimbleby (1986).

Thomas, J. J. *See* Risch, May, Dowson, and Thomas (1996); Wise, Thomas, Pennock, Lantrip, Pottier, Schur, and Crow (1995).

Thomas, J. P. *See* Boff, Kaufman, and Thomas (1986).

Thompson, M. B. *See* Pal and Thompson (1989).

Tichy, W. F. (1985). RCS—A System for Version Control. *Software Practice and Experience, 15*(7), 637–654. . . . . **419**

Tiede, U. *See* Hohne, Pommert, Riemer, Schiemann, Schubert, and Tiede (1995).

Timlin, J. *See* Mihalisin, Timlin, and Schwegler (1991).

Tobler, W. R. (1973). A Continuous Transformation Useful for Districting. *Science, 219,* 215–220. . . . . **359**

Tollis, I. G. *See* Battista, Eades, Tamassia, and Tollis (1994).

Tou, F., Williams, M. D., Fikes, R., A. Henderson, J., and Malone, T. W. (1982). RABBIT: An Intelligent Database Assistant. *Proceedings of AAAI'82.* 314–318. . . . . **233**

Tovée, M. J. (1996). *An Introduction to the Visual System.* Cambridge, UK: Cambridge University Press. **24, 25, 26**

Travers, M. (1989). A Visual Representation for Knowledge Structures. *Proceedings of ACM Hypertext'89 Conference.* 147–158.**156**

Treisman, A. (1986). Features and Objects in Visual Processing. *Scientific American,* Nov. **84**

Truve, S. *See* Ahlberg and Truve (1995).

Tufte, E. R. (1983). *The Visual Display of Quantitative Information.* Cheshire, CT: Graphics Press. **7, 16, 74, 85, 115, 127, 159, 160, 251, 253, 287, 290, 419, 633**

Tufte, E. R. (1990). *Envisioning Information.* Cheshire, CT: Graphics Press.. . . . . **160, 307, 442, 504, 633**

Tufte, E. R. (1994). Graphical Summary of Patient Status. *The Lancet, 344*(8919), 386–389. . . . . **30**

Tufte, E. R. (1997). *Visual Explanations: Images and Quantities, Evidence and Narrative.* Cheshire, CT: Graphics Press. . . . **4, 5, 633**

Tufte, E. R. *See* Powsner and Tufte (1994).

Tukey, J. W. (1977). *Exploratory Data Analysis.* Reading, MA: Addison-Wesley. **7, 85, 95, 598, 617**

Tukey, J. W. *See* Cutting, Karger, Pedersen, and Tukey (1992a).

Turo, D. *See* Asahi, Turo, and Shneiderman (1995).

Tuscany, P. A. (1987). Software Development Environment for Large Switching Projects. *Proceedings of Proceedings of International Switching Symposium'87, ACM Conference on Human Factors in Computing Systems.* 199–214. **419**

Tversky, B. *See* Levy, Zacks, Tversky, and Schiano (1996).

Tweedie, L. A. (1995). Interactive Visualization Artifacts: How Can Abstractions Inform Design? *Proceedings of People and Computers X: The Tenth Conference of the British Computer Society Human-Computer Interaction Specialist Group.* 247–265. . . **277, 620**

Tweedie, L. A. (1997●). Characterizing Interactive Externalizations. *Proceedings of CHI'97, ACM Conference on Human Factors in Computing Systems,* Atlanta. 375–382. . . . . **20, 21, 581**

Tweedie, L. A., Spence, R., Dawkes, H., and Su, H. (1996●). Externalising Abstract Mathematical Models. *Proceedings of CHI'96, ACM Conference on Human Factors in Computing Systems.* 406–412. . . . . **59, 108, 261, 617, 619, 620, 626**

Tweedie, L. A., Spence, R., Williams, D., and Bhogal, R. (1994). The Attribute Explorer. *Conference Companion of CHI'94, ACM Conference on Human Factors in Computing Systems,* New York. 435–436. . . . . **277, 617, 619, 620, 621**

Tweedie, L. A. *See* Dawkes, Tweedie, and Spence (1996).

Tzavaras, I. *See* Apperley, Tzavaras, and Spence (1982).

U.S. Bureau of the Census. (1992). *Statistical Abstract of the United States.* Washington, DC: U.S. Government Printing Office. . **251**

Ullman, J. D. (1980). *Principles of Database Systems.* Rockville, MD: Computer Science Press. **67, 253**

Ungar, D. *See* Chang and Ungar (1993).

Ungar, D. *See* Smith and Ungar (1987).

UNIX Programmer's Manual. (1981). *Unix User's Manual 4.1 BSD.* Vol. June. University of California, Berkeley. **313**

Unwin, A. R., Sloan, B., and Wills, G. J. (1992). Interactive Graphical Methods for Trade Flows. *Proceedings of New Techniques and Technologies for Statistics.* **207, 208, 225**

Upson, C., and Keeler, M. (1988). VBuffer: Visible Volume Rendering. *Proceedings of SIGGRAPH'88, ACM Conference on Computer Graphics.* 59–64. . . . . **47, 49**

Upson, C., Faulhabel Jr., T., Kamins, D., Laidlaw, D., Schegel, D., Vroom, J., Gurwitz, R., and van Dam, A. (1989). The Application Visualization System: A Computational Environment for Scientific Visualization. *IEEE Computer Graphics and Applications, 9*(4 July), 30–42. . . . . **233**

Utting, K., and Yankelovich, N. (1989). Context and Orientation in Hypermedia Networks. *ACM Transactions on Information Systems, 7*(1), 58–84. . . . . **494, 495, 630**

Valdez, J. F. *See* Chignell, Nordhausen, Valdez, and Waterworth (1991).

van Dam, A. *See* Foley, van Dam, Feiner, and Hughes (1990); Herndon, van Dam, and Gleicher (1994); Upson, Faulhabel Jr., Kamins, Laidlaw, Schegel, Vroom, Gurwitz, and van Dam (1989); Yankelovich, Meyrowitz, and van Dam (1985).

VanHeyningen, M. (1994). The Unified Computer Science Technical Report Index: Lessons in Indexing Diverse Resources. *Proceedings of IWWW2, The Second International World Wide Web Conference.* 535–543. . . . . **571**

Vecchi, M. P. *See* Kirkpatrick, Gelatt, and Vecchi (1983).

Veerasamy, A., Hudson, S. E., and Navathe, S. (1995). Querying, Navigating and Visualizing an Online Library Catalog. *Proceedings of DL'95, ACM Conference on Digital Libraries.* **572**

Velleman, P. F. (1985). *The DataDesk Manual.* Ithaca, NY: Data Description Inc. **208, 617, 618**

Vickers, D. L. (1982). Head-Mounted Display Terminal. *Proceedings of ICGC'70,* Silver Spring, MD. 102–109. . . . . **96**

Vincente, K. J., Hayes, B. C., and Williges, R. C. (1987). Assaying and Isolating Individual Differences in Searching a Hierarchical File System. *Human Factors, 29*(3), 349–359. . . . . **153**

Vinge, V. (1981). *True Names.* New York: Dell Books. **205**

Vion-Dury, J., and Santana, M. (1994). Virtual Images: Interactive Visualisation of Distributed Object-Oriented Systems. *Proceedings of OOPSLA'94.* 65–84. . . . . **507**

Vista, D. *See* Consens, Eigler, Hasan, Mendelzon, Noik, Ryman, and Vista (1994).

Visualization Group. (1995). *Vz Visualization Library: User's Guide Version 1.0.* Naperville, IL: AT&T Bell Laboratories. . . . **174, 227**

Vo, K. P. *See* Gansner, Koutsofios, North, and Vo (1993).

VPL. (1989). *EyePhone System Preliminary Specification.* Vol. 4. Redwood City, CA: VPL Research Inc. **96**

VRM. (1980). *Voice Recognition Module Reference Manual.* California: Interstate Electronics Corporation. **335**

Vroom, J. *See* Upson, Faulhabel Jr., Kamins, Laidlaw, Schegel, Vroom, Gurwitz, and van Dam (1989).

Vroomen, L. C. *See* Beaudoin, Parent, and Vroomen (1996).

Wainer, H. (1997). *Visual Revelations.* New York: Copernicus/Springer-Verlag. **626**

Wake, W. *See* Heath, Hix, Nowell, Wake, Averboch, Labow, Guyer, Brueni, France, Dalal, and Fox (1995).

Walker II, J. Q. *See* Beard and Walker II (1990).

Walsby, A. *See* Page and Walsby (1979).

Walsh, P. *See* Monk, Walsh, and Dix (1988).

Walters, T. B. *See* Risch, Rex, Dowson, Walters, May, and Moon (1997).

Ward, M. O. (1994). XmdvTool: Integrating Multiple Methods for Visualizing Multivariate Data. *Proceedings of IEEE Visualization'94 Conference,* San Jose. 326–333. . . . . **108**

Ward, M. O. *See* LeBlanc, Ward, and Wittels (1990).

Ware, C., and Beatty, J. C. (1985). *Using Colour as a Tool in Discrete Data Analysis.* Technical Report CS-85-21. Waterloo, Ontario, Canada: University of Waterloo. **66, 73, 76**

Ware, C., and Franck, G. (1996). Evaluating Stereo and Motion Cues for Visualizing Information Nets in Three Dimensions. *ACM Transactions on Graphics, 15*(2), 121–139. . . . . **634**

Ware, C., Hui, D., and Franck, G. (1993). Visualizing Object-Oriented Software in Three Dimensions. *Proceedings of Gascon'93,* Toronto. 612–620. . . . . **368**

Warger, A. *See* Whiting-O'Keefe, Simbork, Epstein, and Warger (1985).

Watanabe, L. *See* Sanderson, Scott, Johnston, Mainzer, Watanabe, and James (1992).

Waterworth, J. A. *See* Chignell, Nordhausen, Valdez, and Waterworth (1991).

Weil, G. *See* Becker, Cleveland, and Weil (1988b).

Weimer, D., and Ganapathy, S. (1989). A Synthetic Visual Environment with Hand Gesturing and Voice Input. *Proceedings of CHI'89, ACM Conference on Human Factors in Computing Systems,* Austin, TX. 235–240. . . . . **99**

Weinberger, P. J. (1984). Cheap Dynamic Instruction Counting. *AT&T Bell Laboratories Technical Journal, 63*(8), 1815–1826. **419**

Weinreb, D., and Moon, D. (1981). *Lisp Machine Manual.* 4th ed. Cambridge, MA: MIT Artificial Intelligence Laboratory.. . . . **313**

Welsch, R. J. *See* Rowland and Welsch (1983).

Welty, C. (1985). Correcting User Errors in SQL. *International Journal of Man-Machine Studies, 22*(4), 463–477. . . . . **244, 247**

Wenger, K. *See* Livny, Ramakrishnan, Beyer, Chen, Donjerkovic, Lawande, Myllymaki, and Wenger (1997).

White, H. D., and Griffith, B. C. (1981). Author Cocitation: A Literary Measure of Intelligent Structure. *Journal of the American Society for Information Science, 32*(3), 163–171. . . . . **438**

Whitehouse, H. *See* Leckie, Masters, Whitehouse, and Young (1975).

Whiting-O'Keefe, Q. E., Simbork, D. W., Epstein, W. V., and Warger, A. (1985). A Computerized Summary Medical Record System Can Provide Move Information than the Standard Medical Record. *JAMA, 254*(9), 1185–1192. **288**

Whitted, T. *See* Rubin and Whitted (1980).

Whitten, W. B. *See* Reitman, Whitten, and Gruenenfelder (1984).

Widoff, S. *See* Plaisant, Milash, Rose, Widoff, and Shneiderman (1996).

Wijk, J. J. v. *See* Leeuw and Wijk (1993).

Wilcox, C. D. *See* Roman, Cox, Wilcox, and Plun (1992).

Wilhelmson, R. B. (1988). Numerical Simulations of Severe Storms. *Proceedings Fourth International Symposium: Science and Engineering on Cray Supercomputers*. **46**

Wilkinson, L. (1992). Enhancing Scatterplot Matrices. In A. Westlake (ed.), *Survey and Statistical Computing.* New York: Elsevier Science. **617, 620**

Wilks, A. R. *See* Becker and Wilks (1993a, 1993b); Becker, Chambers, and Wilks (1988a); Becker, Cleveland, and Wilks (1987, 1988c); Becker, Eick, and Wilks (1991, 1995); Becker, Eick, Miller, and Wilks (1989b, 1990a, 1990b).

Willett, A. *See* Hemmje, Kunkel, and Willett (1994).

Willett, P. *See* Al-Hawamdeh and Willett (1988).

Williams, D. *See* Tweedie, Spence, Williams, and Bhogal (1994).

Williams, J. *See* Olsen, Korhage, Sochats, Spring, and Williams (1993).

Williams, M. (1984). What Make RABBIT Run? *International Journal of Man-Machine Studies, 21*(4), 333–352. . . . . **248**

Williams, M. D. *See* Tou, Williams, Fikes, A. Henderson, and Malone (1982).

Williamson, C., and Shneiderman, B. (1992). The Dynamic HomeFinder: Evaluating Dynamic Queries in a Real-Estate Information Exploration System. *Proceedings of SIGIR'83, ACM Conference on Research and Development in Information Retrieval,* New York. 339–346. . . . . **11, 237, 245, 277, 623, 628**

Williamson, C. *See* Ahlberg, Williamson, and Shneiderman (1992).

Williges, R. C. *See* Vincente, Hayes, and Williges (1987).

Wills, G. J. (1997). NicheWorks: Interactive Visualization of Very Large Graphs. *Proceedings of Graph Drawing'97*. **467**

Wills, G. J. *See* Cox, Eick, and Wills (1997); Eick and Wills (1993); Unwin, Sloan, and Wills (1992).

Wilner, W. *See* Hollan, Rich, Hill, Wroblewski, Wilner, Wittenburg, and Grudin (1991).

Wilson, J. R. *See* Smith and Wilson (1993).

Winfree, A. T. (1987). *The Timing of Biological Clocks.* New York: Scientific American Books, Inc. **5, 6**

Winkler, K. H., and Norman, M. L. (1986). *Munacolor: Understanding High-Resolution Gas Dynamical Simulations Through Color Graphics, Astrophysical Radiation Hydrodynamics.* Amsterdam: D. Reidel Publishing. 223–243. . . . . **47**

Wise, J. A., Thomas, J. J., Pennock, K., Lantrip, D., Pottier, M., Schur, A., and Crow, V. (1995●). Visualizing the Non-Visual: Spatial Analysis and Interaction with Information from Text Documents. *Proceedings of InfoVis'95, IEEE Symposium on Information Visualization,* New York. 51–58, color plate 140. . . . . **59, 60, 431, 441, 451, 628**

Wish, M. *See* Kruskal and Wish (1979).

Wistrand, E. *See* Ahlberg and Wistrand (1995a, 1995b).

Wittels, N. *See* LeBlanc, Ward, and Wittels (1990).

Wittenburg, K. *See* Hollan, Rich, Hill, Wroblewski, Wilner, Wittenburg, and Grudin (1991).

Wolman, K. *See* Chimera, Wolman, Mark, and Shneiderman (1991).

Wong, A. *See* Salton and Wong (1978); Salton, Yang, and Wong (1975).

Wong, P. C., Crabb, A. H., and Bergeron, R. D. (1996). Dual Multiresolution Hyperslice for Multivariate Data Visualization. *Proceedings of InfoVis'96, IEEE Symposium on Information Visualization.* 74–75. . . . . **18**

Wong, Y. Y. *See* Mandler, Salomon, and Wong (1992).

Wood, A. M. *See* Hendley, Drew, Wood, and Beale (1995).

Wood, D. C. M. *See* Schwartz and Wood (1993).

Wood, D. *See* Bruggeman-Klein and Wood (1989).

Woodruff, A., Landay, J., and Stonebraker, M. (1998). Constant Information Density in Zoomable Interfaces. *Proceedings of AVI'98, Workshop on Advanced Visual Interfaces.* 57–65. . . . . **286**

Woods, D. D. (1984). Visual Momentum: A Concept to Improve Cognitive Coupling of Person and Computer. *International Journal of Man-Machine Studies, 21*(3), 229–244. . . . . **445**

Wright, W. (1995●). Information Animation Applications in the Capital Markets. *Proceedings of InfoVis'95, IEEE Symposium on Information Visualization,* New York. 19–25, color plates 136–137. . . . . **8, 57**

Wroblewski, D. *See* Hill, Hollan, Wroblewski, and McCandless (1992); Hollan, Rich, Hill, Wroblewski, Wilner, Wittenburg, and Grudin (1991).

Wurden, E. H. *See* Leenstra, Wurden, Otis, and Wurden (1996).

Wyatt, J. C. (1994). Clinical Data Systems, Part 1: Data and Medical Records. *The Lancet, 344*(December 3), 1543–1547. . . . . **288, 291, 293**

Wyllys, R. E. *See* Edmundson and Wyllys (1961).

Xerox. (1994). *Visual Recall for Windows.* Palo Alto, CA: Xerox Corporation.. . . . . **256**

Yang, C. S. *See* Salton, Yang, and Wong (1975).

Yang, J. *See* Filo and Yang (1994).

Yankelovich, N., Meyrowitz, N., and van Dam, A. (1985). Reading and Writing the Electronic Book. *IEEE Computer, 18*(10 October), 15–30. . . . . **546, 547**

Yankelovich, N. *See* Utting and Yankelovich (1989).

Yokoyama, T. *See* Miyazawa, Kinoshita, Kobayashi, Yokoyama, and Matsushita (1990).

Yonke, M. D. *See* Zdybel, Greenfeld, and Yonke (1981).

York, J., and Bohn, S. (1995). Clustering and Dimensionality Reduction in SPIRE. *Proceedings of Automated Intelligence Processing and Analysis Symposium,* Tysons Corner, VA. **444**

York, W. *See* Card, Robertson, and York (1996).

Young, D., and Shneiderman, B. (1993). A Graphical Filter/Flow Representation of Boolean Queries: A Prototype Implementation and Evaluation. *Journal of the American Society for Information Science, 44*(6), 327–339. . . . . **147, 239, 301, 572, 618, 620**

Young, F. W., Faldowski, R. A., and McFarlane, M. M. (1993). Multivariate Statistical Visualization. In C. R. Rao (ed.), *Handbook of Statistics.* Vol. 9. . . . . **617, 620**

Young, F. W. *See* Kruskal, Young, and Seery (1973).

Young, L. *See* Leckie, Masters, Whitehouse, and Young (1975).

Yourdon, E. (1989). *Modern Structured Analysis.* Upper Saddle River, NJ: Prentice Hall/Yourdon Press. **160**

Zabusky, N. J. (1984). Computational Synergetics. *Physics Today,* July. **47**

Zacks, J. *See* Furnas and Zacks (1994); Levy, Zacks, Tversky, and Schiano (1996).

Zadeh, L. (1965). Fuzzy Sets. *Information Control, 8,* 338–353. . **255**

Zarmer, C. L. *See* Johnson, Nardi, Zarmer, and Miller (1993); Nardi and Zarmer (1993).

Zdybel, F., Greenfeld, N. R., and Yonke, M. D. (1981). An Information Presentation System. *Proceedings of AAAI'81,* Menlo Park, CA. 978–984.. . . . . **67**

Zeki, S. (1992). The Visual Image in Mind and Brain. *Scientific American, 267*(3 September), 69–76. **85**

Zeleznik, R. C., Herndon, K. P., Robbins, D. C., Huang, N., Meyer, T., Parker, N., and Hughes, J. F. (1993). An Interactive 3D Toolkit for Constructing 3D Widgets. *Proceedings of SIGGRAPH'93, ACM Conference on Computer Graphics.* 81–84.. . . . . **608**

Zeleznik, R. C. *See* Conner, Snibbe, Herndon, and Zeleznik (1992); Stevens, Zeleznik, and Hughes (1994).

Zeltzer, D., Pieper, S., and Sturman, D. (1989). An Integrated Graphical Simulation Platform. *Proceedings of Graphics Interface'89.* 266–274. . . . . **519**

Zeltzer, D. *See* Sturman, Zeltzer, and Pieper (1989).

Zhang, J. (1996). A Representational Analysis of Relational Information Displays. *International Journal of Human-Computer Studies, 45*(1), 59–74. . . . . **616**

Zhang, J., and Norman, D. A. (1994). Representations in Distributed Cognitive Tasks. *Cognitive Science, 18*(1), 87–122. . . . **277, 616, 620**

Zhang, Z. *See* Ross, Zhang, and Choi (1994).

Zimmerman, T., Lanier, J., Blanchard, C., Bryson, S., and Harvill, Y. (1987). A Hand Gesture Interface Device. *Proceedings of CHI+GI'87, ACM Conference on Human Factors in Computing Systems and Graphics Interface,* Toronto. 189–192. . . . . **96**

Zloof. (1975). Query-by-Example. *Proceedings of National Computer Conference'75.* 431–437. . . . . **246**

Zuberec, S. *See* Chignell, Zuberec, and Poblete (1993).

Zulager, D. *See* Marchak and Zulager (1992).

Zuo, Z. *See* Schaffer, Zuo, Bartram, Dill, Dubes, Greenberg, and Roseman (1993, 1996).

Zytkow, J. M. *See* Langley, Simon, Bradshaw, and Zytkow (1987).

Index